SIMON&SCHUSTER
HANDBOOK
FOR WRITERS

LYNN QUITMAN TROYKA

Library of Congress Cataloging-in-Publication Data

Troyka, Lynn Quitman (date)
   Simon & Schuser handbook for writers.

   Includes index.
   1. English language—Rhetoric—Handbooks,
manuals, etc. 2. English language—Grammar—
1950–   —Handbooks, manuals, etc. I. Title.
II. Title: Simon and Schuster handbook for
writers. III. Title: Handbook for writers.
PE1408.T696 1987b   808′.042   86-30455
ISBN 0-13-810433-6 (pbk.)

for David,
who makes it all possible

Editorial/production supervision: *HILDA TAUBER*
Interior and cover design: *LORRAINE MULLANEY*
Manufacturing buyer: *RAY KEATING*
Associate Art Director: *FLORENCE D. SILVERMAN*

Printed in the United States of America
10 9 8 7 6 5 4 3 2 1

ISBN 0-13-810433-6   01

Prentice-Hall International (UK) Limited, *London*
Prentice-Hall of Australia Pty. Limited, *Sydney*
Prentice-Hall Canada Inc., *Toronto*
Prentice-Hall Hispanoamericana, S.A., *Mexico*
Prentice-Hall of India Private Limited, *New Delhi*
Prentice-Hall of Japan, Inc., *Tokyo*
Prentice-Hall of Southeast Asia Pte. Ltd., *Singapore*
Editora Prentice-Hall do Brasil, Ltda., *Rio de Janeiro*

CONTENTS

Preface to
the *Annotated Instructor's Edition*   AIE–vii

These specially commissioned essays appear only in this Annotated Instructor's Edition. *The first three essays summarize current scholarship and include thorough annotated bibliographies. The fourth essay presents many current instructional strategies.*

THE WRITING PROCESS: AN OVERVIEW
JOSEPHINE KOSTER TARVERS, Rutgers University
at New Brunswick   *AIE–1*

THE HISTORY OF RHETORIC: AN OVERVIEW
WILLIAM F. WOODS, Wichita State University   *AIE–9*

LINGUISTICS FOR COMPOSITION TEACHERS:
AN OVERVIEW
ALICE M. ROY, California State University
at Los Angeles   *AIE–15*

HOW TO USE A HANDBOOK: AN OVERVIEW
LOUIS EMOND, Dean Junior College   *AIE–21*

The complete student edition, with its more detailed Table of Contents, appears after the essays in this *Annotated Instructor's Edition.* The annotations, which do not appear in the student edition, include exercise answers, teaching tips, biographies of quoted writers, and a rich variety of other resources.

BRIEF CONTENTS OF STUDENT EDITION

I
Writing an Essay   **1**
1 Thinking About Purposes and Audiences   2
2 Planning and Shaping   12
3 Drafting and Revising   44
4 Writing Paragraphs   73
5 Thinking Critically   113

II
Understanding Grammar   **139**
6 Parts of Speech   140
7 Structures of the Sentence   154
8 Verbs   176
9 Case of Nouns and Pronouns   209
10 Pronoun Reference   221
11 Agreement   230
12 Distinguishing Between Adjectives and Adverbs   247

III
Writing Correct Sentences   **259**
13 Sentence Fragments   260
14 Comma Splices and Fused Sentences   271
15 Sentences that Send Unclear Messages   281

IV
Writing Effective Sentences   **301**
16 Conciseness   302
17 Coordination and Subordination   316
18 Parallelism   330
19 Variety and Emphasis   340

V
Using Effective Words   **354**
20 Understanding the Meaning of Words   355
21 Understanding the Effect of Words   371
22 Spelling and Hyphenation   385

VI
Punctuation and Mechanics   **409**
23 The Period, Question Mark, and Exclamation Point   410
24 The Comma   415
25 The Semicolon   443
26 The Colon   451
27 The Apostrophe   457
28 Quotation Marks   464
29 Other Marks of Punctuation   474
30 Capitals, Italics, Abbreviations, and Numbers   487

VII
Writing Special Assignments   **509**
31 Paraphrasing, Summarizing, and Quoting   510
31 Writing Research   530
33 Observing a Student Writing Research   586
34 Writing in Other Disciplines   614
35 Business Writing   659

Appendix A
Writing Essay Tests   **669**
Appendix B
Using Correct Manuscript Format   **675**
Usage Glossary   **683**
Glossary of Grammatical and Selected
Composition Terms   **699**
Index   **716**

PREFACE TO
THE ANNOTATED INSTRUCTOR'S EDITION

This *Annotated Instructor's Edition* of the *Simon & Schuster Handbook for Writers* represents a major innovation in faculty materials to supplement a textbook for English classes. Moving well beyond the typical instructor's manual, this volume assumes that instructors appreciate having at their disposal a wide array of resources, rather than only answers to exercises and synopses of chapters. This *Annotated Instructor's Edition* is, therefore, a potpourri of information and suggestions. Instructors can browse, select what fits their personal styles of teaching, and add their own special touches as they go along.

I had two purposes in mind when I created this *Annotated Instructor's Edition*. First, I set for myself the challenge of supporting my ongoing contention that effective teaching of composition relies on theory, derived from research. The first section of this volume contains, therefore, four specially commissioned essays written for faculty who teach with the *Simon & Schuster Handbook for Writers*. The essays are intended as catalysts for study and lively discussion among faculty groups, including teaching assistants and part-time and full-time instructors. Three of the essays discuss current scholarship in a major area related to composition studies: the writing process, rhetorical theory, and linguistics. By presenting overviews of theory and research, these essays help set forth the intellectual grounding that supports the *Simon & Schuster Handbook for Writers*. Written by scholar-teachers with experience in synthesizing key concepts, each essay includes a thorough annotated bibliography so that instructors who wish may delve further into the literature. The fourth essay, written by an experienced teacher and department chair, explains how to use a handbook to best advantage in composition courses. This essay includes a variety of course syllabi along with discussions of sentence combining, responding to student writing, and other matters of current interest in the teaching of writing.

My second purpose for creating this *Annotated Instructor's Edition* stems from my interest in offering instructors resources that can add to the pleasure of their teaching. Thus, the second section of this volume reproduces the entire student edition, together with—exclusively for instructors—"marginals" that consist of various teaching resources: answers to exercises, teaching tips, background information on material in the text, quotations about writing, selected brief biographies of authors whose writing serves to illustrate principles in the text, supplementary exercises and their answers, and more. This smorgasbord of theory-based but highly practical resources distills my twenty years' experience as a researcher in the field and as a teacher of writing to college students and to instructors of college students.

This *Annotated Instructor's Edition* is designed for multiple uses. Faculty can turn to it to for information about scholarship and the teaching of writing. Teachers can consult it as they plan their classes and check student work. And, of course, instructors can carry it to their classrooms confident that it includes everything the students have in their edition—and much more.

This volume also is designed for growth. I cordially invite instructors to collaborate on the next edition of this *Annotated Instructor's Edition*. If you have favorite teaching tips, quotations about writing, other items for the marginals, or comments, please send them to me c/o College English Editor, Prentice-Hall, Inc., Englewood Cliffs, NJ 07632. Any item published will carry the byline and, if given, affiliation of its contributor.

My special thanks go to a number of people who helped make this *Annotated Instructor's Edition* a reality. Emily R. Gordon, co-author with me of the *Workbook* and author of the testing package that supplements the *Handbook*, made many useful suggestions throughout the project. The authors of the specially commissioned essays (mentioned here in the sequence their essays appear) gracefully shared their considerable knowledge in this unusual forum: Josephine Koster Tarvers, Rutgers University at New Brunswick; William F. Woods, Wichita State University; Alice M. Roy, California State University at Los Angeles; and Louis Emond, Dean Junior College. At Prentice-Hall, Phil Miller, Executive Editor for Humanities and English Editor, nurtured this book from its inception and continually enhanced my efforts with excellent suggestions. Hilda Tauber, Production Editor, dedicated herself to the book with refreshing skill and unfailing attention to detail.

LYNN QUITMAN TROYKA
Beechhurst, New York

THE WRITING PROCESS: AN OVERVIEW

JOSEPHINE KOSTER TARVERS

Edward Sapir once complained, "All grammars leak." The same complaint can be made about theories of the writing process: they leak, or, more accurately, they leave out possibilities. At the same time, most theories of the writing process overlap; while differing in terminology and in ways of gathering and categorizing information, they suggest common conclusions. In this essay I discuss briefly some of the major research on the writing process, to show you not only where these theories leak and where they overlap, but also what their common conclusions are and how they might help our teaching.

First of all, when we speak of the "writing process," we are amalgamating a number of processes, both psychological and physical. Research suggests that each person's writing process is different and that it changes with the writer's age, experience, and particular writing situation. However, certain stages of the process seem shared: most writers go through a stage of gathering information and noting down ideas, one of "roughing out" those ideas, and one in which the presentation is adjusted according to the writer's intentions and certain conventions of linguistic etiquette. Researchers call these stages planning or prewriting; drafting or writing; revising and editing or rewriting and correcting. Our knowledge of these stages is drawn from the research described below.

Two early studies of the writing process are ethnographic; that is, they study writing behaviors. These were carried out by Janet Emig, then a doctoral candidate at Harvard, and by James Britton and his colleagues at the University of London Institute of Education. Emig, in *The Composing Processes of Twelfth Graders* [item 12 in the Annotated Bibliography, below], conducted case studies of eight twelfth-grade writers of average to above-average ability. They com-

JOSEPHINE KOSTER TARVERS is Assistant Professor of English at Rutgers University, where she teaches writing, grammar theory, history of the language, and other courses in rhetoric and medieval studies. She is also assistant director of the University of North Carolina—Mellon Foundation Summer Writing Workshop for Teachers. Her work has been published in Studies in Philology, Notes and Queries, *and the* North Carolina—Virginia College English Association Newsletter; *she has articles forthcoming on medical writing, linguistic discrimination, and college slang.*

posed aloud in the presence of Emig and a tape recorder, describing their thoughts and feelings as they composed a "writing autobiography" and three short pieces of writing. Emig concluded that these writers wrote both extensively, in response to school assignments, and reflexively, for themselves. In extensive writing, the students spent little time prewriting (often the school situation prevented this), did not revise their work voluntarily, and seemed most concerned with meeting teacher-imposed writing standards (e.g. spelling, grammar, punctuation), since the teacher was to judge the piece of writing. In reflexive writing, the students spent more time prewriting (often "in their heads" rather than on paper), pausing to reflect and contemplate what they had written. They were also more willing to revise and were less concerned with standards of correctness than with "getting it right." Much of Emig's later work, recently collected in *The Web of Meaning* [13], has drawn out the implications of this study, especially those dealing with getting started and thinking out ideas.

Britton and his colleagues undertook a much larger study, one of the largest ever conducted in composition research. In *The Development of Writing Abilities (11–18)* [2] they reported the conclusions drawn from an examination of over two thousand "scripts" (writing assignments) drawn from 85 classes at 65 British secondary schools, concentrating on the relationship of writer to audience and the functions the writings were to perform. Britton calls these functions "expressive" (personal) writing, such as journals, diaries, reflections, and personal letters; "transactional" (action-causing) writings, which informed, advised, persuaded, or instructed an audience; and "poetic" (creative) writing, using language as an art form. Britton's results showed that most writing was for a teacher audience, students having little chance in school situations to write for larger audiences. Students at all ages seemed more comfortable with expressive writing, but were most often required to produce transactional writing. Poetic writing was encouraged briefly in the middle years of school, but then trailed off. Students increasingly had to face audiences of teachers as examiners, and they learned, often by trial and error, to produce writing to satisfy this narrow audience. They were not encouraged to plan and produce writing for larger audiences; this fact seems to have inhibited the students' abilities to write and think speculatively, to produce written reflections of independent thought.

Combinations of Emig's and Britton's techniques have been used in later research on the writing process. Kenneth Kantor [20] has adapted their methods to study seven twelfth graders in a creative writing class in Georgia and to confirm many of their conclusions. Lee Odell and Dixie Goswami have used these methods to study the writing of professionals in a social services agency [30]; they found that those writers "showed a complex awareness of audience, self, and subject" and had clear notions of what constituted acceptable style (including a strong reliance on the passive). While Odell and Goswami understandably could not identify all the factors that contributed to these writers' awareness of the writing process, they suggested that students must learn to adapt their writing processes to different situations and audiences to succeed as writers beyond school.

Many researchers feel that understanding the thinking processes involved in writing will tell us more about the writing process itself. Their cognitive studies have taken a number of forms. In *Pre-Writing* [32], D. Gordon Rohman and Albert O. Wlecke argue that a pre-assimilation of ideas occurs in the mind before writing, and that writers must learn to "picture the process" in order to imitate it consciously. They suggest techniques such as journal-keeping, meditative questions (a problem-solving technique drawn from religious meditation), and the development of analogies through "existential sentences." These existential sentences ask students to explore abstract subjects by constructing sentences in the pattern "Abstraction + linking verb + complement which makes abstraction concrete," such as "Happiness is a warm puppy" or "Comfort is a hot bowl of clam chowder on a cold, rainy day." Rohman and Wlecke insist on the separateness of prewriting from other writing processes, a view later seconded by Mandel (see below).

Other cognitive researchers have drawn on the work of Jean Piaget, who divided all childhood learning experiences into four stages, based on the behaviors children can learn in each stage (*assimilation*) and the changes they can make in those behaviors (*adaptation*) [1]. James Moffett, for example, combines his understanding of Piaget with implications drawn by Britton into a theory of the writing process centered around students' cognitive development [27, 28]. In Moffett's curriculum, students begin by recording experiences (drama) for various audiences, then sequentially learn to report experiences (narratives) and to generalize from them (exposition) until they can theorize about them (argumentation). At each stage students are encouraged to return to the previous stages for help in planning and developing, so that

their writing processes are not separate and linear but recursive and spiraling, drawing on earlier stages to produce new kinds of writing for new audiences.

Some cognitive theoreticians have focused on the prewriting stage of the process. In *Writing Without Teachers* [11], Peter Elbow promotes a technique called "freewriting," which encourages writers to record ideas quickly and continuously, without stopping to worry about spelling and punctuation. He argues that in this way, writers can find and explore ideas—an essential part of the planning process—without jumping ahead to the editing stage. Gregory and Elizabeth Cowan [8] refine Elbow's technique by adding a recursive step called "looping": a piece of freewriting is ransacked for ideas and words the writer finds most interesting, and these become the centers of new pieces of freewriting. The process is repeated until the writer is satisfied that he or she has sufficient material with which to begin drafting.

Brain function research enables Gabriele Lusser Rico to create another prewriting strategy, "clustering" [31]. Like Elbow and the Cowans, she starts with a central important idea. However, instead of writing continuously starting from that idea, writers in Rico's system cluster related ideas around the central one, drawing circles and lines to establish connections and trains of thought. Then they search for recurring patterns of words or images to help organize their ideas in draft form (using information Rico provides about the left and right hemispheres of the brain), and then revise the arranged material by referring back to the original clustered design. Rico encourages clustering to improve creative writing, but the technique may be used with expository writing as well.

The development of plans is central to Linda Flower and John Hayes's research on the writing process [15]. They base their conclusions on an examination of "writing protocols," chronological descriptions of all the activities in which writers engage while completing texts, along with the notes and drafts of those texts. Their model of the writing process consists of three stages, which they call planning, translating, and reviewing. Planning involves generating ideas by probing one's own memory, organizing that information by evaluating and classifying generated material, and setting goals by setting up criteria to judge the completed work. Translating takes the planned material from memory and transforms it into written sentences. Reviewing makes the writer read back over each segment of the translated text and edit it to conform with original purpose and linguistic etiquette.

They use this model to explain how writers solve the problem of moving from the planning to the translating stage by juggling, discarding, or subdividing the constraints on their writing; by drawing on routines or well-learned procedures (such as the five-paragraph theme); and by planning to undertake some action, to include some content, or to write something down, although not in polished form. Flower and Hayes feel that writers who have learned to juggle and control these plans are more successful than those who "plunge into" or "plunge on with" a piece of writing.

Recently, some cognitive researchers have begun to focus on the revising stage. Nancy Sommers [33, 34] has found that student writers frequently confuse revising with correcting, a problem prompted in part by teachers' habits of only marking "mistakes" when evaluating papers. Adult writers, on the other hand, seem more willing to revise for purpose and audience and are less obsessed with getting all the mistakes out. Sommers suggests that learning to distinguish between revising and editing in the writing process is a step in producing better writing.

Another group of researchers has focused not on writers' cognitions but on their intuitions to describe the writing process. Donald Murray, one member of this group, says that the process theory of writing is "the cultivation of surprise," that is, discovering new ideas and new combinations of ideas by writing, learning from one's own errors and experiments [29]. As might be expected, Murray encourages writers to use techniques like freewriting and clustering to explore their intuitions, and to use open-ended plans which lead to further discoveries. Murray recommends a preliminary or "discovery" draft to help writers learn what other kinds of planning and exploring they need to do before beginning a formal draft. Murray puts most emphasis, however, on a writer's intuition; writers, he feels, should write quickly, without recourse to their notes, pausing to read their work aloud to test it by ear. (Notes can be checked later to confirm accuracy.) Revision, in his intuitive theory, is simply the repetition of the stages of collecting, planning, and developing information, done as many times as is needed until the text is ready for editing. Murray concludes his book with a six-page bibliography of sources in which other writers discuss *their* writing processes.

Barrett Mandel, in an essay appropriately titled "Losing One's Mind" [25], takes the notion of intuitive writing one step further. He argues that, our preconceptions aside, the planning stage of writing does not *cause* the drafting step; instead it "bring[s] to consciousness the *intention* to write." Mandel believes drafting enables writers to make discoveries. The final step is binary: writers revise for their own sake and edit for their readers' sake. The latter editing is totally elective—the writer either decides to follow the rules or does not, and must abide by the consequences of that decision.

Another researcher who believes that the writing process draws on a writer's intuitions is William

E. Coles, Jr. In two books, *Composing* [4] and *The Plural I* [5], Coles presents two writing courses which force students to look beyond their preconceptions and use writing as a way of discovering who they are. Writers constantly question their relationships to their subjects, their audiences, and their personae; the "plural I's" are the many personae each writer can adopt. Coles's process demands constant questioning and challenging on the part of the teacher, and constant revision by the writers, as they struggle to answer the question "Who will I be in this paper?" A similar theory of challenge and examination is proposed by Ken Macrorie [23, 24]. He views writing as an attempt to tell the truth about a subject; he encourages writers to freewrite, brainstorm, explore contradictions, until they amaze themselves; the "something amazing" that writers discover leads them to better, more honest writing and less "Engfish" (Macrorie's name for pompous, superficial student prose). Like Elbow and Mandel, Macrorie encourages writers to defy or ignore conventions, following their intuitions instead, and to revise each piece of writing as if it were written by the writer's worst enemy; all of these activities lead to a process of writing in which truth and the writer's own voice become most important.

A final group of writing researchers take some of their cues from Britton's work on audience and function. These "paradigmatic" views, like the traditional modes, set up forms which writers can follow to discover ideas. Kenneth Burke [3] establishes a discovery heuristic (list of questions) based on the old journalistic recipe for a lead story: *what* was done? (act); *where* or *when* was it done? (scene); *who* did it? (agent); *how* was it done? (agency); *why* was it done? (purpose). Burke's "dramatistic" line of questioning is adjusted according to the writer's purpose. If the aim is reporting, then *what* predominates; if the aim is description, then *where* and *when* predominate; and so forth. An expansion of this paradigm, with examples and writing suggestions, can be found in William Irmscher's *Holt Guide to English* [19].

Another paradigmatic theory has been proposed by Frank D'Angelo [9]. He divides the typical patterns of organization into two classes, "static" (fixed in time and space) and "dynamic" (changing over time or through space). Static patterns include description, definition, analysis, enumeration, classification, exemplification, and comparison. Dynamic patterns include narration, process, and cause/effect. D'Angelo provides a general outline of expected development for each pattern; the writers then arrange previously generated material and develop new material to fill in the slots of the outline.

Richard Young, Alton Becker, and Kenneth Pike also produce a set of paradigms for generating and examining ideas; however, their theory encourages writers to view ideas not just as part of one pattern but as parts of many patterns [37]. Their "tagmemic" theory (from the Greek word for *arrangement*) asks writers to view a subject (whether it be an idea, event, or object) from three perspectives: as an unchanging entity, a dynamic process, and a system. Doing this enables the writer to discover how the subject is unique, how much it can change, and how it fits into larger systems. This multifaceted perspective on a subject leads the writer to new discoveries, new clusters of connections, and new ideas for presenting the material to an audience.

Although researchers may disagree on the importance of and connections between the steps, and may use different terms to describe activities, they agree in many respects on what is important in the writing process:

- Writing takes many forms, depending in each case on the writer's purpose and audience. Although a writer may develop certain writing habits, the writing process will vary with every writing occasion.

- Before writers begin writing, they need to find subjects and gather ideas and information to write about. There are many techniques that help writers do this; each writer needs to find the strategy or strategies that work best in a variety of writing situations.

- The need to put ideas on paper "correctly" may inhibit writers. By drafting quickly and suspending editing until a text is nearly complete, many writers can write first drafts closer to their original intentions.

- Many inexperienced writers do not distinguish between revising and editing. Revision allows writers to test drafts against their original intentions and to add, delete, and rearrange what they have produced until it suits their purpose and audience.

- Editing is an act of social etiquette, in which writers decide how closely they wish their texts to conform to accepted conventions of language, and adjust those texts accordingly. Writers who choose to violate these conventions take their audience and purpose into account and accept the consequences.

- Writing processes are recursive, not linear; only in the ideal world of textbooks do writers blithely choose an idea, make a neat outline, develop it, write about it, and make final cosmetic changes before presenting it to an audience. In reality, writers struggle, chew their pencils, cross out, go back, pause, reconsider, find other information, rack their brains, juggle ideas, fling curses, and even start over from scratch in the process of writing a text.

Familiarity with the writing process can make our teaching more productive. Students need to be encouraged to write frequently—and not always for grades—to make their own discoveries about the writing process. We can help by regularly allowing time for writing in class. (Many teachers, for instance, start each class with some writing time.) Students need to learn many different strategies to generate material so that they can find the ones that help them most. By introducing them to freewriting, brainstorming, grouping, paradigms, and other methods (not all at once), we can help them develop better writing habits. Questions of grammar, spelling, punctuation, and "where to start the next paragraph" often hinder students' attempts to draft texts; we can encourage them to postpone those worries until the editing stage, where they are properly addressed. Students also need to learn to revise their papers to suit their purposes and audiences; by scheduling draft review sessions, encouraging peer editing, and holding conferences, we can direct students' attention away from "error-hunting" to questions of arrangement, tone, voice, and so on.

Students will eventually have to learn to write for audiences outside a classroom and for purposes other than theme writing; we can provide them with opportunities to do so by designing our writing assignments to include other possibilities. We can give them time in class not only to write, but to plan, discuss, reflect on, and generate ideas that prompt writing, and can encourage them to practice these activities by collecting their drafts and prewritings when we take up papers for grading. (Of course, these preliminary materials shouldn't be marked or graded, but we can examine them for material to help our students. Students whose papers rely heavily on generalities can be encouraged to do more or different kinds of prewriting to generate concrete information; students who make only cosmetic editing changes can be encouraged to revise as well.) Above all, we can make our students aware of how they work as writers, help them work more efficiently as writers, and help them realize that writings are not merely products, but journeys—journeys of discovery, growth, and sometimes of liberation.

Annotated Bibliography of Suggested Readings

Below I list 37 works that deal, in part or totally, with the views of the writing process discussed above. This is by no means a complete bibliography of the subject, but it will provide the interested teacher with plenty of information and new leads to follow. Abbreviations used are *CCC, College Composition and Communication; CE, College English; RTE, Research in the Teaching of English.*

1. Beard, Ruth M. *An Outline of Piaget's Developmental Psychology for Students and Teachers.* New York: NAL, 1969.

   Contains sections on the development of intelligence, on each of Piaget's four stages of cognitive growth, and on the implications of these theories for teachers.

2. Britton, James, et al. *The Development of Writing Abilities (11–18).* London; Macmillan, 1975.

   A study of about 2,000 pieces of student writing, focusing on the relationships between writer and audience and the functions of the writing produced. Concludes that students are asked to produce types of writing that stifle rather than further learning, and that inhibit creativity and independent thought.

3. Burke, Kenneth. *A Grammar of Motives.* Englewood Cliffs, NJ: Prentice, 1945.

   Thought and language are symbolic forms of action, and can be regarded as dramatic. A "dramatistic pentad" of questions enables us to analyze motives by subdividing action into act, scene, agent, agency, and purpose.

4. Coles, William E., Jr. *Composing: Writing as a Self-Creating Process.* Rochelle Park, NJ: Hayden, 1974.

   A description of a semester's worth (30) of writing assignments centered around teaching and learning, in which students are encouraged to write to discover new information about themselves.

5. ——, *The Plural I: The Teaching of Writing.* New York: Holt, 1978.

   A description of a semester's worth of writing assignments centered around amateurism and professionalism. Students develop a productive self-awareness of themselves as writers in relationship to their subjects and audiences.

6. Comprone, Joseph. "Kenneth Burke and the Teaching of Writing." *CCC* 29 (1978):336–40.

   A restatement or translation of Burke's pentad of questions, with particular attention to ways in which it may be used in the classroom to help generate material.

7. Cooper, Charles R., and Lee Odell, eds. *Research on Composing: Points of Departure.* Urbana, IL: National Council of Teachers of English, 1978.

   Ten essays by well-known specialists, including Britton, Young, Emig, and Murray, covering major topics in the writing process and suggesting possible avenues for research.

8. Cowan, Gregory, and Elizabeth Cowan. *Writing.* New York: Wiley, 1980.

   A text containing numerous prewriting, rewriting, and revising strategies, along with writing assignments and student samples. A second edition by Elizabeth Cowan Neeld appeared in 1985 from Scott, Foresman.

9. D'Angelo, Frank J. *A Conceptual Theory of Rhetoric.* Cambridge, MA: Winthrop, 1975.

   Rhetorical forms are derived from linguistic concepts which reflect the processes of human cognition. These cognitive structures can be described through the use of heuristics which parallel rhetorical structures. D'Angelo's student text, *Process and Thought in Composition,* 3rd ed. (Boston: Little, Brown, 1985), contains on pages 21–30 descriptions of these heuristics and suggestions for their use as prewriting and organizing strategies.

10. Elbow, Peter. *Writing With Power.* New York: Oxford UP, 1981.

    Emphasizes writing as a way of gaining control of one's world; discusses freewriting, revision strategies, and peer editing. Many teaching suggestions, some of which are drawn from "reader response" critical theory.

11. ——, *Writing Without Teachers.* New York: Oxford UP, 1973.

    This brief text encourages writers to break away from traditional writing practices (such as outlining) and to use other means of invention (especially freewriting) to help writing grow. Contains many suggestions for peer revision.

12. Emig, Janet. *The Composing Processes of Twelfth Graders.* Urbana, IL: National Council of Teachers of English, 1971.

A study of the writing of eight twelfth graders, who were asked to compose aloud. Emig concludes that writers begin writing for themselves before they write for others and that they are more willing to spend time on and revise work written for themselves. Her methodology and case study approach are much imitated in later studies.

13. ———, *The Web of Meaning.* Upper Montclair, NJ: Boynton/Cook, 1983.

A collection of Emig's work on the writing process, including studies on getting started, writing as a way of learning, and paradigms for inquiry. Each essay is prefaced by an interview with Emig in which she discusses the concerns raised in that essay.

14. Faigley, Lester, and Stephen Witte. "Analyzing Revision." *CE* 32 (1981): 400–14.

An introductory study which distinguishes between two kinds of revision, surface (correcting minor flaws) and text-based (altering structure, etc.). It argues that students must be encouraged to regard text-based revision as an integral part of the writing process.

15. Flower, Linda, and John R. Hayes. "A Cognitive Process Theory of Writing." *CCC* 32 (1981): 365–87.

A "protocol analysis" of the work of student writers which isolates three important factors in composing: the writing environment, the writer's memory, and the writing process itself, which is "recursive and hierarchical." Further expansions of their work are included as essays in *Cognitive Processes in Writing,* ed. Lee W. Gregg and Erwin R. Steinberg (Hillsdale, NJ: Lawrence Erlbaum, 1980), pp. 3–50, and in *Writing,* vol. 2, ed. Carl H. Frederiksen and Joseph H. Dominic (Hillsdale, NJ: Erlbaum, 1981), pp. 39–58.

16. Foster, David. *A Primer for Writing Teachers: Theories, Theorists, Issues, Problems.* Montclair, NJ: Boynton/Cook, 1983.

As the title suggests, this book covers many issues in teaching writing: the traditional methods of instruction, modern theories of the writing process, testing, remediation, course design, and evaluation.

17. Freedman, Aviva, and Ian Pringle. *Reinventing the Rhetorical Tradition.* Conway, AK: L&S Books for the Canadian Council of Teachers of English, 1980.

Twenty essays exploring research into the writing process, by theoreticians including Emig, Kinneavy, Young, Britton, Murray, Corbett, and many others.

18. Goswami, Dixie, et al. *Writing in the Workplace.* U. Mass. at Boston, Dept. of English, Fall 1983.

Twenty-five unpublished case studies of writing processes of writers outside academe, in business, the sciences, and government.

19. Irmscher, William. *The Holt Guide to English,* 3rd ed. New York: Holt, 1981.

A student text which contains a number of prewriting strategies, including an expansion of Burke's pentad, with further questions and student examples (pp. 26–44).

20. Kantor, Kenneth. "Classroom Contexts and the Development of Writing Intuitions: An Ethnographic Case Study." *RTE* 17 (1983): 72–94.

A study of writing by seven advanced twelfth graders in a creative writing class shows that an emphasis on expressive writing and on revision, in conjunction with peer editing, leads to improved writing.

21. Kneupper, Charles W. "Revising the Tagmemic Heuristic: Theoretical and Pedagogical Considerations." *CCC* 31 (1980): 160–68.

A simplification of Young, Becker, and Pike's tagmemic system into a six-element heuristic which can be used in the classroom.

22. Lindemann, Erika. *A Rhetoric for Writing Teachers.* New York: Oxford UP, 1982.

An overview of theories and research in the teaching of writing, with suggestions for classroom applications. A comprehensive and accessible summary for beginnners and experts alike, with much specific information and a long bibliography.

23. Macrorie, Ken. *Searching Writing.* Rochelle Park, NJ: Hayden, 1980.

A text that encourages students to seek truth, not clichés, to let subjects choose them, to defy rules and follow intuitions, and to seek information that will affect the writers' lives when writing. Contains Macrorie's answer to the research paper: The "I-Search," which stems from students' desire to find answers to questions and problems they confront in their lives.

24. ———, *Writing to be Read,* 2nd ed. Rochelle Park, NJ: Hayden, 1976.

Emphasizes freewriting, truth-telling, and the exploration of striking contradictions, such as signs reading "Slow Men Working" (which Macrorie calls "fabulous realities"), as ways of exploring and developing ideas. Encourages writers to "amaze themselves" and to use writing to gain control over their own lives.

25. Mandel, Barrett. "Losing One's Mind: Learning to Write and Edit." *CCC* 29 (1978): 362–68.

Author says we must put aside our preconceptions about writing and the writing process and admit that prewriting does not *cause* writing to happen; rather it "establishes a frame of mind in which writing is likely to occur." Likewise, editing is not revising, but an expression of the relationship between author and reader; writers who decide not to edit do so at the risk of alienating their readers, and they must be aware of this possibility.

26. ———, "The Writer Writing Is Not at Home." *CCC* 31 (1980): 372–77.

Writers must stop trying to force writing to fit preconceived expectations, and instead experiment with both freewriting and rote writing (imitation of models, especially of eighteenth-century prose styles) to develop new ideas and stylistic devices.

27. Moffett, James. *Teaching the Universe of Discourse.* Boston: Houghton, 1968.

A theory of discourse drawing on students' cognitive development to produce writings on increasingly abstract levels. The relationship between speaker and audience and between speaker and subject is emphasized.

28. Moffett, James, and Betty Jane Wagner. *Student-Centered Language Arts and Reading. K-13,* 3rd ed. Boston: Houghton, 1983.

A complete language arts text based on Moffett's spiraling theory of the writing process, complete with readings, writing assignments, and student examples.

29. Murray, Donald M. *A Writer Teaches Writing,* 2nd ed. Boston: Houghton, 1985.

A book of advice for writers who are teachers, teachers who are writers, and nearly everyone else involved with the writing process. Sections on freewriting, discovery, revision, and many teaching strategies which help students develop their full potentials as writers. Concludes with a long bibliography of readings and writings for and by writers.

30. Odell, Lee, and Dixie Goswami. "Writing in a Nonacademic Setting." *New Directions in Composition Research.* Ed. Richard Beach and Lillian S. Bridwell, New York: Guilford, 1984.

A case study of the writing of eleven employees at a social services agency revealed that these writers had highly developed senses of purpose, audience, and subject and had clear notions of what constituted "acceptable" style for the kinds of writing they composed.

31. Rico, Gabriele Lusser. *Writing the Natural Way: Using Right-Brain Techniques to Release Your Expressive Powers.* New York: Tarcher (St. Martin's), 1983.

A book to help writers learn to "cluster" ideas to generate pieces of writing, and to find patterns and revise the material generated through the use of "right-brain techniques" drawn from cognitive research.

32. Rohman, D. Gordon, and Albert O. Wlecke. *Pre-Writing: The Construction and Application of Models for Concept-Formation in Writing.* USOE Cooperative Research Project No. 2174. East Lansing: Michigan State University, 1964.

The writing process can be separated into three distinct stages: prewriting, writing, and rewriting. Prewriting is a process by which writers learn to consciously imitate cognitive processes of information assimilation; techniques such as journal-keeping, written meditation, and analogy construction help writers imitate those processes.

33. Sommers, Nancy, "Responding to Student Writing." *CCC* 33 (1982): 148–56.

Students confuse revision with correction because teachers' comments have traditionally focused on errors in editing. When teachers focus their comments on matters of arrangement, development, and tone, rather than simply on mechanics, students respond by paying more attention to revision.

34. ———, "Revision Strategies of Student Writers and Experienced Adult Writers. *CCC* 31 (1980): 378–88.

Suggests that major differences between student and experienced writers are the manner and amounts of their revisions; students make few revisions and focus on editing for correctness, while adults are more willing to make revisions and reshape and restructure their material to meet the needs of an audience.

35. Tate, Gary, and Edward P. J. Corbett, eds. *The Writing Teacher's Sourcebook.* New York: Oxford UP, 1981.

Thirty-two essays on composition theory and/or practice, representing the work of many major theorists.

The contents stress the connections between research and classroom applications. Contains many bibliographic references. A second edition is forthcoming.

36. Winterowd, W. Ross, ed. *Contemporary Rhetoric: A Conceptual Background with Readings.* San Diego: Harcourt, 1975.

Twenty-four essays elucidating the theoretical backgrounds of composition teaching; the essays are abstract but readable, and while some of the material has been superseded by more recent work, the essays and bibliographies still provide much useful information.

37. Young, Richard E., Alton L. Becker, and Kenneth L. Pike. *Rhetoric: Discovery and Change.* San Diego: Harcourt, 1970.

A student text which introduces and explains the "tagmemic" way of gaining perspective on a writing subject. Complete with writing assignments, heuristics, and student examples.

THE HISTORY OF RHETORIC: AN OVERVIEW

WILLIAM F. WOODS

From its beginnings in Sicily around 450 B.C., rhetoric has been known as the art or "science" of persuasive discourse, the theory and practice of how to use available means of persuasion to affect the opinions of an audience. The earliest known treatise on rhetoric, by Corax of Syracuse, was a response to the citizens' need to speak well in litigations over land rights. A little more than a century later, Aristotle wrote his famous *Rhetoric* [item 6 in the Annotated Bibliography, below], a work based on a systematic description of persuasive oratory as it was practiced in the law courts and the assembly of Athens. The key to Aristotle's approach to persuasion is *probability*. Logic can demonstrate a truth, but rhetoric can show that a position is worthy or belief—that it has a high probability of being true. Thus, while logical proofs are to be preferred in philosophical or scientific works, the persuasiveness of rhetoric is more effective in speaking or writing about practical affairs, and for a general audience.

Aristotle's *Rhetoric* assumes that there are three modes of appeal that can be used to reach an audience: the appeal to logic or reason (*logos*, in the Greek), the appeal to emotion *(pathos)*, and the appeal to the moral or ethical sense *(ethos)*. In themselves, these modes are only guidelines—ways of orienting the speaker to the task. However, each of the modes was also associated with certain kinds of discourse, as well as with the rhetorical devices proper to that sort of appeal. Perhaps the easiest way to give the flavor of

WILLIAM F. WOODS *is Associate Professor of English at Wichita State University, where he teaches medieval literature and the history of rhetoric. He attended Dartmouth College (B.A.), the University of Chicago (M.A.), and Indiana University (Ph.D.). He has also served aboard the USS Saratoga (CVA-60), attended the Université de Grenoble, and taught at Cleveland State University. Some of his recent published articles are "Nineteenth-Century Psychology and the Teaching of Writing,"* College Composition and Communication 36 *(February 1985): 20–41; "The Reform Tradition in Nineteenth-Century Composition Teaching,"* Written Communication 2 *(October 1985): 377–90; and "The Cultural Tradition of Nineteenth-Century 'Traditional' Grammar Teaching,"* Rhetoric Society Quarterly 15 *(nos. 1–2, 1985): 3–12. At present he is working on a history of composition in America in the nineteenth and twentieth centuries.*

Aristotle's rhetoric is to describe some of the devices he suggests for appealing to the mind, heart, and moral character of an audience.

As Aristotle saw it, the appeal to reason *(logos)* involved the use of certain basic concepts—fundamental, universally recognized formulas for thinking and expressing thought. Aristotle calls them the "common topics," because they are the commonplaces of thought. *Definition,* for example, is the classification of a subject, which in practice means identifying it by placing it in a class with other similar things (e.g., Man is an animal) and then further defining it by pointing out characteristics *(differentiae)* that distinguish it from the other things in that class (Man is a rational animal—"an animal that thinks"). The other topics that belong to the appeal to reason are as familiar and essential to us as definition. *Comparison* brings out the similarity, the difference, and the degree of difference between two subjects. *Relationship* refers to patterns such as cause and effect, antecedent and consequence, contraries, and contradictions. *Circumstance* refers to the process we go through in deciding whether something is or was possible or impossible, given the particular circumstances; here we are defining the subject in relation to its occasion, or context.

These common topics were not originated by Aristotle, of course. He merely gave them names, grouped them, and showed how they function in persuasive discourse. In the history of rhetoric since Aristotle, however, the topics have been one of the most useful and enduring parts of classical rhetorical theory. In the Middle Ages and the Renaissance, they were adapted to theories of logical proof. In the nineteenth and twentieth centuries they have been used mainly as patterns for the development and organization of paragraphs and essays. All of these uses are valid, for the topics are simply a formalized reflection of the ways in which we think, and so they enter into every intellectual task. Indeed, we need to keep in mind that the topics are both fundamental and versatile, hard to pigeonhole. They are handy for organizing one's thoughts, for shaping a paragraph, for arranging an essay—but they can also lend incisive clarity to efforts to revise a piece of writing; they can be a productive guide to the solving of a problem; and they can help writers to think about a subject in ways that will extend the material, unfolding its implications. That is why Aristotle also identified the topics as aids to *invention,* or the *discovery* of arguments for or against a position.

The second kind of appeal Aristotle talks about *(pathos)* is the appeal to the emotions—to the heart. Aristotle recognized that the most powerful appeals are those that harness the primal human emotions, our tendencies to feel protectiveness, anger, envy, pride, fear, desire. Aristotle and the rhetoricians who came after him devoted considerable thought to what we would call "audience psychology"—the types of emotions, and the types of people who experience them—but they also tried to identify the kinds of subjects that would evoke such an emotional response. What are the types of description, they asked, that powerfully involve an audience by helping them to place themselves within an imagined experience? What are the phrases and the words associated with deeply felt issues? And then there were the stylistic effects associated with emotional states. The periodic or suspended sentence, for instance, was thought to create tension and a feeling of building to climax. The "rhetorical" question had its place here, as did the use of exaggeration (hyperbole), metaphor, and various other figures of speech. The study of style has always been closely connected with the appeal to the emotions. That is why the Sophists, professional orators who flourished about the second century A.D., were both praised and condemned for their panegyrics (elaborate eulogies and other ceremonial speeches) which appealed to the emotions but were not always calculated to inspire careful thought.

The third mode of appeal *(ethos)* is best described as a perceived relationship between the character of the speaker or writer, and the social and ethical beliefs of the audience. It is an appeal to ethical values, perhaps, but it also has much to do with the ability of the audience to *identify* with the speaker, to accept him or her as someone who speaks for *them.* This appeal derives as much from the personal qualities of a speaker or writer, perhaps, as its does from the overt content of the discourse. "Is this a person like us, who shares our values, and whose opinion can be trusted?" These are the sorts of questions addressed by the ethical appeal, which has a great deal to do with the *tone* of a piece of writing, and therefore with its syntax and choice of words. Tone also depends on the purpose of the discourse (to explain, persuade, entertain, etc.), and on the level of style adopted by the writer or speaker. Classical rhetoricians after Aristotle liked to identify three levels of style: (1) the high, or grand style (appropriate for epics and for the sublime, highflown passages of persuasive oratory); (2) the middle ("pleasing," ornate) style associated with literary works and with ceremonial oratory; and (3) the low or plain style associated with the language of instruction and everyday affairs. More recently, linguists have tended to identify levels of style by their social function. For instance, Martin Joos [14] identifies five levels of usage: frozen (genteel), formal, consultative, casual, and intimate.

It is worth noting that Aristotle's three modes of appeal—*logos, pathos* and *ethos*—reflect a basic way in which western culture has conceived or "pictured" the mind ever since the days of Plato. We say *mind, body,* and *spirit,*—or *reason, memory, imagination*—as if thought and substance were somehow united by a perceptive consciousness: our bond with the world outside us and the source of our state of being. Indeed, there is a basic "threeness" that runs through classical discussions of art and psychology like a magic thread. For example, beginning, middle, and end stood for the parts of a narrative or dramatic plot (Aristotle again). Invention, arrangement (organization), and style were the three essential phases of composition as classical rhetoricians described it. That is, writers first *discover* and gather together their materials, then they *arrange* them, and finally they *express* them in language that is appropriate to the aim, audience, and circumstances of the discourse. Memory and the techniques of delivery were also included as parts of rhetoric, but they were not directly involved in what we in our industrial age call the "process" of writing. The actual teaching of rhetoric in classical times again took the form of a sequential, three-stage program: *precept,* the learning of principles; *practice,* under the supervision of a grammar or rhetoric teacher; and *imitation* of the style and structure of various model passages.

As oratory gave way to written rhetoric in the seventeenth and eighteenth centuries (a recurrent trend, in the history of rhetoric), it became easier to characterize discourse by its literary form rather than by its appeal to an audience. Whereas ancient oratory had been divided into deliberative (persuasive), epideictic (ceremonial), and judicial (courtroom) oratory, the rhetorical spectrum by the 1700s had broadened to admit formal letters (epistles), history, argument, narration, description, persuasion, and poetry. Since spoken and written discourse were both represented, it was now customary to describe them as the art of "rhetoric and belles lettres" (borrowing a term from French literary criticism, which was then enjoying a period of authority). The theory of rhetoric was also changing. Rhetoricians had followed the empiricist philosophers (e.g., Locke) in assuming that language and thought reflected sense impressions, especially those received through sight. They further assumed that the forms of discourse must derive from the different patterns of language we use to record our perceptions, to form a "point of view," and to influence the opinions (views) of others. For example, we record our perceptions of things (thus, *descriptive* writing); we record our perceptions of events, or "things in action" (*narrative* writing); we interpret the pattern, or "logic" of relationships in the things and events perceived (*expository,* or explanatory writing); finally, we arrange our perceptions as proof, in support of our point of view (*argumentative* writing; "persuasion" generally meant spoken persuasive discourse). Authors of nineteenth-century textbooks on written rhetoric ("composition") found in these four terms, and in the kinds of writing they implied, a comprehensive schema for describing the teaching of writing.

These four "modes of discourse" [15] (which had little or nothing to do with Aristotle's three modes of appeal) where a typical feature of composition textbooks after 1850; they continued to shape teachers' approaches to English composition for at least the next hundred years. Rightly or wrongly, the four modes are now associated with the more conservative side of nineteenth-century composition teaching, which borrowed much from traditional methods of teaching English (and before that, Latin) grammar. There were other emphases, other theories at work in nineteenth-century composition teaching, but that period is remembered mainly for its drills, for the practice of having students memorize principles of grammar and style, for its increasing tendency to stress exposition (essay writing), and for giving first priority to the structuring of sentences, paragraphs, and essays. There was also a pedagogy associated with the rigorous methods and the sometimes endearing eccentricities of writing masters and textbooks writers, such as Alexander Bain, George Quackenbos, and A. S. (Adams Sherman) Hill.

But while the main thrust of nineteenth-century rhetoric and composition teaching was on style and structure, the *character* of the speaker or writer was beginning to receive a new emphasis. In a time when political, religious, and artistic individualism was much respected, the mental nature of the individual thinker, writer, and student became a serious subject of inquiry. The ultimate results of this spirit of romantic individualism, and the studies of child nature that accompanied it, can be seen today in the contemporary work of James Britton [8], a British educator specializing in research on student writing.

Britton's central insight was that written discourse can be described in terms of "function categories" (see Figure One) which represent what the writer is doing, in each case, in the act of writing. Writing is no longer seen as reflecting three aspects of the mind; rather, writing is assumed to represent three basic types of observed language behavior (which may, of course, reflect three types of mental activity).

In Britton's first function category, the *transcactional,* students are participating in a problem, discus-

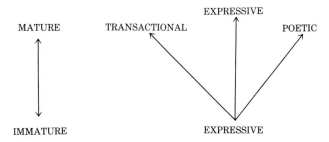

Figure One

sion, or other event: they are getting things done with words. The language relates closely to the needs of the audience and to the features of the task at hand. Language here is seen as a means to an end. In the second category, the *expressive,* the students express their responses to an outside situation in language that relates closely to their own points of view or inner experiences of the situation. Here the language is less a way of getting things done than it is a way of putting feelings into an intelligible form; thus, expressive discourse probably serves the writer's needs more than it does the needs of the audience; or the demands of the task at hand. In the third category, the *poetic,* the writer is a spectator to the problem or situation at hand and uses language that relates closely to the overall concept, or "global context," of what is being done, created, or argued. Here the writer is more a disinterested analyst than a participator in an interactive task or someone trying to verbalize an inner experience.

The striking difference between Britton's system and the classical rhetorics is the centrality of the expressive or personal, aspect of writing. Britton assumes that child language *begins* as expressive discourse and diversifies as the child grows older; the transactional and poetic modes are gradually acquired, and the resources of the expressive mode are further developed. So while Aristotle's three modes of appeal were intended as ways of describing the impact of discourse on an audience, Britton's function categories are ways of identifying the kinds of discourse that emerge from three kinds of writing behavior. To put it another way, while Aristotle's modes are reader-oriented, Britton's categories are writer-oriented, since they describe discourse as the reflection of mental processes associated with certain adaptive social behaviors. Because of this emphasis on behavior, Britton's discussions are helpful to teachers trying to figure out "where students are coming from" in each of the various assignments that they write. Also, Britton's work may be a corrective influence on those who think of expressive discourse as a sloppy aberration from expository writing, or believe it should surface only in creative writing courses. Despite some real differences in theoretical orientation, however, Aristotle and Britton are not mutually exclusive. Teachers who have studied Aristotle's account of the appeals to the reason and the emotions will probably arrive at a better appreciation of Britton's transactional and poetic functions than those who come to Britton with no preparation in rhetoric.

In fact, even though social and historical conditions are vastly different now than they were in ancient Greece, Aristotle's *Rhetoric* continues to stand us in good stead, for the the truth is that there have been no modern Aristotles, and no modern rhetoric has made the impact on rhetorical tradition that Aristotle's work did. James Kinneavy [11] has come as close to that goal as anyone, perhaps, in his attempt to write a comprehensive modern theory of rhetoric, or "discourse," as he calls it, to allow for the enlarged role of writing in modern communication.

Kinneavy's achievement is to distinguish the basic kinds of discourse and describe the forms and characteristics that are essential to each of them. He derives four kinds of discourse from a theory of communication which he expresses by the familiar "communication triangle" (see Figure Two). The three points of the triangle refer to (1) the *writer,* (2) the *audience,* and (3) the *subject* of discourse, while the body of the triangle refers to (4) the *signal,* which is, in this case, the written language that conveys the message.

Each of these four terms is the point of origin for one of the four *aims,* the purposes for which we produce discourse: (1) discourse that derives from the point of view or "inner experience" of the writer is *expressive* (as in Britton's function theory); (2) discourse that is oriented more toward the audience's concerns, ideas, and feelings is called *persuasive* (as in Aristotle's theory of rhetoric); (3) Discourse that is meant to represent accurately a subject of investigation is called *reference* discourse—this aim includes the non-persuasive aspects of most academic and scientific writing, as well as what we call *expository* prose; (4) discourse that is self-referential or mimetic in purpose and that is meant to be used or enjoyed for its own sake is called *literary* discourse or literature (similar to Britton's *poetic* function category but not synonymous with it).

Unlike Britton, Kinneavy is not concerned mainly with the development of students' discourse toward maturity. His emphasis is on the description of the kinds of writing and on their use, rather than on the way they evolve in childhood or the ways they have evolved in history. We can generalize by calling Kinneavy's work a comprehensive, painstaking description of the ways prose writing is used or under-

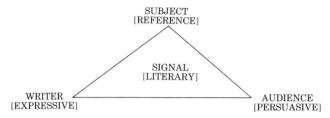

Figure Two (Adapted from Kinneavy)

stood, in the twentieth century. In this sense his work is reminiscent of Aristotle's systematic, analytical description of persuasive oratory in fourth-century Athens. A basic understanding of Kinneavy's four aims lends a perspective on written communication; moreover, it gives us a way of thinking about the entire profession of teaching writing. For example, it makes sense of the differences between the kinds of writing we find in personal experience papers and term papers. It also helps in defining the intellectual tasks we expect students to carry out when they write a particular assignment; for instance, a term paper is predominantly a piece of reference discourse and requires the skills of observation, distinction, comparison, and so forth. In general, teachers who know the four aims, and the features associated with them, can shape their students' writing with more confidence because they will have a better sense of the goals of each assignment. And for those who wish to backtrack Kinneavy's research and pursue their own investigations in one direction or another, full bibliographies are appended to each chapter of his book.

If there is a moral to be drawn from this lightning sketch of a few important works on rhetoric and composition, it is that a little knowledge is not a dangerous thing, but our only salvation. Not one of us has the time or dedication to absorb over two thousand years of rhetorical treatises, debates, and biases; even to desire such a thing is to miss the point badly. Our goal as teachers of writing is rather, by knowing something of the needs, ideas, and practices of former times, to understand more deeply and truly what we are engaged in doing, and where we are tending. Neither Aristotle nor Kinneavy should be adopted as teachers' manuals. These two books, as well as the others that we have examined or that are listed in the bibliography, are parts of the history of our profession, and should be sampled, experimented with, and pondered as we proceed with our own teaching, in our own times, in our own ways. To do so is to use history well; in so doing, we become rhetoricians—and enter history.

Annotated Bibliography of Suggested Readings

I. HISTORIES OF RHETORIC

1. Horner, Winifred, et al. *Historical Rhetoric: An Annotated Bibliography of Selected Sources in English*. Boston: Hall, 1980.

2. Howell, Wilbur S. *Eighteenth-Century British Logic and Rhetoric*. Princeton: Princeton UP, 1971.

3. ———, *Logic and Rhetoric in England, 1500–1700*. Princeton: Princeton UP, 1956.

   The classic study of the changes rhetoric went through in response to the birth of empirical science and the resurgence of classical learning in the period between the early English Renaissance and the end of the seventeenth century. This book, and its sequel, are remarkable for their comprehensive range of scholarship, but readers should be wary of Howell's insistence on logic as the dominant theme of this period in the history of rhetoric.

4. Kennedy, George A. *Classical Rhetoric and Its Classical and Christian Tradition from Ancient to Modern Times*. Berkeley: California UP, 1980.

   A reliable overview of rhetoric in its cultural tradition, but weak in the periods following the Middle Ages. For those interested in Greek and Roman rhetoric, Kennedy's specialized works in those areas are considered standard.

5. Murphy, James J. *Rhetoric in the Middle Ages*. Berkely: California UP, 1974.

   The best survey of medieval rhetoric now available.

II. CLASSICAL THEORIES OF RHETORIC

6. Aristotle. *Rhetoric and Poetics,* trans. Rhys Carpenter and Ingram Bywater. New York: Modern Library, 1984.

   This edition, which competes with the Lane Cooper translation published by Cornell University Press, has the added benefit of a new preface by Edward P. J. Corbett, who edited the volume and contributed some useful bibliographies and notes to the text. Available in paperback.

7. Quintilian. *Institutio Oratoria,* trans. H. E. Butler. Loeb Classical Library. 4 vols. New York: Putnam's, 1921–1922.

   Quintilian was a teacher of rhetoric in Rome, under the Empire. His "Institute" of rhetoric is a thorough-going description of the art as it was practiced and taught during his times. Particularly interesting for our purposes as teachers of writing is his discussion of the kind of education a young orator should receive as a preparation for public life.

III. RHETORIC AND COMPOSITION: DEVELOPMENTAL THEORIES

8. Britton, James, et al. *The Development of Writing Abilities (11–18)*. London: Macmillan Education, 1975.

   Considered one of the classic studies of how writing skills develop in young students. Britton offers a theory of composition based on extensive surveys of children's writing, but the essentials of the theory are not difficult for the average teacher to follow; most people find that Britton's ideas help them think clearly about the flood of data that confronts them in their students' papers.

9. Moffett, James. *Teaching the Universe of Discourse*. Boston: Houghton, 1956.

   Helpful in understanding the neo-progressive or student-centered attitudes toward teaching writing that dominated the Dartmouth Conference (1966) and were later to produce the "open classroom" and other methods that we now associate with the late 1960s and early 1970s.

IV. RHETORIC AND COMPOSITION: THEORIES OF DISCOURSE

10. Hirsch, E. D., Jr. *The Philosophy of Composition*. Chicago: Chicago UP, 1977.

    Known as a conservative approach to the theory of composition, Hirsch's book was nevertheless based on a careful study of the current research on discourse production and deserves a close reading.

11. Kinneavy, James. *A Theory of Discourse*. 1971. New York: Norton, 1980.

    Classifies the kinds of discourse according to purpose and describes the features associated with each of these purposes, or "aims." Kinneavy's book is perhaps the reigning theory of discourse in the profession today because of his attempt to ground it in the scholarship of linguistics, literature, communications, and philosophy. Teachers will probably find Kinneavy's basic theory easy to remember and apply; his extensive descriptions of the kinds of discourse associated with the four aims are somewhat harder going.

12. Young, Richard E., et al. *Rhetoric: Discovery and Change*. San Diego: Harcourt, 1970.

    One of the significant modern attempts to develop a "new" rhetoric that would describe more accurately the processes of inquiry and discovery writers go through in developing a project. This is the place to read about Young's now famous nine-cell matrix, an inventional device that supplements the classical topics of invention.

V. RHETORIC AND COMPOSITION: STYLE

13. Gibson, Walker. *Tough, Sweet, and Stuffy: An Essay on Modern American Prose Styles*. Bloomington: Indiana UP, 1966.

    A readable, yet relatively sophisticated attempt to characterize prose styles by classifying their choice of words, syntax, and other features. Helpful for analyzing the appeal of advertising copy, as well as the "stuffiness" of academic writing.

14. Joos, Martin. *The Five Clocks*. Bloomington: Indiana UP, 1962.

    A modern classification of the levels of style by reference to their use in a social context.

VI. RHETORIC AND COMPOSITION: SECONDARY SOURCES

15. Connors, Robert J. "The Rise and Fall of the Modes of Discourse." *College Composition and Communication* 32 (1981): 444–55.

    A capsule history of the growth and then the decline in popularity of the four "modes": description, narration, exposition, and argumentation. Gives a useful bird's-eye view of the profession of teaching writing during the last two hundred years.

16. Ong, Walter J. "The Writer's Audience Is Always a Fiction." *PMLA* 90 (1975): 9–21.

    In this milestone essay, Ong shows that writers project their own sense of an audience—something that teachers and writers had always suspected but were unable to discuss with any degree of clarity or certainty.

17. Tate, Gary, ed. *Teaching Composition: Ten Bibliographical Essays*. Fort Worth: Texas Christian UP, 1976.

    Comprehensive overview of research in major areas related to composition and rhetoric. A new edition is in press.

18. Tate, Gary, and Edward P. J. Corbett, eds. *The Writing Teacher's Sourcebook*. New York: Oxford UP, 1982.

    A standard aid for background research in rhetoric and composition.

LINGUISTICS FOR COMPOSITION TEACHERS: AN OVERVIEW

ALICE M. ROY

We write in a language. This means that we need to use words, phrases, and sentences that are similar to but not always the same as those we use in speaking a language. Speaking is primary, writing secondary, in that we learn speaking first and also in that it is quite possible to go through life without writing but not "natural" to go through life without speaking. In college, however, writing becomes primary. Our own dialect affects our writing. Further, our communal history of attitudes toward grammar and usage affects readers' perceptions of our writing, and ours of theirs. Still further, how we learn a language, whether a first or second language, affects how we may learn to write or teach others to write. We can get a window on written language by looking at some features of spoken language.

HOW DO SPEAKING AND WRITING DIFFER?

Many years ago Roman Jakobson [item 9 in the Annotated Bibliography, below] described six basic functions of verbal communication. His list of functions is instructive as we consider the amazingly complex task we undertake, trying to do in writing what we achieve so unconsciously in speaking. Jakobson pointed out, first (though these are not in any sense an ordered list), an *emotive* function, through which we transmit an attitude toward what we are speaking about; second, a *connative* function through which we send a request to the hearer about how to respond, such as "Act!" or "Believe" or "Know"; third, a *referential*

ALICE M. ROY is Assistant Professor of Linguistics and English at California State University, Los Angeles, and directs the Freshman Writing Program there. She has Master's Degrees in English and in Linguistics with a concentration in Teaching English as a Second Language and holds a Ph. D. in Linguistics from the University of Michigan. She has published articles on discourse analysis, and her article "Alliance for Literacy" appeared in College Composition and Communication in 1984. She is co-chair of the Committee on English as a Second Language for the Conference on College Composition and Communication and gives workshops on writing and second language acquisition at the national meetings of the Conference. She serves on the editorial boards of College Composition and Communication and the Journal of Basic Writing.

function in that we talk to each other *about* something.

Our speaking also serves to check whether our hearer is listening, understanding, attending to our communication: Jakobson called this the *phatic* function. We can ask actual questions, such as "Do you agree?" but usually we check our listener's state with raised intonation, or with fillers like "Y'know," or with facial expressions and body language such as raised eyebrows, smiles, and hand gestures. The two remaining functions in the communicative act are the *metalingual* and the *poetic*. We use the former when we talk about how we are talking, giving cues such as "What I really meant to say was . . . ." We display the latter when we use language in special ways, playing with the language itself, making puns, and manipulating linguistic resources creatively.

What a richness there is in the shared act of speaking and hearing. How can all this be accomplished in writing? It is clear that speaking and writing are integrally linked, and equally clear that they are not identical. The writer must do in words and structures what the speaker can do with intonation, facial expressions, and body gestures. Further, the speaker can rely on conversational conventions such as those described by conversational analysts. These researchers show that feedback is either immediately forthcoming or can be asked for, a luxury the writer does not have. There is also in the speaking situation a community of shared assumptions: usually we're talking to people who already understand who we are, how we feel about things, and how we're likely to respond to what *they* say when they respond to us—more luxuries the writer doesn't have. Often, particularly in college writing, we're sending something out in an amorphous arena, the "paper" for the college course to the professor who stands for the generalized educated reading public.

When a writer succeeds in communicating phatic, referential, and metalinguistic messages, we say the writer has achieved "reader-based" prose [5]. If a writer relies too much on the shared assumptions of close friends or people in a fairly close cultural community, however, then the writer risks producing "writer-based" prose. In this case, readers who do not know the writer well, or who perhaps are not part of the immediate cultural community, are left out of the communicative interaction. The writer does not succeed in transmitting the message, whether the source of stimulation is the writer's own wish to communicate or an outside assignment, as is normally the case in college writing.

Although there are some difficulties inherent in the differences between speaking and writing, writing offers the tremendous advantage that it can be changed and even erased before it is offered to the world. When thoughts are spoken, they are irrevocable—there's no taking back even when we say "I take it back." The fluidity involved in writing, the flexibility of expression, is especially apparent as we move into the era of writing with word processors.

HOW DOES DIALECT AFFECT WRITING?

Another way that speaking can differ from writing is in the area of dialect. In popular usage, "dialect" is something *other people* speak. Someone else's dialect differs from our own mainly in pronunciation, but we may also notice differences in vocabulary (is it a "hoagie" or a "submarine"? or "seesaw" or a "teeter-totter"?), and we are very aware of differences in grammar. When someone's grammar differs greatly from what we are used to calling "correct" English, we might just say that person doesn't use "good English." Linguists, however, would refer to that person's speech as dialect.

Each of us speaks a dialect—it is impossible not to. Our dialect is a result of many factors: where we lived as a child; where we have lived since childhood; where our parents lived when they were young; our parents' education, occupation, and income; our own age, sex, and ethnicity. Most of us are not surprised to learn that where we live and even where our parents lived contribute a great deal to our way of speaking. These are regional factors and we are familiar with them. The role of socieconomic factors in our speech—education, occupation, and income—is harder to realize and perhaps to accept. We are taught from early grade school that our country was founded on the principle of a "classless" society. However, the work of sociolinguists such as William Labov [11] has shown clearly that these social and economic factors have much to do with how we speak—with our pronunciation and especially with our grammar. In fact, dialect studies have shown that while pronunciation may differ more from region to region, grammar differs more across classes. That is, while someone from Boston may *sound* very different to us compared with someone from Dallas or Philadelphia or Chicago, the *grammar* of middle-class speakers of any one of those cities will be much more like that of middle-class speakers from the other cities than it will be like the grammar

of lower-class speakers in that same city. Grammar, of course, shows up more in writing than pronunciation does. In some instances, however, pronunciation affects grammar. For example, for many speakers of the dialect known as Black English, the second consonant in a "consonant cluster" may not be pronounced. A consonant cluster occurs when two or more consonants appear together, as they do at the end of words such as *cold* or *left*. When we consider that adding the regular past tense to any verb that ends in a consonant is automatically going to create such a cluster—*name* plus *d* gives us a cluster of *m* plus *d* (since the *e* is not pronounced)—we can see that pronunciation and grammar are in many ways interconnected.

Dialect and writing are related also because written standard English, or what some writers call Edited American English (EAE), is a dialect itself, a special form of English. E. D. Hirsch in his *The Philosophy of Composition* [8] explains that no one in fact *speaks* EAE—it exists only in writing. (Hirsch's "readability" formulas have been generally rejected by the writing profession, but his useful discussion of the differences between speaking and writing can be considered separately.) Thus everyone to some extent has to acquire a new dialect in learning to write EAE. For those writers whose spoken dialect is closer at the outset to the grammar used in EAE, the learning task may not be so great as it is for those whose spoken dialect is quite different grammatically. The ease with which a learner apprehends EAE, depends on more than the dialect forms, however, since we know that our dialect is dependent upon our parents' education, occupation, and income, among other factors. While it may seem that dialect depends on education (a good education helps a person learn to speak "better"), in fact the more likely reality is that education depends to a large extent on dialect—what kind of schools are available, what kind of reading and writing activities go on there, and so on. Thus, a speaker of a dialect that differs greatly from EAE may struggle more because of lack of familiarity with literature—with reading and writing as part of a tradition of communication—than merely because of dialect differences.

HOW DO USAGE AND DIALECT AND GRAMMAR INTERACT?

Closely linked to the issue of the relationship of dialect to writing is that of usage. For some people, usage means grammatical features such as the third person singular -s required for subject–verb agreement in standard spoken English; for others, usage includes stylistic options such as the use of an adverb in between the *to* and the verb of an infinitive. For example, on the *Star Trek* television show, and later the

Star Trek movies, the mission of the space voyagers was "to boldly go . . ." where none had gone before. Under the traditional Latinate rule for English usage, such a construction as "to boldly go" would not be acceptable, because a Latin infinitive was all one word and thus could not possibly have an adverb in the middle. As long as Latin was held as the model for English, such usages, though entirely common in normal English speech over many hundreds of years, could not be condoned. How much attention to give "usage" has been a problem for grammarians for many centuries. As far back as Greek and Roman times, we find disagreement among grammarians as to whether usage should be taken into account in describing or defining a language.

In the eighteenth century, because of the high prestige of Latin, which was viewed as an elegant and logical and unchanging language, because of the new middle class wish for how-to books on speaking and writing, and because writers like Jonathan Swift worried that they would not be understood in a hundred years if the language were not protected against change, scholars and grammarians like Samuel Johnson codified many of the grammatical "rules" that have led to the usage problems we struggle with today. For example, Chaucer used the form "It am me," whereas we are now taught (and have been for a couple of hundred years) that we must say "it is *I*." Because Latin required the same ending on the noun or adjective after any form of *be* as that which was attached to the subject (that is, the nominative ending), eighteenth-century grammarians felt that English should also behave that way. Similarly, in earlier periods of our history the use of *they* for the indefinite personal pronoun was quite all right; however, Johnson and other scholars of the time felt that it was illogical to use the plural pronoun referring to a singular antecedent, so they endorsed "Does everyone have *his* ticket?" rather than "*their* ticket." For most of us, "their ticket" remains the most likely choice in speaking, unless we are in a situation that calls for more careful speech, in which case we may be able to think ahead and produce "his," or we may avoid it altogether, or we may correct ourselves part way through. Today especially we feel that the illogic of having the masculine pronoun stand for the female half of the population is at least as serious as the singular–plural disjunction that led to this rule in the first place, and so writers and speakers try to say "his or her," "her or his," and sometimes just "her."

Up to approximately the beginning of the twentieth century, "ain't I," as well as "dropped *g*'s (e.g., *goin'* and *comin'* were quite acceptable in upper-class British English. Now those forms are evaluated differently: *ain't* is always nonstandard, and while speakers of standard English drop *g*'s regularly in normal

speech and never notice it, they consider it inappropriate in formal speaking situations. Similarly, at the time of the colonization of North America, the use of *loan* and *progress* as verbs was common in British English; that use was transported to the colonies, but then the British (unconsciously, of course) stopped using those words as verbs. We find in the literature of the eighteenth century derogatory comments about American English usage because it allowed such barbarisms as "I will loan you some money," even though such usage was quite appropriate in British English of an earlier period. Now we find these items presented as right-or-wrong options in workbooks for students.

These examples let us see that language is always changing and that what people accept at one period may differ from what is seen as appropriate usage, for whatever reasons, at another period. In the United States we have tended to look to our dictionaries for guidance in such issues, assuming that the purpose of a dictionary is to evaluate and prescribe usage. Children used to say in school, enjoying the irony of the form of the utterance, " 'Ain't' ain't in the dictionary." Then, in the 1960s, Webster's *Third International* shocked users by withdrawing its traditional evaluative labels and merely listing what occurred. *Ain't* was now in the dictionary, and so were many other forms, some of which middle-class speakers of standard English *knew* were not acceptable, some of which were genuine issues because people's regular spoken usage didn't match the schoolroom rules and workbook exercises that were remembered imperfectly—they existed, but what was the rule?

The editors of the *American Heritage Dictionary,* published in 1969, thought to redress this problem by empaneling a group of "experts" on English usage. They were writers, editors, educators, businesspeople, and professionals, though later review showed that they were largely of an avowed conservative bent, unsympathetic to accepting change in English usage or allowing common spoken English to affect our legacy of "rules" from eighteenth-century grammarians. Yet even with the conservative nature of the experts selected, there was much disagreement among the panel members. Was it all right to split an infinitive? Some said yes, some said no. In 1944 Leonard Bloomfield [1] had described what he called "tertiary responses" about language. A primary response involves the automatic usage of unconscious rules by native speakers. A secondary response is an utterance about language. Such an utterance may be accurate ("start a sentence with a capital letter"), stylistic ("don't end a sentence with a preposition"), or quite mistaken ("the languages of some primitive tribes have only a few hundred words"). Tertiary responses, Bloomfield said, are heated reactions of English speakers either when someone produces a form they have been taught is improper, or when someone questions a form they consider to be proper. Certainly, a good deal of tertiary response arose during the compilation of the *American Heritage Dictionary,* showing that there remain areas of our language usage not set in cement—they are changing, or have changed, or never quite fit the rules laid out long ago.

The problem remains: even if we decide to include usage in our description of our language, whose usage shall it be? The only way to answer that question is to add, "in what circumstances?" Some usage is appropriate on the playground, some in religious settings, some in the barrio, some in college writing. Linguists sometimes call these different contextually determined types of language "style"; the more common label is "register." Generally, standard English is defined as the usage of educated people in government, business, education itself, and the professions—a middle- and upper-middle-class group. In 1974 the Conference on College Composition and Communication (CCCC) published its statement on "Students' Right to Their Own Language." A main feature of this document was that students have a right to use and maintain "the dialect that expresses their family and community identity." Many teachers and parents feared that this represented an abdication of teachers' responsibility. A few years later the National Council of Teachers of English passed a resolution supporting and clarifying the CCCC statement, affirming "the responsibility of all teachers of English to assist all students in the development of their abilities" in speaking and writing, and "to provide opportunities for all students to learn the conventions of . . . written Edited American English." Today we teachers generally hold that it is inhumane of us to insist that students give up their language or dialect just because that language or dialect does not match standard English. We also agree that we are irresponsible if we do not make available to our students the options of Edited American English. But how is this to be accomplished?

HOW DO WE LEARN LANGUAGE?

Dialect, usage, and edited written English all connect with principles of language learning, and language learning connects with principles of learning in general. We can clearly see the difference between the rote oral memorization used in the one-room schoolhouse of old and our current classroom activities. Recognizing more recent changes in learning theory and methodology is a little harder. Many of us studied a second language in school under the "grammar–trans-

lation" method: each chapter of our book had a short reading selection, a vocabulary list, a grammatical rule or two, and some exercises to be written out. We took vocabulary tests, had dictations, and translated aloud. Under this method, if we didn't "learn" as evidenced by the tests, we simply had not studied enough—with "study" being defined as book study, written exercises, and memorization. Though perhaps not the most efficient method, some of us did learn to read a foreign language under the grammar–translation method.

As the goals for learning a language shifted, however, so did theories of learning. People decided they wanted to be able to speak the new language, an achievement which the grammar-translation method certainly didn't ensure (it was never designed to). At the same time, behavioral psychology was becoming the most powerful theory of how people learned, particularly how they learned language. Anyone who has studied a language since the 1950s may well have experienced the "audiolingual" or "direct" method of language teaching. In this system, a learner memorizes dialogues; spends many hours in language labs, practicing to sound as much like a native speaker as possible; and repeats pattern practices and substitution drills under the leadership of the tutor or teacher. Errors are signs of bad habits developing, and the instructor's job is to protect the student against error by controlling the student's "output." Not learning—as evidenced by being unable to repeat the dialogues, for example—is seen in that model as the result of insufficient drill. "Free" conversation is rarely permitted in such a system, because that's when errors are most likely to occur.

In both these models—grammar–translation and audiolingual—the teacher was in control and was responsible for the progress of the learner. The teacher took the learner through a syllabus of grammar, whether written or spoken, and monitored the learner's performance by identifying and counting errors. Today, however, our model of learning has changed to focus on the process the learner goes through, to focus on the learners themselves. In fact, the model of how we learn *all* things has shifted: rather than being derived from behavioral psychology, it is now based on cognitive psychology. Research on language learning in the past decade and a half has been learner-centered, asking: What do people *do* when they learn language?

This research has led to some important principles. One is the disctinction between language *learning* and language *acquisition,* a concept developed in particular by Stephen Krashen [10]. Although these two categories are not truly discrete, *learning* is applied to formal classroom work, with articulated rules, and *acquisition* is applied to the unconscious development of language, often in a "natural" setting. One of the sources of error in this model—for some linguists perhaps the main source—is "hypothesis testing," sometimes called "creative construction." That is, given sufficient interaction with speakers of the target language (thus "input" to the learner's mental grammar), the learner unconsciously tests out various explanations of forms and uses in the new language. Thus, when a nonnative speaker writes, "I could worked," we do not consider it an unreasonable production. Instead we think that the speaker still has to learn that tense is marked only once in a verb phrase. Linguists see the overgeneralization of the past tense as a constructive stage in the acquisition process. No amount of correction, of control of output, or of prepractice will protect against such errors. In this model, error is seen as the result of not enough interaction between the learner and the speakers and writers of the target language. Acquisition comes from interaction with speakers of the target language over meaningful issues, in situations that meet psychological and social needs.

Thus the principle distinction maintained in the theory of language learning today is that some things can be learned through formal rule and formal practice and some things cannot. A corollary holds that given enough time and interaction with native speakers of the target language, all of language can be acquired unconsiously, or "naturally." Pushed to its logical extent, this tenet might suggest that the teacher is therefore superfluous. Lev Vygotsky [14] and Margaret Donaldson [3], however, have shown us that the learner can move forward sooner and more securely with the help of a teacher. Thus, while we *could* learn everything in language unconsciously, given enough time and interaction with native speakers, we can also learn *some* things consciously with the guidance of a teacher in the role of facilitator. For example, we know that the use of articles in English is an area of language learning that is highly resistant to change, highly unsusceptible to application of rules or practice. On the other hand, past-tense endings are fairly easy to "key on" for advanced speakers in the editing stage of writing. Krashen's term for this sort of "keying" is "monitoring." That is, some rules of language use are easy enough to articulate and keep track of, especially in writing, where there is time to edit what we have written. We need therefore to leave time for students to write without worrying about correctness, whether they come to the writing of Edited American English as speakers of standard English, as speakers of another dialect of English, or as speakers of another language. When we choose exercises and practices for a student, we need to know that mainly we are raising the learner's consciousness about the existence of, or the need for attention to, a particular form; we don't really teach the form with the drill because we cannot affect the unconscious acquistion of language so directly.

Researchers in second language acquisition have found a "natural order" of acquisition of the basic morphemes (for example, endings on nouns and verbs, and function words such as articles, prepositions, and auxiliaries). Roger Brown, in his research on child first-language acquisition [2], found this natural order. When linguists investigated the progress of second-language learners in spoken English, they also found a fairly regular order: *ing* (progressive), plural, forms of *be* as main verb, forms of *be* as auxiliary with progressive, article, irregular past, regular past, third-person singular, possessive. Not only is there a fairly predictable order, but perhaps the most surprising finding is that the order of acquisition does not depend on the learner's first language. That is, even though we are used to thinking of certain problems in English as connected with speakers of certain languages, researchers found that this same order held for speakers of languages as disparate as Spanish, Arabic, and Chinese.

We teachers need to know about principles of language learning because we have to invoke them as we work with students on grammar and usage. Many of us learned "grammar" at school (I walk, you walk, he-she-it walks, we walk, you walk, they walk); we did usage exercises (is it *will* or *shall? lie* or *lay?*); and we learned to rely on the dictionary as a source of firm information about pronunciation, meaning, and correctness. We—or our classmates—were often told and perhaps shown with liberal applications of red ink that our writing wasn't good. Yet it fit the way we—or our classmates—spoke. Many students were left with a feeling of much wrongdoing and a sense of writing as a vast dangerous field, full of traps, pitfalls, and quicksand—how could there be so many possible errors? No wonder now when we tell people we teach English, their frequent response is, "Oh, oh, I'd better watch my grammar!"

When we understand that variety across dialects is legitimate and that change across time is normal, we can have a healthy atttitude toward our students' developing competence at any level of writing skill. As we apply principles of language acquisition to helping our students develop their writing skills, defining our role as facilitators of the process, we can guide students to a healthier sense of language and writing and can thus offer our students access to writing as a liberating experience.

Annotated Bibliography of Suggested Readings

1. Bloomfield, Leonard. "Secondary and Tertiary Responses to Language." *Language* 20 (1944): 45–55.

   Bloomfield describes metalinguistic responses to language use, looking at how distressed we become when someone questions or disagrees with what we think is "correct" usage.

2. Brown, Roger. *A First Language: The Early Stages.* Cambridge, MA: Harvard UP, 1972.

   Brown examines the linguistic development of very young children, finding that language forms are acquired in very similar, regular order.

3. Donaldson, Margaret. *Children's Minds.* New York: Norton, 1978.

   Donaldson, a former student and colleague of Piaget, examines some of Piaget's findings about the relationship of children's maturation and their cognitive abilities. Donaldson shows that with reasonable help from adults, children can do tasks otherwise thought beyond them.

4. Finegan, Edward. *Attitudes Toward English Usage: The History of a War of Words."* New York: Teachers College, 1980.

   Finegan shows how we have arrived at many of our beliefs and prescriptions about our language.

5. Flower, Linda. "Writer Based Prose: A Cognitive Basis for Problems in Writing." *College English* 41 (1979): 19–37.

   Flower shows how some writing successfully contextualizes the message for the reader while other writing is too dependent on the writer's local knowledge and experience.

6. Goelman, Hillel, Antoinette Oberg, and Frank Smith, eds. *Awakening to Literacy.* London: Exeter, 1984.

   Goelman et al. have edited and contributed to this collection of studies of how children acquire literacy. Important information for those who work with young adults and mature writers.

7. Halliday, M. A. K. *Language as Social Semiotic.* Baltimore: E. Arnold, 1978.

   Halliday's work provides an explanation of the concept or "register" and the types and functions of language use.

8. Hirsch, E. D., Jr. *The Philosophy of Composition.* Chicago: Chicago UP, 1977.

   Hirsch's theory of "readability" has not found much support in the writing profession. However, his chapter on differences between writing and reading is useful.

9. Jakobson, Roman. "Linguistics and Poetics." *Essays on The Language of Literature.* Ed. Seymour Chatman and Samuel R. Levin. Boston: Houghton, 1967.

   Jakobson examines linguistic features of poetry and poetics by providing an important schema of the factors, or components, of discourse and their functions.

10. Krashen, Stephen D. *Second Language Acquisition and Second Language Learning.* Oxford: Pergamon, 1981.

    Krashen compiles recent theory and research in second language acquistion, explains the difference between *learning* and *acquisitions,* and sets out the rationale for a natural approach to language acquisition.

11. Labov, William. *Sociolinguistic Patterns.* Philadelphia: Pennsylvania UP, 1972.

    Labov's work on speech features and patterns of Black Vernacular English is a classic in sociolinguistics.

12. Marckwardt, Albert. *American English.* New York: Oxford UP, 1958.

    In this interesting and very readable book, Marckwardt traces the development of English in America: a must for teachers, and enjoyable as well.

13. Wolfram, Walt, and Ralph W. Fasold. *The Study of Social Dialects in American English.* Englewood Cliffs, NJ: Prentice, 1974.

    Wolfram and Fasold present the history, phonology, grammar, and sociology of black English and some other nonstandard dialects such as Appalachian English.

14. Vygotsky, Lev. *Mind in Society: The Development of Higher Psychological Processes.* Ed. Michael Cole, et al. Cambridge, MA: Harvard UP, 1978.

    Vygotsky outlines his concept of the "zone of proximal development," which helps us to see the role of teacher or facilitating adult in a child's learning. This book is also notable for the foreword and afterword by researchers in literacy Schribner and Cole, and John-Steiner and Soberman, which provide readable explanations of Vygotsky's place in current learning theory.

HOW TO USE A HANDBOOK: AN OVERVIEW

LOUIS EMOND

The diversity of ability levels of entering freshmen at two- and four-year colleges makes both the organization of a writing course and the daily instructional process complex to design. Sustaining innovation and motivation in the face of heavy student loads and with students who may have little self-confidence is also quite difficult. Inexperienced teaching assistants, harried part-time instructors running between positions, overloaded full-time instructors with a passion for literature, as well as tenured faculty who have experienced the steady decline of student preparedness levels share the frustrations of trying to design a course sequence that is appropriate for all students.

Because a handbook need not be used sequentially or in its entirety, it is usually included in courses designed for all levels of students. Selected chapters are used for in-class instruction, for in-class exercises, for out-of-class self-instruction, or for essay correction. Chapters and exercises can be assigned to students according to their individual needs. To help you get the best use out of the *Simon & Schuster Handbook for Writers,* this overview shares the experiences and insights of instructors who have successfully utilized composition handbooks in writing courses.

The *Simon & Schuster Handbook for Writers* provides thorough coverage of the writing process (Parts I and VII), it is supportive of all writing process approaches (process, revision, pattern, imitation), and it provides extensive treatment of grammar and punctuation basics.

LOUIS EMOND *is Professor of English and Chair of the Humanities and Communication Arts Department at Dean Junior College in Franklin, Massachusetts. He holds an A.B. and M.A. in English from Providence College and an ME.d. in Reading from Rhode Island College. Emond has published several articles about composition instruction and remedial/developmental education, has made presentations at over thirty regional and national conferences, and has coauthored a Dean Junior College text for developmental reading. His department's Learning Laboratory integrated with the freshman writing program has served as a model for similar innovative programs at other institutions. Emond has consulted in composition and developmental skills. He is a freelance editor and has contributed to several texts in communications/media.*

REPRESENTATIVE COURSE STRUCTURES

Of the many options for organizing a writing skills course, the writing-process-oriented, research-oriented, and language-oriented structures are currently most popular. These approaches are flexible enough for classes with mixed student ability levels.

Writing-Process Syllabus

Writing can be viewed as a continuous process, from prewriting through final draft. Emphasis is placed on each phase of the process, with revision being the most essential. The course objective is to establish a patterned approach to composition that can be adapted to any task. Grammar and punctuation are taught as part of the rewriting phase, and mechanics and rhetorical essay forms become strategies for addressing specific assignments.

This course structure adapts to a wide range of student ability levels. The process approach is highly structured, and the structure is reinforced through repetition, which is beneficial for the low- to average-ability-level students. The writing assignments can be individualized, however, to challenge even the most proficient students.

One-Semester Composition Course: *Essay Emphasis*

Week One	The Prewriting Process: audience, purpose. *S & S* Chapter 1. Single-paragraph assignment.
Week Two	The Prewriting Process: overcoming writer's block, brainstorming, *S & S* Chapters 2–3. Single-paragraph revision.
Week Three	The Writing Process: beginning the essay. From topic to thesis, narrowing the topic, gathering ideas. *S & S* Chapter 2. Single-paragraph assignment and revision.
Week Four	The Writing Process: developing the essay. Body paragraphs. Student essay samples for discussion. *S & S* Chapter 3. First essay assigned.
Week Five	Essay Workshops: overhead transparencies of student essays for group correction. Essay exchanges for peer group

commentary. Revision of first essay assigned. Review *S & S* Chapters 2–3.

Week Six The Writing Process: paragraph development, adding supportive details. *S & S* Chapter 4. Second essay assigned; revision due.

Week Seven The Writing Process: ending the essay. Conclusions and summaries. *S & S* Chapter 4. Second essay due.

Week Eight The Revising Process: variety and detail. Sentence-combining exercises. *S & S* Chapters 3, 13–15, 17–19. Workshop class for beginning third essay.

Week Nine The Revising Process: emphasizing content. Idea development, reasoning, substantiation. Review *S & S* Chapters 3–4. Third essay due. In-class revision of third essay.

Week Ten The Revising Process: correcting prevalent errors. Overhead transparencies of student essays; individual conferences if necessary. *S & S* Chapters 13–16, 22–30 (selected sections as student essays dictate need to cover). Fourth essay assigned.

Week Eleven The Polishing Process: word choice. *S & S* Chapters 20–21. Fourth essay due; fifth essay assigned.

Week Twelve The Polishing Process: phrasing, sentence forms. *S & S* Chapters 7–12, 15–19, as needed. Fifth essay due.

Week Thirteen Applying the Process: focus on types of essays assigned in other disciplines. *S & S* Chapters 2–3, 34–35, as appropriate. Sixth essay assigned.

Week Fourteen Applying the Process: encourage students to bring in assignments from other classes. *S & S* Chapters 2–3, 34–35, as appropriate. Sixth essay due; seventh essay assigned.

Week Fifteen Review of Writing Basics: general review, as well as preparation for taking essay exams. Seventh essay due.

Research-Oriented Syllabus

Writing can be taught as an imitative process, utilizing student and professional models. Emphasis is placed on having students imitate rhetorical and logical essay patterns to learn organizational structure and idea development. Paraphrasing is practiced to teach sentence and paragraph structures. Research writing encourages critical thinking and the inclusion of supporting details.

Students without serious writing skills deficiencies can learn to use a variety of idea development patterns to translate thought into written expression. Students are trained to apply specific expressive patterns to specific writing tasks.

The research-oriented approach requires a reader to provide the models for imitation, a rhetoric for writing process instruction, and a handbook for structuring the research paper.

One-Semester Composition Course: *Essay and Research Emphasis*

Week One Prewriting: audience, purpose, brainstorming. *S & S* Chapters 1–2.

Week Two Writing: topic, thesis, gathering ideas. *S & S* Chapters 2–3. First essay assigned.

Week Three Developing the Essay: body paragraphs, conclusions. *S & S* Chapter 4. First essay due.

Week Four Informative and Persuasive Paragraph Patterns: example. *S & S* Chapter 3. Also Reader: model essays. Example essay assigned.

Week Five Informative and Persuasive Paragraph Patterns: all types. *S & S* Chapters 1 and 4. Reader: model essays. Example essay due. Peer group critique of student essays using overhead transparencies.

Week Six Informative and Persuasive Paragraph and Essay Patterns: all types. *S & S* Chapter 4. Reader: model essays. Comparison/contrast essay assigned.

Week Seven Informative and Persuasive Paragraph and Essay Patterns: cause and effect. *S & S* Chapter 4. Reader: model essays. Comparison/contrast essay due.

Week Eight Informative and Persuasive Paragraph and Essay Patterns: process. *S & S* Chapter 4. Reader: model essays. Process essay assigned. Workshop to start process essay.

Week Nine Focus on Persuasion. *S & S* Chapters 1 and 5. Reader: model essays. Process essay due.

Week Ten Research Writing: library orientation; topic selection. *S & S* Chapters 32 and 33. Research project assigned.

Week Eleven Research Writing: avoiding plagiarism and integrating secondary source material. *S & S* Chapter 31.

Week Twelve Research Writing: search strategy. *S & S* Chapter 32.

Week Thirteen	Research Writing: gathering sources. *S & S* Chapters 32–34.
Week Fourteen	Applying the Patterns: focus on types of essays assigned in other disciplines. *S & S* Chapters 34 and 35. Research paper due.
Week Fifteen	Applying the Patterns: encourage students to bring in assignments from other classes. *S & S* Chapters 34 and 35.

Language-Oriented Syllabus

Writing can also be taught through language skills mastery. Emphasis is placed on a systematic study of grammar, sentence structure, paragraphing, and mechanics as each contributes to the unified process of writing. This approach allows for ongoing sentence-combining exercises as a means of acquainting students with previously unused options for self-expression. It also allows for individualization, with skills exercises selected to match each student's level of proficiency.

This approach is particularly effective for heterogeneous classes and with students who have basic writing skills deficiencies. It requires the integration of a rhetoric, a handbook, and a grammar workbook.

One-Semester Composition Course: *Language Emphasis*

Week One	Prewriting: audience, purpose. *S & S* Chapter 1. Short writing sample assigned.
Week Two	Prewriting: overcoming writer's block, brainstorming. *S & S* Chapters 2–3. In-class writing sample. First-week writing sample due.
Week Three	Sentence Structure. *S & S* Chapter 7. Individualized check sheet of writing skills deficiencies for each student based upon first two writing samples. Narrowing the topic; gathering ideas. *S & S* Chapter 2. Paragraph assigned.
Week Four	Basic Sentence Patterns. *S & S* Chapter 7. Sentence-combining exercises. *S & S* Chapters 16–19. Paragraph revision assigned.
Week Five	Sentence Pattern Variations. Sentence-combining exercises. *S & S* Chapters 16–19. Revised paragraph due. Longer paragraph assigned.
Week Six	Paragraphs: introductory. *S & S* Chapter 4. Longer paragraph due. Introductory paragraph assigned.

Week Seven	Paragraphs: body. Unity and coherence. *S & S* Chapter 4. Introductory paragraph due. Three-to-five paragraph development of introductory paragraph (week six) assigned.
Week Eight	Paragraphs: concluding. *S & S* Chapter 4. Individual conferences to assist with adding a concluding paragraph to the four paragraphs written during weeks six and seven.
Week Nine	Effective Word Choice: tone, inference, connotation. *S & S* Chapters 2, 20–22. Revised essay due.
Week Ten	Punctuation and Mechanics Review. *S & S* Chapters 23–30, as appropriate. New essay assigned.
Week Eleven	Critical Thinking. *S & S* Chapter 5. Essay due. Writing Essay Tests.
Week Twelve	Essay Workshop. *S & S* Chapters 1–3, Appendix on In-class essay followed by supervised revision.
Week Thirteen	Informative Writing: development of essay. *S & S* Chapters 1–3. Essay assigned.
Week Fourteen	Persuasive Writing: development of essay. *S & S* Chapters 1–3, 5. Informative essay due. Persuasive essay assigned.
Week Fifteen	Review. Persuasive essay due.

The key to blending rhetorics, readers, workbooks, and handbooks in a single course is to stress reinforcement. Each student learns in a different way and at a different pace. Many students can find a useful tactile or visual learning experience in a handbook or workbook to supplement the classroom auditory learning experience. The parallels among the texts can be presented to the students as opportunities for learning reinforcement.

IN-CLASS USES FOR A HANDBOOK

Getting Students Started

Assigning an extemporaneous essay during the first class session will provide a writing sample for diagnosis, but the sample will probably be of the students' worst writing. Just as an instructor should try not to assign a reading without previewing the purpose for reading, a writing instructor should try to provide students with a degree of guidance.

A constructive opening series of classes might be directed toward diminishing writer's block. One class could be devoted to having students complete sentences by inserting words or phrases. Since there can be many correct completions, all students can be encouraged to participate. The sentences could be presented as overhead transparencies or as a mimeographed handout.

A second class could use sentence-combining exercises from the handbook to get students used to manipulating word groups and to lessen students' apprehension about phrasing. Students could work in small groups, with the instructor moving among the groups and acting as a member of each for a brief time.

A third class could have students write original sentences as imitations of sentences taken from the handbook. Students can mimic patterns basic to sound structure, so that they can develop in their own writing a sense of what is acceptable. They can work in small groups with different sets of sentences to imitate. The groups can then either exchange materials or make brief presentations of their work.

At the end of the first week, students will have developed a sense of confidence in themselves by succeeding with exercises designed for success. They will also have a greater sense of comaraderie through the group sessions and a more comfortable feeling about the course through the instructor's participating with the groups.

Collaborative Approaches

Although far from new to education, the practice of actively involving students in the learning process through group interaction and peer instruction has recently been revived under the title of "collaborative learning." In its basic form, the collaborative learning process presents a small group of students with a structured learning project which they complete collectively and independently. The students are free to determine the best methodology, to establish realistic time frames, to pool their diverse talents, to criticize each other frankly, and even to evaluate the quality of their results.

Most current applications of the collaborative approach are far more restrictive than the original model. Instructors usually provide strict parameters for methodology and time, select the student group mix, and evaluate the results. Most college freshmen both need and prefer a clearly structured assignment.

The collaborative approach works well with several typical writing course assignments. A few will be discussed in the section on Essay Correction. Others involve one- and two-class writing and grammar skills projects. The simplest is having student groups complete handbook exercises. Not only do students get the opportunity to experience other students' reasoning processes, but they also begin to realize that there can be more than one correct way to resolve many writing dilemmas.

Another approach is to provide students with a poorly written essay (students' name deleted). During the first class students can be asked to identify all of the errors and specify the handbook section that contains the applicable rule. Their homework can be to correct all errors and rewrite the essay. The second class can then be devoted to improving the essay's diction, tone, phrasing, and structure. As always, the instructor can move from group to group acting as a participant both to provide guidance when a group is at an impasse and to make the students more comfortable expressing concerns to their instructor.

For a change of pace, groups can compete to create and correct errors. The instructor asks students to construct three sentences (later paragraphs) that contain a specific grammatical, syntactical, or structural error, making them as difficult to correct as possible. The groups then exchange the sentences and compete to see which group can correct their sentences first. The losing groups can disqualify the winners, however, if they can detect any type of error in the corrected sentences. Thus, the exercise does not encourage focusing on one problem while ignoring all others.

Whether used frequently or only occasionally for variety, collaborative approaches are effective means of shifting students from being passive to active learners. Moving weaker students from group to group and from one role to another can slowly build their self-confidence and enable them to take full advantage of their abilities. Academically strong students can learn to share their expertise and they can also benefit from others' insights and corrections. An important bonus is the changed concept students develop of their instructor, from a distant lecturer/correcter to a more accessible co-learner/learning facilitator.

Sentence Combining

Many educators believe that if students become adept at manipulating the basic sentence elements, they will more quickly achieve control of such stylistic refinements as tone, emphasis, balance, and variety. The basic theory is that sophisticated writing style is the result of one's recognizing and being able to choose among several patterns for expressing each idea. If a student is comfortable altering and interchanging all of the elements in a variety of sentence patterns, then all of those patterns are accessible to the student as vehicles for self-expression.

The objective of sentence-combining exercises is to increase the student's understanding of basic sentence structures and to increase the ability to alter or blend those structures. The exercises progress from the simplest to the most complex alteration of the basic subject–verb–object sentence pattern.

Initial exercises can center on basic grammar variables (e.g., verb tense, noun/pronoun case, active/passive voice). Later exercises can involve combining sentences and sentence elements in a variety of patterns. Thus, punctuation can be used to introduce such modifiers as appositives and parentheticals; the relationship of ideas can be indicated through subordination and coordination; variety can be achieved through changes in sentence length and compound-complex constructions; emphasis can be balanced through parallelism. Sentence-combining exercises work well in a collaborative learning setting as well.

Sentence-combining exercises can be integrated progressively throughout the course syllabus, or they can be assigned periodically as outside work. With either approach, teachers need to let the students see the interrelatedness of the exercises and also the progressive pattern of complexity in the sequence. The ultimate objective of the sentence-combining exercises is to increase the students' options for self-expression.

Individualized Instruction Approach

When confronted with a wide range of ability levels within a single class or group of classes, instructors often aim at the middle ground or teach to the least common denominator. Both approaches ignore the needs of the more skilled students and fail to recognize that limited writing abilities can result from a multitude of individual causes. Weak students may be bright students with a specific learning disability, academically deprived students from a poor school system, visual/tactile learners who have never had demonstration classes, poorly motivated learners, or simply less intellectually gifted students.

An alternative approach is to institute an individualized learning lab within the course. The key element is a checksheet of structural and grammatical skills keyed to the handbook and an appropriate workbook. Each student is given a checksheet of personal problem areas, based upon early writing samples and updated throughout the semester as new problems occur. Allowed to work outside of class at a self-determined pace, the student is expected to use the workbook and handbook to remedy the problems before the established end-of-semester deadline. When the student feels prepared, post tests can be administered in each skill area, with an 80% passing grade. Students who do not pass must confer with the instructor (or student tutor if one is available) for individualized instruction. Post tests can be retaken (different forms recommended) as many times as needed. The workbook and handbook can be supplemented with filmstrip/cassette programs and mimeographed worksheets when appropriate.

Many students simply need to review what was once learned in elementary or high school to remedy basic writing errors. It is counterproductive to consume valuable class time reviewing grammar and syntax rules with an entire class when only a few

commit the errors. However, a few class periods should be open work sessions when students work on their individualized programs while the instructor moves about monitoring progress and offering assistance. Some colleges have formalized this approach for all Freshman English classes and have constructed a separate lab facility where students can work on their

---

LAB WORKSHEET

NAME _____ SECTION/INSTRUCTOR _____

Post Tests	Completed Pass/Fail	S & S Handbook for Writers
1. Comma Splices and Fused Sentences	_____	Chapter 14
2. Fragments	_____	Chapter 13
3. Subjects and Verbs	_____	Chapters 6 and 7
4. Subject–Verb Agreement	_____	Chapter 11
5. Words Frequently Confused:	_____	Chapter 22 and Usage Glossary
accept/except	_____	
affect/effect	_____	
its/it's	_____	
our/are	_____	
then/than	_____	
their/there/they're	_____	
two/too/to	_____	
who's/whose	_____	
your/you're	_____	
_____		
6. Capitalization	_____	Chapter 30
7. Commas	_____	Chapter 24
8. Colons/Semicolons	_____	Chapters 25 and 26
9. Quotation Marks	_____	Chapter 28
10. Spelling	_____	Chapter 22
11. Possessives	_____	Chapters 9 and 22
12. Contractions	_____	Chapter 22
13. Verb Tense	_____	Chapter 8
14. Pronoun Agreement	_____	Chapter 11
15. Pronoun Reference	_____	Chapter 10
16. Dangling Modifiers	_____	Chapter 15
17. Misplaced Modifiers	_____	Chapter 15
18. Parallelism	_____	Chapter 18

Lab assignments must be completed by _____

programs with the assurance of immediate assistance from the lab staff and student tutors.

Handbook As a Reference/Correcting Tool

Many institutions use a handbook in a composition class as an out-of-class reference for student self-instruction. As the following student essay paragraphs (taken from a short story character analysis assignment) illustrate, corrections can be keyed to handbook chapters. The student is then required to study the rules within the chapter to resolve the problem indicated. Students who cannot remedy their problems on their own can be given conference time for instructor assistance.

```
                                the knowledge        unfairly
      The reader will gain ∧ that Lengel is ∧ favoring his
22    16
neice, which is incorrect. As the manager, Lengel should
         experiences an                        toward
think of the store and not his relatives. Sammy learns
         the story of  initiation.  He takes steps to adulthood   15
by
in standing up for his principals. in the consequences of
     es           develops              are that he
losing his job, and ∧ bad feelings towards the girls.
                will be confused by the      22
21    The reader loses insight due to contr∅diction
between Lengel and Sammy.  The fact that Lengel is favoring
      16    22              22
toward his neice shows his irresponsible attitude toward
the job of store manager.  Sammy sees this is going to have
20 negative impact on other
a bad insight on future managers.
      — Study Part V: focus on using the correct words
        and phrases to express your ideas.
```

A further option is to assign specific exercises as part of the correction process. When the exercises are handed in, the instructor can immediately determine whether or not the student has mastered the rule. The following paragraph illustrates how a sentence-combining suggestion can be linked to a specific exercise assignment.

```
      inconsistent verb tenses (8)        Comma splice (14)
The Antagonist (was) Mrs. Barrows, she (is) trying to
have Mr. Martin removed from the company.  She likes to
                            and (17)
be on top of things. She likes to take control. Mr. Martin
           slang (21)
decided to (rub out) Mrs. Ulgine Barrows. The reason for this
was [because he resented all of Mrs. Barrows guesswork and
flashy ideas.] make this an introductory clause
      — Blend these choppy sentences together.
      — Practice blending sentence elements.
      — Do exercise 4, chapter 24.
```

ESSAY CORRECTION AS A STUDENT LEARNING PROCESS

Your purpose for carefully correcting and commenting on students' essays is to inform and suggest. Students should not see the graded essay as being the end of the instructional process, as a measure of success or failure. Instead, they need an opportunity to expand their skills and to experiment with new techniques.

The intent of a writing course, therefore, is to encourage students to change their writing habits. Allowing students to submit revisions to potentially raise their original grade prevents them from seeing grades as an end in themselves and continually "playing it safe" with each writing assignment. In the Essay Evaluation section, methods to accomplish this end without creating an immense volume of correcting work will be discussed.

Revisions are not rewrites, although some instructors use these terms interchangeably. Most students consider a rewrite to be merely a copying-over process; they will rewrite the original essay, with all of the instructor's corrections incorporated, and feel the assignment is complete.

A revision requires returning to the prewriting stage and reworking every step from audience analysis to the finished essay. It is a complete rethinking and recomposition. Ideally, the rewritten original essay would be set aside until the revising process is completed. Then it would be used for comparison. The finished essay would be an assimilation of the best of both.

Students are as much confused by grades as they are intimidated by them. Unless an instructor clearly defines the bases for assigning grades, students tend to equate the quantity of red ink with their final grade.

Ideally, each writing assignment will have a specific skill focus, which will be emphasized in the grading. However, all grading should be consistent with a written set of grading standards which is distributed to the students at the beginning of the course. The standards need not be overly specific, but they should be a clear delineation of instructor expectations.

GRADING STANDARDS

The following standards will be applied to all essays. Additional grading criteria for the research paper will be given to you with the assignment.

A: The content is both unified and coherent. Sufficient supporting details are provided to develop the thesis clearly. There are very few grammar or spelling errors. Sentence patterns are varied, with the pacing controlled throughout. Vocabulary is appropriate for the intended audience.

B: The content is unified and generally coherent. Key ideas are supported with specific details. There are few grammar and spelling errors. Sentence patterns are sufficiently varied to keep the reader interested and alert. Vocabulary and phrasing are appropriate for the intended audience.

C: The content is generally unified and coherent. There are enough supporting details to clarify the thesis. Grammar, spelling, and sentence structure errors are not prevalent enough to distort the meaning of the sentences.

D: The thesis is unclear. Several key ideas are left undeveloped. Generalizations are not supported with details. Several grammatical or sentence structure errors are evident. The vocabulary is inappropriate for the intended audience.

F: The essay is marginally coherent. Few ideas are developed or supported with details. Grammar, spelling, and sentence structures are weak.

Plus and minus grades will be used to indicate slight variations from these standards.

Since idea development (content) and grammatical/structural presentation (form) are viewed differently by many students, it can be helpful to provide split grades for most essays. Doing this can eliminate the frustration for students who say, "I had the same information as John. How come I got a lower grade?" It can also explain why some students can have a lot of red ink on their essays and still get a decent grade. A grade of Content/Form = B/C$^-$ can communicate more than a simple C$^+$, which would be the average.

Given the negative connotations associated with red ink, many instructors have shifted to other colors. No matter what the color, there needs to be a clear contrast between the student's writing and the instructor's comments.

Equally important for the student is the legibility of instructor comments. If necessary, you can print corrections or even type comments at the end of the essay. All student typed essays should be double-spaced and all written essays should be on every other line to allow room for easily readable comments and corrections.

A most important consideration is achieving a balance between positive and negative comments, especially if there are a great number of corrections throughout the essay. Students must be encouraged to build upon their strengths as well as to remedy their weaknesses. They need to recognize your supportive attitude. Even the worst essay has a few redeeming qualities, which might prompt such comments as:

—Although you made numerous comma errors, they fall into only two categories—comma splices and words in series, so check those sections of Chapters 14 and 24.

—You seldom say what you intend because you select the wrong words; read Chapters 20 and 21.

—You have made major structural and syntactical errors, but your basic ideas are sound; see me for a revision conference.

—Most of your fragments result from separating dependent clauses from independent clauses and punctuating them as sentences. Read Chapter 13. As a final check of your essay, try reading every sentence in reverse order, beginning at the end of the essay. That way, you will see and hear each sentence out of context, and you will be able to check sentence completeness more easily.

Too many comments on an essay can disorient students. Specific comments on problem areas of greatest need can indicate the steps to be taken, not just point out weaknesses. A general comment that other, less critical, problems still exist will indicate to the student that the other problems will be addressed later in the course.

Although marking corrections on each essay and adding specific comments to each is still the prevalent method of communicating with student essayists, instructors have devised several productive alternatives. For example, group correcting sessions utilize the collaborative learning technique to involve every student in the correction process. Overhead transparencies are used to project uncorrected, typed, double-spaced copies of student essays (without student names). The students take turns reading and correcting sentences. The students are encouraged to make stylistic and tonal changes collectively after the basic corrections are completed. Some instructors even ask the group to grade the essay. The advantages of this system are that students learn to recognize writing errors, even if they are as yet unsure of how to correct them; that students see correction as a peer process, not the imposition of standards by a superior; and that students learn how imprecise expression can obscure their ideas, even among their friends.

Faculty with large classes or with a desire to impart a personal tone to their corrections use audio tapes for comments. Some make no corrections on the essays; others correct only grammar and spelling. In either case, the audio tapes communicate specific comments to the student, who can replay the tape at his or her convenience. The tapes can be erased and reused, although it is better if students keep a backlog of comments for reference. The disadvantage of this system is that visual learners do not see the corrections. In colleges where word processing is universal and students submit their essays on disk, the instructors usually enter comments and corrections directly on the disk.

Conferences can be used on an individual basis or as a correction system. One-to-one instruction has always been an effective method of assisting students who cannot master the material in a classroom setting. Therefore, students with persistent problems can always be encouraged to utilize faculty office hours to seek extra assistance. However, individual and small group conferences can also be used as the basic correction system. Although time-consuming, these conferences provide an ideal opportunity to discuss an essay line-by-line, to allow students to explain their thought process when composing the essay, and to ensure that the student fully understands the reasons for the corrections.

When there is a formalized conference system, in-class hours are usually reduced by one-third. The released time is replaced by fifteen- or twenty-minute conferences with each student, usually once every other week. The instructor actually commits many more hours to instruction under this system than the released class time represents. The balancing element is that the correction process occurs during the conferences rather than at home or wherever the instructor corrects the essays. The total instruction/correction time should be about the same as when conferences are not used.

When correction loads are extremely heavy, there are a few options available, but these options diminish the quantity and quality of the feedback provided to students. Unless a lot of office time can be made available for individual assistance, these options should be limited to occasional use.

First, correction checklists can be attached to essays to provide a summary of problem areas and even a few specific comments. Since the list does not indicate the location of the errors in the essay, however, the student may have difficulty writing a revision.

Another technique for lessening the correction burden is to correct only one paragraph in detail and provide general comments about the remainder of the essay. This technique allows the instructor to focus student attention on one or two major problems by highlighting a paragraph containing them. However, students are not always capable of locating similar errors in other paragraphs without instructor assistance.

A third option is to train a group of upperclassmen to correct grammar, spelling, punctuation, and structural errors. Comments and suggestions can then be appended to the essay by the instructor based upon the student corrections. These students can also be trained to act as peer tutors, with regularly scheduled drop-in assistance hours if a central tutoring location is available. Compensation can be in the form of academic credits, if a tutoring course exists, or an hourly

---

CHECKLIST

Confer with your student tutor about these problems:

Form	*Content*
_____ subordination	_____ unclear thesis
_____ sentence structure	_____ logical arrangement
_____ word choice	_____ inadequate detail
_____ paragraphing	_____ coherence
_____ spelling	_____ illogical statements
_____ punctuation	_____ unneeded repetition
_____ capitalization	
	_____ _____
	_____ _____

Comments:

---

stipend if departmental or scholarship funds are available.

ESSAY EVALUATION

Even with clearly defined grading standards such as those discussed earlier, it is impossible to eliminate subjectivity from the grading process. Five instructors grading the same essay could arrive at five different assessments. Even one instructor might grade an essay differently at the beginning and the end of a correcting session. How, then, can grading be kept consistent and equitable?

Grading content and form components separately and then averaging them for an overall grade allows the instructor to divide the variables affecting grading. Sharper criteria can be brought to bear on each area, with the average being a less subjective assessment.

Another means for keeping grading as objective as possible is to make each essay assignment detailed and specific.

Write an essay that compares and contrasts the impact on audiences of radio, television, and newspaper advertising. Consider such variables as audience size, immediacy, duration of impact, mode of presentation, and audience receptivity. Begin by deciding on your purpose—to be informative or persuasive. Next, write a clear thesis statement. In your body paragraphs provide specific examples to illustrate each assertion. In your conclusion, suggest which advertising medium achieves the greatest audience impact.

Each objective in the assignment can be used as an assessment criteria. Grades will logically relate to how closely each essay adheres to the assignment. This procedure helps the instructor focus on what is expected of the student.

Course objectives are often established by a department rather than by the individual instructor. It is the instructor's role to formulate grading standards based upon how close each student's essay comes to fulfilling the departmental objectives. In such cases, it is essential that department members regularly hold grading sessions in which selected student essays are corrected and graded, first individually, then collectively. This exchange of grading opinions will produce greater consistency and a more equitable grading pattern.

Whether an instructor chooses to use split form/content grades or single grades, two choices must be made. The first involves using letter grades or number grades. Letters, especially with pluses and minuses, provide a sufficient range for differentiating slight qualitative differences; numbers, of course, provide an even greater range. Letters have immediate meaning for students, whereas numbers must be linked to a range that can be translated into a letter grade (e.g., 94–100 = A). The temptation with numbers is to subtract a set amount for each error, regardless of the seriousness of the error; letter grades require a degree of subjectivity that new instructors may be uncomfortable applying. Number grades can be easily averaged to compute the final grade; letters must first be converted to their decimal equivalents (e.g., B+ = 3.3) before they can be averaged. In effect, there is no "best" system, although the majority of college instructors prefer the more flexible letter grades.

The second choice involves whether to apply consistent standards throughout the course or to increase the severity of the standards as the students become more proficient. The first option usually results in low grades at the beginning of the course, which can have a negative motivational impact on less proficient students. This disadvantage is offset by the enticement of steadily rising grades as the student masters the course content. An added incentive could be the dropping of one or two low grades if the student has shown steady progress.

Increasing the severity of standards as the students theoretically improve provides higher initial grades. However, students can get in a "grade rut,"

even though they are improving, if the standards are raised for each assignment. Allowing the last few assignments to count more heavily toward the final grade is usually an offsetting incentive.

Not all assignments need to be graded. The first few essays could be submitted in draft form for a cursory inspection by the instructor or trained peer tutors. Errors can be circled or highlighted with checkmarks, without instructions for changes. When the essays are returned, the students must determine the nature of the problems indicated and effect corrections. This method teaches students to recognize errors in context and forces them to devise effective changes independently.

This procedure can also be turned into a collaborative learning exercise. The students work in groups of four. Each student prepares three copies of his or her essay and gives them to the other members of the group. Each student therefore corrects three essays and returns them to the owner. The three peer critiques serve as a basis for a revision, which is submitted to the instructor. Each student gains by learning to recognize errors in context and by accepting the corrections of peers.

ATTITUDE IS CRUCIAL

Teaching writing skills is both rewarding and frustrating. An instructor needs to sustain a positive, enthusiastic attitude so that the students are motivated. Communication skills—reading, writing, listening, speaking—are the keys to social and professional success. Writing instructors can be the metal from which one important key is made.

CREDITS

CONTENTS

PREFACE   To the Instructor   xix
         To the Student   xxiv

I

WRITING AN ESSAY   1

1   THINKING ABOUT PURPOSES AND AUDIENCES   2

1a   Understanding the Elements of Writing   3
1b   Understanding Purposes for Writing   4
1c   Understanding Audiences for Writing   8

2   PLANNING AND SHAPING   12

2a   Understanding the Writing Process   12
2b   Thinking About Writing   14
2c   Choosing a Topic for Writing   17
2d   Gathering Ideas for Writing   20
2e   Shaping Ideas for Writing   30

CHAPTER 1
Sets the context for this handbook by explaining college writing from the perspective of writers' purposes and audiences. Discusses features of informative writing (see Checklist, p. 5) and persuasive writing (Checklist, p. 6). Describes academic audiences and ways of identifying them (Checklist, p. 9).

CHAPTER 2
Explains the writing process (see Overview, p. 13) while emphasizing that processes vary and steps often overlap. Six ways to gather ideas. Varied examples of the components of effective thesis statements (see summary, p. 34). Comprehensive coverage of outlining (pp. 37–43).

INSTRUCTOR'S NOTES

CHAPTER 3

Suggests seven ways to get drafting underway (pp. 45–46). Continuing with the students whose work appeared in Chapter 2, shows three drafts of an essay with an informative purpose and the final draft of an essay with a persuasive purpose. Describes the steps and major activities of revision (two summaries, p. 51). Distinguishes between *revising* for ideas and style and *editing* for the correctness of surface features. (Revision Checklist pp. 53–56 and Editing Checklist p. 64).

CHAPTER 4

Presents 64 model paragraphs, numbered for easy reference. Draws from student and professional writing, including male and female and minority-group authors. No model uses *man* as a generic term for *humanity*. Presents an innovative technique for reminding students to develop paragraphs with specific details (pp. 81–82). Offers a complete chart of transitional expressions (p. 84). Discusses and illustrates six ways to arrange sentences within paragraphs and nine patterns for developing paragraphs.

CHAPTER 5

Presents reasoning and logic in the broader context of critical thinking. Emphasizes the importance of critical thinking, especially during reading. Draws parallels between reading and writing (see panel, p. 116). Discusses reading critically with a three-step entry into meaning (see Checklist, p. 120). Applies thinking skills to reasoning processes by explaining five ways to use evidence critically (pp. 125–26) and three ways to evaluate cause-and-effect relationships (p. 130). Makes distinctions between primary and secondary evidence (pp. 126–28) and between inductive and deductive reasoning (see panels pp. 132 and 134). Illustrates fifteen logical fallacies (pp. 135–38).

3 DRAFTING AND REVISING   44

3a Getting Started   44
3b Drafting   46
3c Revising   50
3d Editing   63
3e Proofreading   70
3f Using a Word Processor   71

4 WRITING PARAGRAPHS   73

4a Writing Unified Paragraphs   75
4b Writing Coherent Paragraphs   83
4c Arranging Paragraphs   90
4d Developing Paragraphs   96
4e Writing Special Paragraphs   106

5 THINKING CRITICALLY   113

5a Understanding the Reading Process   114
5b Reading to Think Critically   118
5c Using Evidence to Think Critically   125
5d Evaluating Cause and Effect   130
5e Understanding Reasoning Processes   131
5f Recognizing and Avoiding Logical Fallacies   135

**II
UNDERSTANDING GRAMMAR   139**

6 PARTS OF SPEECH   140

6a Recognizing Nouns   141
6b Recognizing Pronouns   142
6c Recognizing Verbs   144
6d Recognizing Verbals   145
6e Recognizing Adjectives   146
6f Recognizing Adverbs   147
6g Recognizing Prepositions   149

6h Recognizing Conjunctions   151
6i Recognizing Interjections   152
6j Recognizing Expletives   152

7   STRUCTURES OF THE SENTENCE   154

7a Recognizing Subjects and Predicates   155
7b Recognizing Objects   157
7c Recognizing Complements, Modifiers, and Appositives   158
7d Recognizing Phrases   162
7e Recognizing Clauses   165
7f Recognizing Sentence Types   172

8   VERBS   176

Verb forms   177

8a Recognizing Forms of Main Verbs   177
8b Recognizing Regular and Irregular Verbs   180
8c Recognizing Auxiliary Verbs   186
8d Using Intransitive and Transitive Verbs   190

Verb tense   192

8e Using the Simple Present Tense   193
8f Using Perfect Tenses   194
8g Using Progressive Forms of Tenses   195
8h Using Accurate Tense Sequences   197

Mood   202

8i Using Subjunctive Forms   203

Voice   205

8j Using Active and Passive Voices   206

9   CASE OF NOUNS AND PRONOUNS   209

9a Using Pronouns in Compound Constructions   210
9b Matching Case in Nouns and Pronouns   213
9c Using the Subjective Case with Linking Verbs   214
9d Using *who* and *whom*   215

CHAPTER 6

Charts summarize information for easy reference (pp. 141, 143, 145, and 147). Lists common prepositions on p. 150 and conjunctions on pp. 151–52. Connected discourse in exercises, rather than sentences with random content, makes the content resemble real writing.

CHAPTER 7

Fifteen diagramed patterns, tinted for easy reference, illustrate basic points about sentence structures. Patterns maintain one context to ease comparisons among the sentences. Related content for many clusters of examples throughout the chapter (for example, census taking, 7d; Charlie Chaplin, 7f) to increase interest and to reduce distractions caused by a random collection of examples.

CHAPTER 8

Coverage of verbs is particularly accessible with frequent charts for easy retrieval of information. Summarizes key information on *be, do,* and *have* (p. 187); the tenses and progressive forms (p. 193); uses of the present tense (p. 194); and sequences of tenses (pp. 198–99).

CHAPTER 9

Overview of case in two charts (pp. 210 and 215). "Drop test" to teach how to make correct pronoun choices (pp. 211–13, 216). As throughout Parts II–VI of this handbook, uses a dual system of teaching punctuation by offering "punctuation alerts" in addition to full chapters on each mark of punctuation (see p. 210).

9e   Using the Correct Case with *than* and *as*   216
9f   Using the Objective Case with Infinitives   218
9g   Using the Possessive Case with Gerunds   218
9h   Using *-self* Pronouns   220

CHAPTER 10

Stresses the impact on clarity of correct pronoun reference (for example, see discussion and examples on p. 221). Guides students to recognize pronoun uses common in speech but unacceptable in academic writing (for example, see 10e and 10f). Clarifies the many uses of *it* (p. 226).

10   PRONOUN REFERENCE   221

10a   Referring to a Single Antecedent   222
10b   Placing Pronouns Close to Antecedents   222
10c   Referring to a Definite Antecedent   225
10d   Avoiding Overuse of *it*   226
10e   Using *you* for Direct Address   227
10f   Using *who, which,* and *that*   228

CHAPTER 11

Reinforces discussion with visual illustrations of subject-verb agreement: arrows (p. 231) and "fork-in-the-road" device (p. 232). Explains the meaning of *person* in summary form (p. 231). Uses "cross-out" technique to teach students how to use *either/or* constructions correctly (pp. 235–36, 244). Includes a thorough discussion of sexism in pronoun use and offers three ways to avoid the problem (see chart, p. 245).

11   AGREEMENT   230

Subject-verb agreement   *230*

11a   Using Final *-s* and *-es*   232
11b   Ignoring Words Between Subject and Verb   233
11c   Using a Plural Verb When *and* Joins Subjects   234
11d   Using the Right Verb When *or* Joins Subjects   235
11e   Using the Right Verb in Inverted Word Order   236
11f   Using the Right Verb with Indefinite Pronouns   237
11g   Using the Right Verb with Collective Nouns   238
11h   Making a Linking Verb Agree with its Subject   239
11i   Using the Right Verb When *who, which,* or *that* is the Subject   239
11j   Using Singular Verbs with Amounts   240
11k   Using Singular Verbs with Titles   241

Pronoun-antecedent agreement   *242*

11l   Using a Plural Pronoun with *and*   243
11m Using the Right Pronoun with *or*   243
11n   Using the Right Pronoun to Refer to an Indefinite Pronoun   244
11o   Using Pronouns for Collective Nouns   245

INSTRUCTOR'S NOTES

12 DISTINGUISHING BETWEEN ADJECTIVES AND ADVERBS 247

12a Using Adverbs to Modify Verbs 249

12b Using Adverbs to Modify Adjectives and Adverbs 249

12c Avoiding Double Negatives 249

12d Using Adjectives after Linking Verbs 251

12e Forming Comparatives and Superlatives 253

12f Avoiding Too Many Nouns as Modifiers 256

CHAPTER 12

Emphasizes the distinctions between adjectives and adverbs (see p. 248). Features direct and to the point rules and clear examples, and gives special attention to *bad/badly* and *good/well*. Summarizes the discussion of comparisons with two charts (pp. 253, 255).

◼◼‖ III
WRITING CORRECT SENTENCES 259

13 SENTENCE FRAGMENTS 260

13a Testing for Sentence Completeness 261

13b Revising Dependent-Clause Fragments 264

13c Revising Phrase Fragments 267

13d Recognizing Intentional Fragments 269

CHAPTER 13

Helps students to identify fragments by applying a three-question test for sentence completeness (see panel, p. 261). Using many examples, shows specific ways to revise fragments into complete sentences. The connected-discourse exercises replicate student writing and thereby provide useful practice.

14 COMMA SPLICES AND FUSED SENTENCES 271

14a Recognizing Comma Splices and Fused Sentences 272

14b Revising with Periods or Semicolons 274

14c Revising with Coordinating Conjunctions 275

14d Revising with Dependent Clauses 276

14e Punctuating Clauses with Conjunctive Adverbs 278

CHAPTER 14

Explains the three leading causes of comma splices and fused sentences (summarized in chart, p. 273). Helps students learn four different ways to correct errors. Avoids distracting content changes within a set of examples (as on p. 274).

15 SENTENCES THAT SEND UNCLEAR MESSAGES 281

15a Avoiding Unnecessary Shifts 282

15b Avoiding Misplaced Modifiers 288

CHAPTER 15

Uses the context of clear communication to explain problems with shifts, misplaced and dangling modifiers, and mixed and incomplete sentences. Explains why these sorts of errors often slip by writers rereading their prose, and offers four ways to proofread more successfully for these errors (see pp. 281–82).

15c Avoiding Dangling Modifiers   293
15d Avoiding Mixed Sentences   294
15e Avoiding Incomplete Sentences   297

IV
WRITING EFFECTIVE SENTENCES   301

CHAPTER 16
Uses many examples to contrast wordy and consise material so that students can make comparisons easily. Offers a comprehensive Guide for Eliminating Empty Words and Phrases (pp. 311–13) that includes eighteen typical causes of wordiness.

16   **CONCISENESS**   302

16a Eliminating Wordy Sentence Structures   303
16b Eliminating Unneeded Words   309
16c Revising Redundancies   314

CHAPTER 17
Discusses coordination and subordination as two separate options for writing style. Presents the sentence pattern for coordination (p. 317) and various sentence patterns for subordination (pp. 322, 323). Examples from professional writing. "Punctuation alerts" throughout the chapter answer questions as they come up concerning commas (for example, see pp. 318 and 322).

17   **COORDINATION AND SUBORDINATION**   316

Coordination   *317*
17a Showing Relationships with Coordination   318
17b Using Coordination for Effect   318
17c Avoiding Misuse of Coordination   319

Subordination   *322*
17d Showing Relationships with Subordination   324
17e Choosing the Right Subordinating Conjunction   324
17f Avoiding Misuse of Subordination   326
17g Balancing Coordination and Subordination   328

CHAPTER 18
Teaches the principles of writing with parallel elements and stresses the effect of parallelism on meaning and style (for example, see pp. 331–32 for discussions of the Froude and the King examples). Among other exercises, invites students to use the time-proven technique of style imitation so that they can experience the "feel" of parallel rhythms in writing.

18   **PARALLELISM**   330

18a Using Words in Parallel Form   331
18b Using Parallel Phrases and Clauses   332
18c Recognizing Words that Require Parallelism   333
18d Using Parallel Sentences   335
18e Using Parallel Structures in Outlines and Lists   337

INSTRUCTOR'S NOTES

19 VARIETY AND EMPHASIS   340

19a Varying Sentence Length   341
19b Using Questions, Commands, Exclamations   344
19c Choosing Emphatic Sentence Subjects   346
19d Adding Modifiers for Variety and Emphasis   346
19e Inverting Standard Word Order   350
19f Repeating Important Words and Ideas   351

CHAPTER 19
Offers a unified treatment of the principles of sentence variety and emphasis as they affect writing style. Stresses that form and meaning emerge together in effective writing (see p. 340). Explains that techniques of variety and emphasis—as with other stylistic options—are often introduced during the revision process (see p. 341).

■▮‖ V
USING EFFECTIVE WORDS   354

20 UNDERSTANDING THE MEANING OF WORDS   355

20a Using Dictionaries   356
20b Choosing Exact Words   362
20c Increasing Vocabulary   366

CHAPTER 20
In concert with the next chapter, gives thorough coverage to both word meaning and word impact. Explains dictionary usage labels (see summary, p. 358). Contrasts denotation and connotation (see comparison, p. 364) and general and specific language (p. 365).

21 UNDERSTANDING THE EFFECT OF WORDS   371

21a Using Appropriate Language   371
21b Using Figurative Language   377
21c Avoiding Clichés   379
21d Avoiding Artificial Language   380

CHAPTER 21
Shows levels of formality and the tone each communicates (p. 372). The communicative role of Edited American English. Five ways to avoid sexist language (chart, pp. 374–75). Helps students distinguish clichés from "vogue" words and from common word groups (pp. 379–80).

22 SPELLING AND HYPHENATION   385

22a Eliminating Careless Errors   385
22b Learning to Spell Better   386
22c Recognizing Difficult Words and Word Groups   389
22d Spelling Problem Words   397
22e Using Hyphens   403

CHAPTER 22
Helps students recognize patterns in misspellings so that errors are easier to identify and correct (see p. 388). Offers an unusually complete list and definitions of 191 homonyms and other commonly confused words (pp. 389–93). Spelling problems involving eight suffixes (pp. 397–99); six plurals (pp. 401–2); and five major problems associated with hyphens (pp. 404–6).

INSTRUCTOR'S NOTES

■‖ VI
PUNCTUATION AND MECHANICS   409

23   THE PERIOD, QUESTION MARK, AND EXCLAMATION POINT   410

23a   Using a Period to End a Sentence   410
23b   Using Periods in Abbreviations   411
23c   Using a Question Mark in Direct Questions   411
23d   Using a Question Mark for Uncertain Dates   412
23e   Using Exclamation Points Appropriately   412
23f   Avoiding Overuse of Exclamation Points   413

CHAPTER 24
Covers all comma rules, with explanations and examples for students who need to learn the basics and summary charts for students who need only to refresh their memories. Starts with a guide to the chapter (p. 415) so that students can easily locate specific information. Presents six sentence patterns involving commas so that information is offered both visually and verbally. Gives comprehensive attention to restrictive and nonrestrictive elements, using traditional terms and the newer alternate terms "essential" and "nonessential" (24e). For easy retrieval, includes charts for commas with dates, with names and addresses, in letters, and with numbers (pp. 435–37). Summarizes misuses in "comma cautions" throughout the chapter and in a chart (pp. 440–41).

CHAPTER 25
Presents four sentence patterns involving semicolons so that students can learn visually as well as verbally. Uses "comma alerts" to anticipate students' questions about interactions between commas and semicolons. Four exercises of connected discourse give students extensive opportunity for practice.

24   THE COMMA   415

24a   Using a Comma with a Coordinating Conjunction   416
24b   Using a Comma After Introductory Words   420
24c   Using a Comma Between Items in Series   423
24d   Using a Comma Between Coordinate Adjectives   426
24e   Setting off Nonrestrictive Elements   427
24f   Setting off Parenthetical and Other Words   431
24g   Setting off Quoted Words   433
24h   Using Commas in Dates, Names, and Addresses   435
24i   Using Commas to Clarify Meaning   438
24j   Avoiding Misuse of the Comma   439

25   THE SEMICOLON   443

25a   Using a Semicolon Between Independent Clauses   443
25b   Using a Semicolon Between Comma-Containing Clauses   444
25c   Using a Semicolon Before a Conjunctive Adverb   445
25d   Using a Semicolon Between Items in a Series   445
25e   Avoiding Misuse of the Semicolon   446

26 THE COLON 451

26a Using a Colon to Introduce Material 451
26b Using a Colon to Separate Material 453
26c Avoiding Misuse of the Colon 454

27 THE APOSTROPHE 457

27a Using Apostrophes to Form Possessives 457
27b Avoiding Apostrophes with Personal Pronouns 459
27c Using Apostrophes to Form Contractions 460
27d Using Apostrophes with Certain Plurals 461

28 QUOTATION MARKS 464

28a Enclosing Short Direct Quotations 465
28b Enclosing Certain Titles 468
28c Enclosing Certain Words 468
28d Avoiding Misuse of Quotation Marks 470
28e Using Other Punctuation with Quotation Marks 472

29 OTHER MARKS OF PUNCTUATION 474

29a Using the Dash 474
29b Using Parentheses 477
29c Using Brackets 481
29d Using the Ellipses 482
29e Using the Slash 484

30 CAPITALS, ITALICS, ABBREVIATIONS, AND NUMBERS 487

Capitals 487

30a Capitalizing a Sentence's First Word 487
30b Capitalizing Items in a List 489
30c Capitalizing a Direct Quotation 490

CHAPTER 26
Presents three sentence patterns involving colons so that students can learn visually as well as verbally. A "capitalization alert" (p. 453) anticipates students' queries about using capital letters with colons.

CHAPTER 27
Contrasts pronouns and their possessive forms to help students remember when *not* to use apostrophes (p. 459). Presents a complete chart of contractions (p. 460) to refresh students' memories, but encourages avoidance of contractions for formal writing.

CHAPTER 28
Addresses ways of incorporating short and long quotations into documented writing, thus reinforcing the emphasis throughout this handbook on the importance of avoiding plagiarism. Presents the interactions between quotation marks and other marks of punctuation.

CHAPTER 29
Makes clear distinctions among the many uses of the dash (pp. 475–77) and parentheses (pp. 477–80), while showing the contrast between their effects. Examples about brackets and ellipses in quotations show parenthetical references to reinforce the importance of avoiding plagiarism.

CHAPTER 30
Presents a comprehensive Capitalization Guide (pp. 492–96) for easy retrieval of information. Offers an innovative Guide to Underlining (pp. 498–99) that contrasts what should and should not be underlined. Includes a chart of scholarly abbreviations (p. 503)

to help students translate abbreviations they may encounter in their reading and may need to use in their writing. Gives a summary of how to write specific types of numbers in academic papers (pp. 506–7).

CHAPTER 31

How to avoid plagiarism. Major skills needed to work with sources effectively. The role of documentation in writing with chart (p. 513) to guide students to the four different documentation styles covered in this handbook. Augments full discussions of the techniques with many examples.

CHAPTER 32

Emphasizes the ways audience, purpose, and writing process apply to research writing. Augments the discussion with many charts and visual displays: see the sample schedule for planning a research-paper project (p. 532); the flow chart on how to narrow a topic (p. 535); the flow chart explaining a search strategy (p. 541); the chart summarizing equipment necessary for conducting research (p. 537); and guidelines on how to evaluate sources (p. 539). Along with examples of cards from the card catalog (p. 553), includes an annotated excerpt from the Library of Congress Subject Headings (p. 554) and from the computerized database DIALOG (p. 556). Shows student work in a research log (p. 558), on a note card (p. 559), and on bibliography cards (p. 561). Explains drafting a thesis statement (pp. 575–76) and outlining (pp. 576–77) in research writing. Offers comprehensive treatment of MLA documentation: the Works Cited list (pp. 562–74) and parenthetical references (pp. 579–85).

30d Capitalizing *O* and *I*   491
30e Capitalizing Proper Nouns and Adjectives   491

Italics   497

30f Underlining Titles, Words, Letters, Numbers   497
30g Underlining for Special Emphasis   499

Abbreviations   500

30h Using Abbreviations in the Body of a Paper   500
30i Using Abbreviations in Documentation   502

Numbers   505

30j Using Figures and Spelled-Out Numbers   505

■ ‖ **VII**
WRITING SPECIAL ASSIGNMENTS   509

31 PARAPHRASING, SUMMARIZING, AND QUOTING   510

31a Avoiding Plagiarism   511
31b Understanding the Concept of Documentation   512
31c Paraphrasing Accurately   513
31d Summarizing Accurately   519
31e Using Quotations Well   524

32 WRITING RESEARCH   530

32a Understanding a Research-Paper Project   532
32b Choosing and Narrowing a Suitable Topic   533
32c Determining Purpose and Audience   536
32d Preparing to Conduct Research   537
32e Using a Search Strategy   540
32f Keeping a Research Log and Taking Notes   557
32g Making a Bibliography and a Works Cited List   560
32h Drafting a Thesis Statement   575
32i Outlining the Paper   576
32j Drafting and Revising the Paper   577
32k Using Parenthetical References   579

33 OBSERVING A STUDENT WRITING RESEARCH   586

34 WRITING IN OTHER DISCIPLINES   614

34a Recognizing Similarities and Differences Among Disciplines   615

34b Writing in the Humanities   620

34c Writing in the Social Sciences   640

34d Writing in the Natural and Technological Sciences   650

35 BUSINESS WRITING   659

35a Writing and Formatting a Business Letter   659

35b Writing and Formatting a Job-Application Letter   660

35c Writing and Formatting a Résumé   662

35d Writing and Formatting a Memo   662

APPENDIX A   WRITING ESSAY TESTS   669

APPENDIX B   USING CORRECT MANUSCRIPT FORMAT   675

USAGE GLOSSARY   683

GLOSSARY OF GRAMMATICAL AND SELECTED COMPOSITION TERMS   699

INDEX   716

CHAPTER 33
Follows the writing process and presents the written product of Amy Brown, the student whose work was introduced in the previous chapter. In addition to a complete discussion of Brown's research process (pp. 586–89), shows her paper and provides helpful commentary on facing pages (pp. 590–613).

CHAPTER 34
Most complete handbook coverage for students who write in courses other than freshman English. Features six student papers as examples, two each in the humanities (a literary paper and a paper that integrates literature and art); in the social sciences (excerpts from a case study and from a research paper); and in the natural and technological sciences (excerpts from a report of a laboratory experiment and from a research report). Augments Chapter 32's coverage of MLA documentation style using parenthetical references with a brief presentation of the MLA note style (pp. 631–40) and APA style (pp. 648–50).

PREFACE

Scholarship and practice in the teaching of writing have become quite sophisticated today, especially compared to forty-five years ago when handbooks for writers began to be widely used. This *Simon & Schuster Handbook for Writers* weds the best of traditional and contemporary theory to lively, accessible practice. It is a comprehensive handbook that includes all topics usually in handbooks and adds much new material.

- It starts with five chapters about the whole essay, thereby giving students a context for studying writing.
- It sets the scene by devoting a chapter to the concepts of purposes and audiences for writers, thereby explaining the *why* of writing before turning to writing as a process and to written products.
- It explains the writing process, emphasizing that the steps of composing are rarely linear and that the process varies with the writer and the writing situation.

- It offers two student papers to illustrate variations of the writing process. One paper, shown in three drafts, was written with an informative purpose; the other was written with a persuasive purpose.
- It devotes a long chapter to critical thinking, a topic of major importance today. The chapter includes a detailed discussion of critical reading skills for college work and of reasoning and logic.
- It pays extended attention to the problem of plagiarism—with a separate chapter on how to avoid plagiarism and how to paraphrase, summarize, and use quotations correctly.
- It treats the research paper from two perspectives: the research process *and* the writing process, with an illustrative student paper.
- It features the MLA parenthetical system of documentation ("new MLA"), with briefer presentations of the MLA note system ("old MLA"), the APA system, and one system for the sciences.
- It includes a long chapter for "writing across the curriculum," focusing on the similarities *and* differences in assumptions and underlying thought processes that inform the humanities, the social sciences, and the natural and technological sciences; six student samples serve as models.

Rather than preparing a grab bag of isolated components, I have sought to unify this handbook with many elements. Most of all, theory informs practice. For example, I attended to the function of context in writing situations. Therefore, 95 percent of the exercises contain connected discourse rather than random sentences. When students work the exercises, they will experience what writers face when they revise and edit. I chose the content of the exercises for its intrinsic interest, drawn from subjects "across the curriculum." I hope that while students practice skills, they will simultaneously enjoy learning about a variety of subjects. Context was also on my mind when I composed the clusters of examples written especially for this book. Most clusters have related content. This use of context means that students can focus on the instruction instead of being distracted by a new topic with each new example. As with the exercises, I have drawn the content from "across the curriculum"—and all examples are expository to the extent practical.

To reflect my conviction that learning takes place most successfully when students can make connections between disparate elements, I devised a unique dual system of presenting information about selected matters of punctuation. In addition to full chapters on each mark of punctuation, the book uses short "punctutation alerts" to help students make connections between, for example, an aspect of sentence style and the role of a comma. These alerts, and similar ones related to usage, are signaled throughout the text by the same symbol—printed in color.

I am equally convinced that students today are strongly oriented toward the visual. To accommodate this reality, I use two innovations in the *Simon & Schuster Handbook for Writers.* First, I have created over 115 tinted charts and other visual displays. These materials include guidelines, checklists, sentence patterns, summaries, flow charts, illustrations, and more. Each item is designed to help students both learn new material and refresh their memories afterwards when they want to look up information. Second, I use the visual cue of a degree mark (°) with major terms to tell students that a definition of the term appears in the "Glossary of Grammatical and Selected Composition Terms."

A more subtle but no less important concern has been my desire to make the *Simon & Schuster Handbook for Writers* inclusive of all people rather than exclusive. The explanations, the examples I wrote as illustrations, and the examples I chose by professional writers are nonsexist: *man* is not used to stand for the whole human race, and role stereotyping is avoided. Also, an approximately equal number of male and female writers are represented in the professional examples. Student writing is represented by samples of eight student papers, an unprecedented number in a handbook, and by numerous paragraphs by students.

An unusually complete collection of supplementary materials is available with the *Simon & Schuster Handbook for Writers.* The package includes a highly innovative *Annotated Instructor's Edition* which offers a rich array of resources for instructors; the *Simon & Schuster Workbook for Writers,* which is closely coordinated with this handbook; answer keys for both the *Handbook* and *Workbook;* the *Study Guide to Accompany the Simon & Schuster Handbook for Writers;* a collection of diagnostic and competency tests, four reproducible and two on software compatible with IBM and Apple microcomputers; a booklet of 100 transparency masters of important charts and other displays from the text; *Blue Pencil,* interactive editing exercises for IBM and Apple microcomputers; and much more. For information, write College English Editor, Prentice-Hall, Inc., Englewood Cliffs, NJ 07632.

When I was a college student, I never knew that handbooks for writers existed. They were not mentioned by my instructors, nor were they stocked by the campus bookstore. Not until I got to graduate school did I learn how to look up information about written conventions and about how writers make choices; only then did I get the chance to talk through concepts in class and become an independent learner. I have written the *Simon & Schuster Handbook for Writers* for this more enlightened new time, when students are encouraged early to know how to use a handbook, in class and out; when instructors teach not only what writers know but also how writers behave; and when theory can meet practice gracefully in the classroom and on a reference shelf.

Acknowledgments

The writing of this book and its related materials was the most challenging composition assignment I ever undertook. Being able to turn for advice and reactions to a community of colleagues, friends, and family sustained me, affirming once again my conviction that writing is a social act for both writer and reader. Though responsibility for any flaws rests with me, I wish to thank many people for their help.

Emily R. Gordon, Hofstra University and Queensborough Community College of The City University of New York (CUNY), co-author of the *Workbook* and author of the testing package that accompanies this *Handbook,* became a special friend as well as an astute consultant. Judith Stanford, Merrimack College, was my highly valued advisor and friend. Linda Julian, Furman University, made many excellent suggestions in the final stages of the project. The following colleagues generously offered their ideas about teaching writing: Alan Adelson, City College, CUNY; Anne Agee, Anne Arundel Community College; Duncan Carter, Boston University; Karen Anderson, Midway College; Kathleen Shine Cain, Merrimack College; Mary Kay Mahoney, University of Massachusetts at Boston; and Laura Zaidman, University of South Carolina at Sumter. Michael Goodman, Fairleigh Dickinson University, gave me skilled guidance as I prepared the chapter on business writing, a subject I have rarely taught.

For their participation in this book's pivotal "Student Writing Project," whose purpose was to gather a national sample of student writing from which to select the student work in this book, I thank Vivian Brown, Laredo Community College; Jean M. English, Tallahassee Community College; Rodney F. Farnsworth, Indiana University-Purdue University; Christine Hult, Utah State University (formerly at Texas Tech University); Joan Karbach, Indiana University-Purdue University; James E. Porter, Indiana University-Purdue University; John Reedy, State University of New York College at Buffalo; Elizabeth Wahlquist, Brigham Young University;

xxii

Carolyn West, Daytona Beach Community College; and the entire English Department at Dean Junior College. Bonnie Sunstein, Rivier College, also contributed student writing to the pool.

For their attending a Reviewer Conference at Prentice-Hall and making invaluable comments on my evolving text, I owe a special debt to Kenneth Davis, University of Kentucky; Louis Emond, Dean Junior College; Jean M. English, Tallahassee Community College; Elizabeth Penfield, University of New Orleans; and Josephine Koster Tarvers, Rutgers University at New Brunswick. Also, at various stages of the evolution of my manuscript, I had the benefit of excellent suggestions from Gary Acton, Eastern Montana College; Bruce C. Appleby, Southern Illinois University; Dorothy Bankston, Louisiana State University; Vivian Brown, Laredo Junior College; Lennet Daigle, Georgia Southwestern College; Sally Geil, Brevard Community College; G. Dale Gleason, Hutchinson Community College; Mary Ellen Grasso, Broward Community College; Dorothy M. Guinn, Florida Atlantic University; Virginia C. Hinton, Kennesaw College; Albert M. Katz, University of Wisconsin; George E. Kennedy, Washington State University; Mark L. Knapp, University of Texas at Austin; Rosemary Lanshe, Broward Community College; Joyce M. Pair, DeKalb Community College; Edgar V. Roberts, Lehman College, CUNY; Barbara Saigo, University of Northern Iowa; Roy Saigo, University of Northern Iowa; Louise Z. Smith, University of Massachusetts at Boston; Barbara R. Stout, Montgomery College; Carolyn West, Daytona Beach Community College; Stephen Worchel, Texas A&M University.

At Prentice-Hall I have had the privilege of working with a stellar team. Joyce F. Perkins has been the ultimate development editor, nurturing my vision of the book while serving as my invaluable sounding board, shoulder, and—most of all—muse. Phil Miller, Executive Editor for Humanities and English Editor, has woven his way into my creative life with his keen mind, unfailing energy, and gentle optimism. Hilda Tauber, Production Editor, has enhanced the project by giving tirelessly of her vast experience, uncommon skill, and impressive eye for detail. Others at Prentice-Hall who mattered much were Ed Stanford, President of College Book Division, who inspired me to accept the invitation to write this book; Bud Therien, former Executive Editor for the Humanities, who helped me begin; Carol Carter, Marketing Manager for Humanities, who invigorated me with her resourcefulness and enthusiasm; and Jane Baumann, Assistant to Phil Miller, who has magical powers over red tape and knotty problems.

Closer to home, I drew much strength from my colleagues at the *Journal of Basic Writing*, especially Ruth Davis and Marilyn Maiz. Randy and Phil Klein of WORDSERV guided me expertly

xxiii

through the word processing maze of this 150-disk project. Among the many friends who have surrounded me with the special moral support and patience that help a writer thrive were Irving Bieber, Michael and Jayne Brookes, Rita and Hy Cohen, Elliott Goldhush, Myra Kogen, Jo Ann Lavery, Claire Perlmutter, Betty Renshaw, Shirley and Don Stearns, Marilyn Sternglass, Muriel Wolfe, and Gideon Zwas. My parents, Belle and Sidney Quitman, and my sister, Edith Klausner, gave fully of their love and enthusiasm. Above all, I am grateful to my husband, David Troyka, for his discerning reader's eye and the joy of each new day with him.

▮‖ TO THE STUDENT

My purpose in writing this handbook was to give you clear, thorough, up-to-date information about how to write effectively. I discuss the *conventions* of writing—the rules and standard practices concerning grammar, punctuation, spelling, and mechanics. I also discuss *choices* that writers confront—options writers have for shaping their essays and paragraphs, crafting their sentences, and selecting words. To complete the picture of what writing entails, I also discuss how the process of writing works, how writing relates to critical thinking, and what characterizes writing in subjects other than composition.

As with all other tools, the *Simon & Schuster Handbook for Writers* works best when its systems are familiar to the user. Try to take some time right away to get to know the book's format. As you browse through the pages, notice particularly how information is presented in the book's thirty-five chapters. Within each chapter, section headings announce key information. These headings are numbered with a code that includes the chapter number and a letter (*a, b, c,* and so on). The tab at the top of each page carries the code of the nearest section head on the page, so that you can thumb through the book and easily find the section you are searching for.

How do you look up the information you want in this book? You have three ways. On the inside front covers you can see all the main parts of the book at a glance. In the Table of Contents all sections of the book are listed in greater detail, with page numbers. The Index provides an alphabetical listing of all information, referenced both to section numbers and page numbers.

On the inside back covers you will see many of the correction symbols used by instructors, with explanations of the symbols and cross-references to the related sections in this handbook. You will also find a selected list of the key guidelines, checklists, summaries, and sentence patterns which appear in shaded panels in the text.

xxiv

English, like many fields, uses terms not always widely known. The first time I use such a term in this handbook, I define it. Often, however, when I reuse the term later, I do not always have space to redefine it. When you are unsure of the meaning of a term I do not define, you can look it up in the Glossary of Grammatical and Selected Composition Terms. **After a term is introduced and defined, it is marked with a degree symbol (°) to signal that you can find its definition in the Glossary of Grammatical and Selected Composition Terms.** Thus, you can move through material in this book with the confidence that you have easy access to the meaning of unfamiliar terms.

While you are gaining experience as a student writer, you are often likely to want to ask new questions. Sometimes an instructor will be available to answer them, but often the questions will occur to you when you are writing with no one around. I have, therefore, designed this handbook so that you can learn from it with your class as well as on your own. Throughout your college career and beyond, keep this handbook close by so that you can always look up what you need to know. It belongs in your permanent library, alongside your dictionary and other reference books.

If you are like I was in college, you want direct and full answers to your questions. You also want a chance to think about some useful questions that you might have overlooked. I wrote this handbook with you in mind. I hope you will find it a helpful, stimulating, and pleasurable resource now and for many years to come.

LYNN QUITMAN TROYKA
Beechhurst, New York

I ‖ WRITING AN ESSAY

1 Thinking About Purposes and Audiences

2 Planning and Shaping

3 Drafting and Revising

4 Writing Paragraphs

5 Thinking Critically

1
THINKING ABOUT PURPOSES AND AUDIENCES

To start a course in composition, you might ask students to think of instances in their personal experiences that support the four claims about writing that open this chapter. To get things started, you might talk about a few of your experiences that support the claims. Do you recall a college paper you wrote? What do you remember about its contents and the experience of writing it? Have you found that writing about something makes you better able to teach it? Have you ever discovered what you wanted to say—or a connection among the ideas you already had in mind—as the words were formed "at the point of utterance"?

To encourage students to share their experiences, you might ask them first to

Why write? In this age of telephones and tape recorders, television and film, computers and communications satellites, why should you bother with writing? The answer has overlapping parts, starting with the inner life of a writer and moving outward.

Writing is a way of thinking and learning. Writing gives you unique opportunities to explore ideas and acquire information. By writing, you come to know subjects well and make them your own. Even thirty years later, many people can recall details about the topics and content of essays they wrote in college, but far fewer people can recall specifics of a classroom lecture or a textbook chapter. Thus, writing helps you learn and gain authority over knowledge. As you communicate your learning, you are also teaching. When you write for a reader, you play the role of a teacher, someone who knows the material sufficiently well to organize and present it clearly. Little is as hospitable to learning as the act of teaching.

Writing is a way of discovering. The act of writing allows you to make unexpected connections among ideas and language. As you write, thoughts emerge and interconnect in ways unavailable

2

until the physical act of writing began. An authority on writing, James Britton, describes discovery in writing as "shaping at the point of utterance." Similarly, well-known writer E. M. Forster talked about discovery during writing by asking, "How can I know what I mean until I've seen what I said?" You can expect, therefore, many surprises of insight that come only when you write and re-write, each time trying to get closer to what you want to say.

Writing creates reading. Writing creates a permanent, visible record of your ideas for others to read and ponder. Writing is a powerful means of communication, for reading informs and shapes human thought. In an open society, everyone is free to write and thereby to create reading for other people. For that freedom to be exercised, however, the ability to write cannot be concentrated in a few people. All of us need access to the power of the written word.

Writing ability is needed by educated people. Your skill with writing is often considered to reflect your level of education. College work demands that you write many different types of assignments. Most jobs in today's technological society require writing skill for preparing documents ranging from letters and memos to formal reports. Indeed, throughout your life, your writing will reveal your ability to think clearly and use language to express ideas.

 1a

Understand the elements of writing.

What does writing do? Writing is often explained by its elements: *Writing is a way of communicating a message to a reader for a purpose.* Each word in this definition carries important meaning that can help you understand what writing is.

Communicating means sending, so a message must have a destination. The well-known writer and historian Barbara Tuchman says that it takes two to complete the function of the written word.

The **message** of writing is its content. Whether the subject you write about is your choice or is assigned, you must transform it into a message worthy of communication. You need a thesis, a central idea that serves an a unifying focus for your content. You also need sufficient content to support and elaborate that thesis. You can present your message in a variety of ways. Traditionally, forms for writing are divided into *narration, description, exposition,* and *argumentation.* Narration and description are two among many strategies for developing ideas, all of which are presented in Chapter 4. Exposition and argumentation are **purposes** for writing (see 1b). Finally, the **reader** of your writing is your audience (see 1c).

jot down some notes and then participate in a discussion. If the group is large, you might divide them into small groups and give them specific directions (written are more effective than oral) about what to discuss. The directions can ask students to discuss in turn each question in the list in the paragraph above. You can appoint someone to serve as informal chair and someone else as secretary of the group. After a suitable amount of time, you might ask each group to report to the whole class.

TEACHING TIP

You might discuss the "power of the written word" by talking about censorship. A comprehensive discussion of censorship, a bit dated but still compelling is *Dealing with Censorship,* edited by James E. Davis in 1977. It is available for purchase from the National Council of Teachers of English (phone orders with credit cards 1–800–225–NCTE). Its essays include survey results, a list of major titles that have been censored (e.g., Orwell's *Animal Farm, The Autobiography of Malcolm X,* Steinbeck's *The Grapes of Wrath*), and the impact of censorship on textbooks.

QUOTATION ABOUT WRITING

I have always been in a condition in which I cannot *not* write.

—BARBARA TUCHMAN

QUOTATION ABOUT WRITING

Whenever citizens are seen routinely as enemies of their own government, writers are routinely seen to be the most dangerous enemies.

—E. L. DOCTOROW

3

MODES OF DISCOURSE AND PURPOSES FOR WRITING

Writing is sometimes classified according to four modes of discourse: *narration, description, exposition,* and *argumentation.* These modes describe the *what* of writing. They describe characteristics that written products seem to feature, although much overlap exists. A writer can narrate an incident in the service of arguing an opinion; a writer can describe a scene in the service of offering information.

This handbook starts with the *why* of writing. Thus it begins with *purposes* for writing. Purposes are familiar territory for instructors used to modes. Two of the modes are purposes: people write for the purpose of informing (expositing) and for the purpose of persuading (arguing). Purposes are based on the notion that people write for a reason; most college writing is done either to inform or to persuade. Research shows that few writers sit down and say to themselves, "I am going to write a comparison and contrast"; instead they say to themselves, "I want to give my readers some information" or "I want to convince my readers to change their minds." In the service of those purposes, writers compare and contrast, narrate, describe, draw analogy, and so forth.

Narration and description are discussed fully in Chapter 4, "Writing Paragraphs," along with many other writing strategies for idea development, including process, definition, comparison and contrast, cause-and-effect relationship, and analogy.

1b
Understand purposes for writing.

Writing is often defined by its **purpose.** Writing purposes have to do with goals, often referred to as *aims of writing* or *writing intentions.* Thinking about purposes for writing means thinking about the motivating forces that move people to write. Students often think their purpose for writing is to fulfill a class assignment. But the concept of purpose means more: It refers to what the writing seeks to achieve. Purposes for writing, though varied, can be categorized into four major groups.*

- to express yourself
- to provide information for your reader
- to persuade your reader
- to create a literary work

The purposes of writing *to express yourself* and *to create a literary work* contribute importantly to human thought and culture. This handbook, however, concentrates on the two purposes most prominent and practical in your academic life: *to inform your reader* and *to persuade your reader.*

1
Recognize informative writing.

Informative writing seeks to give information and, when necessary, to explain it. This writing is known also as **expository** because it expounds on, or sets forth, ideas and facts. *Informative writing focuses on the subject being discussed.* (In contrast, persuasive writing focuses on the reader, whom the writer wants to influence; see 1b–2.) Informative writing includes reports of observations, ideas, scientific data, facts, statistics. It can be found in textbooks, encyclopedias, technical and business reports, books of nonfiction, newspapers, and magazines.

When you write exposition, you present information. You are expected to offer that information with a minimum of bias, for you are aiming to educate, not persuade. Like all effective teachers, you need to present the information completely and clearly. The material has to be accurate and verifiable by additional reading, talking with others, or personal experience. For example, consider this passage of informative writing.

*Adapted from the ideas of James L. Kinneavy, a modern rhetorician, discussed in *A Theory of Discourse.* 1971; New York: Norton, 1980.

In 1914 in what is now Addo Park in South Africa, a hunter by the name of Pretorius was asked to exterminate a herd of 140 elephants. He killed all but 20, and those survivors became so cunning at evading him that he was forced to abandon the hunt. The area became a preserve in 1930, and the elephants have been protected ever since. Nevertheless, elephants now four generations removed from those Pretorius hunted remain shy and strangely nocturnal. Young elephants evidently learn from the adults' trumpeting alarm calls to avoid humans.

—CAROL GRANT GOULD, "Out of the Mouths of Beasts"

This passage is successful because it *communicates* (sends) a *message* (about young elephants learning to avoid humans) to a *reader* (the general reading public who might be interested in the subject) for a *purpose* (to inform). In this passage, the writer's last sentence states the main idea. Each sentence before the last offers information that builds support for the main idea.

CHECKLIST FOR INFORMATIVE WRITING

1. Is its major focus the subject being discussed?
2. Is its primary purpose to inform rather than persuade?
3. Is its information complete and accurate?
4. Is its information verifiable?
5. Is its information arranged for clarity?
6. Is it interesting to read?

2
Recognize persuasive writing.

Persuasive writing seeks to convince the reader about a matter of opinion. This writing is sometimes called **argumentative** because it argues a position.

As a writer of persuasion, you deal with the debatable, that which has other sides to it. *Persuasive writing focuses on the reader, whom the writer wants to influence.* (In contrast, informative writing focuses on the subject being discussed; see 1b-1.) Persuasive writing seeks to change the reader's mind, to bring the reader's point of view closer to the writer's. Examples of persuasive writing include editorials, letters to the editor, reviews, sermons, business or research proposals, opinion essays in magazines, and books that argue a point of view.

BACKGROUND ON *A THEORY OF DISCOURSE*

A Theory of Discourse by James L. Kinneavy explores the fundamental purposes for which people use language. Kinneavy explains the centrality of the concept of *purpose* in writing:

Purpose in discourse is all important. The aim of a discourse determines everything else in the process of discourse. "What" is talked about, the oral or written medium which is chosen, the words and grammatical patterns used—all of these are largely determined by the purpose of the discourse. (48)

Kinneavy is enthusiastic about the potential for composition as a field of scholarship:

It is the thesis of this work that the field of composition—or discourse as it will presently be termed—is a rich and fertile discipline with a worthy past which should be consulted before being consigned to oblivion, an exciting present, and a future that seems as limitless as either linguistics or literature. (2)

Kinneavy's theories, and ones of similar bent that focus on purposes for writing, are widely accepted today among scholars and teachers. Other modern influential theorists who concentrate writers' purposes include the highly respected James Britton who classifies purposes as *poetic, expressive,* and *transactional.*

5

HISTORY OF RHETORIC
This *Annotated Instructor's Edition* starts with a set of specially commissioned scholarly essays for faculty who want to learn about the theory that underlies this handbook. For an excellent introduction to the history of rhetorical theory, including a full discussion of the contributions of James Kinneavy and James Britton, see the essay by William A. Woods. "The History of Rhetoric: An Overview."

QUOTATION ABOUT WRITING
Unless one is a genius, it is best to aim at being intelligible.
—ANTHONY HOPE HAWKINS

QUOTATION ABOUT WRITING
Writing is making sense of life.
—NADINE GORDIMER

QUOTATION ABOUT WRITING
Writing is a struggle against silence.
—CARLOS FUENTES

QUOTATION ABOUT WRITING
Writing is a dog's life, but the only life worth living.
—GUSTAVE FLAUBERT

QUOTATION ABOUT WRITING
The desire to write grows with writing.
—ERASMUS

To be persuasive, you cannot merely state an opinion. You must offer convincing support for your point of view. To argue well, your reasoning must be logical and sensible (see Chapter 5) and clearly arranged. For example, consider this passage of persuasive writing.

> Scientifically, levels of sound are measured by decibels. Starting with zero, decibels reach a very loud 150 for a jet takeoff. The degree and constancy of exposure to high decibels of noise can be the difference between good and poor health. Repeated exposure to sound levels of 85 or more decibels can cause permanent hearing loss. In the case of our young people who frequent discotheques where the decibels level usually exceeds 115, and who at home have stereo units that play to a damaging 90 decibels, the warning is out. Leading otologists throughout the country have predicted that today's teenagers and those in their early twenties face a grim future with impaired hearing—the price they will pay for their rash disregard of medically proven evidence that music that blares hath no charm whatsoever.
> —SYLVIA RESNICK, "Noise: It Can Kill You"

This passage is successful because it sends a *message* (about damaging sound levels) to a *reader* (especially anyone who listens, or knows people who listen, to loud music) for a *purpose* (to persuade readers that loud music can damage hearing). The writer's last sentence summarizes her opinion. Each sentence before the last offers evidence so that the reader can understand, and perhaps be persuaded to agree with, the author's conclusion. Not all people will heed the warning, but the writer has given sufficient information to sound the alert.

CHECKLIST FOR PERSUASIVE WRITING

1. Is its major focus the reader?
2. Is its primary purpose to convince rather than inform?
3. Does it offer information or reasons to support its point of view?
4. Is its point of view based on sound reasoning and logic?
5. Are the points of its argument arranged for clarity?
6. Does it motivate the reader to action or otherwise evoke the intended response?

UNDERSTANDING PURPOSES FOR WRITING

EXERCISE 1

For each paragraph: (1) Decide if the dominant purpose is *informative* or *persuasive*. (2) Refer back to whichever of the two checklists above corresponds to the purpose you have identified. (3) Answer the questions on the checklist in relation to the paragraph, and explain each of your answers.

A. When most people think of a black hole, the Hollywood image of a spiraling tunnel into alternate dimensions comes to their minds. But we have only theory and speculation as to what a black hole really is. When a star begins to die, the matter that holds it together is burned up. The star looses its bonds and slowly expands from its constant rotation. Eventually, however, it begins to close in on itself until the process is irreversible. The size that the star expanded to before it began to contract is a black circle referred to as an "event horizon." This is what is normally seen in photographs, a black circular void that a beam of light cannot penetrate.

    —David Phillips, student

B. For the past few years, our city has been in a downward slump, especially in terms of its recreational facilities and economy. Our parks and buildings have been the target of considerable vandalism. The lake, which has been sorrowfully neglected, could be improved with more trees, better roads, and additional security. Our unemployment is the highest in the state and our economy the worst. Both situations could be improved by attracting new industries to our city. Reclaiming our land by planting orange trees, onions, and melons would help the farm economy. Our city could be one of the best places to live if it would employ its available manpower to effect these kinds of improvements.

    —Gerardo Antonio Garza, student

C. Twenty-two million American children ride school buses every day, but fewer than 200,000—living in 24 school districts throughout the country—are required to wear seat belts. Figures for the 1982–83 academic year (the latest figures available) reveal that 13 students were killed and approximately 1,500 were injured in school bus accidents. These figures may not be staggering, but they are almost wholly preventable. Seat belts on school buses are a must.

    —Thomas Goldwasser, "Letter to the Editor," *Washington Post*

ANSWERS: EXERCISE 1

A. Dominant purpose is informative. It meets the criteria.

B. Dominant purpose is persuasive. It meets the criteria.

C. Dominant purpose is persuasive, though it uses informative writing to build its case. It meets the criteria.

QUOTATION ABOUT WRITING
I wrote my first novel because I wanted to read it.
—TONI MORRISON

QUOTATION ABOUT WRITING
Many people who want to be writers don't really want to be writers. They want to *have been* writers. They wish they had a book in print.
—JAMES MICHENER

QUOTATION ABOUT WRITING
The role of writers is not to say what we can all say, but what we are unable to say.

—ANAÏS NIN

QUOTATION ABOUT WRITING
Writing is the hardest work in the world not involving heavy lifting.
—PETE HAMILL

QUOTATION ABOUT WRITING
I write books to find out about things.
—REBECCA WEST

INSTRUCTOR'S NOTES

ANSWERS: EXERCISE 2

A. Answers will vary. Samples have to come from a single issue of a newspaper. Editorials, essays, letters to the editor, and reviews can serve as examples of writing with the dominant purpose of being persuasive. News reports can serve as examples of informative writing.

B. Answers will vary, as for above.

ANSWERS: EXERCISE 3:

Answers will vary.

COORDINATED RESOURCES

Alternate examples and exercises for this chapter are available in the *S & S Workbook for Writers,* Gordon and Troyka.

Transparency masters are available for the screened lists in this chapter.

Students can practice and test their knowledge of terms, key concepts, and applications of material in this chapter by using the *Study Guide to the S & S Handbook for Writers,* West.

EXERCISE 2

A. In a single issue of a newspaper, find one informative article and one persuasive article. Explain why you identify them as you do. Next, for each article, go back to the checklist above that corresponds to the purpose you have identified, and answer the questions on the checklist. Explain each answer.

B. Repeat this process with a magazine.

EXERCISE 3

Assume that you have to write on each of these topics twice, once to inform your reader and once to persuade your reader. Be prepared to discuss how your two treatments of each topic would differ.

1. fast-food restaurants
2. studying
3. space exploration
4. cancer signals
5. good manners
6. William Shakespeare
7. pollution
8. endangered species
9. automobile safety
10. Mexico

1c

Understand audiences for writing

Good writing is often judged by its ability to reach its intended **audience.** To be effective, informative and persuasive writing (1b) need to be geared to the fact that someone is "out there" to receive the communication. If you write without considering your audience, you risk communicating only with yourself.

Experienced writers think about the background of their audience as they write. For example, a sales report filled with technical language assumes that its readers know the specialized vocabulary. The general reading public would, of course, have trouble understanding such a report. But if it were rewritten without technical terms, general readers could understand it.

As a writer for an audience, you need to be sensitive to your readers' beliefs and concerns. For example, in writing meant to persuade people to vote for a particular candidate, if you imply disrespect for people who stay home and raise children, you risk losing votes of many homemakers and their spouses. Or, if you want to persuade lawmakers that homemakers should be allowed to draw from the Social Security system, you would need to address some of the lawmakers' practical concerns, such as the impact of your proposal on the federal budget.

The more explicit information you have about your audience, the better you can think about how to reach it. Often, of course, you

8

can only guess at the details. If you know or can take a good guess about even a few characteristics, your chances of reaching your audience improve. Here is a checklist to get your thinking started.

CHECKLIST OF AUDIENCE CHARACTERISTICS

WHO ARE THEY?

age/sex/education?
ethnic background/political philosophy/religious beliefs?
role(s): student/veteran/parent/wage earner/voter/etc.?
employment/economic status?
interests/hobbies?

WHAT INFORMATION DO THEY HAVE?

level of education?
experience with reading academic or business writing?
amount of general knowledge about the subject?
amount of specialized knowledge about the subject?
what preconceptions do they bring to the material?

1
Understand the general reading public.

The **general reading public** is educated, sometimes less and sometimes more than you. Its members are experienced readers, people who frequently read newspapers, magazines, and books. They often have some general information about the subject you are dealing with, but they enjoy a chance to learn something new or see something from a different perspective.

The general reading public expects you to know how to reach them. For example, the general reader expects material to be clear and to be free of advanced technical information. Equally important, the general reading public expects to be treated respectfully. As experienced readers, they are sensitive to your **tone**—the way what you say reflects your attitude toward the subject and the audience. If the tone implies you feel superior to your audience, your tone will be condescending and distasteful. Similarly, if your tone hints that you are uninformed or unsure, readers will lose confidence in your material. Tone is created largely by word choice (see Chapter 21). Although the general reading public enjoys lively language, it is jarred by an overly informal tone in the middle of a

TEACHING TIP
You might find that some students feel inhibited in their writing when they have to think about an audience for their writing. Studies show that some students misunderstand the concept of audience. They think it means that writers should act as if someone is constantly looking over their shoulders. Other students have trouble with the concept of audience because they think that they can never say something that would be unpopular with their audience. Some students might not want to admit these or other misunderstandings of the concept, so you might want to clear up the matter without asking anyone to give you their negative impressions. Once you start talking about the subject, you will often find that the students start chiming in to help you get at their concerns.

The concept of audience is meant to help writers get their message across. The concept is supposed to facilitate, not block. A writer is not expected to tell readers what they want to hear even if the writer disagrees with the readers. A writer is, however, expected to choose words the readers know and to use a tone suitable to the occasion. As writer Gary Provost says in "How to Make the Reader Like You" published in *Writer's Digest* in September 1986:

You need some sense of your reader's knowledge. If you're writing a report for oceanographers, mention the *dorsal carapace* and the *chelipeds* if you must, but if you're writing a brochure for visitors to a public aquarium, please write *shell* and *claws*. Remember that any time, you don't have your entire vocabulary to work with. You have only that portion of your vocabulary that you share with the readers. (37–8)

QUOTATION ABOUT WRITING
QUOTATION ABOUT WRITING
What I want to do is make people laugh so they'll see things seriously.

—WILLIAM ZINSSER

QUOTATION ABOUT WRITING
I started writing because of a terrible feeling of powerlessness: I felt I was drifting and obscure, and I rebelled against that. I didn't see what I could do to change my condition. I wanted to control rather than be controlled, to ordain rather than be ordained, and to relegate rather than be relegated.

—ANITA BROOKNER

QUOTATION ABOUT WRITING
I have tried simply to write the best I can; sometimes I have good luck and write better than I can.

—ERNEST HEMINGWAY

serious presentation of informative or persuasive writing. For example, in a newspaper report about the results of an election, you should not refer to the loser or winner as *guy* or *gal,* no matter how relaxed the candidate's demeanor. Likewise, in the middle of a serious critique, using *pretty* as a synonym for *very* or *fairly* would be out of place (as in "The weak script was helped by some pretty good acting"). An artificial tone is also a mistake (see 21d). Do not, for example, use pretentious phrases such as "the aforementioned occurrence that transpired" when you mean "the event." Also, if your language is biased or slanted (see 21a), your tone will seem underhanded, and your readers will distrust what you say. For more about the writer's role and tone, see 2e-3.

2
Understand your instructor as a reader.

When you write for a class assignment, your audience will almost certainly be your **instructor.** Sometimes, especially when you are planning or revising your work, your instructor might want other students in your class to collaborate as an audience, but your final audience usually remains your instructor.

Your instructor is a member of the general reading public and also someone who recognizes that you are an apprentice. Your instructor knows that few students are experienced writers or complete experts on their subjects. Still, your instructor always expects your writing to reflect that you took time to write well and learn the material thoroughly. In part, therefore, an instructor is a *judge,* someone to whom you must demonstrate that you are doing your best. Instructors are very experienced readers who can quickly recognize minimal efforts or a negative attitude (as when a paper carries a tone that suggests "Tell me what you want and I'll give it to you").

Inexperienced writers wrongly assume sometimes that instructors will fill in mentally what is missing on the page. Instructors expect what they read to include everything that the writer wants to say or imply, so you cannot leave out material. Even if you write immediately after your instructor has heard you give an oral report on the same subject, write as if no one is aware of what you know.

Your instructor is also an *academic,* a member of a group whose professional lives center around intellectual endeavors. You must, therefore, write within the constraints of academic writing. For example, if you are told to write on a topic of your choice, you definitely do not have total freedom to choose. Your topic must have some intrinsic intellectual interest. For example, an essay should

10

not merely give directions on how to cut a wedding cake or use an eraser.

3
Understand specialists as readers.

Specialists are members of the general reading public who have expert knowledge on specific subjects. In writing for specialists, you are expected both to know the specialty and to realize that your readers have advanced expertise.

Specialized readers often share not only knowledge but also assumptions, interests, and beliefs. For example, they may be members of a club that concentrates on a hobby, such as amateur astronomy or orchid raising. They may have similar backgrounds, such as having immigrated from another country or having fought in a particular war. They may have similar views on matters related to religion and politics. You have, therefore, to balance the necessity to be thorough with the demand that you not recapitulate matters such as technical terms and special references.

EXERCISE 4

Each of these passages was written for an instructor, and therefore, for a general reading audience. Read each paragraph and decide (a) if it has the right tone for academic writing and (b) if it assumes knowledge that only a specialist would have.

1. When contrasting Jimmy Connors' style of play to John McEnroe's style, people should remember that Jimmy Connors is a baseline player and John McEnroe is a serve and volley player. Jimmy Connors' game plan is to hit baseline shots until the chance to come to the net is achieved. He also will try to wear down the player by hitting baseline shots until he can hit a winner. In contrast, John McEnroe will serve and come to the net immediately. John comes to the net with the hope that the service return will be poor so that he can hit a winner.

   —DAN DORAN, student

2. If two hockey greats were to be compared, then the unique choice would be to compare Wayne Gretzky and Gordie Howe. Both will be remembered for their hockey prowess. Gordie Howe is now retired, and Wayne Gretzky is probably just entering his prime with the Edmonton Oilers, accumulating records that will probably never be broken again.

   —JOE BROOKS, student

ANSWERS: EXERCISE 4

1. a. The tone is right for academic writing.
   b. This material assumes a specialist reader who would know that the game is tennis and what jargon such as "baseline" means.
2. a. The tone is right for academic writing.
   b. This material does not assume a specialist reader because the writer mentions immediately that the game is hockey and uses nonjargon vocabulary such as "prowess" and "records."

11

2

PLANNING
AND
SHAPING

**BACKGROUND ON THE
WRITING PROCESS**
This *Annotated Instructor's Edition* starts with a set of specially commissioned scholarly essays for faculty who want to learn about the theory that underlies this handbook. For an excellent introduction to theory and research concerning the writing process, see the essay by Josephine Tarvers "The Writing Process: An Overview."

Many people assume that a real writer can pick up a pen (or sit at a typewriter or word processor) and magically write a finished product, word by perfect word. Experienced writers know better. They know that **writing is a process,** a series of activities that start the moment they begin thinking about a subject and end when they complete a final draft. Experienced writers know, also, that good writing is rewriting. Their drafts. are filled with additions, deletions, rearrangements, and rewordings.

For example, on the next page you can see how the paragraph you just read was reworked into final form. Notice that two sentences were dropped, two sentences were combined, one sentence was added, and various words were dropped, changed, or added. Such activities are typical of writing.

▌▌ 2a

Understand the writing process.

Writing is an ongoing process of considering alternatives and making choices. The better you understand the writing process, the better you will write and the more you can enjoy writing. For the

12

plan **2a**

> ~~Chapter One discusses what writing is.~~ ~~This chapter~~
>
> ~~explains how writing happens.~~ Many people assume that a real
>   *pick up a pen*
> writer can ~~put pen to paper~~ (or sit at ~~the keyboard of~~ a
>   *magically—a*
> typewriter or word processor) and write finished product *word*
> *by perfect word.*
> Experienced writers ~~all~~ know better. They know that writing
>
> is a process, ~~Writing is~~ a series of activities that start
>   *they begin*
> the moment thinking about a subject ~~begins~~ and end when they
> *complete* ~~the~~ *a*
> final draft. ~~is complete.~~ Experienced writers know, also,
>
> that good writing is rewriting. *Their drafts are filled with*
> *additions, deletions, rearrangements, and rewordings.*

TEACHING TIP

The facsimile of my writing and revising at the opening of this chapter is completely authentic (though the handwriting is not mine because I tend to scrawl illegibly). I have included this draft to show students that most teachers and professional writers *evolve* a text rather than produce it in one swoop. When I do this in my writing classes, the students never fail to be surprised that their instructor's first draft could be so rough. You might also call attention to the clumsy opening sentences that I deleted and to other revisions that I made in my first draft.

You might also bring in a few examples of your own drafts. A paragraph or two can suffice. And if you use a word processor, as I do, plan ahead and keep those sentences you love to delete with the press of a key. I have found that a few students sometimes think that my rough drafts are better than their final drafts, but I try to emphasize that such a reaction misses the point. After all, I am not as much of an apprentice writer as the students are. And I am trying to better my writing from a base of where I am, not from a base that I started at back in college.

sake of explanation, the parts of the writing process are discussed separately in this chapter. In real life, you will find that the steps overlap, looping back and forth as each piece of writing evolves.

AN OVERVIEW OF THE WRITING PROCESS

Planning calls for you to gather ideas and think about a focus.

Shaping calls for you to consider ways to organize your material.

Drafting calls for you to write your ideas in sentences and paragraphs.

Revising calls for you to evaluate your draft and, based on your decisions, rewrite it by adding, cutting, replacing, moving—and often totally recasting material.

Editing calls for you to check the technical correctness of your grammar, spelling, punctuation, and mechanics.

Proofreading calls for you to read your final copy for typing errors or handwriting legibility.

13

Understanding writing as a multistage process allows you to work efficiently, concentrating on one activity at a time rather than trying to juggle all of the facets of a writing project simultaneously.

As you work with the writing process, rest assured that there is no *one* way to write. When you start, allow yourself to move through each stage of the writing process and see what is involved. Then as you gain experience, begin to observe what works best for you. After you master the differences that separate planning from shaping, drafting from revising, and editing from proofreading, you might want to experiment a little. For example, some people write a "discovery" draft to see what emerges before they begin shaping. Some writers outline immediately and use planning techniques to flesh out points on the outline. Many writers find during revising that they need more ideas, so they use planning techniques once again. Still other writers edit during revision because a grammar or spelling error keeps getting in the way.

Most writers struggle some of the time with ideas that are difficult to express, sentences that will not take shape, and words that are not precise. Do not be impatient with yourself and do not get discouraged. Writing takes time. The more you write, the easier it will be, but remember that experienced writers know that writing never happens magically.

An aside about the words used to discuss writing: Instructors refer to written products in different ways. Often the words are used interchangeably, but sometimes they have specific meanings for specific instructors. Listen closely and ask if you are unsure of what you hear. For example, the words *essay, theme,* and *composition* usually—but not always—refer to writing that runs from about 500 to 1,000 words. This book uses *essay.* The words *report* and *project* usually mean writing that draws on outside sources. The word *paper* can mean anything from a few paragraphs to a long and detailed report of a complex research project. This book uses *paper* to refer to research writing.

■‖ 2b
Think about writing.

Writing begins with thinking. When you are given a writing assignment, you are immediately cast into a **writing situation.** The decisions you make as you write an essay depend on the particulars of each writing situation: topic, purpose, audience, and special requirements.

Underlying all aspects of the writing situation is the **topic.** If you are supposed to choose your own topic or narrow an assigned

14

general topic, you need to keep in mind the constraints of academic writing. If the topic is assigned, you have to write without going off the track. No matter what the topic, *you* are the starting place for your writing. You must draw upon yourself as a source. All writers depend on their accumulated experience and education as they write. Whatever they have seen, heard, read, and even dreamed contributes to their fund of ideas and knowledge. No matter how much you have learned from your reading, going to plays and movies, and watching television, the starting point for your writing is always you, the writer. As you think through and gather ideas (2d) for your topic, your task is to establish a *focus,* or a point of view, about the topic and *support* for that focus.

The writing situation includes the **purpose** for your writing. In college, the major purposes for writing are *to inform* and *to persuade,* as explained fully in 1b. Effective informative and persuasive writing succeed in part because they reflect a clear sense of purpose. Some writing assignments include or clearly imply a statement of purpose. For example, your purpose is informative if you are asked to write about the dangers of smoking. On the other hand, your purpose is persuasive if your assignment calls for an argument against smoking. Many assignments, however, do not stipulate the writing purpose. In such cases, one of your tasks is to choose either an informative or persuasive purpose based on the topic, what you want to say about it (often referred to as the *focus*), and how you develop what you want to say.

The **audience** for your writing is also part of the writing situation. For college writing, your audience is primarily—though not necessarily exclusively—your instructor. Your instructor is both a member of the general reading public and an academic. Your writing needs to be sensitive to such backgrounds, as explained fully in 1c. Sometimes a writing assignment names a very specific audience, such as the head of a major corporation or veterans who have served in Vietnam. These audiences are specialists, people who have more technical knowledge than does the general reading public. You have to write to their level. Sometimes an assignment stipulates that the writing will be read by other students in the class. Students in such situations serve as surrogate instructors, so you are expected to write with the same tone and level of information as you would for your instructor alone.

Special requirements influence every writing situation. These include the time allotted for the assignment, the expected length of the writing, and other practical constraints. If an assignment includes a word count, you have to take it into consideration when you make decisions about topic, purpose, and audience. If an assignment is due in one week, you have to expect that your in-

15

structor wants writing that shows more than one day's work. If research is required, you have to build time for it into your schedule.

Throughout this chapter and the next, you will see the work of two students, Tara Foster and Gary Lee Houseman.

Tara Foster was given this assignment: Write an essay of 500 to 700 words that discusses any important problem facing adult men and women today. Your first and second drafts are due in one week. I will read your second draft as an "essay in progress" and will make comments to help you toward a third draft. Your third draft is due one week after I hand back your second draft.

Gary Lee Houseman was given this assignment: Write a 1,000-word essay in which you argue against some aspect of the destruction of our environment. Your final draft is due in two weeks, but bring your earlier drafts to class for possible discussion.

In analyzing her writing situation, Foster saw that the assignment specified the special requirements of length and time. She decided that her audience would be her instructor. She tentatively choose an informative purpose, knowing that as she got further into planning she might change her mind. Her decision process about the topic is discussed in 2c.

In analyzing his writing situation, Houseman saw that the assignment told him about length, time, and purpose. He realized that the due date of two weeks might imply that research was required, so he asked his instructor. He was told not to use outside sources but to draw on his own fund of knowledge and his personal focus—point of view—about the subject. Once Houseman knew that, he decided that his audience would be his instructor. His decision process about his topic is discussed in 2c.

EXERCISE 1

For each assignment listed below, answer these questions: (a) Is its purpose to inform or to persuade? (b) Is the audience the general reading public or specialists? (c) What special requirements of length and time are stated or implied?

1. *Biology:* You have twenty minutes to list and explain three ways that the circulatory system contributes to homeostasis in the human body.

ANSWERS: EXERCISE 1

1. The purpose is to inform. Because the assignment is for a biology class, the audience will likely be the instructor and perhaps other students in the class; these people are specialists. The assumption about an audience of specialists is further confirmed by the time limit of twenty minutes, which means that the student has to pack in many technical terms and processes in a short period of time. The special requirements include the twenty-minute time limit and, implied by the wording of the assignment, in-class writing.

2. The purpose is to persuade. The audience is the general reading public (such as the course instructor and students in class). The special requirements include a 500 to 700 word limit and a due date of one week.

16

2. *English:* Write a 500- to 700-word essay arguing for or against tougher academic requirements for student athletes. This assignment is due in one week.

3. *Political Science:* Write a 1,000-word essay about television's impact on elections.

4. *English:* Write a 300-word editorial for the student newspaper praising or criticizing the college's library. Draw on your personal experience. Also, interview at least one member of the library staff for his or her reaction to your point of view.

5. *Art:* Write a one-paragraph summary of the difference between a wide-angle lens and a telephoto lens.

▮ 2c
Choose a topic for writing.

Choosing a topic calls for using good judgment and making sound decisions. Experienced writers know that the quality of their writing depends on how they handle a topic. You should, therefore, think through a topic before you rush in and get too deeply involved to pull out within the time allotted. You will write more effectively if your topic is suitable for college writing and if it is one that can be presented and developed well.

Of course, some assignments leave no room for making choices about the topic. You may be given very specific instructions such as "Explain how oxygen is absorbed from the lungs." You may be asked to describe the view from your classroom window or to compare and contrast the personalities of two major characters in a short story. Your job with such assignments is to do precisely what is asked and not go off the topic.

‖ 1
Know how to select a topic on your own.

Some instructors will ask you to write on whatever topic you wish. In such situations, do not assume that all subjects are suitable for informative or persuasive writing in college. Academic settings call for topics that can reflect your ability to think ideas through. For example, the old reliable essay about a summer vacation is probably not safe territory for a college essay if you have nothing extraordinary to report. Your essays need to dive into issues and concepts, and they should demonstrate that you can use specific, concrete details to support what you want to say. The need for spe-

3. A student receiving this assignment has many decisions to make. The purpose can be either informative or persuasive, depending on the student's focus on the topic. The audience can be the general reading public or specialists, according to the student's judgment; if the political science course is advanced, chances are that the instructor expects the writing to be addressed to specialists. The only stated special requirement is a length of 1,000 words. The student should ask the instructor when the assignment is due and if the assignment calls for research. The student might also want to set a purpose and audience and check them with the instructor before proceeding, if time permits.

4. The purpose is to persuade. The audience is readers of the college's student newspaper; they could be considered specialists in that they share the experience of attending the same college, but they are not specialists in technicalities concerning the functioning of college libraries. The special requirements include a 300-word limit, the need to draw on personal experience, and the need to interview a library staff member. The student should ask the instructor when the assignment is due.

5. The purpose is to inform. Because the assignment is only one paragraph and is for an art class, chances are high that the audience is the course instructor and perhaps other students in the class. An assumption of some specialized knowledge is appropriate (unless the instructor says to write the material for people totally unfamiliar with the topic. The special requirements include the one-paragraph limit and, perhaps implied by the wording of the assignment, in-class writing.

cifics should not, however, tempt you to write very technical information, especially for an audience unfamiliar with the particular specialized vocabulary.

When you choose a topic on your own, be careful not to use a very narrow one. You will have little success with topics that give you little to say. For example, for a course in informative and persuasive writing, you might reach a dead end if you tried to write a 500-word essay about what your cat looks like while sleeping, unless you were asked to write an elaborate description of a common sight. Similarly, for the same course, you might find yourself out of ideas if you tried to write 500 words about a single apple. You need to take purpose, audience, and special requirements into account when you make decisions about topics. A cat sleeping might be a fine topic for a zoology course, and an apple might be a suitable topic for a health class.

2
Know how to narrow an assigned topic.

The real challenge in dealing with topics comes when you choose or are assigned a subject that is very broad. You have to *narrow the subject*. This means thinking subdivisions of the subject, of different areas within the subject. Most very broad subjects can be broken down in hundreds of ways, but you need to think of only a few until you come to one that seems possible for an essay. Think it through before rushing in, however. Think about whether the topic as narrowed can be developed well in writing. **What separates most good writing from bad is the writer's ability to move back and forth between general statements and specific details.** A suitably narrowed topic permits such movement.

For example, if the subject is marriage, you might decide to talk about what makes marriages successful. But you cannot depend merely on generalizations such as "In successful marriages husbands and wives learn to accept each other's faults." You need to explain why accepting faults is important, and you need to give concrete illustrations of what you are talking about.

Whenever you narrow a broad subject to obtain a writing topic, keep in mind the writing situation of each assignment: purpose, audience, and special requirements. Think about what you can handle well according to the conditions of each assignment.

SUBJECT	Music
WRITING SITUATION	Freshman composition class
	Informative purpose
	Instructor as audience
	500 words, one week

TEACHING TIP
The concept of a "writing situation" might be new to many students. It is an inclusive term for the combination of topic, purpose, audience, and special requirements such as word or time limits. Each of these four variables influences every decision a writer makes. You might want to ask your students to memorize that short list of key variables: TOPAS (with two letters for "topic") can be an easy memory device for students. These variables are especially important in narrowing a topic, as demonstrated by the inclusion of "writing situation" in the examples for narrowing a topic.

18

POSSIBLE TOPICS	the moods music creates classical music country-western music major classical composers
SUBJECT	Cities
WRITING SITUATION	Sociology Persuasive purpose Students and then instructor as audience 500 to 700 words, one week
POSSIBLE TOPICS	comforts of city living discomforts of city living groups that prefer city life how cities develop
SUBJECT	Mythology
WRITING SITUATION	Humanities course Informative purpose Instructor as audience—a specialist in mythology 1,000 words, two weeks
TOPICS	the purpose of myths mythical views of gods and goddesses myths about the origins of the world

QUOTATION ABOUT WRITING

Since long before the invention of universities, not to mention university programs in creative writing, authors have acquired their authority in four main ways—first, by paying a certain sort of attention to the experience of life as well as merely undergoing it; second, by paying a certain sort of attention to the works of their great and less great predecessors in the medium of written language, as well as merely reading them; third, by practicing that medium themselves, usually a *lot* (Charles Newman, the writer and critic, declares that the first prerequisite for aspiring writers is sufficient motor control to keep their pens moving left to right, line after line, hour after hour, day after day, and I would add year after year, decade after decade); and fourth, by offering their apprentice work for discussion and criticism by one or several of their impassioned peers, or by some more experienced hand, or by both.

—JOHN BARTH

Both Tara Foster and Gary Lee Houseman faced the task of narrowing their topics. Foster's assignment asked for a discussion of "an important problem facing adult men and women today." She knew immediately that "an important problem" was too vague and general, and she realized the assignment implied that she was expected to make it specific and suitably narrow. Being one of today's "adult men and women," she thought of many problems: war, the dangers of nuclear energy, unemployment, divorce. She saw a danger in these topics, however. She knew that she had to avoid what her instructor called *canned rhetoric,* the use of standard statements made commonly by everyone. She wanted to test out what she might say on various topics, so she did some "freewriting" (2d-2). This helped her realize that what interested her most was the problem of divorce. Still, she felt that she did not have enough infor-

19

mation to write a 500- to 700-word essay on the subject. She used divorce as a springboard for "brainstorming" (2d-3). She knew people who had gone through divorce, and she was aware that learning to live alone was a major problem for some. This led her to thinking about many types of people who have to face living alone at one time or another in their lives. She began to think about what they needed to know to be able to live alone. She felt that she had found a good topic, but she confirmed this by asking the "journalist's questions" (2d-4) to see if she would have enough to write about.

Houseman's assignment asked for an argument about "some aspect of the destruction of our environment." Houseman's process of narrowing the subject was very different from Foster's. For a number of years, he had been very interested in conservation issues, and so he had a solid fund of knowledge from having read many newspaper and magazine articles. He thought of choosing the topics of acid rain or toxic wastes or pollution. But the topic he cared about most was the destruction of rain forests. To check whether he could remember many details from his reading, he tried "mapping" (2d-5), and he decided that he had made a good choice for himself.

ANSWERS: EXERCISE 2
Answers will vary.

EXERCISE 2

For each general topic, think of three narrowed topics that would be suitable for a 500- to 700-word essay in a writing course. Assume that each essay is due in one week and that the audience is the general reading public, as represented by the course's instructor. List your three narrowed topics and explain briefly why each is suitable for the writing situation.

1. Computers
2. Movies
3. Political campaigns
4. Health
5. Literature

ANSWERS: EXERCISE 3
Answers will vary.

EXERCISE 3

Think of three subjects that interest you. List them. Then pick one and narrow it to three topics suitable for an essay. Assume that the essay is for a writing class, that it should run from 500 to 700 words, that it is due in one week, and that it will be read by both other students in the class as well as the course's instructor. After you finish listing three topics, explain briefly why each is suitable for the writing situation.

 2d

Gather ideas for writing.

Techniques for gathering ideas, sometimes called *prewriting strategies* or *invention techniques*, can help you while you are narrowing your topic. They help you discover what you know and, often, how much you know about a topic before you decide to write on it. As such, techniques for gathering ideas are important aids for thinking of the ideas and of details to use in essays.

Many techniques for gathering ideas have been developed and used by experienced writers. The ones discussed and illustrated in this chapter are summarized in the following chart.

SUMMARY OF WAYS TO GATHER IDEAS FOR WRITING

Keeping an idea book
Writing in a journal
Freewriting
Brainstorming
Using the journalist's questions
Mapping
Knowing when to read for writing

Students sometimes worry that they have nothing to write about. Often, however, students know far more than they give themselves credit for. The challenge is to uncover what is there but seems not to be. Start with the assumption that you know more than you think, and try some of these techniques for discovering what is not coming easily to mind.

No one technique of generating ideas always works for all writers in all situations. Experiment, therefore, with all these methods. If one does not provide enough useful material, try an alternative. Also, even if one strategy produces some good material, you may still want to try another technique to see what additional possibilities it may turn up.

1
Know how to keep an idea book and write in a journal.

Your ease with writing will grow if you get into some of the habits of mind that typify writers. Professional writers are always on the lookout for ideas to write about and for details to develop their ideas. They listen, watch, talk with people, and generally keep their minds open. For this reason, many writers carry an **idea book**—a pocketsize notebook—with them at all times so that they can jot down ideas that spring to mind. They do not trust their memories because they know that good ideas can melt away like snowflakes. If you keep an idea book handy throughout your college

TEACHING TIP: JOURNALS
Students often have trouble thinking of journal topics. The result is frequently journals that read like parodies of diaries, shopping lists, descriptions of meals or clothes, transcripts of routine conversations. You can avoid this problem if you give students suggested topics. In addition to offering students something to write about, such topics act as models for the creation of original topics. You might distribute this list in groups of five or ten so that they can last for most of a semester.

1. How do you feel about having to keep a journal? How do you feel about writing? Explain.

2. Why are you in college? If there is something else you would rather be doing, what is it? Why are you in school instead?

3. What is your definition of success? Do your friends tend to share your definition or to have a different one? Discuss.

4. Do you think information about sex should be taught at home, in school, or both? Why?

5. How does your religion affect your daily life? Have you ever had to defend or explain your religious beliefs to someone? Do you think you were effective? Why or why not?

6. Do you plan to marry someday? Why? What do you expect married life to be like? (If you are married, were your expectations fulfilled? Why or why not?)

7. What do you want as a career? How are you preparing for it? How did you choose this career? Have you ever had to defend or explain your choice to parents or friends? Do you think you were effective? Why or why not?

8. Is the United States really a melting pot? Should immigrant children be educated in English or in their

JOURNALS (CONT.)

native languages? Should there be non-English radio and television stations in the United States? For each question, why or why not?

9. If you could give advice to your friend(s), what would you say?

10. Where do you go when you feel like being alone? Why?

11. Where do you go when you feel sociable? Why?

12. Does anything make you depressed? What? What do you do when you feel this way? What advice can you give others who feel this way?

13. What is your favorite place? What makes it so special?

14. What do you think your life will be like in the year 2000? What will your family life be like? What work will you be doing? Where will you be living? How will technology have influenced your life?

15. Who is your favorite relative? Why?

16. If you could change one thing about your personality, what would it be? Why?

17. If you could change one aspect of the way you look, what would it be? Why?

18. In what ways is college *not* what you expected? In what ways *is* it what you expected?

19. If you could be given a talent you do not already have, what would it be?

20. What is the most expensive thing you ever bought? Why did you buy it? How did you get the money? Was it worth the money?

21. How would you feel if you were told that you had to cook a healthy dinner for six people, including your-

years, you will find that a ready source of ideas is at hand—and that your powers of observation become increasingly strong.

Like an idea book, a **journal** is a record of your ideas, only the entries are written daily. Many writers, both amateur and professional, write journals. Any size notebook *except* pocketsize can serve well for a journal. Fifteen minutes a day can be enough—before going to bed, between classes, on a bus. When you write in your journal, *you* are your audience. The writing is not for publication, so the content and tone can be as personal and informal as you wish.

When writing in your journal, you can draw on your reading, your observations, your dreams. You can write down and respond to quotations that seem particularly meaningful. You can react to movies, plays, and television programs that are memorable. You can think on paper about your opinions, beliefs, family, friends. Writing in a journal gives you the chance to write about whatever you wish. Unlike a diary, a journal is not merely for listing what you did that day. In a journal you put down your thoughts. Writing is a way of thinking, a way of thinking through ideas that need time to develop, a way of wrestling with problems not given to easy solution. Equally important, writing is a way of discovering, of allowing thoughts to emerge as the physical act of writing moves along.

Keeping a journal can help you in three ways. First, writing every day gives you the habit of productivity. The more you write, the more you get used to the feeling of words pouring out of you onto paper, the easier it will become for you to write in all situations. Second, a journal instills the habit of close observation and thinking. Third, a journal serves as an excellent source of ideas when you need to write in response to an assignment.

Having served overseas in the armed forces before going to college, Gary Lee Houseman was attuned to other places and perspectives. He sometimes wrote in his journal about world issues. When he got the assignment to argue against the destruction of the environment, he looked in his journal for possible starting points. Here is a brief excerpt from Houseman's journal.

October 15

Conservation issues always seem to pop up at me when I am reading or watching TV. I get steamed up. What are they doing to our world? I saw a program on TV last night about rain forests. It confirmed what I've been reading about for the last few years. They are destroying the rain forests in the name of progress. They are robbing *me* of a factory that manufactures oxygen and helps clean the air. One species of plant or animal a day, many of which

22

have potential to give us cures for diseases. I read a year ago that a drug from a plant in a South American rain forest is being used to treat Parkinson's disease.

EXERCISE 4

Write a journal entry about one of these subjects. Write to discover what you have to say or to think though what is already on your mind.

1. Your life ten years from now
2. Thanksgiving Day
3. The homeless
4. Learning to play a sport
5. Cartoons
6. Hiroshima
7. Radios
8. Symphony music
9. Politicians
10. VCR's

2
Know how to use freewriting.

Freewriting is writing nonstop. Freewriting means writing down whatever comes into your mind without stopping to worry about whether the ideas are good or the spelling is correct. When you freewrite, you do nothing to interrupt the flow. Let your mind make all kinds of associations. Do not censor any thoughts or flashes of insight. Do not go back and review. Do not cross out. Some days your freewriting might seem mindless, but other days it can reveal interesting ideas to you.

Freewriting gives you the "feel" of pen moving across paper or of fingers in constant motion on the keyboard of a typewriter or computer. This feeling that comes with the physical act of writing serves you well when you draft and revise your writing.

Freewriting works best if you set a goal, such as writing for fifteen minutes or until you have filled one page. Keep going until you reach that goal, even if you must repeat a word over and over until a new word comes to mind.

If you use a word processor, you can avoid the temptation to stop and criticize your writing by doing "invisible writing." Dim the monitor screen so you cannot see your writing. The computer's memory will still be recording your ideas, but you will not able to see them until you brighten the screen again. The same effect is possible for writing by hand if you use worn-out ballpoint pen and a piece of carbon paper between the paper you are writing on and another piece of paper.

Focused freewriting means starting with a set topic. You may focus your freewriting in any way you like—perhaps with a phrase from your journal or a quotation you like. Use the focus as

JOURNALS (CONT.)

self? Who would you go to for advice or help? What would you serve? How successful do you think the dinner would be?

22. Who are some of the most important people in your life? Why? How do you let these people know how much they mean to you?

23. If you could travel anywhere on this planet, where would you like to go? Why? Where would you least like to go? Why?

24. If you could live in any earlier time period, what would you choose? Why?

25. What is your favorite kind of movie? Why? What are its characteristics? What is the best movie of the kind that you have ever seen?

26. How does the weather affect your mood?

27. Do you enjoy playing a sport? Why or why not? What sport do you enjoy the most? Why?

28. If you were fated to be a public figure, what would you want to be: politician, rock star, movie star, environmental activist, news reporter? Why? What would your life be like? How would you treat people less famous than you?

29. If you were to be reincarnated as an animal that reflected your behavior in this life, what would you be? Why? If you could choose what animal to be, what would you be? Why?

30. What teacher has had a great deal of influence on you? Describe the teacher and his or her effect on you.

23

a starting point for writing down as many of your thoughts as you can until you meet the time or page limit you set. Again, do not censor what you say. Keep moving forward.

As with journals, freewriting can be a source for ideas and details to write about. Here is an excerpt from Tara Foster's focused freewriting. She was thinking about narrowing her topic from the subject "an important problem facing today's adult men and women."

> Well, the assignment says a problem. Let's see if I'm going to write a lot of old junk about things. War. War. War is stupid. Unemployment lines and trying to find a job on this campus. Nuclear energy is too frightening to think about. Anyway, I don't know enough to write about it. I really want to think about divorce. The big D. Why bother getting married if I only have a 50–50 chance of making it? I think I'll be in the 50% that makes it. But many of my friends are not making it. Lives ripped apart. Writing like this gets tiring for my hand. Keep moving, keep moving. Sounds like a movie theater usher. My parents had a great marriage. Since my dad died my mother has had a hard time. She has to live alone now that I am out of the house. It isn't easy for her to get used to a new lifestyle.

EXERCISE 5
Freewrite for five minutes on one of these topics.

1. Worrying
2. Procrastinating
3. A famous person, alive or dead
4. Taking tests
5. Loneliness
6. Mark Twain
7. Libraries
8. Spelling
9. Falling in love
10. Peanut butter

‖ **3**
‖ **Know how to use brainstorming.**

Brainstorming means making a list of all the ideas that come to mind associated with a topic. The ideas can be listed as words or phrases. Listmaking, like freewriting, produces its best results when you let your mind range freely, generating quantities of ideas before analyzing them.

You may find that brainstorming allows you to generate many ideas quickly because the format does not call for sentences or paragraphs. You can brainstorm in one concentrated session or over several days, depending on how much time is available for the as-

24

signment. In courses that use collaborative learning procedures, brainstorming in groups can work especially very well. One person's ideas bounce off the next person's, and collectively more ideas get listed.

Brainstorming is done in two steps. First, you make a list. Then you go back and try to find patterns in the list and ways to group the ideas into categories. The items do not have to be in any particular order within the groups. Set aside any items that do not fit into groups. The areas that have the most items in their lists are likely to be ones you can write about most successfully. If an area interests you but its list is thin, brainstorm on that area alone. If you run out of ideas, ask yourself questions to stimulate your thinking. You might try exploratory questions about the topic, such as: What is it? What is it the same as? How is it different? Why or how does it happen? How is it done? What caused it or results from it? What does it look, smell, sound, feel, or taste like?

Tara Foster used brainstorming while she was narrowing her topic about a problem facing today's adult men and women. She decided to see what she could brainstorm about divorce. The result is shown in her random list. Then she grouped her ideas and discovered that she had more to say about living alone than any other aspect of the topic. She used an asterisk (*) to mark off the items that referred to being alone. A few items did not fit into her grouped list, so she dropped them. She then decided to try writing on the topic of living alone, but first she expanded her ideas by asking the "journalist's questions" (2d-4).

Divorce (random list)

financial problems	arguments
many causes of divorce	being on your own again
personality conflicts	sexual problems
shopping alone	impact of divorce
pressure from parents	buying a car alone
children's reactions	incompatibility
religious laws	splitting up the money
hurt and disappointment	living alone
having to start over	fears of loneliness
finding a lawyer	different tastes

Divorce (grouped list)

causes of divorce	—sexual problems
—financial problems	—pressure from parents
—personality conflicts	—financial problems
—arguments	—incompatability
	—different tastes

QUOTATION ABOUT WRITING
Writing is no trouble: you just jot down ideas as they occur to you. The jotting is simplicity itself—it is the occurring which is difficult.

—STEPHEN LEACOCK

QUOTATION ABOUT WRITING
All you need is a room without any particular interruptions.

—JOHN DOS PASSOS

QUOTATION ABOUT WRITING
I need noise and interruptions and irritation: irritation and discomfort are a great starter. The loneliness of doing it any other way would kill me.

—ANITA BROOKNER

25

results of divorce
—living alone*
—being on your own again*
—shopping alone*
—children's reactions

—splitting up the money
—buying a car alone*
—hurt and disappointment
—having to start over
—fears of loneliness*

ANSWERS: EXERCISE 6

Answers will vary from the one shown here. Class discussion will likely reveal disagreement about the main categories and the distribution of items. Such a discussion can serve to emphasize the role of the individual writer as decision maker.

A. *Leaders' personalities:* ambitious, goal oriented, family life (attitude toward it), inventive, determined.
B. *Leadership style:* welcomes new ideas, inspiring, organized, gets job done, decisive, has charisma, authoritative, dangers of exposure (willingness to accept).
C. *Examples of leaders:* presidents, Susan B. Anthony, John F. Kennedy, Lee Iacocca, generals, Martin Luther King, Mahatma Gandhi, Golda Meir.

The item "personality" became category A. "Natural leaders" and "roles of leadership" do not fit into any of the groups.

ANSWERS: EXERCISE 7

Answers will vary.

EXERCISE 6

Here is a brainstormed list for an assignment in political science. The assignment called for a 500-word essay about what makes a good leader. Look over the list and group ideas. Some items might not fit into any group.

personality	roles of leadership	inventive
ambitious	John F. Kennedy	Mahatma Gandhi
presidents	Lee Iacocca	determined
dangers of exposure	family life	gets job done
natural leaders	inspiring	decisive
goal oriented	organized	Golda Meir
Susan B. Anthony	generals	charisma
welcomes new ideas	Martin Luther King	authoritative

EXERCISE 7

Brainstorm on a subject that interests you. First make a random list. Then group ideas within the list. If you cannot think of a subject, use one from Exercise 4 or 5.

‖ **4**
‖ **Know how to use the journalist's questions.**

Another common means for generating ideas is using the **journalist's questions:** *Who? What? When? Why? Where? How?* Asking these questions forces you to approach a topic from several different perspectives.

To expand her ideas about living alone, Tara Foster used the journalist's questions. She looked over her answers and decided that she had enough details to write an essay.

WHO lives alone?
—students going off to college
—students finish school and move to get a job
—singles leaving the military
—divorced people (1 out of 2 marriages end in divorce)
—widowed people (8 out of 10 married women will be widows)

26

WHAT does living alone entail?
—handling practical things
—balancing a checkbook
—opening a checking or savings account
—locating important papers (will, birth certificate, insurance)
—making necessary major purchases
—making new friends
—getting along socially
—dealing with loneliness
—dealing with depression

WHEN do people have problems living alone?
—when they are used to being taken care of
—when they do not know what to expect
—when they try to hide from the statistics

WHY do people live alone?
—want to (May Sarton's essay on the solitary life)
—have no choice
—prefer to live alone than to be unhappily married or to live with a roommate they dislike

WHERE do people live alone?
—apartments
—houses
—motel rooms
—cities
—suburbs
—rural areas

HOW do people cope with living alone?
—they learn how to take care of themselves
—self-reliance
—they get out and meet new people
—they fight loneliness by staying busy

TEACHING TIP
To teach the journalist's questions effectively, you might bring in (or ask students to bring in) some newspaper articles that cover the *w*'s in the first paragraph.

EXERCISE 8

Ask the journalist's questions about one of these subjects.

1. Learning foreign languages
2. Making friends
3. Exercising
4. Driving defensively
5. Teaching
6. Reading a novel
7. Playing the drums
8. Joking
9. Voting
10. Going to college

ANSWERS: EXERCISE 8
Answers will vary.

27

TEACHING TIP

Mapping is a relatively new concept. It is likely that many of your students—and perhaps even you—have not heard of it before now. Mapping can be a refreshing change of pace in place of or in addition to other more traditional idea-gathering techniques. Because mapping is highly visual, it holds a special appeal for some students. Those who hate to do anything formal (such as an outline or even a list) find the apparent anarchy of a map enticing. Students are often engaged by the bunch of balloons developing on the board. Because entire branches of a map can be omitted from an actual essay, dead ends and short roads are not "errors."

Some students take to mapping readily. Others, especially in the beginning, may prefer to have some guidance, at least in the selection of subtopics. For example, an assignment calling for a persuasive essay about air pollution might benefit from a map based on the senses. Ask students to write an example of air pollution in a circle in the center of the page. Then have them draw a line for each sense and circle the name of that sense (smell, taste, sight, hearing, touch). The students can then draw additional lines and circles for each branch of the map.

ANSWERS: EXERCISE 9

Answers will vary.

5
Know how to use mapping.

Mapping, also called *webbing,* is much like brainstorming, but it is more visual and less linear. A "map" looks quite different from sentences, paragraphs, or lists. Many writers find that mapping frees them to think more creatively, to associate ideas more easily.

When you map, start with your subject circled in the middle of a sheet of unlined paper. Next draw a line radiating out from the center and label it with the name of a major division of your subject. Circle it and from that circle move out further to subdivisions. Keep associating to further ideas and to details related to them. When you finish with one major division of your subject, go back to the center and start again with another major division. As you go along, add anything that occurs to you for any section of the map. Continue the process until you run out of ideas.

Gary Lee Houseman used mapping (p. 29) to check what he knew about rain forests, the topic he wanted to write about for his assignment about the destruction of the environment. After mapping, he felt confident that he could begin shaping and drafting his essay.

EXERCISE 9

Think of a topic about which you have some information. Use mapping to chart what you know.

6
Know when to use reading for writing.

The idea-gathering techniques explained so far in this chapter can help you get onto paper what is stored in your mind as a result of experience, observation, and reading. Reading *after* you receive an assignment is a way to get new information and to confirm what you already know.

But reading is not always part of an assignment. Unless an assignment specifically calls for the use of outside sources, ask your instructor if you can use them. Some instructors want students to use what they know rather than what they learn from new reading at the time of the assignment. Gary Lee Houseman, as explained in 2b, was not sure if research was part of his assignment, so he asked and found out that it was not.

On the other hand, some assignments ask you to read a specific work, such as an essay or short story, and write in reaction to it. Other assignments ask for research writing (see Chapter 32).

28

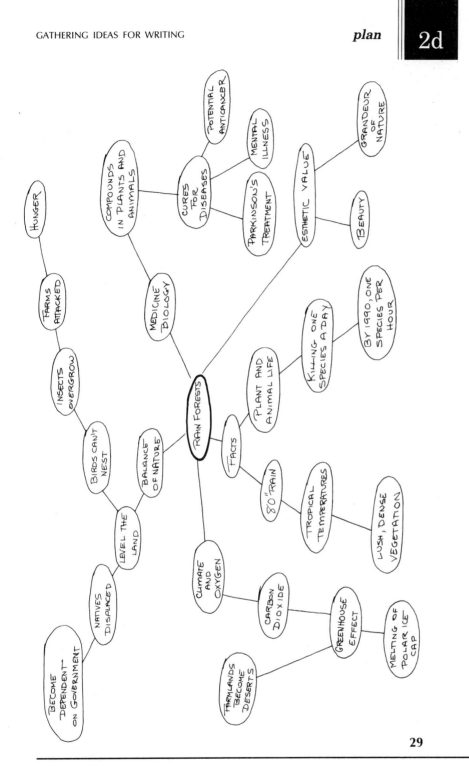

INSTRUCTOR'S NOTES

When you read to write, be sure to *read critically*. Critical reading, a key part of critical thinking, is expected of college students. Both critical thinking and its application to reading are discussed fully in Chapter 5.

‖ 2e
Shape ideas for writing.

Shaping is an important step in making the transition from gathering ideas to drafting an essay. Shaping activities are related to the idea that writing is often called *composing*, the putting together of ideas to create a *composition,* one of the synonyms for *essay.* To shape the ideas that you have gathered, you need to group them, decide on your role and tone, draft a thesis statement, and know how to outline.

As you shape ideas, keep in mind that the form of an essay is related to the ancient notion of a story's having a beginning, a middle, and an end. An essay always has an introduction, a body, and a conclusion. The body consists of a number of paragraphs while the introduction and conclusion are usually one paragraph each. The length of each paragraph is in proportion to the overall length of the essay. Introductory and concluding paragraphs are generally shorter than body paragraphs, and no body paragraph should overpower the others by its length. Chapter 4 discusses and illustrates many types of paragraphs for informative and persuasive writing.

‖ 1
Know how to group ideas.

When you group ideas, your task is to make connections and find patterns. You put related ideas into separate groups. If you used brainstorming (2d-3) or mapping (2d-5) when you were gathering ideas for writing, you have had some experience with the underlying principle of grouping.

When you group material for writing, the concept of *levels of generality* helps you make decisions. One idea is more general than another if it is a larger category—less specific—than the next. For example, "cures for diseases" is more general than "Parkinson's treatment." Also "bank account" is more general than "checking account." In turn, "checking account" is more general than "business checking account" or "regular checking account." And those terms are more general than "account number 221222 at the E–Z Come, E–Z Go Bank." Thus, generality is a relative term. Each idea exists in the context of a whole relationship of ideas. An idea may be general in relationship to one set of ideas, but specific in relation to another set.

Thinking about levels of generality can help you remember that effective writing includes both general statements and specific details. In informative and persuasive writing, general statements must be developed with facts, reasons, examples, and illustrations.

To group ideas, review the material you accumulated while gathering ideas. Then look for general ideas. Next group less general ideas under them. If you find that your notes contain only general ideas, or only very specific details, return again to gathering techniques to supply what you need. One of the standard tools for ordering ideas is making a "subject tree." It shows ideas and details in order from most general at the top to most specific at the bottom. The tree Tara Foster made for her essay on living alone is illustrated. As happens with most writers, Foster did not use every item on the tree when she wrote her essay (she dropped the positive outlook section under "Emotional Life," for example). The material did, however, give her a good start for her drafting.

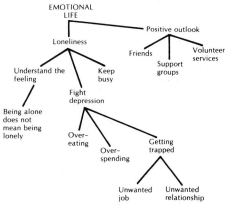

31

ANSWERS: EXERCISE 10
Answers will vary.

EXERCISE 10
Prepare a subject tree on food, on crime prevention, or on another subject of your choice.

2
Order ideas.

Shaping ideas for writing also means ordering them into a logical structure. Writing is a social act, so you have to be sure that you are communicating clearly with your audience. You need to decide what should come first, second, third, and so on, until the last.

Within an essay, and within body paragraphs of an essay, you can order ideas in various ways. Common ones are climactic, chronological, and spatial orders.

Climactic order, also called *emphatic order,* moves from least to most important. Ideas are arranged according to degree of impact on your reader or importance to your subject. The order builds to a climax. You can see examples of such arrangements in Chapter 3: Tara Foster's third draft on living alone and Gary Lee Houseman's essay on rain forests.

Climactic order also refers to structures that move from the simplest to most complex idea or from the most familiar to least familiar idea. For example, you might explain how to drive by starting with physical movements such as turning on the ignition, then talking about distance-awareness such as room to brake and make turns, and finally discussing mental alertness. Such strategies of arrangement are useful not only for ordering major groups of ideas within a large framework, but also for ordering supporting details within each major group.

Chronological order presents ideas according to a time sequence. Chronological order is frequently used in narrating a series of events and in showing a process where steps are normally given in the order in which they occur. For example, you might use chronological order to discuss the career of Martin Luther King or to describe the discovery of the sunken *Titanic*.

Spatial order presents ideas arranged according to their physical locations in relation to one another. This can include top to bottom, near to far, left to right. Spatial order is useful for such topics as describing a stage set or a street scene. Similarly, it would work well for moving from the East Coast to the West Coast when comparing historic preservation programs in New York, Chicago, and San Francisco.

These patterns and others are discussed and illustrated with sample paragraphs in Chapter 4.

32

3
Determine your role and tone.

In all writing situations, you have to play a **role.** Some assignments specify a role, such as being a high school teacher writing to students who have graduated and gone to college. In such cases, you have to imagine what that person would say and would sound like when saying it. Most assignments, however, do not specify a role. You are expected to be yourself.

How you define yourself is important. As an adult writing to an adult audience, you are expected to sound reasonable and moderate. This stance is reflected in your **tone**—*what you say* and *how you say it*. Tone can be broadly described as informal or formal. The tone is informal in the journal entry on page 22 and the freewriting on page 24. As you move from writing for the private you to writing for an audience, you are expected to move toward a more formal tone. This does not mean that you should use overblown language or put on airs that make you sound artificial (see 21d). Most audiences for whom you write expect a tone midway between informal and highly formal. For examples of student writing using a tone appropriate for a general audience, see the third drafts of the essays in Chapter 3; the paragraphs by students in Chapter 4; the research paper in Chapter 33; and various other papers and essays in Chapter 34.

Your tone also has to take into account the writing situation—especially topic, purpose, and audience. For example, if you are supposed to write a humorous piece about current politics, you should inject humor and use a tone that fits what you are saying. On the other hand, if you are asked to discuss how local officials are handling a serious drought or an increase in violent crimes, you should assume that you are supposed to be serious. *Serious* does not mean without spirit, however.

4
Draft a thesis statement.

A **thesis statement** is the central theme of an essay. It is evidence that you have something definite to say about the topic. Because it prepares your reader for the essence of what you discuss in an essay, the thesis statement must accurately reflect the content of the essay. A list of the basic requirements for a thesis statement is on page 34.

Often, instructors ask for more than the basic requirements. For example, you might be required to put your thesis statement at the end of your introductory paragraph. The third draft of the essay

INSTRUCTOR'S NOTES

TEACHING TIP

The notion of *focus* in a thesis statement might be new to some students. A useful analogy can be that the topic is the subject, but the focus is the predicate. Without predication, sentences make no assertion. As Josephine Miles, Professor of English at the University of California at Berkeley, said in her important monograph "Working Out Ideas: Predication and Other Uses of Language": "Sentence making is predication, and to predicate is to assert an idea, selecting and treating facts from a point of view."

BASIC REQUIREMENTS FOR A THESIS STATEMENT

1. It states the essay's main idea—the central point you are making to your readers.
2. It reflects the essay's purpose—either to give your readers information or to persuade your readers to agree with you.
3. It includes a focus—your assertion that conveys your point of view.
4. It *may* briefly state the major subdivisions of the essay's topic.

---

on living alone and the essay on rain forests (Chapter 3) are examples. In addition, many instructors require that the thesis statement be contained in one sentence. Others permit two sentences if the material to be covered warrants such length. All requirements, basic and additional, are designed to help you learn to think in structured patterns that communicate clearly with readers.

In most writing situations, you will not be certain that all parts of a thesis statement accurately reflect what you say in the essay until you have written one or more drafts. To start shaping your essay, however, you need a **preliminary thesis statement**. Often a preliminary thesis statement is too broad ("Rain forests must not be destroyed") or too vague ("Rain forests are important to the human race"). Expect to revise a preliminary thesis statement as you write successive drafts of your essay, but an early version helps you find direction in your writing. When you revise into a **final thesis statement**, make sure that it clearly applies to the content of the essay as it has evolved through its drafts.

Consider the final thesis statement in Tara Foster's essay on living alone (in Chapter 3).

> Chances are high that most adult men and women will have to know how to live alone, briefly or longer, at some time in their lives.

Foster's thesis statement reveals that the *topic* is living alone, the *purpose* is to give information, and the *focus* is that chances are high that most people will have to know how to live alone at some time in their lives.

Here are thesis statements written for 500- to 700-word essays with an **informative purpose.** The ineffective versions resemble some types of preliminary thesis statements. The effective versions are final thesis statements written by students after they had gath-

34

ered and grouped ideas. Note that the good versions contain the first three characteristics listed in the Basic Requirements chart. One of the good versions also includes the major subdivisions of the topic.

TOPIC	houseplants
NO	Houseplants can be harmful.
YES	Certain seemingly innocent household plants can cause serious health problems, even death.
TOPIC	science fiction
NO	There are many types of science fiction.
YES	Science fiction novels range from stories with scary creatures to stories that make serious comments about modern society.
TOPIC	the history of American architecture
NO	The history of American architecture is varied.
YES	American architecture has gone through four major phases: from colonial to federal to victorian to modern.

For a persuasive purpose, Gary Lee Houseman wrote this thesis statement for his essay about rain forests (Chapter 3):

Rain forests must be preserved because they offer the human race many irreplaceable resources.

Houseman's thesis statement reveals that the *topic* is rain forests, the *purpose* is to persuade, and the *focus* is that rain forests must be preserved because they are irreplaceable.

Here are ineffective and effective thesis statements written for 500- to 700-word essays with a **persuasive purpose.** The ineffective versions resemble some types of preliminary thesis statements. The effective versions are final thesis statements written by students after they had gathered and grouped ideas. Note that the good versions contain the first three characteristics listed in the Basic Requirements chart. Two of the good versions also include the major subdivisions of the topic.

TOPIC	industrial pollution
NO	Industrial pollution is a serious hazard in modern society.
YES	Unless industrial pollution is controlled more effectively in the near future, this planet will be poisoned beyond repair.

COORDINATED RESOURCES

Alternate examples and exercises for this chapter are available in the *S & S Workbook for Writers,* Gordon and Troyka.

Transparency masters are available for many of the screened lists and other displays in this chapter.

Students can practice and test their knowledge of terms, key concepts, and applications of material in this chapter by using the *Study Guide to the S & S Handbook for Writers,* West.

35

ANSWERS: EXERCISE 11

1. *Topic:* emphasizing foreign languages in U.S. schools. *Purpose:* to persuade. *Focus:* such knowledge would benefit U.S. culture, business, and politics.
2. *Topic:* babies in their first year of life. *Purpose:* to inform. *Focus:* acquire increasingly sophisticated motor skills as they move from reflexive to nonreflexive activities.
3. *Topic:* successful marriages. *Purpose:* to persuade. *Focus:* have to adjust to the unexpected problems that come along.
4. *Topic:* the earth's surface. *Purpose:* to inform. *Focus:* four major landforms: plains, plateaus, hills, and mountains.
5. *Topic:* programs to eliminate drunk driving. *Purpose:* to persuade. *Focus:* have been somewhat effective but more are needed.

ANSWERS: EXERCISE 12

This exercise refers to the assignment mentioned in Exercise Six: it was a 500-word essay about what makes a good leader. The four thesis statements in this exercise should be evaluated in light of that assignment and the chart of "Basic Requirements for a Thesis Statement" in this chapter.

The fourth thesis statement is successful because it states a main idea (a comparison of power leaders and personality leaders); it reflects a purpose (to inform); it has a focus (that the two types of leaders differ); and it briefly states the major subdivisions of the topic: sources of authority, personal qualities, and leadership skills.

In the first thesis statement the concepts are too broad. The second thesis statement lacks a focus. The third thesis statement is acceptable, although stating the subdivisions of the topic adds interest.

TOPIC	the moods music creates
NO	Music can create many moods.
YES	Music can inspire people to feel romantic, patriotic, or nostalgic.
TOPIC	choosing a major in college
NO	Choosing a major takes much thinking.
YES	College students should choose their majors according to their interests, their personalities, and their financial goals.

EXERCISE 11

Identify the topic, purpose, and focus of each thesis statement.

1. Emphasizing foreign languages in U.S. schools would benefit U.S. culture, business, and politics.
2. Although programs to eliminate drunk driving have been somewhat effective, additional programs are sorely needed.
3. The earth's surface can be divided into four major landforms: plains, plateaus, hills, and mountains.
4. To be successful, marriages have to adjust to unexpected problems that come along.
5. In the first year of life, babies acquire increasingly sophisticated motor skills as they move from reflexive to nonreflexive activities.

EXERCISE 12

Here are several versions of a thesis statement for the material shown in Exercise 6. Identify the characteristics of the final thesis statement based on the Basic Requirements chart on page 34. Then explain why the student rejected each of the first three versions.

1. Not all leaders are the same.
2. There are two basic styles of leadership.
3. Power leaders are different from personality leaders.
4. Power leaders and personality leaders differ in their sources of authority, their personal qualities, and their leadership skills.

EXERCISE 13

Here are writing assignments, narrowed topics, and tentative thesis statements. Evaluate each thesis statement according to the Basic Requirements chart on page 34.

1. *Nursing class assignment:* 700- to 800-word informative report on one non-traditional form of medicine. Audience: Other students and instructor. Topic: Acupuncture. Thesis: Acupuncture differs from Western medicine in its definition of disease, its diagnostic methods, and its style of treatment.

2. *Writing class assignment for a movie review that might be published in the campus newspaper:* 200 words. Audience: instructor and possibly the whole student body. Topic: *Out of Africa.* Thesis: I really liked *Out of Africa.*

3. *Mass Communications class assignment:* Three-page report on job opportunities available in local media. Audience: classmates and instructor. Topic: The *Evening Times.* Thesis: Working for the *Evening Times* looks like it would be a lot of fun.

4. *Writing class assignment:* Simulation: As part of your work-study job in the college's Public Relations Office, you have been asked to prepare a plan for a day's activities for a visiting group of 10 Chinese high school students, all of whom speak English. Audience: instructor and the college's Director of Public Relations. Topic: Follow a typical college student's day. Thesis: As much as possible, the visiting students should share the experiences of typical American students, including their academic and social activities.

5. *Astronomy class:* One- or two-page explanation of the movement of the planets suitable for elementary school students. Audience: instructor. Thesis: While the stars remain fixed on the celestial sphere, the sun proceeds ponderously on its annual ecliptic journey among them, the wandering planets perform convoluted gyrations within the zodiac.

5
Know how to outline.

Many writers find outlining a useful planning strategy. An outline helps pull together the results of gathering and ordering ideas and preparing a thesis statement. It also provides a visual guide and checklist. Some writers always use outlines; others prefer not to outline. Writers who outline do so at various points in the writing process: for example, before drafting, to arrange and organize material; or while revising, to check the logic of an early draft's arrangement and organization. Especially for informative and persuasive writing, outlines can clearly reveal flaws—missing information, undesirable repetitions, digressions from the thesis.

As a college writer, you will likely find that some instructors require outlines. Understandably, they want you to practice the discipline of planning the arrangement and organization of your writ-

ANSWERS: EXERCISE 13

1. The thesis statement is good because it states a main idea, reflects a purpose (to inform), and includes a focus. It also states the major subdivisions of the topic.

2. The thesis statement is weak. It lacks a focus. The audience of a movie review expects a main idea larger than "I liked it."

3. This thesis statement is not appropriate for an assignment that calls for a report on job opportunities in local media. The words "a lot of fun" are too informal and nonspecific to convey a main idea.

4. This thesis statement is good because it states a main idea, reflects a purpose (to persuade), and includes a focus.

5. This thesis statement is poor. The language is not only inappropriate for the audience but also it is overblown and pretentious (more about such word choices in 21d of this book).

TEACHING TIP
If your students have trouble organizing an outline, you might suggest that they write each item on a 3 × 5″ index card. The ability to move the cards around, make piles, and easily eliminate items often facilitates students' work.

37

ing. The more clearly and sensibly your material is presented, the better chance it has of reaching your audience.

Before the final draft of an essay is complete, an outline is only a projection, an estimate of what the essay will say. Once you start writing, the act of writing might lead you to change your plans somewhat. If you are working from an outline and you make changes, be sure to revise your outline at the end. Then check to make sure that your changes have not upset the logic and arrangement of your essay.

An **informal outline** does not have to follow all the formal conventions of outlining. It lists the main ideas of an essay—the major subdivisions of the thesis statement. It also lists subordinate ideas and details, but without attention to levels of generality (see 2e-2). An informal outline is particularly useful for planning when the order within main ideas is still evolving or when topics imply their own arrangement, such as spatial arrangement for describing a room or chronological order for describing an event.

An informal outline can also be a *working plan,* a layout of the major parts of the material intended for an essay. It can be the next logical step after a brainstormed list (2d-3), a map (2d-5), or a subject tree (2e-2). An informal outline can also serve as an early draft of a formal outline. Here is part of an informal outline that served as a working plan for Gary Lee Houseman when he was writing his essay on rain forests. This excerpt includes the thesis and three of the five body paragraphs.

> Thesis statement: Rain forests must be preserved because they offer the human race many irreplaceable resources.
> *Definition of rain forest*
>   80 inches rainfall a year
>   Tropical regions (warm temperatures)
>   Lush, dense vegetation
>   Canopy
>   Branches overlap
>   As high as the trees (I think about 98 feet)
>   Evergreens
>   Plant and insect life thrive
> *Biomedical uses*
>   Over 1,400 plants and animals
>   Compounds for medicines
>   Parkinson's
>   Mental illnesses
>   Anticancer

38

Natural balances
> Level forests ⟶ birds leave ⟶ insects are no longer eaten
> by birds ⟶ insects overgrow and eat crops ⟶ hunger
> Level forests ⟶ natives displaced ⟶ become dependent on
> government ⟶ more pressure on national debt

A **formal outline** follows conventions concerning content and format. The conventions are designed to display material so that relationships among ideas are clear and so that the content is orderly. A formal outline can be a *topic outline* or a *sentence outline*. Each item in a topic outline is a word or phrase; each item in a sentence outline is a complete sentence. Formal outlines never mix the two. Many experienced writers who use formal outlines find that a sentence outline brings them closer to drafting than does a topic outline. Each item in a sentence outline contains a **predicate.** As a grammatical unit, the predicate includes the sentence's verb. As a unit of communication, the predicate states the focus of the sentence. For example, "compounds for medicines" on a topic outline would carry more information on a sentence outline: "Compounds for medicines come from many plants and animals in the rain forests."

PATTERN FOR FORMAL OUTLINE OF AN ESSAY

Thesis Statement: ....
....
  I. First main idea ....
....
    A. First subordinate idea ....
....
      1. First reason or example..
....
      2. Second reason or example ....
....
        a. First supporting detail ....
....
        b. Second supporting detail ....
....
    B. Second subordinate idea...
....
 II. Second main idea..
....

INSTRUCTOR'S NOTES

When writing a formal outline, you are expected to observe the following conventions.

1. **Numbers, letters, and indentations.** All parts of a formal outline are systematically indented and numbered or lettered. Capital roman numerals (I, II, III) signal major subdivisions of the topic. Indented capital letters (A, B) signal the next level of generality. Further indented arabic numbers (1, 2, 3) show the third level of generality. Yet further indented lowercase letters (a, b) show the fourth level, if there is one. The principle here is that within each major subdivision, each succeeding level of the outline shows more specific detail than the one before it. If an outline entry is longer than one line, the second line is indented as far as the first word of the preceding line.

2. **More than one entry at each level.** At all points on an outline, there is no I without a II, no A without a B, and so on. If a category has only one subdivision, you need to either eliminate that subdivision or expand the material to at least two subdivisions.

   No   A. Grown children leaving home
               1. Moving to other cities
           B. Married people not being together forever

   Yes   A. Grown children moving to other cities
           B. Married people not being together forever

   Yes   A. Grown children moving to other cities
               1. Going away to school
               2. Taking jobs
           B. Married people not being together forever

3. **Levels of generality.** All subdivisions are at the same level of generality. A main idea cannot be paired with a supporting detail.

   No   I. Taking care of practical matters
          II. Not overeating
   Yes   I. Taking care of practical matters
          II. Establishing new friendships

4. **Overlap.** Headings do not overlap. What is covered in A, for example, must be quite distinct from what is covered in B.

   No   I. Grown children moving to other cities
           A. Going away to school

40

B. Continuing an education
YES   I. Grown children moving to other cities
    A. Going away to school
    B. Taking jobs

5. **Parallelism.** All entries are grammatically parallel. For example, all items start with *-ing* forms of verbs or all items are adjectives and nouns. For more about parallelism in outlines, see 18e.

NO   I. Taking care of practical matters
    II. New friends
YES   I. Taking care of practical matters
    II. Making new friends
YES   I. Practical matters
    II. New friends

6. **Capitalization and punctuation.** Except for proper nouns°, only the first word of each entry is capitalized. In a sentence outline, end each sentence with a period. Do not punctuate the ends of entries in a topic outline.

7. **Introductory and concluding paragraphs.** The content of the introductory and concluding paragraphs is not part of a formal outline. The thesis statement comes before (above) the roman numeral I entry.

Here is a topic outline of the final draft of Tara Foster's essay on living alone (shown in Chapter 3). A sentence outline follows so that you can compare the two types of outlines.

Thesis Statement: Chances are high that adult men and women will have to know how to live alone, briefly or longer, at some time in their lives.

I. Living alone because of circumstances
  A. Grown children moving to other cities
    1. Going away to school
    2. Taking jobs
  B. Married people not being married forever
    1. One out of two marriages ending in divorce
    2. Eight out of ten married women becoming widowed, usually late in life
II. Taking care of practical matters
  A. Opening a checking account
    1. Comparing bank services

      2. Comparing advantages of different kinds of checking accounts
  B. Making major purchases
      1. Replacing a refrigerator
      2. Buying a car
III. Establishing new friendships
  A. Students getting used to going to classes without old friends
      1. Being able to concentrate better
      2. Being able to meet new friends
  B. Single adults going to the beach or parties
IV. Dealing with loneliness
  A. Understanding the feeling
  B. Avoiding depression
      1. Not overeating
      2. Not overspending
      3. Not getting into unwanted situations
         a. Taking the wrong job
         b. Going into the wrong relationship
  C. Keeping busy

Compare the topic outline you have just read with the following sentence outline of the same material.

Thesis Statement: Chances are high that adult men and women will have to know how to live alone, briefly or longer, at some time in their lives.

I. Circumstances sometimes force people to live alone.
  A. Grown children leave home.
      1. They go to college or graduate school.
      2. They go to other cities to get jobs.
  B. Many married people do not stay married forever.
      1. One out of two marriages end in divorce.
      2. Eight out of ten married women become widowed, usually late in life.
II. People living alone have to take care of practical matters.
  A. Students might have to open a checking account.
      1. They can compare bank services.
      2. They can compare advantages of different kinds of checking accounts.
  B. Divorced or widowed people might have to make major purchases.
      1. A refrigerator might have to be replaced.
      2. A car might not be worth fixing.

III. People living alone can establish new friendships.
 A. Students get used to going to classes without old friends.
  1. One advantage is students might concentrate better.
  2. A second advantage is students can meet new friends.
 B. Single adults get used to going to the beach or parties alone.
IV. People living alone sometimes have to deal with loneliness.
 A. First comes the importance of understanding the feeling.
 B. Second comes the importance of avoiding depression.
  1. Overeating can result.
  2. Overspending can result.
  3. Getting into unwanted situations can result.
   a. People might take the wrong job.
   b. People might go into the wrong relationship.
 C. Third comes the importance of keeping busy.

EXERCISE 14

Here is a sentence outline. Revise it into a topic outline. Decide which form you would prefer as a guide to writing. Explain your decision.

Thesis Statement: Common noise pollution, although it causes many problems in our society, can be reduced.
I. Noise pollution comes from many sources.
 A. Noise pollution occurs in many large cities.
  1. Traffic rumbles and screeches.
  2. Construction work blasts.
  3. Airplanes roar overhead.
 B. Noise pollution occurs in the workplace.
  1. Machines in factories boom.
  2. Machines used for outdoor construction thunder.
 C. Noise pollution occurs during leisure-time activities.
  1. Stereo headphones blare directly into eardrums.
  2. Film soundtracks bombard the ears.
  3. Music in discos assaults the ears.
II. Noise pollution causes many problems.
 A. Excessive noise damages hearing.
 B. Excessive noise alters moods.
 C. Constant exposure to noise limits learning ability.
III. Reduction in noise pollution is possible.
 A. Pressure from community groups can support efforts to control excessive noise.
 B. Traffic regulations can help alleviate congestion and noise.
 C. Pressure from workers can force management to reduce noise.
 D. People can wear earplugs to avoid excessive noise.
 E. Reasonable sound levels for headphones, soundtracks, and discos can be required.

ANSWER: EXERCISE 14

Answer may vary from the following.
I. Sources of noise pollution
 A. Large cities
  1. Traffic
  2. Construction work
  3. Airplanes
 B. Workplace
  1. Factory machines
  2. Outdoor construction machines
 C. Leisure-time activities
  1. Stereo headphones
  2. Film soundtracks
  3. Disco music
II. Problems from noise pollution
 A. Damages hearing
 B. Alters moods
 C. Limits learning ability
III. How to reduce noise pollution
 A. Pressure from community groups
 B. Traffic regulations
 C. Pressure on management by workers
 D. Earplugs
 E. Reasonable sound levels

INSTRUCTOR'S NOTES

3

DRAFTING AND REVISING

In the writing process, drafting and revising follow from planning and shaping, discussed in Chapter 2. **Drafting** means getting ideas onto paper in sentences and paragraphs. In everyday conversation, people usually use the word *writing* when they talk about the activities involved in drafting. In discussing the writing process, however, the word *drafting* is more descriptive. It conveys the idea that the final product of the writing process is the result of a number of versions, each successively closer to what the writer intends and to what will communicate clearly to readers. **Revising** means taking a draft from its preliminary to its final version by evaluating, adding, cutting, moving material, editing, and proofreading.

▌▌ 3a
Know how to get started.

If ever you have trouble getting started when the time arrives for drafting (or for any other part of the writing process), you are not alone. When experienced writers get temporarily stalled, they recognize what is happening and deal with it.

QUOTATION ABOUT WRITING
Writers are notorious for using any reason to keep from working: over-researching, retyping, going to meetings, waxing the floors—anything.
—GLORIA STEINEM

44

If you run into a writing block, make sure that you are not being influenced by any of these common myths about writing.

FALSE   Writers are born, not made.

TRUE   Everyone can write. The key to being a good writer is being a patient rewriter. Rough drafts are not final drafts, but they provide useful starting places.

FALSE   Writers have to be "in the mood" to write.

TRUE   If writers always waited for "the mood" to descend, few would write at all. After all, news reporters have to write to meet deadlines for stories, and professional writers often have to meet deadlines set by their contracts.

FALSE   Writers have to know how to spell every word and to recite the rules of grammar perfectly.

TRUE   One useful definition of a good speller is someone who does not ignore the quiet inner voice that says a word looks wrong and has to be checked. The same principle applies to grammar.

FALSE   Writing can be done at the last minute.

TRUE   Writing takes time. Ideas do not leap onto paper in final, polished form. Not only do writers need to go through the various activities of the writing process, but they also need time to get distance from a draft so that they can revise with fresh eyes.

Once you realize the truths behind myths about writing, you are ready to try the time-proven ways experienced writers get started when they are blocked. The key to getting these suggestions to work is to suspend judgment; do not criticize yourself when you are trying to get underway. The time for evaluation comes during revision, but revising too soon can stall some writers. The writing that results from these ideas is most certainly not a final draft, but having something on paper to work with is a comfort—and can serve as a springboard to drafting.

1. Avoid staring at a blank page. Fill up the paper. Relax your mind and allow your hand to move across the page or keyboard. Write words, scribble, or draw while you think about your topic. The movement of filling the paper while thinking can help stimulate your mind to turn to actual drafting.

TEACHING TIP
Getting started seems hardest for writers at the point when they have to move from planning and shaping to actual writing. Dealing with writer's block is no small matter for writers, instructors of writing, and students. You might take some class time to discuss myths about writing. I am interested in gathering more myths. If you or your students know any, please send me the FALSE/TRUE information for publication—with a byline—in the next edition of this *Annotated Instructor's Edition.* Send the material to me c/o the English Editor, Prentice-Hall, Englewood Cliffs, NJ 07632. (In case of duplicates, we will use the first to arrive.)

QUOTATION ABOUT WRITING
The best time for planning a book is while you're doing the dishes.
—AGATHA CHRISTIE

QUOTATION ABOUT WRITING
I don't wait to be struck by lightning and I don't need certain slants of light in order to write.   —TONI MORRISON

45

TEACHING TIP

Students may be skeptical of the value of picturing themselves working. Share with them these examples of successful people who use visualization: John Ueless, a champion pole-vaulter, used visualization before each meet. He would see himself winning by clearing the bar at a particular height. In his mind, he rehearsed every movement, as well as seeing the crowd and even smelling the grass when pole vaulting out of doors.

Jack Nicklaus says that visualization gives him a "winning feeling": "This gives me a line to the cup just as clearly as if it's been tattooed on my brain. With that feeling, all I have to do is swing the clubs and let nature take its course."

You might want to give students time to visualize in class prior to writing. Tell them to close their eyes and sit comfortably. Tell them to imagine themselves reading a question and realizing they know how they want to respond. Tell them to imagine themselves making a list of notes, rearranging their material, writing. At each stage, remind them to imagine themselves feeling confident and successful. Then have them write. Later, discuss how they felt when writing this time in contrast to their past experiences. This technique often does little for people at first, so try to give your students frequent opportunities to employ visualization techniques.

2. Use "focused freewriting" (see 2d-2). Think about your topic, and write sentences about it nonstop for ten or fifteen minutes or until you fill a few pages. Some of the sentences you write can help you begin actual drafting.

3. Picture yourself writing. Before you get up in the morning, when you are waiting for a bus, or as you are walking to classes, get a full visual image of yourself writing. Imagine yourself in the place where you usually write, with the materials you need, busy at work. Many professional writers say that they write more easily if they picture themselves doing it first.

4. Write your material in a letter to a friend. This gives you a chance to relax and chat on paper to someone you like and feel comfortable with. The letter can be a good beginning for a less informal draft.

5. Write your material as if you are someone else. Take your pick: you can be a friend writing to you, an instructor writing to you or a whole class, your parent writing to you, a person in history writing to you or to someone else. Once you take on a role, you will often feel less inhibited about writing.

6. Switch your method of writing. If you usually typewrite or use a word processor, try writing by hand. If you usually use a pen, switch to a pencil. Whenever you write by hand, especially when you are having trouble getting started, try to treat yourself to good quality paper. The pleasure of writing on smooth, strong paper is considerable and helps many experienced writers want to keep going.

7. Start in the middle. If you do not know what you want to write in your introductory paragraph, start with a body paragraph. Write from the center of your essay out, instead of from beginning to end.

▮‖ 3b
Know how to draft.

Once you have your ideas planned and shaped for an essay, you are ready to **compose** them on paper. When you compose, you put together sentences and paragraphs into a unified whole. A *first draft* is a preliminary draft. First drafts are not meant to be perfect; they are meant to give you something to revise. According to your personal preferences and each writing situation, you can use any of these ways (or your own ways) of writing a first draft.

1. Put aside all your notes from planning and shaping. Write a "dis-

46

covery draft." As you write, be open to discovering ideas and making connections that spring to mind during the physical act of writing. When you finish a discovery draft, you can decide to use it either as a first draft or as part of your notes when you write a structured first draft.

2. Keep your notes from planning and shaping in front of you and use them as you write. Write a structured first draft. Work through all of your material. Depending on the expected length of your essay, draft either the entire essay or blocks of one or two paragraphs at one time.

3. Use a combination of approaches. When you know the shape of your material, write according to that structure. When you feel "stuck" about what to say next, switch to writing as you would for a discovery draft.

The direction of drafting is forward: *keep pressing ahead.* If you are worried about the spelling of a word or a point in grammar, underline the material so that you can come back later and check it—and keep moving ahead. If you cannot think of a word that says precisely what you want, write an easy synonym and circle it so that you will remember to change it later—and move on. If you are worried about your sentence style or the order in which you present the supporting details within a paragraph, write *Style?* or *Order?* in the margin so that you can return to that spot later to revise— and press forward. If you feel that you are running dry, reread what you have written—but only to propel yourself to further writing, not to distract you into rewriting.

As you move into drafting an essay, use the essay's thesis statement as your springboard. A thesis statement has great organizing power. It expresses the central theme that controls and limits what the essay will cover. A thesis statement contains (1) the *topic,* narrowed appropriately for the writing situation; (2) a *focus* which presents what you are saying about the topic; and (3) a *purpose* which is either informative or persuasive as explained in 1b.

As you use your thesis statement, remember that its role is to serve as a connecting thread that unifies the essay. **Unity** is important for communicating clearly to an audience. You achieve unity when all parts of the essay relate to the thesis statement and to each other. Also, an essay is unified when it meets these criteria: (1) The thesis statement clearly ties into all topic sentences. (2) The support for each topic sentence—the paragraph development—contains examples, reasons, facts, and details directly related to the topic and, in turn, to the thesis statement.

QUOTATION ABOUT WRITING
I don't think teaching has ever taken up my writing time. I can't write more than [five hours] a day. That's the energy that I have to give to it. . . . You trade ideas with students. You are forced to articulate your ideas. In all that, there is some benefit to your writing.
—N. SCOTT MOMADAY

QUOTATION ABOUT WRITING
When I sit at my table to write, I never know what it's going to be till I'm under way. I trust in inspiration, which sometimes comes and sometimes doesn't. But I don't sit back waiting for it. I work *every* day.
—ALBERTO MORAVIA

INSTRUCTOR'S NOTES

Equally important, your essay must be **coherent** to communicate clearly to an audience. An essay is coherent when it supplies guideposts that communicate the relations among ideas. Coherence is achieved through the use of transitional expressions, pronouns, repetition, and parallel structures. These techniques operate within paragraphs and to connect paragraphs; they are discussed and illustrated fully in 4b.

When you write, plan your practical arrangements. For example, try to work in a place where you are comfortable and will not be disturbed. If someone comes along and interrupts, you might lose a train of thought or an idea that has flashed into your mind. Also, have enough paper on hand so that you need to use only one side of each sheet of paper. When you revise, you should be able to spread your full draft in front of you so that you can physically see how the parts relate to one another. As you write, leave large margins and plenty of room between lines so that you have space to enter changes when you revise.

This chapter (and Chapter 2) refer to the writing processes of two students, Tara Foster and Gary Lee Houseman, for illustration. Their writing assignments are shown on page 16. Their work in gathering ideas and shaping their material is shown in Chapter 2. In this chapter, you will see three drafts of Foster's essay and the final draft of Houseman's essay.

The dominant purpose of Foster's essay is *informative*. Here is the thesis statement that serves as Foster's central theme:

> Chances are high that most adult men and women will have to know how to live alone, briefly or longer, at some time in their lives.

Here is how Foster used her thesis statement to help her write the first draft of her essay.

BACKGROUND
To gather examples of student writing for the *S & S Handbook,* Prentice-Hall sponsored a project that enlisted the help of faculty across the United States. Dubbed the "Student Writing Project," this search resulted in my being able to draw on a bank of student essays (all in three drafts) and student paragraphs. The names of the participating faculty appear in the handbook's "Preface to the Instructor."

FIRST DRAFT

Lots of people are scared of living alone. They like to live with others. When the statistics catch up with you, therefore, you are never prepared. Chances are high that most adult men and women will have to know how to live alone, briefly or longer, at some time in their lives.

Many grown children move away from their hometowns to get an education or take jobs. Also, married people think they'll always be together, but many marriages

---

end in divorce. The divorce rate is frightening.
People are not making the right choices, or they are
too immature to work out their differences. Fighting
over money, parents, or religion although the underlying
reason is lack of compatability. Divorce brings the
couple and their children a great deal of pain.

I read recently in the newspaper where estimates
are that in the next twety years, 8 out of 10 married
women end up widows. This will happen to most of
them late in life. This statistic is even sadder
than divorce. I feel sorry for any happily married
person whose spouse dies.

People living alone need to establish new friendships.
When single people feel self-reliant. It's easier
for them to start getting out and meeting new people.
Some students are in the habit of always going to classes
with a friend, and they can be find that they can
concentrate better on the course. And also have a chance
to make some new friends. Friends can help people take care
of practical by keeping them company and going with them.

One good way to prepare for living alone is to
learn how to take care of practical matters. Many people
don't know how to do something as simple as opening a
checking account. Making major purchases is something
people have to handle. Such as a refrigerator that can't
be repaired or a useless car. Shop around and make price
comparisons. All decisions are much easier than at first.

Feelings of lonliness are the hardest to take.
I think this is what people fear the most. First,
people have to understand what is going on. Being
alone does not mean being lonely. Second, singles
have to fight depression. Third, they have to keep busy.

People living alone have to handle practical,
social, and emotional problems.

49

3c *draft* DRAFTING AND REVISING

3c
Know how to revise.

To **revise** you must evaluate. You assess your first (or subsequent) draft and decide where improvements are needed. Then you make the improvements and evaluate them alone and in the context of the surrounding material. This process continues until you are satisfied that the essay is in final draft.

To revise successfully you need first to expect to revise. Some people think that anyone who revises is not a good writer. Only the opposite is true. Writing is largely revising. Experienced writers know that the final draft of any writing project shows on paper only a fraction of the decisions made from draft to successive draft. Revision means "to see again," to look with fresh eyes. Good writers are rewriters, people who can truly *see* their drafts and rework them into better form.

To revise successfully you need also to distance yourself from each draft. You need to read your writing with objective eyes. A natural reaction of many writers is to want to hold onto their every word, especially if they had trouble getting started with a draft. If you ever have such feelings, resist them and work on distancing yourself from the material. Before revising, give yourself some time for that rosy glow of authorial pride to dim a bit. The classical writer Horace recommended waiting nine years. Given the hectic pace of modern life, you do not have that much time. But wait a few hours, if at all possible, before going back to look anew at your work.

If time does not help you develop an objective perspective, try reading your draft aloud; hearing the material can give you a fresh new sense of an essay's content and organization. Another useful method is to read the paragraphs in your essay in reverse order, starting with the conclusion; eventually, of course, you must read your essay from beginning to end, but to achieve distance you can temporarily depart from that sequence.

1
Know the steps and activities of revision.

Once you understand the attitudes that underlie the revision process, you are ready to move into actual revising.

As you revise, you are working to improve your draft at all levels: whole essay, paragraph, sentence, and word. A revised draft usually looks quite different from its preceding draft. To revise you need to engage in all the activities in the charts on p. 51. As you

50

STEPS FOR REVISING

1. Shift mentally from suspending judgment (during idea gathering and drafting) to making judgments.
2. Read your draft critically to evaluate it. Be guided by the questions on the Revision Checklist in this chapter or by material supplied by your instructor.
3. Decide whether to write an entirely new draft or to revise the one you have. Do not be overly harsh. While some early drafts serve best as "discovery drafts" rather than first drafts, many early drafts provide sufficient raw material for the revision process to get underway.
4. Be systematic. Do not evaluate at random. You need to pay attention to many different elements of a draft, from overall organization to choice of words. Some writers prefer to consider all elements concurrently, but most writers work better when they concentrate on different elements during separate rounds of revision.

engage in each activity, keep the whole picture in mind. Changes affect more than the place revised. Check that your separate changes operate well in the context of the whole essay or a particular paragraph. Here again, getting distance from your material allows you the chance to be more objective.

MAJOR ACTIVITIES DURING REVISION

Add. Insert needed words, sentences, and paragraphs. If your additions require new content, return to idea-gathering techniques (see 2d).
Cut. Get rid of whatever goes off the topic or repeats what has already been said.
Replace. As needed, substitute new words, sentences, and paragraphs for what you have cut.
Move material around. Change the sequence of paragraphs if the material is not presented in logical order (see 2e-2). Move sentences within paragraphs or to other paragraphs if arrangements seem illogical (see 4c).

Revising is usually separate from editing (3d). During editing you concentrate on important surface features such as correct spell-

TEACHING TIP

You might want to emphasize to your students that the change in attitude is fairly sharp when writers switch from generating prose to revising it. Making this fact conscious often helps students understand and feel comfortable with the notion of writing as a process.

COORDINATED RESOURCES

Transparency masters are available for many of the screened charts, lists, and other displays in this chapter.

Students can practice and test their knowledge of terms, key concepts, and applications of material in this chapter by using the *Study Guide to the S & S Handbook for Writers,* West.

51

ing and punctuation. During revising, you pay attention to the meaning you want your material to deliver effectively.

2
Use the organizing power of your thesis statement and essay title.

When you revise, you need to pay special attention to your essay's thesis statement and title. Both of these features help you stay on the track, and they orient your reader to what to expect.

If your **thesis statement** does not match what you say in your essay, you need to revise either the thesis statement or the essay—and sometimes both. A thesis statement, as explained in 2e-4, must present the topic of the essay, the writer's particular focus on that topic, and the writer's purpose for writing the essay. The first draft of a thesis statement is often merely an estimate of what will be covered in the essay. Early in the revision process, you should check the accuracy of your estimate. You can then use the thesis statement's controling role to bring it and the essay in line with each other.

Each writer's experience with revising a thesis statement varies from essay to essay. Tara Foster wrote a number of versions of her thesis statement before she started drafting. When she checked her thesis statement after she wrote her first draft, Foster decided that her thesis statement communicated what she wanted to say. But she did decide to change parts of her essay to conform more closely to her thesis statement. (For an example of a thesis statement revised after the first draft, see Chapter 33.)

The **title** of an essay also plays an important organizing role. A good title can set you on your course and tell your reader what to expect. A *direct title* tells exactly what the essay will be about. A direct title contains key words under which the essay would be cataloged in a library or a computerized database system. As a result, a direct title is very efficient. The titles of the two essays in this chapter are direct: Tara Foster's "Knowing How to Live Alone" and Gary Lee Houseman's "Rain Forests Must Not Be Destroyed." Each title is specific and prepares the reader for the topic of the essay.

A direct title should not be too broad. An overly broad title implies that the writer has not thought through the essay's content. For example, an unsatisfactory title for Foster's essay would be "Living Alone." On the other hand, a direct title should not be too narrow. An equally unsatisfactory title for Foster's essay would be "Knowing How to Live Alone Is Important for Practical, Social, and Emotional Reasons." Such a title is closer to a thesis statement.

52

An *indirect title* is also acceptable in some situations, according to the writer's taste and instructor's requirements. An indirect title hints at the essay's topic. It presents a puzzle that can be solved when the essay is read. This approach can be intriguing for the reader, but the writer has to be sure that the title is not too obscure. "Solitary Strength," for example, would be a satisfactory indirect title for Tara Foster's essay, but "The Test" would be too indirect.

As you write, plan your essay's title carefully. Do not wait until the last minute to tack on a title. You might write a title before you start to draft or after a first draft while you are revising, but always check as you review your essay and make sure that the title clearly relates to the content of the evolving essay.

Whether direct or indirect, a title stands alone. The opening of an essay should never refer to the essay's title as if it were part of a preceding sentence. For example, after the title "Knowing How to Live Alone," a writer should not begin the essay with the words "This skill is very important" or "Everyone should know how to do this." The title sets the stage, but it is not the first sentence of the essay.

3
Know how to use a revision checklist.

A revision checklist can help you focus your attention as you evaluate your writing. Use a checklist provided by your instructor or compile your own based on the Revision Checklist here. This checklist is comprehensive and detailed; do not let it overwhelm you. Feel free to adapt it to the emphases in each course and writing assignment. Also, tailor it to your personal needs. If you know that you are weak in certain areas, spend more time on them and make the questions even more detailed.

This checklist moves from the whole essay to paragraphs to sentences to words. This progression from larger to smaller elements works well for many writers.

Revision Checklist

The answer to each question on this checklist should be "yes." If it is not, you need to revise. If you are unsure of the meaning of any question, look up the material in this book. The reference numbers in parentheses tell you what chapter or section to consult.

TEACHING TIP
At the other end of the spectrum from nonrevisers are over-revisers. Some students are never satisfied with their work and so never hand it in. This phenomenon is a form of writer's block. Students who suffer from this sort of inhibition often need a little special treatment at first. For example, you might help such students by telling them that for the first few assignments you will consider their work as "in progress," even the final version. You might also share with them these words by Eudora Welty when she was interviewed by *U.S. News and World Report* in August 1986:

I know I can never get it perfect. You just have to know when you've done it the best way. A friend of mine who is a writer said he kept thirteen drafts of a story and put them all in a drawer. Years later he went back, and it was number 7 that was the right one. That taught me a real, true lesson.

PROCESS/PRODUCT DEBATE

Writers are judged in the outside world by their products, not their processes. Teaching students to view writing as process is extremely useful as an instructional technique and as a guide to what real writers do. But telling students that product does not matter is to mislead them about what they will face in other courses and in the workplace.

The call for balance has been made particularly well by one of the editors of the journal *Research in the Teaching of English* in the "Musings" column in May 1984, excerpted here.

Yet that separation has been replaced by another that is likely to be equally unproductive. In the enthusiasm provoked by a focus on process, we have sometimes lost sight of the enterprise in which the process is engaged. Though our best philosophers have always warned us against false dualisms, our best research has often defined itself in reaction to the limitations of previous work. Thus the initial enthusiasm for the study of process was conditioned by a rejection of the earlier preoccupation with product. The research that has followed has been extraordinarily productive, extending both our theoretical understanding and our practical approaches. Yet one characteristic of any new idea is that, in the course of exploring its implications most fully, we learn not only its strengths but also its limitations. The strengths of the process studies of the last decade have been many, and the weaknesses minor relative to the insights we have gained. But as happens with most paradigms, we seem now to be approaching a point where the limitations as well as the advantages of process-oriented research are beginning to be clear.

In particular, the separation of process and product is beginning to reemerge as the unnatural dualism that our past might suggest it would inevitably become. Indeed, when reading, writing, or spoken language processes are separated from the

THE WHOLE ESSAY

1. Is the topic of the essay suitable for college writing and sufficiently narrow? (2c)
2. Does your thesis statement clearly communicate the topic and focus of the essay? (2e-4)
3. Does your thesis clearly reflect the purpose of the essay? (lb)
4. Does the essay reflect an awareness of its audience? (1c)
5. Does the essay take into account the special requirements—the assignment's time limit, word limit, and other factors? (2b)
6. Does your essay have a logical organization pattern? (2e-2)
7. Is the tone of the essay suitable for its audience? Is an appropriate tone consistent throughout? (2e-3)
8. Is your thesis supported well by the main ideas of the paragraphs? (4e-4)
9. Do the paragraphs cover separate but related main ideas? (2e-1 and 2e-5)
10. Have you covered all the material promised by your thesis statement? (2e-4)
11. Are the connections among the paragraphs clear? (4b-1)
12. Does your introduction lead into the thesis statement and the rest of the essay? (4e)
13. Does your conclusion provide a sense of completion? (4e)
14. Have you cut any material that goes off the topic?
15. Is the length of each paragraph in proportion to the whole essay and the length of the other paragraphs? (Remember that an introduction and conclusion are usually shorter than any of the body paragraphs in an essay.)
16. Does your essay have a title? Does it reflect the content of the essay, directly or indirectly?
17. Is your reasoning sound? (5c–5e)
18. Does your essay avoid logical fallacies? (5f)

PARAGRAPHS

1. Does the introduction help your audience make the transition to the body of your essay? (4e)
2. Does each body paragraph express its main idea in a topic sentence as needed? (4a-1)
3. Are the main ideas—and topic sentences—clearly related to the thesis statement of the essay? (4a)
4. Are your body paragraphs *developed?* Is the development sufficient? (4a-2)

54

5. Does each body paragraph contain specific and concrete support for its main idea? Do the details provide examples, reasons, facts? (4d)

6. Are your facts, figures, and dates accurate?

7. Is each body paragraph arranged logically? (4c)

8. Does the conclusion give your reader a sense of completion? (4e)

9. Have you cut any material that goes off the topic?

10. Have you used necessary transitions? (4b-1, 4b-6)

11. Do the paragraphs maintain coherence with pronouns (4b-2), selective repetition (4b-3), parallel structures (4b-4 and Chapter 18)?

12. Do you show relationships between paragraphs? (4b-6)

SENTENCES

1. Are your sentences concise? (Chapter 16)

2. Have you eliminated sentence fragments? (Chapter 13)

3. Have you eliminated comma splices and fused sentences? (Chapter 14)

4. Have you eliminated confusing shifts? (15a)

5. Have you eliminated misplaced modifiers? (15b)

6. Have you eliminated dangling modifiers? (15c)

7. Have you eliminated mixed sentences? (15d)

8. Have you eliminated incomplete sentences? (15e)

9. Do your sentences express clear relationships among ideas? (Chapter 17)

10. Do you use coordination correctly? (17a–17c)

11. Do you use subordination correctly? (17d–17g)

12. Do your sentences avoid faulty parallelism? (Chapter 18)

13. Do you use parallelism as needed to help your sentences deliver their meaning? (Chapter 18)

14. Does your writing style reveal a sensitivity to the need for variety and emphasis? (Chapter 19)

15. Do your sentences vary in length? (19a)

16. Does the structure of your sentences help convey the emphasis you intend? (19c–19f)

WORDS

1. Have you used exact words? (20b)

2. Does your word choice reflect your intentions in denotation and connotation? (20b-1)

ends they serve, we lose the essence of the process itself. Process does not consist of isolated behaviors that operate willy-nilly, but of purposeful activities that lead toward some end for the person who has chosen to engage in them.

Everyone seems to agree that process is good. So do we. The issue we raise is whether any process can ever be looked at alone. This comes from our belief that just as top-down and bottom-up approaches are interactive, so too do all processing behaviors need to be looked at interactively, as they interrelate with their outcomes. For us, process only has meaning as it works toward some end. Examination of *only* the means keeps us from understanding the most interesting complications of the human mind as it works in different ways toward different destinations.

—JUDITH A. LANGER

---

3. Have you used specific and concrete language to bring life to general and abstract language? (20b-2)
4. Does your word choice reflect a level of formality appropriate for your purpose and audience? (21a-1)
5. Do you avoid sexist language? (21a-3)
6. Do you avoid slang and colloquial or regional language not appropriate to your audience and purpose? (21a-4)
7. Do you avoid slanted language? (21a-5)
8. Do you avoid clichés? (21c)
9. Do you avoid artificial language by eliminating pretentious word choice, unnecessary jargon, unnecessary euphemisms, "doublespeak," and bureaucratic prose? (21d)
10. Is your usage correct? (Usage Glossary)

QUOTATION ABOUT WRITING
I do a lot of revising. Certain chapters six or seven times. Occasionally you can hit it right the first time. More often, you don't.   —JOHN DOS PASSOS

When Tara Foster revised her first draft, she concentrated first on the overall essay and then on the paragraphs, the sentences, and the words. As many writers do, sometimes she changed words as she looked at the whole essay, and sometimes she made changes in paragraphs as she looked at her word choice. Nevertheless, she proceeded systematically through the elements so that she was sure she had covered everything.

In working with the larger elements, Foster decided that her thesis statement was working well. But she realized that she needed a title and a better topic sentence in her next-to-last paragraph and that the conclusion sounded "tacked on." She also saw that the sequence of her paragraphs was not logical. In order of importance, she felt that taking care of practical matters came before establishing new friendships, so she rearranged the sequence.

In working at the paragraph level, Foster cut some material that went off the topic. She then decided to integrate what remained into the next paragraph. She also saw that she had insufficiently developed two paragraphs, so she added examples and details to them. To help her readers understand the relations among her ideas, Foster saw that some transitional expressions were called for. She felt that the introduction and conclusion were flat, worked on new ones, and then worked to tie her conclusion more closely to the rest of her essay.

At the sentence and word level, Foster combined sentences to be more concise in discussing a statistic. She also worked for sentence variety by using an occasional short sentence and by transforming one statement into a question. She then changed some words to be more exact. For example, she replaced "what is going on" with "the feeling." As often happens with writers, she did some

56

editing as she was revising: she changed two numerals to spelled-out numbers and she got rid of contractions.

FIRST DRAFT REVISED BY STUDENT

(I need a title)

~~Lots of~~ People are ~~scared~~ *terrified* of living alone. *(I need a better introduction. check Chapter 4.)*

They ~~like to live~~ *are used to living* with others. When the statistics catch up with you, therefore, you are never prepared. Chances are high that most adult men and women will have to know how to live alone, briefly or longer, at some time in their lives.

Many grown children move away from their hometowns to ~~get an~~ *continue their* education*s* or take jobs. ~~Also,~~ ~~M~~arried people ~~think they'll~~ *might feel they will* always be together, but ~~many~~ *currently one out of two* marriages end in divorce. [The divorce rate is frightening. People are not making the right choices, or they are too immature to work out their differences. Fighting over money, parents, or religion although the underlying reason is lack of compatability. Divorce brings the couple and their children a great deal of pain.] *(Cut. I'm off the topic here)*

~~I read recently in the newspaper where~~ Estimates are that in the next twenty years, ~~8~~ *eight* out of ~~10~~ *ten* married women end up widows, ~~This will happen to most of them~~ *usually* late in life. ~~This~~ *An* (statistic) is even sadder, ~~than divorce. I feel sorry for any happily married person whose spouse dies.~~ *(Change order of these two sentences)*

concerns the death of a spouse.

QUOTATION ABOUT WRITING
I don't write easily or rapidly. My first draft usually has only a few elements worth keeping. I have to find out what those are and build from them and throw out what doesn't work, or what simply is not alive.

—SUSAN SONTAG

INSTRUCTOR'S NOTES

[Circled handwritten note:] Move first paragraph down to come after practical matters paragraph

People living alone need to establish new friendships.
When single people feel self-reliant, ~~It's~~ *they can have an* easier *time* ~~for them to start~~ getting out and meeting new people.
For instance, ^Some students are in the habit of always going to classes with a friend, ~~and~~ *but* they can be^ *pleasantly surprised to find* that they can
concentrate better on the course**x** **a**nd also have a chance
to make some new friends. *The idea of going places alone can paralyze* ~~Friends can help people take care~~ *some people. Once you make the attempt, however, you find that everyone* ~~of practical by keeping them company and going with them.~~ *welcomes a new friendly face.*

One good way to prepare for living alone is to
learn how to take care of practical matters. ~~Many people~~ *[circled note: Move this paragraph up]*
For example, they might not ~~don't~~ know how to do something as simple as opening a
checking account.^ *Similarly,* ~~M~~aking major purchases is something
How long can a person manage with people have to handle.^ ~~Such as~~ a refrigerator that ~~can't~~ *cannot*
After some. be repaired or a useless car?^ Shopp**ing** ^around and make price
comparisons. *Most* ~~All~~ decisions are much *less complicated* ~~easier~~ *they seem* than,^ at first.
Probably the most difficult problem for people living alone is dealing with ^*f*eelings of lonliness, ~~are the hardest to take.~~

~~I think this is what people fear the most.~~ First,
the feeling, they confuse people have to understand^ ~~what is going on.~~ *Being*
with alone ~~does not mean~~ being lonely. Second, ~~singles~~ *people living alone*
everyone needs to get involved with have to fight depression. Third, ~~they have to keep busy.~~
activities such as volunteering their services to help others.
People living alone have to handle practical,
social, and emotional problems.

[Boxed handwritten note:] The last paragraph seems boring to me now. I'll look for a more interesting kind of concluding device in Chapter 4

INSTRUCTOR'S NOTES

Foster then typed her second draft neatly and, as required by the assignment, submitted it with the first draft on which she had handwritten her revisions.

SECOND DRAFT

Knowing How to Live Alone

"Alone one is never lonely," says May Sarton. Most people, however, are terrified of living alone. They are used to living with others. When the statistics catch up with you, therefore, you are never prepared. Chances are high that most adult men and women will have to know how to live alone, briefly or longer, at some time in their lives.

Many grown children move away from their hometowns to continue their educations or take jobs. Married people might feel they will always be together, but currently one out of two marriages end in divorce. An even sadder statisitic concerns the death of a spouse. Estimates are that in the next twenty years eight out of ten married women will end up widows, usually late in life.

One good way to prepare for living alone is to learn how to take care of practical matters. For example, they might not know how to do something as simple as opening a checking account. Similarly, making major purchases is something people might have to handle. How long can a person manage with a refrigerator that cannot be repaired or a useless car? After some shopping around and making price comparisons. Most decisions are much less complicated than they seem at first.

People living alone need to establish new friendships. When, single people feel self-reliant they can have an easier

---

59

```
time getting out and meeting new people.  For instance, some
students are in the habit of always going to classes with a
friend, but they can be pleasantly surprised to find that they
can concentrate better on the course and also have a chance to
make some new friends.  The idea of going places alone can
paralyze some people.  Once you make the attempt, however,
you find that everyone welcomes a new friendly face.

    Probably the most difficult problem for people living
alone is dealing with feelings of lonliness.  First, people
have to understand the feeling, they confuse being alone with
being lonely.  Second, people living alone have to fight
depression.  Third, everyone needs to get involved with
activities, such as volunteering their services to help
others.

    People need to ask themselves, "If I had to live alone
starting tomorrow morning, would I know how?"  This is an
important question.
```

4
Know How to Use Criticism.

When criticism is constructive, you can learn a great deal about your writing through the eyes of others. Still, you have much company among writers if your initial reaction to criticism is defensive. Someone else's reactions to your writing can feel like an intrusion at first. Writing is a personal act, even when a writer is trying to communicate with a reader. The more you write, however, the more you will come to welcome constructive criticism.

The eyes of another person, someone who cares to help you improve, can give you an objective view of your material. Useful criticism helps you move your writing closer to what a reader needs to complete the act of communication. In working with comments, look at each one separately. First, make sure that you understand what the comment says. If you are unsure, ask. Next, be open-minded about the comment. If you resist every comment, you will

60

miss many opportunities to improve. Finally, use the comment to make whatever changes you think will improve your draft.

Tara Foster's assignment, shown on page 16, called for Foster to hand in both a first and second draft. Foster's instructor explained that the second draft would be considered an "essay in progress" and all comments would be geared toward helping students write a final draft. When her second draft was returned, Foster saw two types of comments from her instructor: questions to stimulate further writing and codes referring to places in his handbook for Foster to consult. Here is Foster's second draft with comments from her instructor.

SECOND DRAFT WITH INSTRUCTOR'S COMMENTS

How does this interesting quotation tie into your point?
Also, who is Sarton?

Knowing How to Live Alone   *Can you be more specific?*

"Alone one is never lonely," says May Sarton. Most

(15a) people, however, are terrified of living alone. They are

used to living with others. When the statistics catch up *Qualify this statement. (See 5c)*

with you, therefore, you are never prepared. Chances are

high that most adult men and women will have to know how to

live alone, briefly or longer, at some time in their lives. *Can you be more specific?*

Many grown children move away from their hometowns to

continue their educations or take jobs. Married people might

feel they will always be together, but currently *(11a)* one out of *What is your main idea in this paragraph? (See 4a-2)*

two marriages end in divorce. An even sadder *(sp)* statisitic

concerns the death of a spouse. Estimates are that in the

next twenty years eight out of ten married women will end up *informal about topic sentences.)*

widows, usually late in life.   *(10b) unclear pronoun ref.*

One good way to prepare for living alone is to learn how

to take care of practical matters. For example, they might

not know how to do something as simple as opening a checking

account. Similarly, making major purchases is something

people might have to handle. How long can a person manage

How do the points about checking accounts and major purchases tie into your thesis?

TEACHING TIP

Many of us have had the experience of reading what is supposedly a student's revision of an essay we have already read and responded to, only to find that most of our comments have been ignored; the revision turns out to be the original essay with a few spelling errors corrected. Sometimes student do not know how to respond fully to an instructor's comments.

One step in demystifying comments is to have the class collectively respond to the instructor's comments on Tara Foster's second draft. Ask the students to do the following:

Read the instructor's comments on Tara Foster's essay and decide what Foster might do in response to each one.

You might lead a discussion of the options for fixing each problem. As you come to each comment, allow sufficient time for students to think about and draft revisions, or to look up the needed information in their *S & S Handbook for Writers*. Invite students to offer their revisions at each comment, and keep students alert to the many good alternatives that can emerge in response to the instructor's questions. You might also point out that responses are more likely to be identical to the coded comments of the instructor because most of them call for corrections of grammar or punctuation.

An alternative to the class discussion comment-by-comment is to assign the entire revision as a home or class exercise. Then students can discuss their through-through answers and compare their results.

As much as possible, try to use dittoed material or overhead transparencies for the discussion of alternate complete third drafts. Students often cannot follow the discussion if too much relies on memory of various similar versions.

TEACHING TIP

Certainly, all of us sometimes feel that we are drowning in student writing. The battle rages constantly: Do I spend twenty minutes on each short essay or do I spend five minutes and get to respond to more of what my students write?

Given the few minutes that we have for each essay, decisions about what and how to write are important. Codes (abbreviations such as *sp* and *agr;* references to the text, such as *15a*) are a clear, fast way to refer to unambiguous matters in grammar, punctuation, and mechanics. Make sure students know what the symbols mean: you might review the symbols you ordinarily use as part of a follow-up to their receiving back from you their first piece of writing. Along with citing errors, many symbols send a secondary message: "This matter is important but relatively uninspiring. Fix it quickly (and learn the information) and move on to the more interesting aspects of your essay."

Many issues of substance are difficult to discuss exclusively by code. Besides, students like to feel that a real human being is reading their work—and real people ask questions when they are puzzled. Therefore, whenever possible, phrase your reactions as questions. Instead of writing *"unclear,"* ask "How does this relate to your thesis?" If you do not have time to write many questions, try to get at least one in per paper. Psychologically, people can't help but answer questions—at least in their own minds. So, to ask a question is to guarantee an answer. And with the answer in mind a student can revise.

Whenever time permits, a good description deserves more than "nice" scribbled in the margin; you might say "You really made me see the lake at sundown." If a student tells you about a cooking disaster, you might say "You had me laughing in sympathy. The same thing happened to me." Such com-

---

with a refrigerator that cannot be repaired or a useful car? *(1B) parallelism* *(13b) fragment*

[After some shopping around and making price comparisons.] Most decisions are much less complicated than they seem at first. *(24b-1) comma error*

People living alone need to establish new friendships. *How does this main idea* When single people feel self-reliant, they can have an easier *relate to the previous one?* time getting out and meeting new people. [For instance, some students are in the habit of always going to classes with a friend, but they can be pleasantly surprised to find that they *the relationship* can concentrate better on the course and also have a chance to *among* make some new friends.] The idea of going places alone can *these ideas?* *(15a)* *See Chap. 17* paralyze some people. Once you make the attempt, however, *about subordination.* you find that everyone welcomes a new friendly face. *(24d) comma error* *Can you be more specific?*

Probably the most difficult problem for people living *Are there* alone is dealing with feelings of loneliness. First, people *no* *(sp)* *exceptions?* have to understand the feeling, they confuse being alone with *comma splice (14a)* being lonely. Second, people living alone have to fight depression. Third, everyone needs to get involved with *Develop* activities, such as volunteering their services to help *your paragraph* *as explained* others. *in 4a-2.* *number shift and* *agreement problem*

People need to ask themselves, "If I had to live alone *How does this* starting tomorrow morning, would I know how?" This is an *question tie* *into your* important question. *thesis?*

You revised your first draft well, so this second draft shows good progress. Your thesis statement clearly reflects your purpose and focus. Now you are ready to develop your paragraphs more fully. When you revise, think through the questions I ask, and refer to the handbook material I point out. I'm looking forward to reading your final draft. You are writing on a fresh and interesting topic.

EDITING

3d

In some classes you might be asked to share your writing with other students as you revise. In such cases, you can use the reactions of your peers to look at your material with fresh eyes. As much as possible, seek *specific* advice from your peers. To get concrete reactions, ask questions taken from the Revision Checklist in this chapter or worksheets your instructor prepares.

 3d

Know how to edit.

Editing focuses on surface features. When you edit, you check the technical correctness of your writing. You pay attention to correct grammar, spelling, and punctuation, and to correct use of capitals, numbers, italics, and abbreviations.

Editing is a separate part of the writing process because, in contrast to revising (3c), it focuses more on presentation than on meaning. If you edit too soon in the writing process, you might distract yourself from checking to see if your material delivers its meaning effectively. You are ready to edit when you have a final draft that contains suitable content, organization, development, and sentence structure. Your job during editing is not to generate a new draft but to fine-tune the surface features of the draft you have. Once you have polished your work, you are ready to transcribe it into a final copy.

Editing is crucial in writing. No matter how much attention you have paid to planning, shaping, drafting, and revising, slapdash editing will distract your readers and, in writing for assignments, lower your grade.

Editing takes patience. Inexperienced writers sometimes rush editing, especially if they have revised well and feel that they have prepared a good essay. When you edit, resist any impulses to hurry. Matters of grammar and punctuation take concentration—and frequently the time to check yourself by looking up rules and conventions in this handbook. As you edit, be systematic. Use a checklist supplied by your instructor or one you compile from the following Editing Checklist.

Editing checklist

The answer to each question on this checklist should be "yes." If it is not, you need to edit. If you are unsure of the meaning of any question, look up the material in this book. The reference numbers in parentheses tell you what chapter or section to consult.

ments validate students' experiences and also demonstrate compassionate reading.

In many cases, reaction comments are most useful in the final response to an essay. Many students turn to the end of their essays before reading marginal comments. After the grade, this is the part of our response that is most crucial to students. The final comment is our total impression, while the margins represent a kind of running commentary. To be useful, a closing comment needs to clarify our response, not duplicate the grade: a student whose grade has jumped from D to B knows his or her work is "better," so try to be specific.

A useful end comment consists of at least several sentences. A serviceable pattern consists of a personal response, a sentence about the content and organization of the piece (positive as well as negative observations—see the end comment to Foster), and where pertinent a few sentences about a recurring mechanical or grammatical issue (e.g., "Try to hear and pronounce the ends of words. You frequently omit *-s* and *-ed* endings, resulting in tense and number errors that can confuse a reader").

INSTRUCTOR'S NOTES

1. Is the grammar correct? That is, have you used correct verb forms (Chapter 8): Have you used the correct case of nouns and pronouns (Chapter 9); do pronouns refer to clear antecedents (Chapter 10); do subjects and verbs agree (Chapter 11); do pronouns agree with their antecedents (Chapter 11); have you distinguished between adjectives and adverbs (Chapter 12)?

2. Is the spelling correct? (Chapter 22)

3. Have you used hyphens correctly both for compound words and for dividing words at the end of a line? (Chapter 22)

4. Have you correctly used commas? (Chapter 24)

5. Have you correctly used semicolons (Chapter 25), colons (Chapter 26), apostrophes (Chapter 27), quotation marks (Chapter 28)?

6. Have you correctly used other marks of punctuation? (Chapter 29)

7. Have you correctly used capital letters, italics, numbers, and abbreviations? (Chapter 30)

8. Have you followed the format requirements of the assignment? (Manuscript Form Appendix)

Tara Foster revised her work into a final draft based on her instructor's comments and her own sense of what she needed. She then edited it into final form. Here is Foster's final draft.

FINAL DRAFT: ESSAY WITH INFORMATIVE PURPOSE*

Knowing How to Live Alone

Introduction:
Identification
of situation

"Alone one is never lonely," says the poet and author May Sarton in praise of living alone. Most people, however, are terrified of living alone. They are used to living with others--children with parents, roommates with roommates, friends with friends, husbands with wives. When the statistics catch up

Thesis
statement

with them, therefore, they are rarely prepared. Chances are high that most adult men and women will need to know how to live alone, briefly or longer, at some time in their lives.

---

*First draft on pages 48–49; second draft on pages 59–60; second draft with instructor's comments on pages 61–62.

Background: statistics and how they relate to the thesis

In the United States, circumstances often force people to live alone. For example, many high school and college graduates move away from their hometowns to continue their educations or take jobs. Most schools assign roommates, but employers usually expect people to take care of their own living arrangements. Also, married people might feel they will always be together, but currently one out of two marriages ends in divorce. An even sadder statistic concerns the death of a spouse. Estimates are that in the next twenty years eight out of ten married women will become widows, usually late in life. These facts show that most people have to live by themselves at least once in their lives whether they want to or not.

Support: first area

One good way to prepare for living alone is to learn how to take care of practical matters. For example, some students and newly single people might not know how to do something as simple as opening a checking account. When making arrangements alone, they might be too tense to find out that they can compare banks as well as the benefits of various types of accounts. Similarly, making major purchases is something people living alone might have to handle. When divorced or widowed people were married, perhaps the other spouse did the choosing or the couple made the decisions together. But how long can a person manage with a refrigerator that cannot be repaired or a car that will not run? After shopping around and making price comparisons, most people find that these decisions are much less complicated than they seem at first.

Support: second area

The confidence that single people get from learning to deal with practical matters can boost

their chances for establishing new friendships. When
singles feel self-reliant, they can have an easier
time getting out and meeting new people. For
instance, some students are in the habit of always
going to classes with a friend. When they break this
dependency, they can be pleasantly surprised to find
that they can concentrate better on the course and
also have a chance to make some new friends.
Likewise, the idea of going alone to the beach or to
parties can paralyze some singles. Once they make the
attempt, however, people alone usually find that
almost everyone welcomes a new, friendly face.

Support:
third area

Probably the most difficult problem for people
living alone is dealing with feelings of loneliness.
First, they have to understand the feeling. Some
people confuse being alone with feeling lonely. They
need to remember that unhappily married people can
feel very lonely with spouses, and anyone can suffer
from loneliness in a room crowded with friends.
Second, people living alone have to fight any
tendencies to get depressed. Depression can lead to
much unhappiness, including compulsive behavior like
overeating or spending too much money. Depression can
also drive people to fill the feeling of emptiness
getting into relationships or jobs that they do not
truly want. Third, people living alone need to get
involved in useful and pleasurable activities, such as
volunteering their services to help others.

Conclusion:
call for
awareness

People need to ask themselves, "If I had to live
alone starting tomorrow morning, would I know how?"
If the answer is "No," they need to become conscious
of what living alone calls for. People who face up to
life usually do not have to hide from it later on.

INSTRUCTOR'S NOTES

3d

Gary Lee Houseman went through all steps in the writing process as he wrote his essay on rain forests. (See page 16 for the assignment.) His work in gathering ideas is shown in 2d-1 and 2d-5, and his informal outline is shown in 2e-5. The dominant purpose of Houseman's essay is *persuasive*. He used a reliable format for presenting an argument or an opinion. He put his thesis statement at the beginning of the introductory paragraph. Next, he sequenced the body paragraphs by first giving background (along with a definition) of the topic, then supporting his thesis with several main ideas, and then refuting major objections to his position. Finally, he wrote a conclusion that points to the future and calls for awareness. Here is Houseman's final draft.

FINAL DRAFT: ESSAY WITH PERSUASIVE PURPOSE

Rain Forests Must Not Be Destroyed

Introduction:
Identification
of the problem

Developers' bulldozers have been leveling thousands of acres of rain forests every day in recent years. The rain forests of Central and South America, Africa, and the Orient are being destroyed to make way for civilization. As a result, one plant or animal a day is added to the list of extinct species on this planet. By 1990 the number will rise to one life form per hour. Early in the next century,

Thesis
statement

rain forests will disappear forever. This destruction must stop. Rain forests must be preserved because they offer the human race many irreplaceable resources.

Background:
definition
and
description

Rain forests are a special category of forests. They are found only in tropical regions of the world, usually close to the equator. Rainfall averages 80 inches a year, which explains why the forests are identified as <u>rain</u> forests. The rain combined with the warm tropical temperatures creates dense, lush vegetation. The huge evergreen trees are so close together their branches overlap and form an enormous, towering "canopy." Little light gets through to the ground, but on the canopy and immediately below on

---

BACKGROUND: RAIN FORESTS
According to Dr. Terry Erwin, entomologist at the National Museum of Natural History, samplings of the insect life of rain forests indicate that there are probably from 15 to 30 million species of insects on Earth (the previous estimate was from .75 to 1.5 million). This radical shift in our knowledge of insect populations is due to new technology that now enables scientists to study the canopy of a rain forest. (Certainly, analogous findings about new plant life are possible.)

Before Erwin's work, scientists estimated that insects made up 75.9% of the species on Earth (all invertebrates, including insects, 96.7%). Revised figures as of 1986 indicate that invertebrates make up 99.1% of all species. Humans and other vertebrates (all fish, birds, and mammals) make up less than 1% of species. For all the crowding in our cities, people are a tiny minority on this planet.

the trees, plant and insect life are abundant and
rich with benefits for humanity.

Support:
first reason

One major value of rain forests is biomedical.
The plants and animals of rain forests are the source
of many compounds used in today's medicines. A drug
that helps treat Parkinson's disease is manufactured
from a plant that grows only in South American rain
forests. Some plants and insects found in rain
forests contain rare chemicals that relieve certain
mental disorders. Discoveries, however, have only
begun. Scientists say that rain forsts contain over a
thousand plants that have great anticancer potential.
To destroy life forms in these forests is to deprive
the human race of further medical advances.

Support:
second reason

Not only for their medical riches but also for
their role in maintaining global natural balances,
rain forests must be saved. Living organisms exist in
check with each other, so when one is destroyed,
another can overgrow and cause terrible problems. For
example, when developers level rain forests, birds
lose their nesting areas and no longer feed on the
insects there. The insects flourish and attack farm
crops. Then the devastation of agriculture causes an
increase in food prices and a resulting increase in
human hunger world wide. Similarly, when thousands of
acres of rain forest are bought up by developers and
stripped of their vegetation, the natives who support
themselves on the land have no means of subsistence.
Deprived of their livelihood, as well as their
dignity, the natives have to look elsewhere to
survive. People who used to be self-sufficient often
become dependent on their already debt-ridden
governments.

Support:
third reason

Most important, rain forests must be protected
because their trees regulate the planet's oxygen
supply and climate. Rain forests help to balance

conditions in the atmosphere by manufacturing oxygen and absorbing carbon dioxide. As the number of trees decreases, the world has less oxygen. Furthermore, deforestation leads to reduced ability to absorb carbon dioxide. Carbon dioxide creates what is called a "greenhouse effect," a process that is gradually warming the planet. By the middle of the next century, the warming of Earth's atmosphere could cause some melting of the polar ice caps. The sea levels would then rise and put some coastal areas and islands under water. Although the melting would be gradual enough to give people a chance to relocate, the rising ocean would cover such landmarks as the Statue of Liberty and such cities as New Orleans. Also, the greenhouse effect would change rainfall patterns. Areas formerly good for agriculture could become deserts.

Major likely objections and responses to them

Some people see no problem in the destruction of rain forests. These people say that developing the land provides needed raw materials. They point to the hungry demand for firewood for natives and people in third-world countries. In most cases, however, synthetic fuels could be used and the trees spared. The extra cost of such measures would be repaid many times in the benefits from rain forests. Another justification for destroying rain forests is the need for land to farm. This plan is extremely shortsighted because the topsoil in leveled rain forests erodes quickly in the rain and becomes useless for crops of any kind. Land cleared of rain forests usually looks like moonscapes within a few years. An equal lack of foresight is shown by greedy investors who argue for modernizing by building roads and cities at the expense of the forests. They fail to recognize that the economy of the entire world is tied to the balanced natural setting which they want to uproot.

69

Conclusion:
point to the
future and
call for
action

> The demands on rain forests will get worse, not better, in the future. The pessimist says that nothing can be done. The optimist says that people can work together to slow and even reverse the pace of destruction. Anyone who wants to take part can begin by sending a contribution to an organization like Friends of the Earth, an environmental group based in London. They buy seedlings to reforest stripped areas and publicize the dangers of leveling rain forests. No one can afford any longer to be apathetic about the devastating destruction of the world's precious rain forests.

■‖ 3e
Know how to proofread.

When you **proofread,** you check a final version carefully before handing it in. You need to make sure your work is an accurate and clean transcription of your final draft. You then need to proofread, after you revise and edit. If you try to proofread while you edit, one process might distract from the other.

DISTINCTIONS AMONG THE LATER PARTS OF THE WRITING PROCESS	
Revising ⟶	multiple drafts leading to unedited final draft
Editing ⟶	final draft with correct surface features
Proofreading ⟶	final, edited draft with repaired typographical or handwriting errors

Proofreading involves a careful, line-by-line reading of an essay. You may want to proofread with a ruler so that you can focus

70

on one line at a time. Starting at the end also helps you avoid becoming distracted by the content of your paper.

In proofreading, look for letters inadvertently left out of a word or reversed. If you handwrite your material, make sure that your handwriting is legible. If you type, make sure that you have neatly corrected any typing errors. If a page has numerous errors, retype the page. Do not expect your instructor to make allowances for crude typing; if you cannot type well, arrange to have your paper typed properly. No matter how hard you have worked on other parts of the writing process, if your final copy is inaccurate or messy, you will not reach your audience successfully.

◼‖ 3f

Understand the impact of a word processor on your writing process.

Word processors are becoming commonplace today. If you do not have one at your disposal, worry not. The usual methods of writing will continue to serve you well. If you can use a word processor, however, you will likely agree with most writers who rejoice over a new-found flexibility. With a good word-processing program, you can add, cut, replace, and move material with great ease.

As much as possible, try to tailor your use of a word processor to your personal needs. Some experienced writers prefer to use word processors only for preparing the final copy. Others like to do activities such as freewriting (2d-2) and brainstorming (2d-3) by hand and to write all drafts on the computer. Still other writers feel more comfortable writing out drafts by hand and then revising with a computer. Yet others like to use a word processor throughout the writing process. See what works best for you in each writing situation.

To use a word processor to greatest benefit, you need to take the time to learn its various operations. Once you can handle word processing with ease, you will not have to interrupt your writing process to figure out how to do something mechanical. Each program is a little different, and many call their functions by different names. Become familiar with your word processor's jargon so that you can learn from a manual or discuss the program's functions with other people. When starting with a word processor, learn how to create and format a "document." Learn what keys to press to activate various functions such as "insert," "delete," and "move." Also, learn how to "call up" pages that you have already written and want to look at or work on again.

As you write on a word processor, be sure to "save" or

TEACHING TIP
In their monograph "Teaching Writing with a Word Processor, Grades 7–13" published by the National Council of Teachers of English in 1986, Dawn and Raymond Rodrigues list these three assumptions:
1. To teach writing with a word processor most effectively, you must, above all, be comfortable with the tool yourself, writing regularly with it.
2. You can assume that your computer-writing classroom will be different from your traditional classroom.
3. You will be able to adapt some of the ways you currently teach writing to the capabilities of the tool, just as writers who work regularly with a word processor adapt the ways they write to both the power and limitations of the tool.

They then describe many activities such as lesson-file development (with copious examples), electronic journal writing, and collaborative writing with computers.

71

"backup" your material frequently. What appears on the computer screen is stored in a temporary memory. If the electric power goes off, your work vanishes forever. Also, at the end of each work session, "print out" your writing. A printout is often called a *hard copy*. Do not assume that your work is safe simply because it is on a computer disk. Disks are highly vulnerable, especially to magnetism. Place a disk too close to a magnetic source and, quick as a cursor's flash, your hours of work can be irretrievably garbled. In general, disks do not survive well when they have to coexist with dust, cigarettes ashes, food, or humidity.

Relieved of the sometimes tedious work of copying and recopying material, many writers feel more creative when they use a word processor. Their ideas seem to flow more freely when each new thought does not lead to a recopying job. Nevertheless, some writers find that recopying by hand helps them think of new ideas. Be careful, therefore, not to ignore what has always served you well when you wrote by hand. Also, do not let yourself be seduced by the wonders of a word processor. It is only a machine.

4
WRITING PARAGRAPHS

A **paragraph** is a group of sentences that work in concert to develop a unit of thought. Without paragraphs, even a brief essay would be unwieldy for you and your reader. Paragraphing permits you to subdivide material into manageable parts and, at the same time, to arrange those parts into a unified whole that effectively communicates its message.

Paragraphing is signaled by indentation. The first line is indented five spaces in a typewritten paper and one inch in a handwritten paper. (Business letters are sometimes typed in a "block" format, with paragraphs separated by a skipped line between them but no paragraph indentations. The "block" format is not appropriate for essays.)

A paragraph's purpose determines its structure. In college, the most common purposes for writing are *to inform* and *to persuade,* as discussed in 1b. Some paragraphs in informative or persuasive essays serve special roles: they introduce, conclude, or provide transitions. Most paragraphs, however, are **topical paragraphs,** which are also called *developmental paragraphs* or *body paragraphs.* They

TEACHING TIP
Essay paragraphing differs considerably from newspaper-article paragraphing. Anyone can see at a glance that newspapers frequently have paragraphs of a sentence or two. Such paragraphs are rare in essays, except perhaps as transitions. The reason for the difference in the look of essays and articles is the rationale behind each. Essays attempt to present material in a simultaneously logical and dramatic way. They begin with a hook to grab the reader's interest, and then most proceed from point to point until the end (of the narrative or of the list of causes, etc.) is reached. Rarely is the first paragraph used to reveal key information. Essays are written on the assumption that they will be read from beginning to end.

73

TEACHING TIP (CONT.)

In contrast, newspaper articles (not to be confused with essays in newspapers) use few such dramatic devices as suspense. Usually, the only hook is the headline. Then in paragraph 1 the reader gets the *Who, What, Where, When, Why,* and *How.* Subsequent paragraphs reveal additional details, but all the key facts are given in paragraph 1—the opposite of the procedure in the essay's first paragraph. The further one gets into most newspaper articles, the less important the contents. In some cases, a reader can get the idea that the piece doesn't conclude so much as trail off. This is because newspaper articles are written on the assumption that they will *not* be read from beginning to end. Editors may cut off the last few inches of a story to make it fit on a page; readers may only go as far as the first paragraph.

These differences have several implications in the writing classroom. First, most newspaper articles make poor models for paragraphing (unless you are teaching journalism). Second, encouraging students to read a newspaper regularly may make them better informed and expose them to new vocabulary used in complete sentences, but such reading alone is not likely to help them form subconscious ideas about paragraph structure that can be usefully applied to academic writing. To learn to write essays, the students must—at least part of the time—read essays.

One way to show your students the difference between essay paragraphing and newspaper paragraphing is to give them copies of pieces dealing with the same experience: a newspaper account of a fire and an essay (such as an editorial) written in response to the event; a newspaper account of a trial and a magazine essay discussing the case. Ask students to list the differences. At the least, they will mention differences in length, number of paragraphs, and the

consist of (1) a statement of a main idea and (2) specific, logical support for that main idea. Here is an example of a topical paragraph that seeks to inform.

> 1
> The cockroach lore that has been daunting us for years is mostly true. Roaches can live for twenty days without food, fourteen days without water; they can flatten their bodies and crawl through a crack thinner than a dime; they can eat huge doses of carcinogens and still die of old age. They can even survive "as much radiation as an oak tree can," says William Bell, the University of Kansas entomologist whose cockroaches appeared in the movie *The Day After*. They'll eat almost anything--regular food, leather, glue, hair, paper, even the starch in book bindings. (The New York Public Library has quite a cockroach problem.) They sense the slightest breeze, and they can react and start running in .05 seconds; they can also remain motionless for days. And if all this isn't creepy enough, they can fly too.
> —JANE GOLDMAN, "What's Bugging You"

Goldman states her main idea in the first sentence. She then gives concrete examples supporting her claim that there is much truth to the lore about cockroaches. This paragraph relates to the thesis° of the whole essay: "Roaches cannot be banished from the world, but they can be controlled in people's homes and apartments."*

Here is an example of a topical paragraph that seeks to persuade. It, too, consists of a main idea and support.

> 2
> We know very little about pain, and what we don't know makes it hurt all the more. Indeed, no form of illiteracy in the United States is so widespread or costly as ignorance about pain—what it is, what causes it, and how to deal with it without panic. Almost everyone can rattle off the names of at least a dozen drugs that can deaden pain from every conceivable cause—all the way from headaches to hemorrhoids. There is far less knowledge about the fact that about ninety percent of pain is self-limiting, that it is not always an indication of poor health, and that, most frequently, it is the result of tension, stress, idleness, boredom, frustration, suppressed rage, insufficient sleep, overeating, poorly balanced diet, smoking, excessive drinking, inadequate exercise, stale air, or any of the other abuses encountered by the human body in modern society.   —NORMAN COUSINS, *Anatomy of an Illness*

Cousins states his main idea in the first two sentences. The second sentence narrows the focus of the first and sets the stage for the

---

*Throughout this book a degree mark (°) indicates a term that is defined in the Glossary of Grammatical and Selected Compositional Terms.

supporting statements that follow. This paragraph is part of a chapter whose thesis is reflected in the chapter's title: "Pain Is Not the Enemy."

Goldman's and Cousins's paragraphs demonstrate the three major characteristics of a successful paragraph. By having a clear and logical relationship between the paragraph's main idea and the supporting evidence for that main idea, their paragraphs have **unity.** By arranging a smooth progression from one sentence to the next, their paragraphs have **coherence.** By offering detailed, thorough support of the main idea, their paragraphs are **well developed.**

An understanding of paragraph structure can help you at various points during your writing process. Before you start drafting, you might decide to subdivide your material into paragraphs and to develop each in an effective way. If you prefer to plan less at first and instead write a "discovery" or a rough draft that gets all your ideas down on paper, you can later sort out your material and arrange it into manageable paragraphs. When you are revising, you might find that a particular paragraph is weak because it does not clearly state its main idea or it does not develop that idea well. Also, you might notice that although each paragraph is well structured on its own, the paragraphs do not work together very well. This chapter, therefore, offers you paragraphing options to consider as you plan, draft, and revise your writing.

presence of personal opinion. They may also notice the lack of a thesis statement and a conclusion in the newspaper article and the presence of both in the essay.

You might also ask students how satisfied they would be if they were given only the first paragraph of the newspaper article and the essay. The article's introduction will probably be far more satisfying in terms of information, less satisfying in terms of graceful presentation, background, pacing, and the like.

Another way to underscore the difference between the genres is to give students (or assign them to find) a meaty newspaper article—the kind that runs for two pages, usually about a scandal or a major crime. Have them rewrite the article as an essay. Before the students write, you might discuss with them the kinds of changes they anticipate making.

4a

Write unified paragraphs.

A paragraph is **unified** when all its sentences relate to the main idea. Unity is lost if a paragraph goes off the topic by including sentences unrelated to the main idea. Here is a paragraph about data bases, lacking unity because two deliberately added sentences go off the topic.

No   We have all used physical data bases since our grammar school days. Grammar school was fun, but high school was more challenging. Our class yearbooks, the telephone book, the shoebox full of receipts documenting our deductions for the IRS—these are all data bases in one form or another, for a data base is nothing more than an assemblage of information organized to allow the retrieval of that information in certain ways. The IRS requires that taxpayers have documentation to support all but standard deductions.

75

COORDINATED RESOURCES

Alternate examples and exercises for this chapter are available in the *S & S Workbook for Writers,* Gordon and Troyka.

Transparency masters are available for many of the screened charts and/or lists in this chapter.

Students can practice and test their knowledge of terms, key concepts, and applications of material in this chapter by using the *Study Guide to the S & S Handbook for Writers,* West.

In the preceding paragraph, the first sentence states the main idea, and the third sentence expands upon it. But the second and last sentences wander away from the topic of data bases. As a result, unity is lost. A reader quickly loses patience with material that rambles and therefore fails to communicate a clear message. Here is an improved version. All its sentences, including the ones adding interesting details, bear on the subject of data bases.

Yes

3

We have all used physical data bases since our grammar school days. Our class yearbooks, the telephone book, the shoebox full of receipts documenting our deductions for the IRS —these are all data bases in one form or another, for a data base is nothing more than an assemblage of information organized to allow the retrieval of that information in certain ways. A telephone book, for example, assuming that you have the right one for the right city, will enable you to find the telephone number for, say, Alan Smith. Coincidentally it will also give you his address, provided there is only one Alan Smith listed. Where there are several Alan Smiths, you would have to know the address or at least part of it, to find the number of the particular Alan Smith you had in mind. Even without the address, however, you would still save considerable time by the telephone database. The book might list 50,000 names but only 12 Alan Smiths, so at the outset you could eliminate 49,988 telephone calls when trying to contact the elusive Mr. Smith.

—Erik Sanberg-Diment, "Personal Computers"

The sentence that contains the main idea of a paragraph is called the **topic sentence.** Some paragraphs use two sentences to present a main idea. In such cases, the topic sentence is followed by a **limiting or clarifying sentence** which serves to narrow the paragraph's focus. In the paragraph about physical data bases, the first sentence is its topic sentence, and the second sentence is its limiting sentence. The rest of the sentences in the paragraph support the main idea.

1
Know how to use a topic sentence.

Because it contains the main idea of a paragraph, a topic sentence focuses and controls what can be written in the paragraph. The words that create the focus and control usually appear in the sentence's predicate°. To check this, look at the many sample para-

76

graphs in this chapter. Consider, for example, the topic sentence of paragraph 4. The words that create the focus and control for the rest of the paragraph are shown in italics.

> Everyone *must have had at least one personal experience with a computer error by this time.*

The paragraph is developed with examples of computer errors.

Some professional essay writers do not always use topic sentences because they have the skill to carry the reader along without explicit signposts. Understandably, student writers are usually required to use topic sentences so that their essays will be clearly organized and paragraphs will not stray from the controlling power of each main idea.

Topic sentence at the beginning of a paragraph

Most informative and persuasive paragraphs place the topic sentence first so that a reader knows immediately what to expect.

4

> *Everyone must have had at least one personal experience with a computer error by this time.* Bank balances are suddenly reported to have jumped from $379 into the millions, appeals for charitable contributions are mailed over and over to people with crazy-sounding names at your address, department stores send the wrong bills, utility companies write that they're turning everything off, that sort of thing. If you manage to get in touch with someone and complain, you then get instantaneously typed, guilty letters from the same computer, saying, "Our computer was in error, and an adjustment is being made in your account."
> —LEWIS THOMAS, "To Err Is Human"

When the main idea of a paragraph comes first, *deductive reasoning is being used.* Deductive reasoning, as is explained in 5e-2, is a natural thought pattern that starts with a general statement and moves to specific details supporting that general statement (see also 4c).

Sometimes the main idea in the topic sentence starts a paragraph and is then restated at the end of the paragraph.

5

> *Barbie's life is that of the ultimate swinging single.* Although she has no parents to cast shadows into her life of constant boating, skiing, and camping, she also does not seem to have a need for them. Total independence is a central characteristic of Barbie. Although she owns an extensive amount of sporting equipment, Barbie seemingly has no need for employment that allows her to purchase this merchandise. There is no such thing as a Barbie

ALTERNATE EXAMPLE: TOPIC SENTENCE AT BEGINNING

A school that devotes itself totally and unequivocally to salable skills, especially in a time of high unemployment, sending young men and women into the world armed with only a narrow range of skills, is also sending lambs into the lion's den. If those people gain nothing more from their studies than supposedly salable skills, and can't make the sale because of changes in the job market, they have been cheated. But if those skills were more than salable, if study made them better citizens and made them happier to be human beings, they have not been cheated. They will find some kind of job soon enough. It might even turn out that those humanizing and liberating skills are salable. Flexibility, an ability to change and learn new things, is a valuable skill. People who have learned how to learn can learn outside of school. That is where most of us have learned to do what we do, not in school. Learning to learn is one of the highest liberal skills.
—ROBERT A. GOLDWIN, "Is It Enough to Roll with the Times?"

INSTRUCTOR'S NOTES

office in any of the Barbie equipment, nor are there accessories that remotely suggest a job situation for this carefree doll; although Barbie might be in high school or college, there are no accessories that hint at her having to endure the boredom of education. *Life for Barbie appears to be a kind of endless summer vacation, an extended tour of summer homes and resorts, free from school, family, and financial worries.*

—Don Richard Cox, "Barbie and Her Playmates"

Topic sentence at the end of a paragraph

Some informative and persuasive paragraphs reveal the supporting details before the main idea. The topic sentence, therefore, comes at the end of a paragraph. This arrangement reflects *inductive reasoning,* another natural thought pattern, discussed in 5e-1. It starts with specifics and finishes with the generalization (see also 4c). This approach is particularly effective for building suspense and for dramatic effect. Still, this arrangement forces readers to move through all the details before encountering the organizing effect of a main idea.

The next two paragraphs end with a topic sentence. In the first example, the main idea is fairly easy to predict as the concrete details build upon themselves. The main idea in the second example is less predictable—thus more satisfying for some readers but more difficult for others.

6   A combination of cries from exotic animals and laughter and gasps from children fills the air along with the aroma of popcorn and peanuts. A hungry lion bellows for dinner, his roar breaking through the confusing chatter of other animals. Birds of all kinds chirp endlessly at curious children. Monkeys swing from limb to limb performing gymnastics for gawking onlookers. A comedy routine by orangutans employing old shoes and garments incites squeals of amusement. Reptiles sleep peacefully behind glass windows, yet they send shivers down the spines of those who remember the quick death many of these reptiles can induce. *The sights and sounds and smells of the zoo inform and entertain children of all ages.*

—Deborah Harris, student

One of the most common observations anyone can make about honeybees is that they are extraordinarily good at finding honey. Furthermore, not long after one bee finds a source of honey, the whole hive seems to show up to carry it off. A young biologist named Karl von Frisch noted this fact and then asked what seemed to be a very simple question: How does the whole

7   hive find out about a source of honey so quickly? To answer this question completely took him the rest of his life and changed the science of biology in ways still not fully appreciated. Without complicated equipment and with very little laboratory work, von Frisch and his co-workers discovered a whole universe of previously unsuspected senses and behaviors in honeybees. For more than five decades they painstakingly explored the perceptual world of the honeybee, and in recognition of his discoveries and his contribution to the founding of the modern science of animal behavior, Karl von Frisch was awarded the Nobel Prize in physiology and medicine in 1973. *It all began with an observation, a question, and application of the scientific method.*

—ALLEN D. MACNEILL AND LORRIE PENFIELD,
"The Scientific Method in Biology"

Topic sentence implied

Some paragraphs make a unified statement without the use of a topic sentence. Writers must carefully construct such paragraphs, so that a reader can easily discern the main idea.

8   Already, in the nation's heartland—Des Moines or Omaha— you'll find widespread use of Oriental and Mexican vegetables. Houston has some of the best Vietnamese restaurants in the world. The Los Angeles area has more than two hundred Thai restaurants. Mexican fast food has become a $1.6 billion industry covering the whole country—even Barrow, Alaska, north of the Arctic Circle, has a Mexican restaurant. And springing up throughout the land are Ethiopian, Afghan, Brazilian and other exotic ethnic eating places. Indeed, it is no longer enough for a restaurant to be just Chinese; it may be Szechuan, Hunan or Shanghai, but also Suzhou, Hangzhou or some other ethnic specialty within an ethnic specialty.

—NOEL VIETMEYER,
"Exotic Edibles Are Altering America's Diet and Agriculture"

Vietmeyer uses many details to communicate the main idea that exotic foods and restaurants are appearing all across the country. A reader of informative and persuasive writing does not expect to puzzle over material, so implied topic sentences must be very clear, even though they are silent.

EXERCISE 1
Identify all topic sentences, limiting sentences, and topic sentences repeated at the ends of paragraphs. If there is no topic sentence, state an implied one.

79

ANSWERS: EXERCISE 1

A. The topic sentence is the first sentence.

B. The topic sentence is the last sentence.

C. The topic sentence is the first sentence, and the second sentence is a limiting sentence.

D. The topic sentence is implied: The main idea is that because interns are new on July 1st, people should avoid being in a hospital in July.

E. The topic sentence is the first sentence.

BIOGRAPHY

Marilyn Machlowitz (1952–   ) has a Ph.D. from Yale. She has been with the New York Life Insurance Company as a psychologist and manager of human resource development since 1978.

A.   It's not easy to distinguish between the two species, but there are some fairly obvious differences. The northern flying squirrel, at ten to fifteen inches in length and weighing four to eight ounces, is larger than the southern species, which is ten to fifteen inches long and weighs only two to four ounces. The northern species has a thicker pelage and thus

9 tends to look more robust, the face profile in particular appearing more rounded. The tail accounts for forty percent of the animal's total length in both species, but the northern flying squirrel's tail is thicker, more uniformly colored and often has a dark tip. Northern adults vary in color from light tan to rust brown, whereas southern adults tend more toward charcoal gray.

—Nancy Wells-Gosling,
"This Little Squirrel Keeps a Big Trick Hidden in Its Sleeve"

B.   Most people don't lose ten dollars or one hundred dollars when they trade cars. They lose many hundreds or even a thousand. They buy used cars that won't provide them service through the first payment. They

10 overbuy new cars and jeopardize their credit, only to find themselves "hung," unable even to sell their shiny new toys. The car business is one of the last roundups in America, the great slaughterhouse of wheeling and dealing, where millions of people each year willingly submit to being taken.

—Remar Sutton, *Don't Get Taken Every Time*

C.   Education which involves only the gathering of knowledge for its own sake ignores the need of all people to learn to ask larger questions. People may possess a wealth of individual facts, a pile of unrelated names, dates, formulas, structures, and equations, and yet be unable to apply their knowledge to issues such as justice and dignity. For example, it is a fact that more than half the U.S. population is female. Why has

11 the American woman always played a subordinate role in a society where she is the majority? Also, it is a fact that the rate of infant death in the United States is thirteen in every thousand births, a rate higher than that in twelve other countries. How is it possible in a country as wealthy and as technologically advanced as the United States such a cruel problem can exist?

—Amy Dunbar, student

D.   This July 1, more than 13,000 doctors will invade over 600 hospitals across the country. Within minutes they will be overwhelmed. Last

12 July 1, Dr. John Baumann, then twenty-five, walked into Washington, DC's, Walter Reed Army Medical Center, where he was immediately faced with caring for "eighteen of the sickest people I have ever seen."

—Marilyn Machlowitz, "Never Get Sick in July"

80

E.

13

Peanut butter, the pâté of childhood, is the passion of many adults. They eat it in the morning, snack on it at night and, in between, mix it with everything from jellies to exotic spices in recipes that tax a peanut butter lover's inventiveness—and sometimes patience. Some 600 million pounds of peanut butter are eaten annually in what is a $700 million retail market. That's eight pounds of peanut butter per person per year.

—FLORENCE FABRICANT,
"Peanut Butter: An Enduring American Passion"

2
Know how to develop a paragraph.

Because a topic sentence contains a main idea, it is usually a generalization—a general statement or idea. In a topical paragraph, the sentences that support the topic sentence by offering specific, concrete details *develop the paragraph*. Without development, a paragraph is flat and fails to make its point or capture a reader's interest. Compare the following paragraph to the first sample paragraph in this chapter.

No

The cockroach lore that has been daunting us for years is mostly true. Almost every tale we have heard about cockroaches is true. These tales have been disheartening people for generations. No one seems to believe that it is possible to control roaches.

Each sentence merely repeats the first sentence in different words. The paragraph is stalled, going around in circles and failing to develop a main idea.

The key to successful development of topical paragraphs is detail. Details bring generalizations to life by providing concrete, specific illustrations. A paragraph developed with good detail often has one or more "RENNS"—an acronym that stands for *r*easons, *e*xamples, *n*umbers, *n*ames, and appeals to the five *s*enses. You can use RENNS as a memory device to help you check the development of your paragraphs. RENNS does not mean, however, that the details of development must occur in the order of the letters in the acronym. Nor does RENNS mean that every good paragraph has a complete menu of RENNS. A well-developed paragraph usually has only a selection of RENNS.

To see RENNS in action, compare again the two versions of the paragraph about cockroaches: paragraph 1 and the "No" example above. The next paragraph has three of the fives types of RENNS.

81

ANSWERS: EXERCISE 2

A. Focus and control: *hardy worthy of the term "intelligence."* RENNS: Examples include length, weight, fur, tail, and color. Names include northern flying squirrel and southern species. Numbers include 10-to-15 inches in length, two to four ounces in weight, and the tail's being forty percent of the total length. Appeals to the senses include the "look" of the thick fur, the dark tip of the tail, and the colors of light tan to rust brown, and charcoal gray.

B. Focus and control: *one of the last roundups in America . . . where millions of people each year willingly submit to being taken.* RENNS: Examples include buying used cars that do not last through the first payment, and jeopardizing their credit. Numbers include dollars—ten, a hundred, many hundred, even a thousand. Appeal to the senses include "shiny new toys" and "slaughterhouse."

C. Focus and control: *ignores the need of all people to ask larger questions.* RENNS: Examples include the question about the proportion of the population that is female and the question about the rate of infant deaths. Numbers include "majority" and a death rate of thirteen in a thousand births, which is higher than in twelve other countries.

D. The topic sentence is implied. It deals with why people should avoid being in hospitals in July. RENNS: Reasons include the fact that all interns are new (and therefore inexperienced) as of July 1st. Names include Dr. John Baumann and Walter Reed Army Medical Center. Numbers include July 1, 600 hospitals, twenty-five years of age, and eighteen sick people.

E. Focus and control: *passion of many adults.* RENNS: Examples include their eating it in the morning, at night, for snacks in between, and their mixing it into exotic recipes. Numbers include 600 million pounds, $700 million, and eight pounds per person.

14
Whether bad or good, in tune or not, whistling has its practical side. Clifford Pratt is working with a group of speech therapists to develop whistling techniques to help children overcome speech problems through improved breath control and tongue flexibility. People who have a piercing whistle have a clear advantage when it comes to hailing cabs, calling the dog or the children, or indicating approval during a sporting event. And if you want to leave the house and can't remember where you put your keys, there's a key chain on the market now with a beep that can be activated by a whistle: You whistle and the key chain tells you where it is.
—CASSANDRA TATE,
"Whistlers Blow New Life Into a Forgotten Art"

Paragraph 14 succeeds because it does more than merely repeat its topic sentence. It develops the topic sentence by offering concrete, specific illustrations to support the generalization that whistling has its practical side. It has Examples, including treatment for children with speech difficulties; convenience for hailing cabs, dogs, and children, and for sounding off at sporting events; and a signaling key chain. It has Names, such as Clifford Pratt, speech therapists, and children (not the general term *people*), and dogs (not the general term *animals*). It appeals to the Senses by including the feeling of tongue flexibility, the piercing sound of a whistle, the roar at a sporting event, and the sound of a key chain beeping for its owner.

Some well-developed paragraphs have a single extended example to support the topic sentence.

15
He was one of the greatest scientists the world has ever known, yet if I had to convey the essence of Albert Einstein in a single word, I would choose *simplicity.* Perhaps an anecdote will help. Once, caught in a downpour, he took off his hat and held it under his coat. Asked why, he explained, with admirable logic, that the rain would damage the hat, but his hair would be none the worse for its wetting. This knack of going instinctively to the heart of the matter was the secret of his major scientific discoveries—this and his extraordinary feeling for beauty.
—BANESH HOFFMAN, "My Friend, Albert Einstein"

EXERCISE 2
Referring to the paragraphs in Exercise 1, identify the words that give each topic sentence focus and control. Then identify the RENNS in each paragraph.

EXERCISE 3

Using your own words to complete the thought, fill in the blanks. The place can be a city, a spot on campus, a room in your home, an outdoor location, or any other you want.

My favorite place is _____ because it is _____.

Then using this as a topic sentence, write a well-developed paragraph. Be guided by the words that focus and control your development. Use as many RENNS as you need to give the topic sentence concrete, specific support.

 4b

Write coherent paragraphs.

A paragraph is **coherent** when its sentences are related to each other, not only in content but also in grammatical structures and choice of words. Techniques that help to make paragraphs coherent include using transitional expressions, using pronouns, repeating key words, and using parallel structures. Decisions about coherence are often made during revising, after you have written a first draft and can begin to see how your sentence might more effectively relate to one another.

1

Use transitional expressions.

Transitional expressions—words and phrases that signal connections among ideas—can help you achieve coherence in your writing. Each expression is a signal to the reader that explains how one idea is connected to the next. The most commonly used transitional expressions are shown in the chart on the next page.

◗ COMMA ALERT: Transitional expressions are usually set off with commas. ◗

Notice how the transitional expressions (shown in boldface) help to make this paragraph coherent.

> Jaguars, **for example,** were once found in the United States from southern Louisiana to California. Today they are rare north of the Mexican border, with no confirmed sighting since 1971. They are rare, **too,** in Mexico, where biologist Carl Koford estimated their population at fewer than a thousand in a 1972 survey. Some biologists think the number is even smaller today. **Similarly,** jaguars have disappeared from southern Argentina and Paraguay.
>
> —JEFFREY P. COHN, "Kings of the Wild"

16

ANSWERS: EXERCISE 3
Answers will vary. Paragraphs should have some RENNS, though not likely every type.

83

TRANSITIONAL EXPRESSIONS	
SIGNAL	**WORDS**
ADDITION	also, in addition, too, moreover, and, besides, further, furthermore, equally important, next, then, finally,
EXAMPLE	for example, for instance, thus, as an illustration, namely, specifically,
CONTRAST	but, yet, however, on the other hand, nevertheless, nonetheless, conversely, in contrast, on the contrary, still, at the same time,
COMPARISON	similarly, likewise, in like manner, in the same way, in comparison,
CONCESSION	of course, to be sure, certainly, naturally, granted,
RESULT	therefore, thus, consequently, so, accordingly, due to this,
SUMMARY	as a result, hence, in short, in brief, in summary, in conclusion, finally, on the whole,
TIME SEQUENCE	first, firstly, second, secondly, third, fourth, next, then, finally, afterwards, before, soon, later, during, meanwhile, subsequently, immediately, at length, eventually, in the future, currently,
PLACE	in the front, in the foreground, in the back, in the background, at the side, adjacent, nearby, in the distance, here, there,

2
Use pronouns.

When you use pronouns that clearly refer to nouns or other pronouns, you help your reader follow the bridges you build from one sentence to the next. For advice on maintaining clear pronoun reference, see Chapter 10. Notice how the pronouns (shown in bold-face) help make this paragraph coherent.

In the morning, before the sun has broken through, the sandpiper begins to look for food. A tiny thing with gray feathers

84

and a white underbelly, the "peep" looks, front to back, like awl and ball and cotton ball. **He** darts along the wave front, probing the sand for buried flecks of nourishment. Each feeding lasts but seconds and is sneaked in between a departing wave and the one soon to follow. With **his** head poked down into the sand, it seems impossible for the sandpiper to notice the water about to overtake **him.** Yet, at the last possible instant—later than the last possible instant, it sometimes seems—**he** turns, body suddenly erect, and races to higher ground. Rejecting flight, **he** races overland, body perfectly still, feet pounding a noiseless rat-tat-tat-tat-tat into the wet sand. The water is never more than a stride behind **him.**

—RICK HOROWITZ, "The Sandpiper's Politics"

17

3
Use deliberate, selective repetition.

You can achieve coherence by repeating key words in a paragraph. A key word is usually one related to the main idea in the topic sentence or to a major detail in one of the supporting sentences. Repeating a key word now and then helps your reader follow your material. This technique must be used judiciously, however, because you risk being monotonous. The shorter a paragraph, the less likely that repeated words will be effective.

Notice how the careful reuse of the key words *sounds, words, hear,* and *hearing* (shown in boldface) help make this paragraph coherent.

I was then a listening child, careful to **hear** the very different **sounds** of Spanish and English. Wide-eyed with **hearing,** I'd listen to **sounds** more than to **words.** First, there were English (gringo) **sounds.** So many **words** still were unknown to me that when the butcher or the lady at the drugstore said something, exotic polysyllabic **sounds** would bloom in the midst of their sentences. Often the speech of people in public seemed to me very loud, booming with confidence. The man behind the counter would literally ask, "What can I do for you?" But by being so firm and clear, the **sound** of his voice said that he was a gringo; he belonged in public society. There were also the high, nasal notes of middle-class American speech—which I rarely am conscious of **hearing** today because I **hear** them so often, but could not stop **hearing** when I was a boy. Crowds at Safeway or at bus stops were noisy with birdlike **sounds** of *los gringos.* I'd move away from them all—all the chipping chatter above me.

—RICHARD RODRIGUEZ, "Aria: A Memoir of a Bilingual Childhood"

18

BIOGRAPHY
Richard Rodriquez (1944–   ) was born in San Francisco of Mexican parents. He received his Ph.D. from the University of California at Berkeley. In his essay "Aria: A Memoir of a Bilingual Childhood," published in 1981 in *The American Scholar,* he argues against bilingual education and what he considers to be other types of reverse discrimination. Drawing on his experience as a Spanish-speaking child in America, he extends his discussion is his widely acclaimed autobiographical book *Hunger of Memory: The Education of Richard Rodriquez,* published in 1982.

85

4
Use parallel structures.

Parallel structures—grammatically equivalent forms—can help you achieve coherence, especially when used for occasional dramatic effect. Parallelism is discussed in Chapter 18. Using the same form of phrase or clause several times sets up a rhythm that gives unity to the paragraph. Notice how the parallel structures (shown in boldface) make the paragraph coherent as well as dramatic.

19

The world of work into which Jacinto and the other seven-year-olds were apprenticed was within sight and sound of the pueblo. **It was work** under blazing suns, in rainstorms, in pitch-black nights. **It was work** that you were always walking to or walking from, **work without wages** and **work without end. It was work** that gave you a bone-tired feeling at the end of the day, so you learned **to swing a machete, to tighten a cinch, and to walk without lost motion.** Between seven and twelve you learned all this, each lesson driven home when your *jefe* said with a scowl: "Así no, hombre; así." And he showed you how.

—ERNESTO GALARZA, *Barrio Boy*

5
Combine techniques of coherence.

Often techniques of coherence work in unison, though they are shown separately in this chapter for the sake of clear illustration. Indeed, in most of the sample paragraphs in this chapter, many techniques of unity and coherence work together. Notice in the following paragraph by Loren Eiseley how pronouns and deliberate repetition, in particular, combine. The key words, *flower* and *pollen* and their derivatives, are boxed. The repeated pronouns *it* and *its* are circled, and arrows point to the antecedent. A transitional word is underlined.

20

86

When the first simple flower bloomed on some raw upland late in the Dinosaur Age, it was wind pollinated, just like its early pine-cone relatives. It was a very inconspicuous flower because it had not yet evolved the idea of using the surer attraction of birds and insects to achieve the transportation of pollen. It sowed its own pollen and received the pollen of other flowers by the simple vagaries of the wind. Many plants in regions where insect life is scant still follow this principle today. Nevertheless, the true flower—and the seed that it produced— was a profound innovation in the world of life.

—LOREN EISELEY, "How Flowers Changed the World"

BIOGRAPHY
Loren Eiseley (1907–1977) was an American anthropologist, poet, and author recognized for the poetic nature of his writings on scholarly subjects. His works include *The Immense Journey, All the Strange Hours* (autobiographical), and *Darwin's Century*.

6

Show relationships among paragraphs.

Paragraphs in an essay do not stand in isolation. You can use the techniques of coherence discussed in this chapter to communicate relationships among paragraphs in an essay. Transitional expressions, pronouns, deliberate repetition, and parallel structures help you link ideas from paragraph to paragraph throughout an essay.

One excellent way to connect paragraphs is to start a new paragraph with a reference to the previous paragraph. The two student essays discussed in Chapter 3 use this technique. In the final draft of "Knowing How to Live Alone" (pages 64–66), Tara Foster has a paragraph about taking care of practical matters. She suggests that learning to make important practical decisions has positive benefits. Foster then knits the next paragraph, about making new friends, into the essay by referring to the idea of gaining confidence from handling practical matters:

> The confidence that single people get from learning to deal with practical matters can boost their chances for establishing new friendships.

Gary Lee Houseman uses a similar bridging technique in his essay "Rain Forests Must Not Be Destroyed" (pages 67–70). Houseman follows a paragraph about the biomedical benefits of rain forests with one about the role of rain forests in maintaining the balance of nature. He starts the paragraph about maintaining natural balances this way:

> Not only for their medical riches but also for their role in maintaining global balances, rain forests must be saved.

Houseman also links the center of the essay—the reasons why rain forests must be preserved—with words that set up a climactic

87

order. The three paragraphs in which Houseman discusses the importance of rain forests begin this way:

PARAGRAPH PRESENTING FIRST REASON
One major value of rain forests is biomedical.

PARAGRAPH PRESENTING SECOND REASON
Not only for their medical riches but also for their role in maintaining global natural balances, rain forests must be saved.

PARAGRAPH PRESENTING LAST REASON
Most important, rain forests must be protected because their trees control the planet's oxygen supply and climate.

With "Most important," Houseman links three paragraphs and establishes the order he wants readers to use as they evaluate his reasons.

ANSWERS: EXERCISE 4

Students will likely find more examples than the answers given here.

A. *Pronouns:* They, these, their. *Deliberate repetition:* nose(s), they, their. *Parallel structures:* come / go; mapping / probing, sniffing, exploring.

B. *Transitional expressions:* however, in addition, however. *Pronouns:* we, it [cancer], them [factors], us, it [carcinogen that exists]. *Deliberate repetition:* we, we must.

C. *Pronouns:* it [the January wind]. *Deliberate repetition:* it can. *Parallel structures:* all clauses starting with "it can"; the beginning of the last two sentences: On a sunny day, In the cold of a lonely night"; many internal elements: simple forms of verbs, participles as adjectives, etc.

D. *Pronouns:* her, she. *Deliberate repetition:* Kathy, arms, hands, opened, closed. *Parallel structures:* Many parallel clauses starting with "Her shoulders raised"; open hands reaching out and closed hands bringing back.

E. *Transitional expressions:* however. *Pronouns:* their, he, his. *Deliberate repetition:* diving, dive; tail, tail.

EXERCISE 4

Identify the techniques of coherence—words of transition, pronouns, deliberate repetition, and parallel structures—in each paragraph.

A.   Elephant shrews come into the world nose first, and "nose first" they go through the rest of their nervous lives. Ever alert for danger, these **21** tiny mammals depend on their noses as we do our eyes, mapping their twilight world primarily by scent. Their long, flexible noses twitch constantly, probing, sniffing, and exploring every detail of their brushy, dry habitat.   —SUSAN LUMPKIN, "The Elephant Shrew—By a Nose!"

B.   However, we must try even harder to prevent cancer before it starts, since so far it has been difficult to find many biochemical differences between cancer cells and normal cells that can be exploited in therapy. For prevention, we must devise better methods of testing for factors in the environment, including chemicals from industrial processes and possibly food additives, that can cause cancer, and after we find all **22** these factors we must try to remove them. In addition, we must try to understand more of the mechanisms by which chemicals and radiation cause cancer in the hope that such knowledge will make it easier for us to recognize these carcinogens and perhaps to devise means to prevent their action. However, when, as in the case of smoking, we find that a carcinogen exists, we must act to prevent it from entering the environment.   —HOWARD TEMIN, "Editor's Notebook" of the *Wisconsin State Journal*

C.   The January wind has a hundred voices. It can scream, it can bellow, it can whisper, and it can sing a lullaby. It can roar through the leafless oaks and shout down the hillside, and it can murmur in the white

23 pines rooted among the granite ledges where lichen makes strange hieroglyphics. It can whistle down a chimney and set the hearth-flames to dancing. On a sunny day it can pause in a sheltered spot and breathe a promise of spring and violets. In the cold of a lonely night it can rattle the sash and stay there muttering of ice and snowbanks and deep-frozen ponds. —HAL BORLAND, "January Wind"

D.   Kathy sat with her legs dangling over the edge of the side of the hood. The band of her earphones held back strands of straight copper hair, which had come loose from two thick braids that hung down her back. She swayed with the music that only she could hear. Her shoulders raised, making circles in the warm air. Her arms reached out to her side; 24 her opened hands reached for the air; her closed hands brought the air back to her. Her arms reached over her head; her opened hands reached for a cloud; her closed hands brought the cloud back to her. Her head moved from side to side; her eyes opened and closed to the tempo of the tunes. Kathy was motion. —CLAIRE BURKE, student

E.   Diving is perhaps one of their more stupendous feats. The sperm whale is the undoubted master, the only whale that can dive 4,000 feet down—or more. As he prepares to penetrate the depth, he jackknifes 25 with an utter grace--especially his tail movements, which seem desultory and almost casual. His grace, however, is deceptive; the power in that tail is the estimated equivalent of that of a 500-horsepower engine. —JACQUES-YVES COUSTEAU, "Jonah's Complaint"

EXERCISE 5

Reread the paragraphs in Exercise 1 and identify all techniques of coherence—words of transition, pronouns, deliberate repetition, and parallel structures.

EXERCISE 6

Develop three of the following topic sentences into unified paragraphs, with RENNS and techniques of coherence. On a separate sheet of paper, list the RENNS and the techniques of coherence you built into each paragraph.

1. The family photograph I treasure most is _____.
2. Weather often affects people's moods.
3. Television encourages materialism.
4. _____ is the most serious problem facing humanity today.
5. Medical schools should include in their curriculums courses in literature and history.

ANSWERS: EXERCISE 5
Students will likely find more examples than the answers given here.
A. *Pronouns:* which. *Deliberate repetition:* species, flying squirrel, northern, southern, tail. *Parallel structures:* The northern, the southern; ten to fifteen, four to eight, eight to ten, two to four.
B. *Pronouns:* they, them, their, themselves. *Deliberate repetition:* people, cars. *Parallel structures:* They lose, they buy, they overbuy; only to find / even to sell.
C. *Transitional expressions:* for example, also. *Pronouns:* its, their, she. *Deliberate repetition:* people, U.S. and United States. *Parallel structures:* a wealth of individual facts, a pile of unrelated names; dates, formulas, structures, and equations; it is a fact, it is a fact.
D. *Pronouns:* they, he. *Deliberate repetition:* July 1. *Parallel structures:* this July 1, last July 1.
E. *Pronouns:* they, it, that's. *Deliberate repetition:* peanut butter. *Parallel structures:* The pâté of childhood is the passion of many adults; they eat it, snack on it, mix it.

ANSWERS: EXERCISE 6
Answers will vary.

NOTE: Biography of Jacques-Yves Cousteau on p. 90.

BIOGRAPHY

Jacques-Yves Cousteau (1910–   ) is known to most Americans as the face and voice of a series of television programs exploring oceans and waterways around the globe. However, Cousteau is a more complex figure than most imagine. Besides being an explorer and photographer, he is an inventor and writer. Cousteau joined the French Navy in 1930, and became interested in diving in 1936. He began experimenting with underwater breathing apparatus, and in 1942 developed the Aqualung with Emile Gagnan. Between 1946 and 1957 he founded (or cofounded) five oceanographic research centers in Europe and the United States; most continue their research even today.

Cousteau has invented a number of devices that are basic in current undersea research: diving saucers, the Bathygraf cinecamera, deepsea camera sleds, mini-submarines. He has led research expeditions for the National Geographic Society, the French National Research Center, the National Aeronautics and Space Administration, and Texas A & M University.

Dave Schultz is quoted in *Contemporary Authors* as saying of Cousteau:

He is continuously studying the sea, for he feels—no, seriously believes—that the ocean is the last frontier for mankind. This frontier must not be abused the way a number of land areas have been, worldwide, where forests were cleared and wildlife reduced without sufficient consideration of the ecological consequences. If the ocean frontier is tamed with the same wantoness that has marked other pioneering efforts of man, then mankind will be lost, for there is no recovering a dead sea.

Cousteau says of himself "I am not a scientist. . . . I am an impresario of scientists, perhaps. I can speak their jargon, but more important I can make it accessible to the layman."

■∥ **4c**
Know how to arrange a paragraph.

Arranging a paragraph means putting its sentences into an order logical for communicating that paragraph's message clearly and effectively. The choices for arrangement for topical paragraphs are discussed in this section. Introductions, conclusions, and transitions are discussed in 4e. Decisions about arrangement often come during the revising process, after you have written a first draft and can begin to see how your sentences might be arranged for greatest impact.

In informative and persuasive writing, writers have a variety of options for arranging sentences in topical paragraphs. Choices include moving from general to specific, from specific to general, and from least to most important; progressing from problem to solution and sequencing according to location and to time.

From general to specific

An arrangement of sentences from the general to the specific is the most common organization for a paragraph. Seen in many of the examples earlier in this chapter, a general-to-specific arrangement begins with a topic sentence (and perhaps is followed by a limiting or clarifying sentence) and ends with specific details. This arrangement is a reflection of *deductive thinking,* a natural thought pattern discussed in 5e-2.

26

Unwanted music is privacy's constant enemy. There is hardly an American restaurant, store, railroad station or bus terminal that doesn't gurgle with melody from morning to night, nor is it possible any longer to flee by boarding the train or bus itself, or even by taking a walk in the park. Transistor radios have changed all that. Men, women and children carry them everywhere, hugging them with the desperate attachment that a baby has for its blanket, fearful that they might have to generate an idea of their own or contemplate a blade of grass. Thoughtless themselves, they have no thought for the sufferers within earshot of their portentous news broadcasts and raucous jazz. It is hardly surprising that RCA announced a plan that would pipe canned music and pharmaceutical commercials to 25,000 doctors' offices in eighteen big cities—one place where a decent quietude might be expected. This raises a whole new criterion for choosing a family physician. Better to have a second-rate healer content with the sounds of his stethoscope than an eminent specialist poking to the rhythms of Gershwin.

—WILLIAM ZINSSER, *The Haircurl Papers*

From specific to general

A less common arrangement than general to specific moves from the specific to the general. Like paragraphs 6 and 7, the paragraph ends with a topic sentence and begins with the details that support the topic sentence. This arrangement reflects *inductive reasoning*, a natural thought pattern discussed in 5e-1.

27   Suddenly we dipped down and landed on a level meadow near a tiny cluster of tents and tarps. As we stepped out of the chopper our boots sank into eight inches of dark water. The meadow was cluttered with leathery-leafed, knee-high plants with tufts bunched at the top of woody stems. Pitcher plants with cup-shaped leaves and delicate terrestrial orchids protruded from the spongy mire. Little palms rose from the higher ground around the meadow. *The overall impression was tropical lushness gone slightly haywire.*

—DONALD DALE JACKSON, "Scientists Zero in on the Strange 'Lost World' of Cerro de la Neblina"

From least to most important

A sentence arrangement that moves from the least to the most important is also known as *climactic order* because it saves the climax for the end. This arrangement can be effective in holding the reader's interest because the best part comes at the end. In informative and persuasive writing, this type of arrangement usually calls for the topic sentence at the beginning of the paragraph, although sometimes the topic sentence works well at the end. Here is a climactic paragraph that begins with a topic sentence.

28   *But probably the most dumbfounding of nature's extraordinary creations is the horned toad of our Southwest.* A herpetologist once invited me to observe one of these lizards right after it had molted. In a sand-filled glass cage I saw a large male. Beside him lay his old skin. The herpetologist began to annoy the beast with mock attacks, and the old man of the desert with his vulnerable new suit became frightened. Suddenly his eyeballs reddened. A final fast lunge from my friend at the beast and I froze in aston-

BIOGRAPHY

William Zinsser (1922–) served as a writer, editor, and critic for the *New York Herald Tribune* from 1946–59. Zinsser has been a free lance writer since 1959 and has written regular columns for *Look* (1967) and *Life* (1968–72). His civic work includes membership on the Board of Governors of the Brooklyn Museum and on the Board of Directors of the Municipal Art Society of New York. He is now head of the Book of the Month Club. His books include *Any Old Place with You, Seen Any Good Movies Lately?, Search and Research, The City Dwellers, The Haircurl Papers, Pop Goes America, The Paradise Bit* (a novel), *The Lunacy Boom,* and *On Writing Well.*

91

BIOGRAPHY

Jean Craighead George (1919–   ) began her career as a reporter and reporter-artist for various newspapers in Washington, D.C., and New York, but she left that field in 1947 to become well-known as a natural history writer. Her book *My Side of the Mountain* (1960) placed on the International Hans Christian Andersen Award honor list and was a runner-up for the American Library Association's John Newberry medal.

ALTERNATE EXAMPLE: SPATIAL SEQUENCE

The wash [low land that is sometimes flooded, at other times nearly dry] looked perfectly dry in my headlights. I drove down, across, up the other side and on into the night. Glimpses of weird humps of pale rock on either side, like petrified elephants, dinosaurs, stone-age hobgoblins. Now and then something alive scurried across the road: kangaroo mice, a jackrabbit, an animal that looked like a cross between a raccoon and a squirrel—the ringtail cat. Farther on a pair of mule deer started from the brush and bounded obliquely through the beams of my lights, raising puffs of dust which the wind, moving faster than my pickup truck, caught and carried ahead of me out of sight into the dark. The road, narrow and rocky, twisted sharply left and right, dipped in and out of tight ravines, climbing by degrees toward a summit which I would see only in the light of the coming day.
—EDWARD ABBEY, "The Most Beautiful Place on Earth"

ishment—a fine spray of blood shot from the lizard's eye, like fire from a dragon! The beast struck back with a weapon so shocking that it terrifies even the fiercest enemy.
—JEAN GEORGE, "That Astonishing Creature—Nature"

From problem to solution

An effective arrangement can be to present a problem and move quickly to a suggested solution. The topic sentence presents the problem and the next sentence—the limiting or clarifying sentence—presents the main idea of the solution. The rest of the sentences give the specifics of the solution.

> *Burnout is a potential problem for any hard working and persevering student.* A preliminary step for preventing student burnout is for students to work in moderation. Students can concentrate on school every day, provided that they do not overtax themselves. One method students can use is to avoid concentrating on a single project for an extended period of time. For example, if students have to read two books for a midterm history test, they should do other assignments at intervals so that the two books will not get boring. Another means to moderate a workload is to regulate how many extracurricular projects to take on. When a workload is manageable, a student's immunity to burnout is strengthened.

29

—BRADLEY HOWARD, student

According to location

A paragraph arranged according to location is put into a *spatial sequence*. It describes the position of objects relative to one another, often from a central point of reference. The topic sentence usually establishes a location that serves as the orientation for all other places mentioned. The other sentences in the paragraph often use transitional expressions (see page 83) that indicate *place*.

> *About two-hundred feet from where I had waded ashore, the coral rose to a high promontory and I decided to start my exploration there.* I climbed carefully to the top of the ledge and looked around. Only a narrow strait, about the length of a football field, separated me from the nearest island, which I assumed was one of the bird sanctuaries. A submerged reef seemed to join the two islands together. On the other side of the rock ledge was more coral and no sign of sand. As far as I could see, which was no more than a few hundred feet because the island curved sharply, there was nothing but a forest of coconut palms, coral, and the sea. I

30

turned and went back to my arrival point. My government friend had told me there was a sand beach on the island; I decided the best way to find it would be to go inland and come out on the other side.

—CASKIE STINNETT, *Grand and Private Pleasures*

According to time

A paragraph arranged according to time is put into a *chronological sequence*. It tells what happened or what is happening during a period of time.

31 Her name was Aho, and she belonged to the last culture to evolve in North America. Her forebears came down from the high country in western Montana nearly three centuries ago. They were a mountain people, a mysterious tribe of hunters whose language has never been positively classified in any major group. In the late seventeenth century they began a long migration to the south and east. It was a journey toward the dawn, and it led to a golden age. Along the way the Kiowas were befriended by the Crows, who gave them the culture and religion of the Plains. They acquired horses, and their ancient nomadic spirit was suddenly free of the ground. The acquired Tai-me, the sacred Sun Dance doll, from that moment the object and symbol of their worship, and so shared in the divinity of the sun. Not least, they acquired the sense of destiny, therefore courage and pride. When they entered upon the southern Plains they had been transformed. No longer were they slaves to the simple necessity of survival; they were a lordly and dangerous society of fighters and thieves, hunters and priests of the sun. According to their origin myth, they entered the world through a hollow log. From one point of view, their migration was the fruit of an old prophecy, for indeed they emerged from a sunless world.

—N. SCOTT MOMADAY, *The Way to Rainy Mountain*

EXERCISE 7
For each paragraph, arrange the sentences into a logical sequence. Begin by locating the topic sentence and placing it at the beginning of the paragraph.

PARAGRAPH A
1. Handel, through his use of a major key and a dynamic and melismatic melody in the Hallelujah Chorus of his *Messiah,* gives us a sense of hopeful elation.
2. Although defined as "the art of arranging sounds with reference to rhythm, pitch and tone quality" by Funk and Wagnall, music is, in reality, much, much more.

3. Chopin, on the other hand, through his use of the minor mode, bass register and slow tempo, conveys to us the feeling of sullen despair in the third movement of his Second Piano Sonata.

4. There is no doubt that we experience certain feelings when we fall under its hypnotic influence.

5. For example, music is surely the art of creating emotional responses through the skillful manipulation of sounds.

6. Examples of this power can be found among the works of any of the great composers.
—KEVIN KERWOOD, student

PARAGRAPH B

1. Thus, if we only knew how to unlock its secrets, a tree could tell us a great deal about what was happening in its neighborhood from the time of its beginning.

2. The records of past climate that they contain can help us to understand the natural forces that produce our weather, and this, in turn, can help us plan.

3. Trees are living archives, carrying within their structure a record not only of their age but also of precipitation and temperature for each year in which a ring was formed.

4. Trees can tell us what was happening before written records became available.

5. This record might also include the marks of forest fires, early frosts and, incorporated into the wood itself, chemical elements the tree removed from its environment.

6. Trees also have a great deal to tell us about our future.
—JAMES S. TREFIL,
"Concentric Clues from Growth Rings Unlock the Past"

ANSWERS: EXERCISE 8
Students will likely see more than one arrangement in some of these paragraphs. *Note:* You might also ask students to analyze these paragraphs in light of what was previously discussed in this chapter: topic sentence, words in topic sentence that create focus and control (4a–1), development with RENNS (4a–2), and techniques of coherence (4b).
A. general to specific and least to most important
B. problem to solution, time
C. time (and perhaps least to most important)

EXERCISE 8
For each paragraph, first identify the topic sentence. Then identify the arrangement or arrangements that organize the sentences in each paragraph. Choose from general to specific, specific to general, least to most important, problem to solution, question to answer, location, and time.

A.   The dampness clings to the land and everything on the land. In cities like Durham and Richmond and Winston-Salem, it weaves itself into the rich aroma of processed tobacco rising from the cigarette factories. The invisible shroud thus formed drops over the cities, testing the olfactory sense of the natives and reassuring their sense of economic security. In the fields the dampness engulfs the machinery and fertilizes the germ of rust. It bathes and swells the doors of the barn and the privies and the little tenant houses so that the doors will not shut tight, allowing the dampness into the houses. It creeps in on the wind, through cracks

32

94

in the doors and windows and walls. It rises on air currents through the floor. It seeps in with the rain that spatters onto the tin roof and trickles into the nail holes and seam cracks, permeating the tenant houses; and then it attacks the tenants. —DWAYNE E. WALLS, "The Golden Token"

B.   But isn't there a contradiction here? Participation in sports has been increasing since World War II. From 1946 until 1963 the numbers of participants doubled, and a glance at any tennis court or golf course is

33 enough to suggest that the rate of growth since then has accelerated. Unfortunately, only a fraction of the population does most of the participating. The rest of us are spectators. Certainly more than half of all Americans do not exercise enough to do themselves any good, and fifty million adult Americans never exercise at all.

—JAMES F. FIXX, *The Complete Book of Running*

C.   We walked down the path to the well-house, attracted by the fragrance of the honeysuckle with which it was covered. Someone was drawing water and my teacher placed my hand under the spout. As the cool stream gushed over one hand she spelled into the other the word *water*, first slowly, then rapidly. I stood still, my whole attention fixed

34 upon the motions of her fingers. Suddenly I felt a misty consciousness as of something forgotten—a thrill of returning thought; and somehow the mystery of language was revealed to me. I knew then that "w-a-t-e-r" meant the wonderful cool something that was flowing over my hand. That living word awakened my soul, gave it light, hope, joy, set it free! There were barriers still, it is true, but barriers that could in time be swept away. —HELEN KELLER, *The Story of My Life*

D.   I used the verb *to imagine* a moment ago, and now I have some ground for giving it a meaning. *To imagine* means to make images and to move them about inside one's head in new arrangements. When you and I recall the past, we imagine it in this direct and homely sense. The

35 tool that puts the human mind ahead of the animal is imagery. For us, memory does not demand the preoccupation that it demands in animals, and it lasts immensely longer, because we fix it in images or other substitute symbols. With the same symbolic vocabulary we spell out the future—not one but many futures, which we weigh one against another. —JACOB BRONOWSKI, "The Reach of Imagination"

E.   When children begin to play with other children and when they finally go to school, their names take on a public dimension. The child with a "funny" name is usually in for trouble, but most kids are proud of their names and want to write them on their books and pads and home-

D. least to most important, specific to general—after the topic sentence (and perhaps problem to solution)

E. time (and perhaps general to specific)

BIOGRAPHY
Although James Fixx (1932–1984) is best known as the proponent of running who, ironically, died of a heart-attack while running, there is much more to the man. He began his career as a reporter in Sarasota, Florida, and went on to become an editor at several of America's leading publications, among them *Saturday Review* and *Life*. His books include *Games for the Superintelligent* and *More Games for the Superintelligent*, and *The Complete Book of Running*. Of the apparent randomness of his choices of subject, Fixx is quoted in *Contemporary Authors* as writing:

People sometimes ask me how it happens that I've written books on such diverse subjects as human intelligence and physical fitness—i.e., running. They seem to think these an unlikely combination. But they aren't, not really. What I'm most deeply interested in is human limits and potentials. Most people, even quite ordinary people (if there is such a thing), are capable of far more than they dream of. An ordinary middle-aged man like myself can run a grueling 26.2-mile marathon with the requisite training, just as an ordinary person, if he or she works hard enough at it, may occasionally write a line or even a whole quatrain that [John] Donne would have been proud of.

BIOGRAPHY
Jacob Bronowski (1908–1974) is best known to the general public for his PBS series *The Ascent of Man*, but this was just the final project in a productive life. During World War II, he was a researcher and head of statistical units

ANSWERS: EXERCISE 9
Answers will vary according to how each student conceives of each subject. The key is for students to justify their choices satisfactorily.

NOTE: Biography of Miller and Swift on p. 99.

BIOGRAPHY (CONT.)
dealing with the effects of bombings for the British ministry of Home Security. After the war, he was scientific deputy to the British Chiefs of Staff mission to Japan. As he states in *Contemporary Authors,* seeing the ruins of Nagasaki made him reappraise his career. "Coming into that gloomy valley by the sea . . . [I] knew that we had dehumanized the enemy and ourselves in one blow."

In 1964, Bronowski came to San Diego, California, as research professor, fellow, and director of the council for biology in human affairs at the Salk Institute for Biological Studies. He continued in this capacity until his death.

According to John Lenihan in *Books and Bookmen,* quoted in *Contemporary Authors:*

Jacob Bronowski was a man out of his time. . . . Superbly wise in mathematics, physical science, biology and literature, he would have been more at ease in Renaissance Italy than in the world of the twentieth century. . . . [He] had the scholar's gift of illuminating the contemporary world obliquely and sharply by telling about the past. . . . Bronowski saw science as a part of man's cultural heritage: to him the progress of science was not an orderly sequence of logical innovations but a shifting pattern which could be appreciated only by recognising the interwoven strands of history, art, literature and philosophy.

36 work. There was a time when older children carved their names or initials on trees. Now that there are so many people and so few trees, the spray can has taken over from the jackknife, but the impulse to put one's identifying mark where all the world can see it is as strong as ever. The popularity of commercially produced name-on objects of every kind, from tee-shirts to miniature license plates, also attests to the importance youngsters (and a lot of grown-ups too) place on claiming and proclaiming their names.
—CASEY MILLER AND KATE SWIFT, "Women and Names"

EXERCISE 9
What arrangement (one or more) would be effective for discussing each of the listed subjects? Choose from general to specific, specific to general, least to most important, problem to solution, location, and time. Explain your choice.

1. ways to make friends
2. automobile accidents
3. how to combine work and college
4. role of the U.S. Supreme Court
5. *Romeo and Juliet* by William Shakespeare
6. the computer industry
7. getting from home to college
8. earthquakes
9. junk food
10. music

■‖ **4d**
Know patterns for developing a paragraph.

Writing starts with a purpose. In college, most writing is *to inform* and *to persuade.* Patterns for paragraph development in informative and persuasive writing have evolved as writers have sought methods to express their ideas most effectively. By knowing a variety of patterns for paragraph development, you have more choices when you are seeking ways to help your paragraphs deliver their meanings most effectively.

For the purpose of illustration, the patterns shown here are discussed in isolation. In essay writing, however, paragraph patterns often overlap. For example, narrative writing often contains descriptions; explanations of processes often include comparisons and contrasts; and so on. As you write paragraphs of various patterns, you will likely find that many patterns share characteristics. Your goal is to use paragraph patterns in the service of communicating meaning, not for their own sakes.

Narration

Narrative writing tells about what is happening or what happened. In informative and persuasive writing, narration is usually written in chronological sequence. Narrative paragraphs that illustrate other aspects of informative and persuasive writing include paragraphs 15, 18, 19, 28, 30, and 31.

Here is another example of a narrative paragraph. Its main idea appears in the third-from-last sentence when the author asks a question that reveals the focus of her story.

37   When I visited the birthplace of my mother twelve years ago, I was embarrassed by the shiny rented car that took me there. Even in 1974, there were no paved roads in Clonmel, a delicate dot of a mountain village in Jamaica. And despite the breathtaking altitude, you could not get yourself into a decent position for "a view": The vegetation was that dense, that lush, and that chaotic. On or close to the site of my mother's childhood home, I found a neat wood cabin, still without windowpanes or screens, a dirt floor, and a barefoot family of seven, quietly bustling about. I was stunned. There was neither electricity nor running water. How did my parents even hear about America, more than half a century ago? In the middle of the "Roaring Twenties," these eager black immigrants came, by boat. Did they have to borrow shoes for the journey?

—JUNE JORDAN, "Thank You, America!"

Description

Descriptive writing permits you to share your sensual impressions of a person, a place, or an object. Descriptive writing appeals to a reader's senses—sight, sound, smell, taste, and touch. Descriptive paragraphs that illustrate other aspects of informative and persuasive writing include paragraphs 6, 9, 17, 23, 24, 25, 27, and 30.

Here is another example of a descriptive paragraph.

38   Then the bells stopped, and a man with a mandolin stood nearby, and began a quiet rhythmic tune. The master of ceremonies, wearing around his neck a stuffed rabbit clothed in a pink satin jacket, waved the flagging dancers into line, helped the less agile to catch step, and the dancing went on. A jammed and breathless crowd and pilgrims inside the churchyard peered through the iron fence, while the youths and boys scrambled up, over the heads of the others, and watched from a precarious vantage. They reminded one irresistibly of a menagerie cage lined

BIOGRAPHY
June Jordan (1936–   ), poet, essayist, and story writer, was born in Harlem in New York City. After attending Barnard College and the University of Chicago and working for two years as a research writer for New York's Mobilization for Youth, Inc., Jordan began teaching. She has been on the faculty of the City College of New York, Connecticut College (SEEK Program), Sarah Lawrence College, the State University of New York at Stoney Brook, and Yale. She is a member of the board of directors of Teachers and Writers Collaborative, Inc. Her books include *Some Changes* (poems), *Biography of Fannie Lou Hamer, New Days: Poems of Exile and Return, New Room: New Life, Selected Poems of June Jordan: Things That I Do in the Dark, Okay Now.*

As a teacher, Jordan has strong views on student poetry (quoted in *Contemporary Authors*):

A great variety of black people are writing poetry today—it is not any elitist preoccupation but an activity involving everybody. Black youths are finding they don't have to worry about putting together someone else's idea. Frequently, in their own poetic way, they express themselves in classrooms and a teacher will ask, 'What are you trying to say?' Actually, he has already said it—communicated it very well and poetically—but the teacher, who is not tuned in, did not understand it.

97

with young monkeys. They spraddled and sprawled, caught toe-holds and fell, gathered themselves up and shinnied up the railings again. They were almost as busy as the dancers themselves.

—KATHERINE ANNE PORTER, "The Fiesta of Guadalupe"

BIOGRAPHY

Rachel Carson (1907–1964), the woman who alerted America to the timebomb of pollution, received her A.M. degree from Johns Hopkins University in 1932. She did further graduate work at the Marine Biological Laboratory in Woods Hole, Massachusetts.

The Sea Around Us, Carson's second book, was based on extensive research. It took two years to write, but the book's reception indicated that the time had been well-spent. Typical is this comment from the *Saturday Review of Literature,* quoted in *Contemporary Authors.*

Rare indeed is the individual who can present a comprehensive and well-balanced picture of such a complex entity as the sea in an easy and fluent style and in terms anyone can understand. Rachel Carson is such an individual. Many books have been written on the sea, most of them by scholars with a very detailed knowledge of some aspect of oceanography, but with a limited knowledge of popular presentation. Miss Carson's book is different.

Silent Spring is, no doubt, Carson's most famous work—in large part because of its highly controversial stand against the misuse of chemical fertilizers and pesticides. Public pressure in response to *Silent Spring* led President John F. Kennedy to initiate a federal investigation into agricultural chemical abuse. The report of the President's Science Advisory Committee (May 1963) agreed with Carson and called for better control of pesticides and more research into their effects. Shortly after the Committee's report verifying her conclusions, Rachel Carson died of cancer.

Process

Process is a term used for writing that describes a sequence of actions by which something is done or made. Usually a process description is developed in chronological order. To be effective, process writing must include all steps. The amount of detail depends on whether you want to instruct the reader about how to do something or you want to offer a general overview of the process. For examples, see paragraphs 17, 20, and 29. Here is a process description written to give the reader a general picture.

39
> The new earth, freshly torn from its parent sun, was a ball of whirling gases, intensely hot, rushing through the black spaces of the universe on a path and at a speed controlled by immense forces. Gradually the ball of flaming gases cooled. The gases began to liquefy, and Earth became a molten mass. The materials of this mass eventually became sorted out in a definite pattern: the heaviest in the center, the less heavy surrounding them, and the least heavy forming the outer rim. This is a pattern which persists today—a central sphere of molten iron, very nearly as hot as it was two billion years ago, an intermediate sphere of semiplastic basalt, and a hard outer shell, relatively quite thin and composed of solid basalt and granite.
>
> —RACHEL CARSON, *The Sea Around Us*

Here is a process description that gives the reader specific, step-by-step instructions.

40
> Stand or tread water, until you see the right wave far out, gathering momentum. The position yourself—swim farther out or farther in if necessary—so that you are ready to plunge toward shore in the trough created in front of the cresting wave. Once you are in the trough, swim as hard as you can. Ideally, you will be sucked down into the trough. Suddenly the cresting water above you lifts you, holds you, and shoots you forward. At the moment, arch, point, your body with your arms like tensed wings down at your sides, flat and bulletlike. You become a missile projected by the churning, breaking wave. If it works, you are *in,* if you *catch* the wave, you become part of it, the forward part of the cresting wave, like the prow of a boat made somehow of churning foam, and you can ride all the way home to the sand, and come

home *into* the sand like a wedge, grinding into the shore like the wave itself.   —RUTH RUDNER, *Forgotten Pleasures*

Example

A paragraph developed by example uses illustrations to provide evidence in support of the main idea. Examples are highly effective for developing topical paragraphs. They supply a reader with concrete, specific information. Many of the sample paragraphs in this chapter are developed with examples, among them paragraphs 1, 3, 5, 6, 14, and 26. Here is another paragraph with examples used to develop the topic sentence.

41   In fact, mistranslation accounts for a good share of verbal errors. The slogan "Come Alive with Pepsi" failed understandably in German when it was translated: "Come Alive out of the Grave with Pepsi." Elsewhere it was translated with more precision: "Pepsi Brings Your Ancestors Back from the Grave." In 1965, prior to a reception for Queen Elizabeth II outside Bonn, Germany's President Heinrich Lübke, attempting an English translation of *Gleich geht es los* ("It will soon begin"), told the Queen: "Equal goes it loose." The Queen took the news well, but no better than the President of India, who was greeted at the airport in 1962 by Lübke, who, intending to ask "How are you?" instead said: "Who are you?" To which his guest answered responsibly: "I am the President of India."
            —ROGER ROSENBLATT, "Oops! How's That Again?"

Definition

A paragraph of definition develops a topic by explaining the meaning of a word or a concept. A paragraph of definition is an *extended definition*—it is more extensive than a dictionary denotation (although the paragraph may include a dictionary definition). An effective paragraph of definition does not use abstractions to explain abstractions.

Here is a paragraph that offers an extended definition of the concept of democracy.

42   Surely the Board knows what democracy is. It is the line that forms on the right. It is the don't in Don't Shove. It is the hole in the stuffed shirt through which the sawdust slowly trickles; it is the dent in the high hat. Democracy is the recurrent suspicion that more than half of the people are right more than half of the time. It is the feeling of privacy in the voting booths,

BIOGRAPHY

Casey Miller (1919–   ) began her career in publishing, but left in 1964 to become a free-lance writer and editor. She served in the U.S. Naval Reserve on active duty from 1943–46. She is a member of the Women's Institute for Freedom of the Press.

Kate Swift (1923–   ) worked in journalism and public relations until 1953 when she became a science writer for the American Museum of Natural History. She also has served as director of the news bureau at Yale's School of Medicine (1965–70). She has been a free-lance writer and editor since 1970. Swift served in the U.S. Army, Women's Army Corps from 1945–46. She also is a member of the Women's Institute for Freedom of the Press.

Miller and Swift have contributed to magazines, including *New York, Ms.,* and *New York Times Magazine,* and they have co-authored *Words and Women* (1976). In *Contemporary Authors,* they speak about how they came to write on women and language.

We have an editorial partnership known as Miller/Swift, and it was out of our work as free-lance editors that we became interested in the effect of language on women. After writing two articles on the subject ('Desexing the English Language' and 'One Small Step for Genkind') we found we had barely scratched the surface of this topic, which until recently was ignored. *Words and Women* is an expansion of the evidence presented in the articles and is primarily drawn from contemporary sources with historical material as backup. We document many changes occurring in English today as a result of women's changing perceptions of themselves.

99

BIOGRAPHY

E(lywn) B(rooks) White was born in Mount Vernon, New York in 1899. He died in 1985. He began his career as a reporter in Seattle, Washington, and then worked for two years at an advertising agency as a production assistant and copywriter. He joined the *New Yorker* in 1927 as a writer and soon became contributing editor. To many people, White "was" the *New Yorker*. His books include *The Lady Is Cold* (poetry), *Is Sex Necessary?* (essays, with James Thurber), *Ho Hum, Every Day Is Saturday* (commentary), *Quo Vadis?* (essays), *A Subtreasury of American Humor* (edited with his wife, Katherine Sergeant White), *One Man's Meat, The Wild Flag, Here Is New York, Charlotte's Web* (juvenile), and *The Second Tree from the Corner*. He was also editorial supervisor and contributor to the revised edition of William Strunk, Jr.'s *The Elements of Style*.

The reason for White's popularity is well-expressed by Irwin Erdman (quoted in *Contemporary Authors*): "E. B. White is the finest essayist in the United States. He says wise things gracefully; he is the master of an idiom at once exact and suggestive, distinguished yet familiar. His style is crisp and tender, and incomparably his own."

BIOGRAPHY

Jane Temple Howard (1935–   ) worked at the old *Life* magazine as a writer and editor. She has taught at the University of Iowa's Writer's Workshop, the University of Georgia, and Yale University. Her books include *Please Touch: A Guided Tour of the Human Potential Movement* and *A Different Woman*.

the feeling of communion in the libraries, the feeling of vitality everywhere. Democracy is the score at the beginning of the ninth. It is an idea which hasn't been disproved yet, a song the words of which have not gone bad. It's the mustard on the hot dog and the cream in the rationed coffee. Democracy is a request from a War Board, in the middle of the morning in the middle of a war, wanting to know what democracy is.   —E. B. WHITE, "Democracy"

Analysis and Classification

Analysis (sometimes called *division*) divides things up. Classification groups things together. A paragraph developed by analysis divides one subject into its component parts. Paragraphs written in this pattern usually start by identifying the one subject and continue by explaining that subject's distinct parts. For example, here is a paragraph that analyzes new roles families and friends play in our mobile society.

43   The trouble with the clans and tribes many of us were born into is not that they consist of meddlesome ogres but that they are too far away. In emergencies we rush across continents, and if need be, oceans to their sides, as they do to ours. Maybe we even make a habit of seeing them, once or twice a year, for the sheer pleasure of it. But blood ties seldom dictate our addresses. Our blood kin are often too remote to ease us from our Tuesdays to our Wednesdays. For this we must rely on our families of friends. If our relatives are not, do not wish to be, or for whatever reasons cannot be our friends, then by some complex alchemy we must try to transform our friends into our relatives. If blood and roots don't do the job, then we must look to water and branches, and sort ourselves into new constellations, new families.

—JANE HOWARD, "A Peck of Salt"

A paragraph developed by classification groups information according to some scheme. The separate groups must be *from the same class*—they must have some underlying characteristics in common. For example, different types of sports—football, Rugby, and soccer—can be classified together according to their handling of the ball, their playing fields, the placement of their goals, and the like. Here is a paragraph that discusses three classes of sports signals.

Many different kinds of signals are used by the coaches. There are flash signs, which are just what the name implies: the coach may flash a hand across his face or chest to indicate a bunt or hit-and-run. There are holding signals, which are held in one

INSTRUCTOR'S NOTES

44   position for several seconds. These might be the clenched fist, bent elbow, or both hands on knees. Then there are the block signals. These divide the coach's body into different sections, or blocks. Touching a part of his body, rubbing his shirt, or touching his cap, indicates a sign. Different players can be keyed to various parts of the block, so the coach is actually giving several signals with the same sign.   —ROCKWELL STENSRUD, "Who's on Third?"

Comparison and Contrast

Comparison deals with similarities and contrast deals with differences. Paragraphs using comparison and contrast can be structured in two ways. A *point-by-point structure* allows you to move back and forth between the two items being compared. A *block structure* allows you to discuss one item completely before discussing the other.

POINT-BY-POINT STRUCTURE

Student body: college *A,* college *B*
Curriculum: college *A,* college *B*
Location: college *A,* college *B*

BLOCK STRUCTURE

College A: student body, curriculum, location
College B: student body, curriculum, location

Here is a paragraph structured point-by-point for comparison and contrast.

My husband and I constantly marvel at the fact that our two sons, born of the same parents and only two years apart in age, are such completely opposite human beings. The most obvious differences became apparent at their births. Our first born, Mark, was big and bold—his intense, already wise eyes, broad shoulders, huge and heavy hands, and powerful, chunky legs gave us the impression that he could have walked out of the delivery room on his own. Our second son, Wayne, was delightfully different. Rather than having the football physique that Mark was
45   born with, Wayne came into the world with a long, slim, wiry body more suited to running, jumping, and contorting. Wayne's eyes, rather than being intense like Mark's, were impish and innocent. When Mark was delivered, he cried only momentarily, then seemed to settle into a state of intense concentration, as if trying to absorb everything he could about the strange, new en-

101

vironment he found himself in. Conversely, Wayne screamed from the moment he first appeared until the nurse took him to the nursery. There was nothing helpless or pathetic about his cry either—he was damned angry!   —ROSEANNE LABONTE, student

Here is a block-form comparison of the impact of building construction a thousand years ago and now. Notice how the word *today* signals the transition between the two parts of the paragraph.

46

A thousand years ago in Europe, acres of houses and shops were demolished and their inhabitants forced elsewhere so that great cathedrals could be built. For decades, the building process soaked up all available skilled labor; for decades the townspeople stepped around pits in the streets, clambered over ropes and piles of timber, breathed mortar dust, and slept and worked to the crashing noise of construction. The cathedrals, when finished, stood half-empty six days a week, but most of them at least had beauty. Today, the ugly skyscrapers go up, shops and graceful homes are obliterated, their inhabitants forced away, and year after year New Yorkers step around the pits, stumble through wooden catwalks, breathe the fine mist of dust, absorb the hammering noise night and day, and telephone in vain for carpenter or plumber. And the skyscrapers stand empty two days and seven nights a week. This is progress.

—ERIC SEVAREID, *This Is Eric Sevareid*

Analogy

Analogy is a type of comparison. It compares objects or ideas from different classes—things not normally associated. For example, a fatal disease has certain points in common with war. Analogy is particularly effective when you want to explain the unfamiliar in terms of the familiar. Often a paragraph developed with analogy starts with a simile or metaphor (see 21b) to introduce the comparison. Here is a paragraph developed by analogy that starts with a simile and then explains the effect of casual speech by comparing it to casual dress.

Casual dress, like casual speech, tends to be loose, relaxed and colorful. It often contains what might be called "slang words": blue jeans, sneakers, baseball caps, aprons, flowered cotton housedresses, and the like. These garments could not be worn on a formal occasion without causing disapproval, but in ordinary circumstances they pass without remark. "Vulgar words" in dress, on the other hand, give emphasis and get immediate attention in

102

47 almost any circumstances, just as they do in speech. Only the skillful can employ them without some loss of face, and even then they must be used in the right way. A torn, unbuttoned shirt, or wildly uncombed hair can signify strong emotions: passion, grief, rage, despair. They are most effective if people already think of you as being neatly dressed, just as the curses of well-spoken persons count for more than those of the customarily foul-mouthed.

—ALISON LURIE, *The Language of Clothes*

Cause-and-effect analysis

Cause-and-effect analysis involves examining outcomes and reasons for those outcomes. Causes lead to an event or an effect; and effects result from causes. Section 5d describes making reasonable connections between causes and effects. Here is a paragraph developed through a discussion of how television (the cause) becomes indispensable (the effect) to parents of young children.

48 Because television is so wonderfully available as child amuser and child defuser, capable of rendering a volatile three-year-old harmless at the flick of a switch, parents grow to depend upon it in the course of their daily lives. And as they continue to utilize television day after day, its importance in their children's lives increases. From a simple source of entertainment provided by parents when they need a break from child care, television gradually changes into a powerful and disruptive presence in family life. But despite their increasing resentment of television's intrusions into their family life, and despite their considerable guilt at not being able to control their children's viewing, parents do not take steps to extricate themselves from television's domination. They can no longer cope without it.

—MARIE WINN, *The Plug-In Drug*

EXERCISE 10

Identify the pattern or patterns each paragraph illustrates. Choose from narration, description, process, example, definition, analysis, classification, comparison and contrast, analogy, and cause and effect.

A. The way in which culture affects language becomes clear by comparing how the English and Hopi languages refer to H_2O in its liquid state. English, like most other European languages, has only one word—"water"—and it pays no attention to what the substance is used for or its quantity. The Hopi of Arizona, on the other hand, use *pahe* to mean the **49** large amounts of water present in natural lakes or rivers, and *keyi* for the small amounts in domestic jugs and canteens. English, though, makes other distinctions that Hopi does not. The speaker of English is careful to

BIOGRAPHY
Alison Lurie (1926–) has been a member of the English Department at Cornell University since 1968. She has been the recipient of a Rockefeller Foundation grant, a New York State Cultural Council Foundation grant, and the American Academy of Arts and Letters award in literature. Her works include *Love and Friendship, The Nowhere City, Imaginary Friends, Real People, The War Between the Tates,* and *Only Children.*

About her best-known work, *The War Between the Tates,* Julian Jebb writes (quoted in *Contemporary Authors*): "No other writer tells the truth with the sophisticated directness of Alison Lurie; an obsessive hatred of deceit and a minutely exact response to the surface and inner substance of ordinary life go to produce her art."

BIOGRAPHY
Marie Winn (1937–) was born in Czechoslovakia. After she moved to America she received her B.A. from Radcliffe College. In addition to having written many books for children, she has published two well-received and critical studies: *Children Without Childhood* (1983) and *The Plug-In Drug: Television, Children, and the Family* (1977, updated edition 1985).

ANSWERS: EXERCISE 10
Some paragraphs can be interpreted to illustrate more than one pattern. This is a basic list only. *Note:* You might also ask students to analyze these paragraphs in light of what was previously discussed in this chapter: topic sentence, words in topic sentence that create focus and control (4a–1), development with RENNS (4a–2), and techniques of coherence (4b), and arrangement (4c).
A. comparison and contrast—point by point, example

ANSWERS: EX. 10 (CONT.)

B. narration, description, process
C. definition, example, analogy
D. analysis, definition, example
E. narration
F. analogy
G. comparison and contrast—point by point, example

distinguish between a lake and a stream, between a waterfall and a geyser; but *pahe* makes no distinction among lakes, ponds, rivers, streams, waterfalls, and springs.

—PETER FARB, "Man at the Mercy of His Language"

B.   Two days later we had our first storm. It started by the trade wind dying away completely, and the feathery, white trade wind clouds, which were drifting over our heads up in the topmost blue, being suddenly invaded by a thick black cloud bank which rolled up over the horizon from southward. Then there came gusts of wind from the most unexpected directions, so that it was impossible for the steering watch to keep control. As quickly as we got our stern turned to the new direction of the wind, so that the sail bellied out stiff and safe, just as quickly the gusts came at us from another quarter, squeezed the proud bulge out of the sail, and made it swing round and thrash about to the peril of both crew and cargo. But then the wind suddenly set in to blow straight from the quarter whence the bad weather came, and, as the black clouds rolled over us, the breeze increased to a fresh wind which worked itself up into a real storm.   —THOR HEYERDAHL, *Kon-Tiki*

C.   It is Rimsky-Korsakov's bumblebee in its helter-skelter flight, buzzing its way through a summer breeze. It is Greig's "Morning," with the sun peeking over the horizon, its golden rays projecting like spears which prod a world to life, accompanied by sweet birdsong. It is the tumultuous thunder and growling wind of a Beethoven tempest breaking the great solitude of a pastoral scene and it is the gallant fierceness and the ethereal mystique of Wagner's Valkyries, riding their powerful steeds to Valhalla. It is Rodrigo's Madrid, at times bustling, at times serene, and it is Gershwin's Paris, always brilliant and boisterous. It is music.

—KEVIN KERWOOD, student

D.   *Hard*, in terms of wood, really means *harder* to cut, but most hardwoods are also fine and even-grained. They are not apt to split, and they take polish well. For these reasons, they are generally better for small wood carving than the softwoods; most sculptors prefer to use hardwoods for large pieces, too. All the fruitwoods, like cherry, apple, pear, and orange, are hard, and so are oak, mahogany, walnut, birch, holly, and maple. Hardwoods range in color from the almost white of holly to the almost black of walnut. Oak and mahogany are the most open-grained, and therefore more apt to split. They are probably less good for small carvings than the other kinds.

—FLORENCE H. PETTIT, *How to Make Whirligigs and Whimmy Doodles*

E.   They were flat round wafers, slightly browned on the edges and butter-yellow in the center. With the cold lemonade they were sufficient

104

53 for childhood's lifelong diet. Remembering my manners, I took nice little lady-like bites off the edges. She said she had made them expressly for me and that she had a few in the kitchen that I could take home to my brother. So I jammed one whole cake in my mouth and the rough crumbs scratched the insides of my jaws, and if I hadn't had to swallow, it would have been a dream come true.

—MAYA ANGELOU, *I Know Why the Caged Bird Sings*

54 F.   Consider cancer cells and non-cancer cells in the human body. The normal cells are aimed at reproducing and functioning in a way that is beneficial to the body. Cancer cells, on the other hand, spread in a way that threatens and ultimately destroys the whole body. Normal cells work harmoniously, because they "know," in a sense, that their preservation depends upon the health of the body they inhabit. While they are organisms in themselves, they also act as part of the whole body. We might say, metaphorically, that cancer cells do not know enough about self-preservation; they are, biologically, more ignorant than normal cells. The aim of cancer cells is to spread throughout the body, to conquer all the normal cells—and when they reach their aim, the body is dead. *And so are the cancer cells.*   —SYDNEY J. HARRIS, "War Is Cancer of Mankind"

55 G.   Although Littleman, my eleven-year-old poodle, has never been separated from his thirteen-year-old mother, Simone, they are remarkably different. Simone weights in at about ten pounds with very delicate, sophisticated features and coarse, curly hair. Slightly shorter, Littleman tops the scale at no more than seven pounds and is quite handsome with his teddy-bear features and soft wavy hair. Simone was the first dog in the family and is a pedigreed poodle. In many ways she is the picture of a thoroughbred, with her snobby attitude and nonchalant manners. On the other hand, Littleman came into the family a year later with four other puppies of pure breeding, but they were never registered. Unlike his mother, Littleman is very friendly, almost to the point of being pesty at times.   —LINDA NEAL, student

EXERCISE 11
Write three of the following paragraphs.

1. A narrative about your first job (or first day in college).
2. A personal definition of success.
3. A classification of teachers.
4. An analogy about building a friendship.
5. A cause-and-effect analysis about the popularity of music videos.

BIOGRAPHY
Maya Angelou (1928–   ) was born in St. Louis, Missouri and was raised by her grandmother in Stamps, Arkansas. Before receiving wide recognition as a major novelist, she was highly respected as an actress, singer, poet, and playwright. She served as coordinator of the Southern Christian Leadership Conference under Martin Luther King, Jr. Her autobiographical novels have been received well by critics and the public. The books include *I Know Why the Caged Bird Sings* (1970), *Gather Together in My Name* (1974), *Singin' and Swingin' and Gettin' Merry Like Christmas (1976)*, and *The Heart of A Woman* (1981).

ANSWERS: EXERCISE 11
Answers will vary.

EXTRA EXERCISE
Write three of the following paragraphs:
1. A process about making new friends at college.
2. A division of obnoxious people.
3. A comparison and contrast of yourself and a relative.
4. A description of the first meal you ever cooked.
5. A personal definition of privacy.

INSTRUCTOR'S NOTES

▪‖ 4e

Know how to write special paragraphs.

Special paragraphs—**introductory paragraphs, concluding paragraphs,** and **transitional paragraphs**—have special roles in an essay. Introductions prepare a reader for the topical paragraphs that follow; conclusions bring the topical paragraphs to a close for a reader; and transitional paragraphs—usually reserved for longer pieces of writing—help the reader move through complex material. Generally, special paragraphs are proportionately shorter than the topical paragraphs with which they appear.

Effective beginnings and endings are indispensable for successful essays. Good writers know that introductions and conclusions are far from merely "ceremonial," so they expect to plan, draft, and revise them as completely as topical paragraphs.

Introductory paragraphs

In informative and persuasive writing, an introductory paragraph sets the stage and prepares a reader for what lies ahead. Introductions provide a bridge from the reader's mind to yours. For this reason, its introduction must clearly relate to the rest of your essay. If it points in one direction and your essay goes off in another, your reader will be confused—and will likely stop reading.

As you write successive drafts of an essay, you might change your mind about what to say in the introductory paragraph. An early draft might contain an idea that does not belong once your topical paragraphs are written. Indeed, when a subject is new to you, you might decide to write your introduction after having written a "discovery" or first draft of your topical paragraphs. Equally important, once your topical paragraphs are written, you might want to change the *tone* of your introduction. For example, a light-hearted tone would be out of place in an introduction to a serious essay.

In college writing, many instructors require that an introductory paragraph include a statement of the essay's thesis°—the central idea of an essay. Understandably, many instructors want students to demonstrate from the start that all parts of any essay are related. Professional writers do not necessarily include a thesis statement in their introductory paragraphs; with experience comes skill at maintaining a line of thought without overtly stating a central idea. Student writers, however, often need to practice explicitly and demonstrate openly external clues to essay organization.

When instructors require a thesis statement, they often want it to be in the last sentence or two of the introductory paragraph.

106

Here is an example of a student's introductory paragraph with a thesis statement (shown in italics).

56   The age of enlightenment introduced the concept of a free society. What most of us perceive as a free society was first outlined in the seventeenth century by John Locke in "Treatise on Civil Government." *The principles delineated by Locke included freedom of speech, religion, and the press.*

—SYLVIA BERGER, student

Berger's essay then discusses Locke's three principles. Other examples of students' introductory paragraphs that include thesis statements appear on pages 64 and 67.

An introductory paragraph often includes an **introductory device** to lead into the thesis. Introductory devices serve to stimulate a reader's interest in the subject of the essay. Some of the most common introductory devices are listed in the chart. Usually the introductory device precedes the thesis statement. For example, Berger's introduction shown above gives useful background information before stating a thesis.

SELECTED DEVICES FOR INTRODUCTORY PARAGRAPHS

1. Provide relevant background information.
2. Tell an interesting brief story or anecdote.
3. Give a pertinent statistic or statistics.
4. Ask a provocative question or questions.
5. Use an appropriate quotation.
6. Make a useful analogy.
7. Define a term used throughout the essay.

Here is an introduction that uses an anecdote before its two-sentence thesis statement (shown in italics).

57   Bridget and Dorothy are 39-year-old British housewives, identical twins raised apart who first met each other a little over a year ago. When they met, to take part in Thomas Bouchard's twin study at the University of Minnesota, the manicured hands of each bore seven rings. Each also wore two bracelets on one wrist and a watch and a bracelet on the other. *Investigators in Bouchard's study, the most extensive investigation ever made of identical twins reared apart, are still bewitched by the seven rings. Was it coincidence, the result of similar influences, or is this small*

ALTERNATE EXAMPLE
Tom Wolfe has christened today's young adults the "me" generation, and the 1970s—obsessed with things like consciousness expansion and self-awareness —have been described as the decade of the new narcissism. The cult of "I," in fact, has taken hold with the strength and impetus of a new religion. But the joker in the pack is that it is all based on a false idea.

—MARGARET HALSEY, "What's Wrong with 'Me, Me, Me'?"

107

sign of affinity a true, even inevitable, manifestation of the mysterious and infinitely complex interaction of the genes the two women have in common?

—CONSTANCE HOLDEN, "Identical Twins Reared Apart"

The key to the effectiveness of an introductory device is how well it relates to the essay's thesis and to the material in the topical paragraphs. An introductory device must be well integrated into the paragraph, not mechanically slotted in for its own sake. Note how smoothly the message of the quotation in the George Will introduction becomes a dramatic contrast that leads into thesis (shown in italics).

58   In 1895 Sir William Harcourt said to him: "My dear Winston, the experiences of a long life have convinced me that nothing ever happens." *But some things did happen in the stimulating next five decades, in which Winston Churchill was the largest figure.*

—GEORGE F. WILL, "Winston Churchill: In the Region of Mass Effects"

In the following paragraph, the author uses unusual questions to arouse interest and to set the stage for his thesis statement (shown in italics).

59   Today, what respectable person would call a candidate for the highest office in the land a carbuncle-faced old drunkard? A pot-bellied, mutton-headed cucumber? A pickpocket, thief, traitor, lecher, drunkard, syphilitic, a gorilla, crook, anarchist, murderer? *Such charges were commonplace in Presidential contests in the nineteenth century.*

—PAUL F. BOLLER, JR., "Election Fizzle-Gigery"

As Sharon R. Curtin shows, statistics can also serve well in an introduction. The statistical data in the first two sentences help to create a sense of a huge population whose vulnerability comes into focus in the sentence shown in italics.

60   Old men, old women, almost 20 million of them. They constitute 10 percent of the total population, and the percentage is steadily growing. Some of them, like conspirators, walk all bent over, as if hiding some precious secret, filled with self-protection. The body seems to gather itself around those vital parts, folding shoulders, arms, pelvis like a fading rose. *Watch and you see how fragile old people come to think they are.*

—SHARON R. CURTIN, *Nobody Ever Died of Old Age*

108

An effective introduction has no room for self-conscious statements or overused expressions. Guidelines on what to avoid in introductory paragraphs are listed in the chart.

WHAT TO AVOID IN INTRODUCTORY PARAGRAPHS

1. Don't be too obvious. Avoid bald statements such as "In this paper I will discuss the causes of falling oil prices" or "My assignment asks me to discuss Hamlet's inability to take action."
2. Don't apologize. Avoid self-critical statements such as "I do not have much background in this subject," "Of course, other people are more expert in this subject than I am," or "I am not sure if I am right, but here is my opinion."
3. Don't use overworn expressions. Avoid statements such as "Haste makes waste," "A penny saved is a penny earned," "Love is what makes the world go around," and "War is hell."

Concluding paragraphs

In informative and persuasive writing, a conclusion serves to bring your discussion to a logical end. Too abrupt an ending leaves your reader suddenly cut off. Also, a conclusion that is merely tacked onto an essay does not give the reader a sense of completion. On the other hand, an ending that flows gracefully and sensibly from what has come before it reinforces your ideas and enhances your essay.

A concluding paragraph often takes one of several forms. The most common ways of concluding an essay are given in the chart.

SELECTED DEVICES FOR CONCLUDING PARAGRAPHS

1. Use the devices for introductory paragraphs (page 107—but avoid using the same device in the introduction and conclusion of an essay.
2. Summarize the main points of the essay.
3. Call for awareness and/or action.
4. Point to the future.

109

INSTRUCTOR'S NOTES

ANSWERS: EXERCISE 13 (p. 112)

1. Topic sentences

A. first sentence = topic sentence; second = limiting sentence.

B. first sentence

C. last sentence

D. first sentence

E. implied (Cookies were a special treat when I was a child.)

F. first sentence

G. first sentence

2. RENNS

A. *Examples:* all English and Hopi words discussed. *Names:* H₂O, English, Hopi, and—in terms of words being considered names—the words discussed.

B. *Examples:* each event in the storm. *Names:* tradewind clouds, thick black cloudbank, steering watch, stern, crew, cargo.

C. *Examples:* all sentences but the last. *Names:* Rimsky-Korsakov's bumblebee, Grieg's "Morning," Beethoven, Wagner's Valkyries, Valhalla, Rodrigo's Madrid, Gershwin's Paris. *Senses:* buzzing, breeze, golden rays projecting like spears, birdsong, tumultuous thunder, growling wind, tempest breaking solitude of pastoral scene, riding powerful steeds, boisterous.

D. *Reasons:* not even grained, not apt to split, take polish well. *Examples:* fruitwoods, cherry, apple, pear, orange, oak, mahogany, walnut, birch, holly, maple. *Senses:* white of holly, almost black of walnut.

E. *Senses:* slightly browned on the edges, butter-yellow in the center, cold lemonade, lady-like bites, rough crumbs scratched the insides of my jaws.

F. *Examples:* normal cells, cancer cells—and the aim of normal cells to reproduce and of cancer cells to destroy.

WHAT TO AVOID IN CONCLUDING PARAGRAPHS

1. Don't go off the track. Avoid introducing an entirely new idea or adding a fact that belongs in the body of the essay. Your conclusion should flow from the rest of your essay.
2. Don't reword your introduction. Avoid simply listing the main idea in each topic sentence or restating the thesis. While a summary can refer to those points, it msut tie them into what was covered in the essay. A good test is to check if the introduction and conclusion are interchangeable. If they are, you need to revise.
3. Don't announce what you have done. Avoid statements such as "In this paper I have tried to show the main causes for the drop in oil prices."
4. Don't make absolute claims. Avoid statements such as "This proves that . . ." and "If we take this action, the problem will be solved." Always qualify your message with expressions such as "This seems to prove . . ." and "If we take this action, we will begin working toward a solution of the problem."
5. Avoid logical fallacies. Conclusions are particularly vulnerable to errors in reasoning. Logical fallacies are explained and illustrated in 5f.
6. Don't apologize. Avoid casting doubt on your material by making statements such as "I may not have thought of all the arguments, but . . ." and "Even though I am not an expert, I feel that what I have said is correct."

Here is a concluding paragraph that summarizes a persuasive essay about the problem of teenagers getting married for the wrong reasons.

> **61** Teenagers may contemplate marriage for a variety of reasons—most of them misguided. Before they pledge their lifelong devotion to their "one and only," however, teenagers should secure the counsel of an impartial party, and they should seriously consider their options.
>
> —ADRIAN GONZALEZ, student

The essay for which the following conclusion was written is a condemnation of racism as demonstrated by the existence of urban ghettos. This concluding paragraph reinforces the message of the essay by calling for awareness and, by extension, action.

110

62   It is a terrible, an inexorable, law that one cannot deny the humanity of another without diminishing one's own: in the face of one's victim, one sees oneself. Walk through Harlem and see what we, this nation, have become.
—JAMES BALDWIN, "Fifth Avenue, Uptown: A Letter from Harlem"

The following conclusion ends an essay that discusses the failure of public schools to educate students well. The author points to the future and calls for action.

63   Our schools provide a key to the future of society. We must take control of them, watch over them, and nurture them if they are to be set right again. To do less is to invite disaster upon ourselves, our children, and our nation.
—JOHN C. SAWHILL, "The Collapse of Public Schools"

An effective conclusion does not detract from the central message of an essay. Refer to the chart for a list of what to avoid when writing concluding paragraphs.

Transitional paragraphs

A transitional paragraph provides one or two sentences to help a reader move from one major point to another. Transitional paragraphs often restate a main idea briefly. Transitional paragraphs are uncommon in short essays.

Swedish director Ingmar Bergman uses a transitional paragraph in a fairly long essay about the art of filmmaking. He leads the reader from a complex discussion of how to create patterns from pictures to an equally complex discussion of how rhythm is created by the relation of one picture to another.

64   This is an almost impossible task.
—INGMAR BERGMAN, "Introduction" to Four Screenplays

Other typical one-sentence transitional paragraphs convey ideas such as "Much more is at stake, however, than people's comfort" or "Let us examine individually each malfunction in the system."

Here is a two-sentence transitional paragraph written as a bridge between a discussion of people's gestures and people's eating habits. This paragraph is followed by a number of paragraphs each of which discusses a different type of eater.

Like gestures, eating habits are personality indicators, and even food preferences and attitudes toward food reveal the inner

BIOGRAPHY
James Baldwin (1924–   ) was born in Harlem in New York City. After serving as a lay preacher in America, he moved to France for ten years. He returned to America in 1957 and became active in the civil rights movement. His widely acclaimed novels include *Go Tell It On the Mountain* (1953), *Giovanni's Room* (1956), and *If Beale Street Could Talk* (1974). His essay collection *Notes of a Native Son* (1955) and his nonfiction work including *The Fire Next Time* (1963) are frequently quoted.

ANSWERS: EX. 13 (CONT.)
G. *Examples:* Littleman and Simone, their features, hair, and personalities. *Numbers:* eleven-year-old, thirteen-year-old, ten pounds, seven pounds, four other puppies.

3. Techniques of coherence. In this order, if they appear: transitional expressions *(te)*, pronouns *(p)*, deliberate repetition *(dr)*, and parallel structures *(ps)*.
A. *te:* on the other hand, though; *dr:* English, Hopi, water
B. *te:* then; *p:* it; *dr:* wind, gusts, as, we, our, us; *ps:* all verbs in past tense, dying away / drifting / being, as quickly / just as quickly, stiff / safe
C. *dr* it is; *ps:* buzzing / peeking / growling / breaking / riding / bustling
D. *te:* too, therefore; *p:* they, other kinds; *dr:* hardwoods, apt; *ps:* all verbs in simple present, they are
E. *p:* they, I, my, she, them, me
F. *te:* on the other hand; *p:* they, their, we; *dr:* cancer, cells, body, normal; *ps:* all verbs in simple present, to spread / to conquer

111

65 self. Food plays an important role in the lives of most people beyond its obvious one as a necessity.

——Jean Rosenbaum, m.d., *Is Your Volkswagon a Sex Symbol?*

ANSWERS: EXERCISE 12
Answers will vary.

EXERCISE 12

Write an introduction and conclusion for each essay informally outlined below.

A. Violence on Television
Thesis: Violence on television is harmful to children.
Topical paragraph 1: cartoons
Topical paragraph 2: series
Topical paragraph 3: made-for-television movies

B. Starting a new job
Thesis: Starting a new job demands much concentration.
Topical paragraph 1: learning or adapting skills
Topical paragraph 2: fitting in with co-workers
Topical paragraph 3: adjusting to the surroundings

ANSWERS: EX. 13 (CONT.)
See pp. 110-111.

G. *te:* on the other hand; *p:* my, his, she, her; *dr:* Littleman, mother, Simone; *ps:* Simone weighs / Littleman tops, Simone was / Littleman came

4. Paragraph arrangement
A. general to specific
B. time
C. specific to general
D. general to specific
E. time
F. general to specific and least to most important
G. general to specific

EXERCISE 13

Reread the paragraphs in Exercise 10 and do the following.

1. Referring to Section 4a-1, identify all topic sentences, limiting sentences, and implied topic sentences.
2. Referring to Section 4a-2, identify all RENNS.
3. Referring to Section 4b, identify all techniques of coherence.
4. Referring to Section 4c, identify paragraph arrangements.

INSTRUCTOR'S NOTES

5
THINKING CRITICALLY

Thinking is not something you choose to do, any more than a fish "chooses" to live in water. To be human *is* to think. But while thinking may come naturally, awareness of *how* you think does not. Thinking about thinking is the key to thinking critically. When you think critically, you take control of your conscious thought processes. Without such control, you risk being controlled by the ideas of others. Indeed, critical thinking is at the heart of a liberal (from the Latin word for *free*) education.

The word **critical** here has a neutral meaning. It does not mean taking a negative view or finding fault, as when someone criticizes another person for doing something wrong. The essence of critical thinking is thinking beyond the obvious—beyond the flash of visual images on a television screen, the alluring promises of glossy advertisements, the evasive statements by some people in the news, the half-truths of some propaganda, the manipulations of slanted language and faulty reasoning.

Critical thinking is an attitude as much as an activity. If you face life with curiosity and a desire to dig beneath the surface, you are a critical thinker. If you do not believe everything you read or hear, you are a critical thinker. If you find pleasure in contemplating the puzzle of conflicting ideologies, theories, personalities, and facts, you are a critical thinker.

113

Activities of the mind and higher-order reasoning—the core of a college education—are processes of contemplation and deliberation. These processes take time. They contrast with the glorification of speed in today's culture: fast foods, instant mixes, self-developing film, short-spurt images in movies and videos. If you are among the people who assume that speed is a measure of intelligence, consider this true anecdote about Albert Einstein. The first time that Banesh Hoffman, a scientist, was expected to talk about his work to Albert Einstein, Hoffman was speechless and overawed. Einstein instantly put Hoffman at ease when he said: "Please go slowly. I don't understand things quickly."

The components of critical thinking differ slightly from discipline to discipline, but all critical thinking is rooted in the principles of **analysis** (taking ideas apart), **synthesis** (making connections among ideas), and **evaluation** (determining the quality of the ideas). These principles apply to reading and writing for your English classes and for all other disciplines.

This chapter first discusses reading as a process that leads to critical thinking, and then looks at the reasoning processes so readers may recognize them and writers may use them critically.

QUOTATION ABOUT READING
Reading is to the mind what exercise is to the body
—JOSEPH ADDISON and RICHARD STEELE

■‖ 5a

Understand the reading process.

Reading, like writing, helps you to come to "know," to compose meaning. In college you get many reading assignments that assume you have the ability to analyze, synthesize, and evaluate. If you understand the reading process, you can use it to fullest advantage to think critically.

Reading is not a passive activity. It involves more than looking at words. Reading is an active process—a dynamic, meaning-making encounter among page, eye, and brain. When you read, your brain actively makes connections between what you know already and what is new to you. You comprehend and learn new material by associating it with material you already know.

Experts who have researched the reading process report that the key activity in reading is *making predictions*. As you read, your brain is always involved in guessing what is coming next. Once it discovers what comes next, it either confirms or revises its prediction and moves on. For example, if you encountered a chapter title "The Heartbeat," your predictions could be diverse, ranging from romance to how the heart pumps blood. As you read on, you would confirm or revise your prediction according to what you found—you would be in the realm of romance if you encountered a paragraph

114

about two lovers and roses, and you would be in the realm of biology if you encountered material that included diagrams of the physiology of the heart. Predicting during reading happens at split-second speed without the reader's being aware of it. Without predictions, the brain would have to consider infinite possibilities for assimilating every new piece of information; with predictions, the brain can narrow its expectations to reasonable proportions. Predicting keeps the reader sane.

1
Know your purpose in reading.

Purposes for reading vary. Most reading in college is for the purpose of learning new information, appreciating literary works, or reviewing notes on classes or readings. These types of reading involve much *rereading;* one encounter with the material rarely suffices. Vladimir Nabokov, a respected novelist and lecturer on literature, observed: "Curiously enough, one cannot *read* a book: one can only reread it. A good reader, a major reader, an active and creative reader is a rereader."

Your purpose in reading determines the speed at which you can expect to read. When you are hunting for a particular fact in an almanac, you can skim the material until you come to what you want. When you read about a subject you know well, your brain is familiar with the material, so you can move somewhat rapidly through most of it, slowing down when you come to new material. When you are unfamiliar with the subject, your brain needs time to absorb the new material, so you have to slow down.

2
Use a system for reading to learn.

Three universals about reading to learn hold for all material. These universals have parallels in the writing process, with slightly different labels, as explained in the chart on the next page. These universals help you use what you know about the reading process to study and think critically. Various structured systems for applying these universals have been suggested by experts in reading. Here is one widely endorsed system, popularly known by its acronym: SQ3R.*

*Originated by Francis P. Robinson in 1946, the system has been adapted by many others since. The version here is adapted for college students.

QUOTATION ABOUT READING
Rereading books is an antisocial habit. If I keep it up, I'm not going to be invited out anymore. It's a pity, because rereading books has become a sort of addiction. If a book is really good, it deserves to be read again, and if it's great, it should be read at least three times.

It's not a question of paying homage to the book, but of doing it justice. In a first reading, you're distracted by pleasure, excitement, curiosity. The book may so seize you that you rush through it in a kind of delirium. In my own case, the more I like a book, the more slowly I read, and this has its distractions too. When you read slowly, as the speed-reading courses point out, you have time to free-associate to the material, and this blurs your recollection of it, confusing stimulus and response. Yet I wouldn't want to give up these associations, this spontaneous talking back to a book, because it's one of the things that makes reading so valuable. In mingling your ideas and feelings with the author's, you raise and complicate the level of your own imagining.

—ANATOLE BROYARD, "About Books: Reading and Other Excesses"

115

COORDINATED RESOURCES

Alternate exercises for this chapter are available in the *S & S Workbook for Writers,* Gordon and Troyka.

Transparency masters are available for many of the screened charts and/or lists in this chapter.

Students can practice and test their knowledge of terms, key concepts, and applications of material in this chapter by using the *Study Guide to the S & S Handbook for Writers,* West.

UNIVERSALS IN READING TO LEARN	
SKIM	Like *planning°* in the writing process, skimming means getting ready to read.
READ	Like *drafting°* in the writing process, reading means moving through the material, according to your purpose for reading.
REIN-FORCE	Like *revising°* and *editing°* in the writing process, reinforcing means rereading, clarifying, fine tuning, and getting into final form.

S = *Survey:* Surveying is part of *skimming.* You survey to get an overview of the material before you start reading closely. As you survey, your brain begins unconsciously to make predictions about the material.

If you are surveying a textbook, first quickly survey the entire text, and then as you need each chapter, survey it more slowly. If the material has headings, subheadings, words in italics or boldface, or visuals, use them as a road map during your surveying. If you are reading a book that has no headings, (1) read the title; (2) establish a general sense of the length of the material you need to read; (3) read the opening and closing paragraphs—unless you do not want to know the ending—and, if the material is long, glance over some intervening paragraphs.

Q = *Question:* Questioning is part of *skimming.* Asking questions stimulates your brain to prepare for learning. Experiments have shown that college students who actively use structured questioning before reading improve dramatically in comprehension and in recall over both short and long periods of time. Question in small chunks, in contrast to covering large amounts of material during surveying. If you are reading a textbook, it is best to question when you encounter each new subsection. Working in small chunks allows your brain to narrow its focus and to make more accurate predictions about what is coming next.

Ask questions deliberately and consciously. Here are some examples, based on the first three pages of this chapter.

TITLE	Thinking Critically
QUESTION	What is thinking critically?
KEY WORD	critically

116

QUESTION	What does "critically" mean here?
HEADING	Understand the reading process.
QUESTIONS	What is the reading process? What should I understand about it?

Answers during questioning do not necessarily have to be precise. The goal is to get your thinking started so that your brain will be alerted to focus on key matters as you read.

R = *Read.* Reading is the core activity. The speed at which you read depends on your purpose. Your comprehension—making meaning out of the written word—will be enhanced if you have surveyed and questioned before you start reading. The full meaning of written material emerges on three levels—the literal, inferential, and evaluative (these levels are described in 5b).

Comprehension can break down for a number of reasons: (1) If you are reading about a totally unfamiliar subject, your brain might not be able to associate so much new material to what you already know. In such a situation, take the time to build up your store of information by reading easier material in other sources on the subject; of course, for academic work you must return as quickly as possible to the more difficult material you are required to read. (2) Comprehension can elude you if your mind wanders, thus taking up some of your brain's activity with extraneous material. If this happens, you must be fiercely determined to concentrate and resist the appeal of other thoughts. Do whatever it takes: arrange for silence or music, for being alone or in a crowded library's reading room, for studying at your best time of day—some people concentrate better in the morning, others in the evening. (3) You cannot comprehend new material if you have not allotted sufficient time to work with it. College students are pulled in many different directions and have to discipline themselves to balance their class, study, social, and job—if any—schedules with the unavoidable and time-consuming demands of a reading and studying schedule. Nothing prevents learning so much as lack of time.

R = *Recite.* Reciting is part of *reinforcing.* Reciting calls for you to look away from the page and repeat the main points, aloud or to yourself. For best success, recite in chunks—subsections of textbook chapters, for example. Do not try to cover too much material at once. Knowing ahead of time that when you finish a section you will have to recite stimulates your concentration during reading. If you cannot recite the main points of the material, reread it and try again. If you still have trouble, go back to surveying and questioning and then reread.

117

QUOTATION ABOUT READING
The one thing I regret is that I will never have time to read all the books I want to read.

—FRANÇOISE SAGAN

R = *Review.* Reviewing is part of *reinforcing.* When you finish reading, survey again. This process refreshes your memory about the initial overview you got during surveying. It also gives you a larger framework into which to fit new material you have just learned. Be honest with yourself about what you cannot recall and need to reread. The next day, and again about a week later, repeat your review—always adding whatever new material you have learned since the previous review. As much as your time permits, review again at set intervals during a course. The more reinforcement, the better.

Collaborative learning can help you reinforce what you learn from reading. Ask a friend or classmate who knows the material well to discuss it with you, even test you. Conversely, offer to teach the material to someone, and you will know quickly whether or not you have mastered it sufficiently to communicate it.

Writing can help you reinforce your learning. There is little that promotes authority over knowledge as does writing about it. Keep a learning log: draw a line down the center of your notebook page; on one side take notes on the reading material, and on the other side list key words, ask questions, make connections among ideas, and have a "conversation on paper" with the material. Also, you can master difficult sections by writing paraphrases, the techniques of which are described in 31b.

ANSWERS: EXERCISE 1
The answers will vary somewhat, depending on the material each student selects.

EXERCISE 1
(1) List the steps you usually go through when you read a textbook. (2) Next, apply SQ3R to reading a chapter in a textbook. (3) Observe your SQ3R reading process and list the steps you go through. (4) Compare the two lists— note how they are alike and how they are different. (5) Write a brief discussion that compares the two lists and that explains which steps in either or both lists helped you learn most successfully from your reading.

 5b

Read to think critically.

During the reading process, the full meaning of a passage emerges on three levels: the **literal,** the **inferential,** and the **evaluative.** If you are like most readers, you stop reading at the literal level. Unless you move to the next two levels, however, your critical thinking skills will suffer.

1
Read for literal meaning.

Reading for literal meaning, sometimes called reading *on the line,* calls for you to understand what is said. It does not include impressions or opinions about the material. Depending on the discipline in which you are reading, the literal level has to do with (1) the key facts, the central points in a line or argument, or the central details of plot and character; and (2) the minor details that lend texture to the picture. If you do not understand the literal meaning of a passage, you cannot move beyond it to the next levels crucial for critical thinking.

2
Read to make inferences.

Reading to make inferences, sometimes called reading *between the lines,* means understanding what is implied but not stated. Often you have to infer information, or background, or the author's purpose. Consider this passage:

> How to tell the difference between modern art and junk puzzles many people although few are willing to admit it. The owner of an art gallery in Chicago had a prospective buyer for two sculptures made of discarded metal and put them outside his warehouse to clean them up. Unfortunately, some junk dealers, who apparently didn't recognize abstract expressionism when they saw it, hauled the two 300-pound pieces away.
> —ORA GYGI, "Things Are Seldom What They Seem"

The literal meaning is that many people cannot tell the difference between art and junk, so two abstract metal sculptures were carted away as junk when an art dealer left them outside a warehouse to clean them.

Now read the material inferentially. You can begin with the unexplained statement, "few are willing to admit" they do not know the difference between art and junk. Reading between the lines, you realize that people feel embarrassed *not* to know; they feel uneducated, or without good taste, or perhaps left out. With this inference in mind, you can move to the last two sentences, in which the author offers not only the literal irony of the art's being carted away as junk, but also the implied irony that the people who carted it away are not among those who might feel embarrassed. This im-

QUOTATION ABOUT READING
A reflection on having once read 800 pages of *War and Peace* in one day:

It took me a long time to forget the way I read that book. For a long time it seemed to me I had betrayed reading itself. Coming back to it now, I still find it disturbing. Something had been sacrificed in my quick dash through the book—another reading altogether. I had limited myself to the story at the expense of a deep, receptive, non-narrative reading of Tolstoy's writing itself. It was as though I had realized that day, once and for all, that a book consists of two layers: on top, the readable layer I had read that day on the train, and underneath, a layer that was inaccessible. You only sense its existence in a moment of distraction from the literal reading, the way you see childhood through a child. It would take forever to tell what you see, and it would be pointless.

—MARGUERITE DURAS, "On Tolstoy, Racine, and Reading by the Light of the Book"

QUOTATION ABOUT READING
Books rule the world, or at least those nations which have a written language; the others do not count.

—VOLTAIRE

plied irony suggests that the people either do not care if they know the difference between art and junk (after all, they assumed it was junk and went on their way) or they "apparently" (a good word for inference making) want to give the impression that they do not know the difference. Thus, it is the art dealer who ends up being embarrassed, for it is he who created the problem by leaving the sculptures outdoors unattended.

The process of inferring is a critical thinking skill that adds not only texture but also invaluable background for the interpretation of any passage.

> CHECKLIST FOR MAKING INFERENCES DURING READING
>
> 1. What is being said beyond the literal level?
> 2. What alternate interpretation is implied rather than stated?
> 3. What words suggest more than one interpretation?
> 4. What information does the author expect me to have before I start to read the material?
> 5. What does the author seem to assume are my biases?
> 6. What information does the author expect me to have about his or her background, philosophy, and the like?
> 7. What do I need to be aware of concerning author bias?

3
Read to evaluate.

Evaluative reading, sometimes called *reading beyond the lines,* is essential for critical thinking. Once you know an author's literal meaning and you have drawn as many inferences as possible from the material, you must evaluate.

Evaluative reading calls for many skills, including knowing how to recognize faulty reasoning (5c-5e), logical fallacies (5f), slanted language (21a-5) and artificial language (21d). Evaluative reading also demands the ability to recognize the impact of an author's tone, to detect prejudice, and to differentiate fact from opinion.

Recognizing an author's tone

An author's tone reveals the author's attitude toward the material and the reader. Tone is communicated by all aspects of a piece of writing, from its choice of words to•the content it uses to communicate its message.

120

Most writers use a serious tone, but sometimes they use humor to get their point across; if you read such material exclusively for its literal meaning, you will miss the point. Here is a passage from an argument against the destruction of buildings that house small, friendly neighborhood stores and their replacement by large, impersonal buildings.

> Every time an old building is torn down in this country, and a new building goes up, the ground floor becomes a bank. The reason for this is that banks are the only ones who can afford the rent for the ground floor of the new buildings going up. . . . Most people don't think there is anything wrong with this, and they accept it as part of the American free-enterprise system. But there is a small group of people in this country who are fighting for Bank Birth Control.
>
> —ART BUCHWALD, "Birth Control for Banks"

Buchwald clearly respects his readers, for he expects that they will realize that (1) although he is talking only of banks, the banks stand for many aspects of urban renewal; (2) the first sentence is an exaggeration intended to elicit a smile—Buchwald is being slightly ridiculous to get across his point; and (3) the group "Bank Birth Control" does not exist—it is Buchwald's creation to advance his argument.

Most readers are wary of a highly emotional tone whose purpose is not to give information but to incite the reader.

> Urban renewal must be stopped! Urban redevelopment is ruining this country. Money-hungry capitalists are robbing treasures from law-abiding citizens! Corrupt politicians are murderers, caring nothing about people being thrown out of their homes into the streets.

Writers of such material do not respect their readers, for such writers assume that readers do not recognize screaming in print when they see it. Discerning readers instantly know the tone here is emotional and unreasonable. The exaggerations (robbing treasures, politicians as murderers) hint at the truth of some cases, but they are generalizations too extreme to be taken seriously.

On the other hand, if a writer's tone sounds reasonable and moderate, readers are more likely to pay attention.

> Urban renewal is revitalizing our cities, but it has caused some serious problems. While investors are trying to replace

QUOTATION ABOUT READING
Books: The most effective weapon against intolerance and ignorance.
—LYNDON BAINES JOHNSON

121

slums with decent housing, they must also remember that they are displacing people who do not want to leave their familiar neighborhoods. Surely a cooperative effort between government and the private sector can lead to creative solutions.

Detecting prejudice

Writers often express opinions, which readers should expect to be based on sound reasoning (see 5c-5f). **Prejudice** is revealed in negative opinions based on beliefs rather than on facts or evidence. Negative opinions might be expressed in positive language, but the underlying assumptions are negative. Prejudicial statements are like these: *Poor people like living in crowded conditions because they are used to the surroundings, Women are not aggressive enough to succeed in business, Men make good soldiers because they enjoy killing.* Often writers imply their prejudices rather than state them outright. Detecting underlying negative opinions is important for critical reading, because discerning readers must call into question any argument that rests upon a weak foundation. (See also Hasty Generalization in 5f.)

Differentiating fact from opinion

An author sometimes intentionally blurs the difference between fact and opinion, and a discerning reader must be able to tell the difference. Sometimes that difference is quite obvious.

A. A woman can never make a good mathematician.
B. Although fear of math is not purely a female phenomenon, girls tend to drop out of math sooner than boys, and adult women experience an aversion to math and math-related activity that is akin to anxiety.

Because of the word *never,* statement *A* is clearly an opinion, whereas statement *B* at least seems to be factual. Knowing who made these statements helps confirm judgments: Statement *A* is by a male Soviet mathematician living in Russia, as reported by David K. Shipler, a well-respected veteran reporter on Russian affairs for the *New York Times;* statement *B* is in a book called *Overcoming Math Anxiety* by Sheila Tobias, a university professor who has undertaken research studies to find out why many people dislike math.

One aid in differentiating between fact and opinion is to *think beyond the obvious.* For example, is "Strenuous exercise is good for your health" a fact? Although the statement has the ring of truth, it is not a fact. People with severe arthritis or heart trouble could

122

be harmed by some forms of exercise. Also, what does "strenuous" mean—a dozen pushups, jogging, aerobics, or playing singles in tennis?

A second aid in differentiating between fact and opinion is to *remember that facts sometimes masquerade as opinions, and opinions sometimes try to pass for facts.* Evaluative reading demands concentration and a willingness to deal with matters that are relative and sometimes ambiguous. For example, in an essay for or against capital punishment, you would likely evaluate the argument differently if you knew that the author is currently on death row, or a victim of a crime committed by someone on death row, or a disinterested party with a philosophy to discuss.

At times, however, the stance of the author is less obvious. Consider these statements:

> C. The common wart usually occurs on the hands, especially on the backs of the fingers, but they may occur on any part of the skin. These dry, elevated lesions have numerous projections on the surface.
>
> D. Warts are wonderful structures. They can appear overnight on any part of the skin, like mushrooms on a damp lawn, full grown and splendid in the complexity of their architecture.

Both statements are about warts. Judging only from the words—often all the evidence available—and without knowing who the authors are, we might say that *C* is fact and *D* is opinion.

Information about the authors, however, can make your judgments more subtle and therefore more reliable. Statement *c* is from a respected medical encyclopedia; thus it can be confirmed as fact. Statement *D* is by Lewis Thomas, a distinguished physician, hospital administrator, researcher, and writer who won the National Book Award for his popular essays revealing the intricacies of biology to laypeople. Given this information and the comparatively benign nature of the material, the words in *D* move into the realm of fact—fact cast in metaphoric language. The author is trying to bring the facts to life by looking at them in a new way and explaining them inventively.

EXERCISE 2

Decide if each statement is a fact or an opinion. When the author and source are provided, explain how that information influences your judgment.

1. Only seven of the poems of Emily Dickinson, a famous and prolific American poet who lived from 1830 to 1886, were published during her lifetime.

ANSWERS: EXERCISE 2
1. fact

123

ANSWERS: EX. 2 (CONT.)
2. opinion
3. opinion, though clearly the judgment of an authority
4. For some people this is a fact, for others an opinion.
5. fact

2. Emily Dickinson is the best American-born female poet, living or dead.
3. "Beethoven is the supreme architect in music." (Joseph Machlis, professor of music, in *The Enjoyment of Music*)
4. "We are, after all, a resourceful people in a nation that has been blessed with abundance." (Lee Iacocca, President of Chrysler Corporation, in his autobiography *Iacocca*)
5. "Capitalism is an economic system based on private property, free enterprise, self-interest as a motivating force, competition, a price system, and a limited government role." (Robert T. Justis, professor at the University of Nebraska—Lincoln, in *Dynamics of American Business*)

ANSWERS: EXERCISE 3
Answers may vary somewhat, but here is a fairly complete list of possibilities:
Literal information
1. Gandhi envisaged a constitution and government for an independent India.
2. The constitution was spelled out at the forty-fifth convention of the All-India Congress.
3. The Congress began at Karachi on March 27, 1931.
4. The Congress was a political convention.
5. The Congress was attended by some 350 leaders.
6. The leaders were both men and women.
7. The leaders were just out of jail.
8. The leaders squatted in the heat under a tent in a semicircle at Gandhi's feet.
9. They all worked at spinning wheels.
10. They made up the so-called Subjects Committee, which was selected from the 5,000 delegates.
11. Gandhi wrote most of the resolutions and moved their adoption.

EXERCISE 3
After you read this passage, (1) list all literal information, (2) list all implied information, and (3) list the opinions stated.

EXAMPLE   The study found many complaints against the lawyers were not investigated, seemingly out of a "desire to avoid difficult cases."
—Norman F. Dacey

Literal information: Few complaints against lawyers are investigated. *Implied information:* The words "difficult case" imply a coverup: lawyers, or others in power, hesitate to criticize lawyers for fear of being sued, or for fear of a public outcry if the truth about abuses and errors were revealed. *Opinions:* None—all is factual because it refers to, and contains a quote from, a study.

The kind of constitution and government Gandhi envisaged for an independent India was spelled out at the forty-fifth convention of the All-India Congress, which began at Karachi on March 27, 1931. It was a party political convention the like of which I had not seen before—nor seen since—with its ringing revolutionary proclamations acclaimed by some 350 leaders, men and women, just out of jail, squatting in the heat under a tent in a semicircle at Gandhi's feet, all of them, like Gandhi, spinning away like children playing with toys as they talked. They made up the so-called Subjects Committee, selected from the five thousand delegates to do the real work of the convention, though in reality, it was Gandhi alone who dominated the proceedings, writing most of the resolutions and moving their adoption with his customary eloquence and surprising firmness.
—WILLIAM L. SHIRER, *Gandhi: A Memoir*

■|| 5c
Use evidence to think critically.

The cornerstone of all reasoning is evidence. Readers expect writers to provide solid evidence for any assertion made or conclusion reached. Writers who successfully communicate their messages use evidence well to support their assertions or conclusions. Evidence consists of facts, statistical information, examples, and opinions of experts. Keep these guidelines in mind as you gather, evaluate, and use evidence.

1. **Evidence should be ample.** In general, the more evidence, the better. A survey that draws upon a hundred respondents is likely to be more reliable than a survey involving only ten. As a writer, you may convince your reader that violence is a serious problem in the high schools on the basis of two specific examples, but you will be more convincing if you can give five examples—or, better still, statistics for the whole school district.

2. **Evidence should be representative.** Readers expect as much objectivity and fairness as possible. People should not trust an assertion or conclusion if it is based on only some members of a group being discussed; it must be based on a truly *representative*, or typical, sample of the group. A political pollster would not get representative evidence by asking questions of the first 1,500 people to walk by a street corner in Austin, Texas, because no such group would truly represent the various regional, racial, political, and ethnic subgroups of the American electorate. Leading political and media pollsters, like those who do the Gallup polls and the Nielsen ratings, use sophisticated sampling techniques to try to ensure that their evidence is representative.

3. **Evidence should be relevant.** Determining relevance can demand subtle thinking. If you heard evidence that one hundred students who had watched television for more than two hours a day throughout their high school years earned significantly lower scores on the Scholastic Aptitude Test than one hundred students who had not, you might conclude that students who watch less television perform better on achievement tests. Yet closer examination of the evidence might reveal other, more important differences between the two groups—differences in geographical region, family background, socioeconomic group, even

ANSWERS: EX. 3 (CONT.)
Implied information
1. India was not independent before March 27, 1931.
2. Even though the Congress had met 45 times, India was still not independent.
3. The Congress took more than one day—it only "began" on March 27, 1931.
4. Most of the leaders likely were revolutionaries who had been political prisoners—because all were "just out of jail."
5. The leaders were very dedicated—they were willing to squat in the heat under a tent.
6. The ruling government did not provide the basic amenities for a convention: room in a building, decent ventilation, chairs, tables, and so forth.
7. The leaders' sitting at Gandhi's feet implies how they respected him.
8. Gandhi often worked at a spinning wheel as he spoke.
9. Everyone's spinning implies that they wanted to imitate Gandhi.
10. Five thousand people is too large a group to get policy matters decided.
11. Gandhi dominated the proceedings because everyone respected him so much.

Opinions
1. The author had not seen before—or since—a political convention like this one in achievement and tone.
2. The revolutionary proclamations were "ringing."
3. The leaders were spinning away like children playing with toys as they talked.
4. Gandhi dominated the proceedings.
5. Gandhi wrote and spoke with his customary eloquence and surprising firmness.

125

quality of schools attended. Your evidence would be both ample and representative, but your conclusion would not be *relevant to* the evidence.

4. **Evidence should be qualified.** Rarely does evidence allow claims that use words such as *all, certainly, always,* or *never.* Conclusions are more reasonable if they are qualified with words such as *some, many, a few, probably, possibly, perhaps, may, usually,* and *often.*

5. **Evidence should be accurate.** Evidence must come from reliable sources, either *primary* or *secondary,* as explained below.

Here is a summary of what to remember when you use evidence.

GUIDELINES FOR USING EVIDENCE EFFECTIVELY

1. Use ample evidence.
2. Use representative evidence.
3. Use relevant evidence.
4. Qualify the claims you make based on the evidence.
5. Use accurate evidence.

Primary evidence, first-hand evidence provided by your own (or someone else's) direct observation, has the greatest impact on a reader. Consider this eyewitness account:

> Poverty is dirt. . . . Let me explain about housekeeping with no money. For breakfast I give my children grits with no oleo or cornbread without eggs and oleo. This does not use up many dishes. What dishes there are, I wash in cold water and with no soap. Even the cheapest soap has to be saved for the baby's diapers. Look at my hands, so cracked and red. Once I saved for two months to buy a jar of Vaseline for my hands and the baby's diaper rash. When I had saved enough, I went to buy it and the price had gone up two cents. The baby and I suffered on. I have to decide every day if I can bear to put my cracked sore hands into the cold water and strong soap. But you ask, why not hot water? Fuel costs money. If you have a wood fire it costs money. If you burn electricity, it costs money. Hot water is a luxury. I do not have luxuries. . . .
>
> —Jo Goodwin Parker, in *America's Other Children*

Remember, both as a reader and as a writer, that not all eyewitness accounts are equally reliable. What is it about Parker's ac-

126

count that makes you trust what she says? She is specific. She is also authoritative. It is doubtful that anyone would have invented the story about being two cents short of the price of a jar of Vaseline. As a writer of personal observations, you need to be as specific as possible—to prove that you truly saw what you say you saw. Use language that appeals to all five senses: describe sights, sounds, and experiences that could have been seen, heard, or experienced only by someone who was there. Show your readers *your* cracked, red hands.

Primary evidence can also come from a reported observation. Few will ever see the surface of the moon or the top of Mt. Everest. People rely, therefore, upon the reports of the astronauts and mountain climbers who have been there. History depends heavily on letters, diaries, and journals—the reports of eyewitnesses. Consider this reported observation:

> The immediate causes of death from nuclear attack are the blast wave, which can flatten heavily reinforced buildings many kilometers away, the firestorm, the gamma rays and the neutrons, which effectively fry the insides of passersby. A school girl who survived the American nuclear attack on Hiroshima, the event that ended the Second World War, wrote this first-hand account:
>
>> Through a darkness like the bottom of hell, I could hear the voices of the other students calling for their mothers. And at the base of the bridge, inside a big cistern that had been dug out there, was a mother weeping, holding above her head a naked baby that was burned bright red all over its body. . . . But every single person who passed was wounded, all of them, and there was no one, there was no one to turn to for help. And the singed hair on the heads of the people was frizzled and whitish and covered with dust. They did not appear to be human, not creatures of this world.
>
> —CARL SAGAN, *Cosmos*

As with the eyewitness account, the strength or value of reported observation hinges on the reliability of the observer. That reliability is a function of how specific, accurate, and authoritative the observations are.

Surveys, polls, and experiments are means by which people extend their powers of observation beyond what can be "seen" in the everyday sense of the word. These surveys, polls, and experiments must be carefully controlled—through weighing, measuring, or quantifying information that would otherwise not be available. Jo Parker could look at her hands, as the Japanese schoolgirl could

127

see the singed hair of passersby, but who can see, for example, the attitude of the American public toward marriage, toward a presidential candidate, toward inflation? For evidence on these matters, polls or surveys are necessary.

Secondary evidence is provided by the opinions of experts. Here the old maxim, "consider the source," becomes crucial. Expertise comes from long familiarity with primary evidence. An expert's reputation must stem from some special experience (as the prisoner of war is an "expert" on prison camps) or training (as the history professor is an authority on the Civil War). To discover who is a reliable source, notice what names keep coming up when you read about your subject.

CHECKLIST FOR EVALUATING A SECONDARY SOURCE

1. Is the source written by an expert on the subject?
2. Is the source mentioned in various other sources when you read about the subject?
3. Is the source's material based on primary evidence?
4. Is the source's language relatively objective (therefore more reliable) or slanted (therefore likely not reliable)?
5. Is the material still current (therefore more reliable) or outdated (therefore likely not reliable)?
6. Do the statements appear in a reputable publication—in a book published by an established publisher or a respected journal or magazine (therefore more reliable)?

ANSWERS: EXERCISE 4

1. *Primary evidence:* Reported observation by Lillian Schlissel about eyewitness account by Mrs. John Kirkwood (This is reliable evidence because it is first-hand from a diary.

2. *Primary evidence:* Results of a poll (This information seems reliable because of the facts, although if Futrell later includes information about the design of the poll—the sample size, the representativeness of the sample, other questions that might have influenced these answers,—the argument will be even more reliable.)

EXERCISE 4

(a) Is each passage based on primary or secondary evidence? (b) Is the evidence acceptable? Why or why not?

1. Marriages on the frontier were often made before a girl was half through her adolescent years, and some diaries record a casualness in the manner in which such decisions were reached. [As] Mrs. John Kirkwood recounts:

> The night before Christmas, John Kirkwood . . . the path finder, stayed at our house over night. I had met him before and when he heard the discussion about my brother Jasper's wedding, he suggested that he and I also get married. I was nearly fifteen years old and I thought it was high time that I got married so I consented.
> —LILLIAN SCHLISSEL, *Women's Diaries of the Westward Journey*

128

2. In the fall of 1982, only 4.7 percent of first-year college students indicated an interest in elementary or secondary teaching as a career. In 1970 that percentage was more than 19 percent. And there are other equally disturbing statistical measures. More than a third of the nation's teachers have told pollsters that if they had to start their own careers over again, they would not select teaching. Thirteen out of every 100 teachers say they *certainly* would not become teachers again, and 30 more maintain they *probably* would not do so.

—MARY HATWOOD FUTRELL, "Towards Excellence"

3. Periods of widespread hunger are not new [to Ethiopia]. Famine was first recorded in the ninth century, and ten major famines occurred within the two centuries following the expulsion of the Muslim invaders in 1540. The great famine of 1888–1889 caused widespread death and devastation. More localized but no less lethal famines occurred in 1916–20, 1927–28, and 1934–35.

—ALLAN HOBEN, "The Origins of Famine"

4. Back in the days when large families were desired for their labor, at least children knew they were really needed. Today's child, overwhelmed with possessions and catered to endlessly by parents, is struggling with feelings of worthlessness. Even with labor-saving devices, big families are a lot of work. My children know they have to pitch in, and they know we appreciate their help. Maybe I don't have time to read to the three-year-old, but the eight-year-old does—to the benefit of them both.

—SARA L. SMITH, "Big Families Can Be Happy, Too"

5. I had read about the giant water bug, but never seen one. "Giant water bug" is really the name of the creature, which is an enormous, heavy-bodied brown beetle. It eats insects, tadpoles, fish, and frogs. Its grasping forelegs are mighty, and hooked inward. It seizes a victim with these legs, hugs it tight, and paralyzes it with enzymes injected during a vicious bite. That one bite is the only bite it ever takes. Through the puncture shoot the poisons that dissolve the victim's muscles and bones and organs—all but the skin—and through it the giant water bug sucks out the victim's body, reduced to a juice. This event is quite common in warm water. The frog I saw was being sucked by a giant water bug. I had been kneeling on the island grass; when the unrecognizable flap of skin settled on the creek bottom, swaying, I stood up and brushed the knees of my pants. I couldn't catch my breath.

—ANNIE DILLARD, *Pilgrim at Tinker Creek*

ANSWERS: EX. 4 (CONT.)

3. *Secondary evidence:* Historical report (This information seems reliable because of the abundance of evidence, the fact that the information can be verified by consulting other sources, and the objective language in which it is written.)

4. *Primary evidence:* Eyewitness account (This argument is based on some assumptions that the reader might not share: For example, are all of today's children "struggling with feelings of worthlessness"? On the other hand, Smith is a suitable expert to discuss the effects of a large family on her children's needing to pitch in and help. Additional specific examples about Smith's family and testimony from people in other big families would strengthen this argument.)

5. *Both secondary and primary:* Secondary in that Dillard reports her reading about the giant water bug; primary in that Dillard sees the frog skin sink to the creek bottom. (This evidence is reliable because of the detail Dillard uses in relating what she learned from her reading, and because of the first-hand report confirming what she read.)

129

5d
Evaluate cause and effect to think critically.

Cause and effect is a type of thinking that seeks to establish some relationship, or link, between two or more specific pieces of evidence. You may seek to understand the effects of a known cause (say, studying two more hours each night):

$$\text{More studying} \longrightarrow \text{produces} \longrightarrow \text{?}$$

Or you may attempt to determine the cause or causes of a known effect (say, your recurrent headaches):

$$\text{?} \longrightarrow \text{produces} \longrightarrow \text{recurrent headaches}$$

Regardless of whether you begin your thinking with a cause or an effect, you are working with this basic pattern:

$$\text{Cause A} \longrightarrow \text{produces} \longrightarrow \text{effect B}$$

If you want to use reasoning based on a relationship of cause and effect, evaluate the connections carefully. Keep these guidelines in mind as you evaluate cause-and-effect relationships.

GUIDELINES FOR EVALUATING CAUSE AND EFFECT

1. **Clear relationship.** Causes and effects normally occur in chronological order: *first* a door slams, *then* a pie that is cooling on a shelf falls. But suppose you are walking down the sidewalk when, first, a car backfires, and then the person walking in front of you falls to the ground. Does this mean that the backfire is related to the fall? A cause-and-effect relationship must be linked by more than chronological sequence. The fact that *B* happens after *A* does not prove that it was caused by *A*.

2. **A pattern of repetition.** To establish the relationship of *A* to *B*, there must be proof that every time *A* was present, *B* occurred—or that *B* never occurred unless *A* was present. The need for a pattern of repetition explains why the Food and Drug Administration performs thousands of tests before declaring a new food or medicine safe for human consumption.

3. **No oversimplification.** The basic pattern of cause and effect— single cause, single effect—rarely gives the full picture. Most complex social or political problems have **multiple causes,** not a single cause and a single effect.

130

Cause 1 ⎫
Cause 2 ⎬ ⟶ produce ⟶ effect B
Cause 3 ⎭

It is oversimplifying to assume that high schools were the only cause of the nationwide decline in scores on the Scholastic Aptitude Test between 1964 and 1984. Not only would it be unfair to high schools, it would also be ignoring a variety of other possible important causes, such as television viewing habits, family life, level of textbooks, and so on. Similarly, one cause can produce **multiple effects:**

Cause A ⟶ produces ⟶ { effect 1 / effect 2 / effect 3 }

Some felt that medical researchers were guilty of this form of oversimplification when they first released an arthritis medicine for public consumption. They had proven that the pill helped control arthritis, but they had not given enough attention to its side effects.

Here is a summary of what to remember when you evaluate cause-and-effect relationships.

GUIDELINES FOR EVALUATING CAUSE-AND-EFFECT RELATIONSHIPS

1. Establish a clear relationship between events.

2. Determine whether the events can be repeated.

3. Avoid oversimplifying: Look for multiple causes and/or effects.

■‖ 5e

Understand reasoning processes to think critically.

To think critically—to think about thinking—you need to be able to understand reasoning processes so that you can (1) recognize and evaluate them in your reading and (2) use them correctly in your writing. **Induction** and **deduction** are reasoning processes.

131

They are natural thought patterns that people use every day to think through ideas and to make decisions.

COMPARISON OF INDUCTIVE AND DEDUCTIVE REASONING	INDUCTION	DEDUCTION
ARGUMENT BEGINS	with specific evidence	with a general claim
ARGUMENT CONCLUDES	with a general claim	with a specific statement
CONCLUSION IS	reliable or unreliable	true or false
USE IT	to discover something new	to apply what is known

1
Recognize and use inductive reasoning.

Induction is the process of arriving at general principles from particular facts or instances. Suppose that you go the Registry of Motor Vehicles to renew your driver's license, and you have to stand

SUMMARY OF INDUCTIVE REASONING

1. Inductive reasoning moves from the specific to the general. It begins with the evidence of specific facts, observations, or experiences and moves to a general conclusion.

2. Inductive conclusions are considered *reliable* or *unreliable*, not true or false. An inductive conclusion indicates probability, the degree to which the conclusion is likely to be true. Frustrating though it may be for those who seek certainty, inductive thinking is, of necessity, based only on a sampling of the facts.

3. An inductive conclusion is held to be reliable or unreliable in relation to the quantity and quality of the evidence supporting it (see 5c).

4. Induction leads to new "truths." Induction allows you to make statements about the unknown on the basis of what is known.

TEACHING TIP
Using analogy is a way to think inductively. An analogy compares two dissimilar objects, ideas, or experiences by focusing on what they have in common. For example, some people make an analogy between the role of a teacher and that of a coach. Like coaches, teachers train people in fundamentals through repetition and practice, recommend changes in technique, and try to inspire excellence. However, despite points of similarity, two dissimilar items remain dissimilar.

First, coaches work primarily with the body rather than the mind, developing physical rather than mental skills. Second, team coaches praise the team player while good teachers reward independence and originality. Thus the analogy between teachers and coaches breaks down at some point.

In the absence of other evidence, an analogy will not *prove* anything. Nevertheless, although an analogy can always be shown as flawed under close scrutiny, it can still help explain a point and thus help persuade an audience.

132

INSTRUCTOR'S NOTES

in line for two hours until you get the document. Then a few months later, when you return to the Registry for new license plates, a clerk gives you the wrong advice, and you have to stand in two different lines for three hours. Another time you go there in response to a letter asking for information, and you discover that you should have brought your car registration form, although the letter failed to mention that fact. You conclude that the Registry is inefficient and seems not to care about the convenience of its patrons. You have arrived at this conclusion by means of induction.

2
Recognize and use deductive reasoning.

If several unproductive visits to the Registry of Motor Vehicles have convinced you that the Registry cares little about the convenience of its patrons (as the experiences described in 5e-1 suggest), you will not be happy the next time you are forced to return. Your reasoning might go something like this:

The Registry wastes people's time.
I have to go to the Registry tomorrow.
Therefore, tomorrow my time will be wasted.

You reached the conclusion—"therefore, tomorrow my time will be wasted"—by means of deduction.

Deductive arguments have three parts: two **premises** and a **conclusion.** This structure is known as a **syllogism.**

PREMISE 1   When it snows, the streets get wet.
PREMISE 2   It is snowing.
CONCLUSION   Therefore, the streets are wet.

The first premise of any deductive argument is an assumption. The second premise of any deductive argument can be a statement of fact (It is snowing), or it can be a second assumption that has to be defended with evidence. The conclusion follows logically from the premises.

A deductive argument has to be **valid.** The deductive argument above is valid. Validity has to do with the form, or structure, of the argument. A deductive argument is valid when the conclusion logically follows from the premises. Otherwise it is invalid.

INVALID   When it snows, the streets get wet.
The streets are wet.
Therefore, it is snowing.

EXTRA EXERCISE
Each analogy here can be defended. Like all analogies, each can also be attacked. First, defend each one—give one or more arguments to show that the two parts of the analogy are similar and are relevant to the claim being made. Second, attack each one by pointing out how they are not similar. Finally, offer other types of evidence that would help make the claim ultimately more convincing.
1. Like warfare, the aim of a football is to destroy.
2. Don't bother to take your books home over vacation. Vacation is like a "study date"—no studying ever takes place.
3. Taking care of a group of young children is like trying to string beads without a knot on the end of the string.
4. The atom is like a small solar system, with its own "sun" and its own satellites.
[Answers on page 137.]

ALTERNATE EXAMPLES
Invalid:
Some circular things are bubbles.
Some human heads are circular things.
Some human heads are bubbles.
Valid:
All mammals are animals.
All whales are mammals.
Therefore, all whales are animals.

133

INSTRUCTOR'S NOTES

This invalid argument has two acceptable premises, but its conclusion is wrong because it ignores the fact that streets can get wet from rain, from street-cleaning trucks that spray water, from people using hoses to cool off the pavement or wash off cars, and so on. The first syllogism given above is valid because its conclusion follows logically from the premises.

In any deductive argument, beware of premises that are implied but not stated—called **unstated assumptions.** Often they are wrong. For example, suppose a corporation argued that it should not be required to install pollution control devices because the cost would cut into their profits. This argument rests on the unstated assumption that no corporation should be asked to do something that would lower its profits. That assumption is wrong, and so is the argument. Similarly, if someone says that certain information has to be correct because it was printed in a newspaper, the person's deductive reasoning would be flawed. Here the unstated assumption is that everything in a newspaper is correct—which is not true. Whenever there is an unstated assumption, supply it and then check to make sure it is true.

ANSWERS: EXERCISE 5

In discussing the answers, note that the assignment is to determine the *validity of the conclusions,* not to debate the truth of the premises.

1. *Invalid.* The conclusion is not contained in the premises. It is impossible to tell whether Stuart is part of the group "some."

2. *Valid.* The claim made in the conclusion is contained in the premises. If E. B. White was a great writer, anything true of all great writers must be true of him. (People can challenge the premises: It is likely that not all writers write many drafts of their work, and White's greatness as a writer is a matter of opinion.)

3. *Invalid.* As with item 1, it is impossible to tell whether the U.S. Post Office is part of the group "some."

4. *Invalid.* This is an example of the "fallacy of the shared characteristic." The son's sharing one characteristic with terrorists does not mean that the son is a terrorist.

5. *Invalid.* This is an example of the "fallacy of the converse." The uncle could have eaten for many reasons aside from being hungry: he was visiting someone who offered food and he did not want to seem impolite, he was nervous or bored so he decided to eat, and so on. Here is a revised syllogism:

   VALID. When my uncle is hungry, he eats.
   My uncle is hungry.
   Therefore, my uncle will eat.

SUMMARY OF DEDUCTIVE REASONING

1. Deductive reasoning moves from the general to the specific. It begins with a general statement, then moves to a specific instance, and then moves to a conclusion formed from that instance.

2. Deductive conclusions are considered *true* or *false.* This is the strength of deductive reasoning.

3. If deductive reasoning is structured properly—that is, if it is *valid* (see below)—the conclusion must be true.

4. Deductive reasoning applies what you already know. Though it does not yield anything new, it builds stronger arguments than does induction because it offers the certainty of a conclusion's being true or false.

EXERCISE 5

Ignoring for the moment whether the premises seem to you to be true, determine if each conclusion is valid. Explain your answer.

1. Some students are not wealthy.
   Stuart is a student.
   Stuart is not wealthy.

2. All great writers write many drafts of their work.
   E. B. White was a great writer.
   E. B. White wrote many drafts of his work.

3. Some government bureaucracies are inefficient.
   The U.S. Post Office is run by a government bureaucracy.
   The U.S. Post Office is inefficient.

4. Terrorists defy the established order.
   My son defies me.
   My son is a terrorist.

5. When my uncle is hungry, he eats.
   My uncle just finished eating.
   Therefore, he was hungry.

 ## 5f

Recognize and avoid logical fallacies.

Logical fallacies are flaws in reasoning that lead to illogical statements. They tend to occur most often when ideas are being argued, although they can be found in all types of writing. Most logical fallacies masquerade as reasonable statements, but they are in fact attempts to manipulate readers by reaching their emotions instead of their intellects, their hearts rather than their heads. Most logical fallacies are known by labels; all indicate a way that thinking has gone wrong during the reasoning process.

Hasty generalization

A **hasty generalization** occurs when someone generalizes from inadequate evidence. If the statement "My hometown is the best place in the state to live" is supported with only two examples of why it is pleasant, the generalization is hasty. **Stereotyping** is a type of hasty generalization that occurs when someone makes prejudiced, sweeping claims about all of the members of a particular religious, ethnic, racial, or political group: "Everyone from country X is dishonest."

False analogy

A **false analogy** is a comparison in which the differences outweigh the similarities, or the similarities are irrelevant to the claim the analogy is intended to support. "Old Joe Smith would never make a good President because an old dog cannot learn new tricks." Home-spun analogies like this often seem to have an air of wisdom about them, but just as often they fall apart when examined closely.

TEACHING TIP
Many students enjoy finding and correcting logical fallacies in newspaper editorials and opinion columns, as well as in the work of their peers. You might distribute copies of works containing fallacies, as a spur to class discussion or for revision. A less adept class might benefit from a preliminary lesson based on a list of logical fallacies you can cull from assorted sources (newspapers, political literature, advertisements, student papers, etc.); tell them all the passages are illogical and have them explain why, as a prelude to revision (oral or written, as time allows).

Your analytically minded students may be interested in additional logical fallacies:

A question-begging phrase (sometimes called *alleged certainty*) presents something as certain that is open to debate: "Everyone knows" and "It is obvious that" are typical phrases that beg the question. This statement is flawed: "It is common knowledge that jobs in Texas pay more than do jobs in Idaho"; this statement is logical: "A recent government survey revealed that, on the average, workers in the oil fields of Texas are paid more than are loggers in the timber industries of Idaho." *To correct:* Drop the phrase and substitute evidence that supports your claim.

5f | log

TEACHING TIP (CONT.)

A *complex question* (also known as a *loaded question*) contains one or more unproven assumptions: "Are you still spending time with known drug addicts?" Notice what happens when you try to answer such a question. If you say "yes," you are guilty. If you say "no," you are still guilty, because you are admitting that you used to spend time with drug addicts. *To correct:* Split the question into its parts ("Are you still spending time with those people?" "Are those people drug addicts?") and deal with each separately.

Appeal to fear uses scare tactics instead of legitimate evidence. Such an argument implies danger: "Anyone who stages a protest against the government is a communist, so we must outlaw all protests."

Appeal to the people (also known as *ad populum*) draws on whatever the people hold dear—for example, country, religion, or family. This approach tries to sway people by using a favorable label instead of providing reasons: "A vote for Joe Smith is a vote for the flag."

Name-calling attaches an unpleasant label to something or someone. Consider how a label can stop people from thinking: "Jane Jones was once an alcoholic, so she cannot possibly say anything of value about politics."

Appeal to pity attempts to arouse sympathy: "He embezzled $1,500 of company money, but after all, his wife recently died and his child needs surgery."

The genetic fallacy, a special form of *hasty generalization,* predicts something about a person based on that person's origins: "Joe Smith is from New York City, so he knows how to deal with street crime." Often this fallacy involves a person's religion, sex, race, or economic status.

Learning the role of the President is hardly comparable to a dog's learning new tricks.

Circular argument

A **circular argument,** sometimes called a **circular definition,** is an assertion merely restated in slightly different terms: "Boxing is a dangerous sport because it is unsafe." Here, "unsafe" conveys the same idea as "dangerous" rather than adding something new. This "begs the question" because the conclusion is the same as the premise.

Non sequitur

Non sequitur in Latin translates as "does not follow," meaning a conclusion does not follow from the premises: "Jane Jones is a forceful speaker, so she will make a good mayor." It does not follow that someone's ability to be a forceful speaker means that person would be a good mayor.

Post hoc, ergo propter hoc

Post hoc, ergo propter hoc—which means "after this, therefore because of this"—results when someone assumes that sequence alone proves something. This cause-and-effect fallacy is very common: "Because a new weather satellite was launched last week, it has not stopped raining."

Self-contradiction

Self-contradiction occurs when two premises are used that cannot simultaneously be true: "Only when nuclear weapons have finally destroyed us will we be convinced of the need to control them." This statement is self-contradictory in that no one will be around to be convinced after everyone has been destroyed.

Red herring

A **red herring,** sometimes referred to as **ignoring the question,** sidetracks an issue by bringing up a totally unrelated issue: "Why worry about pandas becoming extinct when we should be concerned about the plight of the homeless?" Someone who introduces an irrelevant issue hopes to distract the audience as a red herring might distract bloodhounds from a scent.

Appeal to the person

An **appeal to the person,** also known as **ad hominem,** attacks the appearance, personal habits, or character of the person

136

involved instead of dealing with the merits of the issue at hand: "We could take her plea for money for the homeless seriously if she were not so nasty to the children who live next door to her."

Bandwagon

Bandwagon, also known as **going along with the crowd,** implies that something is right because everyone is doing it, that truth is determined by majority vote: "Smoking must not be bad for people because millions of people smoke."

False or irrelevant authority

Using **false or irrelevant authority,** sometimes called **ad verecundiam,** means citing the opinion of an "expert" who has no claim to expertise about the subject at hand. This fallacy attempts to transfer prestige from one area to another. Many television commercials rely on this tactic—a famous tennis player praising a brand of motor oil or a popular movie star lauding a brand of cheese.

Card-stacking

Card-stacking, also known as **special pleading,** ignores evidence on the other side of a question. From all the available facts, the person arguing selects only those that will build the best (or worst) possible case. Many television commercials use this strategy. When three slim, happy consumers rave about a new diet plan, they do not mention (a) the plan does not work for everyone and (b) other plans work better for some people. The makers of the commercial selected evidence that helped their cause, ignoring any that did not.

The either–or fallacy

The either–or fallacy, also known as **false dilemma,** offers only two alternatives when more exist: "Either go to college or forget about getting a job." This statement implies that a college education is a prerequisite for all jobs.

Taking something out of context

Taking something out of context separates an idea or fact from the material surrounding it, thus distorting it for special purposes. If a critic writes about a movie saying, "The plot was predictable and boring but the music was sparkling," and an advertisement for the movie says, "Critic calls this movie 'sparkling,'" the critic's words have been taken out of context—and distorted.

ANSWERS: EXTRA EX. (p. 133)
Answers will vary. Answers here are intended to be suggestive.

1. *Pro:* Both involve uniformed "teams" inflicting injury upon each other in pursuit of territorial gain. *Con:* football is played according to rules, with clear time limits, for entertainment. *To Revise:* Add statistics to actual injuries inflicted upon high school, college, and professional football players, as well as evidence of asocial attitudes (if any) developed by players.

2. *Pro:* In both cases, serious intentions readily give way to the pursuit of pleasure. *Con:* A study date ostensibly has a serious purpose whereas vacation, by definition, is unstructured free time. *To Revise:* Add eyewitness accounts or reported observations about how time was spent on actual study dates, actual vacations.

3. *Pro:* Both are nearly impossible to control. The moment you get one "on the string," the others fall off. *Con:* Beads are much easier to control. *To Revise:* Eyewitness accounts of babysitting experiences.

4. *Pro:* Both have large centers with smaller objects orbiting them. *Con:* The sun is chemically more complex than the nuclei of atoms; plants orbit the sun because of gravity rather than electrical charge. *To Revise:* Other than listing additional similarities, the analogy cannot be made stronger—the properties of the solar system and of the atom are what they are.

Appeal to ignorance

Appeal to ignorance assumes that an argument is valid simply because there is no evidence on the other side of the issue: "Since no one has proven that depression does not cause cancer, we can assume that it does." The absence of opposing evidence, however, proves nothing.

Ambiguity and Equivocation

Ambiguity and **equivocation** describe expressions that are not clear because they have more than one meaning. An ambiguous expression may be taken either way by the reader. A statement such as "They were entertaining guests" is ambiguous. Were the guests amusing to be with or were people giving hospitality to guests? An equivocal expression, by contrast, is one used in two or more ways within a single argument. If someone argued that the President *played an important role* in arms control negotiations and then, two sentences later, accused him of *merely playing a role*, the person would be equivocating.

ANSWERS: EXERCISE 6
1. appeal to ignorance
2. red herring
3. hasty generalization
4. *post hoc ergo propter hoc*
5. *ad hominem.* The end of the story is that the lawyer took her case to court and got this ruling: "While [her] living arrangement may be unorthodox and unacceptable to some segments of the society, this conduct bears no rational connection to her fitness to practice law."
6. circular argument
7. either-or
8. self-contradiction

EXERCISE 6

Identify and explain the fallacy in each item. If the item is correct, circle its number.

EXAMPLE   We cannot use coal for energy because its fumes will pollute our environment. [This is an *either-or fallacy* because it assumes that technology offers us no way to contain or "clean" the fumes.]

1. UFO's must exist because no reputable studies have proven conclusively that they do not.
2. Politics should not interfere with participation in the Olympics because many athletes are not old enough to vote in their countries.
3. I just saw my first Tennessee Williams play, *The Glass Menagerie.* He's the twentieth century's greatest playwright, I'm positive.
4. Water fluoridation affects the brain. Citywide, students' test scores began to drop five months after fluoridation began.
5. (This incident is real.) A 34-year-old female lawyer working in Washington, D.C., for the federal government was denied permission to take the bar examination to practice law in her home state because she was living with a man who was not her husband. What fallacy is working here?
6. Plagiarism is unethical because it is dishonest.
7. Seat belts are the only hope for reducing the death rate from automobile accidents.
8. Medicare is free; the government pays for it from taxes.

138

II UNDERSTANDING GRAMMAR

6 Parts of Speech

7 Structures of the Sentence

8 Verbs

9 Case of Nouns and Pronouns

10 Pronoun Reference

11 Agreement

12 Distinguishing Between
Adjectives and Adverbs

6

PARTS OF SPEECH

Knowing grammar helps you understand how language works. Grammar describes the way words deliver meaning. Grammar also describes components of language and standard rules for using language. Still, grammar is only a tool. You need to know more than labels and rules to be able to write. You need to gain control of larger matters as well, all discussed in this handbook: understanding the writing process°; developing and supporting a thesis°; organizing material°; and using words, sentences, and paragraphs to carry out your writing purposes successfully.

When you learn the parts of speech, you gain a basic vocabulary. You can identify words, think about words and the structures they form, and communicate with other people about language. This chapter presents each part of speech—noun, pronoun, verb, adjective, adverb, conjunction, and interjection—to help you identify words and their functions. **Function** is an important aspect of grammar, for the same word can function in more than one way. To identify a word's part of speech, you must see the word functioning in a sentence.

We ate **fish.** [*Fish* is a noun. It names a thing.]

We **fish** on weekends. [*Fish* is a verb. It names an action.]

140

6a

Recognize nouns.

A **noun** names a person, place, thing, or idea.

NOUNS		
PROPER	Names specific people, places, or things (first letter is always capitalized)	John Lennon Paris Buick
COMMON	Names general groups, places, people, or things	singer city car
CONCRETE	Names things that can be seen, touched, heard, smelled, tasted	landscape pizza thunder
ABSTRACT	Names things *not* knowable through the five senses	freedom shyness
COLLECTIVE	Names groups	family team committee
MASS	Names "uncountable" things	water time

Most nouns change form to show number°: *idea, mouse* (singular); *ideas, mice* (plural). Nouns also change form for the possessive case°: *the **pilot's** hometown.* Nouns function as subjects°, objects°, and complements°.

Linda ate **pizza** in **Paris** [*Linda* = subject, *pizza* = direct object, *Paris* = object of preposition]

Linda is a **singer** [*Linda* = subject, *singer* = subject complement].

141

QUOTATIONS ABOUT WRITING

Language, like the body, is so comfortable and familiar that we hardly notice its presence or complexity. Yet once examined closely, the accomplishment of any ordinary speaker is rather astonishing. He can produce and understand an indefinite number of new sentences—sentences he has never encountered previously.

—RICHARD OHMANN, "Grammar and Meaning"

WHERE TO FIND INFORMATION RELATED TO NOUNS

Nouns as subjects	7a-1
Nouns as objects	7b-1, 7b-2
Nouns as complements	7c-1
Noun clauses	7e-3
Making subjects and verbs agree	11a–11k
Avoiding too many nouns as modifiers	12f
Finding and correcting fragments that need subjects	13
Avoiding unnecessary shifts of subject	15a-2
Forming plurals of nouns	22d-4
Spelling compound words: e.g., *grocery store, supermarket, brother-in-law*	22e-3
Making nouns possessive: *s, s', s's*	27a
Capitalizing nouns	30e

Articles often appear with nouns. These little words—*a, an, the*—are also called **limiting adjectives, noun markers,** or **noun determiners.** *A* and *an* "limit" a noun less than *the* does: **a** *plan,* **the** *plan.* Of *a* and *an, a* is the right word to use when the word following it starts with a consonant sound: **a** *carrot,* **a** *broken egg,* **a** *hip. An* is the right word to use when the word following it starts with a vowel sound: **an** *egg,* **an** *old carrot,* **an** *honor.*

■‖ 6b

Recognize pronouns.

A **pronoun** takes the place of a noun.

David is an accountant. [noun]

He is an accountant. [pronoun]

The word (or words) a pronoun replaces is called its **antecedent.**

Some pronouns have different singular and plural forms: *I, her, himself* (singular) and *we, their, themselves* (plural), for example. Some pronouns change form to show case° changes: *I, me, mine; who, whom, whose,* for example.

WHERE TO FIND INFORMATION RELATED TO PRONOUNS

Using correct case forms: e.g., *we* or *us, who* or *whom*	9b–9h
Using pronouns and antecedents clearly	10
Making pronouns and antecedents agree	11l–11o
Understanding the difference between *its* and *it's*	27b

142

PRONOUNS		
PERSONAL *I, you, they, we, her, its, ours,* and others	Refers to people or things	I saw **her** take your book to **them.**
RELATIVE *who, which, that, what, whoever,* and others	Introduces certain noun clauses and adjective clauses	**Whoever** took the book **that** I left must return it.
INTERROGATIVE *who, whose, what, which,* and others	Introduces a question	**Who** called?
DEMONSTRATIVE *this, these, that, those*	Points out the antecedent	Is **this** a mistake?
REFLEXIVE; INTENSIVE *myself, yourself, herself, themselves,* and all *-self* or *-selves* words	Reflects back to the antecedent; intensifies the antecedent	They claim to support **themselves.** I **myself** doubt it.
RECIPROCAL *each other, one another*	Refers to individual parts of a plural antecedent	We respect **each other.**
INDEFINITE *all, anyone, each,* and others	Refers to nonspecific persons or things	**Everyone** is welcome here.

ANSWERS: EXERCISE 1

1. She^P joined (the) Auxiliary Territorial Service^N in 1944.
2. At (the) time^N, she^P was still (a) princess.
3. Her^P supervisors^N treated her^P like all (the) others^P, though.
4. When she^P started, she^P did not know how to drive.
5. (The) princess^N quickly learned to strip and repair many kinds^N of engines^N.

EXERCISE 1

Underline and label all nouns (N) and pronouns (P). Circle all articles.

EXAMPLE
$$\overset{N}{\underline{\text{Queen Elizabeth II}}}, \text{ served as } @ \overset{N}{\underline{\text{driver}}}, \text{ and } \overset{N}{\underline{\text{mechanic}}}, \text{ in}$$
$$\overset{N}{\underline{\text{World War II}}}.$$

1. She joined the Auxiliary Territorial Service in 1944.
2. At the time, she was still a princess.
3. She was treated like all the others, though.
4. When she started, she did not know how to drive.
5. The princess quickly learned to strip and repair many kinds of engines.

■|| 6c

QUOTATION ABOUT WRITING

It is not the business of grammar . . . to give law to the fashions which regulate our speech. On the contrary, from its conformity to these, and from that alone, it derives all its authority and value.

—GEORGE CAMPBELL

COORDINATED RESOURCES

Alternate examples and exercises for this chapter are available in the *S & S Workbook for Writers*, Gordon and Troyka.

Students can practice and test their knowledge of terms, key concepts, and applications of material in this chapter by using the *Study Guide to the S & S Handbook for Writers*, West.

6c
Recognize verbs.

Main verbs express action, occurrence, or state of being.

I **dance**. [action]

The audience **became** silent. What **happened?** [occurrence]

You **were** wonderful, but the show **seemed** too long. [state of being]

A **linking verb** is a main verb that connects a subject° with a subject complement°—a word (or words) that renames or describes the subject.

George Washington **was** President. [*George Washington* = subject, *was* = linking verb, *President* = complement; *President* renames *George Washington*.]

George Washington **grew** old at Mount Vernon. [*George Washington* = subject, *grew* = linking verb, *old* = complement; *old* describes *George Washington*.]

Auxiliary, or **helping, verbs** are forms of *be, do, have, can, may, will,* and others; they combine with main verbs to make verb phrases.

Clothing prices **have soared** recently. [*have* = auxiliary verb, *soared* = main verb, *have soared* = verb phrase]

Leather shoes **can cost** hundreds of dollars. [*can* = auxiliary verb, *cost* = main verb, *can cost* = verb phrase]

WHERE TO FIND INFORMATION RELATED TO VERBS

Verb forms and principal parts	8a
Learning irregular verbs	8b-2
Forms of *be, do, have*	8c
Using *be, do, have* as auxiliaries	8c
Using *can, may, will* (modal auxiliaries)	8c
Using *lie, lay; sit, set; rise, raise*	8d
Showing time with verbs	8e–8h
Making subjects and verbs agree	11a–11k

EXERCISE 2
Underline all verbs.

EXAMPLE Albert Einstein <u>was offered</u> the presidency of Israel.

1. When Israel's first president died in office, an Israeli newspaper suggested that Einstein become the next president.
2. Many people felt that he could be elected easily.
3. Everyone expected that he would continue his scientific research even if he won the office.
4. Nevertheless, he refused the nomination.
5. He said that he lacked the talent and experience that were needed for politics.

ANSWERS: EXERCISE 2
1. died, suggested, become
2. felt, could be elected
3. expected, would continue, won
4. refused
5. said, lacked, was needed

■|| 6d

Recognize verbals.

Verbals are verb parts functioning as nouns, adjectives, or adverbs.

VERBALS		
INFINITIVE *to* + simple form of verb	1. Noun: names an action, state, or condition 2. Adjective or adverb: describes or modifies.	**To eat** now is inconvenient. Still, we have far **to go**
PAST PARTICIPLE *-ed* form of regular verb or equivalent in irregular verb	Adjective: describes or modifies	**Boiled, filtered** water is usually safe to drink.
PRESENT PARTICIPLE *-ing* form of verb	1. Adjective: describes or modifies 2. Noun; see *Gerund,* below	**Running** water may not be safe.
GERUND *-ing* form of verb	Noun: names an action, state, or condition	**Eating** in turnpike restaurants can be an adventure.

INSTRUCTOR'S NOTES

QUOTATION ABOUT WRITING

Grammarians are not necessarily writers, but writers must always be grammarians, whether they are conscious of what they are doing or not.

—WILLIAM F. IRMSCHER, *Teaching Expository Writing*

WHERE TO FIND INFORMATION RELATED TO VERBALS

Making verbs show accurate time sequences with verbals	8h-2
Putting pronouns into the right case with infinitives	9f
Finding and correcting fragments that have verbals, not verbs	13

■‖ 6e
Recognize adjectives.

Adjectives modify—that is, describe or limit—nouns, pronouns, and word groups functioning as nouns.

> I saw a **green** tree. [*Green* modifies noun, *tree.*]
>
> It was **leafy** and **healthy.** [*Leafy* and *healthy* modify pronoun, *it.*]
>
> The flowering trees were **beautiful.** [*Beautiful* modifies noun phrase, *the flowering trees.*]

Descriptive adjectives, like *healthy, leafy,* and *green,* can show levels of intensity: *green, greener, greenest; beautiful, more beautiful, most beautiful.*

Some words quite different from descriptive adjectives still function to limit nouns, so they are classified as adjectives. Articles, one type of these **limiting adjectives,** are discussed in 6a. The chart lists other types.

Because most of these words also function as pronouns, you must see each word functioning in a sentence to identify its part of speech.

> **That** car belongs to Harold. [*that* = demonstrative adjective]
>
> **That** is Harold's car. [*that* = demonstrative pronoun]

Proper adjectives are formed from proper nouns: *American, Victorian.* See 30e for advice about capitalizing them.

WHERE TO FIND INFORMATION RELATED TO ADJECTIVES

Avoiding double negatives	12c
Good and *well*	12d
Bad and *badly*	12d
Forming comparatives and superlatives: *-er, more; -est, most*	12e
Using adjectives, instead of nouns, as modifiers	12f

146

LIMITING ADJECTIVES

DEMONSTRATIVE *this, these, that, those*	**Those** students rent **that** house.
INDEFINITE *any, each, other, some,* and others	**Few** films today have complex plots.
INTERROGATIVE *what, which, whose*	**What** answer did you give?
NUMERICAL *one, first, two, second,* and others	The **fifth** question was tricky.
POSSESSIVE *my, your, their,* and others	My violin is older than **your** cello.
RELATIVE *what, which, whose, whatever, whichever, whosever*	We don't know **which** road to take.

Spelling compound words: e.g., *well-known* or *well known*	22e-3
Using commas with two or more adjectives	24c, 24d
Capitalizing proper adjectives	30e

EXERCISE 3
Underline all adjectives.

Answers on p. 148.

EXAMPLE   Thomas H. Holmes was the father of <u>modern</u> embalming.

1. Holmes experimented with embalming while in medical school.
2. Later, he moved to New York and became one of the first professional embalmers in this country.

147

INSTRUCTOR'S NOTES

ANSWERS: EXERCISE 3
1. medical
2. first professional
3. Civil, government, dead Union
4. wealthy, embalming, rich
5. strict

3. During the Civil War, he received a government contract to embalm dead Union soldiers.

4. He became wealthy because he limited his embalming practice to the officers whose families were rich enough to pay his fee of $100.

5. He gave strict instructions that he was not to be embalmed.

▮‖ 6f
Recognize adverbs.

An **adverb** modifies—that is, describes or limits—verbs, adjectives, other adverbs, and entire sentences.

> Good cooks plan meals **carefully.** [*Carefully* modifies verb, *plan.*]
>
> They know vegetables provide **very** important vitamins. [*Very* modifies adjective, *important.*]
>
> Potato chips are often **too** highly salted. [*Too* modifies adverb, *highly.*]
>
> **Fortunately,** people are learning that salt can be harmful. [*Fortunately* modifies the entire sentence.]

Many adverbs are easy to recognize because they are formed by adding -*ly* to adjectives: *sadly, loudly, normally, happily.* Still, some adjectives end in -*ly: brotherly, lovely,* and *oilly,* for example. Also, many adverbs do not end in -*ly: very, much, always, not, yesterday, so,* and *well* are just a few that do not. For a complete explanation of how to distinguish between adverbs and adjectives, see Chapter 12.

Conjunctive adverbs modify by creating logical connections in meaning between independent clauses°.

CONJUNCTIVE ADVERBS	
SHOWING ADDITION	*also, furthermore, moreover, besides*
SHOWING CONTRAST	*however, still, nevertheless, conversely, nonetheless, instead*
SHOWING COMPARISON	*similarly, likewise*
SHOWING RESULT OR SUMMARY	*therefore, thus, consequently*
SHOWING TIME	*next, then, meanwhile, finally, subsequently*
SHOWING EMPHASIS	*indeed, certainly*

INSTRUCTOR'S NOTES

Descriptive adverbs can show levels of intensity, usually by adding *more* (or *less*) and *most* (or *least*): *more happily, least clearly.*

WHERE TO FIND INFORMATION RELATED TO ADVERBS

Well and *good*	12d
Badly and *bad*	12d
Punctuation with conjunctive adverbs	24f, 25c

EXERCISE 4

Underline all adverbs.

EXAMPLE   Niagara Falls is eroding <u>rapidly.</u>

1. The falls are already 12,000 years old.
2. Erosion has steadily destroyed seven miles of land.
3. Not less than one foot of land disappears annually.
4. In about 35,000 years, the falls will likely merge with Lake Erie, which is now twenty miles away.
5. Recently, the rate of erosion has diminished very slightly, as water has been diverted to hydroelectric plants.

ANSWERS: EXERCISE 4

1. already
2. steadily
3. Not less than, annually
4. about, likely, now, away
5. Recently, very slightly

6g
Recognize prepositions.

Prepositions function with other words, in **prepositional phrases.** A prepositional phrase always has a preposition and a noun or pronoun object. It may contain modifying words too. Prepositional phrases often set out relationships in time or space: *in April, under the orange umbrella.*

In the fall, we will hear a concert **by our favorite tenor.**

WHERE TO FIND INFORMATION RELATED TO PREPOSITIONS

Using pronouns as objects: *me, him, whom,* etc.	9b–9h
Recognizing and revising sentence-fragment phrases	13
Placing phrases carefully	15b, 15c
Punctuating introductory phrases	24b
Punctuating nonrestrictive phrases	24e

149

EXPLETIVES (6J)

These two amusing essays make clear the differences between two kinds of expletives.

There, There

by WILLIAM SAFIRE

"There's no *there* there" was Gertrude Stein's classic slander of the city of Oakland, Calif. That was the last time a sentence was started successfully with a pronominal, impersonal *there*.

There is an inclination among weak writers to use *there* at the beginning of sentences. Look at the slow-starting agglomeration of words in the previous sen-

Continued on p. 151.

ANSWERS: EXERCISE 5

1. The first major construction job to employ Mohawks was a bridge (across) the St. Lawrence River (in) Canada.
2. Because Mohawks (from) the Caughnawaga reservation worked skillfully (at) huge heights, builders (in) the area hired them (for) additional projects.
3. They did their most famous work (during) the New York City building boom (of) the 1920s and 1930s.
4. They traveled (by) subway (from) their homes (in) Brooklyn to work (on) the Empire State Building and Rockefeller Center.
5. Probably thousands of Mohawks have worked (on) projects (in) many North American cities (over) the years.

COMMON PREPOSITIONS

about	concerning	onto
above	despite	on top of
according to	down	out
across	during	out of
after	except	outside
against	except for	over
along	excepting	past
along with	for	regarding
among	from	round
apart from	in	since
around	in addition to	through
as	in back of	throughout
as for	in case of	till
at	in front of	to
because of	in place of	toward
before	inside	under
behind	in spite of	underneath
below	instead of	unlike
beneath	into	until
beside	like	up
between	near	upon
beyond	next	up to
but	of	with
by	off	within
by means of	on	without

EXERCISE 5

Circle the prepositions and underline the prepositional phrases.

EXAMPLE   Much (of) New York City's famous skyline was built (by) Mohawk Indians.

1. The first major construction job to employ Mohawks was a bridge across the St. Lawrence River in Canada.
2. Because Mohawks from the Caughnawaga reservation worked skillfully at great heights, builders in the area hired them for additional projects.
3. They did their most famous work during the New York City building boom of the 1920s and 1930s.
4. They traveled by subway from their homes in Brooklyn to work on the Empire State Building and Rockefeller Center.
5. Probably thousands of Mohawks have worked on projects in many North American cities over the years.

150

6h

Recognize conjunctions.

A **conjunction** connects words, phrases°, or clauses°. **Coordinating conjunctions** join two or more grammatically equivalent structures.

COORDINATING CONJUNCTIONS
and   nor   so
but   or   yet
for

And, but, and *or* can join structures of any kind: two or more nouns, pronouns, verbs, adjectives, adverbs, phrases, or clauses. As a coordinating conjuction, *yet* can do the same.

Oregon and **Washington** are north of California. [nouns]

We **hike** and **camp** there every summer. [verbs]

The air is **fresh** and **clean.** [adjectives]

I love the outdoors, and **my family does too.** [independent clauses]

As coordinating conjunctions, *for* and *so* can connect only independent clauses.

My vacation is in May, so **we will go camping then.** [independent clauses]

We will take warm clothing, for **the outdoors will be cold.** [independent clauses]

Correlative conjunctions function in pairs, joining equivalent grammatical structures.

CORRELATIVE CONJUNCTIONS
both . . . and
either . . . or
neither . . . nor
not only . . . but (also)
whether . . . or

Both English **and** Spanish are spoken in many homes in the United States.

Subordinating conjunctions begin certain dependent (adverb) clauses°.

tence: it's a wet noodle of a sentence, putting the reader to sleep before coming to life with the word *weak.* Compare that "pronominal there" pap to this vigorous alterntive: "Weak writers are inclined to use *there* at the beginning of sentences."

Ah, you say, what about Shakespeare's "There is a tide in the affairs of men. . . ."? Face it: even the Bard had his bad days. If he had a chance, Shakespeare would pick up the phone and say: "Hello, Rewrite? I want to change Brutus's line that begins *There is a tide* to *A tide exists. . . .* No, hold on—make that *Great tides appear. . . .* Yes, same iambic pentameter, and putting the noun up closer to the front gives it a little zing. *There is* is a weak way to start any speech."

Rewrite would say: "But how about the *there* in Hamlet's 'Ay, there's the rub!' That *there* sounds pretty strong to me."

Shakespeare would then patiently point out to Rewrite that *there,* when meaning a place or an intensifier for *that,* is a powerful word. (So *there!*) Moreover, when used to mean "thither" or "yon" (as in "Cassius over there has a lean and hungry look"), *there* has its place. And when meant as "at or to that point," it serves a real purpose. (What is the point of this piece? I'm getting there.) But when used in writing, as a mere "function" word for writers reluctant to bite into the subject without first fiddling around, *there* is a sign of weakness, irresolution and pusillanimity. (Brutus was, deep down, weak; maybe Shakespeare was sending a signal. O.K., on that basis, leave the *there is* bit in.)

The linking verb that follows the lazy writer's pronominal impersonal is also weak; sentences that start *There is* stagger to the starting line. Compare the wimpish *There are a couple of reasons I like to hide behind 'there is.' . . .* to the forceful *The reasons I reject 'there is' include. . . .*

Continued on p. 152.

151

EXPLETIVES (CONT.)
A Taxi Bill of Rights
by FRED M. HECHINGER

The first thing I saw on entering the taxi was a large sign, "No Smoking." The second thing was the driver lighting up. Then he turned on the radio, full blast.

A few days later, having lucked upon a taxi after a performance at Lincoln Center, we had not yet settled down when the driver, a formidable woman, announced that she was going to smoke and if we didn't like it we had better get out. Demoralized by the long wait for a cab, we chose to suffer in silence. But that was a vain hope. The misanthrope at the wheel gave us a shrieking, profanity-packed account of that [expletive deleted] female passenger she had picked up at the airport who threatened to report her if she failed to put out her cigarette.

Finally our driver's attention was mercifully diverted by a cabbie occupying the part of the street on which she had set her heart. More expletives deleted. For the remainder of the ride, she proved she could screech her brakes as well as her speech.

All this raises a modest question about the relationship between New York's cab drivers and their passengers. Let statesmen ponder reforms on a grand scale; I cannot expect any mayor to eradicate the tyranny of the taxicab medallions or even to find the ones misplaced at the Taxi Commission. I suggest only a slight reform, perhaps enforceable with suitable withholding of the tip. Require a clear sign outside each cab that reads "Smoking" or "No Smoking." And perhaps, if it will not offend the fragile psyches of the drivers, a second sign: "Silent Car" or "Disco on Wheels."

SUBORDINATING CONJUNCTIONS

after	so that
although	though
as	unless
because	until
before	when
even though	where
if	whether
once	while
since	

Because the floods eroded the shore, the foundations of many buildings along the coast have been weakened.

WHERE TO FIND INFORMATION RELATED TO CONJUNCTIONS

Using commas with coordinating conjunctions	24a
Punctuating independent clauses linked by coordinating conjunctions	24a, 25b
Punctuating clauses that start with subordinating conjunctions	24b-1
Punctuating series	24c, 25d
Using semicolons with coordinating conjunctions	25b
Using the right coordinating conjunction	p. 317

■‖ 6i
Recognize interjections.

An **interjection** is a word or expression that conveys surprise or another strong emotion. Alone, an interjection is usually punctuated with an exclamation point. As part of a sentence, an interjection is set off with a comma (or commas). In academic writing, use interjections sparingly, if at all.

> Alas!
> Hooray! I got the promotion.
> Oh, they are exasperating.

■‖ 6j
Recognize expletives.

An **expletive** is not a part of speech, but the term describes a function of the words *there* and *it*. As expletives, *there* and *it* combine with a form of the verb *be* to postpone the subject of a sentence. Used this way, *there* and *it* have no meaning of their own.

There will be a new dean of students next term.
It is the trustees' job to interview final candidates.

Expletives are usually wordy and weak. See 16a-1 for advice on how to revise expletives for conciseness.

The word *expletive* also refers to an oath or exclamation. When you see "Expletive deleted," you can be sure that the words omitted were neither *it* nor *there*.

EXERCISE 6

Identify the part of speech of each word in italics. Choose from noun, pronoun, verb, adjective, adverb, preposition, coordinating conjunction, and subordinating conjunction.

One[1] of the most devastating *natural*[2] *disasters*[3] *of*[4] recorded history *began*[5] on April 5, 1815, *when*[6] Mount Tambora, located *in*[7] present-day Indonesia, erupted. The *volcano*[8] blew off the top 4,000 feet of the mountain, creating a seven-mile-wide crater. Twelve thousand people *were killed*[9] *immediately*,[10] *and*[11] 80,000 died *later*[12] of starvation because the ash *from*[13] the volcano *destroyed*[14] farmland. The *blast*,[15] eighty times stronger than that of Mount St. Helens, was heard over 900 miles away. The cloud of *volcanic*[16] ash *circled*[17] the globe, reaching North America the following summer. The cloud *was*[18] *so*[19] thick that even the sun's rays could not penetrate *it*.[20] *Freezing*[21] temperatures and snow continued through the *entire*[22] summer, resulting in crop failures and death.

ANSWERS: EXERCISE 6

Instructors can require students to identify the part of speech of any word in this paragraph, in addition to those with superscript numbers.

1. pronoun
2. adjective
3. noun
4. preposition
5. verb
6. subordinating conj.
7. preposition
8. noun
9. verb
10. adverb
11. coordinating conj.
12. adverb
13. preposition
14. verb
15. noun
16. adjective
17. verb
18. verb
19. adverb
20. pronoun
21. adjective
22. adjective

7

STRUCTURES OF THE SENTENCE

To understand the art of writing, writers often observe how sentences are formed. Although an infinite variety of sentences can be composed, all sentences share a basic structure. This chapter presents the basic structure and explains each of the parts.

The sentence has several definitions, each of which views it from a different perspective. On its most mechanical level, a sentence starts with a capital letter and finishes with a period, question mark, or exclamation point. A sentence can be defined according to its purpose. Most sentences are **declarative;** they make a statement: *Sky diving is dangerous.* Some sentences are **interrogative;** they ask a question: *Is sky diving dangerous?* Some sentences are **imperative;** they give a command: *Be careful.* Some sentences are **exclamatory:** *How I love sky diving!* Grammatically, a sentence contains an independent clause, a group of words that can stand alone as an independent unit: *Sky diving is dangerous.* Sometimes a sentence is described as a "complete thought," but the concept of "complete" is too subjective to be reliable.

The most practical way for you to begin a study of the sentence is to consider its structure.

154

7a

Recognize subjects and predicates.

A sentence consists of two basic parts: a subject and a predicate.

1

Recognize subjects.

The **simple subject** is the word or group of words that acts, is described, or is acted upon.

> The **telephone** rang. [Simple subject, *telephone,* acts.]
>
> The **telephone** is red. [Simple subject, *telephone,* is described.]
>
> The **telephone** was being connected. [Simple subject, *telephone,* is acted upon.]

The **complete subject** is the simple subject and its modifiers—all the words that describe or limit it.

SENTENCE I

THE SENTENCE

COMPLETE SUBJECT	+	COMPLETE PREDICATE
The red telephone		rang.

↑
SIMPLE SUBJECT

> The **lawyer** listened. [simple subject = *lawyer*]
>
> **The wise lawyer** listened. [complete subject = *the wise lawyer*]

A subject can be **compound,** consisting of two or more nouns or pronouns and their modifiers.

SENTENCE II

THE SENTENCE

COMPLETE SUBJECT	+	COMPLETE PREDICATE
The telephone and the doorbell		rang.

COMPOUND SUBJECT

> **The lawyer and her client** met.

INSTRUCTOR'S NOTES

WORD HISTORY

Sentence comes from the Latin *sententia,* a way of thinking, an opinion, a sentiment. In Latin, *sententia* also referred to a formally expressed opinion or a pithy saying, such as a maxim or aphorism, and *sentence* was used in this way by the fourteenth century. The more limited use of *sentence* to describe a grammatically complete passage began in the fifteenth century.

COORDINATED RESOURCES

Alternate examples and exercises for this chapter are available in the *S & S Workbook for Writers,* Gordon and Troyka.

Transparency masters are available for many of the screened charts in this chapter.

Students can practice and test their knowledge of terms, key concepts, and applications of material in this chapter by using the *Study Guide to the S & S Handbook for Writers,* West.

‖ 2
Recognize predicates.

The **predicate** is the part of the sentence that contains the verb. The predicate tells what the subject is doing or experiencing or what is being done to the subject.

The telephone **rang.** [*Rang* tells us what the subject, *telephone,* did.]

The telephone **is** red. [*Is* tells what the subject experiences—being red.]

The telephone **was** being connected. [*Was being connected* tells what was being done to the subject.]

The **simple predicate** contains only the verb. The **complete predicate** contains the verb and its modifiers as well as any objects° or complements° and their modifiers.

SENTENCE III

THE SENTENCE

COMPLETE SUBJECT	+	COMPLETE PREDICATE
The red telephone		rang loudly.
SIMPLE SUBJECT		SIMPLE PREDICATE (VERB)

The lawyer **listened.** [simple predicate = *listened*]

The lawyer **listened carefully.** [complete predicate = *listened carefully*]

A predicate can be **compound,** consisting of two or more verbs and any objects or modifiers.

SENTENCE IV

THE SENTENCE

COMPLETE SUBJECT	+	COMPLETE PREDICATE
The red telephone		rang loudly and startled everyone
		COMPOUND PREDICATE

EXERCISE 1

Use a slash to separate the complete subject from the complete predicate.

EXAMPLE   Ordinary water / is essential for all life.

1. Water evaporates constantly.
2. Evaporation alternates with condensation in the water cycle.
3. Water vapor enters the air by evaporation from water surfaces, such as the oceans.
4. Oceans and other bodies of water cover more than seventy percent of our planet.
5. Molecules of water in the air condense and fall as rain or snow.

EXERCISE 2

Draw a single line under the complete subject and a double line under the complete predicate. Circle the verbs.

EXAMPLE   Rain and snow (are) visible stages in a mostly invisible process.

1. The water passes through the ground to evaporation sites.
2. Water also enters the air from the transpiration of plants.
3. In transpiration, water evaporates from leaf surfaces and passes out through leaf openings called *stomata*.
4. Evaporation and transpiration purify the water of its salts.
5. Only water molecules pass into the air.

■‖ 7b

Recognize objects.

Objects occur in the predicate of a sentence.

‖ 1

Recognize direct objects.

A **direct object** receives the action—completes the meaning—of a transitive verb (see 8d).

SENTENCE V		
THE SENTENCE		
COMPLETE SUBJECT	**+**	**COMPLETE PREDICATE**
The caller		offered money.
		↑ ↑
		VERB DIRECT OBJECT

ANSWERS: EXERCISE 1

1. Water / evaporates constantly.
2. Evaporation / alternates with condensation in the water cycle.
3. Water vapor / enters the air from water surfaces, such as the oceans.
4. Oceans and other bodies of water / cover more than seventy percent of our planet.
5. Molecules of water in the air / condense and fall as rain or snow.

ANSWERS: EXERCISE 2

1. The water passes through the ground to evaporation sites.
2. Water also enters the air from the transpiration of plants.
3. In transpiration, water evaporates from leaf surfaces and passes out through leaf "cells" known as *stomata*.
4. Evaporation and transpiration purify the water of its salts.
5. Only water molecules pass into the air.

157

To find a direct object, make up a *whom?* or *what?* question about the verb. The caller offered what? *Money.*

2
Recognize indirect objects.

An **indirect object** answers a *to whom?* or *for whom?* question about the verb.

ANSWERS: EXERCISE 3
1. The government needed the gardeners to serve as soldiers.
2. The sheep attracted tourists.
3. Mrs. Wilson gave the Red Cross money from the sale of their wool.
4. More recently, the U.S. Army gave goats the task of trimming the lawns at ammunition dumps.
5. If you tell people this fact, they may not believe you.

EXERCISE 3
Draw a single line under all direct objects and a double line under all indirect objects.

EXAMPLE   President Woodrow Wilson bought the White House gardeners sheep to serve as lawnmowers during World War I.

1. The government needed the gardeners to serve as soldiers.
2. The sheep attracted tourists.
3. Mrs. Wilson gave the Red Cross money from the sale of their wool.
4. More recently, the U.S. Army gave goats the task of trimming the lawns at ammunition dumps.
5. If you tell people this fact, they may not believe you.

▮‖ 7c
Recognize complements, modifiers, and appositives.

1
Recognize complements.

A **complement** occurs in the predicate of a sentence. It renames or describes a subject or an object.

A **subject complement** is a noun or adjective that follows a **linking verb.** (Linking verbs—such as *was* and *seems*—operate like an equal sign, signaling that the subject is being renamed or described.)

The caller was **a sophomore** [noun *sophomore* = subject complement]

The student seemed **nervous.** [adjective *nervous* = subject complement]

Some systems of grammar use the term **predicate nominative** for a noun used as a subject complement and the term **predicate adjective** for an adjective used as a subject complement.

An **object complement** is a noun or an adjective that immediately follows a direct object and either describes or renames it.

The student called himself **a pawn.** [noun *pawn* = object complement renaming *student*]

The student considered the situation **hopeless.** [adjective *hopeless* = object complement describing *student*]

159

ANSWERS: EXERCISE 4
1. native (subject complement)
2. member (subject complement)
3. three feet tall, fat, and clumsy (subject complements)
4. incapable (subject complement)
5. gone (subject complement)
6. a myth (object complement)

EXERCISE 4

Underline all complements and identify each as a subject complement or an object complement.

EXAMPLE   The dodo is <u>extinct</u>. (subject complement)

1. The dodo was a native of Mauritius, an island in the Indian Ocean.
2. It was a member of the dove family.
3. It was three feet tall, fat, and clumsy.
4. The dodo was incapable of flight or fight.
5. By 1681, all the dodos were gone.
6. In the eighteenth century, many people thought the dodo a myth.

2
Recognize modifiers.

Modifiers are words or groups of words that describe other words. There are two basic kinds of modifiers, adjectives and adverbs.

Adjectives modify only nouns or words acting as nouns, such as pronouns, noun phrases°, or relative clauses°. Adjectives can appear in the subject or the predicate of a sentence.

> **SENTENCE IX**
>
> **THE SENTENCE**
>
> **COMPLETE SUBJECT**   +   **COMPLETE PREDICATE**
>
> The red telephone   rang.
>   ↑
>   ADJECTIVE

The **large red** telephone rang. [adjectives *large* and *red* modifying the noun *telephone*]

The **worried** student needed a **good** lawyer. [adjective *worried* modifying the noun *student;* adjective *good* modifying the noun *lawyer*]

Adverbs modify verbs, adjectives, other adverbs, and independent clauses°. They can appear in the subject or the predicate of a sentence.

160

The lawyer answered **quickly.** [adverb *quickly* modifying the verb *answered*]

The student was **extremely** upset. [adverb *extremely* modifying adjective *upset*]

The student spoke **very quickly.** [adverb *very* modifying the adverb *quickly*]

Therefore, the lawyer spoke quietly. [adverb *therefore* modifying the independent clause *the lawyer spoke quietly*]

3
Recognize appositives.

An **appositive** is a word (or words) that renames a noun or words functioning as a noun. ▌ PUNCTUATION ALERT: Use a comma to separate a nonrestrictive appositive° from what it renames. ▌

The student's **story, a tale of broken promises,** was complicated. [*A tale of broken promises* renames the noun *story.*]

EXTRA EXERCISE A

Fill in the blanks with appropriate subject or object complements. Then on the numbered line below the exercise, indicate if you added a subject complement (SC) or an object complement (OC) and identify each as a noun or an adjective.

EXAMPLE

They elected her *treasurer.* [OC, noun]
1. The pickpocket was _____. [_____]
2. He seemed _____. [_____]
3. The judge called him _____. [_____]
4. The pickpocket considered himself _____. [_____]
5. The pickpocket's name was _____. [_____]

ANSWERS: EXTRA EXERCISE A

Answers will vary. Possibilities are:
1. The pickpocket was *caught.* [SC, adjective]
2. He seemed *poor.* [SC, adjective]
3. The judge called him *a tramp.* [OC, noun]
4. He considered himself *a free spirit.* [OC, noun]
5. The pickpocket's name was *Joe.* [SC, noun]

> SENTENCE XII
>
> ### THE SENTENCE
>
> COMPLETE SUBJECT   +   COMPLETE PREDICATE
>
> The student   asked to speak to his lawyer, Ms. Smythe.
>
>
> APPOSITIVE

The lawyer consulted an **expert, her law professor.** [*Her law professor* renames the noun *expert*.]

EXERCISE 5

Identify whether each italicized word or group of words is an adjective, adverb, or appositive.

EXAMPLE   William Bligh, *Captain of the H.M.S. Bounty* (appositive), was involved in a total of *three* (adjective) mutinies.

In 1789, *Master's Mate*[1] Fletcher Christian took command and set Bligh and *eighteen*[2] *loyal*[3] crewmen adrift in an *open*[4] boat. Bligh sailed 3,618 miles in *six*[5] weeks, *miraculously*[6] arriving *safely*[7] in the East Indies. In 1797, Bligh, *now commander of the H.M.S. Director,*[8] was involved in the mutiny of the *whole*[9] fleet at The Nore, England. While governor of New South Wales, Australia, Bligh took some unpopular measures, *punishing drunkenness and limiting liquor sales.*[10] *These*[11] actions set off the Rum Rebellion, and Bligh was *again*[12] held in custody by mutineers.

■‖ 7d
Recognize phrases.

A **phrase** is a group of related words that does not contain a subject or a predicate. A phrase cannot stand alone as an independent unit. Phrases function as parts of speech.

A **noun phrase** functions as noun in a sentence.

The **modern population census** dates back to the **seventeenth century.**

A **verb phrase** functions as a verb in a sentence.

Two military censuses **are mentioned** in the Bible.

ANSWERS: EXERCISE 5

1. adjective	7. adverb
2. adjective	8. appositive
3. adjective	9. adjective
4. adjective	10. appositive
5. adjective	11. adjective
6. adverb	12. adverb

TEACHING TIP

Students sometimes feel that phrases are peculiar constructions invented by the writers of grammar books. As an antidote to this misconception, you might find it useful to reproduce and distribute copies of a newspaper article on a popular subject (e.g., Dear Abby or a sports column). Ask the students to identify noun phrases, verb phrases, and prepositional phrases. As absolute phrases rarely occur in informal writing, it is perhaps best to omit them from this assignment. Students will be amazed at how often phrases appear in "real" writing. Class discussion might next cover the functions of the noun phrases and prepositional phrases (subject, object, complement, adjective, adverb).

162

The Romans **had been conducting** censuses every five years to establish tax liabilities.

A **prepositional phrase,** which always starts with a preposition, functions as an adjective or an adverb.

After the collapse **of Rome,** the practice was discontinued **until modern times.**

William the Conqueror conducted a census **of landowners in newly conquered England in 1086.** [three prepositional phrases in a row]

An **absolute phrase** consists of a subject and a participle°. It functions as a modifier of the entire sentence to which it is attached.

Census-taking being the fashion, Quebec and Nova Scotia took sixteen counts between 1665 and 1754.

Eighteenth-century Sweden and Denmark had complete records of their populations, **each adult and child having been accounted for.**

EXERCISE 6

Identify whether each italicized word or group of words is a noun phrase, verb phrase, prepositional phrase, or absolute phrase.

PREPOSITIONAL PRHASE

EXAMPLE   In animals, eighty to ninety percent   *of the food*   digested

VERB PHRASE

is used   to supply energy.

Many specific organic and inorganic substances[1] are necessary *for the growth and maintenance*[2] *of the body.*[3] Nutritional needs vary from species to species, but *the same general principles*[4] apply *in all cases.*[5] *Body tissue constantly being rebuilt,*[6] proteins, vitamins, and minerals *are always needed.*[7] *The average adult human*[8] requires only 45 to 60 grams, 1½ to 2 ounces,[9] *of protein*[10] daily. Protein *is broken down*[11] *during digestion*[12] into *its amino acids,*[13] which *are used*[14] *by the body*[15] to provide the nourishment it needs.

A **verbal phrase** is a word group that contains a verbal. Verbals are infinitives°, past participles°, and present participles°. **Gerund phrases** function as nouns. A gerund is the *-ing* form of a verb—its present participle. **Infinitive phrases** function as nouns or modifiers. An infinitive is the simple form° of a verb, usually preceded by *to,* but not always.

EXTRA EXERCISE B

Label the italicized words and phrases as adjectives (ADJ) or adverbs (ADV).

EXAMPLE

The *record*[ADJ] score on the computer game Asteroids is over 30 million.
1. The game lasted *two* days.
2. People play over *20 billion* games at arcades every year.
3. That is a 49 percent increase *since 1980.*
4. *They spend about $5 billion a year* on video games.
5. *Before video games were invented,* people played pinball.
6. Pinball was *especially* popular in the 1930s.
7. The *first* big pinball success was Baffle Ball in 1930.
8. It was *soon* followed by Ballyhoo.
9. Flippers became a feature of pinball machines *for the first time* in 1947.
10. There was *one* problem.
11. In *some* places, players received money for winning.
12. *Many* people considered this gambling.
13. In 1942, New York City banned the game as a *corrupting* influence.
14. Pinball was declared legal there again only *a few years ago.*
Answers on p. 167.

ANSWERS: EXERCISE 6

1. noun phrase	9. noun phrase
2. prep. phrase	10. prep. phrase
3. prep. phrase	11. verb phrase
4. noun phrase	12. prep. phrase
5. prep. phrase	13. prep. phrase
6. absolute phrase	14. verb phrase
7. verb phrase	15. prep. phrase
8. noun phrase	

163

TEACHING TIP

To give students a sense of the range of uses for *-ing* words, you might hand out a list of *-ing* words and ask your students to use each in three different sentences: in one as a noun, in another as an adjective, and in a third as part of a verb phrase. Then you can collect the sentences and select 25 to 30 to reproduce and distribute. As an exercise or quiz, you can ask the students to identify each *-ing* word as a noun, an adjective, or part of a verb phrase. Often the author of a sentence is eager for others to get the identification correct and is therefore quite willing to explain the answer. You might use these *-ing* words or any others: (1) swimming, (2) painting, (3) flying, (4) reading, (5) cooking.

Here are some possible responses (the words appear first as nouns, then as adjectives, and finally as parts of verb phrases):

1. *Swimming* is fun. The *swimming* pool is crowded. She is *swimming* laps.
2. Oil *painting* requires an eye for detail. The *painting* equipment is in the shed. We will be *painting* the bedroom this weekend.
3. He likes *flying*. The *flying* squirrel leaped out of sight. Are you *flying* to Vancouver?
4. *Reading* is the basis of many other skills. The *reading* room at the library has comfortable chairs. What are you *reading*?
5. *Cooking* is a creative experience. The *cooking* class meets on Wednesday evenings. I am *cooking* something special for your birthday.

ANSWERS: EXERCISE 7

1. infinitive phrase
2. participial phrase
3. participial phrase
4. participial phrase
5. gerund phrase
6. infinitive phrase

In 1624, Virginia began **to count its citizens** in a census. [infinitive phrase = direct object]

The first U.S. census was conducted without **asking anyone's occupation, birthplace, marital status, or exact age.** [gerund phrase = object of preposition *without*]

Understanding the questions on a census is important. [gerund phrase = subject]

Participial phrases function as adjectives or adverbs. Participial phrases can be formed from a verb's present participle—its *-ing* form—as well as from its past participle—the *-ed* form of a regular verb.

> **Going from door to door,** census takers interview millions of people. [participial phrase = adjective modifying *census takers*]
>
> When I was a census taker, I listened **engrossed by people's answers.** [participial phrase = adverb modifying *listened*]

Telling the difference between a gerund phrase and a participial phrase using a present participle can be tricky because both use the *-ing* verb form. The key is to determine how the verbal phrase is functioning: a gerund phrase functions only as a noun, and a participial phrase functions only as a modifier.

> **Wanting to win the trivia contest** was an obsession. [gerund phrase]
>
> **Wanting to win the trivia contest,** Abby studied the faces of her opponents. [participial phrase]

EXERCISE 7

Identify whether each italicized verbal phrase is an infinitive phrase, a participial phrase, or a gerund phrase.

EXAMPLE   The body is not capable of *making vitamins*. (gerund phrase)

To function properly,[1] the human body must take in small amounts of vitamins. *Supplying important amino acids,*[2] vitamins are essential to human growth and natural functioning. *Used to power crucial reactions in humans,*[3] vitamins must be absorbed into the cells. On the other hand, green plants, *manufacturing all the vitamins they need,*[4] are not dependent upon absorbed vitamins. For humans, *eating a wide range of plant and animal foods*[5] is the best way *to ensure good health.*[6]

164

EXERCISE 8

Combine each set of sentences into a single sentence, converting one sentence in each set into a phrase. Choose from among noun phrases, verb phrases, prepositional phrases, absolute phrases, infinitive phrases, participial phrases, and gerund phrases. You can omit, add, or change words. Most sets can be combined in several equally correct ways, but be sure to check that your combined sentence makes sense.

EXAMPLE The word *chauvinism* comes from the name of Nicholas Chauvin, a retired French soldier. Chauvin was obsessed with Napoleon's greatness.

The word *chauvinism* comes from the name of Nicholas Chauvin, a retired French soldier obsessed with Napoleon's greatness.

1. Chauvin was wounded in battle at least seventeen times. When he retired he received a medal, a ceremonial sword, and a pension of about $40.
2. Chauvin turned away from bitterness. He became a champion of Napoleon and France.
3. Napoleon was defeated. Chauvin became even more fanatical in his support.
4. Word of his hero worship spread beyond his village. Chauvin was used as a character in a comedy.
5. Other playwrights also used Chauvin as a character. That made his name synonymous with excessive dedication to one's country.
6. Many other words started out as someone's name. These include *sandwich* and *bloomer*.
7. Other words enter the language in other ways. Some words were originally slang. Some words have actually been voted into existence.
8. The number *googol* is a one followed by a hundred zeroes. Milton Sirotta made up the word when he was nine years old.
9. His mathematician uncle used the word in a book in 1940. It caught on.

ANSWERS: EXERCISE 8

Answers may vary. For the instructor's information, each type of clause is identified. The example sentence is a participial phrase.

1. *Wounded in battle at least seventeen times,* Chauvin received a medal, a ceremonial sword, and a pension of about $40 when he retired. (participial phrase)
2. Chauvin turned away from bitterness *to champion Napoleon and France.* (infinitive phrase)
3. *Napoleon having been defeated,* Chauvin became even more fanatical in his support. (absolute phrase)
4. *Word of his hero worship having spread beyond his village,* Chauvin was used as a character in a comedy. (participial phrase)
5. *Other playwrights' using Chauvin as a character* soon made his name synonymous with excessive dedication to one's country. (gerund phrase)
6. Many other words, *including sandwich and bloomer,* started out as someone's name. (noun phrase)
7. Other words enter the language *from slang* or by being voted *into existence.* (two prepositional phrases)
8. The number *googol, a word made up by Milton Sirotta when he was nine years old,* is a one followed by a hundred zeroes. (noun phrase)
9. *Used in a book in 1940 by his mathematician uncle,* the word caught on. (participial phrase)

■‖ 7e

Recognize clauses.

A **clause** is a group of words that contains a subject and a predicate. Clauses are divided into two categories: **independent clauses** (also known as **main clauses**) and **dependent clauses** (also known as **subordinate clauses**).

A HUMOROUS NOTE

Each year the number of children coming to the mall to see Santa Claus grew larger, so the store owners decided to hire additional Santas and station them around the mall. The most experienced Santa was in charge. He referred to the trainees as his "Subordinate Clauses."

1

Recognize independent clauses.

An **independent** (or **main**) **clause** contains a subject and a predicate. It can stand alone as a sentence because it is an independent grammatical unit.

SENTENCE XIII

THE SENTENCE

INDEPENDENT CLAUSE

COMPLETE SUBJECT	+	COMPLETE PREDICATE
The telephone		rang.

QUOTATION ABOUT WRITING

A *dependent clause* is like a dependent child: incapable of standing on its own but able to cause a lot of trouble.

—WILLIAM SAFIRE, "About Language"

2

Recognize dependent clauses.

A **dependent clause** contains a subject and a predicate and usually starts with a word that makes the clause unable to stand alone as a sentence. A dependent clause must be joined to an independent clause°.

Some dependent clauses start with **subordinating conjunctions.** Each subordinating conjunction implies a relationship

---

SUBORDINATING CONJUNCTIONS AND THE RELATIONSHIPS THEY IMPLY

TIME	after, before, once, since, until, when, whenever, while
REASON OR CAUSE	as, because
RESULT OR EFFECT	in order that, so, so that, that
CONDITION	if, even if, provided that, unless
CONCESSION	although, even though, though, whether
LOCATION	where, wherever
CHOICE	rather than, than, whether

166

between the meaning in the dependent clause and the meaning in the independent clause.

Clauses that start with subordinating conjunctions function as adverbs. **Adverb clauses** modify verbs, adjectives, other adverbs, and entire independent clauses. Adverb clauses may appear in different parts of sentences, but they always begin with subordinating conjunctions. They usually answer some question about the independent clause: *how? why? when?* or *under what conditions?*

> **If the bond issue passes,** the city will install sewers. [The adverb clause modifies the verb *install;* it explains "under what conditions."]
>
> They are drawing up plans as quickly **as they can.** [The adverb clause modifies the adverb *quickly;* it explains "how."]
>
> The homeowners feel happier **because they know the flooding will soon be better controlled.** [The adverb clause modifies the adjective *happier;* it explains "why."]

▍ PUNCTUATION ALERT: When an adverb clause comes before its independent clause, separate the clauses with a comma. ▍

> **After gold was discovered at Sutter's Mill,** miners flocked to California.

Most **adjective clauses** start with relative pronouns or *when, where,* or *why.* Relative pronouns include *who, that, which, whom, whose, whoever, whomever, whichever, what,* and *whatever.* Another name for these clauses is **relative clauses.**

ANSWERS: EXTRA EXERCISE B

1. adjective	8. adverb
2. adjective	9. adverb
3. adverb	10. adjective
4. adverb	11. adjective
5. adverb	12. adjective
6. adverb	13. adjective
7. adjective	14. adverb

167

INSTRUCTOR'S NOTES

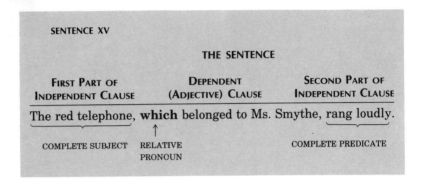

The word starting an adjective clause refers to something—a specific antecedent°—in the independent clause.

> The car **that Jack bought** is practical. [The adjective clause describes the noun *car; that* refers to *car.*]
>
> The day **when I can buy my own car** is getting closer. [The adjective clause modifies the noun *day; when* refers to *day.*]

▌ USAGE ALERT: Use *who, whom, whoever, whomever,* and *whose* when the antecedent is a person or a special, intelligent animal. Use *which* or *that* when the antecedent is a thing or an animal. Of *which* and *that,* use *that* or *which* for restrictive° adjective clauses and *which* for nonrestrictive° ones. ▌

> The Smythes, **who collect cars,** are wealthy.
>
> The Cadillac, **which is very expensive,** is not as costly as some imported cars.
>
> The place **where I will look for my first car** is the want ads.

▌ PUNCTUATION ALERT: When an adjective clause is nonrestrictive°, use commas to separate it from the independent clause. ▌

Sometimes, *that* can be omitted from a sentence. For purposes of grammatical analysis, however, the omitted *that* is considered to be implied and therefore present.

> The car [that] **I buy** will have to get good mileage.
>
> The review [that] **he wrote** praised the car's performance well.

EXERCISE 9
Underline the dependent clauses. Write (ADJ) at the end of adjective clauses and (ADV) at the end of adverb clauses.

168

EXAMPLE The scientists <u>who discovered (disease carrying bacteria</u> (ADJ) did so <u>in the second half of the nineteenth century.</u>(ADV)

1. The bacteria that led to typhoid fever and cholera were spread when water was contaminated by solid human waste.
2. Sewers were built so that water supplies could be protected.
3. Waste water pipes from the sewers were connected to storm drainage systems, which took the waste to distant rivers.
4. The people who constructed these systems believed this practice to be safe because a river can purify itself.
5. They were wrong because the rivers cannot renew themselves as quickly as we can pollute them.

EXERCISE 10

Combine each set of sentences into a single sentence by converting some sentences into adjective or adverb clauses. You can add, omit, or change a few words, but do not make major changes. Most sets can be combined in several equally correct ways, but be sure to check that your combined sentences communicate a clear message.

EXAMPLE The detailed workings of sewage treatment plants vary. The basic steps of the operation are the same in most plants.

Although the detailed workings of sewage treatment plants vary, the basic steps of the operation are the same in most plants.

1. A first treatment takes out suspended solids. Second and third treatments remove small particles.
2. Early in the first treatment waste water is screened through a row of iron bars set one inch apart. Large material, such as rags and wood, is filtered immediately.
3. This material must be removed. It could damage the more delicate machinery used later in the process.
4. The water is slowed down. Sand and other suspended particles fall to the bottom. They are removed and used for landfill.
5. The water is allowed to become almost still in the second treatment. Particles settle to the bottom. Oil gathers on top.
6. Chemicals are added at this point. The chemicals cause particles to clump. Clumped particles settle more rapidly.
7. This settled material, along with oil, is considered raw sludge. The settled material is mechanically removed.

ANSWERS: EXERCISE 9

1. The bacteria *that led to typhoid fever and cholera*^{ADJ} were spread *when water was contaminated by solid human waste*^{ADV}.
2. Sewers were built *so that water supplies could be protected*^{ADV}.
3. Waste water pipes from the sewers were connected to storm drainage systems *which took the waste to distant rivers*^{ADJ}.
4. People *who constructed these systems*^{ADJ} believed this practice to be safe *because a river can purify itself*^{ADV}.
5. They were wrong *because the rivers cannot renew themselves*^{ADV} as quickly *as we can pollute them*^{ADV}.

ANSWERS: EXERCISE 10

Answers may vary from those shown here.

1. A first treatment takes out suspended solids while second and third treatments remove small particles.
2. Since early in the first treatment waste water is screened through a row of iron bars set one inch apart, large material, such as rags and wood, is filtered immediately.
3. This material must be removed because it could damage the more delicate machinery used later in the process.
4. As the water is slowed down, sand and other suspended particles fall to the bottom where they are removed and used for landfill.
5. When the water is allowed to become almost still in the second treatment, particles settle to the bottom while oil gathers on top.
6. Chemicals which cause particles to clump and settle more rapidly are added at this point.
7. This settled material, which, along with oil, is considered raw sludge, is mechanically removed.

169

ANSWERS: Ex. 10 (cont.)

8. The third treatment is called "biological treatment" because it uses organisms to eliminate remaining organic contaminants by eating them.

9. It is important to realize that no method of treatment can remove all dissolved contaminants, which include fertilizer chemicals, phosphates from detergents, heavy metals, and synthetic compounds.

8. The third treatment is called the "biological treatment." It uses organisms to eliminate remaining organic contaminants by eating them.

9. No method of treatment can remove all dissolved contaminants. The contaminants include fertilizer chemicals, phosphates from detergents, heavy metals, and synthetic compounds. This is important to realize.

Noun clauses function as subjects°, objects°, or complements°. Noun clauses begin with many of the same words as adjective clauses: *that, who, which,* and their derivatives, as well as *when, where, whether, why,* or *how.* Noun clauses do not *modify.* They replace a noun with a clause.

> **Promises** are not always dependable. [noun]
>
> **What politicians promise** is not always dependable. [noun clause]
>
> The electorate often cannot figure out the **truth.** [noun]
>
> The electorate often cannot know **what the truth is.** [noun clause]

Because they start with similar words, it is easy to confuse noun clauses and adjective clauses. A noun clause *is* a subject, object, or complement. An adjective clause *modifies* a subject, object, or complement. The word at the start of an adjective clause has a specific antecedent elsewhere in the sentence. The word that starts a noun clause does not.

> Politicians understand **whom they must please.** [noun clause = direct object]
>
> Politicians **who make promises** sometimes fail to keep them. [adjective clause modifying *politicians*]

Elliptical clauses are grammatically incomplete for the deliberate purpose of concise prose. The elliptical clause gets its name from the word *ellipsis,* meaning "omission." An elliptical clause delivers its meaning only if the missing elements can be filled in from context. The relative pronouns *that, which,* or *whom* in adjective clauses, the subject and verb in adverb clauses, and the second half of a comparison are common omissions.

> Engineering is one of the majors [**that**] **she considered.** [relative pronoun omitted]
>
> **After [he was granted]** a retrial, he was released. [subject and verb omitted]
>
> Broiled fish tastes better **than boiled fish [tastes].** [second half of the comparison omitted]

TEACHING TIP
Elliptical clauses: To enhance students' appreciation of their options, you might ask them whether they prefer the elliptical or full forms of the text's sentences—and why. Here are alternate examples to use also.
Living in Spain was one of the best experiences [that] Carol had during college. When [she was] living with a family in Spain, Carol started to feel like a native. Air travel is faster than sea [travel].

EXERCISE 11

Identify each italicized clause as an adjective clause, an adverb clause, a noun clause, or an elliptical clause.

EXAMPLE   No one knows *how the creative mind works.* (noun clause)

1. In 1964, a freighter was raised in Kuwait harbor *when Karl Kroyer filled the hull with 27 billion polystyrene balls.*
2. *Because lighter than water,* the balls made the ship float.
3. Kroyer, a Danish manufacturer, got his inspiration from an old comic book *in which Donald Duck raised a boat by filling it with Ping-Pong balls.*
4. Until 1959, the world's largest camera was the Mammoth, *which weighed 1400 pounds.*
5. Photographer George R. Lawrence built it for the Chicago and Alton Railway, *whose management wanted pictures of their luxury train, the Alton Limited.*
6. That train must have been very special *since a crew of fifteen was needed to operate the camera.*
7. The Paris Exposition was *where those 4½ by 8 foot pictures were first shown.*
8. In 1959, Rolls-Royce built a larger camera, *which weighed 30 tons.*
9. Which would you prefer to own, the camera by Rolls-Royce *or the car?*

ANSWERS: EXERCISE 11

1. adverb clause
2. elliptical clause
3. adjective clause
4. adjective clause
5. adjective clause
6. adverb clause
7. noun clause (*Note:* this functions as a complement)
8. adjective clause
9. elliptical clause

EXERCISE 12

Combine each of the following pairs of sentences using some of the subordinating conjunctions and relative pronouns from this list. Some pairs may be combined in a variety of ways. Create at least one elliptical clause. Subordinators may be used more than once, but try to use as many different ones as possible.

| which | because | of which | since | if |
| while | as | how | that | although |

EXAMPLE   Famine occurs. Insects or rodents destroy crops or stored food.

When insects or rodents destroy crops or stored food, famine occurs.

1. Destruction of crops has been a problem for ages. The human race has an equally long history of trying to eliminate pests.
2. The earliest pesticides were not very effective. The earliest pesticides included sulfur, lead, mercury, and arsenic.
3. We now realize something. These original pesticides are poisonous.
4. They accumulate in the soil. They can limit or stop plant growth.

ANSWERS: EXERCISE 12

Answers will vary somewhat; at least one elliptical is required by the directions.

1. While destruction of crops has been a problem for ages, the human race has an equally long history of trying to eliminate pests.
2. The earliest pesticides, which included sulfur, lead, mercury, and arsenic, were not very effective. (An elliptical alternative is: Not very effective, the earliest pesticides included sulfur, lead, mercury, and arsenic.)
3. We now realize that these original pesticides are poisonous. (An elliptical alternative is to drop *that.*)
4. If they accumulate in the soil, they can limit or stop plant growth.

INSTRUCTOR'S NOTES

5. Because some pests develop immunity to the chemicals, the pests are never completely destroyed.

6. Since the surviving pests reproduce quickly, passing on resistant genes, a new generation of resistant pests takes the place of those killed.

7. New pesticides are manufactured organic chemicals of which the most famous is DDT, dichlorodiphenyltrichloroethane.

8. No one thought about how DDT would contaminate and threaten the entire planet. (An elliptical alternative is to drop *about how.)*

TEACHING TIP
The class discussion of compound sentences may be a good time to review compounding of all sorts. A series of examples to show compound subjects, objects, verbs, adjectives, adverbs, phrases, and clauses may help your students see the compound sentence as the final step in a logical progression.

John F. Kennedy and Richard M. Nixon were the candidates in the 1960 presidential election. [compound subject] Kennedy won the election because of his popularity in *the South and the East.* [compound object of preposition] *Many people admired his energy and his*

5. Some pests develop immunity to the chemicals. The pests are never completely destroyed.

6. The surviving pests reproduce quickly, passing on resistant genes. A new generation of resistant pests takes the place of those killed.

7. New pesticides are manufactured organic chemicals. The most famous is DDT, dichlorodiphenyltrichloroethane.

8. No one thought about something. DDT would contaminate and threaten the entire planet.

▉ 7f
Recognize sentence types.

Sentences can be **simple, compound, complex,** and **compound-complex.**

1
Recognize simple sentences.

A **simple sentence** is composed of a single independent clause° with no dependent° clauses. It has one subject and one predicate (either or both may be compound). It can contain modifying words or phrases.

> Charlie Chaplin was born in London on April 16, 1889. He specialized in pantomime and became famous for his character "The Tramp."

2
Recognize compound sentences.

A **compound sentence** is composed of two or more independent clauses° joined by a coordinating conjunction *(and, but, for, or, nor, yet,* or *so.)* or a semicolon. Compound sentences operate according to principles of **coordination,** a technique of writing style discussed in Chapter 17. ▉ PUNCTUATION ALERT: Use a comma before any coordinating conjunction that connects two independent clauses. ▉

> His father died early, **and** his mother often had to spend time in mental hospitals.
> Chaplin lived in orphanages or boarding schools, **but** sometimes he left them to perform in theaters.

3
Recognize complex sentences.

A **complex sentence** is composed of one independent clause° and one or more dependent clauses°. Many complex sentences operate according to the principles of **subordination,** a technique of writing style discussed in Chapter 17. ▌ PUNCTUATION ALERT: Always use a comma after a dependent clause when it occurs before an independent clause. ▌

> **When times were bad,** Chaplin lived in the streets. [dependent clause starting *when;* independent clause starting *Chaplin*]
>
> **When Chaplin was performing with a troup which was touring the United States,** he was hired by Max Sennett, **who owned the Keystone Comedies.** [dependent clause starting *when;* dependent clause starting *which;* independent clause starting *he;* dependent clause starting *who*]

4
Recognize compound-complex sentences.

A **compound-complex sentence** joins a compound sentence and a complex sentence. It contains two or more independent clauses° and one or more dependent clause°. ▌ PUNCTUATION ALERT: (1) Use a comma before a coordinating conjunction that joins two independent clauses. (2) Use a comma after an adverb clause° that comes before an independent clause. (3) Always use commas to set off a nonrestrictive clause° from the rest of a sentence. ▌

> Chaplin's comedies were immediately successful, **and** his salaries were huge **because of the enormous popularity of his tramp character, who was famous for his tiny mustache, baggy trousers, big shoes, and trick derby.** [independent clause starting *Chaplin's;* independent clause starting *his salaries;* dependent clause starting *because;* dependent clause starting *who*]
>
> **Once studios could no longer afford him,** Chaplin co-founded United Artists, **and** then he was able to produce and distribute his own films. [dependent clause starting *Once;* independent clause starting *Chaplin;* independent clause starting *then he was able*]

wholesomeness. [compound object] *He made* respected cabinet appointments *and sponsored* far-sighted legislation. [compound verb] The first months of his administration were *smooth-running and successful.* [compound adjectives] *However, the period quickly and unexpectedly* came to an end. [compound adverbs] There were many successes: *establishment of the Alliance for Progress to aid Latin America, increased foreign aid to underdeveloped nations, the development of the Peace Crops, and reduced tariffs to encourage foreign trade.* [compound noun phrases] *Yet within a few months, an attempt by Cuban exiles to invade Cuba failed, Communist forces expanded their operations in Laos and Vietnam, and the East Germans built the Berlin Wall.* [compound independent clauses, which comprise a compound sentence]

This is probably also a good time to point out the difference between sentences such as these: John F. Kennedy was President of the United States and a hero to many young people. [compound subject complement] John F. Kennedy was President of the United States, *and he was* a hero to many young people. [compound sentence]

INSTRUCTOR'S NOTES

ANSWERS: EXERCISE 13

1. complex	6. simple
2. compound	7. simple
3. compound	8. complex
4. complex	9. compound-complex
5. compound	10. simple

EXERCISE 13

Identify each sentence as simple, compound, complex, or compound-complex.

EXAMPLE   The teachings of Voltaire, Montesquieu, and Rousseau contributed to the French Revolution. (simple)

1. Each helped to convince middle-class French intellectuals that the monarchy was corrupt and that they could create a better government.
2. Voltaire considered many social institutions insensitive; his favorite target was the Catholic Church.
3. Voltaire saw the Church as narrow-minded and unsympathetic to the people, so he sought its elimination from politics.
4. The Baron de Montesquieu was a political theorist who traveled all over Europe studying various governments.
5. Montesquieu popularized the English system of checks and balances among the branches of government, and this ideal was adopted as a model by the writers of the American constitution.
6. He also argued that people should select their form of government, an idea of appeal to the French as well as the Americans.
7. Jean Jacques Rousseau saw humanity as pure and good.
8. Rousseau, who was born in Switzerland but lived in France, believed that children are born in a natural and unspoiled state but that civilization corrupts people.
9. Because of private ownership of property, people become selfish, and they must be taught to act for the common good.
10. Rousseau's ideas have had a strong impact on modern socialist and communist thought.

EXERCISE 14

Combine each set of sentences into a sentence of the type given in parentheses.

EXAMPLE   Nine people were killed in London on October 17, 1814. A vat in a brewery burst, releasing 3,500 barrels of beer. (complex)
Nine people were killed in London on October 17, 1814, *when* a vat in a brewery burst, releasing 3,500 barrels of beer.

ANSWERS: EXERCISE 14

Answers will vary somewhat. Here is one set of possibilities.
1. Because the neighborhood was flat, run-off accumulated in the basements of local buildings.
2. Rescuers had to wade through waist-high beer, but no one got drunk.

1. The neighborhood was flat. Run-off accumulated in the basements of local buildings. (complex)
2. Rescuers had to wade through waist-high beer. No one got drunk. (compound)

174

3. A flood of molasses killed 21 people in Boston. This happened in 1919. (simple)

4. The Food and Drug Administration (FDA) allows cola makers to keep "essential ingredients" secret. Rival companies have to rely on chemists to try to duplicate secret formulas. (complex)

5. The original secret ingredient of Coca-Cola was known to fewer than ten people. That ingredient made up less than one percent of the drink. (complex)

6. The original secret ingredient in Seven Up was lithium carbonate. Lithium carbonate is now used to treat severe manic depressive behavior. (complex)

7. Seven Up was a big success during the Depression. Some people suggest something. The suggestion is that Seven Up was popular during the Depression because lithium had a calming effect that people very much needed during those hard times. (compound-complex)

8. In the 1940s lithium was taken out of Seven Up. Lithium was restricted by the FDA. The drink remains a favorite today. (compound-complex)

3. A flood of molasses killed 21 people in Boston in 1919.

4. Because the Food and Drug Administration (FDA) allows cola makers to keep "essential ingredients" secret, rival companies have to rely on chemists to try to duplicate secret formulas.

5. The original secret ingredient of Coca-Cola, which was known to fewer than ten people, made up less than one percent of the drink.

6. The original secret ingredient in Seven Up was lithium carbonate, which is now used to treat severe manic depressive behavior.

7. Seven Up was a big success during the Depression, and some people suggest that this was because lithium had a calming effect that people very much needed during those hard times.

8. In the 1940s lithium was taken out of Seven Up because it was restricted by the FDA, but the drink remains a favorite today.

INSTRUCTOR'S NOTES

8
VERBS

Some students may feel overwhelmed by verb tenses—which they may perceive to be infinite in number—with the result that they refuse to face the fearsome verb and thus pick a form at random (or so it seems to us). It may be helpful to show them the basic distinction between tense and aspect.

Time can be divided into past, present, and future. *Tense* refers to the reflection of one of these times in a verb. Therefore, there are three basic tenses: past, present, future. *Aspect* says something about the way the action is experienced. The progressive aspect *(to be + -ing)* shows an action still in progress, and the perfect aspect *(has, have,* or *had* + past participial) shows a completed action or one being continued into the present from a specific point in the past. *Mood,* which describes conditions such as certainty, necessity, and possibility,

Verbs convey information about what is happening, what has happened, and what will happen. In English, a verb tells of an action *(eat, wrestle, argue),* an occurrence *(become, change, happen),* or a state of being *(be, seem, feel, exist).*

> The earth **rotates** on its axis approximately every twenty-four hours. [action]
> Mother's Day **falls** on the second Sunday in May. [occurrence]
> The cockroach still **exists** after hundreds of millions of years. [state of being]

Verbs do more work than this, however. By means of endings, internal form changes, combinations of main verbs° with other verbs called auxiliary verbs°, and interactions with nouns and pronouns, they also convey the following information:

Person: who or what acts or experiences an action—first (the one speaking), second (the one being spoken to), or third (the person or thing spoken about)

Number: how many subjects act or experience an action—one (singular) or more than one (plural)

176

Tense: when an action occurs—in the past, present, or future

Mood: what attitude the writer or speaker is expressing toward the action—indicative, imperative, or subjunctive

Voice: whether the subject acts (active) or is acted upon (passive)

Understanding verb forms, tense, mood, and voice can give you control of these most important words for delivering meaning.

is a separate issue, and so is *voice.* A verb can show all four qualities, but you might want to focus on the interplay of tense and aspect first.

It may be useful to go over a chart, such as the one at the bottom of this page, with your students, discussing the possible uses of each tense.

▌▐ VERB FORMS

A verb usually changes form by adding an ending *(change, chang**es**, chang**ing**, chang**ed**.)* Some verbs change forms more extensively *(eat, ate; be, is)*. Changes in form help verbs deliver information about tense and, in a limited way, about person and number.

▌▐ 8a
Recognize the forms of main verbs.

A **main verb** names an action, an occurrence, or a state of being: *earth* **rotates,** *Mother's Day* **fell,** *the cockroach* **existed.** Main verbs are distinguished from **auxiliary verbs.** Main and auxiliary verbs together form **verb phrases.**

> earth **is rotating** [*is* = auxiliary verb, *rotating* = main verb, *is rotating* = verb phrase]
>
> the cockroach **will have been existing** [*will have been* = auxiliary verbs, *existing* = main verb, *will have been existing* = verb phrase]

Auxiliary verbs help to deliver information about tense, mood, and voice. See 8c for more about auxiliary verbs.

▌ 1
Identify a main verb's three principal parts.

Every main verb has three principal parts: a **simple form,** a **past tense,** and a **past participle.**

Other terms for the simple form are **dictionary form** (because it is the form given first in the dictionary entry for a verb) and **base form.** The simple form shows action (or occurrence or state of being)

177

TO LOVE					
Time	*Form*	*Tense*	*Time*	*Form*	*Tense*
present	love	simple present	future	will love	future
	am, is, are loving	present progressive		will be loving	future progressive
past	loved	simple past		will have loved	future perfect
	was, were loving	past progressive		will have been loving	future perfect prog.
	has, have loved	present perfect			
	had loved	past (or pluperfect)			
	has, have been loving	present perfect prog.			
	had been loving	past (or pluperfect) prog.			

EXAMPLE: VERBS IN CONTEXT
Despite the popular idea that the human brain *is* a very delicate organ, scientific eficence *indicates* that the brain *can continue* functioning even after much of it *has been damaged* or even when as much as half of it *has been removed* by surgery. It *seems* that although brain functions *are* localized, sometimes other parts of the brain *take* over the work of damaged or removed areas. Even in cases where half the brain *was removed* in order to control life-threatening seizures, people *were* able to live normal lives. In fact, in one case removal of the right half of the brain *led* to an increase of over twenty points in a patient's IQ (as reported when he *was tested* fifteen years later). Apparently loss of the right half of the brain *did* not *interfere* with his ability to think and learn, and removal of the diseased area *allowed* him to live free from distracting seizures. We *do* not *know* how the brain *compensates* for such losses, but researchers *hope* they *will find* an answer soon.

taking place now, in the present, for *I, you, we,* and *they.* That is, the simple form occurs in the first and second person° for a singular subject and in the first, second, and third person for a plural subject: *I learn, they go.* The simple form is also the basis for the future tense, with *will* or *shall* (I will *learn,* they will *go*).

For the present-tense third-person singular, most verbs add a final *s* or *es* to the simple form: *she learns, he goes.* ❚❚ VERB ALERT: *Be, have,* and **modal** auxiliary verbs ("helping" verbs like *can* and *would*) are exceptions. ❚❚ See 8a-2 for more about the *-s* form and 8c for more about *be, have,* and the modal auxiliary verbs.

The **past-tense** form is the second principal part. It indicates an action or occurrence or state of being completed in the past. The past tense of all regular verbs adds final *-ed* or *-d* to the simple form. Many verbs, however, are irregular. That is, their past-tense form, and very often their past participle as well, either change in spelling or make use of different words instead of adding *-ed* or *-d: sing, sang, sung; go, went, gone.* The principal parts of common irregular verbs are listed on pages 183–85.

Except for the past tense of *be* (8c), past-tense forms do not change with changes of person and number:

> We *learned* the way to the library. You *learned* the way too. [*learn* = regular verb]
>
> I *completed* survival training. The cadets *completed* it too. [*complete* = regular verb]
>
> She *swam* three miles. You *swam* three miles. [*swim* = irregular verb]

The **past participle** is the third principal part. In regular verbs, the past participle uses the same form as the past tense. However, these forms differ in many irregular verbs, so you must simply memorize the principal parts of irregular verbs (see pages 183–85).

To function as a verb, a past participle must combine with an auxiliary verb° (see 8c) in a **verb phrase.** Verb phrases formed with past participles make the perfect° tenses (8g) and passive° constructions (page 205).

> I have learned. [*have* = auxiliary verb, *learned* = past participle, *have learned* = verb phrase]
>
> They were startled. [*were* = auxiliary verb, *startled* = past participle, *were startled* = verb phrase]

Used alone, past participles function as adjectives, modifying nouns or pronouns: *crumbled* cookies, *fallen* trees. Alone, a past participle can never function as a verb.

178

Verbs also have a **present participle,** formed by adding *-ing* to the simple form: *eating, falling, learning.* Like the past participle, the present participle needs an auxiliary verb to function as a verb. With the various forms of *be,* present participles make **progressive forms** in all the tenses.

> I **am getting** a headache. [progressive form in the present tense; *am* = auxiliary verb, *getting* = present participle]
>
> The sun **was setting.** [progressive form in the past tense; *was* = auxiliary verb, *setting* = present participle]
>
> The senators **will be meeting.** [progressive form in the future tense; *will* and *be* = auxiliary verbs, *meeting* = present participle]

Used alone, a present participle functions as an adjective (a *diving* board, the *boiling* broth, a *thinking* person) or a noun (*swimming* is fun; *leaving* can be painful). When it functions as a noun, a present participle is called a **gerund.** Alone, a present participle can never function as a verb.

The **infinitive** is another verb form that functions as a noun or an adjective but not as a verb. Infinitives use the simple form and usually, but not always, *to.*

> **To dance** is my dream. [*to dance* = infinitive functioning as noun subject°]
>
> I expected you **to leave.** [*to leave* = infinitive as noun object°]
>
> I heard you **leave.** [*leave* = infinitive, without *to,* as noun object°]

Participles and infinitives functioning as nouns or modifiers are called **verbals.** They are also called **nonfinite verbs,** in contrast to **finite verbs. Finite verbs** are the verb forms that convey information about tense°, mood°, voice°, person°, and number° while they deliver meaning about an action, occurrence, or state of being.

2
Use the -s form correctly.

Except for *be* and *have,* all verbs in the present tense—that is, all verbs whose action (or occurrence or state of being) is taking place now—add an *-s* or *-es* ending to the simple form when the subject is third-person singular. (Third-person singular subjects are singular nouns; the pronouns *he, she,* and *it;* and indefinite pronouns—words like *one, everybody,* and *someone.*)

COORDINATED RESOURCES

Alternate examples and exercises for this chapter are available in the *S & S Workbook for Writers,* Gordon and Troyka.

Transparency masters are available for many of the screened charts and/or lists in this chapter.

The software program *Blue Pencil,* available from Prentice-Hall, offers students additional practice coordinated with this chapter.

Students can practice and test their knowledge of terms, key concepts, and applications of material in this chapter by using the *Study Guide* to the *S & S Handbook for Writers,* West.

WORD HISTORY
Infinitive comes from the Latin *infinitivus,* meaning *unlimited* or *indefinite.* This is appropriate, since the infinitive shows no person or number. Coming from the same Latin verb, *finire (to limit),* the term *finite verb* refers to a verb that is limited by person and number. In contrast, a *nonfinite verb* (also known as a *verbal*) is not limited in these ways.

TEACHING TIP

Some of your students may speak a non-standard English dialect. Black English is perhaps the most discussed of these, but nonblack rural and inner-city students and students (of any color) from former British colonies and U.S. protectorates may also speak nonstandard dialects.

Two-dialect students can pick up changes in vocabulary comparatively easily. Their verbs, however, might need to be monitored with care. You might consider reviewing the following chart with such students:

NONSTANDARD ENGLISH   STANDARD ENGLISH

Present Tense

I
you } loves
we
they
he, she, it *love*

I
you } love
we
they
he, she, it *loves*

Past Tense

I
you } *love*
we
they
he, she, it

I
you } *loved*
we
they
he, she, it

ANSWERS: EXERCISE 1

1. He also protects
2. He cures
3. The shaman is
4. The shaman has
5. Shamans still exist

The **rabbit travels** faster than the tortoise.
She chooses a rapid pace.
The slow **one,** however, often **wins** the race.

Be and *have*—irregular verbs° (all forms are given on page 187)—do not use their simple forms in third-person singular of the present tense. Instead, *be* uses *is* and *have* uses *has*.

The **rabbit is** unarguably quick.
The **tortoise has** more stamina.

Some dialects of English use forms such as *he be, the rabbit have* for third-person singular in the present tense. Academic writing requires *is* and *has*. Also, if you tend to drop the *-s* or *-es* ending when you speak, you may forget to use it when you write. Be sure to proofread your writing to make sure you have used the *-s* form correctly. (Also see Subject–Verb Agreement, Chapter 11.)

EXERCISE 1

Rewrite each sentence, changing the subject to the word given in parentheses. Change the form of the verb to match this new subject. Keep all sentences in the present tense.

EXAMPLE   In many cultures, shamans heal the sick. (a shaman)
          In many cultures, *a shaman heals* the sick.

1. They also protect the community from danger. (he)
2. They cure patients by calling on supernatural powers. (he)
3. Some shamans are extremely rich. (The shaman)
4. Some shamans have great political power. (The shaman)
5. Shamanism still exists in societies of the far north, such as those in Siberia, Alaska, and Canada. (Shamans)

■‖ **8b**

Recognize regular and irregular verbs.

A **regular verb** is one that forms its past tense° and past participle° by adding *-ed* or *-d* to the simple form°. Most verbs in English are regular.

SIMPLE FORM	PAST TENSE	PAST PARTICIPLE
enter	entered	entered
smile	smiled	smiled

180

Some English verbs are **irregular.** They form the past tense and past participle in a number of different ways.

SIMPLE FORM	PAST TENSE	PAST PARTICIPLE
bring	brought	brought
swim	swam	swum

Regular verbs will give you few problems once you understand the use of the *-ed* or *-d* ending and you learn a few spelling guidelines (such as when to change a verb's final *-y* to *-i* with *-ed,* as explained in 8b-1). Irregular verbs are easy to use once you learn the principal parts (see 8b-2).

1

Form the past tense and past participle of a regular verb by adding *-ed* or *-d.*

Adding *-ed* or *-d* to the simple form makes the past tense and past participle of any regular verb. Some verbs that end in a vowel followed by a consonant double the consonant before adding *-ed: occur, occurred; transfer, transferred.* Others do not: *label, labeled; focus, focused.* Many are spelled either way: *travel, traveled, travelled; program, programed, programmed.* You will find advice in 22d-1. You can also confidently follow the preferred spelling shown in an up-to-date college dictionary.

Regular verbs with the simple form ending in *-y* are more consistent. If the final two letters of the simple form are a vowel followed by *y,* simply add *-ed: obey, obeyed; display, displayed.* If the final two letters are a consonant followed by *y,* change the *y* to *i* before you add *-ed: spy, spied; reply, replied.* For more about spelling verbs, see Chapter 22.

Speakers often skip over the *-ed* sound in the past tense, hitting it lightly or not at all. If you are unused to hearing or pronouncing this sound, you may forget to add it when you use the past tense and past participles. Nevertheless, written English requires the *-ed* ending, so be sure to proofread your writing for *-ed* endings.

No	He **promise** to pay me by Tuesday.
Yes	He **promised** to pay me by Tuesday.
No	We were **suppose** to study adverbs for class today.
Yes	We were **supposed** to study adverbs for class today.
No	The conquerors were **prejudice** against the natives.
Yes	The conquerors were **prejudiced** against the natives.

181

TEACHING TIP
Leaving the *-s* off verbs is a common error, even among students who can quote the rule for its use. Many of these students speak or have studied second languages that have much more complex systems of verb endings. A discussion of the English *-s* in the context of other languages the students know may reduce the number of carelessly omitted *-s*'s. You can let students know, jokingly, that anyone who accurately writes and speaks French, Spanish, or Italian and still doesn't bother to keep track of "one little *-s*" is too strange to be believed.

Here is a comparison of the verb *speak* (present tense) in four languages, with endings shown in boldface. When no pronouns are given, the pronoun is communicated by the verb's ending.

ENGLISH
Singular	*Plural*
I speak	we speak
you speak	you speak
he, she, it speaks	they speak

SPANISH
hablo	hablamos
hablas	habláis
habla	hablan

ITALIAN
parlo	parliamo
parli	parlate
parla	parlano

FRENCH
je parle	nous parlons
tu parles	vous parlez
il, elle, on parle	ils, elles parlent

ANSWERS: EXERCISE 2

1. owned
2. stabilized
3. provided
4. strengthened
5. participated; created

EXERCISE 2

Rewrite each sentence, changing the italicized verb to the past tense.

EXAMPLE The religious beliefs of many agricultural societies *include* the worship of family and tribal ancestors.

The religious beliefs of many agricultural societies *included* the worship of family and tribal ancestors.

1. In these societies, extended family groups often *own* the land.
2. Ancestor worship *stabilizes* social and economic relationships.
3. It *provides* continuity from generation to generation.
4. It *strengthens* family structures.
5. The belief that long-dead family members *participate* in daily life *creates* a bond between generations.

∥ 2

Memorize the principal parts of irregular verbs.

About two hundred of the most common verbs in English are **irregular:** They do not add *-ed* or *-d* to form the past tense and past participle. Some irregular verbs change an internal vowel to make past tense and past participle: *sing, sang, sung.* Some change an internal vowel and add an ending other than *-ed* or *-d; grow, grew, grown.* Some use the simple form throughout: *read, read, read.*

Unfortunately, a verb's simple form provides no clue about whether the verb is irregular or regular. If you do not know the principal parts of a verb you are using, you can find them in a college dictionary. Most college dictionaries use the simple form for the dictionary entry, listing after it the past-tense form and the past participle only if the verb is irregular. If only the simple form is given, you will know the verb is regular and adds *-ed* or *-d.* If the simple form and only one other form are given, you will know that both the past-tense form and the past participle use the second form *(buy, bought).*

Although you can always look up the principal parts of any verb, memorizing them is much more convenient in the long run. The following chart lists most of the common irregular verbs. If you do not find the verb you need here, look it up in the dictionary and then add its principal parts to this list.

182

COMMON IRREGULAR VERBS

SIMPLE FORM	PAST TENSE	PAST PARTICIPLE
arise	arose	arisen
awake	awoke *or* awaked	awaked *or* awoken
be (is, am, are)	was, were	been
bear	bore	borne *or* born
beat	beat	beaten
become	became	become
begin	began	begun
bend	bent	bent
bet	bet	bet
bid (offer)	bid	bid
bid (command)	bade	bidden
bind	bound	bound
bite	bit	bitten *or* bit
blow	blew	blown
break	broke	broken
bring	brought	brought
build	built	built
burst	burst	burst
buy	bought	bought
cast	cast	cast
catch	caught	caught
choose	chose	chosen
cling	clung	clung
come	came	come
cost	cost	cost
creep	crept	crept
cut	cut	cut
deal	dealt	dealt
dig	dug	dug
dive	dived *or* dove	dived
do	did	done
draw	drew	drawn
drink	drank	drunk
drive	drove	driven
eat	ate	eaten
fall	fell	fallen
feed	fed	fed
feel	felt	felt
fight	fought	fought
find	found	found
flee	fled	fled

SIMPLE FORM	PAST TENSE	PAST PARTICIPLE
fling	flung	flung
fly	flew	flown
forbid	forbade *or* forbad	forbidden
forget	forgot	forgotten *or* forgot
forgive	forgave	forgiven
forsake	forsook	forsaken
freeze	froze	frozen
get	got	got *or* gotten
give	gave	given
go	went	gone
grow	grew	grown
hang (suspend)*	hung	hung
have	had	had
hear	heard	heard
hide	hid	hidden
hit	hit	hit
hurt	hurt	hurt
keep	kept	kept
know	knew	known
lay	laid	laid
lead	led	led
leave	left	left
lend	lent	lent
let	let	let
lie	lay	lain
light	lighted *or* lit	lighted *or* lit
lose	lost	lost
make	made	made
mean	meant	meant
pay	paid	paid
prove	proved	proved *or* proven
quit	quit	quit
read	read	read
rid	rid	rid
ride	rode	ridden
ring	rang	rung
rise	rose	risen
run	ran	run
say	said	said
see	saw	seen

*When it means to execute by hanging, *hang* is a regular verb: "In wartime, armies routinely **hanged** deserters."

184

SIMPLE FORM	PAST TENSE	PAST PARTICIPLE
seek	sought	sought
send	sent	sent
set	set	set
shake	shook	shaken
shine (glow)*	shone	shone
shoot	shot	shot
show	showed	shown *or* showed
shrink	shrank	shrunk
sing	sang	sung
sink	sank	sunk
sit	sat	sat
slay	slew	slain
sleep	slept	slept
sling	slung	slung
speak	spoke	spoken
spend	spent	spent
spin	spun	spun
spring	sprang *or* sprung	sprung
stand	stood	stood
steal	stole	stolen
sting	stung	stung
stink	stank *or* stunk	stunk
stride	strode	Stridden
strike	struck	struck
strive	strove	striven
swear	swore	sworn
sweep	swept	swept
swim	swam	swum
swing	swung	swung
take	took	taken
teach	taught	taught
tear	tore	torn
tell	told	told
think	thought	thought
throw	threw	thrown
understand	understood	understood
wake	woke *or* waked	waked *or* woken
wear	wore	worn
wring	wrung	wrung
write	wrote	written

*When it means to polish, *shine* is a regular verb: "We **shined** our shoes."

185

ANSWERS: EXERCISE 3
1. came
2. made
3. spread; were
4. grew
5. became
6. left
7. found; had
8. forsook; kept
9. built
10. led

EXERCISE 3

In each blank, write the correct past-tense form of the verb in parentheses. Use the list of irregular verbs on pages 183–85.

EXAMPLE   The first people in the New World, the Paleo-Indians, (bring) _____ their Old World culture with them.

The first people in the New World, the Paleo-Indians, *brought* their Old World culture with them.

1. These people (come) _____ mainly from eastern Siberia into the North American territory that is now Alaska.
2. Once across the Aleutian bridge, they (make) _____ their way south.
3. Scientists believe that the Paleo-Indians (spread) _____ rapidly, at least partly because they (be) _____ curious.
4. Each time a group entered an uninhabited area with abundant resources, the number of people (grow) _____.
5. Food, water, and building materials soon (become) _____ scarce, forcing some people to move on.
6. Those who (leave) _____ moved to new territory, where the pattern started over again.
7. In each new place, the settlers (find) _____ different conditions, so they (have) _____ to modify old ways or invent new ones.
8. For example, the mammoth hunters of the western United States (forsake) _____ certain hunting methods as they (keep) _____ traveling eastward into the territory of the smaller bison.
9. Paleo-Indian groups in the eastern United States (build) _____ cultures based on fishing, plant gathering, and small-game hunting.
10. Anthropologists wonder whether the expansion of these peoples (lead) _____ to the extinction of the mammoths, wild horses, camels, and mastodons that roamed the continent.

WORD HISTORY

An *auxiliary verb* is also called a *helping verb,* and, not surprisingly, *auxiliary* comes from *auxiliarius,* a Latin word for *help.* Linking verbs were, until recently, often called *copulative verbs.* This usage dates back to the seventeenth century and comes from the Latin *copulativus,* meaning *connective.*

■ 8c

Recognize *be, do, have,* and other auxiliary verbs.

The verbs *be, do,* and *have* function both as main verbs° and as auxiliary verbs°. *Be,* the most common verb in English, is the most irregular verb. *Do* and *have* are not as irregular as *be.*

As a main verb°, *be,* along with its forms, is a **linking verb.** These join a subject° to a **subject complement**—a word or group of words that renames or describes the subject.

THE FORMS OF *BE*	
SIMPLE FORM	be
PAST TENSE	was, were
PAST PARTICIPLE	been
-s FORM	is
PRESENT PARTICIPLE	being

PERSON	PRESENT TENSE	PAST TENSE
I	am	was
you (singular)	are	were
he, she, it	is	was
we	are	were
you (plural)	are	were
they	are	were

THE FORMS OF *DO* AND *HAVE*			
SIMPLE FORM	do	SIMPLE FORM	have
PAST TENSE	did	PAST TENSE	had
PAST PARTICIPLE	done	PAST PARTICIPLE	had
-s FORM	does	*-s* FORM	has
PRESENT PARTICIPLE	doing	PRESENT PARTICIPLE	having

High blood pressure **is** a leading cause of chronic illness. [*is* = linking verb, *high blood pressure* = subject, *cause* = subject complement]

A low-salt diet is important for reducing blood pressure. [*low-salt diet* = subject, *is* = linking verb, *important* = subject complement]

▮ USAGE ALERT: Academic writing requires standard forms and uses of *be*. ▮

No   He driving his car to work. [missing *be* form]

No   He **be** driving his car to work. [nonstandard *be* form]

Yes   He **is** driving his car to work. [standard form of *be* supplied]

WORD HISTORY

The word *conjugation* has been used since the early sixteenth century to refer to all the forms of a particular verb. *Conjugation* and *conjugate* both come from the Latin *conjugāre*, basically meaning *to join together*. In Latin, a list of the forms of a verb was called a *conjugatio*, and *conjugata verba* (literally *joined words*) referred to words that were etymologically related.

TEACHING TIP

Although *to be* is always a linking verb, others verbs may or may not be, depending upon how they are used in a given sentence. When in doubt, try substituting a form of *to be*: If the sentence makes sense, it contains a linking verb; if it no longer makes sense, it does not contain a linking verb.

He *seems* ill. / He *is* ill.
[The *to be* verb makes sense, so *seems* is a linking verb.]
Daisies *grow* in the park. / Daisies *are* in the park.
[The *to be* verb makes sense, so *grow* is a linking verb.]
Joyce *grows* orchids. / Joyce *is* orchids.
[The *to be* verb does not make sense, so *grows* is not a linking verb.]

INSTRUCTOR'S NOTES

Used alone, as main verbs, *have* is transitive and *do* can be transitive. **Transitive verbs** must be followed by a direct object° to deliver full meaning, as explained in 8d.

> Most people **have hobbies.** [*have* = main verb, *hobbies* = direct object]
>
> I **do** a crossword **puzzle** every Sunday. [*do* = main verb, *puzzle* = direct object]

Combined with the present or past participle of main verbs, forms of *be* and *have* are **auxiliary verbs** or **helping verbs,** that help the participles to show tense (see page 192) and mood (see page 202).

> I **am listening.** [auxiliary verb *am* + present participle *listening* = progressive present tense]
>
> Several reasons for low birth weight in infants **have been discovered.** [auxiliary verb *have* + auxiliary verb *been* + past participle *discovered* = present perfect tense in the passive voice]

The auxiliary verbs *will* and *shall* help to create two tenses, the **future** *(he will look, you will go)* and, with *have* and past participles of main verbs, the **future perfect** *(we shall have looked, you will have gone). Will* and *shall* never change form. *Shall* is less used than *will.* Formal writing, however, reserves *shall* for the first person *(I, we)* and *will* for all other persons *(you, she, he, it, they).*

> I **shall strive** for excellence.
>
> **You will strive** for excellence.

The verbs *can, could, may, might, should, would, must,* and *ought to* are called **modal auxiliary verbs.** Modal auxiliary verbs have only one form; they do not change, no matter what constructions they appear in.

I, you, he, she, it, we, you, they

- can
- could
- may
- might
- should
- would
- must
- ought to

Modal auxiliaries add to the main verb a sense of needing, wanting, or having to do something, a sense of possibility, likelihood, obligation, permission, or ability.

188

Exercise **can lengthen** lives. [possibility]

The exercise **must occur** regularly. [requirement]

Most of us **should take** better care of our bodies. [obligation]

May I exercise? [permission]

She **can** jog for five miles. [ability]

EXERCISE 4

Using auxiliary verbs from the list below, fill in the blanks. For some sentences, more than one correct answer is possible, but use each auxiliary only once.

are	can	may	must	should	will

EXAMPLE   When firefighters search the scene of a fire, they _____ first find where the fire originated.

When firefighters search the scene of a fire, they *must* first find where the fire originated.

1. In searching for the point of origin, a keen investigator _____ look for the telltale signs of arson.

2. For example, there _____ be evidence that the fire had multiple points of origin, or *streamers,* trails of gasoline that were used to spread the fire from area to area.

3. The discovery of containers that _____ hold an accelerant is another clue.

4. Ignition devices, from a simple candle to complex electronic mechanisms, _____ convincing evidence of arson.

5. Investigators _____ also look for signs of breaking and entering or theft.

EXERCISE 5

Using each of the auxiliary verbs listed below just once, fill in the blanks. For some sentences, more than one correct answer is possible. Use up all the words by the end of the exercise.

are	do	may	should	will
can	have	ought	were	

1. The first pet fish were probably goldfish, which _____ kept captive in China over a thousand years ago.

2. You _____ forget the stresses and strains of everyday life as you watch your fish swim about.

3. Fish are unlike any other pets because they _____ not make noise, eat much, or scratch the furniture.

4. Landlords who prohibit other pets _____ permit people to have aquariums.

ANSWERS: EXERCISE 4
Answers may vary slightly. A possible set is:

1. will	4. are
2. may	5. should
3. can	

ANSWERS: EXERCISE 5
Answers may vary slightly. A possible set is:

1. were	4. may	7. have
2. can	5. will	8. should
3. do	6. ought	9. are

INSTRUCTOR'S NOTES

5. Maintaining an aquarium may seem complicated, but if you follow a few simple steps, you _____ find it rather easy.
6. You _____ to buy the largest tank possible, based on your available space and money.
7. Fish thrive when they _____ been placed in a relatively roomy tank.
8. The smallest tank in which you _____ invest is a ten-gallon tank.
9. Rectangular glass tanks with stainless steel frames _____ recommended by most experts.

■‖ 8d

Use intransitive and transitive verbs correctly, especially *sit* and *set, lie* and *lay, rise* and *raise.*

The difference between *I sing loudly* and *I sing a song* is that the first sentence tells how the subject° does something while the second points to what the subject does. The second sentence points out the goal—or object—of the action the verb tells about. In the first sentence, the verb is **intransitive.** In the second sentence, the verb is **transitive**—the action of the verb carries over to whatever is named in a **direct object**°. Many verbs in English can be either intransitive or transitive.

INTRANSITIVE (NO OBJECT)	TRANSITIVE (WITH AN OBJECT)
The cat **sees** in the dark. [*In the dark* is not a direct object; it is a modifier°.]	The cat **sees** the dog. [*dog* = direct object]
I can **hear** well. [*Well* is not a direct object; it is a modifier°.]	I can **hear** you. [*you* = direct object]
We **teach** tomorrow. [*Tomorrow* is not a direct object; it is a modifier°.]	We **teach** French. [*French* = direct object]

Three important pairs of verbs, which happen to look and sound very much alike, are not so flexible. In these pairs—*sit* and *set, lie* and *lay, rise* and *raise*—one verb is intransitive, the other transitive. If you do not already know the forms of these verbs, memorize them.

To *sit* means to seat oneself; to *set* means to place something else down.

INTRANSITIVE	I **sit** there. I **sat** there. [*there* = modifier, not a direct object]
TRANSITIVE	I **set** the books down. [*books* = direct object]

190

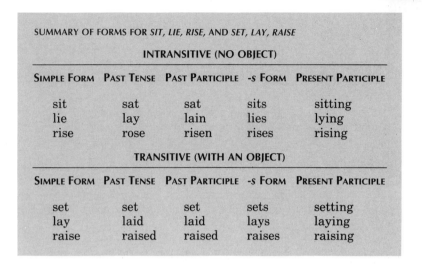

SUMMARY OF FORMS FOR *SIT, LIE, RISE*, AND *SET, LAY, RAISE*

INTRANSITIVE (NO OBJECT)

SIMPLE FORM	PAST TENSE	PAST PARTICIPLE	-*S* FORM	PRESENT PARTICIPLE
sit	sat	sat	sits	sitting
lie	lay	lain	lies	lying
rise	rose	risen	rises	rising

TRANSITIVE (WITH AN OBJECT)

SIMPLE FORM	PAST TENSE	PAST PARTICIPLE	-*S* FORM	PRESENT PARTICIPLE
set	set	set	sets	setting
lay	laid	laid	lays	laying
raise	raised	raised	raises	raising

Set does have one specialized intransitive meaning—the passing of a celestial body below the horizon: *The sun set.*

To *lie* means to recline or place oneself down or to remain; to *lay* means to place something down.

> INTRANSITIVE   Vern **lies** down for a nap. Vern **lay** down for a nap. [*down for a nap* = modifier, not a direct object]

> TRANSITIVE   Vern **lays** tiles in the kitchen. Vern **laid** tiles in the kitchen. [*tiles* = direct object]

To *rise* means to stand up, get up out of bed, or elevate oneself in some other way or to ascend; to *raise* is to lift up or elevate someone or something else.

> INTRANSITIVE   Lee **rises** every morning at 6:00. Lee **rose** every morning at 6:00. [*every morning at 6:00* = modifier, not a direct object]

> TRANSITIVE   Lee **raises** the cup high. Lee **raised** the cup high. [*cup* = direct object]

EXERCISE 6
Select the appropriate verb from each pair in parentheses.

EXAMPLE   One day I was (laying, lying) on my towel at the beach.
          One day I was *lying* on my towel at the beach.

191

ANSWERS: EXERCISE 6

1. raised; setting   5. lain; rising
2. lie; rises; sets   6. rose
3. laid; raised; sitting   7. sat; lain
4. sat; rising

1. When I woke up after a nap, I (raised, rose) my head and saw the sun (sitting, setting) in the east.

2. I was about to (lay, lie) down again when it occurred to me that the sun (rises, raises) in the east and (sets, sits) in the west.

3. So I (lay, laid) my book down and (rose, raised) myself into a (sitting, setting) position.

4. As I (set, sat) there surrounded by sand and the (raising, rising) surf, I thought about this puzzling situation.

5. I had (lain, laid) down for a nap in the late afternoon as the humidity was (raising, rising), but something was now wrong.

6. Then an idea (rose, raised) out of my subconscious.

7. I now (sat, set) with the water in front of me, while before my nap it had (laid, lain) at my back. The sun had not changed positions during my nap: I had.

▪‖ VERB TENSE

Tense conveys when the action, occurrence, or state of being expressed by a verb takes place. Verbs are the only group of words that change form to express time. The time changes are indicated by the addition of final *-ed* or *-d* to the simple form° of the verb; by the use of *be, have,* and *will* and *shall* as auxiliary verbs°; and by other form changes.

English has six verb tenses, divided into simple and perfect groups. The three **simple tenses** divide time into present, past, and future. The **present tense** describes what is happening, what is true at the moment, and what is consistently true.

Rick **wants** to speak Spanish fluently.
Rick **takes** advanced Spanish now.

The **past tense** tells of an action completed or a condition ended. It uses the past-tense form (8a-1 and, for irregular verbs, 8b).

He **wanted** to improve rapidly.
He **took** a language placement test to qualify.

The **future tense** indicates action yet to be taken or a condition not yet experienced. The future tense uses the auxiliary verbs *will* or *shall* and the simple form (8c).

Next year Rick **will want** to progress even further.
Rick **will take** a course in the contemporary South American novel.

192

SUMMARY OF TENSES—INCLUDING PROGRESSIVE FORMS

SIMPLE TENSES

	REGULAR VERB	IRREGULAR VERB	PROGRESSIVE FORM
PRESENT	I talk	I eat	I am talking, I am eating
PAST	I talked	I ate	I was talking, I was eating
FUTURE	I will talk	I will eat	I will be talking, I will be eating

PERFECT TENSES

PRESENT PERFECT	I have talked	I have eaten	I have been talking, I have been eating
PAST PERFECT	I had talked	I had eaten	I had been talking, I had been eating
FUTURE PERFECT	I will have talked	I will have eaten	I will have been talking, I will have been eating

The **perfect tenses** also divide time into present, past, and future. They show more complex time relationships than do the simple tenses. The perfect tenses are discussed in 8f.

All six tenses also have **progressive forms.** These forms show an ongoing or continuing dimension to whatever the verb describes. Progressive forms add auxiliary verbs to the *-ing* form (the present participle). Progressive forms are discussed in 8g.

◼‖ 8e

Use the simple present tense correctly.

The **simple present tense** describes what is happening or what is true at the moment. It also has special functions, summarized below.

SUMMARY OF USES FOR THE SIMPLE PRESENT TENSE

DESCRIBING WHAT IS HAPPENING NOW, IN THE PRESENT

You **work** efficiently.
The gale **rattles** the windows.

DESCRIBING A HABITUAL OR REGULARLY OCCURRING ACTION

My accounting class **meets** at 10:00 on Tuesdays.
Horror movies **give** him nightmares.

EXPRESSING A GENERAL TRUTH OR WIDELY HELD OPINION

A kilogram **is** roughly 2.2 pounds.
Good fences **make** good neighbors.

DESCRIBING A FIXED-TIME FUTURE EVENT

The semester **ends** on May 30.
The ship **leaves** port at midnight.
His birthday **falls** on a Sunday this year.

DISCUSSING "TIMELESS" EVENTS AND ACTIVITIES AND INTENTIONS OF THOSE WHO CREATE THEM

Jay Gatsby **wants** it all.
Luke Skywalker and Han Solo repeatedly **save** Princess Leia.
Einstein **speaks** of matter as something that **is** interchangeable with energy.

■‖ 8f

Use the three perfect tenses correctly.

The **perfect tenses** generally describe actions or occurrences that have already been completed or that will be completed before a more recent point in time. In fact, the name "perfect" comes from the Latin *perfectus,* meaning "completed."

The **present perfect tense** shows that action begun and completed in the past also continues—or its effects continue—into the present.

194

Eric **has learned** to drive. [action completed but condition still in effect]

Severe drought **has created** terrible hardship for the people of Africa. [condition completed and still prevailing]

I **have** always **believed** in freedom of speech. [condition true once and still true]

The **past perfect tense** indicates that an action was completed before another one took place.

The tornado **had swept** through the town before the warning **could be given.**

Bella **had** barely **mastered** Swedish when her father **was sent** to Greece.

The **future perfect tense** indicates that an action will be complete before some specified or predictable time.

The eggs **will have hatched** before winter comes.

World population **will have reached** 8 billion by the year 2000.

▌▌ 8g

Use the progressive form of each tense correctly.

The **progressive form** uses the present participle° preceded by the various forms of *be* and other auxiliary verbs° appropriate to the tense. It shows that an action or condition is ongoing. This continuing action or state is not infinite, however. The sentence itself often states an explicit time.

The **present progressive** indicates something taking place at the time it is written or spoken about.

The damp weather **is making** her arthritis worse.

Fewer young people **are studying** Latin these days.

The **past progressive** shows the continuing nature of a past action, sometimes within stated or implied limits.

Computers **were selling** well this Christmas season.

The crack in the dam **was getting** larger.

The citizens of Pompeii **were going** about their business when Vesuvius erupted.

The **future progressive** shows that a future action will continue for some time. Often, this future action depends on another action or condition stated in the sentence.

195

If wholesale prices go down, retail prices **will be falling.**

Now that the first quake is over, we **shall be experiencing** an aftershock.

When he returns from vacation, he **will be looking** more relaxed.

The **present perfect progressive** describes something ongoing in the past that is likely to continue in the future.

The baby **has been crying** ever since his parents brought him home.

Real estate prices **have been rising** steadily.

The **past perfect progressive** describes an ongoing condition in the past that has been ended by something stated in the sentence.

Houses **had been selling** well until home mortgage interest rates went up.

He **had been playing** the saxophone long before he took up the flute.

The **future perfect progressive** describes an action or condition ongoing until some specific future time.

I **shall have been sleeping** for hours by the time you get home.

In May, our college's radio station **will have been operating** for twenty years.

ANSWERS: EXERCISE 7

1. had fallen
2. remained
3. have been compared *or* compare
4. leads
5. have had
6. require
7. ranks
8. vote
9. suggest *or* have suggested
10. have said
11. crossed
12. have led *or* have been leading

EXERCISE 7

Select the verb in parentheses that best suits the meaning. If there is more than one possible answer, be prepared to explain the differences in meaning among them.

EXAMPLE   In the United States in 1964, only 64.4 percent of eligible voters (turned, had turned, had been turning) out to vote.

              In the United States in 1964, only 64.4 percent of eligible voters *turned* out to vote.

1. By the 1970 congressional elections, this figure (fell, had fallen, was falling, had been falling) to about 50 percent.
2. The figure (remained, has remained, had remained) at about 50 percent through the mid-1980s.
3. These low turnouts (compare, have compared, are comparing, have been compared) poorly to the voting records of many other countries.

196

4. The USSR (leads, has led, has been leading) the world, with an impressive 99.6 percent reported voter turnout.

5. Many other countries (had, have had, were having, have been having) voter turnouts of over 95 percent, including Czechoslovakia, East Germany, and Hungary.

6. Many countries (require, have required, have been requiring) their citizens to vote.

7. Of the countries that require their citizens to vote, however, only the Netherlands (ranks, has ranked, is ranking, has been ranked) in the top twenty countries, at 92.1 percent.

8. In Argentina, despite mandatory voting, fewer people (vote, have voted, are voting, have been voting) than in the United States.

9. Some authorities say that Americans cannot vote because they are at work, and these people (are suggesting, have suggested, had suggested, suggest) that voting take place on Sundays.

10. Other authorities (have said, have been saying) that complicated residency laws are the problem.

11. In 1855, despite only 2,000 registered voters in Kansas, 6,000 ballots were cast in an election when people from neighboring Missouri (crossed, had crossed, were crossing, had been crossing) the state line to vote for candidates in sympathy with Missouri's policies.

12. Episodes like this (have led, were leading, have been leading) to the enactment of strict residency laws.

■ ‖ 8h

Use verbs in accurate tense sequences.

Sentences often have more than one verb, and these verbs often refer to actions taking place at different times. Showing the right time relationships—that is, using accurate tense sequences—is important. Always check tense sequences carefully in your writing to be sure that your sentences are delivering accurate meaning about the actions, occurrences, and states you intend those verbs to express.

‖ 1
Use accurate tense sequences in complex sentences.

Complex sentences use dependent clauses° as well as independent clauses°. The tense of the verb in an independent clause determines the possibilities for verb tense in that sentence's dependent clauses.

197

EXTRA EXERCISE A

Select the verb in parentheses that best suits the meaning. If there is more than one possible answer, be prepared to explain the differences in meaning.

EXAMPLE

In the United States in 1964, only 64.4 percent of the eligible voters (turned, had turned, were turning, had been turning) out to vote. In the United States in 1964, only 64.4 percent of eligible voters *turned* out to vote.

1. By the 1970 congressional elections, this figure (fell, had fallen, was falling, had been falling) to about 50 percent.

2. The figure (remained, has remained, had remained) at about 50 percent through the mid 1980s.

3. These low turnouts (compare, have compared, are comparing, have been compared) poorly to the voting records of many others countries.

4. The USSR (leads, has led, is leading, has been leading) the world, with an impressive 99.6 percent reported voter turnout.

5. Many other countires (had, have had, were having, have been having) voter turnouts of over 95 percent, including Czechoslovakia, East Germany, and Hungary.

6. Many other countries (require, have required, are requiring, have been requiring) their citizens to vote.

7. Of the countries that require their citizens to vote, however, only the Netherlands (ranks, has ranked, is ranking, has been ranked) in the top twenty countries, at 92.1 percent.

8. In Argentina, despite mandatory voting, fewer people (vote, have voted, are voting, have been voting) than in the United States.

SUMMARY OF SEQUENCE OF TENSES

WHEN INDEPENDENT-CLAUSE VERB IS IN THE SIMPLE PRESENT TENSE, FOR THE DEPENDENT-CLAUSE VERB:

- Use the present tense to show same-time action.

  The director **says** that the movie **is** a tribute to Chaplin.
  I **avoid** shellfish because I **am** allergic to it.

- Use the past tense to show earlier action.

  I **am** sure that I **deposited** the check.

- Use the present perfect tense to show a period of time extending from some point in the past to the present.

  They **claim** that they **have visited** the planet Venus.

- Use the future tense for action to come.

  The book **is** open because I **will be reading** it later.

WHEN INDEPENDENT-CLAUSE VERB IS IN THE PAST TENSE, FOR THE DEPENDENT-CLAUSE VERB:

- Use the past tense to show earlier action.

  I **ate** dinner before you **offered** to take me out for pizza.

- Use the past perfect tense to show earlier action.

  The sprinter **knew** she **had broken** the record.

- Use the present tense to state a general truth.

  Christopher Columbus discovered that the world **is** round.

WHEN INDEPENDENT-CLAUSE VERB IS IN THE PRESENT PERFECT OR PAST PERFECT TENSE, FOR THE DEPENDENT-CLAUSE VERB:

- Use the past tense.

  The agar plate **has become** moldy since I **poured** it last week.
  Sugar prices **had** already **declined** when artificial sweeteners first **appeared.**

WHEN INDEPENDENT-CLAUSE VERB IS IN THE FUTURE TENSE, FOR THE DEPENDENT-CLAUSE VERB:

- Use the present tense to show action happening at the same time.

    You **will be** rich if you **win** the prize.

- Use the past tense to show earlier action.

    You **will** surely **win** the prize if you **remembered** to mail the entry form.

- Use the present perfect tense to show future action earlier than the action of the independent-clause verb.

    The river **will flood** again next year unless we **have built** a better dam by then.

WHEN THE INDEPENDENT-CLAUSE VERB IS IN THE FUTURE PERFECT TENSE, FOR THE DEPENDENT-CLAUSE VERB:

- Use either the present tense or the present perfect tense.

    Dr. Chang **will have delivered** 5,000 babies by the time she **retires.**

    Dr. Chang **will have delivered** 5,000 babies by the time she **has retired.**

▌ USAGE ALERT: When an independent-clause verb is in the future tense, using a future-tense verb in the dependent clause is redundant. ▌

No   You **will be** rich if you **will** win the lottery.

Yes   You **will be** rich if you **win** the lottery.

No   The river **will flood** again next year unless we **will build** a better dam.

Yes   The river **will flood** again next year unless we **build** a better dam.

9. Some authorities say that Americans cannot vote because they are at work, and these people (are suggesting, have suggested, had suggested, suggest) that voting take place on Sundays.
10. Other authorities (say, have said, have been saying) that complicated residency laws are the problem.
11. In 1855, despite only 2,000 registered voters in Kansas, 6,000 ballots were cast in an election when people from neighboring Missouri (crossed, had crossed, were crossing, had been crossing) the state line to vote for candidates in sympathy with Missouri's policies.
12. Episodes like this (led, have led, were leading, have been leading) to the enactment of strict residency laws.

ANSWERS: EXTRA EXERCISE A
Other answers than these may be possible.
1. fell *or* had fallen
2. remained
3. compare *or* have been compared
4. leads *or* is leading
5. have had
6. require
7. ranks *or* has ranked [implies this is no longer true], has been ranked
8. vote
9. have suggested *or* suggest
10. say *or* have said
11. crossed
12. led *or* have led

INSTRUCTOR'S NOTES

EXTRA EXERCISE B

Revise these sentences so that the verb sequence is logical. If more than one answer is possible, be prepared to discuss their different meanings. If a sentence is correct, circle its number.

EXAMPLE

The history of geology, sadly, includes the stories of people who distort evidence to fit their theories. The history of geology, sadly, includes the stories of people who *distorted* evidence to fit their theories.

1. One of the most amazing of these men was Dr. Albert Koch, who regularly had combined fossil bones to create new prehistoric animals.

2. In 1840, while he had visited America from his native Germany, Dr. Koch announced a major find.

3. He would claim that he had discovered in Missouri the skeleton of a gigantic animal which he would have called the Missouri Leviathan.

4. Actually it had been the remains of a mastodon.

5. Dr. Koch had been inserting extra vertebrae, so that the backbone of the specimen appeared far longer than it really had been.

6. Koch writes that he had been identifying the Leviathan from its description in the Book of Job.

7. The skeleton has probably ended up in the British Museum, although no one knows for certain.

8. In 1845, Dr. Koch strikes again.

9. He announced finding a skeleton in Alabama that he had called "the longest of all fossil skeletons found either in the new or old world."

10. This time by inserting extra vertebrae again, he had turned an ordinary Mesozoic seagoing mammal into a 114-foot long sea serpent.

Answers on p. 205

2

Use correct tense sequences with infinitives and participles.

The present infinitive—*to* and the simple form of the verb—names or describes an activity or an occurrence simultaneous with or coming after the time expressed in the main verb.

> I **hope to buy** a second-hand car. [*To buy* comes later than the hoping.]
>
> I **hoped to buy** a second-hand car. [*To buy* comes at the same time as the hoping.]
>
> I **had hoped to buy** a second-hand car. [The hoping came before the attempt to buy.]

The present participle—a verb's *-ing* form—describes simultaneous action.

> **Walking** into his office, the detective **saw** his car keys on his desk. [The walking and the seeing happen at the same time.]

To describe an action that occurs before the action in the main verb, use the perfect infinitive *(to have eaten, to have worried)*; the past participle° (a regular verb's *-ed* form); or the present perfect participle *(having eaten, having worried)*.

> Raoul Wallenberg **is said to have saved** a hundred thousand people from the Nazis. [The perfect infinitive, *to have saved*, comes earlier in time than the saying.]
>
> **Pleased** with the short story, Candida **sent** it off to several magazines. [Candida was pleased before she mailed the story.]
>
> **Having sold** one short story, Candida **invested** in a word processor. [Candida sold the story before she bought the machine.]

EXERCISE 8

Select the verb form in parentheses that best suits the sequence of tenses. Be prepared to explain your choices.

EXAMPLE   Count Dracula, the subject of so many books and movies, (was, is) based on a real Transylvanian noble named Vlad II.

Count Dracula, the subject of so many books and movies, *is* based on a real Transylvanian noble named Vlad II.

1. Vlad's family name (had been, was) *Dracul,* which (means, was meaning) "devil," "son of devil," or "dragon" in Romanian.

2. Also known as Vlad Tepesh (or Vlad the Impaler), he (earned, had earned) this nickname because he (had, had had) a policy of impaling everyone who offended him.

3. Vlad (impaled, will have been impaling) anyone he suspected of any crime, from treason to rudeness.

4. Throughout his life, Vlad (received, had received) respect because he (defended, had defended) Christianity against the Turks.

5. Nevertheless, he (was, had been) a Turkish ally at one time.

6. Although most of his victims (were, having been) Turkish soldiers, he also impaled many of his own people simply for saying the wrong thing.

7. One man was impaled when he (commented, had commented) on the stench of the bodies rotting on stakes around the outdoor banquet he was attending.

8. It (is, was) also reported that when Turkish ambassadors (refused, were refusing) to remove their turbans in his presence, Vlad had the turbans nailed to their heads.

9. Local peasants also (tell, having told) of an exquisite gold cup that Dracula (placed, had placed) near a mountain spring.

10. As long as Dracula (lived, had been living), people were allowed to use the cup if they replaced it.

11. No one (dared, had dared) to steal the cup since impalement would have been swift and certain.

12. Although Vlad's bloodthirsty reputation (has been documented, was documented), there (is, was) no evidence that he was ever a vampire.

ANSWERS, EXERCISE 8
1. was; means
2. earned; had
3. impaled
4. received; had defended
5. had been
6. were
7. commented
8. is; refused
9. tell; placed
10. lived
11. dared
12. has been documented; is

EXERCISE 9

The verbs in each of the following sentences are in correct sequence. For each sentence, change the main verb as directed in the parentheses. Then adjust dependent verbs, infinitives, or participles if necessary to maintain correct verb sequence. Some sentences may have several correct answers.

EXAMPLE   The resemblance of electric sparks and lightning flashes led some people to believe they were the same. (Change *led* to *leads.*)

The resemblance of electric sparks and lightning flashes *leads* some people to believe they *are* the same.

1. For lightning to occur, there must be a great electrical pressure caused by large opposite charges on the clouds and the earth. (Change *to occur* to *to have occurred.*)

ANSWERS: EXERCISE 9
1. For lightning to have occurred there must have been a great electrical pressure caused by large opposite charges on the clouds and the earth.

INSTRUCTOR'S NOTES

ANSWERS: EX. 9 (CONT.)

2. In most storms, the earth will have a positive charge and the low-lying clouds will have a negative charge.

3. The electrical charges involved can be so tremendous that lightning flashes of five miles from cloud to earth, or of ten miles from cloud to cloud, can occur frequently.

4. The thunderclap that follows the flash is caused by inrushing air when the air that has been expanded by the hot lightning bolt cools and contracts, creating a partial vacuum that sucks in the surrounding air.

5. Ben Franklin's lightning rod works by providing an easy way for the lightning's charge to reach the ground, bypassing the building itself.

2. In most storms, the earth has a positive charge and the low-lying clouds have a negative charge. (Change *has* to *will have*.)

3. The electrical charges involved are so tremendous that lightning flashes of five miles from cloud to earth, or of ten miles from cloud to cloud, occur frequently. (Change *are* to *can be*.)

4. The thunderclap that followed the flash was caused by inrushing air when the air that had been expanded by the hot lightning bolt had cooled and contracted, creating a partial vacuum that sucked in the surrounding air. (Change *followed* to *follows*.)

5. Ben Franklin's lightning rod worked by providing an easy way for the lightning's charge to reach the ground, bypassing the building itself. (Change *worked* to *works*.)

▮▮ MOOD

Mood refers to the ability of verbs to convey a writer's attitude toward a statement.

By far the most common mood in English is the **indicative mood.** It is used for statements about real things, or highly likely ones, and for questions about fact.

INDICATIVE   The door opened.

In walked the student.

Do you need a tutor?

The **imperative mood,** which always uses the simple form° of the verb, expresses commands and direct requests. When the subject is omitted in an imperative sentence—and it often is—the subject is assumed to be either the singular or plural *you* or the indefinite pronouns *anybody, somebody,* or *everybody.*

IMPERATIVE   Please shut the door.

Fasten your seatbelts.

Watch out!

▮ PUNCTUATION ALERT: A strong command is followed by an exclamation point; a mild command is followed by a period. ▮▮

The **subjunctive mood** expresses conditions including wishes, recommendations, indirect requests, and speculations. The subjunctive mood is used less often in English than it once was. For example, the subjunctive in the following sentence is correct.

202

SUBJUNCTIVE   Whether it be now or later, he must eventually pay his tax bill.

But many people now use the indicative to express the same idea:

INDICATIVE   Whether he does it now or later, he must eventually pay his tax bill.

Soon or later, he must pay his tax bill.

8i
Use correct subjunctive forms.

The present subjunctive uses the simple form° for all persons° and numbers°.

The grand jury asks that **she testify** [not *testifies*] again.

When she does, it is important that **her lawyer be** [not *is*] with her.

Except for the verb *be*, the past subjunctive uses the same form as the simple past tense in the indicative mood: *I wish that I had* a car. The past subjunctive of *be* is *were* for all persons and numbers.

I wish that **I were** [not *was*] taller.

They asked if **she were** [not *was*] leaving.

1
Use the subjunctive in *if* clauses and some *unless* clauses for speculations or conditions contrary to fact.

In dependent clauses introduced by *if* and sometimes *unless*, the subjunctive describes speculations or conditions contrary to fact.

If **my party were** [not *was*] in power, we would run the city well.

If **it were** [not *was*] to rain, voter turnout would be low.

In an *unless* clause, the subjunctive signals that what the clause says is very unlikely.

Unless **war were** [not *was*] to break out, the elections will be held on Tuesday.

BACKGROUND
William Safire recently quoted Robert Burchfield, overseer of the new four-volume *Oxford English Dictionary*, on the supposed death of the subjunctive mood: "'This very useful verbal distinction is not at all tottering toward extinction.'" Safire adds:

If it were not for the subjunctive, we would be less able to express desire, supposition, doubt; more important, we would find it hard to set up a situation contrary to fact—a shocker, something ridiculous—to see how we would deal with it.

Then he gives a complex but thought-provoking example:

A law professor testified at a recent Congressional hearing that Senator John C. Danforth's product-liability bill "reads as though it were written by James Joyce." Obviously, the bill was not written by the long-dead author of the punctuation-disdaining novel "Ulysses," which meant that the witness's don't-you-believe-it subjunctive *were* was necessary; if the indicative, here-comes-a-fact *was* had been used, hordes of illiterate legislators would have been led to assume that James Joyce was a Danforth staffer.

203

8i *v*

2
Use the subjunctive for conjectures introduced by *as if* or *as though*.

The subjunctive expresses conditions that are possible but cannot be confirmed.

This refrigerator sounds as if **it were** [not *was*] broken, but it is still running.

If the **telephone were** [not *was*] to have rung, we would have heard it.

3
Use the subjunctive in *that* clauses for wishes, indirect requests, recommendations, and demands.

Things that people wish for, ask for, or demand have not yet become reality. Use the subjunctive to express these unrealized goals.

I wish that this **week were** [not *was*] over.

It is important that the **doctor finish** [not *finishes*] the examination because someone is demanding that **she go** [not *goes*] to the clinic.

4
Use the subjunctive in certain standard expressions. Some subjunctive constructions appear in everyday language.

If I **were** you . . .	**Come** what may . . .
Please let me **be**.	If only I **were** there . . .
Be that as it may . . .	Far **be** it from me . . .

EXERCISE 10

Fill in the blanks with the appropriate subjunctive form of the verb in parentheses.

EXAMPLE   It is important that something (to be) _____ done about the rising rate of arson in America.

It is important that something *be* done about the rising rate of arson in America.

1. Criminologists insist that arsonists (to be) _____ caught and punished as a deterrent to others.

204

2. It is crucial that the arson investigator (to examine) _____ the fire scene for signs of arson immediately, because gasoline and kerosene can evaporate within hours.

3. Also public safety may require that cleanup (to begin) _____ almost immediately.

4. Once evidence evaporates or is moved, it is as if it never (to exist) _____.

5. The United States Supreme Court has ordered that arson investigations (to take) _____ precedence over any search warrant requirements.

6. If all arsonists (to be) _____ caught, our fire insurance rates might come down.

▌▌ VOICE

Voice refers to verbs' ability to show whether a subject° acts or receives the action named by the verb. English has two voices: active and passive. In the **active voice,** the subject performs the action.

> Most clams live in salt water.
> They burrow into the sandy bottoms of shallow waters.

In the **passive voice,** the subject is acted upon, and the person or thing doing the acting often appears as the object° of the preposition *by.*

> Clams have long been considered a delicacy by many people. [*people* = object of the preposition]
> They are also admired by crabs and starfish. [*crabs and starfish* = object]

The passive voice uses a past participle° to name the action and a form of *be* to specify person°, number°, and tense°.

> He **is respected** by his co-workers. [present tense of *be* + past participle = present passive]
> She **was insulted** by their ignorance of her work. [past tense of *be* + past participle = past passive]
> We **were being photographed** as we walked along the beach. [past progressive of *be* + past participle = past progressive passive]

Misusing voice usually creates problems of writing style rather than problems of incorrect grammar. To make your writing

ANSWERS: EXTRA EX. B (p. 200)

1. One of the most amazing of these men was Dr. Albert Koch, who regularly *combined* fossil bones to create new prehistoric animals.

2. In 1840, while he *was visiting* America from his native Germany, Dr. Koch announced a major find.

3. He *claimed* that he had discovered in Missouri the skeleton of a gigantic animal which he *called* the Missouri Leviathan.

4. Actually it *was* the remains of a mastodon.

5. Dr. Koch *had inserted* extra vertebrae, so that the backbone of the specimen appeared far longer than it really *was.*

6. Koch *wrote* that he *had identified* the Leviathan from its description in the Book of Job.

7. The skeleton probably *ended up* in the British Museum, although no one *knows* for certain.

8. In 1845, Dr. Koch *struck* again.

9. He announced finding a skeleton in Alabama that he *called* "the longest of all fossil skeletons found either in the new or old world."

10. Correct

205

clear, use voice consistently in sentences on the same topic. (See 15a-2 for ways to identify and correct confusing shifts in voice.)

■‖ 8j

Write in the active rather than the passive voice except to convey special types of emphasis.

Because the active voice emphasizes the doer of an action, active constructions have a more direct and dramatic effect. Active constructions also use fewer words than passive constructions. It makes sense, therefore, to use the active voice wherever you can. Most sentences in the passive voice can easily be converted to the active voice.

PASSIVE   African tribal masks are often imitated by Western sculptors.

ACTIVE   Western sculptors often imitate African tribal masks.

The passive voice does have some uses. If you learn what they are, you can use the passive to advantage.

‖ 1
Use the passive voice when the doer of the action is unknown or unimportant.

When no one knows who or what did something, you have to use the passive voice.

The lock **was broken** sometime after four o'clock. [Who broke the lock is unknown.]

When the doer of an action is unimportant, writers often use the passive voice.

In 1899, the year I was born, **a peace conference was held** at The Hague. [The doers of the action—holders of the conference—are unimportant to White's point.]

—E. B. WHITE, "Unity"

‖ 2
Use the passive voice to focus attention on the action rather than on the doer of the action.

The passive voice emphasizes the action, while the active voice focuses on the doer of the action. For example, in a passage about

ALTERNATE EXAMPLE:
NECESSARY PASSIVE VOICE
In the days of Aristotle, air was believed to be one of four fundamental substances that could not be further subdivided into constituent components.
—Frederick K. Lutgens and Edward J. Tarbuck, *The Atmosphere*

INSTRUCTOR'S NOTES

important contributions to the history of science, you might want to emphasize a doer by using the active voice.

ACTIVE   **Joseph Priestley discovered** oxygen in 1774.

But in a passage summarizing what is known about oxygen, you may want to emphasize what was done.

PASSIVE   **Oxygen was discovered** in 1774 by Joseph Priestley.

The passive voice is an important feature of some writing in the sciences. (For more about writing in the sciences, see Chapter 34.)

> Most of the oxygen in the blood is carried by the red blood cells. The amount of oxygen that can be transported is directly related to the number of red blood cells and the hemoglobin level within them.
>
> —MALINDA MURRAY, *Fundamentals of Nursing*

Your choices about audience° and purpose° greatly influence the voice you should choose for a sentence.

PASSIVE   The news that the dictator had fled was received before the order to attack the palace could be given. [Here the emphasis is on events, not on the doers of the action.]

ACTIVE   Before he could give the order to attack, the commander received the news that the dictator had fled the palace. [Here the emphasis is on the people rather than the actions.]

EXERCISE 11

First, determine whether each of these sentences is in the active or the passive voice. Second, rewrite the sentence in the other voice. Some sentences will require two changes.

EXAMPLE   The justices of the Supreme Court consider cases that raise questions of constitutional interpretation. [*active voice*]

Cases that raise questions of constitutional interpretation are considered by the justices of the Supreme Court.

1. The Supreme Court's decisions establish a basis for public policy until changing circumstances require new interpretations.
2. The Supreme Court's decisions have always been based on the Justices' reading of the Constitution or interpretations of it.

ANSWERS: EXERCISE 11
Rewrites may vary somewhat from the possibilities shown here.
1. *Active; rewrite in the passive:* A basis for public policy is established by the Supreme Court's decisions until new interpretations are required by changing circumstances.
2. *Passive; rewrite in the active:* The Supreme Court has always based its decisions on the Justices' reading of the Constitution or interpretations of it.

207

ANSWERS: EX. 11 (CONT.)

3. *Active; rewrite in the passive:* Just what the writers of the Constitution meant by what they wrote must be understood by each member of the Court, however, before he or she can interpret the Constitution.

4. *Passive; rewrite in the active:* Several problems make any question of what the framers of the Constitution intended—or would have intended—difficult to answer.

5. *Passive; rewrite in the active:* In many places the authors chose vague or open-ended language.

6. *Passive; rewrite in the active:* The Constitution's framers seemed to have focused on theoretical principles rather than concrete applications.

7. *Passive; rewrite in the active:* No one can guess at the private thoughts that motivated each person involved in drafting, rewriting, amending, and ratifying the document two hundred years ago.

8. *Active; rewrite in the passive:* Any court is prevented from imposing its will on other branches of government by the uncertainties that also prevent it from making absolute decisions.

9. *Passive; rewrite in the active:* The margin for flexibility of interpretation guarantees that judicial powers will remain limited.

10. *Active; rewrite in the passive:* Although the constitution will never be interpreted with absolute certainty by any court, balance between democratic processes and the authority of law is encouraged by this very uncertainty.

3. Before he or she can interpret the Constitution, however, each member of the Court must understand just what the writers of the Constitution meant by what they wrote.

4. Any question of what the framers of the Constitution intended—or would have intended—is made difficult to answer by several problems.

5. Vague or open-ended language was chosen by the authors in many places.

6. Theoretical principles rather than concrete applications seem to have been focused on by the Constitution's framers.

7. The private thoughts that motivated each person involved in drafting, rewriting, amending, and ratifying the document two hundred years ago cannot be guessed at by anyone.

8. The uncertainties that prevent any court from making absolute decisions also prevent it from imposing its will on other branches of government.

9. That judicial powers will remain limited is guaranteed by the margin for flexibility of interpretation.

10. Although no court will interpret the Constitution with certainty, this very uncertainty encourages a balance between democratic processes and the authority of law.

208

9

CASE OF NOUNS AND PRONOUNS

Case refers to word form changes to deliver information. The case of a noun or a pronoun communicates how that word relates to other words in a sentence. For example, *I, me,* and *mine* are three different cases of the singular first-person pronoun (Although *I* wanted a small wedding like my sister's, my parents asked *me* to invite all their friends to *mine*).

English has three cases: *subjective, objective,* and *possessive.* This chapter presents the cases of pronouns and nouns and explains how case operates, with special emphasis on the pronouns that writers sometimes find troublesome. See Chapter 27 for using *-s* and apostrophes to form the possessive case of nouns.

Personal pronouns, the most common type of pronouns, have a full range of cases that show changes in **person** (first, second, and third person) and **number** (singular and plural).

A pronoun in the **subjective case** functions as a subject°.

We were going to get married. [*We* is the subject.]

John and **I** wanted an inexpensive band to play at our wedding. [*I* is part of a compound° subject.]

A resourceful couple, **he** and **I** found a one-person band we could afford. [*He* and *I* are compound° subjects.]

LANGUAGE FACTS
Many languages have noun and/or pronoun case systems. The smallest number of cases is two, as in the Masai language of East Africa. In contrast, Sanskrit has eight cases. Latin has six; Greek has five. The prize, however, goes to Finnish, with fifteen noun cases.

209

TEACHING TIP

English has the same pronoun for both the singular and plural second person: *you*. This seems strange to many people, and some speakers use the nonstandard *you all* in an effort to show they are addressing more than one person. Most other languages have separate forms for the singular and plural second-person pronoun. However, in some cases the singular is reserved for family members and friends (whether one or more), while the plural is used as an indication of respect for the person or persons addressed. This split occurred in English with *thou/thee* and *you* in the thirteenth century. French makes a similar distinction between *tu* and *vous*. If you have French-speaking students, you might ask them to explain the difference to the class. Spanish uses *tu* (singular)/*vosotros* (plural) informally and *Usted* (singular)/*Ustedes* (plural) formally to mean *you*. The formal pronouns are always capitalized. Again, you might wish to have your bilingual students explain the difference. (Incidentally, *Usted* and *Ustedes* take third-person verbs.)

CASES OF PERSONAL PRONOUNS						
	SUBJECTIVE		**OBJECTIVE**		**POSSESSIVE**	
PERSON	SING.	PLUR.	SING.	PLUR.	SING.	PLUR.
First	I	we	me	us	my/mine	our/ours
Second	you	you	you	you	your/yours	your/yours
Third	he she it	they	him her it	them	his her/hers its	their/theirs

A pronoun in the **objective case** functions as a direct object° or an indirect object°.

> We saw **him** perform in a public park. [*Him* is the direct object.]
>
> We showed **him** our budget. [*Him* is the indirect object.]
>
> He understood and shook hands with a very happy bride, **me.** [*Me* is an appositive° that renames *bride*, the object of the preposition *with*.]

A pronoun in the **possessive case** indicates possession or ownership. ▊ PUNCTUATION ALERT: Do not use an apostrophe for a personal pronoun in the possessive case, as is explained in Chapter 27. ▊

> The signatures appearing quickly on the written agreement were **ours.** [*Ours* indicates possession.]
>
> **His** followed. [*His*, which indicates possession, also implies the inclusion of the noun *signature*.]

The pronouns *who* and *whoever* also change form for case changes. Using *who* and *whoever* is discussed in 9d.

▊ 9a

For pronouns in compound constructions, use the same cases as for single constructions.

A compound construction contains more than one subject or object.

> **He** saw the eclipse of the sun. [single subject]
>
> **He and I** saw the eclipse of the sun. [compound subject]

210

That eclipse astonished **us.** [single object]

That eclipse astonished **him and me.** (compound object)

A compound construction has no effect on the choice of pronoun case. A compound subject uses the subjective case, and a compound object uses the objective case. Sometimes, however, people make the mistake of switching cases for compounds. If you sometimes are unsure which case to use, try the "drop test."

Here is a three-step drop test for compound constructions to help you stay in the appropriate case: Temporarily drop *all of the compound element except the pronoun in question,* and then you will be able to tell which pronoun case is needed. Here is how the method works for compound subjects.

EXAMPLE	**Janet and (me, I)** read that the moon has one-eightieth the mass of the earth.
STEP 1	Drop "Janet and."
STEP 2	Which reads correctly: "**Me** read that the moon has one-eightieth the mass of the earth" or "**I** read that the moon has one-eightieth the mass of the earth"?
STEP 3	Answer: Janet and **I** read that the moon has one-eightieth the mass of the earth.

This "drop test" works also when both parts of the compound subject are pronouns: *She* and *I* [not *Her* and *me*] *read that the moon has one-eightieth the mass of the earth.*

The same "drop test" works for compound objects:

EXAMPLE	The instructor told **Janet and (I, me)** that the moon has one-fiftieth the volume of the earth.
STEP 1	Drop "Janet and."
STEP 2	Which reads correctly: "The instructor told **I** that the moon has one-fiftieth the volume of the earth" or "The instructor told **me** that the moon has one-fiftieth the volume of the earth"?
STEP 3	Answer: The instructor told Janet and **me** that the moon has one-fiftieth the volume of the earth.

This "drop test" works also when both parts of the compound object are pronouns: *The instructor told* **her** *and* **me** [not *she* and *I*] *that the moon has one-fiftieth the volume of the earth.*

TEACHING TIP

If your students have trouble choosing the appropriate pronoun in compound constructions, you can do the drop test using these additional sentences.

Compound subjects

Someday (she, her) and (I, me) will travel there as scientists. [She, I]

(We, Us) and other pioneers will lead the people of Earth into space. [We]

Compound objects

The instructor told (we, us) and the other students that volume is not the same as mass. [us]

The instructor explained to (I, me) and (she, her) that volume is size, but mass is related to weight and gravity. [me, her]

INSTRUCTOR'S NOTES

LANGUAGE HISTORY

Nowadays the pronouns *thou* and *thee* linger only among some religious sects. In fact, they had disappeared almost entirely by the start of the eighteenth century. However, they have an interesting history that reflects changes that occurred simultaneously in many European languages. These pronouns were originally second-person singular pronouns (subjective and objective cases); they were replaced by *you*, which was originally the second-person plural pronoun.

As Joseph M. Williams explains in *Origins of the English Language* (New York: Free Press, 1975: 248-49), the change is rooted in the Roman Empire of the fourth century A.D. At that time there were two emperors, one in Rome and one in Constantinople. People speaking to either emperor were required to use the plural form of address. The practice of using the plural as a sign of respect slowly spread to France, where *tu* is the second-person singular pronoun and *vous* the plural. During the thirteenth century, in imitation of the *tu/vous* of the French nobles who occupied their country, the English began using *thee* (objective), *thou* (subjective), and *you* the same way. *You* become a mark of mutual respect in conversations among the elite and a sign of deference when a person spoke to a social superior. In contrast, *thee/thou* became a sign of intimacy among members of the same family or among those who believed in the same things.

ANSWERS: EXERCISE 1

1. we	7. we
2. me	8. us
3. us	9. we
4. she	10. I
5. I	11. me
6. us	

When pronouns in a prepositional phrase° occur in compound constructions, inexperienced writers sometimes allow pronouns to slip into the wrong case. A prepositional phrase always has an object°, so any pronouns that follow words such as *with, to, from, for, after, between* must be in the objective case.

No	The instructor gave an assignment **to Sam and I.** [*I* is in the subjective case and cannot follow a preposition.]
Yes	The instructor gave an assignment **to Sam and me.** [*Me* is in the objective case, so it is correct.]
No	The instructor spoke **with he and I.**
No	The instructor spoke **with him and I.**
Yes	The instructor spoke **with him and me.**

Between is a preposition that frequently leads people to pronoun error; a pronoun after *between,* like other prepositions, must always be in the objective case.

No	The instructor divided the work **between Sam and I.** [*I* is in the subjective case and cannot follow a preposition.]
Yes	The instructor divided the work **between Sam and me.** [*Me* is in the objective case, so it is correct.]

If you are in doubt when you use pronouns in prepositional phrases, use the "drop test" shown on page 211.

EXERCISE 1

From each pair of pronouns in parentheses select the correct one and circle it.

EXAMPLE   My sister and (*I,* me) decided to buy our brother a lizard for his birthday.

(We, Us)[1] went to an exotic pet store where the owner showed my sister and (I, me)[2] a variety of lizards. The owner kept trying to give (we, us)[3] lizards to hold, but (she, her)[4] and (I, me)[5] refused. Then across from (we, us)[6] (we, us)[7] spotted a Gila monster. Although it did not appeal to (we, us)[8], (we, us)[9] were sure it would make an unusual pet. My sister and (I, me)[10] asked about buying it, but the owner said, "Between you and (I, me),[11] I don't advise you to get it for your brother—its bite can be fatal."

212

▪▮ 9b
Match noun and pronoun cases.

When *we* (subjective) occurs with a noun, the noun must be functioning as a subject°; when *us* (objective) occurs with a noun, the noun must be functioning as an object°. The drop test shown in Section 9a can be adapted here. Temporarily drop the noun following the pronoun and see which pronoun reads correctly.

> **(We, Us)** tennis players practice hard.

No   **Us** practice hard.

Yes   **We** practice hard.

Yes   **We** tennis players practice hard. [*Tennis players* functions as a subject, so the pronoun must be in the subjective case.]

> Our coach tells **(we, us)** tennis players to practice hard.

No   Our coach tells **we** to practice hard.

Yes   Our coach tells **us** to practice hard.

Yes   Our coach tells **us** tennis players to practice hard. [*Tennis players* functions as an object, so the pronoun must be in the objective case.]

The same principles hold when pronouns occur in an **appositive**—a word or group of words that renames the noun or noun phrase° preceding it. The drop test shown in Section 9a can be adapted here. Drop the noun and test each pronoun separately to see if it is correct.

No   The winners, **her** and **me**, advanced to the finals. [*Her and me* rename the subject, *the winners,* so objective pronouns are incorrect.]

Yes   The winners, **she** and **I**, advanced to the finals. [*She and I* rename the subject, *the winners,* so subjective pronouns are correct.]

No   The crowd cheered the winners, **she** and **I**. [*She and I* rename the object, *the winners,* so subjective pronouns are incorrect.]

Yes   The crowd cheered the winners, **her** and **me**. [*Her and me* rename the object, *the winners,* so objective pronouns are correct.]

TEACHING TIP

If your students have trouble choosing the appropriate pronoun for use in appositives, you can do the drop test using these additional sentences.

Subjective case

The gymnasts, (he, him) and (she, her), were ignored. [he, she]

They, especially (he, him), missed being the center of attention. [he]

Objective case

The gymnastics coach cheered up the disheartened athletes, (I, me) and (they, them). [me, them]

The coach told the people on the trampoline, (he, him) and (she, her), her plans for a big win at the next competition. [him, her]

213

◼‖ 9c

After linking verbs, use the subjective case.

A **linking verb** connects a subject° to a word that renames it. Linking verbs indicate a state of being (*am, is, are, was, were,* etc.), relate to the senses (*look, smell, taste, sound, feel*), or indicate a condition (*appear, seem, become, grow, turn, remain,* and *prove*).

Because a pronoun coming after any linking verb renames the subject, the pronoun must be in the subjective case.

> The contest winner was **I.** [*I* renames *the contest winner,* the subject, so the subjective case is required.]
>
> The ones who will benefit are **they** and **I.** [*They* and *I* rename *the ones who will benefit,* the subject, so the subjective case is required.]
>
> May I please speak to Guy? This is **he.** [*He* renames *this,* the subject, so the subjective case is required.]
>
> Who is there? It is **I.** [*I* renames *it,* the subject, so the subjective case is required.]

In speech and informal writing, the objective case is sometimes substituted in the two constructions shown in the last two examples above, but avoid these usages in academic writing.

ANSWERS: EXERCISE 2
1. I
2. me
3. she
4. we
5. We
6. I
7. I
8. me
9. she
10. me
11. I
12. us
13. him
14. he

EXERCISE 2

Circle the correct pronoun in each pair in parentheses.

EXAMPLES   Bob Soak, Jr.: Sally and (I , me) lent a friend five hundred dollars, but we have no proof.

Bob Soak, Sr.: Between you and (I, me), son, you are in an awkward situation.

Jr.: The two of us, Sally and (I, me),[1] know. To make matters worse, another friend told Sally and (I, me)[2] today that our friend has moved to another city.

Sr.: Don't you know better, you and (she, her)[3], not to give someone cash and forget to ask for a receipt?

Jr.: It was (we, us)[4] who did exactly that.

Sr.: (Us, We)[5] Soaks are usually more careful, but I think that together you and (I, me)[6] can work out a solution.

Jr.: Sally and (I, me)[7] would truly appreciate your help, and I will not forget that one of the people who created this problem is (I, me).[8]

214

Sr.: Here is what to do. You and Sally write your friend a letter saying that you and (she, her)[9] have an emergency and need the one thousand dollars back right away.

Jr.: Between you and (I, me),[10] Dad, he will think I am crazy because Sally and (I, me)[11] lent him only five hundred dollars.

Sr.: Give (we, us)[12] experienced folks a little credit. When your friend reads that you expect one thousand dollars from (he, him),[13] he will write quickly to say that (he, him)[14] is the person who owes you five hundred dollars. Then you will have your proof in writing.

■|| 9d

Use *who* and *whoever* when the subjective case is needed; use *whom* and *whomever* when the objective case is needed.

The pronouns *who* and *whoever* are in the subjective case, and *whom* and *whomever* are in the objective case. Within each case, the pronouns do not change form for singular or plural or for first, second, or third person.

CASES OF RELATIVE AND INTERROGATIVE PRONOUNS		
SUBJECTIVE	**OBJECTIVE**	**POSSESSIVE**
who whoever	whom whomever	whose -----

|| 1
Know how to use *who, whoever, whom,* and *whomever* in dependent clauses.

A **dependent clause** (also called a **subordinate clause**) contains a subject° and predicate° and starts with a word that makes the clause unable to stand alone as a sentence. Pronouns such as *who, whoever, whom* or *whomever* start many dependent clauses.

To determine what pronoun case° is correct in a dependent clause, it is not necessary to determine whether the entire clause is functioning as a subject or an object in the sentence. All that matters is how the pronoun functions in its own clause. Making this determination can sometimes be prickly for inexperienced writers, especially because informal, spoken English tends to blur distinctions between *who* and *whom*.

COORDINATED RESOURCES

Alternate examples and exercises for this chapter are available in the *S & S Workbook for Writers,* Gordon and Troyka.

Transparency masters are available for many of the screened charts in this chapter.

Students can practice and test their knowledge of terms, key concepts, and applications of material in this chapter by using the *Study Guide* to the *S & S Handbook for Writers,* West.

215

TEACHING TIP

If your students have trouble choosing the appropriate relative pronoun in dependent clauses, you can do the drop test using these additional sentences.

Subjective case

I found out (who, whom) needed a lift to the polls. [who]

I was willing to pick up (whoever, whomever) lived in my neightborhood. [whoever]

Objective case

Discuss your vote with your family and friends, but do not let them pick (who, whom) you will vote for. [whom]

It is important to vote in private, so you can vote for (whoever, whomever) you choose, without pressure. [whomever]

A variation of the drop test shown in Section 9a can be adapted here to a four-step method. Temporarily drop everything in the sentence up to the pronoun in question, and then make substitutions—remembering that *he, she, they, who,* and *whoever* are subjects, and *him, her, them, whom,* and *whomever* (the *-m* forms and *her*) are objects. Here is how the method works for the subjective case:

EXAMPLE	**I wondered (who, whom) would vote.**
STEP 1	Omit "I wondered."
STEP 2	Test the sentence with *he* and *him* (or *she* and *her*): "**He** would vote" or "**Him** would vote."
STEP 3	Answer: "**He** would vote."
STEP 4	Therefore, because *he* is subjective, *who*, which is also the subjective, is correct: "I wondered **who** would vote."

This four-step drop test works also for *whoever.*

Voter registration drives attempt to enroll **whoever** is eligible to vote. ["*He* (not *him*) is eligible to vote" proves that the subjective case of *whoever* is needed.]

The subjective case is called for even when expressions such as *I think* or *he says* come between the subject and verb. Ignore these expressions when you are trying to determine the correct pronoun.

She is the candidate who [I think] will get my vote.

The same four-step drop test works for the objective case:

EXAMPLE	**Volunteers go to senior citizen centers hoping to enroll people (who, whom) others have ignored.**
STEP 1	Omit "Volunteers . . . people."
STEP 2	Test the sentence with *they* and *them:* "Others have ignored **they**" or "Others have ignored **them**."
STEP 3	Answer: "Others have ignored **them**."
STEP 4	Therefore, because *them* is objective, *whom*, which is also objective, is correct: "Volunteers go to senior citizen centers hoping to enroll people **whom** others have ignored."

216

This four-step drop test works also for *whomever:*

Such transportation means that the senior citizens can vote for **whomever** they wish. ["The senior citizens can vote for *him*" proves that the objective case of *whomever* is needed.]

2
Know how to use *who* and *whom* in questions.

At the beginning of questions, use *who* if the question is about the subject° and *whom* if the question is about the object°. To determine if the case is subjective or objective, recast the question as a statement.

Who watched the space shuttle lift-off? ["*I* watched the space shuttle lift-off" uses the subjective pronoun *I*, so *who* is correct.]

Ann admires **whom?** ["Ann admires *her*" uses the objective pronoun *her,* so *whom* is correct]

Whom does Ann admire? [Same as above.]

To **whom** does Ann speak about becoming an astronaut? ["Ann speaks to *them* about becoming an astronaut" uses the objective pronoun *them,* so *whom* is correct.]

EXERCISE 3
Circle the correct pronoun in each pair in parentheses.

EXAMPLE   Experts say that our personal philosophies depend largely upon ((who) , whom) or what has been important in our lives.

1. For example, many people vote for (whoever, whomever) their parents prefer.
2. Parents transmit to us their ideas about politics and (who, whom) to respect in government.
3. In general, adults treat the world as they were treated by (whoever, whomever) raised them.
4. Research shows that children (who, whom) have been overprotected often become adults for (who, whom) life is difficult beyond the protective family circle.
5. Adults (who, whom) were consulted as children about some family decisions, such as (who, whom) to invite to dinner or what to name the dog, usually are more active politically than people (who, whom) had no voice in family matters.
6. In totalitarian countries, schools indoctrinate youngsters (who, whom) have learned never to question authority, so adults believe that trouble waits for (whoever, whomever) challenges the system.

217

TEACHING TIP
If your students have trouble choosing the appropriate pronoun in questions, you might offer practice with these questions:

(Who, Whom) is the best candidate for governor? [Who]

(Who, Whom) do you think will win? [Who]

The Republicans nominated (who, whom)? [whom]

(Who, Whom) did the Republicans nominate? [Whom]

To (who, whom) can we turn for advice about the issues? [whom]

(Who, Whom) are you going to vote for? [Whom]

ANSWERS: EXERCISE 3
1. whomever
2. whom
3. whoever
4. who, whom
5. who, whom, who
6. who, whoever

TEACHING TIP

If your students have trouble choosing the appropriate pronoun after *than* or *as,* you might try expanding elliptical comparisons with them to verify the best choice. Here are a few practice sentences.

> Your appetite for ice cream is bigger than (me, mine). [mine]
>
> You devour more Rocky Road ice cream than (I, me). [I]
>
> You love Rocky Road ice cream more than (I, me). [Both are correct, but the meanings are very different.]

■‖ 9e

After *than* or *as,* use the pronoun case that reflects your intended meaning.

A sentence of comparison often can be clear even though some of the words following *than* or *as* are implied but not directly stated. For example, the word *are* does not have to be expressed at the end of this sentence: *My two-month-old Saint Bernard is larger* **than** *most full-grown dogs.*

When a pronoun follows *than* or *as,* the pronoun case carries essential information about what is being said. For example, these two sentences convey two very different messages, simply because of the choice between the words *me* and *I* after *than.*

1. My sister loved that dog more **than me.**
2. My sister loved that dog more **than I.**

Sentence 1 means "My sister loved that dog more *than she loved me.*" On the other hand, sentence 2 means "My sister loved that dog more *than I loved it.*" To make sure that any sentence of comparison delivers its message clearly, either include all words in the second half of a comparison or mentally fill in the words to check that you have chosen the correct pronoun case.

■‖ 9f

When a pronoun is the subject or the object of an infinitive, use the objective case.

An **infinitive** is the simple form° of a verb usually, but not always, following *to: to laugh, to dance.* Objective pronouns occur as both subjects and objects of infinitives.

> Our tennis coach expected John and **me** *to beat* Jimmy and **her.** [*Me* is the subject of the infinitive *to beat,* and *her* is the object of the infinitive; both are in the objective case.]

■‖ 9g

Before gerunds, use the possessive case.

A **gerund** is a verb's *-ing* form functioning as a noun. (**Brisk walking** *is excellent exercise.*) When a noun or pronoun precedes a gerund, the possessive case is called for (**Kim's brisk walking** *built up her stamina.* **Her brisk walking** *built up her stamina.*) In con-

218

trast, a present participle—a form that also ends in *-ing*—functions as a modifier. It does not take the possessive case. *(Kim,* **walking briskly,** *caught up to me.)*

The possessive case, therefore, communicates important information. Consider these two sentences which convey two different messages, entirely as a result of the possessive:

1. The detective noticed the **man staggering.**
2. The detective noticed the **man's staggering.**

Sentence 1 means that the detective noticed the man; sentence 2 means that the detective noticed the staggering.

The same distinction applies to pronouns:

1. The detective noticed **him** staggering.
2. The detective noticed **his** staggering.

In conversation, the distinction is often ignored, but readers of academic writing expect that information will be precise. Consider the difference in the following two examples:

GERUND (AS A SUBJECT)	The **governor's calling for a tax increase** surprised her supporters.
PARTICIPLE (MODIFIER)	The governor, **calling for a tax increase,** surprised her supporters.

EXERCISE 4
Circle the correct pronoun in each pair in parentheses.

EXAMPLE   Sam Houston, leader of the drive for Texas's independence, is less well-known for (*his* him) championing of the rights of the Cherokees.

1. Houston's concern grew out of (him, his) living with the Cherokees for three years in his late teens.
2. From 1817 to 1818 he served as a government subagent helping to settle some Cherokees on a reservation, but a reprimand from Secretary of War John C. Calhoun persuaded (he, him) to resign.
3. Calhoun was angry about (Houston, Houston's) wearing Indian clothing to meet (he, him).
4. Not only as tall and energetic as Andrew Jackson, Houston was also as popular as (he, him).
5. Houston served as congressman and later governor of Tennessee until his wife of three months left (he, him).
6. (She, Her) leaving prompted (he, him) to resign the governorship.

ANSWERS: EXERCISE 4
1. his
2. him
3. Houston's, him
4. he
5. him
6. her, him
7. him
8. them

219

INSTRUCTOR'S NOTES

7. He lived again with the Cherokees, who decided to adopt (he, him) as a member of their nation.

8. Later, he went to Washington on behalf of the Cherokees to help (them, they) protest the fraud of some government agents.

EXTRA EXERCISE

From each group of pronouns in parentheses, select the correct word.

EXAMPLE:

My softball teammates and (myself, me, *I*) are confident we will make the finals this year.

1. I am so certain that I have already bought (me, myself) a new glove to celebrate.

2. Every practice session the coach tells the others and (me, myself) that we are getting better and better.

3. The sponsor (himself, hisself), Big Al of Big Al's Used Cars, even comes to games now.

4. The other women and (I, myself) are glad that our hard work has paid off.

5. We had an exhibition game against our husbands, who tired (theirselves, themselves) out and lost by four runs.

ANSWERS: EXTRA EXERCISE

1. myself
2. me
3. himself
4. I
5. themselves

◼‖ 9h

Reserve *-self* forms of pronouns for reflexive or intensive use.

Reflexive pronouns reflect back on the subject° or object°.

The detective disguised **himself.**
He had to rely on **himself** to solve the mystery.

Reflexive pronouns should not be used as substitutes for subjects or objects.

The detective and **I** (not *myself*) had a long talk.
He wanted my partner and **me** (not *myself*) to help him.

Intensive pronouns provide emphasis by making another word more intense in meaning.

The detective felt that his career **itself** was at stake.

Avoid these nonstandard forms of reflexive and intensive pronouns in academic writing: *hisself,* nonstandard for *himself; theirself, theirselves, themself,* and *themselfs,* nonstandard for *themselves.*

10
PRONOUN REFERENCE

The term **pronoun reference** refers to the fact that the meaning of a pronoun comes from its **antecedent,** the noun or pronoun to which the pronoun refers. For your writing to communicate its message clearly, each pronoun must relate directly to an antecedent. This chapter describes clear pronoun reference and alerts you to ways in which unclear pronoun reference can occur.

Consider these sentences in which each pronoun has a clear referent.

> **Facts** do not cease to exist just because **they** are ignored.
> —ALDOUS HUXLEY

> **Martyrdom** does not end something; **it** is only the beginning.
> —INDIRA GANDHI

When pronoun reference is unclear, meaning gets muddled. For example, consider this passage, which contains unclear pronoun reference.

> In 1911, **Roald Amundsen** reached the South Pole just thirty-five days before **Robert F. Scott** arrived. **He** [who? Amundsen or Scott?] had told people that **he** was going to sail for the Arctic, but **he** turned south for the Antarctic. Then on the journey home, **he** [who? Amundsen or Scott?] and **his** party froze to death just a few miles from safety.

WORD HISTORY

Antecedent comes from the Latin *ante,* meaning *before,* and *cedere,* meaning *to go.* Thus the *antecedent* is the word that "goes before" the pronoun.

BIOGRAPHY

Indira Gandhi was born in Allahabad, India, the only child of Jawaharlal Nehru, the first prime minister of an independent India. Her parents were fiercely nationalistic, and their periodic imprisonments during her childhood served as a model for her own dedication to an autonomous India. She first

Continued on p. 222

221

BIOGRAPHY (CONT.)

served as prime minister from 1966 to 1977. During this time, she implemented several unpopular social and political policies (including large-scale birth control by sterilization and declaring a state of emergency, which entailed the arrest of opposition leaders and complete press censorship). As a result of such policies, she was badly defeated in the 1977 elections. However, the Janata party, which succeeded her, collapsed, and Gandhi was restored to power in 1980.

The most serious problem of her second administration was agitation by the Sikhs (a religious minority) for an independent state in the Punjab, a major agricultural region of India. The Sikhs threatened to withhold badly needed food crops from the rest of the country, so Gandhi ordered troops to take the Sikhs' headquarters and holiest shrine, the Golden Temple at Amritsar. Hundreds were killed. Soon after, Gandhi was assassinated on October 31, 1984, by Sikh members of her own bodyguard.

10a

Make a pronoun refer clearly to a single antecedent.

To be understood, a pronoun must refer clearly to a single nearby antecedent. Often the same pronoun is used to serve as a referent to more than one antecedent. For example, in the paragraph above, *he* in different places refers to two different men, thus creating confusion for the reader. You can clarify such a passage by replacing some pronouns with nouns so that all the remaining pronouns clearly refer to single antecedent.

> In 1911, **Roald Amundsen** discovered the South Pole just thirty-five days before **Robert F. Scott** arrived. **Amundsen** had told people that **he** was going to sail for the Arctic but then **he** turned south for the Antarctic. On the journey home, **Scott** and **his** party froze to death just a few miles from safety.

More than one pronoun can appear in a sentence, but each must have a clear antecedent.

> **Robert F. Scott** used **horses** for **his** assault on the Pole, but **they** perished quickly because **they** were unsuited for travel over ice and snow.

Said and *told,* when used with pronouns that refer to more than one person, are particularly prone to creating confusion for readers. Quotation marks and slight rewording can clarify meaning.

No   Her mother told her she was going to visit Alaska.

Yes   Her mother told her, "You are going to visit Alaska."

Yes   Her mother told her, "I am going to visit Alaska."

10b

For clarity, place pronouns close to their antecedents.

If too much material comes between a pronoun and its antecedent, even though they may be logically related, unclear pronoun reference results. Readers lose track of the meaning of a passage if they have to trace back too far to find the antecedent of a pronoun.

222

No **Alfred Wegener,** a highly trained German meteorologist and professor of geophysics and meteorology at the University of Graz in Austria, was the first person to suggest that all the continents on earth were originally part of one large land mass. According to this theory, the supercontinent broke up long ago and the fragments drifted apart. **He** named this supercontinent Pangaea. [Although *he* can refer only to *Wegener,* too much material intervenes between the pronoun and its antecedent.]

Yes **Alfred Wegener,** a highly trained German meteorologist and professor of geophysics and meteorology at the University of Graz in Austria, was the first person to suggest that all the continents on earth were originally part of one large land mass. According to **his** theory, the supercontinent broke up long ago and the fragments drifted apart. **Wegener** named this supercontinent Pangaea.

EXERCISE 1

Rewrite each passage so that each pronoun has a single, nearby antecedent. Either replace pronouns with nouns or restructure a sentence to clarify pronoun reference. If you consider a passage correct as written, circle its number.

EXAMPLE Dag Hammarskjold was born in Jonkopin, Sweden, on July 29, 1905. He became a diplomat, economist, and United Nations official. People considered him a tactful and energetic leader. After his death, he was awarded the Nobel Peace Prize.

    (To correct, replace the last *he* with *Hammarskjold.*)

1. He was given the Nobel Peace Prize in 1961. His father, Hjalmar Hammarskjold, a former Swedish prime minister, had been head of the Nobel Prize Foundation from 1929 to 1947. He died eight years before his son was awarded the prize, so no family influence could have been involved.

2. In 1952 Dag Hammarskjold was appointed head of Sweden's delegation to the United Nations General Assembly. In April 1953 he was elected Secretary-General of the United Nations, succeeding the popular Trygve Lie, a Norwegian diplomat. He had served as Secretary-General since 1946.

3. Around the time of his unanimous reelection for a second five-year term in 1957, Hammarskjold became deeply involved in the Middle East, especially the Suez Canal crisis. He made several trips to confer with Arab and Israeli leaders.

ANSWERS: EXERCISE 1

Answers may vary somewhat. Some students may think that some of the *he*'s replaced here with nouns are acceptable, but clarity is the issue—avoiding intervening information that distracts the reader, unambiguous references, and so on. Possible answers are:

1. *Dag Hammarskjold* was given the Nobel Peace Prize in 1961. His father, Hjalmar Hammarskjold, a former Swedish prime minister, had been head of the Nobel Prize Foundation from 1929 to 1947. *Hjalmar Hammarskold* [or *The father*] died eight years before his son was awarded the prize, so no family influence could have been involved.

2. In 1952, Dag Hammarskjold was appointed head of Sweden's delegation to the United Nations General Assembly. In April 1953, he was elected Secretary-General of the United Nations, succeeding Trygve Lie, a Norwegian diplomat. *Lie* had served as Secretary-General since 1946.

3. Correct

INSTRUCTOR'S NOTES

ANSWERS: EX 4 (CONT.)

4. Hammarskjold met with Soviet Premier Nikita Khrushchev on March 27, 1959, to discuss world peace. *Hammarskjold* [or *The Secretary General*] found the meeting productive for furthering his goals as leader of the United Nations.

5. In 1960, war broke out in what was then called the Belgian Congo. Hammarskjold sent United Nations troops in an effort to restore peace and unity. Khrushchev denounced this move and demanded Hammarskjold's resignation. *Hammarskjold* maintained that he [or *his action*] was justified, and he refused to resign.

6. Tragically, *Hammarskjold* was killed soon after when his plane crashed while he was on a peace mission for the United Nations to the new Republic of the Congo.

4. Hammarskjold met with Soviet Premier Nikita Khrushchev on March 27, 1959, to discuss world peace. He found the meeting productive for furthering his goals as leader of the United Nations.

5. In 1960, war broke out in what was then called the Belgian Congo. Hammarskjold sent United Nations troops in an effort to restore peace and unity. Khrushchev denounced this move and demanded Hammarskjold's resignation. He maintained that he was justified, and he refused to resign.

6. Tragically, he was killed soon after when his plane crashed while he was on a peace mission for the United Nations to the new Republic of the Congo.

10c
Make a pronoun refer to a definite antecedent.

The antecedent of a pronoun must be clear or your writing will not succeed in delivering its intended message.

1
Do not let a pronoun refer to a noun's possessive form.

A pronoun cannot have as an antecedent a noun's possessive form.

No   Geologists think that about one hundred of the **earth's** biggest craters are the result of large asteroids colliding with **it**. [*It* cannot refer to the possessive *earth's*.]

Yes   Geologists think that about one hundred of the **earth's** biggest craters are the result of large asteroids colliding with **our planet**.

2
Do not let a pronoun refer to an adjective.

An adjective° serves as a modifier and cannot therefore serve double duty as a noun to which a pronoun can refer.

No   Avery likes to study **geological** records. **That** will be her major. [*That* cannot refer to the adjective *geological*.]

Yes   Avery likes to study **geological** records. **Geology** will be her major.

224

3

Make *it, that, this,* and *which* refer to only one antecedent.

Pronouns such as *it, that, this,* and *which* are particularly prone to creating unclear pronoun reference. As you write and revise, check carefully to see that the referent of these pronouns can be determined easily by your readers.

No　　Comets usually fly by the earth at 100,000 m.p.h., whereas asteroids sometimes collide with the earth. **This** interests scientists. [What does *this* refer to? . . . the speed of the comets? . . . comets flying by the earth? . . . asteroids colliding with the earth?]

Yes　　Comets usually fly by the earth at 100,000 m.p.h., whereas asteroids sometimes collide with the earth. **This difference** interests scientists.

No　　A fireball, caused by the impact of either a comet or an asteroid, rose twelve miles above central Siberia in 1908, but **it** is still unknown. [What does *it* refer to?]

Yes　　A fireball, caused by the impact of either a comet or an asteroid, rose twelve miles above central Siberia in 1908, but **the source of the explosion** is still unknown.

No　　According to some scientists, a rain of comets lasting hundreds of centuries hits the earth every 26 million years. Maybe **that** is how the dinosaurs perished in a mass extinction 65 million years ago. [What does *that* refer to?]

Yes　　According to some scientists, a rain of comets lasting hundreds of centuries hits the earth every 26 million years. Maybe **such a bombardment of comets killed the dinosaurs** in a mass extinction 65 million years ago.

No　　I told my friends that I was going to major in geology, **which** annoyed my parents. [What does *which* refer to?]

Yes　　My parents were annoyed because I discussed my major with my friends.

Yes　　My parents were annoyed because I chose to major in geology.

BACKGROUND

Many people are aware that the dinosaurs became extinct, apparently suddenly, about 65 million years ago. Fewer people realize that more than half of all the other kinds of animals and plants on earth also became extinct at that time. The theory that a gigantic comet or asteroid was responsible for this mass extinction was first proposed in 1980 by Nobel Prize-winning physicist Dr. Luis Alvarez and his geologist son, Dr. Walter Alvarez. They claimed that the collision of a comet or asteroid with the Earth sent up clouds of dust that hid the sun for months or even years, causing vegetation, and the animals dependent on it for food, to die.

Their theory remains controversial, but evidence is accumulating in its support. For example, in an effort to determine the nature of the object that might have hit the earth, scientists collected from sites around the wrold carbon particles deposited at the time of the supposed impact. Surprisingly, all the samples contained more than 10,000 times the amount of carbon expected. The pattern of the carbon was peculiar too—of the kind made only by burning vegetation.

Some scientists say the Alvarez hypothesis must be modified. They state that the impact probably occurred in the Bering Sea, gouging out a crater 100 miles across. A 3000°F fireball, moving at the speed of sound, ignited the forests of Europe, Asia, and North America. Hundreds of billions of tons of plants and animals were burned, creating huge clouds of smoke that joined the original impact dust in the atmosphere. This dark mixture encircled the earth, blocking the sun. Many plants and large animals were killed by the impact blast, the fire, and clouds of carbon monoxide; and many others could not withstand the climatic changes caused by the lack of sunlight.

INSTRUCTOR'S NOTES

COORDINATED RESOURCES

Alternate examples and exercises for this chapter are available in the *S & S Workbook for Writers,* Gordon and Troyka.

The software program *Blue Pencil,* available from Prentice-Hall, offers students additional practice coordinated with this chapter.

Students can practice and test their knowledge of terms, key concepts, and applications of material in this chapter by using the *Study Guide to the S & S Handbook for Writers,* West.

EXTRA EXERCISE (FOR 10F)

Select a relative pronoun to fill in each blank.

Example

Alaska, <u>which</u> is the largest state, has the lowest population density: one person for every two square miles.

1. New Jersey, _____ is the fifth smallest state, has the highest population density.
2. California is home to 3.5 million residents born outside the United States, _____ makes it the new melting pot, replacing New York.
3. Half of the 450,000 Indochinese refugees _____ came here after the Vietnam War live in California.
4. Automobile "lemon laws," _____ protect car buyers, had their beginnings in California.
5. The state _____ leads the country in pharmaceuticals is New Jersey.

4
Use *it* and *they* precisely.

In speech, common statements are *It said on the radio* or *In Washington they say,* but such expressions are inexact and wordy. They should be avoided in academic writing.

The newspaper reports [not *It said in the newspaper*] that minor earthquakes occur almost daily in California.

Californians say [not *In California they say*] that no one feels a minor earthquake.

5
Do not use a pronoun in the first sentence of a work to refer to the work's title.

A piece of writing has to stand on its own, so when referring to a title, be sure to repeat or reword whatever part of the title you want to use.

TITLE   Geophysics as a Major

NO   It unites the sciences of physics, biology, and ancient life.

YES   Geophysics unites the sciences of physics, biology, and ancient life.

■ 10d

Avoid overusing *it.*

It has three different uses in English.

1. *It* is a personal pronoun: *Doug wants to visit the 18-inch Schmidt telescope, but* **it** *is on Mount Palomar.*
2. *It* is an expletive, a word that postpones the subject: **It** *is interesting to observe the stars.*
3. *It* is part of idiomatic expressions of weather, time, or distance: **It** *is sunny.* **It** *is midnight.* **It** *is not far to the hotel.*

226

All of these uses are acceptable, but combining them in the same sentence can create confusion.

No   Because our car was overheating, **it** came as no surprise that **it** broke down just as **it** began to rain. [*It* is overused here even though all three uses—2, 1, and 3 above, respectively—are acceptable.]

Yes   It came as no surprise that our overheating car broke down just as the rain began to fall.

▉‖ 10e

Use *you* only for direct address.

In academic writing, *you* is not a suitable substitute for specific words that refer to people, situations, and occurrences. Exact language is always preferable. Also, *you* used for other than direct address tends to lead to wordiness.

No   Uprisings in prison often occcur when **you allow** overcrowded conditions to continue. [Are you, the reader, allowing the conditions to continue?]

Yes   Uprisings in prison often occur when **the authorities allow** overcrowded conditions to occur.

No   In many states, **you have prisons** with few rehabilitation programs. [Do you, the reader, have few programs?]

Yes   In many states, **prisons have** few rehabilitation programs.

No   In the Soviet Union **you** usually have to stand in long lines to buy groceries. [Are you, the reader of this handbook, planning to do your grocery shopping in the Soviet Union?]

Yes   Soviet consumers usually have to stand in long lines to buy groceries.

6. The forests and farmlands _____ make up two thirds of New Jersey give it its nickname: The Garden State.
7. Pennsylvania was founded in 1681 by William Penn, _____ was a Quaker.
8. Pennsylvania's leading cities are Philadelphia, _____ played a great role in U.S. history, and Pittsburgh, _____ was the first major industrial center of the Midwest.
9. States _____ were explored by travelers from Tennessee include Alabama, Mississippi, Arkansas, Louisiana, and Texas.
10. The mainland state _____ has the longest coastline is Florida.
11. Although anyone _____ glances at a map may think California's coast is longer, it is an optical illusion.

ANSWERS: EXTRA EXERCISE
1. which
2. which
3. who
4. which
5. that *or* which
6. that *or* which
7. who
8. which; which
9. that *or* which
10. that *or* which
11. who

227

ANSWERS: EXERCISE 2
Answers will vary somewhat. Possibilities are:
1. No one is certain how the brain stores information, but [drop *they claim*] the particular way *people* [not *you*] store and recall it.
2. *Clearly* [not *it is clear*], storing material is a complicated process.
3. Sir Frederick Bartlett, an early student of memory, suggested that a person's [not *your*] prior knowledge makes *the learning of new material possible* [not *it possible for new material to be learned*].
4. Correct
5. Correct
6. *These experiments prove* [not *it proves*] that [drop *this means*] *people* [not *you*] can use patterns in sets of information lists to help *them* [not *you*] remember.
7. *Tulving's findings are* [not *It is*] very interesting.
8. *As a result of these findings* [not *In this way*], students' beliefs that *people* [not *they*] can cram large amounts of material just before a test have been proven wrong.
9. Cramming does not work because no time is available for *the* [not *your*] brain to find patterns into which to fit new information.

EXERCISE 2
Rewrite each sentence so that all pronoun references are clear. If you consider a passage correct as written, circle its number.

EXAMPLE It says the term "memory storage" refers to a not-yet-understood process that helps memory work. (Replace *It* with *My psychology text*.)

1. No one is certain how the brain stores information, but they claim the particular way you organize material affects the way you store and recall it.
2. It is clear that it is a complicated process to store material.
3. Sir Frederick Bartlett, an early student of memory, suggested that your prior knowledge makes it possible for new material to be learned.
4. Bartlett claimed that each person's memory has its own unique features.
5. Endel Tulving, another expert, found that no matter how a given list of words was arranged, people participating in experiments always learned the words by regrouping them into the same categories.
6. It proves that this means you can use patterns in sets of information to help you remember them.
7. It is very interesting.
8. In this way, students' beliefs that they can cram large amounts of material just before a test have been proven wrong.
9. Cramming does not work because no time is available for your brain to find patterns into which to fit new information.

■‖ 10f
Use *who*, *which*, and *that* correctly.

Who refers to people or animals with names or special talents.

Theodore Roosevelt, who served from 1901 to 1909 as the twenty-sixth President of the United States, inspired the creation of the stuffed animal, the "teddy bear."

Lassie, the famous movie and TV collie, **who** was known for her intelligence and courage, was actually played by a series of male collies.

Which and *that* refer to animals, things, and sometimes anonymous or collective groups of people. The choice between *which* and *that* depends on whether the clause introduced by the pronoun is restrictive° or nonrestrictive°. (A restrictive clause is essential to limit meaning; a nonrestrictive clause is nonessential. See 24e for a full discussion.) Use *that* or *which* with restrictive clauses and *which* with nonrestrictive clauses. Use *who,* for people, in both kinds of clauses. ▮COMMA CAUTION: Set off nonrestrictive clauses with commas. ▮

> In modern zoos, **animals that** are dangerous are exhibited so that the public can observe them from monorails or other types of moving cages for humans.
>
> Modern **zoos that** are being built or renovated today provide natural habitats for their animals.
>
> **Giant pandas, which** are native to China, are in danger of extinction.
>
> **Bamboo, which** is their primary food source, recently has become scarce in many areas of China.
>
> **Children, who** virtually all enjoy zoos, especially enjoy "petting zoos," where they can touch animals safely.
>
> **Children who** like animals usually grow up to be affectionate adults.

EXERCISE 3

Fill in the blanks with *who, which,* or *that.*

EXAMPLE   Sometimes words __that__ [*or* __which__] look alike may have several different meanings.

1. One such word is *hydra,* _____ refers to a monster, an island, and a group of animals.
2. In Greek legend, Hydra was a gigantic monster _____ had nine heads, each of _____ grew back two new heads as soon as one was cut off.
3. Hercules was given twelve supposedly impossible tasks, one of _____ was to destroy the monster.
4. Hercules, _____ found killing the creature difficult, was finally successful when he burned out the roots as he cut off each head.
5. Hydra was also the old name of the Greek island now called Idhra, _____ is located in the Aegean Sea.
6. This is an island _____ was largely settled in the seventeenth century by Albanians _____ were fleeing the Turks.
7. In zoology, hydras, _____ are small, tentacled polyps, are found in fresh water throughout the world.
8. They capture food by means of stingers located in tentacles _____ carry the food to a centrally located mouth.

ANSWERS: EXERCISE 3

Note: As the text mentions, distinctions between *that* and *which* are becoming less rigid, although many writers reserve *that* for restrictive clauses and *which* for nonrestrictive clauses. Because of common practice in academic writing today, in this exercise both words are shown as acceptable for the example and for items 6 and 8. However, if you prefer to reserve *that* for restrictive clauses and *which* for nonrestrictive clauses, the answer to the example and to items 6 (first blank) and 8 is *that.*

1. which
2. who, that, or which; which
3. which
4. who
5. which
6. that or which; who
7. which
8. that or which

11
AGREEMENT

The concept of *agreement* in human affairs rests on matching knowledge and opinions. Grammatical agreement is also based on matching. Before language can work properly, certain parts of speech that change number°, person°, and, less often, gender° must match each other in form when they work together. Although the rules governing agreement are not difficult, their applications can seem tricky. Indeed, almost everyone has to consult a handbook once in a while to check one or another of the rules for agreement. This chapter discusses agreement in (1) subjects and verbs and (2) pronouns and antecedents—the only two combinations in which questions of matching forms arise.

■‖ SUBJECT–VERB AGREEMENT

Subject–verb agreement occurs at least once per sentence. To be grammatically correct, subjects and verbs must match in number (singular or plural) and in person (first, second, or third).

The **firefly glows** with luminescent light. [*firefly* = singular subject in the third person; *glows* = singular verb in the third person]

Fireflies glow with luminescent light. [*fireflies* = plural subject in the third person; *glow* = plural verb in the third person]

This **insect is** nocturnal.

These **insects are** nocturnal.

A QUICK REVIEW OF "PERSON" FOR AGREEMENT

The **first person** is the speaker or writer. *I* (singular) and *we* (plural) are the only subjects that occur in the first person.

SINGULAR	**I** see a field of fireflies.
PLURAL	**We** see a field of fireflies.

The **second person** is the person spoken or written to. *You* (both singular and plural) is the only subject that occurs in the second person.

SINGULAR	**You** see a shower of sparks.
PLURAL	**You** see a shower of sparks.

The **third person** is the person or thing being spoken or written of. Most rules for subject–verb agreement involve the third person. A subject in the third person can vary widely—for example, *student* and *students* (singular and plural people), *table* and *tables* (singular and plural things), and *it* and *they* (singular and plural pronouns).

SINGULAR	The **scientist sees** a cloud of cosmic dust.
	She (he, it) sees a cloud of cosmic dust.
PLURAL	The **scientists see** a cloud of cosmic dust.
	They see a cloud of cosmic dust.

ALTERNATE EXAMPLE
Notice how many subject–verb pairs are in the following passage from *Our Space Environment* by Phillip D. Stern:

It is common to refer to the sky as blue. Actually, the *sky is* black and our *atmosphere is* blue. *That is* because the tiny particles of *dust* and little moisture *droplets* in the air *are* small enough to interfere with and scatter the shorter wavelengths of the sun's light, the blue and violet colors, to produce an illusion of a blue sky. *Astronauts*, circling our planet at heights of hundreds of miles, *report* the *sky is* black and that the *sun, moon, stars,* and *planets can be seen* in the daytime hours.

INSTRUCTOR'S NOTES

EXTRA EXERCISE A

Fill in the blank with the correct present-tense form of the verb in parentheses.

Example

Psychologists often (to use) _____ projective tests to investigate clients' unconscious memories and drives. [*use*]

1. Psychologists sometimes (to present) _____ their clients with questions to which there are no correct answers.
2. The client then (to tell) _____ what he (to see) _____, thus showing the psychologist some of his inner self.
3. The popular *Rorschach Psychodiagnostic Inkblot Test* (to require) _____ the client to examine ten cards containing symmetrical inkblots and say what he (to think) _____ each means.
4. Next, the client (to point) _____ out where in the blot he (to find) _____ each image or idea.
5. Several scoring systems (to exist) _____ to help psychologists interpret clients' responses.

ANSWERS: EXTRA EXERCISE A

1. present
2. tells; sees
3. requires; thinks
4. points; finds
5. exist

11a

Use the final *-s* or *-es* for plural subjects or for singular verbs.

Subject–verb agreement often involves one letter: *s*. The key is the distinction between the *-s* added to subjects and the *-s* added to verbs.

We form most **plural subjects** by adding an *-s* or *-es* (*lip, lips; princess, princesses*). Exceptions include most pronouns (*they, who*); a few nouns that do not change form (*deer, deer*); and a few nouns that change in other ways (*mouse, mice; child, children*). We form **singular verbs** in the present tense of the third person by adding *-s* or *-es* to the simple form°— (*laugh* becomes *laughs, kiss* becomes *kisses*)—with the exceptions of *be (is)* and *have (has)*. (*Is* and *has* have an *-s* ending, but they are not formed from the simple form.)

Here is a memory device to help you to visualize how, in most cases, the *s* works in agreement. The *-s* (or *-es* when the word ends in *s*) can take only one path at a time, either the top or bottom.

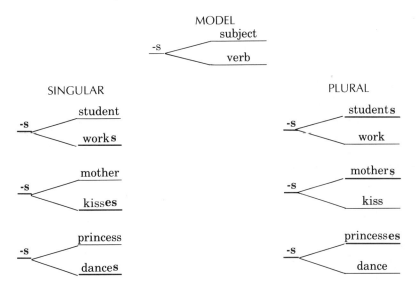

Even though some plural subjects do not have a final *s*, the principle of the memory device holds. The final *s* does not appear in some plural nouns (such as *people, children*), in plural personal pronouns (*we, you, they*), in the plural demonstrative pronouns (*these* and *those*), or in certain indefinite pronouns when they are used as plurals (*few, some, more, many, most,* and *all*).

232

The **child enjoys** watching cartoons.

Children enjoy watching cartoons.

We watch cartoons every Saturday morning.

They reflect rudimentary human impulses.

Most involve a startling amount of violence.

▌ USAGE ALERT: Do not add *-s* to the third person singular main verb after a modal auxiliary verb—a helping verb like *can, might, must, would*—see 8c. ▌

No   The coach **must thinks** every student likes swimming.

Yes   The coach **must think** every student likes swimming.

EXERCISE 1

Using the subject and verb in each set shown, write two complete sentences—one with the subject as a singular and one with the subject as a plural. Keep all verbs in the present tense.

1. boat
  race
	2. flag
	  fly
		3. man
		  applaud
			4. woman
			  cheer

5. chorus
  sing
	6. baby
	  burp
		7. judge
		  might decide
			8. winner
			  kiss

■▌ 11b

For the purposes of agreement, ignore words that come between a subject and verb.

Words that separate the subject from the verb can cause confusion about what a verb should agree with. This intervening material often appears as a prepositional phrase°. To locate the subject of a sentence, eliminate any prepositional phrases from consideration.

No   The **winners** in the state competition **goes** to the national finals. [*Winners* is the subject with which the verb must agree; *in the state competition* is a prepositional phrase.]

Yes   The **winners** in the state competition **go** to the national finals.

No   The **sponsor** of the concerts **pay** all expenses. [*Sponsor* is the subject with which the verb must agree; *of the concerts* is a prepositional phrase.]

Yes   The **sponsor** of the concerts **pays** all expenses.

COORDINATED RESOURCES

Alternate examples and exercises for this chapter are available in the *S & S Workbook for Writers*, Gordon and Troyka.

A transparency master is available for the screened chart in this chapter.

The software program *Blue Pencil*, available from Prentice-Hall, offers students additional practice coordinated with this chapter.

Students can practice and test their knowledge of terms, key concepts, and applications of material in this chapter by using the *Study Guide to the S & S Handbook for Writers*, West.

ANSWERS: EXERCISE 1

Answers will vary. Each set of sentences must use the subject once as a singular and once as a plural, and the verbs must agree accordingly.

233

EXTRA EXERCISE B
Fill in the blank with the correct present-tense form of the verb in parentheses.

Example

In the eyes of many people, the Rorschach Inkblots (to be) _____ the psychologists' standard tool for getting at clients' hidden thoughts and feelings. [*are*]

1. Yet either the Holtzman Inkblot Technique or the Thematic Apperception Test (TAT) (to be) _____ given by psychologists who feel the Rorschach is unreliable.
2. Not only does the Holtzman series have more inkblots (45) than the Rorschach (10), but it also (to have) _____ a more standardized system of administration.
3. The TAT (to use) _____ a series of pictures showing people engaged in a wide range of activities.
4. Although the pictures show people in realistic situations, there (to be) _____ many possible acceptable answers.
5. It (to be) _____ the task of the person interpreting the picture to make up a story, deciding what has occurred and what the characters are thinking and feeling.

ANSWERS: EXTRA EXERCISE B

1. is
2. has
3. uses
4. are
5. is

Also, to locate the subject of a sentence, eliminate any phrases that start with *including, together with, along with, accompanied by, in addition to, except,* and *as well as.*

No	**The moon,** as well as Venus, **are** visible in the night sky. [*The moon* is the subject with which the verb must agree; ignore *as well as Venus.*]
Yes	**The moon,** as well as Venus, **is** visible in the night sky.
No	**The Big Dipper,** along with many other constellations, **are** easy to learn to find. [*The Big Dipper* is the subject with which the verb must agree; ignore *along with many other constellations.*]
Yes	**The Big Dipper,** along with many other constellations, **is** easy to learn to find.

■‖ 11c

Use a plural verb for subjects connected by *and.*

When two or more subjects are joined by *and,* they become plural as a group; therefore, they need a plural verb.

The moon and Venus are visible in the night sky.
The Big Dipper and the constellation Orion are easy to learn to find.
Herb and Phyllis like to gaze at the stars.

However, if the word *each* or *every* precedes a singular subject, use a singular verb.

Each human hand and foot leaves a distinctive print.
Every police chief, sheriff, and federal marshall in the country has used these prints to identify people.

But when *each* or *every* follows subjects joined by *and,* they do not affect the basic rule: use a plural verb for subjects joined by *and.*

The Splitting Devil and the Masked Madman each claim to be the meanest wrestler alive.
Memphis and St. Louis each claim to be the birthplace of the blues.

234

The one exception to the *and* rule occurs when the parts combine to form a single thing or person.

Ham and cheese is our best-selling sandwich.
My best friend and neighbor feeds my cat when I go away.

EXERCISE 2

Supply the correct present-tense form of the verb in parentheses.

EXAMPLE   Increased heartbeat, rapid breathing, muscular tension, and sweaty palms (to be) _____ physical signs of fear.

Increased heartbeat, rapid breathing, muscular tension, and sweaty palms *are* physical signs of fear.

1. Every man, woman, and child in every culture (to experience) _____ fear from time to time.
2. An internal state of tension and generalized nameless worry accompanied by physical changes and irrational behavior (to be) _____ called *anxiety*.
3. A person who (to feel) _____ anxiety, as well as fear, often (to feel) _____ a need to escape from some imagined danger.
4. Anxiety, as it is expressed in disordered behaviors, (to take) _____ several forms.
5. Sigmund Freud, one of the founders of modern psychoanalysis, (to be) _____ said to have been the first to call these disorders *neuroses*.
6. Anxiety can (to make) _____ a sufferer very uncomfortable.

ANSWERS: EXERCISE 2
1. experiences
2. is
3. feels; feels
4. takes
5. is
6. make

▮‖ 11d

When subjects are joined by *or, nor,* or *not only . . . but (also),* the verb should agree with the subject closest to it.

When you join subjects with *or* or *nor* or correlative conjunctions°, *either . . . or, neither . . . nor, not only . . . but (also),* make the verb agree with the subject closest to it. Unlike *and*, these conjunctions do not automatically create plurals. For the purposes of agreement, ignore everything before the final subject.

~~Either a spider or~~ **a fly makes** a nice treat for a frog.
~~Either my sisters or~~ **my brother plans** to get a pet frog.

235

~~Not only the spider but also all other~~ **arachnids have** four pairs of legs.

~~Neither spiders nor~~ **flies tempt** my appetite.

~~Six clam fritters, four blue crabs, or one steamed~~ **lobster tempts** my appetite.

If the final example sounds awkward, rearrange the items so that the plural subject is next to the verb: *One steamed lobster, four blue crabs, or six clam fritters tempt my appetite.*

■‖ 11e

With inverted word order, make sure the verb agrees with its subject.

In English, the subject of a sentence normally precedes its verb: *Astronomy is interesting.* Inverted word order occurs primarily in two situations: in questions, and in sentences using *there* or *it* in expletive° constructions.

In questions, the auxiliary verb that has to agree with the subject often comes before the subject. Be sure to look ahead to check that the subject and verb agree.

Is astronomy interesting?

What **are** the **requirements** for the major?

Do John and Mary study astronomy?

Expletive constructions postpone the subject. Expletives using *there* or *it* plus a form of the verb *be* can be tricky because the form of *be* must agree with the sentence subject. Check ahead in such sentences to identify the subject, and make the form of *be—is, are, was, were,* for example—agree with the subject.

There are nine **planets** in our solar system. [The verb *are* agrees with the subject, *planets.*]

There is probably no **life** on eight of them. [*Is* agrees with *life.*]

The introductory *it* plus a form of the verb *be* can be an expletive construction as well, but one that always takes a singular verb.

It is astronomers who want to talk about the possibility of life in other galaxies.

It was the Viking mission to Mars ten years ago that ruled out any possibility of life on Mars.

236

For advice on making sentences more direct and concise by eliminating expletives, see 16a-1.

   You may occasionally want to write a statement in inverted word order for special effect (see 19e). Be sure to locate the subject and make the verb agree with it.

> Into deep space **shoot** probing **satellites.** [*Shoot* agrees with the inverted subject, *satellites*.]

> On the television screen **appears** an **image** of Saturn. [*Appears* agrees with the inverted subject, *image*.]

EXERCISE 3

Supply the correct present-tense form of the verb in parentheses.

EXAMPLE   Either sales and marketing or finance (to provide) _____ the basic training for most top corporate executives.

                Either sales and marketing or finance *provides* the basic training for most corporate executives.

1. To an outsider, the chief executive officer (CEO) of a company or conglomerate of companies (to seem) _____ to be an independent decision-maker.
2. Neither the economic climate nor a business's social responsibilities (to permit) _____ independance today, however.
3. There (to be) _____ many conflicting demands to reconcile from both stockholders and consumers.
4. Not only daily operations but also the public image of the corporation (to set) _____ the environment for a CEO.
5. The finance people, along with the public relations department, (to decide) _____ on the corporation's short-term goals.
6. Either the members of the board of directors or the CEO (to attempt) _____ to influence the government agencies that regulate business.

■ ‖ 11f

Use singular verbs for most indefinite pronouns.

   Indefinite pronouns do not refer to any particular person, thing, or idea. In context, however, they take on very clear meanings. Most indefinite pronouns are singular and therefore take singular verbs. (See 11n for a discussion of masculine pronouns with indefinite pronouns as antecedents.) Following is a list of indefinite pronouns.

ANSWERS: EXERCISE 3
1. seems
2. permit
3. are
4. sets
5. decide
6. attempts

BACKGROUND ON LANGUAGE
Most of us spend a fair proportion of our time reminding students that indefinite pronouns (with the exception of *all, any, some,* and *none*) are always singular. Yet widespread informal usage does not adhere to this rule, and we hardly seem to make a dent in our students' habit of following *everyone, anybody,* and the like with *their.*

   According to Martha Kolln of Pennsylvania State University, we shouldn't be too concerned about this usage. In "Everyone's Right to Their Own Language" (*College Composition and Communication,* Feb. 1986, 100-2), she looks at the issue. Most handbooks treat this usage as, at best, informal, while some continue to label it an outright error. Yet, Kolln points out, studies of usage

Continued on p. 238

237

BACKGROUND (CONT.)

patterns indicate that *everybody* has been treated as a plural for over four hundred years and *everyone* for over two hundred, appearing this way in the works of Cardinal Newman, Shakespeare, and Swift. Despite this evidence (available since 1957), the rule stands—at least on the record.

Kolln argues for treating indefinite pronouns as we treat collective nouns. A collective noun such as *crowd* takes a singular verb but takes a plural pronoun when it clearly refers to more than one person. She gives as an example:

> At first *the crowd* was singing; then *they* began to laugh.

Kolln gives this example for indefinite pronouns:

> At first *everyone* in the room was singing; then *they* began to laugh.

In fact, a singular pronoun would be out of place in the second clause. She demonstrates that the same applies when the indefinite pronoun appears as the direct object or as the subject of a tag question.

Kolln ends by calling for the acceptance of the plural possessive pronoun *(their)* after collective indefinite pronouns:

> These dicta that designate all indefinite pronouns as singular have no basis either in actual usage or in the rules of logic. Yet the current handbooks apply the same rule to all of the indefinite pronouns, whether they are collective or not, whether singular or not. (102)

Whether you agree or disagree with Kolln, the issue is certainly worth discussion.

another	either	neither	somebody
anybody	every	nobody	someone
anyone	everybody	no one	something
anything	everyone	nothing	
each	everything	one	

Everything about that intersection **is** dangerous.

But whenever **anyone says** anything, **nothing is** done.

Everyone knows that **something** terrible **is** likely to happen.

A few indefinite pronouns—*none, some, more, most, any,* and *all*—may be either singular or plural, depending on the meaning of the sentence.

Some of our streams **are** polluted. [*Some* refers to more than one stream.]

Pollution is always a threat, but **some is** easy to reverse. [*Some* refers to a portion of *pollution,* so it is singular and the verb *is* is used.]

All he asks **is** a chance. [*Chance* is singular; therefore, *all* is singular, and *is* is a singular verb.]

All are gone. [*All* here refers to more than one, so the verb *are* is correct.]

11g

With collective nouns, use singular or plural verbs according to context.

A **collective noun** names a group of people or things: *family, group, audience, class, number, committee, team,* and the like. When the group acts as one unit, use a singular verb. When the members of the group act individually, thus creating more than one action, use a plural verb.

The senior class nervously **awaits** final exams. [*Class* is acting as a single unit, so the verb is singular.]

The senior class were fitted for their graduation robes today. [Each member was fitted individually, and because there is more than one action, the verb is plural.]

The couple in red **is** invited. [*Couple* refers to a single unit, so the verb is singular.]

The couple say their vows tomorrow. [The two people will take a separate action, so there will be more than one action, and the verb is plural.]

238

■‖ 11h

Make sure a linking verb agrees with the subject—not the subject complement.

A **linking verb**° acts like an equal sign between a subject and a word that renames the subject—its **subject complement**°.

> You **seem** angry. [*you* = *angry; you* is the subject and *angry* is the subject complement]

The subject complement that follows a linking verb may differ in number° from the subject. When it does, the verb agrees with the subject, regardless of the number of the complement.

No   **The worst part** of owning a car **are** the bills.

Yes   **The worst part** of owning a car **is** the bills.

However, notice what happens when the subjects and complements are reversed:

No   **Bills is** the worst part of owning a car.

Yes   **Bills are** the worst part of owning a car.

■‖ 11i

With *who, which,* and *that* as subjects, use verbs that agree with the antecedents of these pronouns.

Who, which, and *that* have the same form in singular and plural. Find their antecedents—words to which the pronouns refer—before deciding whether the verb is singular or plural.

> The scientist will share the income from her new patent with the graduate **students who work** with her. [*Who* refers to *students,* so the verb *work* is plural.]
>
> George Jones is **the student who works** in the science lab. [*Who* refers to *student,* so the verb *works* is singular.]

Be especially careful to identify the antecedent of *who, which,* or *that* when you see *one of the* or *the only one of the* in a sentence.

> George Jones is one of the lab assistants **who deserve** recognition. [*Who* refers to *lab assistants,* so *deserve* is plural.]
>
> George Jones is the only one of the lab assistants **who deserves** recognition. [*Who* refers to *one,* so *deserve* is singular.]

TEACHING TIP
Many students have trouble selecting the appropriate verb form after *who.* In most cases, selection is simple: the verb agrees with the same noun that serves as the antecedent of *who.*

> The professor *who* teaches French comes from Haiti.
> The professors *who* teach French come from Haiti.

Yet when the word *one* is the subject and it is followed by a prepositional phrase, application of this rule becomes more difficult.

> One of the professors who *teach/teaches* French *comes/come* from Haiti.

The trick is to be sure that the verb in the dependent clause (*teach/teaches*) agrees with the subject of its own clause—which is often not the same as the subject of the main clause. In the above example, *one* is the subject of the main clause, but *professors* is the antecedent of *who* and hence is the implied subject of the dependent clause. Thus, we ought to write:

> One of the professors who *teach* French comes from Haiti.

239

When you write a sentence with *one . . . who, one . . . which,* or *one . . . that,* decide whether the relative pronoun° refers to *one* or to the group named after *one of the.* If the pronoun refers to *one,* use a singular verb. If the pronoun refers to what comes after *one of the,* use a plural verb.

ANSWERS: EXERCISE 4
1. feels
2. watches (or, if individuals in a family: watch)
3. is
4. affects; have
5. have
6. requires
7. have

EXERCISE 4
Supply the correct present-tense form of the verb in parentheses.

EXAMPLE   Everyone (to experience) ＿＿＿ anxiety from time to time, but some people (to have) ＿＿＿ difficulty controlling their feelings.

Everyone *experiences* anxiety from time to time, but some people *have* difficulty controlling their feelings.

1. In free-floating anxiety, often someone (to feel) ＿＿＿ as if an inescapable danger were imminent.
2. The family (to watch) ＿＿＿ the victim go through attacks of sweating, dizziness, heart palpitations, and shortness of breath.
3. Of all the anxieties, none (to be) ＿＿＿ as startling as a sudden panic attack.
4. A severe group of symptoms (to affect) ＿＿＿ axiety-ridden people when they (to have) ＿＿＿ to appear in public or to be in large open spaces.
5. Psychiatrists are medical doctors who (to have) ＿＿＿ completed at least three years of clinical training beyond the M.D. degree.
6. The program for psychoanalysts is one that (to require) ＿＿＿ the psychoanalysis of the doctor in training.
7. Social workers who (to have) ＿＿＿ taken advanced studies may become psychiatric social workers.

■‖ 11j

Use singular verbs with subjects that specify amounts and with singular subjects that are in plural form.

Subjects that refer to sums of money, distance, or measurement are considered singular and take singular verbs.

Ninety cents is the current bus fare.
Three hundred dollars is the price.
Three-quarters of an inch is all we need.
Two miles is a short sprint for a serious jogger.

240

Many words that end in *-s* or *-ics* are singular in meaning despite their plural appearance. They include *news, ethics, economics, mathematics, physics* (as a course of study), *politics, sports, measles, statistics,* as a group of data).

> The **news gets** better each day.
>
> Experts say that **sports builds** character.
>
> **Statistics is** required of math and science majors. [Here *statistics* is a source of study.]
>
> **Statistics indicate** a coming shortage of teachers. [Here *statistics* refers to a body of data, not a discipline or course.]

There are also some words treated as plural, even though they refer to one thing; they include *jeans, pants, scissors, clippers, tweezers, eyeglasses, thanks, riches.*

> **Eyeglasses fog up** in damp weather, so **my thanks go** to the inventor of contact lenses.
>
> My **slacks need** pressing. [But: My *pair* of slacks *needs* pressing.]

Series and *means* have the same form in singular and plural, so the meaning determines whether the verb is singular or plural.

> **The new series begins** on Sunday night.
>
> **A series of disasters are plaguing** our production.

■‖ 11k

Use singular verbs for titles of written works, companies, and words as terms.

Even though plural and compound nouns occur in a title, the title itself signifies one work or entity. Therefore, these subjects are singular and always take singular verbs.

> *Cider House Rules* by John Irving **is** a popular novel.
>
> *Dreamgirls* **was** a major Broadway hit.

Even if a word is plural, when you refer to it as a term, it takes a singular verb.

> *Our* implies that I am included.
>
> During the Vietnam War, *protective reaction strikes* **was** a euphemism used by the United States government to mean *bombing.*

241

ANSWERS: EXERCISE 5
1. study; strive; give
2. say; is
3. change
4. asks; are
5. is; shows
6. reveals; is
7. does
8. is; appears
9. is; gives
10. are

EXERCISE 5
Supply the correct present-tense form of the verb in parentheses.

EXAMPLE   Palmistry, also known as hand reading, (to go) _____ back to the ancient Chinese and Egyptians.

Palmistry, also known as hand reading, *goes* back to the ancient Chinese and Egyptians.

1. Advocates believe that if they (to study) _____ the weaknesses revealed in their palms and (to strive) _____ to correct them, then they (to give) _____ new meaning to the expression "Your fate is in your hands."
2. Contrary to popular belief, people who read palms (to say) _____ that nothing revealed in palms (to be) _____ irreversible.
3. Believers in palmistry also claim that people's hands (to change) _____ to reflect their lives.
4. Everybody who is curious about palmistry (to ask) _____ which hand is read; both (to be) _____.
5. According to believers, if someone (to be) _____ right-handed, the left hand (to show) _____ inherited characteristics and potential.
6. The other hand (to reveal) _____ how the person (to be) _____ using what is given to him or her.
7. Supposedly, either the right hand or the left hand alone (to do) _____ not give a complete reading.
8. Palm readers claim that there (to be) _____ a "poison line" that (to appear) _____ in the hands of chronic drug users.
9. Five dollars (to be) _____ is the usual fee for a basic reading; even fifteen minutes at lunch hour (to give) _____ a person enough time to get a quick reading.
10. I would think that eyeglasses (to be) _____ a necessity for a nearsighted palm reader.

▮|| PRONOUN-ANTECEDENT AGREEMENT

The form of most pronouns depends on **antecedents**—nouns, noun phrases, or other pronouns to which the pronouns refer. The connection between a pronoun and its antecedent must be clear if writing is to be clear and coherent (see Chapter 10 for advice on pronoun reference). These connections are achieved by agreement in number (singular or plural), person (first, second, or third), and gender (male or female).

Pronouns must match their antecedents in number (singular pronouns refer to singular antecedents, and plural pronouns to plural antecedents).

Loud music has **its** harmful side effects.
Many musicians suffer damage to **their** auditory nerves.

▚▎ 11l

Use a plural pronoun when its antecedents are joined by *and*.

Two or more antecedents joined by *and* require a plural pronoun, even if the antecedents are singular.

The United States and Canada maintain **their** border as the longest open frontier in the world.
Although **France and Spain are** friendly nations, **they** control access across **their** common border.

When *each* or *every* precedes singular nouns joined by *and,* use a singular pronoun.

Every American and Canadian may cross the border without showing **his or her** passport.
Each car and truck that comes through the border station has **its** contents inspected.

When the singular nouns joined by *and* refer to a single person or thing, use a singular pronoun.

Our guide and translator told us to watch out for scorpions as she took us into the tomb.

▚▎ 11m

When antecedents are joined by *or* or *nor,* make the pronoun agree with the antecedent closest to it.

Antecedents joined by the conjunction° *or, nor,* or correlative conjunctions° (such as *either . . . or, neither . . . nor),* often mix the masculine and feminine or singular and plural. For the purposes of agreement, ignore everything before the final antecedent.

ALTERNATE EXAMPLE
Notice how each pronoun (P) refers to its antecendent (A).

Studies done on [A]*identical twins* separated at birth indicate that [P]*they* often have much in common. Twins Oskar Stohr and Jack Yute were separated at birth. [A]*Oskar* was raised as a Catholic by [P]*his* grandmother in Germany under the Nazis. [A]*Jack* was raised as a Jew in the Caribbean and spent time with [P]*his* father on a kibbutz in Israel. Yet when the [A]*brothers* met years later [P]*they* were dressed similarly (wire-rimmed glasses, two-pocket shirts with epaulets), had mustaches, and were found to have similar eating, sleeping, reading, and toilet habits. [P]*Their* [A]*mother* would have been surprised [P]*herself* to have seen how alike [P]*her* [A]*boys* were, but the records do not indicate whether [P]*she* ever saw either of [P]*them* after giving Oskar to [P]*her* mother.

EXTRA EXERCISE C
Rewrite this paragraph so that pronoun-antecedent agreement in person and number is maintained. It may also be necessary to change verbs or other words.

Buying stock involves many steps. Once a stockbroker receives an order, they call their firm's telephone clerk, who is located near the edge of the trading area. The telephone clerk summons his firm's floor broker by flashing their code number on a large electronic board posted in the trading area. Seeing their number, the floor broker goes to the telephone clerk and picks up the buy order. You then go to the small area set

Continued on p. 244

INSTRUCTOR'S NOTES

~~Either the waitress or~~ **the waiter** will seat you in **his** section.
~~Either the waiter or~~ **the waitress** will seat you in **her** section.
~~Neither Chef Jacques nor~~ **the waiters** eat **their** dinners early.
~~Neither the waiters nor~~ **Chef Jacques** eats **his** dinner early.

■ 11n
Use a singular pronoun to refer to most indefinite-pronoun antecedents.

Indefinite pronouns (see 11f for a list) do not refer to any particular person, thing, or idea. In context, however, they take on very clear meanings. Indefinite pronouns are usually singular, so the pronouns that refer to them should also be singular.

Anyone who knows the answer should raise **his or her** hand.
Everybody hopes **he or she** will find it.

1
Use a plural pronoun when an indefinite-pronoun antecedent is plural.

Some indefinite pronouns can be singular or plural *(none, some, more, most, any, all)*, depending on the meaning of the sentence. When an indefinite pronoun is plural, the pronouns that refer to it should be plural.

2
Use masculine pronouns appropriately.

Until the 1960s, grammatical convention specified using masculine pronouns to refer back to indefinite pronouns and nouns and pronouns naming general categories to which any person might belong: *"Everyone* **should** admit *his* mistakes." Today people are more conscious that *he, his, him,* and *himself* exclude women, who make up over half the population. Experienced writers try to avoid using masculine pronouns to refer to the entire population. The chart shows three ways to avoid using masculine pronouns to refer to males and females together. For advice on how to avoid other types of sexist language, see 21a-3.

244

HOW TO AVOID USING ONLY THE MASCULINE PRONOUN TO REFER TO MALES AND FEMALES TOGETHER

Solution 1: Use a pair—but try to avoid a pair more than once in a sentence or in many sentences in a row.

> **Everyone** hopes that **he or she** will win the scholarship.
> **A successful doctor** knows that **he or she** has to work long hours.
> With the explosion of knowledge, no **doctor** can read much outside **his or her** specialty.

Solution 2: Revise into the plural.

> **Many people** hope that **they** will win the scholarship.
> **Successful doctors** know that **they** have to work long hours.
> With the explosion of knowledge, few **doctors** can read much outside **their** specialties.

Solution 3: Recast the sentence.

> Everyone hopes to win the scholarship.
> Successful doctors should expect to work long hours.

11o

Use singular or plural pronouns according to context to match collective-noun antecedents.

A **collective noun** names a group of people or things: *family, group, audience, class, number, committee, team,* and the like. When the group acts as one unit, use a singular pronoun to refer to it. When the members of the group act individually, thus creating more than one action, use a plural pronoun.

> **The audience** is cheering as **it** stands to applaud the performers. [The audience is acting as one unit, so the pronoun is singular.]

> **The audience** put on **their** coats and walk out. [Here the audience is acting as individuals, so all the actions collect to become plural. The verbs *put* and *walk* must be plural as well as the pronoun *their*.]

> The **family is** spending **its** vacation in Maine. [All the family members went to one place together.]

> The **family are** spending **their** vacations in Maine, Hawaii, and Rome. [Each family member went to a different place.]

245

INSTRUCTOR'S NOTES

EXTRA EXERCISE D
In these sentences, pronouns already agree with their antecedents. For each sentence, make the change requested in brackets, being sure also to change any other words that may be needed to maintain noun-pronoun and subject-verb agreement.
Example

Political scientist David Truman has a theory about interest groups. He believes that "wherever there are people, there exists the potential for an interest group, and the people will organize into such a group whenever it becomes necessary for them to take action." [Change *political scientist David Truman* to *political scientists.*]
Political scientists have a theory about interest groups. *They believe* that . . . .

1. The theory credits interest groups with a major role in the workings of any democracy. [Change *the theory* to *theorists.*]

2. Organized special interest groups, such as the National Rifle Association, influence policies as a result of their time, effort, and resources. [Change *organized special interest groups* to *an organized special interest group.*]

3. Because of its extensive network of interest groups, Truman considers the United States a pluralist democracy. [Change *the United States* to *many Western nations.*]

4. These are countries in which a large number of interest groups, supporting such concerns as health and housing, want their own cause supported. [Change *countries* to *a country.*]

Continued on p. 246

ANSWERS: EXERCISE 6

1. *their* aims
2. *its* leaders
3. *it seeks*
4. *its* claim
5. *is* more focused on *its*
6. *their* goal
7. *their*

EXTRA EX. D (CONT.)

5. By compromising on their demands, such groups are able to make progress toward their goals, while they are prevented from imposing their wills on everyone. [Change *such groups* to *such a group.*]

ANSWERS: EXTRA EXERCISE D

1. *Theorists credit* interest groups with a major role in the workings of any democracy.
2. *An organized special interest group,* such as the National Rifle Association, *influences* policies as a result of *its* time, effort, and resources.
3. Because of *their* extensive network of interest groups, Truman considers *many Western nations* pluralistic *democracies.*
4. *This is a country* in which a large number of interest groups, supporting such concerns as health and housing, want their own cause supported.
5. By compromising on *its* demands, *such a group is* able to make progress towards *its* goals, while *it is* prevented from imposing *its* will on everyone.

EXERCISE 6

Revise each sentence so that all pronouns agree with their antecedents. When necessary, change verbs and other words to maintain subject–verb agreement. Most sentences have more than one solution.

EXAMPLE   All political interest groups aim to advance the interests of its members while affecting public policy.

All political interest groups aim to advance the interests of *their* members while affecting public policy.

1. Interest groups differ from political parties in its aims, structure, and number.
2. Unlike political parties, each group selects their leaders without elections.
3. The interest group is concerned only with one or two issues, such as gun control or crop subsidies, and they seek no official representative in government.
4. For example, the American Tobacco Institute tries to gain support for their claim that cigarette smoking is not dangerous.
5. Even the membership of a diverse special interest group, such as the Sierra Club, are more focused on their specific goals than are members of the large political parties.
6. Many fast-food chains have pushed hard for its goal of a reduced minimum wage for teenagers.
7. The United States Senate and House of Representatives in its meetings is constantly hearing pleas from these thousands of groups.

12
DISTINGUISHING BETWEEN ADJECTIVES AND ADVERBS

Both adjectives and adverbs are **modifiers**—words or groups of words that describe other words. Distinguishing between adjectives and adverbs is sometimes troublesome for writers.

ADJECTIVE   *The* **brisk** *wind blew.*

ADVERB   *The wind blew* **briskly.**

This chapter explains that the key to distinguishing between adjectives and adverbs is understanding that they modify different words or groups of words. The chart on the next page will help you to remember these distinctions.

In spite of these essential differences, inexperienced writers sometimes interchange adjectives and adverbs because of the *-ly* ending. In many cases, an adverb is formed by adding *-ly* to an adjective: *smooth* and *smoothly, beautiful* and *beautifully, busy* and *busily.* Even though many adverbs end in *-ly* (eat *swiftly,* eat *frequently,* eat *hungrily*), some do not (eat *fast,* eat *often,* eat *little*). To complicate matters further, some adjectives end in *-ly* (*lovely* flower, *friendly* dog). The *-ly* ending, therefore, is not a reliable way to identify adverbs.

WORD DERIVATION
Adjective comes from the Latin *adjectus,* meaning *that is added,* and *adverb* comes from the Latin *adverbus,* meaning *to a word.* Both etymologies reflect the use of adjectives and adverbs as enhancers of other words' meanings.

LANGUAGE HISTORY
Adverbs in Old English and Middle English were formed differently than they are today: to make an adverb, an *-e* was simply added to an adjective. The modern *-ly* ending for adverbs comes from an adjective ending, *-lice* (meaning *like*), which became softened to *-ly* and was somehow reinterpreted as an adverb signal. Some modern adjectives ending in *-ly* (such as *friendly* and *heavenly*) are descendants of those old *-lice* adjectives.

247

INSTRUCTOR'S NOTES

SUMMARY OF DIFFERENCES BETWEEN ADJECTIVES AND ADVERBS	
WHAT ADJECTIVES MODIFY	**EXAMPLE**
nouns° pronouns°	The **busy** *lawyer* rested. *She* felt **triumphant.**
WHAT ADVERBS MODIFY	**EXAMPLE**
verbs° adverbs° adjectives°	The lawyer *spoke* **quickly.** The lawyer spoke **very** *quickly.* The lawyer was **extremely** *busy*.
independent clauses°	**Therefore,** the lawyer rested.

ANSWERS: EXERCISE 1

ADV   ADJ
1. Many American teenagers
   ADV   ADV ADV
   always worked very hard
      ADJ   ADJ
   part-time jobs high school
      ADJ   ADJ
   greater percentage teenage students

        ADJ
2. Reliable statistics
   ADV   ADJ
   almost one third of all
   ADJ   ADJ
   ninth and tenth graders and
   ADV   ADJ
   almost one half of
   ADJ   ADJ
   all eleventh and twelfth graders

        ADV
3. Interestingly, they are
   [whole clause] ─────────→
                 ADJ
   working longer hours than the
      ADJ
   high school students of
      ADJ
   twenty-five years ago.
   ADJ   ADJ
4. Some determined students
      ADV   ADJ
   earn more two hundred dollars

To determine whether a specific occasion calls for an adjective or an adverb, see how the word functions in its sentence. If a noun or pronoun is being modified, use an adjective; if a verb, adjective, or other adverb is being modified, use an adverb. Also, you can consult your dictionary for the word's part of speech.

EXERCISE 1

First underline and label all adjectives (ADJ) and adverbs (ADV). Then go back and draw an arrow from each adjective and adverb to the word or words it modifies.

ADJ───→   ADV───→
EXAMPLE Do American teenagers frequently take jobs while attending
         ADJ───→
         high school?

1. Many American teenagers have always worked very hard at part-time jobs while going to high school, but a greater percentage of teenage students work today than ever before.

2. Reliable statistics reveal that almost one-third of all ninth and tenth graders and almost one-half of all eleventh and twelfth graders are employed.

3. Interestingly, they are working longer hours than the high school students of twenty-five years ago.

4. Some determined students earn more than two hundred dollars a month.

5. Not surprisingly, the number of hours worked greatly influences school performance.

6. An important study conducted recently at the University of California disclosed that most eleventh and twelfth graders can manage a weekly work schedule of twenty hours without damaging their grades.

248

■‖ 12a

Use adverbs—not adjectives—to modify verbs.

Only adverbs modify verbs. Using adjectives as adverbs is nonstandard.

No   He drove **careless.** [Adjective *careless* cannot modify verb *drove.*]

Yes   He drove **carelessly.** [Adverb *carelessly* modifies verb *drove.*]

■‖ 12b

Use adverbs—not adjectives—to modify adjectives and other adverbs.

Only adverbs can modify adjectives and other adverbs. Here again, using adjectives as adverbs is nonstandard.

No   The candidate felt **unusual** energetic today. [Adjective *unusual* cannot modify adjective *energetic.*]

Yes   The candidate felt **unusually energetic** today. [Adverb *unusually* modifies adjective *energetic.*]

No   The candidate spoke **exceptional forcefully** today. [Adjective *exceptional* cannot modify adverb *forcefully.*]

Yes   The candidate spoke **exceptionally forcefully** today. [Adverb *exceptionally* modifies adverb *forcefully.*]

■‖ 12c

Do not use double negatives.

A **double negative** is a statement that contains two negative modifiers, the second of which repeats the message of the first. (This form, nonstandard today, was standard in the days of Chaucer and Shakespeare.) Negative modifiers include *no, neither, not, none, nothing, never, hardly, scarcely,* and *barely.*

No   The union members did **not** have **no** money in reserve.

Yes   The union members did **not** have **any** money in reserve.

5. ADV   ADV
Not surprisingly, the number of
[whole clause] ⟶
ADV
hours worked greatly influences
ADJ
school performance.

6. ADJ   ADV
important study conducted recently
ADJ   ADJ
eleventh and twelfth graders
ADJ
twenty hours

249

LANGUAGE HISTORY

The rule banning double negatives in English is a relatively new one. Double, triple, and even quadruple negatives were acceptable in Old English and Middle English, just as they are in many modern languages. In the eighteenth century the first attempts were made to regularize English. The first English dictionaries and usage books were written. One of these was Robert Lowth's *Short Introduction to English Grammar,* in which he stated that "two Negatives in English destroy one another, or are equivalent to an affirmative." The new rich of the merchant class, eager to fit in by speaking and writing correctly, accepted Lowth's rule, and it became the standard despite the thousand-year history of acceptable double negatives in English.

No	The factory workers will **never** vote for **no** strike.
Yes	The factory workers will **never** vote for a strike.
No	The factory workers will **not never** vote for a strike.
Yes	The factory workers will **not ever** vote for a strike.
Yes	The factory workers will **not** vote for a strike.
No	The office workers will **not** be hurt **none** by a strike.
Yes	The office workers will **not** be hurt by a strike.

Not—No—Nothing

The words *not, no,* and *nothing* are particularly prone to creating double negatives.

No	He did **not** hear **nothing.**
Yes	He did **not** hear **anything.**
No	The trees do **not** have **no** leaves.
Yes	The trees do **not** have **any** leaves.
Yes	The trees have **no** leaves.

When the word *not* is used in a contraction°, such as *isn't, don't,* or *haven't,* the negative message carried by *not* tends to slip by some inexperienced writers. They add a second—incorrect—negative. If you use contractions, which many writers prefer to avoid in their academic writing, be especially careful not to use double negatives.

No	He did**n't** hear **nothing.**
Yes	He did**n't** hear **anything.**
No	She **couldn't scarcely** hear the music.
Yes	She **could scarcely** hear the music.
No	She **couldn't hardly** hear the music.
Yes	She **could hardly** hear the music.

250

■‖ 12d

After linking verbs, use adjectives—not adverbs— as complements.

Linking verbs indicate a state of being or a condition. They include *be (am, is, are, was, were);* verbs related to the senses, including *look, smell, taste, sound,* and *feel;* and verbs such as *appear, seem, become, grow, turn, remain,* and *prove.* Linking verbs connect the subject° to a complement, a word that renames or describes the subject. You can think of a linking verb as an equal sign between a subject and its complement.

The guests looked **happy.** [subject *guests* = adjective *happy*]

The party was **successful.** [subject *party* = adjective *successful*]

Problems can arise with verbs that are sometimes linking verbs and sometimes action verbs, depending on the sentence. As linking verbs, these verbs use adjectives in complements. As action verbs, they use adverbs.

Anne **looks** happy. [*looks* = linking verb]

Anne **looks** happily at the sunset. [*looks* = action verb]

He **grows happy** when he sees Emily. [*grows* = linking verb]

He **grows** flowers **happily.** [*grows* = action verb]

Bad—Badly

The words *bad* (adjective) and *badly* (adverb) are particularly prone to misuse with verbs such as *feel, grow, smell, sound, taste.* Only the adjective *bad* is correct when a verb is functioning as a linking verb.

FOR DESCRIBING A FEELING

No   The student felt **badly.**

Yes   The student felt **bad.**

FOR DESCRIBING A SMELL

No   The food smelled **badly.**

Yes   The food smelled **bad.**

COORDINATED RESOURCES

Alternate examples and exercises for this chapter are available in the *S & S Workbook for Writers,* Gordon and Troyka.

Transparency masters are available for many of the screened charts and/or lists in this chapter.

Students can practice and test their knowledge of terms, key concepts, and applications of material in this chapter by using the *Study Guide to the S & S Handbook for Writers,* West.

Good—Well

Good and *well* can be especially tricky, for *well* functions both as an adverb and as an adjective. *Good* is always an adjective. *Well* is an adjective referring to good health. When it is describing anything other than good health, *well* is an adverb.

You look **well** = You look in good health. [*well* = adjective]

You write **well** = You write skillfully. [*well* = adverb]

Except when *well* is an adjective referring to health, use *good* only as an adjective and *well* only as an adverb.

No She sings **good.** [*sings* = action verb; adverb, not adjective, required]

Yes She sings **well.** [*well* = adverb]

EXERCISE 2

Revise these sentences to eliminate double negatives and to make the use of all adjectives and adverbs suitable for academic writing.

Example Does love come natural?

Does love come *naturally*?

1. Is romance thriving good in America?
2. If sales of Valentine's Day cards are any indication, many Americans do not never want to forget to say "I love you" on February 14.
3. Sure people think the Valentine's Day idea is good because every year the cards sell brisk.
4. Americans buy from 900 million to 1.1 billion Valentine's Day cards yearly, proving that people are powerful eager to express affection.
5. Interestingly, adults frequent send and receive only 20 percent of all the cards; children buy enormous numbers of them for any good friends or teachers they consider unusual fine.
6. Even though many spouses and sweethearts feel strong about their mutual love, they easy send more Valentine's Day cards to their mothers than to each other.
7. For many centuries, people have reacted positive to a day that honors love.
8. The ancient Romans honored careful their clear popular tradition of holding a "love lottery" in mid-February.
9. An unmarried man would draw random the name of an unmarried woman from a secure guarded box, and then the couple would court polite to see if they liked each other good enough to get married.

ANSWERS: EXERCISE 2

1. Is romance thriving *well* in America?
2. If sales of Valentine's Day cards are any indication, many Americans *do not want/do not want ever/want never* to forget to say "I love you" on February 14.
3. *Surely* people think the Valentine's Day idea is good because every year the cards sell *briskly.*
4. Americans buy from 900 million to 1.1 billion Valentine's Day cards yearly, proving that people are *powerfully* eager to express affection.
5. Interestingly, adults *frequently* send and receive only 20 percent of all the cards; children buy enormous numbers of them for any good friends or teachers they consider *unusually* fine.
6. Even though many spouses and sweethearts feel *strongly* about their mutual love, they *easily* send more Valentine's Day cards to their mothers than to each other.
7. For many centuries, people have reacted *positively* to a day that honors love.
8. The ancient Romans honored *carefully* their *clearly* popular tradition of holding a "love lottery" in mid-February.
9. An unmarried man would draw *randomly/at random* the name of an unmarried woman from a *securely* guarded box, and then the couple would court *politely* to see if they liked each other *well* enough to get married.

■‖ 12e
Use correct comparative and superlative forms of adjectives and adverbs.

When comparisons are made, descriptive adjectives and adverbs often carry the message. Adjectives and adverbs, therefore, have forms that communicate relative degrees of intensity.

‖ ### 1
Use correct forms of comparison for regular adjectives and adverbs.

Most adjectives and adverbs show degrees of intensity by adding *-er* and *-est* endings or by combining with the words *more* and *most*. (All adjectives and adverbs show diminishing or negative comparison by combining with the words *less* and *least: less jumpy, least jumpy; less surely, least surely*.) A few adjectives and adverbs are irregular; see 12e-2.

FORMS OF COMPARISON FOR REGULAR ADJECTIVES AND ADVERBS	
FORM	**FUNCTION**
Positive	Used for a statement when nothing is being compared
Comparative	Used when only two things are being compared—with *-er* ending or *more* (or *less*)
Superlative	Used when three or more things are being compared—with *-est* ending or *most* (or *least*)

Here is a list that contrasts the three forms. Consider the messages of comparison in the sentences after the list.

POSITIVE	COMPARATIVE	SUPERLATIVE
green	greener	greenest
happy	happier	happiest
selfish	less selfish	least selfish
beautiful	more beautiful	most beautiful

Her tree is **green.**
Her tree is **greener** than his tree.
Her tree is the **greenest** tree on the block.

EXTRA EXERCISE

Underline the adjectives and adverbs. If any adjective or adverb is in an incorrect form, write the correct form above it.

Example

The music played *loud* in the disco than in the restaurant.

1. The Joneses have the bigger tree on the block.
2. Colorado has some of the most prettiest scenery in the country.
3. Which of the sick twins has the highest fever?
4. Juan is friendlier than his cousin.
5. The more faster runner received a ribbon.
6. The red blouse is the most attractive in the store.
7. Leontyne Price sings good.
8. That is the worse coffee shop in town.
9. Spain is near to Africa than most people realize.
10. Marc Chagall is the more famous modern artist from Russia.

ANSWERS: EXTRA EXERCISE

1. biggest
2. prettiest (drop *most*)
3. higher
4. Correct
5. faster or fastest (drop *more*)
6. Correct
7. well
8. worst
9. nearer
10. most famous

His flower garden is **beautiful.**

His flower garden is **more beautiful** than her flower garden.

His flower garden is the **most beautiful** on the block.

The choice of whether to use *-er, -est* or *more, most* depends largely on the number of syllables in the adjective or adverb. With **one-syllable words,** the *-er, -est* endings are most common: *large, larger, largest* (adjective); *far, farther, farthest* (adverb). With **three-syllable words,** *more, most* are used. With **adverbs of two or more syllables,** *more, most* are used: *easily, more easily, most easily.* With **adjectives of two syllables,** practice varies: some take the *-er, -est* endings; others combine with *more* and *most.* One general rule covers two-syllable adjectives ending in *-y:* use the *-er, -est* endings after changing the *-y* to *i.* For other two-syllable adjectives, often you will form comparatives and superlatives intuitively, based on what you have heard or read for a particular adjective. If neither form "sounds" natural for a given adjective, use whichever form your dictionary advises.

Be careful not to use a **double comparative** or **double superlative.** The words *more* or *most* cannot be used if the *-er* or *-est* ending has been used.

NO	He was **more younger** than his brother.
YES	He was **younger** than his brother.
NO	Her music was the **most snappiest** on the radio.
YES	Her music was the **snappiest** on the radio.
NO	People danced **more easier** [or **more easilier**] to her music.
YES	People danced **more easily** to her music.

2
Use correct forms of comparison for irregular adjectives and adverbs.

Some comparative and superlative forms are irregular. Learn the short list in the chart on the opposite page.

The Perkinses saw a **good** movie.

The Perkinses saw a **better** movie than the Smiths did.

The Perkinses saw **the best** movie that they had ever seen.

The Millers had **little** trouble finding jobs.
The Millers had **less** trouble finding jobs than the Smiths did.
The Millers had **the least** trouble finding jobs of everyone.

IRREGULAR COMPARATIVES AND SUPERLATIVES		
POSITIVE (1)	COMPARATIVE (2)	SUPERLATIVE (3+)
good (adjective)	better	best
well (adjective and adverb)	better	best
bad (adjective)	worse	worst
badly (adverb)	worse	worst
many	more	most
much	more	most
some	more	most
little	less	least

▌ USAGE ALERT: Do not use *less* and *fewer* interchangeably. *Less* refers to amounts or values that form one whole. *Fewer* refers to numbers or anything that can be counted. *They consumed fewer calories; the sugar substitute had less aftertaste.* ▐

WORD HISTORIES

Common irregular adjectives (and adverbs) can be confusing to students because the comparative and superlative forms seem unconnected to the positive form. The realization that these irregularities are only accidents of history rather than the product of difficult rules can make them less intimidating.

For example, *good* comes from the Old English *god*, related to the German *gut*, both of which come from the Indo-European word meaning *to be suitable; better* and *best* come from Old English *betera* and *betst* respectively, based on the Indo-European word meaning *good*.

Another example is *worse* and *worst*, which come from their Old English synonyms: *wiersa* and *wyrsta*. However, *bad* does not come from *yfel*, the Old English word for *bad* or *evil*, but from Old English *baeddel*, meaning *hermaphrodite*. Perhaps your students would like to theorize about why this happened.

EXERCISE 3

First complete this chart. Next, write sentences that set a context for each word in the completed chart.

EXAMPLE   Weighing 270 pounds and standing seven feet tall, he is big, even for a football player.

POSITIVE (1)	COMPARATIVE (2)	SUPERLATIVE (3+)
big	_____	_____
_____	_____	hungriest
_____	more hungry	_____
quickly	_____	_____
important	_____	_____
_____	thicker	_____
_____	_____	most thirsty

Sentences: Answers will vary, but each sentence should set a context for the use of each word. (For example, *He is big* is less satisfactory than *Weighing 270 pounds and standing seven feet tall, he is big, even for a basketball player.*)

ANSWERS: EXERCISE 3

big	bigger	biggest
hungry	hungrier	hungriest
hungry	more hungry	most hungry
quickly	more quickly	most quickly
important	more important	most important
thick	thicker	thickest
thirsty	more thirsty	most thirsty

ANSWERS: EXERCISE 4

1. Passengers say that often the chicken sauce is *thicker* than glue, the beef is *better* suited to feeding dogs than humans, and the pasta is soggier than a wet sponge.

2. The *most* popular joke seems to be about a cabin attendant who announced, "You can choose chicken, beef, or pasta for dinner tonight. But please don't get upset if we run out of your choice because one is no *better* than the other."

3. Of the more than a dozen caterers who supply airline food, the *largest* prepares 90 million meals a day.

4. Controlling quality might be *easier* if the numbers were less *large.*

5. Still, some airlines are trying *harder:* One large American airline offers the choice of a low-cholesterol meal with a *less* fatty grade of meat.

6. A recent survey, however, revealed that frequent flyers consider food *less* important compared to on-time records.

7. Airline executives are *little* motivated to upgrade food if passengers are willing to settle for the *cheapest* meals an airline can serve.

EXERCISE 4

Revise these sentences so that all comparative and superlative forms are suitable for academic writing.

EXAMPLE   Most people say that airlines serve the worse food they have ever tasted.

Most people say that airlines serve the *worst* food they have ever tasted.

1. Passengers say that often the chicken sauce is more thick than glue, the beef is best suited to feeding dogs than humans, and the pasta is soggier than a wet sponge.

2. The more popular joke seems to be about a cabin attendant who announced, "You can choose chicken, beef, or pasta for dinner tonight. But please don't get upset if we run out of your choice because one is no more better than the other."

3. Of the more than a dozen caterers who supply airline food, the larger prepares 90 million meals a day.

4. Controlling quality might be more easier if the numbers were less larger.

5. Still, some airlines are trying hardest: One large American airline offers the choice of a low-cholesterol meal with a least fatty grade of meat.

6. A recent survey, however, revealed that frequent flyers consider food least important compared to on-time records.

7. Airline executives are less motivated to upgrade food if passengers are willing to settle for the most cheapest meals an airline can serve.

▉‖ 12f

Avoid using too many nouns as modifiers.

Sometimes nouns can modify other nouns: *truck driver, train track, security system.* These very familiar terms create no problems. However, when nouns pile up in a sequence of modifiers, it can be difficult to know which nouns are being modified and which nouns are doing the modifying. As a result, the style puts too much burden on the reader to decipher the writer's message. Depending on the particular sentence, writers have several routes to revision: (1) rewrite the sentence, (2) change a noun to an adjective, (3) change a noun to the possessive case°, or (4) change a noun to a modifying phrase.

256

(1) SENTENCE REWRITTEN

No   I asked my advisor to write **two college recommendation** letters for me.

YES   I asked my advisor to write **letters of recommendation** to **two colleges** for me.

(2) AND (3) ONE NOUN CHANGED TO POSSESSIVE CASE AND ANOTHER TO ITS ADJECTIVE FORM

No   Some students might take the **United States Navy examination** for **navy engineer training.**

YES   Some students might take the **United States Navy's examination** for **naval engineer training.**

(4) NOUN CHANGED TO PREPOSITIONAL PHRASE

No   Our **student advisement program** has won awards for excellence.

YES   Our **program in student advisement** has won awards for excellence.

EXERCISE 5

Revise the following sentences so that they are suitable for academic writing. Apply all the material covered in this chapter.

EXAMPLE   Increasing in recent years, bankrupt businesses are being rescued by their employees who think creative.
Increasingly in recent years, bankrupt businesses are being rescued by their employees who think *creatively.*

1. Workers who want bad to keep their jobs pool their money careful and become worker-owners.
2. Typical each worker-owner buys a share in the business and participates democratic in its operations.
3. The resulting "cooperative" often has unusual enthusiastic workers and the most happiest customers.
4. Cooperatives most frequent run supermarkets, but they have also taken over sewing factories, tool manufacturing plants, and even a steel mill.
5. Worker-owner rescue actions can be exciting when new.
6. The worker-owners, however, work the hardest than they ever did because they must do their original jobs good and spend extra time on management.
7. Because collective decision-making does not never work well if the worker-owners number over 400, most larger cooperatives hold democratic run elections to choose managers.

ANSWERS: EXERCISE 5

1. Workers who want *badly* to keep their jobs pool their money *carefully* and become worker-owners.
2. *Typically* each worker-owner buys a share in the business and participates *democratically* in its operations.
3. The resulting "cooperative" often has *unusually* enthusiastic workers and the *happiest* customers.
4. Cooperatives most *frequently* run supermarkets, but they have also taken over sewing factories, tool manufacturing plants, and even a steel mill.
5. *Worker-owners* rescue actions can be exciting when new.
6. The worker-owners, however, work *harder* than they ever did, because they must do their original jobs *well* and spend extra time on management.
7. Because collective decision-making does *not ever/not* work well if the worker-owners number over 400, most larger cooperatives hold *democratically* run elections to choose managers.

INSTRUCTOR'S NOTES

8. Unless all goes well, there are *not any/no* profits to share, and sometimes the workers cannot be paid *any* salary until the business gets on its feet.

9. *Widely* publicized examples of successfully run cooperatives, many in *severely* economically depressed areas, give encouragement to groups having *less* success than others.

10. *Cooperatively* managed businesses are seen by some experts as the *best* hope for the future of small, *locally* owned businesses in America.

8. Unless all goes well, there are not no profits to share, and sometimes the workers cannot be paid no salary until the business gets on its feet.

9. Wide publicized examples of successfully run cooperatives, many in severe economically depressed areas, give encouragement to groups having little success than others.

10. Cooperative managed businesses are seen by some experts as the better hope for the future of small, local owned businesses in America.

III ‖ WRITING CORRECT SENTENCES

13 Sentence Fragments

14 Comma Splices and Fused Sentences

15 Sentences that Send Unclear Messages

13

SENTENCE FRAGMENTS

A **sentence fragment** is a portion of a sentence that is punctuated as though it were a complete sentence. Most sentence fragments are phrases° or dependent clauses°. You can avoid writing sentence fragments if you recognize the difference between a fragment and a complete sentence.

FRAGMENT	The telephone with two outside lines. [no verb]
REVISED	The telephone has two outside lines.
FRAGMENT	Rang loudly for ten minutes. [no subject]
REVISED	The telephone rang loudly for ten minutes.
FRAGMENT	At midnight. [no verb or subject]
REVISED	The telephone rang at midnight.
FRAGMENT	**Because** the telephone rang loudly. [dependent clause with subordinating conjunction]
REVISED	Because the telephone rang loudly, the family was awakened.

260

FRAGMENT	The telephone **that** I answered. [dependent clause with relative pronoun]
REVISED	The telephone that I answered woke the family.

 ## 13a
Know how to test for sentence completeness.

If you write sentence fragments frequently, you need a system to check that your sentences are complete. Here is a test to use if you suspect that you have written a sentence fragment.

TEST FOR SENTENCE COMPLETENESS

1. **Is there a verb?** If no, there is a sentence fragment.
2. **Is there a subject?** If no, there is a sentence fragment.
3. **Do the subject and verb start with a subordinating word—and lack an independent clause to complete the thought?** If yes, there is a sentence fragment.

QUESTION 1: Is there a verb?

If there is no verb, you are looking at a sentence fragment. Verbs convey information about what is happening, what has happened, or what will happen. In testing for sentence completeness, you need to find a verb that can change form to communicate a change in time.

> Yesterday, the telephone **rang.**
> Now the telephone **rings.**

Verbals° do not function as verbs. Do not, therefore, mistake a verbal for a verb. Verbals are present participles°, past participles°, and infinitives°.

FRAGMENT	Yesterday, the students registering for classes.
REVISED	Yesterday, the students **were** registering for classes.

TEACHING TIP
One useful way to introduce discussion of sentence fragments is to speak to the class in fragments. For example, you might enter the class one morning and make the following, unembellished announcement: "Before we discuss the midterm." Students will, of course, be confused. Feign ignorance when they ask what you mean: Wasn't my announcement clear?"

Finally, someone might tell you that your announcement was not clear because the thought was incomplete. Tell that student that he or she has just given one definition of a sentence fragment. If no one can tell what is wrong, you can write your original announcement on the board, and have students identify the problem. Then you can ask students to supply (at the board or orally) whatever they feel is needed to complete the statement. Most will add independent clauses. Use these revisions of your announcement to explain (or review) the Three-Step Test for Sentence Completeness.

TEACHING TIP

You might find it useful to distribute typed copies of several student paragraphs containing fragments, without student names. Have students work in teams to identify and correct fragments. The groups can submit one revision of each paragraph, for a common grade, or a spokesperson from each group can lead a class discussion of the group's different paragraph, identifying fragments and weighing the relative merits of various revisions.

FRAGMENT	Now the students registering for classes.
REVISED	Now the students **are** registering for classes.
FRAGMENT	Yesterday, told about an excellent teacher.
REVISED	Yesterday, I **was** told about an excellent teacher.
FRAGMENT	Yesterday, the students to register for classes.
REVISED	Yesterday, the students **wanted** to register for classes.
FRAGMENT	Now the students to register for classes.
REVISED	Now the students **want** to register for classes.

In the sentences above, *were, are, was, wanted,* and *want* are verbs that change form to indicate time. They are examples of complete-sentence verbs.

QUESTION 2: Is there a subject?

If there is no subject, you are looking at a sentence fragment. To find a subject, ask the verb "who?" or "what?"

FRAGMENT	Studied hard for the test. [Who studied? unknown]
REVISED	The students studied hard for the test. [Who studied? students]
FRAGMENT	Contained some difficult questions. [What contained? unknown]
REVISED	The test contained some difficult questions. [What contained? the test]

Every sentence must have its own subject. A sentence fragment without a subject often occurs when the missing subject is the same as the subject in the preceding sentence.

NO	World War II ended in 1945 for most people. **Continued for others, however, until the end of their lives.**
YES	World War II ended in 1945 for most people. **It continued for others, however, until the end of their lives.**

262

Imperative statements—commands and some requests—are an exception. Imperative statements imply the word "you" as the subject.

Run! = (You) run!
Think fast. = (You) think fast.
Please return my books. = (You) please return my books.

QUESTION 3: Do the subject and verb start with a subordinating word—and lack an independent clause to complete the thought?

If the answer is "yes," you are looking at a sentence fragment. Clauses that begin with subordinating words are called **dependent clauses,** and they cannot stand alone as independent units. A dependent clause must be joined to an independent clause to be part of a complete sentence. One type of subordinating word is a **subordinating conjunction.** The most frequently used are:

after	even though	until
although	if	when
as	since	whenever
because	though	where
before	unless	wherever

FRAGMENT   **Because** she returned my books.

REVISED   **Because** she returned my books, I can study.

FRAGMENT   **When** I study.

REVISED   I have to concentrate **when** I study.

▌ PUNCTUATION ALERT: When a dependent clause starting with a subordinating conjunction comes before an independent clause, a comma always separates the clauses. ▌
Another type of subordinating word is a **relative pronoun.** The most frequently used relative pronouns are *who, which, that, what, whoever,* and *whatever.*

FRAGMENT   The test **that** we studied for.

REVISED   The test **that** we studied for was cancelled.

FRAGMENT   The professor **who** taught the course.

REVISED   The professor **who** taught the course was ill.

TEACHING TIP
To discuss fragments, you might ask students to bring in samples of public writing that contain fragments. Fruitful sources include advertisements, mail solicitations, and memos from companies where the students work. Collect, reproduce, and distribute a sampling of the passages. Ask students to identify all fragments and to determine which, if any, are acceptable. Then have them revise the passages to eliminate the unacceptable fragments.

This lesson can be enlivened by the use of an overhead projector. Prepare transparencies of the original passages, and use a series of overlays to record and compare student revisions.

263

FRAGMENT	**Whoever** registered early.
REVISED	**Whoever** registered early got a good schedule.

Questions are an exception—they can begin with words such as *when, where, who,* and *which* without being sentence fragments: *When do you want to study? Where is the library? Who is your professor? Which class are you taking?*

ANSWERS: EXERCISE 1

Two pieces of information are given for each item: the reason for the sentence fragment and the number of the question in the "Test for Sentence Completeness" that explains what has caused each sentence fragment. (Exercise 3 asks students to correct the sentence fragments in this exercise.)

1. No verb; question 1
2. No verb; question 1
3. No verb; question 1
4. No subject; question 2
5. Complete sentence
6. Starts with a subordinating word—without an independent clause to complete the thought; question 3
7. Starts with a subordinating word—without an independent clause to complete the thought; question 3
8. Has a subordinating word—without an independent clause to complete the thought; question 3
9. Starts with a subordinating word—without an independent clause to complete the thought; question 3
10. Complete sentence

EXERCISE 1

Check each word group according to the Test for Sentence Completeness on page 261. If a word group is a sentence fragment, explain what makes it incomplete. If a word group is a complete sentence, circle its number.

EXAMPLE   The rescue of thousands of whales. [no verb; Question 1 on the Test]

1. A Soviet icebreaker trying to rescue the whales.
2. Thousands of ten-foot-long whales struggling for air in the thick ice.
3. In the Arctic Ocean in the winter of 1983.
4. Raced to reach the whales.
5. The icebreaker arrived in time.
6. Because the whales were afraid of the ship.
7. Although the ship wanted to cut a path through the ice.
8. A crew member who found a solution.
9. Classical music which he played over the ship's loud speaker.
10. The whales then followed the ship to the open sea.

◼‖ 13b

Revise dependent clauses punctuated as sentences.

A **dependent clause** contains both a subject and verb but starts with a subordinating word and is thus unable to stand on its own as a sentence. Subordinating words include subordinating conjunctions and relative pronouns (listed on page 263).

To correct a dependent clause punctuated as a sentence, you can do one, or sometimes either, of two things. (1) You can join the dependent clause to an independent clause that comes directly before or after; sometimes you will need to add words so that the combined sentence makes sense. (2) You can drop the subordinating word and, if necessary, add words to create an independent clause.

264

FRAGMENT	Many people over twenty-five years of age are deciding to get college degrees. **Because they want the benefits of an advanced education.**
REVISED	Many people over twenty-five years of age are deciding to get college degrees because they want the benefits of an advanced education. [joined into one sentence]
REVISED	Many people over twenty-five years of age are deciding to get college degrees. They want the benefits of an advanced education. [subordinating conjunction dropped to create an independent clause]
FRAGMENT	College is an attraction for many older people. **Who could not attend upon graduation from high school.**
REVISED	College is an attraction for many older people who could not attend upon graduation from high school. [joined into one sentence]
REVISED	College is an attraction for many older people. They could not attend upon graduation from high school. [relative pronoun dropped and *they* added to create an independent clause]

When trying to identify dependent clauses, be especially careful with words that indicate time – such as *after, before, since,* and *until*. In some sentences they function as subordinating conjunctions, but in other sentences they function as adverbs° and prepositions°. Do not automatically assume when you see these words that you are looking at a dependent clause.

> Before, the class was never full. Now it is overfilled. [These are two complete sentences. In the first sentence, *before* is an adverb modifying the independent clause *the class was never full*.]

> Before this semester, the class was never full. [This is a complete sentence. *Before* is the preposition in the prepositional phrase° *before this semester*.]

> Before the professor arrived. [This is a sentence fragment. *Before* is a subordinating conjunction.]

> Before the professor arrived, the room was empty. [This is a complete sentence. The dependent clause precedes an independent clause.]

COORDINATED RESOURCES

Alternate examples and exercises for this chapter are available in the *S & S Workbook for Writers,* Gordon and Troyka.

A transparency master is available for the screened list in this chapter.

The software program *Blue Pencil,* available from Prentice-Hall, offers students additional practice coordinated with this chapter.

Students can practice and test their knowledge of terms, key concepts, and applications of material in this chapter by using the *Study Guide to the S & S Handbook for Writers,* West.

INSTRUCTOR'S NOTES

When you use time-indicator words such as *before,* consider the context of the sentence before you decide if you are looking at a sentence fragment.

ANSWERS: EXERCISE 2

Answers will vary. Here is one set of possible answers.

1. The ancient Egyptians valued silver more than gold because silver was easier to mine and work with.

2. Greyhounds, which are the fastest dogs, have been clocked running 42 miles per hour.

3. Although it consumes 25 percent of the blood's oxygen supply, the human brain is motionless. If it is deprived of oxygen for four to five minutes, it will die.

4. In 1911, Bobby Leech went on a worldwide lecture tour. After surviving a barrel ride over Niagara Falls which broke many of his bones, he slipped on a banana peel in New Zealand and died of his injuries.

5. Many Vietnamese immigrants to the United States have been high school valedictorians in recent years. Because education is important in their culture, Vietnamese families expect their children to study hard.

6. People who refuse to wear seat belts in spite of the evidence about safety should realize that fatalities involving nonbelted occupants have been recorded at 12 miles per hour. That is the approximate speed in a large parking lot.

7. Even though everyone knows that confronting the unpleasant is inevitable, procrastination affects nearly everyone at some time. Many people are expert at knowing how to postpone cleaning, paying bills, and other chores.

EXERCISE 2

Find and correct any sentence fragments.

EXAMPLE   Headlights help drivers see and be seen. When it rains, sleets, or snows, no matter what time of day. Drivers should always turn on their headlights.
Headlights help drivers see and be seen. *When it rains, sleets, or snows, no matter what time of day, drivers should always turn on their headlights.*

1. The ancient Egyptians valued silver more than gold. Because silver was easier to mine and work with.

2. Greyhounds which are the fastest dogs. They have been clocked running 42 miles per hour.

3. Although it consumes 25 percent of the blood's oxygen supply, the human brain is motionless. If it is deprived of oxygen for four to five minutes. It will die.

4. In 1911 Bobby Leech went on a worldwide lecture tour. After surviving a barrel ride over Niagara Falls. Which broke many of his bones. He slipped on a banana peel in New Zealand and died of his injuries.

5. Many Vietnamese immigrants to the United States have been high school valedictorians in recent years. Because education is important in their culture. Vietnamese families expect their children to study hard.

6. People who refuse to wear seat belts in spite of the evidence about safety. They should realize that fatalities involving non belted occupants have been recorded at 12 miles per hour. That is the approximate speed in a large parking lot.

7. Even though everyone knows that confronting the unpleasant is inevitable. Procrastination affects nearly everyone at some time. Many people are expert at knowing how to postpone cleaning, paying bills, and other chores.

8. The world's largest diamond which was found in 1905. After, it was cut into 105 stones. Each was considered especially valuable.

9. Whoever refuses to walk under a ladder in fear of bad luck. The person is perpetuating an ancient superstition.

10. Selling and buying babies has become a big business in the United States. Although this route to adopting a child is illegal. Unfortunately, many people who lose their life savings hoping to get a baby. They pay their money and never see the "agency representative" again.

13c

Revise phrases punctuated as sentences.

A phrase is a group of words that lacks a subject, a verb, or both. A phrase, therefore, is not a sentence. To revise a phrase into a complete sentence, you can either rewrite it to become an independent clause, or you can join it to an independent clause that comes directly before or after.

A verbal phrase contains a verbal. Verbals are present participles°, past participles°, and infinitives°.

FRAGMENT	The mayor called a news conference last week. **To announce new programs for crime prevention and care for the homeless.**
REVISED	The mayor called a news conference last week to announce new programs for crime prevention and care for the homeless. [joined into one sentence]
REVISED	The mayor called a news conference last week. She wanted to announce new programs for crime prevention and care for the homeless. [rewritten]
FRAGMENT	**Introduced by her assistant.** The mayor began with an opening statement.
REVISED	Introduced by her assistant, the mayor began with an opening statement. [joined into one sentence]
REVISED	The mayor **was** introduced by her assistant. She then began with an opening statement. [rewritten]
FRAGMENT	**Hoping for strong public support.** She gave many examples of problems everywhere in the city.
REVISED	Hoping for strong public support, she gave many examples of problems everywhere in the city. [joined into one sentence]
REVISED	She hoped for strong public support. She gave many examples of problems everywhere in the city. [rewritten]

A **prepositional phrase** contains a preposition° (for a complete list, see 6g), its object°, and any modifiers°.

8. The world's largest diamond was found in 1905. After, it was cut into 105 stones, each of which was considered especially valuable.

9. Whoever refuses to walk under a ladder in fear of bad luck is perpetuating an ancient superstition.

10. Selling and buying babies has become a big business in the United States although this route to adopting a child is illegal. Unfortunately, many people lose their life savings hoping to get a baby. They pay their money and never see the "agency representative" again.

267

FRAGMENT	Cigarette smoke made the conference room seem airless. **During the long news conference.**
REVISED	Cigarette smoke made the conference room seem airless during the long news conference. [joined into one sentence]
REVISED	Cigarette smoke made the conference room seem airless. It was hard to breathe during the long news conference. [rewritten]

An **appositive** is a word or word group that renames a noun or a group of words functioning as a noun.

FRAGMENT	Most people respected the mayor. **A politician with fresh ideas and practical solutions.**
REVISED	Most people respected the mayor, a politician with fresh ideas and practical solutions. [joined into one sentence]
REVISED	Most people respected the mayor. She seemed to be a politician with fresh ideas and practical solutions. [rewritten]

Compound predicates contain two or more verbs along with any objects and modifiers. To be part of a complete sentence, a predicate must have a subject. If the second half of a compound predicate is punctuated as a separate sentence, it is a sentence fragment.

FRAGMENT	The reporters asked the mayor many questions about the details of her program. **And then discussed her answers at length among themselves.**
REVISED	The reporters asked the mayor many questions about the details of her program and discussed her answers at length among themselves. [joined into one sentence]
REVISED	The reporters asked the mayor many questions about the details of her program. Then the reporters discussed her answers at length among themselves. [rewritten]

EXERCISE 3

Go back to Exercise 1 and revise any sentence fragments into complete sentences.

EXERCISE 4

Correct all sentence fragments.

New words coming into American English constantly. Many start out as slang. For example, *preemie* meaning "a prematurely born infant." Unknown until a few years ago. Another word rarely heard was "humongous." Indicating something of enormous size. Other words fade from the language. And disappear from use. Rudolph Flesch, the author of *Lite English: Popular Words That Are O.K. to Use*. A book explaining that the American language is changing every day. Just like the American people.

 13d

Recognize intentional fragments.

Professional writers sometimes intentionally use fragments, sparingly, for emphasis and effect.

> The cars were jammed for 30 miles along the Karagatch road. Water buffalo and cattle were hauling carts through the mud. **No end and no beginning. Just carts loaded with everything they owned.** The old men and women, soaked through, walked along keeping the cattle moving.
> —Ernest Hemingway, *In Our Time*

The ability to judge the difference between an acceptable and unacceptable sentence fragment comes from much exposure to reading the work of skilled writers. Many instructors, therefore, often do not accept sentence fragments in student writing until a student can demonstrate the firm ability to write well-constructed complete sentences.

EXERCISE 5

Revise this paragraph to eliminate any sentence fragments. In some cases, you can join word groups to create complete sentences; in other cases, you have to revise the word groups into complete sentences. In the final version, check not only the individual sentences but also the clarity of the whole paragraph.

ANSWERS: EXERCISE 3

Answers will vary. Here is one set of possible answers.

1. A Soviet icebreaker was trying to rescue the whales.
2. Thousands of ten-foot-long whales were struggling for air in the thick ice.
3. The whales were stranded in the Arctic Ocean in the winter of 1983.
4. Complete sentence—join with item 5
5. The icebreaker raced to reach the whales and arrived in time.
6. Because the whales were afraid of the ship, they stayed away from it.
7. Although the ship wanted to cut a path through the ice, the whales did not understand.
8. A crew member found a solution.
9. Classical music which he played over the ship's loudspeaker instilled confidence in the whales.
10. Complete sentence

ANSWERS: EXERCISE 4

Answers will vary. Here is one possible revision.

New words are coming into American English constantly. Many start out as slang. For example, one new word is *preemie* meaning "a prematurely born infant." The word was unknown until a few years ago. Another word rarely heard was "humongous." It indicates something of enormous size. Other words fade from the language and disappear from use. Rudolph Flesch is the author of *Lite English: Popular Words that Are O.K. to Use*. His book explains that the American language is changing every day. American English changes just like the American people.

269

ANSWERS: EXERCISE 5

Answers will vary. Here is one set of possible answers.

Students looking for jobs need more than the "Help Wanted" section of a newspaper. One major tool is a carefully written resumé. A resumé should be written in a standard form (see Chapter 35) and proofread carefully to eliminate errors in spelling, punctuation, or grammar. For the content of the resumé students should analyze all types of experiences. A resumé can include not only paid jobs but also volunteer positions and extracurricular activities. Students have a better chance of getting a job if they have supervised other people, handled money, or taken on highly responsible tasks such as participating in political campaigns or chairing major committees at school. Many employers will consider student resumés, especially when the resumés include names of the students' supervisors.

ANSWERS: EXERCISE 6

Answers will vary. Here is one set of possible answers.

When most people need to earn a living, they look for a job. When interviewing for a job, people should demonstrate punctuality, a very important trait. On the other hand, arriving too early is not wise either. Job candidates should greet the interviewer pleasantly and use a firm handshake. They should refrain from smoking. When called upon to discuss their backgrounds and experience, job applicants should, above all, emphasize their strengths and try to appear self-confident, without a trace of conceit. Interviewers appreciate people who answer questions directly and specifically. Job candidates should know when to leave and should thank the interviewer for his or her time. When the choice is between two candidates with similar credentials, a follow-up letter can sometimes make the difference between getting a job or not.

Students looking for jobs need more than the "Help Wanted" section of a newspaper. One major tool, a carefully written resumé. A resumé should be written in a standard form (see Chapter 35). And proofread carefully to eliminate errors in spelling, punctuation, or grammar. For the content of the resumé. Students should analyze all types of experiences. A resumé including not only paid jobs but also volunteer positions and extracurricular activities. Students have a better chance of getting a job. If they have supervised other people, handled money, or taken on highly responsible tasks. Such as participating in political campaigns or chairing major committees at school. Many employers will consider student resumés. Especially when the resumés include names of the students' supervisors.

EXERCISE 6

Revise this paragraph to eliminate any sentence fragments. In some cases, you can join word groups to create complete sentences; in other cases, you have to write new sentences. In the final version, check not only the individual sentences but also the clarity of the whole paragraph.

When most people need to earn a living. They look for a job. Interviewing for a job. Punctuality, a very important trait. Although arriving too early is not wise. Job candidates should greet the interviewer pleasantly. And use a firm handshake. To refrain from smoking. Called upon to discuss their backgrounds and experience. Job applicants should, above all, emphasize their strengths. To appear self-confident, without a trace of conceit. Interviewers appreciate people who answer questions directly and specifically. Job candidates who know when to leave. And thank the interviewer for his or her time. When the choice is between two candidates with similar credentials. A follow-up letter which can sometimes make the difference between getting a job or not.

14

COMMA SPLICES AND FUSED SENTENCES

A **comma splice,** also known as a **comma fault,** occurs when a comma by itself joins independent clauses°. The only time that a comma is correct between two independent clauses is when the comma is followed by a coordinating conjunction (*and, but, for, or, nor, yet,* and *so*). The word *splice* means "to fasten ends together." The end of one independent clause and the beginning of another cannot be fastened together with a comma alone.

> COMMA SPLICE   The hurricane intensified, it turned toward land.

A **fused sentence** occurs when two independent clauses are not separated by punctuation or joined by a comma with a coordinating conjunction. The word *fused* means "to unite as if by melting together." Two independent clauses cannot be united as if melted together. A fused sentence is also known as a **run-on sentence** or a **run-together** sentence.

> FUSED SENTENCE   The hurricane intensified it turned toward land.

Comma splices and fused sentences are two versions of the same problem: incorrect joining of two independent clauses. A fused

271

COORDINATED RESOURCES

Alternate examples and exercises for this chapter are available in the *S & S Workbook for Writers,* Gordon and Troyka.

A transparency master is available for the screened charts in this chapter.

The software program *Blue Pencil,* available from Prentice-Hall, offers students additional practice coordinated with this chapter.

Students can practice and test their knowledge of terms, key concepts, and applications of material in this chapter by using the *Study Guide to the S & S Handbook for Writers,* West.

sentence, however, reveals less awareness of the need for a separation between the independent clauses. Comma splices and fused sentences can be corrected in a variety of ways.

The hurricane intensified. It turned toward land. [period]

The hurricane intensified; it turned toward land. [semicolon]

The hurricane intensified, and it turned toward land. [comma and coordinating conjunction]

As the hurricane intensified, it turned toward land. [the first independent clause revised into a dependent clause°]

The hurricane intensified as it turned toward land. [the second independent clause revised into a dependent clause°]

The hurricane intensified; then it turned toward land. [semicolon and conjunctive adverb]

■‖ **14a**

Know how to recognize comma splices and fused sentences.

To recognize comma splices and fused sentences, you need to be able to recognize an independent clause. As was explained in 7e-1, an independent clause contains a subject° and predicate°. Also, an independent clause can stand alone as a sentence because it is an independent grammatical unit.

SUBJECT	PREDICATE
Thomas Edison	was an American inventor.

If you tend to write comma splices, here is a useful technique for proofreading your work. Cover all the words on one side of the comma and see if the words remaining constitute an independent clause. If they do, cover that clause and uncover all the words on the other side of the comma. If the second side of the comma is also an independent clause, you have written a comma splice. To further help yourself avoid writing comma splices, become familiar with correct uses for commas, explained in Chapter 24. Experienced writers sometimes use a comma to join very brief parallel° independent clauses: *Mosquitos do not bite, they stab.* Many readers, including most instructors, consider this form an error; therefore, use a semicolon or period instead of the comma.

If you tend to write fused sentences, you are ignoring the need to signal the end of one sentence before another one starts. If you

272

RECOGNIZING COMMA SPLICES AND FUSED SENTENCES   *cs,fs*   14a

---

LEADING CAUSES OF COMMA SPLICES AND FUSED SENTENCES

1. **Pronouns.** A comma splice or fused sentence often occurs when the second independent clause starts with a pronoun.

   No   Thomas Edison was a productive inventor, **he** held over 1,300 U.S. and foreign patents.

   Yes   Thomas Edison was a productive inventor. **He** held over 1,300 U.S. and foreign patents.

2. **Conjunctive adverbs and other transitional expressions.** A comma splice or fused sentence often occurs when the second independent clause starts with a conjunctive adverb° (see page 148 for a list) or other transitional expression° (see page 84 for a list). Remember that these words are *not* coordinating conjunctions, so they cannot work in concert with a comma to join two independent clauses.

   No   Thomas Edison was a brilliant scientist, **however,** his schooling was limited to only three months of his life.

   Yes   Thomas Edison was a brilliant scientist. **However,** his schooling was limited to only three months of his life.

3. **Explanations or examples.** A comma splice or fused sentence often occurs when the second independent clause explains or gives an example of the information in the first independent clause.

   No   Thomas Edison was the genius behind many inventions, the phonograph and the incandescent lamp are among the best known.

   Yes   Thomas Edison was the genius behind many inventions. The phonograph and the incandescent lamp are among the best known.

---

are making this error because you are unsure about how to identify a complete sentence, use the Test for Sentence Completeness given in 13a.

You will also learn to avoid writing comma splices and fused

TEACHING TIP

Students who write comma splices and/or fused sentences have a better chance of finding and correcting their errors if they can find a pattern in them. To help students detect patterns, set aside one class or conference session to have students review all the paragraphs and essays they have written for the course. First, if they have not already done so, they should correct all comma splices and fused sentences. Then they should tally the *types* of sentences involved, using for reference the chart, Leading Causes of Comma Splices and Fused Sentences. Encourage students to create additional categories, if needed, for their errors that do not fit the three basic patterns. Make yourself available to answer questions, and encourage students to ask advice of their peers. At the end of the exercise have students submit a review statement. Here is a student's response:

Of the twelve comma splices and fused sentences I have written this semester, seven involved a second independent clause starting with a pronoun, four involved conjunctive adverbs, and one involved an explanation. I need to be careful, when I use a pronoun as the subject of an independent clause, to punctuate that clause as a sentence.

An explicit statement of results will force students to do the analysis, and the "I need to be careful . . ." sentence will force them to verbalize a plan of attack. Both steps work to overcome students' perhaps fuzzy perceptions of punctuation errors as being random and uncontrollable.

You can then keep the statements on file (1) to help you determine who needs to work on a particular kind of comma splice or fused sentence; and (2) as a contract between you and each student acknowledging that he or she knows what to do—and will do it.

TEACHING TIP

You might want to liven up a class by running a "revision contest." Divide the class into an even number of teams, each composed of four students. Tell the students that in preparation for the competition, everyone is to bring to class two paragraphs containing comma splices and fused sentences: (1) a published paragraph that the student has intentionally edited to have three such errors; and (2) an original paragraph written for the competition, containing three intentional comma splices or fused sentences. Ask each student to supply two copies of each paragraph: one for the contest and one filled in as an answer key.

On the day of the competition, pair up teams and have them exchange paragraphs. Collect the answer keys. Give the teams thirty minutes to revise the paragraphs they have received. When they finish, compare their revisions with the answer keys. Here is one way to score.

+5 points	for each correct revision
+2 points	for each minute by which a team beats the time limit
−5 points	for each incorrect revision, missed comma splice, or missed fused sentence
+5 points	added to the *finder's* team score for each unintentional error in end punctuation found in a contest paragraph (fragments, missing question marks, etc.)
−10 points	deducted from the *writer's* team score for each unintentional error in end punctuation in a contest paragraph
+10 points	bonus for a perfect response

Team scores can be adjusted along a curve, if you wish, for group grades.

sentences if you become aware that the majority of such errors occur for one of the three reasons listed on page 273.

■‖ 14b

Use a period or semicolon to correct comma splices and fused sentences.

You can use a period or semicolon to correct comma splices and fused sentences. For the sake of sentence variety and emphasis, however, do not always choose punctuation to correct this type of error. Other methods are discussed in 14c and 14d. Strings of too many short sentences rarely establish relationships and levels of importance among ideas.

A **period** can separate the independent clauses in a comma splice or fused sentence.

COMMA SPLICE	The Muir Woods National Monument is located in central California, its dominant tree is the coast redwood.
FUSED SENTENCE	The Muir Woods National Monument is located in central California its dominant tree is the coast redwood.
CORRECTED	The Muir Woods National Monument is located in central California. Its dominant tree is the coast redwood.

A **semicolon** can separate independent clauses that are closely related in meaning. See also 25a.

COMMA SPLICE	The coast redwood is named "Sequoia" after a Cherokee Indian, he developed the first alphabet used by that tribe.
FUSED SENTENCE	The coast redwood is named "Sequoia" after a Cherokee Indian he developed the first alphabet used by that tribe.
CORRECTED	The coast redwood is named "Sequoia" after a Cherokee Indian; he developed the first alphabet used by that tribe.

The question mark and exclamation point also signal the ends of independent clauses.

274

▮‖ 14c
Use coordinating conjunctions to correct comma splices and fused sentences.

When ideas in independent clauses are closely related and grammatically equivalent, you might decide to connect them with a coordinating conjunction. If you are correcting a comma splice, you can insert a coordinating conjunction and retain the comma. In correcting a fused sentence, you must insert a comma if you use a coordinating conjunction.

When using a coordinating conjunction, you need to be sure that it fits the meaning of the material. *And* signals addition; *but* and *yet* signal contrast; *for* and *so* signal cause; and *or* and *nor* signal alternatives. A sentence consisting of two independent clauses joined by a coordinating conjunction and a comma is called a **compound sentence** (7f-2). ▮‖ PUNCTUATION ALERT: Use a comma before a coordinating conjunction that links independent clauses (see 24a). ‖▮

COMMA SPLICE	Redwood trees can grow to over 300 feet in height and up to 16 feet in diameter, their seeds are only a sixteenth of an inch long.
FUSED SENTENCE	Redwood trees can grow to over 300 feet in height and up to 16 feet in diameter their seeds are only a sixteenth of an inch long.
CORRECTED	Redwood trees can grow to over 300 feet in height and up to 16 feet in diameter, **but** their seeds are only a sixteenth of an inch long.
COMMA SPLICE	The foot-thick bark of the redwood tree is a barrier to destructive insects, the bitter chemicals and tannins in the bark further discourage insects and fungi.
FUSED SENTENCE	The foot-thick bark of the redwood tree is a barrier to destructive insects the bitter chemicals and tannins in the bark further discourage insects and fungi.
CORRECTED	The foot-thick bark of the redwood tree is a barrier to destructive insects, **and** the bitter chemicals and tannins in the bark further discourage insects and fungi.

275

ANSWERS: EXERCISE 1

Answers will vary. Here is one set of possible revisions.

1. Today cattle rustling remains a thriving business, but it does not depend on horses and cowboys.
2. Modern rustlers are a far cry from their Old West predecessors. They use helicopters instead of horses.
3. Some cattle thieves even use computers; this modern technology helps them to steal more than $30 million worth of livestock per year.
4. Ranchers try to fight back, often by offering money for information, and they also hire guards to patrol grazing land from airplanes.
5. Like the rustlers, ranchers take advantage of modern technology. Some of them "brand" their cattle by implanting electronic computer chips which can be detected by portable sensors.

EXERCISE 1

Revise any comma splices or fused sentences by using a period, a semicolon, or a coordinating conjunction (and a comma, if the sentence is fused). If an item is correct, circle its number.

EXAMPLE   Cattle rustlers were common figures in the Old West, they wore eye masks and rode dark horses.
Cattle rustlers were common figures in the Old West. They wore eye masks and rode dark horses.

1. Today cattle rustling remains a thriving business, it does not depend on horses and cowboys.
2. Modern rustlers are a far cry from their Old West predecessors they use helicopters instead of horses.
3. Some cattle thieves even use computers, this modern technology helps them to steal more than $30 million worth of livestock per year.
4. Ranchers try to fight back, often by offering money for information, they also hire guards to patrol grazing land from airplanes.
5. Like the rustlers, ranchers take advantage of modern technology, some of them "brand" their cattle by implanting electronic computer chips which can be detected by portable sensors.

■‖ 14d

Revise one of two independent clauses into a dependent clause to correct a comma splice or fused sentence.

You can revise a comma splice or fused sentence by changing one of two independent clauses into a dependent clause. This method is suitable when one idea can be logically subordinated to the other. Sentences composed of one independent clause and one or more dependent clauses are called **complex sentences** (see 7f-3). ▮ PUNCTUATION ALERT: If you put a period after a dependent clause that is not attached to an independent clause, you will create the error called a sentence fragment (see Chapter 13). ▮

One way to create a dependent clause is to insert a subordinating conjunction in front of the subject and verb. When using a subordinating conjunction, be sure that it fits the meaning of the material. For example, *as* and *because* signal reason, *although* signals concession, *if* signals condition, and *when* signals time (see page 166 for a fuller list. ▮ PUNCTUATION ALERT: Always use a comma after an introductory dependent clause that starts with a subordinating conjunction. (see 24b-1). ▮

276

COMMA SPLICE	Gertrude Stein wanted to support struggling artists in the 1920s, she bought many paintings by Picasso and others.
FUSED SENTENCE	Gertrude Stein wanted to support struggling artists in the 1920s she bought many paintings by Picasso and others.
CORRECTED	**Because Gertrude Stein wanted to support struggling artists in the 1920s,** she bought many paintings by Picasso and others.

COMMA SPLICE	Gertrude Stein wrote many novels, short stories, essays, poems, plays, and one opera, she is better known for her art collection.
FUSED SENTENCE	Gertrude Stein wrote many novels, short stories, essays, poems, plays, and one opera she is better known for her art collection.
CORRECTED	Gertrude Stein wrote many novels, short stories, essays, poems, plays, and one opera **although she is better known for her art collection.**

A relative pronoun can also create a dependent clause. Commonly used relative pronouns are *who, which,* and *that.* ▌ PUNCTUATION ALERT: Use commas to set off nonrestrictive—nonessential—elements (see 24e). ▌

COMMA SPLICE	Gertrude Stein moved from America to Paris in 1902, she quickly became fascinated by impressionist painting.
FUSED SENTENCE	Gertrude Stein moved from America to Paris in 1902 she quickly became fascinated by impressionist painting.
CORRECTED	Gertrude Stein, **who moved from America to Paris in 1902,** quickly became fascinated by impressionist painting.

EXERCISE 2
Revise any comma splices or fused sentences.

Some legendary creatures such as leprechauns and vampires are strictly imaginary they cannot be accounted for by science. One fabled creature likely can be explained by reality, however, the facts have been distorted through the centuries. Unicorns are probably based on mountain goats viewed from far away. Goats sometimes lose a horn during a fight or in an

BIOGRAPHY
Although Gertrude Stein was born in Allegheny, Pennsylvania, in 1874, she spent little time in the United States once she had completed her education. She attended Radcliffe from 1893 to 1897, and Johns Hopkins Medical School from 1897 to 1902. In 1903 she went to Paris, where she stayed. Her writing was considered unusual: repetitious and sometimes nonsensical. According to Edmund Wilson, "Widely ridiculed and seldom enjoyed, she has yet played an important role in connection with other writers who have become popular." For forty years her home was a gathering place for famous and not-yet-famous artists and writers: Henri Matisse, Pablo Picasso, Juan Gris, Wyndham Lewis, Sherwood Anderson, Ezra Pound, Ernest Hemingway, André Gide, Paul Robeson.

Answers to Exercise 2 on p. 278

INSTRUCTOR'S NOTES

ANSWERS: EXERCISE 2

Answers will vary. Here is one possible revision.

Some legendary creatures such as leprechauns and vampires are strictly imaginary. They cannot be accounted for by science. One fabled creature likely can be explained by reality; however, the facts have been distorted through centuries. Unicorns are probably based on mountain goats viewed from far away. Goats sometimes lose a horn during a fight or in an accident. From a distance, the remaining horn appears to be centered on the goat's head. Another creature, the zombie, has origins in old West Indian superstitions, but it can be explained by recent research on a fish common to West Indian waters. A zombie, which is supposedly a human corpse, roams around in a trance-like state ready to do the will of someone who has power over it. Pufferfish, also known as blowfish, contain a potent toxin that paralyzes nerves if the fish is cooked improperly. Then a person who eats the fish will act like the traditional "living dead."

accident, from a distance, the remaining horn appears to be centered on the goat's head. Another creature, the zombie, has origins in old West Indian superstitions, it can be explained by recent research on a fish common to West Indian waters. A zombie is supposedly a human corpse it roams around in a trance-like state ready to do the will of someone who has power over it. Pufferfish, also known as blowfish, contain a potent toxin that paralyzes nerves if the fish is cooked improperly, then a person who eats the fish will act like the traditional "living dead."

■‖ 14e

Use a semicolon or a period before a conjunctive adverb or other transitional expression between two independent clauses.

Conjunctive adverbs and other transitional expressions link ideas between sentences. Remember, however, that these words are *not* coordinating conjunctions, so they cannot work in concert with commas to join independent clauses. Conjunctive adverbs and other transitional expressions require that the previous sentence end in a period or semicolon.

Conjunctive adverbs include such words as *however, therefore, also, next, then, thus, furthermore,* and *nevertheless* (see page 148 for a fuller list). ■‖ PUNCTUATION ALERT. Use a comma after a conjunctive adverb at the beginning of a sentence. ‖■

COMMA SPLICE	Car theft has increased alarmingly in most major cities, **however,** one city has decided to fight back.
FUSED SENTENCE	Car theft has increased alarmingly in most major cities **however,** one city has decided to fight back.
CORRECTED	Car theft has increased alarmingly quickly in most major cities. **However,** one city has decided to fight back.

Transitional expressions include *for example, for instance, in addition, in fact, of course,* and *on the other hand* (see page 84 for a fuller list). ■‖ PUNCTUATION ALERT: Use a comma after transitional words at the beginning of a sentence. ‖■

COMMA SPLICE	In Boston stolen car reports are broadcast over the radio, **in fact,** a police officer "deputizes" about 500,000 listeners to be on the alert for stolen vehicles.

278

FUSED SENTENCE In Boston stolen car reports are broadcast over the radio **in fact,** a police officer "deputizes" about 500,000 listeners to be on the alert for stolen vehicles.

CORRECTED In Boston stolen car reports are broadcast over the radio. **In fact,** a police officer "deputizes" about 500,000 listeners to be on the alert for stolen vehicles.

A conjunctive adverb or other transitional expression can appear in more than one location within an independent clause. In contrast, a coordinating conjunction can appear only between the independent clauses it joins.

Car theft has increased alarmingly in most major cities.
One city, **however,** has decided to fight back.
Car theft has increased alarmingly in most major cities.
One city has decided, **however,** to fight back.
Car theft has increased alarmingly in most major cities.
One city has decided to fight back, **however.**
Car theft has increased alarmingly in most major cities, **but** one city has decided to fight back.

EXERCISE 3

Revise any comma splices or fused sentences caused by a conjunctive adverb or other transitional expression. If an item is correct, circle its number.

EXAMPLE Old comic books can be very valuable, therefore, many people collect them.
Old comic books can be very valuable. Therefore, many people collect them.

1. Comic strips and comic books have been loved by some, however, others have viewed them as dangerous and degrading.
2. In recent years, television has been named as a bad influence on children; consequently, comics have not gotten as much attention.
3. In the 1950s, however, many parents believed that reading "Superman" and "Tales from the Crypt" would cause their children to grow up with distorted minds therefore, comic books were forbidden in many homes.
4. Some communities banned the sale of comic books, teachers and clergy, in addition, complained about the negative effects of comic books.
5. Comic books, nevertheless, have continued to be popular in fact, people are often amazed to discover that comic books were once objected to so fiercely.

ANSWERS: EXERCISE 3
Answers will vary. Here is one set of possible revisions.
1. Comic strips and comic books have been loved by some; however, others have viewed them as dangerous and degrading.
2. Correct
3. In the 1950s, however, many parents believed that reading "Superman" and "Tales from the Crypt" would cause their children to grow up with distorted minds. Therefore, comic books were forbidden in many homes.
4. Some communities banned the sale of comic books. Teachers and clergy, in addition, complained about the negative effects of comic books.
5. Comic books, nevertheless, have continued to be popular. In fact, people are often amazed to discover that comic books were once objected to so fiercely.

INSTRUCTOR'S NOTES

ANSWERS: EXERCISE 4

Answers will vary. Here is one set of possible revisions.

1. Children learn penmanship by conscious practicing how to form each letter. In a few years, however, their handwriting becomes automatic.
2. As people mature, their handwriting takes on unique traits, and the slight variations in angles, slope, speed, and pressure become enormous.
3. Handwriting experts know how to recognize minute differences in letter and word spacing, in comparative sizes of letters, and in finger dexterity; furthermore, experts can see patterns in how people spell, punctuate, and use certain phrases.
4. Handwriting specialists working on criminal cases prefer not to make judgments based on a short sample because they know that it gets harder to maintain a forged handwriting with each successive word.
5. Correct

ANSWERS: EXERCISE 5

Answers will vary. Here is one possible revision.

Most baseball fans know many amusing stories and wild tales about Casey Stengel. He could be a clown on the ball field but a great strategist behind the scenes. Stengel was born in Kansas City, Missouri in 1890, and he died in Glendale, California, in 1975. He had eighty-five years in between to devote to baseball. He claimed that he did not play golf or go to the movies, so baseball was all that was left. In 1929, he was managing a last-place team called the Toledo Mud Hens. He was not, of course, very happy with their performance. He told the players that they should all get interested in the stock market; in fact, he told them to invest in Pennsylvania Railroad stock. He told the team that they had to improve, or otherwise they would be riding trains out of town. The railroad would get many new customers. Therefore, Stengel reasoned, the stock would go up. Baseball history does not reveal whether the players bought the stock, but they did start playing better.

EXERCISE 4

Revise all comma splices or fused sentences, using a different method of correction for each one. If an item is correct, circle its number.

EXAMPLE   No two adults have exactly the same handwriting therefore, handwriting analysis can help solve crimes.
No two adults have exactly the same handwriting. Therefore, handwriting analysis can help solve crimes.

1. Children learn penmanship by consciously practicing how to form each letter, in a few years, however, their handwriting becomes automatic.
2. As people mature, their handwriting takes on unique traits, the slight variations in angles, slope, speed, and pressure become enormous.
3. Handwriting experts know how to recognize minute differences in letter and word spacing, in comparative sizes of letters, and in finger dexterity, furthermore, experts can see patterns in how people spell, punctuate, and use certain phrases.
4. Handwriting specialists working on criminal cases prefer not to make judgments based on a short sample they know that it gets harder to maintain a forged handwriting with each successive word.
5. Clifford Irving tried to forge the signature of Howard Hughes, and although the signatures look alike to most untrained eyes, trained investigators found many of Irving's personal handwriting traits in his forgery.

EXERCISE 5

Revise any comma splices and fused sentences, using as many different methods explained in this chapter as you can.

Most baseball fans know many amusing stories and wild tales about Casey Stengel, he could be a clown on the ball field but a great strategist behind the scenes. Stengel was born in Kansas City, Missouri, in 1890 he died in Glendale, California, in 1975, he had eighty-five years in between to devote to baseball. He claimed that he did not play golf or go to the movies, baseball was all that was left. In 1929 he was managing a last-place team called the Toledo Mud Hens, he was not, of course, very happy with their performance. He told the players that they should all get interested in the stock market; in fact, he told them to invest in Pennsylvania Railroad stock. He told the team that they had to improve, otherwise they would be riding trains out of town. The railroad would get many new customers, therefore, Stengel reasoned, the stock would go up. Baseball history does not reveal whether the players bought the stock, they did start playing better.

280

15

SENTENCES THAT SEND UNCLEAR MESSAGES

A sentence can seem structurally correct at first glance—as if no grammatical principles of English have been violated—but still have internal flaws that keep it from delivering a sensible message. To help you sort through the various ways that sentences can send unclear messages, here is a summary of the material covered in this chapter:

Section 15a Shifts in person and number, subject and voice, tense and mood, and direct and indirect discourse

Section 15b Misplaced modifiers

Section 15c Dangling modifiers

Section 15d Mixed sentences

Section 15e Incomplete sentences

Most sentence flaws can be hard to spot because of the way the human brain works. When writers know what they mean to say, they sometimes misread what is on the paper for what they intend. The brain unconsciously "adjusts" an error or "fills in" missing material. Readers, on the other hand, see only what is on paper.

281

COORDINATED RESOURCES

Alternate examples and exercises for this chapter are available in the *S & S Workbook for Writers,* Gordon and Troyka.

The software program, *Blue Pencil,* available from Prentice-Hall, offers students additional practice for 15b and 15c.

Students can practice and test their knowledge of terms, key concepts, and applications of material in this chapter by using the *Study Guide to the S & S Handbook for Writers,* West.

No	Heated for 30 seconds, you get bubbles on the surface of the mixture. [This sentence says *you* are heated for 30 seconds.]
Yes	After the mixture is heated for 30 seconds, bubbles form on the surface.
No	After you boil the mixture for two minutes, it is cooled in a test tube. [This sentence shifts from *you* to *it* and from the active to the passive voice.]
Yes	After you boil the mixture for two minutes, you cool it in a test tube.
Yes	After the mixture is boiled for two minutes, it is cooled in a test tube.
No	The chemical reaction taking place rapidly creates a salt. [Does *rapidly* refer to the pace of the reaction or to the speed at which the salt is created?]
Yes	The chemical reaction takes place rapidly and creates a salt.
Yes	The chemical reaction rapidly creates a salt.

If you make such errors and have trouble noticing them, what can you do to get yourself to "see" the flaws? Here are some suggestions.

1. Finish your revision well before its deadline so that you can put it aside and go back to it with fresh eyes that will pick up flaws more easily as you proofread.
2. Proofread by working backwards, from your last sentence to your first; this can help you see each sentence as a separate unit free of context that might trick your brain into overlooking flaws.
3. Ask your instructor or other experienced readers to check you, and then look over their findings and try to raise your consciousness about what went wrong.
4. Proofread an extra time exclusively for any error that you tend to make more than any other.

■‖ 15a

Avoid unnecessary shifts.

Shifts within sentences blur meaning quickly. Readers expect to stay on the track you started them on. If you switch to another track, your readers become confused. Few readers have the patience to read material that seems garbled.

Unless the meaning or grammatical structure of a sentence requires it, always avoid shifting between person and number, subject and voice, and tense and mood. Also do not shift from indirect to direct discourse within a sentence without using punctuation and grammar to make the changes clear.

1
Stay consistent in person and number.

Person in English consists of the *first person* (I, we), who is the speaker; the *second person* (you), who is the person spoken to; and the *third person* (he, she, it, they), who is the person or thing being spoken about. Do not shift person within a sentence or a longer passage unless the meaning calls for a shift.

No   **They** enjoy feeling productive, but when a job is unsatisfying **you** usually become depressed. [*They* switches to *you*.]

Yes   **They** enjoy feeling productive, but when a job is unsatisfying **they** usually become depressed.

Number refers to one (singular) and more than one (plural). Do not start to write in one number and then shift suddenly to the other. Such shifting gives your sentences an unstable quality and your message becomes fuzzy.

No   By the year 2000, most **people** will live longer, and **an employed person** will retire later. [The plural *people* shifts to the singular *person*.]

Yes   By the year 2000, most **people** will live longer, and **employed people** will retire later.

A common cause of inconsistency in person and number is shifts to the second-person *you* from the first-person *I* or a third-person noun such as *person, the public,* or *people*. You will avoid this error in academic writing if you remember to reserve *you* for sentences that directly address the reader and to use third-person pronouns for general statements.

No   **I** enjoy reading forecasts of the future, but **you** wonder which will turn out to be correct. [*I*, first person, shifts to *you*, second person.]

Yes   **I** enjoy reading forecasts of the future, but **I** wonder which will turn out to be correct.

BACKGROUND
English emphasizes the number of every noun or pronoun in a sentence. In fact, it is impossible to talk or write about anything in English without signaling its number. English speakers take such information for granted, but the system is not universal. In Chinese, for example, the speaker decides if it is necessary to mention whether an item is singular or plural. Usually, number is considered irrelevant, and few sentences make any reference to it.

283

ANSWERS: EXERCISE 1

Answers may vary somewhat because of the alternate ways to eliminate shifts in person and number.

(1) Hyperactivity in children is a problem that affects up to 6 percent of young boys and girls, although *boys are* more likely to be affected than *girls.* (2) Teachers can find teaching hyperactive children difficult, especially if *the teachers* do not know how to recognize the characteristics of such *children.* (3) In one study, teachers called as many as 30 percent of their students hyperactive. (4) In school, these children may daydream excessively, fidget a great deal, or talk constantly. (5) *They show* other traits including tactlessly blurting out whatever is on their minds or racing around charging into people. (6) *Hyperactive children are* often impatient, cannot wait *their turns,* and are unable to follow directions. (7) New studies recently have been published. (8) They indicate that a key element in hyperactivity is a short attention span, possibly because *these children* eat too much sugar.

WORD HISTORY

According to the *Oxford English Dictionary (OED),* the word *voice* comes from the Latin word *vox,* meaning *voice* or *sound.* The earliest recorded statement in English using *voice* as a grammatical term is from 1382. Wyclif: "A participle of a present tens, either preterit, or actif vois, eithir passif."

No   By the year 2000, **Americans** will pay twice today's price for a car, and **you** will get twice the gas mileage. [*Americans,* third person, shifts to *you,* second person.]

Yᴇs   In 2000, **Americans** will pay twice today's price for a car, and **they** will get twice the gas mileage.

EXERCISE 1

Eliminate shifts in person and number. Be alert to shifts between, as well as within, sentences.

(1) Hyperactivity in children is a problem that affects up to 6 percent of young boys and girls, although a boy is more likely to be affected than a girl. (2) Teachers can find teaching hyperactive children difficult, especially if you do not know how to recognize the characteristics of such a child. (3) In one study, teachers called as many as 30 percent of their students hyperactive. (4) In school, these children may daydream excessively, fidget a great deal, or talk. (5) He shows other traits including tactlessly blurting out whatever is on their minds or racing around charging into people. (6) A hyperactive child is often impatient, cannot wait your turn, and are unable to follow directions. (7) New studies recently have been published. (8) It indicates that a key element in hyperactivity is a short attention span, possibly because we eat too much sugar.

‖ 2
Stay consistent in subject and voice.

The **subject** of a sentence is the word or group of words that acts, is acted upon, or is described: *People laugh, people were entertained, people are nice.* A subject can shift within a sentence only if the meaning justifies the shift.

People look forward to the future, but **the future** holds many secrets.

Shifts in subjects, however, are rarely justified when they are accompanied by a shift in voice. The **voice** of a sentence is either **active** *(People expect changes in the future)* or **passive** *(Changes are expected in the future).* The active voice emphasizes the doer of an action, and the passive voice does not. Unnecessary shifts in subject and voice reflect a lack of planning that causes a sentence or longer stretch of writing to drift out of focus.

No   Most of **the people polled expect** major improvements by the year 2000, but some **hardships are anticipated.** [The subject shifts from *people* to *hardships,* and the voice shifts from active to passive.]

Yes   Most of **the people polled expect** major improvements by the year 2000, but **they anticipate** some hardships.

No   When some **respondents consider** the year 2000, very optimistic **predictions are made.** [The subject shifts from *respondents* to *predictions,* and the voice shifts from active to passive.]

Yes   When some **respondents consider** the year 2000, **they make** very optimistic predictions.

Yes   Some **respondents consider** the year 2000 very optimistically.

3
Stay consistent in tense and mood.

Tense refers to the ability of verbs to show time. Tense changes are required when time movement is described: *We will go to the movies after we finish dinner.* If tense changes are illogical, sentence clarity suffers. (See 8h for guidance about correct sequences of tenses.)

No   The campaign in the United States to clean up the movies **began** in the 1920s as civic and religious groups **try** to ban sex and violence from the screen. [The tense shifts from the past *began* to the present *try.*]

Yes   The campaign in the United States to clean up the movies **began** in the 1920s as civic and religious groups **tried** to ban sex and violence from the screen.

No   Producers and distributors **created** a film Production Code in the 1930s. At first, violating its guidelines **carried** no penalty. Eventually, however, films that **fail** to get the board's Seal of Approval **are not distributed** widely. [This shift occurs between sentences: the past tense *created* and *carried* shift to the present tense *fail* and *are not distributed.*]

ALTERNATE EXAMPLES: VOICE SHIFTS

No   The campers *planned* on staying in the woods for a week, but the lack of bathrooms *had* not *been anticipated.* [Who had not anticipated the lack of bathrooms?]

Yes   The campers *planned* on staying in the woods for a week, but they *had* not *anticipated* the lack of bathrooms.

No   After three days, they *wanted* showers because poison ivy *had been contracted.* [Who had poison ivy?]

Yes   After three days, they *wanted* showers because all of them *had contracted* poison ivy.

No   The League of Women voters *has organized* presidential debates in the last few general elections, hoping to inform the public, clarify the issues, and stimulate voter turnout. Along the way, women *have been encouraged* to vote their consciences. [Who encouraged these women? The shift to the passive *have been encouraged* leaves this unclear.]

Yes   The League of Women Voters *has organized* presidential debates in the last few general elections, hoping to inform the public, clarify the issues, and stimulate voter turnout. Along the way, the League *has encouraged* women to vote their consciences. [Now the League's role is clear because of the active voice, *has encouraged.*]

Note: An extra exercise on logical tense sequence appears on pp. 298–9.

YES   Producers and distributors **created** a film Production Code in the 1930s. At first, violating its guidelines **carried** no penalty. Eventually, however, films that **failed** to get the board's Seal of Approval **were not distributed** widely.

Mood refers to whether a sentence is a statement or question (indicative° mood), a command or request (imperative° mood), or a conditional or other-than-real statement (subjunctive° mood). Shifts among moods blur your message. The most common error in shifts is between the imperative and indicative, though other types sometimes occur.

No   The Production code included two guidelines about violence. **Do not show** the details of brutal killings, and **movies should not be** explicit about how to commit crimes. [The verbs shift from the imperative mood *do not show* to the indicative mood *movies should not be.*]

YES   The Production code included two guidelines about violence. **Do not show** the details of brutal killings, and **do not be** explicit about how to commit crimes.

YES   The Production code included two guidelines about violence. **Movies should not show** the details of brutal killings, and **should not be** explicit about how to commit crimes.

No   **If a movie were going to be shown** outside the United States, the **guidelines are** less strict. [The verbs shift from the subjunctive mood *if a movie were going to be shown* to the indicative mood *guidelines are.*]

YES   **If a movie were going to be shown** outside the United States, the **guidelines would be** less strict.

WORD HISTORY

According to the *Oxford English Dictionary (OED),* the term *mood* has been used since the sixteenth century to refer to verb forms that indicate commands or wishes. The earliest recorded use of the word in this way dates back to 1573, when a scholar named Golding asked a question that still concerns our students: "How shall men directly fynde the Coniugation, Nomber, Person, Tence, and Moode of Verbes togither in their kynde?"

When we speak of the *mood* of a verb, we are not discussing its emotional state. *Mood* when it refers to a mental state is related to Latin *mos,* meaning *custom.* In contrast, *mood* used to discuss verbs is an alteration of *mode,* which comes from the Latin *modus,* meaning *measure, moderation,* or (most relevant here) *manner.* The earliest use of *mode* to refer to verbs dates back to 1520: "Sometyme of the infinytyve mode folowynge." Other early references make it clear that *mood/mode* was originally used for discussions of Greek and Latin, rather than of English.

4
Avoid unmarked shifts between indirect and direct discourse within the same sentence.

Indirect discourse reports speech or conversation and is not enclosed in quotation marks. **Direct discourse** repeats speech or conversation exactly and encloses the spoken words in quotation marks. Sentences that merge indirect and direct discourse without quotation marks and other markers, confuse readers and distort the message.

286

No   Professor Anderson attributed acid rain specifically to carbon fuels but **are we ready to give them up?** [The first clause is indirect discourse; the second shifts to unmarked direct discourse.]

Yes   Professor Anderson attributed acid rain specifically to carbon fuels but **asked whether we are ready to give them up.** [This revision sustains indirect discourse.]

Yes   Professor Anderson attributed acid rain specifically to carbon fuels but **asked, "Do we really want to give them up?"** [This revision uses direct and indirect discourse correctly because the quotation marks and grammatical structures clearly signal which is which.]

EXERCISE 2

Revise these sentences to eliminate all incorrect shifts discussed so far in this chapter. Some sentences have several possible revisions.

EXAMPLE   British physicist J. H. Fremlin speculated that some day the world might be housed in a continuous 2,000-story building and did we understand that the building would cover our entire planet?

British physicist J. H. Fremlin speculated that some day the world might be housed in a continuous 2,000-story building *and asked whether we understood that the building would cover our entire planet.*

1. In 8000 B.C., five million people lived on earth, but about 10,000 years later the population grows to 500 million.

2. One expert pointed out that the population doubled only once every thousand years between 8000 B.C. and A.D. 1650 and did we realize that such a rate presented no problem in those days?

3. In 1850 the earth's population reaches one billion; it had doubled in 200 years.

4. The world needed only 80 years to double again by 1930, and you saw the next doubling 35 years later in 1965.

5. Some people think that space colonies will eventually relieve crowding on earth, but that possibility is doubted by me.

EXERCISE 3

Revise this paragraph to eliminate incorrect shifts. Be alert to shifts between, as well as within, sentences.

(1) The twentieth-century intercontinental traveler faces different challenges than their ancestors a hundred years ago. (2) The traveler a hundred

ANSWERS: EXERCISE 2

1. [Corrected shift in verb tense] In 8000 B.C., five million people *lived* on earth, but about 10,000 years later the population *grew* to 500 million.

2. [Corrected shift between direct and indirect discourse] One expert pointed out that the population doubled only once every thousand years between 8000 B.C. and A.D. 1650, *and he asked whether we realized* that such a rate presented no problem in those days.

3. [Corrected tense shift] In 1850 the earth's population *reached* one billion; it *had doubled* in 200 years.

4. [Corrected shift in person] The world needed only 80 years to double again by 1930, and it saw the next doubling 35 years later in 1965.

5. [Corrected subject and voice shift] Some people think that space colonies will eventually relieve crowding on earth, but I doubt that possibility.

Answers to Exercise 3 on p. 288

INSTRUCTOR'S NOTES

ANSWERS: EXERCISE 3

Answers might vary somewhat. The final result must avoid all shifts. One possibility is:

(1) Twentieth-century intercontinental *travelers face* different challenges than their ancestors a hundred years ago. (2) *Travelers* a hundred years ago crossed oceans on slow *ships* that *took* weeks to arrive at their destination. (3) Today's *travelers*, on the other hand, *ride* on a jet airliner that takes only hours. (4) Nineteenth-century voyagers often encountered delays because of ocean storms, but *today's travelers experience problems caused* by the speed of jet planes. (5) If travelers cross through several time zones in a few hours, *they may experience* jet lag. (6) Victims of jet lag often feel weak, and sometimes *they* may be disoriented for days following the trip. (7) To help prevent jet lag, avoid alcoholic beverages while in flight. (8) Also, *get* plenty of sleep the day before your interncontinental trip.

years ago crossed oceans on a slow ship that takes weeks to arrive at their destination. (3) Today's traveler, on the other hand, rides on a jet airliner that took only hours. (4) Nineteenth-century voyagers often encountered delays because of ocean storms, but today problems are caused for travelers by the speed of jet planes. (5) If travelers cross through several time zones in a few hours, jet lag may be experienced. (6) Victims of jet lag often feel weak, and sometimes you may be disoriented for days following the trip. (7) To help prevent jet lag, avoid alcoholic beverages while in flight. (8) Also you should get plenty of sleep the day before your intercontinental trip.

■‖ 15b
Avoid misplaced modifiers.

A **modifier** is a word, phrase°, or clause° that describes other words, phrases, or clauses. A **misplaced modifier** is a description incorrectly positioned in a sentence, thus distorting your meaning. As you write and revise, always check to see that your modifiers are placed as close as possible to what they describe so that your reader will attach the meaning where you intend it to be.

‖ 1
Avoid ambiguous placements.

With **ambiguous placement,** a modifier can refer to two or more words in a sentence.

Little limiting words (such as *only, just, almost, hardly, nearly, even, exactly, merely, scarcely, simply*) can change meaning according to where they are placed. When you use such words, position them precisely. Consider how the placement of *only* changes the meaning of this sentence: *Professional coaches say that high salaries motivate players.*

Only professional coaches say that high salaries motivate players. [No one else says this.]

Professional coaches **only** say that high salaries motivate players. [The coaches probably do not mean what they say.]

Professional coaches say **only** that high salaries motivate players. [The coaches say nothing else.]

Professional coaches say that **only** high salaries motivate players. [Nothing except high salaries motivates players.]

Professional coaches say that high salaries **only** motivate players. [High salaries do nothing other than motivate players.]

288

Professional coaches say that high salaries motivate **only** players. [No others on the team, such as coaches and managers, are motivated by high salaries.]

Squinting modifiers also cause ambiguity. A squinting modifier can describe both what precedes and what follows it. Since a modifier cannot do double duty, either move the modifier to a position where its meaning will be precise or revise the sentence.

No   The high school star being recruited **actively** believed each successive offer would be better. [What was active—the recruitment or the star's belief?]

Yes   The high school star being recruited believed **actively** that each successive offer would be better.

Yes   The **actively** recruited high school star believed each successive offer would be better.

2
Avoid wrong placements.

With **wrong placement,** modifying words are misplaced in a sentence, thus garbling the meaning.

No   The history of college athletics sheds light on current policies and practices of college football **beginning in the nineteenth century.** [This sentence says that current policies and practices, not the history, started in the nineteenth century.]

Yes   The history of college athletics, **beginning in the nineteeth century,** sheds light on current policies and practices of college football.

No   Most college athletic departments in the 1920s evolved from academic divisions, **especially those with large football programs.** [This sentence says that academic divisions, not athletic departments, had football programs.]

Yes   Most college athletic departments in the 1920s, **especially those with large football programs,** evolved from academic divisions.

3
Avoid awkward placements.

Awkward placements are interruptions that seriously break the flow of a message.

TEACHING TIP
If your students feel that modifier placement is a slapdash business, you might ask them to look at some ludicrous sentences and have them try to draw what is written. Here are a few to use:
1. When people first saw whales, they were still wearing animal skins and had stone axes.
2. The man kissed the baby with a beard.
3. Walking down the street, the Eiffel Tower came into view.
4. The wildlife specialist said that most bears are dangerous on television.
5. Poison ivy is common in the forest which gives many people an itchy rash.

EXTRA EXERCISE B
Add an independent clause to each modifier, taking care to avoid misplaced modifiers.
Example
with great care

Calligraphy must be done with great care.
 1. in the yard
 2. above the horizon
 3. who grow strawberries
 4. when night fell
 5. worn in one ear
 6. in front of the fruit stand
 7. rather slowly
 8. lasting a lifetime
 9. if prices drop
10. winding up to pitch

ANSWERS: EXTRA EXERCISE B
Answers will vary considerably. Make sure that each answer is an independent clause. Check especially for misplaced modifiers.

289

A **split infinitive** is one type of awkward placement. An **infinitive** is a verb form that starts with *to: to convince, to create.* When material comes between the *to* and its verb, it can interrupt meaning, particularly when the intervening material could easily go before or after the infinitive.

> **No** Orson Welles's radio drama "War of the Worlds" managed **to,** on October 30, 1938, **convince** listeners that they were hearing an invasion by Martians.
>
> **Yes** On October 30, 1938, Orson Welles's radio drama "War of the Worlds" managed **to convince** listeners that they were hearing an invasion by Martians.

Often the intervening word that splits an infinitive is an adverb ending in *-ly.* Many such adverbs sound awkward unless they are placed either before or after the infinitive.

> **No** People feared they would no longer be able **to happily live** in peace.
>
> **Yes** People feared they would no longer be able **to live happily** in peace.

Nevertheless, sometimes an adverb seems awkward in any position except between *to* and the verb. Many readers, therefore, accept split infinitives like these:

> The starship Enterprise on "Star Tek" was charged **"to boldly go. . . ."**
>
> Welles wanted **to realistically portray** a Martian invasion for the radio audience.

If you think your readers prefer that infinitives never be split, you can usually revise the sentence to avoid the split:

> Welles wanted his "Martian invasion" to sound realistic to the radio audience.

Interruptions of **subjects and verbs** by highly complex phrases° or clauses° disturb the smooth flow of a sentence.

> **No** **The announcer,** because the script, which Welles wrote himself, called for perfect imitations of emergency announcements, **opened** with a warning that included a description of the "invasion."
>
> **Yes** Because the script, which Welles wrote himself, called for perfect imitations of emergency announcements, **the announcer opened** with a warning that included a description of the "invasion."

290

When a **verb phrase** (a group of words that functions as verb in a sentence: *was kissed, had been kissed*) is interrupted by words unrelated to the time sequence of the verb, the sentence lurches instead of flows.

No   People who tuned in late to "The War of the Worlds" believed that New Jersey **had,** by Martians bent on destruction, **been invaded.**

Yes   People who tuned in late to "The War of the Worlds" believed that New Jersey **had been invaded** by Martians bent on destruction.

No   Police switchboards **were,** not surprisingly, **jammed** with frantic phone calls.

Yes   Not surprisingly, police switchboards **were jammed** with frantic phone calls.

When a verb and its object are interrupted by words that should modify both those elements, clarity often suffers.

No   Many churches **held** for their frightened communities **"end of the world" prayer services.**

Yes   Many churches **held "end of the world" prayer services** for their frightened communities.

EXERCISE 4

Revise these sentences to correct any ambiguous, wrong, or awkward placements. If a sentence is correct, circle its number.

EXAMPLE   Experience makes only college registration easier.
               Only experience makes college registration easier.

1. Many students have, before they begin college, an ideal image of college life.
2. The first challenge is to, without feeling hesitant or losing your temper, enroll in required classes.
3. At some colleges, freshman courses because of overenrollment fill up very quickly.
4. If a course you want has, in spite of your having planned to take it, been closed, you have to think of alternatives.
5. You might consider bringing your problem, even though it is unlikely to be solved unless you are an isolated case, to the registrar.
6. The registrar, in consultation with each department, plans the number of sections that will be offered for each class in advance.

ANSWERS: EXERCISE 4
Answers may vary somewhat. Possibilities are:

1. Before they begin college, many students have an ideal image of college life.
2. The first challenge is to enroll in required classes without feeling hesitant or losing your temper.
3. At some colleges, freshman courses fill up very quickly because of overenrollment.
4. In spite of your having planned to take a course, if the course you want has been closed, you have to think of alternatives.
5. You might consider bringing your problem to the registrar even through it is unlikely to be solved unless you are an isolated case.
6. In consultation with each department, the registrar plans in advance the number of sections that will be offered for each class.

INSTRUCTOR'S NOTES

7. Therefore, as much as prerequisites will permit, you should go to registration with alternate plans for your schedule.

8. Colleges that regularly use on-line computer registration have easier procedures for students.

9. Upper-class students, because they must take course in their majors, have to be sure to get into the classes they need.

10. Correct, or: Once classes begin, any long lines, frustrations, and disappointments at registration often fade into memory.

ANSWERS: EXERCISE 5

1a. Frequently, the microbiologist used old methods to explore new problems.

1b. The microbiologist used old methods to explore new problems frequently.

1c. To explore new problems, the microbiologist used old methods frequently.

1d. To explore new problems frequently, the microbiologist used old methods.

2a. To become a biomedical engineer, the student studied engineering and medicine together.

2b. The student studied engineering and medicine together to become a biomedical engineer.

3a. Eagerly, the computer specialists worked only to solve problems in artificial intelligence.

3b. The computer specialists worked eagerly only in artificial intelligence to solve problems.

3c. Only the computer specialists worked eagerly in artificial intelligence to solve problems.

7. Therefore, you should, as much as prerequisites will permit, go to registration with alternate plans for your schedule.

8. Colleges that use on-line computer registration regularly have easier procedures for students.

9. Upper-class students have to, because they must take courses in their majors, be sure to get into the classes they need.

10. Once classes begin, registration, with its long lines, frustrations, and disappointments, often fades into memory.

EXERCISE 5

Combine each list of words or word groups to create all the possible logical sentences. Each list offers more than one possibility. Explain any differences in meaning among the alternatives you create.

EXAMPLE   college graduates
              on the average
              than do high school graduates
              earn more money

a. On the average, college graduates earn more money than do high school graduates.

b. College graduates earn more money, on the average, than do high school graduates.

c. College graduates, on the average, earn more money than do high school graduates.

1. the microbiologist
   frequently
   new
   to explore
   old
   used
   problems
   methods

2. to become
   engineering
   medicine
   the student
   a biomedical engineer
   studied
   successfully
   and

3. eagerly
   the computer specialists
   to solve problems
   worked
   artificial intelligence
   in
   only

4. know
   scientists
   that
   smoking
   lung
   not
   causes
   only
   cancer

292

15c

Avoid dangling modifiers.

A **dangling modifier** modifies what is implied but not stated in a sentence. Dangling modifiers can be hard for a writer to spot, because the writer's brain tends to supply the missing material, thereby allowing the error to go unnoticed.

> **No**   **Reading Faulkner's short story "A Rose for Emily,"** the ending surprised us.

This sentence says that the ending is doing the reading. The implied subject of the modifier is *we,* but nowhere is that subject stated—thus the modifier dangles. You can correct a dangling modifier by revising the sentence so that the intended subject is expressed.

> **Yes**   **Having read Faulker's short story "A Rose for Emily," we** were surprised by the ending.
>
> **Yes**   We read Faulkner's short story "A Rose for Emily" and were surprised by the ending.

> **No**   **Shocked by her father's death, the family home** became a refuge for Emily. [*The family home* cannot be shocked.]
>
> **Yes**   **Shocked by her father's death, Emily** took refuge in the family home.

> **No**   **When courting Emily, the townspeople** gossiped about her. [*The townspeople* were not courting Emily.]
>
> **Yes**   **When Emily and Homer Barron were courting, the townspeople** gossiped about her.

Dangling modifiers sometimes result from unnecessary use of the passive voice°.

> **No**   **To earn money, china-painting lessons** were offered by Emily to wealthy young women. [*China-painting lessons* cannot earn money.]
>
> **Yes**   **To earn money, Emily** offered china-painting lessons to wealthy young women.

3d. The computer specialists worked eagerly in artificial intelligence only to solve problems.

4a. Not only scientists know that smoking causes lung cancer.

4b. Scientists know that smoking causes not only lung cancer.

4c. Scientists know that not only smoking causes lung cancer.

EXTRA EXERCISE C
Add an independent clause after each modifier, taking care to avoid dangling modifiers.
Example
washing the car
Washing the car, I noticed signs of rust.
1. to juggle successfully
2. opening the door
3. because scared
4. broken into pieces
5. setting off an alarm
6. to get an interview
7. in playing soccer
8. while an Olympic diver
9. flagging down the police car
10. before locking your suitcase

ANSWERS: EXTRA EXERCISE C
Answers will vary considerably. Make sure each answer is an independent clause. Check especially for dangling modifiers.

ANSWERS: EXERCISE 6

Answers may vary somewhat. One set of possibilities is:

1. To be successful, the student journalist must plan carefully.
2. Being tense, an inexperienced journalist might begin on the wrong note.
3. Until relaxed, the student journalist should mention only neutral topics.
4. Correct
5. With a list of questions, the interviewer can make the process go more smoothly for everyone involved.
6. Although easy to answer, factual questions are sometimes answered incorrectly by a hostile interviewee.
7. By being analytic and evaluative, an experienced journalist can learn a great deal from those mistakes.
8. Knowing how to pace an interview, a journalist will more likely get honest answers to hard questions after he or she has caught the interviewee off guard.
9. Correct
10. Essential information might be revealed when the journalist is leaving.

EXERCISE 6

Identify and correct any dangling modifiers in these sentences. If a sentence is correct, circle its number.

EXAMPLE   Assigned to interview an unfriendly person, the experience can be instructive to a student journalist.
Assigned to interview an unfriendly person, *a student journalist can find the experience instructive.*

1. To be successful, careful plans must be made by the student journalist.
2. Being tense, the interview might begin on the wrong note for an inexperienced journalist.
3. Until relaxed, questions should mention only neutral topics.
4. After the journalist is more at ease, the person being interviewed might also relax.
5. With a list of questions, the interview process goes more smoothly for everyone involved.
6. Although easy to answer, mistakes are sometimes made on factual questions by a hostile interviewee.
7. By being analytic and evaluative, those mistakes can reveal a great deal to an experienced journalist.
8. Knowing how to pace an interview, the hard questions are more likely to be answered honestly after the interviewee has been caught off guard.
9. Until an interview is complete, the seasoned journalist always remains alert.
10. Essential information might be revealed when leaving.

15d
Avoid mixed sentences.

A **mixed sentence** has two or more parts that do not make sense together.

1
Revise mixed constructions.

A **mixed construction** starts out taking one grammatical form and then changes, derailing the meaning of the sentence.

No   Because television's first transmissions in the 1920s included news programs became popular with the public. [The opening subordinate clause is fused with the inde-

294

pendent clause that follows. What does the writer want to emphasize—the first transmissions or the popularity of news programs?]

Yes Television's first transmissions in the 1920s included news programs, which quickly became popular with the public. [The idea of the first transmissions is now emphasized. *Because* has been dropped, making the first clause independent; and *which* has been added, making the second clause subordinate and logically related to the first.]

No By doubling the time allotment for network news to thirty minutes increased the prestige of network news programs. [A prepositional phrase, such as *by doubling*, cannot be the subject of a sentence.]

Yes Doubling the time allotment for network news to thirty minutes increased the prestige of network news programs. [Dropping the preposition *by* clears up the problem.]

Yes By doubling the time allotment for network news to thirty minutes, the network executives increased the prestige of network news programs. [Inserting a logical subject, *the network executives,* clears up the problem; an independent clause is now preceded by a modifying prepositional phrase.]

The phrase *the fact that* is sometimes the cause of a mixed sentence. Most writers prefer to avoid the expression.

No The fact that quiz show scandals in the 1950s prompted the networks to produce even more news shows.

Yes The fact is that quiz show scandals in the 1950s prompted the networks to produce even more news shows.

Yes Quiz show scandals in the 1950s prompted the networks to produce even more news shows.

‖ 2

‖ Revise faulty predication.

Faulty predication, sometimes called **illogical predication,** occurs when a subject and its predicate (the part of the sentence that says something about the subject) do not make sense together.

295

No	The **purpose** of television **was invented** to entertain people.
Yes	The **purpose** of television **was** to entertain people.
Yes	**Television was invented** to entertain people.

One key cause of illogical predication is a breakdown in the connection between a subject and its complement. A **complement** renames or describes the subject; it follows a form of a verb such as *be*, which acts like an equal sign: *The student is happy* (student = happy).

No	Walter Cronkite's outstanding characteristic as a newscaster was credible.

The subject of this sentence is *characteristic*. While *credible* can rename (and would complement) a person, it cannot rename (or complement) a characteristic. A suitable renaming of a characteristic is *credibility*.

Yes	Walter Cronkite's outstanding characteristic as a newscaster was credibility.

Illogical predication is the problem in most constructions that begin **is when** or **is where.** Avoid these constructions in academic writing.

No	A disaster **is when** television news shows get some of their highest ratings.
Yes	Television news shows get some of their highest ratings during a disaster.

Similarly, avoid **reason . . . is because** in academic writing.

No	**One reason** television news captured national attention **is because** it covered the Vietnam War thoroughly.
Yes	**One reason** television news captured national attention **is that** it covered the Vietnam War thoroughly.
Yes	Television news captured national attention **because** it covered the Vietnam War thoroughly.

EXERCISE 7

Revise the mixed sentences below so that the beginning of each sentence fits logically with its end. If a sentence is correct, circle its number.

EXAMPLE   As a result of an archaeologist's discovery of an ancient grave site often provides important physical evidence of a past society.
An archaeologist's discovery of an ancient grave site often provides important physical evidence of a past society.

1. Archaeology is when you study the material remains, relics, artifacts, and monuments of past human life.
2. The reason that grave sites are important is because archaeologists can infer a great deal about a society from the way it buried its dead.
3. By comparing grave sites of other civilizations with burial places of North American civilization suggests interesting hypotheses about our society.
4. Among the conclusions such a study will produce include noting how democratic modern-day burials have become.
5. In an Egyptian pharaoh's desire to please the gods might demand as much as 40 percent of his country's gross national product to be spent on his burial.
6. By contrast, less that 0.2 percent of the gross national product of the United States is spent each year for all funerals.
7. The fact that China's first emperor, Qin Shihuangdi, was buried surrounded by an army of 7,500 terra cotta figures the extravagant interments favored by the ancient Chinese.
8. When George Washington, America's first president, was buried a simple ivy-covered tomb is a symbol of his country's values.
9. The fact that the Duke of Wellington was buried inside four nested coffins in a manner that the British felt would honor their beloved military hero.
10. Future archaeologists might compare Wellington's burial with burials in Arlington National Cemetery is where American military heroes are interred.

2. Grave sites are important because archaeologists can infer a great deal about a society from the way it buried its dead.
3. The comparison of grave sites of other civilizations with burial places of North American civilization suggests interesting hypotheses about our society.
4. The conclusions such a study will produce include noting how democratic modern-day burials have become.
5. An Egyptian pharaoh, in his desire to please the gods, might demand as much as 40 percent of his country's gross national product to be spent on his burial.
6. By contrast, less than 0.2 percent of the gross national product of the United States is spent each year for all funerals.
7. China's first emperor, Qin Shihuangdi, was buried surrounded by an army of 7,500 terra cotta figures, which suggests the extravagant interments favored by the ancient Chinese.
8. George Washington, America's first president, was buried in a simple ivy-covered tomb, a symbol of his country's values.
9. The Duke of Wellington was buried inside four nested coffins in a manner that the British felt would honor their beloved military hero.
10. Future archaeologists might compare Wellington's burial with burials in Arlington National Cemetery, where American military heroes are interred.

■‖ 15e
Avoid incomplete sentences.

An **incomplete sentence** has missing words, phrases°, or clauses° necessary for grammatical correctness or sensible meaning. Such omissions quickly blur meaning.

INSTRUCTOR'S NOTES

EXTRA EXERCISE A
LOGICAL TENSE SEQUENCE
(15a–3, pp. 285–6)

In each of these sentences, one or more verbs are out of sequence with the italicized verb. Correct each sentence so that the verb sequence is logical. Some sentences may have several correct answers.

Example

For a company *to have analyzed* marketing opportunities in a given area, it must be aware of a number of conditions.

For a company *to analyze* marketing opportunities in a given area, it *must be* aware of a number of conditions.

1. Because federal, state, and local governments *are concerned* with fostering competition and protecting the consumer, they imposed regulations to restrict some business practices.

2. Regulation was not always a problem, as some businesses *prosper* by manufacturing articles required by the government (such as safety goggles).

3. Consumer groups representing social and ecological interests *have exerted* great influence upon government agencies, and their actions resulted in great difficulties for some companies, most recently those who dumped or stored toxic wastes in unauthorized areas.

4. The mass media *influence* public opinion and played a major role in shaping market opportunities.

5. In addition, because the media *carry* advertisements for products and services, consumers could be-

1
Use elliptical constructions carefully.

An **elliptical construction** deliberately leaves out words that have already appeared in the sentence: *I have my book and Joan's* [*book*]. The paramount rule for an elliptical construction is that the words that are left out must be exactly the same as the words that do appear in the sentence.

No   The first important jazz **period belongs** to Dixieland, and the later **periods** to diverse styles ranging from ragtime to classical. [The word *belongs* cannot take the place of *belong*, needed in the second clause.]

Yes   The first important jazz **period belongs** to Dixieland, and the later **periods belong** to diverse styles ranging from ragtime to classical.

No   During the 1920s in Chicago, the cornetist Manuel Perez **was leading** one outstanding jazz group, Tommy and Jimmy Dorsey another. [The words *was leading* cannot take the place of *were leading*, needed in the second clause.]

Yes   During the 1920s in Chicago, the cornetist Manuel Perez **was leading** one outstanding jazz group; Tommy and Jimmy Dorsey **were leading** another.

Yes   During the 1920s in Chicago, the cornetist Manuel Perez **led** one outstanding jazz group; Tommy and Jimmy Dorsey another. [The verb *led* works in both clauses, so it can be omitted from the second clause.]

No   The period of the big jazz dance bands **began** and **lasted through** World War II. [This construction implies *began through* in the first clause, but *began* requires *in*, not *through*.]

Yes   The period of the big jazz dance bands **began in** and **lasted through** World War II.

2
Make comparisons complete, unambiguous, and logical.

In writing a comparison, be sure to include all words needed to make clear the relationship between the items or ideas being compared.

No   Individuals with high concern for achievement make better business executives. [*Better* indicates a comparison, but none is stated.]

Yes   Individuals with high concern for personal achievement make better business executives than do people with little interest in getting ahead.

No   Most personnel officers value high achievers more than risk takers. [Not clear: more than risk takers value high achievers, or more than personnel officers value high achievers?]

Yes   Most personnel officers value high achievers more than they value risk takers.

Yes   Most personnel officers value high achievers more than risk takers do.

No   An achiever's chance of success in business is greater than a gambler. [*Chance* is compared to *a gambler;* a thing cannot be compared logically to a person.]

Yes   An achiever's chance of success in business is greater than a gambler's. [A correct elliptical construction, with the word *chance* omitted]

No   Achievers value success as much, if not more than, a high salary. [Comparisons using *as . . . as* require the second *as*.]

Yes   Achievers value success as much as, if not more than, a high salary.

No   Achievers have such a reputation for success. [In academic writing, intensifiers such as *such, so,* and *too* must be completed.]

Yes   Achievers have such a reputation for success that often they are offered jobs before they complete their formal educations.

3
Proofread carefully to catch inadvertently omitted articles, pronouns, conjunctions, and prepositions.

Small words—articles, pronouns, conjunctions, and prepositions—that are needed to make sentences complete, sometimes slip into the cracks. If you tend inadvertently to omit words, proofread your work an extra time solely to find them.

come aware of what is available to them.

6. The overall health of the economy will have a direct effect on marketing opportunities and, in fact, *can determine* the success or failure of a company.

7. A company that easily *would succeed* under certain economic conditions failed under others.

8. Companies *need to have* research and development departments in order to have kept abreast of breakthroughs in science and technology that could have led to the production of new or improved products.

9. Failure to keep up with developments could have been costly or even fatal, as many small computer companies *are finding* out these days.

10. People expected the best for their money, and companies whose products were out of date as soon as they reach the market *are* doomed.

ANSWERS: EXTRA EXERCISE A
1. governments *are concerned;* they *impose* regulations
2. Regulation *is;* businesses *prosper*
3. *have exerted;* actions *have resulted;* those who *dump* or *store*
4. The mass media *influence; play*
5. media *carry;* customers *can* become aware
6. economy *has; can determine*
7. A company that easily *would succeed; fails (may fail)*
8. Companies *need to have; keep* abreast; *can lead*
9. developments *can be;* companies *are finding*
10. People *expect;* products *are; are* doomed.

No   On May 2, 1808, citizens Madrid rioted against French soldiers.

Yes   On May 2, 1808, **the** citizens **of** Madrid rioted against French soldiers.

No   On following day, captured rioters were taken into country and shot.

Yes   On **the** following day, captured rioters were taken into **the** country and shot.

No   The Spanish painter Francisco Goya recorded both the riot the execution in a pair of pictures painted 1814.

Yes   The Spanish painter Francisco Goya recorded both the riot **and** the execution in a pair of pictures painted **in** 1814.

EXERCISE 8

Revise this paragraph for correct elliptical constructions and complete comparisons. Also, insert any missing small words.

(1) Trained criminal investigators often value bits of glass as evidence more than eyewitness reports about crimes. (2) Information about the force and direction the impact that broke the glass creates a unique identification. (3) The chances of finding useful fingerprints at the scene of a robbery are less than glass from a broken window or glassware. (4) Often, glass fragments cling to robbers' clothes or a shard of glass to their shoes. (5) In many hit-and-run accidents, investigators use pieces of headlights or windshields evidence. (6) Because glass is so common in our society, being able to physically fit together pieces of glass offers best possibility of useful evidence, while making chemical matches the least.

ANSWERS: EXERCISE 8

(1) Trained criminal investigators often value bits of glass as evidence more than *they value* eyewitness reports about crimes. (2) Information about the force and direction *of* the impact that broke the glass creates a unique identification. (3) The chances of finding useful fingerprints at the scene of a robbery are less than *those of finding* glass from a broken window or *broken* glassware. (4) Often, glass fragments cling to robbers' clothes or a shard of glass *clings* to their shoes. (5) In many hit and run accidents, investigators use pieces of headlights or windshields *as* evidence. (6) Because glass is so common in our society, being able to physically fit together pieces of glass offers *the* best possibility of useful evidence, while making chemical matches *offers* the least.

300

IV WRITING EFFECTIVE SENTENCES

16 Conciseness

17 Coordination and
    Subordination

18 Parallelism

19 Variety and Emphasis

16
CONCISENESS

Trim sentences, like trim bodies, usually require far more effort than flabby ones. But though striving toward a lean and graceful style involves hard work, it can also be fun—like swimming or running.

—CLAIRE KEHRWALD COOK

Conciseness describes writing that is direct and to the point. Writing that is not concise is wordy. It forces readers to clear away excess words before sentences can deliver their messages.

WORDY PARAGRAPH

Every once in a while you will find that there is a day when everything seems to run very smoothly and even the riskiest of ventures seems to have come out exactly right. You may exclaim as a result of this, "This seems to be a lucky day for me!" Then, as an afterthought after such an utterance, you may say to yourself, "Knock on wood!" Of course, it is not really a situation where you believe that danger would actually be warded off if you happen to knock on wood. Still, you can be given a slight uneasy feeling because of boasting about your own luck, and so you go ahead and see that the little protective ritual is carried out. If someone were to challenge you at that moment, probably you would quickly rush to say, "Oh, that's nothing. Just an old superstition."

302

Wordy, indirect writing irritates readers. In contrast, concise writing, appeals to readers because it is direct.

CONCISE ORIGINAL PARAGRAPH

Once in a while there is a day when everything seems to run smoothly and even the riskiest venture comes out exactly right. You exclaim, "This is my lucky day!" Then as an afterthought you say, "Knock on wood!" Of course, you do not really believe that knocking on wood will ward off danger. Still, boasting about your own good luck gives you a slightly uneasy feeling—and you carry out the little protective ritual. If someone challenged you at that moment, you would probably say, "Oh, that's nothing. Just an old superstition."

—MARGARET MEAD AND RHODA METRAUX, "New Superstitions for Old"

Good writers stand behind the principle of conciseness—and illustrate it as well.

If it is possible to cut out a word, then always cut it out.
—GEORGE ORWELL, "Politics and the English Language"

Omit unnecessary words.
—WILLIAM STRUNK JR. AND E. B. WHITE, *The Elements of Style*

■‖ 16a

Eliminate wordy sentence structures.

Wordy sentence structures, including expletive and passive constructions, can make writing seem abstract and uninteresting.

‖ 1

Revise unnecessary expletive constructions.

An **expletive** postpones the subject and diminishes its effect by putting *it* or *there* plus a form of the verb *be* before the subject. If you remove the expletive and revise slightly, you give the subject—and the entire sentence—greater power.

No   It is necessary for students to fill out both registration forms.

YES   Students must fill out both registration forms.

TEACHING TIP
You might find it effective to take a passage of good prose (professional or student writing) and clutter it up. Distribute copies, and ask students to delete all unnecessary words, phrases, and clauses. Discuss their cuts. End by distributing copies of the original for students to compare with their versions. The discussion can become particularly lively if students question the conciseness of the original or champion the value of your padding.

COORDINATED RESOURCES
Alternate examples and exercises for this chapter are available in the *S & S Workbook for Writers,* Gordon and Troyka.

A transparency master is available for the screened chart in this chapter.

Students can practice and test their knowledge of terms, key concepts, and applications of material in this chapter by using the *Study Guide to the S & S Handbook for Writers,* West.

No	There are three majors offered by the computer science department.
Yes	Three majors are offered by the computer science department.
Yes	The computer science department offers three majors.

2
Revise unnecessary passive constructions.

In the **active voice,** the subject of a sentence *does* the action named by the verb.

Active	In *My Fair Lady*, **Professor Higgins teaches** Eliza to speak "proper" English. [*Professor Higgins* is the subject, and he does the action: he *teaches*.]

In the **passive voice,** the subject of a sentence *receives* the action named by the verb.

Passive	In *My Fair Lady*, **Eliza is taught** to speak "proper" English by Professor Higgins. [*Eliza* is the subject, and she receives the action: she *is taught*.]

For most writing, the active voice adds liveliness as well as conciseness. One way to revise from the passive to the active voice is to make the doer of the action the subject of the sentence. For example, when a passive construction names the doer of an action, it does so in a phrase starting with *by*. Therefore, make the noun or pronoun in the *by* phrase the sentence subject.

No	Volunteer work **was done by the students** for credit in sociology. [The students are doers of the action, but they are not the subject of the sentence.]
Yes	The **students did** volunteer work for credit in sociology.
No	The new spending bill **was vetoed by the governor.** [The governor is the doer of the action, but he is not the subject of the sentence.]
Yes	The **governor vetoed** the new spending bill.

Sometimes you can revise a sentence from passive to active by finding a new verb, especially when you want to keep the same subject.

304

PASSIVE	Britain **was defeated** by the United States in the war of 1812.
ACTIVE	Britain **lost** the war of 1812 to the United States.
PASSIVE	Hundreds of soldiers **were stricken** with yellow fever.
ACTIVE	Hundreds of soldiers **caught** yellow fever.

Writers use the passive voice when the doer of an action is unknown or when naming the doer would disrupt the focus they want a sentence to have. (The passive voice occurs often in science writing, as is discussed in Chapter 34.) In situations that do not call for the passive voice, writers sometimes deliberately use it for sentence after sentence in the mistaken belief that it sounds "mature" or "academic." When the doers of the action are important, as in the following example, you should use the active voice.

NO	One very important quality developed by an individual during a first job is self-reliance. This strength was gained by me when I was allowed by my supervisor to set up and conduct my own survey project.
YES	During their first job, many individuals develop the very important quality of self-reliance. I gained this strength when my supervisor allowed me to set up and conduct my own survey project.
YES	During a first job, many people develop self-reliance, as I did when my supervisor let me set up and conduct my own survey project.

One important caution about the passive voice: Do not use it to hide information about who acts. For example, a report might say this:

Cracks in the foundation of the structure had been found in 1984, but these problems were not considered serious.

Left out of this sentence is possibly important information about who found cracks and who decided the cracks were not serious. Such omissions may be intentional; writers may choose the passive voice to sound impersonal or objective. In most cases, however, use of the passive voice creates distorting omissions of information. For more advice on acceptable uses of the passive voice, see Voice, page 205.

305

TEACHING TIP
One way to demonstrate how conciseness is achieved is to show students how we work toward it in our own writing. Telling a student, "I always revise to eliminate wordiness" rarely works. Instead, you might try one of these two approaches:

1. Distribute copies of a first, messy draft and a final version of one of your current projects. Invite students to trace the changes you made, as you took out unnecessary words and passages, wavered between synonyms, adjusted verb tenses, and so forth. Some rhetorical readers contain facsimile pages from writers' manuscripts that can be used in the same way. Students are likely to take the process more seriously, however, if they see your work. A page from Keats or Faulkner is not as immediate as one from their own teacher's current project.

2. You might distribute three or four versions of a piece (each successively more concise) without noting their order of composition. Ask the students to guess which came earlier or later, and how they know. This activity helps prove that revising for conciseness produces noticeable results.

TEACHING TIP
In class you might ask the students to exchange papers. Direct them to read the papers looking for unnecessary words. You can structure this lesson in several ways:

1. Have pairs of students write directly on one another's papers. You then collect the paragraphs, add your own comments, and return them the next class.

2. Have pairs or trios of students confer on papers one at a time and arrive at a consensus. You can circulate around the room, answering questions, and give credit for each paragraph completed.

3. Have authors number their lines in the margin. Ask students to pass their assignments to the left. The students write comments on a separate sheet of paper, keying each comment to a line number. After five minutes, students sign their comments and pass the paragraphs and comment sheets to the left again. Repeat as time and class interest allow. At the end of the class, give the comment sheets to the authors. For homework, students can review the responses to their work and incorporate whichever comments they feel are valid. At the next class, you can collect the revised paragraphs and comment sheets.

3

When possible, combine sentences, reduce clauses to phrases, and reduce phrases to words.

Clarity is among your main concerns during revision. Often when you see the need for conciseness, you can combine sentences or reduce a clause to a phrase or reduce a phrase to a single word. When you aim for conciseness, often you also achieve better clarity.

Combining sentences

When you revise, look carefully at sets of sentences in your draft. You may be able to reduce the information in one sentence to a group of words that you can include in another sentence.

TWO SENTENCES
The *Titanic* was discovered seventy-three years after being sunk by an iceberg. The wreck was located in the Atlantic by a team of French and American scientists.

COMBINED SENTENCE
Seventy-three years after being sunk by an iceberg, the *Titanic* was located in the Atlantic by a team of French and American scientists.

TWO SENTENCES
These scientists used several million dollars worth of equipment to locate the wreck. This electronic equipment included sonar devices.

COMBINED SENTENCE
These scientists used several million dollars worth of electronic equipment, including sonar devices, to locate the wreck.

TWO SENTENCES
The stern of the ship was missing and there was some external damage to the hull. Otherwise, the Titanic seemed to be in excellent condition.

COMBINED SENTENCE
Aside from its missing stern and external damage to its hull, the *Titanic* seemed to be in excellent condition.

You will find more advice about reducing sentence structures and combining and subordinating information in Chapter 17.

Reducing clauses

You can often reduce adjective clauses (7e-2) to phrases, sometimes just by dropping the opening relative pronoun° and its verb.

The *Titanic,* **which was a huge ocean liner,** sank in 1912.
The *Titanic,* **a huge ocean liner,** sank in 1912.

Sometimes you can reduce the clause to a single word.

The scientists held a memorial service for the passengers and crew members **who had died.**
The scientists held a memorial service for the **dead** passengers and crew members.

Creating elliptical constructions° is another way to reduce clauses, but be sure to omit only clearly implied words.

When they were confronted with disaster, some passengers behaved heroically, **while others behaved selfishly.**
Confronted with disaster, some passengers behaved heroically, **others selfishly.**

Keep your meaning clear when you reduce clauses. Making your writing concise should never make it hard to understand.

Reducing phrases

Sometimes you will be able to reduce phrases to shorter phrases or to single words.

Although loaded with luxuries, the liner was thought to be unsinkable.
The **luxury** liner was thought to be unsinkable.

Over fifteen hundred **travelers on that voyage** died in the shipwreck.
Over fifteen hundred **passengers** died in the shipwreck.

Objects found inside the ship **included unbroken** bottles of wine and expensive **undamaged** china.
Found undamaged inside the ship were bottles of wine and expensive china.

EXTRA EXERCISE
Unnecessary words have been added to this paragraph. Cross out any words you think do not belong.

When I first started to begin writing, I thought I was doing something kind of wrong. I would look at the first drafts I had written with all the cross-outs, write-ins, and notes I had written to myself, and in a very real sense I would think that it should come more easily to me than it did. I would worry and be anxious that I was working too hard at it. Then one day I was up in the Great Books section of the New York Public Library on Fifth Avenue in New York City and I saw something that, in fact, amazed and stunned me. I located and looked at the actual, rough drafts of the pages of the poet Walt Whitman's poem *Leaves of Grass,* and I saw for myself that it was filled and covered with the same false starts, the same cross-outs, and the same write-ins that covered my own writing that I was doing.

ANSWER: EXTRA EXERCISE
When I first stared writing I thought I was doing something wrong. I would look at the first drafts with all the cross-outs, write-ins, and notes to myself, and I would think that it should come more easily to me. I would worry that I was working too hard at it. Then one day I was in the Great Books section of the New York Public Library on Fifth Avenue and I saw something that amazed me. I looked at the actual, rough drafts of the poet Walt Whitman's *Leaves of Grass,* and I saw that it was filled with the same false starts, the same cross-outs, and the same write-ins that covered my own writing.
PATRICK FENTON, quoted in
The Writer's Craft

307

4
Use strong verbs and avoid nouns formed from verbs.

Your writing will have more impact when you choose strong verbs—verbs that directly convey an action. *Be* and *have* are not strong verbs. When you revise weak verbs to strong ones, you will often reduce the number of words in your sentences.

WEAK VERB
The proposal before the city council **has to do with** locating the sewage treatment plant outside city limits.

STRONGER VERB
The proposal before the city council **suggests** locating the sewage treatment plant outside city limits.

WEAK VERBS
The board members **were of the opinion** that the revisions in the code **were not** changes they could accept.

STRONGER VERBS
The board members **said** they **could not accept** the revisions in the code.

When you look for weak verbs to revise, look too for nominals—nouns derived from verbs, often by adding suffixes° such as *-ance, -ment,* or *-tion.* To achieve conciseness, try turning a nominal back into a verb, thus reducing words and gaining impact.

No   We **oversaw the establishment of** a student advisory committee.

YES   We **established** a student advisory committee.

No   The building **had the appearance of** being renovated.

YES   The building **appeared** to be renovated.

ANSWERS: EXERCISE 1
Answers may vary. Here is one set of possibilities:
1. In the late 1800s, Leadville, Colorado, developed because of the discovery of silver.
2. Leadville, like other gold and silver mining towns, grew rapidly.
3. Thousands of people flocked into Leadville, among them some colorful characters.

EXERCISE 1
Combine each set of sentences. Eliminate wordy constructions, such as expletives and unnecessary passives, and condense clauses and phrases.

EXAMPLE   An occurrence in the nineteenth century in America was the springing up of various mining towns across the United States. These towns were noted by all as being usually both flamboyant and short-lived.

A variety of flamboyant, short-lived mining towns sprang up in nineteenth-century America.

308

1. It was in the late 1800s that a town which was known as Leadville developed in Colorado. The town developed as the result of the discovery of silver.

2. Other towns in various areas of the country grew rapidly as the result of gold and silver mines. It can be seen that Leadville was no exception to this general rule.

3. There were thousands of people flocking into Leadville. As was the case in many other mining towns, a large variety of colorful characters were soon to be seen.

4. One of the most famous citizens to be found in Leadville was H. A. W. Tabor. He was originally a citizen of Vermont. He and two other men all owned a mine called the Little Pittsburg. The mine brought fortunes to all three men.

5. It was because of the Little Pittsburg that Tabor grew very wealthy. After that he continued to prosper in other investments. He was eventually elected by the citizens of Colorado to be their Lieutenant Governor.

6. But eventually Tabor, like many other men, was made bankrupt by a silver panic in the 1980s. Before he died, he warned his second wife, Elizabeth, not to sell a mine they still owned called the Matchless Mine. He told her that someday it would make her another fortune.

7. But Tabor was wrong. When the formerly wealthy Elizabeth McCourt Doe Tabor died, she was living in great poverty in a cabin by the Matchless Mine. She died in her eighties.

8. The life story of the Tabors was colorful enough that it was captured in an opera. The opera was called *The Ballad of Baby Doe,* and it was written by Douglas Moore.

9. Many well-known names are associated with Leadville, which seems to have been visited by a wide range of people in the nineteenth century. They included the poet and playwright Oscar Wilde, suffragette Susan B. Anthony, and the well-known western figure Doc Holliday.

10. Leadville was, however, a typical mining town in what happened to it. It sprang up suddenly, it had for a short time a vivid and exciting history, and then it faded away. Now the town of Leadville can be seen as being a shadow of its former self, but there is still the memory of its former more colorful days.

4. One of the most famous citizens of Leadville was H. A. W. Tabor, originally from Vermont. Tabor and two other men made fortunes as joint owners of a mine called the Little Pittsburg.

5. Tabor grew very wealthy from the Little Pittsburg and other investments, and he was eventually elected Lieutenant Governor of Colorado.

6. But eventually Tabor, like many others, lost his money in a silver panic in the 1890s. Before he died, he warned his second wife, Elizabeth, not to sell the Matchless Mine because it would make her another fortune.

7. But Tabor was wrong. When she died in her eighties, the formerly wealthy Elizabeth McCourt Doe Tabor was living, alone and impoverished, in a cabin by the Matchless Mine.

8. The colorful story of the Tabors was captured in a opera by Douglas Moore, called *The Ballad of Baby Doe.*

9. Many famous people visited Leadville in the nineteenth century, including the poet and playwright Oscar Wilde, suffragette Susan B. Anthony, and the well-known Western figure Doc Holliday.

10. Like other mining towns, Leadville sprang up quickly, had a vivid and exciting history, and then faded away. Leadville is now a shadow of its earlier self, but the memory of its more colorful days still remains.

▮‖ 16b

Eliminate unneeded words.

Unneeded words clutter your writing. Always eliminate them to achieve conciseness. Also, imprecise language creates wordiness.

309

A writer may use six inexact words when one precise word would work better.

When a writer tries to write very formally or tries to reach an assigned word limit, **padding** usually results. Sentences are loaded down with **deadwood**—empty words and phrases that increase the word count but lack meaning. Deadwood never substitutes for more ideas or more evidence. If you find deadwood, clear it away.

PADDED   ~~In fact~~, the television station ~~which was situated in the local area~~ had won ~~a great~~ many awards ~~as a result of its having been involved in the~~ coverage of ~~all kinds of~~ controversial issues.

CONCISE   The local television station had won many awards for its coverage of controversial issues.

PADDED   ~~In a manner of speaking,~~ the PTA ~~could be seen as having~~ cancelled the play ~~due to the pressure~~ of financial problems.

CONCISE   The PTA cancelled the play because of financial problems.

PADDED   The bookstore ~~entered the order for~~ the books ~~that the instructor has said will be utilized in~~ the course ~~sequence~~.

CONCISE   The bookstore ordered the books for the course.

Clearing out deadwood may require a few structural changes in sentences, such as the addition of *because* in the example about the PTA. Still, the final version is shorter than the original.

Sentences loaded with empty words can damage an entire paragraph by hiding the message in distracting language.

WORDY VERSION

Computers are good at some things, and people are good at some things, but as a matter of fact, the things people and computers are good at tend to be rather different. It is clear that computers have good memories. It is also true that computers are fast, consistent, and reliable. However, as of yet, it appears that computers are not creative and they are also not able to adapt readily to novel and unusual situations. It can be seen that people have memories that are poor. People are also slow, seldom do something in the same manner twice, and are unreliable in nature,

310

but they can also be viewed as adaptable and full of creativity. Computers seem on the whole to belong to a totally different race when considered in comparison with people. It would be a wonderful ideal to consider the possibility of designing and creating systems wherein these two groups can complement and wed together the talents which each one of them has.

CONCISE ORIGINAL VERSION

What computers are good at and what people are good at tend to be different. Computers have good memories and are fast, consistent, and reliable but as yet are not creative or readily able to adapt to novel situations. People have poor memories, are slow, seldom do things the same way twice, and are unreliable, but they are adaptable and creative. Computers are a different race from people. It is a wonderful ideal to design systems wherein these two can complement and wed their talents.

—THOMAS B. SHERIDAN, "Computer Control
and Human Alienation"

Here is a list of worst-offender empty words, showing how they are often used and how they can be revised.

GUIDE FOR ELIMINATING EMPTY WORDS AND PHRASES

EMPTY WORD OR PHRASE	WORDY EXAMPLE	REVISION
as a matter of fact	*As a matter of fact*, statistics show that many marriages end in divorce.	Statistics show that many marriages end in divorce.
because of the fact that	*Because of the fact that* a special exhibit is scheduled, the museum will be open until ten o'clock.	Because of a special exhibit, the museum will be open until ten o'clock.
case	*In the case of* the proposed water tax, residents were very angry.	Residents were very angry about the proposed water tax.

311

EMPTY WORD OR PHRASE	WORDY EXAMPLE	REVISION
exist	The crime rate that *exists* is unacceptable.	The crime rate is unacceptable.
factor	The project's final cost was an essential *factor* to consider.	The project's final cost was essential to consider.
for the purpose of	Work crews were dispatched *for the purpose* of fixing the potholes.	Work crews were dispatched to fix the potholes.
in a very real sense	*In a very real sense,* the drainage problems caused the house to collapse.	The drainage problems caused the house to collapse.
in fact	*In fact,* the physicist published her results yesterday.	The physicist published her results yesterday.
in view of the fact that	*In view of the fact* that the rainfall was so heavy, we had flooding.	Because the rainfall was so heavy, we may have flooding.
manner	The child touched the snake in a reluctant *manner.*	The child touched the snake reluctantly.
nature	His comment was of an offensive *nature.*	His comment was offensive.
seems	It *seems* that the union called a strike over health benefits.	The union called a strike over health benefits.
tendency	The team had a *tendency* to lose home games.	The team often lost home games.
that is to say	*That is to say* that we cannot afford a strike.	We cannot afford a strike.

INSTRUCTOR'S NOTES

the point I am trying to make	*The point I am trying to make* is that news reporters should not invade people's privacy.	News reporters should not invade people's privacy.
to get to the point	*To get to the point,* the crime rate is going up.	The crime rate is going up.
type of	Gordon took a relaxing *type of* vacation.	Gordon took a relaxing vacation.
what I mean to say	*What I mean to say* is that I expect a bonus.	I expect a bonus.

EXERCISE 2

Eliminate unnecessary words or phrases. Be especially alert for empty words that add nothing to meaning.

EXAMPLE   If in fact it seemed that you had to be the one to award a prize to the most famous detective in the world, which one would you choose?

If you had to award a prize to the world's most famous detective, which one would you choose?

In a very real sense, Sherlock Holmes is probably the best known fictional detective in all the world. Readers and moviegoers alike are in fact likely to feel a sense of recognition when they hear the phrase "Elementary, my dear Watson," or see a pipe and deerstalker cap. Sherlock Holmes, of course, is widely noted for his ability to combine a variety of obscure clues and come to a correct conclusion which is of such a nature as to totally astound his readers. His companion, Dr. Watson, is unfortunately remembered for his tendency to jump to conclusions and the situation of his complete inability to understand what Holmes is doing. Sherlock Holmes was born, that is to say he was created by the pen of Sir Arthur Conan Doyle, in 1887 with the publication of *A Study in Scarlet.* It seems that Holmes's popularity with his readers grew very quickly. Doyle tried to kill off his creation by a type of a situation in which it seemed that Holmes had been killed by his chief foe, Professor Moriarty, but fans in several countries protested. Eventually Sherlock Holmes was brought back by his creator. In fact, Doyle himself is now long since dead, but Holmes continues to capture the hearts of readers with his exploits.

ANSWERS: EXERCISE 2

Answers will vary somewhat, but at the least students should revise the underlined words.

In a very real sense, Sherlock Holmes is probably the best known fictional detective in all the world. Readers and moviegoers alike are in fact likely to feel a sense of recognition when they hear the phrase "Elementary, my dear Watson," or see a pipe and deerstalker cap. Sherlock Holmes, of course, is widely noted for his ability to combine a variety of obscure clues and come to a correct conclusion which is of such a nature as to totally astound his readers. His companion, Dr. Watson, is unfortunately remembered for his tendency to jump to conclusions and the situation of his complete inability to understand what Holmes is doing. Sherlock Holmes was born, that is to say he was created by the pen of Sir Arthur Conan Doyle, in 1887 with the publication of *A Study in Scarlet.* It seems that Holmes' popularity with his readers grew very quickly. Doyle tried to kill off his creation by a type of a situation in which it seemed that Holmes had been killed by his chief foe, Professor Moriarty, but fans in several countries protested. Eventually Sherlock Holmes was brought back by his creator. In fact, Doyle himself is now long since dead, but Holmes continues to capture the hearts of readers with his exploits.

INSTRUCTOR'S NOTES

▪️ 16c
Revise redundancies.

Planned repetition can create a powerful rhythmic effect (see 18f), but the dull drone of unplanned repetition can undermine writing. Unplanned repetition is called **redundancy.** A redundant phrase gives your message at least twice.

No   Bringing the project to **final completion** three weeks early, the new manager earned our **respectful regard.**

Yes   **Completing** the project three weeks early, the new manager earned our **respect.**

No   **Astonished,** the architect **circled around** the building in **amazement.**

Yes   **Astonished,** the architect **circled** the building.

Yes   The architect **walked around** the building **in amazement.**

Notice how redundancies deaden a sentence's impact.

No   The council members **proposed a discussion** of the amendment, but that **proposal for a discussion** was voted down after they had **discussed** it for a while.

Yes   The council members' proposal to discuss the amendment was eventually voted down.

No   The package, **rectangular in shape,** lay on the counter.

Yes   The rectangular package lay on the counter.

No   We need **an addition** on the math building for **additional space.**

Yes   The math building needs an addition.

EXERCISE 3
Eliminate redundant words and phrases. Then revise the paragraph so that it is concise.

EXAMPLE   The possibility that brain development continues into adulthood has fascinated and intrigued many scientists, but yet clear proof has continued to be difficult to find.

The possibility that brain development continues into adulthood has intrigued many scientists, but proof is difficult to find.

ANSWERS: EXERCISE 3
Answers will vary somewhat, but at the least students should revise the underlined words and recast sentences as needed.

For a long period of many years, many people have believed that the brain reaches its height and peak of development and growth sometime in late childhood. But recent studies with rats, however, suggest the implication that a stimulating environment can cause positive changes and transformations in brain cells. This is to an extent due to experiments in California involving rats. These experiments used rats which were in terms of rat age equivalent to humans in their seventies in age. Some of the rats were placed in bare, lonely cages, while the other rats were placed in cages where there were also to be found other rats and a variety of toys. The rats living in the stimulating environment with toys and other rats were the ones whose brains showed positive changes. It still does seem nevertheless to be true that the effect of a challenging environment on the brain decreases as the brain gets older. But these new and innovative theories about later brain development suggest that the brain is far more flexible than was usually thought by most people.

For a long period of many years, many people have believed that the brain reaches its height and peak of development and growth sometime in late childhood. But recent studies with rats, however, suggest the implication that a stimulating environment can cause positive changes and transformations in brain cells. This is to an extent due to experiments in California involving rats. These experiments used rats which were in terms of rat age equivalent to humans in their seventies in age. Some of the rats were placed in bare, lonely cages, while the other rats were placed in cages where there were also to be found other rats and a variety of toys. The rats living in the stimulating environment with toys and other rats were the ones whose brains showed positive changes. It still does seem nevertheless to be true that the effect of a challenging environment on the brain decreases as the brain gets older. But these new and innovative theories about later brain development suggest that the brain is far more flexible than was usually thought by most people.

EXERCISE 4
Rewrite this paragraph, making it clear and concise.

Among the authors of detective fiction who are popular and well-known is the British writer Agatha Christie. In Christie's books, she generally writes about one of her two major detectives, Hercule Poirot and Jane Marple. These two detectives both have their own fans among detective fiction readers, but the two of them are actually quite different as far as personality and temperament are concerned. Poirot it seems does his detective work as a private detective who sees as the basis and foundation of his investigations the use of method, order, and mental kinds of activity—what he calls the "little grey cells." The other detective, Jane Marple, on the other hand, is quite different. She is a seemingly fragile elderly woman who is shown as living alone in the small English village of St. Mary Mead. Whereas Poirot is the type of person who is hired by clients to investigate specific cases, murder seems to be inevitably drawn toward the person of Jane Marple. Her assistance is sought by friends, relatives, and some police detectives, and she always manages as a matter of fact to provide the answer to the puzzle. It often happens in the novels that she is able to see through the confusion of tricky and misleading clues because of the fact that she compares events and people linked to the crime to events and people she is familiar with in St. Mary Mead.

ANSWERS: EXERCISE 4
Answers will vary somewhat, but at the least students should revise the underlined words.

Among the authors of detective fiction <u>who are popular and well-known</u> is the British writer Agatha Christie. <u>In Christie's books</u>, she generally writes about one of her two major detectives, Hercule Poirot and Jane Marple. <u>These two detectives both have their own fans among detective fiction readers</u>, but the <u>two of them are actually</u> quite different <u>as far as personality and temperament are concerned</u>. Poirot <u>it seems</u> does his <u>detective</u> work as a private detective who <u>sees as the basis and foundation of</u> his investigations the use of method, order, and mental <u>kinds of</u> activity—what he calls the "little grey cells." <u>The other detective</u>, Jane Marple, on the other hand, <u>is quite different</u>. <u>She</u> is a seemingly fragile elderly woman who <u>is shown as</u> living alone in the small English village of St. Mary Mead. Whereas Poirot is <u>the type of person who is</u> hired by clients to investigae specific cases, murder seems to be inevitably drawn toward <u>the person of</u> Jane Marple. Her assistance <u>is sought by</u> friends, relatives, and <u>some</u> police detectives, and she always manages <u>as a matter of fact</u> to provide the answer to the puzzle. <u>It often happens</u> in the novels that she <u>is</u> able to see through the confusion of <u>tricky and</u> misleading clues <u>because of the fact that</u> she compares events and people linked to the crime to events and people she is familiar with in St. Mary Mead.

INSTRUCTOR'S NOTES

COORDINATION AND SUBORDINATION

Coordination and subordination help writers communicate relationships between two or more ideas. **Coordination** uses grammatical equivalency to communicate a balance or sequence in ideas. **Subordination** puts an idea to which the writer wants to give less importance in a dependent clause° and puts the more important idea in an independent clause°.

TWO IDEAS	The sky became dark gray. The air stilled ominously.
COORDINATED VERSION	The sky turned dark gray, and the air stilled ominously.
SUBORDINATED VERSION	As the sky turned dark gray, the air stilled ominously. [The *air* is the focus.]
SUBORDINATED VERSION	As the air stilled ominously, the sky turned dark gray. [The *sky* is the focus.]

This chapter explains how coordination and subordination make it possible for your writing style to work in concert with the meaning that you want to deliver.

■ ‖ COORDINATION

A **coordinate sentence** is also known as a **compound sentence.** It consists of grammatically equivalent independent clauses° joined by a semicolon or a coordinating conjunction *(and, but, for, or, nor, yet,* or *so).* Coordination can produce harmony by bringing together related but separate elements to function smoothly in unison. The compounding of a sentence must be justified by its meaning, for coordinate sentences communicate balance or sequence in ideas they contain.

COORDINATE (COMPOUND) SENTENCE

Independent clause	, and	independent clause.
	, but	
	, for	
	, nor	
	, or	
	, so	
	, yet	
	;	

MEANING OF THE COORDINATING CONJUNCTIONS

CONJUNCTION	MEANING	FUNCTION
and	also, in addition to	to join
but	however	to contrast
for	because	to show cause
nor	an additional negative	to make the second element negative
or	an alternative	to show more than one possibility
so	therefore	to show result
yet	nevertheless	to contrast

written, it is a less important idea.

On the other hand, if Scott had been writing on marriage customs, he could have used subordination to provide a different emphasis:

Although rice is one of the world's most important and versatile foods, many Americans value it most as a good-luck symbol for newlyweds.

Here the independent clause stresses the connection of rice with weddings, and the food value of rice is mentioned as a less central point.

QUOTATION ABOUT WRITING
It is the nature of the healthy organism to delight in fine coordination. We all know the sense of satisfaction, of fulfilment, which comes from more than usual order or coherence of any kind. It may be purely intellectual—a lucid scientific exposition, for example; or a complex organization of human material towards practical efficiency, as in a ship's crew, or a big business; or it may be emotional. We all know people, very often people of no education at all, whose human, emotional nature seems to possess perfect control, balance and beauty. And this sense of satisfaction in the presence of successful coordination, is matched by a sense of frustration and disharmony when we meet disorder or muddle, from the discomfort we feel at the blurred presentation of a simple argument, up to the passion of rebellion which can seize us at the warpings and distortions of the human soul.

—ELIZABETH DREW, *Discovering Poetry*

COORDINATED RESOURCES

Alternate examples and exercises for this chapter are available in the *S & S Workbook for Writers,* Gordon and Troyka.

Transparency masters are available for many of the screened charts and/or lists in this chapter.

Students can practice and test their knowledge of terms, key concepts, and applications of material in this chapter by using the *Study Guide to the S & S Handbook for Writers,* West.

Each coordinating conjunction has a specific meaning that establishes the relationship between the ideas in a coordinate sentence.

> The sky became dark gray, **and** the air stilled ominously.
> The November morning had just begun, **but** it looked like dusk.
> Shopkeepers closed their stores early, **for** they wanted to get home.

▮ PUNCTUATION ALERT: Always use a comma before a coordinating conjunction that joins two independent clauses. ▮▮

▮▮ 17a

Use coordinate sentences to show relationships.

Coordination communicates relationships among ideas more effectively than does a group of separate sentences—except when you want occasionally to use a string of short sentences for impact. (For advice on how to handle such a technique well, see 19a.)

UNCLEAR RELATIONSHIPS
We decided not to go to class. We planned to get the notes. Everyone else had the same plan. Most of us ended up failing the quiz.

CLEAR RELATIONSHIPS
We decided not to go to class, **but** we planned to get the notes. Everyone else had the same plan, **so** most of us ended up failing the quiz.

Be sure to employ coordination sparingly so that you do not bore your reader with an unbroken rhythm. Also use subordination.

▮▮ 17b

Use coordinate sentences for occasional effect.

Consider the following passage in which the writers use coordinate sentences to communicate an unfolding of events.

> The first semester of my junior year at Princeton University is a disaster, **and** my grades show it. D's and F's predominate, **and** a note from the dean puts me on academic probation. Flunk one more course, **and** I'm out.
> —JOHN A. PHILLIPS and DAVID MICHAELS, "Mushroom: The Story of an A-Bomb Kid"

Coordinate structures can be effective for joining ideas not ordinarily associated, thus surprising or amusing the reader. Consider the irony communicated through coordination in this passage.

> On August 27, 1947, a multimillionaire and a bull killed each other in Linares, Spain, and plunged an entire nation into deep mourning. The bull's name was Islero, **and** he was of the miura strain. The man's name was Manolete, **and** he was the essence of everything Spanish.
>
> —Barnaby Conrad, *La Fiesta Brava*

F. Scott Fitzgerald (as well as Ernest Hemingway) often used coordination in his fiction to achieve dramatic effect. Consider this passage by Fitzgerald in which coordination underlines the contrasts in the scene.

> It was a hidden Broadway restaurant in the dead of night, **and** a brilliant and mysterious group of society people, diplomats, and members of the underworld were there. A few minutes ago the sparkling wine had been flowing, **and** a girl had been dancing gaily upon a table, **but** now the whole crowd were hushed and breathless.
>
> —F. Scott Fitzgerald, "The Freshest Boy"

■‖ 17c
Avoid misusing coordination.

‖ 1
Avoid illogically coordinated sentences.

Coordination is illogical when ideas in the compounded independent clauses are not related. Your reader expects one part of a coordinate construction to lead logically to the other.

No   Computers came into common use in the 1970s, and they sometimes make costly errors.

The statement in each independent clause is true, but the ideas are not related. The date computers became commonly used is unrelated to their making errors. The two ideas should not be coordinated.

Yes   Computers came into common use in the 1970s, but they have not been improved sufficiently to prevent occasional costly errors.

BIOGRAPHY

Francis Scott Key Fitzgerald, an American novelist famous for his portraits of life in the Roaring Twenties, was born in St. Paul, Minnesota, in 1896. He came from a middle-class family but was sent to private schools catering to the wealthy. He must have felt a perennial outsider—near money, but never having it—and this dilemma turned into a recurring theme in his work.

He left Princeton to join the Army in 1917. Hoping to see action, he was disappointed, for he was never sent overseas. Instead, he used his free time, while stationed in Alabama, to write his first (semi-autobiographical) novel. The book was originally rejected by publishers, but Fitzgerald revised it, and *This Side of Paradise* became a huge success in 1920. He married Zelda Sayre, whom he had met while in the Army, and spent his time writing a second novel and short stories for magazines. However, Fitzgerald did not reach his full power until 1925 with *The Great Gatsby.* It combined the Jazz Age portraits of the magazine stories with an examination of the American soul and mind—and its protagonist was, like Fitzgerald, an outsider trying desperately to get into the golden circle.

The next eight years were difficult ones for Fitzgerald: He traveled abroad, drank heavily, and tried to cope with the deepening insanity of his wife. He wrote and destroyed thousands of pages while writing *Tender Is the Night* (1934), considered by some his best work. The novel, was poorly received—and Fitzgerald turned to more lucrative projects, such as writing for the movies. He described his agony in *Esquire,* in a series of essays called "The Crack-Up" (1936). He died on December 21, 1940. His incomplete novel about Hollywood was published, together with his notes, as *The Last Tycoon* (1941).

Soap operas have earned a bad name,
and they don't always deserve it. Some
people may watch too many programs,
or some people may take the plots too
seriously, but that does not make the
programs themselves unworthy. Years
ago the soap opera viewer was regarded
as unintelligent, but today studies show
that many professionals take time each
day to relax with their favorite continuing story. Some hospitals tell patients
to watch soap operas to pass the time,
or therapists sometimes urge their emotionally disturbed patients to watch certain programs. Later the patients
discuss the characters' problems, and
therapists encourage the patients to relate those problems to their own, and often the patients are helped by this process.

2
Avoid overusing coordination.

Like all good techniques, coordination can be used too often.
Overused coordination can create "babble"—the writing that results
from putting down whatever comes into a writer's head, without
later revision to ensure that the meaning justifies the compounding.
Readers become impatient with "babble." They quickly lose interest
when they have to figure out what the writer meant, or indeed if
the writer had a clear idea in mind in the first place.

No   Dinosaurs could have disappeared for many reasons, and
      one theory holds that the climate suddenly became cold,
      and another theory suggests that a sudden shower of me-
      teors and asteroids hit the earth, so the impact created a
      huge dust cloud that caused a false winter. The winter
      lasted for years, and the dinosaurs died, for most of the
      vegetation they lived on died out.

Yes   Dinosaurs could have disappeared for many reasons. One
      theory holds that the climate suddenly became cold, and
      another suggests that a sudden shower of meteors and
      asteroids hit the earth. The impact created a huge dust
      cloud that caused a false winter. The winter lasted for
      years, killing most of the vegetation that dinosaurs used
      for food.

In the corrected version, the sentences deliver their meanings
clearly.

Writers also overuse coordination if they fail to feature some
ideas more prominently than others. Such undifferentiated writing
tends to drone monotonously.

No   Laughter seems to help healing, so many doctors are pre-
      scribing humor for their patients, and some hospitals are
      doing the same. Comedians have donated their time to
      several California hospitals, and the nurses in one large
      hospital in Texas have been trained to tell each patient
      a joke a day.

Yes   Laughter seems to help healing. Many doctors and hos-
      pitals are prescribing humor for their patients. Comedi-
      ans have donated their time to several California hospi-
      tals, and the nurses in one large hospital in Texas have
      been asked to tell each patient a joke a day.

In the corrected version, some ideas are kept separate and some are
put into a coordinate sentence.

320

EXERCISE 1

Revise these sentences to eliminate illogical or overused coordination. If you think a sentence needs no revision, circle its number.

EXAMPLE　Automation has come to many American factories, so computer-driven robots do the work, and the job gets done quickly, but fewer people are needed in those factories.

Automation has come to many American factories. Computer-driven robots do the work. The job gets done quickly, but fewer people are needed in those factories.

1. General Electric has a new automated locomotive plant, and it is located in Erie, Pennsylvania, and it is an example of what American factories will look like in the twenty-first century.

2. Tools are selected for machining, and they are inserted into machines, and then 2,500-pound castings are made, but no employees work in this section of the factory.

3. General Electric employs 8,000 workers, but the machining operation at the locomotive plant requires only a computer technician and two semi-skilled workers.

4. To do the same work, the factory used to employ seventy workers, and they had to work sixteen days to do each casting, but now computers and robots do all the work, and the company produces the same item in just sixteen hours.

5. American factories use robots, and as of 1985 they had about 13,000 robots in operation, but the Japanese were leading the world in robot production, for they already had more than 40,000 in use.

EXERCISE 2

Revise this paragraph. Choose which ideas seem to have equal weight and could therefore be contained in compound sentences. Your final version should have no more than two compound sentences—all other sentences should be left as they are.

　　Many modern couples choose traditional weddings. Some do not. Some couples are very sentimental about how they met. They decide to have unique marriage ceremonies. For example, a firefighter and his fiancée exchanged vows in a burning building. Two marathon runners got married while participating in a race. An adventurous couple said "I do" as they parachuted from an airplane. One modern wedding reportedly took place in a California hot tub. The guests and the Justice of the Peace got into the water with the bride and groom. Perhaps the next unusual wedding will be in outer space.

ANSWERS: EXERCISE 1

Answers will vary somewhat. One set of possibilities is:

1. General Electric has a new automated locomotive plant. Located in Erie, Pennsylvania, it is an example of what American factories will look like in the twenty-first century.

2. Tools are selected for machining. They are inserted into machines, and then 2,500-pound castings are made. No employees work in this section of the factory, however.

3. Correct

4. To do the same work, the factory used to employ 70 workers. They had to work 16 days to do each casting. Now computers and robots do all the work, and the company produces the same item in just 16 hours.

5. As of 1985 American factories had about 13,000 robots in operation. The Japanese, however, were leading the world in robot production, for they already had more than 40,000 in use.

ANSWERS: EXERCISE 2

Answers will vary somewhat. Students have to choose ideas best given to effective compounding. They are to choose which ideas seem to have equal weight and could therefore be contained in compound sentences. Their final version should have no more than two compound sentences—all other sentences should be left as they are.

　　Many modern couples choose traditional weddings, *and* some do not. Some couples are very sentimental about how they met, *so* they decide to have unique marriage ceremonies. For example, a firefighter and his fiancée exchanged vows in a burning building. Two marathon runners got married while participating in a race. An adventurous couple said "I do" as they parachuted from an airplane. One modern wedding reportedly took place in a California hot tub. The guests and the Justice of the Peace got into the water with the bride and groom. Perhaps the next unusual wedding will be in outer space.

EXTRA EXERCISE A

Revise this paragraph, using subordination to combine short, choppy sentences into better sentences that show the relationships among ideas. You may want to use coordination for some ideas so that you have some variety in your sentence types.

> The Anasazi Indians built cities in Colorado. These Indians disappeared in the thirteeth century. They left behind an advanced culture. Archaeologists have been able to study them carefully. Their beautiful buildings gleam in the afternoon sun. Historians believe these structures may have started the legend of golden cities. In 1540 Francisco de Coronado tried to find the fabled cities of gold. He found no treasure.

ANSWERS: EXTRA EXERCISE A

Answers may vary. One possibility is:

> Although the Anasazi Indians built cities in Colorado, these Indians disappeared in the thirteenth century. They left behind an advanced culture, and archaeologists have been able to study them carefully. Because their beautiful buildings gleam in the afternoon sun, historians believe these structures may have started the legend of golden cities. Although in 1540 Francisco de Coronado tried to find the fabled cities of gold, he found no treasure.

SUBORDINATION

A sentence with some information **subordinated** contains (1) an **independent clause,** which stands on its own as a complete grammatical unit and (2) one or more phrases or clauses that cannot stand alone as a sentence. (When a sentence contains one independent and at least one **dependent clause,** it is called a **complex sentence.**)

Subordination weaves elements together so that one idea is featured, in the independent clause, and others are subordinated. What information you choose to subordinate depends on what meaning you want a sentence to deliver.

Adverb clauses are dependent clauses that start with **subordinating conjunctions,** such words as *after, before, until, when, so that,* and *although.* An adverb clause usually occurs before or after the independent clause.

SENTENCES WITH ADVERB CLAUSES

Adverb clause, independent clause.
Independent clause, **adverb clause.**
Independent clause **adverb clause.**

After the sky grew dark, the air stilled ominously.
Birds stopped singing, **as they do during an eclipse.**
The shopkeepers closed early **because they wanted to get home before the storm began.**

PUNCTUATION ALERTS: (1) When a dependent clause that starts with a subordinating conjunction occurs before the independent clause, separate the clauses with a comma. (2) When an adverb clause follows the independent clause, separate these clauses with a comma *unless* the adverb clause is essential to the meaning of the independent clause. (See 24e.)

Each subordinating conjunction has a specific meaning that establishes a relationship between the clause and the independent clauses.

Another pattern of subordination is created by **relative pronouns°,** such as *who, which,* and *that. Who* refers to people (and

322

SUBORDINATING CONJUNCTIONS AND THE RELATIONSHIPS THEY IMPLY	
TIME	*after, before, once, since, until, when, whenever, while*
REASON OR CAUSE	*as, because*
RESULT OR EFFECT	*in order that, so, so that, that*
CONDITION	*if, even if, provided that, unless*
CONCESSION	*although, even though, though, whether*
LOCATION	*where, wherever*
CHOICE	*rather than, than, whether*

sometimes to animals with names or special talents); *which* refers to animals or things; *that* refers to animals, things, and sometimes to a collective or anonymous group of people. **Adjective clauses** start with relative pronouns. Adjective clauses are dependent clauses. They either follow or interrupt the independent clauses they modify.

SENTENCES WITH ADJECTIVE CLAUSES
Independent clause **restrictive adjective clause.**
Independent clause, **nonrestrictive adjective clause.**
Beginning of independent clause **restrictive adjective clause** end of independent clause.
Beginning of independent clause, **nonrestrictive adjective clause,** end of independent clause.

The weather forecasts warned of a storm **that might bring a thirty-inch snowfall.**

Spring is the season for tornados, **which terrify me.**

Anyone **who lives through a tornado** recalls the experience.

The sky, **which had been clear,** was turning gray.

▌ PUNCTUATION ALERT: When an adjective clause is nonrestrictive—that is, when the clause is not essential to the meaning of the sentence—separate it from the independent clause with commas. ▌

TEACHING TIP

Here is a way you might find useful for illustrating to your students the contrast between coordination and subordination. Ask them to consider these two ideas: (1) Flow-Through Plumbers do high-quality work on small repair and emergency jobs. (2) They do poor work on major projects. Then discuss the fact that a writer dealing with these two ideas should make a choice: to present both ideas to the reader as equally important or to focus the reader's attention on one idea more than on the other.

Here is a treatment of the two ideas that reveals a writer who has not made such a choice.

Flow-Through Plumbers do small repair and emergency jobs. Their work is high-quality. Their work on larger projects, such as replacing entire plumbing systems in old houses, is not as good. Contractors rarely recommend them for major projects. Flow-Through Plumbers are experts at fixing faucets and clearing out clogged pipes.

This writer did not choose a core message, so the material simply meanders along without focus. The reader has to flip back and forth between good and bad impressions of the plumbers, and ends up without a clear sense of the writer's point.

Using **coordination,** a writer can communicate that both ideas about the plumbers are equally important.

Flow-Through Plumbers do small repair and emergency jobs, *and* their work is high-quality. They are good at fixing faucets and clearing out clogged pipes, *but* they do not specialize in larger projects, such as replacing entire plumbing systems in old houses.

Continued on p. 324

INSTRUCTOR'S NOTES

TEACHING TIP (cont.)

Using **subordination,** a writer can minimize one idea and stress the other: This version stresses what the plumbers do well.

When Flow-Through Plumbers do small repair and emergency jobs, they do high-quality work. *While they do not specialize in larger projects, such as replacing entire plumbing systems in old houses,* they are good at fixing faucets and clearing out clogged pipes.

Here is another version using subordination. This version stresses what the plumbers do not do well.

When Flow-Through Plumbers do small repair and emergency jobs, they do high quality work. *While they are good at fixing faucets and clearing out clogged pipes,* they do not specialize in larger projects, such as replacing entire plumbing systems in old houses.

BIOGRAPHY

Eric Arthur Blair (better known by his pseudonym, George Orwell) was born at Motihari, Bengal, in 1903. He was educated in England and came back to Asia in 1922. From then until 1927 he served as police officer in Burma. Upon his return to Europe, he lived in poverty while writing his first two books, including *Down and Out in Paris and London* (1933).

He had no patience with writers whose politics struck him as insincere. Although he was a leftist, he detested the Communists. He had seen their methods while he was fighting in the Spanish Civil War, and he abhorred them (*Homage to Catalonia,* 1938). When he returned from Spain, he moved to Hertfordshire, where he raised hens and grew vegetables while writing his best-known works. These also re-

■|| 17d
Use subordination to show relationships.

Subordination directs your readers' attention to the idea in the independent clause while at the same time using the idea in the dependent clause to provide context and support. Consider these examples (the dependent clauses are in boldface).

> **As soon as I saw the elephant,** I knew with perfect certainty that I ought not to shoot it.
> —GEORGE ORWELL, "Shooting an Elephant"

> **When I think of hills,** I think of the upward strength I tread upon. **When water is the object of my thought,** I feel the cool shock of the plunge and the quick yielding of the waves that crisp and curl and ripple above my body.
> —HELEN KELLER, *The World I Live In*

Subordination usually communicates relationships among ideas more effectively than does a group of separate sentences. (You may want to use an occasional string of short sentences for impact. For advice on how to handle short sentences well, see 19a.)

UNCLEAR RELATIONSHIPS

In 1888, two cowboys had to fight a dangerous Colorado snowstorm. They were looking for cattle. They came to a canyon. They saw outlines of buildings through the snow. Survival then seemed certain.

CLEAR RELATIONSHIPS

In 1888, two cowboys had to fight a dangerous Colorado snowstorm **while they were looking for cattle. When they came to a canyon,** they saw outlines of buildings through the snow. Survival then seemed certain.

In the clearer version the first four short sentences have been combined into two subordinate sentences. The last sentence is left short for dramatic impact.

■|| 17e
Choose the subordinate conjunction appropriate to your meaning.

Subordinating conjunctions are your allies in communicating the relationship between major and minor ideas in sentences. Refer

324

to the chart on page 323 for the relationship implied by various subordinating conjunctions. Each of the following sentences, deals with a similar idea. However, each has a different meaning because of the influence of the subordinating conjunction.

> **After you have handed it in,** you cannot make any changes in your report. [time limit]
>
> **Because you have handed it in,** you cannot make any changes in your report. [reason]
>
> **Unless you have handed it in,** you cannot make any changes in your report. [condition]
>
> **Although you have handed it in,** you can make changes in your report. [concession]
>
> I want to read your report **so that I can evaluate it.** [purpose]
>
> **Since you handed in your report,** three more people have handed in theirs. [time]
>
> **Since I have not seen the report,** I cannot comment on it. [condition]

EXERCISE 3

Combine each pair of sentences, using an adverb clause to subordinate one idea. Then revise each sentence so that the adverb clause becomes the independent clause. Refer to the list of subordinating conjunctions on page 323.

EXAMPLE   The days of Captain Hook are gone forever. Pirates still sail the oceans.

>   a: *Although the days of Captain Hook are gone forever, pirates still sail the oceans.*
>
>   b: *Although pirates still sail the oceans, the days of Captain Hook are gone forever.*

1. Blackbeard has been dead for over a hundred years. His modern counterparts tyrannize today's shipping companies.
2. Modern pirates feel free to use commando tactics. No ship is safe from these buccaneers.
3. Pirates of yesteryear looked for gold. Modern buccaneers often look for drugs as their treasure.
4. People thought that government ships were safe from pirate raids. A Navy cargo ship was robbed of nearly $20,000.
5. The raiders were silent and stealthy. None of the crew ever saw them.

flected his war experiences. *Animal Farm* (1945) shows his opinion of Stalinism, and *Nineteen Eighty-Four* (1949) shows his hatred of powerful political parties.

Orwell volunteered to fight in World War II but he was rejected, so he joined the British Broadcasting Company and worked in India.

ANSWERS: EXERCISE 3
Ask students to discuss the differences in emphasis between *a* and *b* in each item.

1. a: Although Blackbeard has been dead for over a hundred years, his modern counterparts tyrannize today's shipping companies.
   b: Blackbeard has been dead for over a hundred years, although his modern counterparts tyrannize today's shipping companies.

2. a: Because no ship is safe from modern pirates, these buccaneers feel free to use commando tactics.
   b: Because modern pirates feel free to use commando tactics, no ship is safe from these buccaneers.

3. a: While pirates of yesteryear looked for gold, modern buccaneers often look for drugs as their treasure.
   b: While modern buccaneers often look for drugs as their treasure, pirates of yesteryear looked for gold.

4. a: People thought that government ships were safe from pirate raids until a Navy cargo ship was robbed of nearly $20,000.
   b: A Navy cargo ship was robbed of nearly $20,000, although people thought that government ships were safe from pirate raids.

5. a: Because the raiders were silent and stealthy, none of the crew ever saw them.
   b: The raiders were silent and stealthy so that none of the crew ever saw them.

325

ANSWERS: EXERCISE 4

Ask students to discuss the differences in emphases between *a* and *b* in each item.

1. a: Rembrandt had a vibrant talent that was demonstrated early in his life.
   b: Rembrandt's talent, which was demonstrated early in his life, was vibrant.
2. a: Rembrandt, who was happily married, was financially successful and creatively vigorous.
   b: Rembrandt, who was financially successful and creatively vigorous, was happily married.
3. a: "The Night Watch," which became one of Rembrandt's most famous canvases, was commissioned in 1642.
   b: "The Night Watch," which was commissioned in 1642, became one of Rembrandt's most famous canvases.
4. a: For centuries "The Night Watch" was a misunderstood and neglected painting that became covered with yellowish varnish and layers of dirt.
   b: "The Night Watch," which for centuries was a misunderstood and neglected painting, became covered with yellowish varnish and layers of dirt.
5. a: Experts, who thoroughly cleaned and restored the huge thirteen-foot canvas to its original brilliance and detail, finally came into possession of the painting after World War II.
   b: The experts who finally came into possession of the painting after World War II thoroughly cleaned and restored the huge thirteen-foot canvas to its original brilliance and detail.

EXERCISE 4

Combine each pair of sentences, using an adjective clause to make one idea subordinate to the other. Then revise each sentence so that the adjective clause becomes the independent clause. Use the relative pronoun given in parentheses.

EXAMPLE Rembrandt was a seventeenth-century Dutch painter. Rembrandt is probably the most widely known artist of the baroque period. (who)

   a: *Rembrandt, who was a seventeenth-century Dutch painter, is probably the most widely known artist of the baroque period.*

   b: *Rembrandt, who is probably the most widely known artist of the baroque period, was a seventeenth-century Dutch painter.*

1. Rembrandt had a vibrant talent. Rembrandt's talent was demonstrated early in his life. (that)
2. Rembrandt was happily married. Rembrandt was financially successful and creatively vigorous. (who)
3. "The Night Watch" became one of Rembrandt's most famous canvases. "The Night Watch" was commissioned in 1642. (which)
4. For centuries "The Night Watch" was a misunderstood and neglected painting. "The Night Watch" became covered with yellowish varnish and layers of dirt. (which)
5. Experts finally came into possession of the painting after World War II. The experts thoroughly cleaned and restored the huge thirteen-foot canvas to its original brilliance and detail. (who)

▮ 17f
Avoid misusing subordination.
1
Avoid illogical subordination.

Subordination is illogical when the subordinating conjunction does not make clear the relationship between the independent and dependent clause.

No   Because he was deaf when he wrote them, Beethoven's final symphonies were masterpieces.

The above sentence is illogical because it was not Beethoven's deafness that led to his writing symphonic masterpieces.

Yes   Although Beethoven was deaf when he wrote his final symphonies, they are musical masterpieces.

EXTRA EXERCISE B

Evaluate these paragraphs to see if they have excessive subordination or coordination. If they do, revise to achieve a balance.

1. Many people are amazed when they learn that there are women in the United States who control estates and businesses which are worth hundreds of millions of dollars. For example, Iphigene Ochs Sulzberger, whose wealth is estimated at $400 million, is particularly noteworthy because she has served on the board of the *New York Times* while at the same time she has presided over the *Times*' other publications and stations. Mary Kay Ash left her sales career in order to start her own cosmetic company, which is now highly successful and which is said to be worth $100 million. By comparison to these two women, Jackie Kennedy Onassis, who now works as an editor for Doubleday Publishers, can be considered poor because she has a fortune estimated at only $25 million.

2. We hear many complaints about rising costs, and statistics show those complaints are justified. Food costs have gone up, and house costs have increased, but hospital costs have skyrocketed. In 1974 one-half gallon of milk cost $.78, and in 1984 one-half gallon of milk cost $1.13. An average house cost $35,800 in 1974, but in 1984 the same house cost $86,400. The real shock comes from hospital costs, for they have increased 229 percent. In 1974 one day in the hospital cost an average of $113.49, but in 1984 an average day cost $373.62.

2
Avoid overusing subordination.

Like all good writing techniques, subordination can be overused. Too many images or ideas may crowd together, confusing readers and making them lose track of the message. If you have used more than two subordinating conjunctions or relative pronouns in a sentence, check carefully to see if your meaning is clear.

No   A new technique for eye surgery, which is supposed to correct nearsightedness, which previously could be corrected only by glasses, has been developed, although many doctors do not approve of it because it can create unstable eyesight.

Yes   A new technique for eye surgery, which is supposed to correct nearsightedness, has been developed. Previously, nearsightedness could be corrected only by glasses. Because it can create unstable eyesight, many doctors do not approve of it, however.

In the revised version the first sentence has a relative clause, the second is a simple sentence°, and the third has a dependent clause starting *Because*. Some words have been moved to new positions. The revision communicates its message more clearly because it provides a variety of sentence structures (see 19a) while avoiding the density of overused subordination.

EXERCISE 5
Correct illogical or excessive subordination in this paragraph. As you revise, use not only some short sentences but also some correctly constructed adverb clauses. Also, you can apply the principles of coordination discussed in 17a–17c.

Although some experts question the value of traditional fairy tales, most parents continue to read their old favorites to their children. For instance, some experts think that fairy tales are too scary because they have characters like witches and dragons which often frighten little children who are not yet mature enough to understand the difference between fantasy and reality, while other experts object to the theme of the "handsome prince and beautiful princess" theme which many fairy tales feature because the princess is always shown as weak while the prince always depicted as infallibly strong so that children get a distorted impression about what they should expect of themselves and the opposite sex.

ALTERNATE EXAMPLE: EXCESSIVE SUBORDINATION
Soap operas have earned a bad name, which they do not always deserve. Although some people may watch too many programs, and although some people may take the plots too seriously, that does not make the programs themselves unworthy. Although years ago the soap opera viewer was regarded as unintelligent, today studies show that many professionals take time each day to relax with their favorite continuing story. While some hospitals tell their patients to watch soap operas to pass the time, therapists sometimes urge their emotionally disturbed patients to watch certain programs so that later the patients can discuss the characters' problems while the therapists encourage the patients to relate those problems to their own which can often help the patients.

ANSWERS: EXERCISE 5
Answers will vary considerably. Here is one possiblility:

Although most parents continue to read their old favorites to their children, some experts question the value of traditional fairy tales. For instance, some experts think that fairy tales are too scary because they have characters like witches and dragons. These characters often frighten little children who are not yet mature enough to understand the difference between fantasy and reality. Other experts object to the theme of the "handsome prince and beautiful princess" which many fairy tales feature. The princess is always shown as weak, and the prince is always depicted as infallibly strong. Thus, children get a distorted impression of what they should expect of themselves and the opposite sex.

327

ALTERNATE EXAMPLE: BALANCE OF COORDINATION AND SUBORDINATION

Soap operas have earned a bad name, which they do not always deserve. Although some people may watch too many programs or take the plots too seriously, that does not make the programs themselves unworthy. Years ago the soap opera viewer was regarded as unintelligent, but today studies show that many professionals take time each day to relax with their favorite continuing story. Some hospitals tell their patients to watch soap operas to pass the time. Some therapists urge their emotionally disturbed patients to watch certain programs. Later the patients discuss the characters' problems, while the therapists encourage the patients to relate those problems to their own. This process can often help the patients.

ANSWERS: EXERCISE 6

Answers may vary somewhat. One set of possibilites is:

1. Five-figure prices, which are shocking to buyers of new cars, may keep you away from the showrooms.
2. Perhaps you should lease your next car because you may pay less as a down payment, and you may pay less each month.
3. If you are a potential customer, you should shop carefully, because you may find a particularly good arrangement that might save you money.
4. Although ten years ago only one in every ten private cars was leased, in 1984 one of every six private cars was leased, and by now many more drivers favor car leasing.

■‖ 17g

Achieve a balance between subordination and coordination.

Coordination and subordination are not always used in separate sentences. Compound-complex sentences°, for example, combine coordination with subordination.

> **When two Americans look searchingly into each other's eyes,** emotions are heightened, and the relationship tipped toward greater intimacy.
> —Flora Davis, "How to Read Body Language"

Varying sentence types improves your ability to emphasize key points in your writing. Consider the following paragraph which demonstrates a good balance between simple sentences, compound sentences°, and sentences with dependent, as well as independent, clauses:

> As a paleoanthropologist—one who studies the fossils of human ancestors—I am superstitious. Many of us are because the work we do depends a great deal on luck. The fossils we study are extremely rare, and quite a few distinguished paleoanthropologists have gone a lifetime without finding a single one. I am one of the more fortunate. This was only my third year in the field at Hadar, and I had already found several. I know I am lucky, and I don't try to hide it. That is why I wrote "feel good" in my diary. When I got up that morning, I felt it was one of those days when you should press your luck.
> —Donald Johanson, *Lucy: The Beginnings of Humankind*

EXERCISE 6

Using subordination and coordination, combine these sets of short, choppy sentences.

Example　Some people love their cars. Some people give their cars pet names.

Because some people love their cars, they like to give them pet names.

1. Five-figure prices are for new cars. The prices are shocking. The prices may keep you away from the showrooms.
2. Perhaps you should lease your next car. You may pay less as a down payment. You may pay less each month.

328

3. You are a potential customer. Potential customers should shop carefully. You may find a particularly good arrangement. The arrangement might save you money.

4. Ten years ago only one in every ten private cars was leased. In 1984, one of every six private cars was leased. By now many more drivers favor car leasing.

5. Leasing has become popular with many drivers. It is particularly popular with young professionals. They want to save their money for necessities or other luxuries.

6. You may want a particular make of car. You can lease it from a new car dealer. You can lease it from a company. The company specializes in leasing.

EXERCISE 7
Using topics of your choosing, imitate the style of two different examples shown in this chapter. Choose from Fitzgerald, Keller, or Johanson.

5. Leasing has become popular with many drivers, but it is particularly popular with young professionals who want to save their money for necessities or other luxuries.

6. If you want a particular make of car, you can lease it either from a new car dealer or from a company that specializes in leasing.

ANSWERS: EXERCISE 7
Students use a topic of their own to imitate the styles of two different examples shown in this chapter. They can choose from Fitzgerald, Keller, or Johanson. Imitation has a proud tradition as a learning tool. The classic rhetoricians said that versatility in style came from (1) a study of principles, (2) practice in writing, and (3) imitation of the practice of others. For a modern interpretation of classical rhetoric, see Edward P. J. Corbett, *Classical Rhetoric for the Modern Student* (New York: Oxford UP, 1971), especially pages 416 and 496–538.

18
PARALLELISM

WORD HISTORY
The Complete Oxford English Dictionary (OED) has seven columns on *parallel* and related words. The OED reports the first use of *parallel* in 1549 concerning geometry. *Parallelism* was used to describe biblical poetry in 1800 when Paley wrote of "correspondences between the Gospel of Mark and of Luke in sentences, words, and order of words."

Parallelism, related to the concept of parallel lines in geometry, calls for the use of equivalent grammatical forms to express equivalent ideas.

To line up a putt correctly, **examine** the grin of the grass, **observe** the contours of the green, and **gauge** the slope between the ball and the cup. [The same part of speech—all verbs in the present tense—introduces each parallel word group.]

An **equivalent grammatical form** is a word or group of words that matches—is parallel to—the structure of a corresponding word or group of words. When you are expressing similar information or ideas in your writing, parallel sentence structures echo that fact.

PARALLEL WORDS

ALTERNATE EXAMPLE
I have nothing to offer but blood, toil, tears, and sweat.
   —WINSTON CHURCHILL, *Their Finest Hour*

Recommended exercise includes
running,
swimming,
and
cycling.

The *ing* words are parallel in structure and equal in importance.

330

INSTRUCTOR'S NOTES

PARALLEL PHRASES

Exercise helps people
to maintain healthy bodies
and
to handle mental pressures.

‖ The phrases are parallel in structure and equal in importance.

PARALLEL CLAUSES

Many people begin to exercise
because they want to look healthy,
because they need to have
stamina,
and
because they hope to live longer.

‖ The clauses starting with *because they* are parallel in structure and equal in importance.

This chapter explains how parallelism helps you avoid the error of **faulty parallelism**—using nonequivalent grammatical patterns—and lets you strengthen your writing with the style and grace of parallel forms.

▌‖ 18a
Use words in parallel form.

Words in parallel structures must occur in the same grammatical form. Be sure to use matching forms for parallel items.

No   The strikers had tried **pleading, threats,** and **shouting.**

Yes   The strikers had tried **pleading, threatening,** and **shouting.**

Yes   The strikers had tried **pleas, threats,** and **shouts.**

Parallelism offers you a writing style that uses rhythm to help deliver the meaning of a sentence.

Briefly, solemnly, and **sternly,** they delivered their awful message.
—JAMES ANTHONY FROUDE, "The Execution of Queen Mary"

If Froude had expressed the same idea without using parallelism, his message would have been weaker. If he had used an ordinary sentence such as "They were stern and solemn as they delivered their awful message," his words would have lost their opportunity

ALTERNATE EXAMPLE
Some books are to be tasted, others to be swallowed, and some few to be chewed and digested.
—SIR FRANCIS BACON,
"Essay: Of Studies"

ALTERNATE EXAMPLE
We are saddened; we are stunned; we are perplexed.
—EARL WARREN, on the death
of John F. Kennedy

TEACHING TIP
To teach *faulty parallelism,* you might show students nonparallel examples in contrast to the ones given. For demonstrating the problem of *faulty parallelism,* you might find nonparallel examples useful. Contrasting the parallel examples that start this chapter, you might show these or other nonparallel versions:
Words: Recommended exercises include running, swimming, and some people like to go cycling.
Phrases: Exercise helps people maintain healthy bodies and with coping with mental pressures.
Clauses: Many people begin to exercise because they want to look healthy, hoping they can build up their stamina, and to live longer.

TEACHING TIP
A useful technique for giving students experience in writing parallel structures is to give sentences that need completion. Here are two examples:
Moving into one's first apartment can be expensive; you need to buy _____, _____, and _____. Settling into a new apartment can be tiring: hanging curtains, _____, _____, and _____.

to unfold ominously to the reader—just as surely as did the "awful message" to Queen Mary. Froude's placing the three parallel words first in his sentence also contributed to their impact.

◼‖ 18b
Use phrases and clauses in parallel form.

Phrases and clauses in parallel structures must occur in the same grammatical form. Be sure to use matching forms for parallel items.

No   The committee members **read the petition, were discussing its arguments,** and **the unanimous decision was to ignore it.**

Yes   The committee members **read the petition, discussed its arguments,** and **decided to ignore it.**

1
Use the rhythm of parallel phrases and clauses for impact.

Deliberate repetition of word forms, word groups, and sounds creates a rhythm that underlines the message your sentence delivers. This technique can be highly effective as long as you do not overuse it.

> Go back to Mississippi, go back to Alabama, go back to South Carolina, go back to Georgia, go back to Louisiana, go back to the slums and ghettos of our northern cities, knowing that somehow this situation can and will be changed.
> —MARTIN LUTHER KING, JR., "I Have a Dream"

If King had expressed the same idea without parallelism, his message would have been weaker. His words reinforce the power of his message. An ordinary sentence would have been less effective: "Return to your homes in Mississippi, Alabama, South Carolina, Georgia, Louisiana, or the cities, and know that the situation will be changed."

332

2
Arrange parallel elements from least to most important.

Arranging elements from least to most important is called **climactic order** because the material builds to a climax. Parallel structures in climactic order are particularly effective.

> You can fool some of the people all of the time, and all of the people some of the time, but you cannot fool all of the people all of the time. —ABRAHAM LINCOLN

3
Use parallel forms in balanced sentences.

Balanced sentences use parallel structures to enhance the message of compared or contrasted ideas.

> The limits of my language stand for the limits of my world. —LUDWIG WITTGENSTEIN

> Ask not what your country can do for you, but what you can do for your country. —JOHN F. KENNEDY

18c
Be aware that certain words call for parallel structures.

1
Use parallel forms with coordinating conjunctions.

Whenever you join words, phrases, or clauses with coordinating conjunctions *(and, but, for, or, nor, yet, so),* be sure that they occur in parallel form.

> You come to understand what to expect when you **tease a cat, or toss a pebble** in a pool, **or touch a hot stove.** —ANN E. BERTHOFF, *Forming, Thinking, and Writing*

ALTERNATE EXAMPLE
He gave us of his love that we, too, might give. He gave that we might give of ourselves, that we might give to one another until there would be no room, no room at all, for the bigotry, the hatred, the prejudice, and the arrogance which converged in that moment of horror to strike him down.
—SENATOR MIKE MANSFIELD, on the death of John F. Kennedy

ALTERNATE EXAMPLE
It is my purpose, as one who lived and acted in these days, first to show how easily the tragedy of the Second World War could have been prevented; how the malice of the wicked was reinforced by the weakness of the virtuous; how the structure and habits of democratic states, unless they are welded into larger organisms, lack those elements of persistence and conviction which can alone give security to humble masses; how, even in matters of self-preservation, no policy is pursued for even ten or fifteen years at a time. We shall see how the counsels of prudence and restraint may become the prime agents of mortal danger; how the middle course adopted from desires for safety and a quiet life may be found to lead direct to the bull's-eye of disaster. We shall see how absolute is the need of a broad path of international action pursued by many states in common across the years, irrespective of the ebb and flow of national politics.
—WINSTON CHURCHILL, *The Gathering Storm*

INSTRUCTOR'S NOTES

QUOTATION ABOUT WRITING

Every competent writer has to know how to write a concise sentence and how to edit a long one down to comprehensible length. But a writer has also to know how to manage a long sentence gracefully, how to make it as clear and as vigorous as a series of short ones.

—JOSEPH M. WILLIAMS, *Ten Lessons in Clarity and Grace."*

BIOGRAPHY

Charles Dickens (1812–1870) has been called by some the greatest English novelist, and even people who do not particularly care for Victorian novels are often enthralled by his view of the world and his distinctive characters. The England of the 1800s that Dickens describes is not the one that we see in the history books. Dickens was deeply hurt by his parents' financial difficulties: the family moved often to avoid bill collectors, his mother opened a school that failed, and finally his father was sent to debtor's prison while Charles was sent to work in a blacking (shoe polish) factory. Dickens often portrays people in poor financial straits *(Nicholas Nickleby, Oliver Twist, David Copperfield)* as well as people who have postponed life or altered it in expectation of a better financial situation *(Bleak House, Great Expectations)*. He drew upon his childhood recollections of his father's imprisonment to write about prison life in *The Pickwick Papers* and *Little Dorrit.*

2
Use parallel forms with paired words (correlative conjunctions).

Be sure to use parallel form when you link elements of a sentence with pairs of words known as **correlative conjunctions,** such as *both . . . and, not only . . . but also, either . . . or, neither . . . nor.*

Writing permits us to understand **not only** the world **but also** the self.

—ERIKA LINDEMANN, *A Rhetoric for Writing Teachers*

3
Repeat certain words to begin parallel elements.

To enhance the effect of parallelism, you can intentionally repeat certain words that begin parallel phrases or clauses. Such words include prepositions°, articles *(a, an, the),* and the *to* of the infinitive°.

To assign unanswered letters their proper weight, **to free us** from the expectations of others, **to give us** back to ourselves—here lies **the great, the singular** power of self-respect.

—JOAN DIDION, "On Self-Respect"

Because repetition can create dull prose, the technique has to be used carefully. The Didion passage avoids monotony by mixing parallel repetition with much variety in her other word choices. Consider the rich combination in this famous passage:

It was the best of times, it was the worst of times, it was the age of wisdom, it was the age of foolishness, it was the epoch of belief, it was the epoch of incredulity, it was the season of Light, it was the season of Darkness, it was the spring of hope, it was the winter of despair, we had everything before us, we had nothing before us, we were all going direct to Heaven, we were all going direct the other way.

—CHARLES DICKENS, *A Tale of Two Cities*

Dickens mixes repetition *(it was the)* with variety *(times, age, epoch, season)* and with contrasts *(best* and *worst, wisdom* and *foolishness, belief* and *incredulity, Light* and *Darkness, spring* and *winter, hope* and *despair, everything* and *nothing, Heaven* and *the other way).*

334

4

Use parallel clauses beginning with *and who, and whom,* or *and which* when they follow clauses beginning with *who, whom* or *which.*

I have in my own life a precious friend, a woman of 65 **who has** lived very hard, **who is** wise, **who listens** well, **who has** been where I am and can help me understand it; **and who represents** not only an ultimate ideal mother to me but also the person I'd like to be when I grow up.

—JUDITH VIORST, "Friends, Good Friends—and Such Good Friends"

■ ‖ 18d

Use parallel sentences in longer passages for impact.

Parallel sentences in longer passages create a dramatic unity through carefully controlled repetition of words and word forms. Consider this rich passage of repeated words, concepts, and rhythms.

You ask me what is **poverty? Listen** to me. Here I am, dirty, **smelly,** and with no "proper" underwear on and with the **stench** of my rotting teeth near you. I will tell you. **Listen** to me. **Listen** without pity. I cannot use your pity. **Listen** with understanding. Put yourself in my dirty, worn-out, ill-fitting shoes, and hear me.

Poverty is getting up every morning from a dirt- and illness-stained mattress. The sheets have long since been used for diapers. **Poverty** is living in a **smell** that never leaves. **This is a smell** of urine, sour milk, and spoiling food sometimes joined with the strong **smell** of long-cooked onions. Onions are cheap. If you have **smelled** this **smell,** you did not know how it came. **It is the smell** of the out-door privy. **It is the smell** of young children who cannot walk the long dark way in the night. **It is the smell** of the mattresses where years of "accidents" have happened. **It is the smell** of the milk which has gone sour because the refrigerator long has not worked, and it costs money to get it fixed. **It is the smell** of rotting garbage. I could bury it, but where is the shovel? Shovels cost money.

—JO GOODWIN PARKER, "What Is Poverty?"

BIOGRAPHY

Judith Viorst has had a varied writing career. She is a poet (*It's Hard to Be Hip over Thirty and Other Tragedies of Married Life, How Did I get to Be Forty and Other Atrocities*), a writer of children's books (*Rosie and Michael*), a contributing editor to *Redbook* magazine, and an Emmy Award winner (1970) for monologs written for a television special. She credits her husband and children with the inspirations for her poems and juvenile fiction. For example, she says that she wrote one book to cheer up a son who was being picked on by his big brother. Viorst resents the fact that her poems are usually referred to as light verse, because it creates the impression they are written quickly. In fact, "I sit and think about a poem all day and then throw it in the wastebasket at night. I care about it very much and I respect it and I just keep on working on things until they sound right to me." In 1986 she published *Necessary Losses: The Loves, Illusions, Dependencies, and Impossible Expectations That All of Us Have to Give Up in Order to Grow* (Simon & Schuster), based on her training at the Washington Psychoanalytic Institute.

COORDINATED RESOURCES

Alternate examples and exercises for this chapter are available in the *S & S Workbook for Writers,* Gordon and Troyka.

Students can practice and test their knowledge of terms, key concepts, and applications of material in this chapter by using the *Study Guide to the S & S Handbook for Writers,* West.

335

ANSWERS: EXERCISE 1

Elements of parallelism in Parker's passage not shown in boldface are: *Repetitions:* you, me, I, dirty (dirt), pity, onions, mattress(es), urine (privy, "accidents"), long, it, shovels. *Paired words:* with / with. *Imperatives (mild commands):* Listen, Put, hear. *Contrasts:* pity and understanding, with / without. *Words in a series:* my dirty, worn-out, ill-fitting shoes; smell of urine, sour milk, and spoiling food.

ANSWERS: EXERCISE 2

Students use topics of their own to imitate the parallel style of three of the passages shown in this chapter: by King, Lincoln, Didion, Dickens, Viorst, or Parker. Style imitation has a proud tradition as a learning tool. The classical rhetoricians said that versatility in style came from (1) a study of principles, (2) practice in writing, (3) and imitation of the practice of others. For a modern interpretation of classical rhetoric see Edward P. J. Corbett *Classical Rhetoric for the Modern Student* (New York: Oxford UP, 1971), especially pages 416 and 496–538. For more information, see Teaching Tip p. 338.

ANSWERS: EXERCISE 3

Answers may vary. One set of possibilities is:
1. The Space Camp is open *to adults* and *to children* over ten years.
2. The "campers" are people *who want to experience a three-day educational fantasy, who can pay the $350 tuition,* and *who are willing to take part in serious role-playing.*
3. Jerry Hill, the camp director, says that many participants always wanted *to be astronauts* or *to learn science and space.*
4. On the first day, participants take tests that determine *what roles they will play* and *whether they will work in mission control or in the shuttle simulator.*
5. The people assigned to the shuttle simulator *perform scientific experiments* and *complete tasks in extravehicular work using the Five Degrees of Freedom Chair and the Manned Maneuvering Unit.*
6. Everyone agrees that *the adults take their roles seriously and professionally* but *the children like to joke around more.*

EXERCISE 1

Reread the Jo Goodwin Parker passage above. Discover all parallel elements in addition to those shown in boldface.

EXERCISE 2

Using topics of your choosing, imitate the writing style of three different passages shown in this chapter. Choose from King, Lincoln, Didion, Dickens, Viorst, or Parker.

EXERCISE 3

Revise these sentences to eliminate any errors in parallel structure.

EXAMPLE   The Alabama Space and Rocket Center offers a Space Camp where participants hear lectures, are sampling astronaut training, and fly simulated missions.

The Alabama Space and Rocket Center offers a Space Camp where participants hear lectures, *sample* astronaut training, and fly simulated missions.

1. The Space Camp is open to adults, and children over ten years can attend.
2. The "campers" are people who want to experience a three-day educational fantasy, who can pay the $350 tuition, and they are willing to take part in serious role-playing.
3. Jerry Hill, the camp director, says that many participants always wanted to be astronauts, or learning about science and space is another reason many attend.
4. On the first day, participants take tests that determine what roles they will play and whether work in mission control or in the shuttle simulator will be their assignment.
5. The people assigned to the shuttle simulator perform scientific experiments, and then there is the Five Degrees of Freedom Chair and the Manned Maneuvering Unit in which they have to complete tasks as part of the extravehicular work.
6. Everyone agrees that the adults take their roles seriously and professionally, but liking to joke around is more of what the children do.

EXERCISE 4

Combine these sentences using techniques of parallelism.

EXAMPLE   Many United States Presidents are famous for their political skill. Some of their unusual ways are not well known.

Many United States Presidents are famous *for* their political skill *but not for* their unusual ways.

336

1. John Quincy Adams, sixth U.S. President, read his Bible to start each day. Swimming in the nude each morning was also a daily routine.

2. William McKinley, twenty-fifth U.S. President, thought the red carnation he wore each day would bring him luck. It was also supposed to protect him from harm.

3. On September 6, 1901, after McKinley gave his lucky carnation to a little girl, an assassin stalked him. The assassin's shot wounded the President. He was killed.

4. The glare from a portrait of John Quincy Adams was annoying to Calvin Coolidge, thirtieth U.S. President. Coolidge called in an artist to paint hairs on Adams's shiny head.

5. William Henry Harrison, ninth U.S. President, gave the longest inaugural speech on record. It contained 8,500 words. Delivering it took two hours.

6. During Harrison's inauguration ceremonies it snowed. Harrison spoke without a coat. He was also hatless. He died one month later from pneumonia.

■‖ 18e

Use parallel structure for formal outlines and lists.

Items in formal outlines and lists must be parallel in structure. If the parallelism is faulty, the information fails to be clear to the reader and fails to communicate that the items are equally important. (For information about developing outlines, see pages 37–43.)

OUTLINE NOT IN PARALLEL FORM

Reducing Traffic Fatalities

I. Stricter laws
  A. Top speed on any highway should be 50 m.p.h.
  B. Higher fines
  C. Repeat offenders sentenced to jail
II. Legislating installation of safety devices
  A. All automobiles should be required to have safety belts in both front and back seats
  B. Making seat belt use mandatory for all drivers
  C. We should force auto manufacturers to offer airbags as an option in all cars

ANSWERS: EXERCISE 4
Answers will vary. One set of possibilities is:

1. Every morning, John Quincy Adams, sixth U.S. President, *read* his Bible **and** *swam* in the nude. [parallel verbs with coordinating conjunction *and*]

2. William McKinley, twenty-fifth U.S. President, thought the red carnation he wore each day **not only** *would bring him luck* **but also** would *protect him from harm.* [paired words with parallel verb phrases]

3. On September 6, 1901, after McKinley gave his lucky carnation to a little girl, an assassin *stalked, shot,* **and** *killed* him. [parallel verbs with coordinating conjunction *and*]

4. *Calvin Coolidge,* thirtieth U.S. President, *was annoyed* by the glare from a portrait of John Quincy Adams, **and** *Coolidge called in* an artist to paint hairs on Adams's shiny head. [parallel subjects and verbs with coordinating conjunction *and*]

5. William Henry Harrison, ninth U.S. President, gave the longest inaugural speech on record, **which** *contained 8,500 words* **and which** *took two hours to deliver.* [parallel clauses of past-tense verbs with *which / and which*]

6. During the inauguration ceremonies *it snowed, Harrison spoke without a coat* **or** *hat,* **and** *he died* one month later from pneumonia. [parallel independent clauses in a series from least to most important]

INSTRUCTOR'S NOTES

TEACHING TIP

Classical rhetoric teaches that successful speaking or writing comes, in part, from the imitation of good examples. This imitation can take the form of copying passages verbatim or of imitating particular sentence patterns. Classical rhetoricians are not the only ones who have written about the benefits of imitation. Benjamin Franklin writes in his *Autobiography* (1771) of using essays in *The Spectator* as models for organization, sentence structure, and vocabulary. Malcolm X writes in his *Autobiography* of the benefits he gained from simply copying the dictionary in longhand. Winston Churchill and Somerset Maugham also write of the lessons they learned by imitating written models.

A possible first step in imitation is copying verbatim passages from favorite writers. This is not as brainless as it seems, for done properly it enables students to observe the details of an author's style. For this exercise to succeed, students should follow these guidelines adapted from Corbett *Classical Rhetoric for the Modern Student* (New York: Oxford UP, 1971):

1. Students should read a piece through before beginning to copy it, in order to see the purpose and style of the whole. While working, they should read each sentence before beginning to write it. Once the passage has been completed, students should read their transcriptions in order again to "get a sense of the passage as a whole."

2. Students should copy for fifteen minutes per session. If they copy much longer, their minds will no longer focus on the work and the copying will become mechanical.

3. Students should copy by hand. Typing is too fast to allow students to see the qualities of a writer's style. Writing lets students work slowly enough to see the selection and placement of words, and the lengths and types of sentences.

4. Students should copy from a variety of authors. If they concentrate on one author to the exclusion of others, they may end up aping a single style rather than getting the feel of a variety of styles.

5. Students should copy patiently and with care. Too much speed can make the exercise meaningless. One way of controlling speed is to require that work be legible.

OUTLINE IN PARALLEL FORM

Reducing Traffic Fatalities

I. **Passing** stricter speed laws
   A. **Making** 50 m.p.h. top speed on any highway
   B. **Raising** fine for first-time speeding offenders
   C. **Requiring** jail sentences for repeat offenders
II. **Legislating** installation and use of safety devices
   A. **Requiring** all automobiles to have safety belts in front and back seats
   B. **Making** seat belt use mandatory for all drivers
   C. **Forcing** auto manufacturers to offer airbags as an option in all cars

Although the faulty outline might be useful as a scratch outline for a writer's private purposes in the early stages of the writing process, only the parallel outline communicates clearly to a reader. The parallel outline fills in the gaps of information and communicates equivalencies. The same principles apply to lists.

LIST NOT IN PARALLEL FORM

Workaholics share the following characteristics:

1. They are intense, energetic, competitive, and driven.
2. Strong self-doubters.
3. Labor is preferred to leisure by workaholics.
4. Workaholics: work any time and anywhere.
5. Making the most of their time.
6. Workaholics will blur the distinction between business and pleasure.

LIST IN PARALLEL FORM

Workaholics share the following characteristics:

1. **They are** intense, energetic, competitive, and driven.
2. **They have** strong self-doubts.
3. **They prefer** labor to leisure.
4. **They can—and do—work** any time and anywhere.
5. **They make** the most of their time.
6. **They blur** the distinction between business and pleasure.

The list not in parallel format appears disorganized and is more difficult and unpleasant to read. The list in parallel format carries the unspoken message that all these items are equivalent and contribute equally to the definition of a workaholic.

338

A second kind of imitation exercise uses sentences as patterns. The students duplicate the *kind, number,* and *order* of clauses and phrases in the model.

The aim of this exercise is not to achieve a word-for-word correspondence with the model but rather to achieve an awareness of the variety of sentence structures of which the English language is capable. The reason why many students never venture outside their puerile, monotonous sentence structure is that they have never attempted sophisticated sentence patterns. Writing such patterns according to models will increase the student's syntactical resources. (Corbett 533)

EXERCISE 5
Revise this outline into parallel form.

Problems in Weather Forecasting

I. Information unavailable from some areas
  A. Politics lead some countries not to cooperate.
  B. If war breaks out, no one communicates about the weather.
  C. Cost
II. Computer problems
  A. Computer repairs not easily available in remote areas.
  B. Unreliable computers send garbled messages.
III. Unstable atmosphere
  A. The weather is harsh.
    1. South Pole
    2. The North Pole is extremely cold and windy.
  B. Conditions shift suddenly.
  C. There is a lack of reliability over time.

EXERCISE 6
Find the parallel elements in the following examples. Next, using your own topics, imitate the style of two of the examples.

1. Our earth is but a small star in a great universe. Yet of it we can make, if we choose, a plane unvexed by war, untroubled by hunger or fear, undivided by senseless distinctions of race, color, or theory.
—STEPHEN VINCENT BENÉT

2. Difficult choices arise for all those who have promised to keep secret what they have learned from a client, a patient, or a penitent. How to deflect irate fathers asking whether their daughters are pregnant and by whom; how to answer an employer inquiring about the psychiatric record of someone on his staff; how to cope with questions from the press about the health of a Congressional candidate: such predicaments grow more common than ever.
—SISSELA BOK, *Lying*

3. I think I learned more from the town dump than I learned from school: more about people, more about how life is lived, not elsewhere but here, not in other times but now.
—WALLACE STEGNER, "The Town Dump"

4. I have never been lonely in a cemetery. They are perfect places to observe the slow changing of the seasons, and to absorb human history—the tragedies and anguishes, the violences and treacheries, and always the guilts and sorrows of vanished people.
—WILLIE MORRIS, "A Love That Transcends Sadness"

ANSWERS: EXERCISE 5
I. Information unavailable from some areas
  A. Politics
  B. Wars
  C. Cost
II. Computer problems
  A. Computer repairs not easily available in remote areas
  B. Garbled messages from unreliable computers
III. Unstable atmosphere
  A. Weather harsh
    1. South pole
    2. North pole
  B. Sudden shifts
  C. Lack of reliability over time

ANSWERS: EXERCISE 6
Answers will vary. See answer to Exercise 2 for commentary on imitation as a learning device.

INSTRUCTOR'S NOTES

19
VARIETY AND EMPHASIS

Your writing style has **variety** when your sentence lengths and patterns vary. Your writing style is characterized by **emphasis** when your sentences are constructed to communicate the relative importance of the ideas. This chapter discusses both variety and emphasis. Together they affect how form and meaning are unified.

Consider the following passage, which successfully employs key techniques of variety and emphasis. The authors vary their sentence length (19a), include a variety of structures (19b), and use different kinds of modifiers in various positions (19d).

> Henri Poincaré, a famous mathematician who lived in the nineteenth century, devised an exercise in imagination to help people understand the relativity of measures. Imagine that one night while you were asleep everything in the universe became a thousand times larger than before. Remember this would include electrons, planets, all living creatures, your own body, and all the rulers and other measuring devices in the world. When you awoke, could you tell that anything had changed? Is there any experiment you could make to prove that some change had occurred? According to Poincaré there is no such experiment.
>
> —JUDITH AND HERBERT KOHL, *The View from the Oak*

340

The techniques of variety and emphasis rarely emerge from a writer's pen (or fingers on a keyboard) in final form. Most writers attend to such matters during the revision process.

19a

Vary sentence length.

If you vary your sentence length, you communicate clear distinctions among ideas so that your readers can understand the focus of your material. Also, you avoid the unbroken rhythm of monotonous sentence length—a trait that eventually lulls a reader into losing attention.

1

Revise strings of too many short sentences.

Strings of too many short sentences rarely establish relationships and levels of importance among ideas. Readers cannot discern distinctions between major and minor points. Such strings, unless deliberately planned in a longer piece of writing for occasional impact, suggest that the writer has not thought through the material and decided what to emphasize. The style tends to read like that of young children.

No   There is a legend. This legend is about a seventeenth-century Algonquin Indian. It says that he was inspired. He had an idea about popcorn. He transformed it into a gift. It was the first gift to a hostess in American history. He was invited to the Pilgrims' harvest meal. He brought along a bag of popcorn. This was a demonstration of good will. The occasion is honored to this day with Thanksgiving dinner.

The ten short sentences above range from four to eleven words. The sentence structures do not feature significant ideas over unimportant ones.

Yes   According to legend, in the seventeenth century an inspired Algonquin transformed popcorn into the first hostess gift in history. Invited to the Pilgrims' harvest meal, the Indian brought along a bag of popcorn as a demonstration of good will. The occasion is honored today with Thanksgiving dinner.
            —Patricia Linden, "Popcorn"

TEACHING TIP
Students sometimes cannot perceive the contrast between short and long sentences. One helpful technique is to use highlighter pen on a typewritten copy, to make either the short or the long sentences stand out from the rest of the passage. Also, if you can make a transparency of your typewritten copy, you can ask the students to participate in deciding what sentences are long and short—and then underline or circle one type.

ALTERNATE EXAMPLE
This sentence has five words. This is five words, too. Five-word sentences are fine. But several together become monotonous. Listen to what is happening. The writing is getting boring. The sound of it drones. It's like a stuck record. The ear demands some variety. Now listen. I vary the sentence length and I create music. Music. The writing sings. It has a pleasant rhythm, a lilt, a harmony. I use short sentences. And I use sentences of medium length. And sometimes when I am certain the reader is rested I will engage him with a sentence of considerable length, a sentence that burns with energy and builds with all the impetus of a crescendo, the roll of the drums, the crash of the cymbals, sounds that say, "Listen to this; it is important."
            —Gary Provost, "Sound Advice"

BIOGRAPHY

Lewis Thomas, a popular writer on the interconnections of science and everyday life, was born in Flushing, New York, in 1913. He graduated Harvard Medical School in 1937. As a physician, researcher, teacher, and hospital administrator, he wrote scholarly articles for years. Then in 1971 he began a column for the *New England Journal of Medicine:* "Notes of a Biology Watcher." In 1975 his book *The Lives of a Cell: Notes of a Biology Watcher* (a collection of his columns) won a National Book Award for Arts and Letters. His other books include *The Medusa and the Snail: More Notes of a Biology Watcher* and *Late Night Thoughts on Listening to Mahler's Ninth Symphony.*

ALTERNATE EXAMPLE

It may seem to you that the population can go up a long, long time before it reaches the point where there are 30,000,000,000,000 times as many people in the world as there are today. *Let's think about that, though.* Let us suppose that the population growth-rate stays at 2.0 percent so that the number of people in the world continues to double every 35 years. How long, then, will it take for the world's population to weigh as much as the entire planet?

—ISAAC ASIMOV, *Earth: Our Crowded Spaceship*

In the revised version above, the sentence structures permit the key ideas to be featured. (In addition, this version employs techniques of conciseness discussed in Chapter 16: ten sentences reduce to three and 73 words reduce to 47.) The two versions use almost the same short last sentence, but because the improved version leads up to it with longer, carefully textured sentences, the message in the last sentence is emphasized.

2
Revise a string of too many compound sentences.

A **compound sentence**° consists of independent clauses° which present closely related and equally important ideas. The compounding of a sentence must be justified by its meaning. Too often, compound sentences only are short sentences strung together with *and* or *but,* without consideration of the relationships among the ideas.

> **No**   Science fiction writers are often thinkers, and they are often dreamers, so they let their imaginations wander. Jules Verne was such a writer, and he predicted space ships and atomic submarines, but most people did not believe airplanes were possible.

> **Yes**   Science fiction writers are often thinkers and dreamers who let their imaginations wander. Jules Verne was one such writer. He predicted space ships and atomic submarines before most people believed airplanes were possible.

In the revised version the relationships among the ideas are clear and key ideas are featured. In the last sentence a particularly obscure connection is clarified. (In addition, this version employs techniques of conciseness discussed in Chapter 16: one independent clause is reduced to a word, *dreamers;* another is reduced to a relative clause, *who let their imaginations wander;* another starts a new sentence, *He predicted . . .;* and another is reduced to a subordinate clause, *before most people . . . possible.*)

3
Revise for a suitable mix of sentence lengths.

You can emphasize one idea among many others by expressing it in a sentence noticeably different in length or structure from the

342

sentences surrounding it. Consider this passage, which carries its emphasis in one short sentence among longer ones:

> Today is one of those excellent January partly cloudies in which light chooses an unexpected landscape to trick out in gilt, and then shadow sweeps it away. **You know you are alive.** You take huge steps, trying to feel the planet's roundness arc between your feet. Kazantzakis says that when he was young he had a canary and a globe. When he freed the canary, it would perch on the globe and sing. All his life, wandering the earth, he felt as though he had a canary on top of his mind, singing.
> —ANNIE DILLARD, *Pilgrim at Tinker Creek*

A long sentence among shorter ones is equally effective.

> Mistakes are not believed to be part of the normal behavior of a good machine. **If things go wrong, it must be a personal, human error, the result of fingering, tampering, a button getting stuck, someone hitting the wrong key.** The computer, at its normal best, is infallible. I wonder whether this can be true.
> —LEWIS THOMAS, "To Err Is Human"

EXERCISE 1

Revise these sets of sentences to vary the sentence lengths effectively.

1. Horror tales are not new. *Frankenstein* was written in the nineteenth century. It was written by Mary Shelley. She was the wife of the poet Percy Bysshe Shelley. *Frankenstein* tells the story of a scientist. He makes a monster. He makes it from a human corpse.

2. Another famous horror tale of the nineteenth century is "The Monkey's Paw," by W. W. Jacobs, and it tells about an old English couple with a teenage son, and they get a monkey's paw. It has the power to grant three wishes, so the father wishes for 200 pounds, but the money comes because their son is killed in an accident at work. The mother uses the second wish to bring her son back, and soon there is a knocking at their door, and the mother rushes to unbolt it, but the father is terrified of seeing a walking, rotting corpse, so he uses the last wish, and the knocking stops.

3. After radios became common, horror programs broadcast their tales of terror into the living rooms of America which were filled with families that included children of all ages who were grouped around the radio while they listened for the latest story of monsters and strange events. The many programs, which included *The Inner Sanctum*, which featured a creaking door, and *The Fat Man* who had a madman's laugh, scared and delighted the audience who came from different parts of the country, from different occupations, and from different economic and social groups.

ANSWERS: EXERCISE 1

In this exercise, the first item has too many short sentences, the second too many compounds, the third long and complicated sentences. Students will revise in various ways. Here is one set of possibilities:

1. Horror tales are not new. *Frankenstein* was written in the nineteenth century by Mary Shelley, the wife of the poet Percy Bysshe Shelley. *Frankenstein* tells the story of a scientist who makes a monster from a human corpse.

2. Another famous horror tale of the nineteenth century is "The Monkey's Paw," by W. W. Jacobs. It tells about an old English couple, parents of a teenage son, who get a monkey's paw. The paw has the power to grant three wishes. The father wishes for 200 pounds, but the money comes because their son is killed in an accident at work. The mother uses the second wish to bring her son back. Soon there is a knocking at their door. The mother rushes to unbolt it, but terrified of seeing a walking, rotting corpse, the father uses the last wish. The knocking stops.

3. After radios became common, horror programs broadcast their tales of terror into the living rooms of America. Many families, including children of all ages, grouped around the radio while they listened for the latest story of monsters and strange events. The many programs included *The Inner Sanctum*, which featured a creaking door, and *The Fat Man*, who had a madman's laugh. The scared, delighted audience came from different parts of the country, different occupations, and different economic and social groups.

BIOGRAPHY

Isaac Asimov is likely best known to students as a science fiction writer, but he is much more than that. Born in the U.S.S.R. in 1920, he came to the United States in 1923 and was naturalized in 1928. He received his B.S., M.A., and Ph.D. (1948) from Columbia University, and he began supporting himself and his family by teaching at Boston University's School of Medicine.

Throughout his years of formal education, Asimov had written science fiction stories. In fact, under the tutelage of John W. Campbell (a pioneer science fiction author and editor), he had published over a dozen pieces by the time he was 21. His first nonfiction work was a medical textbook, *Biochemistry and Human Metabolism* (1950), which he co-authored with two senior colleagues from the medical school. As he says of himself, he "can read a dozen dull books and make one interesting book out of them." He states, "I'm on fire to explain, and happiest when it's something reasonably intricate which I can make clear step by step. It's the easiest way I can clarify things in my own mind."

Asimov has written and edited hundreds of books. In fact, for the last thirty years his writing has averaged one book every six weeks. He accomplishes this by working twelve hours a day, rarely taking vacations. Despite his heavy writing schedule, Asimov handles everything himself.

I have no assistants of any kind. I have no agent, no business manager, no research aides, no secretary, no stenographer. I do all my own typing, all my own proofreading, all my own indexing, all my own research, all my own letter writing, all my own telephone answering. I like it that way. Since I don't have to deal with other people, I can concentrate more properly on my work, and get more done.

19b

Use an occasional question, mild command, or exclamation.

To vary your sentence structure and to emphasize material, you can call on four basic sentence types. The most typical English sentence is **declarative**: it makes a statement—it declares something. Declarative sentences offer an almost infinite variety of structures and patterns, as described in other sections of this chapter.

A sentence that asks a question is called **interrogative**. Occasional questions help you involve your reader.

A sentence that issues a mild or strong command is called **imperative**. Occasional mild commands are particularly helpful for gently urging your reader to think along with you. A sentence that makes an exclamation is called **exclamatory**. ▌ PUNCTUATION ALERT: A mild command ends with a period, whereas a strong command or an exclamation ends with an exclamation mark. ▌

Consider the following examples from *Change!* by Isaac Asimov, a writer who often uses different sentence types to keep his material lively and to focus attention on what he wants to emphasize.

QUESTION	The colonization of space may introduce some unexpected changes into human society. **For instance, what effect will it have on the way we keep time?** Our present system of time-keeping is a complicated mess that depends on accidents of astronomy and on 5,000 years of primitive habit.
MILD COMMAND	**Consider the bacteria.** These are tiny living things made up of single cells far smaller than the cells in plants and animals.
EXCLAMATION	**The amazing thing about the netting of the coelanth was that till then zoologists had been convinced the fish had been extinct for 60 million years!** Finding a living dinosaur would not have been more surprising.

INSTRUCTOR'S NOTES

EXERCISE 2

The paragraph below effectively varies sentence lengths and uses a question and a command. The result emphasizes the key points. Write an imitation of this paragraph, closely following all aspects except the topic. Choose your own topic.

EXAMPLE   If your topic were pets, your first sentence might be: *Why do most people buy expensive pure-bred dogs or cats when they want pets?*

Why do most people imagine hurricanes or bombs when they think of disasters? Consider the worst disaster in history. In 1347–1351, the black death killed over 75 million victims. A snow avalanche in Peru killed 25,000 in 1970, and a panic in an air raid shelter in Chungking, China, claimed 4,000 in 1941. Yet, the strangest disaster of all happened at the coronation of Czar Nicholas II when 5,000 were trampled to death in the stampede for free beer that was part of the celebration.

EXERCISE 3

In each passage, change one sentence to a question, a command, or an exclamation. Choose the sentence to change according to what you think should be emphasized.

EXAMPLE   You can think about race horses. They have become some of the most valuable animals in the world.

   Think about race horses. They have become some of the most valuable animals in the world.

1. In October 1980, Easy Jet, a multi-race winner, was sold for 30 million dollars. That is more than the average combined yearly income of a town of 2,000 people.
2. We may wonder what the popularity of horse racing might suggest about the American national character. We may be a nation of gamblers. On the other hand, we may simply want the chance to become financially independent.
3. Lotteries have become as popular as horse racing. Many states run lotteries to raise money for services that used to be provided from taxes. You may not know that in many states school books are purchased with funds gambled on lottery tickets.
4. Some television commercials for lotteries show winners riding in limousines and dressed in expensive clothing. Most lottery ticket holders lose, though. That tempting chance to win a million dollars has odds worse than a million to one.

ANSWERS: EXERCISE 2

Students use a topic of their own to imitate the variety of sentence lengths and types in the paragraph shown. Imitation has a proud tradition as a learning tool. The classic rhetoricians said that versatility in style came from (1) a study of principles, (2) practice in writing, and (3) imitation of the practice of others. For a modern interpretation of classical rhetoric, see Edward P. J. Corbett *Classical Rhetoric for the Modern Student* (New York: Oxford UP, 1971), especially pages 416 and 496–538.

ANSWERS: EXERCISE 3

Answers may vary. One set of possibilities is:

1. In October 1980, Easy Jet, a multi-race winner, was sold for 30 million dollars. That is more than the average combined yearly income of a town of 2,000 people!
2. What might the popularity of horse racing say about the American national character? We may be a nation of gamblers. On the other hand, we may simply want the chance to become financially independent.
3. Lotteries have become as popular as horse racing. Many states run lotteries to raise money for basic services that used to be provided from taxes. Did you know that in many states school books are purchased with funds gambled on lottery tickets?
4. Some television commercials for lotteries show winners riding in limousines and dressed in expensive clothing. Most lottery ticket holders lose, though. That tempting chance to win a million dollars has odds worse than a million to one!

INSTRUCTOR'S NOTES

19c
Choose the subject of your sentence according to your intended emphasis.

The subject° of a sentence establishes the focus for that sentence. The subject you choose should therefore correspond to the emphasis you want to communicate to your reader.

The following sentences, each of which is correct grammatically, contain the same information. Consider, however, how changes of the subject (and its verb) influence meaning and impact.

1. **Our study showed** that 25 percent of college students' time is spent eating or sleeping.
2. **College students eat or sleep** 25 percent of the time, according to our study.
3. **Eating or sleeping occupies** 25 percent of college students' time, according to our study.
4. **Twenty-five percent** of college students' time **is spent** eating or sleeping, according to our study.

Sentence 1 focuses on the study, 2 on the students, 3 on eating and sleeping, and 4 on percentage of time. Each sentence provides a different emphasis. You would use whichever version most effectively delivers your message in relation to your purpose: for example, sentence 4 seems more suitable for a statistical report while sentence 2 might work well in an article for a college newspaper.

19d
Add modifiers to basic sentences for variety and emphasis.

A **modifier** is a word, phrase°, or clause° that describes other words, phrases, or clauses. A basic message is delivered by the subject and verb of a simple declarative sentence°—a sentence that consists of a single independent clause°: *The river rose.* Adding modifiers to basic sentences permits you to expand a simple subject and verb into a rich variety of sentence patterns.

346

ADDING MODIFIERS   *var/emph* || 19d

1
Expand basic sentences with modifiers.

Sentences that consist only of a subject and verb usually seem very thin. Except when you choose to use a very short sentence for its dramatic effect in emphasizing an idea, you can expand basic sentences with modifying words, phrases, and clauses, as shown in boldface below.

BASIC SENTENCE	The river rose.
ADJECTIVE	The **swollen** river rose.
ADVERB	The river rose **dangerously.**
PREPOSITIONAL PHRASE	**In April,** the river rose **above its banks.**
PARTICIPIAL PHRASES	**Swollen by melting snow,** the river rose, **flooding the farmland.**
ABSOLUTE PHRASE	**Trees swirling away in the current,** the river rose.
ADVERB CLAUSE	**Because the snows had been heavy that winter,** the river rose.
ADJECTIVE CLAUSE	The river, **which runs through vital farmland,** rose.

Your decision to expand a basic sentence or to add information to any sentence will depend on the focus of each sentence and how it works in concert with its surrounding sentences.

EXERCISE 4
Expand each sentence by adding (a) an adjective, (b) an adverb, (c) a prepositional phrase, (d) a participial phrase, (e) an absolute phrase, (f) an adverb clause, and (g) an adjective clause. For guidance, refer to the expansion list above.

1. We went to register for classes.
2. The lines were long.
3. The students seemed edgy.
4. The staff remained calm.
5. Both of us got the schedules we wanted.

ANSWERS: EXERCISE 4
Students are to expand each sentence by adding (a) an adjective, (b) an adverb, (c) a prepositional phrase, (d) a participial phrase, (e) an absolute phrase, (f) a subordinate clause, and (g) a relative clause. They can refer for guidance to the expansion example shown in 19d-1. The answers will vary considerably. Here is a possible set of answers for item 1:

a. We went to register for *our college* classes.
b. We went *eagerly* to register for classes.
c. We went to register for classes *at the college.*
d. *Forced to wait until the storm passed,* we went to register for classes, *hoping we were not too late.*
e. *Clothing still unpacked in our dormitory,* we went to register for classes.
f. *As soon as we got to the college,* we went to register for classes.
g. We, *who had never attended college before,* went to register for classes.

INSTRUCTOR'S NOTES

2
Position modifiers to create variety and emphasis.

Brain research suggests that readers are more likely to retain the message at the very beginning or the very end of a sentence. Although you do not have unlimited choices about where to place modifiers, you do have some. Try to place them according to the emphasis you want to achieve. At the same time, you must place your modifiers precisely within sentences so that you avoid the error of misplaced modifiers°.

A sentence that starts with a subject and verb is called a **cumulative sentence.** You add information by placing modifiers after the subject and verb. This is the most common sentence structure. Its name derives from the notion that information accumulates. Sometimes it is referred to as a **loose sentence** because it lacks the tightly planned structure of other sentence varieties. Although such sentences are easy to read because they reflect how humans receive and pass on information, cumulative sentences often do not provide impact.

In contrast, a **periodic sentence** (sometimes called a **climactic sentence**) is highly emphatic. It builds up to the period of the sentence, reserving the main idea for the end. It draws the reader in as it builds to its climax.

PERIODIC	At midnight last night, on the road from Las Vegas to Death Valley Junction, **a car hit a shoulder and turned over.**
	—JOAN DIDION, "On Morality"
CUMULATIVE	**A car hit a shoulder and turned over** at midnight last night on the road from Las Vegas to Death Valley Junction.
PERIODIC	**The driver,** very young and apparently drunk, **was killed instantly.**
	—JOAN DIDION, "On Morality"
CUMULATIVE	**The driver, killed instantly,** was very young and apparently drunk.

Periodic sentences can be very effective, but if you overuse them they lose their punch. For this reason, Joan Didion follows the two periodic sentences presented above with a cumulative sentence: *His girl was found alive but bleeding internally, deep in shock.*

BACKGROUND
Periodic and cumulative sentences work by placing the weight of a sentence's message at one end. On the other hand, the balanced sentence, using the concept of parallel structure, presents two equally weighted pieces of meaning. Usually a punctuation mark and/or a coordinating conjunction acts as a centerpoint upon which the meaning balances, much like a see-saw on its base.

Freedom is the right to be wrong, not the right to do wrong.
—JOHN DIEFENBAKER

BIOGRAPHY
Joan Didion, novelist and essayist, was born in Sacramento, California, in 1934. Her books include *Play It As It Lays* (1971), *A Book of Common Prayer* (1977), and *The White Album* (1979). She has written for publications as diverse as *Vogue,* the *Saturday Evening Post,* and the *National Review,* and also co-authored the screenplay for the movie *True Confessions.* She says that she became a writer to come to terms with " 'images that shimmer around my mind.' "

Another way to vary your sentence structures is to start sentences with introductory words, phrases, or clauses.

WORD	**Indeed,** Henry Wallace once said, "Certain books are more powerful by far than any battle."
PHRASE	**Along with cereal boxes and ketchup labels,** comic books were the primers that taught me how to read. —GLORIA STEINEM
CLAUSE	**Long before I wrote stories,** I listened for stories. —EUDORA WELTY, *One Writer's Beginnings*

Positioning modifiers in two or more places can also lend your writing style both variety and emphasis—as long as you avoid overly complicated sentences.

On our half-acre or three-quarters we can raise enough tomatoes **for our salads** and assassinate enough beetles **to satisfy the gardening urge.**

—PHYLLIS McGINLEY, "Suburbia, Of Thee I Sing"

Television, **by its emphasis on movement and activity, by its appetite for incident,** has become **by far** the most potent instrument **in creating this overexcited atmosphere, this barely recognizable world.**

—HENRY FAIRLIE, "Can You Believe Your Eyes?"

EXERCISE 5

Combine each set of sentences by changing one sentence to a clause, phrase, or word that will modify the other sentence.

EXAMPLE Computer fraud has been rapidly increasing. This increase has been since 1964.

Since 1964, computer fraud has been rapidly increasing.

1. Students have found the code to college computers. This happened even at large universities with sophisticated technology.
2. Students at one college changed their grades to all "A's." They did this without going to any classes.
3. Computer fraud happens more often than robberies. This happens when banks have weak security.
4. A man was arrested by the FBI in 1978. He was charged with defrauding a Los Angeles bank of $10.2 million.

ANSWERS: EXERCISE 5
Answers will vary. One set of possibilities is:
1. Even at large universities with sophisticated technology, students have found the code to college computers.
2. Without going to any classes, students at one college changed their grades to all A's.
3. When banks have weak security, computer fraud happens more often than robberies.
4. Charged with defrauding a Los Angeles bank of $10.2 million, a man was arrested by the FBI in 1978.

INSTRUCTOR'S NOTES

5. Between 1964 and 1973, over 64,000 fake insurance policies were created on the Equity Funding Corporation computer.

6. Gradually, the Equity Funding Corporation lost over $2 million.

7. Although fraudulent use of computers in education and in business is serious, even more terrifying possibilities exist.

8. Invading vital health records at a hospital, teenagers seriously endangered the lives of many patients.

9. As the film *War Games* suggests, a problem could result from the misuse of military computers.

10. In the film, the computer gets the wrong message and almost starts a nuclear war.

5. Over 64,000 fake insurance policies were created on the Equity Funding Corporation computer. It happened between 1964 and 1973.

6. The Equity Funding Corporation lost over $2 million. This happened gradually.

7. Fraudulent use of computers in education and in business is serious. Even more terrifying possibilities exist.

8. Teenagers seriously endangered the lives of many patients. They invaded vital health records at a hospital.

9. The film *War Games* suggests a problem. The problem could result from the misuse of military computers.

10. There is a computer in the film. The computer gets the wrong message and almost starts a nuclear war.

EXERCISE 6

Revise each set of sentences—a new set starts at each number in parentheses—by combining them. Choose one sentence in each set to be the main focus, and reduce the other(s) to modifying clauses, phrases, or words.

EXAMPLE   Characters in folklore are usually strong. Many of them perform daring acts. They are often described as bigger than people in real life.

Characters in folklore are usually described as strong, daring, and bigger than people in real life.

(1) Molly Brown was a tough settler of the American Frontier. She is remembered for bravery because she saved some of the *Titanic* passengers. (2) Don Diego was a hero who lived on a hacienda in Southern California. He opposed a cruel governor. (3) He wore a mask and assumed the name *Zorro*. He would take unfairly gained riches from the Governor's friends. Then he would return the goods to the poor. (4) Then there was John Henry. He was a man. He worked building the railroads. He could drive steel spikes very fast. He could drive them faster than anybody else. (5) Sacajawea was a Native American. She knew how to find mountain passages. No one else could find these passages. Because of this skill, she was chosen to guide an expedition. The expedition was important. The expedition was led by Lewis and Clark.

■‖ 19e
Invert standard word order.

Standard word order in the English sentence calls for the subject to be followed by the verb: *The mayor walked into the room.* Because this pattern is so common, it is set in people's minds, and any varia-

ANSWERS: EXERCISE 6

Answers will vary. One set of possibilities is:

(1) Molly Brown, a tough settler of the American Frontier, is remembered for bravery because she saved some of the *Titanic* passengers. (2) A hero who lived on a hacienda in Southern California, Don Diego opposed a cruel governor. (3) Wearing a mask and assuming the name *Zorro,* Diego would take unfairly gained riches from the Governor's friends and would return the goods to the poor. (4) John Henry, a man who worked building the railroads, could drive steel spikes faster than anybody in the world. (5) Sacajawea, a Native American, was chosen to guide an important expedition led by Lewis and Clark because she knew how to find mountain passages that no one else could find.

350

tion automatically creates emphasis. Used too often, inverted word order can be distracting, but used sparingly, it can be very effective.

STANDARD	**The mayor walked** in. **The governor walked** out.
INVERTED	In **walked the mayor.** Out **walked the governor.**
STANDARD	**The house** that shelters a friend **is happy.**
INVERTED	**Happy is the house** that shelters a friend.

                                               —RALPH WALDO EMERSON

◼‖ 19f

Repeat important words or ideas to achieve emphasis.

Repeating carefully chosen words can help you emphasize your meaning. Choose for repetition only words that contain a main idea or that use rhythm to focus attention on a main idea. Consider this passage, which uses deliberate repetition along with a variety of sentence lengths to deliver its meaning.

> Coal is **black** and it warms your house and cooks your food. The night is **black,** which has a moon, and a million stars, and is beautiful. Sleep is **black** which gives you rest, so you wake up **feeling good.** I am **black.** I **feel** very **good** this evening.
>   —LANGSTON HUGHES, "That Word *Black*"

Hughes repeats the word *black,* each time linking it to something related to joy and beauty. The incantation that results from the rhythm of deliberate repetition of *black* and *good* emphasizes Hughes's message and helps the reader remember it.

    While deliberate repetition is a good ally when you use it occasionally to achieve variety and emphasize selected ideas, it can be misused. Be sure to use deliberate repetition sparingly, with central words, and only when your meaning justifies such a technique. Consider this passage, which misuses repetition:

| No | **An insurance agent** can be an excellent adviser when you want to buy a **car. An insurance agent** has records on most **cars. An insurance agent** knows which **models** tend to have most accidents. **An insurance agent** can tell you which **models** are the most expensive to repair if they are in a collision. **An insurance agent can** tell you which **models** are most likely to be stolen. |

BIOGRAPHY

Langston Hughes was born in Joplin, Missouri, in 1902 and went on to become a major figure in the Harlem Renaissance of the 1920s. He began writing poetry as a youth, but unable to get his work published, he traveled the country doing odd jobs to support himself. In 1925, poet Vachel Lindsay "discovered" Hughes, who was then working as a busboy. One year later Hughes was a published author (a poetry collection, *The Weary Blues*) and enrolled in college. Hughes devoted the rest of his life to his craft, often using dialect or jazz rhythms in his novels, plays, and poems depicting the black American experince. His poems, especially, have remained popular. He died in 1967, but his work still stands as an important expression of today's black culture.

INSTRUCTOR'S NOTES

ANSWERS: EXERCISE 7

Answers will vary. In the version below, the word *dreams* is deliberately repeated, many short sentences are combined, the second half of the compound sentence becomes a single sentence for particular emphasis, and the word order is rearranged in the last sentence.

Dreams come in many forms, some pleasing and others distressing. Dreams can be about the future or past successes or joys. Sometimes they are bizarre. According to researchers, some dreams recur over and over again, such as those about flying or falling. Many people dream they are failing tests or unable to make an important telephone call. Experts have suggested various explanations for some dreams, which makes a person's dreams seem objective and impersonal. They are not. Special is the dream, no matter how common, to its dreamer.

ANSWERS: EXERCISE 8

Using their own topics, students imitate the variety and emphasis of two different passages shown in this chapter. They can choose from Kohl, Asimov, Thomas, or Hughes. For a discussion of the technique of imitation, see the answer to Exercise 2.

TEACHING TIP

Having students imitate the style of the examples in the text or in the margins of this chapter can be an excellent teaching device. For some background, see the discussion of imitation in the margins of Chapter 18.

The repetition in this passage seems merely the result of a limited vocabulary and a dull, unvaried style. Although there are few synonyms for the words *an insurance agent, car,* and *model,* there are some. Also, the writer could have achieved variety in sentence structure. The passage's content does seem to call for the rhythmic effect of deliberate repetition.

YES If you are thinking of buying a new car, an insurance agent can be an excellent adviser. An insurance broker has complete records on most automobiles. For example, he or she knows which models are accident prone. Did you know that some car designs suffer more damage than others in a collision? If you want to know which automobiles crumple more than others and which are least expensive to repair, ask an insurance agent. Similarly, some models are more likely to be stolen, so find out from the person who specializes in dealing with claims.

EXERCISE 7

Revise this paragraph to achieve emphasis through varied sentence length and deliberate repetition. You can reduce or increase the number of sentences.

Dreams come in many forms. Some are pleasing. They also can be distressing. They can be about the future. They can be about past successes or joys. Sometimes, they are bizarre. According to researchers, some visions during sleep recur over and over again. Typical ones are about flying or falling. Many people see themselves failing tests. Being unable to make an important telephone call is also common. Experts have suggested various explanations for some dreams. This makes a person's dreams seem objective and impersonal, but they are not. No matter how common, a dream is special to the dreamer.

EXERCISE 8

Using topics of your choosing, imitate the variety and emphasis of two different passages shown in this chapter: choose from Kohl, Dillard, Thomas, or Hughes.

EXERCISE 9

Using the techniques of variety and emphasis discussed in this chapter, revise the following paragraph.

Many amazing events in bathtubs have taken place. Three different women died by drowning in the bathtub while they were married to George Joseph Smith of England. There was great surprise at Mr. Smith's trial when

INSTRUCTOR'S NOTES

the fact that he now had a fourth wife, Edith, was revealed. Edith testified at the trial that she remembered George's taking only one bath during the whole time they were married. Other things besides gory murders, however, happen in the bathtub. For example, French author Edmond Rostand took baths while he was writing plays like *Cyrano de Bergerac* to escape interruptions from friends. Also, many people know that the discovery of the scientific theory of displacement by Archimedes took place in the bathtub. Archimedes shouted "Eureka!" jumped out of his bath, and ran through the streets in the nude because he was so excited by his discovery. A modern example of the importance of the bathtub is illustrated by what happened to astronaut John Glenn. There was going to be an election for senator in Ohio, but Glenn had to withdraw from the race because he hurt himself when he fell in a bathtub.

ANSWERS: EXERCISE 9
Answers will vary. This is a summary exercise, and so it should reflect many of the techniques of variety and emphasis discussed in the chapter. Here is one possible answer.

Did you know that bathtubs have been the setting for many amazing events? While married to George Joseph Smith of England, three different women died by drowning in the bathtub. Mr. Smith's trial revealed that he now had a fourth wife, Edith. During the whole time they were married, Edith testified at the trial, she remembered George's taking only one bath. More than gory murders happen in the bathtub, however. For example, to escape interruptions from friends, French author Edmond Rostand took baths while he was writing plays like *Cyrano de Bergerac*. Also, Archimedes discovered the scientific theory of displacement in the bathtub. Jumping out of his tub, Archimedes shouted "Eureka!" and ran through the streets in the nude because he was so excited by his discovery. Astronaut John Glenn provides a modern example of the importance of the bathtub. Glenn was planning to run for senator in Ohio, but he hurt himself when he fell in the bathtub. He had to withdraw from the race!

INSTRUCTOR'S NOTES

V USING EFFECTIVE WORDS

20 *Understanding the Meaning of Words*

21 *Understanding the Effect of Words*

22 *Spelling and Hyphenation*

20

UNDERSTANDING THE MEANING OF WORDS

American English, evolving over centuries into a rich language, reflects the many cultures that have merged in our melting-pot society. The earliest varieties of American English can be traced from sixteenth-century Elizabethan English—the language of Shakespeare. As the United States expanded, so did American English. Changes from Elizabethan forms occurred in vocabulary, spelling, and syntactic patterns. Distinctly American words originated colloquially—in spoken language—and words from all the cultures settling the United States became part of the language. Food names, for example, show how other languages and cultures loaned words to English. Africans brought the words *ham, okra, gumbo,* and *goober* (peanut). Spanish and Latin American peoples contributed *tortilla, taco, burrito,* and *enchilada.* From German we got *hamburger, wiener,* and *pretzel;* Italian supplied *spaghetti, pasta, pizza,* and *antipasto;* and Yiddish is responsible for *gefilte fish, tsimmes,* and *bagel.* American English creates a truly international *smorgasbord,* a Scandinavian word meaning "a wide variety of appetizers and other tasty foods."

Etymology is the study of a word's origins and historical development—its changes in form and meaning. For example, *alphabet* originates from the names of the first two letters in Greek: *a* =

Note: See the margins of Chapter 22 for a series of "Language History" items, related to spelling and to the origins of American English.

WORD DERIVATION
The Greeks felt all foreigners were savages, speaking crude, primitive languages. *Barbarous* and *barbaric* come from the nonsense syllables the Greeks used in imitation of foreign speech: *barbar.*

355

WORD DERIVATION
Arkansas comes from the French adaptation of a Siouan tribal name believed to have meant "downstream people."

WORD DERIVATION
The name *California* originally referred to an imaginary island in a Spanish romance written by Montalvo in 1510.

WORD DERIVATION
Florida was named by explorer Ponce de León. The name is Spanish for "abounding in flowers."

WORD DERIVATION
Georgia was named for King George II of England. *Virginia* was named for Elizabeth I, who was known as the Virgin Queen. Naming new territories after monarchs and their family members was a common practice among explorers who wanted to gain favor or give thanks for patronage.

WORD DERIVATION
Kentucky comes from the Iroquoian words for "level land."

WORD DERIVATION
Louisiana comes from *La Louisianne.* The French, who had controlled the Mississippi Valley before selling the area to the United States in 1803, had named the area after their king, Louis XIV.

alpha, b = beta. Nice shows how a word's meaning can change with time. As W. Nelson Francis points out in *The English Language, nice* "has been used at one time or another in its 700-year history to mean . . . foolish, wanton, strange, lazy, coy, modest, fastidious, refined, precise, subtle, slender, critical, attentive, minutely accurate, dainty, appetizing, agreeable."

The fact that American English is a growing, changing language affects you as a writer. To write well, you need to use words accurately. Three important steps toward using American English effectively are knowing what kinds of information dictionaries hold (20a), understanding denotation *and* connotation of words (20b), and actively building your own vocabulary (20c).

■|| 20a
Learn to use dictionaries.

Good dictionaries show how language has been used and is currently being used. Such dictionaries give at each entry not only the word's meaning but also much additional important information. Many dictionaries also include essays on the history and use of language.

|| 1
Understand the information in a dictionary entry.

A good dictionary entry includes items 1 through 8 listed below, and sometimes items 9 through 12.

1. Spelling
2. Word division into syllables (syllabication)
3. Pronunciation
4. Functions (parts of speech)
5. Grammatical forms (plural, parts of verb including irregular forms, etc.)
6. Etymology
7. Meanings
8. Related words (nouns, adjectives)
9. Synonyms (and often antonyms)
10. Word used in context
11. Usage label
12. Idioms that include the word

356

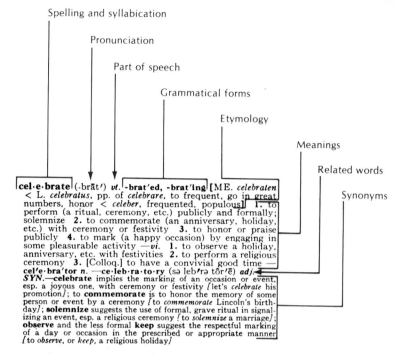

Spelling and syllabication

Pronunciation

Part of speech

Grammatical forms

Etymology

Meanings

Related words

Synonyms

cel·e·brate (-brāt′) *vt.* **-brat′ed, -brat′ing** [ME. *celebraten* < L. *celebratus,* pp. of *celebrare,* to frequent, go in great numbers, honor < *celeber,* frequented, populous] **1.** to perform (a ritual, ceremony, etc.) publicly and formally; solemnize **2.** to commemorate (an anniversary, holiday, etc.) with ceremony or festivity **3.** to honor or praise publicly **4.** to mark (a happy occasion) by engaging in some pleasurable activity —*vi.* **1.** to observe a holiday, anniversary, etc. with festivities **2.** to perform a religious ceremony **3.** [Colloq.] to have a convivial good time — **cel′e·bra′tor** *n.* —**ce·leb·ra·to·ry** (sə leb′rə tôr′ē) *adj.* **SYN.**—**celebrate** implies the marking of an occasion or event, esp. a joyous one, with ceremony or festivity [let's *celebrate* his promotion]; to **commemorate** is to honor the memory of some person or event by a ceremony [to *commemorate* Lincoln's birthday]; **solemnize** suggests the use of formal, grave ritual in signalizing an event, esp. a religious ceremony [to *solemnize* a marriage]; **observe** and the less formal **keep** suggest the respectful marking of a day or occasion in the prescribed or appropriate manner [to *observe,* or *keep,* a religious holiday]

Look at the entry above for the word *celebrate* from *Webster's New World Dictionary, Second College Edition.* The spelling is given first, with the word divided into syllables by a centered dot. The pronunciation follows, in parentheses. Here you will sometimes see unusual symbols, such as /ə/, the *schwa* or "uh" sound. Pronunciation symbols are explained in a pronunciation key in the dictionary's introductory pages. Some dictionaries also include a shortened version of the key at the bottom of each right-hand page. The accented syllable is shown by the stress mark /′/. Next you see the part of speech: *vt.* in the entry for *celebrate,* standing for *transitive verb.* Inflected forms (in regular verbs, the *-ed* form for past tense and past participle, the *-ing* form for the present participle) come before the bracketed etymology (word history). Definitions and related forms of the word are then given. Also note these features:

> *Celebrate* comes from a Middle English (ME) word, which is derived from the Latin *celeber,* meaning "populous"; one celebrates with numbers of other people at the same ceremony or festivity, according to the original meaning of the word.

> The numbered definitions reflect current usage by educated speakers and writers of English.

WORD DERIVATION

Nevada is a shortening of the Spanish *Sierra Nevada* ("snowy range"), a mountain range in eastern California.

WORD DERIVATION

New Mexico is a literal translation of the Spanish *Nuevo Méjico. Méjico* is the Spanish rendering of *Mexitli,* the name of an Aztec war god.

WORD DERIVATION

The state of *Pennsylvania* is named after a man and the local geography. *Sylvania* means "wooded land" in Latin. The *Penn* part is less clear. Some say that the *Penn* is William Penn, the colonist to whom King Charles II of England gave the land. Others say that under orders from King Charles, Penn named the land after his own late father, an English admiral. In either case, the admiral had died before the king could repay a debt of 16,000 pounds. The king gave the land to William Penn in settlement of the debt—and to keep the religious activist out of England.

WORD DERIVATION

*Rhode Island'*s etymology is a mystery. There are two theories. According to one, Italian explorer Giovanni da Verrazano saw a resemblance between the island on which the city of Newport is now located and the Greek island of Rhodes. According to the second, Dutch explorers named the area *Roode Eylandt* ("red island") because of its red clay soil.

357

Following the four meanings of the transitive verb are three meanings of the intransitive verb, and then noun and adjective forms with their pronunciations.

A discussion of synonyms starts at *SYN*. Here the differences among four words close in meaning to *celebrate* are pointed out; each word is defined and used in context.

Usage labels in a dictionary give much important information. See [Colloq.] at the third definition of *celebrate* as an intransitive verb. The most common usage labels are shown in the chart below. All labels and their abbreviations used in your dictionary are identified in its opening pages.

Besides usage labels, meanings specific to a particular field of knowledge or activity are so labeled. For example, one meaning of *carrier* is specific to chemistry ("a catalytic agent that causes an element or radical to be transferred from one compound to another") and is preceded by the label *Chem.* Another meaning of *carrier* is specific to electronics ("a steady transmitted wave whose amplitudes, frequency, or phase is modulated by the signal") and is labeled *Elec.*

ANSWERS: EXERCISE 2

Usage labels here are from *Webster's New World Dictionary, Second College Edition* and *Webster's New World Compact School and Office Dictionary*. For the student sentences, answers will vary.

1. colloquial for "without exaggeration"; slang for "pleasing" and for "emotionally uninvolved"
2. slang for "a mongrel dog" or "a stupid person"
3. obsolete for "long ago"
4. slang for "money"
5. colloquial for "a concluding or summarizing statement"
6. archaic or dialect for "near"
7. colloquial for "surely"
8. slang for someone who is "very dull and ineffective"
9. archaic or dialect for "yonder"
10. colloquial for "to fail"
11. slang for "speak in a way that is exaggerated or insincere, in an effort to mislead"
12. poetic for "meadow or grassy field"
13. colloquial for "unconventional or unusual"
14. dialect or colloquial for "person or animal regarded as objectionable or troublesome"
15. colloquial for "accessories or trimmings"

USAGE LABELS

LABEL	DEFINITION	EXAMPLE
Colloquial	Characteristic of conversation and informal writing	**pa** [father] **ma** [mother]
Slang	Not considered part of standard language, but sometimes used in informal conversation	**whirlybird** [helicopter]
Archaic or *Obsolete*	No longer used; occurred in earlier writing	**betimes** [promptly, quickly]
Poetic	Found in poetry or poetic prose	**o'er** [for *over*]
Dialect	Used only in some geographical areas	**poke** [Southern: a bag or sack]

EXERCISE 1

Use a dictionary that has entries which include a list of synonyms and some labels, as in the entry for *celebrate* on page 357. Then, assuming as your audience a student unfamiliar with such entries, write an explanation of each part.

EXERCISE 2

Consult a dictionary that gives usage labels. First, for each word below, give the usage label or labels: colloquial, slang, archaic or obsolete, poetic, or dialect. Then use the word in a sentence to show the meaning clearly.

1. *cool* (adj.) not referring to temperature
2. *mutt*
3. *yore*
4. *bread* (noun) not referring to food
5. *a wrapup*
6. *nigh*
7. *sure* (adv.)
8. *nerd*
9. *yon*
10. *flunk*
11. *jive* (verb)
12. *lea* (noun) not referring to yarn
13. *offbeat* (noun) not referring to music
14. *varmint*
15. *fixings*

EXERCISE 3

Consult a college dictionary for the etymology of the following words.

1. *current*
2. *pasteurize*
3. *mausoleum*
4. *nicotine*
5. *boycott*
6. *Taoism*
7. *erotic*
8. *olympic*
9. *popular*
10. *chauvinism*

2
Know about unabridged dictionaries.

Unabridged means "not shortened." Unabridged dictionaries have the most in-depth, accurate, complete, and scholarly entries of the various kinds of dictionaries. They give many examples of a word's current uses and changes in meanings over time. They include infrequently used words that abridged (shortened) dictionaries may omit. The most important and comprehensive unabridged dictionary of English is the *Oxford English Dictionary (OED)*. The *OED* has fifteen volumes plus supplements with more than 500,000 entries. These volumes comprise the definitive dictionary of the English languages. The *OED* traces the history of each word and

ANSWERS: EXERCISE 1
Answers will vary.

ANSWERS: EXERCISE 3
1. From the Latin *currere* meaning "to run"
2. After L. Pasteur, a nineteenth-century French bacteriologist
3. After the tomb of King Mausolus in ancient Asia Minor
4. After J. Nicot, a sixteenth-century French diplomat who introduced tobacco to France
5. After Captain Boycott of Ireland whose neighbors refused to do business with him
6. From the Chinese *tao* meaning "the way"
7. From the Greek *erós* meaning "love"
8. From *olympia*, the plain in Greece which was the site of the ancient games
9. From the Latin *populus* meaning "the people"
10. After N. Chauvin, a fanatical French patriot

359

gives dated quotations to illustrate changes in meaning and spelling. The 1986 supplement to the *OED* shows that American words are the greatest source of new words in the English language. The *OED* is particularly useful for people with an intense or scholarly interest in language.

For most college students *Webster's Third New International Dictionary of the English Language* will provide any needed information. This highly respected, one-volume work has more than 450,000 entries and is especially strong in new scientific and technical terms. It uses quotations to show various meanings, and its definitions are given in order of their appearance in the language.

Random House Dictionary of the English Language is another one-volume work. The newest unabridged dictionary, it has more than 260,000 entries. It is the least expansive and least expensive of the three unabridged dictionaries and has an atlas with color maps as well as a list of reference books in appendixes.

3
Know about abridged dictionaries.

Abridged means "shortened." Abridged dictionaries contain the most commonly used words. They are convenient in size and economical to buy. They serve as the most practical reference books for writers and readers. Many good abridged dictionaries are referred to as "college" editions because they serve the needs of most college students.

Webster's New World Dictionary of the American Language, 2nd edition, has more than 158,000 entries and gives detailed etymologies. It lists all entries in alphabetical order, with names of people, places, abbreviations, and foreign expressions in the main body of the work (rather than in appendixes). Its precise, easy-to-read definitions appear in chronological order of their acceptance into the language. *Webster's New World Dictionary* has a contemporary American emphasis. It uses a star symbol (☆) for Americanisms—words that first became part of the language in the United States. It gives the origins of American place names (cities, states, rivers, and so on). It supplies usage labels for many words and gives thorough synonymies. Its appendixes cover punctuation, mechanics, and manuscript form (footnotes, bibliography, proofreading marks, scholarly terms). Its introductory material includes essays on language, etymology, and Americanisms.

Although not itself a "college edition," *Webster's New World Compact School and Office Dictionary* is based on *Webster's New World Dictionary, Second College Edition.* Far more complete than

360

"pocket" dictionaries, this compact version of *Webster's New World Dictionary* has 56,000 entries, clearly and precisely defined. Its coverage of frequently encountered terms from the sciences, arts, business, technical, and professional fields is thorough and up-to-date. It contains pronunciation and spelling guidance, common abbreviations, foreign words and phrases often used in English writing, and etymologies. *Webster's New World Compact* gives tables of weights and measures, a dictionary of geography, a list of Presidents and Vice-Presidents of the United States, and lists of principal cities in the United States and in the rest of the world.

The American Heritage Dictionary of the English Language has more than 200,000 entries and 3,000 photographs, illustrations, and maps. This dictionary lists a word's most common meaning first, departing from the traditional practice of listing the oldest meaning first. *The American Heritage Dictionary* has especially thorough guidance on usage and extensive notes in its synonymies to distinguish subtle differences among words of similar meaning. Its introductory material contains essays on language, culture, and usage, as well as sections on grammar, spelling, and pronunciation. Biographical and geographic-names entries are in separate sections, and a list of Indo-European roots appears in an appendix.

Random House Dictionary of the English Language, based on the unabridged *Random House Dictionary,* has more than 155,000 entries. It gives a word's most common definition first and has full synonymies. It includes recent technical words and is generously illustrated. *The Random House Dictionary of the English Language* does not separate biographical and geographic entries from other entries. Its introductory section presents essays on usage, dialects, and functional varieties of English; its appendixes include a style manual.

4
Know about specialized dictionaries of English.

A specialized dictionary focuses on a single area, such as slang, word origins, synonyms, usage, or almost any other aspect of language.

SYNONYMS
*New Roget's Thesaurus of the English Language in
    Dictionary Form*

SLANG
Dictionary of Slang and Unconventional English, ed. Eric
    Partridge

361

Dictionary of American Slang, ed. Harold Wentworth and Stuart Berg Flexner

ETYMOLOGIES
Dictionary of Word and Phrase Origins, ed. William Morris and Mary Morris
Origins: A Short Etymological Dictionary of Modern English, ed. Eric Partridge

USAGE
Modern American Usage, ed. Jacques Barzun

REGIONALISMS
Dictionary of American Regional English, ed. Frederic Cassidy

■‖ 20b
Choose exact words.

Experienced writers pay close attention to **diction**—word choice. To choose the most appropriate and accurate word, a writer must understand the word's *denotation* and *connotation.*

‖ 1
Understand denotation and connotation.

Denotation is the explicit dictionary meaning of a word—its definition. When you look up a new word in the dictionary to find out what it means, you are looking for its denotation. For example, the denotation of the word *semester* is "a period of time of about eighteen weeks that makes up part of a school or college year."

Readers expect words to be used according to their established meanings for their established functions. Exactness is essential. Thus dangers, as well as benefits and pleasures, arise when you use a thesaurus or dictionary of synonyms. Be aware that subtle shades of meaning differentiate words with the same general definitions. These subtle differences in meaning allow you to be very precise in choosing just the right word, but they also oblige you to make sure you know what meanings your words convey. For instance, describing a person famous for praiseworthy achievements in public life as *notorious* would be wrong. Although *notorious* means "well-known" and "publicly discussed"—which renowned people are likely to be—*notorious* means "unfavorably known or talked about." George

BACKGROUND
Good news arrived in December 1985 for linguists, folklorists, and run-of-the-mill browsers. After an incubation period of almost one hundred years, volume one (A–C) of the *Dictionary of American Regional English (DARE)* arrived. Upon completion, *DARE* will contain over 60,000 regional words and expressions.

The roots of *DARE* go back to 1889 and the founding of the American Dialect Society. The Society's purpose was to sponsor and record data for an American dialect dictionary. It had its own journal, which continues today as *The Publication of the American Dialect Society.* Compilation of a master file of entries for the dictionary began in 1917, and the society participated along the way in several other, smaller dialect dictionaries (the incomplete *Linguistic Atlas of the United States and Canada* and the *American Dialect Dictionary* [1944]).

In 1963, the society appointed Frederic G. Cassidy (editor of *The Dictionary of Jamaican English*) the *DARE* editor. He and his staff had at their disposal a hundred years of accumulated scholarship: the files of the American Dialect Society, linguistic and folklore journals, regional publications, diaries and other materials in library archives, records of folk speech, historical dictionaries, and linguistic atlases.

Astonishingly, Cassidy chose to go beyond the written word, and the *DARE* benefits from five years of original fieldwork aimed at finding out how people speak in their daily lives. Eighty-two trained fieldworkers, most of them graduate students in linguistics or the history of English, went across the

INSTRUCTOR'S NOTES

Washington is *famous,* not *notorious.* Al Capone, on the other hand, is *notorious.*

Here is another example. *Obdurate* means "not easily moved to pity or sympathy," and its synonyms include "inflexible, obstinate, stubborn, hardened." You could correctly use *obdurate* in sentences like the following:

YES   The supervisor remained *obdurate* in refusing to accept excuses.

YES   My roomates, *obdurate* people who are unwilling to compromise, want me to get rid of my pet boa constrictor, Alphonse.

However, the synonym *hardened* may prompt someone unfamiliar with *obdurate* to use the word incorrectly.

NO   Footprints showed in the *obdurate* concrete.

As a final example of the importance of explicit meaning, suppose a writer who is describing the location of a mine shaft has used the word *deep* several times. Searching for a synonym, the writer consults a thesaurus and finds, among other alternatives, the word *profound.* The writer then states: "Shaft 4, outside Woodville, is the most profound in the state." Because *profound* means "deep" in reference to thoughts or ideas, it cannot be used in reference to a mine shaft.

Connotation refers to the ideas implied, but not directly indicated, by a word. Connotations convey associations as emotional overtones beyond a word's direct, explicit definition. What first comes to mind when you see the word *home?* Probably *home* evokes more emotion than does its denotation, "a dwelling place," and its synonym *house. Home* may have very pleasant connotations of warmth, security, the love of family. Or *home* may have unpleasant connotations of an institution for elderly or disabled people. Good writers understand the additional layer of meaning connotations deliver. Connotations are never completely fixed, for the associations to a word often are individual. Still, people can communicate effectively because most words have relatively stable connotations and denotations in most contexts.

Being sensitive to the differences between a word's denotation and connotation is essential for critical thinking. Critical thinkers must first consider material at its literal level (5b-1). Doing so calls for dealing with the denotation of words. Next, critical thinkers must move to the inferential level (5b-2)—to what is implied, although not explicitly stated. Here the connotations of words often

United States conducting personal interviews.

The 2,777 informants represented 1,002 communities across the United States. The informants were chosen to create a balance of male and female, city and country, black and white, North and South. However, in order to preserve vanishing words, about two-thirds of the informants were sixty years old or older. Each questionaire contained 1,847 questions. One questionaire was filled in for each community. In some cases, one informant answered all the questions; in others, the questions were divided among a number of informants. The fieldworkers also brought back 1,843 tape recordings of conversations: a total of two million oral responses and 900 hours of tape-recordings.

TEACHING TIP
To underscore the importance of subtle shades of meaning and connotation, you might ask your students how they would react to each of the statements below. Once their egos are involved, students will quickly see that all synonyms are not created equal.

You are wrong.
You are incorrect.
What you say is false.
You are inaccurate.
You are imprecise.
You are evil.
You are improper.
You are unethical.
You are unrighteous.
You are bad.
You are willfully misleading.

363

carry the message. Consider these comparisons of denotation and connotation:

WORD	DENOTATION	CONNOTATION
additive	an added substance	in food, a preservative, but perhaps also harmful to health
cheap	inexpensive	of products, low quality; of people, stingy
nuclear accident	unintentional meltdown of fuel rods in nuclear reactor	release of dangerous radiation; possibility of imminent death or eventual cancer; poisoning of food chain

ANSWERS: EXERCISE 4

The response to this exercise is likely to elicit much debate, given that shades of connotative meaning are often fairly personal. The list here is the result of a poll of the students in a half-dozen classes; some votes were very close.

1. *Positive:* portly; *Neutral:* rotund, large-sized, overweight; *Negative:* fat, fleshy, stout, chubby, plump, obese, corpulent, heavy, paunchy, rolypoly
2. *Positive:* lean, lanky, slender, slim; *Neutral:* thin, slight; *Negative:* skinny, gaunt, scrawny, rawboned, skin and bones
3. *Positive:* mentor, scholar, educator; *Neutral:* teacher, lecturer, instructor, professor; *Negative:* pedant, pedagogue
4. *Positive:* senator, representative, leader; *Neutral:* politician, lawmaker; *Negative:* demagogue, rabble rouser
5. *Positive:* loyal, dedicated, devoted, determined; *Neutral:* firm; *Negative:* stubborn, unyielding

EXERCISE 4

Separate the words in each set of words into one of three columns: *Neutral* if you think the word has no connotations; *Positive* if you think it has good connotations; *Negative* if you think it has bad connotations.

EXAMPLE alibi, excuse, pretext, reason, explanation

Positive	*Neutral*	*Negative*
explanation	reason	alibi
		pretext
		excuse

1. fat, fleshy, stout, portly, rotund, chubby, plump, obese, corpulent, heavy, paunchy, overweight, rolypoly, large-sized.
2. thin, lean, lanky, skinny, gaunt, scrawny, rawboned, slender, slim, slight, skin and bones.
3. teacher, lecturer, instructor, professor, pedant, pedagogue, mentor, scholar, educator.
4. politician, lawmaker, senator, representative, leader, demagogue, rabble-rouser.
5. loyal, dedicated, devoted, determined, stubborn, firm, unyielding.

‖ **2**

‖ **Use specific and concrete language to bring life to general and abstract language.**

Specific words identify individual items in a group *(Oldsmobile, Honda, Ford)*. **General** words relate to an overall group *(car)*.

364

Concrete words identify persons and things that can be perceived by the senses—seen, heard, tasted, felt, smelled (the *black padded vinyl dashboard* of my car). **Abstract** words denote qualities, concepts, relationships, acts, conditions, ideas *(transportation)*. Writers must use all these types of words: specific and concrete as well as general and abstract. Effective writers, however, make sure to supply enough specific details and examples to substantiate and illustrate generalizations and abstractions. For example, compare the general sentences with the more specific versions:

GENERAL	My car has a great deal of power, and it is very quick.
SPECIFIC	My Trans Am with 135 horsepower can go from zero to fifty in six seconds.
GENERAL	The car gets good gas mileage.
SPECIFIC	The Dodge Lancer gets about 35 mpg on the highway and 30 mpg in the city.
GENERAL	Her car is comfortable and easy to drive.
SPECIFIC	Her Buick Regal has an 8-way adjustable leather seat, cruise control, tilt steering wheel, and automatic transmission.
GENERAL	His car has the latest technology for a smooth ride
SPECIFIC	His Toyota Celica has four-wheel independent suspension, stabilizer bars, and rack-and-pinion steering for stability and controllability.

Usually, good writing combines general and abstract words and ideas with specific and concrete words and ideas. In the following sentences from a paper comparing American-made and imported cars, the combination works effectively.

GENERAL   SPECIFIC   SPECIFIC   ABSTRACT
My car, a **135-horsepower Trans Am,** is **quick.** It accelerates from

SPECIFIC   SPECIFIC   SPECIFIC
0 to 50 miles per hour in **6 seconds**—but it gets only **18 miles** per gallon. The

SPECIFIC   ABSTRACT   GENERAL
Dodge Lancer, on the other hand, gets **very good** gas **mileage:** about

SPECIFIC   GENERAL   SPECIFIC   SPECIFIC   GENERAL
35 mpg in **highway driving** and **30 mpg** in **stop-and-go driving conditions.**

COORDINATED RESOURCES

Alternate examples and exercises for this chapter are available in the *S & S Workbook for Writers,* Gordon and Troyka.

Transparency masters are available for many of the screened charts and/or lists in this chapter.

Students can practice and test their knowledge of terms, key concepts, and applications of material in this chapter by using the *Study Guide to the S & S Handbook for Writers,* West.

Note that specific language is not always preferable to general language, and concrete language is not always preferable to abstract language. For example, in a paper about how to change a washer in a faucet, readers who are looking for information do not care that the faucet is a 1984 model Kohler stainless steel flange handle with lucite ribs. All those readers need to know is how to put the washer in the faucet so that the faucet works driplessly. Although the directions must include specific details about installing the washer, using ultraspecific language to describe the faucet would create an annoying distraction for do-it-yourself plumbers.

EXERCISE 5
Revise the following paragraph by providing specific and concrete words to explain and enliven the general and abstract words.

I enjoy good food. I do not like to eat greasy foods or foods made with more artificial ingredients than real ones. To me, good food starts with sweet, delicious desserts. I am also fond of many ethnic dishes. Bread is one of my other favorites. As long as I watch my weight, I can look forward to years of pleasure from good food.

20c
Increase your vocabulary.

A larger and richer vocabulary is one of the most rewarding outcomes of a college education. Dictionaries, of course, are a logical source of new words, as well as of new meanings for familiar words. In addition, you can use a few routine practices to build into your vocabulary new words you encounter.

1
Know prefixes and suffixes.

Prefixes are syllables in front of a **root** word that modify its meaning. *Ante-* (before) placed before the root *bellum* (war) gives *antebellum,* which means "before the war." *Antebellum* refers to the time before the Civil War. **Suffixes** are syllables added to the end of a root word that modify its meaning. For example, *excite* (formed by adding the prefix *ex,* "out," to the past participle of *cierce,* "to summon," has the various forms of adjective, adverb, and noun when suffixes are added: *excited, exciting, excitedly, excitement.* A word's part of speech is often signaled by the suffix.

366

TECHNIQUES FOR BUILDING YOUR VOCABULARY

1. Using a highlighter pen, mark all unfamiliar words in your textbooks and other reading material you own. Then define the words in the margin so you can study the meaning in context. Copy new words onto index cards or into a special notebook.
2. Listen carefully to learn how speakers use the language. Jot down new words and later look them up and write each word and its definitions on an index card or in a special notebook.
3. Set aside time each day to study the new words. You can carry your cards or notebook in your pocket to study in spare moments during the day.
4. Use mnemonics to memorize words (see 22b-2). Set a goal of learning *and using* 8 to 10 new words a week.
5. Every few weeks go back to the words from the previous weeks. Make a list of any words you still do not remember and study them again.

Roots are the central parts of words to which prefixes and suffixes are added. Once you know, for example, the Latin root *bene* ("well, good"), you can decipher various forms: **bene**ign, **bene**factor, **bene**diction, **bene**ficial, **bene**ficiary, **bene**volent, **bene**fit.

Knowing common prefixes and suffixes is an excellent way to learn to decode unfamiliar words and increase your vocabulary.

PREFIXES

Prefix	Meaning	Example
anti-	against	*antiballistic*
contra-	against	*contradict*
extra-	more	*extraordinary*
hyper-	more	*hyperactive*
super-	more	*supernatural*
ultra-	more	*ultraconservative*
dis-	not	*disagree*
il-	not	*illegal*
im-	not	*immoral*
in-	not	*inadequate*
ir-	not	*irresponsible*
mis-	not	*misunderstood*

INSTRUCTOR'S NOTES

TEACHING TIP

Knowledge of prefixes and suffixes can help students figure out the meaning of many words. If this skill is coupled with the ability to recognize root words, however, many students power to decipher new words can increase dramatically. Fundamentally, a root word is a base to which prefixes and suffixes can be added. For example, *-graph* (from the Greek *-graphos,* "to write") refers to something that writes or records, such as a *telegraph* or *graphite,* or something written, such as a *paragraph* or the *graphic arts; graphology* is the study of handwriting.

Here are a few of the most common Greek and Latin roots, their meanings, and a sample word built from each root.

LATIN

<u>aequs</u>	equal (equiva-lent)
<u>amare</u>, <u>amatum</u>	to love (amiable)
<u>dicere</u>, <u>dictum</u>	to say, to speak (diction)
<u>manus</u>	hand (manuscript)
<u>omnis</u>	all (ominpotent)
<u>portare</u>, <u>portatum</u>	to carry (porter)
<u>scribere</u>, <u>scriptum</u>	to write (scribble)
<u>sentire</u>, <u>sensum</u>	to feel (sense)
<u>spirare</u>, <u>spiratum</u>	to breathe (inspi-ration)
<u>verbum</u>	word (verb)

GREEK

<u>bios</u>	life (biology)
<u>chronos</u>	time (chronology)
<u>gamos</u>	marriage (bigamy)
<u>geo-</u>	earth (geology)

Continued on p. 369.

PREFIXES

Prefix	Meaning	Example
non-	not	*noninvolvement*
un-	not	*unhappy*
semi-	half	*semicircle*
mono-	one	*monopoly*
uni-	one	*uniform*
poly-	many	*polygamy*
ante-	before	*antebellum*
pre-	before	*prehistoric*
post-	after	*postscript*
re-	back	*return*
retro-	back	*retroactive*
sub-	under	*submissive*
trans-	across	*transportation*
inter-	between	*interpersonal*
intra-	inside	*intravenous*
auto-	self	*autobiography*
mal-	poor	*malnutrition*

SUFFIXES

NOUNS

Suffix	Meaning	Example
-tion	act of	*integration*
-hood	state of	*childhood*
-ness	state of	*kindness*
-ship	state of	*friendship*
-tude	state of	*solitude*
-dom	state of	*freedom*

VERBS

Suffix	Meaning	Example
-ate	to make	*integrate*
-ify	to make	*unify*
-ize	to make	*computerize*

368

SUFFIXES		
	ADJECTIVES	
Suffix	*Meaning*	*Example*
-able	able to be	*comfortable*
-ible	able to be	*compatible*
-ate	full of	*fortunate*
-ful	full of	*tactful*
-ous	full of	*pompous*
-y	full of	*gloomy*
-less	without	*penniless*

TEACHING TIP (cont.)

krates (-crat)	member of a group (democrat)
metron	to measure (thermometer)
pathos	suffering, feeling (sympathy)
phobos	fear (agoraphobia)
photos	light (photograph)
podos	foot (tripod)

EXERCISE 6

Add a prefix to each italicized word to match the definition given. Consult a dictionary if necessary.

EXAMPLE not *happy* = *unhappy*

1. not *logical*
2. not *athletic*
3. not *decent*
4. excessively *sensitive*
5. below the *conscious*
6. against the *freeze*
7. *dated* after
8. one *rail*
9. *existing* before
10. *consider* again

ANSWERS: EXERCISE 6

1. illogical
2. unathletic
3. indecent
4. hypersensitive
5. subconscious
6. antifreeze
7. postdated
8. unirail
9. preexisting
10. reconsider

EXERCISE 7

Add a suffix to each italicized word to match the definition given. Notice that you will be changing the form of the word to match the exact definition.

EXAMPLE state of being *lazy* = *laziness*

1. state of being *happy*
2. act of *flirting*
3. full of *room*
4. able to *agree*
5. to make *beautiful*
6. to make *ideal*
7. state of being *grateful*
8. full of *courage*
9. to make *original*
10. state of being *contented*

ANSWERS: EXERCISE 7

1. happiness
2. flirtation
3. roomy
4. agreeable
5. beautify
6. idealize
7. gratitude
8. courageous
9. originate
10. contentment

369

2
Use context clues to deduce word meanings.

The familiar words that surround an unknown word can give you hints about the new word's meaning. Such **context clues** include four main types.

1. **Restatement context clue:** You can figure out an unknown word when a word you know repeats the meaning. *He jumped into the* fray *and enjoyed every minute of the fight. Fray* means "fight." The restatement may be set off with punctuation, such as commas, dashes, or parentheses: Et al. *("and others") is used in a bibliography to indicate other authors of a work.* But often a restatement is not set off: Et al. *indicates that other authors' names have been omitted.*

2. **Contrast context clue:** You can figure out an unknown word when an opposite or contrast is presented: *We feared that the new prime minister would be a* menace *to society, but she turned out to be a great peacemaker. Menace* means "threat." The explanatory contrast is *but she turned out to be a great peacemaker.*

3. **Example context clue:** You can figure out an unfamiliar word when an example or illustration relating to the word is given: *They were* conscientious *workers, making sure that everything was done correctly and precisely. Conscientious* means "motivated by a desire to do what is right." You get close to that definition with "done correctly and precisely."

4. **General sense context clue:** An entire passage can convey a general sense of particular difficult words. For example, in *Nearly forty million Americans are overweight; obesity has become an* epidemic. You can deduce that *epidemic* refers to something happening to many people.

Sometimes a "general sense context clue" may fail to make clear a word's exact denotation. In clue 4 above, for instance, you might guess that *epidemic* indicates a widespread threat, but you might miss the connection of the word *epidemic* with the concept of disease. Interpreting a word's meaning from the general sense of a passage can nevertheless make you miss the subtle variations that distinguish one word from another. When you believe you have deciphered a meaning from any of these context clues, check the exact definition in a dictionary. Then add the word to your vocabulary.

370

21
UNDERSTANDING THE EFFECT OF WORDS

Words do not exist in a vacuum. They communicate meaning and so have an effect on the people reading or hearing them. As a writer, therefore, use words carefully both for their correct meaning (Chapter 20) and for their effect.

Using words well depends on making good choices. Sometimes the choices are either right or wrong, but sometimes the choices are subtler. Your awareness of your purpose in writing, your audience, and the situation in which you are writing should influence your choice of words. Your choice of words affects the *tone* of your writing. A chummy tone is fine for a letter to a friend but inappropriate for an essay written for a college course. A humorous tone might be fine for an essay about the time you wore an unmatched pair of shoes to an interview, but a serious tone would be needed in your letter of application for a job. This chapter discusses the many options available when you choose words for the effect they will have on your audiences.

■‖ 21a
Use appropriate language.

Good writers pay special attention to **diction**—word choice—making certain that the words they use will communicate their meaning as clearly and convincingly as possible.

371

1
Be aware of levels of formality in language use.

Informal and highly formal levels of writing use different vocabulary and sentence structures, and they differ clearly in **tone.** Tone in writing means the attitude of the writer toward the subject and toward the audience. Tone may be highly formal, informal, or somewhere in between. Different tones are appropriate for different audiences, different subjects, and different purposes. An informal tone occurs in casual conversation or letters to friends. A highly formal tone, in contrast, occurs in sermons and proclamations, treatises and treaties.

Informal language, which creates an informal tone, may include slang, colloquialisms, and regionalisms. In addition, informal writing may include sentence fragments, contractions, and other forms that approximate casual speech. **Medium** language level uses general English—not too casual, not too scholarly. Unlike informal language, medium-level language is acceptable for academic writing. This level uses standard vocabulary (for example, *learn* instead of *wise-up*), conventional sentence structure, and few or no contractions. A **highly formal** language level uses a multisyllabic Latinate vocabulary (*edify* instead of *learn*) and often stylistic flourishes such as extended or complex figures of speech. Academic writing and most writing for general audiences should range from medium to somewhat formal levels of language.

INFORMAL	Ya know stars? They're a gas!
MEDIUM	Gas clouds slowly changed into stars.
FORMAL	The condensations of gas spun their slow gravitational pirouettes, slowly transmogrifying gas cloud into star.
	—CARL SAGAN, "Starfolk: A Fable"

INFORMAL	Basically, we're ex-chimps.
MEDIUM	The human race's genes evolved in a manner similar to that of other reproducing things on earth.
FORMAL	And then one day there came to be a creature whose genetic material was in no major way different from the self-replicating molecular collectives of any of the other organisms on his planet, which he called Earth.
	—CARL SAGAN, "Starfolk: A Fable"

As these examples show, the choice of informal, medium, or formal language establishes the *tone,* the way the writer regards the audience and the subject. The informal examples would be appropriate in a letter to a close friend or in a journal; the writer's attitude toward the subject is playful and humorous. Word choice and sentence structure assume great familiarity between writer and audience. The medium examples would be appropriate in most academic and professional situations. It is easy to see an instructor as the audience for these sentences; the writer's attitude toward the subject is serious and straightforward. The formal examples are addressed to an audience with considerable interest in and knowledge of scientific phenomena—perhaps readers of a science journal or magazine.

2
Use edited American English for most writing.

The language standards you are expected to use in academic writing are those of **edited American English**—the accepted written language of a book like this handbook or a magazine like *Newsweek* or *Harper's.* Such language is called *standard English* because it conforms to established rules of grammar, sentence structure, punctuation, and spelling. When referring to writing, this language is also called *edited American English* because it is often the result of careful revision into standard forms from quickly drafted informal writing. Because advertising language and other language intended to reach and sway a large audience often ignores conventional usage, readers *do* encounter English that varies from the standard. However, do not let these published departures from edited English influence you into believing they are acceptable in academic writing. Edited English is not a fancy dialect for the elite; it is a practical form of the language that most educated people use. When you use edited American English in your academic writing, you will not risk distracting your readers from the message you want to communicate.

3
Do not use sexist language.

Sexist language assigns roles or characteristics to people on the basis of sex. Such practices unfairly limit or discriminate

TEACHING TIP
If you have any doubts about whether encouraging nonsexist language is worth the effort, consider this passage from the introduction to "Guidelines for Nonsexist Use of Language in NCTE [National Council of Teachers of English] Publications":

"Sexism" may be defined as words or actions that arbitrarily assign roles or characteristics to people on the basis of sex. Originally used to refer to practices that discriminated against women, the term now includes any usage that unfairly delimits the aspirations or attributes of either sex. Neither men nor women can reach their full potential when men are conditioned to be only aggressive, analytical, and active and women are conditioned to be only submissive, emotional, and passive. The man who cannot cry and the woman who cannot command are equally victims of their socialization.

Language plays a central role in socialization, for it helps teach children the roles that are expected of them. Through language, children conceptualize their ideas and feelings about themselves and their world. Thought and action are reflected in words, and words in turn condition how a person thinks and acts. Eliminating sexist language will not eliminate sexist conduct, but as the language is liberated from sexist usages and assumptions, women and men will begin to share more equal, active, caring roles. (1)

373

against both sexes. Sexist language inaccurately assumes all nurses and homemakers are female (and therefore refers to them as "she") and all physicians and wage earners are male (and therefore refers to them as "he"). One of the most widespread occurrences of sexist language is the use of the pronoun *he* to refer to someone of unidentified sex. Although tradition holds that *he* is correct in such situations, using only masculine pronouns to represent the human species excludes females—a distortion of reality. You can avoid this problem by following the suggestions in the chart below.

HOW TO AVOID SEXIST LANGUAGE

1. Avoid using only the masculine pronoun to refer to males and females together by using a pair of pronouns, but try to avoid strings of pairs in a sentence or in several consecutive sentences.

   No A doctor cannot read much outside **his** specialty

   Yes A doctor cannot read much outside **his or her** specialty.

   Revise into the plural.

   No A successful doctor knows that **he** has to work long hours.

   Yes Successful doctors know that **they** have to work long hours.

   Recast the sentence to omit the gender-specific pronoun.

   No Everyone hopes that **he** will win the scholarship.

   Yes Everyone hopes to win the scholarship.

2. Avoid the use of *man* when men and women are clearly intended in the meaning.

   No **Man** is a social animal.

   Yes **People** are social animals.

   No A **man's** best friend is a dog.

   Yes A **person's** best friend is a dog.

3. Avoid stereotyping jobs and roles by gender when men and women are included.

TEACHING TIP

In addition to the techniques given in the chart How to Avoid Sexist Language, here are a few additional tactics.

1. When appropriate, use the first person or the second person.

   NO A person should always keep an eye on his luggage in airports.

   YES I should always keep my eye on my luggage in airports.

   YES We should always keep an eye on our luggage in airports.

   YES Keep an eye on your luggage in airports.

2. Repeat a noun or use a synonym in place of the troublesome pronoun.

   NO A preoccupied traveler is an easy target for thieves, who can pick his pocket in a second.

   YES A preoccupied traveler is an easy target for thieves, who can pick a traveler's pocket in a second.

   YES A preoccupied traveler is an easy target for thieves, who can pick a tourist's pocket in a second.

3. Use *who.*

   NO A traveler has little to worry about, if he stays alert.

   YES A traveler who stays alert has little to worry about.

INSTRUCTOR'S NOTES

No	chairman; policeman; businessman; statesman
Yes	chair, chairperson; police officer; businessperson, business executive; diplomat, prime minister, statesperson
No	teacher . . . **she**; principal . . . **he**
Yes	teachers . . . **they**; principals . . . **they**

4. Avoid expressions that exclude one sex.

| No | mankind; the common man; man-sized sandwich; old wives' tale |
| Yes | humanity; the average person; huge sandwich; superstition |

5. Avoid using demeaning and patronizing labels.

| No | lady lawyer; gal Friday; career girl; coed |
| Yes | lawyer; assistant; professional woman; student |

| No | My girl will help you. |
| Yes | My secretary will help you. Jane Baumann will help you. |

EXERCISE 1
Revise the following sentences using a medium level of formality consistently and changing sexist language to nonsexist language.

1. After Professor John Smith lectured brilliantly for ninety minutes on the urbanization of the South, he was too pooped to answer questions.
2. I told my friend, "You know, that was the most sagacious blab I've ever heard."
3. That professor learned me a lesson about stereotyping Southerners.
4. Some Northerners think that a Southerner don't know nothing because of his Southern drawl—slow talking gotta mean slow thinking.
5. The Northerner may claim that he is right smarter than the Southerner.
6. When a Northerner runs into people with southern accents, he often forgets the lowdown about Southerners.
7. Some of America's brightest businessmen and statesmen have come from the South.

BACKGROUND
This editor's note appeared in the *New York Times* on Friday, June 20, 1986.

Beginning today, the *New York Times* will use "Ms." as an honorific in its news and editorial columns.

Until now, "Ms." had not been used because of the belief that it had not passed sufficiently into the language to be accepted as common usage. The Times now believes that "Ms." has become a part of the language and is changing its policy.

The Times will continue to use "Miss" or "Mrs." when it knows the marital status of a woman in the news, unless she prefers "Ms."

"Ms." will also be used when a woman's marital status is not known, or when a married woman wishes to use it with her prior name in professional or private life.

ANSWERS: EXERCISE 1
Answers will vary. Here is one set of possibilities:
1. change "pooped" to "exhausted"
2. change "sagacious blab" to "intelligent talk"
3. change "learned" to "taught"
4. Revise to: Some Northerners think that Southerners do not know anything because of their Southern accent—slow talking is taken to mean slow thinking.
5. Revise to: Northerners may claim that they are intellectually superior to Southerners.
6. Revise to: When Northerners meet people with southern accents, they often forget the truth about Southerners.
7. Some of America's brightest people in business and politics have come from the South.

4

Avoid slang, colloquial, or regional language for most expository writing.

Slang consists of coined words and new or extended meanings attached to established terms. Slang words and phrases usually pass out of use quickly. Occasional slang terms become accepted into standard usage. **Colloquial** language is characteristic of casual conversation and informal writing: *The student flunked chemistry* instead of *the student failed chemistry*. **Regional (dialectal) language** is specific to some geographic areas: *They have nary a cent.*

Although slang and colloquial words and regional language are neither substandard nor illiterate, they are not appropriate for academic writing. Replacing slang, colloquial, and regional language with general English in your college writing allows you to communicate clearly with the large number of people who speak and write in medium or somewhat formal levels of langauge. Slang, colloquial, and regional expressions can have a place in narratives in which you describe the exact speech of individuals, however.

Slang words are only used in very informal situations. Sometimes slang terms are inventions: *hippie* from the 1960s and its 1980 counterpart *yuppie* are examples. Sometimes slang terms are redefinitions of existing words: *psyched* or *wired* to mean "enthusiastic" are examples. Slang varies according to time and place. Consider, for instance, these expressions defined in a 1983 *New York Times* article, "City Teenagers Talking Up a 'Say What?' Storm": *chill out* meaning "relax, be cool"; *say what?* for "excuse me?"; *box* for "radio"; *gear* for "stylish clothing." These expressions communicated their meanings colorfully and accurately among teenagers in New York in 1983. They might not have communicated the same meanings to teenagers in California in 1983 or to teenagers anywhere in 1987. And they certainly would not communicate accurate meanings in an academic paper or business report in New York in 1983 nor in any other time or place. Slang is fun, informal, and personal; it rarely has a place in writing for college.

Dialects are different from slang because dialectic differences correlate with both geographical regions and socioeconomic status. Although no regional or social dialect can be designated as the one "correct" form of a language, dialects spoken by educated people usually hold the attention of educated people more than do the speech patterns of others. Using a dialect when writing for the general reading public tends to shut some people out of the communi-

376

cation. One way to assess the appropriateness of dialect is to remember that the best form of language is whatever language most clearly communicates to a given audience.

5
Avoid slanted language.

To communicate clearly, you need to choose words that convince your audience of your fairness as a writer. When you are writing about a subject on which you hold strong opinions, it is easy to slip into biased or emotionally loaded language. Such **slanted language** usually does not convince a careful reader to agree with your point. Instead, it makes the reader wary or hostile. For example, suppose you are arguing against the practice of scientific experimentation on animals. If you use language such as "laboratory Frankensteins" who "routinely and viciously maim helpless kittens and puppies," you are using slanted language. A neutral audience will doubt your ability to write fairly about the subject. Especially in persuasive writing, you want to use words that make your side of an issue the more convincing one. Once you start using slanted, biased language, however, readers feel manipulated rather than reasoned with. Only those who already agree with you will be convinced. Those who disagree will be annoyed. And those who might have been persuaded will start to think of rebuttals to your unfair, slanted presentation.

▪▮ 21b
Use figurative language.

Figures of speech use words for more than their literal meanings. Figurative language creates comparisons and connections that use one idea or image to enhance or explain another. The most common figures of speech are similes and metaphors.

A **simile** states a direct comparison between otherwise dissimilar things. It sets up the comparison by using the words *like* or *as*. The famous black poet Langston Hughes says that a deferred dream dries up *like a raisin in the sun*.

A **metaphor** implies a comparison between otherwise dissimilar things without using *like* or *as: the soldier tulips march in even rows*. Many words are used metaphorically almost as often as they are used literally. With common metaphoric words, writers must be especially careful not to create an unintentionally impossible im-

WORD DERIVATIONS
Metaphor comes from *metapherein* (Greek for "to transfer"), a combination of *pherein* ("to carry") and *meta* ("over"). A metaphor carries over the meaning. The first recorded use of the word in English was by Henry VIII in 1533: "And rather then men would note a lye when they know what is meant, they will sooner by allegory or metaphor draw the word to the truth."

Simile comes from *similis* (Latin for "like"). Similes always contain *like* or *as*, making the comparison explicit. *Simile* was first used in 1393 in William Langland's "Piers Plowman."

INSTRUCTOR'S NOTES

TEACHING TIP

Sports have been a fertile field of metaphor in America. You might remind your students of these common metaphors. What does each mean within its sport? What does each mean in a general context? You might also ask students if they can add to the lists or start lists for other sports or interests. Many metaphors listed here are discussed in Tim Considine's "Starting from Scratch" (*New York Times,* June 8, 1985).

Soccer
kick off
get the ball rolling

Baseball
right off the bat
off base
touch base with
go to bat for
out of left field
drop the ball
in there pitching
ballpark figure
southpaw

Football
huddle
chalk talk
a flag on the play
Monday morning quarterback
all-American

Boxing
answer the bell
a low blow
below the belt
on the ropes
down for the count
roll with the punch
saved by the bell
throw in the towel

Answers to Exercise 2 on p. 379

age. Consider this sentence for example: *The rush-hour traffic bled out of all the city's major arteries.* Cars are not at all like blood and their movement is not similar to the flow of blood, so the metaphor ends up being confusing rather than clarifying. Words with metaphorical meanings can also create **mixed metaphors,** incongruously combined images: *Milking the migrant workers for all they were worth, the supervisors bled them dry.* Here the initial image is of taking milk from a cow; but the final image has blood, not milk, as the result of the supervisors' evil actions.

Other types of figurative language include:

Understatement, or using a very restrained style
    It gets warm when the temperature goes above 101 degrees.

Personification, or giving human traits to nonhuman things
    The *book begged* to be read.

Irony, or suggesting the opposite of the usual sense
    Told that the car repair would cost $1,000 and take at least two weeks, she muttered, "A bargain!"

Onomatopoeia, or using words to imitate the sound they denote
    I heard a *hiss* of steam

Metonymy, or using a name associated with something to refer to anything in that class
    The White House [the President] had no comment.

Synecdoche, or substituting a part for the whole (or vice versa)
    The *pen* [discourse] is mightier than the *sword* [warfare].

Oxymoron, or combining opposites for a seeming contradiction or paradox
    The *silence* was *thunderous.*

EXERCISE 2

Identify each figure of speech. Revise any mixed metaphors.

1. The challenger, another Goliath, fell with the first blow.

2. She went inside the house, shutting the door like a clam snapping shut its shell.

3. The ocean screamed its fury.

4. Triple bypass heart surgery is no tea party.

5. In tilling his land, Henry David Thoreau wanted the earth to say "beans" instead of "grass."

6. The beaver buzz-sawed through the tree trunk.

7. The world ended when his parents divorced.

8. The champion was like a cobra ready to strike.

378

9. The soft mountains shone in the sun.
10. Changing a flat tire is exactly how I love to spend my time.

■‖ 21c
Avoid clichés.

A **cliché** is an overused, worn-out expression that has lost its capacity to communicate effectively. Some comparisons, once clever, have grown trite: *dead as a doornail, gentle as a lamb, straight as an arrow.* If you have heard words over and over again, so has your reader. If you cannot think of a way to rephrase a cliché, delete the phrase entirely.

The word *cliché* is often used to describe both overused expressions and overused words. But a single word cannot really be a cliché, although it can become tiresome and trite. Such words are called **vogue words** by linguists. For a while you hear and see them everywhere; their use is a kind of fad. Like fads, vogue words soon lose their popularity, and then they once again take their place as useful, but not overused, terms. Examples of vogue words are *relevant* which in the early 1970s was used to describe everything from school curricula to political party platforms. Occasionally a perfectly useful phrase will also enjoy a span of overpopularity and become a vogue phrase. For example, during the period following World War II "in our time"—perhaps echoing Churchill's ringing conviction that there would be "peace in our time"—became popular and was overused by the journalists and newscasters of that period. Now the phrase has receded to its former status, and a writer can use it without fear of being thought unoriginal.

The difference between a vogue phrase and a cliché is that although a vogue phrase can return to being a useful part of the language, a cliché cannot. The language loses its punch *(happily ever after, face the music, ripe old age)* and new ways of expressing the ideas are needed. Nevertheless, clichés are not created simply by being repeated or by becoming overly familiar. English is full of word groups that are very common and are frequently used, yet they do not become clichés: We can always say "up and down" and "in and out." Adjectives also fall into certain patterns. We usually say "a tiny blue book" or "a gigantic yellow moon" rather than "a blue, tiny book" or a "yellow, gigantic moon." Such common patterns are not clichés and you should not try to alter them in the search for fresh language.

ANSWERS: EXERCISE 2
1. metaphor
2. mixed metaphor (change "like a clam snapping shut its shell" to "firmly" or another appropriate word or image)
3. personification
4. understatement
5. metaphor
6. onomatopoeia (and perhaps personification)
7. overstatement
8. simile
9. oxymoron
10. irony

379

Like vogue phrases, **proverbs** are also often confused with clichés. However, although both proverbs and clichés are used frequently, they are very different. Proverbs are lean and economical phrases that express a great deal with a few words. A true proverb cannot be shortened or edited. For example, "Don't count your chickens before they hatch" or "a stitch in time saves nine" communicates its message in the most economical way possible. A cliché, on the other hand, can easily be turned into a more direct expression. For instance, "hit the books" translates to "study" and "keep your nose to the grindstone" becomes "work hard." A proverb sums up accumulated experience and observation; a cliché lacks the permanent power of a proverb.

ANSWERS: EXERCISE 3:
Answers will vary.

EXERCISE 3
Revise these clichés. Use the idea in each cliché for a sentence of your own in plain English.

1. If you want a sale, you have to take the bull by the horns.
2. You can't be shrinking violets when it comes to getting a sale.
3. Being aggressive means knocking the socks off prospective buyers with an impressive sales pitch.
4. To stay cool as a cucumber, you have to know your onions.
5. To make customers as happy as a lark, give them a good product and good service.
6. Slowly but surely they realize that you are there to help them.
7. Last but not least, be sure to get the buyers to put their John Hancocks on the dotted line.
8. Her sales pitch hit the nail on the head.
9. She felt ready to climb the ladder of success.
10. Nevertheless, she knew that was easier said than done.

■|| 21d

Avoid artificial language.

Sometimes a beginning writer thinks that using ornate words and complicated sentence structures makes writing impressive. Most experienced writers, on the other hand, work hard to communicate as clearly and directly as they can. These writers do not spend time looking for long, fancy words to explain a point. Instead, they try to make what they are saying as accessible as possible to

380

their readers. Extremely complex ideas or subject areas may require complex terms or phrases to explain them, but in general the simpler the language, the more likely it is to be understood.

1
Avoid pretentious language.

Pretentious language is too showy, calling undue attention to itself with complex sentences and polysyllabic words. College writing does not call for big words used for their own sake. Plain English that communicates clearly is far better than embellished English that makes the reader aware that you are trying to be "fancy" for no reason. "The clearer, the better" is good advice. Overblown words are likely to obscure your message.

> I hate it when he tries ostentatiously to flaunt his accoutrements recently acquired in the haberdashery shop. [*Translation: I hate it when he tries to show off his new clothes.*]

> The raison d'être for my matriculation in this institution of higher learning is the acquisition of a better education. [*Translation:* The reason I am in college is to get a better education.]

2
Avoid unnecessary jargon.

Jargon is specialized vocabulary of a particular group—words that an outsider unfamiliar with this field would not understand. Whether or not a word is considered jargon depends on purpose and audience. For example, when a sportswriter uses words such as *gridiron, sacked, TD,* and *safety,* a football fan understands them with no difficulty. Specialized language evolves in every field: professions, academic disciplines, commerce, even hobbies. However, using jargon unnecessarily is pretentious, showy, and artificial. Instead of communicating, jargon may shut readers out. Whenever you must use jargon for a general audience, be sure to explain the specialized meanings.

ACCEPTABLE SPECIALIZED LANGUAGE

As the lake eutrophicates, it gradually fills until the entire lake will be converted into a terrestrial community. Eutrophic changes (or eutrophication) is the nutritional enrichment of the water, promoting the growth of aquatic plants.
—DAVIS AND SOLOMON, *The World of Biology*

381

Subroutines may call other subroutines. That is, subroutines may be "nested." Nesting can be carried out to any desired depth. You must remember, though, that the RETURN statement in a subroutine will cause the program to return to the statement immediately following the GOSUB statement which the computer executed last.

—MARIO V. FARINA, *Programming in Basic*

These examples show acceptable specialized language. They are from college textbooks which expect that students either know or can decipher the meaning of *eutrophication, eutrophic, subroutines,* and *nesting.*

3
Avoid euphemisms.

The word *euphemism* comes from the Greek meaning "words of good omen" (*eu-,* "good" + *pheme,* "voice"). Euphemisms attempt to avoid the harsh reality of truth by using more pleasant-sounding, "tactful" words. Although they are sometimes necessary for tact in social situations, euphemisms can drain meaning from truthful writing. People use unnecessary euphemisms to describe socially unacceptable behavior: "Johnny has a wonderfully vivid imagination" instead of "Johnny lies." They use euphemisms to hide unpleasant facts: "She is between assignments" instead of "She lost her job." Euphemisms like these fool no one, and they are unlikely to spare feelings.

ANSWERS: EXERCISE 4:
Answers will vary.

EXERCISE 4
Revise each example of pretentious language, jargon, or euphemism.

1. It is of utmost importance that students prioritize their hours in the day in a type of apportionment to fulfill all their academic obligations.
2. She came within the venue of the law enforcement establishment.
3. It is with grave misgivings that I undertake this endeavor to instruct myself in the intricacies of computer programming.
4. Her occupation is domestic engineering.
5. His conversation was full of amusing thoughts concisely expressed with humor.
6. She announced herself to be in favor of terminating the employment of the sales representative.
7. The administrative assistant typed an epistle for his superior.

382

8. She is awaiting a little bundle of joy from heaven.
9. I recall the time in my past when the school I matriculated at was razed by an incendiary event.
10. Their cat passed away and is now reposing in the Slumber Haven Pet Cemetery.

4
Avoid "doublespeak."

Doublespeak is artificial, evasive language. Moreover, it can be grossly unfactual, deceptive, confusing, and self-contradictory. For example, people who strip and sell stolen cars might call themselves "auto dismantlers and recyclers" selling "predismantled, previously-owned parts." A toothpick has been called a "wood interdental stimulator," and a bribe was once described as a "rebate . . . one of the clearest instances of the free market at work." Such language is distorting and dishonest. To use doublespeak is to use words to hide the truth, a highly unethical practice that tries to control people's thoughts. So severe is the doublespeak problem today that the National Council of Teachers of English yearly awards a "Doublespeak Award" for the "best" example of language that is purposely deceptive or grossly unfactual. In so doing, the Council wants to call attention to distorting language. In 1984 the award went to the U.S. State Department for announcing it will no longer use the word *killing* in its official reports about human rights in other countries. *Killing* was replaced with *unlawful or arbitrary deprivation of life*. Such misuses of language have devastating social and political consequences for a free society that seeks truth, rather than evasion, distortion, self-contradiction, and confusion.

5
Avoid bureaucratic language.

Like doublespeak, **bureaucratic language** is distorting. Unlike doublespeak, it is not intended to mislead. Rather, it is carelessly written, stuffy, overblown language.

> You can include a page that also contains an Include instruction. The page including the Include instruction is included when you paginate the document but the included text referred to in its Include instruction is not included.

ALTERNATE EXAMPLES: DOUBLESPEAK

The following verbal machinations have been reported in the *Quarterly Review of Doublespeak*, published by the National Council of Teachers of English.

Sun Oil Company, one of the nations ten largest oil companies, is *not* laying off about forty of the 550 people employed at its headquarters. "We don't characterize it as a layoff," said company spokesman Kurt Van Vlandren. "We're managing our staff resources. Sometimes you manage them up, and sometimes you manage them down."
—*Philadelphia Inquirer,*
19 December 1985

First National Bank of Chicago had $23 million in overdrafts by a currency exchange and gold dealer in Jordan. The overdrafts were classified as "non-performing assets in the bank's fourth-quarter financial statement."
—*Chicago Tribune,* 5 February 1986

The National Transportation Safety Board in FAA Accident Investigation Records calls an airplane crash "controlled flight into terrain."

383

BACKGROUND

P.T. Barnum, the great showman, wanted people to move through his sideshow more quickly than they were doing on their own. The exhibits were too successful, causing people to stay too long and prevent the entry of new paying customers. To solve his problem, Barnum hung a sign in front of a doorway: "This way to the Egress." Eager to see what kind of monster an egress might be, people passed through the door—to find themselves in an alley on the other side of the exit.

The irony here is that the writer seems to be trying to communicate very precisely. Bureaucratic language (or *bureaucratese*, the coined word to describe the style) is marked by jargon, euphemism, and unnecessary complexity. Such writing becomes meaningless because it is evasive, ambiguous, and wordy.

EXERCISE 5

Rewrite into plain English these examples of doublespeak and bureaucratic language.

1. The government will add a user fee to the cost of gasoline.
2. In 1983 when the Soviets shot down Korean Airlines Flight 007, killing all aboard, they said, "The interceptor fight plane of the anti-aircraft defenses fulfilled the order of the command post to stop the flight."
3. For fire safety, all homes must have a "combustion enunciator" to warn people of smoke.
4. At a commercial postal delivery service, the "least-best" drivers are the ones who have poor driving and/or delivery records.
5. That explanation is no longer operative.

ANSWERS: EXERCISE 5:

Answers will vary

22
SPELLING
AND
HYPHENATION

One reason English spelling can be difficult is that English words originate from several sources. Some come from Latin, some from Greek, some from French (the French invaded Britain in the eleventh century). Many words have come into the language recently from technical jargon; nobody spoke of *lasers* or *bytes* thirty years ago. These various origins and the various ways English-speaking people pronounce words make it almost impossible to rely on pronunciation in spelling a word. What you *can* rely on, however, is a system of proofreading, studying, and learning spelling rules. With a little time and effort, English spelling can be mastered.

■‖ 22a
Eliminate careless errors.

Many spelling errors are not *spelling* errors at all. They are the result of illegible handwriting, slips of the pen, or typographical errors. Although you may not be able to change your handwriting, you can make it legible enough so that readers know what words you are writing. Catching "typos" requires careful proofreading. Try these techniques:

LANGUAGE HISTORY
Before the earliest form of English came to be spoken, Britain was the home of the Celts. Their language was the ancestor of modern Welsh and Gaelic, still spoken in parts of Ireland and Scotland. In 55 B.C. Julius Caesar led a successful Roman invasion of Britain. The Romans ruled for about 400 years, leaving to fight barbarians who were attacking the Empire. Although the early Romans had a large impact on local law, roadways, and architecture, they apparently had little impact on the language. Their major contribution is the Latin word for *camp, castra,* which lives on in the names of cities such as *Lancaster* and *Winchester*.

385

1. Read the page *backwards*, from the last sentence to the first. This method forces you to look at the words themselves by depriving you of the sense of a paragraph or sentence.
2. Use a ruler or other device to focus on only one line at a time.

See the manuscript form appendix for advice on correcting typos with proofreaders' marks.

ANSWERS: EXERCISE 1

1. stolen
2. supermarket
3. having
4. melt
5. lemonade
6. circles
7. previous
8. enough

LANGUAGE HISTORY

Soon after the Romans left Britain, three Germanic tribes—the Jutes, the Angles, and the Saxons—began crossing the English Channel. Over a period of about 200 years they drove the Celts into hiding in the mountains of Wales and Scotland. The common language of these Germanic warriors is called Anglo-Saxon or Old English. It was the first native ancestor of modern English. Although Anglo-Saxon does not look or sound much like the language we know, many of our words for basic concepts are descended from it: *faeder (father), sittan (sit), hring (ring), hund (hound), hūs (house),* and *Englaland (England, "land of the Angles").*

At this point, English contained few foreign words. The Anglo-Saxons had picked up a small number of Latin words before migrating to Britain: *wine, cup.* Other Latin words entered Old English through the work of Christian missionaries: *paegel (pail), pott (pot), munuc (monk), catt (cat), leahtric (lettuce), purs (purse), discipul (disciple), son* (musical *sound), schol (school), cometa (comet).*

EXERCISE 1

Proofread this paragraph, using one or both of the methods described above. Eight typos of various sorts occur. Underline each typo and write the correction above it.

I'll never forget the day I thought my car had been stollen. I had just finished an hour-long ordeal in the super market after haveing spend three hours studying. As I stepped out of the 68° air-conditioned store in the 97° Kansas sunshine, I headed for the car as quickly as I could. Not only was I about to mealt, but the two bowls of low-calorie non-dairy whipped topping and the four cans of frozen lemonad were already dripping in the bag. When I reached the spot where I knew I had parked the car, all I saw were three cricles of motor oil, a discarded popsicle stick oozing orange-red goo, and a crumpled ticket from the prevous week's lottery. Not an orange Vega in sight. Do you know what my first thought was? "Who could be fool enogh to steal a '76 Vega?"

◼◼‖ 22b

Train yourself to improve your spelling.

‖ **1**
‖ **Use the dictionary and be alert for new words.**

Not all good spellers automatically know how to spell every word, but most good spellers know when to consult the dictionary for help. If you are unsure of how to spell a word but you know how it starts, look it up in the dictionary. The first spelling listed in most college dictionaries is the *preferred* spelling; use it. (The dictionary will also tell you whether the word can be divided, and if it can be, where to hyphenate it.) If you have no idea of how a word is spelled or if you do not know how to spell the beginning of a word, think of a synonym you can spell and look that word up in a thesaurus. Chances are you will find the original word listed.

Unfamiliar words often cause problems. When you come across key terms in a textbook, highlight or underline them as you read. (Do not underline *all* unfamiliar words; stick to the terms that are essential to the subject.) Then, *after you have finished reading,* memorize the spelling of those words. Writing unfamiliar words on 3 × 5″ cards can be especially helpful, because an isolated word on a card stands out far more clearly than one item on a long list. You may wish to write the word twice on the card, once regularly and once dividing it into parts that will simplify your learning. For example, you may find it easier to spell *perseverate* if you isolate the *sever: per sever ate.*

‖ 2

Use visuals and mnemonic devices to help you spell.

The 3 × 5″ card system described in 22b-1 can also help you learn how to spell familiar words. As you discover words you frequently misspell, print each carefully on a card, highlighting the problem area by using larger print, a different-colored ink, or a pastel highlighter.

democRACY   neCESSary

Mnemonic devices—techniques to improve memory—can also help you to remember the spelling of difficult words. Remember "the principal is your pal" line from high school? That mnemonic has helped many students distinguish between *principle* and *principal* by associating the latter word with a simple, familiar word. Memory techniques allow your brain to do more than simply memorize letters. For example, if you have trouble with the homonyms *stationary* and *stationery* try this: *Station**a**ry* means st**a**nding still, while *station**e**ry* is used to writ**e** on." The *a* and the *e* are the problem letters here, so by associating the *a* in *stationary* with the *a* in the word *stand*, you can remember more easily. The same principle holds for the *e* in *stationery*. Here are two more examples: *an e**mi**grant l**e**aves, and an **i**mmigrant comes **in**; the weather is cle**a**r, and wh**e**ther is wh**a**t*. Try to make up similar mnemonics for words you misspell.

‖ 3

Look for patterns in your misspelled words and keep a spelling chart.

Misspellings usually occur in patterns. Many people, for example, are confused by words containing *ei* or *ie*. You will find it easier to learn the rule for these words than to try to memorize each

INSTRUCTOR'S NOTES

portions *of* the water and grain mixture on *pieces of* hot stone over a fire. The first *raised* breads *were* probably made *by* accident when someone *waited* before baking. People learned a *lesson.* Delayed baking had the *effect* of producing bread *which* was soft and light. The Egyptians realized this was the *right* way *to proceed.* They soon made over fifty different kinds *of* bread. Although wheat was *their principal* grain, they used barley *too.* As *their* baking skills grew, the Egyptians went on *to* invent a *new device:* the oven. *For* all this time, they *were* the only humans *to know* how *to* bake at all. It *seems* the Romans did not begin *to* bake *their* own bread until thousands *of* years had *passed.*

LANGUAGE HISTORY

During the ninth century the Danes (Vikings) attacked Britain in such numbers that by A.D. 878 the English had to give them the eastern half of the country to get peace. These Vikings had a similar language and culture to those of the Anglo-Saxons, so there was easy transference between the two.

The Danes contributed a number of words to English, many of them containing the *sk* sound: *skull, sky, skill, skin, scrape,* and *skirt; band, bull, dirt, down* (feathers), *egg, sister, slaughter, gift, want, awkward, low.* The personal pronouns *they, their,* and *them* also came from the Danes, replacing Anglo-Saxon words. By the year 1000, the Danes had been completely assimilated, but not before they had contributed almost 1,000 words to English.

word separately. Here are some of the many patterns of misspellings:

DOUBLING CONSONANTS	**coming** not *comming* (22d-1)
ADDING SYLLABLES	**athletic** not *atheletic*
DELETING SYLLABLES	**mathematics** not *mathmatics*
USING APOSTROPHES FOR PLURALS	ten **boys** not ten *boy's*
DROPPING FINAL e	**management** not *managment* (22d-1)
RETAINING FINAL e	**debatable** not *debateable* (22d-1)
RETAINING FINAL y	**merriment** not *merryment* (22d-1)
BLENDING SOUNDS	**length** not *lenth*
OMITTING SILENT LETTERS	**wealthy** not *welthy*
TRANSPOSING LETTERS	**relevant** not *revelant*
COMBINING SEPARATE WORDS	**a lot** not *alot* (22c-3)
USING IMPROPER FORMS	the **vanquished** enemy, not the *vanquish* enemy (22h-3)

Not all these patterns correspond to rules listed in the handbook. Patterns are often related simply to memory and not to stated rules. In fact, many people have their own particular misspelling patterns, unlike those of any other writer. Whatever your misspelling patterns, remember that your brain can handle five different *patterns* more easily than fifty-five different *words.* Not only is the number more manageable, but the concept of a pattern makes it easier for your brain to recognize possible misspelled words.

The most effective way to group your spelling errors into patterns is to keep a spelling chart. List on the chart all of the words you misspell, their correct spelling, the problem area, and the corresponding handbook section or pattern. Your chart should be set up like this:

RECOGNIZING DIFFICULT WORDS AND WORD GROUPS   *sp*   22c

INCORRECT	CORRECT	PROBLEM AREA	RULE OR PATTERN
recieve	receive	ie/ei	22d-2
writting	writing	tt/t	22d-1
labratory	laboratory	ra/ora	deleted syllable
immediatly	immediately	tly/tely	22d-1
Febuary	February	ua/rua	missing letter

22c

Solve spelling problems that arise from difficult words and word groups.

1
Recognize homonyms and commonly confused words.

Homonyms are words that sound exactly like others (*its/it's, morning/mourning*). Many other words sound almost alike so they are often confused for each other. The best way to distinguish between homonyms or other commonly confused words is to use mnemonic devices, like ones mentioned in 22b-2.

HOMONYMS AND COMMONLY CONFUSED WORDS

accept	to receive
except	with the exclusion of
advice	recommendation
advise	to recommend
affect	to produce an influence on *(verb)*; an emotional response *(noun)*
effect	result *(noun);* to bring about or cause *(verb)*
aisle	space between rows
isle	island
allude	to make indirect reference to
elude	to avoid
allusion	indirect reference
illusion	false idea, misleading appearance
already	by this time
all ready	fully prepared
altar	sacred platform or place
alter	to change
altogether	thoroughly
all together	everyone or everything in one place

LANGUAGE HISTORY

In 1066 England was invaded yet again. This time the invaders were the Normans. The Normans' ancestors were Vikings, who had settled in France in the eighth and ninth centuries and adopted the local customs and language. Led by William the Conqueror, the Normans overran England in just one year. They killed many of the Saxon nobles and divided up the land among themselves. Norman French was declared the official language: businesses, schools, law courts, and the government used French for the next 200 years. Literature was written in French or Latin; English was considered too barbaric to be used for such an elevated purpose. The Normans never bothered to control what the masses spoke, however, so although French was the official language, English remained the language of daily activity among most people.

Eventually, the Normans were cut off from France. They remained bilingual, but speaking pure French became less important. English began to reappear in schools as well as in business and legal papers. By 1400 Chaucer's *The Canterbury Tales* showed that English was suitable for literature after all.

389

INSTRUCTOR'S NOTES

LANGUAGE HISTORY

During the Renaissance, many scholars believed that English needed an infusion of Greek and Latin words. This need became apparent when translators from the classics to English found there was often no English equivalent for key Greek or Latin words. Others felt that English was not sufficiently elegant for scholarship. Among the borrowings from Latin at that time were *adjacent, allegory, custody, frustrate, genius, history, homocide, include, individual, infancy, legal, limbo, lunatic, mechanical, necessary, nervous, picture, polite, popular,* and *solitary.*

Another part of this deliberate effort to expand English was the borrowing of Greek and Latin roots, prefixes, and suffixes rather than entire words—enabling us, even today, to coin new words for new occasions.

angel	supernatural being, good person
angle	the shape made by joining two straight lines at one end
are	plural form of *to be*
hour	sixty minutes
our	plural form of *my*
ascent	the act of rising or climbing
assent	consent
assistance	help
assistants	helpers
bare	nude, unadorned
bear	to carry; an animal
board	piece of wood
bored	uninterested
breath	air taken in
breathe	to take in air
brake	device for stopping
break	destroy, make into pieces
buy	to purchase
by	next to, through the agency of
canvas	heavy cloth
canvass	to poll
capital	major city
capitol	government building
choose	to pick
chose	past tense of *to choose*
cite	to point out
sight	vision
site	a place
clothes	garments
cloths	pieces of fabric
coarse	rough
course	path; series of lectures
complement	something that completes
compliment	praise, flattery
conscience	sense of morality
conscious	awake, aware
corps	regulated group
corpse	dead body
council	governing body
counsel	advice
dairy	place where milk products are collected, manufactured, and/or sold
diary	personal journal
descent	downward movement
dissent	disagreement

390

RECOGNIZING DIFFICULT WORDS AND WORD GROUPS

dessert	final, sweet course in a meal
desert	to abandon; dry, sandy area
device	a plan; an implement
devise	to create
dominant	commanding, controlling
dominate	to control
die	to lose life; one of a pair of dice
dye	to change the color of something
dyeing	changing the color of something
dying	losing life
elicit	to draw out
illicit	illegal
eminent	prominent
immanent	living within; inherent
imminent	about to happen
envelop	to surround
envelope	container for a letter or other papers
fair	light-skinned; just, honest
fare	money for transportation; food
formally	conventionally, with ceremony
formerly	previously
forth	forward
fourth	number four
gorilla	animal in ape family
guerilla	soldier specializing in unconventional, surprise attacks
hear	to sense sound by ear
here	in this place
heard	past tense of *to hear*
herd	group of animals
hole	opening
whole	complete; an entire thing
human	relating to the species *homo sapiens*
humane	compassionate
its	possessive form of *it*
it's	contraction for *it is*
know	to comprehend
no	negative
later	after a time
latter	second one of two things
lead	heavy metal substance; to guide
led	past tense of *to lead*
lessen	to decrease
lesson	something learned and/or taught
lightning	storm-related electricity
lightening	making lighter

LANGUAGE HISTORY

During the period of colonization, English continued to expand. From the American Indians, we learned *tomahawk, wigwam, squaw,* and place names, such as *Nebraska, Allegheny, Kentucky, Seattle,* and *Dakota.* From the Spanish in the New World: *mustang, ranch, patio, bonanza, rodeo, vigilante, sombrero.* From India: *thug, loot, pajamas, bandana.* From Germany: *kindergarten, semester, delicatessen, frankfurter, hamburger.*

Borrowing continues unabated. Recent borrowings have come from Italian *(casino, malaria, studio);* Spanish *(cigar, canyon, cafeteria);* German *(pumpernickel, iceberg, protein);* Slavic *(pogrom, soviet, robot);* Arabic *(genie, candy, safari);* Hebrew *(hallelujah, kosher);* Persian *(spinach, lilac, bazaar);* Tibeto-Chinese *(tea, ketchup);* and Japanese *(zen, karate).*

Over the centuries, the Anglo-Saxons' vocabulary of 50,000 words has expanded to more than 600,000 words. Irregular spellings is the price we pay for this acquired richness and flexibility.

INSTRUCTOR'S NOTES

	loose	unbound, not tightly fastened
	lose	to misplace
	maybe	perhaps
	may be	might be
	meat	animal flesh
	meet	to encounter
	miner	a person who works in a mine
	minor	under age
	moral	distinguishing right from wrong; the lesson of a fable, story, or event
	morale	attitude or outlook, usually of a group
	of	preposition indicating origin
	off	away from
	passed	past tense of *to pass*
	past	at a previous time
	patience	forbearance
	patients	people under medical care
	peace	absence of fighting
	piece	segment or part of a whole; musical arrangement
	personal	intimate
	personnel	employees
	plain	simple, unadorned
	plane	to shave wood; aircraft
	precede	to come before
	proceed	to continue
	presence	being at hand; attendance at a place or in something
	presents	gifts
	principal	foremost (adjective); administrator of a school (noun)
	principle	moral conviction, basic truth
	quiet	silent, calm
	quite	very
	rain	water drops falling to earth; to fall like rain
	reign	to rule
	rein	strap to guide or control an animal (noun); to guide or control (verb)
	raise	to lift up
	raze	to tear down
	respectfully	with respect
	respectively	in that order
	reverend	title given to clergy; deserving reverence or respect
	reverent	worshipful
	right	correct; opposite of *left*
	rite	ritual
	write	to put words on paper

road	path
rode	past tense of *to ride*
scene	place of an action; segment of a play
seen	viewed
sense	perception, understanding
since	measurement of past time; because
stationary	standing still
stationery	writing paper
straight	unbending
strait	narrow waterway
taught	past tense of *to teach*
taut	tight
than	besides
then	at that time; next
their	possessive form of *they*
there	in that place
they're	contraction for *they are*
through	finished; into and out of
threw	past tense of *to throw*
thorough	complete
to	toward
too	also
two	number following one
track	course, road
tract	pamphlet
waist	midsection of the body
waste	discarded material; to squander, to fail to use up
waive	forgo, renounce
wave	flutter, move back and forth
weak	not strong
week	seven days
weather	climatic condition
whether	if
where	in which place
were	past tense of *to be*
which	one of a group
witch	female sorcerer
whose	possessive form of *who*
who's	contraction for *who is*
your	possessive form of *you*
you're	contraction for *you are*
yore	long past

INSTRUCTOR'S NOTES

ANSWERS: EXERCISE 2

1. our	13. whose
2. council	14. dye
3. passed	15. clothes
4. waste	16. to
5. sites	17. waived
6. their	18. already
7. choose	19. too
8. no	20. to
9. accept	21. all together
10. breathe	22. through
11. no	23. your
12. to	

EXERCISE 2

From each group in parentheses, select the appropriate homonym.

Last week (are, our) county's governing (council, counsel) (passed, past) a new ordinance. As of July 1, no hazardous (waist, waste) dumping (cites, sights, sites) may be built within three miles of any populated area. Local factories will now have to ship (their, there, they're) refuse to another county or (choose, chose) to dispose of it in another way. We will (know, no) longer (accept, except) living in fear of poisons we might (breath, breathe). We are (know, no) longer willing (to, too, two) allow our water to be polluted. For example, a company (who's, whose) main branch is in our county is presently manufacturing (die, dye) for women's (clothes, cloths). The owners might try (to, too, two) have the regulations (waived, waved) for businesses (all ready, already) in existence, but the issue is (to, too, two) serious (to, too, two) permit any exceptions. Would you want a creek mixing red, blue, and green (all together, altogether) running (threw, through) (your, you're) backyard?

2
Know American versus British spellings and other preferred forms.

Many English words have two correct spellings: one British, one American. The variations often involve the following word endings:

AMERICAN		BRITISH	
-or	(vig**or**)	-our	(vig**our**)
-ize	(apolog**ize**)	-ise	(apolog**ise**)
-tion	(connec**tion**)	-xion	(conne**xion**)
-ed	(dream**ed**)	-t	(dream**t**)
-ment	(acknowledg**ment**)	-ement	(acknowledg**ement**)
-led	(reve**led**)	-lled	(reve**lled**)

In the United States, use American spellings. American college dictionaries differ in the ways they show variant spellings. Read your dictonary's introductory pages to find out its method. As a general rule, any entry that is fully defined and not otherwise noted as a variant form is a word's most common (and usually preferred) form. In order to remain consistent, use one dictionary and stick to its preferred forms. Always use the same form throughout a paper.

394

EXERCISE 3

First underline the seven words spelled according to British rules. Then, write the preferred American form above each.

My friends often criticise me for my strange taste in ice cream. My favourite flavor is rum-berry-raisin, a magnificent concoction to be savoured only by the most ardent lovers of ice cream. This delicacy is too precious to be wasted on the ordinary ice cream fancier. To prevent even a drop of it from being spilt on a "Grandma's Little Angel" T-shirt, children should not be allowed near it. I consider this flavor food for the gods. I have travelled miles to taste the best rum-berry-raisin, and my judgement is impeccable. And I have the greatest respect for those who share my taste, because I consider good taste in ice cream to be a reflexion of one's overall character and zest for life.

3
Learn to tell apart words with multiple forms.

Some expressions may be written either as one word or two, depending on meaning:

An **everyday** occurrence is something that happens **every day.**
The guests were there **already** by the time I was **all ready.**
When we were **all together,** there were five of us **altogether.**
We were there **a while** when the host said dinner would be
    awhile longer.
Maybe the main course will be sushi, but it **may be** tofuburgers.
When we went **in to** dinner, he walked **into** the table.

Memorize the two expressions that are always written as two words: *all right* (not *alright*), and *a lot* (not *alot*).

4
Avoid spelling problems based on faulty pronunciation.

Pronunciation can cause spelling problems for a number of reasons. Sometimes people have trouble hearing the differences between two forms of the same word. If you know what form of the word you need for the meaning you want your sentence to deliver, you can decide on the correct spelling. For example, *prejudice* can be a noun, *prejudiced* an adjective ("I am guilty of *prejudice* [noun]

ANSWERS: EXERCISE 3

1. criticize	5. traveled
2. favorite	6. judgment
3. savored	7. reflection
4. spilled	

395

WORDS OFTEN MISSPELLED

Here is a collection of commonly misspelled words. To help you locate the words your students have difficulty with, the lists are organized in these categories: Word Endings (Suffixes), *ei/ie*, Double Consonants, Unstressed Syllables, Silent Letters and Blended Sounds, and Other Commonly Misspelled Words. It's a good idea to assign words for study in groups of 25 at a time.

Word Endings (Suffixes)

acceptable	commitment
accessible	competent
accidentally	competition
accuracy	completely
acreage	confident
actually	consistent
admission	continuous
affectionately	convenient
aggression	coolly
announcement	criticism
apparent	criticize
appearance	cruelty
approximately	curiosity
arguing	decision
argument	definitely
assassination	description
attendance	desirable
barbarous	desperate
basically	despicable
beautiful	
beginning	
beneficial	disastrous
biggest	discussion
bureaucracy	dormitory
business	easily
	elaborately
	entirely
calculator	environment
carrying	equipment
changeable	especially
changing	evidently
characteristic	existence
Christianity	experiment

if I am a *prejudiced* [adjective] person"). *Advice* is a noun, *advise* a verb ("If I *advise* [verb] you, I hope you will take my *advice* [noun]").

Some expressions are often mispronounced. Here are three: **used to,** not *use to;* **supposed to,** not *suppose to;* **should have,** not *should of.*

Imprecise pronunciation often leads to misspelling familiar words. Some people, for example, add an extra syllable to the word *athletic,* spelling it with an extra *e.* On the other hand, some people delete a syllable from the word *privilege,* spelling it without the second *i.*

ask	not	*aks* or *axe*
athlete	not	*athelete*
disastrous	not	*disasterous*
environment	not	*enviorment* or *enviroment*
especially	not	*expecially*
etcetera	not	*eksetera*
February	not	*Febuary*
grievous	not	*grevious*
height	not	*heighth*
mischievous	not	*mischevious*
nuclear	not	*nucular*
prescribe	not	perscribe
privilege	not	privlege
represent	not	*repersent*
strength	not	*strenth*
width	not	*with*

Distinguishing between pronoun forms can also create spelling problems. Always consider the meaning of a pronoun. In general, the form containing an apostrophe is a contraction:

it's	=	*it is*
they're	=	*they are*
who's	=	*who is*
you're	=	*you are*

Note carefully that there is no word *its'*. The forms without contractions are possessive forms of the pronouns:

its	is the possessive form of *it*
their	is the possessive form of *they*
whose	is the possessive form of *who*
your	is the possessive form of *you*

396

22d

Solve spelling problems within words.

1

Spell suffixes (word endings) carefully.

A **suffix** is an ending added to the basic (root) form of a word. For example, suffixes can change a present-tense verb to past tense *(talk, talked)*, an adjective to an adverb *(quick, quickly)*, a verb to a noun *(govern, government)*, and a noun to an adjective *(courage, courageous)*. Spelling problems can arise when different suffixes sound alike or when changes must be made in the base word before the suffix is added.

-d ending

The *-d* ending changes many present-tense verb forms into past tense and past participle forms *(change, changed)*. Spelling problems may arise if the *-d* ending is not clearly pronounced and therefore not written. Although you may hear "use to," write *used to*. Do not count on the way words sound in conversation to guide your spelling.

-able, -ible

The two *-ble* suffixes cause problems primarily because no consistent, reliable rules for their use exist. More words end in *-able: advisable, comfortable, culpable, inalienable, insurmountable, probable, treatable, washable*. Still, some common words end in *-ible: audible, forcible, fusible, irresistible*. The best rule to follow with these two endings is, "When in doubt, look it up."

-ally, -ly

Both *-ally* and *-ly* endings turn words into adverbs. The suffix *-ally* is added to words ending in *ic: logic + ally = logically; tragic + ally = tragically*. The suffix *-ly* is added to adjectives not ending in *ic: quick + ly = quickly; slow + ly = slowly*.

-ance, -ence, -ant, -ent

The *-nce* and *-nt* endings do not occur according to any rule. Some words end in *-ance: compliance, defiance, dissonance, observance, reluctance, resistance*. Other words end in *ence: convenience, correspondence, dissidence, existence, independence, prevalence*.

explanation
extremely
finally
financially
generally
government
governor
guidance
happily
hindrance
hoping
humorous
hungry

hurriedly
hypocrisy
ideally
idiosyncrasy
ignorant
illogical
imaginary
immediately
immensely
incalculable
incidentally
incredible
independent
indispensable
individually
influential
innocuous
insurance
intelligent
interference
irrelevant
irresistible
irritated
likelihood
listening

liveliest
livelihood
lying
magnificent
maintenance
manageable

management
marriage
meanness
mischievous
mysterious
narrative
naturally
necessary
noticeable
noticing
nuisance
numerous
occasionally
occurrence
occurring
official
omission
omitting
opponent

opportunity
opposite
oppression
optimism
ordinarily
originally
particularly
peaceable
peculiar
performance
permanence
permissible
politician
possession
practicality
predominant
preparation
prevalent
prisoner
probably
professor
prominent
pronunciation
publicly
pursuing

397

questionnaire
rarity
reality
realize
really
recession
recommend
referring
regulate
rehearsal
religious
remembrance
repetition
representative
resemblance
ridiculous
scarcity
scenery
secretary
senseless
shining
shrubbery
significant
simply
sincerely

skiing
strenuous
stubbornness
studying

suburban
succession
sufficient
summary
superintendent
supersede
suppress
surely
susceptible
suspicious
swimming
technical
temporary
tendency
tragedy
tremendous
truce
unanimous
unconscious
undoubtedly
usage

using
usually
valuable
various
vegetable
vengeance
violence
visible
writing
written

If a noun ends in *ance*, its adjective form ends in *-ant: compliance, compliant; defiance, defiant; resistance, resistant.* Similarly, if a noun ends in *-ence*, the adjective form ends in *-ent: confidence, confident; convenience, convenient; existence, existent; prevalence, prevalent.* Be careful of the spelling of the word *confident.* The similar word *confidant* is pronounced differently and has an entirely different meaning: *Confident* means "self-assured" and *confidant* means "a person confided in."

-cede, -ceed, -sede

Only one word ends in *-sede: supersede.* Three words end in *-ceed: exceed, proceed,* and *succeed.* All other words whose endings sound like these suffixes end in *-cede:* for example, *accede, concede, intercede, precede.* A very common misspelling involves *proceed:* its noun form drops an *e* from *-ceed* and is spelled *procedure.*

Final e

The basic rule for final *e* is this: drop it before a suffix beginning with a vowel, but retain it if the suffix begins with a consonant. Consider the word *require,* for example. If *-ing* is added to the word, the final *e* is dropped: *requiring.* If, however, *-ment* is added, the final *e* is retained: *requirement.* Other examples include *abate + ment = abatement; like + ly = likely; oblige + ation = obligation; tribe + al = tribal.*

Some words retain final *e* to prevent confusing them with other words. For example, *dye + ing* is *dyeing* to avoid confusion with *dying (die + ing).*

For the few exceptions to the basic rule for final *e,* simply memorize their spelling: *argument, awful, truly,* and *wisdom,* for example.

Final y

When final *y* is preceded by a consonant, change the *y* to *i* before adding a suffix (unless the suffix begins with *i.*) For example, when adding *-ed* to the word *fry,* change the final *y* to *i: fried.* When *-ing* is added to a final *y,* however, the *y* is retained: *frying,* Here are other examples: *comply + ance =* compliance, *comply + ing =* complying; *supply + er = supplier, supply + ing = supplying.* If the final *y* is preceded by a vowel, retain the *y* when you are adding any suffixes: *destroy + er = destroyer, employ + ed = employed, joy + ous = joyous, stay + ing = staying.*

SPELLING PROBLEM WORDS   *sp* 22d

Doubling final consonants

When should you double a final consonant? If a one-syllable word ends in a consonant preceded by a single vowel, then double the final consonant before adding a suffix. For example, if you add *-ing* to the word *flip,* double the *p: flipping.* Here are more examples: *blot, blotted; cram, cramming; pit, pitted; quit, quitting.*

With two-syllable words, an additional rule applies: double the final consonant only if the last syllable is stressed. If you add *-ing* to *refer,* you should double the final consonant: *referring.* However, if you add *-ence,* do not double the final consonant: *reference.* The difference here is in pronunciation. In *referring,* the accent is on the last syllable of *refer,* while in *reference* the accent is on the first syllable. Here are more examples: *abut, abutting; control, controlled; omit, omitting; prefer, preferring.*

2
Know the *ie, ei* rule and exceptions.

The old rhyme for *ie* and *ei* is usually true: "*I* before *e,* except after *c,* or when sounded like *ay,* as in *neighbor* and *weigh.*"

IE   believe, field, grief

EI   ceiling, conceit, eight, neigh, receive, vein

Because there are so few exceptions, they are worth memorizing.

IE   conscience, financier, science, species

EI   counterfeit, either, foreign, forfeit, height, leisure, neither, seize, sleight, weird

WORDS OFTEN MISSPELLED
ei/ie

achievement	forfeit
apiece	height
atheist	leisure
belief	lenient
believed	niece
ceiling	receive
chief	relief
conceited	relieve
conceive	review
conscientious	seize
eighth	view
foreign	weird

Double Consonants

accommodate	equipped
accompanied	fulfill
accomplish	happened
accordion	harass
accustomed	interrupt
address	
annihilate	mirror
appoint	missile
appreciate	occasion
appropriate	occurred
arrest	parallel
bulletin	processes
commercial	quizzes
committee	satellite
controlled	stepped
different	succeed
disappear	suppose
disappoint	surround
disapprove	tyranny
efficient	villain

EXERCISE 4

A. Add *-able* or *-ible* to each word.

1. contempt_____

2. resist_____

3. adore_____

4. believe_____

5. reverse_____

6. adapt_____

7. dispense_____

8. use_____

Answers to Exercise 4 on p. 400

399

ANSWERS: EXERCISE 4

A. 1. contemptible
2. resistible
3. adorable
4. believable
5. reversible
6. adaptable
7. dispensable
8. usable (also useable)

B. 9. relevant
10. attendant
11. variant
12. imminent
13. reliant
14. resistant

C. 15. changeable
16. changing
17. management
18. managing
19. revision
20. revising
21. repulsive
22. repulsion
23. creation
24. creating
25. completely
26. completion
27. notable
28. noting
29. including
30. included

D. 31. playful
32. playing
33. studying
34. studious
35. merriment
36. supplied
37. varying
38. various

E. 39. writing
40. stopped
41. starting
42. trotted
43. beginning
44. opened

F. 45. relief
46. brief
47. deceive
48. niece
49. conceive
50. sleigh
51. pierce
52. freight

B. Add -*ant* or -*ent* to each word.

9. relev_____
10. attend_____
11. vari_____
12. immin_____
13. reli_____
14. resist_____

C. Add the given ending to each word, dropping final *e* as needed.

15. change + able
16. change + ing
17. manage + ment
18. manage + ing
19. revise + ion
20. revise + ing
21. repulse + ive
22. repulse + ion
23. create + ion
24. create + ing
25. complete + ly
26. complete + ion
27. note + able
28. note + ing
29. include + ing
30. include + ed

D. Add the given ending to each word, changing final *y* to *i* as needed.

31. play + ful
32. play + ing
33. study + ing
34. study + ous
35. merry + ment
36. supply + ed
37. vary + ing
38. vary + ous

E. Add the given ending to each word, doubling the final consonant as needed.

39. write + ing
40. stop + ed
41. start + ing
42. trot + ed
43. begin + ing
44. open + ed

F. Fill in the spaces correctly with *ie* or *ei*.

45. rel_____f
46. br_____f
47. dec_____ve
48. n_____ce
49. conc_____ve
50. sl_____gh
51. p_____rce
52. fr_____ght

|| 3
Know how to use prefixes.

Prefixes are syllables placed in front of words, either changing or adding to the word's meaning. For example, the prefixes *un-* and

400

in- turn a word into its opposite (**un***cooperative,* **in***admissible*); *re-* adds the meaning "again" to a word (**re***create,* **re***incarnation*); and *pre-* adds the meaning "before" to a word (**pre***cook,* **pre***destination*). A prefix does not alter the spelling of the word to which it is added: for example, *un + reliable = unreliable; re + locate = relocate.* Some prefixes, however, do require hyphens, as is explained in 22e. For a complete list of prefixes, see 20c.

4
Know how to form plurals.

Plurals in English are formed in a number of different ways, but they are relatively easy to learn because the rules are fairly consistent:

Regular plurals (-s/-es)

In general, add *-s* to form a plural: *leg, legs; desk, desks; elephant, elephants; shoe, shoes.*

If a word ends in *-ch, -s, -sh, -x,* or *-z,* however, adding simply *-s* would cause pronunciation problems. Add *-es* to such words: *beach, beaches; iris, irises; ash, ashes; tax, taxes; topax, topazes.*

Most words ending in *o* become plural with the addition of *-s: alto, altos; radio, radios; cameo, cameos; tobacco, tobaccos.* A few words ending in *o* become plural with the addition of *-es* (those that do so have a consonant before the final *o*): *hero, heroes; tomato, tomatoes; potato, potatoes; veto, vetoes.* A few words ending in *o* preceded by a consonant take either *-s* or *-es* (always be consistent in the form you use): *cargo, cargoes, cargos; volcano, volcanoes, volcanos; tornado, tornadoes, tornados; zero, zeroes, zeros.*

Words ending in f or fe

In general, change *f* to *v* before adding *-s* or *-es: leaf, leaves, loaf, loaves; life, lives; wife, wives.*

Three exceptions to this rule come up often: *belief, beliefs; motif, motifs; safe, safes.* These exceptions avoid confusion with the singular verbs *believes* and *saves* and with the plural noun *motives.*

When a word ends in *ff* or *ffe,* simply add *-s: giraffe, giraffes; staff, staffs.*

Compound words

In general, add *-s* or *-es* at the end of a compound word: *capful, capfuls; player-coach, player-coaches; nurse-midwife, nurse-midwives.* If, however, the major word in the compound is the first word, add the *-s* or *-es* to the first word: *mile per hour, miles per*

WORDS OFTEN MISSPELLED
Unstressed Syllables (including syllables frequently not pronounced)

adolescent	heroes
alcohol	holiday
amateur	hundred
analysis	imagine
angel	imitate
apology	integrate
article	
aspirin	
average	interest
bargain	introduce
boundary	laboratory
cafeteria	liable
calendar	luxury
category	magazine
cemetery	manual
census	mathematics
certain	medicine
challenge	miniature
channel	particle
children	perhaps
chocolate	persuade
chosen	physical
coarsely	pigeon
concentrate	pitiful
controversial	pleasant
	poison
	practical
curious	prepare
decorate	privilege
delicate	propaganda
despair	pumpkin
destroy	purpose
develop	pursue
disease	
dispel	
divide	pursuit
divine	quandary
ecstasy	rebel
embarrass	recognize
enemy	regular
escape	remember
everything	reproduce
exercise	resources
family	restaurant
favorite	sacrifice
grammar	saxophone

(Cont. on p. 404)

WORDS OFTEN MISSPELLED
Silent Letters and Blended Sounds

acquainted	muscle
acquire	pamphlet
condemn	psychology
contradict	quantity
courteous	receipt
crowd	reminisce
dealt	rhythm
descend	safety
distinct	sandwich
empty	schedule
fascinate	sergeant
February	shoulder
foresee	source
foretell	souvenir
gauge	straight
group	strength
gruesome	stretch
guaranteed	strict
guard	technique
initiative	themselves
instead	though
knowledge	thought
length	through
library	trouble
meant	twelfth
mortgage	vacuum

ANSWERS EXERCISE 5

1. vetoes	11. bacteria
2. brothers-in-law	12. heroes
3. wolves	13. spoonfuls
4. district attorneys	14. tomatoes
5. marches	15. shelves
6. stresses	16. comrades-in-arms
7. deer	17. lives
8. teeth	18. trout; trouts
9. children	19. patios
10. selves	20. monkeys

hour; professor emeritus, professor**s** emeritus; sister-in-law, sister**s**-in-law.

Internal changes

Some words change internally to form the plural: *child, children; foot, feet; man, men; mouse, mice; ox, oxen.* Fortunately, these plurals sound so different that they do not cause spelling problems, except in the case of *woman* and *women.* If you remember that these words add *wo-* to *man* and *men,* you should be able to spell them correctly.

Foreign plurals

Latin words ending in *-um* usually form their plurals by changing the *-um* to *-a; curriculum, curricul**a**; datum, data; medium, media; stratum, strat**a**.*

For Latin words ending in *-us,* the plural is *-i: alumnus, alumni; syllabus, syllabi.* Less common Latin forms and words borrowed from other languages usually form their plurals according to the rules of the language: *alumna, alumnae; criterion, criteria; axis, axes; thesis, thes**e**s.*

Plurals retaining singular form

Some words are spelled the same whether they are being used in a singular or plural sense. Usually they are the names of animals or grains: *deer, elk, fish, quail, rice, wheat.*

EXERCISE 5
Form the plurals of these words.

1. veto	11. bacterium
2. brother-in-law	12. hero
3. wolf	13. spoonful
4. district attorney	14. tomato
5. march	15. shelf
6. stress	16. comrade-in-arms
7. deer	17. life
8. tooth	18. trout
9. child	19. patio
10. self	20. monkey

■‖ 22e
Use hyphens correctly.

‖ 1
Learn when and how to divide a word at the end of a line.

Unless the last word on a line would use up most of the right margin of your paper, do not divide it. If you absolutely must divide a word, remember not to divide the last word on the first line of a paper, the last word in a paragraph, or the last word on a page. When you must divide a word, follow these guidelines:

Never divide single-syllable words or very short words. No matter how long a word is, if it has only one syllable or is pronounced as one syllable, do not divide it—for example, *cleansed, drought, screamed, wealth.* Do not divide short words, even ones that have two or more syllables—for example, *area, every, envy.*

Always divide words between syllables. The dictionary listing of a word shows its syllables clearly. The dictionary shows *distinction,* for example, as *dis-tinc-tion,* so you should divide it after the *s* or after the *c,* but nowhere else.

Never leave or carry over only one or two letters. This guideline means that words like *alive* and *ocean* are not divided at all. It also means that a word like *he-li-cop-ter* can be divided after the *i* or the *p,* but not after the *e.*

Follow rules for double consonants. Suffixes (word endings) usually add syllables. If a base word ends in a double consonant, divide the word after the double consonant: *access-ible,* not *acces-sible; success-ful,* not *succes-sful; trespass-ing,* not *trespas-sing.* On the other hand, when you double a consonant only to add a suffix, divide the word between the double consonants: *omit-ting,* not *omitt-ing; regret-table,* not *regrett-able; swim-ming,* not *swimm-ing.*

Never violate pronunciation when you divide words. Not all word endings add pronounceable new syllables. The *-ed* ending, for example, often simply adds a *d* sound to the end of a word. If you divide such a word at the *ed,* a reader will read a syllable that the word's pronunciation does not reflect. For example, *cleared* should not be divided and *compelled* should be divided *com-pelled,* not *compel-led.* Also, do not divide a word like *issue,* because both its syllables are pronounced differently separated than they are together: *is-sue.*

403

BACKGROUND
A single missing hyphen cost U.S. citizens $18.5 million in 1962. Mariner I, a U.S. space exploration rocket, went off course and had to be destroyed. The reason: a missing hyphen in its computer-run flight program.

COORDINATED RESOURCES
Alternate examples and exercises for this chapter are available in the *S & S Workbook for Writers,* Gordon and Troyka. The software program *Blue Pencil,* available from Prentice-Hall, offers students additional practice coordinated with 22e.

Students can practice and test their knowledge of terms, key concepts, and applications of material in this chapter by using the *Study Guide to the S & S Handbook for Writers,* West.

Unstressed syllables (cont.)

sentence	temperature
separate	therefore
several	thorough
sheriff	tobacco
similar	together
sophomore	tomorrow
specimen	typical
sponsor	vitamins
statistics	Wednesday
strategy	woman
surprise	women

Other Commonly Misspelled Words

absence	material
across	mere
always	minutes
among	morning
ancestry	nevertheless
anxiety	nineteen
anywhere	ninety
authentic	ninth
awkward	nuclear
bachelor	omit
benefited	opinion
birthday	paid
compel	parole
consensus	pastime
cylinder	penetrate
defer	pertain
disagree	phase
disturb	prairie
exceed	pretty
expense	prevail
familiar	restaurant
forty	science
forward	speak
furniture	speech
grandeur	temperature
hesitate	until
hypocrite	vicious
intercede	wherever
laid	whether
license	wholly

2

Divide words with prefixes and suffixes correctly.

Most prefixes form **closed words,** or words written as one (*semi* + *sweet* = *semisweet*). When you divide a word that has a prefix of three or more letters, divide after the prefix rather than between other syllables: *mis-understand,* not *misunder-stand; non-conformist,* not *noncon-formist; super-impose,* not *superim-pose.*

Some prefixes must be followed by hyphens separating them from the base word. These prefixes fall into the following categories:

all-, ex-, quasi-, and self-

The prefixes *all-, ex-, quasi-,* and *self-* usually take hyphens: *all-inclusive, all-knowing, ex-husbamd, ex-president, quasi-judicial, quasi-psychological, self-assured, self-confidence.*

Selfish and *selfless* do not have hyphens because in each case *self* is a base word followed by a suffix, *-ish* and *-less,* respectively. Only when *self* is a prefix is it followed by a hyphen. It is never hyphenated when it is a suffix *(herself).*

Proper nouns and numbers

When the main word is a proper noun or a number, the prefix is followed by a hyphen: *all-American, anti-Communist, pro-Republican, pre-1950.*

Compound main words

When the main word is a compound, the prefix is followed by a hyphen: *anti-gun control, mini-baby boom, post-middle age.* Often, such compounds are not very clear, and you should revise, not so much to solve a hyphen problem as to make your meaning unambiguous for readers.

Avoiding confusion

Sometimes it is necessary to hyphenate a prefix in order to avoid confusion in meaning or pronunciation. If a prefix added to a word causes it to look exactly like another word, a hyphen after the prefix should help a reader understand which word you mean. For example, the hyphen in *re-dress* signals a reader that you mean "dress again" rather than "set right" *(redress).*

If the last letter of a prefix is the same as the first letter of the main word, or if adding a prefix results, in three vowels in a row, you may use a hyphen after the prefix: *anti-intellectual, re-*

INSTRUCTOR'S NOTES

ionize, semi-intensive. Some words are commonly spelled without this hyphen— *cooperation, preeminent,* and *reexamine,* for example.

Suspended hyphens

When you use two prefixes with one base word in a sentence, you may choose to write the base word only once, after the second prefix. But follow *both* prefixes with a hyphen: *pre- or post-test, pre- and post-war eras, two- and four-year colleges.* Note that the first hyphen is separated from the next word by a space.

3
Spell compound words correctly.

Many writers, professionals as well as students, have difficulty with compound words. Some terms, called **open compounds,** are written as two words: *cedar shingles, night shift, executive secretary, student union.* In compounds like these, the first term acts as an adjective modifying the second. Do not confuse open compounds with adjective-noun combinations such as *Central America* and *thatched roof.*

Other compounds, called **closed compounds,** are written as one word: *handbook, housewife, northeast, sunburn.*

The third type of compound is known as a **hyphenated compound.** Examples are *comparison-contrast, nurse-practitioner, secretary-treasurer, tractor-trailer.* In general, when terms of compound words are new or are coined for a specific purpose, they are spelled as open compounds. Once their use is widespread, however, they often come to be spelled as closed compounds. For example, the term *mini van* came into the language in the early 1980s. By the middle of the decade, *minivan* was the accepted spelling.

Some compounds require hyphens, either to make the meaning clearer or to make the compound easier to read. When a compound acts as a modifier° *before* a noun, it is usually hyphenated:

fast-paced lecture	soft-sided luggage
long-term commitment	twenty-page report

Usually, that same modifier is not hyphenated if it comes *after* the noun, however.

The lecture seems fast paced.	That luggage is soft sided.
My commitment is long term.	The report was twenty pages.

405

Some familiar terms are unambiguous and easy to understand and so do not require hyphens: for example, *genetic engineering laboratory, health insurance policy, junior high school, state sales tax.*

When the first word in a compound is an *-ly* adverb, when the first word is a comparative° or superlative°, or when the compound is a foreign phrase, the hyphen is omitted: **happily** *married couple*, **better** *fitting dress*, **least** *expected results*, **ex post facto** *law*.

Use a hyphen between the two components of a combined **unit of measurement:** for example, *degree-days, kilowatt-hours, light-years.*

Although most compound titles are not hyphenated *(state senator, vice principal)*, many are. Hyphenated titles usually are nation names, actual double titles, or three-word titles: Anglo-Irish, Italian-American, broker-analyst, ambassador-at-large, father-in-law, forget-me-not.

4
Use hyphens correctly in spelled-out numbers.

Fractions

Use a hyphen between the numerator and denominator of a fraction, unless a hyphen already appears in either or both: *three-hundredths* (3/100), but *two three-hundredths.* (2/300).

Double-digit numbers

Use hyphens between the two components of numbers from twenty-one through ninety-nine only. This rule holds whether those numbers are written alone or as part of larger numbers: *thirty-five, sixty-two, two hundred thirty-five, five hundred sixty-two.*

Combined numbers and words

When numbers and words are combined to form one idea or modifier, use a hyphen between the number and the word: for example, *50-minute class, 3-to-1 odds, 10-kilometer race.* If the word in the modifier is possessive, however, omit the hyphen: *5 days' vacation, 8 hours' pay, 1 week's work.*

ANSWERS: EXERCISE 6
1. pre-World War I
2. Eastern Europeans
3. Anti-Soviet

EXERCISE 6
Write the correct form of the word in parentheses according to the way it is used in the sentence.

1. In (pre World War I) _____ America, a "red scare" gripped the nation.
2. Americans grew suspicious of foreigners, especially Slavs and (Eastern Europeans) _____.

406

VI PUNCTUATION AND MECHANICS

23 *The Period, Question Mark, and Exclamation Point*

24 *The Comma*

25 *The Semicolon*

26 *The Colon*

27 *The Apostrophe*

28 *Quotation Marks*

29 *Other Marks of Punctuation*

30 *Capitals, Italics, Abbreviations, and Numbers*

23

THE PERIOD, QUESTION MARK, AND EXCLAMATION POINT

The period, question mark, and exclamation point are called **end punctuation** because they occur at the end of sentences.

I love you.
I love you!
Do you love me?

■‖ 23a
Use a period at the end of a statement, a mild command, or an indirect question.

Unless a sentence asks a direct question (23c) or issues a strong command or emphatic declaration (23e), it ends with a period.

STATEMENT	A journey of a thousand leagues begins with a single step. —LAO-TSU
MILD COMMAND	Put a gram of boldness into everything you do. —BALTASAR GRACIAN

410

INDIRECT QUESTION   They wondered how many attempts have
                           been made to climb Mt. Everest. [Com-
                           pare with a direct question, which ends
                           in question mark: *How many attempts
                           have been made to climb Mt. Everest?*]

▋ ‖ 23b
Use periods with most abbreviations.

Most **abbreviations** call for periods, but some do not. Typical
abbreviations that include periods and that are acceptable in academic writing include *Dr., Mr., Ms., Mrs., Ph.D., M.D., R.N.,* and
a.m. and *p.m.* with exact times such as *2:15 p.m.* Abbreviations not
requiring periods include: address abbreviations for states, such as
CA and *NY;* names of some organizations and government agencies,
such as *CBS* and *FBI;* and acronyms (initials pronounced as words),
such as *NASA* and *CARE.*

Ms. Yuan, who works at NASA, lectured to Dr. Arias's physics
class yesterday at 9:30 A.M.

For a list of abbreviations and a discussion of their uses, see Chapter 30. ▋‖ PUNCTUATION ALERTS: (1) Abbreviations of academic
degrees should usually be set off with commas. When they follow
city names, abbreviations of states are set off with commas. (2)
When the period of an abbreviation falls at the end of a sentence,
the period serves also to end the sentence. ▋‖

▋ ‖ 23c
Use a question mark after a direct question.

A **direct question** asks a question, in contrast to an **indirect
question,** which reports a question and ends with a period (23a). A
question mark follows a direct question.

What would life be if we had no courage to attempt anything?
                                               —VINCENT VAN GOGH

How many attempts have been made to climb Mt. Everest? [Com-
pare with an indirect question: *They wondered how many attempts have been made to climb Mt. Everest.*]

BIOGRAPHY (P. 410)
Lao-Tsu (also known as Lao-Tse) rivals
his contemporary, Confucius, as an influence on traditional Chinese life. He is
credited with having founded Taoism, a
naturalistic philosophy with millions of
followers. No one is certain of just who
Lao-Tsu was, but the consensus holds
that he was born about 600 B.C. and
lived as a recluse, although he served as
librarian (or treasurer) to the Chou Dy-
nasty, until he left the royal court to
disappear somewhere into the west. He
left behind the *Tao* (meaning "the
way"), his philosophical writings. This
document, a shaper of Far Eastern philosophy, art, and literature for twenty
centuries, deals with the unchanging,
all-inclusive *way* of Nature. However,
the language is imprecise, and over 700
commentaries have been written in an
attempt to explain what Lao-Tsu meant
in the *Tao.*

BIOGRAPHY (P. 410)
Baltasar Gracían y Morales was a major seventeenth-century Spanish author,
famous for his educational and literary
theories and noted as a rhetorician. A
Jesuit whose superiors disapproved of
his writing, Gracián tried to leave the
order, but his petition was denied, and
he was punished for his work.

▌ PUNCTUATION ALERT: Do not combine a question mark with a comma, a period, or an exclamation point. ▐

No   She asked, "How are you?."

Yes   She asked, "How are you?"

Questions in a series are each followed by a question mark, whether or not each question is a complete sentence.

> The mountain climbers wondered whether they would reach the summit. Would they have good weather? Would they avoid accidents? Would everyone stay healthy?

> After the fierce storm had passed, the mountain climbers debated what to do next. Turn back? Move on? Rest for a while?

If a request is phrased as a question, it does not always require a question mark.

> Would you please send me a copy.

> Would you please tell her I called.

▌ 23d

Use a question mark in parentheses for a doubtful date or number.

When **information is unknown or doubtful** according to your very best research, you can use (?).

> Mary Astell, an English author who was born in 1666 (?) and died in 1731, wrote pamphlets on women's rights.

The word *about* is often a graceful substitute for (?) within a sentence: *Mary Astell was born about 1666.*

Use language, not (?), to communicate irony or sarcasm.

No   Suffering from the flu is a delightful (?) experience.

Yes   Suffering from the flu is as pleasant as having a tooth drilled.

▌ 23e

Use an exclamation point to issue a strong command or an emphatic declaration.

A **strong command** gives a very firm order, and an **emphatic declaration** makes a shocking or surprising statement.

412

BACKGROUND

Mary Astell was an English writer and early champion of women's rights. In *A Serious Proposal to the Ladies for the Advancement of Their True and Greatest Interest* (1694–1697) she offered a plan for a women's college, but her goal was not fulfilled and her ideas brought her public ridicule. Your students might be interested in a small sampling of her writing.

> Women are from their very Infancy debarr'd those advantages [of education] with the want of which they are afterwards reproached, and nursed up in those vices with which will hereafter be upbraided them. So partial are Men as to expect Bricks when they afford no straw.
>
> —MARY ASTELL

> The poor lady, having passed the prime of her years in gaiety and company . . . and having all this while been so over-careful of her body, that she had no time to improve her mind, which therefore affords her no safe retreat, now she meets with disappointments abroad, and growing every day more and more sensible that the respect which used to be paid her decays as fast as her beauty.
>
> —MARY ASTELL

Help!

John! Look out behind you!

"Oh no! There's been an accident!" cried my mother.

Mild commands, however, end with a period.

Don't worry about it.

▮ PUNCTUATION ALERT: Do not combine an exclamation point with a comma, a period, or a question mark. ▮

No   "You may not do that again!," ordered my mother.

Yes   "You may not do that again!" ordered my mother.

▮‖ 23f

Do not overuse exclamation points.

In academic writing your choice of words, not exclamation points, is expected to communicate the strength of your message. Reserve exclamation points, therefore, for dialogue or, very rarely, for a short declaration within a longer passage.

What a new face courage puts on everything!
—Ralph Waldo Emerson

Your writing will lose its punch if you use exclamation points more than very rarely, because your reader will think that your judgment of urgency is exaggerated.

No   Mountain climbing can be dangerous! You must learn correct procedures! You must have the proper equipment. Take rope! Wear spiked boots! Carry special picks designed for mountaineering.

Yes   Mountain climbing can be dangerous. Without knowing correct procedures, climbers quickly can turn an outing into a disaster. Absolute necessities for anyone mountaineering include rope, spiked boots, and special picks.

Similarly, use language, not (!), to communicate amazement or sarcasm.

No   At 29,141 feet (!), Mt. Everest is the world's highest mountain.

Yes   At a majestically staggering 29,141 feet, Mt. Everest is the world's highest mountain.

413

COORDINATED RESOURCES
Alternate examples and exercises for this chapter are available in the *S & S Workbook for Writers,* Gordon and Troyka.

The software program *Blue Pencil,* available from Prentice-Hall, offers students additional practice coordinated with this chapter.

Students can practice and test their knowledge of terms, key concepts, and applications of material in this chapter by using the *Study Guide to the S & S Handbook for Writers,* West.

ANSWERS: EXERCISE 1

1. "When will women be encouraged to serve?" many people asked.
2. During World War II, the Women's Army Corps, known as the WACs, was established.
3. Over 100,000 women became WACs. (! is acceptable)
4. Jeanne M. Holm, a native of Portland, OR, moved up through the ranks and became a captain.
5. Correct
6. After World War II, she joined the U.S. Air Force and began to increase women's career opportunities.
7. She became Director of Women and fought to revise policies that discriminated against women
8. Soon she was promoted to major. (! is acceptable)
9. In 1980, Major Holm had the pleasure of watching as about 200 women received active commissions upon graduation from military academies.
10. Women now serve in every branch of the American armed services. Some people wonder if women will ever be given combat duty.

ANSWERS: EXERCISE 2

During World War II, U.S. soldiers' mail was censored. Specially trained people read the mail. Many people wanted to know why this was necessary. The censors had to make sure that no military information was disclosed. Return addresses often read "Somewhere in the Pacific Area" to keep strategic positions secret. Have you ever heard the story about the soldier who could not write his sweetheart for many months but finally had time? He wrote her a long letter explaining the delay and telling her that he loved her very much. All the woman received, however, was a tiny slip of paper that read: "Your boyfriend is fine. He loves you. He also talks too much! Sincerely, The Censor."

EXERCISE 1

Insert any needed periods, question marks, and exclamation points. Also, delete any unneeded ones.

EXAMPLE   Until World War II, few women were in the US military!
Until World War II, few women were in the U.S. military.

1. "When will women be encouraged to serve" many people asked.
2. During World War II, the Women's Army Corps, known as the WACs (!), was established.
3. Over 100,000 women became WACs!
4. Jeanne M Holm, a native of Portland, OR., moved up through the ranks and became a captain!
5. Captain Holm commanded a women's training regiment.
6. After World War II, she joined the US Air Force and began to increase women's career opportunities.
7. She became Director of Women and fought (?) to revise policies that discriminated (!) against women
8. Soon she was promoted to major!
9. In 1980, Major Holm had the pleasure of watching as 200 (?) women received active commissions upon graduation from military academies.
10. Women now serve in every branch of the American armed services. Some people wonder if women will ever be given combat duty?

EXERCISE 2

Insert needed periods, question marks, and exclamation points.

During World War II, US soldiers' mail was censored Specially trained people read the mail Many people wanted to know why this was necessary The censors had to make sure that no military information was disclosed Return addresses often read "Somewhere in the Pacific Area" to keep strategic positions secret Have you ever heard the story about the soldier who could not write his sweetheart for many months but finally had time He wrote her a long letter explaining the delay and telling her that he loved her very much All the woman received, however, was a tiny slip of paper that read: "Your boyfriend is fine He loves you He also talks too much Sincerely, The Censor."

414

24

THE COMMA

The comma is the most frequently used mark of punctuation, occurring twice as often as all other marks of punctuation combined. Rules for comma use abound because the comma *must* be used in certain places, it *must not* be used in other places, and it is *optional* in still other places. To help you sort through the various rules and get an overview of the uses of the comma, here is a summary of the material covered in this chapter.

AN OVERVIEW OF THE USES OF THE COMMA

Section 24a Comma before coordinating conjunction° linking independent clauses°

Section 24b Comma after an introductory clause°, phrase°, or word

Section 24c Commas to separate items in a series

Section 24d Commas to separate coordinate adjectives°

Section 24e Commas to set off nonrestrictive° (nonessential) elements

Section 24f Commas to set off parenthetical and transitional expressions°, contrasts, words of direct address, and tag questions

Section 24g Commas with quoted words

Section 24h Commas in names, dates, addresses, and numbers

Section 24i Commas to clarify meaning

Section 24j Commas misused or overused

415

TEACHING TIP

A surprising number of students, especially those inexperienced with academic writing, tend to equate writing ability with knowledge of spelling and rules for the comma. (Not all students who have these ideas admit them freely, but often such notions emerge on anonymous questionnaires or in teacher-student conferences.) You might deal with this misperception about comma rules in a variety of ways. First, you can put commas in their place by referring to the writing process, especially the different concerns that occupy a writer during drafting, during revision, and during editing—students can reread Chapters 2 and 3 to refresh their memories about these activities. Second, you can invite students to circle any comma in their writing about which they have a question—or any spot where they have not written a comma and have a question—and to jot the question in the margin. This helps students avoid getting snagged on commas while at the same time being able to get answers to their questions when you return their work. You will likely find that students have used most commas correctly (a fact when pointed out enhances students' confidence) and that you can organize the areas of confusion and thus clarify them for the students. Finally, after students have studied topics such as coordination, subordination, parallelism, and variety and emphasis, you can offer a tutorial review of commas—and students will be happy to discover how much they already know.

The role of the comma is to group and separate sentence parts, helping to create clarity for readers. Consider how hard it is to understand the following paragraph, which contains all the punctuation it needs except commas.

> NO Among publishers typographical errors known as "typos" are an embarrassing fact of life. In spite of careful editing reviews and multiple readings few books are perfect upon publication. Soon after a book reaches the marketplace and reports of errors embarrassments to authors and editors alike start to come in. Everyone laughed therefore although no one thought it was funny when an English textbook was published with this line: "Proofread your writing carefullly."

Here is the same paragraph with commas included.

> YES Among publishers, typographical errors, known as "typos," are an embarrassing fact of life. In spite of careful editing, reviews, and multiple readings, few books are perfect upon publication. Soon after, a book reaches the marketplace, and reports of errors, embarrassments to authors and editors alike, start to come in. Everyone laughed, therefore, although no one thought it was funny, when an English textbook was published with this line: "Proofread your writing carefullly."

In the second paragraph, meaning is clear. Each comma is used for a specific reason according to a comma rule. Be guided by the comma rules, discussed in this chapter, to figure out when to use commas. Be wary of two practices that get inexperienced writers into trouble with commas: (1) As you are writing, do not insert a comma because you happen to pause to think before moving on; (2) as you reread your writing, do not insert commas according to your personal habits of pausing. Although a comma alerts a reader to a slight pause (except in dates and other conventional material), pausing is not a reliable guide for writers, because people's breathing spans, accents, and thinking stretches vary greatly.

■‖ 24a
Use a comma before a coordinating conjunction that links independent clauses.

The **coordinating conjunctions**—*and, but, or, nor, for, so,* and *yet*—can link two or more independent clauses° to create **compound sentences**°. Use a comma before the coordinating conjunction.

416

PATTERN FOR COMMAS WHEN COORDINATING CONJUNCTIONS LINK INDEPENDENT CLAUSES		
Independent clause,	**and** **but** **for** **or** **nor** **so** **yet**	independent clause.

BACKGROUND
A comma once saved a man's life. Czar Alexander III had signed a death warrent reading: "Pardon impossible, to be sent to Siberia." Being sent to Siberia inevitably led to death. However, Czarina Maria Fyodorovna saved the man by altering the message to read: "Pardon, impossible to be sent to Siberia."

The sky was dark gray, **and** the air stilled ominously.

The November morning had just begun, **but** it looked like dusk.

Shopkeepers closed their stores early, **for** they wanted to get home.

Soon high winds would start, **or** thick snow would begin silently.

Farmers had no time to continue harvesting, **nor** could they round up their animals in distant fields.

The firehouse whistle blew four times, **so** everyone knew a blizzard was closing in.

People on the road tried to reach safety, **yet** a few unlucky ones were stranded.

When each independent clause° contains only a few words, writers sometimes omit the comma before the coordinating conjunction.

The storm ended **and** life returned to normal.

▮▮ COMMA CAUTION: Don't put a comma *after* a coordinating conjunction that links independent clauses°. ▮▮

NO   The November morning had just begun **but,** it looked like dusk.

YES   The November morning had just begun, **but** it looked like dusk.

▮▮ COMMA CAUTION: Don't use a comma when a coordinating conjunction links two words, phrases°, or dependent clauses°. (See 24c for information about commas with coordinating conjunctions in a series of three or more words, phrases, or clauses.) ▮▮

NO   Learning a new language demands time, and patience.

YES   Learning a new language demands time and patience.

417

No   Each language has a beauty of its own, and forms of expression which are duplicated nowhere else.

Yes   Each language has a beauty of its own and forms of expression which are duplicated nowhere else.
                                              —MARGARET MEAD, "Unispeak"

▮▌ COMMA CAUTION: To avoid creating a comma splice°, don't use a comma to separate independent clauses unless they are linked by a coordinating conjunction. ▐▮

No   Five inches of snow fell in two hours, one inch of ice built up when the snow turned to freezing rain. [The comma alone is insufficient. A coordinating conjunction must follow when the comma is used here.]

Yes   Five inches of snow fell in two hours, **and** one inch of ice built up when the snow turned to freezing rain. [The co-ordinating conjunction *and* links the two independent clauses.]

Yes   Five inches of snow fell in two hours. One inch of ice built up when the snow turned to freezing rain. [Independent clauses can become two separate sentences.]

No   The weight of the ice broke power lines, consequently, only places with their own generators had electricity. [*Consequently,* a conjunctive adverb°, must be preceded by a semicolon or a period when it comes between two independent clauses.]

Yes   The weight of the ice broke power lines; consequently, only places with their own generators had electricity.

When independent clauses containing other commas are linked by a coordinating conjunction, you can use a semicolon before the coordinating conjunction.

Because temperatures remained low all winter, the snow could not melt until spring; **and** some people wondered when they would see grass again.

EXERCISE 1

Insert commas before coordinating conjunctions that link independent clauses. If a sentence is correct, circle its number.

EXAMPLE   You and I make telephone calls almost every day yet we rarely think about the men and women who keep the telephone system functioning.

You and I make telephone calls almost every day, yet we rarely think about the men and women who keep the telephone system functioning.

418

1. Some people might say that anyone can be a directory assistance operator but only people with patience and a sense of humor can succeed.

2. Some callers whisper so that they can hardly be heard yet others shout commands in angry tones.

3. Callers may speak another language or they may use pedantic words or the latest slang.

4. Some people request a number and then they ask the operator to hold on while they get a pencil or answer the doorbell.

5. Many callers who want to reach a business number do not know the company's exact name nor do they know the address.

6. A few callers require very gentle and tactful treatment for their requests reveal that they have special needs.

7. An elderly woman called and asked the operator to sing "Happy Birthday" to her.

8. The operator lowered her voice and sang for the depressed and lonely sounding woman.

9. One young boy needed help with his homework so he called the operator to ask how to spell *Czechoslovakia*.

10. Operators say that the callers who take the cake are the ones who start cooking and then call an operator for advice about the recipe.

EXERCISE 2

Combine each pair of sentences using the coordinating conjunction shown in parentheses. When necessary, you can rearrange words. Insert commas before coordinating conjunctions that separate independent clauses.

EXAMPLE   Jurors usually believe eyewitness testimony. Eyewitnesses often give unreliable information. (yet)

Jurors usually believe eyewitness testimony, yet eyewitnesses often give unreliable information.

1. Someday you might be a juror or be accused of a crime. It is important to understand the ways in which eyewitnesses can be wrong. (so)

2. Eyewitnesses remember less accurately and completely than they think. They become more convinced and self-assured the more they are asked to repeat their information. (but)

3. One eyewitness viewed a lineup just after having glanced at a photograph on a detective's desk. The eyewitness promptly picked out the person in the picture—who was a suspect in another case and was in jail when the crime the eyewitness saw had taken place. (and)

4. A hypnotized eyewitness may describe the number and pattern of freckles or scars on a mugger's nose. The person who is eventually caught and confesses to the crime has neither freckles nor scars. (yet)

419

INSTRUCTOR'S NOTES

ANSWERS: EXERCISE 1

1. Some people might say that anyone can be a directory assistance operator, but only people with patience and a sense of humor can succeed.

2. Some callers whisper so that they can hardly be heard, yet others shout commands in angry tones.

3. Callers may speak another language, or they may use pedantic words or the latest slang.

4. Some people request a number, and then they ask the operator to hold on while they get a pencil or answer the doorbell.

5. Many callers who want to reach a business number do not know the company's exact name, nor do they know the address.

6. A few callers require very gentle and tactful treatment, for their requests reveal that they have special needs.

7. Correct

8. Correct

9. One young boy needed help with his homework, so he called the operator to ask how to spell Czechoslovakia.

10. Correct

ANSWERS: EXERCISE 2

1. Someday you might be a juror or perhaps be accused of a crime, so it is important to understand the ways in which eyewitnesses can be wrong.

2. Eyewitnesses remember less accurately and completely than they think, but they become more convinced and self-assured the more they are asked to repeat their information.

Continued on p. 420

ANSWERS: EX 2. (CONT.)

3. One eyewitness viewed a lineup just after having glanced at a photograph on a detective's desk, and the eyewitness promptly picked out the person in the picture—who was a suspect in another case and was in jail when the crime the eyewitness saw had taken place.

4. A hypnotized eyewitness may describe the number and pattern of freckles or scars on a mugger's nose, yet the person who is eventually caught and confesses to the crime has neither freckles nor scars.

5. Most eyewitnesses strongly believe what they are saying is true, or they would never go to the trouble of giving information to the police or offering testimony at a trial.

6. After all, it is no treat to watch a crime being committed, nor is it any pleasure to take the witness stand and undergo possible nasty cross-examination.

7. A suspect's family or friends who insist that a suspect was with them often fail to convince a jury, for jurors usually believe the testimony of eyewitnesses.

5. Most eyewitnesses strongly believe what they are saying is true. They would never go to the trouble of giving information to the police or offering testimony at a trial. (or)

6. After all, it is no treat to watch a crime being committed. It is not any pleasure to take the witness stand and undergo possibly nasty cross-examination. (nor)

7. A suspect's family or friends who insist that a suspect was with them often fail to convince a jury. Jurors usually believe the testimony of eyewitnesses. (for)

■|| 24b
Use a comma after an introductory clause, phrase, or word.

When clauses°, phrases°, or words introduce an independent clause°, use a comma to signal the end of the introductory element and the beginning of the independent clause.

PATTERN FOR COMMAS WITH INTRODUCTORY CLAUSES, PHRASES, AND WORDS

Introductory clause,
Introductory phrase, —————independent clause.
Introductory word,

Some writers omit the comma when an introductory element is very short and the sentence is clear without the comma. If you are in doubt, use the comma; it is always correct.

|| 1
Use a comma after an introductory adverb clause.

An adverb clause cannot stand alone as an independent unit because it starts with a subordinating conjunction. (Adverb clauses are discussed in 7e-2.) Subordinating conjunctions include *after, although, because, before, if, since, unless, until, when,* and *where.* When an adverb clause precedes the independent clause, separate the clauses with a comma.

When it comes to eating, you can sometimes help yourself more by helping yourself less.   —RICHARD ARMOUR

Although most of us don't realize it, the foods of the future are already with us.

> —LILA PERL, *Junk Food, Fast Food, Health Food*

When an adverb clause follows the independent clause, do not use a comma unless the adverb clause is long and complex.

The chimney made fearful sounds of protest **as it was invaded by the urgent gusts.**

> —MAYA ANGELOU, *I Know Why the Caged Bird Sings*

Somehow he felt betrayed, **as he had when as a child he grew to discover that his father was dead.**

> —RALPH ELLISON, "Flying Home"

2
Use a comma after an introductory phrase.

A **phrase** is a group of words that cannot stand alone as an independent unit; it lacks a subject, a predicate, or both. Use a comma to set off a phrase that introduces an independent clause.

Next to sugar, salt is the nation's leading food additive. [prepositional phrase°]

> —JANE E. BRODY, Introduction to *Craig Claiborne's Gourmet Diet*

Beginning in infancy, we develop lifelong tastes for sweet and salty foods. [participial phrase°]

To satisfy a craving for ice cream, timid people sometimes brave midnight streets. [infinitive phrase°]

Eating being enjoyable, we tend to eat more than we need for fuel. [absolute phrase°]

3
Use a comma after an introductory word.

Conjunctive adverbs° and **transitional expressions** carry messages of a relationship between ideas in sentences and paragraphs. Transitional expressions include *for example* and *in addition* (complete list on page 84). Conjunctive adverbs include *therefore* and *however* (complete list on page 148). When these introductory words appear at the beginning of a sentence, follow them with a comma.

TEACHING TIP
Some adverbs that double as prepositions are likely to cause confusion when placed before the subject of a sentence unless they are set off by commas. You can advise students to apply common sense to avoid confusion. This issue is discussed fully in 13b.

NO Below the submarine checked the water for mines. [Was something below the submarine?]

YES Below, the submarine checked the water for mines.

NO After the crew expected to escort the president's ship. [Then what?]

YES After, the crew expected to escort the president's ship.

INSTRUCTOR'S NOTES

For example, fructose is fruit sugar, lactose is milk sugar, and maltose is malt sugar.

Therefore, no matter what their names, all sugars are metabolized into blood sugar.

Interjections convey surprise or other emotions. Typical interjections are *well* and *oh*. Interjections are uncommon in academic writing. Most interjections stand alone and are punctuated with an exclamation point. Use a comma after an interjection at the beginning of a sentence. If the interjection is meant to convey strong emotion, you may use an exclamation point after it. If you use an exclamation point, start the first word following it with a capital letter.

Oh, I did not realize you are allergic to cats.

Well, you didn't have to throw the cat outside.

Yes! Your sneezing annoys me.

EXERCISE 3

Insert commas where needed after introductory words, phrases, and clauses. If a sentence is correct, circle its number.

EXAMPLE   Although everyone values a car for transportation few people realize that a car can help them survive danger.

Although everyone values a car for transportation, few people realize that a car can help them survive danger.

'(1) To protect your life in certain life-threatening circumstances your car offers many resources. (2)ᵗSurprisingly it contains many items that can help you survive. (3) For example a car's horn can alert rescuers as far as a mile downwind. (4)ᵗTo dig trenches or throw up an earth screen in a severe storm you can use the flat top of the air cleaner. (5)ᵗ A reservoir of oil is available under the hood. (6) Burned in a hubcap a quart will spew a miniature cloud visible for miles. (7) While some people know that any hose in the car can be used as a siphon to get at gasoline few realize that windshield washer tubing can be used for a life-saving tourniquet. (8) When you need a fire that will not go out for three to four hours you can burn a tire. (9)ᵗIn most situations your car can serve as a bunkhouse. (10) Yes survival experts know that giving people this information saves lives.

ANSWERS: EXERCISE 3

(1) To protect your life in certain life-threatening circumstances, your car offers many resources. (2) Surprisingly, it contains many items that can help you survive. (3) For example, a car's horn can alert rescuers as far as a mile downwind. (4) To dig trenches or throw up an earth screen in a severe storm, you can use the flat top of the air cleaner. (5) A reservoir of oil is available under the hood. (6) Burned in a hubcap, a quart will spew a miniature cloud visible for miles. (7) While some people know that any hose in the car can be used as a siphon to get at gasoline, few realize that windshield washer tubing can be used for a life-saving tourniquet. (8) When you need a fire that will not go out for three to four hours, you can burn a tire. (9) In most situations, your car can serve as a bunkhouse. (10) Yes, survival experts know that giving people this information saves lives.

INSTRUCTOR'S NOTES

EXERCISE 4

Combine each set of sentences into one sentence that starts according to the directions in parentheses. You can add, delete, and rearrange words as needed. Be sure to use commas after introductory elements in the combined sentences.

EXAMPLE   You might be someone who is dieting for weight loss. You likely need to shed poor eating habits along with pounds. (clause beginning *if*)

If you are someone who is dieting for weight loss, you likely need to shed poor eating habits along with pounds.

1. You might want to lose weight very rapidly. Crash diets can endanger your health. (clause beginning *although*)

2. You need to diet wisely. You should begin with information about protein, vitamins, and minerals. (phrase beginning *to diet*)

3. Some dieters skip breakfast. They think they are saving calories. (clause beginning *when*)

4. You start the day with a balanced meal. Your body will soon demand food for energy. (clause beginning *unless*)

5. You have an empty stomach. You are more likely to snack before lunch. (phrase beginning *with*)

6. You might be tempted to eat a morning snack of doughnuts and coffee. You might be tempted at the office. (begin with *for example*)

7. Doughnuts are high in calories and low in nutrition. Other types of junk food are the same. (phrase beginning *along with*)

8. Some dieters like fad diets. Some fad diets consist of only one or two foods. (begin with *unfortunately*)

9. The nutrients in fad diets are very limited. You will weaken your body's ability to function well and fight illness. (clause beginning *because*)

10. Forget shortcuts and quick fixes. Your chances of losing weight and keeping it off are greatly increased. (phrase beginning *without*)

ANSWERS: EXERCISE 4

Answers may vary slightly.

1. Although you might want to lose weight very rapidly, crash diets can endanger your health.

2. To diet wisely, you should begin with information about protein, vitamins, and minerals.

3. When some dieters skip breakfast, they think they are saving calories.

4. Unless you start the day with a balanced meal, your body will soon demand food for energy.

5. With an empty stomach, you are more likely to snack before lunch.

6. For example, you might be tempted to eat a morning snack of doughnuts and coffee at the office.

7. Along with doughnuts, other types of junk food are high in calories and low in nutrition.

8. Unfortunately, some dieters like fad diets which consist of only one or two foods.

9. Because the nutrients in fad diets are very limited, you will weaken your body's ability to function well and fight illness.

10. Without shortcuts and quick fixes, your chances of losing weight and keeping it off are greatly increased.

■‖ 24c

Use commas to separate items in a series.

A **series** is a group of three or more elements—words, phrases, or clauses—that match in grammatical form and in importance in the same sentence.

INSTRUCTOR'S NOTES

COORDINATED RESOURCES

Alternate examples and exercises for this chapter are available in the *S & S Workbook for Writers,* Gordon and Troyka.

Transparency masters are available for many of the screened charts and/or lists in this chapter.

The software program *Blue Pencil,* available from Prentice-Hall, offers students additional practice coordinated with this chapter.

Students can practice and test their knowledge of terms, key concepts, and applications of material in this chapter by using the *Study Guide to the S & S Handbook for Writers,* West.

PATTERN FOR COMMAS IN A SERIES

word, word, and word
word, word, word
phrase, phrase, and phrase
phrase, phrase, phrase
clause, clause, and clause
clause, clause, clause

Many **artists, writers, and composers** have indulged in daydreaming and reverie.

—EUGENE RAUDSEPP, "Daydreaming"

Culture is a way of **thinking, feeling, believing.**

—CLYDE KLUCKHOHN, *Mirror for Man*

A university should be a place **of light, of liberty, and of learning.**

—BENJAMIN DISRAELI

For real recreation I spent my slack afternoons and long evenings **reading, playing Chinese checkers, and writing lies in my diary.**

—PHYLLIS THEROUX

The bearded vulture and the people survive there, the Egyptian flourishes, and the great griffon swarms.

—JOHN D. STEWART, "Vulture Country"

We have been taught **that children develop by ages and stages, that the steps are pretty much the same for everybody, and that to grow out of the limited behavior of childhood,** we must climb them all.

—GAIL SHEEHY, *Passages*

Some writers omit the comma before the coordinating conjunction between the last two items of a series, but many do not. To avoid misleading a reader, always use a comma unless the items in the series are short and the way words are grouped is clear.

In a construction that repeats the coordinating conjunction in a series of three or more words, writers usually omit the commas.

They were experts with hypersensitive powers of **sight and smell and hearing.**

—ALAN MOOREHEAD, "A Most Forgiving Ape"

424

When the items in a series contain commas or other punctuation, or when the items are long and complex, separate them with semicolons instead of commas.

> If it's a bakery, they have to sell cake; if it's a photography shop, they have to develop films; **and** if it's a dry-goods store, they have to sell warm underwear.
> —ART BUCHWALD, "Birth Control for Banks"

Numbered or lettered lists within a sentence are items in a series. Use commas (or semicolons if the items are long) to separate them.

> To file your insurance claim, please enclose (1) a letter requesting payment, (2) a police report about the robbery, and (3) proof of purchase of the items you say are missing.

▍ COMMA CAUTION: Don't use a comma before the first item or after the last item in a series unless a different rule makes it necessary. ▍

YES	If we wanted **to find such a language, outfit it as a universal second language, launch it by satellite,** we could have the world speaking it in a decade. [The comma after *satellite* separates the introductory clause° *If we wanted . . .* from the independent clause°.] —MARGARET MEAD, "Unispeak"
NO	Many artists, writers, and composers, have indulged in daydreaming and reverie.
YES	Many artists, writers, and composers have indulged in daydreaming and reverie.
NO	Such dreamers include, Miró, Debussy, Dostoevsky, and Brahms.
YES	Such dreamers include Miró, Debussy, Dostoevsky, and Brahms.

EXERCISE 5

Insert commas to separate items in series. If a sentence needs no commas, circle its number.

EXAMPLE   Car fumes industrial smoke and jet aircraft exhaust contribute to urban air pollution.

Car fumes, industrial smoke, and jet aircraft exhaust contribute to urban air pollution.

425

ANSWERS: EXERCISE 5

1. Governments, industries, and universities have attempted to find common ground for agreement about pollution control.
2. Experts compile statistics, take photographs, or run experiments to provide evidence about pollution.
3. Some businesspeople apply varying standards, pursue different goals, and offer diverse solutions concerning pollution.
4. Scientists discussing pollution point out that one part pollutant per million is equivalent to one inch in sixteen miles, one minute in two years, one penny in $10,000, or one adult mouthful over a lifetime.
5. Correct
6. A clinic in Florida has treated more than 5,000 birds suffering from illnesses, deformities, and injuries similar to those found in humans exposed to the same pollutants.
7. Many prominent people are trying to combat pollution because they know that sources of pollution are multiplying, that too few people are taking the problem seriously, and that the human race faces a serious threat to its well-being.

1. Governments industries and universities have attempted to find common ground for agreement about pollution control.
2. Experts compile statistics take photographs or run experiments to provide evidence about pollution.
3. Some businesspeople apply varying standards pursue different goals and offer diverse solutions concerning pollution.
4. Scientists discussing pollution point out that one part pollutant per million is equivalent to one inch in sixteen miles one minute in two years one penny in $10,000 or one adult mouthful over a lifetime.
5. Pollution is affecting animals that are suffering from diseases related to human illnesses and are dying in greater numbers than ever before.
6. A clinic in Florida has treated more than 5,000 birds suffering from illnesses deformities and injuries similar to those found in humans exposed to the same pollutants.
7. Many prominent people are trying to combat pollution because they know that sources of pollution are multiplying that too few people are taking the problem seriously and that the human race faces a serious threat to its well-being.

■‖ 24d
Use a comma to separate coordinate adjectives.

Coordinate adjectives are two or more adjectives that equally modify a noun or noun group. Separate coordinate adjectives with commas or coordinating conjunctions.

> **PATTERN FOR COMMAS WITH COORDINATE ADJECTIVES**
>
> **coordinate adjective, coordinate adjective** noun

The **large, restless** crowd waited impatiently for the concert to begin.

Adjectives are coordinate if *and* can be inserted between them or if their order can be reversed without changing the meaning of the sentence. Meaning does not change when the example sentence says *large and restless crowd* or *restless, large crowd*. ▊ COMMA CAUTIONS: (1) Don't put a comma after a final coordinate adjective and the noun it modifies—note that no comma comes between *restless* and *crowd* in the above example. (2) Don't put a comma between adjectives that are not coordinate.▐

The program featured *several new* bands.

426

EXERCISE 6

Insert commas to separate coordinate adjectives. If a sentence needs no commas, circle its number.

EXAMPLE A lively bright chimpanzee named Kanzi can communicate with humans.

A lively, bright chimpanzee named Kanzi can communicate with humans.

1. Kanzi communicates using a keyboard filled with complex geometric symbols.

2. Kanzi was not taught how to use the sophisticated intricate system.

3. The bright curious young chimp quickly and efficiently learned on his own by watching his mother being taught.

4. Kanzi has the most advanced linguistic abilities of any animal on record.

5. Kanzi sometimes can be an exasperating stubborn student who teases his teachers by doing exactly the opposite of what is asked.

6. He is not above giving his infant half-sister a sharp startling pinch if she is getting too much attention.

7. Most of the time, however, Kanzi is a cheerful alert spirited student with remarkable unending desire to learn.

ANSWERS: EXERCISE 6

1. Correct
2. sophisticated, intricate system
3. bright, curious young chimp
4. Correct
5. exasperating, stubborn student
6. sharp, startling pinch
7. cheerful, alert, spirited student

■‖ 24e

Use commas to set off nonrestrictive (nonessential) elements. Don't set off restrictive (essential) elements.

Restrictive and nonrestrictive elements are modifiers°. A **nonrestrictive element** is also called a **nonessential element** because the information it provides about the modified term is "extra." Although the extra information adds texture to the meaning, if a nonrestrictive element is dropped, a reader will still understand the full meaning of the modified term. Nonrestrictive elements are set off with commas.

PATTERN FOR COMMAS WITH NONRESTRICTIVE (NONESSENTIAL) ELEMENTS

Nonrestrictive element, independent clause.

Beginning of independent clause, **nonrestrictive element,** end of independent clause.

Independent clause, **nonrestrictive element.**

TEACHING TIP

The words *restrictive* and *nonrestrictive* are being replaced in many classrooms with the words *essential* and *nonessential*. For this reason, this chapter uses the more grammatically descriptive terms and then gives in parentheses the terms more accessible to nongrammarians. No matter what words you use in your teaching, the concept of restriction is a helpful one for students to understand. To illustrate this concept, you might focus on the differences between the words *the* and *a* in these sentences, as they affect restriction and the role of the commas.

I took the bus, which made many stops, to get here.

I took a bus that made many stops to get here.

INSTRUCTOR'S NOTES

BACKGROUND

The power of the comma was demonstrated at the 1984 Republican National Convention. An item proposed for the party platform read "The Convention opposes any form of tax increase which would hurt the economy." Someone called for the addition of a comma, so that the item would read, "The Convention opposes any form of tax increase, which would hurt the economy."

That comma was a reflection of the conservative economic position of its proposer. In the first version of the sentence, *which* begins a restrictive clause. The author of the proposal was talking only of harmful tax increases and implying that nonharmful increases would be acceptable. In the second version, *which* begins a nonrestrictive clause. This author saw all tax increases as the same—harmful.

An eighteenth-century Englishman, Thomas Sedall grew the largest potato on record. [The nonrestrictive phrase *An eighteenth-century Englishman* adds information about Thomas Sedall, but the information is not essential for a reader to understand which Thomas Sedall is meant.]

Sedall dug the potato, which weighed 18.25 pounds, from his garden in 1795. [The reader can understand what potato is meant without the information about weight in the nonrestrictive clause.]

We can only imagine the reactions of his neighbors, who had never seen so large a potato.

When the nonrestrictive information in these examples is eliminated, the meaning of the modified terms does not change.

> Thomas Sedall grew the largest potato on record.
> Sedall dug the potato from his garden in 1795.
> We can only imagine the reactions of his neighbors.

A **restrictive element** is essential to meaning. Notice what happens to the sentence *Sedall dug the potato, which weighed 18.25 pounds, from his garden in 1795* when we change *the potato* to *a potato* and *which* to *that*:

> Sedall dug a potato that weighed 18.25 pounds from his garden in 1795.

In this sentence, the clause about weight specifies exactly which potato is meant of all the potatoes in the garden: the one weighing 18.25 pounds. The clause *that weighed 18.25 pounds* restricts the meaning of *potato* to one particular potato; it is essential to the meaning of *potato*. The clause is restrictive.

▮▮ COMMA CAUTION: A restrictive element is essential, not extra. Don't set it off from the rest of the sentence. ▮▮

> Scientists **who study food production** experiment with many different growing conditions. [The noun *scientists* is limited by the restrictive element to only those scientists who study food production.]

> Food **grown in the laboratory** is sometimes chemically produced without soil or water. [The noun *food* is limited to include only that grown in the laboratory.]

If you are unsure whether an element is nonrestrictive (non-essential) or restrictive (essential), consider it in the context of the whole sentence. If a term does not fully communicate your message without the modifier, the modifier is probably restrictive. On the other hand, if the modifier adds texture—interesting but not basic for your reader's comprehension—it is very likely a nonrestrictive element.

1
Use commas to set off nonrestrictive clauses and phrases.

Adjective clauses° modify nouns or pronouns and usually begin with *who, whom, that, which, when, where,* or *why.* When adjective clauses are nonrestrictive, set them off with commas.

NONRESTRICTIVE CLAUSES

Farming, **which is a major source of food production,** may not always be dependent on the weather. [Farming in this sentence is not meant to be restricted by *which is a major source of food production,* so the information is not essential and commas are used.]

Someday, food may be grown in places like Death Valley, **where temperatures of 120° have been recorded for 43 consecutive days.** Organic farmers, **who use only natural substances to produce food,** are appalled by the widespread use of chemicals in commercial agriculture.

RESTRICTIVE CLAUSES

Much food **that is canned or frozen** is grown by the same large companies **that process it for consumption.** [The first restrictive clause limits the general word *food* to only food that is canned or frozen; the second one restricts the large companies to only those that process the food for consumption. The information in both cases is essential.]

Cooling on the window might be a peach pie **whose steaming crust was made with bear grease.**
—EDWARD A. HOEY, "More Need for Elbow Room"

A **phrase** is a group of related words without a subject, a predicate, or both. Set nonrestrictive phrases off with commas.

Anyone who can improve a sentence of mine by the omission or placing of a comma is looked upon as my dearest friend.

—GEORGE MOORE

429

QUOTATION ABOUT WRITING
All morning I worked on the proof of one of my poems, and I took out a comma; in the afternoon I put it back.
                                        —OSCAR WILDE

NONRESTRICTIVE PHRASES

Farmers, **using pesticides and fertilizers,** try to enhance their crops' growth. [*Farmers* in this sentence is not meant to be limited by the phrase *using pesticides and fertilizers,* so the information is not essential and commas are used.]

Chemical pollutants affect all life forms, **including people.**

With their potential to harm human life, these chemicals create a serious health hazard.

RESTRICTIVE PHRASES

Farmers **retaining complete control over their land** are very hard to find these days. [The sense of *farmers* in this sentence is meant to be narrowed to only those retaining complete control over their land, so the information is essential.]

Corporations in agribusiness exercise considerable control over their farm investments.

2
Use commas to set off nonrestrictive appositives.

An **appositive** is a word or group of words that renames the noun or noun group preceding it. A **nonrestrictive appositive** is not essential for the identification of what it is renaming; it is set off by commas.

NONRESTRICTIVE APPOSITIVE

The agricultural scientist, **a new breed of farmer,** controls the farming environment so that food can be grown almost anywhere.

Most appositives are nonrestrictive. Once the name of something is given, words renaming it are not usually necessary to specify or limit it even more. In some cases, however, appositives are restrictive and are not set off with commas.

RESTRICTIVE APPOSITIVES

My parents **the farmers** dislike corporate control, but my parents **the investors** expect their shares to earn good dividends. [In the context of this sentence, the appositives *the farmers* and *the investors* specify essential information about what they rename—*my parents*—so they are restrictive and are not set off with commas.]

430

EXERCISE 7

Using your knowledge of restrictive and nonrestrictive clauses and phrases, insert commas as needed.

EXAMPLE   Farming which people developed about 10,000 years ago remains a major means of food production for the world's population.

Farming, which people developed about 10,000 years ago, remains a major means of food production for the world's population.

1. Farmers always chose seeds from the plants that were the strongest and most productive for the next season's crop.
2. In the 1860s, the few plant breeders who understood genetics started crossing varieties within the same species to create hybrids.
3. Modern farming particularly in the United States has become as technological as is the business world.
4. The tangelo a citrus fruit available in many modern markets is an example of such crossbreeding.
5. This fruit is a hybrid cross between two others, the orange and the tangerine.
6. Crossbreeding wheat an important practice in agricultural genetics has produced even more important results.
7. Some strains of wheat supported by the use of chemicals and irrigation yield enough grain to make underdeveloped nations nutritionally self-sufficient.
8. Research into the genetic makeup of plants which is almost as complex as the cellular coding found in humans promises to eliminate world hunger in the twenty-first century.
9. Scientists once limited to crossbreeding within a plant species are now transferring genetic material from one species to another to create new kinds of foods.
10. Scientists having spliced protein genes into potato cells hope to create a "meatato" that will contain the nutritional value of a whole meal.

ANSWERS: EXERCISE 7

1. None [restrictive relative clause]
2. None [restrictive relative clause]
3. Modern farming, particularly in the United States has become as technological as is the business world [nonrestrictive phrase].
4. The tangelo, a citrus fruit available in many modern markets, is an example of such crossbreeding. [nonrestrictive appositive]
5. This fruit is a hybrid cross between two others, the orange and the tangerine. [nonrestrictive appositive]
6. Crossbreeding wheat, an important practice in agricultural genetics, has produced even more important results. [nonrestrictive appositive]
7. Some strains of wheat, supported by the use of chemicals and irrigation, could yield enough grain for underdeveloped nations to feed all their inhabitants. [nonrestrictive participial phrase]
8. Research into the genetic makeup of plants, which is almost as complex as the cellular coding found in humans, promises to eliminate world hunger in the twenty-first century. [nonrestrictive clause]
9. None [restrictive participial phrase]
10. Scientists, having spliced protein genes into potato cells, hope to create a "meatato" that will contain the nutritional value of a whole meal. [nonrestrictive participial phrase]

■|| 24f

Use commas to set off transitional and parenthetical expressions, contrasts, words of direct address, and tag questions.

Words, phrases, or clauses that interrupt a sentence but do not change its essential meaning should be set off, usually with

INSTRUCTOR'S NOTES

commas. (Parentheses or dashes—see Chapter 29—also set material off.)

Conjunctive adverbs such as *however* and *therefore* and **transitional expressions** such as *for example* and *in addition* sometimes express connections within sentences. When they do, they are set off with commas.

> The American midwest, **therefore,** is the world's breadbasket.
> California and Florida are important food producers, **too.**

▌ COMMA CAUTION: When a transitional expression links independent clauses°, use a semicolon or a coordinating conjunction°. A comma alone will create a comma splice. ▌

Parenthetical expressions are "asides," additions to sentences that the writer thinks of as extra.

> American farmers, **according to U.S. government figures,** export more wheat than they sell at home.

Expressions of contrast are set off with commas.

> Feeding the world's population is a serious problem, **but not an intractable one.**
> We must work against world hunger continuously, **not just when emergencies develop.**

Words of direct address and tag questions, too, should be set off with commas.

> Join me, **brothers and sisters of one world,** to end hunger. [direct address]
> Worldwide response to the Ethiopian famine was impressive, **wasn't it?** [tag question]

EXERCISE 8

Add necessary commas to set off transitional, parenthetical, and contrasting elements, words of direct address, and tag questions. If a sentence is correct, circle its number.

EXAMPLE   Malaria according to recent World Health Organization reports is back on the list of epidemic diseases.

Malaria, according to recent World Health Organization reports, is back on the list of epidemic diseases.

1. Malaria is caused by organisms that mosquitoes carry not by malnutrition.

432

2. Almost eliminated in the 1960s to be sure malaria is reappearing in many parts of the world.

3. Mosquitoes are becoming resistant to pesticides not intended for them.

4. Insecticide on the crops originally succeeded in killing most malaria-carrying mosquitoes too.

5. Some mosquitoes survived however because they had developed immunity to the chemicals.

6. The immune mosquitoes sad to say began spreading malaria anew.

7. Agricultural specialists who were trying to solve the problem of malnutrition in underdeveloped nations unintentionally created as serious a problem with malaria didn't they?

 ## 24g

Use commas to set off quoted words from explanatory words.

Use a comma to set off quoted words from short explanations in the same sentence. This rule holds whether the explanatory words come before, between, or after the quoted words.

PATTERNS FOR COMMAS WITH QUOTED WORDS

Explanatory words, "Quoted words."

"Quoted words," explanatory words.

"Quoted words begin," explanatory words, "quoted words continue."

Speaking of ideal love, the poet William Blake wrote, "Love seeketh not itself to please."

"Happy I, that love and am beloved," said William Shakespeare about reciprocated love.

"I love no love," proclaimed poet Mary Coleridge, "but thee."

This is an especially important rule for reporting conversations or other direct discourse. Explanatory words like *she said, they replied,* and *he answered* are called **speaker tags,** and they are always set off from immediately following words of direct discourse in the ways shown in the pattern box.

433

ANSWERS: EXERCISE 8

Answers may vary slightly.

1. Malaria is caused by organisms that mosquitoes carry, not by malnutrition.

2. Almost eliminated in the 1960s, to be sure, malaria is reappearing in many parts of the world.

3. Correct

4. Insecticide on crops originally succeeded in killing most germ-carrying mosquitoes, too.

5. Some mosquitoes survived, however, because they had developed immunity to the chimicals.

6. The immune mosquitoes, sad to say, began spreading malaria anew.

7. Agricultural specialists who were trying to solve malnutrition problems in underdeveloped nations unintentionally created as serious a problem with malaria, didn't they?

BACKGROUND

Here is the complete poem by William Blake quoted in 24g.

The Clod and the Pebble

"Love seeketh not itself to please,
Nor for itself hath any care,
But for another gives its ease,
And builds a Heaven in Hell's despair."

So sung a little Clod of Clay
Trodden with the cattle's feet,
But a Pebble of the brook
Warbled out these metres meet:

"Love seeketh only self to please,
To bind another to its delight,
Joys in another's loss of ease,
And builds a Hell in Heaven's despite."

BACKGROUND

Here is the complete poem by Mary Coleridge quoted in 24g.

*My True Love Hath My Heart
and I Have His*

None ever was in love with me but grief.
    She wooed me from the day that I was born;
She stole my playthings first, the jealous thief,
    And left me there forlorn.

The birds that in my garden would have sung,
    She scared away with here unending moan;
She slew my lovers too when I was young,
    And left me there alone.

Grief, I have cursed thee often—now at last
    To hate the name I am no longer free;
Caught in thy bony arms and prisoned fast,
    I love no love but thee.

When explanatory words have *that* just before the quoted words, however, do not use a comma after *that*.

Shakespeare also wrote that "Love's not Time's fool."
Shaw quipped that "Love is a gross exaggeration of the difference between one person and everybody else."

For information about capitalization in quotations, see 30c.

▌▌ COMMA CAUTION: When quoted words end with a question mark or an exclamation point, keep that punctuation even if explanatory words follow. ▐█

QUOTED WORDS	"O, Romeo! Romeo!"
NO	"O, Romeo! Romeo!," called Juliet as she stood at her window.
NO	"O, Romeo! Romeo," called Juliet as she stood at her window.
YES	"O, Romeo! Romeo!" called Juliet as she stood at her window.

QUOTED WORDS	"Wherefore art thou Romeo?"
NO	"Wherefore art thou Romeo?," continued Juliet as she yearned for her new-found love.
NO	"Wherefore art thou Romeo," continued Juliet as she yearned for her new-found love.
YES	"Wherefore art thou Romeo?" continued Juliet as she yearned for her new-found love.

EXERCISE 9

Punctuate the following dialogue correctly. If a sentence is correct, circle its number.

EXAMPLE "Has anyone called an ambulance?," shouted a bystander at the scene of an accident.

"Has anyone called an ambulance?" shouted a bystander at the scene of an accident.

434

1. "Let me through" said a man who was trying to push into the crowd.
2. A woman close to the victim said "First we have to loosen his collar and belt."
3. "I've had first-aid training! I'll do it" exclaimed the man.
4. "Excuse me" said the woman, tapping his shoulder.
5. "When you get to the part in your training where you call a doctor" she said "don't bother. I'm already here."

■‖ 24h
Use commas in dates, names, addresses, and numbers according to accepted practice.

When you write dates, names, and numbers, be sure to use commas according to accepted practice.

RULES FOR COMMAS WITH DATES

1. Use a comma between the date and the year: **July 20, 1969.**
2. Use a comma between the day and the date: **Sunday, July 20, 1969**
3. Within a sentence, use commas after the day *and* the year in a full date.

   Everyone wanted to be near a television set on **July 20, 1969,** to watch Armstrong emerge from the lunar landing module.

4. Don't use a comma in a date that contains the month with only a day or a year or that contains only the season and year.

   The major news story during **July 1969** was the moon landing; news coverage was especially heavy on **July 21.**

5. An inverted date takes no commas: **20 July 1969.**

   People stayed near their television sets on **20 July 1969** to watch the moon landing.

ANSWERS: EXERCISE 9

1. "Let me through," said a man who was trying to push into the crowd.
2. A woman close to the victim said, "First we have to loosen his collar and belt."
3. "I've had first-aid training! I'll do it!" exclaimed the man.
4. "Excuse me," said the woman, tapping his shoulder.
5. "When you get to the part in your training where you call a doctor," she said, "don't bother. I'm already here."

435

RULES FOR COMMAS WITH NAMES, PLACES, AND ADDRESSES

1. When an abbreviated title (Jr., M.D., Ph.D.) comes after a person's name, use a comma between the name and the title—**Rosa Gonzales, M.D.**—and also after the title if it is followed by the rest of the sentence:

   The jury heard the expert testimony of **Rosa Gonzales, M.D.,** last week.

2. When you invert a person's name, use a comma to separate the last name from the first: **Troyka, David.**

3. Use a comma between a city and state: **Philadelphia, Pennsylvania.** In a sentence, use a comma after the state, as well:

   The Liberty Bell has been on display in **Philadelphia, Pennsylvania,** for many years.

4. When you write a complete address as part of a sentence, use a comma to separate all the items, with the exception of the zip code. The zip code follows the state after a space without a comma. A comma does not follow the zip code.

   I wrote to Mr. U. Lem, 10-01 Rule Road, Englewood Cliffs, New Jersey 07632 for the instruction manual.

RULES FOR COMMAS WITH LETTERS

1. For the opening of an informal letter, use a comma: **Dear Betty,**
   (The opening of a business or formal letter takes a colon.)

2. For the close of a letter, use a comma: **Sincerely yours, Love, Best regards, Very truly yours,**

RULES FOR COMMAS WITH NUMBERS

1. Counting from the right, put a comma after every three digits in numbers over four digits: **72,867** **156,567,066**

2. In a number of four digits, a comma is optional for money, distance, and most other measurements and amounts as long as you use a consistent style within a given piece of writing.

$1776	$1,776
1776 miles	1,776 miles
1776 hours	1,776 hours
1776 cartons	1,776 cartons
1776 potatoes	1,776 potatoes

3. Don't use a comma for a four-digit year—**1990** (but **25,000 B.C.**); in an address of four digits or more—**12161 Dean Drive;** or in a page number of four digits or more—**see page 1338.**

4. Use a comma to separate related measurements written as words: **five feet, four inches**

5. Use a comma to separate a scene from an act in a play: **Act II, scene iv**

6. Use a comma to separate a reference to a page from a reference to a line: **page 10, line 6**

EXERCISE 10

Insert commas where they are needed. If a sentence is correct, circle its number.

EXAMPLE Perhaps Eden Texas offers people an earthly paradise.

Perhaps Eden, Texas, offers people an earthly paradise.

1. Eden Texas lies 165 miles north of San Antonio Texas and has a population of 1400.

2. A researcher reported in the summer of 1983 that there are 16 Edens listed in the zip code book.

3. Eden Prairie Minnesota must be an attractive spot, for its population soared between January 1 1970 and January 1 1980 from 6938 to 16263.

ANSWERS: EXERCISE 10

1. Eden, Texas, lies 165 miles north of San Antonio, Texas, and has a population of 1,400 [or 1400].

2. Correct

3. Eden Prairie, Minnesota, must be an attractive spot, for its population soared between January 1, 1970, and January 1, 1980, from 6,938 [or 6938] to 16,263.

4. Correct

5. The citizens of Edenton, North Carolina, publish a brochure saying their town is the "South's Prettiest Town."

6. The brochure reports that the town is 135 miles from Raleigh, North Carolina, and has a population of 5,264 [or 5264].

7. You can explore all the Edens by visiting them alphabetically throughout the United States—from Eden, Arkansas, to Eden, Wyoming.

4. The people of North Carolina's Edenton used a slight variation of the Eden name.

5. The citizens of Edenton North Carolina publish a brochure saying their town is the "South's Prettiest Town."

6. The brochure reports that the town is 135 miles from Raleigh North Carolina and has a population of 5264.

7. You can explore all the Edens by visiting them alphabetically throughout the United States from Eden Arkansas to Eden Wyoming.

■‖ 24i

Use commas to clarify meaning.

Sometimes you will need to use a comma to clarify the meaning of a sentence, even though no other rule calls for one.

No	Of the gymnastic team's twenty five were injured.
Yes	Of the gymnastic team's twenty, five were injured.
No	Those who can practice many hours a day.
Yes	Those who can, practice many hours a day.
No	George dressed and performed for the sellout crowd.
Yes	George dressed, and performed for the sellout crowd.

ANSWERS: EXERCISE 11

1. Using specially prepared tape, recorders communicate hidden messages to listeners.

2. Some people who want to, learn supposedly without effort by listening to the tape.

3. Correct

4. Of the twenty, nine reported pilferage had decreased by about 37 percent.

5. Correct

EXERCISE 11

Insert commas to prevent misreading. If a sentence is correct, circle its number.

EXAMPLE   Though controversial subliminal learning appeals to many people.
Though controversial, subliminal learning appeals to many people.

1. Using specially prepared tape recorders communicate hidden messages to listeners.

2. Some people who want to learn supposedly without effort by listening to the tape.

3. To prevent shoplifting, twenty major department stores started using subliminal tapes.

4. Of the twenty nine reported pilferage had decreased by about 37 percent.

5. Many people worry that governments or businesses might use subliminal learning to control people against their wills.

24j

Avoid misusing the comma.

Don't overuse commas by inserting them where they don't belong. Common misuses are discussed throughout this chapter, signaled by COMMA CAUTION. A summary list of comma cautions begins on page 440.

Besides the misuses of commas listed in the cautions, writers sometimes unnecessarily separate major sentence parts with commas.

No   Orville and Wilbur Wright, made their first successful airplane flights on December 17, 1903. [As a rule, don't let a comma separate a subject from its verb.]

Yes   Orville and Wilbur Wright made their first successful airplane flights on December 17, 1903.

No   These inventors enthusiastically tackled, the problems of powered flight and aerodynamics. [As a rule, don't let a comma separate a verb from its object.]

Yes   These inventors enthusiastically tackled the problems of powered flight and aerodynamics.

No   Flying has become, both an important industry and a popular hobby. [As a rule, don't let a comma separate a verb from its complement.]

Yes   Flying has become both an important industry and a popular hobby.

No   Airplane hobbyists visit Kitty Hawk's flight museum from, all over the world. [As a rule, don't separate a preposition from its object.]

Yes   Airplane hobbyists travel to Kitty Hawk's flight museum from all over the world.

Clauses and phrases that function as subjects, objects, or complements can be confusing. They may look like adjective clauses° or adverb clauses° or phrases°—modifiers—that should be set off with commas. When a clause or a phrase is doing the work of a noun, though, don't set it off. (See 7e-2 for a discussion about noun clauses.)

ANSWERS: EXERCISE 13 (p. 442)
(1) In the United States, [*insert: introductory phrase*] disastrous tornadoes, [*insert: series of words*] hurricanes, [*insert: series of words*] floods, [*insert: series of words*] fires, [*insert: series of words*], earthquakes, [*insert: series of words*] and volcanic eruptions [*omit: not after final series item; not between a subject and verb*] cause yearly damage estimated up to $7 billion of insured property. (2) In addition, [*insert transitional expression*] such dangerous, [*insert: coordinate adjectives*] destructive catastrophes have killed thousands of people [*omit: not between two phrases linked by a coordinating conjunction*] and left other thousands homeless in the past twenty years. (3) In spite of such devastation, [*keep: introductory phrase*] most communities hit by a disaster [*omit: modifier is restrictive; not between a subject and verb*] rebuild within one or two years. (4) "People bend," [*insert:*

Continued p. 440

INSTRUCTOR'S NOTES

ANSWERS: CONT:
P. 442

quoted words] according to one leader of
the American Red Cross, *[insert: quoted
words]* "but they do not break." (5) Nevertheless, *[keep: introductory transitional expression]* one place *[omit: restrictive clause]* that never recovered
[omit: restrictive clause] is Baytown, *[in-
sert: between city and state]* Texas,
*[keep: conventional after state in city–
state name; nonrestrictive clause]* which
was hit by hurricane Alicia in 1 *[omit:
not in a four-digit year]* 983. (6) The
wreckage was so complete that the federal government declared it unsafe, *[in-
sert: series of phrases]* purchased the
land from its residents, *[insert: series of
phrases]* and created a park. (7) Compared with many other countries, *[in-
sert: introductory phrase]* the United
States handles catastrophes well, *[in-
sert: open parenthetical transition]* however, *[insert: close parenthetical transi-
tion]* because of modern *[keep:
coordinate adjectives]* expertly coordinated systems for early warning *[omit:
not between two phrases linked by a coordinating conjunction]* and for emergency medical care. (8) Although hurricanes alone killed 1947 people in the
United States between 1940 *[omit: not
between two nouns—years—joined by a
coordinating conjunction]* and 1985,
*[keep: end of introductory subordinate
clause]* a single cyclone that struck
Bangladesh in 1970 *[omit: not after a
year by itself, unless another rule makes
it necessary; ends restrictive clause]*
killed 300, *[insert: number of six digits]*
000 people. (9) What surprised some
people, *[omit: do not separate subject
noun clause from verb]* was that anyone
survived the cyclone.

No   What appeals to many people about flying, is the pan-
oramic views. [The noun clause functions here as the
sentence subject. No comma should separate it from
the verb.]

YES   What appeals to many people about flying is the panora-
mic views.

No   Hang gliders try, to find strong updrafts for long flights.
[The infinitive phrase° functions as an object. No comma
should separate it from the verb.]

YES   Hang gliders try to find strong updrafts for long flights.

No   Their objectives are, soaring long times and covering
long distances. [The gerund phrases° function as complements. No comma should separate them from the
verb.]

YES   Their objectives are soaring long times and covering long
distances.

Because the comma occurs so frequently, advice against overusing it sometimes clashes with a rule requiring it. In such cases,
follow the rule that calls for the comma.

Kitty Hawk, North Carolina, attracts thousands of tourists each
year. [Although the comma after *Carolina* separates the subject
and verb, using it is required.]

SUMMARY OF COMMA CAUTIONS

1. Don't use a comma *after* a
coordinating conjunction that
links two independent clauses.   See 24a, page 417

2. Don't use a comma when a
coordinating conjunction links
two words, phrases, or
dependent clauses.   See 24a, page 417

3. Don't use a comma to separate
independent clauses unless they
are linked by a coordinating
conjunction.   See 24a, page 418

INSTRUCTOR'S NOTES

4. Don't use a comma *before* the first item or *after* the last item in a series, unless a different rule makes it necessary. See 24c, page 425

5. Don't use a comma after a final coordinate adjective and the noun it modifies. See 24d, page 426

6. Don't use a comma between noncoordinate adjectives. See 24d, page 426

7. Don't set off a restrictive element See 24e, page 428

8. When a transitional exression links independent clauses, use a semicolon or coordinating conjunction rather than a comma. See 24f, page 432

9. When quoted words end with a question mark or an exclamation point, do not substitute a comma, even if explanatory words follow the quotation. See 24g, page 434

10. Don't use commas to separate subjects from their verbs or verbs from their objects or complements See 24j, page 439

ANSWERS: EXERCISE 12

1. Wilbur [omit: coordinating conjunction joining two nouns] and Orville Wright proved that people could fly in 1903.

2. By 1943, [*optional omit: the introductory phrase is short*] U.S. engineers were building rocket planes for research.

3. The planes were built to withstand the intense air pressure, [*omit: clause is restrictive*] that is present at Mach 1, [*omit: joining two infinitive phrases*] and to provide the necessary power to break the sound barrier.

4. Mach 1, [*omit: don't separate subject and verb*] is defined as the speed of sound, [*keep: opens nonrestrictive clause*] which is approximately 738 miles per hour, [*omit: restrictive phrase*] at sea level, [*keep: closes nonrestrictive clause and also separates two independent clauses linked by* "and"] and the term "sound barrier" applies to the resistance, [*omit: participial phrase introduced by* experienced *is restrictive*] experienced by planes as they near the speed of sound.

5. Finally, [*optional keep: one-word transition*] the Bell X-1, [*keep: open nonrestrictive appositive*] the product of many engineering challenges, [*keep: close nonrestrictive appositive*] was perfected.

EXERCISE 12

Some commas have been deliberately misused and overused in these sentences. Delete or add commas as needed.

EXAMPLE   Airplanes started as little more than motorized, double-winged, gliders, and have advanced to supersonic transportation in less than a century.

Airplanes started as little more than motorized, double-winged gliders and have advanced to supersonic transportation in less than a century.

INSTRUCTOR'S NOTES

**ANSWERS: EX 12
(CONT. FROM P. 441)**

6. In 1947, [*optional omit: the introductory phrase is short*] Air Force Captain, [*omit: restrictive appositive*] Charles E. Yeager, [*omit: restrictive appositive*] broke the sound barrier, [*omit: restrictive prepositional phrase*] in a Bell X-1 rocket plane.

7. This, [*omit: do not separate subject and verb*] was the first supersonic flight, [*omit: restrictive phrase*] in history.

8. At first, [*optional omit: the introductory phrase is short*] all supersonic jets were military, [*keep: coordinating conjunction joining two independent clauses*] but Russia initiated commercial supersonic transport (SST), [*omit: contextually restrictive*] in 1968.

9. England and France, [*keep: open parenthetical*] you may remember, [*keep: close parenthetical*] cooperated with each other to build an SST, [*keep: open appositive*] the Concorde.

10. Landings of the Concorde SST at American airports, [*omit: do not separate subject and verb*] has been a topic, [*omit: do not separate verb from object*] of much debate, [*keep: coordinating conjunction joining two independent clauses*] for no one knows, [*omit: do not separate verb from noun clause functioning as direct object*] what long-term damage such planes might inflict on areas around the airports.

NOTE: Answers to Exercise 13 on pp. 439–40

1. Wilbur, and Orville Wright proved that people could fly in 1903.

2. By 1943, U.S. engineers were building rocket planes for research.

3. The planes were built to withstand the intense air pressure, that is present at Mach 1, and to provide the necessary power to break the sound barrier.

4. Mach 1, is defined as the speed of sound, which is approximately 738 miles per hour, at sea level, and the term "sound barrier" applies to the resistance, experienced by planes as they near the speed of sound.

5. Finally, the Bell X-1, the product of many engineering challenges, was perfected.

6. In 1947, Air Force Captain, Charles E. Yeager, broke the sound barrier, in a Bell X-1 rocket plane.

7. This, was the first supersonic flight, in history.

8. At first, all supersonic jets were military, but Russia initiated commercial supersonic transport (SST), in 1968.

9. England and France, you may remember, cooperated with each other to build an SST, the Concorde.

10. Landings of the Concorde SST at American airports, has been a topic, of much debate, for no one knows, what long-term damage such planes might inflict on areas around the airports.

EXERCISE 13

Following the rules in this chapter, insert needed commas and delete misused ones. Some commas may be correct.

(1) In the United States disastrous tornadoes hurricanes floods fires earthquakes and volcanic eruptions, cause yearly damage estimated up to $7 billion of insured property. (2) In addition such dangerous destructive catastrophes have killed thousands of people, and left other thousands homeless in the past twenty years. (3) In spite of such devastation, most communities hit by a disaster, rebuild within one or two years. (4) "People bend" according to one leader of the American Red Cross "but they do not break." (5) Nevertheless, one place, that never recovered, is Baytown Texas, which was hit by hurricane Alicia in 1,983. (6) The wreckage was so complete that the federal government declared it unsafe purchased the land from its residents and created a park. (7) Compared with many other countries the United States handles catastrophes well however because of modern, expertly coordinated systems for early warning, and for emergency medical care. (8) Although hurricanes alone killed 1947 people in the United States between 1940, and 1985, a single cyclone that struck Bangladesh in 1970, killed 300000 people. (9) What surprised some people, was that anyone survived the cyclone.

442

25

THE SEMICOLON

Most often used between two independent clauses°, the **semicolon** communicates greater separation than a comma but less than a period. A semicolon signals to a reader that the material on both sides is closely related in meaning.

■‖ 25a

You can use a semicolon between closely related independent clauses.

When independent clauses are related in meaning, you can separate them with a semicolon instead of a period.

> SEMICOLON PATTERN I
>
> Independent clause ; independent clause.

The choice is yours in relation to the meaning you want your material to deliver. A period signals complete separation between in-

BACKGROUND
The semicolon was used in Classical Greek to indicate a question.

QUOTATION ABOUT WRITING
It is almost always a greater pleasure to come across a semicolon than a period. The period tells you that that is that; if you didn't get all the meaning you wanted or expected, anyway you got all the writer intended to parcel out and now you have to move along. But with a semicolon there, you get a pleasant little feeling of expectancy; there is more to come; read on; it will get clearer.

—LEWIS THOMAS, "Notes on Punctuation"

INSTRUCTOR'S NOTES

QUOTATION ABOUT WRITING

Punctuation contributes to art as well as to correctness, to style as well as to styling. Make it work for you, not just to develop prose that is "clear enough"—not just to prevent confusion—but to help you express yourself, or your characters express themselves. Don't lean on it; don't shy away from it; just *use* it—and in doing so, let it help you convey nuances too subtle for words alone to convey; let it help you evoke effects so delicate that talk would shatter them. And remember that if you frequently use more marks than usual—or fewer than usual—you will call attention to your craft, with the results possibly seeming artful rather than artistic, posturing rather than expressive. Nor do I for a moment suggest that punctuation can, or should, be charged with sole responsibility for effectiveness: descriptive detail, diction, sentence length, sentence rhythm, paragraph structure, timing—these and other elements of style can and must share the load.

—ROBERT M. PIERSON, "Punctuation as Art"

dependent clauses; a semicolon tells readers that the separation is softer.

> Knowledge is not a rock that we inherit from a geological past; it is a living, growing organism constantly in need of nourishment and renewal.
>
> —DANIEL J. BOORSTIN, Librarian of Congress,
> Congressional testimony, February 1986

> Our Constitution is in actual operation; everything appears to promise that it will last; but in this world nothing is certain but death and taxes. —BENJAMIN FRANKLIN

> This powerful sense of history constantly in the making, forever unfinished, is equally tangible in the 365 churches that dot the landscape surrounding the city of Choluda; they rise on the razed sites of an identical number of pre-Columbian temples.
>
> —CARLOS FUENTES, "Mexico"

▌ COMMA CAUTION: Do not use only a comma between independent clauses, or you will create the error called a comma splice (see Chapter 14). ▌

■▌ 25b

Use a semicolon between related independent clauses that contain commas, even if a coordinating conjunction joins the independent clauses.

You will usually use a comma to separate independent clauses linked by a coordinating conjunction *(and, but, or, nor, for, yet, so)*. When the independent clauses already contain commas, however, use a semicolon instead. The semicolon makes plain to your reader where one independent clause ends and the next begins.

SEMICOLON PATTERN II

Independent clause, one that contains commas; coordinating conjunction independent clause.

Independent clause; coordinating conjunction independent clause, containing commas.

Independent clause, one that contains commas; coordinating conjunction independent clause, one that contains commas.

444

The U.S. Fish and Wildlife Service, after conducting its wildlife "census" in 1935, estimated the California condor population to be 60; but the 1985 count numbered only 6.

For anything worth having one must pay the price; and the price is always work, patience, love, self-sacrifice.

—JOHN BURROUGHS

▬‖ 25c

You can use a semicolon when conjunctive adverbs or other transitional expressions connect independent clauses.

Use a semicolon between two independent clauses when the second clause begins with a conjunctive adverb (*therefore, however,* and others, listed on page 148) or other transitional expressions (page 84). Your other option is to use a period, creating two sentences.

SEMICOLON PATTERN III

Independent clause; conjunctive adverb or other transition expression, independent clause.

The average annual rainfall in Death Valley is about two inches; **nevertheless,** hundreds of plant and animal species survive and even thrive there.

Patient photographers have spent years recording desert life cycles; all of us have, **as a result,** watched barren sands flower after a spring storm.

▮‖ COMMA ALERTS: (1) Do not use only a comma between independent clauses connected by a conjunctive adverb or other words of transition, or you will create the error called a comma splice, as explained in Chapter 14. (2) Use a comma *after* a conjunctive adverb or a transitional expression. Some writers omit the comma after short words, such as *then, next, soon.* (3) When you position a conjunctive adverb or a transitional expression somewhere after the first word in an independent clause, set it off with commas. See the example with *as a result,* above. ▮‖

▬‖ 25d

Use a semicolon between long or comma-containing items in a series.

When a sentence contains series of words, phrases°, or clauses°, commas usually separate one item from the next. When

445

COORDINATED RESOURCES

Alternate examples and exercises for this chapter are available in the *S & S Workbook for Writers,* Gordon and Troyka.

Transparency masters are available for many of the screened charts in this chapter.

The software program *Blue Pencil,* available from Prentice-Hall, offers students additional practice coordinated with this chapter.

Students can practice and test their knowledge of terms, key concepts, and applications of material in this chapter by using the *Study Guide to the S & S Handbook for Writers,* West.

the items are long and contain commas for other purposes, you can make your message much easier for readers to understand by using semicolons instead of commas to separate items. The semicolons show exactly where one item ends and the next begins.

> **SEMICOLON PATTERN IV**
>
> Independent clause that includes a series of items, each or all of which contain commas; another item in the series; another item in the series.

Everyone also remembers a few of the observances of childhood— wishing on the first star; looking at the moon over the right shoulder; avoiding the cracks in the sidewalk on the way to school while chanting, "Step on a crack, break your mother's back"; wishing on white horses, on loads of hay, on covered bridges, on red cars; saying quickly, "Bread and butter" when a post or a tree separated you from the friend you were walking with.

—MARGARET MEAD, *A Way of Seeing*

Functioning as assistant chefs, the students chopped onions, green peppers, and parsley; sliced chicken and duck meat into strips; started a delicious-smelling broth simmering; and filled a large, low, long-handled pan with oil before the head chef moved up to the stove.

■‖ 25e
Avoid misusing the semicolon.

1
Don't use a semicolon between a dependent clause and an independent clause.

No   Although the new computers had arrived at the college;
      the computer lab was still being built.

YES   Although the new computers had arrived at the college,
      the computer lab was still being built.

446

2
Don't use a semicolon to introduce a list; use a colon.

No   The newscast featured three stories; the latest pictures of Uranus, a speech by the president, and a series of brush fires in Nevada.

Yes   The newscast featured three major stories: the latest pictures of Uranus, a speech by the president, and a series of brush fires in Nevada.

EXERCISE 1
Insert semicolons where they are needed. If a sentence is correct, circle its number.

Example   The dangers of toxic wastes were first recognized over eight years ago today we face a serious environmental emergency.

The dangers of toxic wastes were first recognized over eight years ago; today we face a serious environmental emergency.

1. In 1980 Congress created a "superfund" of $1.6 billion, this money was earmarked to clean up thousands of dumps which were leaking toxic wastes.
2. The lawmakers' action seemed an excellent way to address the problem, however, the law providing the funds expired in 1985.
3. Meanwhile, fears about toxic wastes continue to grow because each day more and more communities discover that they are living on or near ground that has been contaminated, each day chemicals with names like dioxin, vinyl chloride, PBB, and PCB leach into the ground, each day lead, mercury, and arsenic poisoning threaten more households.
4. The Office of Technology Assessment (OTA) contends that there may be at least 10,000 hazardous-waste sites in the United States, not surprisingly, these dumps pose a serious threat to public health.
5. Cleanup costs, OTA estimates, could reach $100 billion, more than $1,000 per U.S. household.
6. The United States faces other grave environmental risks acid rain, smoggy skies, and lethal gases escaping from industrial plants are all threats to human, animal, and plant life.
7. The disposal of toxic wastes, however, is clearly the most pressing concern.
8. In the handling and production of chemicals, more than 1,500 people have been injured, 135 have died.

ANSWERS: EXERCISE 1
1. billion; this
2. problem; however, the law
3. contaminated; each day / ground; each day
4. United States; not surprisingly, these
5. Correct
6. risks; acid rain
7. Correct
8. injured; 135
9. Correct [*or* others; and each]
10. up; otherwise

447

9. Knowing where to place the blame is difficult because each government agency blames the others, and each administration blames the one before it.

10. Placing blame is less important than cleaning up, otherwise, we will all suffer.

ANSWERS: EXERCISE 2

Answers may vary slightly. Here is one set of possibilities:

1. Some postcards offer colorful views of exotic places; others reproduce famous paintings or portraits of famous persons.

2. On postcard racks today you can find a wide variety of selections; you may find a classic scene from a Bogart film or a giant cactus with sunglasses.

3. There are dinosaurs fighting Martians and great Olympic moments; there are also perennial favorites that say such things as "Greetings from Fargo" or "Having a wonderful time in Hicksville."

4. Postcards have been popular for a long time; however, the so-called "Golden Age of Postcards" lasted from the turn of the century to the Great Depression.

5. Today postcard sales are booming again; for example, in 1983 more than 2.5 billion cards were mailed to Americans, which was an increase of more than 100 million from the previous year.

6. Postcards are a popular means of communication for many reasons; for instance, postcards, costing from 15 cents to $1, represent a bargain.

7. You may also send postcards for practical reasons; they give you a chance to show your friends who are shoveling snow how much you are enjoying the sun.

8. Some rare postcards are extremely valuable; for instance, a signed original by the artist Alphonse Mucha recently sold for $3,000.

EXERCISE 2

Combine each set of sentences into one sentence containing two independent clauses. Use a semicolon between the two clauses. You may omit, add, revise, or rearrange words. More than one answer may be correct.

EXAMPLE   Postcards are more than a means of communication. They are miniature works of art. Some of them can be quite valuable.

Postcards are more than a means of communication; they are miniature works of art, some of them quite valuable.

1. Some postcards offer colorful views of exotic places. Some cards reproduce famous paintings. Others feature portraits of famous persons.

2. On postcard racks today you can find a wide variety of selections. You may find a classic scene from a Bogart film. On the other hand, you may see a giant cactus with sunglasses.

3. There are dinosaurs fighting Martians. There are great Olympic moments. There are also perennial favorites. These perennial favorites say such things as "Greetings from Fargo" or "Having a wonderful time in Hicksville."

4. Postcards have been popular for a long time. However, there was a so-called "Golden Age of Postcards." That lasted from the turn of the century to the Great Depression.

5. Today postcard sales are booming again. For example, in 1983 more than 2.5 billion cards were mailed to Americans. That was an increase of more than 100 million from the previous year.

6. Postcards are a popular means of communication for many reasons. Postcards cost from 15 cents to $1. That represents a bargain.

7. You may also send postcards for practical reasons. They give you a chance to show that you are enjoying the sun. Your friends who are shoveling snow get the message very quickly.

8. Some rare postcards are extremely valuable. A signed original by the artist Alphonse Mucha is a good example. One of these cards recently sold for $3,000.

448

INSTRUCTOR'S NOTES

9. The first postcard was designed in 1869. It was designed by Emmanuel Hermenn. Four years later the U.S. government began issuing specially designed "postal cards." These cards had an illustration on one side and a space for an address and stamp on the other.

EXERCISE 3
Insert needed semicolons in the following sentences, and delete unnecessary ones. If a sentence is correct, circle its number.

1. The sound of Muzak has invaded our banks, supermarkets, and elevators, furthermore, it often assaults our ears when we are placed on hold on a busy telephone line.

2. Muzak plays in government offices, in the White House, in the Pentagon, in Congress, it played during the Olympics, and it even played in the Apollo XI spaceship carrying Neil Armstrong to the moon.

3. The Muzak Corporation, now part of Westinghouse; estimates that its recordings are heard by 80 million people every day, and the company and its affiliates take in more than $150 million annually.

4. Not all listeners appreciate Muzak novelist Vladimir Nabokov, artist Ben Shahn, and composer Philip Glass have used adjectives such as "horrible," "abominable," "offensive," and "tormenting" to describe it.

5. The Muzak system was the creation of an unusual general, George Owen Squier; a West Pointer who devoted much of his army career to science.

6. During World War I, Squier invented a system for transmitting several messages simultaneously over electric power lines, in the era following the war, he took his ideas and patents to the North American Company, a utilities combine.

7. The company backed him in launching Wired Radio, Inc.; a kind of competitor to the booming fad for wireless radio.

8. The company wanted a catchy new name for this product; therefore, they combined the sound of the word "music" with the name of the manufacturer of popular cameras, Kodak.

9. The first customers for Muzak were residents of Cleveland however, a series of experiments in the late 1930s opened a much larger market.

10. These tests proved that Muzak could get more work out of people and animals, in factories, absenteeism was reduced, early departures were curbed, and morale was raised, on farms, cows gave more milk and chickens laid more eggs.

---

9. The first postcard was designed in 1869 by Emmanuel Hermenn; four years later the U.S. government began issuing specially designed "postal cards" with an illustration on one side and a space for an address and stamp on the other.

ANSWERS: EXERCISE 3

1. The sound of Muzak has invaded our banks, supermarkets, and elevators; furthermore, it often assaults our ears when we are placed on hold on a busy telephone line.

2. Muzak plays in government offices, in the White House, in the Pentagon, in Congress; it played during the Olympics; and it even played in the Apollo XI spaceship carrying Neil Armstrong to the moon.

3. The Muzak Corporation, now part of Westinghouse, estimates that its recordings are heard by 80 million people every day; and the company and its affiliates take in more than $150 million annually.

4. Not all listeners appreciate Muzak; novelist Vladimir Nabokov, artist Ben Shahn, and composer Philip Glass have used adjectives such as "horrible," "abominable," "offensive," and "tormenting" to describe it.

5. The Muzak system was the creation of an unusual general, George Owen Squier, a West Pointer who devoted much of his army career to science.

6. During World War I, Squier invented a system for transmitting several messages simultaneously over electric power lines; in the era following the war, he took his ideas and patents to the North American Company, a utilities combine.

Continued on next page.

INSTRUCTOR'S NOTES

ANSWERS: Ex. 3 (cont.).

7. The company backed him in launching Wired Radio, Inc., a kind of competitor to the booming fad for wireless radio.

8. Correct

9. The first customers for Muzak were residents of Cleveland; however, a series of experiments in the late 1930s opened a much larger market.

10. These tests proved that Muzak could get more work out of people and animals; in factories, absenteeism was reduced, early departures were curbed, and morale was raised; on farms, cows gave more milk and chickens laid more eggs.

ANSWERS: EXERCISE 4

1. Our inner clocks help determine our times of elation and depression; they also regulate our times of patience, irritability, precision, and carelessness.

2. We need to understand how these clocks work and what they are; we need to know how they interact and how they can be thrown off schedule.

3. Understanding these principles can help us to organize our lives so that we will be able to maximize performance and pleasure; we will not waste energy fighting the body's natural inclinations.

4. Some valuable facts about the internal time clocks are already known; for example, people are least likely to be alert after they have eaten lunch, and calories consumed at breakfast are less likely to turn to body fat than those eaten at supper.

5. Many people find certain other facts useful; for instance, a high-protein breakfast enhances alertness while a high-carbohydrate supper helps induce sleep.

EXERCISE 4

Combine each set of sentences into one sentence containing two independent clauses. Use a semicolon between the independent clauses. You may omit, add, revise, or rearrange words.

EXAMPLE   Some people live by the clock on the wall. All of us are governed by internal clocks. These clocks regulate hundreds of biological functions.

Some people live by the clock on the wall; however, all of us are governed by internal clocks which regulate hundreds of biological functions.

1. Our inner clocks help determine our times of elation and depression. They also regulate our times of patience and irritability. Our inner clocks also regulate our precision and carelessness.

2. We need to understand how these clocks work. We need to know what they are. We need to know how they interact. We also need to know how they can be thrown off schedule.

3. Understanding these principles can help us to organize our lives. We will be able to maximize performance and pleasure. We will not waste energy fighting the body's natural inclinations.

4. Some valuable facts about the internal time clocks are already known. People are least likely to be alert, for example, after they have eaten lunch. In addition, calories consumed at breakfast are less likely to turn to body fat than those eaten at supper.

5. Many people find certain other facts useful. A high-protein breakfast enhances alertness. A high-carbohydrate supper helps induce sleep.

26
THE COLON

In sentence punctuation, the colon introduces what comes after it: a quotation, a summary or restatement, or a list. The colon has the effect of pointing a bit dramatically to what follows it. The colon has a few special separating functions as well.

■‖ 26a
Use a colon to introduce quotations, summaries, lists.

Use a colon at the end of your words introducing a formal quotation.

COLON PATTERN I

Independent clause containing words that introduce a quotation: "Quoted Words."

451

26a :

TEACHING TIP

To distinguish between the colon and the semicolon, your students may find it helpful to think of the colon as often introducing some kind of an explanation of the preceding clause. In contrast, the semicolon connects equal elements. The explanatory nature of the colon can be seen in these three examples.

A trip to the Galápagos changes you in an essential way: nature, which is everywhere threaded through our complicated lives, becomes more visible and meaningful.

—JOEL MEYEROWITZ, "Galápagos Unretouched"

Sarah Brady, whose husband, White House Press Secretary James Brady, was shot through the head during the assassination attempt on President Reagan, says: "I ask why it is possible for the John Hinckleys of this world to walk into a store, buy a handgun and go out and shoot people because they hear voices or have strange visions."

—HAROLD EVANS, "High Noon on Gun Control"

The world outside looks dead in winter: lifeless brown grass on stonehard earth, bare tree skeletons. The fields and woods are quiet as death: no buzz of insects, no burbling of birdsong, no smells of moist earth or flowers. The cold is painful to the skin, and sensible people stay indoors.

—JO ELLEN TUTHILL, "The Bugs of Winter"

Autumn is equally busy, as Eleanor Perenyi states in *Green Thoughts:* "As the natural world prepares to shut up shop, the gardener may be inclined to do the same. But as most of us know, fall is the busiest season of the year" (14).

E. B. White writes of his annual surge of interest in gardening: "We are hooked and are making an attempt to kick the habit."

—MARIE WINN, *The Plug-In Drug*

Your words introducing a quotation may be very short, but they should be a complete independent clause°. ▌PUNCTUATION ALERT: When your words introducing a quotation are not an independent clause, use a comma between the introductory words and the quotation (see 24g). For advice on working quoted words smoothly into your writing, see 28a. ▌

You can use a colon to introduce statements that summarize, restate, or explain what is said in an independent clause.

COLON PATTERN II

Independent clause : summarizing or restating words.

The two-year-old rejects carrots, squash, pumpkin, segments of an orange, and apricot halves, but she accepts spinach, apples, celery, nuts, and slices of egg: She is rejecting the color orange, not food in general.

Perhaps it is this specter that most haunts working men and women: the planned obsolescence of people that is of a piece with the planned obsolescence of the things they make.

—STUDS TERKEL, *Working*

Anthropology provides a scientific basis for dealing with the crucial dilemma of the world today: How can peoples of different appearance, mutually unintelligible languages, and dissimilar ways of life get along peaceably together?

—CLYDE KLUCKHOHN, *Mirror for Man*

You can use a colon to lead into a final appositive—a word or group of words that renames or restates a noun or a pronoun.

The Metropolitan Museum in New York City now owns the best-known works of Louis Tiffany's studio: those wonderful stained-glass windows. [*Stained-glass windows* renames *best-known works.*]

452

Use a colon to introduce a list or a series of items announced by an independent clause°.

COLON PATTERN III

Independent clause**:** listed items.

If you really want to lose weight, you need give up only three things: breakfast, lunch, and dinner.

Laboratory experiments prove that tarantulas can distinguish three types of touch: pressure against the body walls, stroking of the body hair, and riffling of certain very fine hairs on the legs called trichobothria.
—ALEXANDER PETRUNKEVITCH, "The Spider and the Wasp"

When you use phrases like *the following* or *as follows,* a colon is usually required. A colon is not called for with the words *such as* or *including* (see 26c).

The students' demands included the following: an expanded menu in the cafeteria, better janitorial services, and more up-to-date textbooks.

▌ CAPITALIZATION ALERTS: (1) Use a capital letter to start a quotation introduced by a colon. (2) Use a lower-case letter for a list, an appositive, or any other set of words *not* an independent clause°—unless the first word after the colon is a proper noun. (3) Either a capital letter or a lowercase letter is correct for the first word of an independent clause or a question following a colon. Whichever practice you choose, be consistent throughout a paper. ▌

▌ 26b
Use a colon to separate standard material.

TITLE AND SUBTITLE

The Aquarian Conspiracy: Personal and Social Transformations in the 1980s
Charles Dickens: His Tragedy and Triumph

HOURS, MINUTES, AND SECONDS

The plane took off at 7:15 P.M.
She passed the halfway point at 1:23:02.

QUOTATION ABOUT WRITING
Remember that colons—perhaps the mark we exploit least—generally mean that what is to come will explain what has just gone by. They imply identity, whereas semicolons imply "separate but equal" status. "I have just learned three facts: that St. Pual is the capital of Minnesota; that Helena is the capital of Montana; and that Lincoln is the capital of Nebraska." Everything after the colon adds up to "three facts"—whereas the three statements of fact, though they have much in common, are not identical (there are three, not one). Colons can also save words and create special effects. Compare:
√I admire her poetry. Its imagery is magnificent.
√I admire her poetry for its magnificent imagery.
√I admire her poetry: its imagery is magnificent.
All three versions are "correct." The first is emphatic and probably clear—or clear enough: *Probably* your reader will realize that the second sentence explains the first. The second version is clearer, and it flows along smoothly. The third is clearer than the first and just as clear as the second, and it gives us a unique kind of silence—not just a break (the period did *that*) but mild suspense. Your job is to decide which way of punctuating best expresses what *you* want to express.
—ROBERT M. PIERSON, "Punctuation as Art"

COORDINATED RESOURCES

Alternate examples and exercises for this chapter are available in the *S & S Workbook for Writers,* Gordon and Troyka.

Transparency masters are available for many of the screened charts in this chapter.

The software program *Blue Pencil,* available from Prentice-Hall, offers students additional practice coordinated with this chapter.

Students can practice and test their knowledge of terms, key concepts, and applications of material in this chapter by using the *Study Guide to the S & S Handbook for Writers,* West.

CHAPTERS AND VERSES OF THE BIBLE

> Psalms 23:1–3
>
> Luke 3:13

MEMO FORM

> To: Dean Kristen Olivero
> From: Professor Daniel Black
> Re: Student Work-Study Program

SALUTATION OF FORMAL OR BUSINESS LETTER

> Dear Ms. Beins:

MLA BIBLIOGRAPHIC FORMAT: CITY OF PUBLICATION AND PUBLISHER (BOOK)

> Atwood, Margaret. *The Handmaid's Tale.* Boston: Houghton, 1986.

MLA BIBLIOGRAPHIC FORMAT: YEAR FROM PAGES (ARTICLE)

> McGrath, Anne, "Books that Speak for Themselves." *U.S. News & World Report.* 14 July 1986: 49.

■‖ 26c

Avoid misusing the colon.

A complete independent clause° must precede a colon except when the colon separates standard material (26b). Especially with listed items, take care that lead-in words make a grammatically complete statement. When they do not, do not use a colon.

No   The small boy bought: eggs, milk, cheese, and bread.

Yes   The small boy bought eggs, milk, cheese, and bread.

The words *such as* and *including* can be tricky: Do not let them lure you into using a colon incorrectly.

No   The health board discussed a number of problems, such as: water quality, the inefficiency of the sewage treatment system, and the lack of a backup water supply.

Yes   The health board discussed a number of problems, such as water quality, the inefficiency of the sewage treatment system, and the lack of a backup water supply.

454

YES The health board discussed a number of problems: water quality, the inefficiency of the sewage treatment system, and the lack of a backup water supply.

No Five dates were chosen, including: April 3, May 6, May 17, June 11, and July 6.

YES Five dates were chosen, including April 3, May 6, May 17, June 11, and July 6.

YES Five dates were chosen, including the following: April 3, May 6, May 17, June 11, and July 6.

Do not use a colon to separate a dependent clause° from an independent clause°.

No After the drought ended: the mayor appointed a commission to plan water-saving measures for the future.

YES After the drought ended, the mayor appointed a commission to plan water-saving measures for the future.

EXERCISE 1

Insert colons where they are needed. If a sentence is correct, circle its number.

EXAMPLE Most gamblers ignore how slim their chances are of hitting the jackpot in a slot machine, about one in 2,000.

Most gamblers ignore how slim their chances are of hitting a jackpot in a slot machine: about one in 2,000.

1. Researchers at Washington University have discovered a startling new fact, not only do you dream approximately every 90 minutes when you are asleep, but you daydream approximately every 90 minutes when you are awake.

2. Among the forgers who have committed these crimes for hundreds of years, three continue to interest experts, William Henry Ireland, who forged a series of letters he claimed were written by Shakespeare; Hans Van Meegeren, who produced amazingly accurate copies of Jan Vermeer's paintings; and Clifford Irving, who convinced a New York publisher that he had been hired to ghost-write Howard Hughes's autobiography.

3. Writing about the problems of leadership, Barbara Tuchman reaches this conclusion "As witnesses of the twentieth century's record, comparable to the worst in history, we have little confidence in our species."

ANSWERS: EXERCISE 1
1. fact: Not only
2. experts: William Henry
3. concludes: "As witnesses
4. Correct
5. Tess of the D'Urbervilles: A Virtuous Woman
6. 11:00
7. 85:10
8. work: his
9. places: napkins,
10. fact: You

455

4. The worst insurance risks in the United States include astronauts, drivers of hydroplanes, race drivers in the Indianapolis 500, and drivers in Grand Prix auto races.

5. Many proper Victorians were shocked by Thomas Hardy's novel *Tess of the D'Urbervilles; A Virtuous Woman.*

6. Halley's comet made its predicted return in 1986, passing nearest to the sun on February 9, just before 1100 A.M. Greenwich time.

7. The text was based on Psalms 85,10, "Mercy and truth are met together: righteousness and peace have kissed each other."

8. Two characteristics aided Einstein in his work, his curiosity and his ability to concentrate.

9. Wills have been written in unusual places, napkins, wallpaper, hospital charts, and even the side of a corncrib.

10. For those who think there must be a pleasant way to lose weight, consider the following fact, you have to kiss 389 times to lose one pound.

27

THE APOSTROPHE

The apostrophe plays three major roles: it helps to form the possessive of nouns and a few pronouns; it stands for one or more omitted letters; and it helps to form the plurals of letters and numerals. It does *not* help form plurals of nouns or the possessive case of personal pronouns.

▀‖ 27a

Use an apostrophe to form the possessive case of nouns and indefinite pronouns.

The **possessive case** serves to communicate ownership or close relationship.

OWNERSHIP	The writer's pen
CLOSE RELATIONSHIP	The novel's plot

Possession in nouns and certain indefinite pronouns can be communicated by an apostrophe in combination with an *-s* (*the instructor's comments*) or by phrases beginning with *of the* (*the comments of the instructor*).

457

COORDINATED RESOURCES

Alternate examples and exercises for this chapter are available in the *S & S Workbook for Writers*, Gordon and Troyka.

A transparency master is available for the screened list in this chapter.

The software program *Blue Pencil*, available from Prentice-Hall, offers students additional practice coordinated with this chapter.

Students can practice and test their knowledge of terms, key concepts, and applications of material in this chapter by using the *Study Guide to the S & S Handbook for Writers*, West.

1

When nouns and indefinite pronouns do *not* end in -s, add -'s to show possession.

The **dean's** duties included working closely with the resident assistants. [*dean* = singular noun not ending in -*s*]

In one more year I will receive my **bachelor's** degree. [*bachelor* = singular noun not ending in -*s*]

They care about their **children's** futures. [*children* = plural noun not ending in -*s*]

The accident was really **no one's** fault. [*no one* = indefinite pronoun not ending in -*s*]

2

When singular nouns end in -s, add -'s to show possession.

The tour **bus's** passengers switched to a train in Athens.
Chris's hand shook.
Lee **Jones's** insurance was cancelled.
Charles **Dickens's** story "A Christmas Carol" is a perennial favorite at Christmas time.
That **business's** system for handling complaints is inefficient.

3

When a plural noun ends in -s, use only an apostrophe to show possession.

The **boys'** bicycles are stored in the basement.
The **visitors'** comments included high praise for the park rangers at Yellowstone.
The newspapers have publicized several **medicines'** severe side effects recently.

4

In compound words, add -'s to the last word.

His **mother-in-law's** corporation just bought out a competitor.
The **tennis player's** strategy was brilliant.
They wanted to hear **somebody else's** interpretation of the rule.

5
In individual possession, add -'s to each noun.

Olga's and Joanne's books are valuable. [Olga and Joanne each own some of the valuable books; but they do not own the books together.]

After the fire, **the doctor's and the lawyer's** offices had to be rebuilt. [The doctor and the lawyer had separate offices.]

6
In joint or group possession, add -'s to only the last noun.

Olga and Joanne's books are valuable. [Olga and Joanne own the books together.]

Anne and Glen Smith's article on solar heating interests me. [More than one Smith wrote the article.]

■‖ 27b
Do not use an apostrophe with the possessive forms of personal pronouns.

Some pronouns have specific possessive forms. Do not use an apostrophe with these forms.

PRONOUN	POSSESSIVE FORM(S)
he	his
she	her, hers
it	its
we	our, ours
you	your, yours
they	their, theirs
who	whose

Be especially alert to *it's* and *its,* as well as *who's* and *whose,* which occur often in English and are frequently confused. (*It's* stands for *it is; its* is a personal pronoun showing possession. *Who's* stands for *who is; whose* is a personal pronoun showing possession.)

No ⠀⠀⠀⠀The government has to balance **it's** budget.

Yes ⠀⠀⠀The government has to balance **its** budget.

N0	This briefcase is mine and that one is **your's**.
Yes	This briefcase is mine and that one is **yours**.
N0	The professor **who's** class was canceled is at a convention.
Yes	The professor **whose** class was canceled is at a convention.

▮ APOSTROPHE CAUTION: The following forms do not exist in English, so do not use them: *its', his', hers', yours', theirs', whos'.* ▮

▮ 27c
Use an apostrophe to stand for omitted letters, numbers, or words in contractions.

Contractions are words from which one or more letters have been intentionally omitted and in which apostrophes are inserted to signal the omission. Contractions are common in speaking and in informal writing, but many readers dislike them in formal writing. Always consider your proposed audience and the degree of formality you want to convey when you choose between a contraction and the full phrase.

COMMON CONTRACTIONS

I'm = I am
he's, she's, it's = he is, she is, it is
you're, we're, they're = you are, we are, they are
isn't = is not
aren't = are not
wasn't = was not
weren't = were not
he'll , she'll = he will, she will
you'll, we'll, they'll = you will, we will, they will
won't = will not
didn't = did not
I'd = I would
I've, we've = I have, we have
you've, they've = you have, they have
who's = who is
there's = there is
let's = let us
can't = can not or cannot
o'clock = of the clock

460

Contractions can help to show informal speech or dialect, especially in dramatic or fictional writing.

> Scout yonder's been **readin'** ever since she was born, and she **ain't** even started school yet. You look right puny for **goin'** on seven.
>
> —HARPER LEE, *To Kill a Mockingbird*

Apostrophes also indicate the omission of the first two numerals in years. Use this contraction only in informal writing.

The class of '50 is having a reunion this year.
They moved to Florida after the blizzard of '78.

▮‖ 27d
Use an apostrophe to form plurals of letters, numerals, symbols, and words used as terms.

Billie always has trouble printing **W's**.
The address includes six **6's**.
The **for's** in the paper were all misspelled as **four's**.
When the keys jammed, a series of **&'s** showed on the computer screen.

▮ UNDERLINING ALERT: Always underline letters as letters and words as words. In printed material, they are set in italic type; underlining is the way to show this distinction in typewritten or handwritten material. ▮

Most of the first-graders consistently had trouble making <u>8</u>'s and trying to pronounce <u>eight</u>'s phonetically.

For the plural form of years, two styles are acceptable: with an apostrophe (1980's) or without (1980s). Whichever form you prefer, use it consistently.

EXERCISE 1
Rewrite these sentences to insert *'s* or an apostrophe alone to make the words in parentheses show possession. Delete the parentheses.

1. At Pablo (Picasso) birth, two (midwives) errors nearly allowed him to be left for dead.
2. Luckily for Picasso, his cigar-smoking (uncle) quick act saved him.
3. The uncle filled his (nephew) lungs with a blast of much-needed, yet smoke-filled, air.

ANSWERS: EXERCISE 1
1. Picasso's midwives'
2. uncle's
3. nephew's
4. Paris's
5. painting's, Madame Gautreau's
6. Max Jacob and Pablo Picasso's
7. Picasso's, experts', Jacob's, Picasso's
8. anyone's
9. children's, others'
10. contemporaries'

4. When (Paris) most celebrated beauty, Mme. Virginie Gautreau, was depicted by the painter John Singer Sargent as vain and immodest in a portrait entitled "Madame X," those who knew her agreed with the portrayal.

5. Nevertheless (the painting) notoriety and Madame (Gautreau) hysterics forced Sargent to leave for London.

6. (Max Jacob and Pablo Picasso) shared Paris apartment caused them some problems.

7. (Picasso) work habits included leaving paintings all over the floor, and many years later art (experts) skills were needed to remove (Jacob) footprints from (Picasso) valuable canvases.

8. The American painter Charles Willson Peale believed that (anyone) desire to paint could be fulfilled.

9. He acted on his belief and helped to develop his seventeen (children), and many (other), artistic talents.

10. His faith was rewarded: his sons Rembrandt and Raphaelle both earned their (contemporaries) praise.

ANSWERS: EXERCISE 2

1. Athletic competition is encouraged in accordance with the participants' age and ability.

2. These athletes' training takes place in schools and other institutions.

3. Participants' handicaps do not prevent them from competing in sports from basketball to gymnastics and ice skating to wheelchair exercise.

4. The program's sponsor is the Joseph P. Kennedy, Jr., Foundation, which first sponsored the event in 1968.

5. The foundation's true beneficiary is American society, for a democracy's aim is equal opportunity and participation for all its members.

EXERCISE 2

Rewrite these sentences so that each contains a possessive noun.

EXAMPLE   The Special Olympics is an international program promoting the physical fitness of mentally retarded children and adults.

The Special Olympics is an international program promoting mentally retarded children's and adults' physical fitness.

1. Athletic competition is encouraged in accordance with the age and ability of the participants.

2. The training of these athletes takes place in schools and other institutions.

3. Handicaps of the participants do not prevent them from competing in sports from basketball to gymnastics and ice skating to wheelchair exercise.

4. The sponsor of the program is the Joseph P. Kennedy, Jr., Foundation, which first sponsored the event in 1968.

5. The true beneficiary of the foundation is American society, for the aim of a democracy is equal opportunity and participation for all its members.

EXERCISE 3

Correct any errors in the use of apostrophes in the paragraph below.

(1) One of Albert Einsteins biographers tells about the famous physicists encounter with a little girl in his' neighborhood. (2) The little girl stared at Einstein's soaking wet feet and said, "Mr. Einstein, youve come out with-

462

out you'r boots again!'' (3) Einstein laughed and, pulling up his trousers, replied, ''Yes, and Ive forgotten my socks, too.'' (4) Most people arent as forgetful as Einstein, but sometimes our memories' let all of us down. (5) We may not be able to remember if our first job started in '81 or 82; we may forget whether our employers' husband spells his name with two ts or with one. (6) No one is absolutely sure how memory works. (7) Dr. Barbara Jones study of memory suggests that personality style's affect memory. (8) People with rigid personalities who's livelihoods depend on facts tend to have good memories. (9) Mr. Harry Lorayne and Dr. Laird Cermak's studies of memory each provide a different approach to improving that useful faculty. (10) Mr. Lorayne suggest's relating what you want to remember to something verbal or visual. (11) For instance, if you want to remember that your sister's-in-law's name is Rose, you would picture her wearing a rose corsage. (12) Dr. Cermaks suggestions include consideration of physiological factors. (13) He notes that doctors' are currently developing drugs that will prevent older people from losing the memories that are rightfully their's.

ANSWERS: EXERCISE 3
(1) One of Albert Einstein's biographers tells about the famous physicist's encounter with a little girl in his neighborhood. (2) The little girl stared at Einstein's soaking wet feet and said, "Mr. Einstein, you've come out without your boots again!" (3) Einstein laughed and, pulling up his trousers, replied, "Yes, and I've forgotten my socks, too." (4) Most people aren't as forgetful as Einstein, but sometimes our memories let all of us down. (5) We may not be able to remember if our first job started in '81 or '82; we may forget whether our employer's husband spells his name with two *t*'s or with one. (6) No one is absolutely sure how memory works. (7) Dr. Barbara Jones' study of memory suggests that personality styles affect memory. (8) People with rigid personalities whose livelihoods depend on facts tend to have good memories. (9) Mr. Harry Lorayne's and Dr. Laird Cermak's studies of memory each provide a different approach to improving that useful faculty. (10) Mr. Lorayne suggests relating what you want to remember to something verbal or visual. (11) For instance, if you want to remember that your sister-in-law's name is Rose, you would picture her wearing a rose corsage. (12) Dr. Cermak's suggestions include consideration of physiological factors. (13) He notes that doctors are currently developing drugs that will prevent older people from losing the memories that are rightfully theirs.

INSTRUCTOR'S NOTES

28
QUOTATION MARKS

Most commonly, quotation marks enclose **direct quotations**—spoken or written words from an outside source. Quotation marks also set off some titles, and they can call attention to words used in special senses.

Always use quotation marks in pairs, and be especially careful not to omit the second (closing) quotation mark. **Double quotation marks** (" ") are standard. **Single quotation marks** (' ') are used only for quotation marks within quotation marks. In print, opening and closing quotation marks look slightly different from each other, but they look identical when made on a typewriter or computer printer. You will find examples of both print and of typewritten quotation marks in this chapter.

For information about the functions in quotations of brackets, see 29c; of the ellipsis, see 29d; of the slash, see 29e. For information about capital letters with quotations, see 30c.

When you quote the words of others in your writing, be sure to remain alert to these important matters:

- Incorporate quotations correctly and smoothly into your writing: see 31e.
- Avoid plagiarism—the use of another person's words as if they were your own: see Chapter 31.

464

- Document direct quotations correctly: for the MLA parenthetical system, see 32k; for the APA parenthetical system, see 34c-4; for a footnote or endnote system, see 34b-4.

28a

Enclose direct quotations of not more than four lines in quotation marks.

Direct quotations are exact words copied from a print source or transcribed from a nonprint source.

1

Use double quotation marks to enclose short quotations.

A quotation is considered "short" if it can be typed or handwritten to occupy no more than four lines on a page. Short quotations are enclosed in double quotation marks. Longer quotations are not enclosed in quotation marks—they are **displayed.** A displayed quotation starts on a new line, and all typewritten lines indent ten spaces. (In the examples, parenthetical documentation is used—see 32k.)

SHORT QUOTATIONS

Hall explains the practicality of close conversational distances:
"If you are interested in something, your pupils dilate; if I say
something you don't like, they tend to contract" (47).

Personal space "moves with us, expanding and contracting according
to the situation in which we find ourselves" (Fisher, Bell, and
Baum 149).

LONG QUOTATION

Robert Sommer, an environmental psychologist, uses literary
and personal analogies to describe personal space:

> Like the porcupines in Schopenhauer's fable, people like
> to be close enough to obtain warmth and comradeship but
> far enough away to avoid pricking one another. Personal
> space . . . has been likened to a snail shell, a soap
> bubble, an aura, and "breathing room." (26)

See the Manuscript Form appendix for a complete discussion of displaying quotations.

465

TEACHING TIP
As the study summarized in the margins of Chapter 31 points out, many students think that they are not plagiarizing as long as they use quotation marks to indicate material taken from sources. These students do not realize that they must also document the source. Now that MLA recommends a system of parenthetical references, the direction to "use footnotes" no longer can help college instructors deal easily with documentation. You might find it useful, therefore, to take some time to explain the word *documentation,* which in contrast to *footnotes,* is not widely known to students inexperienced in writing research papers. You might also explain that the placement of the parenthetical reference depends on the length of the quotation. If the quotation is "run in," the parenthetical reference comes before the period; if the quotation is displayed, the parenthetical reference comes after the period.

TEACHING TIP
You might point out to your students that typewriter face is used in 28a-1 so that writers can see how such material should look on their typed papers. All material is double spaced. A short quotation is "run in" with the writer's prose; a long quotation is displayed. For additional examples in typewriter face, you might direct your students' attention to the student research paper in Chapter 33. In particular, you might point out that paragraphs are indented five spaces and displayed quotations are indented ten spaces for all lines.

2

Use single quotation marks for quotations within quotations.

When you want to quote four lines or less and the original words already contain quotation marks, use double quotation marks at the start and end of the directly quoted words. Then, substitute single quotation marks ('   ') wherever there are double quotation marks in the original source.

ORIGINAL SOURCE
Personal space . . . has been likened to a snail shell, a soap bubble, an aura, and "breathing room."

—ROBERT SOMMER, *Personal Space:*
The Behavioral Bases of Design, page 26

SINGLE QUOTATION MARKS WITHIN DOUBLE QUOTATION MARKS
Robert Sommer, an environmental psychologist, lists comparisons of personal space to "a snail shell, a soap bubble, an aura, and 'breathing room' " (26).

If there are quotation marks in a quotation of more than four lines, display it without enclosing it in quotation marks. But be sure to use any quotation marks that appear in the original source. See the Manuscript Form appendix for a complete discussion of displayed quotations.

3

Use quotation marks correctly for short quotations of poetry and for direct discourse.

A quotation of poetry is "short" if it is no more than three lines of the poem. As with short prose quotations, use double quotation marks to enclose the material. If you quote more than one line of poetry, use a slash with one space on each side to show the line divisions (see 29e).

As W. H. Auden wittily defined personal space, "some thirty inches from my nose / The frontier of my person goes. . . ."

See the Manuscript Form appendix for a complete discussion of displayed quotations of poetry. ▌CAPITALIZATION ALERT: When you quote lines of poetry, follow the capitalization of the version you are quoting. ▌

Quotation marks are also used to enclose speakers' words in **direct discourse.** Whether you are reporting the exact words of a

TEACHING TIP
One pleasant way to review the use of quotation marks is to have students "translate" passages of indirect discourse found in short stories into dialogues. Alternatively, students can be given a short scene from a play they enjoy and asked first to rewrite it as if it were a chapter in a short story. They set the scene and present the dialogue as conversation, following the conventions of the short story rather than those of the play. Then they can rewrite the scene using indirect discourse in all the conversations.

466

real speaker or making up dialogue in, for example, a short story, quotation marks let your readers know which words belong to the speaker and which words do not. Use double quotation marks at the beginning and end of a speaker's words, and start a new paragraph each time the speaker changes.

> "I don't know how you can see to drive," she said.
> "Maybe you should put on your glasses."
> "Putting on my glasses would help you to see?"
> "Not me; you," Macon said. "You're focused on the windshield instead of the road."
>
> —ANNE TYLER, *The Accidental Tourist*

Indirect discourse reports what a speaker said, in contrast to direct discourse, which presents a speaker's exact words. Do not enclose indirect discourse in quotation marks.

DIRECT DISCOURSE
The mayor said, "I cannot attend the conference in San Antonio."

INDIRECT DISCOURSE
The mayor said that he could not attend the conference in San Antonio.

See 15a-4 for advice on revising incorrect shifts between direct and indirect discourse.

EXERCISE 1
Correct the use of double and single quotation marks in the following sentences. If a sentence is correct, circle its number.

EXAMPLE According to J. F. Perkins, "O. Henry "solves" most of his short story plots with surprise endings.
According to J. F. Perkins, "O. Henry 'solves' most of his short story plots with surprise endings."

1. Canfield and Lebson write, No one understands the sleeping habits of these sharks.
2. In the last two lines of the poem, Dickinson creates a powerful contrast: Parting is all we know of heaven, / And all we need of hell.
3. "One can put up with "Service with a Smile" if the smile is genuine and not mere compulsory toothbaring," wrote Cornelia Otis Skinner. She did not, on the other hand, advocate 'Service with a Snarl.'
4. "Promises," said Hannah Arendt, are the uniquely human way of ordering the future.

COORDINATED RESOURCES
Alternate examples and exercises for this chapter are available in the *S & S Workbook for Writers,* Gordon and Troyka.

The software program *Blue Pencil,* available from Pentice-Hall, offers students additional practice coordinated with this chapter.

Students can practice and test their knowledge of terms, key concepts, and applications of material in this chapter by using the *Study Guide to the S & S Handbook for Writers,* West.

ANSWERS: EXERCISE 1
1. Canfield and Lebson write, "No one understands the sleeping habits of these sharks."
2. In the last two lines of the poem, Dickinson creates a powerful contrast: "Parting is all we know of heaven, / And all we need of hell."
3. "One can put up with 'Service with a Smile' if the smile is genuine and not mere compulsory toothbaring," wrote Cornelia Otis Skinner. She did not, on the other hand, advocate "Service with a Snarl."
4. "Promises," said Hannah Arendt, "are the uniquely human way of ordering the future."

5. According to Henry James, "Nothing . . . will ever take the place of the good old fashion of 'liking' a work of art or not liking it."

6. Pauline Kael, the movie critic, notes that "certain artists can, at moments in their lives, reach out and unify the audience" and in so doing give people the opportunity for "a shared response."

7. "Don't let anyone convince you that you can't fulfill your ambitions," warned the speaker, "or you surely won't."

8. "Why have women passion, intellect, moral activity—these three—and a place in society where no one of the three can be exercised?" asked Florence Nightingale in the 1850s.

9. "In seven cases," the report continued, "outlets with the lowest prices had the highest percentages of defective merchandise."

10. Leslie Hanscom reports about the latest volume of the *Oxford English Dictionary*, "Most of the new words are originating in the USA."

Answers to Exercise 2 on p. 469

5. According to Henry James, "Nothing . . . will ever take the place of the good old fashion of "liking" a work of art or not liking it."

6. Pauline Kael, the movie critic, notes that "certain artists can, at moments in their lives, reach out and unify the audience" and in so doing give people the opportunity for "a shared response.

7. Don't let anyone convince you that you can't fulfill your ambitions, warned the speaker, or you surely won't.

8. Why have women passion, intellect, moral activity—these three—and a place in society where no one of the three can be exercised? asked Florence Nightingale in the 1850s.

9. "In seven cases, the report continued, outlets with the lowest prices had the highest percentages of defective merchandise.

10. Leslie Hanscom reports about the latest volume of the *Oxford English Dictionary,* Most of the new words are originating in the USA.

EXERCISE 2

Indicate whether each sentence is direct or indirect discourse. Then rewrite each sentence in the other form.

EXAMPLE   In 1928 an elderly woman contacted a London auctioneer and asked, "Would you be interested in selling this manuscript?

(Direct discourse)

In 1928 an elderly woman contacted a London auctioneer and asked if he would be interested in selling a manuscript.

1. The auctioneer said that his company did sell manuscripts, but only original ones by famous authors.

2. "This manuscript is original," the woman replied.

3. "The author inscribed it with these words—'A Christmas gift to a dear child'—and I was that child," she continued.

4. Astonished, the auctioneer said, "Is this manuscript what I think it is?"

5. The woman acknowledged that it was the original Lewis Carroll manuscript of *Alice in Wonderland*.

▪‖ 28b

Enclose certain titles in quotation marks.

When you refer to certain types of works by their titles, enclose the titles in quotation marks. Use quotation marks around the titles of short published works, like poems, short stories, essays, articles from periodicals, pamphlets, and brochures. Also use them around song titles and individual episodes of television or radio series.

> Discuss the rhyme scheme of Andrew Marvell's "Delight in "Disorder." [poem]
>
> Have you read "Young Goodman Brown"? [short story]
>
> One of the best sources I found is "The Myth of Political Consultants," [magazine article]
>
> "Shooting an Elephant" describes George Orwell's experience in Burma. [essay]

Underlining (for italics) is used for titles of many other types of works, such as books and plays. A few titles are neither underlined nor enclosed in quotation marks. You will find useful lists showing how to present titles in 30e and 30f.

Do not put the title of your own paper in quotation marks either on a title page or at the top of a page. See 28d.

EXERCISE 3
Make the use of quotation marks correct in the following sentences. If a sentence is correct, circle its number.

1. Almost everyone who has had to make a difficult choice in life can relate to Robert Frost's poem The Road Not Taken.
2. On a *Twilight Zone* episode called Healer, the main character steals a magic artifact.
3. In her essay titled "In Search of Our Mothers' Gardens, Alice Walker says that she found her own garden because she was guided by a "heritage of a love of beauty and a respect for strength.
4. Unable to get enough peace and quiet to write songs, such as his famous Over There and You're a Grand Old Flag, George M. Cohan would sometimes hire a Pullman car drawing room on a train going far enough away to allow him to finish his work.
5. A snake gives Sherlock Holmes the clue he needs to solve a puzzling murder in the mystery story The Speckled Band.

∎‖ 28c

Words used in special senses or for special purposes may be enclosed in quotation marks.

Writers sometimes enclose in quotation marks words or phrases meant ironically or in some other nonliteral way.

ANSWERS: EXERCISE 2
Answers may vary in the rewritten sentences. Here is one set of possibilities.
1. *Indirect discourse.* The auctioneer said, "My company does sell manuscripts, but only original ones by famous authors."
2. *Direct discourse.* The woman replied that the manuscript was original.
3. *Direct discourse.* She said that the author inscribed it with the words "A Christmas gift to a dear child" and that she was that child.
4. *Direct discourse.* Astonished, the auctioneer asked if the manuscript was what he thought it was.
5. *Indirect discourse.* The woman said, "Yes, it is the original Lewis Carroll manuscript of *Alice in Wonderland.*"

ANSWERS: EXERCISE 3
1. Almost everyone who has had to make a difficult choice in life can relate to Robert Frost's poem "The Road Not Taken."
2. On a *Twilight Zone* episode called "Healer," the main character steals a magic artifact.
3. In her essay titled "In Search of Our Mothers' Gardens," Alice Walker says that she found her own garden because she was guided by a "heritage of a love of beauty and a respect for strength."
4. Unable to get enough peace and quiet to write songs, such as his famous "Over There" and "Your're a Grand Old Flag," George M. Cohan would sometimes hire a Pullman car drawing room on a train going far enough away to allow him to finish his work.
5. A snake gives Sherlock Holmes the clue he needs to solve a puzzling murder in the mystery story "The Speckled Band."

The proposed tax "reform" is actually a tax increase.

The "wonderful companion for children" snarled menacingly.

Writers sometimes put technical terms in quotation marks and define them the first time they are used. No quotation marks are used once such terms have been introduced and defined.

"Plagiarism"—the unacknowledged use of another person's words or ideas—can result in expulsion. Plagiarism is a serious offense.

The translation of a word or phrase can be enclosed in quotation marks. (Underline words or phrases that require translation.)

My grandfather usually ended arguments with *de gustibus non disputandum est* ("there is no disputing about tastes").

Words being referred to as words can be either enclosed in quotation marks or underlined. Follow consistent practice throughout a paper.

YES   Many people confuse "affect" and "effect."

YES   Many people confuse *affect* and *effect*.

28d
Avoid misusing quotation marks.

Writers sometimes enclose in quotation marks words they are uncomfortable about using, such as slang in formal writing or a cliché. Do not use quotation marks around language you sense is inappropriate to your audience or your purpose. Take the time to find accurate, appropriate, and fresh words instead.

No   They "eat like birds" in public, but they "stuff their faces" in private.

YES   They eat very little in public, but they consume enormous amounts of food in private.

Do not enclose a word in quotation marks merely to call attention to it.

No   "Plagiarism" can result in expulsion.

YES   Plagiarism can result in expulsion.

470

In papers, when you refer to published or performed works by title, you will often need quotation marks (28b) or underlining (30f) to set the title off. When you put the title of your paper at the top of a page or on a title page, however, do not enclose the title in quotation marks.

No   "The Elderly in Nursing Homes: A Case Study"

Yes   The Elderly in Nursing Homes: A Case Study

The only exception is if the title of your paper refers to another title or a word that requires setting off.

No   Character Development in Shirley Jackson's The Lottery

Yes   Character Development in Shirley Jackson's "The Lottery"

Do not put a nickname in quotation marks unless you are giving a nickname with a full name. When a person's nickname is widely known and used, you do not have to give both the nickname and the full name. For example, use *Senator Ted Kennedy* or *Senator Edward Kennedy*, whichever is appropriate to your audience and purpose. You do not have to write *Senator Edward "Ted" Kennedy*.

EXERCISE 4

Make the use of quotation marks correct in the following sentences. If a sentence is correct, circle its number.

Example   Many people confuse the spellings of "there," *their,* and *they're.*

         Many people confuse the spellings of "there," "their," and "they're."

1. "Accept" and *except* sound enough alike to confuse many listeners.
2. "Mickey" Mantle, "Yogi" Berra, and Whitey Ford helped make the Yankees champions in the 1950s.
3. Although the district attorney thought it would be an "open and shut case," she found out that "life is full of surprises."
4. An "antigen" is any substance from outside the body that activates the body's immune system. Today scientists are focusing intensive research on "antigens."
5. *Valross,* whale-horse, is the Norwegian word from which we get *walrus.*

ANSWERS: EXERCISE 4

1. "Accept" and "except" sound enough alike to confuse many listeners. [or *Accept* and *except* sound enough alike to confuse many listeners.]
2. Mickey Mantle, Yogi Berra, and Whitey Ford helped to make the Yankees champions in the 1950s.
3. Correct
4. An "antigen" is any substance from outside the body that activates the body's immune system. Today, scientists are focusing intensive research on antigens.
5. *Valross,* "whale-horse," is the Norwegian word from which we get *walrus.*

INSTRUCTOR'S NOTES

28e
Follow accepted practices for other punctuation with quotation marks.

1

Place commas and periods inside closing quotation marks.

> Because the class enjoyed F. Scott Fitzgerald's "The Freshest Boy," they were looking forward to his longer works.
> Ms. Rogers said, "Don't stand so close to me."
> Edward T. Hall coined the word "proxemics."

2

Place colons and semicolons outside closing quotation marks.

> We have to know "how close is close": we don't want to offend.
> Some experts claim that the job market now offers "opportunities that never existed before"; others disagree.

3

Place question marks, exclamation points, and dashes inside or outside closing quotation marks, according to the context.

If a question mark, exclamation point, or dash belongs with the words enclosed in quotation marks, put that punctuation mark *inside* the closing quotation mark.

> "Did I Hear You Call My Name?" was the winning song.
> "I've won the lottery!" he shouted.
> "Who's there? Why don't you ans—"

If a question mark, exclamation point, or dash belongs with words that are *not* included in quotation marks, put the punctuation *outside* the closing quotation mark.

> Have you read Nikki Giovanni's poem "Knoxville, Tennessee"?
> If only I could write a story like Erskine Caldwell's "The Rumor"!
> Weak excuses—"I have to visit my grandparents" is a classic—change little from year to year.

472

EXERCISE 5

Make the use of quotation marks and other punctuation with quotation marks correct in the following sentences. If a sentence is correct, circle its number.

1. One of the most famous passages in Shakespeare is Hamlet's soliloquy, which begins with the question ''To be, or not to be''?

2. ''Take this script'', Rudyard Kipling said to the nurse who had cared for his first-born child'', and someday if you are in need of money you may be able to sell it at a handsome price.''

3. Ernest Hemingway claimed this was the source of his famous phrase ''a lost generation:'' in conversation with ''Papa'' Hemingway, a garage owner used the words to describe the young mechanics he employed.

4. After lulling the reader with a description of a beautiful dream palace in his poem Kubla Khan, Coleridge changes the mood abruptly: And 'mid this tumult Kubla heard from far / Ancestral voices prophesying war.

5. Syndicated disk jockey Dr. Demento offers this possibility for the worst song title of all time'': I've Got Those Wake Up at Seven Thirty, Wash Your Ears They're Dirty, Eat Your Eggs and Oatmeal Rush to School Blues''.

ANSWERS: EXERCISE 5

1. One of the most famous passages in Shakespeare is Hamlet's soliloquy, which begins with the question "To be, or not to be?"

2. "Take this script," Rudyard Kipling said to the nurse who had cared for his first-born child, "and someday if you are in need of money you may be able to sell it at a handsome price."

3. Ernest Hemingway claimed that this was the source of his famous phase "a lost generation": in conversation with Papa Hemingway, a garage owner used the words to describe the young mechanics he employed.

4. After lulling the reader with a description of a beautiful dream palace in his poem "Kubla Khan," Coleridge changes the mood abruptly: "And 'mid this tumult Kubla heard from far / Ancestral voices prophesying war."

5. Syndicated disc jockey Dr. Demento offers this possibility for the worst song title of all time: "I've Got Those Wake Up at Seven Thirty, Wash Your Ears They're Dirty, Eat Your Eggs and Oatmeal Rush to School Blues."

INSTRUCTOR'S NOTES

29

OTHER
MARKS
OF
PUNCTUATION

This chapter explains the uses of the dash, parentheses, brackets, ellipses, and slash.

◼‖ 29a
Use the dash to emphasize interruptions in sentences.

The dash, or a pair of dashes, lets you interrupt a sentence's structure to add information—an explanation, examples, a definition, even a personal comment or reaction. Dashes are like parentheses in this function of setting off "asides," or extra material (see 29b for parentheses). Such asides can come at the beginning, in the middle, or at the end of a sentence. Unlike parentheses, dashes emphasize the interruptions. Use dashes sparingly—if you do use them—so that their impact is not diluted by overexposure.

In typed papers, make a dash by hitting the hyphen key twice. Don't put a space before, between, or after the hyphens. In handwritten papers, make a dash slightly longer than a hyphen, using one unbroken line for each dash.

474

1
Use a dash or dashes to emphasize explanations, including appositives°, examples, and definitions.

APPOSITIVES

On television, a cattle drive or a cavalry charge or a chase—the climax of so many a big movie—loses the dimensions of space and distance that made it exciting, that sometimes made it great.

—PAULINE KAEL, *Kiss Kiss Bang Bang*

Two of the strongest animals in the jungle are vegetarians—the elephant and the gorilla.

—DICK GREGORY, *The Shadow that Scares Me*

EXAMPLES

The care-takers—those who are helpers, nurturers, teachers, mothers—are still systematically devalued.

—ELLEN GOODMAN, "Just Woman's Work?"

Life, Look, the *Saturday Evening Post*—each went to its grave, later to undergo resurrection as a small-circulation ghost of its former self.

—ALVIN TOFFLER, "The De-Massified Media"

DEFINITIONS

From this analogy with sexism and racism I suppose the name for this malady is "speciesism"—the prejudice that there are no beings so fine, so capable, so reliable as human beings.

—CARL SAGAN, *Broca's Brain*

Personal space—"elbow room"—is a vital commodity for the human animal, and one that cannot be ignored without risking serious trouble.

—DESMOND MORRIS, *Manwatching*

Be sure to place the words you set off in dashes next to or near to the words they explain. Otherwise, the interruption will distract or confuse your reader.

No   The current argument is—one that parents, faculty, students, and coaches all debate fiercely—whether athletes should have to meet minimum academic standards to play their sports.

YES   The current argument—one that parents, faculty, students, and coaches all debate fiercely—is whether athletes should have to meet minimum academic standards to play their sports.

475

BIOGRAPHY

Ellen Goodman's column for the *Boston Globe,* which is syndicated in over 200 newspapers, won her the 1980 Pulitzer Prize for Commentary. Her columns have been collected and published in several volumes: *Turning Points, Close to Home,* and *At Large.*

BIOGRAPHY

Alvin Toffler has worked as a Washington correspondent for various newspapers and has been an associate editor of *Fortune,* a faculty member of the New School for Social Research in New York, and a visiting professor at Cornell University. He is the author of a number of books that investigate the shape of the future and how people can best adapt to it. These books include *Future Shock* (1970) and *The Third Wave* (1980).

ALTERNATE EXAMPLE: DASH OF DEFINITION

Futuristic novels with a bleak vision of the prospects for the free individual characteristically portray a society in which history—knowledge of the past—has been systematically eliminated.

—DIANE RAVITCH, "Decline and Fall of Teaching History"

ALTERNATE EXAMPLE: DASH OF DEFINITION

Dinner at the Huntercombe's possessed only two dramatic features—the wine was a farce and the food a tragedy.

—ANTHONY POWELL

2
Use a dash or dashes to emphasize a contrast.

Tampering with time brought most of the house tumbling down, and it was this that made Einstein's work so important—and controversial.

—BANESH HOFFMANN, "My Friend, Albert Einstein"

Today a majority of men in this part of the country, especially in Texas, wear some type of "Western" hat—and so do a number of the women.

—ALISON LURIE, *The Language of Clothes*

3
Use a dash or dashes to emphasize an "aside."

"Asides" are writers' comments, within the structure of a sentence or a paragraph, on something they have written. Especially in writing that is otherwise meant to seem objective, asides let writers introduce their personal views or convey their attitudes. Writers who want to emphasize asides set them off with dashes.

These five passages have not been picked out because they are especially bad—I could have quoted far worse if I had chosen—but because they illustrate various of the mental vices from which we now suffer.

—GEORGE ORWELL, "Politics and the English Language"

In a world governed solely by the principle of "dog eat dog"—if indeed there ever was such a world—how many children a family had would not be a matter of public concern.

—GARRETT HARDIN, "The Tragedy of the Commons"

If the words you put between a pair of dashes would take a question mark or an exclamation point written as a separate sentence, use that punctuation before the second dash.

A first date—do you remember?—stays in the memory forever. Commas, semicolons, colons, and periods are not used next to dashes.

4
Use a dash to show hesitating or broken-off speech.

"Naturally," said Mr. Lorry. "Yes—I—"

After a pause, he added, again settling the crisp flaxen wig at the ears, "It is very difficult to begin."

—CHARLES DICKENS, *A Tale of Two Cities*

EXERCISE 1
Supply dashes in the following sentences.

EXAMPLE　In the Middle Ages nearly everyone believed as Aristotle had that the intellect was located in the heart.

In the Middle Ages nearly everyone believed—as Aristotle had—that the intellect was located in the heart.

1. The adult blue, or lycaenid, butterfly is tiny about big enough to cover a 20 cent stamp.
—MATTHEW DOUGLAS, "The Butterfly Connection"

2. This personality so runs the erroneous belief will be revealed in all its splendor if the individual just forgets about courtesy. . . .
—MARGARET HALSEY, "What's Wrong with 'Me, Me, Me'?"

3. They wanted to be moved, excited, inspired, consoled, uplifted in short, led!
—MICHAEL KORDA, "What It Takes to Be a Leader"

4. Per capita, Japan has a twentieth of the lawyers and crime of America.
—JOHN TRAIN, *Preserving Capital and Making It Grow*

5. Different as they were in background, in personality, in underlying aspiration these two great soldiers had much in common.
—BRUCE CATTON, "Grant and Lee: A Study in Contrasts"

ANSWERS: EXERCISE 1
1. The adult blue, or lycaenid, butterfly is tiny—about big enough to cover a 20 cent stamp.
—MATTHEW DOUGLAS, "The Butterfly Connection"

2. This personality—so runs the erroneous belief—will be revealed in all its splendor if the individual just forgets about courtesy . . .
—MARGARET HALSEY, "What's Wrong with 'Me, Me, Me'?"

3. They wanted to be moved, excited, inspired, consoled, uplifted—in short, led!
—MICHAEL KORDA, "What It Takes to Be a Leader"

4. Per capita, Japan has a twentieth of the lawyers—and crime—of America.
—JOHN TRAIN, *Preserving Capital and Making It Grow*

5. Different as they were—in background, in personality, in underlying aspiration—these two great soldiers had much in common.
—BRUCE CATTON, "Grant and Lee: A Study in Contrasts"

■‖ 29b

Use parentheses to enclose interrupting material in sentences, as well as for a few special purposes.

Parentheses let you interrupt a sentence's structure to add information of many kinds. Parentheses are like dashes in this function of setting off extra or interrupting words. Unlike dashes, which make interruptions stand out, parentheses deemphasize what they enclose.

DASHES　　　　The books and journals—and tapes, filmstrips, even the people you want to interview—are all too often unavailable when you are ready.

PARENTHESES　The books and journals (and tapes, filmstrips, even the people you want to interview) are all too often unavailable when you are ready.

Do not use parentheses too frequently in any one piece of writing. They can be very distracting for readers.

477

BIOGRAPHY

S. I. (Samuel Ichiyé) Hayakawa has had a notable public career; he was president of San Francisco State College and served as a U.S. Senator. However, he is known best as a scholar and educator. Born in Canada, Hayakawa entered academe as a professor of English. He has gone on to become a leader in the field of general semantics—the study of the (sometimes) changing meanings of words and how they influence speakers. One of his books, *Language in Thought and Action* (1941), has been widely used as a writing and philosophy textbook. In addition to scholarly works, Hayakawa often writes popular articles on social themes, applying the lessons of general semantics to day-to-day problems. A selection of these articles was published in 1979 as *Through the Communciation Barrier*.

ALTERNATE EXAMPLE

We demand that people should be true to the picture we have of them, no matter how repulsive those pictures may be: we prefer the true portrait (as we have conceived it), in all its homgeneity, to one with a detail added which refuses to fit in.

—PAMELA HANSFORD JOHNSON

1

Use parentheses to enclose interrupting words, including explanations, examples, and asides.

EXPLANATIONS

For a really big job of dictionary-writing, such as the *Oxford English Dictionary* (usually bound in about twenty-five volumes), millions of such cards are collected, and the task of editing occupies decades.

—S. I. HAYAKAWA, *Language and Thought in Action*

In *division* (also known as *partition*) a subject commonly thought of as a single unit is reduced to its separate parts.

—DAVID SKWIRE, *Writing with a Thesis*

EXAMPLES

Though other cities (Dresden, for instance) had been utterly destroyed in World War II, never before had a single weapon been responsible for such destruction.

—LAURENCE BEHRENS and LEONARD J. ROSEN, *Writing and Reading Across the Curriculum*

ASIDES

"Dreamlike and fantastic" is how Schell (correctly) dismisses the prospect of a pre-emptive Soviet missile attack on the U.S.'s supposedly vulnerable land forces.

—STROBE TALBOTT, "A Grim Manifesto on Nuclear War"

The sheer decibel level of the noise around us is not enough to make us cranky, irritable, or aggressive. (It can, however, affect our mental and physical health, which is another matter.)

—CAROL TAVRIS, *Anger: The Misunderstood Emotion*

2

Use parentheses for certain numbers and letters of listed items.

When you number listed items within a sentence, enclose the numbers (or letters) in parentheses.

These four items are on the agenda for tonight's meeting: (1) current membership figures, (2) current treasury figures, (3) the budget for renovations, and (4) the campaign for public contributions.

■ PUNCTUATION ALERT: Separate items of a run-in list (a list within the structure of a sentence) with commas or semicolons. ▮

478

3

In business and legal writing, use parentheses to enclose a numeral repeating a spelled-out number.

The monthly rent is three hundred sixty-five dollars ($365).

We are confirming that your order of fifteen (15) gross was shipped today.

4

Use a question mark enclosed in parentheses for a doubtful date or number.

When information is unknown or doubtful despite your best attempts to determine it, you can use (?) after the number or fact. Using the word *about* is equally acceptable.

Sappho was born in 612 (?) B.C.

Sappho was born about 612 B.C.

5

Know how to use other punctuation with parentheses.

Never put a comma before an opening parenthesis even if what comes before the parenthetical material requires a comma. Put the parenthetical material in, and then use the comma immediately after the closing parenthesis.

No   Although radically different from my favorite film, *(Ben Hur) Citizen Kane* is an important film and one worth studying.

Yes   Although radically different from my favorite film *(Ben Hur), Citizen Kane* is an important film and one worth studying.

You can use a question mark or an exclamation point with parenthetical words that occur within the structure of a sentence.

Looking for clues (did we really expect to find any?) wasted four entire days.

Use a period, however, only when you enclose a complete statement in parentheses outside the structure of another sentence. In this case, use a capital letter as well.

COORDINATED RESOURCES

Alternate examples and exercises for this chapter are available in the *S & S Workbook for Writers,* Gordon and Troyka.

The software program *Blue Pencil,* available from Prentice-Hall, offers students additional practice coordinated with 29a and 29b.

Students can practice and test their knowledge of terms, key concepts, and applications of material in this chapter by using the *Study Guide to the S & S Handbook for Writers,* West.

479

No Looking for clues (now I wonder whether we really expected to find any.) wasted four entire days.

Yes Looking for clues wasted four entire days. (Now I wonder whether we really expected to find any.)

Yes Looking for clues (now I wonder whether we really expected to find any) wasted four entire days.

ANSWERS: EXERCISE 2

Answers may vary slightly.

1. The four basic elements that make up all but one percent of terrestrial matter (carbon, hydrogen, nitrogen, and oxygen) are also the basic elements of the Milky Way.

2. A "shell" of television and radio signals carrying old radio and television programs (for example, *Gangbusters, The Lone Ranger,* and *Howdy Doody*) is expanding through the cosmos at the speed of light.

3. The first automobile to cross the United States took fifty-two days (in 1903) to go from San Francisco to New York.

4. There are half a million (500,000) more automobiles in Los Angeles than there are people.

5. The most sensational thefts in history include (1) the theft of the British Crown Jewels from the Tower of London; (2) the Great Train Robbery near Cheddington, England, which netted the crooks over $7,368,715 in cash; and (3) the theft of the Mona Lisa from the Louvre in Paris on August 21, 1911.

6. Ts'ai Yen, who was born in A.D. 162 (?) and who lived until about A.D. 239 is considered by many experts to be the first great Chinese female poet.

7. Dashes (see Section 29a) can sometimes, but not always, serve the same function as parentheses.

8. At the Safety Evaluation Conference (called *Safecon*) of the National Intercollegiate Flying Association, college flying teams compete in events such as (1) precision landing, (2) message drops, (3) navigation, and (4) accuracy with flight computers.

EXERCISE 2

Supply needed or useful parentheses.

EXAMPLE The universe is so large in relation to the matter it contains that it can be compared to a building of huge proportions twenty miles long, twenty miles high, and twenty miles wide that holds only a single grain of sand.

The universe is so large in relation to the matter it contains that it can be compared to a building of huge proportions (*twenty miles long, twenty miles high, and twenty miles wide*) that holds only a single grain of sand.

1. The four basic elements that make up all but one percent of terrestrial matter carbon, hydrogen, nitrogen, and oxygen are also the basic elements of the Milky Way.

2. A "shell" of television and radio signals carrying old radio and television programs for example, *Gangbusters, The Lone Ranger,* and *Howdy Doody* is expanding through the cosmos at the speed of light.

3. The first automobile to cross the United States took fifty-two days in 1903 to go from San Francisco to New York.

4. There are half a million 500,000 more automobiles in Los Angeles than there are people.

5. The most sensational thefts in history include 1 the theft of the British Crown Jewels from the Tower of London; 2 the Great Train Robbery near Cheddington, England, which netted the crooks over $7,368,715 in cash; and 3 the theft of the Mona Lisa from the Louvre in Paris on August 21, 1911.

6. Ts'ai Yen, who was born in 162 A.D. ? and who lived until about 239 A.D. is considered by many experts to be the first great Chinese female poet.

7. Dashes see Section 29a can sometimes, but not always, serve the same function as parentheses.

8. At the Safety Evaluation Conference called *Safecon* of the National Intercollegiate Flying Association, college flying teams compete in events such as 1 precision landing, 2 message drops, 3 navigation, and 4 accuracy with flight computers.

480

29c

Use brackets to enclose insertions into quotations or into parentheses.

1

Use brackets to enclose words you insert into quotations.

When you work quoted words into your own sentences (see 31e), you may have to change a word or two to make the quoted words fit into the structure of your sentence. Enclose any changes you make in square brackets.

ORIGINAL
Surprisingly, this trend is almost reversed in Italy where males interact closer and display significantly more contact than do male/female dyads and female couples.
—ROBERT SHUTER, "A Field Study of Nonverbal Communication in Germany, Italy, and the United States," page 305

QUOTATION WITH BRACKETS
Although German and American men stand farthest apart and touch each other least, "[this phenomenon] is almost reversed in Italy where males interact closer and display significantly more contact than do male/female dyads and female couples" (Shuter 305).

The same technique—enclosing your words in brackets—lets you add explanations and clarifications to quoted material.

ORIGINAL
This sort of information seems trivial, but it does affect international understanding. Imagine, for example, a business conference between an American and an Arab.

QUOTATION WITH BRACKETS
"This sort of information seems trivial, but it *does* affect international understanding [italics mine]."

Now and then you may find that an author or a typesetter has made a mistake in something you want to quote—a wrong date, a misspelled word, an error of fact. You cannot change another writer's words, but you do not want readers to think you made the error. You can show that you know about the error by inserting the Latin

INSTRUCTOR'S NOTES

word *sic,* in brackets, next to the error. Meaning "so" or "thus," *sic,* in brackets says to a reader, "it is thus in the original."

> In the report, the construction supervisor points out one unintended consequence of doubling the amount of floor space: "With that much extra room per person, the tennants [sic] would sublet."

2

Use brackets to enclose very brief parenthetical material inside parentheses.

> From that point on, Thomas Parker simply disappears. (His death [c. 1441] is unrecorded officially, but a gravestone marker is mentioned in a 1640 parish report.)

■ 29d

Use an ellipsis to signal omissions from quotations or to show hesitating or broken-off speech.

An **ellipsis** is a set of three spaced dots (use the period key on a typewriter). Its most important function is to show that you have left out some of the original writer's words in material you are quoting. Ellipses can also show hesitant or broken-off speech, as does the dash (29a-4).

1

Use an ellipsis to show that you have omitted words from material you are quoting.

ORIGINAL
Personal space is not necessarily spherical in shape, nor does it extend equally in all directions. (People are able to tolerate closer presence of a stranger at their sides than directly in front.) It has been likened to a snail shell, a soap bubble, an aura, and "breathing room."

—ROBERT SOMMER, *Personal Space:*
The Behavioral Bases of Design, page 26

SOME MATERIAL USED IN A QUOTATION
Surprisingly, Sommer has been able to define its dimensions: "Personal space . . . not necessarily spherical in shape . . . has been likened to a snail shell, a soap bubble, an aura, and 'breathing room' " (26).

482

If an omission occurs at the beginning of your quoted words, you do not need to use an ellipsis to show the omission. Also you do not need to use an ellipsis at the end as long as you end with a complete sentence. (Otherwise, almost everything you quote would require an ellipsis.)

> According to Sommer, it may not be "spherical in shape, nor does it extend equally in all directions" (26).

If you select for quotation two or more sentences separated by material you do not want to quote, show the omission with (1) the period that ends the sentence before the omission and (2) the three spaced periods of an ellipsis. Use this procedure for sentences in the same paragraph or in sequential paragraphs.

> Sommer explains, "Personal space is not necessarily spherical in shape, nor does it extend equally in all directions. . . . It has been likened to a snail shell, a soap bubble, an aura, and 'breathing room' " (26).

If you stop quoting before the end of the sentence in the original and your own sentence continues, you may use an ellipsis to show that the quoted sentence continues.

> Personal space "has been likened to a snail shell, a soap bubble, . . ." (Sommer 26), but the shape varies among cultures.

When a quotation comes at the end of your sentence but the quoted words are *not* the end of a sentence in the original source, you must use an ellipsis. If the quotation is not followed by parenthetical documentation, use (1) a sentence period after the last quoted word, (2) three spaced dots for the ellipsis, and then (3) closing quotation marks.

> **ELLIPSIS AT END OF SENTENCE WITHOUT PARENTHETICAL DOCUMENTATION**
> Still, on that same page Sommer says people have described personal space as "a snail shell, a soap bubble, an aura. . . ."

But if the quotation is followed by parenthetical documentation, use (1) three spaced dots for the ellipsis, (2) closing quotation marks, (3) the parenthetical reference, and then (4) the sentence period.

> **ELLIPSIS AT END OF SENTENCE WITH PARENTHETICAL DOCUMENTATION**
> Sommer says people have described personal space as "a snail shell, a soap bubble, an aura . . ." (26).

When you delete words immediately after an internal punc-

483

ALTERNATE EXAMPLE: ELLIPSES

They ate frozen meat, frozen fried potatoes, and frozen peas. Blindfolded, one could not have identified the peas, and the only flavor the potatoes had was the flavor of soap. It was the monotonous fare of the besieged . . . but . . . where was the enemy?

—JOHN CHEEVER

tuation mark in the quotation, include that mark in your sentence and then add the three spaced dots for the ellipsis.

> It has been likened to a snail shell, . . . and "breathing room."

|| 2
Use an ellipsis to show broken-off speech.

Like the dash (29a-4), an ellipsis shows a speaker's broken-off or interrupted speech.

> "And, anyway, what do you know of him?"
> "Nothing. That is why I ask you . . ."
> "I would prefer never to speak of him."
> —UMBERTO ECO, *The Name of the Rose*

■|| 29e
Use the slash correctly for quoting poetry lines, for numerical fractions, and for *and/or*.

|| 1
Use the slash to separate up to three lines of quoted poetry.

If you quote more than three lines of a poem in writing, set the poetry off with space and indentations as you would a prose quotation of more than four lines (see 28a and the Manuscript Form appendix). For three lines or less, quote poetry—enclosed in quotation marks—in sentence format, with a slash to divide one line from the next. Leave a space on each side of the slash.

> Consider the beginning of Anne Sexton's poem "Words": "Be careful of words, / even the miraculous ones."

Capitalize and punctuate each line as it is in the original, with this exception: End your sentence with a period, even if the quoted line of poetry does not have one.

|| 2
In typed manuscripts, use the slash for numerical fractions.

If you have to type numerical fractions, use the slash to sepa-

BIOGRAPHY

Anne Sexton (1928–1974) began writing poetry in her late twenties. She composed a large body of work, much of it focused on domestic and personal crises and on nature. Among her works are *To Bedlam and Part Way Back* (1960), *Live or Die* (1967), and *The Awful Rowing Towards God* (1975). In her poetry, Sexton struggled to overcome mental illness and suicidal urges—unfortunately, those ugres were too strong and she died, a suicide, in 1974.

484

rate numerator and denominator and a hyphen to tie a whole number to its fraction: *1/16, 1-2/3, 2/5, 3-7/8*. (See 30j for advice on using spelled-out and numerical forms of numbers.)

3
Use the slash for *and/or*.

You will not use word combinations like *and/or* often for writing in the humanities, but where use is acceptable, separate the words with a slash. Leave no space before or after the slash.

In the humanities, listing both alternatives in normal sentence structure is usually better than separating choices with a slash.

No	The best quality of reproduction comes from 35mm slides/direct positive films.
Yes	The best quality of reproduction comes from 35mm slides or direct positive films.

EXERCISE 3

Supply needed dashes, parentheses, brackets, ellipses, and slashes. If a sentence is correct as written, circle its number.

EXAMPLE   Every year in the United States, four times the amount of money spent on baby food is spent on pet food $1.5 billion.

Every year in the United States, four times the amount of money spent on baby food is spent on pet food ($1.5 billion).

1. Albert Einstein's last words they were spoken in his native German will never be known because his attending nurse spoke only English.
2. During one five-week span in 1841, three different men served as President of the United States: 1 Martin Van Buren finished his term on March 3; 2 William Henry Harrison Van Buren's successor was inaugurated on March 4; and 3 John Tyler who assumed the Presidency when Harrison died on April 6 after only thirty-two days in office.
3. Gold is so malleable that a single ounce can be beaten out into a thin film less than 1 282,000th of an inch that would cover 100 square feet.
4. To get at every ounce of gold, miners have dug as deep as 2-1/2 miles.
5. The American portrait artist Charles Willson Peale made George Washington an innovative set of dentures elks' teeth set in lead.
6. Henri Matisse's painting *Le Bateau* once hung in New York's Museum of

ANSWERS: EXERCISE 3
Answers may vary slightly.
1. Albert Einstein's last words—they were spoken in his native German—will never be known because his attending nurse spoke only English. [parentheses also acceptable]
2. During one five-week span in 1841, three different men served as President of the United States: (1) Martin Van Buren finished his term on March 3; (2) William Henry Harrison—Van Buren's successor—was inaugurated on March 4; and (3) John Tyler—who assumed the Presidency when Harrison died on April 6 after only thirty-two days in office.
3. Gold is so malleable that a single ounce can be beaten out into a thin film (less than 1/282,000th of an inch) that would cover 100 square feet. [dashes also acceptable]
4. Correct
5. The American portrait artist Charles Willson Peale made George Washington an innovative set of dentures—elks' teeth set in lead.
6. Henri Matisse's painting *Le Bateau* once hung in New York's Museum of Modern Art for forty-seven days (not to mention being viewed by about 116,000 people) before someone noticed that it was hung upside down. [dashes also acceptable]

485

7. When Thomas Edison learned that one of the batteries his company manufactured was defective, he offered a refund to all buyers—a pledge made good by $1 million from his own pocket.

8. In 1816 a strange chain of events (beginning with a volcanic eruption in the Dutch East Indies [now Indonesia]) caused New England to experience snow in June and killing frosts through July and August.

9. Although the identity of the famous Jack the Ripper was never proven, when the convicted murderer Dr. Thomas Cream was hanged his last words were the unfinished sentence, "I am Jack the —" [the . . ." also acceptable]

10. Maxine Kumin—the winner of the 1973 Pulitzer Prize for Poetry—wrote these memorable lines about calves as they are being born: "They come forth with all four legs folded in / like a dime-store card table." [parentheses also acceptable]

ANSWERS: EXERCISE 4
Answers will vary greatly. When checking them, note whether the directions were followed.

1. only three lines of the sonnet, with slash marks between the first and second and between the second and third lines—quoted in a sentence.

2. parentheses to enclose the numbers 1–4 that label the list within a sentence

3. an ellipses to indicate an omission from a quotation, with the meaning of the whole still clear

4. dashes to set off a definition in a sentence

5. parentheses to enclose a brief example in a sentence

Modern Art for forty-seven days not to mention being viewed by about 116,000 people before someone noticed that it was hung upside down.

7. When Thomas Edison learned that one of the batteries his company manufactured was defective, he offered a refund to all buyers a pledge made good by $1 million from his own pocket.

8. In 1816 a strange chain of events (beginning with a volcanic eruption in the Dutch East Indies (now Indonesia) caused New England to experience snow in June and killing frosts through July and August.

9. Although the identity of the famous Jack the Ripper was never proven, when the convicted murderer Dr. Thomas Cream was hanged his last words were the unfinished sentence, "I am Jack the."

10. Maxine Kumin the winner of the 1973 Pulitzer Prize for Poetry wrote these memorable lines about calves as they are being born: "They come forth with all four legs folded in / like a dime-store card table."

EXERCISE 4
Follow the directions for each item. Use dashes, parentheses, ellipses, and slashes as needed.

EXAMPLE   Write a sentence using dashes that exclaims about love.
I am in love—again!

1. Write a sentence that quotes only three lines of Sonnet XLIII by Elizabeth Barrett Browning:
How do I love thee? Let me count the ways.
I love thee to the depth and breadth and height
My soul can reach, when feeling out of sight
For the ends of Being and ideal Grace.
I love thee to the level of every day's
Most quiet need, by sun and candlelight.
I love thee freely, as men strive for Right;
I love thee purely, as they turn from Praise.
I love thee with the passion put to use
In my old griefs, and with my childhood's faith.
I love thee with a love I seemed to lose
With my lost saints,—I love thee with the breath,
Smiles, tears, of all my life!—and, if God choose,
I shall but love thee better after death.

2. Write a sentence that includes a list of four numbered items.

3. Quote a few sentences from a source. Choose one from which you can omit a few words without losing meaning. Correctly indicate the omission. At the end, give the source of the quotation.

4. Write a sentence in which you use dashes to set off a definition.

5. Write a sentence in which you use parentheses to enclose a brief example.

486

30

CAPITALS, ITALICS, ABBREVIATIONS, AND NUMBERS

Capital letters, italics (shown as underlining in handwritten or typed material), abbreviations, and styles of writing numbers are sometimes referred to as **mechanics.** Knowing which forms to use and when to use them, however, is far from mechanical. Issues of mechanics involve making choices: Does a word start with a capital letter or a lower-case one? Does a group of words need to be underlined, put in quotation marks, or left alone? Is an abbreviation acceptable in a given case? When is a figure used rather than a number spelled out in words?

■|| CAPITALS

■|| 30a
Capitalize the first word of a sentence.

Always capitalize the first letter of the first word in a sentence, a question, or a command.

INSTRUCTOR'S NOTES

TEACHING TIP

A useful capitalization activity is to dictate a passage containing a mix of proper and common nouns, leaving capitalization up to the students. Grading can be based only on use of capitals or on overall correctness. If you do not want to test punctuation, read all punctuation marks as you go along; this practice helps students focus their attention on capitalization. Here are two passages to use from *The Height of Your Life* by Ralph Keyes (Boston: Little, Brown, 1980).

Covering the victory celebration of 6′5″ former basketball player Bill Bradley after his nomination for the U.S. Senate, a New Jersey television commentator noted how much easier his job was when a candidate's head stood so high above the mob. "It's always easier with tall guys," an advance man once explained as he funneled voters over to his candidate—New York's 6′5″ U.S. senator-to-be Daniel Patrick Moynihan. Prior to working for Moynihan the same aide had worked for 6′3″ New York Mayor John Lindsay. (214-15)

When Sylvester Stallone was filming *Rocky II* in Philadelphia, I followed him around for an afternoon and was impressed both by his two-inch heels and by the way his pant cuffs were cut low in back to drape over them. . . . Heavyweight boxer Ken Norton was originally expected to play Rocky's opponent Apollo Creed. But next to Norton's hefty 6′3″ frame, Stallone looked like a middleweight. So the part went to Stallone's size-mate Carl Weathers. Other supporting roles were filled with even smaller actors, such as Burgess Meredith, Burt Young, and Talia Shire. By contrast Rocky looked huge. (263)

Records show that snow fell in Antarctica while the thermometer registered minus 65 degrees.

Does it ever get too cold to snow?

Verify that temperature immediately.

Practice varies for starting each question in a series of questions with a capital letter.

YES   What facial feature would most people change if they could? Their eyes? Their ears? Their mouths?

YES   What facial feature would most people change if they could? their eyes? their ears? their mouths?

Whichever practice you choose, be consistent throughout a piece of writing. Of course, if the questions are complete sentences, start each with a capital letter.

Practice also varies for using a capital letter for a complete sentence following a colon.

YES   I need advice about what to do: The instructions give contradictory commands.

YES   I need advice about what to do: the instructions give contradictory commands.

Whichever practice you choose, be consistent throughout a piece of writing.

A complete sentence enclosed in parentheses may stand alone or may fall within the structure of another sentence. Those that stand alone start with a capital letter. Those that fall within the structure of another sentence do not start with a capital letter. ▌‖ PUNCTUATION ALERTS: (1) When a complete sentence within parentheses stands alone, always end it with a period, question mark, or exclamation point—as needed for meaning. (2) When a complete sentence within parentheses falls within the structure of another sentence, use only a question mark or an exclamation point at the end if meaning calls for either; if meaning calls for a period, omit it. Both types of parenthetical sentences occur in the first example below. ‖▌

I didn't know till years later that they called it the Cuban Missile Crisis. But I remember Castro. (We called him Castor Oil and were awed by his beard—beards were rare in those days.) We might not have worried so much (what would the Communists want with our small New Hampshire town?) except that we lived 10 miles from an air base.

—JOYCE MAYNARD, "An 18-Year-Old Looks Back on Life"

The journey from the first clues to the final interpretation was a long one (it took six years), and the route was not straightforward.

—EVELYN FOX KELLER, *A Feeling for the Organism*

When you quote lines of poetry, follow the practice of the version you quote from concerning capital letters at the beginning of lines and within lines. (See 28a-3 for advice on formats for quoted poetry.)

■‖ 30b

Capitalize listed items correctly.

In a **run-in list,** the items are worked into the structure of a sentence or a paragraph rather than being set up vertically with each item on a new line. When the items in a run-in list are complete sentences, capitalize the first letter of each item.

We found three reasons for the delay: (1) Bad weather held up delivery of raw materials. (2) Poor scheduling created confusion and slowdowns. (3) Lack of proper machine maintenance caused an equipment failure.

When the items in a run-in list are not complete sentences, do not begin them with capital letters.

The reasons for the delay were (1) bad weather, (2) poor scheduling, and (3) equipment failure.

In a **displayed list,** the items are set up vertically, one below the other. Capitalize the first letter of all items in a displayed list if any item is a complete sentence. ■‖ PARALLELISM ALERT: Make list items parallel in structure. If one item must be a sentence, make all the items sentences. ‖ If the items are not sentences, you may either start all of them with capital letters or start all of them with lower-case letters. Whichever practice you choose, be consistent throughout a piece of writing.

TEACHING TIP
You might find that students overcapitalize in their writing. Comparison can be a useful tool in getting them to distinguish between common and proper nouns. First, review the basic rule: proper (capitalized) nouns name specific people, places, or things; common (uncapitalized) nouns refer to nonspecific people, places, or things. Then give students series of paired noun phrases, one of which contains a proper noun and one a common noun. Omit all capitals. Ask students to identify and capitalize the proper noun: president Washington, the president of the country; hunter high school, the high school band; a new car, a lincoln continental; psychological testing, psychology 101. Augment this list with pairs representing your students' most common errors.

Your students will probably find this rather easy, because contrast highlights the specific nouns. The next step can be to make up or edit a paragraph to eliminate all capital letters except those that begin sentences. Ask students to capitalize the first letters of all proper nouns. Upon completion, you might have students exchange papers and discuss the correct answers. Then students can correct one another's exercises and you can collect the papers to review or record grades.

INSTRUCTOR'S NOTES

YES   The reasons for the delay are as follows:
    1. Bad weather
    2. Poor scheduling
    3. Equipment failure

YES   The reasons for the delay are as follows:
    1. bad weather
    2. poor scheduling
    3. equipment failure

In a **formal outline,** each item must start with a capital letter (see 2e-5).

TEACHING TIP

Students are prone to confuse *O* and *oh.* They are not interchangeable. *Oh* is capitalized only when it begins a sentence. It is an exclamation: *Oh, I am late. O* is always capitalized. It is used in words as a digression within a speech):

O Caesar, what a wounding shame is this.
—Cleopatra, in Shakespeare's *Antony and Cleopatra*

30c

Capitalize the first letter of an introduced quotation.

If you have made quoted words part of the structure of your own sentence, do not capitalize the first quoted word.

> Mrs. Saintonge says that when students visit a country whose language they are trying to learn, they "absorb a good accent with the food."
> Doris Lessing believes that "the way to learn a language is to breathe it in."

If the words in your sentence serve only to introduce quoted words or if you are directly quoting speech, capitalize the first letter of the quoted words.

> Mrs. Saintonge says, "Students should always visit a country when they want to learn its language. They'll absorb a good accent with the food."
> According to Doris Lessing, "The way to learn a language is to breathe it in."

Do not capitalize a quotation you resume within a sentence, and do not capitalize a partial quotation.

> "Persistence," says my supervisor, "is more important than quickness for this task."
> Winking, she encouraged me to try "very speedy persistence."

See Chapter 28 for full coverage of quotation marks.

490

■‖ 30d
Capitalize the interjection *O* and the pronoun *I*.

I would drink from the river, which I would meet again and again.

> —Maxine Hong Kingston, *The Woman Warrior*

Temper, O fair Love, Love's impetuous rage.

> —John Donne, "On His Mistress"

■‖ CAPITALIZATION CAUTION: Do not capitalize *oh* unless it starts a sentence or unless it is capitalized in poetry you are quoting. ‖■

■‖ 30e
Capitalize nouns and adjectives according to standard practice.

Capitalize **proper nouns** (nouns that name specific people, places, or things) and **proper adjectives** (adjectives formed from proper nouns).

Proper Nouns	Proper Adjectives
Mexico	Mexican literature
Rome	the Roman legions
Shakespeare	a Shakespearean comedy

Notice that articles *(the, a, an)* in front of proper nouns or adjectives are not capitalized.

Do not capitalize common nouns (nouns that name general classes of people, places, or things) unless they start a sentence.

Common Nouns

a state	people
the car	tomatoes
team	an exercise

■‖ CAPITALIZATION CAUTION: A proper noun or adjective sometimes takes on a "common" meaning, losing its very specific "proper" word associations. When that happens, the word loses its capital letter as well. Examples include *arabic numeral, derringer, french fry, india ink, italics, oriental rug, panama hat, pasteurize.* ‖■

Many common nouns are capitalized when names or titles are added to them. For example, *lake* is not ordinarily capitalized, but when a specific name is added, it is: *Lake Ontario.* Without the spe-

COORDINATED RESOURCES

Alternate examples and exercises for this chapter are available in the *S & S Workbook for Writers,* Gordon and Troyka.

Transparency masters are available for the screened charts and/or lists in this chapter.

The software program *Blue Pencil,* available from Prentice-Hall, offers students additional practice coordinated with 30f and 30g.

Students can practice and test their knowledge of terms, key concepts, and applications of material in this chapter by using the *Study Guide to the S & S Handbook for Writers,* West.

cific name, however, even if the specific name is implied, the common noun is not capitalized.

NO Canada and the United States cleaned up Lake Ontario in the 1970s, for the **Lake** was near death from industrial pollution.

YES Canada and the United States cleaned up Lake Ontario in the 1970s, for the **lake** was near death from industrial pollution.

The Capitalization Guide can help you with capitalization questions. Although it cannot cover all possibilities, you can apply what you find in the list to similar items.

This chapter shows you capitalization guidelines for academic writing in the humanities. In your reading, you will sometimes see capitalized words you are told here *not* to capitalize. How writers capitalize has a good deal to do with audience and purpose. A corporation's annual report will refer to *the Board of Directors* and *the Company,* not the *board of directors* and *the company.* The administrators of your school probably write *the Faculty* and *the College* or *the University,* words you would not capitalize in a paper. Capitalization is one convention you may need to adapt if you write for and about a particular group. The conventions set out here—and in dictionaries—apply to writing for a general audience.

CAPITALIZATION GUIDE		
	CAPITALS	**LOWER-CASE LETTERS**
NAMES	Nikki Giovanni	
	Bob Ojeda	
	Mother Theresa	my mother (*relationship*)
	Doc Holliday	the doctor (*role*)
TITLES	Chief Justice Earl Warren	the chief justice
	President Truman the President (*who is now in office*)	a president

	CAPITALS	LOWER-CASE LETTERS
	Democrat (*a party member*)	democrat (*a believer in democracy*)
	Representative Marge Roukema	the congressional representative
	Senator Dole	the senator
	Professor Roberts	the professor
	Pope John XXIII	the pope
	Rabbi Gale Weiss	the rabbi
	the Reverend Allan Risden	the minister
	Queen Elizabeth II	the queen
GROUPS OF HUMANITY	Caucasian (*race*)	white (*also* White)
	Negro (*race*)	black (*also* Black)
	Oriental (*race*)	
	Muslim	
	Jewish	
ORGANIZATIONS	Congress	congressional
	the Ohio State Supreme Court	the state supreme court
	the Communist Party	the party
	the Rotary Club	the club
	Xerox Corporation	the corporation
	Eastman Kodak Company	the company
PLACES	Los Angeles	
	India	
	the South (*a region*)	turn south (*a direction*)
	Main Street	the street
	Hunter Avenue	the avenue
	Atlantic Ocean	the ocean
	the Atlantic	
	Orinoco River	the river
	the Gobi Desert	the desert
	the Australian continent	the continent

493

	CAPITALS	LOWER-CASE LETTERS
BUILDINGS	the Capitol (in Washington, D.C.)	the state capitol
	Union High School	the high school
	China West Cafe	the restaurant
	Highland Hospital	the hospital
SCIENTIFIC TERMS	Mars, Martian	
	Earth (*the planet*)	the earth (*where we live*)
	the Milky Way	the galaxy
		the moon
		the sun
	Streptococcus aureus	a streptococcal infection
	Amanita muscaria	fly amanita mushroom
	Gresham's law	the theory of relativity
LANGUAGES, NATIONALITIES	Spanish	
	Vietnamese	
	Chinese	
SCHOOL COURSES	Chemistry 342	the chemistry course
	History of the American Revolution	my history class
NAMES OF THINGS	the *St. Louis Post-Dispatch*	the newspaper
	Time	the magazine
	Purdue University	the university
	Campbell's vegetable soup	
	the Dodge Colt	

	CAPITALS	LOWER-CASE LETTERS
TIME NAMES	Friday August	
SEASONS		spring, summer, fall, autumn, winter
HISTORICAL PERIODS	World War II the Great Depression (*in the 1930s*) the Reformation	the war the cold war the depression (*any economic depression*) an era, an age the eighteenth century fifth-century manuscripts the civil rights movement
RELIGIOUS TERMS	God Buddhism the Torah the Koran the Bible	a god, a goddess
LETTER PARTS	Dear Ms. Tauber: Sincerely yours, Yours truly,	
TITLES OF WORKS	"The Lottery" *A History of the United States to 1877* *Catcher in the Rye*	[Capitalize the first word and all other words except articles°, short prepositions°, and short conjunctions°]

INSTRUCTOR'S NOTES

ANSWERS: EXERCISE 1

A slash indicates no capital is needed. A capitalized italicized word indicates that a capital is needed.

1. President Abraham Lincoln's *S*ecretary, whose name was Kennedy, and President John F. Kennedy's *S*ecretary, whose name was Lincoln, advised these ill-fated presidents not to go out just before their assassinations.

2. The first child of European *P*arents to be born in *North* America was Snorro, whose *M*other was the *W*idow of Leif Erickson's *B*rother.

3. The *A*ncient Egyptians, the first to embalm their *D*ead *C*itizens, also embalmed their *D*ead *C*rocodiles.

4. In 1659 Massachusetts outlawed *Christmas* and fined anyone celebrating the *H*oliday five *S*hillings.

5. Mark Twain, the author of *"The* Celebrated *Jumping Frog* of Calaveras *County,"* once refused to invest in a friend's invention, calling it a *"W*ildcat speculation." *The* invention was the telephone!

6. An artificial hand invented in 1551 by a *Frenchman* (his name was Ambroise Tare) had *F*ingers that moved by cogs and levers, thus enabling a handless member of the *C*avalry to grasp the reins of his horse.

7. "Take care, *O* traitor," roared the hero, *"O*r your *V*illainy will do you in!"

8. Researchers at the Institute for *Policy Studies* of Harvard *University* discovered that the following jobs are considered most boring by those who hold them: (1) *A*ssembly line worker, (2) elevator operator, (3) pool typist, (4) *B*ank *G*uard, (5) *H*ousewife.

	CAPITALS	**LOWER-CASE LETTERS**
COMPOUND WORDS	un-American post-Victorian Mexican-American native American Indo-European	
ACRONYMS	IRS FBI NATO UCLA AFL-CIO IBM NAACP CUNY	

EXERCISE 1

Add needed capital letters and change incorrect capitals to lower-case letters.

1. President Abraham Lincoln's Secretary, whose name was Kennedy, and President John F. Kennedy's Secretary, whose name was Lincoln, advised these ill-fated Presidents not to go out just before their assassinations.

2. The first child of European Parents to be born in north America was Snorro, whose mother was the Widow of Leif Erickson's Brother.

3. The Ancient Egyptians, the first to embalm their Dead Citizens, also embalmed their Dead Crocodiles.

4. In 1659 Massachusetts outlawed christmas and fined anyone celebrating the Holiday five Shillings.

5. Mark Twain, the author of "the Celebrated jumping frog of Calaveras county," once refused to invest in a friend's invention, calling it a "Wildcast speculation." the invention was the Telephone!

6. An artificial hand invented in 1551 by a frenchman (His name was Ambroise Tare) had Fingers that moved by cogs and levers, thus enabling a handless member of the Cavalry to grasp the reins of his Horse.

7. "Take care, o traitor," roared the hero, "Or your Villainy will do you in!"

8. Researchers at the Institute for policy studies of Harvard university discovered that the following jobs are considered most boring by those

who hold them: (1) Assembly line worker, (2) elevator operator, (3) pool typist, (4) Bank Guard, (5) Housewife.

9. What is the most common item in a family medicine chest? Is it Aspirin? adhesive bandages? a thermometer? an antibacterial agent?

10. "I don't care what you do, my dear," the Actress mrs. Patrick Campbell is supposed to have said, "as long as you don't do it in the Street and frighten the horses!"

9. What is the most common item in a family medicine chest? Is it Áspirin? *Adhesive* bandages? *A* thermometer? *An* antibacterial agent? [no capitals for *adhesive, a,* and *an* also acceptable]

10. "I don't care what you do, my dear," the Áctress *Mrs.* Patrick Campbell is supposed to have said, "as long as you don't do it in the Street and frighten the horses!"

■‖ ITALICS (UNDERLINING)

In printed material, **roman type** is the standard; type that slants to the right is called **italic.** Words in italics contrast with standard roman type, so italics create an emphasis readers can see. In typewritten and handwritten manuscripts, underlining stands for italics.

HANDWRITTEN

TYPED   Catch 22

TYPESET   *Catch 22*

■‖ 30f

Follow standard practice for underlining titles and other words, letters, or numbers.

Underlining is conventional for titles of long written works, names of ships and some aircraft, film titles, titles of television series, titles of works of graphic art and sculpture, and titles of long musical compositions, such as operas. Underlining also calls the reader's attention to words in languages other than English and to letters, numbers, and words that are mentioned as such. For examples, refer to the Guide to Underlining. The list also points out which titles call for quotation marks. It gives standard treatments for titles in notes and bibliographies. For other treatments of titles in documentation, consult Chapters 32–34.

INSTRUCTOR'S NOTES

GUIDE TO UNDERLINING

TITLES

UNDERLINE	DO NOT UNDERLINE
<u>The Bell Jar</u> [a novel]	
<u>Death of a Salesman</u> [a play]	
<u>Collected Works of O. Henry</u> [a book]	"The Last Leaf" [one story in the book]
<u>Simon & Schuster Handbook for Writers</u> [a book]	"Thinking Critically" [one chapter in the book]
<u>Contexts for Composition</u> [a collection of essays]	"Science and Ethics" [one essay in the collection]
<u>The Iliad</u> [a long poem]	"Nothing Gold Can Stay" [a short poem]
<u>The African Queen</u> [a film]	

the <u>Los Angeles Times</u> [a newspaper. Note: Even if *The* is part of the title printed on a newspaper, don't use a capital letter and don't underline it in your paper. In documentation°, omit the word *The*.]

<u>Scientific American</u> [a magazine]	"The Molecules of Life" [an article in a magazine]
<u>The Barber of Seville</u> [title of an opera] <u>Symphonie Fantastique</u> [title of a long musical work]	Concerto in B-flat Minor Symphony No. 8 in F [identification of a musical work by form, number, and key. Use neither quotation marks *nor* underlining]
<u>Twilight Zone</u> [a television series]	"Terror at 30,000 Feet" [an episode of a television series]
<u>The Best of Bob Dylan</u> [a record album or a tape]	"Blowin' in the Wind" [a song or a single selection on an album or a tape]

OTHER WORDS

UNDERLINE	DO NOT UNDERLINE
the <u>Intrepid</u> [a ship; don't underline preceding initials like U.S.S. or H.M.S.]	aircraft carrier [a general class of ship]

498

Voyager 2 [names of specific aircraft, spacecraft, and satellites]

Boeing 747 [general names shared by classes of aircraft, spacecraft, and satellites]

summa cum laude [term in a language other than English]

burrito, chutzpah [widely used and commonly understood words from languages other than English]

What does our imply? [a word referred to as such]

the abc's; confusing 3's and 8's [letters and numbers referred to as themselves]

▪‖ 30g
Underline sparingly for special emphasis.

Professional writers use italics to clarify a meaning or stress a point.

> Many people we *think* are powerful turn out on closer examination to be merely frightened and anxious.
> —MICHAEL KORDA, *Power!*

Meanings can change when the emphasized word changes.

> *Isabella* ordered Ferdinand to outfit the ships.
> Isabella *ordered* Ferdinand to outfit the ships.
> Isabella ordered *Ferdinand* to outfit the ships.

Instead of counting on underlining to deliver impact, try to make word choices and sentence structures convey emphasis. Excessive underlining makes writing seem immature.

No   One hundred and fifty years ago in England working men were *not allowed* to wear moustaches. The moustache was a privilege reserved *exclusively* for aristocrats. When some feisty tradesmen *defied* tradition by growing moustaches, members of the upper class were *furious*. They called the popularization of the moustache a *profound threat* to national institutions.

499

ANSWERS: EXERCISE 2

1. The first rule in an old book about rules of etiquette reads, "Do not eat in mittens."
2. When he originated the role of Fonzie in the television series *Happy Days,* Henry Winkler earned about $750 per episode.
3. The *Monitor* and the *Merrimac* were the first iron-hulled ships to engage in battle.
4. Iowa's name comes from the Indian word *ayuhwa,* which means "sleepy ones."
5. The *New York Times* does not carry comic strips.
6. Judy Garland was the second lowest paid star in the film classic *The Wizard of Oz;* only the dog who portrayed Toto was paid less.
7. For distinguished accomplishments of people over age 70, we should look to Goethe, who finished the novel *Faust* at age 80; Verdi, who wrote the song "Ave Maria" at age 85; and Tennyson, who wrote the short poem "Crossing the Bar" at age 80.
8. Handwriting experts say personality traits affect the way an individual dots an *i* and crosses a *t.*
9. The Italian word *ciao* is both a greeting and a farewell.
10. A sense of danger develops slowly in Shirley Jackson's short story "The Lottery."

EXERCISE 2

Cross out unneeded underlining and quotation marks and add needed underlining. Correct capitalization if necessary.

1. The first rule in an old book about <u>Rules of Etiquette</u> reads, "Do not eat in mittens."
2. When he originated the role of <u>Fonzie</u> in the television series "Happy Days," Henry Winkler earned about $750 per episode.
3. The Monitor and the Merrimac were the first iron-hulled ships to engage in battle.
4. <u>Iowa's</u> name comes from the Indian word <u>ayuhwa</u>, which means "sleepy ones."
5. The New York Times does not carry comic strips.
6. Judy Garland was the second lowest paid star in the film classic The Wizard of Oz; only the dog who portrayed <u>Toto</u> was paid less.
7. For distinguished accomplishments of people over age 70, we should look to Goethe, who finished the novel "Faust" at age 80; Verdi, who wrote the song "Ave Maria" at age 85; and Tennyson, who wrote the short poem "Crossing the Bar" at age 80.
8. Handwriting experts say personality traits affect the way an individual dots an i and crosses a t.
9. The <u>Italian</u> word <u>ciao</u> is both a greeting and a farewell.
10. A sense of danger develops slowly in Shirley Jackson's short story <u>The Lottery</u>.

■‖ ABBREVIATIONS

■‖ 30h

Use abbreviations in the body of a paper according to standard practice.

What you are writing and who will read that writing affect whether you should abbreviate or spell a word out. A few abbreviations are standard in any writing circumstances.

A.M. AND **P.M.** WITH SPECIFIC TIMES
    7:15 a.m.   3.47 p.m.

A.D. AND **B.C.** WITH SPECIFIC YEARS
A.D. 977 [A.D. precedes the year]
12 B.C. [B.C. follows the year]

TITLES OF ADDRESS BEFORE NAMES

Dr. D. K. Gooden   Ms. S. R. Odell
Mr. Charles Piatagorski   Mrs. Edna Cheek

ACADEMIC DEGREES AFTER NAMES

D. K. Gooden, Ph.D.   S. R. Odell, M.D.
Charles Piatagorski, J. D.   Edna Cheek, M.S.W.

▍ ABBREVIATION CAUTION: Don't use a title of address before a name *and* an academic degree after the name. Use one or the other. ▍

NO   Dr. Joyce A. Brown, M.D.

YES   Dr. Joyce A. Brown

YES   Joyce A. Brown, M.D.

If you use a long name or term frequently in a paper, you can abbreviate it. The first time you use it, give the full term, with the abbreviation in parentheses right after the spelled-out form. After that you can use the abbreviation alone.

Spain recently voted to continue as a member of the North Atlantic Treaty Organization (NATO), to the surprise of most other NATO members.

You can use *USSR* without giving the spelled-out form first. You can abbreviate *U.S.* as a modifier (the U.S. ski team, a U.S. government official); spell out *United States* when you use it as a noun, however.

NO   Lousiana is one of the few places in the **U.S.** where rice can be grown.

YES   Louisiana is one of the few places in the **United States** where rice can be grown.

TEACHING TIP

The letters B.C. follow a date, while the letters A.D. precede a date. William Safire, essayist on language for the *New York Times,* reports in his column of June 22, 1986 that a plaque left on the moon by the first Americans reads: "July 1969, A.D." He further reports that at the time he was a speechwriter at the White House and he approved the wording. He writes:

In a century or so, I hope some descendant of mine will take a sharp stylus on some weekend rocket to the moon and, while awaiting a transfer rocket to Mars, will draw a little circle around the *A.D.* and put an arrow placing it in front of the word *July.* This will show that human beings in the early days of space were grammatically fallible; that mankind (since changed to *humankind,* but you can leave it the old way on the plaque, Junior) is forever editing, and that a little precision is a dangerous thing.

TEACHING TIP

You might want to refer your students to Section 23b for a discussion of the use of periods with abbreviations.

501

Other than these cases, you should seldom use abbreviations in the body of a paper you write for a course in the humanities.

NO   Robt. Frost taught at Amherst Col. in Amherst, Mass., where Doctor Eliz. Adams (my lit. prof.) taped an interview with him in Sept. 1957.

YES   Robert Frost taught at Amherst College in Amherst, Massachusetts, where Dr. Elizabeth Adams (my professor of literature) taped an interview with him in September 1957.

▌ABBREVIATION CAUTION: If you include a full address—street, city, and state—in the body of a paper, you can use the postal abbreviation for the state name (see 30i for a list), but spell out any other combination of a city and a state. ▐

NO   The Center for Disease Control in **Atlanta, GA,** sometimes quarantines livestock.

YES   The Center for Disease Control in **Atlanta, Georgia,** sometimes quarantines livestock.

Abbreviations in documentation° are common in the humanities. See 30i for a list. In the social and natural sciences, abbreviations are common in the body of a paper as well as in documentation. For guidance, see the *Publication Manual of the American Psychological Association,* 3rd edition, the *CBE Style Manual,* 5th edition, or ask instructors.

Like other abbreviations, symbols are seldom used in the body of papers written for courses in the humanities. You can use a percent symbol (%) or a cent sign (¢), for example, in a table, graph, or other illustration, but in the body of the paper spell out *percent* and *cent.* You can, however, use a dollar sign with specific dollar amounts: $23 billion, $7.85. As with other decisions, let common sense and your readers' needs guide you. If you mention temperatures once or twice in a paper, spell them out: *ninety degrees, minus twenty-six degrees.* If you mention temperatures throughout a paper, use figures and symbols: 90°, −26°.

■║ **30i**

Use abbreviations in documentation according to standard practice.

Documentation styles are discussed in Chapters 32 (for English composition) and 34 (for the humanities, social sciences, and natural sciences). The list of scholarly abbreviations below gives forms you may find in the sources you consult as well as those you will need to document your own work. Use the postal abbreviations and month abbreviations as needed in your lists of works cited.

SCHOLARLY ABBREVIATIONS

anon.	anonymous
b.	born
c. *or* ©	copyright
c. *or* ca.	about (with dates)
cf.	compare
col., cols.	column, columns
d.	died
ed.; eds.	editor, edited by; editors
e.g.	for example
esp.	especially
et al.	and others
f., ff.	and the following page, pages
i.e.	that is
ms., mss.	manuscript, manuscripts
n.b.	note carefully
n.d.	no date (of publication, for a book)
p., pp.	page, pages
pref.	preface
rept.	report, reported by
sec., secs.	section, sections
v. *or* vs.	versus (legal case)
vol., vols.	volume, volumes

POSTAL ABBREVIATIONS

AL	Alabama	IL	Illinois
AK	Alaska	IN	Indiana
AZ	Arizona	IA	Iowa
AR	Arkansas	KS	Kansas
CA	California	KY	Kentucky
CO	Colorado	LA	Louisiana
CT	Connecticut	ME	Maine
DE	Delaware	MD	Maryland
DC	District of Columbia	MA	Massachusetts
FL	Florida	MI	Michigan
GA	Georgia	MN	Minnesota
HI	Hawaii	MS	Mississippi
		MO	Missouri
ID	Idaho	MT	Montana

503

NB	Nebraska	RI	Rhode Island
NV	Nevada	SC	South Carolina
NH	New Hampshire	SD	South Dakota
NJ	New Jersey	TN	Tennessee
NM	New Mexico	TX	Texas
NY	New York	UT	Utah
NC	North Carolina	VT	Vermont
ND	North Dakota	VA	Virginia
OH	Ohio	WA	Washington (state)
OK	Oklahoma	WV	West Virginia
OR	Oregon	WI	Wisconsin
PA	Pennsylvania	WY	Wyoming

ANSWERS: EXERCISE 3

1. All of the world's ten [*or* 10] largest cities are in the USSR. [Students who do not use the abbreviation for USSR are not "wrong" even though the text recommends this abbreviation.]

2. The ice over the Arctic Ocean is seven or more feet thick in most places.

3. Did you know that more births and deaths occur in the morning [*or* before noon] and more growth hormone is produced at night while people sleep?

4. After an extended study, Dr. Derel L. Abrams and Dr. Norton G. Waterman of the University of Louisville School of Medicine in Kentucky found almost half the paper dollars they tested to be contaminated with germs.

5. If the age of the earth were one year, humans would have lived on it for only fifteen [*or* 15] minutes.

6. President Harry Truman was the first U.S. president to travel in a submerged submarine.

MONTH ABBREVIATIONS

Jan.	January	July	
Feb.	February	Aug.	August
Mar.	March	Sept.	September
Apr.	April	Oct.	October
May		Nov.	November
June		Dec.	December

EXERCISE 3

Make needed changes so that abbreviations are used correctly.

1. All of the world's ten largest cities are in the Union of Soviet Socialist Republics.

2. The ice over the Arctic Ocean is seven or more ft. thick in most places.

3. Did you know that more births and deaths occur in the a.m. and more growth hormone is produced in the p.m. while people sleep?

4. After an extended study, Doctor Derel L. Abrams and Dr. Norton G. Waterman, M.D., of the U. of Louisville Sch. of Med. in KY found almost half the paper $'s they tested to be contaminated with germs.

5. If the age of the earth were one yr., humans would have lived on it for only fifteen mins.

6. Pres. Harry Truman was the first U.S. pres. to travel in a submerged submarine.

7. He made his trip in a captured German sub. on Nov. 21, 1946.

8. At 20,300 ft., McKinley is the highest mt. in No. America.

9. When the ms. of his book on the Fr. Revolution was used to feed a fire, the great Eng. historian Thomas Carlyle rewrote every page from memory.

10. Some political analysts believe that SE Asia will be the area of greatest economic growth in the twenty-first century.

7. He made his trip in a captured German submarine on November 21, 1946.

8. At 20,300 feet, McKinley is the highest mountain in North America.

9. When the manuscript of his book on the French Revolution was used to feed a fire, the great English historian Thomas Carlyle rewrote every page from memory.

10. Some political analysts believe that Southeast Asia will be the area of greatest economic growth in the twenty-first century.

■‖ NUMBERS

■‖ 30j

Use figures and spelled-out numbers according to standard practice.

Depending on how often numbers occur in a paper and what they refer to, you will sometimes express the numbers in words and sometimes in figures. The guidelines here, like those in the *MLA Handbook for Writers of Research Papers,* 2nd edition, are suitable for writing in the humanities. For the guidelines other disciplines follow, ask your course instructors or consult other style manuals. The *Publication Manual of the American Psychological Association,* 3rd edition, and the *CBE Style Manual,* 5th edition, will guide you for the social sciences and natural sciences respectively.

If conveying numerical exactness to your readers is not a prime purpose in your paper and if you mention numbers only a few times, you may spell out numbers that can be expressed in one or two words.

Emma O'Brien was twenty-six years old when she emigrated to the United States.

Iceland's population increases by more than one percent a year, but that gain translates into fewer than three thousand individuals.

■‖ HYPHENATION ALERT: Use a hyphen between spelled-out two-word numbers from *twenty-one* through *ninety-nine.* ‖■

If you use numbers fairly frequently in a paper, spell out numbers from *one* to *nine* and use figures for numbers *10* and above.

TEACHING TIP
Some writers mix suffixes with numerals: *1st, 33rd.* Traditional practice calls for the spelled-out word (the *first* robin), except for days, when only the numeral without a suffix should be used (November 1). When you clarify this for students, you might also want to point out that this is among the few cases in English in which formal spoken practice differs from formal written practice. That is, a person can say in a formal talk: "The crisis occurred on November 21st." In written form, however, the formal convention is: November 21.

505

Never start a sentence with a figure. If a sentence starts with a number, spell it out.

Three hundred seventy-five dollars per credit is the tuition rate for nonresidents.

Nineteen twenty-nine saw the stock market crash, wiping out speculators and conservative investors alike.

In practice, you can usually revise a sentence so that the number does not come first.

The tuition rate for nonresidents is $375 per credit.

The stock market crashed in 1929, wiping out speculators and prudent investors alike.

Do not mix spelled-out numbers and figures in a paper when they both refer to the same thing. Use figures for all the numbers.

No   In four days, our volunteers increased from five to eight to 17 to 233.

Yes   In four days, our volunteers increased from 5 to 8 to 17 to 233. [All the numbers referring to volunteers are given in figures, but *four* is still spelled out because it refers to a different quantity—days.]

Give specific numbers—dates, addresses, measurements, identification numbers of many kinds—in figures. The following list shows examples in major categories.

DATES   August 6, 1941
              1732–1845
              34 B.C. to A.D. 230

ADDRESSES   10 Downing Street
              237 North 8th Street
              Export Falls, MN 92025

TIMES   8:09 a.m.; 3:30 [but *six o'clock*, not 6 *o'clock*]

DECIMALS AND 5.55; 98.6; 3.1416; 7/8; 12-1/4 [but *three*
FRACTIONS   *quarters*, not *3 quarters*]

TEACHING TIP

Some students may need a review of Roman numerals. The major ones are: I = 1. V = 5. X = 10. L = 50. C = 100. D = 500. M = 1000.

In academic writing, Roman numerals have few uses. They designate the major divisions in outlines; sometimes they are used in lists. They are used as parts of names and titles: *Peter Brown III, Queen Elizabeth II, Rocky IV*. You might remind students that Roman numerals are not interchangeable with arabic (regular) numerals in addresses, dates, or measurements.

TEACHING TIP

William Safire, essayist on language for the *New York Times*, pointed out in his column of April 23, 1986 that practice varies greatly on how to write *noon* or *midnight* when the number 12 is involved. Some people use 12:00 A.M. for midnight, while others use 12:00 P.M. The same is true for noon. Safire suggests using *12 noon* and *12 midnight* for greatest clarity.

506

USING FIGURES AND SPELLED-OUT NUMBERS   *num* **30j**

CHAPTERS AND PAGES	Chapter 27, page 245
SCORES AND STATISTICS	a 6-0 score; a 5 to 3 ratio; 29 percent
IDENTIFICATION NUMBERS	94.4 on the FM dial; call 1-212-555-0000
MEASUREMENTS	2 feet; 67.8 miles per hour; 1.5 gallons; 2 level teaspoons, 3 liters; 8-1/2″ × 11″ paper or 8-1/2 × 11-inch paper
ACT, SCENE, AND LINE NUMBERS	act II, scene 2, lines 75–79
TEMPERATURES	43° F; 4° Celsius
MONEY	$1.2 billion; $3.41; 25 cents

EXERCISE 4

Revise so that numbers are in correct form—spelled out or in figures.

1. The film *Quo Vadis* used thirty thousand extras and 63 lions.
2. The best time to use insecticides is four p.m. because that is when insects are most susceptible.
3. People in the United States spend six hundred million dollars a year on hot dogs.
4. 4/5 of everything alive on this earth is in the sea.
5. The earliest baseball game on record was played in 1846 on June nineteenth for a final score of 23 to one in 4 innings.
6. Aaron Montgomery Ward started the first mail order company in the United States in 1872 at eight hundred twenty-five North Clark Street in Chicago.
7. The record for a human's broad jump is about twenty-eight feet, one-quarter inch, and the record for a frog's broad jump is 13 feet, 5 inches.
8. 250 words per minute is the reading speed of the typical reader.
9. The yearly income of the average family in the United States in nineteen fifteen was six hundred and eighty-seven dollars.
10. 3 out of 4 people who wear contact lenses are between 12 and 23 years of age.

ANSWERS: EXERCISE 4

1. The film *Quo Vadis* used 30,000 extras and 63 lions. [*or,* thirty thousand extras and sixty-three lions.]
2. The best time to use insecticides is 4:00 p.m. because that is when insects are most susceptible.
3. People in the United States spend $600 million a year on hot dogs. [Also correct are the spelled-out form, *$600,000,000,* and *600,000,000 dollars,* but *$600 million* is most appropriate for academic writing.]
4. Four fifths of everything alive on this earth is in the sea.
5. The earliest baseball game on record was played in 1846 on June 19 [or *19th*] for a final score of 23 to 1 in four innings.
6. Aaron Montgomery Ward started the first mail order company in the United States in 1872 at 825 North Clark Street in Chicago.
7. The record for a human's broad jump is about 28 feet, one quarter inch, and the record for a frog's broad jump is 13 feet, 5 inches.
8. Two hundred fifty words per minute is the reading speed of the typical reader. [*or:* The typical reader reads 250 words per minute.]
9. The yearly income of the average family in the United States in 1915 was $687. [spelled-out form for money also correct.]
10. Three out of four people who wear contact lenses are between 12 and 23 years of age.

VII ‖ WRITING SPECIAL ASSIGNMENTS

31 Paraphrasing, Summarizing, and Quoting

32 Writing Research

33 Observing a Student Writing Research

34 Writing in Other Disciplines

35 Business Writing

31
PARAPHRASING, SUMMARIZING, QUOTING

The core of every writing project is its content. In many writing assignments, the source of that content is expected to be your own thinking. For many other assignments, however, you are expected to draw upon outside sources—such as books, articles, films, and interviews—to explain and support your ideas. **Paraphrasing, summarizing,** and **quoting** are three techniques that writers use both to take notes from sources and to incorporate into their own writing the ideas and sometimes the words of sources—always according to accepted academic practice.

CORRECT PRACTICES FOR USING OUTSIDE SOURCES IN YOUR WRITING

1. Avoid plagiarism by always attributing ideas and words that are not yours to their source.
2. Document sources accurately and completely.
3. Know how and when to use the techniques of paraphrase, summary, and quotation.

510

∎‖ 31a
Avoid plagiarism.

To plagiarize is to present another person's words or ideas as if they were your own. Plagiarism is like stealing. The word *plagiarize* comes from the Latin word for kidnapper and literary thief. Plagiarism is a serious offense that can be grounds for failure of a course or expulsion from a college. Plagiarism can be intentional, as when you deliberately incorporate the work of other people in your writing without mentioning and documenting the source. Plagiarism can also be unintentional—but no less serious an offense—if you are unaware of what must be acknowledged and how to go about documenting. All college students are expected to know what plagiarism is and how to avoid it. If you are not absolutely clear about what is involved, take time *now* to learn the "rules of the game" so that you never expose yourself to charges of plagiarism.

What do you *not* have to document? You are not expected to acknowledge information that is considered *common knowledge*—for example, that Columbus's ships landed in America in 1492 or that Einstein's theory of relativity is represented in the formula $E = mc^2$. You might have to look up and remind yourself about the date on which the Titanic sunk or Neil Armstrong walked on the moon, but such material is common knowledge nevertheless. Similarly, you do not document *personal knowledge*—for example, that your mother was born June 6, 1906, or that a blizzard crippled your city last January for 48 hours.

What should you document? You must acknowledge the source of any words you quote. Along with your documentation, you must always use quotation marks or, if the material is more than three lines, an indented format. For an example of a paragraph that uses quotation marks for some material and an indented format for other material, see paragraph 3 of the research paper in Chapter 33.

In addition, you must acknowledge your source when you paraphrase or summarize someone else's ideas. Writing the words of others in your own words does not release you from your obligation to attribute the material to its originator. When you write a paper that draws on outside sources, you are expected to use your own thinking to formulate the thesis and to organize your material, but when you use outside sources in support of your thesis, you are expected to document. For an example of a paper that has these characteristics, see the student research paper in Chapter 33. Note that the student, Amy Brown, presents her own thesis but uses outside sources—all of which she acknowledges through correct documentation—to support her ideas.

511

the number of teachers who taught when to document sources and the students' avoidance of plagiarism. Students who reported that all their teachers explained how to credit sources were far more likely to understand the concept of plagiarism and to avoid copying reports than their peers who received such instruction from just a few of their teachers.

Only forty-seven percent of the students questioned understood, when they were seniors in high school, how to write an unplagiarized report. Among the untrained students, some felt that putting ideas into their own words and providing a bibliography (no parenthetical references or footnotes) was sufficient. Others felt that copying was fine provided that they supplied either footnotes, parenthetical references, or a bibliography (no quotation marks). Almost six percent had no idea what "plagiarism" meant. Not surprisingly, over sixty percent of the students in these three groups reported having copied high school reports.

QUOTATION ABOUT WRITING
Borrowed thoughts, like borrowed money, only show the poverty of the borrower.

—MARGUERITE GARDINER

QUOTATION ABOUT WRITING
Plagiarists are always suspicious of being stolen from.

—SAMUEL TAYLOR COLERIDGE

Plagiarism can slip into your work unless you keep careful notes as you look for supporting material from outside sources. (For guidelines on evaluating sources, see 32d-2. For guidelines on selecting material for notetaking, see 32f.) Here are practices that help assure researchers that they will avoid plagiarism.

1. *Use a consistent note-taking system.* Good notes give you more than a report of what you have read. **To avoid the risk of plagiarism, you must always be able to tell what in the notes is yours and what belongs to an outside source.** You must keep three things separate: (1) material you have paraphrased or summarized; (2) quotations from a source; and (3) your own thoughts triggered by what you are reading. For quotations, always write very large quotation marks that you have no chance of missing later. Color coding can help you keep material separate. Stores stock different colors of cards, inks, highlighter pens, and clips. A more cluttered but acceptable method is to underline one type of material, circle another, and leave the third unmarked.

2. *Record complete documentation information.* Become entirely familiar with the documentation style you intend to use in your paper (31b). Make a master list of the documentation facts required for each source.

3. *Record documentation information as you go along.* Never forget to write down documentation facts as you take notes. Use very clear handwriting. Do not expect to retrace your steps and get documentation facts after you finish taking notes or writing your paper. **Your chances of unintentional plagiarism increase sharply if you have to recreate your research process. Do not expect to be able to relocate your sources or to reconstruct what came from the source and what was your own thinking.** In addition to increasing your risk of plagiarizing, retracing your steps wastes your time. You also risk not being able to find a source again—someone else might be using it.

■‖ 31b

Understand the concept of documentation.

Basic to paraphrasing, summarizing, and quoting is the concept and practice of **documentation**—acknowledging your sources

512

by giving full and accurate information about the author, title and date of publication, and related facts.

Documentation styles vary among the disciplines. Some use a system of footnotes or endnotes, and others place reference information in parentheses within the text. Some styles abbreviate and capitalize differently than others; and each style sequences information and punctuates it a little differently. In each course for which you write using outside sources, find out what documentation style you are expected to use. Chapters 32 and 34 explain and illustrate documentation styles you may be required to use. Here is a chart to help you locate what you need for the discipline in which you are writing.

DOCUMENTATION STYLES DISCUSSED IN THIS HANDBOOK

FOR ENGLISH AND OTHER SUBJECTS IN THE HUMANITIES

Parenthetical system (MLA)	pages 562–74; 579–85
Endnote or footnote system	pages 631–40

FOR THE SOCIAL SCIENCES

Parenthetical system (APA)	pages 647–50

FOR NATURAL SCIENCES AND TECHNOLOGIES

Varies; see pages 650–58

 31c
Paraphrase accurately.

When you **paraphrase,** you make a detailed restatement of someone else's words in your own. The word *paraphrase* combines the Greek word for "tell" with the Greek prefix *para-,* meaning "alongside." Thus, *paraphrase* describes a parallel text, one that goes alongside an original writing. When you paraphrase, you precisely restate in your own words a passage written by another author (or spoken by someone interviewed, or heard on a film). Your paraphrasings offer an account of what various authorities have to say, not in their words but in yours. (For advice about identifying authoritative sources in a subject, see 32d-2.) The ideas of authorities can give substance and credibility to your message, and they can offer support for your thesis°.

Equally important, the process of writing a paraphrase helps

513

you untangle difficult passages and gain domination over a thought. Paraphrasing forces you to read closely and to extract precise meaning from complex passages. The process of paraphrasing helps you come to know material on at least two levels of reading: the literal and the inferential (both are explained in Chapter 5).

Select for paraphrase only the passages that carry ideas that you will need to reproduce in detail. Because paraphrase calls for very close approximation of a source, it is not practical to paraphrase whole chapters—or indeed much more than a page. Usually, two or three paragraphs in a chapter is the most you should attempt to translate in the detail required by paraphrase; use summary (31d) for the rest.

1
Restate the material completely.

When you paraphrase, you restate the material—and no more. You do not skip points, you do not guess at meaning, and above all, you do not insert your own opinions or interpretations. The source's thinking is paramount, in both order and emphasis.

You may later select what parts you want to use in your writing, but do not make those decisions when you are taking the notes. Recast the source's message just as it appears. If the source's words trigger your own thinking, do not lose your thought or assume you will recall it later. *Be sure, however, to write down your thought so that it is physically separate from your paraphrase:* put it in the margin, use an alternate color ink, or circle it clearly so that you will know it does not belong in the paraphrase.

2
Use your own words, not the source's.

To paraphrase, translate the writer or speaker's language into your own. If you do not use your own words, you will be quoting, not paraphrasing. Use words that come naturally to you. Use synonyms for the source's words wherever you can, and then always read over your sentences to be sure that your paraphrase makes sense and does not distort the meaning.

Sometimes, synonyms are not advisable. For example, if you are dealing with basic concepts such as *water* or *politics,* synonyms such as *aqua* or *the science and art of political government* might make the material seem strained. Consider how each synonym fits into the flow of your sentence. Also, do not rename terms that the author identifies as coined; quote them. For example, in paragraph 2

514

of the student research paper in Chapter 33, no synonym is used for Edward Hall's word "proxemics," because he originated it. When you use someone else's special terms in a paraphrase, be certain to put the words in quotation marks and then to give a definition in your own words enclosed in parentheses.

In paraphrasing, the farther you get from the original phrasing, the more likely you are to sound like yourself. Do not be surprised, therefore, to find that when you change language you might also have to change word order, sentence length and style, punctuation, verb tense, and voice°.

As you turn someone else's words into your own, you can expect your material to be as long as or longer than the source's. To paraphrase well, you must use as many words as you need to extract every drop of meaning. Authors are usually forced to condense their material as they polish it for publication. Conciseness is a virtue in writing (see Chapter 16), but it runs counter to the nature of paraphrase. Your paraphrase should be accurate and complete, not necessarily concise.

3
Avoid plagiarizing when you paraphrase.

Be sure to recast your source material so that you are not plagiarizing. Compare these three passages: an original, a paraphrase that plagiarizes, and an acceptable paraphrase that uses many synonyms and some alternate sentence structures.

SOURCE
Smith, Hedrick. *The Russians*. New York: Quadrangle, 1976: 260.*

ORIGINAL
The fact that power and authority derive from above, not below, has made Soviet society far more rank-and-hierarchy conscious than Western societies—strange as that may seem for a state that preens itself as the protagonist of the proletariat. The crucial test, in Lenin's blunt formula, is *Kto-Kogo?*, literally, "Who-Whom" but more meaningfully "Who can do what to whom?" It is an unspoken question Russians have in mind constantly as they deal with each other. Hence the enormous attention paid to the pecking order at all levels of Soviet society. It is the inordinate care that the Soviet leadership itself devotes to de-

*Source information throughout this chapter is adapted from MLA style for bibliographic entries.

TEACHING TIP
As Charles Bazerman (*The Informed Writer,* Boston: Houghton Mifflin, 1981, p. 14) says, "there are . . . ways . . . of appearing to read while not really reading": (1) We may open a book with the assumption that it is worthless—and spend our time and energy looking for errors. As no book can be all things to all people, finding an error of some sort is easy, and it is then even easier to dismiss the book. In doing so, unfortunately, we also dismiss whatever valuable insights there may be. (2) We may assume a book means what we wish it to mean. A few familiar phrases may encourage us to misinterpret an entire argument; we may go as far as not to see important words, *not, sometimes, rarely.* At the least, we may gloss over details that do not fit our notion of what the book ought to say. (3) We may misinterpret words, such as abstractions and jargon, or ignore the context of words—all in an effort to see what we want to see. (4) We may fail to see how pieces of the argument fit together, giving undue or insufficient weight to material in proportion to how it suits our ideas. Once students are aware of these pitfalls, they are more likely to avoid them.

515

QUOTATION ABOUT WRITING

You could compile the worst book in the world entirely out of selected passages from the best writers in the world.

—G. K. CHESTERTON

ciding who stands where in official photographs or on top of the Lenin Mausoleum which gave birth to the Western art of Kremlinology.

UNACCEPTABLE PARAPHRASE (ITALICIZED WORDS ARE PLAGIARIZED)

Power and authority derive from above which has led Soviet society to be *more conscious of rank-and-hierarchy than Western societies.* This is surprising because Soviet society *preens itself as the protagonist of the proletariat.* The major point is what Lenin called *"Kto-Kogo?"* which means *"Who can do what to whom?"* This is the silent question Russians think about *constantly as they deal with each other.* As a result, they pay a great deal of attention to "the pecking order at all levels of Soviet society." The *Soviet leadership use inordinate care* to determine who will stand where in *official photographs or on top of the Lenin Mausoleum which gave birth to the Western art of Kremlinology.* (Smith 260)*

ACCEPTABLE PARAPHRASE

Power and rank come from above in Soviet society. Russians are more concerned with status than are people from Western societies. This is surprising in light of the communists' bragging that the state represents the interests of the common people—those with the lowest status in the society. The major point is what Lenin called *"Kto-Kogo?"* which means "What can anyone do to anyone else?" In interpersonal dealings, everyone thinks about this question. As a result, people always think about "the pecking order at all levels of Soviet society." For example, Soviet leaders spend much time determining who will stand where in official photographs or at ceremonies at the Lenin Mausoleum. In the Western world, this fact provides the basis of the study of the government, foreign policy, and related matters in the Soviet Union. (Smith 260)

The first attempt to paraphrase fails because the writer has simply changed a few words here and there. What remains contains much plagiarized material because the passage keeps most of the original's language and sentence structure. Of course, the Russian Word *"Kto-Kogo"* had to be used because no English-speaking student would be expected to know a synonym.

The second paraphrase is acceptable. It captures the essence of the original in the student's own words. A distinctive phrase from the original is placed in quotation marks. No one would charge this student with plagiarism.

*Unless otherwise noted, parenthetical references are in MLA style. This documentation system is fully described in Chapter 32.

GUIDELINES FOR WRITTING A PARAPHRASE

1. Say what the source says, but no more.
2. Reproduce the source's order of ideas and emphases.
3. Use your own words and phrasing to restate the message. If certain synonyms are awkward, quote the material—but resort to this very sparingly.
4. Read over your sentences to make sure that they make sense and do not distort the source's meaning.
5. Expect your material to be as long as, and possibly longer than, the original.
6. Avoid plagiarism.
7. Write down all documentation facts so that you can document your source when you use it in your writing.

Here are two more examples of acceptable paraphrase. Both were written by the student doing research for the paper in Chapter 33.

Source
Morris, Desmond. *Manwatching*. New York: Abrams, 1977: 131.

Original
　　Unfortunately, different countries have different ideas about exactly how close is close. It is easy enough to test your own "space reaction": when you are talking to someone in the street or in any open space, reach out with your arm and see where the nearest point on his body comes. If you hail from western Europe, you will find that he is at roughly fingertip distance from you. In other words, as you reach out, your fingertips will just about make contact with his shoulder. If you come from eastern Europe you will find you are standing at "wrist distance." If you come from the Mediterranean region you will find that you are much closer to your companion, at little more than "elbow distance."

Acceptable paraphrase
　　People from different nations think that "close" means different things. You can easily see what your reaction is to how close to you people stand by reaching out the length of your arm to measure how close someone is as the two of you talk. When people from Western Europe stand on the street and talk together, the space between them is the distance it would take one person's fingertips to reach to the other person's shoulder. People

COORDINATED RESOURCES
Alternate examples and exercises for this chapter are available in the *S & S Workbook for Writers*, Gordon and Troyka.

Transparency masters are available for many of the screened charts and/or lists in this chapter.

Students can practice and test their knowledge of terms, key concepts, and applications of material in this chapter by using the *Study Guide to the S & S Handbook for Writers*, West.

517

from Eastern Europe converse at a wrist-to-shoulder distance. People from the Mediterranean, however, prefer an elbow-to-shoulder distance. (Morris 131)

SOURCE

Worchel, Stephen, and Joel Cooper. *Understanding Social Psychology* 3rd ed. Homewood, IL: Dorsey, 1983: 535. (The material from Worchel and Cooper shows the APA style of parenthetical documentation. APA style is described in Chapter 34.)

ORIGINAL

One of the more consistent findings in the personal-space literature is that females have smaller personal spaces than males (Willis, 1966; Aiello & Aiello, 1974; Edwards, 1972; Heckel & Hiers, 1977; Evans & Howard, 1973). Further, smaller personal space zones are found between male–female pairs than between same-sex pairs. We can speculate about the reasons for these differences. In Western cultures there are strong taboos against homosexuality, especially male homosexuality. Children are often punished by their parents for touching or caressing another child of the same sex. However, direct teaching and available models inform children that heterosexual behavior is accepted. Hence, children's spatial behavior may result in part as a response to norms about permitted sexual behavior. Children learn, however, that such behavior with members of the opposite sex is all right under some circumstances.

In light of this speculation, it is interesting to note that stable personal-space norms do develop around the time that the child reaches puberty. Investigations reveal that children do not begin to exhibit consistent spatial behavior before the age of four or five (Eberts & Lepper, 1975). After that age, the size of personal space increases until the age of 12 or 13 when it stabilizes (Aiello & Aiello, 1974; see Figure 13–2).

ACCEPTABLE PARAPHRASE

People do differ as to how much private space they need around them, depending on whether they are male or female and on how old they are. Many scientists have confirmed that men feel more comfortable with more space around them while women maintain less private space. It is also true that between any two people, a male and a female will approach each other more closely, each person maintaining less personal space, than a male will approach a male or a female, a female. Why do these differences exist? In the West, society clearly forbids homosexual behavior, among men in particular. Many parents punish their children if they catch them behaving in any intimate way with others of the same sex.

Until children reach the beginning of sexual maturity, they do not settle into consistent patterns with regard to how much private space they need and how far they should keep from males and females until they approach sexual maturity in their early teens. Before they are four or five, children act in all sorts of different ways with regard to how near they come to people. After four or five, they gradually seem to expand their private space until they are twelve or thirteen. After that, their behavior changes very little (Worchel and Cooper 535).

EXERCISE 1

A. For a paper proposing that drug and chemical companies have rushed too fast into the new technology of genetic engineering, paraphrase this paragraph. End your paraphrase with this parenthetical reference to the source that conforms to the MLA documentation style explained in Chapter 32: (DeDeuve 362–63).

> Some of the initial objections to genetic engineering arose largely from the fear that some bacteria, unwittingly transformed into highly pathogenic species, might escape into the environment. This risk appeared particularly hazardous because the most widely used bacterium is E. coli, a normal inhabitant of the human digestive track. At first, strict physical containment of the facilities used was imposed as a safeguard against such conjectural accidents. Nowadays, reliance is put mostly on biological containment, itself a product of genetic manipulation (by conventional procedures). Mutant strains of E. coli have been produced that have strict temperature and nutritional requirements, absolutely incompatible with their survival in the human body, or in any environment other than the highly specialized conditions provided in the culture vats.
> —Christian DeDeuve, *A Guided Tour of the Living Cell*

B. Write a paraphrase of a paragraph of at least 150 words from one of the sources you are using for a paper assigned in one of your courses. If you have no such assignment, choose any material suitable for a college-level paper.

 ## 31d

Summarize accurately.

A **summary** reviews the main points of a passage and gets at the gist of what an author or speaker says. A summary condenses

ANSWERS: EXERCISE 1

A. Answers will vary, but here is one acceptable paraphrase: One of the first protests lodged against experimental changes in the normal genetic structures of organisms—known as genetic engineering—was based on the worry that altered bacteria might become extremely dangerous without anyone's knowing it. The worry also involved the concern that the bacteria might somehow get out of the laboratory and into the environment. The danger feared the most had to do with E. coli, a bacteria frequently used in genetic engineering. E. coli is a common bug that lives in the human intestines. When work on genetic engineering began, the rooms in laboratories where this experimentation went on were kept under strict quarantine to protect against any imaginable disasters. At the present time, the type of safeguard has changed—it is now biological. Certain altered types of E. coli have been created that cannot survive unless they are exposed to specific temperatures and foods. These very special conditions are available exclusively in laboratory tanks. The mutant bacteria cannot live in the environment or in the human body or anywhere else. (DeDeuve 362–3)

B. Answers will vary.

the essentials of someone else's thought in a few general statements.

Writing summaries is probably the most frequently used technique for taking notes and for incorporating sources into your writing. To summarize a paragraph, a chapter, or a statement, isolate its separate points and, in your own words, write a statement that digests the material. To do this, you must discover the material's main ideas and their relation to one another. The length of your summary should be in proportion to the length of the passage you are summarizing: a general guide is one sentence per paragraph, though sometimes more is needed when the material is particularly complex. In a formal summary—the type to use in your writing— you are expected to tie together your summarizing sentences with appropriate transitional expressions°. In an informal summary—the type you use to take notes—you can pay less attention to transitions, but you still need to record connections among ideas so that the material is clear to you when you consult it at a later time.

As you likely know from experience, writing summaries of your lecture notes or your chapter assignments in preparation for a test helps you study. Writing summaries is an excellent way to learn material because the process helps you lock information into your memory. Summarizing forces you to read closely and to comprehend clearly.

1
Isolate the main points.

A summary must capture the entire sense of a paragraph in very little space, so you must read through (or listen to) all the content before you write. A good summary reports only the main points contained in a passage. Isolating the main points involves making decisions. These are the controlling questions: What is the subject? What is said about it? You have to take in the complete message, and then you must differentiate between main ideas and supporting facts, examples, or reasons. A summary excludes more than it includes, so you must make substantial deletions.

Sometimes, but not often, the points for your summary are available in topic sentences°. If so, you must rewrite the topic sentences in your own words, and you must make sure that the connections among the ideas are clear. If you find no topic sentences, your summary serves to supply their equivalent.

Condensing information into a table is another option you can use to summarize, particularly when you are summarizing numerical data. For an example, see paragraph 5 of the sample research paper in Chapter 33: Table 1 summarizes ten pages of a source.

2
Condense without losing meaning.

As you summarize, you will be tracing a line of thought. This involves deleting peripheral ideas and sometimes transposing certain points into an order more suited to summary. A summary is always significantly shorter than the original. In fact, it should reduce the original by at least half. The essential content should take no more than one or two sentences per paragraph. If your summary is too long, summarize it.

Until you are experienced at writing summaries, you will likely have to revise them more than once. Always be firm in your resolve to see that any summary accurately reflects the source and its emphases.

As you summarize, you may be tempted to interpret something the author says or make some judgment about the value of the argument. Your own opinions do not belong in a summary, but you do not have to lose a good thought. Jot down your ideas immediately, but *be sure to place them in your notes so that they are physically separate from your summary*—in the margin, an alternate color ink, or clearly circled so they stand out.

3
Avoid plagiarizing when you summarize.

In summarizing, use your own language. If you have no alternative but to use a source's key terms because synonyms would not work, be sure to use quotation marks. When you copy exact words from a source, use quotation marks written large. If you do not, you will surely forget whose words are whose when you incorporate your summary into your paper—and your summary will be plagiarizing words from the author.

Compare these three passages: an original, a summary that plagiarizes, and an acceptable summary.

SOURCE
Smith, Hedrick. *The Russians*. New York: Quadrangle, 1976: 16.

ORIGINAL
What makes the Soviet false fronts so much more misleading than those of other countries is the lack of public controversy and independent information to provide a corrective context. The

521

visitor can peer in vain at power stations, truck factories, or private cars for an understanding of Soviet Russia. It is not a monolith, but it can wear a pretty monolithic facade, and the outsider can miss entirely the intangibles and the invisible mechanisms that set it and its people apart from America, the West, and even Eastern Europe.

UNACCEPTABLE SUMMARY (ITALICIZED WORDS ARE PLAGIARIZED)
Soviet false fronts are misleading especially because no *corrective context* is available from public debate or *independent information* (Smith 16).

ACCEPTABLE SUMMARY
The outsider cannot get behind the "false fronts" in Soviet Russia because public debate is not permitted and confirming evidence from independent sources is not available (Smith 16).

The unacceptable summary does isolate the main point, but it plagiarizes because the writer has taken almost all the language from the source. The only substitute is "debate" for the source's "controversy" in "public controversy."

The second summary is acceptable because it not only isolates the main idea but also recasts it in the student's words. One phrase, "false fronts" is borrowed, but it is set off in quotation marks. No one would charge this student with plagiarism.

4
Turn long paraphrases into summaries to use in your writing.

When a paraphrase is too long and involved to use in your paper, condense your paraphrase by summarizing it. Here is a summary written from the paraphrase of the Worchel and Cooper material on page 518–19. You can see it in its final form in paragraph 8 of the student research paper in Chapter 33.

People have different needs for interpersonal space, depending on their sex and age. Males need more space than females, and males in pairs keep farther apart than they do when with a female; females keep farther apart when paired together and approach males more closely. This may be because same-sex intimacy is forbidden by Western cultures. In fact, until children are four or five, they seem to be unaware of personal space boundaries, but after that they become more aware until they reach puberty, when their behavior conforms to cultural standards (Worchel and Cooper 535).

> **GUIDELINES FOR WRITING A SUMMARY**
>
> 1. Identify the main points.
> 2. Condense the main points without losing the essence of the material.
> 3. Use your own words to condense the message. If certain synonyms are awkward, quote the words.
> 4. Keep your summary short.
> 5. Avoid plagiarism.
> 6. Write down all documentation facts so that you can document your source when you use it in your writing.

Here is a summary written for the sample research paper in Chapter 33.

SOURCE

Hall, Edward T. *The Hidden Dimension*. New York: Doubleday, 1966: 109.

ORIGINAL

The general failure to grasp the significance of the many elements that contribute to man's sense of space may be due to two mistaken notions: (1) that for every effect there is a single and identifiable cause; and (2) that man's boundary begins and ends with his skin. If we can rid ourselves of the need for a single explanation, and if we can think of man as surrounded by a series of expanding and contracting fields which provide information of many kinds, we shall begin to see him in an entirely different light. We can then begin to learn about human behavior, including personality types. . . . Concepts such as these are not always easy to grasp, because most of the distance-sensing process occurs outside the awareness. We sense other people as close or distant, but we cannot always put our finger on what it is that enables us to characterize them as such. So many different things are happening at once it is difficult to sort out the sources of information on which we base our reactions.

ACCEPTABLE SUMMARY

Human beings make the mistake of thinking that events have single causes and that people are limited by the boundaries of their bodies. Most people are unaware of the "distance-sensing process," nor do they know that the concept of interpersonal dis-

523

ANSWERS: EXERCISE 2

A. Answers will vary, but here is one possible summary: Genetic engineering makes it possible for scientists to insert new genes into organisms and thus make many farm products resistant to major diseases and insects.

B. Answers will vary, but here is one possible summary: To counteract an initial public fear that genetically altered organisms would become highly dangerous, escape from laboratories and cause unimaginable harm to the population and environment, tight security was used wherever genetic engineering took place. These safeguards have been relaxed since gene-splicing has made it possible to create new mutant species of organisms that can live only under specific conditions that do not exist outside laboratories.

C. Answers will vary.

QUOTATION ABOUT WRITING
Quotations are the wisdom of the wise and the experience of ages.

—ISAAC D'ISRAELI

QUOTATION ABOUT WRITING
Stay at home in your mind. Don't recite other people's opinions. I hate quotations. Tell me what you know.

—RALPH WALDO EMERSON

tance exists and contributes to their reactions to other people (Hall 109).

EXERCISE 2

A. For a paper defending the potential benefits to farming from genetic engineering, summarize this material. End your summary with this parenthetical reference to the source that conforms to the MLA documentation style explained in Chapter 32: (Schneiderman 52).

With genetic engineering, scientists can take one or several genes from one organism—a corn plant or an animal—and insert them into a completely different organism, such as a bacterium, to produce a bacterium with those new genes. Each new gene inserted into the bacterium carries instructions to manufacture a new protein. It is now commonplace, for example, to insert the human gene for insulin, a protein native only to humans, into bacteria to produce insulin by the pound for fermentation tanks. Plant breeding has provided plants with resistance to major diseases and to some insect pests. But genetic engineering will be able to accelerate plant breeding and confer traits such as resistance to insects on soybeans, wheat, corn, rice, alfalfa, and cotton.
— H. A. SCHNEIDERMAN, "Altering the Harvest"

B. Write a summary of your paraphrase of the DeDeuve material in Exercise 1. End it with the parenthetical reference given.

C. Write a summary of one or two paragraphs, totaling about 200 words. Take it from a source you are using for a paper assigned in one of your courses, or select material suitable for a college-level paper.

■‖ 31e
Use quotations well.

Quotations are the exact words of a source—in written form set off in quotation marks. (See Chapter 28 for rules on using quotation marks.) Quotations lend special credibility and support to your statements. If you choose quotations for their particularly apt language and if you use them in moderation, quotations add impact to your paper. Whereas paraphrase and summary distance your reader one step from your source, quotations give your reader the chance to encounter directly the words of your source.

When you use quotations in your writing, however, you confront two conflicting demands. You want the effect and support of quotations, but you also want your writing to be fluent, coherent, and readable. You gain authority by quoting experts on the topic, but if you use too many quotations, you lose coherence, as well as control of your own paper. Rather than a single piece of carefully woven fabric, you get a patchwork quilt. As a general rule, if more than a quarter of your paper consists of quotations, your instructor and other readers will assume that you have done little thinking on your own. A paper overloaded with quotations becomes what some people call a "scotch tape special." Your words and thinking about the subject are paramount. Use quotations sparingly, therefore. When you want to draw on support from an authority, rely mostly on paraphrase and summary. (In contrast, when you write a literary analysis which rests on examination of specific passages, you are expected to use fairly extensive quotation; for an example see pages 623–25.)

Well-chosen quotations should support, not make, your points. Draw on authorities to confirm what you are saying, not to deliver the message of your thesis or main ideas. Use quotations only when (1) the language is especially striking, (2) the thought is particularly difficult to rephrase accurately, (3) the authority conveyed by the quotation is especially important for your thesis or main ideas, or (4) the source's words could be open to alternate interpretations, so your reader needs direct access to the words.

1
Quote accurately.

Be very careful not to misquote a source. Always check your quotations against the originals—and then recheck. It is very easy to make mistakes when you are copying from the source into your notes or from your notes into your paper. If you photocopy material, be sure to mark off on the copy the exact place that caught your attention; otherwise, you might forget your impressions and will have to spend time trying to reconstruct your thought processes.

If you have to add a word or two to a quotation so that it fits in with your prose, put those words in brackets (see 29c) and make sure that your additions do not distort the meaning of the quotation. The student writer of the sample research paper in Chapter 33 added *North* to *American* in paragraph 13 to make it clear that the source was not referring to South Americans or Central Americans. The student's addition helps the reader understand the material, but the added words do not intrude on the source's meaning.

> If the [North] American moves away, the Arab feels that the American is being cold and hostile, while the American finds the Arab, who keeps moving closer, is being pushy and aggressive (Charles G. Morris 516).

QUOTATION ABOUT WRITING
I quote others only the better to express myself.

—MONTAIGNE

QUOTATION ABOUT WRITING
I often quote myself. It adds spice to my conversation.

—GEORGE BERNARD SHAW

525

Similarly, if for the sake of conciseness and focus, you delete a portion of a quotation, indicate the omission with an ellipsis (see 29d). When using ellipses, make sure that the remaining words accurately reflect the source's meaning. Also, make sure that the sentence structure does not become awkward. The author of the sample research paper in Chapter 33, wanted to quote only some of Robert Sommer's words on page 26 of *Personal Space: The Behavioral Bases of Design.*

ORIGINAL
: Like the porcupines in Schopenhauer's fable, people like to be close enough to obtain warmth and comradeship but far enough away to avoid pricking one another. Personal space is not necessarily spherical in shape, nor does it extend equally in all directions. (People are able to tolerate closer presence of a stranger at their sides than directly in front of them.) It has been likened to a snail shell, a soap bubble, an aura, a "breathing room." (Sommer 26)

WITH ELLIPSES
: Like the porcupines in Schopenhauer's fable, people like to be close enough to obtain warmth and comradeship but far enough away to avoid pricking one another. Personal space . . . has been likened to a snail shell, a soap bubble, an aura, a "breathing room." (Sommer 26)

2

Select quotations that are from accepted authorities and that fit your meaning.

Whom you choose to quote is as important as the words you choose. Your message is enhanced only when you use authorities who bring credibility to your discussion. For example, the student author of the research paper in Chapter 33 about personal space correctly included Edward T. Hall. If she had not, she would have been missing a basic source because Hall founded the field of "proxemics." Any paper that ignores a key figure in a field under discussion is missing something crucial. (For advice on how to select sources when doing research, 32d-2.)

Similarly, the words you choose to quote are important. They must fit your context. Never hunt for a quotation simply because you want to include a person's words, and don't resort to a quotation because you do not want to take the time to paraphrase or summarize. If you force a quotation to fit your material, your reader will quickly discern the manipulation.

526

3
Keep long quotations to a minimum.

When you use a quotation, your purpose is to supply evidence or support your assertion, not to reconstruct someone else's argument. Occasionally, however, you may need to present a complicated argument in detail and thus quote long passages. Make sure every word in the quotation counts. Edit out irrelevant parts (using an ellipsis to indicate deleted material) while maintaining proper sentence structure.

When you must use a long quotation, prepare your reader by explaining its importance. Otherwise, chances are your reader will simply skip over it.

4
Work quotations smoothly into your own prose.

The greatest risk you take when you use quotations is that you will end up with choppy, incoherent sentences in which the quoted portions do not quite mesh with the style, grammar, or logic of your prose. Guard against this possibility by reading the combined material aloud. Listen and try to hear whether the language flows smoothly and gracefully.

> While the genetic [engineering] gold rush was getting under way, Apple happened to read an article about plant breeding. "It clicked in my mind that this was the big opportunity in genetic engineering," he says. "Everyone else was thinking about medical applications." Having started a medical-instruments company while a college student, Apple decided to travel the entrepreneurial path once again. He wrote a plan for a research institute, focusing on the idea of transplanting a protein gene into potato cells to create a "meatato" full of valuable protein—equivalent, he says, "to having lamb chops grow on trees."
> —STEPHEN SOLOMON, "Green Genes"

Equally important, avoid tossing disembodied quotations into your paper. Help readers concentrate on your message by mentioning the author's name as you introduce a quotation. If the flow of language is not seriously interrupted, also give the title of the source you are quoting. Moreover, if the source is an eminent figure, you can give additional authority to your message by referring to his or her credentials as part of this introductory tag.

527

TEACHING TIP

To give your students practice in note taking before they are assigned research paper topics, you might distribute copies of a newspaper or magazine article on a popular subject and ask your students to take notes in support of a particular thesis.

Once they (and you) are sure of their skills, the students can move on to more complex issues with confidence, but at first keeping to popular subjects will help interest students.

Encourage students to paraphrase, summarize, and quote as they feel necessary, and to take as many (or as few) notes as they feel would be useful in supporting a thesis. Then collect their notes and distribute copies of all or some sets of notes. As a class (or in groups), discuss the notes one set at a time.

1. Do all the notes support the thesis?
2. Are paraphrases accurate?
3. Are summaries accurate?
4. Are quotations appropriate and accurate?
5. Are quoted words within paraphrases and summaries placed in quotation marks?
6. Would any material be better presented in a different kind of note?

NAME

As Adam B. Ulam argues, "For some time now, the United States and Russia have been struggling not so much against each other as against phantoms, their own fears of what each might become unless it scored points over the other. . . ."

NAME AND BOOK TITLE

As Adam B. Ulam argues in *The Rivals,* "For some time now, the United States . . . ."

NAME, CREDENTIALS, AND BOOK TITLE

As Adam B. Ulam, Harvard University Professor of Government, argues in *The Rivals,* "For some time now . . . ."

Occasionally quotations speak for themselves, but often they do not. The chances are that you have seen the words you are quoting as part of a larger piece, so connections may be obvious to you; however, they might not be clear to your reader, who may have to puzzle over why you included the quotation. Avoid this problem by giving a brief introductory analysis that tells your readers what you want them to notice about the quotation:

GUIDELINES FOR WORKING QUOTATIONS INTO YOUR WRITING

1. Set off quotations with quotation marks—otherwise you will be plagiarizing.
2. Do not use quotations in more than a third of your paper; rely mostly on paraphrase and summary to report information from sources.
3. Use quotations to *support* what you say, not to present your thesis and main points.
4. Choose a quotation if:
   a. its language is particularly apt.
   b. its thought is particularly difficult to rephrase accurately.
   c. the authority of the source is especially important to support for your thesis and main ideas.
   d. the source's words are open to interpretation.
5. Quote accurately.
6. Select quotations from authorities in your subject.
7. Select quotations that fit your meaning.
8. Keep long quotations to a minimum.
9. Work quotations smoothly into your writing.
10. Document your source.

528

NAME AND INTRODUCTORY ANALYSIS

But Adam B. Ulam does not think that the tension between the superpowers is based on objective information: "For some time now, the United States . . . ."

A good variety of verbs is available to help you weave quotations into your writing smoothly, without any strain of style. Many are used in the student research paper starting on page 594. Some of these verbs have rather specific meanings while others are general enough to use in most situations, so choose them according to the meaning you want your sentences to deliver:

allege	conclude	insist	reveal	think
argue	deduce	maintain	say	volunteer
assert	describe	note	show	write
claim	explain	observe	speculate	
complain	find	offer	suggest	
concede	grant	report	suppose	

EXERCISE 3

A. For a paper explaining that the science of genetic engineering has advanced dramatically in recent years, write a three- to four-sentence passage that includes your own words and a quotation from this material. After the quoted words, use this parenthetical reference to the source that conforms to the MLA documentation style explained in Chapter 32: (Lax 32).

"We used to do genetics with our eyes closed," [Ron] Cape [founder and chief executive officer of the Cetus Corporation] says late one afternoon in his office. "Now we can do it with our eyes open. We can redesign genes, not at random but actually knowing the genetic coding material. It's unfortunate that people use the term 'genetic genes' as a flip joke, because it's accurate. The genetic code is almost precisely as an engineer would have designed it. It's almost impossible to communicate the wonder and yet simplicity of it."
                              —ERIC LAX, "Banking on the Biotech Industry"

B. For a paper that urges cautious control of genetic engineering, write a three- to four-sentence passage that includes your own words and a quotation from the DeDeuve material in Exercise 1.

C. Write a three- to four-sentence passage that includes your own words and a quotation from a source you are using for a paper assigned in one of your courses. If you have no such assignment, choose any material suitable for a college-level paper.

ANSWERS: EXERCISE 3

A. Answers will vary, but here is one possibility: Genetic engineering has advanced dramatically in recent years. Methods used to be crude, but by now techniques are extremely precise. As Ron Cape, founder and chief executive officer of the Cetus Corporation, has explained, "We used to do genetics with our eyes closed. Now we can do it with our eyes open. We can redesign genes, not at random but actually knowing the genetic coding material" (Lax 32).

B. Answers will vary, but here is one possibility: We must be cautious in controlling genetic engineering. Accidents can happen causing mutant bacteria bred in laboratories to get out and cause great harm. Christian DeDeuve reports that there used to be "strict physical containment" but now "reliance is put mostly on biological containment" (362). What backup system do we have if the biological controls fail?

C. Answers will vary.

INSTRUCTOR'S NOTES

32
WRITING RESEARCH

Conducting research for the purpose of writing helps you gain authority over knowledge and join yourself to groups of people recognized as experts. *Research* literally means repeated *(re-)* going over or looking through to find something *(search)*. Research is, therefore, a process that seeks to answer a question—to move from the known to the unknown. Seeing research as a quest for an answer makes clear that you cannot know whether you have found something unless you know what it is you are looking for.

Not all research assignments in college are given in the form of questions, but all imply that you will need to search for answers. Research questions, explicit or implicit, and the processes needed to answer them vary widely. You might be asked to explain information: "How does penicillin destroy bacteria?" You might be asked to argue one side of an issue: "Is Congress more important than the Supreme Court in setting social policy?"

To attempt to answer such questions, you must conduct exper-

530

iments or track down information from varied sources. *Attempt* is an important word in relation to research. Not all research questions lead to a final, definitive answer. The question about penicillin, for example, leads to a definitive answer—the antibiotic destroys the cell walls of some bacteria (though researchers did not learn this information until the electron microscope was invented). The question about social policy, on the other hand, does not lead to a definitive answer. It invites an informed opinion based on evidence gathered from research.

Some research assignments, like the one about penicillin, may require you to conduct experiments and make direct observations. Such activities are called *primary research*. The reports written from such research are one type of **primary source.** Primary sources include original works of an author—novels, poems, short stories, autobiographies, diaries, first-hand reports of observations and of research, and so on. When you use primary sources, no one comes between you and your direct exposure to the author's own words. For many research assignments, primary sources provide invaluable information and offer excellent material for quotation, paraphrase, and summary (techniques explained in Chapter 31).

Secondary sources, also important for writing research, talk about someone else's original work. The information comes to you second-hand, influenced by the intermediary between you and the primary source. Secondary sources explain events, analyze information, and draw conclusions. The question about social policy, for example, calls for an informed opinion based on your reading of secondary sources. Consulting secondary sources gives you the opportunity to read closely—and listen closely, if you interview authorities—and thereby work to understand what scholars and other experts know about your subject. But some caution is needed also, for you want to avoid distorted reports and biased analyses..

Whether you use primary or secondary sources, or a combination, research is an engrossing and creative activity. By gathering information and composing a synthesis of it, you come to know your subject deeply. You make fresh connections and gain unexpected insights. Equally important, you sample the pleasures of being an independent learner. Little is more rewarding than the realization that you have the self-discipline and intellectual resources to locate and understand information on your own.

This chapter shows you methods for doing secondary research and writing research papers about it. To help you further, Chapter 33 presents a student research paper and a commentary on it and the research that produced it.

TEACHING TIP

According to Robert A. Schwegler and Linda K. Shamoon ("The Aims and Process of the Research Paper," *College English,* Dec. 1982, 817–24), students often have trouble writing research papers that fulfill instructors' expectations because the two groups have very difficult views of the purposes and stylistic conventions of research writing.

Students view the research paper as a close-ended, informative, skills-oriented exercise written for an expert audience by novices pretending to be experts. No wonder then that students' papers often roam freely over the subject area, are devoid of focus, and loaded down with quotes. Academics, on the other hand, view the research paper as open-ended and interpretive, written for an audience of fellow inquirers who have specific expectations of logic, structure, and style. Academic research papers reflect this view by being narrowly focused, aware of the scholarly audience, and frequently tentative in advancing a conclusion (820).

Although some features (such as methods of documentation) vary from discipline to discipline, most features of academic research papers are constant. In teaching the freshman research unit then, we can go a long way toward preparing our students for the papers they will be writing in their majors.

The aim of the academic research paper is twofold, reflecting the duality of the research process it aims to represent. The research paper is at once open-ended and limited—exploratory and demonstrative. It begins with the known, as defined by current scholarship, and moves into the unknown, attempting to pursue an admittedly elusive truth (821).

32a

■∥ 32a

Understand what a research-paper project involves.

A "research paper," sometimes called a "library paper" or a "term paper," involves two processes. You conduct the research, and you write the paper based upon it. Both processes take time. If you are aware of the steps involved in a research-paper project, you will be able to plan ahead and budget your time intelligently.

SAMPLE SCHEDULE FOR A RESEARCH-PAPER PROJECT

FINISH BY

Assignment received (date) _____

1. Choose a suitable topic (32b). _____
2. Determine purpose and audience (32c). _____
3. Prepare to conduct research.
   a. Gather equipment (32d-1). _____
   b. Know how to evaluate sources (32d-2). _____
   c. Determine documentation style (32d-4). _____
4. Use a search strategy (32e), keep a research log (32f–1), take notes (32f-2), and make bibliographic cards (32g). *Use whichever steps fit the situation.*
   a. Get a broad overview (32e-1). _____
   b. Draft a preliminary thesis statement (32h). _____
   c. Decide whether to interview experts (32e-2). _____
   d. Decide whether to send for information (32e-3). _____
   e. Use reference books (32e-5). _____
   f. Use indexes to periodicals and read periodicals (32e-6). _____
   g. Use the card catalog and read books (32e-7). _____
   h. Use computerized databases (32e-8). _____
5. Compile a bibliography (32g). _____
6. Draft and revise a final thesis statement (32h). _____
7. Outline as required (32i). _____
8. Draft paper (32j). _____
9. Use parenthetical references (32k). _____
10. Revise paper (32j). _____

11. Assignment due (date) _____

The processes of researching and of writing are interwoven throughout a research-paper project. The **writing process** for a research paper is much like the writing process for all academic papers. As discussed in Chapter 1 of this book, you begin by thinking about your paper's purpose, audience, and sources. As discussed in Chapters 2 and 3, you plan, draft, revise, edit, and proofread. The **research process** is an added dimension to consider throughout. In planning, you are involved in choosing a suitable topic, refining it into a research question, using a search strategy to find sources of information, evaluating those information sources, and taking notes on useful sources. In drafting and revising, you are involved in integrating sources into the paper by paraphrasing, summarizing, and quoting. (These techniques are the subject of Chapter 31.) Also, during revising, you are watching for sections that need additional support from sources.

Once you know what is involved, you can design your research-paper project according to the limits of time and information resources available. As soon as your instructor gives a research-paper assignment, work out a schedule for finishing each step. You might need one day for a number of steps and two weeks for another. For example, if your assignment gives the topic and specifies the sources, you do not have to choose or narrow a suitable topic. If interim deadlines are part of your assignment, plan your work around them. The more you do research-paper projects, the more skilled you will become at mapping out the work and handling it efficiently. The schedule shown here lists typical steps in a research-paper project (the parentheses give the section in which each step is discussed). No two research-paper projects are alike. The steps do not proceed in a straight line, but often loop back or work in concert. This chapter covers all major steps, but you have to adapt them to your assignment and personal work style.

■‖ 32b
Choose and narrow a topic suitable for a research-paper project.

Instructors assign research-paper topics in different ways. Some assign the specific topic that they want you to research. Others expect you to find a suitable topic. Still others assign a general subject area but expect students to narrow it to a limited, researchable topic. Whenever you are responsible for choosing a topic or for narrowing a general subject area into a researchable topic, remember that not every topic is suitable for a research-paper project.

BACKGROUND
As we struggle to teach the Research Paper, we may sometimes wonder if we are struggling alone. According to James E. Ford and Dennis R. Perry ("Research Paper Instruction in the Undergraduate Writing Program," *College English*, Dec. 1982, 825–31), we are definitely not alone.

Research paper instruction is currently being offered in 84.09% of freshman composition programs and in 40.03% of advanced composition programs. In general this high level of occurrence is fairly uniform in all types and sizes of institutions and in all regions of the country. There is, however, a slight tendency for research paper instruction to decrease as the size of the school increases (down to 71.06% in the large schools). Also, occurrence is highest in the Rocky Mountain region (91.66% and . . . lowest on the Pacific coast (72.40%). Instruction in the research paper is required in 78.11% of freshman composition programs offering it and 42.35% of advanced writing programs where it is offered. Although 4.16% of the schools not offering instruction in the research paper at the basic level indicated their reason for omitting it as "faculty think it unnecessary," the most common reason given for not offering it came under the "other" category, checked by 12.12%. About half of these (that is, about 6% of the total respondents) said the course was already too full to allow time for such instruction.
. . . No institution surveyed had eliminated a research paper requirement during the past five years and only two now have plans to do away with it. (827)

Ford and Perry also say:

Not surprisingly, research paper instruction is offered more in freshman programs (50.56%) during the second semester of the freshman year, but it also is included in a

533

BACKGROUND (CONT.)

significant number of courses offered during the first semester (41.57%). It is a feature in both semesters at 15.17% of the institutions. Such instruction on the advanced level most often comes during the sophomore year, (63.83%) but it is common also during the junior year (46.81%). . . . Whenever it is offered, research paper instruction constitutes, on the average, a very considerable 34.66% of one basic course and 36.71% of an advanced course. (828)

1
Choose a sufficiently narrow topic.

Two characteristics make a topic sufficiently narrow. First, the topic must work within the time allotment and word limit set by your instructor. For example, in five weeks and 1500 to 2000 words, you could not do justice to the history of skyscrapers—or even to the history of all the skyscrapers in San Francisco. A sufficiently narrow topic would relate to the question: "How have new San Francisco skyscrapers been built to withstand earthquakes?"

Second, a topic must be specific enough to allow for sufficient detail to make your paper more than a collection of generalizations. For example, in a paper of 1500–2000 words, you could include too few details if your topic covered all aspects of the risks and benefits of nuclear energy. Your topic would still be too broad if it were in response to the question: "What are the effects on unborn children of overexposure to radiation?" The word *effects* needs to be narrowed, as does *children,* and *radiation.* Sufficient detail would be possible if you narrowed the topic to answer this question: "What were the birth defects in children born in Hiroshima up to eight months after the atomic bomb was dropped?"

Communication was the general topic assigned to Amy Brown, the student who wrote the paper in Chapter 33. Her instructor required a paper of 1800 to 2000 words to be written in five weeks based on about twelve secondary sources. To get started, Brown borrowed two textbooks from a friend, one an introduction to psychology and the other an introduction to business communications. Browsing through the textbooks helped Brown make her first major choice. She decided to focus on *nonverbal communication.* To further narrow her focus, Brown read a book that a psychology professor recommended during an interview. She then began to concentrate on *personal space,* a topic that particularly caught her interest. She was fascinated to learn that cultures have unspoken standards for the accepted distances between people who are conversing and interacting. Brown also liked the topic of personal space because her college had excellent sources to which she could refer. As she began to read closely on the topic, Brown evolved her research question: "How do standards for personal space differ among cultures?" The flow chart (p. 535) illustrates Brown's process of narrowing the topic. Although this chart makes each decision look as if it flowed smoothly from the one before, the process looks clear-cut only after all the thinking, debating, and choosing is over. The process in action is rarely neat and tidy. As you think through your topic, do not be surprised if you have to back out of dead ends and make some

534

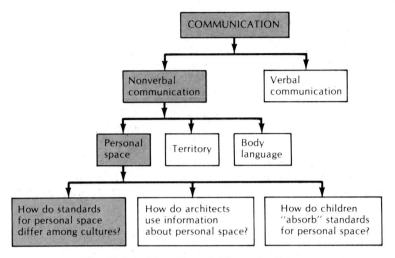

Flow Chart of Amy Brown's Narrowing Process

TEACHING TIP
All too often, the Research Paper looms over Freshman Composition like a thundercloud. It requires much time, students resent "doing" it, and the results are dismal. James Strickland ("The Research Sequence: What To Do Before the Term Paper," *College Composition and Communication,* May 1986, pages 233–36) offers a useful semester plan that incorporates the research project into the ongoing concerns of Freshman Composition.

The sequence begins with an opinion paper in the form of a letter to the editor. No research is required, and Strickland encourages students to submit the letters to local papers (with a publication rate of almost fifty percent and a concomitant increase in students' self-esteem).

Strickland next splits the class into groups of readers whose jobs are to go over one another's letters and indicate what points need support to be more convincing. Wanting to close the holes in their arguments, students are now ready to learn the research skills they need.

As periodicals are the most likely source for the information students need, Strickland begins with the use of periodical indexes. Students must locate and read several articles bearing on their subjects to see if their "original position was accurate and/or reasonable." Students at this stage learn to decipher periodical indexes, to make bibliography notecards, and to paraphrase and take notes.

Based on their research, students now write "documented essays" on the subjects of their original letters to the editor. They are asked to imagine that, on the basis of their letters, they have been asked to write 750 word essays for the Sunday newspaper's magazine section.

Continued on page 536

sharp turns to new avenues. To help yourself define your choices and find a suitable path to a research question, try charting your decision process as you go along.

2
Choose a topic neither too narrow nor too current.

Extremely specific topics are usually so narrow that an extensive search will turn up only a few fragments of information. Imagine looking at your general subject area with a zoom lens. You can survey the whole terrain, zoom in part way, look around for a point of interest, and zoom in yet closer. If, however, you zoom in yet again, you might be focusing on a small detail. You will know you are being overly specific if your topics resemble these: "The Doves in the Altarpieces of Guarineto di Arpo" or "The Effect of Muddy Infields During the 1974 Baltimore Orioles Season."

Also, avoid topics that have suddenly come to public attention in current newspapers or magazines. They tend to move in and out of vogue quickly. Most of all, they cannot lead you to the diversity of sources you need to represent a thorough search.

This warning does not mean that you should avoid current publications to provide support for what you are saying. Indeed, you might well refer to a current event—for example, a recent accident at a nuclear power plant—as an example of a point you are making.

These two to three page essays provide an opportunity to revise the thrust of the original letters, and to use quotation and paraphrase in support of a thesis. Several parenthetical references or endnotes and a bibliography are standard.

The next step is a "researched paper," using more thorough research and fuller documentation. This time students are asked to imagine that they have been invited to expand their Sunday newsmagazine piece into a full-size article (14–24 pages) for a major national magazine. Each student serves as "editor" to another student, in addition to writing his or her own article. The editor's job is to point out places in the essay where additional evidence is needed or where logic is unclear or faulty. The students explore a variety of heuristics as they seek to fill developmental gaps and correct logical flaws.

Overall, Strickland feels, the sequence has resulted in superior papers, exhibiting better documentation skills than papers written by students before he used this sequence. Student attitude has also changed in a positive way: students are more willing to go to the library, are more confident in their ability to do research, and complain less about assignments.

3
Choose a topic worth researching.

When choosing a topic, do not rush. Keep in mind that a good research topic should give you the chance to investigate related ideas or bring together conflicting concepts. The topic should not be too trivial for a college-level research paper. For example, recent marriages among Hollywood stars is not suitable for a research-paper project. Such a subject not only lacks importance but also prevents you from demonstrating that you can grapple with ideas and their implications.

A topic worth researching has a number of characteristics. First, it allows you to draw from varied sources rather than one or two books or articles. Second, it gives you the chance to delve into material worth time and attention from you and your reader. Third, it is complex enough to stimulate you to think critically (see Chapter 5) and gain new insight.

When considering topics, try to find one that interests you sufficiently to spend time on it. You might select an aspect of a major you are considering (or have chosen) so that you can get to know it better. You might select a worthwhile topic that you wish you knew more about but have not had the time to get to know well. If you cannot think of a topic, try browsing in the library to find books and articles that catch your attention.

32c
Determine your paper's purpose and audience.

Your research process involves making decisions about your paper's purpose and audience. Purposes and audiences for writing are discussed extensively in Chapter 1, which you might want to review at this time.

The two major purposes for writing academic papers are *to inform* and *to persuade*. The question that guides your research process helps determine your paper's purpose. If the question asks for facts or information, your purpose is to inform. The question "How do standards for personal space differ among cultures?" requires an answer that calls for informative writing. On the other hand, if the question raised by a topic asks for an informed opinion supported with evidence, your purpose is to persuade. The question "Why should people be aware of intercultural differences in standards for personal space?" calls for persuasive writing. A paper's purpose may shift during the research process. Remain open-minded as you work.

536

32d

By the time you are writing your paper, however, be sure to have defined your purpose.

The audience for your college writing is primarily (but perhaps not exclusively) your instructor. When you think of writing for your instructor, remember that he or she is both a member of the general reading public and a person responsible to see how well you have learned your material and the forms for presenting it. Sometimes the audience for a research paper includes other people—students in your class or even specialists on your topic. For a fuller understanding of writing for various audiences, see 1c.

■|| 32d
Prepare to conduct your research.

Before you start your research, you need to prepare. You need equipment to facilitate your work. You need also to be familiar with

---

BASIC EQUIPMENT FOR CONDUCTING RESEARCH

1. A copy of your assignment.
2. A separate notebook to use for a research log. This important tool is explained in 32f.
3. Pens—several different colors—for taking notes. Writing in pencil tends to blur when notes are shuffled and handled often.
4. Index cards for two purposes. Cards that measure 4 × 6″ give you more room for notes. The 3 × 5″ size is fine for bibliographic data. Use one index card per source to record bibliographic information (see 32d-4 and 32g). Also, use a separate index card for each idea you take down in notes. (See 32f about taking notes, and see Chapter 31 for avoiding plagiarism by learning to paraphrase, summarize, and quote sources.) Index cards give you flexibility in moving information around; pages in a notebook do not.
5. Dimes, quarters, or whatever coins you need for the library's copying machines. (See 32f about the uses and limitations of photocopying.)
6. Paper clips, a small stapler, or rubber bands to help you organize index cards and other papers.
7. A book bag if you intend to check out books from the library. Librarians joke about researchers with wheelbarrows. You might need a backpack.

TEACHING TIP
Students might feel overwhelmed if they had to do a research paper on, say, the role of the media in shaping public attitude toward the Vietnam war or the impact of wheat sales to Russia on the American farmer. The problem has more to do with students' fears than the actual complexity of such assignments. Students' confidence can be built as research skills are developed if "accessible" topics are assigned—especially for preliminary exercises in library skills and note taking. Here are a few possible assignments:

1. Write a biography of someone you would like to know more about: a sports figure, a cartoonist, a movie director, a state legislator, a deposed dictator.
2. Write an essay recommending a particular type or model of some fairly expensive consumer item that you are interested in buying yourself, such as a car, a VCR, or a microwave oven.
3. Write an essay recommending and explaining an eating regimen that can help someone lose weight, train for a sport, or control a health problem (e.g., diabetes or high blood pressure).
4. Imagine you are a travel agent who has been asked to plan a tour of Asia or Africa. Money is no object. You have been told to arrange stops in all countries with which the United States has friendly relations. Advise your clients of (1) entry requirements such as a visa and limitations on what they may bring in to each country; (2) health precautions that they ought to take including innoculations; and (3) local laws or customs that they must not violate such as the non-use of alcohol or drugs.

two key concepts in research—evaluating sources and using headings or key words.

1
Equip yourself.

Experienced researchers use equipment that helps them work efficiently. Gather the materials listed in the chart on page 537 and keep them separate from your regular books and materials so that you can locate them easily.

Color coding is an option many researchers find helpful in establishing categories for information. For example, you might use one color of index cards or colored clips for notes and another for bibliographic information. You might use one color ink for summarized information, another for quotations taken from sources, and a third for your own comments on a source.

2
Know how to evaluate sources.

A source is any information-providing person, book, article, document, or other form of communication. But not all sources are equally valuable. Before you start to gather information from sources, learn how to evaluate them. Follow the guidelines on page 539. If you are using a secondary source, also see the Checklist for Evaluating a Secondary Source in 5c.

3
Start to compile a list of headings or key words.

Researchers use headings and key words to look up information. **Headings** are subject categories in books and periodicals. **Key words**—sometimes called *descriptors* or *identifiers*—identify subject categories in periodicals and computerized databases.

Knowing how to locate headings and key words is central to the research process. The people who prepare reference books, catalog cards, and indexes to periodicals do not have the resources to maintain an infinite number of headings. In fact, their job is to group information into categories and arrange efficient retrieval systems. Your paper constructs its own category of information. Your job, therefore, is to locate the headings and key words that lead you to books and articles on your topic. For example, the topic *nuclear energy* is identified with various headings or key words: *energy, nuclear; atomic energy; energy, atomic; nuclear power; power, nuclear;* and so on. You have to "break the code" to figure out what

GUIDELINES FOR EVALUATING SOURCES

1. **Authoritative:** Check encyclopedias, textbooks, articles in academic journals, and bibliographies, and ask experts. If a particular name or a specific work is mentioned often, that source is probably recognized as an authoritative one on your topic. Also, to check if the author of a source has a background that makes him or her an authority, consult one of the biographical references listed on pages 546–47.

2. **Reliable:** Check different sources. If the same information appears, the material is likely to be reliable.

3. **Well Supported:** Check that each source supports assertions or information with sufficient evidence. If the material expresses the source's point of view but offers little to back up that position, turn to another source.

4. **Balanced Tone:** Read a source critically, as explained in Chapter 5. If the tone is unbiased and if the reasoning is logical, consider the source to be balanced.

5. **Current:** Check that the information is up-to-date. Sometimes long-accepted information is replaced or modified by new research. Check indexes to journals or computerized databases to see if anything newer has come along.

words identify the category you are seeking in each source. As you conduct your research, keep an ongoing list in your research log of headings and key words that relate to your topic. Then when you approach a new source, your search process will be more efficient.

4
Determine your documentation style.

The term **documentation style** refers to various systems for providing information about the sources you have used in a research paper. Documentation styles vary among the disciplines. Some styles use footnotes or endnotes; others put reference information in parentheses within the text. Styles also differ in requirements for the complete list of sources at the end of a paper.

Before you start consulting sources, know what documentation style you will be using in your paper. If your assignment does not specify a documentation style, ask your instructor which to use. Be

539

aware of what information the style calls for about each source. Then as you take notes on each source, keep a record of that information so that you can document your sources correctly and fully.

The **Modern Language Association (MLA)** has developed the documentation styles used most often in the humanities. Before 1984, "MLA style" called for footnotes or endnotes, and the list of sources was named Bibliography. Current MLA style, introduced in 1984, calls for parenthetical references instead of footnotes or endnotes. It also changed the name of the list of sources used to Works Cited. If your instructor tells you to use MLA style, see 32k to find out how to use parenthetical references and see 32g about the Works Cited list. If your instructor tells you to use a footnote or endnote system of documentation, see 34b-4.

The **American Psychological Association (APA)** has developed another documentation system commonly used for research papers, especially in the social sciences. Like MLA style, APA style uses parenthetical references and a list of sources. If your instructor tells you to use APA style, see 34c-4.

■‖ 32e
Use a search strategy to conduct your research.

Inexperienced researchers can easily feel overwhelmed by a seemingly limitless choice of source. Researchers can interview experts, send for information by mail, and—most of all—use the resources of a library. Experienced researchers use a **search strategy** for working systematically through these sources. A search strategy is an organized procedure that leads step-by-step from general to specific sources. A structured approach helps you use time efficiently and cover the necessary territory. No two research processes are exactly alike, so the search strategy explained here should serve as a guide to your personally tailored strategy. A search strategy is rarely as tidy as it seems to be when described in a textbook. Expect to adapt the explanation here to your needs in each research project.

‖ 1
Get a broad overview and narrow your topic.

If you have to choose a topic of your own or narrow a subject into a researchable topic, start by getting a broad overview. For advice on how to think about narrowing a topic, see 32b.

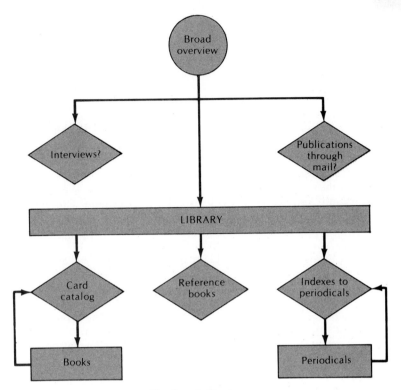

The Search Strategy

SUGGESTIONS FOR GETTING A BROAD OVERVIEW

1. Confer briefly with a professor in your general field of interest (psychology, biology, literature, and so on). Ask for advice in narrowing your topic. Also ask for names of major books and authorities on your topic.

2. Browse through a textbook in your field of interest. Look for material that points toward ways to narrow your topic. Also look for names of major books and authorities on your topic.

3. Read an encyclopedia article about your field of interest or subcategories of the field. Get basic information that might help you narrow your topic. Look for the names of major books and authorities. *Do not, however, stop with the encyclopedia.* College-level research demands a thorough search of a variety of sources.

541

32e

2
Decide whether to interview experts.

As you pursue a broad overview, you might decide to interview experts on your subject, either in person or on the telephone. An expert can often offer valuable leads or advice. If your topic relates to an event that your family or friends lived through, they qualify as experts, and access to them will likely be easy. If you want to interview other people, start early. It takes time to set up appointments and fit your research needs into other people's schedules. You may not always be granted the interviews you seek. Still, many people remember their own experiences doing research in school or college and try to help.

The faculty at your college or nearby colleges have special expertise about many topics. Corporations and professional organizations can often suggest experts in many fields. (When you call a large company, ask to be connected with the public relations department or its equivalent.) Public officials are sometimes available for interviews. Many federal and state government offices have employees who specialize in providing information to the public.

Carefully evaluate any information you get from interviewing experts, using the guidelines in 32d-2. Even the information of experts may be slanted to suit special interests. For example, what are your chances of getting unbiased information about the dangers of smoking from the executive of a tobacco company?

Prepare questions that use time efficiently. Know why you are interviewing the person and what you want to know. Ask questions that elicit information, not merely a "yes" or "no" answer. Be constructive and avoid language that shows bias or a hostile attitude. For example, if you are researching toxic waste disposal, a good question to ask a government official is "What long-range plans are being made to dispose of toxic wastes?" A loaded question not likely to yield useful information is: "Why doesn't the government or your office do anything about the proper disposal of toxic wastes?"

Always follow up an interview, no matter how short, with a brief note of thanks. Aside from its being polite, this courtesy helps pave the way for the next student who might ask for an interview.

3
Decide whether to send for information.

As a result of getting a broad overview, you might decide to send for publications or other kinds of information available by mail. A month or more can go by before your inquiry is processed,

542

so send early and leave time in your schedule to use the material. Never depend entirely on mail-order sources for your research. The material might not arrive in time or might turn out to be unsuitable. Also, a well-handled research-paper project draws on a variety of sources, including those found in a library.

When researching a question about business, you might write to companies involved with matters related to your topic. Target your request to the material you need. If you are unsure of what is available, call the company and talk with someone in its public relations office (or the equivalent). Evaluate the material carefully for bias and promotion of special interests. To be useful, corporate publications must go well beyond the kinds of information usually written for consumers. Large libraries sometimes have corporate reports and specialized technical reports on file, so check with a reference librarian *before* you order through the mails.

United States government publications are available in an almost astounding variety. You can get information on population figures, weather patterns, agriculture, national parks, and much more. Large libraries often have many government documents on file, so ask a reference librarian before you order. To find out what publications are available and how to order them, consult one of these directories in the reference section of a large library.

The *Monthly Catalog of United States Government Publications* is an up-to-date listing of all offerings. Items are cataloged according to subject.

American Statistics Index (ASI) is published in two volumes. The *Index* catalogues all statistical documents produced by government departments. The *Abstracts* gives concise summaries of the documents' contents.

CIS, published by the Congressional Information Service, indexes all the papers produced by congressional panels and committees. These documents include the texts of hearings (for example, testimony about the plight of the homeless) and reports (for example, a comparative study of temporary shelters for the homeless.)

4
Be ready to use all the resources of the library.

Using the library as a resource for a research-paper project takes time. In his work as Chief of the General Research Division of the New York Public Library, Rodney Phillips has become extremely familiar with the time needed to prepare a good undergrad-

543

BACKGROUND

Some very famous people have been librarians. A few of them may even have helped students with term papers.

- German philosopher-mathematician and diplomat Gottfried Von Liebniz (1646–1716) served two terms as a librarian.

- British philosopher, economist, and historian David Hume (1711–1776) spent five years as a librarian at the Library of the Faculty of the Advocates at Edinburgh while writing his *History of England.*

- The infamous Casanova (1725–1798) served as a private librarian to royalty for thirteen years at the end of his life.

- Pope Pius XI (1857–1939) spent nineteen years at the Ambrosian Library in Milan, and he was then appointed chief librarian. In 1911, he began reorganization and updating of the Vatican Library, and in 1915 was named prefect of the Vatican Library. He went on to become pope in 1922.

- Archibald MacLeish (1892–1982), poet, playwright, Assistant Secretary of State, and three-time Pulitzer Prize winner, served as Librarian of Congress under Franklin D. Roosevelt.

- Mao Tse-Tung (1893–1976) at one time was assistant to the chief librarian of the University of Peking.

- J. Edgar Hoover (1895–1964) was a messenger and cataloguer in the Library of Congress as a young man.

uate research paper. Division staff receives an average of 2,000 inquiries per day, and many of them are from students like you who want to know how to find information for their papers. To do a decent job, Mr. Phillips says, you will want to gather and look over at least 25 different items. Some you will need to skim, and some you will need to read slowly. You will need to take notes on many. "Plan to spend at least 15 hours in the library," Mr. Phillips says. "You will sometimes be frustrated to find that others have been there before you and taken books you want. Then you'll have to look further, just as they probably did. You will find that titles you thought were promising will not give you what you were after. Other sources might pay off enormously." Mr. Phillips says the typical undergraduate, new to research writing, expects to obtain a paper from one book and two or three other sources. These students, he states flatly, are not budgeting anywhere near the time they need to do a good job.

Librarians are information experts. They are highly skilled at searching for and finding information. Reference librarians seek to help people learn how to use library resources well. Nevertheless, the research task remains yours. Professor Mary Cope, chief of the reference division of the library at the City College of the City University of New York, says she holds "reference interviews" with students "to determine what they want to learn. We direct them, then, to the resources and tell them to return if they need more guidance." Professor Cope thinks that the best assistance she offers is to point out different aspects of subjects covered in reference sources. By doing so, she helps students narrow their topics.

Many college and large public libraries prepare written guides to their resources. Find out if your library has such a guide. With or without a guide, get to know your library well. Wander around and browse. Libraries differ slightly from each other, in physical layout and in the breadth and depth of resources.

5
Know how to use reference books.

Reference books range from general sources to specialized ones. Reference books summarize or list much important information. You can choose from encyclopedias, yearbooks and almanacs, atlases, dictionaries, biographies, bibliographies, indexes, and other reference books. Some of these are general references; others focus on a particular subject.

Eugene P. Sheehy's *Guide to Reference Books* is a valuable resource. It covers reference works in all fields, describing general

544

ones first, and then specialized ones. This book, or another like it, is worth getting to know well.

Encyclopedias

Articles in general encyclopedias summarize information about a wide variety of subjects. The articles are most useful for a broad overview but not as major sources for college-level research. They are written by specialists for nonspecialist readers. Many articles end with a brief bibliography of major works on the subject. Because encyclopedias take long to write and publish, some kinds of information in them—about technology, for example—quickly becomes outdated. Look for up-to-date editions and annual supplements. Even so, general encyclopedias are not the place to look for reports on recent events or current research.

Collier's Encyclopedia, Encyclopaedia Britannica, and *Encyclopedia Americana* are among the respected multivolume general encyclopedias. They are all widely available.

One-volume general encyclopedias cover subjects very briefly. You may want to consult one, such as *The New Columbia Encyclopedia* or the *Random House Encyclopedia,* to see whether a general subject area interests you enough for further research. A one-volume encyclopedia may also be useful when something comes up in your research that you need not explore fully but do need to understand in a general way.

Specialized encyclopedias exist in many fields. See the list (pp. 547–50) of specialized reference works arranged by academic discipline.

Almanacs, Yearbooks, Fact Books

Almanacs—books such as *The World Almanac and Book of Facts*—briefly present a year's events and data in government, politics, sports, economics, demographics, and many other categories. *Facts on File* covers world events in a weekly digest and in an annual one-volume *Yearbook.*

Congressional Record and *Statistical Abstract* contain a wealth of data about the United States. *Demographic Yearbook* and *United Nations Statistical Yearbook* carry worldwide data. Other specialized yearbooks and handbooks are named in the list of reference works below, arranged by academic discipline.

Atlases

Atlases contain maps—and remember that seas and skies and even other planets have been mapped. You have probably looked up places in a geographical atlas, such as *National Geographic Atlas of*

BACKGROUND
The Nuremberg Chronicle (1493) was the world's first encyclopedia. Its three volumes were written by one man, Hartmann Schedel, using his extensive personal library for most of his research. Schedel did overlook one event, though: Columbus's discovery of the New World one year earlier.

BACKGROUND
German Johann Georg Krünitz (1728–1796), a philosopher and medical doctor, wrote a 242 volume encyclopedia all by himself. In his spare time, he wrote over 400 other books.

BACKGROUND
Denis Diderot spent over twenty years writing and editing his *Encyclopédie.* In twenty-eight volumes, he and famous contributors, such as Rousseau and Voltaire, collected all the scientific thinking of the Age of Reason. The project began as a commission from a French publisher to translate a one-volume British encyclopedia into French. Diderot earned about $12 a week while working on the encyclopedia. When the project was complete, he was forced to sell his library in order to provide his daughter with a dowry. Catherine II, Empress of Russia, paid him $5,000—and also allowed him access to the books for the rest of his life.

545

BACKGROUND

The Guinness Book of World Records was founded as a result of the curiosity of Sir Hugh Beaver, the managing director of Arthur Guinness, Son and Co., Ltd. One day in 1954, Sir Hugh went bird hunting. He shot at some plovers—and missed. He started wondering if plovers were the fastest game birds, and he tried to satisfy his curiosity in the encyclopedia. Neither it nor any other reference work had the answer.

As a result, Sir Hugh decided that people needed a book that would accurately list record sizes, speeds, and durations. His plan was to have a copy of the book in every pub that sold Guinness stout, as an aid in settling bets. He set about finding someone to author such a book, and one of his executives recommended the McWhirter brothers. Trivia history was made.

Norris and Ross McWhirter, identical twin sons of a newspaper writer, had grown up around newspapers, magazines, and reference books. Their childhood hobby had been to collect information of the very type Sir Hugh was seeking. They had frequently found contradictions in their sources, and so as adults they had founded a company to verify these statistics and to "supply facts and figures to newspapers, yearbooks, encyclopedias, and advertisers."

Four months after Sir Hugh had interviewed them, the McWhirters published the first book in the series. The 198 page bet-settler became England's number one non-fiction best seller in only four months. Immediately, readers began submitting their own fantastic facts. The McWhirters collected and checked these submissions, and soon an updated volume was on the way. Norris and Ross McWhirter acted as co-editors until 1975.

the World. These comprehensive books contain many kinds of geographic information: topography, climates, populations, migrations, natural resources, crops, and so on.

Dictionaries

Dictionaries define words and terms. The kinds of dictionaries described in Chapter 20 define words in the English language and give various other information about these words. As a reference work, no other dictionary is more comprehensive or scholarly than the *Oxford English Dictionary.* Unless you are researching word origins, however, you will likely find the other dictionaries discussed in Chapter 20 sufficient. They give extensive definitions and also report information on usage, slang, regional forms, and other categories of English.

Specialized dictionaries exist in many fields, among them literature, music, folklore, economics, and the sciences. These dictionaries define the words and phrases specific to a field. For specialized dictionaries, see the reference works below arranged by academic discipline.

Biographies

Biographical reference books give brief information about the major events in many famous people's lives. Various *Who's Who* series cover noteworthy people, male or female, living or dead. *Current Biography: Who's News and Why*—well-described by its title—is published monthly, with six-month and annual cumulative editions. *Dictionary of American Biography* and *Webster's Biographical Dictionary* are very widely available.

Specialized biographical reference books focus on artists, musicians, important people of various historical periods or nationalities, and so on. See the list below of specialized reference works arranged by academic discipline.

Bibliographies

Bibliographies name books. *Books in Print* lists all books in print—that is, available through their publishers and sometimes other sources—in the United States. This multivolume work classifies its entries by author name, by title, and by general subject headings, but it does not describe a book's content in any way.

The *Book Review Digest* excerpts book reviews. If a book has been reviewed in major newspapers and magazines, you can find out what those critics thought of it. These excerpts can help you evaluate a source (see also 32d-2). This digest is published every year.

546

The reviews appear in the volume that corresponds to the year a book was published or the one immediately following. The *Book Review Index* and *Current Review Citations* list *where* reviews have appeared but do not carry the actual reviews.

Consulting specialized bibliographies—ones that list many books on a particular subject—can be very helpful in your research process. Annotated or critical bibliographies describe and evaluate the works they list and so are especially useful. You will find some specialized bibliographies in the following list of reference works arranged by academic discipline.

Specialized Reference Works

As you work into a research topic, you should look for increasingly specific and focused information. First, get an overview from general reference works, and then consult specialized ones. Here are some titles, grouped by general academic disciplines.

BUSINESS AND ECONOMICS

Accountant's Handbook, Lee. J. Seidler and Douglas R. Charmichael
A Dictionary of Economics, Harold S. Sloan and Arnold Zurcher
Encyclopedia of Advertising, Irwin Graham
Encyclopedia of Banking and Finance, G. G. Munn
The Encyclopedia of Management, Carl Heyel, ed.
Handbook of Modern Marketing, Victor P. Buell, ed.

FINE ARTS

Bryan's Dictionary of Painters and Engravers, Michael Bryan
Crowell's Handbook of World Opera, Frank L. Moore
The Dance Encyclopedia, Anatole Chujoy and P. W. Manchester
Dictionary of Contemporary Music
Dictionary of Contemporary Photography
Encyclopedia of Painting
Encyclopedia of World Architecture, Henri Stierlin
Harvard Dictionary of Music, Willi Apel
International Cyclopedia of Music and Musicians, Oscar Thompson
    and N. Slonimsky
The Lives of the Painters, John E. Canaday
New Dictionary of Modern Sculpture, Robert Maillard, ed.
Oxford Companion to Art, Harold Osborne
Oxford Companion to Music, Percy A. Scholes
Popular Music: An Annotated List of American Popular Songs

HISTORY AND POLITICAL SCIENCE

Cambridge History of China, John K. Fairbank and Denis Twitchett

547

A Biblographic Guide to the History of Indian-White Relations in the United States, Francis P. A. Prucha
Dictionary of American Biography
Dictionary of American History
Encyclopedia of American History
An Encyclopedia of Latin-American History, Michael R. Martin et al.
An Encyclopedia of World History, William L. Langer
Foreign Affairs Bibliography
Harvard Guide to American History, Frank Freidel and Richard K. Showman, eds.
The Literature of Political Science, Clifton Brock
The Negro in America: A Bibliography, Elizabeth W. Miller and Mary Fisher
New Cambridge Modern History
Political Handbook and Atlas of the World
Political Science Bibliographies, Robert W. Harmon
The Study of the Middle East: Research and Scholarship in the Humanities and Social Sciences, Leonard Binder, ed.

LITERATURE

American Authors, 1600–1900, S. F. Kunitz and Howard Haycraft
Cassell's Encyclopedia of World Literature
Columbia Dictionary of Modern European Literature
Contemporary Authors
The Contemporary Novel: A Checklist of Critical Literature on the British and American Novel Since 1945, Irving Adelman and Rita Dworkin
Dictionary of Literary Biography
A Dictionary of Literary Terms
European Authors, 1000–1900, S. J. Kunitz and Vineta Colby
Funk & Wagnall's Guide to Modern World Literature
A Handbook to Literature, C. Hugh Holman
Harvard Guide to Contemporary American Writing, Daniel Hoffman, ed.
Literary History of the United States: Bibliography, Robert E. Spiller
MLA International Bibliography of Books and Articles on the Modern Languages and Literature
Modern Drama: A Checklist of Critical Literature on the Twentieth Century Plays, Irving Adelman and Rita Dworkin
New Cambridge Bibliography of English Literature, George Watson, ed.
The Oxford Companion to American Literature, James D. Hart, ed.
The Oxford Companion to English Literature, Margaret Drabble, ed.
The Oxford Companion to the Theatre, Phyllis Hartnoll, ed.
Poetry Explication, Joseph M. Kuntz
The Reader's Encyclopedia, William Rose Benet

548

MYTHOLOGY

Bulfinch's Mythology, Thomas Bulfinch

Funk & Wagnall's Standard Dictionary of Folklore, Mythology, and Legend

Larousse World Mythology

PHILOSOPHY AND RELIGION

The Concise Encyclopedia of Western Philosophy and Philosophers Dictionary of the Bible, F. C. Grant and H. H. Rowley

Eastern Definitions: A Short Encyclopedia of Religions of the Orient, Edward Rice

Encyclopedia of Judaica

Encyclopedia of Philosophy, Paul Edwards, ed.

An Encyclopedia of Religion, Vergilius Ferm

New Catholic Encyclopedia

The Oxford Dictionary of the Christian Church, F. L. Cross and E. A. Livingston

A Reader's Guide to the Great Religions, Charles Adams, ed.

Twentieth-Century Encyclopedia of Religious Knowledge

SCIENCE AND TECHNOLOGY

American Men and Women of Science

Biological Abstracts

Chamber's Technical Dictionary

Dictionary of Physics

A Dictionary of Science Terms, G. Speck and B. Jaffe

The Encyclopedia of the Biological Sciences, Peter Gray, ed.

Encyclopedia of Chemistry, Douglas M. Considine and Glenn D. Considine

Encyclopedia of Computer Science and Technology, J. Belzer et al., eds.

The Encyclopedia of Oceanography, Rhodes W. Fairbridge, ed.

Encyclopedia of Physics

Handbook of Chemistry and Physics

Introduction to the History of Science, George Sarton

The Larousse Encyclopedia of Animal Life

McGraw-Hill Encyclopedia of Science and Technology

Universal Encyclopedia of Mathematics

Van Nostrand's Scientific Encyclopedia

SOCIAL SCIENCES

The American Negro Reference Book, John P. Davis, ed.

Dictionary of Anthropology, Charles Winnick

Dictionary of Education, Carter V. Good

Encyclopedia of Human Behavior: Psychology, Psychiatry, and Mental Health

Encyclopedia of Psychology, Hans Jurgen Eysenck
International Encyclopedia of the Social Sciences, David L. Sills, ed.
Reference Encyclopedia of the American Indians, Barry T. Klein, ed.
Sources of Information in the Social Sciences, Carl Milton White et al.
Women: A Bibliography of Bibliographies, Patricia K. Ballou

Television and Film
International Encyclopedia of Film
International Television Almanac, C. S. Aaronson, ed.
New York Times Film Reviews, 1913–1970
World Encyclopedia of the Film, Tim Cawkwell and John Milton
Smith, eds.

6
Know how to use indexes to periodicals.

Periodicals are magazines and journals published at set periods during a year. **Indexes to periodicals** list articles written between the dates on the cover on each edition. Many indexes are kept up-to-date with supplements between editions. Some indexes include abstracts—brief summaries—of each article. Classification systems vary among indexes, so take time to learn how to decipher the codes and abbreviations in the index you need. Most indexes include a guide for readers in the front or back of each volume and supplement. As you learn to use an index, update your list of headings and key words (32d-3) for future reference.

Indexes are packaged in a variety of ways. Some are in print, with yearly bound volumes and interim paperback updates. Some indexes are on microfilm or microfiche—film strips or film cards with miniature reproductions of the print pages. Machines called *readers* project the pages full size or larger onto a screen. Get to know how these machines work. Some machines come with an instruction diagram; if you need help, ask a librarian. Many indexes are also part of computerized databases (see 32e-8).

General Indexes

General indexes list articles in magazines and newspapers. Headings and key words on the same subject vary among indexes, so think of every possible way to look up the information you seek. Large libraries have many general indexes. Almost all libraries have these two major indexes:

The *New York Times Index* catalogs all articles that have been printed in this encyclopedic newspaper since 1851. Supplements are published every two weeks in paperbound volumes. The supplements are organized into volumes (bound or on microfilm) periodically.

The *Readers' Guide to Periodical Literature* is the most widely used index to over 100 magazines and journals with general (rather than specialized) readers. Paperback supplements are published every two weeks. These supplements are organized into volumes (bound or on microfilm) periodically. This index does not include scholarly journals, so its uses are often limited for college-level research. It can be useful, however, for getting a broad overview and for ways to narrow a subject. Illustrated is an entry from *Readers' Guide* showing listings for Communication, the subject of Amy Brown's research-paper assignment.

COMMUNICATION, Nonverbal ———————— Subject heading
Does your body *parle francais*? French body ——— Title of article
   language; teaching methods of L. Wylie) pors ——— Author
   Time 113:107 + My 14 '79
Feminine intuition: fact or fiction? work of
   Judith Hall. il Seventeen 38:59 Mr '79 ——— Periodical title
How to know what everybody's really thinking.
   il Mademoiselle 85:184-5 N '79
People who read people: Neurolinguistic Pro-
   gramming workshops; work of R. Bandler and
   J. Grinder. J. Goleman bibl il Psychol Today —— Has bibliography,
   13:66-7 + Jl '79   illustrations
Watching your every move: what you reveal
   about yourself without saying a word. J.
   Marks. Teen 23:36 + Jl '79 ——————— Vol. 23, p. 36 +, July 1979
When tensions talk—listen! Subtle motion tells
   a story. E. Hamilton por Sci Digest 85:30-2 + —— Has portrait
   Ap '79
Women smile less for success; study of job
   success by Wendy McKenna and Florence
   Denmark. M. B. Parlee. Psychol Today 12:16
   Mr '79
      See also
Eye—Movements
Gesture
Sign language ——————————————— Related subject
Touch   headings

Annotated Excerpt from *Readers' Guide to Periodical Literature*

BACKGROUND
During the Middle Ages, the libraries of Western Europe were affiliated with religious houses and cathedrals. The few private libraries belonged to bishops. The clergy were the only people who could read, and even if the level of literacy was sometimes low, the church maintained the tradition of schools and libraries. These religious libraries were quite small by twentieth-century standards. The largest (at Canterbury and Bury St. Edmunds) had 2,000 volumes each, but libraries of only a few hundred volumes were the rule. The libraries contained theological and biblical works, law books, classical texts, medical and historical works. Contemporary histories, written in monasteries, remain the best records of what happened during the period. In the thirteenth and fourteenth centuries, the rise of the new universities, the rediscovery of Aristotle (from Arabic), and the position of the friars as university teachers undermined the dominance of the monastic libraries. Although the university libraries were not open to undergraduates, the Franciscan friars opened their own libraries (some still survive in England), and they printed small, portable books which contrasted with the bulky illuminated manuscripts of the monasteries. The monastic libraries of England were destroyed in 1536–40) (during Henry VIII's reign) and their books dispersed. In 1550, university libraries, schools, and churches were purged. Many treasures saved during the 1000 years of the Dark Ages were lost.

BACKGROUND
João de Barros (1496–1570), a Portuguese historian, wrote *Décadas da Ásia,* a history of the Portuguese Empire. King John III was more than satisfied—he was thrilled. So he gave de Barros 130,000 square miles of land—the Brazilian state of Maranhão.

Specialized Indexes

Specialized indexes list articles published in academic and professional periodicals. When researching a college-level paper, you will often find the material in specialized indexes more appropriate than that in general indexes. Many specialized indexes carry an abstract (a summary) of each listed article.

Depending on their resources, libraries stock many or few specialized indexes. Commonly available specialized indexes include *America: History and Life,* published every four months; *Applied Science and Technology Index,* published monthly; *Art Index,* published every three months; *Biological Abstracts,* published monthly; *Biological and Agricultural Index,* published monthly; *Business Periodicals Index,* published monthly; *Education Index,* published monthly; *General Science Index,* published monthly and cumulative editions published every three months; *Humanities Index,* published every three months. (Before 1974, it was part of the *Social Sciences and Humanities Index.* Before 1965, the *Social Sciences and Humanities Index* was called the *International Index.*); *MLA International Bibliography of Books and Articles in the Modern Languages and Literatures,* published annually; *Music Index,* published monthly; *Psychological Abstracts,* published monthly.

BACKGROUND
Before it was burnt down in the third century A.D., the famous library at Alexandria, Egypt contained as many as 700,000 scrolls. Under the Ptolemies (third century B.C. on) the library became a depository for copies of all important texts. Books were edited into a standard format, and systems of punctuation and accents were introduced. Textual scholarship, revisions of books to incorporate new knowledge, and the writing of new books went on constantly. Most of the books have been lost. Only those works which were widely copied and distributed have managed to survive. For example, evidence indicates that Aeschylus, Sophocles, Euripides, and Aristophanes wrote about 330 plays in total; only 43 remain.

7
Know how to use the card catalog.

The **card catalog** is a record of all books—and most periodicals—available in a library. Information is organized alphabetically in three categories: authors' names, book titles, and subjects. In some libraries, authors and titles are in one file, subjects in another. In other libraries, the three types of information are filed together.

Each card from the card catalog contains much useful information. The **call number** is most important. Be sure to copy it down *exactly* as it appears, with all numbers, letters, and decimal points. The call number tells where the book is located in the stacks. If you are working in a library with open stacks (one where you can go into the book collection yourself), the call number leads you to the area in the library where all books on the same subject can be found. Being there is an excellent search strategy in itself, even though some books might have been checked out and other books might be at the reserve desk. The call number is also crucial in a library with closed stacks. In this case, to get a book, you must fill in a call slip, hand it in at the call desk, and wait for the book to arrive. If you have filled in the wrong number or an incomplete number, your wait will be in vain.

32e

Libraries classify books according to one of two systems. You can tell what system a particular library uses from the call numbers on the catalog cards. Cards in the **Library of Congress system** have call numbers that start with a letter. Each letter indicates a major classification of information: *A* stands for general works, *B* for philosophy, *C* and *D* for history, and so on. Cards in the **Dewey Decimal system** have call numbers that start with three-digit numbers. Each number indicates a major classification of information: 0–99 signals general works, 100–199 philosophy, 200–299 religion, and so on. Find out what system your library uses and ask for a complete list of the classifications.

Tracers are another important feature of cards in the card catalog. Tracers are words, numbered and in fine print below a book's publication data. Tracers give other headings used to classify information related to the subject of the card. They are valuable hints for other topics to look up in the subject file of the card catalog when you want to find more about a subject. As you find tracers, be sure to add them to your list of headings and key words (see 32d-3).

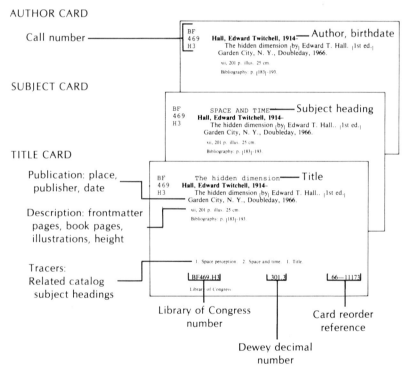

AUTHOR CARD

Call number ——— Author, birthdate

SUBJECT CARD

— Subject heading

TITLE CARD

Publication: place, publisher, date

Description: frontmatter pages, book pages, illustrations, height

Tracers: Related catalog subject headings

— Title

Library of Congress number

Dewey decimal number

Card reorder reference

Library of Congress Catalog Cards

BACKGROUND
Melvil Dewey (1851–1931) is famous for the Dewey Decimal System of book classification (1876). He was also a founder and editor of the *Library Journal* and of the American Library Association. In 1883, he became librarian at Columbia University, New York City, and founded its school of library economy, the first program to train and certify librarians. Dewey and the school moved to Albany, New York, where it became the State Library school. Dewey served as director of the New York State library (1899–1906), secretary of the University of the State of New York (1899–1900), and state Director of Libraries (1904–6). He remade the state library into one of the most efficient in the country, and he set up traveling libraries and picture collections. His innovations were widely copied in the United States and abroad.

BACKGROUND
Benjamin Franklin organized the Library Company of Philadelphia in 1731. It was the first American subscription library. Its original purpose was to provide ready access to books for members of the Junto Club, a public service group to which Franklin belonged. Franklin himself said that he spent time at the library almost daily, learning foreign languages or reading for general knowledge.

At libraries that use the Library of Congress cataloging systems, the multi-volume *Library of Congress Subject Headings (LCSH)* is an excellent guide. Available in the reference or reserve section of a library, it is a catalog of the subject headings (not title or author) used in the card catalog.

This valuable resource helps you in three ways. First, you can look up your subject without having to go through the cards. Second, if the term you are using is not in the card catalog, it might be in the *LCSH* with a cross reference to the term used in the card catalog. The expense and time is enormous to change subject headings in the card catalog, so the terms are not always up-to-date. For example, until recently, sources related to "World War I" were filed in the card catalog under "The European War." People who consulted the *LCSH* easily found out that the old term for "World War I" was still in effect, and they could continue with their research. Third, at each subject heading, you can find a list of tracers—related headings that can lead you to additional sources. As a bonus, the *LCSH* also lists related terms (marked by *x*) that are *not* used to classify information in the system; knowing these terms will help you avoid unproductive searching. All the terms in the *LCSH* suggest alternate key words you can use when searching through other sources. Amy Brown, whose research paper appears in Chapter 33,

Library of Congress Subject Headings

(E) INDEX

(G) FOCUS KNOB

(F) MANUAL KNOB

(D) FAST BUTTONS

(A) ON/OFF SWITCH

(B) FILE SELECTOR SWITCH

(C) INSTRUCTIONS

The COMCAT (Computer Output Microform CATalog)

found this when she looked up "nonverbal communication" as well as "personal space," the two entries shown in the illustration.

Many libraries today have card catalogs "on-line." These computerized access systems often list millions of titles, some of which are in the library you are using. On-line systems vary, so if your library has one, learn how to use it to best benefit. (See also 32e-8.)

Many libraries today have transferred their card catalogs from cards in drawers to alphabetical listings on microfilm. The microfilm entries have exactly the same information that would appear on a card in a drawer. Some libraries offer a mixture of cards and microfilm. To use microfilm, you need to operate a machine called a *reader*. Learn how to turn it on and off, focus the picture, and search at fast and slow speeds. Many such readers are currently on the market. *Comcat,* shown in the illustration, is a widely used one.

8
Know how to use computerized databases.

A **computerized database** is a bibliographic computer file of articles, reports, and—less often—books. Each item in a computerized database provides information about title, author, and pub-

555

lisher. If the database catalogs articles from scholarly journals, the entry might also provide a summary—called an *abstract*—of the material. Once you locate an entry that seems promising for your research, you must then locate the source itself. A computerized database entry is only the beginning.

The idea of letting a computer do the work is very attractive, but for a computerized database to be useful, you as a researcher have to lay much groundwork. To use a database, you must know how to search by consulting a list of key words (as explained in 32d-3). Cast a net too widely and you can get far too many entries; cast a net too narrowly and you can get too few. Most computerized databases are complicated to use, so you likely will need a reference librarian to guide you at first.

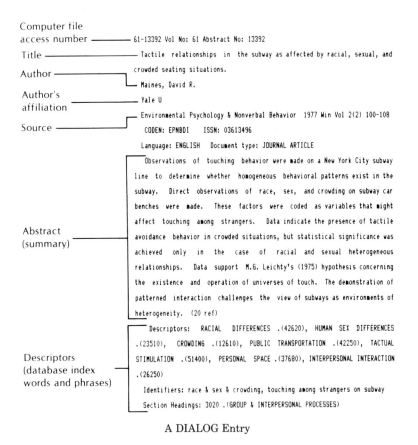

Computer file access number ——— 61-13392 Vol No: 61 Abstract No: 13392

Title ——— Tactile relationships in the subway as affected by racial, sexual, and crowded seating situations.

Author ——— Maines, David R.

Author's affiliation ——— Yale U

Source ——— Environmental Psychology & Nonverbal Behavior 1977 Win Vol 2(2) 100-108
    CODEN: EPNBDI   ISSN: 03613496
    Language: ENGLISH Document type: JOURNAL ARTICLE

Abstract (summary) ——— Observations of touching behavior were made on a New York City subway line to determine whether homogeneous behavioral patterns exist in the subway. Direct observations of race, sex, and crowding on subway car benches were made. These factors were coded as variables that might affect touching among strangers. Data indicate the presence of tactile avoidance behavior in crowded situations, but statistical significance was achieved only in the case of racial and sexual heterogeneous relationships. Data support M.G. Leichty's (1975) hypothesis concerning the existence and operation of universes of touch. The demonstration of patterned interaction challenges the view of subways as environments of heterogeneity. (20 ref)

Descriptors (database index words and phrases) ——— Descriptors: RACIAL DIFFERENCES .(42620), HUMAN SEX DIFFERENCES .(23510), CROWDING .(12610), PUBLIC TRANSPORTATION .(42250), TACTUAL STIMULATION .(51400), PERSONAL SPACE .(37680), INTERPERSONAL INTERACTION .(26250)
    Identifiers: race & sex & crowding, touching among strangers on subway
    Section Headings: 3020 .(GROUP & INTERPERSONAL PROCESSES)

A DIALOG Entry

556

Most computerized databases are operated by commercial companies. Libraries pay a fee for computer time and for each entry. Often that charge is passed on to the user—you. Find out the arrangement at your library. The cost of locating entries can vary from nothing to over one dollar per entry, with a set minimum charge. The cost of a printout is extra per entry.

Amy Brown, the student who wrote the research paper in Chapter 33, used the DIALOG Information System to search for sources. DIALOG contains over 100 million references—mostly journal articles and reports—combined from over 200 smaller databases in the humanities, the social sciences, business, the sciences and technology, medicine, economics, and current events. A librarian helped Brown choose key words. Brown's topic was *personal space,* an area of nonverbal communication. Brown started with *nonverbal communication,* but the librarian soon discovered that the term was too general. It would have yielded 1,486 citations. The expense of such a list, as well as its lack of focus, led Brown to limit her search to the journal *Psychological Abstracts* (called *PsycINFO* in the DIALOG system). To get the number of entries down to manageable size, Brown crossed *nonverbal communication* with other key words such as *conversation, personal space, social perception,* and *ethnic values.* One of those citations is illustrated here, with an explanation of its parts.

32f

Keep a research log and take useful notes.

Your research process includes locating sources, taking notes on them, and recording your ideas along the way.

1
Keep a research log.

A **research log** is like a diary. Keep it in a notebook reserved exclusively for your research project. A thorough research log helps you think about your evolving material. Your log is a history of your search strategy and ideas that occur to you during the research process. It keeps you from having to retrace your steps or reconstruct your thoughts unnecessarily. It is *not* for notes about content of sources: put notes on index cards, as explained in 32f-2. Rereading your log can help you make decisions about the next research step or about the content of your paper. Although much of your log will not find its way into your paper, its entries become valuable

QUOTATION ABOUT RESEARCH
One of the skills of research is knowing when you have enough information; in considering too many side issues or too many perspectives, you may lose the main thread of your subject.

—CHARLES BAZERMAN,
The Informed Writer

QUOTATION ABOUT RESEARCH
Research means to give each and every element its final value by grouping it in the unity of an organized whole.

—PIERRE T. DE CHARDIN

> Nov. 15: Found Sommer and made a biblio. card. Excellent source. He is an environmental psychologist. Tone is calm, seems to be unbiased. I now realize that I was overlapping two concepts: territory and personal space. Territory refers to the places we carve out as our own — a chair in a classroom, a room in a house. Personal space is the "bubble" of space we carry around with us. We don't like intrusions in our bubbles. Sommer's description on page 26 is the best I've seen. I photocopied the page and marked off the part I will probably quote in my paper.

Excerpt from Amy Brown's Research Log

aids when you move from gathering material to organizing information to writing the paper. An entry from Amy Brown's log is shown above.

2
Take useful notes.

Taking good notes is the key to using sources well in your research paper. Together with your research log and bibliography cards, your notes give you a complete record of your research and the information you found.

Notetaking is a decision-making process. The first decision concerns whether a source related to your topic is worth taking notes on. To decide, evaluate it according to the guidelines in 32d-2. If it seems to be a good source, take notes. If it does not, record its title and location in your research log—along with a message to yourself about why you rejected it. What seems useless one day might have potential if you revise your focus or narrow your topic.

The second decision concerns what to put into your notes. Knowing how to select material for notes comes with experience.

558

Dive in and get that experience. Use critical reading skills (as explained in Chapter 5) to sort out major information from minor information as it relates to your topic. Do not get bogged down in unimportant details. At the same time, do not overlook important material. Try for a reasonable balance.

When you begin, if you have only a general sense of your topic, read and take notes widely. Stay alert for ways to narrow your topic. Use your research log to keep track of your thoughts—ideas tend to pop in and out of mind during a selection process. Topic narrowing takes time and patience (for advice, see 32b). Do not get discouraged. All researchers cast about at first. Once you have narrowed your subject, take notes focused within the boundaries of your choice.

The third decision in the notetaking process concerns the form of your notes. **You must use procedures that prevent plagiarism.** This matter is so important that Chapter 31 is devoted to the skills of paraphrasing, summarizing, and quoting. To plagiarize is to steal someone else's words and pass them off as your own. To avoid the risk of plagiarism, always be able to tell from your notes what is yours and what belongs to a source.

To take notes, use index cards. You can write more on a 4 × 6″ than on a 3 × 5″ card. Cards, in contrast to pages in a notebook, provide flexibility for organizing information to write your paper. Never put notes from more than one source on the same index card.

QUOTATION ABOUT RESEARCH
Research is the ability to investigate systematically and truly all that comes under your observation in life.
—MARCUS AURELIUS

Hall, _Hidden_, p. 109

Awareness of personal space

Summary: Most people are unaware that interpersonal distances exist and contribute to peoples' reactions to one another.

A Note Card Summarizing a Source

559

Sommer, p.26

I'll paraphrase this

The best way to learn the location of invisible boundaries is to keep walking until somebody complains. Personal space refers to an area with invisible boundaries surrounding a person's body into which intruders may not come. [Like the porcupines in Schopenhauer's fable, people like to be close enough to obtain warmth and comradeship but far enough away to avoid pricking one another. Personal space ~~is not necessarily spherical in shape, nor does it extend equally in all directions. (People are able to tolerate closer presence of a stranger at their sides than directly in front.) It~~ has been likened to a snail shell, a soap bubble, an aura, and "breathing room."] There are major differences between cultures in the distances that people maintain—Englishmen keep further apart than Frenchmen or South Americans. Reports

I'll quote this with ellipses

Photocopy of Source, with Annotations

If your notes on a source require more than one index card, number the cards sequentially. (If, for example, you use the labels "1 of 2" and "2 of 2" for two cards, you will know each card's number and the total number of cards in your records). If you take notes on more than one idea or topic from a particular source, start a new card for each new area of information. Head each index card with identifying information that clearly relates to one of your bibliographic cards. Include the source's title and the number of the page or pages from which you are taking notes. Also, clearly identify the *type* of note on the card: paraphrase, summary, or quotation. Think of note cards as one half of a set of cards—the second half is the bibliographic card. Without bibliographic information you cannot write parenthetical references (32k) or a final bibliography. A note card written by Amy Brown, the student whose paper is in Chapter 33, is shown on page 559.

Photocopying can save you time if you want a word-for-word record of a source. Photocopying, however, can be a seductive trap for researchers. It is a waste of time and money to photocopy everything you come across. Write your paraphrases and summaries as you go along. When you do photocopy, always mark the paper with (1) identifying information and (2) notations about what you consider important and why. Do not merely pile up stacks of photocopies without any record of your thought processes. A photocopy Amy Brown made and annotated is shown above.

■‖ 32g
Make a working bibliography and include a final list of sources in your paper.

Informing readers about the sources you have used for a research paper is an important part of documentation. A working bibliography helps you to keep careful track of all sources you take notes on. A list of sources submitted with your research paper gives readers bibliographic facts for the evidence you use.

1

Make a bibliographic card for each source you take notes on.

To create a working bibliography, write out a bibliographic card for every source you take notes on (*Bibliography* literally means "description of books.") Include on each card all the bibliographic information you need to fulfill the requirements of the documentation style you are using (see 32d-4). Also, for each card on a library source, write the call number in the upper lefthand corner,

> HM
> 285
> H3
>
> Hall, Edward J. *The Hidden Dimension.*
> New York: Doubleday, 1969.

> Martin, Judith. "Here's Looking at You."
> *Newsday* 27 Jan. 1981,
> Section 2: 9–13

WORD HISTORY
According to the *Oxford English Dictionary*, *bibliography* comes from the Greek word meaning *book writing*. In the sense that we use the word with undergraduate students (a list of the books of a particular author or publisher, or those in a particular subject), it is relatively new, going back just to 1869. However, the word earlier meant *the writing of books* (1678). In the early 19th century, *bibliography* was first used to refer to "the systematic description and history of books, their authorship, printing, publication, editions, etc." or a book about such matters.

BACKGROUND
Nicolás Antonio (1617–1684) is credited with the creation of modern bibliography and the shaping of literary history into a scholarly discipline. His *Bibliotheca Hispana* is an index in Latin of Old World and New World Spanish writers after 1500. It also contains a history of earlier Spanish literature.

being careful to copy it exactly. When the time comes to compile a final list of sources for your research paper, you can easily arrange bibliographic cards in correct order. Two of Amy Brown's bibliographic cards are shown, one for a book and one for an article.

As you organize and write your paper, you may find that you have not drawn on certain sources at all, even though you took notes on them. In MLA documentation, presented in this chapter, and APA documentation, presented in 34c-4, include only the sources you mention in your paper. If you are *not* using either MLA or APA documentation, ask your instructor whether your source list should include all the sources you consult or only sources you refer to.

2
Compile a Works Cited list according to MLA guidelines.

In Modern Language Association (MLA) documentation style, a final list of sources is called Works Cited. (See 34c-4 about the References list in American Psychological Association—documentation style and 34d-4 for information about other styles.) Works Cited is a list of all sources referred to in your paper and arranged alphabetically by author name. The list includes only the sources from which you use paraphrases or summaries or quotations. It does not include sources you consulted but did not actually refer to in the paper. This list follows any endnotes* and begins on a new page, numbered sequentially with the rest of the paper. Entries are alphabetized according to the author's last name. If the author's name is unknown, the entry is alphabetized by the first significant word of the title (not by *A, An,* or *The*). Each entry starts at the left margin, and the second and any subsequent lines indent five spaces. Double spacing is used within and between entries. Citations include information to help a reader easily locate a source.

The following pages present examples of patterns for citing various sources in a Works Cited list. If you have further questions about citations or parenthetical references, consult Joseph Gibaldi and Walter S. Achtert, *MLA Handbook for Writers of Research Papers,* 2nd ed., New York: MLA, 1984.

---

*MLA style calls for notes not for documentation purposes, but for commentary or other information that would interrupt the discussion in your paper. See page 585.

Citing books

Citations for books have three main parts: author, title, and publication information (place of publication, publisher, and date of publication). Each part is followed by a period and two spaces.

```
Didion, Joan.  Salvador.  New York: Simon, 1983.
```

Many sources need additional items of information included in the citation.

```
Chester, Laura, and Sharon Barba, eds.  Rising Tides:

    Twentieth Century American Women Poets.

    Intro. Anäis Nin.  New York: Simon, 1973.
```

You can find most of this information on the title page or copyright page (reverse of the title page). If several cities are listed for the place of publication, give only the first. If the city might be unfamiliar to a reader, add an abbreviation of the state, Canadian province, or country. You can shorten the publisher's name as long as the shortened version is easily identifiable. (*Prentice-Hall* can be *Prentice; Oxford University Press* can be *Oxford UP, Simon & Schuster* can be *Simon.*) Give the latest copyright date for the edition you are using. If the book has had several printings (rather than editions), use the original publication date. The examples of various book citations on the following pages show and explain this format.

BOOK WITH ONE AUTHOR

```
Welty, Eudora.  One Writer's Beginnings.  Cambridge:

    Harvard UP, 1984.
```

This citation follows the basic pattern of author (last name first, for alphabetizing), full title, and publication information (place, publisher, and date). Each part is followed by a period and then two spaces before entering the next part. Note the abbreviation of *University Press* as *UP*.

BOOK WITH TWO OR THREE AUTHORS

```
Leghorn, Lisa, and Katherine Parker.  Woman's Worth.

    Boston: Routledge, 1981.
```

563

```
Kelly, Alfred H., Winfred A. Harbison, and Herman Belz.

     The American Constitution: Its Origins and

     Development.  6th ed.  New York: Norton, 1983.
```

Give only the first author's name in reversed order; give other authors' names in normal order. Use commas to separate authors' names, including a comma before the *and* preceding the last name in the series. Give the names in the order they appear on the title page of the book; note that authors' names are not always listed alphabetically on the title page. Note the shortened version of the publisher's name.

BOOK WITH MORE THAN THREE AUTHORS

```
Moore, Mark H., et al.   Dangerous Offenders: The Elusive

     Target of Justice.  Cambridge: Harvard UP, 1984.
```

Use only the first author's name, in reversed order; *et al.* ("and others") indicates the other three or more authors' names.

TWO OR MORE BOOKS BY THE SAME AUTHOR(S)

```
Morris, Desmond.  Manwatching: A Field Guide to Human

     Behavior.  New York: Abrams, 1977.

---, ed.  Primate Ethology.  London: Wiedenfeld, 1967.
```

When citing two or more books by the same author(s), give the name(s) in the first entry only. In the second and subsequent entries, use three hyphens to stand for exactly the same name(s). If the person served as author of subsequent books, put a period and two spaces following the three hyphens. If the person served as editor or translator, put a comma and the appropriate abbreviation (ed. or trans.) following the three hyphens. Alphabetize the works listed according to book title, regardless of such labels as *ed.* or *trans,* and regardless of the chronological order in which they were published.

BOOK BY A CORPORATE AUTHOR

```
The Boston Women's Health Collective.  Our Bodies,

     Ourselves.  New York: Simon, 1986.
```

Cite the full name of the corporate author first. If the author is also the publisher, the name may be abbreviated.

564

ANONYMOUS BOOK

> <u>The Chicago Manual of Style</u>. 13th ed. Chicago:
>
> U of Chicago P, 1982.

If there is no author's name on the title page, begin the citation with the title. Alphabetize the entry according to the first significant word of the title (not *A, An,* or *The*).

ANTHOLOGY OR COLLECTION

> Valdez, Luis, and Stan Steiner, eds. <u>Aztlan: An</u>
>
> <u>Anthology of Mexican American Literature</u>.
>
> New York: Knopf, 1972.

The name of the editor follows the same pattern as book authors, but after the name place a comma, a space, and the abbreviation *eds.*

ONE SELECTION FROM AN ANTHOLOGY OR A COLLECTION

> Galarza, Ernesto. "The Roots of Migration." <u>Aztlan:</u>
>
> <u>An Anthology of Mexican American Literature</u>.
>
> Ed. Luis Valdez and Stan Steiner. New York:
>
> Knopf, 1972. 127-132.

Give the author and title of the selection first. Place titles of essays, short stories, or short poems in quotation marks. Underline the title of a book or a play. Then give the full title of the anthology. Follow it with the editor(s). Note that the editors' names are preceded by *Eds.* (you would use *Ed.* for only one editor) and are given in normal order. End the citation with the inclusive page numbers of the selection. Just put the number(s); do not use the abbreviation *p.* or *pp.*

TWO SELECTIONS FROM ONE ANTHOLOGY OR COLLECTION

> Gilbert, Sandra M., and Susan Gubar. <u>The Norton Anthology</u>
>
> <u>of Literature by Women</u>. New York: Norton, 1985.
>
> Kingston, Maxine Hong. "No Name Woman." Gilbert
>
> and Gubar 2337-2347.
>
> Morrison, Toni. "The Bluest Eye." Gilbert and
>
> Gubar 2067-2184.

If you cite more than one selection from the same anthology, you can avoid repeating all the bibliographic facts. List the anthol-

565

ogy as a separate entry, complete with all the publication information. Also list each selection from the anthology by author and title of the selection, but then give only the names of the editor(s) of the anthology and the page number(s) of the selection.

ARTICLE IN A REFERENCE BOOK

```
Holt, Robert R.  "Freud, Sigmund."  International Encyclopedia

    of the Social Sciences.  Ed. David L. Sills.  18 vols.

    New York: Macmillan, 1968.

"Ireland."  Encyclopaedia Britannica.  1974 ed.
```

Treat articles in an encyclopedia and dictionary entries like selections in an anthology. If no author is named, give the title first. If articles are alphabetically arranged in the work, omit the volume and page numbers. If the reference book is frequently revised, give only the edition and year of publication. If a reference book is probably not well known, however, give full publication information.

BOOK WITH AN AUTHOR AND AN EDITOR

```
Brontë, Emily.  Wuthering Heights.  Ed. David Daiches.

    London: Penguin, 1985.

Daiches, David, ed.  Wuthering Heights.  By Emily Brontë.

    London: Penguin, 1985.
```

If what you refer to in your paper is the work of the book's author, begin the citation with the author's name. If you are citing instead the work of the editor, begin the citation with the editor's name.

TRANSLATION

```
Freire, Paulo.  Pedagogy of the Oppressed.  Trans. Myra

    Bergman Ramos.  New York: Seabury, 1970.
```

Cite the author's name first, and then cite the work's title. Then put Trans. followed by the translator's name.

WORK IN SEVERAL VOLUMES OR PARTS

```
Jones, Ernest.  The Last Phase.  Vol. 3 of The Life and

    Work of Sigmund Freud.  3 vols.  New York:
    Basic, 1957.

Randall, John Herman, Jr.  The Career of Philosophy.  2 vols.

    New York: Columbia UP, 1962.
```

566

If the work has two or more volumes, state the total number of volumes between the title and the publication information or between the editor and the publication information. If you are citing only one volume of a multivolume work, place this information after the publication date. For example:

```
New York: Columbia UP, 1962.  Vol. 1.
```

If you are citing one volume of a multivolume work that has its own title, state that title first and then state the volume number of the work. Note that the MLA recommends using arabic numerals, even if the source uses roman numerals *(Vol. 6* for *Vol. VI)*.

EDITION

```
Mandell, Maurice I.  Advertising.  4th ed.  Englewood

     Cliffs, NJ: Prentice, 1984.
```

When a book is not the first edition, the edition number appears on the title page. Place this information between the title and the publication information. An edition may also mean an edition of a particular author's work, involving an author and an editor (see the citation for a book with an author and an editor). If there is an edition number as well as a citation for an editor, that number should follow the editor's name.

REPRINT OF AN OLDER BOOK

```
Hurston, Zora Neale.  Their Eyes Were Watching God.  1937.

     Urbana: U of Illinois P, 1978.
```

A republished book may be the paperback version of a book originally published as a hardbound, or it may be the reissuing of a book. Republishing information can be found on the copyright page. Give the date of the original version before the publication information for the version you are citing.

INTRODUCTION, PREFACE, FOREWORD, OR AFTERWORD

```
Mead, Margaret.  Preface.  Patterns of Culture.  By Ruth

     Benedict.  1934.  Boston: Houghton, 1959.
```

If you are citing an introduction, preface, foreword, or afterword, give its author's name first and then the name of the part cited. Capitalize the first letter of the part cited, but do not underline it nor put it in quotation marks. If the writer of the introduction, preface, foreword, or afterword is different from the author of the book,

567

give that author's full name after the title. Give the inclusive page numbers of the part you are citing after the publication information. Note that such prefatory page numbers are in roman numerals just as they appear in the work.

BOOK IN A SERIES

> McClave, Heather. <u>Women Writers of the Short Story</u>.
>
>   Twentieth Century Views Series. Englewood Cliffs,
>
>   NJ: Prentice, 1980.

Place the title of the series, found on the title page, between the title of the work and the publication information.

BOOK WITH A TITLE WITHIN A TITLE

> Lumiansky, Robert M., and Herschel Baker, eds. <u>Critical</u>
>
>   <u>Approaches to Six Major English Works: Beowulf Through</u>
>
>   <u>Paradise Lost</u>. Philadelphia: U of Pennsylvania P, 1968.

When a book title includes the title of another work that is usually underlined (such as a novel, play, or long poem), do *not* underline the incorporated title. If the incorporated title is usually enclosed in quotation marks (such as a short story or short poem), keep the quotation marks and underline the complete title of the book.

GOVERNMENT PUBLICATION

> United States. Cong. House. Committee on the Judiciary.
>
>   <u>Immigration and Nationality with Amendments and Notes</u>
>
>   <u>on Related Laws</u>. 7th ed. Washington: GPO, 1980.

If such a publication has no stated author, use the government, governmental body, and/or government agency as the author, with periods and two spaces separating the parts. "GPO" is the standard abbreviation for Government Printing Office.

PUBLISHED PROCEEDINGS OF A CONFERENCE

> Harris, Diana, and Laurie Nelson-Heern, eds. <u>Proceedings of</u>
>
>   <u>NECC 1981: National Educational Computing Conference</u>.
>
>   17-19 June 1981. Iowa City: Weeg Computing Center,
>
>   U of Iowa, 1981.

568

Treat published proceedings of a conference like a book. Add any important information, such as the date of the conference, which does not appear in the title.

Citing articles

Like citations for books, citations for articles in periodicals (such as journals, magazines, and newspapers) contain three major parts: author, title of article, and publication information. For articles, however, the publication information usually includes the periodical title, volume number, year of publication, and inclusive page numbers.

```
Maines, David R.  "The Sand and the Castle: Some Remarks

     Concerning G. P. Stone's Critique of Small Group Research."

     Studies in Symbolic Interaction 5 (1984): 23-24.
```

In the citation for an article, each part is followed by a period and two spaces. Additional items of information may be required, depending on the source. In citations for articles, arrange information in the following order:

1. Author's name
2. Title of the article
3. Name of the periodical
4. Series number or name
5. Volume number
6. Date of publication
7. Page numbers

You can usually find this information on the cover and/or title page of the periodical and sometimes on the first page of the article. Examples of various citations on the following pages show and explain this format.

ARTICLE IN A JOURNAL WITH CONTINUOUS PAGINATION

```
Cochran, D. D., W. Daniel Hale, and Christine P. Hissam.

     "Personal Space Requirements in Indoor versus Outdoor

     Locations."  Journal of Psychology 117 (1984): 132-133.
```

To cite an article in a journal with continuous pagination, follow the basic format of author (last name first), title of the article, and publication information (journal title, volume number, year of pub-

569

lication in parentheses followed by a colon, and inclusive page numbers). Separate each part with a period and two spaces. If a journal pages its issues continuously through an annual volume, give only the volume number, not the issue number, and the page numbers. (*National Geographic* is such a journal. If the first issue of a volume ends on page 224, for example, the second issue starts on page 225.) Notice that all numbers, even the volume, are arabic numerals.

ARTICLE IN A JOURNAL THAT PAGES EACH ISSUE SEPARATELY

```
Wacker, J. F., and R. K. Teas.  "Starting Salaries of the
     College of Business Graduates."  Review of Business and
     Economic Research 15.1 (1979): 70-81.
```

Some journals page each issue of an annual volume separately. (Each issue begins with page 1.) To cite articles from such journals, give both the volume number and the issue number (15.1 because 15 is the volume and 1 is the issue).

ARTICLE FROM A WEEKLY OR BIWEEKLY MAGAZINE OR NEWSPAPER

```
Randolph, Barbara.  "Hailing the Eureka Factor."  Time 21
     Feb. 1986: 65.
```

If a periodical is published every week or every two weeks, cite the complete date in place of the volume and issue number. Cite the year of publication without parentheses. First cite the day, then the month (abbreviated if necessary), and finally, the year. Always drop an introductory *A, An,* or *The* from the title of a periodical.

ARTICLE FROM A MONTHLY OR BIMONTHLY PERIODICAL

```
Hogan, Patti.  "Setting the Pace."  Ms.  Aug. 1985: 20-32.
```

If a periodical is published monthly or every two months, cite the month(s) and year instead of volume and issue numbers and year of publication.

ARTICLE FROM A DAILY NEWSPAPER

```
Dullea, Georgia.  "Literary Folk Look for Solid Comfort."
     New York Times 16 April 1986: C14.
"Hospitals, Competing for Scarce Patients, Turn to
     Advertising."  New York Times 20 April 1986: 47.
```

If an author's name appears, give the author's name, last name first. If no author's name is given, begin the entry with the title. As with books, alphabetize the entry according to the first main word of the title. Cite the title of the newspaper exactly as it appears on the masthead, omitting any introductory *A* or *The* (Boston Globe, New York Times). If the city of publication is not in the title of the periodical, add it in square brackets after the title, not underlined: for example, Patriot Ledger [Quincy, MA]. The day, month, and year of the issue are given instead of volume and issue numbers. Be sure to give the section letter as well as the page number, if appropriate: for example, C14. If an article does not run on consecutive pages (if, for example, it starts on 23 and continues on 42), give the first page number and add a plus sign (23 +).

ARTICLE FROM A COLLECTION OF REPRINTED ARTICLES

Ryan, Bill. "Nuclear Waste Crisis--Don't Dump on Us." In

Social Issues Resources Series. Pollution. Vol. 3 Article

14. Boca Raton, FL: Social Issues Resources Series, 1984.

EDITORIAL, LETTER TO THE EDITOR, REVIEW

Childress, Glenda Teal. Letter. Newsweek 9 June 1986: 10.

Linebaugh, Peter. "In the Flight Path of Perry Anderson."

Rev. of In the Tracks of Historical Materialism,

by Perry Anderson. History Workshop 21 (1986):

141-46.

"Prayer Meetings in Public School?" Editorial. Washington

Post 27 March 1986: A20.

To cite editorials, letters to the editor, and reviews, follow the same format as for previous citations. In addition, add descriptive labels *(Editorial, Letter,* or *Rev.)* to identify the kind of work clearly.

ABSTRACT FROM *Dissertation Abstracts* OR *Dissertation Abstracts International*

Huber, Elaine Clare. "Women and the Authority of Inspiration."

DAI 45 (1984): 315A. U of California, Berkeley.

Dissertation Abstracts (DA) became *Dissertation Abstracts International (DAI)* with volume 30 (1969). The letter at the end of the

571

page number (3691A) indicates which paginated series (humanities, social sciences, or European dissertations) is being cited. Give the degree-granting institution at the end of the citation.

UNPUBLISHED DISSERTATIONS OR ESSAYS

> Geissinger, Shirley Burry. "Openness versus Secrecy in
>
> Adoptive Parenthood." Diss. U. of North Carolina
>
> at Greensboro, 1984.

To cite an unpublished dissertation or essay (your own or another person's), state the author's name first, then the title in quotation marks (not underlined), then a descriptive label (such as *Diss.* or *Unpublished essay*), then the degree-granting institution (for dissertations), and finally the date.

Citing other sources

Citations for computer software, films, or maps are treated similarly to printed books and articles. The particular nature of each source dictates what information is available and what items of information should be included.

PUBLISHED AND UNPUBLISHED LETTERS

> Lapidus, Jackie. Letter to her mother. 12 Nov. 1975.
>
> Between Ourselves: Letters Between Mothers & Daughters.
>
> Ed. Karen Payne. Boston: Houghton, 1983. 323-26.

Treat a published letter like a selection in an anthology, adding a descriptive label (if there is no title), the date of the letter, and the number (if one is assigned in the text). For unpublished letters, cite the author, a descriptive label, and the date.

INTERVIEW

> Atwood, Margaret. Telephone interview. 4 Feb. 1984.

For personal interviews, cite the person interviewed, a descriptive label, and the date.

572

COMPUTER SOFTWARE

> <u>SuperCalc</u>. Computer software. Sorcim, 1981. CP/M-based
>
> microcomputer, disk.

To cite computer software, give the writer of the program (if known), the title (underlined), a descriptive label, the distributor, and the year of publication. Add any other important information, such as the computer on which the program can be used, number of kilobytes or units of memory, the operating system, and the form of the program (cartridge, cassette, or disk).

INFORMATION SERVICE

> Beam, Paul. <u>COMIT English Module</u>. ERIC ED 167 189.

To cite material from an information service, give the writer, the title, full details of original publication (if published previously), and the name of the service and identifying number within the service.

MAPS AND CHARTS

> <u>The Caribbean & South America</u>. Map. Falls Church,
>
> VA: AAA, 1982.

Begin the citation for a map or chart with the title. Name the type of visual (map or chart) between the title and the publication information.

RADIO AND TELEVISION PROGRAMS

> <u>The Little Sister</u>. Writ. and dir. Jan Egleson. With
>
> Tracy Pollan and John Savage. Prod. Rebecca Eaton.
>
> American Playhouse. PBS. WGBH, Boston. 7 April 1986.

To cite radio or television programs, include all information shown in the example: the title of the program (underlined); the network; the local station and its city; and the date of the broadcast. For a series also supply the title of the specific episode (in quotation marks) before the title of the program and the title of the series (neither underlined nor in quotation marks).

INSTRUCTOR'S NOTES

RECORDINGS

```
Handel, George Frederick.  Water Music.  Cond. Pierre Boulez.

    Hague Philharmonic Orch.  Nonesuch, H-71127, n.d.

Turner, Tina.  "Show Some Respect."  Private Dancer.

    Capitol, ST-12330, 1983.
```

Begin the citation of a recording with either the composer, conductor, or performer, depending on whom or what you are emphasizing in your paper. Then give the information shown in the examples.

FILMS

```
Erendira.  Writ. Gabriel Garcia Marquez.  Dir. Ruy Guerra.

    With Irene Pappas.  Miramax, 1984.
```

To cite a film, include the title (underlined), the director, the distributor, and the year of issue. Add any other pertinent information about the writer or actors after the title. Begin the citation with the title or the director, the writer, or the performer, depending on what or whom you are emphasizing in your paper.

LIVE PERFORMANCE

```
The Real Thing.  By Tom Stoppard.  Dir. Mike Nichols.  With

    Jeremy Irons and Glenn Close.  Plymouth Theatre, New

    York.  3 June 1984.
```

To cite a performance (stage play, concert, ballet, or opera) include the title; pertinent information about the playwright, conductor, performers; the theater, city, and the date of the performance. Begin with the title or a particular individual (for example, writer, conductor, or director) depending on the emphasis in your paper.

WORKS OF ART

```
Cassatt, Mary.  La Toilette.  Art Institute of Chicago,

    Chicago.
```

To cite a work of art (painting or sculpture), give the artist's name (last name first), the title (usually underlined), and the institution housing the work (for example, a museum, private collection) and its city.

■‖ 32h
Draft a thesis statement

A **thesis statement** in a research paper is like the thesis statement in any essay: it tells the central theme. (Thesis statements are discussed thoroughly in 2e.) Any paper must fulfill the promise of its thesis statement. Because readers expect unified material, the theme of the thesis must serve as a connecting thread throughout a paper.

The research process and the writing process are interwoven throughout a research-paper project, as explained in 32a. Drafting a thesis statement for a research paper is the beginning of the transition between the research process and the writing process. Some researchers draft a **preliminary thesis statement** before or during their research process. They know that they will revise the thesis somewhat after their research, but they use the preliminary version as a useful focus while they search for sources. Other researchers draft a thesis statement after the research process.

No matter at what point you draft your thesis statement, expect to write many alternatives. Your goal is to craft the thesis carefully so that it delivers the message you intend. In writing any **revised thesis statement,** take charge of your material. Reread your research log. Reread your notes. Look for categories of information. Rearrange your note cards into logical groupings. Begin to impose a structure on your material. (For an example, see how Amy Brown accomplished these processes in Chapter 33.)

In addition to presenting the central theme of a paper, a thesis statement reflects a writing purpose—*to inform* or *to persuade* (see 32b). Also, a thesis statement implies the amount of expertise in the subject expected from an audience. For example, when writing for people who likely have little background about your topic, your thesis cannot be too technical.

To check your thesis statement, go back to the research question that guided your research process. Your thesis statement should be one answer to the question. Here are examples of subjects narrowed to topics, then focused into research questions, and then cast as thesis statements. The thesis statements are written on the assumption of a nonspecialist audience.

SUBJECT	Rain forests
TOPIC	The importance of rain forests
RESEARCH QUESTION	What is the importance of rain forests?

575

THESIS STATEMENT (informative)	Rain forests provide the human race with many resources.
THESIS STATEMENT (persuasive)	Rain forests must be preserved because they offer the human race many irreplaceable resources.
SUBJECT	Nonverbal communication
TOPIC	Personal space
RESEARCH QUESTION	How do standards for personal space differ among cultures?
THESIS STATEMENT (informative)	Everyone has expectations concerning the use of personal space, but accepted distances for that space are determined by each person's culture.
THESIS STATEMENT (persuasive)	To prevent intercultural misunderstandings, people must be aware of cultural differences in standards for personal space.

As you draft a thesis statement, remember that one of your major responsibilities in a research paper is to support the thesis. Be sure that the material gathered during the research process offers effective support. If it does not, revise your thesis or conduct further research, or both. Never stray from the unifying effect of your thesis. Do not move too far afield from the material in your notes.

 32i
Know how to outline your paper.

Outlining is explained in detail in Chapter 2; you might want to review that material. To organize your evidence, you can make an **informal outline.** Look over your note cards and group them into piles of related information. You likely started this process in preparation for writing your thesis statement. If the content of one note relates to more than one category, make a new card that contains the material so that each topic's pile of cards will be complete.

Make a list of the categories of information represented by the piles. Then look over the list to see if material needs to be regrouped. During this process, you might find that you lack sufficient material for some categories. If so, go back to your sources or research new sources to fill in what you need. Once you feel com-

576

fortable with your list, look within each pile for subcategories of information. Group the subcategories. Then list them and regroup as needed.

Your instructor may ask you to submit a **formal outline** with your research paper. Writing a formal outline before drafting helps some people plan. Writing a formal outline after drafting helps some people check a paper's organization. Do the main ideas clearly relate to each other? Do the subordinate ideas offer support clearly connected to their main ideas?

A formal outline is headed with the title of the paper and followed by the paper's thesis statement. It can be a **topic outline,** a format that requires words or phrases for each item. It can be a **sentence outline,** a format that requires full sentences for each item. It cannot be a mixture of the two types. See Chapter 33 for a sentence outline of Amy Brown's research paper on personal space. A sentence outline has the advantage of having complete thoughts in its items. A reader can tell not only what topics are covered but also what is said about those topics.

A formal outline uses rankings for levels of information. It goes into detail according to the material it covers. If you outline only main and subordinate ideas, your outline has entries for Roman numeral and capital letters. If you go into more detail, your outline includes lower-case letters. Always follow one important principle: subdivide information only when you have at least two entries to make. In a formal outline, you cannot have an *A* without a *B,* a *1* without a *2,* and so on.

    I. Main idea
      A. Subordinate idea
      B. Subordinate idea
        1. Example of subordinate idea
        2. Example of subordinate idea
          a. Supporting detail
          b. Supporting detail
   II. Main Idea

32j
Draft and revise your paper.

Drafting and revising a research paper have much in common with the processes for writing any type of paper. (See Chapters 2 and 3.) But more is demanded. You must demonstrate that you have followed the research steps in this chapter. You must demonstrate an understanding of the information you have located. You must organize for effective presentation. You must integrate sources into your writing without plagiarizing, by properly using the techniques of paraphrase, summary, and quotation described in Chapter 31. And you must use parenthetical references (32k) to document your sources. These special demands take extra time for drafting, thinking, redrafting, and rethinking.

Expect to write a number of drafts of your paper. Successive drafts help you to gain authority over the information you learn from your research. The **first draft** is your initial attempt to structure your notes into a unified whole. It is also a chance to discover new insights and fresh connections. Only the act of writing makes such discovery possible. A first draft is a rough draft. It is a prelude to later work at revising and polishing. Here are some alternative ways to write the first draft of a research paper.

1. Some researchers work with their notes in front of them. They use the organized piles made for drafting a thesis statement (32h) and for outlining (32i). They spread out each pile and work according to the categories of information that have emerged from their material. They proceed from one pile to the next. They expect this process to take time, but they are assured of a first draft that includes much of the results of their research.

2. Some researchers gather all their information and then set it aside to write a **partial first draft,** a quickly written first pass at getting the material under control. Writing this way helps researchers get a broad view of the material. The second step is to go back and write a **complete first draft** with research notes at hand. They go over their partial draft slowly to correct information, add material left out, and—most important—insert parenthetical references (32k).

3. Some researchers write their first draft quickly to get words down on paper when they feel "stuck" about what to say next. When they have a clear idea of how to proceed, they slow down and use their notes.

Your **second and subsequent drafts** are the results of reading your first draft critically and revising it. If at all possible, get some distance from your material by taking a break of a few days (or few hours, if you are pressed for time). Then, reread your first draft and get a fresh look at it. Think how it can be improved. You also might ask friends or classmates to read it and react.

Some researchers photocopy their first drafts and cut up the paper to move paragraphs and sentences around. If the researchers

578

like a new order that suggests itself, they tape the paper together in its new form.

Here are some questions to guide your reading and revising of each draft. If any answer is "no," you need to rework your material.

Are you fulfilling the promise of the thesis statement?

Do the ideas follow from one another?

Do you stay on the topic?

Are important questions answered?

Do you avoid bogging down the paper with irrelevent or insignificant information?

Do you avoid leaving gaps in information?

Have you integrated source material without plagiarizing?

Have you used paraphrases, summaries, and quotations well?

Do not try to talk yourself out of uneasy feelings. Pay attention to those instincts and work on refining your drafts. Good writing is rewriting.

The **final draft** shows that you have revised well. It shows also that you have edited and proofread for correct grammar, spelling, and punctuation. No amount of careful research and good writing can make up for a sloppy manuscript. Strive to make the paper easy to read. If any page is messy with corrections, retype it. If your instructor accepts handwritten papers, use ruled white paper that has *not* been torn out of a spiral notebook. (If at all possible, however, type your work because it will present itself better.) Use black or blue ink and write very legibly.

For an example of the writing process in action for research writing, and for a sample research paper, see Chapter 33.

▊‖ 32k
Know how to use parenthetical references in MLA style.

As you draft and revise your research paper, be sure to use parenthetical references. The purpose of parenthetical references is to lead your readers to the sources you have used. In the past, you may have used footnotes or endnotes to document your paraphrases, summaries, and quotations of sources. In the MLA style mentioned throughout this chapter, brief **parenthetical references** within the text of papers replace footnotes or endnotes. (A note system of documentation is explained in 34b-4.)

579

1
Understand the MLA system of parenthetical references.

In the MLA system of parenthetical references, you may still use footnotes or endnotes for certain explanatory purposes, as discussed on page 585. In general, this MLA system of parenthetical references and the Works Cited list (described in 32g-2) are simpler and more efficient for both writers and readers.

Parenthetical references within a paper have three functions:

1. They signal places in your paper where you have paraphrased, summarized, or quoted ideas or words from another source.
2. They say exactly where that material is located in the source.
3. They often give information enabling a reader to find the source in the Works Cited (32g-2) list.

When you quote fewer than four handwritten or typewritten lines, you integrate the quoted material into your own sentence or paragraph.

SHORT QUOTATIONS

```
Political economists have identified two main categories
of corporate women: "Those who have corporate positions in
major industrial enterprises and those who own their own
business" (Berch 151).
```

```
Because Berch recognizes that housework has traditionally
been defined by many people as "just puttering around the
house" (92), she provides detailed tables to demonstrate
the time required to keep a household running efficiently.
```

In the first example, the author's name and the page number are cited in parentheses after the quotation marks but before the period. The author's name, which is usually what a reader needs to find in an entry in the Works Cited list, is provided in the parenthetical reference because it is not mentioned anywhere else in the sentence. No punctuation separates the author's name from the page number.

580

In the second example, only the page number is given as a parenthetical reference because the author's name is mentioned in the sentence. The page number is placed at the end of the quoted words but before the comma. Placing the page reference immediately after the quotation signals that the rest of the sentence does not paraphrase or summarize Berch; it is the paper-writer's own words.

When you quote more than four hand-written or typewritten lines, you set the quoted material off from your own writing by indenting it ten spaces from the left margin and double-spacing it. You do not put quotation marks around a long, indented quotation.

LONG QUOTATION

```
Bettina Berch suggests self-employment to be one of the

most promising developments for women:

          Self-employed women are engaged in businesses, from

          the mundane to the spectacular.  There are the free-

          lance inventors and writers as well as the more

          straightforward businesses, ranging from banks to

          record companies.  Of course, not all of these

          businesses are all-female, but they do offer a growing

          number of women the satisfaction of trying out their

          ideas, without unnecessary interference.  While self-

          employment is difficult financially, it may provide

          women with some needed autonomy in the future.  (205)
```

This example shows how to document a quotation that is set off from the rest of the text. The reference is in parentheses at the end of the quotation and *after* the final period. Again, because the author's name is mentioned in the sentence that introduces the quotation, it is not given in the parenthetical reference. Only the page number is supplied in parentheses.

The quotations above all come from one book. The entry for this book in the Works Cited (32g-2) list looks like this:

```
                    Works Cited
Berch, Bettina.  The Endless Day: The Political Economy
     of Women and Work.  New York: Harcourt, 1982.
```

Make parenthetical references brief and accurate. When you are deciding what information to include in a reference, you need to

581

consider what information about the source already appears in the sentence or the immediate context. Sometimes you may mention an author and refer to the entire work being cited in the sentence. Then *no* parenthetical reference is necessary.

```
Bettina Berch's careful research, which she presents in
every chapter of The Endless Day, makes a significant
contribution to our understanding of women's work.
```

Most references are not as straightforward as these examples, however. Some sources name multiple authors or corporate authors or even no author. Some sources have several volumes or are reprinted from another source. Always consider such factors so that you can identify sources and the uses you make of them briefly and accurately. To avoid lengthy parenthetical references, get in the habit of putting into your sentence or the immediate context enough information about a source so that readers can locate it in the Works Cited list.

The following cases discuss format and methods for handling long citations within a paper. All the works mentioned in these examples are shown as Works Cited entries in 32g-2.

Works by more than one author

Suppose you have used a source written by more than one author, such as one book by Lisa Leghorn and Katherine Parker. You have the option of providing the names in the parenthetical reference—(Leghorn and Parker 115)—or providing the names in the sentence itself, followed by just the page number in parentheses. If a book is by two or three authors, you must give all the names. If a book is by more than three authors, such as Mark Moore, et al., you can use the author's last name plus *et al.* either in the parenthetical reference—(Moore, et al. 275)—or in the sentence. *Et al.* means "and others." Notice that there is never a period after *et* (because it is the complete Latin word for *and*); however, there is always a period after *al.* (because it is an abbreviation of the Latin word *alii,* meaning "others").

An author with two or more works

Suppose you have used several works by Desmond Morris in your paper. To refer to one of those works, supply the author's last name, an abbreviated title of the work, and the relevant page numbers—(Morris, Manwatching 95). Notice that a comma separates the author and underlined title, but no punctuation separates

582

the title and page number. To shorten the parenthetical reference, use the author's name and the title of the work in your sentence and give only the page number in parentheses.

Two or more authors with the same last name

Suppose your list of works cited contains sources by Edith Johnson and Samuel Johnson. To cite either source, you must supply the author's first and last names—(Edith Johnson 278–81). Notice that no comma separates the author from the page numbers. To shorten the parenthetical reference, you can include the author's complete name in the sentence itself and give only the relevant page numbers in parentheses—(278–81).

Corporate authors

Suppose you are referring to a source by the Boston Women's Health Collective. The author's name is the name of the corporation. A parenthetical reference might use the corporate author's name and relevant page number—(Boston Women's Health Collective 11). Whenever possible, however, follow the MLA's recommendation to incorporate long names in your sentence to avoid a long parenthetical reference. The parentheses will contain only the relevant page number—(11).

Works cited by title

Suppose you have used a source with anonymous authors, such as The Chicago Manual of Style. Substitute the title or abbreviated title for the author's name in the parenthetical reference—(Chicago 305)—or in the text itself. Notice that the title is underlined. If you use a shortened version of the title, be sure it starts with the word by which the source is alphabetized in the Works Cited list.

Multivolume works

Suppose you have used both volumes of a work by John Herman Randall, Jr. To cite a reference from one volume, indicate the volume number as well as the page number in the parenthetical reference—(Randall 1:64). Notice that a colon and a space separate the volume number and the page number. If the entry in the Works Cited list refers only to one volume of a multivolume work, give only the page number, not volume number too, in the parenthetical citation—(Byron 130). If you include the author's name in your sentence, supply only the page number—(130)—or the volume and page number in the parenthetical reference—(1:64).

583

Literary works

Suppose you are referring to an edition of a classic novel, play, or poem. Because there are usually multiple editions of such classic literary works, the MLA recommends that you give more information than a page reference. (Readers might be using other editions.) For prose works, in addition to a page number to your edition, give additional information about parts, sections, or chapters—(3; pt. 1, ch. 1). Notice that a semicolon separates the page number from other information. Use standard abbreviations, such a *pt.* (part); *sec.* (section); and *ch.* (chapter). For classic verse, plays, and poems, the MLA recommends that you omit page references altogether and cite divisions (canto, book, part, act, or scene and line), using periods to separate the various numbers:

> Il. 9.19 [book 9, line 19 of Homers *Iliad*]
>
> King Lear 4.1.5–6 [act 4, scene 1, lines 5–6 of Shakespeare's *King Lear*]

Never use the lower-case letter *l* to abbreviate *lines* in reference to poetic works, since these abbreviations may be confused with the numeral "one" (1). As in the reference to *King Lear,* the MLA recommends the use of arabic rather than roman numerals; however, some instructors still prefer roman numerals for citing acts and scenes—King Lear IV.i.

References to more than one source

Suppose more than one source has contributed to an idea or opinion in your paper. To acknowledge multiple sources, put all necessary information for each source in the parenthetical reference, and separate the sources with a semicolon—(Morris, Intimate 193; Mead 33). Because multiple references tend to interrupt the flow of your prose, the MLA recommends that you put them in footnotes or endnotes.

Article in a book

Suppose you quote an article that appears in a book. Cite the name of the author of the article, not the editor of the book. If you were quoting from Ernesto Galarza's "The Roots of Migration," which appears in a book edited by Luis Valdez and Stan Steiner, you would use the following citation form: (Galarza 127).

An indirect source

Suppose you are quoting an author who has been quoted by another author. Indicate both names: (Cather qtd. in Mc-

584

Clave). This form tells the reader that you are quoting the words of Willa Cather, that you found them in McClave's work, and that the Works Cited entry is in McClave's name.

**2
Understand how to use notes with the MLA system of parenthetical references.**

In MLA's system of parenthetical references, footnotes or endnotes serve two specific purposes. You can use them for commentary that does not fit into your paper but is still worth relating.

TEXT OF PAPER

> Eudora Welty's literary biography, <u>One Writer's</u>
> <u>Beginnings</u>, shows us how both the inner world of self
> and the outer world of family and place form a writer's
> imagination.[1]

ENDNOTE WITH COMMENTARY

> [1] Welty, who values her privacy, has resisted
> investigation of her life. However, at the age of 74,
> she chose to present her own autobiographical
> reflections in a series of lectures at Harvard University.

You can also put into notes extensive lists of bibliographic information supporting points you make in a paper. Otherwise, such information interrupts the flow of your paper.

TEXT OF PAPER

> Barbara Randolph believes that enthusiasm is contagious
> (65).[2] Many psychologists have found that panic, fear,
> and rage spread more quickly in crowds than positive
> emotions do, however.

ENDNOTE WITH ADDITIONAL SOURCES

> [2] Others agree with Randolph. See Thurman 21, 84,
> 155; Kelley 421-25; and Brookes 65-76.

585

33
OBSERVING
A STUDENT
WRITING
RESEARCH

This chapter explains Amy Brown's processes of conducting research and writing a research paper based on her findings. This chapter also shows Brown's paper with annotations that draw your attention to its key elements. Here is the assignment Brown worked from.

ASSIGNMENT FOR A RESEARCH PAPER

This assignment for a research paper will involve you in two interrelated processes. One process calls for you to conduct research according to the procedures explained in Chapter 32 of the *Simon & Schuster Handbook for Writers*. In particular, you will (1) narrow the subject of the assignment to a suitable topic and research question; (2) determine your purpose and audience; (3) use a search strategy to yield information—mostly from sources in the library—that answers your research question; and (4) take notes so that you have a record of information and can avoid plagiarism.

586

The second process calls for you to write a paper based on your research findings. To do this, you have to integrate your researched information into your writing. Carefully consult Chapter 31 of the *Simon & Schuster Handbook for Writers,* which explains how to avoid plagiarism and how to use the techniques of paraphrase, summary, and quotation.

The general subject for this assignment is "communication." Your paper should be 1,800 to 2,000 words based on about twelve different sources. It is due in five weeks. Use MLA documentation style presented in the *Simon & Schuster Handbook for Writers,* sections 32g and 32k. Interim deadlines for parts of your work will be announced.

Brown made many decisions as she worked on this assignment. First, she set up a project schedule like the one in 31a. Next, she narrowed the subject of communication to a suitable topic. She decided to concentrate on nonverbal communication because she had heard the expression "body language," and the idea of unspoken messages among people interested her.

The memory of a personal experience helped Brown narrow the topic further. She remembered how she felt when a cousin had come for a weekend and stayed three weeks while looking for a new job. Brown's family lived in a small apartment. Brown liked her cousin and wanted to help, but she felt she had lost her "space." Brown remembered this reaction when she read Edward T. Hall's *The Hidden Dimension,* the book recommended by a professor when Brown was getting a broad overview of her subject. Hall talks about the concept of personal space. Personal space concerns the amount of physical distance people expect during social interaction. Hall discusses the fact that cultures differ in their standards for personal space. Although the topic of personal space was not directly related to the crowding Brown felt during her cousin's visit, the idea of space as a part of communication interested Brown. She therefore chose personal space as her topic. She decided that her research question would focus on intercultural differences: "How do standards for personal space differ among cultures?" (For a flow chart that shows Brown's narrowing process, see 32b.)

Next Brown thought about her purpose and audience. She chose a general audience (rather than a specialized one) because she assumed her readers would know little about the topic. Brown's choice of purpose was more complicated. She started with one and later switched. At first, she wanted to argue that people from different cultures can have trouble communicating unless they are aware of varying expectations concerning personal space. While conduct-

587

ing her research, however, Brown decided to change from persuasive writing to informative writing. She found that she could not explain basic concepts *and* argue a position within the assignment's length and time limits.

While narrowing her topic, Brown had already begun her search strategy. (For a discussion and flow chart of a search strategy, see 32e.) Brown had looked over two textbooks and had talked with a professor who recommended Hall's book. Reading Hall helped Brown narrow her topic and formulate her research question.

While knowing that Hall would be an important source in her paper, Brown started to search for additional sources. Hall called the study of personal space *proxemics.* Brown assumed it was a key word (for an explanation of key words, see 32d-3) and went to the library to look for books and articles. She drew several blanks. Nowhere could she find the term *proxemics,* not in the *Readers' Guide,* in any of the encyclopedias, or in any dictionary. Hall had evidently made up the term himself based on the word *proximity.* Finally, Brown had a breakthrough. The *Social Sciences Index* listed proxemics in a cross-reference: "See personal space." She did, and there were numerous articles exploring aspects of the topic.

The key words *personal space* produced an important title from the library's card catalog: Robert Sommer's *Personal Space: The Behavioral Basis of Design.* Brown also looked in the card catalog under the key words *body language* and found the book *Body Language* by Julius Fast. At the back of Fast's book she found a bibliography of key references. She was delighted to find Hall's book and Sommer's book listed. This helped her confirm that Hall and Sommer were authoritative and reliable sources. (For guidelines on evaluating sources, see 5c and 32d-2.)

To find more articles on personal space, Brown used the computerized databased system called DIALOG. She searched the *Psychological Abstract Index*—called PsycINFO in the DIALOG system. (For a description of this search and a sample from DIALOG, see 32e-8.) Two articles that Brown found became references in her paper.

Now Brown had a working bibliography. Using MLA documentation style, she had made bibliography cards on three key books, fifteen articles, and two textbooks. It was time to read closely and take notes. Brown carefully headed each index card with the author of the source. Making sure to avoid plagiarism, she paraphrased, summarized, and copied quotations according to the techniques described in Chapter 31 of this handbook. Whenever she used an author's exact words, Brown wrote oversized quotation marks so that she would be sure to see them when using her notes.

588

While taking notes, Brown realized that some of the articles she had found were not as useful as she had thought. Later as she was writing her paper she dropped a few more. She ended up with fourteen references.

In organizing her paper, Brown looked through her notes and saw that they fell into two piles: standards for personal space in North America and standards in other countries. She tried to outline the material, and quickly realized that she had to start with a definition of personal space. Going back through her cards, she created a third pile for definitions. Her thesis statement was next. Brown knew that her thesis statement would be the last sentence of her introductory paragraph. She drafted a number of versions to answer her research question, and revised the thesis further as she drafted her paper. Here is an early draft of Brown's introduction:

```
    People know unconsciously how close is close when they

    stand near other people during conversations. This relates

    to the concept of personal space—the amount of physical

    distance people expect during social interaction. Stand-

    ards for personal space vary among cultures.
```

Brown knew that the paragraph was flawed. It lacked interest, the word "this" was a vague pronoun reference, and the thesis statement did not give a full picture of the paper. She showed her draft to three friends and asked them to react. One friend who was majoring in psychology had a newspaper clipping in his files that gave Brown the opening she needed. Then as Brown worked on drafts of her paper, she refined her thesis statement. For the result, see page 1 of Brown's paper.

In writing her paper. Brown composed three drafts. In addition to rewriting her opening paragraph, Brown made other improvements as she revised. Her first draft lacked clear signals to readers about the material's organization. In her second draft, Brown used topic sentences to start many of her paragraphs. Her first draft relied too much on quotation. In her second draft, Brown used paraphrase and summary—techniques explained in Chapter 31 of this handbook. She used quotations only when an author's language was particularly apt. In her third draft, Brown polished her word choice, corrected her grammar and spelling, and reworked her conclusion. Brown wanted the conclusion to be a "call to action," urging people to become sensitive to the concept of personal space and thereby avoid intercultural misunderstandings. In her first and second drafts, her concluding paragraph was quite long, so in her final draft she divided it into two and added a particularly relevant quotation.

589

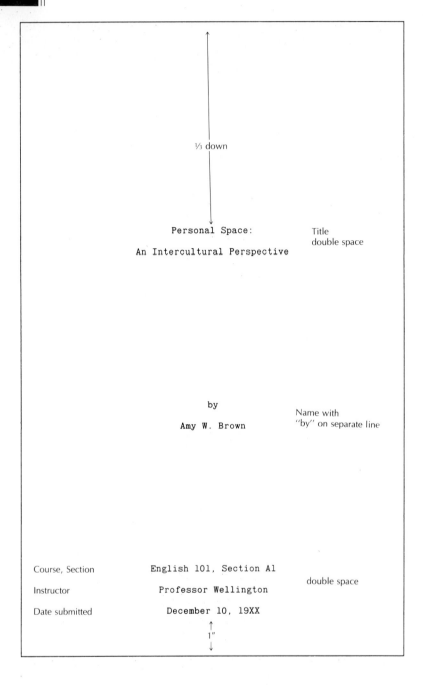

⅓ down

Personal Space:

An Intercultural Perspective

Title
double space

by

Amy W. Brown

Name with
"by" on separate line

Course, Section   English 101, Section A1

Instructor   Professor Wellington

Date submitted   December 10, 19XX

double space

1"

OBSERVING A STUDENT WRITING RESEARCH

Cover page. If your instructor requires a cover page, use the format and types of information shown on the opposite page. Then on page 1 of your paper, repeat only the paper's title.

First page. If your instructor does not require a cover page, follow the Modern Language Association style shown below for heading your first page. If you use a cover page, omit this heading and put the title at the top of page 1. Always leave a quadruple space between the title and the first line of your paper.

HEADING FOR FIRST PAGE WITHOUT COVER PAGE   1

Amy W. Brown   Name

Professor Wellington   Instructor

English 101, Section A1   Course, Section

10 December 19XX   Date submitted

                                              double space

              Personal Space:

          An Intercultural Perspective

                                              quadruple
                                              space

     When she returned home after a year in South America,

Judith Martin, a North American writer, began to have a

problem. People kept interpreting her behavior as

flirtatious, but she was not flirting. Fairly soon she

INSTRUCTOR'S NOTES

Brown i

Outline

<u>Thesis statement</u>: Everyone has expectations concerning the use of personal space, but accepted distances for that space are determined by each person's culture.

I. Observations about personal space began about twenty years ago.

   A. Most people are unaware that interpersonal distances exist.

   B. Personal space depends on invisible boundaries.

   C. Personal space moves with people as they interact.

   D. People do not like anyone to trespass on their personal space.

II. Research reveals North Americans' expectations for personal space.

   A. Hall identified four zones.

      1. "Intimate" is the smallest zone.

      2. "Personal" is next.

      3. "Social" is next.

      4. "Public" is the largest zone.

   B. Subcultures help determine expectations for personal space.

   C. Age affects how people use personal space.

   D. Gender influences people's use of personal space.

III. Research reveals standards for personal space in countries other than the United States.

   A. Conversational distances vary.

      1. Western Europeans use a fingertip-to-shoulder distance.

592

```
                                                    Brown ii

        2. Eastern Europeans use a wrist-to-shoulder

           distance.

        3. Mediterraneans use elbow-to-shoulder distances.

     B. Permitted amounts of touching vary.

     C. Arabs prefer close interpersonal distances.

     D. Japanese do not prefer close interpersonal

        distances.
```

Outline. Brown uses a formal outline. It is also a sentence outline, in that all items are complete sentences. (For information about outlining, see 32i.) Outline pages precede page 1 of the paper, so they are numbered in lower-case roman numerals; the student's last name is also given.

Note that in Brown's paper, Section I corresponds to paragraphs 2 through 4; Section II corresponds to paragraphs 5 through 8; Section III corresponds to paragraphs 9 through 12. The conclusion consists of the last two paragraphs.

A   1

B

Personal Space:

An Intercultural Perspective

C

1   When she returned home after a year in South America, Judith Martin, a North American writer, began to have a problem. People kept interpreting her behavior as flirtatious, but she was not flirting. Fairly soon, she figured out what was happening. When most South Americans talk to each other face-to-face, they stand closer together than do North Americans. Martin had not readjusted to North American distances (9). She had forgotten about the phenomenon known as "personal space"— the amount of physical distance people expect during social interaction. Everyone has expectations concerning the use of personal space, but accepted distances for that space are determined by each person's culture.

D

2   Observations about personal space began about twenty years ago. Anthropologist Edward T. Hall was a pioneer in the field. He conducted research to find out precisely what distances were acceptable when people interacted. In his aptly titled book <u>The Hidden Dimension</u>, Hall coined the word "proxemics" to describe people's use of space as a means of communication (1). As Hall's book title indicates, most people are unaware that interpersonal distances exist and contribute to people's reactions to one another (109).

E

F

594

General Note: Amy Brown has followed the new MLA Style for format and documentation (see 32g and 32k).

A. **Page number.** In the upper righthand corner Brown typed the number 1; on continuation pages, the page number is preceded by her last name.

B. **Title.** Brown's title prepares readers for the paper in two important ways. It gives the paper's major term (personal space) and the focus of the paper's discussion (more than one culture). In an earlier draft, Brown's title was "Proxemics: An Intercultural Perspective on the Need for Space." She rejected it because "space" was too general and "proxemics" was too technical. She then tried "Being Close: An Intercultural Perspective." She liked the second half because it was an accurate description of her focus, but the first half had multiple meanings.

C. **Introductory device.** In her introductory paragraph, Brown uses an anecdote. (Introductory devices are discussed in 4e.) She felt the ancedote served four functions: to make the abstract concept of personal space concrete and familiar; to tie into the paper's title; to lead into the thesis statement; and to capture readers' interest.

D. **Thesis statement.** The last sentence of Brown's introductory paragraph is the paper's thesis statement. The thesis presents the central idea of the paper. Emerging from the paper's title and opening anecdote, the thesis prepares readers for what to expect—a discussion of expectations concerning personal space and how those expectations differ among cultures.

E. **Evaluation of source:** Brown establishes Hall as an expert by identifying him as an anthropologist and as a pioneer on the subject of personal space.

F. **Parenthetical reference to author and book named in the text.** Brown uses two sources by Edward T. Hall (see "Works Cited" on Brown's page 10). When referring to the two works, Brown has to be sure to keep them separate. In this paragraph, therefore, she mentions Hall's name and the title of the work she is referring to. Her two parenthetical references, therefore, include only the page numbers. They are inserted before the periods that end the sentences. Brown uses quotation marks to set off the coined word "proxemics," but she uses no other quotation marks because she has summarized the material. The other work by Hall is cited in paragraph 11.

595

Brown 2

3   Personal space depends on invisible boundaries.
Those boundaries move with people as they interact.
Personal space "moves with us, expanding and contracting
according to the situation in which we find ourselves"
(Fisher, Bell, and Baum 149). Robert Sommer, an
environmental psychologist, uses literary and visual
analogies to describe personal space:

> Like the porcupines in Schopenhauer's fable,
> people like to be close enough to obtain warmth
> and comradeship but far enough away to avoid
> pricking one another. Personal space . . . has
> been likened to a snail shell, a soap bubble,
> an aura, a "breathing room." (26)

4   People do not like anyone to trespass on their
personal space. As Worchel and Cooper explain, invasions
of personal space elicit negative reactions that range
from mild discomfort to retaliation to walking out on the
situation (539-40). The poet W. H. Auden threatened a
uniquely negative reaction to intrusions in his space.

> Some thirty inches from my nose
> The frontier of my Person goes
> And all the untilled air between
> Is private pagus or demesne
> Stranger, unless with bedroom eyes
> I beckon you to fraternize
> Beware of rudely crossing it
> I have no gun but I can spit.
>
> (qtd. in Worchel and Cooper 539)

G

H

I

J

K

596

G. **Quotation within sentence.** Brown fits a quotation into her prose. She uses quotation marks to avoid plagiarism.

H. **Parenthetical reference to author not named in the text.** The source of the definition (author and page) is added in parentheses.

I. **A long quotation.** A quotation of more than four typewritten lines, is set off from the rest of the text. Brown introduces it with a colon because she has written a complete sentence (compare with paragraph 13). She indents the material 10 spaces and does not paragraph indent the first line. In the fourth line Brown uses a three-dot ellipsis to indicate the place where she omitted words (the full original source is shown on page 560). The page reference for the quotation is given in parentheses after the punctuation that ends the quotation. The words "breathing room" are in quotation marks because they appear this way in the original source.

J. **Use of an unexpected source.** Brown realizes that W. H. Auden is not a likely expert on personal space. She uses his poem nonetheless because (a) she discovered it reprinted in a discussion of personal space by social psychologists, so she decided its content had credibility for her paper, and (b) she decided that it would suit her audience well, given the paper was for her freshman English class.

K. **Parenthetical reference for an indirect source.** Brown did not find the poem in its original source. After she found it, she tried to locate the book in which the poem was first published, but her library did not have a copy. So she relied on the indirect source. In her parenthetical reference, she used *qtd. in,* the abbreviation for "quoted in."

597

Brown 3

5   Research provides information about the distances that North Americans prefer when interacting. The pioneering work was done by Hall. He observed the behavior of a group of middle-class adults in business and professions in the northeastern United States. He saw four zones of personal space; they are summarized and explained in Table 1.

Table 1   **L**

Hall's "Distance Zones"[a]

	Intimate	Personal	Social	Public
Close	0 to 6″	1½′ to 2½′	4′ to 7′	12′ to 25′
Far	6″ to 1½′	2½′ to 4′	7′ to 12′	25′ +

Source: Discussion in Hall, <u>Hidden</u> 110–20; also Henley 32–33; Fisher, Bell, and Baum 153.   **M**

[a]Selected illustrations of each zone are: <u>Close Intimate</u>: lovers, children with parents; <u>Far Intimate</u>: strangers in crowds; <u>Close Personal</u>: husband and wife talking on the street; <u>Far Personal</u>: friends talking on the street; <u>Close Social</u>: boss and subordinate at a meeting; <u>Far Social</u>: receptionist and people in a large waiting room; <u>Close Public</u>: teacher and students in a classroom; <u>Far Public</u>: actors or public speakers with audiences.

INSTRUCTOR'S NOTES

L. **Table.** A table is an excellent way to summarize complex information that involves numbers and/or repeated categories. A table should be placed as close as possible to the paragraph in which it is first mentioned. If a table cannot fit in the space remaining on the page, it can be placed on the following page after the end of the first paragraph on that page. Some instructors permit students to put tables on a separate page at the end of the paper, before "Notes," if any, or before "Works Cited." Brown uses the format described in the *MLA Handbook:* the table number and title at the left margin, a lettered—not numbered—footnote, and source information immediately below the data, before the footnote.

M. **Source identification.** Because Brown uses two works by Hall, she includes a shortened title *(Hidden)* so that readers will know which Hall work she is referring to. Semicolons are used to separate each item in a series of multiple references. The other Hall work is cited in paragraph 11.

Brown 4

6   Researchers working with Hall's data found that accepted interpersonal distances in the United States also depend on other factors. For example, subcultures help determine expectations concerning personal space. Fisher, Bell, and Baum report that groups of Hispanic-Americans generally interact more closely within their subculture than Anglo-Americans do within theirs. They further explain that in general "subcultural groups tend to interact at closer distances with members of their own subculture than with nonmembers", (158).

7   Age also affects how people use personal space. North American children seem unaware of boundaries for personal space until the age of four or five, according to Worchel and Cooper. As the children get older, however, they become more aware of standards for personal space. By the time they reach puberty, they have completely adapted to their culture's standards for interpersonal distances (535-37).

8   Gender also influences people's use of personal space. For example, North American males' most negative reaction is reserved for invasions of their personal space that come directly in front of them. Females, on the other hand, feel most negative about approaches from the side (Worchel and Cooper 535). Also, females have smaller interpersonal distances than do males, although same-sex pairs communicate across larger spaces than do male-female

N

N

O

INSTRUCTOR'S NOTES

N. **Placement of parenthetical references.** Parenthetical references go immediately after a quotation or after the end of a set of information.

O. **Paraphrase of original source.** In paragraph 8, Brown paraphrases Worchel and Cooper, page 535. The original reads: "Males responded most negatively to frontal invasions of their space, whereas females reacted most negatively to invasions from the side." Brown uses her own words for almost all words except "males," "females," and "from the side."

601

Brown 5

pairs (Worchel and Cooper 535–537). The gender factor
shifts, however, in high density situations such as
crowded subways or elevators in the United States. As
Maines reports, when people have some choice about where
they stand or sit in crowded settings, they gravitate to
people of the same sex (100).

9   Expectations concerning personal space exist in all
cultures, but such expectations vary greatly from culture
to culture (Fast 29). Research reveals standards for
personal space in countries other than the United States.
For example, conversational distances vary between people   **P**
from different countries, according to Desmond Morris, a
British zoologist. He notes that when people from Western
Europe stand on the street and talk together, the space
between them is the distance it would take one person's
fingertip to reach the other's shoulder. People from
Eastern Europe converse at a wrist–to–shoulder distance.
People from the Mediterranean, however, prefer elbow–to–
shoulder distance (131).

10   Permitted amounts of touching also illustrate   **Q**
intercultural differences in standards for personal space.
Touching while conversing differs in Germany, Italy, and
the United States, reports Robert Shuter, a communications
specialist. His research shows that Germans and North
Americans behave alike in that males stand farther apart
and touch less when talking than do male–female pairs or

P. **Summary of original source.** In paragraph 9, Brown summarizes Desmond Morris, page 131. Here is the original, which uses British—not American English—conventions for quotation marks.

> Unfortunately, different countries have different ideas about exactly how close is close. It is easy enough to test your own 'space reaction': when you are talking to someone in the street or in any open space, reach out with your arm and see where the nearest point on his body comes. If you hail from western Europe, you will find that he is at roughly fingertip distance from you. In other words, as you reach out, your fingertips will just about make contact with his shoulder. If you come from eastern Europe you will find you are standing at 'wrist distance'. If you come from the Mediterranean region you will find that you are much closer to your companion, at little more than 'elbow distance'.

Q. **Transferring information from note to paper.** In paragraph 10, Brown uses the summary from her notes. Here is her note card:

> *Shuter*, p. 305
> _Intercultural differences_
> Summary:
> Germans and N. Americans behave alike in that males stand farther apart and touch less while talking than do male-female pairs. The opposite is true in Italy, where males interact more closely and touch more during conversations than do male-female pairs or female pairs. Thus, Italian males expect to use personal space as females do in Germany and the United States.

female pairs. The opposite is true in Italy, where males
interact more closely and touch more during conversations
than do male–female pairs or female pairs. Shuter
concludes that Italian males expect to use personal space
as females do in Germany and the United States (305). In
another experiment, adults were asked to put dolls in
position for what was called "comfortable interaction."
People from Italy and Greece placed the dolls closer
together than did people from Sweden, Scotland, or the
United States (Worchel and Cooper 536). Also, in doctors'
waiting rooms, Australians were less likely to start
conversations with strangers than were Indonesians
(Worchel and Cooper 536).

11   Arabs prefer close interpersonal distances. Polhemus
explains that Arab students move close together more
often, confront each other directly, and touch each other
frequently when talking than do American students (21).
In an interview called "Learning the Arabs Silent
Language," Hall explains that Arabs know the practicality
of close conversational distances: "If you are
interested in something, your pupils dilate; if I say
something you don't like, they tend to contract" (47).[1]   **R**
Conversational distances of two feet—that preferred by
many Arabs—permits people to see each other's pupils
better than does the typical North American distance of
five feet (48).

R. **Comment in an endnote.** Brown uses an endnote to comment on her information. She wants to make a related observation about the use of sunglasses. Because the point does not fit into her paragraph, she uses an endnote. The number for the endnote is raised slightly above the line after the period ending the sentence. The endnote is on Brown's page 9.

INSTRUCTOR'S NOTES

Brown 7

12   Japanese do not prefer close interpersonal distances.
Because the island of Japan is quite small for its
population of about 120 million, public places are often
very crowded. To cope, the people remain formal and aloof
even when in very close proximity to one another (Fast 38).

13   People can easily be misunderstood if they are   **S**
insensitive to how people from another culture use
personal space. Clearly, what is considered obnoxious in
one culture might be considered polite in another (Fisher,
Bell, and Baum 167). As Hall explains, virtually
everything people are and do

        is associated with the experience of space. . . .   **T**
        Therefore, people from different cultures, when
        interpreting each other's behavior, often
        misinterpret the relationship, the activity, or
        the emotions. This leads to alienation in
        encounters or distorted communications. (<u>Hidden</u>
        171)

In the next few years, more studies will be undertaken to
uncover information about cultural differences in matters
such as personal space (Davis and Skupien, xix). The
information will be important. International
understanding cannot thrive unless people recognize and
accept such disparities, according to Charles G. Morris, a
professor of psychology:

S. **Concluding device.** In paragraphs 13 and 14, Brown concludes her paper with a "call for action" (concluding devices are discussed in 4e).

T. **Combined quotation from two paragraphs in original source.** Brown combines into one quotation material from two paragraphs in Hall. She uses no punctuation to lead into the quotation (compare to colon used before next quotation). She does this because her lead-in is an incomplete sentence that is completed by the quotation. Brown uses a four-dot ellipsis to show that the quotation is taken from two paragraphs. Here is the original source (Hall, *Hidden* 171):

> This book emphasizes that virtually everything that man is and does is associated with the experience of space. Man's sense of space is a synthesis of many sensory inputs: visual, auditory, kinesthetic, olfactory, and thermal. Not only does each of these constitute a complex system—as, for example, the dozen different ways of experiencing depth visually—but each is molded and patterned by culture. Hence, there is no alternative to accepting the fact that people reared in different cultures live in different sensory worlds.
>
> We learn from the study of culture that the patterning of perceptual worlds is a function not only of culture but of *relationship, activity,* and *emotion.* Therefore, people from different cultures, when interpreting each other's behavior, often misinterpret the relationship, the activity, or the emotions. This leads to alienation in encounters or distorted communications.

Brown 8

This sort of information seems trivial, but it does affect international understanding. Imagine, for example, a business conference between a [North] American and an Arab. The American prefers to have about three or four feet between them, while the Arab is inclined to stand closer.[2] If the American moves away, the Arab feels that the American is being cold and hostile, while the American finds that the Arab, who keeps moving closer, is being pushy and aggressive. (516)

U

14   As international travel and commerce increase, intercultural contact is becoming commonplace. Soon, perhaps, cultural variations in expectations for personal space will be as familiar to everyone as are cultural variations in food and dress. Until then, people need to make a special effort to learn one another's expectations concerning personal space. Once people are sensitive to such matters, they can stop themselves from taking the wrong step--either away from or toward a person from another culture.

U. **Words inserted in a quotation.**   Brackets are used to show words that do not appear in the original quotation. Brown inserts the word "North" to clarify that Morris is talking about North Americans, not South Americans. She inserts it the first time only, assuming that each subsequent use of "American" will be read as "North American."

INSTRUCTOR'S NOTES

½″

Brown 9   **V**

1″

Notes

[1] This explains why some Arab leaders wear sunglasses indoors.

[2] Both Morris and Hall agree that North Americans prefer larger conversational distances than do Arabs. They do not, however, seem to agree on the precise distances. Morris says the distance is three to four feet. Hall says five feet. These differences do not detract, however, from the central point concerning the contrasts in cultural preferences.

Brown 10

Works Cited

Davis, Martha, and Janet Skupien, eds. <u>Body Movement and</u>   **A**

    <u>Nonverbal Communication: An Annotated Bibliography</u>

    <u>1971–1981</u>. Bloomington, IN: Indiana UP, 1982.

Fast, Julius. <u>Body Language</u>. New York: Evans, 1970.   **B**

Fisher, Jeffrey D., Paul A. Bell, and Andrew Baum. <u>Envi-</u>   **C**

    <u>ronmental Psychology</u>. 2nd ed. New York: Holt, 1984.

INSTRUCTOR'S NOTES

V. **Comment notes.**   On a separate numbered page headed "Notes," Brown provides commentary that does not fit into the text of her paper. Contents notes in MLA style can comment upon, explain, or clarify material written in the text. Each note starts with a number raised a half line and indented five spaces, paragraph style. Double spacing is used within and between all comment notes.

General Format.   A bibliography, called "Works Cited," is used in MLA documentation style (see 32g). Entries are in alphabetical order by author's last name, with a 5-space indention after the first line of each entry. Punctuation and spacing between words and lines are as shown. Double spacing is used within and between entries. Two spaces occur after each period in an entry.

A. **Entry for edited book.**   Inverted order for name of first editor (last name, first name), but regular order for second name. *University Press* abbreviated *UP*.

B. **Entry for book by a single author.**

C. **Entry for book by three authors.**   Inverted order (last name, first name) for name of first author, but regular order for others. [*Note:* In a work with three or fewer authors, all names are listed; in a work by four authors or more, the first author is followed by *et al.*] *Second edition* abbreviated to *2nd ed.* Publisher abbreviated from *Holt, Rinehart and Winston* to *Holt*.

611

Hall, Edward T. The Hidden Dimension. New York:

Doubleday, 1966.

---. Interview. "Learning the Arabs Silent Language."

With Kenneth Friedman. Psychology Today Aug. 1979:

44–54.

Henley, Nancy M. Body Politics: Power, Sex, and Nonverbal

Communication. Englewood Cliffs: Prentice, 1977.

Maines, David R. "Tactile Relationship in the Subway as

Affected by Racial, Sexual, and Crowded Seating

Situations." Environmental Psychology and Nonverbal

Behavior 2 (1977): 100–108.

Martin, Judith. "Here's Looking at You." Newsday 27 Jan.

1981, sec. 2: 9+.

Morris, Charles G. Psychology: An Introduction. 4th ed.

Englewood Cliffs: Prentice, 1982.

Morris, Desmond. Manwatching: A Field Guide to Human

Behavior. New York: Abrams, 1977.

Polhemus, Ted. "Social Bodies." The Body as a Medium of

Expression. Ed. Jonathan Benthall and Ted Polhemus.

New York: Dutton, 1975. 13–35.

Shuter, Robert. "A Field Study of Nonverbal Communication

in Germany, Italy, and the United States."

Communication Monographs 44 (1977): 298–305.

Sommer, Robert. Personal Space: The Behavioral Bases of

Design. Englewood Cliffs: Prentice, 1969.

Worchel, Stephen, and Joel Cooper. Understanding Social

Psychology. 3rd ed. Homewood, IL: Dorsey, 1983.

D
E

F

G

H

I

J

D. **Second work by same author.** Three hyphens and a period stand for the repetition of the preceding author's name. [*Note:* In such instances, works by the same author are listed alphabetically by title, not chronologically according to date of publication.]

E. **Entry for an interview published in a magazine.** Entry listed by person interviewed, not by the person doing the interviewing. The page numbers are not preceded by *pp.*

F. **Entry for an article in a journal with continuous pagination.** Article title in quotation marks. Journal title underlined. Then volume number, year (in parentheses), and page numbers without *pp.*

G. **Entry for article in a daily newspaper.** Title of article in quotation marks. Name of newspaper underlined. Date of newspaper in this order: day, month (abbreviation permitted), year. Then newspaper section, columns, and page numbers without *pp.*

H. Publisher abbreviated from *Prentice-Hall* to *Prentice.*

I. **Entry for article in a book.** Author of article heads the entry. Editors of book, with names in regular order, follow book title. Title of article in quotation marks. Title of book underlined. Page numbers—without *pp.*—after city of publication and publisher.

J. **Entry for book by two authors.** Inverted order (last name, first name) for name of first author, but regular order for second name. Place of publication includes city *and* two-letter postal abbreviation for state because many readers might not know that Homewood is in Illinois.

613

WRITING IN OTHER DISCIPLINES

QUOTATION ABOUT WRITING
You can write about *anything,* and if you write well enough, even the reader with no intrinsic interest in the subject will become involved.

—TRACY KIDDER

Writing assignments are given in most college courses. A literature instructor may require you to write an analysis of a poem or a research paper on literary critics' reactions to Ernest Hemingway's *The Sun Also Rises;* a psychology instructor may require you to write a case study based on your observations of a person or write a research report that synthesizes various experts' observations about the causes of divorce or the problems of the homeless; a biology instructor may require you to write a laboratory report or a formal scientific paper.

When college instructors give writing assignments, they assume that you have the requisite reading and writing skills to complete college-level assignments. Instructors also expect your writing to conform to the standards for content, style, and format common to each separate discipline. This chapter discusses standards for writing—especially research writing—in academic disciplines other than English composition.

614

34a
Recognize similarities and differences among the disciplines.

Each field of study—the humanities, social sciences, and natural and technological sciences—has its own perspectives on the world and its own philosophies about academic thought and research. To understand some of the differences among the disciplines, consider these three quite different paragraphs about a mountain.

HUMANITIES

The mountain stands above all that surrounds it. Giant timbers—part of a collage of evergreen and deciduous trees—conceal the expansive mountain's slope, where cattle once grazed. At the base of the mountain, a cool stream flows over rocks of all sizes, colors, and shapes. Next to the outer bank of the stream stands a shingled farmhouse, desolate, yet suggesting its active past. Unfortunately, the peaceful scene is interrupted by billboards and chairlifts, landmarks of a modern, fast-paced life.

SOCIAL SCIENCES

Among the favorite pastimes of American city dwellers is the "return to nature." Many outdoor enthusiasts hope to enjoy a scenic trip to the mountains, only to be disappointed. They know they have arrived at the mountain that they have traveled hundreds of miles to see because huge billboards are directing them to its base. As they look up the mountain, dozens of people are riding over the treetops in a chairlift, littering the slope with paper cups and food wrappers. At the base of the mountain stands the inevitable refreshment stand, found at virtually all American tourist attractions. Land developers consider such commercialization a way to preserve and utilize natural resources, but environmentalists are appalled.

SCIENCES

The mountain is approximately 5,600 feet in height. The underlying rock is igneous, of volcanic origin, composed primarily of granites and feldspars. Three distinct biological communities are present on the mountain. The community at the top of the mountain is alpine in nature, dominated by very short grasses and forbs. At middle altitudes, a typical northern boreal coniferous forest community is present, and at the base and lower altitudes, deciduous forest is the dominant community. This commu-

QUOTATION ABOUT WRITING

Writing represents a unique mode of learning—not merely valuable, not merely special, but unique. . . . Writing serves learning uniquely because writing as process-and-product possesses a cluster of attributes that correspond uniquely to certain powerful learning strategies.

—JANET EMIG, "Writing as a Mode of Learning"

QUOTATION ABOUT WRITING

But liberal learning does not permit us to hold on to any single answer for too long. As soon as you find one answer, you discover that that answer leads to other questions. Liberal learning can be unsettling. People like certainty, the right answer, the only way. Because of this desire for certainty and security, people can find themselves living with answers that other people have imposed upon them. In a free society, people learn to cultivate inquiring minds. They see that in broad areas of life there are no single right answers, that knowledge has a peculiar way of generating more questions, and that the world is more ambiguous than it appears. Liberal learning frees the mind to experience a sense of wonder at this ambiguous and fascinating world. F. Scott Fitzgerald writes, "The test of a first-rate intelligence is the ability to hold two opposed ideas in the mind at the same time, and still retain the ability to function." A liberally educated person learns to use this first-rate intelligence to function—even to prevail—in the midst of ambiguity.

—ELAINE P. MAIMON, ET AL.
Writing in the Arts and Sciences

nity has, however, been highly affected by agricultural development along the river at its base and, more recently, by recreational development.

Though such examples cannot demonstrate all differences among the disciplines, they do show clearly that each discipline has its writing traditions and preferences. The paragraph written for the humanities describes the mountain from the individual perspective of the writer—a perspective both personal and yet representative of a general human response. The paragraph written for the social sciences focuses on the behavior of people as a group. The paragraph written for the sciences reports observations of natural phenomena.

SIMILARITIES AND DIFFERENCES IN WRITING FOR VARIOUS DISCIPLINES

SIMILARITIES

1. Consider your purpose and audience.	Chapters 1–2
2. Use the writing process to plan, shape, draft, revise, edit, and proofread.	Chapters 2–3
3. Develop a thesis.	Chapters 2–3
4. Arrange and organize your ideas.	Chapter 2
5. Use supporting evidence.	Chapters 2–4
6. Develop paragraphs thoroughly.	Chapter 4
7. Think critically, and use correct reasoning and logic.	Chapter 5
8. Write effective sentences.	Chapters 16–19
9. Choose words well.	Chapters 20–21
10. Use correct grammar.	Chapters 6–15
11. Spell correctly.	Chapter 22
12. Use correct punctuation and mechanics.	Chapters 23–30

DIFFERENCES

1. Conduct research and select sources according to the discipline.
2. Select a style of documentation appropriate to the discipline.
3. Follow special format requirements, if any, in each discipline.
4. Use specialized language, when it is needed, in each discipline.

No matter what differences exist among the disciplines, all subject areas interconnect and overlap. When you study biology in your biology class, literature in your literature class, and psychology in your psychology class, you will likely notice that distinctions among fields of study are not absolutely rigid. For example, in a humanities class you might read *Lives of a Cell,* a collection of essays about science and nature, by Lewis Thomas, both a noted physician and prize-winning author, but you will also be thinking deeply about biology and other sciences. Similarly, if you write a research paper on senility for your psychology class, you might refer to medical texts and scientific journals for some information.

Writing is the one activity that unites all the disciplines. You will have to write often for most of your college courses. Writing is the principal means of communication between you and your instructor, and writing is a way for you to learn material and gain authority over knowledge.

The chart on the opposite page summarizes similarities and differences in writing for different disciplines.

1

Conduct research and select sources according to the discipline.

Research methods differ among the disciplines when **primary sources** are used. Primary sources offer you first-hand exposure to information. No one comes between you and the exciting experience of discovering and confronting material on your own. No one else's interpretation or description can color your reactions when you confront primary sources "raw." In the humanities, existing documents are primary sources; the task of the researcher is to analyze and interpret these primary sources. Typical primary-source material for research could be a poem by Dylan Thomas, the floor plans of Egyptian pyramids, or early drafts of music manuscripts. In the social and natural sciences, primary research involves the design and undertaking of experiments involving direct observation. The task of the researcher in the social and natural sciences is to conduct the experiments or to read the first-hand reports of experiments and studies written by people who conducted them.

Secondary sources—articles and books about a primary source—are also important in all disciplines. In the humanities, you can learn much from the examples of others who have analyzed and interpreted primary sources. In the social sciences, secondary sources can usefully synthesize findings in many areas and draw parallels that offer new insights. In the natural sciences, if some

QUOTATION ABOUT WRITING
In schools where the lessons taught in English classes are not repeated and emphasized in the student's other classes, the knowledge and skills learned in those lessons tend to atrophy. We believe language skills deserve more conscious attention from teachers in all academic disciplines, and that teachers who recognize the role played by these "elementary" skills can help students increase their learning ability, improve their communication skills, and enhance their cognitive and emotional growth.

—TOBY FULWILER AND ART YOUNG,
Language Connections

QUOTATION ABOUT WRITING
Problem solving is common ground for all the disciplines and fundamental to all human activities. . . . The discovery function of writing in the content areas, particularly in the scientific and technological fields, can help students become aware of the processes they use to solve problems.

—CAROL BERKENKOTTER, "Writing and
Problem Solving"

617

QUOTATION ABOUT WRITING
The main assumption behind Writing Across the Curriculum seems to embody a resurrected sense of the responsibility of entire faculties and administrative bodies for the literary competence of the graduate. . . . Literacy is the concern of all faculty members since it is the cornerstone of education. Another assumption is that some rhetorical principles—careful description, explanation and proof, problems of definition and classification, and consideration of style and audience—transcend departments. Everyone can teach writing in a way. All faculty members can learn some general writing-teaching skills.

—JAMES KINNEAVY, interview, December 1984

TEACHING TIP
You might want to explain that formats are of major importance in many disciplines other than English composition. The formats constitute "genres" which readers expect. The formats ease communication because readers know where to look for specific information: background, data, conclusions.

primary sources are outdated by the time they are published, review articles and monographs can be useful for making connections among studies and bringing major questions into focus.

Because a secondary source puts one step or more between you and the primary source, many instructors prefer that whenever possible you work with primary sources for certain assignments. At other times, instructors assign secondary sources so that you can get a more comprehensive perspective. Secondary sources can even be worth investigating or analyzing in their own right. For example, reading nineteenth-century reviews for the reactions of his contemporaries to Edgar Allen Poe's early writing might lead you to try to determine whether this criticism influenced Poe's later works. Similarly, a fifty-year-old anthropological study can highlight changes in a group you are studying today.

2
Select a style of documentation appropriate to the discipline.

Writers use **documentation** to give credit to the sources they have used. A writer who does not credit a source is guilty of **plagiarizing**—a serious academic offense discussed at length in Chapter 31. Styles of documentation differ among the disciplines. The major styles are presented in this handbook, as indicated in the chart on the opposite page.

3
Follow special format requirements, if any, in each discipline.

Because of the differences among disciplines, different formats are expected in each for presentation of material. These special formats have evolved to communicate a writer's purpose, to emphasize content by eliminating distracting variations in format, and to make the reader's work easier. Writing in the humanities (34b) is less often subject to set formats, although your writing is expected to be well organized and accepted documentation formats are expected. Writing in the social sciences (34c) and natural sciences (34d) often calls for using fixed special formats for specific types of writing. For example, if you are writing a case study (for a sample, see pages 644–45) or a laboratory report (for a sample, see pages

618

DOCUMENTATION STYLES DISCUSSED IN THIS HANDBOOK

FOR ENGLISH AND OTHER SUBJECTS IN THE HUMANITIES

Parenthetical system (MLA)　　　　pages 562–74;
　　　　　　　　　　　　　　　　　579–85

Endnote or footnote system　　　　pages 631–40

FOR THE SOCIAL SCIENCES

Parenthetical system (APA)　　　　pages 647–50

FOR NATURAL SCIENCES AND TECHNOLOGIES

Varies; see pages 650–58

654–56), you are expected to use the formats always used for such writings.

4
Use specialized language, when it is needed, in each discipline.

All disciplines use specialized language to some degree. The specialized terms in the natural and social sciences are generally more technical and less accessible to nonspecialists than are those in the humanities. The more important observable or theoretical exactness is to a discipline, the more likely there will be many words with very special meanings. For example, consider the word *niche*. It has two generally known meanings: "a place particularly suitable to the person or thing in it," and "a hollowed space in a wall for a statue or vase." *Niche* in the natural sciences, however, has a very specialized meaning: "the set of environmental conditions—climate, food sources, water supply, enemies—that permit an organism or species to survive." The extent to which you define the specialized language in your writing depends on your readers' level of expertise. (For more about audience awareness, see 1c.)

The acceptability of the active voice° or passive voice° in writing varies with the disciplines. Writers in the humanities generally prefer the active voice *(John Priestley discovered oxygen in 1774)*, while writers in the social and natural sciences often use the passive voice *(Oxygen was discovered in 1774)* to report facts and ob-

TEACHING TIP
In 1984, the Modern Language Association (MLA) changed its recommended documentation style from a note system to a parenthetical system. Often, therefore, the MLA parenthetical system is called "new MLA" or "1984 MLA." You might want to point out to your students that the change in documentation style has implications for writing style. With the MLA note system, readers often had to get all source information in the note; with the parenthetical system, readers do not expect to have to divert their eyes (and attention) to learn about the source. The new preference is for writers to include as much information as gracefully as possible in the text, with the balance left for parentheses.

TEACHING TIP
One way for students to demonstrate mastery of a subject is to be able to explain it in several different ways rather than parroting the textbook or the professor. This technique is useful in any discipline. For example, an engineering student might be asked to explain to a variety of audiences how radar works. In a series of short written assignments, the student explains radar to (1) a classmate who has missed several lectures but shares the same science background; (2) his nonscientist parents, who want to know what he is learning; (3) a group of sixth-graders.

619

servations. The use of the passive voice in the sciences occurs when a writer wishes to emphasize the observation rather than the observer: "The gorillas were observed in their natural setting" focuses on the gorillas, not on the person observing the gorillas. In science writing when the focus can be on the observer, however, the writer uses the active voice: "Susan Kohn Green observed Lulu and Patty Cake, mother and daughter gorillas in New York City's Central Park Zoo, for one and a half years." (For a full discussion of active and passive voices, see 8j and 16a-2.)

 34b
Understand writing in the humanities.

Disciplines in the humanities include literature, language, philosophy, religion, and other subject areas. (Some colleges consider history to be part of the humanities, while other colleges consider it part of the social sciences; similarly, art and music are sometimes included in the humanities and sometimes not.)

1
Understand methods of inquiry in the humanities.

The humanities are concerned with questions that focus on human values. Reading, writing, and discussing—sometimes referred to as *discourse*—are key activities in the pursuit of answers to questions in the humanities. From the perspective that the well-reasoned thoughts of one person are typical of a general human response, the humanities draw on individual engagement and personal point of view. Thinking critically (Chapter 5) is crucial; for inquiry in the humanities seeks to locate "truth" based on values, ideas, and interpretations that relate to the human condition. Such inquiry must avoid emotionalism in favor of balanced, unbiased exploration.

Some questions in the humanities ask you to deal with material in its literal level. You might be asked what a passage says, or to describe the major tenets of a particular religion or philosophy. Other questions in the humanities call for inferential and evaluative thinking—looking "between the lines" and "beyond the lines," as explained in 5b. You might be asked to discuss the relative merits of abstract and representational art or your personal interpretation of Jean-Paul Sartre's statement "life is absurd." Your answers must be thorough, well-reasoned, and informed by knowledge of the material and the major issues at hand.

620

2
Understand writing purposes and practices in the humanities.

The major purposes of writing in the humanities are to inform and to persuade. **Informative writing** includes explaining what a passage means or what constitutes the key features of a philosophy. **Persuasive writing** includes arguing the merits of an opinion or interpretation. To those ends, writers synthesize, analyze, interpret, and evaluate.

In the humanities, some instructors ask students to use first person *(I, we, our)* to write about their own points of view or personal evaluations, and the third person *(he, she, it, they)* for all other assignments. Other instructors prefer students to write always in the third person. Be sure to inquire about and adapt to your instructor's requirements. In research papers for the humanities, the first person is generally acceptable only when you present your personal experience, your own conclusions, or your personal views contrasted with those of the sources you consult and document.

As discussed in Chapter 31, the techniques of paraphrasing and summarizing the words of others—with proper documentation so that plagiarism is avoided—are called upon frequently by writers in the humanities. For example, if you are assigned a review or a report, you often cannot assume that your readers have read or seen the work you are referring to, so you must provide a short summary of the work.

3
Recognize different types of papers in the humanities.

The types of papers in the humanities described in this section focus on literary works, but you can adapt the principles to other works as well. Before you write a paper that asks you to refer or react to a literary work, be sure to read the work closely. To read well, use your understanding of the reading process (5a) and critical reading skills (5b).

Analyses and Reviews

Analysis, the examination of the relationship of a whole to its parts, is a common method of development in writing about litera-

TEACHING TIP
You might want to refer students to the information on "cue words" in Appendix A. The words are typical not only of essay tests but also of writing assignments in various disciplines.

621

COORDINATED RESOURCES

Transparency masters are available for many of the screened charts and/or lists in this chapter.

Students can practice and test their knowledge of terms, key concepts, and applications of material in this chapter by using the *Study Guide to the S & S Handbook for Writers,* West.

ture (as well as films, plays, works of art, architecture, and music). In a literary analysis, you discuss your well-reasoned ideas about a work of fiction, poetry, or drama. To get to know the work well and to gather ideas for your analysis, you read closely—reading thoroughly again and again while being *on the lookout for patterns in all the aspects of literary analysis* listed on the chart below. Look up or consult with other people about any word, reference, allusion, or idea you do not understand. Keep notes as you go along so that you have a record both of the patterns you find in the material and of your reactions to the patterns and the whole work.

Use this brief list of major aspects of literary works as an introductory guide to what to look for, think about, and seek to understand in a literary work.

MAJOR ASPECTS OF LITERARY WORKS TO ANALYZE	
PLOT	The story and its emphases
THEME	Central idea or message
STRUCTURE	Organization and relationship of parts to each other and to the whole
CHARACTER(S)	Traits, thoughts, and actions of the person(s)
SETTING	Time and place of the action
POINT OF VIEW	Perspective or position from which the material is presented—sometimes by a narrator or a main character
STYLE	How words and sentence structures present the material
IMAGERY	The pictures created by the words (similes, metaphors, figurative language)
TONE	The attitudes expressed through the choice of words and the imagery
SYMBOLISM	The meaning beneath the surface of the words and images
RHYTHM AND RHYME	Beat, meter, repetition of sounds, etc.

QUOTATION ABOUT WRITING

Great writers leave us not just their works, but a way of looking at things.

—ELIZABETH JANEWAY

Starting on the next page, you will find an example of literary analysis. The student writer decided from a close reading of Alfred Lord Tennyson's poem "Break, Break, Break" that the poet was using indirect techniques to convey emotions. To support this thesis, the student analyzes the poem's imagery and style.

622

SAMPLE LITERARY ANALYSIS PAPER

Chris Johns

Professor Perkins

English 105

April 22, 19XX

Emotion in Alfred Lord Tennyson's

"Break, Break, Break"

1   In Tennyson's "Break, Break, Break," the poet avoids direct description of his feelings of grief. Instead he allegorizes, alludes to, and only suggests his essential emotion. Tennyson uses two vehicles to convey his feelings: sea imagery and personal musings. These personal musings are not descriptions of what Tennyson is feeling, but rather are statements of what he is thinking: "But the tender grace of a day that is dead / Will never come back to me."[1] From the knowledge of these thoughts the reader can infer the content and intensity of Tennyson's feelings.

2   The imagery also suggests the poet's feelings. This is obvious from the line structure of the poem and from the quality of the image. In the first, third, and fourth stanzas the imagery is presented in the first two lines, while Tennyson's thoughts are given in the second two lines (which are also the last lines, because each verse is composed of four lines). In the second stanza the relationship between the imagery and Tennyson's thoughts is closest: All four lines are devoted to Tennyson's reaction to an image:

[1] All quotations in this paper are from Tennyson's poem "Break, Break, Break." The complete poem is shown in the Appendix.

623

TEACHING TIP
This chapter includes six student papers, two complete and four excerpted. The purpose is to show students specific examples of what is expected of them in courses other than English composition. Some students will not need the information offered here until they move beyond their freshman year in college, so you might vigorously encourage students to keep their handbooks throughout their college years.

O well for the fisherman's boy

Johns 2

That he shouts with his sister at play!

O well for the sailor lad

That he sings in his boat on the bay!

3   Every element in the poem is designed to define and modify Tennyson's grief. The images are controlled and simple and always clear. Tennyson deals with each image separately; there is no pictorial confusion. In the first and last verses the image is clearly of breaking waves:

Break, break, break,

On thy cold gray stones, O Sea!

. . . . Indicates
skipped lines

Break, break, break

At the foot of thy crags, O Sea!

The third verse's image is equally specific: "And the stately ships go on / To their haven under the hill; . . ."

4   Images rather than direct statement of feeling are Tennyson's resource:

Break, break, break,

On thy cold gray stones, O Sea!

I would that my tongue could utter

The thoughts that arise in me.

As the waves beat against the rocks, so does Tennyson's grief beat against his heart; as the rocks can find no refuge, so Tennyson's tongue cannot release the feelings from his heart. The reader can sense the intensity of Tennyson's grief and can then construct the pain and what lies behind it.

Johns 3

Start new page

Appendix

Break, Break, Break

Alfred Lord Tennyson

Break, break, break,

  On thy cold gray stones, O Sea!

And I would that my tongue could utter

  The thoughts that arise in me.

O well for the fisherman's boy

  That he shouts with his sister at play!

O well for the sailor lad,

  That he sings in his boat on the bay!

And the stately ships go on

  To their haven under the hill;

But O for the touch of a vanished hand,

  And the sound of a voice that is still!

Break, break, break,

  At the foot of thy crags, O Sea!

But the tender grace of a day that is dead

  Will never come back to me.

Interpretations

An interpretation discusses either what the author means by the work or what the work means personally to the reader. When you are writing an interpretation paper, always consider these questions.

625

QUESTIONS FOR AN INTERPRETATION PAPER
1. What is the theme of the work?
2. How are particular parts of the work related to the theme?
3. If patterns exist in various elements of the work, what do they mean?
4. What message does the author convey through the work's setting, characters, narrator, etc.?
5. What symbols are used, and what do they mean?
6. Why is the ending what it is?

Book reports

A book report informs readers about the content of a book—by summarizing its plot and its theme and by discussing (1) the book's significance and purpose, (2) how the book presents its content, and (3) who might be most interested in the book. Your discussion of the book's significance should relate to your field of study. For example, if the book is a classic in children's literature, your focus for a literature class would differ somewhat from your focus for a course in psychology or education.

Reaction papers

A reaction paper presents the writer's thoughts, reactions, and feelings about a work of literature, or about an idea or an interpretation related to a work (or group of works). In a reaction paper, you might ask and try to answer a central question that the work made you think about, criticize a point of view in the work, or present a problem that you see in the work. For example, if you are asked to respond to a play, you might write about why you did or did not enjoy reading the play, how the play does or does not relate to your personal experience or to your view of life, what the play made you think about and try to puzzle through. You can focus on the entire play or on a particular scene, character, or set of lines.

Research papers

In a research paper for the humanities, you consult outside sources to learn what they have to say about a subject or a work of literature. After reading and perhaps talking with experts, you then evolve a thesis° whose purpose is either to inform or to persuade (see Chapter 1). In writing your research paper, you must draw on

626

the sources to support your thesis° and help develop its main points. To do this, you draw heavily on the techniques of paraphrase, summary, and quotation, as explained in detail in Chapter 31.

Research in the humanities always calls for you to use library resources to obtain books and articles other people have written about your topic. You will find a list of reference works for subjects in the humanities in 32e-5. For a complete discussion of conducting research for writing, see Chapters 32 and 33. Remember that when your research subject concerns written works of literature, you have to read them closely—reading thoroughly again and again to evolve your thesis and then to find material that specifically supports it.

Starting below you will find a student paper written for a humanities course. The student's thesis is that the Greek myth of Icarus has strongly influenced other works of art and literature.

This paper uses a note system of documentation, as is required in some humanities courses. In most English courses, the MLA parenthetical system of documentation is used. It is presented and explained in Chapter 32.

TEACHING TIP

As an exercise, ask your students to revise the documentation style in Shannon's paper "The Influence of the Myth of Icarus" from a note style to the MLA parenthetical style explained in Chapter 32. Point out that the students should try to integrate some source information into their sentences (to the extent that they can without having access to the sources). Point out also that they will need to revise the "Bibliography" into a "Works Cited" list.

SAMPLE HUMANITIES RESEARCH PAPER

Theresa A. Shannon

Professor Anderson

Humanities 32

March 10, 19XX

The Influence of the Myth of Icarus

1   We cannot know exactly why the Greeks included the myth of Icarus in their mythology or why Ovid wrote the myth down and included it in the Metamorphoses.[1] However, the importance of the myth is evident by its obvious influence on other works of art and literature. These influences can be seen in Brueghel's painting Landscape with the Fall of Icarus[2] and in Stephen Spender's poem "Icarus."[3] Even psychologists

Shannon 2

have named a personality that exhibits a particular pattern of behavior the Icarus complex.[4] The fact that the Icarus myth has generated so many other works indicates that it is more than an interesting story.

2   According to the myth, Daedalus, Icarus' father, designs wings of wax and feathers for himself and his son so that they may fly to freedom. Daedalus warns Icarus to fly directly between the sun and the ocean to prevent damage to the wings from either of these elements. Icarus ignores his father's warning and flies too close to the sun, causing the wax to melt. Icarus then plunges into the ocean and drowns. After Icarus' death, Daedalus offers a sacrifice of appeasement to the sun god, Apollo.

3   Pieter Brueghel's painting, Landscape with the Fall of Icarus, is not merely a representation of Icarus' death. Brueghel shows Icarus falling from the sky on a typical day near an average village. A ploughman either does not notice Icarus falling or chooses to ignore the event. A nearby sailing ship continues on its route. The poet W. H. Auden interpreted the painting as a representation of human suffering. In "Musée des Beaux Arts," a poem about Brueghel's painting of Icarus, Auden writes about suffering: "they were never wrong, / The Old Masters: how well they understood / Its human position."[5] He continues to describe the ploughman's reaction to Icarus' fall: "But for him it was not an important failure;" and observes how the ship "Had somewhere to go and sailed calmly on."[6]

Shannon 3

4   Stephen Spender's poem, on the other hand, focuses on Icarus instead of on those who observed his death. He presents Icarus as a bold and arrogant boy who "almost had a War on the sun." He writes:

> This aristocrat, superb of all instinct,
>
>   With death close linked
>
> Had paced the enormous cloud, almost had won
>
>   War on the sun.[7]

5   Although these are not the only allusions in art and literature to the myth of Icarus, they are representative of the importance of the myth as an influence to artists. The myth of the fall of Icarus, like any other myth, serves to educate us, not just to entertain us. Artists will undoubtedly continue to interpret the myth according to their own insights, perhaps viewing it from a perspective that only the future can offer.

Start new page   Shannon 4

Notes

[1] Publius Ovidius Naso, "Icarus and Daedalus," in Metamorphoses (Amsterdam: Wetstein and Smith, 1932), I, 257–260.

[2] Pieter Brueghel, Landscape with the Fall of Icarus, Musée des Beaux Arts, Brussels, Belgium.

629

[3] Stephen Spender, "Icarus," in The Norton Anthology of Poetry, eds. Richard Ellman and Robert O'Clair (New York: W. W. Norton and Company, 1973), p. 790.

[4] Daniel Ogilvie, "The Icarus Complex," Psychology Today, 20, No. 6 (1976), 31–4, 67.

[5] W. H. Auden, "Musée des Beaux Arts," in The Norton Anthology of English Literature, eds. M. H. Abrams et al. (New York: W. W. Norton and Company, 1979), p. 2396.

[6] Auden, p. 2397.

[7] Spender, p. 790.

Start new page   Bibliography   Shannon 5

Auden, W. H. "Musée des Beaux Arts." In The Norton
     Anthology of English Literature. Eds. M. H. Abrams
     et al. New York: W. W. Norton and Company, 1979,
     pp. 2396–2397.

Brueghel, Pieter. Landscape with the Fall of Icarus.
     Musée des Beaux Arts, Brussels, Belgium.

Ogilvie, Daniel. "The Icarus Complex." Psychology
     Today, 20, No. 6 (1976), 31–4, 67.

Ovidius Naso, Publius. "Icarus and Daedalus." In
     Metamorphoses. Amsterdam: Wetstein and Smith, 1932,
     pp. 257–260.

Spender, Stephen. "Icarus." In The Norton Anthology of
     Poetry. Eds. Richard Ellman and Robert O'Clair. New
     York: W. W. Norton and Company, 1973, p. 790.

630

4
Know documentation style in the humanities.

Writers use **documentation** to give credit to the sources they have used. (A writer who does not credit a source is guilty of **plagiarizing**—a serious academic offense discussed at length in Chapter 31.) Styles of documentation differ among the disciplines. A very commonly used documentation style is the so-called parenthetical system developed by the Modern Language Association (MLA), an organization of scholars and teachers in language and literature. This system is discussed and illustrated in Chapters 32 and 33. Some humanities instructors require the documentation system developed by the American Psychological Association (APA). See 34c-4 for APA documentation. Some humanities instructors require a note system of documentation. Such a system, based on the Modern Language Association system before 1984, is explained here.

GUIDELINES FOR NOTE NUMBERS IN A PAPER

1. Put the number as near as possible to whatever you are referring to: at the end of a quotation, either direct or indirect, but after any punctuation that goes with whatever you are quoting.
2. Raise these numbers a little above the line of words.
3. Leave no extra space before a number.
4. Leave one space after the number except at the end of a sentence. Leave two spaces after the number before starting a new sentence.

EXAMPLE

We cannot know exactly why the Greeks included the myth of Icarus in their mythology or why Ovid wrote the myth down and included it in the Metamorphoses.[1] However, the importance of the myth is evident by its obvious influence on other works of art and literature. These influences can be seen in Brueghel's painting "Landscape with the Fall of Icarus"[2] and in Stephen Spender's poem "Icarus."[3]

GUIDELINES FOR FORMATTING ENDNOTES

1. Center the word *Notes* two inches from the top of a separate page at the end of the paper. Do not put *Notes* in quotation marks, and do not underline it.
2. Skip four lines before starting the first note.
3. Indent the first line of each note five character spaces, but if a note has more than one line, start the second line (and any following lines) at the left margin.
4. Raise each note number a little above the words.
5. Leave one space between the note number and the first word.
6. Double space within *and* between endnotes.
7. Do not number the first page of endnotes, but number the second page and any other pages in continuous sequence with the text of your paper.

EXAMPLE

Notes

¹ Publius Ovidius Naso, "Icarus and Daedalus," in <u>Metamorphoses</u> (Amsterdam: Wetstein and Smith, 1932), I, 257–260.

² Pieter Brueghel, <u>Landscape with the Fall of Icarus</u>, Musée des Beaux Arts, Brussels, Belgium.

³ Stephen Spender, "Icarus," in <u>The Norton Anthology of Poetry</u>, eds. Richard Ellman and Robert O'Clair (New York: W. W. Norton and Company, 1973), p. 790.

Put documenting information in notes either at the bottom of pages (footnotes) or on a separate page or pages following the end of your paper (endnotes). The content is the same, whether you use footnotes or endnotes. Unless your instructor requires footnotes, use endnotes because they are easier to manage when you are typing a paper. Consecutive numbers raised a little above the words alert readers to the information you are documenting in a note.

Here are guidelines for inserting note numbers in a paper and for formatting endnotes and footnotes. To illustrate each set of guidelines, an example is shown from the student paper that begins on page 627.

GUIDELINES FOR FORMATTING FOOTNOTES AND FITTING THEM ON PAGES

1. Be aware that footnotes differ from endnotes in only one way: single space within footnotes and double space between them.
2. Be prepared to allot space at the bottom of each page for footnotes.
3. Estimate space on each page this way: Each time you use a footnote number in the text of your paper, know that you will need room at the bottom of the page for four lines (the space required between text and the first note) *plus* three lines for each note. Stop typing text and start your footnotes according to your estimate.
4. Retype a page if a footnote runs more than two or three lines short or long.
5. Remember that four spaces are required between the end of the text and the start of the footnotes.
6. If the content of a footnote runs more than six or eight lines, you can continue the note on the next page. On the new page (but not on the page where the content note started), type a line across the page, one line below the text. Then skip four more lines before beginning the first line of the continued note.

EXAMPLE

¹ Publius Ovidius Naso, "Icarus and Daedalus," in Metamorphoses (Amsterdam: Wetstein and Smith, 1932), I, 257–260.

² Pieter Brueghel, Landscape with the Fall of Icarus, Musée des Beaux Arts, Brussels, Belgium.

If your paper refers to only one or two sources, you may be permitted to use simplified documentation. (Such papers typically are about one or two works of literature, like the student paper beginning on page 623.) In such cases, keep the documentation as simple as possible. A single note tells where quotations come from. For example, this note tells that the entire work is given in the paper's appendix:

633

> but rather are statements of what he is thinking: "But the
> tender grace of a day that is dead / Will never come back
> to me."[1]
>
>
>   [1] All quotations are from Tennyson's poem "Break,
> Break, Break." A copy of the full text is in the appendix
> at the end of this paper.

If the poem were not included with the paper, the note would give full publication information:

>   [1] All quotations are from Alfred Lord Tennyson,
> "Break, Break, Break," in <u>Literature: An Introduction to
> Reading and Writing</u>, Edgar V. Roberts and Henry E. Jacobs.
> Prentice-Hall, 1986, p. 629.

In either case, a separate list of sources is unnecessary. When a paper refers to two or three sources, the following system works well:

> the similarities between Frost's "The Onset" and "Stopping
> by Woods" and Aiken's "Winter for a Moment Takes the
> Mind."[1]
>
>
>   [1] Quotations from "The Onset" are followed by (1);
> those from "Stopping by Woods" by (2); and from "Winter
> for a Moment Takes the Mind" by (3). The versions re-
> ferred to are collected in <u>The Pocket Book of Modern
> Verse</u>, Oscar Williams, ed. (New York: Pocket Books, 1954),
> pp. 233-34, 240, 360-62.

First-reference note form

In a note system of documentation, the first time you refer to a source in your writing, the note gives complete bibliographic facts as well as the specific place you are referring to or quoting from in that source. Here are first-reference note forms for common sources.

BOOK WITH ONE AUTHOR

[1] Joan Didion, <u>Salvador</u> (New York: Simon & Schuster, 1983), p. 64.

BOOK WITH TWO OR THREE AUTHORS

[2] Irving Wallace, David Wallechinsky, and Amy Wallace, <u>Significa</u> (New York: Dutton, 1983), p. 177.

BOOK WITH A CORPORATE AUTHOR

[3] Music Educators' National Conference, <u>Music in the Senior High School</u> (Washington: Music Educators' National Conference, 1959), 42.

WORK IN SEVERAL VOLUMES OR PARTS

[4] Robert Kelley, <u>The Shaping of the American Past</u>, II (Englewood Cliffs, NJ: Prentice-Hall, 1975), 724-25.

WORK IN AN ANTHOLOGY OR A COLLECTION

[5] Wayne Tosh, "Computer Linguistics," in <u>Linguistics Today</u>, ed. Archibald A. Hill (New York: Basic Books, 1969), p. 200.

ARTICLE IN A REFERENCE WORK

[6] "Fraudulence in the Arts," <u>The New Encyclopaedia Britannica</u>, 1979 ed.

635

ARTICLE FROM A JOURNAL WITH CONTINUOUS PAGINATION

⁷ William A. Madden, "<u>Wuthering Heights</u>: The Binding Passion," <u>Nineteenth—Century Fiction</u>, 27 (1972), 151.

ARTICLE FROM A JOURNAL THAT PAGES EACH ISSUE SEPARATELY

⁸ Michael C. T. Brookes, "A Dean's Dilemmas," <u>Journal of Basic Writing</u>, 5, No. 1 (1986), 65.

ARTICLE FROM A WEEKLY OR BIWEEKLY MAGAZINE OR NEWSPAPER

⁹ Barbara Randolph, "Hailing the Eureka Factor," <u>Time</u>, 21 April 1986, p. 65.

ARTICLE FROM A MONTHLY PERIODICAL

¹⁰ Patti Hogan, "Setting the Pace," <u>Ms.</u>, Aug. 1985, p. 20.

ARTICLE FROM A DAILY NEWSPAPER

¹¹ Georgia Dullea, "Literary Folk Look for Solid Comfort," <u>New York Times</u>, 16 April 1986, Sec. 3, p. 6, col. 5.

FILM

¹² Bernardo Bertolucci, dir., <u>Last Tango in Paris</u>, with Marlon Brando, United Artists, 1972.

INTERVIEW

¹³ Personal interview with professor Shirley Stearns, 17 July 1985.

WORK REPRINTED IN ANOTHER WORK

¹⁴ W. H. Auden, "Prologue: The Birth of Architecture," <u>About the House</u> (New York: Random; London: Faber and Faber), 1965; rpt. in <u>Understanding Social Psychology</u>, 3rd ed., Stephen Worchel and Joel Cooper (Homewood, IL: Dorsey, 1983), p. 539.

INSTRUCTOR'S NOTES

Note forms for second and subsequent references

After the first note for a source, you should shorten all further references to the source. If you are citing only one work by the author, the author's last name and the page references are enough:

^{15} Hogan, p. 31.

If you are citing more than one work by the same author, you must include a shortened form of the title of the particular book—along with the author's last name and the page reference.

^{16} Didion, Salvador, p. 45.

^{17} Didion, Common Prayer, pp. 92–94.

List of sources

Bibliographies list all sources consulted for a research paper, not just the sources referred to or quoted from. Because first-reference notes give full bibliographic data for each source, your instructor may not require you to submit a separate list of sources. If your instructor requires a list of sources, ask whether you should include in it all sources consulted or only those cited. You can follow the format here for a list of *all* sources consulted. Follow the advice in 32g-2 for a list of only sources cited.

GUIDELINES FOR FORMATTING A BIBLIOGRAPHY

1. Center the word *Bibliography* two inches from the top edge of the paper. Leave four lines of space before starting the list.
2. Arrange the entries alphabetically by author's last name.
3. In general, give this information: author's last name, author's first name (if more than one author, use first–last order for the second and other authors); title; and publishing data. Follow each block of information with a period.
4. Start each item at the left margin, but if the item has two or more lines, indent all lines after the first line five spaces.
5. Double-space within *and* between entries.

INSTRUCTOR'S NOTES

6. If you use endnotes, place the bibliography on a new page after them. If you use footnotes, put the bibliography on a new page after the end of the text of your paper.
7. Do not number the first page of the bibliography, but number second and subsequent pages in continuous sequence with the text of your paper.

EXAMPLE

Bibliography

Thurman, Judith. Isak Dinesen: The Life of a Storyteller. New York: St. Martin's, 1982.

Zigrosser, Carl. The Book of Fine Prints, revised ed. New York: Crown, 1966.

Below are bibliographic entries for the note forms shown on pages 635–37.

BOOK WITH ONE AUTHOR

Didion, Joan. Salvador. New York: Simon & Schuster, 1983.

BOOK WITH TWO OR THREE AUTHORS

Wallace, Irving, David Wallechnsky, and Amy Wallace, Significa. New York: Dutton, 1983.

BOOK WITH A CORPORATE AUTHOR

Music Educators' National Conference. Music in the Senior High School. Washington: Music Educators' National Conference, 1959.

WORK IN SEVERAL VOLUMES OR PARTS

Kelley, Robert. The Shaping of the American Past, 2 vols.
Englewood Cliffs, N.J.: Prentice—Hall, 1975.

WORK IN AN ANTHOLOGY OR A COLLECTION

Tosh, Wayne. "Computer Linguistics." In Linguistics Today.
Ed. Archibald A. Hill. New York: Basic Books, 1969,
pp. 198—206.

ARTICLE IN A REFERENCE WORK

"Fraudulence in the Arts," The New Encylopaedia Britannica,
1979 ed.

ARTICLE FROM A JOURNAL WITH CONTINUOUS PAGINATION

Madden, William A. "Wuthering Heights: The Binding Passion."
Nineteenth—Century Fiction, 27 (1972), 127—154.

ARTICLE FROM A JOURNAL THAT PAGES EACH ISSUE SEPARATELY

Brookes, Michael C. T. "A Dean's Dilemmas." Journal of Basic
Writing, 5, No. 1 (1986), 65—76.

ARTICLE FROM A WEEKLY OR BIWEEKLY MAGAZINE OR NEWSPAPER

Randolph, Barbara. "Hailing the Eureka Factor." Time, 21
April 1986, p. 65.

ARTICLE FROM A MONTHLY PERIODCAL

Hogan, Patti. "Setting the Pace." Ms., Aug. 1985, pp. 20—32

ARTICLE FROM A DAILY NEWSPAPER

Dullea, Georgia. "Literary Folk Look for Solid Comfort." New
York Times, 16 April 1986, Sec. 3, p. 1, col. 1; p. 6,
cols. 1—6.

639

FILM

Bertolucci, Bernardo, dir. <u>Last Tango in Paris</u>. With Marlon
Brando. United Artists, 1972.

INTERVIEW

Stearns, Shirley. Personal interview. 17 July 1985.

WORK REPRINTED IN ANOTHER WORK

Auden, W. H. "Prologue: The Birth of Architecture." In <u>About
the House</u>. New York: Random; London: Faber and Faber),
1965. Rpt. in <u>Understanding Social Psychology</u>, 3rd ed.,
Stephen Worchel and Joel Cooper. Homewood, IL: Dorsey,
1983, p. 539.

◼‖ 34c
Understand writing in the social sciences.

Disciplines in the social sciences include subject areas such as
economics, education, geography, political science, psychology, and
sociology.

‖ 1
Understand methods of inquiry in the social sciences.

The social sciences ask questions that focus on the behavior of
people as individuals and in groups. As researchers and writers,
social scientists—such as economists and psychologists—want to
know what people do and why. To find out, they usually follow a
procedure that involves observation, investigation, and collection of
data.

Observation is a common method for research in the social sciences (as well as the natural sciences). If social scientists want to study how aggression emerges in small children, for example, they might observe a group of children at play. If you are asked to make observations, take along whatever tools or equipment you might need in order to work: writing or sketching materials, and perhaps recording or photographic equipment. As you make your observations, take very accurate and complete notes about what you see. If you use your own system of abbreviations to speed your note taking, make sure you can go back to your notes and understand them when the time comes to write up your observations. In your report, be sure to indicate what tools or equipment you took along and how you used it—because your method might have influenced what you saw (for example, taking photographs may make people too self-conscious to act as they usually do).

Interviewing is another common technique that social scientists use for collecting information. They are useful for gathering people's opinions and impressions of events. Remember, however, that interviews are not always a reliable way to gather factual information because people's memories are not precise. If your only source for facts is interviews, be sure to interview as many people as possible so that you can cross-check the information. As with observation, if you have scheduled an interview, be prepared with

GUIDELINES FOR WRITING QUESTIONS FOR A QUESTIONNAIRE

1. Know clearly what you want to find out.

2. Make questions easy to understand.

3. Make the questions fair—do not use slanted language (see 21a-5) or imply to people what *you* want to hear.

4. Test your questions on a small group of people before you use them for gathering data. If any question turns out to be hard for people to understand, or if it can be interpreted in more than one way, revise and retest it.

5. Use a sufficient number of people when you administer the final form of the questionnaire. You cannot generalize from small samples.

whatever note-taking tools you might need. Practice with those tools so they do not intrude on the interview process.

Questionnaires are often useful for gathering information in the social sciences. If you are asked to write questions for a questionnaire, you need to make sure that you get the information you are looking for. The way you phrase the questions will determine if your data are a true reflection of what people are thinking.

2
Understand writing purposes and practices in the social sciences.

Social scientists write to inform and to persuade by classifying, analyzing, or explaining a human problem or condition. They most often use rhetorical strategies such as definition, analogy, and analysis of a problem and its solution.

Definition is extremely important in the social sciences when ambiguous social issues and terms are the topic of discussion. For example, if you are writing a paper on substance abuse in the medical profession, you first have to define *substance* and *medical profession*. By *substance* do you mean alcohol and drugs or only drugs? When you refer to the medical profession, are you including nurses and lab technicians or just doctors? Without defining these terms, you can confuse your readers or lead them to the wrong conclusions.

Analogy helps social scientists make unfamiliar ideas clearer to their readers. When an unfamiliar idea is compared with one that is more familiar, the unfamiliar idea becomes easier to understand. For example, when sociologists talk of the "culture shock" that people feel when they live in a society very new to them, they might compare it to the reaction someone living today might have when moving suddenly hundreds of years into the future or the past.

Analysis can be helpful when social scientists write about problems and their solutions. For example, an economist studying a major automobile company in financial difficulties might analyze the situation to define a problem and ultimately to offer a solution. The economist might break the situation into parts, analyzing employee salaries and benefits, the selling price of cars, costs of doing business, and other aspects, to show how these parts relate to the financial status of the whole company. Then the economist might speculate about how specific changes in these parts would contribute to solving the automobile manufacturer's financial problems.

In college courses in the social sciences, some instructors ask students to write their personal reactions to information or experiences, in which case the first person *(I, we, our)* is acceptable. In most writing for the social sciences, however, writers use the third person *(he, she, it, they)*. Also, because the emphasis is on people or groups being observed rather than on the person doing the observing, the passive voice° is a frequent characteristic of such writing. An economist is likely to write, "The audits of The Frazzle Company were studied for indications of mismanagement and waste" instead of "I studied the audits of The Frazzle Company for indications of mismanagement and waste." Nevertheless, some material can be written about in the less austere active voice°: "The Frazzle Company seems eager to improve its methods of operation" and "The audits revealed that The Frazzle Company needs major overhauling."

3
Recognize different types of papers in the social sciences.

Two major types of papers in the social sciences are case studies and research papers.

Case studies

A case study is an intensive study of one group or individual. It is usually presented in a relatively fixed format, but the specific parts and order of case study formats vary. Most case studies contain the following components: (1) basic identifying information about the individual or group; (2) a history of the individual or group; (3) observations of the individual's or group's behavior; and (4) conclusions and perhaps recommendations as a result of the observations.

On pages 644–45 are parts of the first and last sections of a case study written by a student. Omissions are noted in the paper. The purpose of the case study was to determine if a young child was having trouble socializing in her day-care center.

643

SAMPLE CASE STUDY (EXCERPTS)

Case Study: Child Observation

Theresa L. Cox

<u>Basic Information</u>

Name: Molly

Setting: Early Education Center

Age: 3 years

Sex: Female

Time: 10:30 to 11:00 A.M.

Date: 6-30-85

Activity: Painting and play

<u>Observations</u>

Molly stretched her arms out and stated "Me" as the teacher was giving another child a paint pencil. She watched as the other child began painting, reached for this child's paint pencil and then turned to the teacher and stated "Me want some." Molly painted with a paint pencil, squeezed the paint pencil, and periodically touched the paint with her finger. She observed the other children frequently. Molly made marks on another girl's paper, and after being reprimanded, she returned to her paper. Molly marked another girl's arm and smiled broadly, until she was reprimanded. Molly then marked on the same child's arm a second time and placed in "time-out." She crossed her arms, looked down, frowned, and muttered "I'm mad."

[A section on background omitted here]

<u>Conclusion</u>

Molly expressed her independence and demonstrated a self-centered attitude in practically everything she did. She often

Cox 2

returned to activities for which she had earlier been

reprimanded, thus nonverbally (and sometimes verbally)

objecting to what she was told. Cognitively, Molly is

progressing from the sensorimotor stage to the stage of

symbolic thought. She frequently observed her environment,

was very expressive and imitative, and showed imagination in

her play. Molly's actions primarily met her needs, but she did

alter her behavior at times to avoid punishment. Overall, Molly

exemplifies the behavior of one type of typical toddler.

The case study begins with basic information and moves to a detailed account of Molly's activities. The study concludes with an interpretation of Molly's actions as compared to those of other children her age. The information in the observation section is actual observed activities. The conclusion contains ideas and interpretations of the observer based on the observed activities.

In writing a case study, always be sure to differentiate between the things you observed and the things you conclude or surmise—facts versus opinions. For example, if you are observing patients in a nursing home and you notice that several of them lie in bed in the afternoon facing the door, describe the situation; do not interpret it by saying that the patients are watching for visitors. The fact could be that medicines are administered by injection in the right hip every afternoon and the patients are therefore more comfortable if they lie on the left hip, causing them to face the door.

Research papers

Research papers are common in the social sciences. In some social science courses you may conduct an experiment or do other **primary research** that offers you first-hand exposure to information. Papers that report primary research often have fixed formats, depending on the subject area; be sure to ask your instructor if a specific format is required.

You may also be assigned a research paper based on your consulting **primary** and **secondary sources**—articles and books that report, summarize, and otherwise discuss the findings of primary research. You will find a list of reference works for subjects in the social sciences in 32e-5.

645

SAMPLE SOCIAL SCIENCE RESEARCH PAPER (EXCERPT)

America's Street People

Douglas Franklin

The number of homeless people in the cities of the United States is a social problem that has grown larger over the last few years. Estimates range from 250,000 (Huntley and Thorton, 1985) to 2-3 million (Bassuk, 1984; Fustero, 1984) people living in the streets of the United States. One fact experts agree on, however. The stereotypical "skid-row bum" is being replaced by a large assortment of people (Bassuk). As Fustero (1984) reports, the homeless now include "runaway children, immigrants, bag ladies, displaced families, a growing number of unemployed, alcoholics and drug abusers, and the mentally ill" (p. 58).

These changes in the size and nature of the homeless population have many causes. Two stand out. First, the deinstitutionalization of the mentally ill (Bassuk; Fustero) led to a huge outpouring of people unable to take care of themselves. This trend of releasing people from mental institutions "followed the widespread introduction in the 1950s of psychoactive drugs, which seemed to offer the possibility of rehabilitating psychotic people within a community setting" (Bassuk, p. 41). Second, availability of low-cost housing in the cities has dropped sharply since single-room occupancy and other modest facilities have given way to urban development projects (Fustero).

INSTRUCTOR'S NOTES

Franklin 6

References

Bassuk, E. L. (1984, July). The homelessness problem. _Scientific American_, pp. 40–45.

Fustero, S. (1984, February). Home on the street. _Psychology Today_, pp. 56–63.

Huntley, S., & Thorton, J. (1985, December 9). Shielding the homeless from a deadly winter. _U.S. News and World Report_, p. 79.

Here is an excerpt from a social science research paper by a student. It uses the style of documentation established by the American Psychological Association (APA), described in detail in 34c-4. Its purpose is to inform readers about the problem of homeless people living in cities of the United States.

4
Know documentation style in the social sciences.

Writers use **documentation** to give credit to the sources they have used. (A writer who does not credit a source is guilty of **plagiarizing**—a serious academic offense discussed at length in Chapter 31.) Styles of documentation differ among the disciplines.

In the social sciences, the American Psychological Association (APA) style is a common method of documentation. APA style uses parenthetical citations to refer briefly to a source and a References list to give detailed information on all sources referred to in the paper. All citations in your paper must have equivalent entries listing bibliographic facts in the References list, and no items can appear in References that have not been cited in your paper. Notes serve only to convey content information not included in your paper.

INSTRUCTOR'S NOTES

Here are basic guidelines to help you use APA parenthetical citations and references. For complete information covering all types of citations, see the *Publication Manual of the American Psychological Association* (1983, or later if available).

GUIDELINES FOR PARENTHETICAL CITATIONS IN APA STYLE

1. If a parenthetical citation comes at the end of your sentence, place the sentence's period after the parentheses.
2. If you are paraphrasing or summarizing material and you do *not* mention the name of the author in your text, do this: (Jones, 1982).
3. If you are quoting and you do *not* mention the name of the author in your text, do this: (Jones, 1982, p. 65).
4. If you are paraphrasing, summarizing, or quoting material and *do* mention the name of the author in your text, do this: (p. 65).
5. If you use more than one source written in the same year by the same author(s), assign letters (*a, b,* etc.) to the works in the References list and do this for a parenthetical reference: (Jones, 1983a).
6. If you refer to a work more than once, give the author's name and year only the first time; then use only the name.
7. If you cite several sources in one place, put them in alphabetical order by authors' last names and separate the sources with a semicolon: (Bassuk, 1984; Fustero, 1984).

GUIDELINES FOR THE APA REFERENCES LIST

1. Arrange the list of sources cited alphabetically by author's last name. For two or more works by an author, arrange the works by date, most recent first.
2. Start with an author's last name, followed by initials for the author's first and middle names. If there is more than one author, name them all (up to six authors)—again starting with the last name and using initials for first and middle names. If there are over six authors, use only the first author and the words *et al.*
3. Put the date of publication in parentheses immediately after the author's name. If you list two works by the same author published in the same year, assign letters (*a, b,* etc.) to the year: (1984a), (1984b).

648

4. Put the title after the year of publication. Capitalize only the first word and any proper names in a title or subtitle. Do not put articles in quotation marks. Underline titles.
5. Put the city of publication and the publisher next. Use short forms for the names of well-known publishers: New York: Harper.
6. Put page numbers next, but use *p.* or *pp.* only for page numbers of articles in newspapers or popular magazines. Do not use *p.* or *pp.* with page numbers of articles in professional journals. In contrast, parenthetical references to specific pages, always include *p.* or *pp.*—no matter what type of source.
7. Start each item at left margin, but if the item has two or more lines, indent all lines after the first line five spaces.

Here are sample references in APA style for common types of source material.

BOOK WITH ONE AUTHOR

> Toynbee, A. (1939). <u>A study of history</u>. New York: Oxford
> University Press.

BOOK WITH TWO OR THREE AUTHORS

> Smith, R. E., Sarason, I. G., & Sarason, B. R. (1982).
> <u>Psychology: The frontiers of behaviors</u>. New York:
> Harper.

WORK IN AN ANTHOLOGY OR A COLLECTION

> Ambrose, J. A. (1961). The development of the smiling
> response in early infancy. In B. M. Foss (Ed.),
> <u>Determinants of infant behavior</u>. New York: Wiley.

ARTICLE IN A REFERENCE WORK

> Family and marriage. (1979). <u>Encyclopaedia Britannica</u>.

649

A BOOK WITH A CORPORATE AUTHOR

U.S. Department of Commerce. (1985) <u>Statistical abstract of</u>
<u>the United States</u>. Washington, DC: U.S. Government
Printing Office.

ARTICLE FROM A JOURNAL WITH CONTINUOUS PAGINATION

Bernstein, B. (1960). Language and social class. <u>British</u>
<u>Journal of Sociology</u>, <u>11</u>, 271–276.

ARTICLE FROM A JOURNAL THAT PAGES EACH ISSUE SEPARATELY

Maines, D. R. (1977) Tactile relationships in the subway as
affected by racial, sexual, and crowded seating
situations. <u>Environmental Psychology and Nonverbal</u>
<u>Behavior</u>. <u>2</u>(2), 100–109.

**AN ARTICLE FROM A WEEKLY, BIWEEKLY, OR MONTHLY MAGAZINE, OR
WEEKLY NEWSPAPER**

Jarmulowski, V. (1985, February). Blended families: A
growing American phenomenon . . . Who are they?
<u>Ms.</u>, pp. 33–34.

ARTICLE FROM A DAILY NEWSPAPER

Castillo, A. (1980, November 2). Mystery resurfaces. <u>The</u>
<u>Courier-Journal</u>, p. A22.

■|| 34d
Understand writing in the natural and technological sciences.

Disciplines in the natural and technological sciences include
astronomy, biology, chemistry, engineering, geology, physics, computer science, health sciences, and electrical or mechanical technology.

650

1
Understand methods of inquiry in the sciences.

The natural and technological sciences ask questions about natural phenomena. The sciences adhere to key principles of research: observation, collection, and organization of physical and factual material. The purpose of scientific investigation is discovery; scientists observe and attempt to explain natural phenomena. To do this, scientists formulate and test hypotheses in order to explain cause and effect systematically and objectively.

The **scientific method,** commonly used in the sciences to make discoveries, is a procedure for gathering information related to a specific hypothesis. A hypothesis is a tentative explanation for an observed phenomenon. In an attempt to confirm or reject the hypothesis, scientists do one or all of these: collect data related to the hypothesis, test the hypothesis through experimentation, form further hypotheses and investigate them. Scientists then draw conclusions about the hypothesis based on the data from their observations. The information gathered by observing natural events is known as **empirical evidence.** Ideas or opinions, even those stated by experts, never constitute empirical support for a scientific report. Here is a basic guide to the scientific method:

GUIDELINES FOR USING THE SCIENTIFIC METHOD

1. Formulate a hypothesis or question, defined as specifically as possible.
2. Collect "known" (previously published) information related to the hypothesis or question.
3. Plan a method of investigation to uncover unknown information.
4. Experiment, exactly following the investigative procedures you have outlined.
5. Analyze the results of the investigation.
6. Apply the results to the hypothesis or question and arrive at conclusions—and perhaps suggest additional hypotheses.

2

Understand writing purposes and practices in the sciences.

Scientists usually write to inform their audiences about some piece of research or to relate factual information about some topic. Sometimes a scientific paper's thesis is implied in the paper's statement of purpose. For example, when a geologist describes a rock formation for other geologists who are not able to visit the formation themselves, the writer's purpose is to inform, not to present the writer's own ideas or hypotheses. Similarly, a chemist describes an experiment in detail so that others may evaluate the scientific procedure or may duplicate the experiment to compare results.

Exactness is extremely important in scientific writing. Readers expect precise descriptions of procedures and findings, free of personal biases. Scientists expect to be able to *replicate*—repeat step-by-step—the experiment or other process and get the same outcome as the writer.

Completeness is another essential characteristic of scientific writing. A scientist who makes an observation does not always know what information might become important at a later date. For example, a researcher describing observations of the types of food brought to baby robins by their parents also should report other information, such as the times feedings occur, the behavior of the nestlings when food is presented, and the identity of the parent offering the food. Having recorded all this information, the researcher may gain unexpected insights. For example, the researcher may realize that food types tell only part of the story because the food presented depends on the parents' hunting preferences, the food available at a specific time of day, or the nestlings' preference. Unless complete information is available, the researcher and the readers can come to wrong conclusions about what determines the diet of nestling robins.

Because the sciences generally focus on the experiment rather than the experimenter, and on objective observation rather than subjective interpretation, scientific report writing is often written in a style that distances a subject from both writer and reader. As a result, the passive voice° is common in scientific and technical reports because the observer of the action is often either unimportant or understood to be present. Therefore, do not refer to *the experimenter* or *the technician* unless that person is the focus of the discussion. For example, readers expect to see "The robins were observed feeding over a 24-hour period" rather than "I observed the robins over a 24-hour period." Unless you are writing a personal-reaction paper for a college course, generally avoid the first person *(I, we, our)*.

652

When writing for the sciences, often you are expected to follow fixed formats, which are designed to summarize a project and its results efficiently. Even though the format establishes the overall organization, you must organize the presentation of information within each section. Also, writers in the sciences often use charts, graphs, tables, diagrams, and other illustrations to present material to readers. In fact, illustrations sometimes show complex material more clearly than words can.

3
Recognize different types of papers in the sciences.

Two major types of papers in the sciences are scientific reports and scientific review papers.

Scientific reports

Scientific reports tell about observations and experiments. A formal scientific report must accurately represent the procedures and results. Imprecise or inexact reports mislead other researchers. Formal reports include the seven sections (plus the title) described below; less formal reports, such as are sometimes assigned in introductory college courses, might not include an abstract or a review of the literature. Be sure to ask your instructor which sections to include if you are assigned a scientific report. Here are the sections of a scientific report, listed in the order in which they should appear.

The **title** should be exact and should include the main idea of your research. If the work gets published, it will be catalogued according to its key words. If your title is not descriptive of your main point, your work will not be found when other scientists do library research.

An **abstract** is a very condensed summary of the report. Its purpose is to give the reader a rapid overview and understanding of the contents without the reader's having to go through the entire presentation of methods, data, and conclusions.

The **introduction** states the purpose of the research, explains the problem addressed by the hypothesis, states the hypothesis, and gives the reasons for investigating the problem. The introduction also may include two other matters: any background information necessary to explain the hypothesis or to interpret the research, and a "review of the literature," which presents previous references that relate to the hypothesis. In some courses students are not required to include a literature review.

The **methods and materials** section describes the equipment, materials (such as chemicals), and procedures used in the experiment or investigation.

653

The **results** section provides information obtained from experiments, tests, and observations. (In some reports this section is combined with the discussion section.) For ease of reading, the information is presented from most-to-least important or—less frequently—chronologically. Charts, graphs, and photographs can be included as needed to explain material.

The **discussion** section evaluates the results and examines what the experiment means. The section starts with a statement that reports whether the hypothesis was supported by the research. Questions underlying the rest of the discussion might include: (1) Do the results agree with the results of previous experiments discussed in references? (2) If the results do not support the hypothesis, what reasons can be suggested? (3) If the experiment failed, how did it happen and why? All general statements here must be supported by concrete evidence.

The **conclusions** section lists conclusions about the hypotheses and the outcomes, with particular attention to any theoretical implications that can be drawn from the work. Also this section can include *specific* suggestions for further research, but it should avoid vague statements such as "further research is suggested."

References cited lists references cited in the review of the literature in a report's introduction. Its format conforms to the requirements of the documentation style in the discipline (see 34d-4). Students are sometimes not required to review the literature and therefore do not give a reference list.

SAMPLE SCIENCE REPORT (EXCERPTS)

An Experiment to Predict Vestigial Wings

in an F_2 Drosophila Population

by Avery Bird

INTRODUCTION

The purpose of this experiment was to observe second filial generation (F_2) wing structures in Drosophila. The hypothesis was that abnormalities in vestigial wing structures would follow predicted genetic patterns.

654

METHODS AND MATERIALS

On February 7, four <u>Drosophila</u> (P_1) were observed. Observation was made possible by etherizing the parents (after separating them from their larvae), placing them on a white card, and observing them under a dissecting microscope. The observations were recorded on a chart.

On February 14, the larvae taken from the parents on February 7 had developed to adults (F_1) and they were observed as on February 7. The observations were recorded on the chart started on February 7.

On February 19, the second filial generation (F_2) was supposed to be observed. This, however, was impossible because they did not hatch. The record chart had to be discontinued.

RESULTS

No observations of F_2 were possible. For the F_1 population it is interesting to note that according to the prediction, no members should have had vestigial wings. According to the observations, however, some members of F_1 did have vestigial wings.

[Discussion section omitted]

CONCLUSIONS

Two explanations are possible to explain vestigial wings in the F_1 population. Perhaps members from F_2 were present from the F_1 generation that was observed. This is doubtful since the incubation period is 10 days, and the time between observations was only 8 days. A second possible explanation is that the genotype of the male P_1 was not WW (indicating that both genes were for normal wings) but rather heterozygous (Ww). If this were true the following would be the first filial products:

655

```
        P₁   Ww × ww

        F₁   Ww ww      in a 1:1 ratio.
```

Thus, the possibility for vestigial wings would exist. The problem remains, however, that according to the observations the ratio was not 1:1 2:1 (i.e., 24 normal to 12 abnormal). One explanation could be that the total number was not large enough to extract an average. This experiment should be repeated to get F₂ data. Also, a larger F₁ sample should be used to see if the F₁ findings reported here are repeated.

Scientific reviews

A scientific review is a paper about published information on a scientific topic or issue. The purpose of the review is to inform readers about the current knowledge about the topic or issue. Sometimes the purpose of a scientific review is to suggest a new interpretation of the old material. Any reinterpretation is based on a synthesis of old information with new, more complete information. In such reviews, the writer must marshal evidence to persuade readers that the new interpretation is valid.

If you are assigned a review, do this: (1) choose a very limited scientific issue currently being researched; (2) use information that is current—the more recently published the articles, books, and journals you consult, the better; (3) accurately summarize and paraphrase material—as explained in Chapter 31; and (4) document your sources, as explained in 34d-4. You will find a list of reference works for the sciences in 32e-5. You can use headings to help your reader understand your paper's organization and progression of ideas.

4
Know documentation style in the sciences.

Writers use **documentation** to give credit to the sources they have used. (A writer who does not credit a source is guilty of **pla-**

giarizing—a serious academic offense discussed at length in Chapter 31.) Styles of documentation differ among the disciplines.

The documentation styles of the various fields within the natural and technological sciences may vary slightly from one another. Many fields have manuals (see list below) that explain the documentation style common to their professional journals. If you are writing in a field that does not have a style manual, refer to a journal in the field and imitate its documentation style. Most style manuals also provide useful information about writing practices in the field, covering such matters as abbreviations, spelled-out numbers versus numerals, special formats, literature citation, writing standards, and format issues.

In each course, ask your instructor what documentation style is required. If the choice is yours, use the style of your major field so that you can practice it, or follow the style of the subject of your course. Here is a list of some style manuals in the sciences.

BIOLOGY

Council of Biology Editors Style Manual Committee. *CBE Style Manual*. 5th ed. Bethesda, MD: Council of Biology, 1983.

CHEMISTRY

American Chemical Society. *Handbook for Authors of Papers in American Chemical Society Publications*. Washington, DC: American Chemical Society, 1978.

GEOLOGY

U.S. Geological Survey. *Suggestions to Authors of Reports of the United States Geological Survey*. 6th ed. Washington, DC: Department of the Interior, 1978.

PHYSICS

American Institute of Physics. *Style Manual for Guidance in Preparation of Papers*. 3rd ed. New York: American Institute of Physics.

To take an example, the *CBE Style Manual* suggests documentation much like the American Psychological Association (APA) system explained on pages 647–50. Brief information about a reference is given in parentheses in the text, and full bibliographic information is given in a Literature Cited list at the end of the paper.

On the next page is a paragraph and part of a reference list from a student paper that follows conventions given in the *CBE Style Manual*. Notice that in the paragraph scientific names are underlined, and that the genus is capitalized and the species is not *(Passer griseus)*. Name–year parenthetical references are given

657

within the text—except in the last sentence, where only the year of publication is given because the source author's name is part of the sentence.

In the Literature Cited, notice that (1) the entries are typed "block style" (without indentations); (2) single spacing is used within a reference and double spacing is used between the references; (3) the list is alphabetical according to author's last name; (4) titles are neither underlined nor put in quotation marks; (5) only the first word and proper names are capitalized in titles; and (6) only initials are used for author's first and middle names.

SAMPLE SCIENCE RESEARCH (EXCERPT)

Brian D. Anderson

The genus <u>Passer</u> is believed to have arisen on the African savanna during the late Miocene or early Pliocene (Johnston and Klitz 1977). Ten species occur in Africa, seven of these in Africa exclusively. Consequently, an African origin seems reasonable. Morphologically, all are similar and are primarily adapted for grain and seed eating. One might reasonably expect a group such as this to have arisen in a savanna biotope. Summers-Smith (1963) suggested that the ancestor form may have been very much like <u>Passer griseus</u> (Gray-headed sparrow), which currently inhabits the sub-Saharan grasslands.

Literature Cited

Johnston, R. F.; Klitz, J. Variations and evolution in a grainivorous bird: the house sparrow. In: Pinowski, J.; Kendeigh, S. C., eds. Grainivorous birds in ecosystems. Cambridge, England: University press; 1977.

Summers-Smith, J. D. The house sparrow. Cambridge, England: University Press; 1963.

35
BUSINESS WRITING

Business writing requires of you what other kinds of writing call for: understanding your audience and your purpose. When you write for the business world—perhaps a letter asking for a job interview or a memo or report for an employer—keep five points in mind.

- Consider your audience's needs and expectations.
- Show that you understand the purpose for a business communication and the context in which it takes place.
- Put essential information first.
- Make your points clearly and directly.
- Use conventional formats.

▮‖ 35a

Understand how to write and format a business letter.

Business letters are clear, usually short communications written to give information, to build good will, or to establish a foundation for discussions or transactions. Experts in business

TEACHING TIP
Some students expect business writing to involve rules about margins, indentations, and abbreviations. While such concerns do matter, they should take only a small part of your time. Format can be taught in just a few lessons; the emphasis in business writing is on audience, tone, and organization.

Audience: Business writers need to keep acutely aware of their audiences. As business correspondence is aimed at a particular individual or limited group of individuals, rather than the general audience of essays, in certain aspects business writing differs markedly from essay writing. The most obvious difference is that the use of *you* and *I/we* is preferable to the third person often used in essays.

Tone: The tone of business correspondence needs to be adjusted to suit the

659

35b

TEACHING TIP (CONT.)

actual relationship between author and audience. It is perfectly conceivable that a business person might write a very formal memo to the staff of one department about lax security and a minute later write a relatively friendly memo to another department congratulating it for exceeding production goals. The key word in deciding on the appropriate tone is *relationship*. Your students can judge the nature of the relationship by asking themselves a few questions as they prepare to write: Who is this person? How long and under what circumstances have we known one another? What do I want him or her to do? No matter what the relationship, correspondence should be written in standard, clear, and honest English. See Chapter 21 for discussions of levels of formality and artificial language.

and government agree that the letters likely to get results are short, simple, direct, and human. As part of International Paper Company's series of advertisements "The Power of the Printed Word," Malcolm Forbes of *Forbes* magazine gave these recommendations for effective business letters:

1. Call the person by name.
2. Tell what your letter is about in the first paragraph.
3. Be honest.
4. Be clear and specific.
5. Use accurate English.
6. Be positive and natural.
7. Edit ruthlessly.

For business letters and envelopes, you can use the standard formats shown on pages 664 and 665.

▆ǁ 35b

Understand how to write and format a job-application letter.

One important type of business letter is the job-application letter. (See the sample job-application letter written by a student, Lee Franco, on page 666.) Specific advice about each part of the letter is given in the chart below.

COORDINATED RESOURCES

Transparency masters are available for many of the screened charts and/or lists in this chapter.

Students can practice and test their knowledge of terms, key concepts, and applications of material in this chapter by using the *Study Guide to the S & S Handbook for Writers*, West.

GUIDELINES FOR JOB APPLICATION LETTERS	
YOUR ADDRESS	To the right, type your address as you would on an envelope. Be sure to give as your address a place where you can be reached **by letter.** Be sure to give the zip code.
DATE	Put the date below your address.

35b

INSIDE ADDRESS	(1) Direct your letter to a specific person. You can phone a company to find out the name of the personnel director or a department head, if you know what department the job is in. (2) Be accurate. With a misspelled name or the wrong address, your letter may never get to its destination. If it does, inaccuracies make you seem careless.
SALUTATION	Again, be accurate. No one likes to see his or her name misspelled. If you are replying to an ad that gives only a post-office box number (no personal or company names), omit the salutation. Start the opening paragraph right below the inside address.
INTRODUCTORY PARAGRAPH	State your purpose for writing and the source of your information about the job.
BODY PARAGRAPH(S)	Interest the reader in the skills and talents you offer by mentioning whatever personal experience you have that relates to the job. Say that you have enclosed your resume, but do *not* summarize it.
CLOSING PARAGRAPH	Suggest an interview, stating when you are available for one and when you will call to make arrangements.
CLOSING	*Sincerely* is generally appropriate for a job-application letter.
NAME LINES	Type your full name below your signature.
NOTATION	If you are enclosing any other materials with your letter of application, type *Enc.:* and briefly list what you are enclosing.

TEACHING TIP

Few letters are as difficult for students to write as those they send in hopes of getting a job interview. The following suggestions can be adapted to any job-seeking situation.

Before writing a letter of application, the student should already have prepared a stock résumé, one that can be used for any job in the student's area of interest. A properly written résumé will be good for six months to a year or more. As it lists the basics of a career to date, it should not have to be redone for each job sought.

In the cover letter, students should tell a prospective employer what they can bring to the job, why they feel they are qualified—not why they want the job. This is the place to expand upon the information listed in the résumé. Do not, however, summarize or repeat large parts of the résumé.

In paragraph 1, students should tell how they found out about the job (ad, friend with the company). In paragraphs 2 to 4, students should pick three skills or personal qualities that they know are needed for the job. These may include, but are not limited to, using office machines, driving a delivery truck, preparing a payroll, speaking a second language, being available for night shifts or out-of-town travel.

In the next paragraph, students should discuss their specific qualifications. They can draw upon work experience, education, volunteer work, family responsibilities, and hobbies. In the final paragraph, students should thank the reader for taking the time to consider the application. They should also express a wish for an interview at the employer's convenience and include a phone number and address.

661

■‖ 35c

Understand how to write and format a résumé.

A **résumé** is an easy-to-read, factual document that presents your qualifications for employment. (The résumé that Lee Franco enclosed with her job-application letter is shown on page 667.) All résumés cover certain standard items:

> name, address, phone number; education; past experience; skills and talents; publications, awards, honors, membership in professional organizations; list of references or a statement that they are "available upon request."

A résumé gives you an opportunity to present a positive picture of yourself to a prospective employer. You are expected to give information about your skills, your experience, and your education. Employers understand that college students may have limited experience in the business world. Think of headings that allow you to emphasize your strengths. For example, if you have never done paid work, do not use *Business Experience*. You can use *Work Experience* if you have done volunteer or other unpaid work. If the experience you can offer an employer is that you have run school or social events, you might use *Organizational Experience*. If your greatest strength is your academic record, put your educational attainments first.

You may choose to arrange your résumé with the most important information first and the least important last. Lee Franco's is a good example of an emphatic résumé. Or you may choose to arrange information in chronological (time) order, a sequence that is good for showing a steady work history or solid progress in a particular field. Stephen Schmit's résumé (see page 668) is chronological.

■‖ 35d

Understand how to write and format a memo.

A **memo** can call for action or document action; it can provide a written record of a conversation; it can make a brief, informal report. A sample memo, its parts labeled, is shown. You can follow it for format guidance. When you are writing a memo, determine who should receive the information by evaluating the audience and deciding the memo's goals. At the **"to" line** list the person or people who need to act on the information in the memo. List for **distribution** anyone else you think should be informed.

662

Use the **subject line** to define and limit the memo's contents. The subject line should also set the tone for the message, signaling to the reader your attitude toward the subject. A subject line is like an essay title.

In the **message,** give the most important information first. Give additional information or secondary points in decreasing order of importance, but include them only if they are essential to the picture. If you expect action of some kind from the memo, end the memo with a clear statement of your expectations—about the action and about the time the action should take place.

MEMO FORMAT

Date	12 March 19XX
"To" Line	To: Len DeBeers
Sender	From: Ann Soukolov
Subject Line	Subject: Annual Meeting Publications Support

Message   For the annual meeting of our stockholders on April 3 we need the active participation of the following people:

  —speech writer
  —graphic artist
  —graphics production specialist
  —one copy editor
  —typists and proofreaders

We will use the office space on the second floor of the office building next to the auditorium. Word processing equipment should be in place by Monday. Six phones were installed today.

Art Smith, the meeting manager, will be here on Monday for a kick off meeting at 10:00 a.m.

Please prepare a detailed list of critical items for that meeting.

Typist's
Notation   AS/ls

Distribution   Dist: A. Adams
              R. Traub
              T. Ziff-Smith

TEACHING TIP

Some people are fascinated by those initials and abbreviations they see in letters, at the left margin a few lines below the signature. Few of our students have any need to use these on a regular basis, but in case you are asked about these symbols, here's a quick review.

AB:cd The writer's initials followed by the typist's initials (known as reference initials). Practice varies in the use of capital and lowercase letters.

Enclosures: 2 Typed below the reference initials, this notation alerts the opener of the mail to the presence of additional material: brochures, résumés, photographs. A multi-page enclosure counts as one. Sometimes this notation is written out as "Enclosed: résumé and letter of reference."

cc: Elliott Goldhush Typed below the reference initials (and below any enclosure notation), the abbreviation *cc* indicates that a carbon copy has been sent. Carbon paper is passé, but the abbreviation lingers. The notation is followed by a name or initials.

P.S. A postscript may be added after everything else to highlight a point made within the letter or to add a brief personal message. Do not use a postscript to add important information that you forgot to include in the letter; rewrite the letter. Strings of postscripts (P.P.S., etc.) are definitely not suitable for business writing.

INSTRUCTOR'S NOTES

TEACHING TIP: SALUTATIONS

The salutation is the first thing a reader sees, so it must be suitable if the letter is to be taken seriously. In most situations the salutation presents no problem, but sometimes the writer has to make a difficult decision. Here are some guidelines:

1. When the recipient's name is known: *Dear Mr. ____; Dear Ms. ____; Dear Mrs. ____; Dear Miss ____.*

2. When the writer normally calls the recipient by his or her first name and when the letter is relatively informal: *Dear Heidi; Dear Elliot.*

3. When the letter is going to a position within an organization and the writer has not been able to get an individual's name: *Manager, Customer Service Department; Dear Manager.*

4. When the writer does not know the sex of the recipient: *Dear Mr. or Ms. Gery; Dear Director; Dear Mr. or Ms. Director.*

5. When the recipient is a group: *Dear Members of ____; Dear Committee Members.*

6. When there will be many anonymous recipients: *Dear Homeowners; Dear Student; Dear Customer.*

BUSINESS LETTER FORMAT

AlphaOmega Industries, Inc.
123456 Motor Parkway
Fresh Hills, CA 55555 — Letterhead

December 28, 19xx — Date

Ron R. London, Sales Director
Seasonal Products Corp.
5000 Seasonal Place
Wiscasset, ME 00012 — Inside address

Subject: Spring Promotional Effort — Subject line

Dear Ron: — Salutation

Since we talked last week, I have completed plans for the Spring promotion of the products that we market jointly. AlphaOmega and Seasonal Products should begin a direct mailing of the enclosed brochure on January 28th.

I have secured several mailing lists that contain the names of people who have a positive economic profile for our products. The profile and the outline of the lists are attached. — Message

Do you have additional approaches for the promotion? I would like to meet with you on January 6 to discuss them, and to work out the details of the project.

Please call me and let me know if a meeting next week at your office accomodates your schedule.

Sincerely, — Closing

Alan Stone — Signature

Alan Stone, Director of Special Promotions — Name, Title

AS/kw — Typist's notation

Copy to: Ken Lane, V.P. Marketing
Encl.: Brochure; Mailing Lists; Customer Profile — Other notations

BUSINESS ENVELOPE FORMAT

```
AlphaOmega Industries, Inc.
123456 Motor Parkway
Fresh Hills, CA 55555


          Ron R. London, Sales Director
          Seasonal Products Corp.
          5000 Seasonal Place
          Wiscasset, ME 00012
```

GUIDELINES FOR BUSINESS LETTER AND ENVELOPE

LETTERHEAD	If printed stationery is not available, type the company name and address centered at top of opaque white paper, 8½ × 11″.
DATE	Place the date at left margin under letterhead, when typing in block form as shown in the example. If using paragraph indentations, type date to end at right margin.
INSIDE ADDRESS	Direct the letter to a specific person. Be accurate in spelling the name and in the address. If unsure of your information, call the company and ask questions.
SUBJECT LINE	Type to end at right margin. Be concise; in a few words inform your reader of the subject.
SALUTA-TION	Use a first name only if you know the person. Otherwise, use *Mr.* or *Ms.* or whatever title is applicable.
CLOSING	*Sincerely* is generally appropriate unless you know the person very well and wish to use *Cordially*. Leave about four lines for your signature.
NAME LINES	Type your name and title. The title can be on the same line as your name or on the next line.
ENVELOPE	Use block form. If printed envelope is not available, type the company name and return address in the upper left corner of a 9½ × 4″ envelope. In the center of envelope, type the name and address of the person to receive your letter.

665

JOB-APPLICATION LETTER

422 Broward
University of Texas at Arlington
Arlington, Texas 75016
May 15, 19XX

Rae Clemens, Director of Human Resources
Taleno, Ward Marketing, Inc.
1471 Summit Boulevard
Houston, Texas 78211

Dear Ms. Clemens:

I am answering the advertisement for a marketing trainee
that Taleno, Ward placed in today's Houston Chronicle.

Marketing has been one of the emphases of my course work
here at the University of Texas, Arlington, as you will
see on my enclosed résumé. This past year, I gained some
practical experience as well, when I developed marketing
techniques that helped to turn my typing service into a
busy and profitable small business.

Successfully marketing the typing service (with flyers,
advertisements in college publications, and even a two-
for-one promotion) makes me a very enthusiastic novice. I
can think of no better way to become a professional than
working for Taleno, Ward.

I will be here at the Arlington campus through August 1.
You can reach me by phone at 555-1976. Unless I hear from
you before, I'll call on May 25 about setting up an
interview.

Sincerely,

Lee Franco

Lee Franco

Enc.: Résumé

EMPHATIC RÉSUMÉ

MARKETING TRAINEE

Lee Franco
422 Broward
University of Texas at Arlington
Arlington, Texas 75016

713:555-1976

The experience I acquired marketing my typing service
provided me with a good practical background for a
position as a marketing trainee.

MARKETING EXPERIENCE (program for campus typing service)
Evaluated typing-service capabilities; analyzed market
for service; drew up and implemented marketing plan;
produced 2-color flyer, designed print ads and wrote
copy, developed and ran special promotion. August 19XX
to February 19XX

BUSINESS EXPERIENCE
Type-Right Typing Service: Ran campus typing service
for two years. Duties included word processing
(Wordstar, Displaywrite, SuperCalc), proofreading,
billing and other financial record-keeping, and
customer contact. August 19XX to present

Archer & Archer Advertising: Worked as general
assistant in the copy department under direct
supervision of John Allen, Director. Duties included
proofreading, filing, direct client contact. June 19XX
to August 19XX

ADDITIONAL EXPERIENCE
Coordinated student-employment service at Hawthorne
High School, Baton Rouge, Louisiana. Duties included
contacting students to fill jobs with local employers,
arranging interviews, and writing follow-up reports on
placements.

EDUCATION
University of Texas, Arlington
B.A. May 19XX, Psychology, Marketing

EXTRACURRICULAR
Marketing Club, Computer Graphics Society

References available upon request.

CHRONOLOGICAL RÉSUMÉ

STEPHEN L. SCHMIT
5230 ST. STEPHENS STREET
BOSTON, MASSACHUSETTS 02188
617–555–8165

CAREER QUALIFICATIONS
    Technical writer trained in preparation of technical
    definitions and descriptions, manuals, catalogues, part
    lists, and instructional materials. Experienced in eval-
    uating and editing computer documentation containing
    syntax formats.

WORK EXPERIENCE
    Northeastern University, Boston, Massachusetts
    Reading and Writing Specialist, English Language Ctr.
    March–July 1987, January–March 1988

        Created individual lesson plans for each student as-
        signed to the Reading and Writing Laboratory. Designed
        materials for use in the Laboratory. Ran the Laboratory
        for approximately one hundred students for twenty hours
        each week, maintained records of students' work, and
        prepared written and oral reports on student progress
        and the operation of the Laboratory.

    Tutor of Foreign Students, September 1985–Present

        Integrated foreign students into a large urban school
        and community while being a positive role model educa-
        tionally and socially.

    William M. Mercer, Incorporated Boston, Massachusetts,
    September–December 1984

        Data Processing and general office duties. Initiated and
        implemented a CRT search system for office personnel.

    American Architect Magazine, New York, N.Y., 1981–1984
        Student intern.

SPECIAL SKILLS
    BASIC programming. PASCAL, Editing and Graphics courses to
    be completed June 1988.

EDUCATION
    Northeastern University, Boston, Massachusetts
    Bachelor of Arts, June 1986

    Concentration: English with minors in Technical Communica-
    tions and Economics.
    Activities: Selected to serve on the Residence Judicial
    Board, an impartial group of faculty, staff and students
    who adjudicate discipline problems; Northeastern News;
    Northeastern Yearbook staff.

668

APPENDIX A
WRITING ESSAY TESTS

Writing answers for essay tests is one of the most important writing tasks in college. Essay tests give you the chance to synthesize and apply your knowledge, thereby helping your instructor determine what you have learned.

Common in the social sciences and humanities, essay tests are becoming increasingly common in the natural sciences as well. Essay tests demand that you recall information and also put assorted pieces of that information into contexts that lead to generalizations you can support. For example, from your reading and lecture notes, you may know many facts about the battles in the Korean War, but the facts become significant when you use them to show one side's superior military strength, or a general's brilliant tactics, or a pattern of defeats from seemingly inconsequential misjudgments.

Most essay questions contain what is sometimes called a **cue word,** a word of direction that tells what the content of your answer is expected to emphasize. Knowing the major cue words and their meanings can increase your ability to plan efficiently and to write effectively. Be guided by the following list of cue words and sample essay-test questions.

669

CUE WORDS FOUND IN QUESTIONS FOR ESSAY TESTS

Analyze means to separate something into parts and discuss the parts.

> Analyze Socrates' discussion of "good life" and "good death."

Clarify means to make clear.

> Clarify T. S. Eliot's idea of tradition.

Classify means to arrange into groups on the basis of shared characteristics.

> Classify the different types of antipredator adaptations.

Compare and contrast means to show similarities and differences.

> Compare and contrast the reproductive cycles of a moss and a flowering plant.

Criticize means to give your opinion concerning the strengths and weaknesses of something.

> Criticize the architectural function of the modern football stadium.

Define means to give the definition of something and in so doing to separate it from similar things.

> Define the term "yellow press."

Describe means to explain features to make clear an object, procedure, or event.

> Describe the chain of events that constitutes the movement of a sensory impulse along a nerve fiber.

Discuss means to consider and evaluate as many details as possible concerning an issue or event.

> Discuss the effects of television viewing on modern attitudes toward violence.

Evaluate means to give your opinion about the value of something.

> Evaluate Margaret Mead's contribution to the field of anthropology.

Explain means to give reasons for something.

> Explain how the amount of carbon dioxide in the blood regulates rates of heartbeat and breathing.

Illustrate means to give examples of something.

> Illustrate the use of symbolism in Richard Wright's novel *Native Son*.

Interpret means to explain the meaning of something.

> Give your interpretation of Robert Frost's poem "Fire and Ice."

Justify means to show or prove that something is valid or correct.

> Justify the existence of labor unions in today's economy.

Prove means to present evidence that cannot be refuted logically or with other evidence.

> Prove that smoking is a major cause of lung cancer.

Relate means to show the connections between two or more things.

> Relate increases in specific crimes in 1932-33 to the prevailing economic conditions.

Review means to reexamine, summarize, or reprise something.

> Review the structural arrangements in proteins to explain the meaning of the term *polypeptide*.

Show means to point out or demonstrate something.

> Show what effects the second law of thermodynamics predicts for Halley's comet.

Summarize means to repeat briefly the major points of something.

> Summarize the major benefits of compulsory education.

Support means to argue in favor of something.

> Support the position that passage of the equal rights amendment must occur at the national rather than the state level.

671

Each essay question also has one or more **key words** that tell you the information, topics, and ideas you are to write about. For example, in the question "Criticize the architectural function of the modern football stadium," the key words are "architectural function" and "football stadium." To answer the question successfully, you must define "architectural function," then describe the typical modern football stadium (mentioning major variations when important), and then you must discuss how well the typical football stadium meets the principles you named in your definition of "architectural function." Similarly, in the question, "Classify the different types of antipredator adaptations" you need to define "antipredator adaptions" by dividing them into groups based on their shared characteristics.

Here are two answers to the question, "Classify the different types of antipredator adaptations." The first one is successful; the second is not. The sentences are numbered for your reference.

Answer 1

(1) Although many antipredator adaptations have evolved in the animal kingdom, they all can be classified into four major categories according to the prey's response to the predator. (2) The first category is hiding techniques. (3) These techniques include cryptic coloration and behavior in which the prey assumes characteristics of an inanimate object or part of a plant. (4) The second category is early enemy detection. (5) The prey responds to alarm signals from like prey or other kinds of prey before the enemy can get too close. (6) Evasion of the pursuing predator is the third category. (7) Prey that move erratically or in a compact group are displaying this technique. (8) The fourth category is active repulsion of the predator. (9) The prey kills, injures, or sickens the predator, establishing that it represents danger to the predator.

Answer 2

(1) Antipredator adaptations are the development of the capabilities to reduce the risk of attack from a predator without too much change in the life-supporting activities of the prey. (2) There are many different types of antipredator adaptations. (3) One type is camouflage, hiding from the predator by cryptic coloration or imitation of plant parts. (4) An example of this type of antipredator adaptation is the praying mantis. (5) A second type is the defense used by monarch butterflies, a chemical protection that makes some birds ill after eating the butterfly. (6) This protection may injure the bird by causing it to vomit, and it can educate the bird against eating other butterflies. (7) Detection and evasion are also antipredator adaptations.

672

Here is an explanation of what happens, sentence by sentence, in the two responses.

	ANSWER 1	**ANSWER 2**
Sentence 1	Sets up classification system and gives number of categories based on key word	Defines key word
Sentence 2	Names first category	Throwaway sentence—accomplishes nothing
Sentence 3	Defines first category	Names and defines first category
Sentence 4	Names second category	Gives an example for first category
Sentence 5	Defines second category	Gives an example for second (unnamed) category
Sentence 6	Names third category	Continues to explain example
Sentence 7	Defines third category	Names two categories
Sentence 8	Names fourth category	
Sentence 9	Defines fourth category	

Answer 1 sets about immediately answering the question by introducing a classification system as called for by the cue word, *classify*. Answer 2, on the other hand, defines the key word, a waste of time on a test that will be read by an audience of specialists. Answer 1 is tightly organized, easy to follow, and to-the-point, whereas answer 2 rambles, never manages to name the four categories, and says more around the subject than on it.

Remember that your purpose in answering essay exam questions is to show your instructor what you know in a clear, direct, and well-organized way. Most essay tests have a time limit, so you will do well to use well-developed strategies. Try to follow this plan:

673

STRATEGIES FOR WRITING ESSAY TESTS

1. Do not start writing immediately.

2. If the test has more than one question, read them all at the start. If you know from the beginning what you will have to answer, you will know what to expect and you will have a better sense of how to budget your time by either dividing it equally or allotting more for some questions. If you have a choice, select questions about which you know the most—and the ones whose cue words you can work with best.

3. Reread each question you are going to answer and then underline the cue and key words to determine exactly what the question asks for.

4. Use the writing process as much as possible within the constraints of the time limit. Try always to find time to plan and revise. For a one-hour test of one question, take about 10 minutes to jot down preliminary ideas about content and organization, and save at least 10 minutes to reread your answer and to revise and edit it. For a one-hour test with more than one question, divide your time for planning, drafting, and revising accordingly. If you suddenly become pressed for time— but try to avoid this—consider skipping a question you cannot answer well or a question that counts less on your total score.

5. Organize and develop your answer to provide what a question's cue and key words ask for.

The more you use these strategies, the better you will be able to use them to your advantage. Try to practice them, making up questions that might be on your test and timing yourself as you write the answers. Doing this offers you another benefit: if you study by anticipating possible questions and writing out the answers, you will be very well prepared if one or two of them show up on the test.

APPENDIX B
USING CORRECT MANUSCRIPT FORMAT

■∥ B1
Follow standard practices for typing or handwriting marks of punctuation.

PERIOD, QUESTION MARK, EXCLAMATION POINT . ? ! .?!

Do not space before these marks. Space twice after each mark when it ends a sentence.

```
I do.  Do you?  You do!  I know you do.
```

In typing initials used in personal names, leave one space after each period.

```
B. A. Jones
W. E. B. Du Bois
```

Practice varies both for the use of periods and for spacing after periods in other abbreviations. An up-to-date dictionary can guide you.

675

Comma, Semicolon, Colon   , ; :   , ; :

Do not space before these marks. Space once after them in sentences. (See 26b for cases where the colon separates numbers with no space before or after.)

```
Usually, I call first; however, I failed to do so today.  My
reason is this: I saw you peeking through the curtains.
```

Apostrophe   '   '

Do not space before or after an apostrophe within a word.

```
Isn't that Ken's car?
```

Space once after a final apostrophe followed by another word.

```
He must be using the Clarks' garage.
```

When an apostrophe ends the word that ends a sentence, do not leave a space between the apostrophe and the final period, question mark, or exclamation point. Put the apostrophe before the final mark of punctuation.

```
Those cars in the driveway are the Clarks'.
```

Quotation marks   " "   ' '   " "   ' '

Do not space between quotation marks and whatever they enclose. Do not space between double and single quotation marks.

```
I said, " 'Here Comes the Sun' makes me smile whenever I hear
it."
```

Space once after a closing quotation mark unless it ends a sentence. In that case, space twice.

```
He said "plaster."  I heard "blister," but I guess I was wrong.
```

Hyphen   –   –

Do not space before or after a hyphen except to use one space after a "suspended" hyphen—that is, a hyphen showing that two prefixes or suffixes refer to one root word.

```
Many athletes trade the agony of defeat for pre- and post-game
shows.
```

676

When a hyphen occurs at the end of a line, always make it the last mark on the line. Do not carry the hyphen over to start a new line.

Dash -- ▬

In typed manuscripts, make a dash by striking the hyphen key twice, with no space between. In handwritten manuscripts, make a dash with a single line a little longer than a hyphen. Do not space before or after a dash.

```
All of us--all of us!--think sentimentally about adolescence.
```

Slash / /

Do not space before or after a slash except when you use the slash to separate no more than three lines of quoted poetry.

```
and/or    1/16
```

When separating lines of poetry, space once before and once after the slash.

```
Consider these lines from Shakespeare's "Sonnet 30": "When to
the sessions of sweet silent thought / I summon up remembrance
of things past."
```

Brackets, Parentheses [ ] ( )   [ ] ( )

Do not space between brackets or parentheses and whatever they enclose.

```
The letter continued, "Parrish was borne [sic] June 30, 1830. At
least that's what Ada Jencks (my great grandmother) wrote."
```

Ellipses . . .   . . .

Use three evenly spaced dots for an ellipsis. Use one space before, between, and after the dots.

```
"Turning away . . . they began to laugh."
```

Use four dots to indicate the omission of one or more sentences. Because the first dot is the period at the end of the sentence, leave no space before it. After the first dot, use three evenly spaced dots.

```
"The shopper felt crowded. . . . Moving away was natural."
```

677

See 29d for information about using other punctuation with ellipses.

UNDERLINING (ITALICS)

When you underline more than one word, you may use either style shown here—with or without breaks between words. Whichever style you choose, use it consistently throughout a paper.

Zen and the Art of Motorcycle Maintenance

Zen and the Art of Motorcycle Maintenance

■‖B2

Follow standard practices when you prepare the final copy of a paper.

The appearance of a paper sends important messages to your instructor. Although no paper will earn an *A* only because it looks exceptionally neat and shows your attention to the conventions of manuscript format, a first-rate appearance suggests to the instructor that you took the assignment seriously and that you value what you have written.

APPEARANCE

Paper: For typed papers, use 8-1/2 × 11-inch white, standard typing paper. Do not use onionskin or erasable paper: onionskin is for copies only, and erasable paper smudges easily and resists handwritten corrections. Type on only one side of each sheet of paper.

If your instructor accepts handwritten papers, use ruled 8-1/2 × 11-inch standard white, lined paper. Do not use colored paper or paper torn from a spiral-bound notebook. Write on only one side of each sheet of paper. Write on every other line, so that you will have space to make neat corrections and so that your instructor will have space to make comments.

Ink: Use a black typewriter ribbon, and keep the typewriter keys clean so that the letters will be clear, not blurred.

For handwritten papers, use dark blue or black ink, not red, green, brown, or other colors. Do not use pencil.

Computer printouts: If a printer has both capital and lowercase letters and produces an easy-to-read type, most instructors accept papers prepared on word processors. Ask first, however. When you submit the paper, tear off the hole-punched edges and separate the pages.

678

FORMATS

First page: In this appendix you will find reproduced a paper's first page with the endorsement (name, date, course, and other information your instructor may specify) in MLA-recommended spacing; a later page with name and page number at the top and a long prose quotation; and the first page of a Works Cited list. Note the 5-character indent for paragraphs and for second and subsequent lines of Works Cited entries.

Formats for long quotations: Set off a prose quotation of four or more lines by starting the quotation on a new line. Indent this first line and all other lines of the quotation ten spaces from the left. See the examples in this appendix, in 28a, and in 33.

When you quote more than three lines of poetry, set the quotation off from your own words. Start a new line and lay the quoted poetry out so that it looks as much as possible like the printed version you are quoting from. If indenting ten spaces from the left causes you to have to break lines, you can indent less than ten spaces or not at all.

```
O Captain! my Captain! our fearful trip is done,
The ship has weather'd every rack, the prize we sought is won,
The port is near, the bells I hear, the people all exulting,
While follow eyes the stead keel, the vessel grim and daring;
    But O heart! heart! heart!
      O the bleeding drops of red,
        Where on the deck my Captain lies,
          Fallen cold and dead.
```

You will find other examples in 33 and 34b-3.

WHERE TO FIND DOCUMENTATION FORMATS

Parenthetical MLA documentation	32g, 32k
Footnotes or endnotes	34b-4
APA documentation	34c-4
CBE (natural sciences) documentation	34d-4

■‖ B3

Make careful handwritten corrections and insertions in typed papers.

Your typewriter may lack special characters, such as accent marks. If you need them, you will have to handwrite them. You can

679

also make a few handwritten corrections in a paper you intend to hand in (see list below). But if you have more than three handwritten corrections on a page, you should retype the page.

Draw one line through words you want to take out.

These ~~extra words~~ are deleted.

To insert words, make a caret ($\wedge$) where the missing words should be, and then write them in above the caret.

A caret shows *where words* should be inserted.

To transpose letters, use a mark like this:

squiggel

You can transpose words in a similar way:

Transpose in the words wrong order.

You can indicate the start of a new paragraph like this:

Molly's actions primarily met her needs. Overall, Molly exemplifies the behavior of one type of typical toddler.

You can close up space between letters this way:

Avoid in correct spacing.

You can open space between letters this way:

Leave one space between words ina sentence.

You can drop a letter and close up the remaining letters this way:

Some spellers have trouble with doubble letters.

680

FIRST PAGE WITHOUT COVER PAGE

Amy W. Brown   **Name**

Professor Wellington   **Instructor**

English 101, Section A1   **Course, Section**

10 December 19xx   **Date submitted**

                                                  } **Quadruple space**

                    Personal Space: } **Double space**

              An Intercultural Perspective

                                                  } **Quadruple space**

     When she returned home after a year in South America,

Judith Martin, a North American writer, began to have a

problem. People kept interpreting her behavior as flirta-

tious, but she was not flirting. Fairly soon she figured

                                        ↕ 1″   ↕ ½″
                                                   Brown 7

personal space. Clearly, what is considered obnoxious in

one culture might be considered polite in another (Fisher,

Bell, and Baum 167). As Hall explains, virtually every-

thing people are and do

10 space   is associated with the experience of space. . . .
indent for
displayed   Therefore, people from different cultures,
quotation
                       when interpreting each other's behavior, often

                       misinterpret the relationship, the activity,

                       or the emotions. This leads to alienation in

                       encounters or distorted communications.

                    (Hidden 171)

In the next few years, more studies will be undertaken to

uncover information about cultural differences in matters

681

↕ ½"

Indent 5 spaces after
first line of entry

Brown 10

Works Cited

**Double space
throughout**

Davis, Martha, and Janet Skupien, eds. <u>Body Movement and</u>

<u>Nonverbal Communication: An Annotated Bibliography</u>

<u>1971–1981</u>. Bloomington, IN: Indiana UP, 1982.

Fast, Julius. <u>Body Language</u>. New York: Evans, 1970.

Fisher, Jeffrey D., Paul A. Bell, and Andrew Baum.

<u>Environmental Psychology</u>. 2nd ed. New York:

Holt, 1984.

Hall, Edward T. <u>The Hidden Dimension</u>. New York:

Doubleday, 1966.

———. Interview. "Learning the Arabs' Silent Language."

With Kenneth Friedman. <u>Psychology Today</u> Aug. 1979:

44–54.

Henley, Nancy M. <u>Body Politics: Power, Sex, and Nonverbal</u>

<u>Communication</u>. Englewood Cliffs: Prentice, 1977.

682

USAGE
GLOSSARY

A **glossary** is a list of words or phrases singled out for special attention. This glossary relates to **usage,** the customary manner of using particular words or phrases.

The term "customary manner" refers to usage by educated people, as demonstrated especially in books, newspapers, and speeches. "Customary manner," however, is not as firm in practice as the term implies. Indeed, little demonstrates as dramatically as does a usage glossary that standards for language use change. Some words slip away from usage: for example, *thee* and *thou* are no longer used in everyday life. Some constructions considered nonstandard a decade ago are accepted as standard today; for example, *shall* used to be required for the first-person future *(I **shall** finish the work tomorrow),* but today most dictionaries and usage surveys report that *shall* and *will* can be used interchangeably in such constructions.

This Usage Glossary, which contains over 200 entries in alphabetical order, reflects customary practice for academic writing—as of the date this handbook was published. If you think that any information reported here might have changed, consult one of the dictionaries discussed in Chapter 20 with a publication (or revision) date later than this handbook's. The entries in this Usage Glossary cover matters of usage as well as many frequently confused homonyms and commonly confused words. Additional homonyms and commonly confused words appear in Chapter 22.

You will find this glossary easier to use if you understand two terms used frequently in the discussion: *Informal* indicates that the word or

683

phrase occurs commonly in speech but should be avoided in academic writing. *Nonstandard* indicates that the word or phrase is unacceptable for standard spoken English and for writing.

This glossary can help you in at least two ways: (1) You can browse through it to become familiar with the words and phrases that are subject to usage constraints in academic writing. (2) You can consult it as a reference when you are editing your writing to make sure that you are using the words or phrases correctly.

As in the rest of this book, words marked here with a degree symbol (°) are defined in the Glossary of Grammatical and Selected Composition Terms.

a, an Use *a* before words beginning with consonant sounds: ***a** dog*, ***a** grade*, ***a** harbor*. Also, use *a* before words beginning with vowels that sound like consonants: ***a** unit*, ***a** one-page paper*, ***a** European*. Use *an* before words beginning with vowel sounds or a silent *h*: ***an** apple*, ***an** onion*, ***an** hour*.

accept, except To *accept* means "to agree to" or "to receive." To *except* (verb°) means "to exclude or leave out"; *except* (preposition°) means "leaving out."

> **Except** [preposition] for one or two details, the striking workers were ready to **accept** management's offer. The workers wanted the no-smoking rule **excepted** from the contract.

advice, advise *Advice* (noun°) means "recommendation"; to *advise* (verb°) means "to give a recommendation".

> I **advise** you to follow your doctor's **advice.**

affect, effect To *affect* means "to influence" or "to arouse the emotions"; to *effect* means "to bring about"; *effect* (noun°) means "result or conclusion."

> One **effect** of the weather is that it **affects** some people's moods. We **effected** some changes in our system for weather forecasting.

aggravate, irritate *Aggravate* is used colloquially to mean *irritate*. Use precisely: to *aggravate* means "to intensify or make worse"; to *irritate* means "to annoy or make impatient".

> The executive was **irritated** by her assistant's carelessness, for it further **aggravated** the company's financial problems.

ain't is a nonstandard contraction for *am not, is not, are not, has not,* and *have not.*

all ready, already *Already* means "before or by this time"; *all ready* means "completely prepared."

> The athletes were **all ready;** the warmup had **already** begun.

all right is two words, never one (not *alright*).

all together, altogether *All together* means "in a group, in unison"; *altogether* means "entirely or thoroughly."

> The sopranos, altos, and tenors were supposed to sing **all together,** but the outcome was not **altogether** successful.

allude, elude To *allude* means "to refer to indirectly or casually"; to *elude* means "to escape notice of."

> The researchers **alluded** to budget cuts when they discussed why the identification of the virus had **eluded** them.

684

allusion, illusion An *allusion* is an indirect or casual reference; an *illusion* is a false impression or idea.

> The candidate wanted to create the **illusion** that he was sympathetic to the poor, so he made a snide *allusion* to his rival's wealth.

a lot (two words, not *alot*) is informal for *a great deal* or *a great many* and should be avoided in academic writing.

a.m., p.m. (or **A.M., P.M.**) are used only with numbers, not as substitutes for the words *morning, afternoon,* or *evening.*

> Our class, which usually meets early in the **morning** [not *a.m.*], will meet at 7:10 **p.m.** tomorrow.

among, between Use *among* for three or more people or things; use *between* for two people or things.

> The problem was discussed **among** the three students. They had to choose **between** staying in school and getting full-time jobs.

amount, number Use *amount* for concepts or things that are collective rather than separate (wealth, work, happiness); use *number* for anything that can be counted (coins, jobs, joys).

> A large **number** of people had to do a great **amount** of work.

an, and *An* is an article° (see *a, an*) and should not be confused with *and,* which is a conjunction°.

> They saw **an** eagle **and** its chicks in the nest.

and/or occurs in business or legal writing when either one or both of the items it connects can apply.

anybody, any body *Anybody* is any person not specified; *any body* is a specific person, object, or group.

> The purity of **any body** of water can be tested by **anybody** with the correct materials.

anyone, any one. See *anybody, any body.*

anyplace is informal for *any place* or *anywhere.* Avoid it in academic writing.

anyways, anywheres are nonstandard for *anyway, anywhere.*

apt, likely, liable See *likely, apt, liable.*

as, like, as if
1. Use *like,* not *as,* in a comparison when resemblance but not equivalence is suggested.

> Mexico, **like** [not *as*] Argentina, is a Spanish-speaking country.

2. Use *as,* not *like,* in a comparison when equivalence is suggested—that is, when the subject equals the description.

> John served **as** [not *like*] the chef at our barbecue. [John = the chef]

3. *As* functions as a subordinating conjunction° or a preposition°, depending on the meaning of the sentence. *Like* functions only as a preposition. To start a clause°, *as* is required.

> That hamburger tastes good, **as** [not *like*] a hamburger should. [subordinating conjunction]
>
> That hamburger tastes **like** chopped leather. [preposition]

685

---

4. Use *as if*, not *like*, with the subjunctive mood.°
> This hamburger tastes **as if** [not *like*] it has been grilled for an hour.

assure, ensure, insure To *assure* means "to promise or convince"; to *ensure* or to *insure* means "to make certain." *Insure* is reserved for financial or legal certainty, especially related to insurance.
> The insurance agent **assured** me that I could **insure** my life, but he explained that no one could **ensure** that I would have a long life.

as to should be avoided as a substitute for *about*.
> The pilot was unsure **about** [not *as to*] the airplane's safety.

awful, awfully *Awful* (adjective°) means "causing fear" or "inspiring awe"; it should not be used as a substitute for intensifiers such as *very* or *extremely*. *Awfully* (adverb°) is informal for *very* or *extremely* and should be avoided in academic writing.
> The cyclone was an **awful** phenomenon to watch. It caused serious [not *awful*] damage. It came **very** [not *awfully*] close to our house.

a while, awhile *A while* is an article° and a noun°; it functions as a subject° or object°. *Awhile* is an adverb°; it modifies verbs°. In a prepositional phrase°, the correct form is *a while: for* **a while**, *in* **a while**, *after* **a while**.
> We waited **awhile** for our friends to arrive, but after **a while** we had to leave.

bad, badly *Bad* is an adjective° (*bad* feelings); it is used after linking verbs° such as *feel* or *felt* (*He felt* **bad**). *Badly* is an adverb° and is nonstandard after linking verbs. For more information, see 12d.
> The farmers felt **bad** [not *badly*]. [*Felt* in this example is a linking verb.]
> The **bad** drought had **badly** damaged the crops.

been, being *Been* is the past participle° of *to be; being* is the progressive form° of *to be.*
> *Alcohol abuse has* **been** [not *being*] on the rise recently. We see lives **being** [not *been*] ruined by drinking.

being as, being that are nonstandard for *because* or *since*.
> **Because** [not *being as* or *being that*] the catcher injured his arm, he had to leave the game.

beside, besides *Beside* (preposition°) means "next to or by the side of "; *besides* (when functioning as a preposition) means "other than or in addition to"; *besides* (when functioning as an adverb°) means "also or moreover."
> With keys in her hand, she stood **beside** the new car. No one **besides** her had a driver's license. **Besides,** she owned the car.

better, had better Used in place of *had better, better* is informal. Avoid it in academic writing.
> We **had better** [not *we better*] be careful.

between, among See *among, between.*

breath, breathe *Breath* is a noun°; *breathe* is a verb°.
> The jogger had to rest and **breathe** rapidly before he could catch his **breath.**

686

bring, take Use *bring* for movement from a distant place to a near place; use *take* for any other movement.

> The coach will **bring** her team to our college, and then she will **take** the team on a tour of the campus.

broke is nonstandard for past participle° *broken*. Avoid it in academic writing, except as the past tense°.

> The jogger's ankle was **broken** [not *broke*]. He **broke** it yesterday.

burst, bust To *burst* means "to break apart suddenly and violently"; its principal parts are *burst, burst, burst,* (not *burst*). To *bust* is slang for to *burst* and should be avoided in academic writing.

> The bubble **burst** [not *busted* or *bursted.*].

but, however, yet Use *but, however,* and *yet* alone, not in combination with each other.

> The economy is strong, **but** [not *but yet* or *but however*] unemployment is still high.

but that, but what are nonstandard for *that.* Avoid them in academic writing.

> The supervisor does not doubt **that** [not *but that* or *but what*] the job can be done.

calculate, figure, reckon are informal for *imagine* or *expect.* Avoid such informal uses in academic writing.

> The farmers **expect**]not *figure* or *reckon*] that they will have a good crop.

can, may *Can* indicates ability or capacity; *may* requests or grants permission. In the negative, however, *can* is acceptable in place of *may.*

> **May** I leave the room so that I **can** have a cigarette?
> Why **can't** I?

can't hardly, can't scarcely are double negatives and are nonstandard; use *hardly* and *scarcely* only. For more information, see 12c.

> They can **hardly** [not *can't hardly* or *can't scarcely*] see through the fog.

censor, censure To *censor* means "to judge" or "to delete objectional material"; to *censure* means "to condemn or officially reprimand."

> The town council **censured** the mayor for permitting a citizen's committee to **censor** books in the public library.

chairman, chairperson, chair Usage is changing concerning *chairman,* which has a masculine implication. The gender-free terms *chairperson* and *chair* often are preferred, although *chair* seems to be more widely used at this time.

choose, chose *Choose* is the simple form of *to choose; chose* is the past tense of *to choose.*

> Today I will **choose** the college I will attend. Yesterday she **chose** the college she will attend.

cloth, clothe *Cloth* (noun°) means "fabric"; to *clothe* (verb°) means "to dress" or "to cover with garments."

> The king wanted to **clothe** himself with garments made of fine **cloth.**

687

complement, compliment To *complement* means "to complete" or "to supplement"; to *compliment* means "to express praise or flattery."

> The instructor **complimented** the student for her research project, saying that it **complemented** work done twenty years before.

conscience, conscious *Conscience* (noun°) means "a sense of right or wrong"; *conscious* (adjective°) means "being aware or awake."

> The thief was **conscious** that his **conscience** was bothering him.

consensus of opinion is a redundant phrase. Use *consensus* only.

continual, continuous *Continual* is occurring repeatedly; *continuous* is going on without interruption in space or time.

> Although all essential systems of the spacecraft were expected to operate **continuously,** the astronauts **continually** checked their instrument panels.

> The washing machine **continually** breaks down, and then it makes a **continuous** humming sound.

couple, couple of are nonstandard for *a few* or *several.*

> You should rest for **a few** [not *a couple* or *a couple of*] minutes before you begin again.

data is the plural of *datum,* a rarely used word. Informal usage now treats *data* as singular, but it should be treated as plural in academic writing.

> **These** [not *this*] **data show** [not *shows*] that the virus is spreading.

different from, different than *From* is the preferred preposition after *different,* although *than* is commonly used in speech.

> Football is **different from** [not *different than*] soccer.

disinterested, uninterested *Disinterested* means "impartial"; *uninterested* means "indifferent or not concerned with."

> They were **uninterested** in hearing my side of the story, so we agreed to ask a **disinterested** person to settle our dispute.

done is a past participle°; it cannot substitute for the past tense *did.*

> The farmers raised [not *done* raised] a fine crop. They **did** [not *done*] a good job.

don't is a contraction for *do not,* not for *does not (doesn't).*

> She **doesn't** [not *don't*] like loud music.

due to is informal as a preposition° meaning "because of." *Due to* is always acceptable after a form of *to be.*

> He was late **because of** [not *due to*] an accident. [There is no noun for *due to* to modify.] His lateness was **due to** an accident. [*Due to* modifies *lateness.*]

emigrate from, immigrate to See *immigrate to, emigrate from.*

ensure, assure, insure See *assure, ensure, insure.*

enthused as an adjective° is nonstandard for *enthusiastic.*

> The student was **enthusiastic** [not *enthused*] about going to college.

especially, specially *Especially* and *specially* are not interchangeable. *Especially* means "mainly or particularly"; *specially* is for a special purpose.

688

Because the quarterback was **especially** tired, he could not attend the **specially** organized party celebrating his team's victory.

etc. is the abbreviation for the Latin *et cetera*, meaning *and the rest.* Do not use it in academic writing; acceptable substitutes are *and the like, and so on,* or *and so forth.*

everyday, every day *Everyday* is an adjective°; it means "daily" and modifies nouns. *Every day* is an adjective-noun combination that functions as a subject° or object°.

I missed the bus **every day** last week. Arriving at work late has become an **everyday** occurrence.

everywheres is nonstandard for *everywhere.*

except, accept See *accept, except.*

explicit, implicit *Explicit* means "directly stated or expressed;" *implicit* means "implied or suggested."

The warning on cigarette packs is **explicit:** Smoking may be dangerous to your health. The warning's **implicit** message is that people should not smoke.

farther, further are used interchangeably, although many writers prefer to use *farther* for geographical distances and *further* for all other cases.

fewer, less Use *fewer* for anything that can be counted (**fewer** *dollars,* **fewer** *jobs,* **fewer** *joys*); use *less* for concepts or things thought of collectively, not separately (**less** *money,* **less** *work,* **less** *happiness*).

figure, calculate, reckon See *calculate, figure, reckon.*

fine, find *Fine* is an adjective° *(She bought a **fine** electric drill)*; it is nonstandard for *well* or any other adverb° (not *The new electric drill worked* **fine**). *Find* is the simple form of the verb *to find (We **find** the defendant "not guilty").*

former, latter When two ideas or things are referred to, *former* refers to the first of the two, and *latter* refers to the second of the two. When more than two ideas or things are referred to, do not use these words.

Brazil and Ecuador are two Latin American countries. The **former** is Portuguese-speaking, the **latter** Spanish-speaking.

gender, sex *Gender* is attributed to words, *sex* to people and animals.

Today, many writers prefer to use **gender-free** not [*sex-free*] language, like *chair* instead of *chairman.*

given, giving *Given* is the past participle° of *to give; giving* is the progressive° form.

A reward was **given** to a citizen for **giving** the police valuable help in preventing a robbery.

goes, says *Goes* is nonstandard for *says.*

He **says** [not *goes*] we will have a test tomorrow .

gone, went *Gone* is the past participle° of *to go; went* is the past tense° of *to go.*

They **went** [not *gone*] to the concert after their friends **had gone** [not *had went*] home.

689

good and is nonstandard for *very*.
> *He was* **very** [not *good and*] sorry.

good, well *Good* is an adjective° (***good*** *idea*); it is nonstandard as an adverb; *well* is an adverb° (*run* ***well***). For more information, 12d.
> The **good** writer spoke **well**.

got, have *Got* is the past tense° of *to get* (*He* **got** *an A*) and is also one of the past participles° of *to get* (*She has* **got**—*or* **gotten**—*excellent grades*). *Got* is nonstandard in place of *have; got to* is nonstandard as a substitute for an intensifier such as *must*.
> What do we **have** [not *got*] for dinner?
> You **must** [not *got to*] help me.

great is an informal adjective meaning "good," "wonderful," "skillful," or "clever." Reserve it for its precise meaning: "a high degree of," "eminent," "large," "grand."
> No   She has a **great** personality.
> YES   Einstein was a **great** scientist.
> YES   Her work gave her **great** satisfaction.

had best, had better are nonstandard for *ought* or *should*.
> She **ought** to [not *had best* or *had better*] call home.

had ought, hadn't ought are nonstandard for *ought* and *ought not*.
> He **ought** [not *had ought*] to call home.

hanged, hung Use *hanged* only to refer to executions (*The prisoner was* **hanged** *this morning*). Use *hung* for all other meanings.

have, got See *got, have*.

have, of *Have*, not *of*, should be used after such verbs as *could, may, might, must, should*.
> They *could* **have** [not *of*] telephoned. They *may* **have** [not *of*] tried to call.

he, she, he or she Using *he* to refer to both males and females is avoided by many people today. Many writers use *he or she* or, if it's at all possible for the meaning of the sentence, they switch to plural nouns and pronouns. For more information, see 21a-3.
> If **they** want [not *he* wants] to avoid accidents, **drivers** [not *a driver*] should drive defensively.

himself, herself See *myself, yourself, himself, herself*.

hisself is nonstandard for *himself*.

hopefully means "with hope"; it is nonstandard if used to mean "it is hoped that."
> No   **Hopefully,** the plane will land safely.
> YES   They waited **hopefully** for her safe return.

however, yet, but See *but, however, yet*.

hung, hanged See *hanged, hung*.

if, whether *If* is a subordinating conjunction°. *Whether occurs in three situations:* (1) in an indirect question (*She asked* **whether** *I had heard from the hikers*), (2) to express doubt (*She was not sure* **whether** *they would be safe*

690

in the storm), and (3) to express alternatives with or without *or not (I did not know **whether** [or whether or not] to search for them)*.

illusion, allusion See *allusion, illusion.*

immigrate to, emigrate from To *immigrate to* means "to enter a new country to live there"; to *emigrate from* means "to leave one country to live in another."

> After the ballet star **emigrated from** Russia, he **immigrated to** the United States to start a new life.

implicit, explicit See *explicit, implicit.*

imply, infer To *imply* means "to hint or suggest without stating outright"; to *infer* means "to draw a conclusion from what has been written or said." Speakers and writers *imply;* listeners and readers *infer.*

> The governor **implied** that she might not seek reelection, and the reporters **inferred** that she had decided to run for president.

incredible, incredulous *Incredible* means "extraordinary" or "not believable"; *incredulous* means "unable or unwilling to believe." A person would be *incredulous* in response to something that is *incredible.*

> Their families were **incredulous** as the freed hostages told of the **incredible** cruelty they had suffered while captives.

illusion See *allusion, illusion.*

individual, person, party are not interchangeable in academic writing. Use *individual* to emphasize the uniqueness of a single human being; otherwise use *person.* Use *party* only for a group of people.

> The Constitution guarantees every **individual** certain rights.
> Each **person** received a written invitation.
> The governor and his **party** entered the room together.

infer, imply See *imply, infer.*

inside of, outside of See *outside of, inside of.*

insure, assure, ensure See *assure, ensure, insure.*

irregardless is nonstandard for *regardless.*

irritate, aggravate See *aggravate, irritate.*

is when, is where In giving definitions, *is* should not be followed by *when* or *where.*

> Defensive driving means that [not *is when*] drivers stay on the defense against accidents that might be caused by other drivers.

its, it's *Its* is a personal pronoun in the possessive case. *(The dog lost **its** bone). It's* is a contraction of *it is (**It's** a warm day).*

-ize is a suffix used to change a noun° or adjective° to a verb° *(hospital + ize = hospitalize, brutal + ize = brutalize).* Be careful not to attach *-ize* indiscrimiately to create new words rather than using good words that already exist. When in doubt, check your dictionary to see if a word ending in *-ize* is acceptable.

kind, sort are singular words and should therefore be paired with *this,* not *these. These* can be paired with *kinds* or *sorts.*

691

kind of (a), sort of (a) *Kind of* and *sort of* are nonstandard if used as adverbs° meaning "in a way" or "somewhat." Also, the *a* with these phrases is nonstandard.

> The hikers were **somewhat** [not *kind of*] tired when they got home.
> That **kind of** [not *kind of an*] exercise is healthy.

later, latter *Later* means "after some time" or "subsequently;" *latter* refers to the second of a pair of ideas or things.

> That restaurant opens **later** than we had thought. It serves lunch and dinner, the **latter** starting at 7 p.m.

latter, former See *former, latter*.

lay, lie *Lay* (principal parts: *laying, laid*) is always followed by a direct object°. As a substitute for *lie* (principal parts: *lying, lay, lain*), *lay* is nonstandard. For more information, see 8d.

> **Lay** the blanket on the beach so you can **lie** [not *lay*] down and rest.

learn, teach *Learn* is nonstandard for *teach*. Students *learn;* teachers *teach*.

> *The instructor will* **teach** us [not *learn us*] chemistry.

leave, let To *leave* means "to depart"; to *let* means "to permit." *Leave* is nonstandard for *let* unless *leave* is followed by *alone*.

> I had to **leave** the classroom early because I was ill. My instructor will **let** [not *leave*] me take a retest tomorrow. She will have to find a proctor, because she cannot **leave** a student **alone** during an exam.

likely, apt, liable *Likely* and *apt* are loosely interchangeable. Strictly, however, *apt* is used to indicate a tendency or inclination; and *likely* is used to indicate a reasonable expectation that something will happen. *Liable* means "having undesirable consequences."

> Although the roads are **apt** to be icy, you **likely** will arrive on time. However, you are **liable** to have an accident if you speed on icy roads.

loose, lose, loss *Loose* means "not tight;" to *lose* means "to be unable to find"; *loss* means "that which cannot be found or retrieved."

> Before I **lose** this **loose** belt, I had better tighten it.
> The **loss** from the fire included most of his clothing.

lots, lots of, a lot of are informal for *many, much, a great deal of*.

> **Many** [not *lots of*] bees were in the hive.

may, can See *can, may*.

may be, maybe *May be* is a verb phrase°; *maybe* is an adverb°.

> Our team **may be** out of practice, but **maybe** we will win anyway.

media is the plural of *medium* and therefore requires a plural verb.

> The **media** *cover* [not *covers*] the elections, but the **medium** that reaches most people is television.

mighty is a nonstandard substitute for *extremely* or *very*.

mind, mine *Mind* is a noun° *(She had a good* **mind***); mine* is a personal pronoun° *(That key is* **mine***).*

morale, moral *Morale* (noun°) means "a mental state relating to courage, confidence, or enthusiasm." *Moral* (noun) means "the conclusion of, or lesson from, a story"; *moral* (adjective°) means "right in conduct or character."

692

The president's good **moral** character boosted the country's **morale**.
The **moral** of that story is that people should be kind to animals.

most is nonstandard for *almost*.

Ms. is the title free of reference to marital status for women; it is equivalent to the male title *Mr.* Unless a woman specifically requests *Miss* or *Mrs.*, use *Ms.*

myself, yourself, himself, herself are reflexive pronouns° *(I told **myself** to stay home)* and intensive pronouns° *(I **myself** will volunteer)*. They are nonstandard when used as a subject° or an object in a prepositional phrase.°

The dean and **I** [not *myself*] will explain the facts to the president. First, however, the class has to explain them to the dean and **me** [not *myself*].

nothing like, nowhere near are nonstandard for *not nearly*.

Last month's rain was **not nearly** [not *nowhere nearly*] enough.

nowheres is nonstandard for *nowhere*.

number, amount See *amount, number*.

of, have See *have, of*.

off of is nonstandard for *off*.

He fell **off** [not *off of*] the chair.

OK, O.K., okay are acceptable, but avoid them in academic writing in favor of a word more specific to the meaning of the sentence.

The weather was *satisfactory* [not *okay*] for the race. Course officials gave the *approval* [not *okay*] for the final lap.

on account of is wordy for *because, because of*.

Because of [not *on account of*] the rainy weather, we stayed home.

outside of, inside of are nonstandard when used with *of (She waited **outside** [not *outside of*] the dormitory)*. Also, *inside of* is nonstandard when referring to time *(She waited **about** [not *inside of*] five minutes)*.

party, individual, person See *individual, person, party*.

per The Latin word *per* is reserved for technical terms *(miles **per** hour, **per** capita income)*. Use English equivalents in academic writing.

He earned $200 **a** [not *per*] month **as explained in** [not *per*] your letter.

percent, percentage *Percent* is used with specific numbers *(two percent, 95 percent)*. *Percentage* is used with descriptive words or phrases (a *small percentage*), but only for amounts that have been expressed as percentages. Do not use it as a synonym for *part, portion, number, amount,* or other words denoting quantity

Several people in my class are bilingual [not *A percentage* of my class is bilingual].

A large **percentage** of the voters watch the presidential debates on television.

693

person, individual, party See *individual, person, party*.

photocopy, Xerox® To *photocopy* (verb°) means "to make a copy on a copier machine"; *photocopy* (noun°) is the copy. *Xerox®* is a registered trademark, not a synonyn for either the noun or the verb *photocopy*.

plenty is nonstandard for words such as *quite* and *very (She was* **very** *(not plenty) tired from the workout).* When used as a noun meaning *a large amount,* plenty must be followed by *of (They must have* **plenty of** *food for the winter).*

plus is a preposition° meaning "in addition to" *(She had talent* **plus** *good work habits). Plus,* however, is nonstandard (1) as a substitute for *and* between independent clauses and (2) as a transitional word such as *besides, moreover, in addition.*

> He studied hard, **and** [not *plus*] he played hard. **In addition** [not *plus*], he had a long commute between his home and campus.

p.m., a.m. See *a.m., p.m.*

practical, practicable *Practical* means "useful or sensible"; *practicable* means "capable of being put into practice."

> The mayor wanted a **practical** evacuation plan, but none of the proposals was **practicable** for a large city.

precede, proceed To *precede* means "to come before"; to *proceed* means "to continue."

> The attorney **preceded** her client to court and then **proceeded** to unpack her briefcase.

pretty is informal for words such as *rather, quite, very,* and *somewhat.* Avoid such use in academic writing.

> The flu epidemic was **quite** [not *pretty*] severe.

principal, principle *Principle* means "a basic truth or rule." *Principal* (noun°) means "chief person" or "main or original amount"; *principal* (adjective°) means "most important."

> The school **principal** paid interest on the **principal** of her bank loan. One of the **principal** values in the United States is the **principle** of free speech.

raise, rise *Raise* (principal parts: *raised, raising*) needs a direct object° *(Please* **raise** *your hand); rise* (principal parts: *rose, risen, rising*) does not take a direct object *(The run will* **rise***).* Using these verbs interchangeably is nonstandard. For more information, see 8d.

> The governor will **rise** [not *raise*] to speak after we **raise** [not *rise*] the flag.

rarely ever is an informal expression for *rarely* or *hardly ever;* avoid it in academic writing.

> He **rarely** [not *rarely ever*] came to class, so I **hardly ever** (not *rarely ever*) saw him.

real is nonstandard for intensifiers such as *really* (informal) or *very.*

really is informal for intensifiers such as *very* and *extremely.*

reason is should not be used in combination with *because.*

> The **reason is** [not *the reason is because*] we want to lower taxes.

694

reason why is redundant; drop *why*.

> The **reason** [not *reason why*] they left home is a mystery.

reckon, calculate, figure See *calculate, figure, reckon.*

regarding, in regard to, with regard to are used in some legal and technical writing but are too stiff for most academic writing. Useful substitutes are words such as *about* and *concerning.*

> The committee members asked **about** [not *regarding, in regard to,* or *with regard to*] the plan for a new park.

respectful, respectfully; respective, respectively *Respectful* and *respectfully* relate to showing respect; *respective* and *respectively* refers to items that are in the given sequence.

> The staff **respectfully** requested that the dean hear their complaints. He suggested that the typist and telephone operators go back to their desk and switchboards, **respectively.** They then returned to their **respective** jobs.

right is nonstandard for intensifiers such as *very* or *extremely.*

> The workers were **very** [not *right*] pleased to hear that the factory will reopen.

says, goes See *goes, says.*

seen is a nonstandard substitute for *saw. Seen* is the past participle° of *to see* and must be used with an auxiliary verb° such as *have, has,* or *had.*

> They **saw** [not *seen*] the film. I **had seen** [not *I seen*] it last week.

set, sit *Set* (principal parts: *set, setting*) is nonstandard as a substitute for *to sit* (principal parts: *sat, sitting*). *Set* means "to place" and is followed by a direct object°. *Sit* means "to be seated." For more information, see 8d.

> After you carefully **set** [not *sit*] the rare Chinese vase on the table, please **sit** [not *set*] down.

sex, gender See *gender, sex.*

shall, will Use *shall* for questions in the first person **(Shall I leave?)** or in very formal settings *(The judge **shall** render her verdict after hearing the testimony)*. In all other cases, *will* is now accepted for the future tense in first, second, and third persons.

should, would Use *should* to express obligation *They **should** practice what they preach)* or condition *(If you **should** need advice, call me)*. Use *would* to express a wish *(I wish my family **would** buy a VCR)* or habitual action *(I **would** tape all the comedy specials)*.

sit, set See *set, sit.*

so is colloquial as an intensifier like *very* and *extremely.*

some is both nonstandard and vague as a substitute for modifiers such as *somewhat, a little,* and *remarkable.*

> That was **a remarkable** [not *some*] performance.

somebody, some body See *anybody, any body.*

someone, some one See *anybody, any body.*

sometime, sometimes, some time *Sometime* means "at an unspecified future time"; *sometimes* means "now and then"; *some time* is a span of time.

695

Sometime next semester we have to take qualifying exams.
Sometimes I worry about the tests. I need **some time** to get used to the pressure.

somewhereas is nonstandard for *somewhere.*

sort, kind See *kind, sort.*

sort of (a), kind of (a) See *kind of (a), sort of (a).*

specially, especially See *especially, specially.*

stationary, stationery are not interchangeable. *Stationary* means "standing still"; *stationery* refers to paper and related products.

such is informal and overused as an intensifier such as *very* or *extremely.* Avoid it in academic writing, unless it is part of a comparison including *that.*

No It was **such** a poorly written play.
Yes It was a **very** poorly written play.
Yes It was **such** a poorly written play **that** no one went to see it.

supposed to, used to The final *d* is essential in both expressions.
The weather is **supposed to** [not *suppose to*] improve. It **used to** [not *use to*] be sunny this time of year.

sure is nonstandard when used an an adverb° meaning *surely* or *certainly.*
I **surely** [not *sure*] hope to go to college.

take, bring See *bring, take.*

teach, learn See *learn, teach.*

than, then *Than* indicates comparison (*One is smaller* **than** *two*). *Then* relates to time (*He tripped and* **then** *fell*).

that there, then there, this here, these here are nonstandard for *that, those, this,* and *these,* respectively.

that, which Use *that* with restrictive (essential) clauses°; *which* can be used today for both restrictive and nonrestrictive (nonessential) clauses°, but most writers prefer to use it only with nonrestrictive (nonessential) clauses.
We visited the house **that** Jack built. Jack built the house, **which** is on Beanstalk Street, for his large plant collection.

their, there, they're *Their* is possessive; *there* means "in that place" or serves as an expletive°; *they're* is a contraction of *they are.*
The students attended **their** classes in the lecture hall, which is over **there.** At this college, **there** are many courses to take, but **they're** all scheduled in the morning.

theirself, theirselves, themself are nonstandard for *themselves.*

them is nonstandard when used for *these* or *those.*
Let's buy **those** [not **them**] *strawberries.*

then, than See *than, then.*

thusly is nonstandard for *thus.* Because *thus* is already an adverb°, the *-ly* ending is not needed.

696

till, until are both acceptable, although most writers prefer *until* in academic writing. Avoid the contraction *'til* in academic writing.

to, too, two *To* is a preposition°; *too* is an adverb°; *two* is the number.
> They went **to** the game. They ate at a restaurant, **too.** The check was not **too** expensive for the **two** of them.

toward, toward, are both acceptable, although some writers prefer *toward.*

try and, sure and are nonstandard for *try to* and *sure to.*
> She wanted to **try to** [not *try and*] get a part-time job. Therefore, she had to be **sure to** [not *sure and*] prepare a résumé.

type is nonstandard for *type of.*

uninterested, disinterested See *disinterested, uninterested.*

unique is an absolute word and therefore cannot be modified by intensifiers such as *very* or *most.*
> Her talent was **unique** [not *very unique* or *most unique*].

used to, supposed to See *supposed to, used to.*

wait on is informal for *wait for.*

ways is colloquial for *way.*
> California is a long **way** [not *ways*] from New York.

well, good See *good, well.*

went, gone See *gone, went.*

what is nonstandard when used for *that* or *who.*
> The house **that** [not **what**] Jack built contains a beanstalk.

where is nonstandard when used for *that.*
> I read in the newspaper **that** [not *where*] tuition will be increased.

where . . . . at is redundant; drop *at.*
> **Where** is the house [not *house at*]?

whether, if See *if, whether.*

which, that See *that, which.*

which, who Use *which* to refer to things or ideas; use *who* to refer to people.

who, whom Use *who* for the subjective case° (*The person who can type has an easier time in school*). Use *whom* for the objective case° (*I asked to whom my professor was speaking*). For more information, see 9d.

who's, whose *Who's* is the contraction of *who is; whose* is possessive.
> **Who's** going to run for mayor?
> **Whose** campaign is well organized?

will, shall See *shall, will.*

-wise The suffix *-wise* means "in a manner, in a direction, or in a position" (*clockwise, sidewise*). Be careful not to attach *-wise* indiscriminately to create new words rather than using good words that already exist. When in doubt, check your dictionary to see if a word ending in *-wise* is acceptable.
> The **weather** [not *Weatherwise, the*] outlook is excellent.

would, should See *should, would.*

697

Xerox®, photocopy See *photocopy, Xerox®*

Xmas is an abbreviation for *Christmas;* avoid using it in academic writing.

yet, however, but See *but, however, yet.*

your, you're *Your* is possessive; *you're* is the contraction of *you* are.

    You're generous to share **your** food with us.

yourself, See *myself, yourself, himself, herself.*

INSTRUCTOR'S NOTES

GLOSSARY
OF GRAMMATICAL
AND SELECTED
COMPOSITION
TERMS

The first time that a term is used in this handbook, it is defined. After that when the term is used, it is marked with a degree symbol (°) to signal that it is defined in this glossary. Also, when a definition in this glossary uses terms that are themselves defined here, the terms are marked with a degree symbol. In addition, each definition concludes with a reference, in parentheses, to the handbook section(s) or chapters where the term is most fully discussed.

abstract A condensed summary of a report, especially used in research papers in the social sciences and in theses and dissertations. (34d-3)

abstract noun A noun° that names things not knowable through the five senses: *idea, guilt.* (6a)

absolute phrase A phrase containing a subject° and a participle° and modifying an entire sentence: *Summer being over,* we left the seashore. (7d)

acronym A word made up of the first letters of other words that acts as an abbreviation for those words: *NASA.* (30h)

active voice The form of a verb° in which the subject° performs the action named by the verb. This voice° emphasizes the doer of the action, in contrast to the passive voice°, which emphasizes the action. (8j)

adjective A word that describes or limits (modifies) a noun° or pronoun° or word group functioning as a noun: *silly, three.* (6e, 12)

699

adjective clause A dependent clause° that usually begins with a relative pronoun° and that modifies nouns° or pronouns°. (7e-2)

adverb A word that describes or limits (modifies) verbs°, adjectives°, other adverbs, or whole sentences: *wearily, very.* (6f, 12)

adverb clause A dependent clause° that begins with a subordinating conjunction° and that modifies verbs°, adjectives°, adverbs°, or whole sentences. (7e-2)

agreement The match in expressing number° and person° required between a subject° and its verb° or a pronoun° and its antecedent°. For pronouns and antecedents, expressions of gender° must match as well. (11)

analogy An explanation of the unfamiliar in terms of the familiar, analogy compares objects or ideas from different classes, things not normally associated with each other. Analogy is also a method of developing one or more paragraphs. (4d, 34c-2)

analysis A thinking process, analysis divides something into its component parts to make clear the relationship between the whole and the parts. Sometimes called *division*, analysis is also a method of developing one or more paragraphs. (4d)

antecedent The noun° or pronoun° to which a pronoun refers. (10)

agreement The match in expressing number° and person° required between a subject° and its verb° or a pronoun° and its antecedent°. For pronouns and antecedents, expressions of gender° must match as well. (11)

appositive A word or group of words that renames a noun° or words functioning as a noun: *my favorite month,* **October.** (7c-3)

argumentative writing See *persuasive writing.*

articles The words *a, an,* and *the.* Also called *limiting adjectives, noun markers* or *noun determiners.* (6a)

audience The readers to whom a piece of writing is directed. Knowledge of the educational level, age, cultural background, interests, economic status, political philosophy, and religious beliefs of the audience can help the writer shape the message so that it will effectively inform or persuade the reader. (1c)

auxiliary verb Also known as a *helping verb,* an auxiliary verb is a form of *be, do, have, can, may, will,* and others that combine with main verbs° to make verb phrases°. Auxiliary verbs help main verbs to express tense°, mood°, and voice°. (6c, 8a, 8c)

balanced sentence A sentence that uses parallelism° to enhance the message of similar or dissimilar ideas. (18b-3)

base form See *simple form.*

brainstorming An invention technique° that calls for listing all the ideas that come to mind in connection with a topic and then grouping the ideas according to patterns that emerge. (2d-3)

700

bureaucratic language Stuffy, overblown language that tries to impress by sounding important and official when, in fact, it is wordy, ambiguous, and often evasive. (21d-5)

case The way a noun° or pronoun° changes form to show whether it is functioning as a subject°, an object°, or a possessor: *she, her, hers*. (9)

cause-and-effect analysis Examination of the relationship between outcomes (effects) and the reasons for them (causes). Cause-and-effect analysis can be used to develop one or more paragraphs°. (4d, 5d)

chronological order An arrangement of ideas according to a time sequence. Paragraphs, essays, and larger works may be in chronological order. Narrations and descriptions of processes are usually in chronological order. (2e-2, 4c)

clarifying sentence See *limiting sentence.*

classification A method of developing a paragraph° or a larger piece of writing in which separate categories that share some characteristics are grouped together. Classification is often used along with analysis°. (4d)

clause A group of words containing a subject° and a predicate°. A clause that delivers full meaning is called an *independent clause°* (or main clause). A clause that needs another sentence structure to deliver full meaning is called a *dependent clause°* (or subordinate clause). (7e)

cliché An overused, worn-out phrase that has lost its capacity to communicate effectively: *smooth as silk, ripe old age.* (21c)

climactic order An arrangement of ideas in a paragraph° or larger piece of writing from least important to most important. Climactic order is sometimes called *emphatic order.* (2e-2, 4c)

climactic sentence See *periodic sentence.*

coherence The clear progression from one idea to another in a piece of writing. Transitional expressions°, pronouns°, selective repetition, and parallelism° enhance coherence. A piece of writing is coherent when its parts relate to one another not only in content but also in terms of grammatical structures and choice of words. (3b, 4b)

collective noun A noun° that names a group of people or things: *family, pride* (of lions). (6a, 11g, 11o)

colloquial language Language characteristic of conversation and informal writing. (21a-4)

comma fault See *comma splice.*

comma splice The error that occurs when only a comma connects two independent clauses°. (14)

common noun A noun° that names general groups, places, people, or things: *dog, house.* (6a)

comparative The form of an adjective° or adverb° that reflects a different degree of intensity between two: *bluer, more easily.* See also *positive* and *superlative.* (12e-1)

701

comparison and contrast A pattern for developing a paragraph° or whole essay in which the writer considers the similarities (comparison) and differences (contrast) of subjects. (4d)

complement A word or group of words in the predicate° of a sentence that renames or describes a subject° or object° in that sentence. (7c-1)

complete predicate See *predicate.*

complete subject See *subject.*

complex sentence A sentence containing one independent clause° and one or more dependent clauses.°. (7f-3)

compound-complex sentence A sentence containing at least two independent clauses° and one or more dependent clauses°. (7f-4)

compound predicate See *predicate.*

compound sentence A sentence containing two or more independent clauses° joined by a coordinating conjunction. (7f-2)

compound subject See *subject.*

concrete noun A noun° that names things that can be seen, touched, heard, smelled, or tasted: *smoke, sand.* (6a)

conjunction A word that connects words, phrases°, or clauses°, including coordinating conjunctions°, correlative conjunctions°, and subordinating conjunctions°. (6h)

conjunctive adverb A kind of adverb° that creates logical connections between independent clauses°: *therefore, however.* (6f)

connotation The emotional associations suggested by a word that, along with its denotation°, make up its complete meaning. (20b)

coordinate adjectives Two or more adjectives that equally modify a noun° or pronoun°. They are separated by a comma: *heavy, round* paperweight. (24d)

coordinating conjunction A conjunction that joins two or more grammatically equivalent structures. The seven coordinating conjunctions are *and, or, for, nor, but, so,* and *yet.* (6h)

coordination The technique of using grammatically equivalent forms to show a balance or sequence of ideas. (17)

corelative conjunction A pair of words that joins equivalent grammatical structures, including *both . . . and, not only . . . but also, either . . . or, neither . . . nor,* and *whether . . . or.* (6h)

cumulative sentence A sentence that begins with the subject° and verb° and then adds modifiers°—the most common kind of sentence. Also known as a *loose sentence.* (19d-2)

dangling modifier A modifier° that describes something implied but not stated: ***Walking down the street,*** *the Sears Tower came into view.* (15c)

deadwood Empty words and phrases that increase the word count but do not add to the meaning. Also called *padding.* (16b)

declarative sentence A sentence that makes a statement: *I walked home.* (7)

702

deduction The process of reasoning from general claims to a specific instance. (5e-2)

demonstrative pronoun A pronoun° that points out the antecedent°. The demonstrative pronouns are *this, these, that,* and *those.* (6b)

denotation The dictionary definition of a word. (20b)

dependent clause A clause° that cannot stand alone as an independent grammatical unit, usually preceded by a relative pronoun° or subordinating conjunction°. (7e-2)

descriptive adjective An adjective° that describes the condition or properties of the noun° it modifies and has comparative° and superlative° forms: *round, rounder, roundest.* (6e)

descriptive adverb An adverb° that describes the qualities of the verb° and has comparative° and superlative° forms: *happily, more happily, most happily.* (6f)

diction Word choice. (20a, 20b)

dictionary form A term relating to verbs. See *simple form.*

direct discourse In writing, words that repeat speech or conversation exactly, requiring the use of quotation marks. (15a-4, 28a-3)

direct object A noun° or pronoun° or group of words functioning as a noun that receives the action—that is, completes the meaning—of a transitive verb°. (7b, 8d)

direct question A sentence that asks a question and ends with a question mark: *Are you going?* (23c)

direct quotation Spoken or written words from an outside source; such words must be enclosed in quotation marks. (28a, 31e)

division See *analysis.*

documentation Acknowledging the sources used in any piece of writing, by giving full and accurate information about the source's author, title, and the work's date of publication, and related facts. (31-b, 32d-4)

documentation style Any of various systems for providing information about the sources other than oneself used in writing others read. Some cite information in parentheses at appropriate places within the text; others use footnotes or endnotes. The form of the bibliography also varies from one style of documentation to another. Two of the most widely used styles are those of the Modern Language Association (MLA) and the American Psychological Association (APA). (31b, 32d-4)

doublespeak Evasive language intentionally used to hide the truth. (21d-4)

double negative A nonstandard statement that contains two negative modifiers°, the second of which repeats the message of the first. (12c)

drafting A part of the writing process° in which writers compose ideas in sentences and paragraphs. (2a, 3b)

edited American English Also called *standard English,* the language that conforms to established rules of grammar, sentence structure, punctuation, and spelling. (21a-2)

703

---

editing A part of the writing process° in which writers check the technical correctness of their grammar, spelling, punctuation, and mechanics°. (2a, 3d)

elliptical clause See *elliptical construction.*

elliptical construction A sentence structure, such as a clause° or phrase°, that deliberately omits words that have already appeared in the sentence and can be inferred from the context. (7e-2, 15e-1)

euphemism Language that attempts to avoid the harsh reality of some truths by using more pleasant-sounding, "tactful" words. (21d-3)

evaluative reading A part of the reading process in which the reader determines the author's tone, differentiates between fact and opinion, and assesses the author's reasoning. (5b-3)

evidence Facts, statistical information, examples, and opinions of others used by a writer to support assertions and conclusions. (5c)

exclamatory sentence A sentence that expresses strong emotion by making an exclamation: *That's ridiculous!* (7, 19b)

expletive A term that describes the function of *there* and *it* when they combine with a form of the verb *to be* to postpone the subject of the sentence: ***It is** Harold whom we must convince.* (6j, 11e)

expository writing See *informative writing.*

extended definition A definition that includes in addition to the denotation° of a word or phrase, its connotations° as well as concrete details to clarify abstract terms. An extended definition may require an entire paragraph° or essay. (4d)

faulty predication An error that occurs when a subject° and its predicate° do not make sense together. (15d-2)

finite verb A verb° form that shows tense°, mood°, voice°, person°, and number° while expressing an action, occurrence, or state of being. (8a-1)

first person See *person.*

freewriting Writing nonstop for a specified time in order to generate ideas by free association of thoughts. Freewriting that starts with a set topic is called "focused freewriting." As an invention technique°, freewriting often helps writers discover interesting ideas or patterns of thought to develop. (2d-2)

fused sentence The error of running independent clauses° together without a semicolon or a comma and a coordinate conjunction° between them. Also called a *run-on* or *run-together sentence.* (14)

future perfect progressive tense The form of the future perfect tense° that describes an action or condition ongoing until some specific future time: *they will have been talking.* (8g, p. 193)

future perfect tense The tense° indicating that an action will have been completed or a condition will have ended by a specified point in the future: *they will have talked.* (8f, p. 193)

future progressive tense The form of the future tense° showing that a future action will continue for some time: *they will be talking.* (8g, p. 193)

704

future tense The form of a verb, made with the simple form° and either *shall* or *will,* expressing an action yet to be taken or a condition not yet experienced: *they will talk.* (8c, p. 193)

gender Concerning languages, the labeling of nouns° and pronouns° as masculine, feminine, or neutral, a division in English only in third person singular personal pronouns *(he, she, it)* and in a few nouns *(prince, princess).*

gerund A verbal°, the present participle° functioning as a noun°: **Walking** *is good exercise.* (6d)

gerund phrase A verbal° phrase functioning as a noun° and containing a gerund° and its modifiers°. (7d, 8a-1)

helping verb See *auxiliary verb.*

highly formal level of language A level of language characterized by multisyllabic Latinate words and stylistic flourishes such as extended or complex figures of speech. (21a-1)

homonyms Words spelled differently that sound alike: *to, too, two.* (22c)

illogical predication See *faulty predication.*

imperative mood The mood° that expresses commands and direct requests: *Go.* It uses the simple form° of the verb. (8h-2)

imperative sentence A sentence that gives a command: *Go home now.* (7)

indefinite pronoun A pronoun° that refers to nonspecific persons or things but that takes on meaning in context: *any, few.* (6b, 11f)

independent clause A clause° that can stand alone as an independent grammatical unit. (7e-1)

indicative mood The mood° of verbs° used for statements about real things, or highly likely ones, and questions about fact: *I think Grace will be there.* (page 202)

indirect discourse Discourse that reports speech or conversation and is not enclosed in quotation marks because it does not give the speaker's exact words. (15a-4, 28a-3)

indirect object A noun° or pronoun° or group of words functioning as a noun that tells *to whom* or *for whom* the action expressed by a transitive verb° was done. (7b-2)

indirect question A sentence that reports a question and ends with a period: *I wonder whether you are going.* Also see *direct question.* (23c)

induction The process of arriving at general principles from particular facts or instances. (5e-1)

inferential meaning The meaning gained in the part of the reading process when a reader reads "between the lines," understanding what is implied but unstated. (5b-2)

infinitive A verbal° made of the simple form° of a verb and usually, but not always, *to.* It functions as a noun°, adjective°, or adverb°. (6d, 8a-1, 9g)

infinitive phrase An infinitive° and its modifiers°. It functions as a noun°, adjective°, or adverb°. (7d)

705

informal language Word choice that creates a tone° appropriate for casual conversation or letters to friends. The words may be slang°, colloquial language°, or regional language°. (21a-1)

informative writing Also known as *expository writing,* informative writing gives information and, when necessary, explains it. In contrast to persuasive writing°, informative writing focuses on the subject being discussed rather than the reader's reaction to the information. (1b-1)

intensive pronoun A *-self* form of a pronoun°, which intensifies the antecedent. (6b, 9h)

interjection A word (or words) conveying surprise or another strong emotion. (6i)

interrogative pronoun A pronoun° that asks a question, such as *whose* or *what.* (6b)

interrogative sentence A sentence that asks a question: *Did you see that hat?* (7)

intransitive verb A verb that does not take a direct object° and is not a linking verb°. (8d)

invention techniques Ways writers gather ideas. Some techniques are keeping an idea book or journal, freewriting°, brainstorming°, using the journalist's questions, mapping°, and reading. (2d)

irony Suggesting the opposite of the usual sense of the words. (21b-4)

irregular verb A verb that forms the past tense and past participle° in some way other than by adding *-ed* or *-d: see, seen, seen.* (8b)

jargon Specialized vocabulary of a particular field or group that people outside the group would not understand. The unnecessary use of jargon creates pretentious language°. (21d-2)

limiting adjective An adjective° that limits the noun° it modifies by pointing out, questioning, enumerating, showing possession, or showing its relation to other words in the sentence. (6a, 6e)

limiting sentence A sentence that follows the topic sentence in a paragraph and narrows the focus of the paragraph; sometimes called a clarifying sentence. (4a-1)

linking verb A main verb° that connects a subject° with a subject complement°. Linking verbs indicate a state of being, relate to the senses, or indicate a condition. (6c, 11h, 12d)

literal meaning The meaning gained in the reading process, when a reader reads "on the line," getting information from facts, points in an argument, or details of plot or character. It does not include inferential meaning° or opinions about the material. (5b-1)

logical fallacies Flaws in reasoning that leads to illogical statements. Common fallacies are hasty generalization, false analogy, circular reasoning, *non sequitur, post hoc,* self-contradiction, red herring, *ad hominem,* bandwagon, appeal to false authority, special pleading, the either-or fallacy, taking something out of context, appeal to ignorance, and ambiguity and equivocation. (5f)

706

loose sentence See *cumulative sentence.*

main clause See *independent clause.*

main verb A verb that expresses action, occurrence, or state of being. It shows mood°, tense°, voice°, number°, and person°. (6c, 8a)

mapping An invention technique° for generating ideas. This process is also called *webbing.* (2d-5)

mass noun A noun° that names "uncountable" things: *furniture, weather.* (6a)

mechanics Conventions regarding the use of capital letters, italics, abbreviations, and styles of writing numbers. (30)

medium level of formality A level of language that is neither too scholarly nor too casual. This level, which uses standard vocabulary, conventional sentence structure, and few or no contractions, is acceptable for academic writing. (21a-1)

metaphor A comparison between otherwise dissimilar things. It does not use a word like *like* or *as* to form the comparison, as a simile° does, but directly equates the things being compared. (21b)

metonomy A figure of speech that uses a name associated with something to refer to anything in that class. (21b)

misplaced modifier A modifier° that is incorrectly positioned in a sentence, thus distorting meaning. (15b)

mixed construction A sentence that begins by setting up one grammatical form but switches unintentionally to another, thus garbling the meaning of the sentence. (15d-1)

mixed metaphors Incongruously combined images. (21b)

modal auxiliary verbs Auxiliary verbs° that have only one form: *can, could, may, might, should, would, must,* and *ought.* They add a sense of needing, wanting, or having to do something, a sense of possibility, likelihood, obligation, permission, or ability. (8c)

modifier A word or group of words that describes or limits other words, phrases°, or clauses°. The most common modifiers are adjectives° and adverbs°. (7c-2)

mood The ability of verbs° to convey the attitude that the writer or speaker is expressing toward the action. English has three moods: indicative°, imperative°, and subjunctive°. (8i)

nonessential element See *nonrestrictive element.*

nonfinite verb A participle° or infinitive° functioning as a noun° or modifier°. Also known as a *verbal°.* (8a-1)

nonrestrictive element A limiting or descriptive word, phrase°, or dependent clause°. that provides information not essential to understanding the element it modifies. A nonrestrictive element, sometimes called a *nonessential element,* is set off by commas. (24-e)

nonsexist language See *sexist language.*

INSTRUCTOR'S NOTES

noun The name of a person, place, thing, or idea. Nouns can be classified as proper°, common°, concrete°, abstract°, collective°, or mass°. Nouns function as subjects°, objects°, and complements°. (6a)

noun clause A dependent clause° that functions as a subject°, object°, or complement°. (7e-2)

noun phrase A noun° and its modifiers° functioning as a subject°, object°, or complement°. (7d)

number Relates to how many subjects act or experience an action, one (singular) or more than one (plural). (page 176)

object complement A noun° or adjective° that immediately follows a direct object° and either describes or renames it. (7c-1)

objective case The case° of the pronoun° functioning as direct object°, indirect object°, object of a preposition°, or object of a verbal°. (9)

object A noun° or pronoun° or group of words functioning as a noun or pronoun that receives the action of a verb° (direct object°), tells to whom or for whom something is done (indirect object°), or completes the meaning of a preposition° (object of a preposition°). (7b, 6g)

onomatopoeia The use of a word or words to imitate the sound the word denotes: *the **rat-a-tat** of a woodpecker*. (21b)

oxymoron The technique of combining opposites for a seeming contradiction or paradox: *the burning winter wind*. (21b)

padding See *deadwood.*

paragraph A group of sentences that work together to develop a unit of thought. Introductory paragraphs° prepare the reader for what will follow in a piece of writing. Concluding paragraphs° bring a sense of completion to a piece of writing. Transitional paragraphs° link major sections within a piece of writing. Most paragraphs are topical paragraphs°, stating a main idea and offering specific, logical support of that idea. (4)

paragraph development The arrangement and organizational pattern a writer chooses to elaborate on or to support the topic° of a paragraph°. Methods of paragraph development include general to specific, specific to general, climactic order°, problem to solution, spatial order°, chronological order°, narration, description, process, example, definition, analysis°, classification°, comparison and contrast°, analogy°, and cause-and-effect analysis°. (4)

parallelism The use of equivalent grammatical forms or matching sentence structures, to express equivalent ideas. (18)

paraphrase A restatement of someone else's ideas in language and sentence structure different from those of the source. (31c)

parenthetical documentation Information enabling a reader to identify the source of ideas or of direct quotations°. This information is placed in parentheses close to that quotation or information, usually at the end of the sentence in which the material appears. (32k)

parenthetical reference See *parenthetical documentation.*

708

participial phrase A phrase containing a present participle° or past participle°, and any modifiers, that functions as an adjective° or adverb°. (7d)

passive construction See *passive voice.*

passive voice The form of a verb° in which the subject° is acted upon. If the subject is mentioned in the sentence, it usually appears as the object of the preposition° *by.* This voice° emphasizes the action, in contrast to the *active voice°,* which emphasizes the doer of the action. (8j)

past participle The third principal part° of the verb°. In regular verbs°, it adds *-d* or *-ed* to the simple form° and is identical to the past tense°. In irregular verbs°, it often differs from the simple form and the past tense. To function as a verb, it must have an auxiliary verb°. Used alone, it functions as an adjective°. (6d, 8a-1)

past perfect progressive tense The past perfect tense° form that describes an ongoing condition in the past that has been ended by something stated in the sentence: *I had been talking.* (8g)

past perfect tense The tense° that describes a condition or action that started in the past, continued for a while, and then ended in the past: *I had talked.* (8f)

past progressive tense The past tense form° that shows the continuing nature of a past action: *I was talking.* (8g)

past tense form The second principal part of the verb°. It shows an action or occurrence or state of being completed in the past. The past tense of regular verbs° add *-ed* or *-d* to the simple form°: *watched.* The past tense of irregular verbs° changes in spelling or uses a different word than the simple form°: *written.* (8a-1)

perfect tenses The three tenses—the present perfect°, the past perfect°, and the future perfect°—that show complex time relationships in the present, past, and future. (8f)

periodic sentence A sentence that begins with modifiers° and ends with the independent clause°, thus saving the main idea—and the emphasis—for the end of the sentence. Also called *climactic sentence.* (19d-2)

person Who or what acts or experiences an action. First person is the one speaking *(I, we);* second person is the one being spoken to *(you, you);* and third person is the person or thing spoken about *(he, she, it; they).* (page 231)

personal pronoun A pronoun° that refers to people or things, such as *I, you, them, hers,* and *it.* (6b, 9)

personification A type of figurative language that gives human traits to non-human things: *Mother earth.* (21b)

persuasive writing Also known as argumentative writing, persuasive writing seeks to convince the reader about a matter of opinion. It focuses on the reader, whom the writer wants to influence. (1b-2)

phrase A group of related words that does not contain a subject° and predicate°, and thus cannot stand alone as an independent grammatical unit. A phrase functions as a noun°, verb°, or modifier°. (7d)

709

INSTRUCTOR'S NOTES

plagiarism A serious offense, like stealing. A form of intellectual dishonesty that can lead to failure or expulsion, plagiarism occurs when a writer presents another person's words or ideas without giving credit to that person. Writers must use documentation° to give proper credit to their sources.

planning An early part of the writing process° in which writers gather ideas, often using invention strategies°. Along with shaping°, planning is sometimes called *prewriting*°. (2a–2d)

plural See *number.*

positive The form of an adjective° or adverb° when it is not being compared. Also see *comparative, superlative.* (12e-1)

possessive case The case° of a noun° or pronoun° that shows ownership or possession. (9)

predicate The part of the sentence that contains the verb° and tells what the subject° is doing or experiencing or what is being done to the subject. A *simple predicate* contains only the main verb° and auxiliary verb°, if any. A *complete predicate* contains the verb and all its modifiers°, objects°, and other related words. A *compound predicate* contains two or more verbs and their objects and modifiers. (7a-2)

predicate adjective An adjective° used as a subject complement°. (7c-1)

predicate nominative See *subject complement.*

prefix One or more syllables in front of a root word° that modify its meaning. (20c, 22d-3)

premise In the syllogism of a deductive argument, the first premise is an assumption and the second premise is either a fact or another assumption based on evidence. These two premises are followed by a conclusion. (5e-2)

preposition A word that shows a relationship between a noun° or pronoun° and other words in the sentence. A preposition is followed by a noun or pronoun object°. (6g)

prepositional phrase A preposition° and its object° and any modifiers° of its object. A prepositional phrase often shows a relationship in time or space. Prepositional phrases function as adjectives° or adverbs°. (6g)

present participle Used with one or more auxiliary verbs° in a main verb phrase°, shows action, occurrence, or state of being: *I am running.* As a verbal°, the *-ing* form of the verb° functioning as an adjective° (*running* water) or a noun° (*running* pleases me). (6d, 8a-1)

present perfect progressive tense The present perfect tense form° that describes something ongoing in the past that is likely to continue into the future. *I have been talking.* (8g)

present perfect tense The tense° indicating that an action or its effects continue into the present though begun or perhaps completed in the past: *I had talked.* (8f)

present progressive tense The present tense° form of the verb° that indicates something taking place at the time it is written or spoken about: *I am talking.* (8g)

710

present tense The tense that describes what is happening, what is true at the moment, and what is consistently true. It uses the simple form° *(I talk)* and in the third person singular, it uses the *-s* form° *(she talks).* (8a-1, 8a-2, 8d)

pretentious language Showy, overblown writing that calls attention to itself with complex sentences and long words for their own sakes. (21d-1)

prewriting A term for all activities in the writing process before drafting°. See *planning* and *shaping*.

primary evidence First-hand evidence from direct observation by the writer or an authoritative reporter. (5c)

primary source An original work of an author—novels, poems, short stories, autobiographies, diaries—and first-hand reports of observations and of research. (32)

progressive forms Verb forms made in all tense° with the present participle° and forms of *to be*. These forms show that an action is ongoing. (8g)

pronoun A word that takes the place of a noun°. Types of pronouns are personal°, relative°, interrogative°, demonstrative°, reflexive°, intensive°, reciprocal°, and indefinite°. Pronouns function in the same ways that nouns° do. (6b)

pronoun-antecedent agreement The match in expressing number°, person°, and gender° required between a pronoun° and its antecedent°. (11l–11o)

pronoun case The way a pronoun changes in form to reflect its use as the agent of action (subjective case°), the thing being acted upon (objective case°), or the thing showing ownership (possessive case°). (9b–9h)

pronoun reference The relationship between a pronoun° and its antecedent°. (10)

proofreading The final step in the writing process°, proofreading calls for the writer to read the final copy a piece of writing to find and correct typing errors or handwriting illegibility. (2a, 3e)

proper adjective An adjective° formed from a proper noun°: *Victorian, American.* (6e, 30e)

proper noun A noun° that names a specific person, place, or thing: *St. Louis, Toni Morrison, Corvette.* (6a, 30e)

purpose The goal or aim of a piece of writing: to express oneself, to provide information, to persuade, or to create a literary work. (1b)

quotation The use in written form of words another person has spoken or written. Direct quotation° repeats the words of the source exactly and encloses them in quotation marks. Indirect quotation° reports what the source said, without the requirement for using quotation marks unless some of the source's words are repeated as well. Quotation requires documentation° of the source. (31)

reciprocal pronoun A pronoun° that refers to individual parts of a plural antecedent°: *each other, one another.* (6b)

reflexive pronoun A *-self* form of the pronoun° that reflects the antecedent°. A reflexive pronoun cannot substitute for subjects° or objects°. (9h)

711

regional language Language specific to a geographic area. (21a-4)

regular verb A verb° that forms its past tense° and past participle° by adding -*ed* or -*d* to the simple form°. Most English verbs are regular. (8b)

relative clause See *adjective clause.* (7e-2)

relative pronoun A pronoun° that introduces certain noun clauses° and adjective clauses°, for example, *who, which, that, what,* and *whomever.* A relative pronoun is a subordinating word°. (6b, 7e-2)

restrictive appositive An appositive° renaming a noun° or pronoun° by giving information that is essential to distinguish it from other things in its class: *my brother* **John.**

restrictive clause A dependent clause° that limits a noun° or pronoun° by giving information necessary to distinguish it from others in its class. In contrast to a nonrestrictive clause°, this kind of dependent clause is never set off with commas. (24e)

restrictive element A word, phrase°, or dependent clause° that provides information essential to the understanding of the element it modifies. Restrictive elements are never set off by commas. (24c)

revision A part of the writing process° in which writers evaluate their rough drafts and, based on their decisions, rewrite by adding, cutting, replacing, moving, and often totally recasting material. (2a, 3c)

rhetoric The area of discourse that focuses on arrangement of ideas and choice of words as a reflection of the writer's purpose° and sense of audience°. (1)

root word The central part of a word to which a prefix° and/or suffix° is added. (20c-2)

run-on (run-together) sentence See *fused sentence.*

second person See *person.*

secondary evidence Evidence° from experts, reliable sources in their fields. Reliable secondary evidence appears in respected publications, is current, and is stated in relatively objective language. (5c)

secondary source A source that talks about someone else's original work. It explains events, analyzes information, and draws conclusions. (32)

sentence See *simple sentence, compound sentence, complex sentence, compound-complex sentence.*

sentence fragment A portion of a sentence that is punctuated as though it were a complete sentence. (13)

sexist language Language that unfairly assigns roles or characteristics to people on the basis of sex. Language that avoids stereotying according to sex is called *nonsexist language* (21b-3)

shaping An early part of the writing process° in which writers consider ways to organize their material. Along with planning°, shaping is sometimes called prewriting°. (2e)

712

simile A comparison, using *like, as,* or *as if,* between otherwise dissimilar things. (21b)

simple form The form of the verb° that shows action (or occurrence or state of being) taking place in the present for first and second person° singular and for first, second, and third persons plural. It is also the first principal part° of a verb. The simple form is also known as the *dictionary form* or *base form.* (8a-1)

simple predicate See *predicate.*

simple sentence A single independent clause° with no dependent clauses°. The subject° or predicate° or both may be compound. (7f-1)

simple subject See *subject.*

simple tenses The present°, past°, and future tenses°, which divide time into present, past, and future. (8e)

singular See *number.*

slang Coined words and new or extended meanings for established words, which quickly pass in and out of use. Inappropriate for any but the most informal communications. (21a-4)

slanted language Biased or emotionally loaded language. (21a-5)

spatial order A description of objects according to their physical relationship to one another, often in terms of a central reference point. Spatial order is a pattern that may be used to organize a paragraph°. The topic sentence° usually establishes a location that serves as the orientation for all other places mentioned. (2e-2, 4c)

speaker tag Explanatory words that identify the speaker of directly quoted words: *"Stay,"* **said the trainer.** (24g)

standard English See *edited American English.*

subject The word or group of words in a sentence that acts, is acted upon, or is described by the verb°. A *simple subject* includes only the noun° or pronoun°. A *complete subject* includes the noun or pronoun and all its modifiers°. A *compound* subject includes two or more nouns or pronouns and their modifiers. (7a-1)

subject complement Also called a *predicate nominative,* a noun° or adjective° that follows a linking verb° and describes or renames the subject° of the sentence. (7c-1, 8c)

subject-verb agreement The match of the subject° and verb° in expressing number° and person° required between a subject° and its verb°. (11a–11k)

subjective case The case° of the pronoun° functioning as subject°. (9)

subjunctive mood The verb mood° that expresses wishes, recommendations, indirect requests, and speculations: *I wish I* **were going.** (8i)

subordinate clause See *dependent clause.*

subordinating conjunction A conjunction that introduces an adverbial clause°, showing its relationship to the independent clause°. (6h, 7e-2)

713

subordination The technique of using grammatical structures to reflect the relative importance of ideas. A sentence with subordinated information contains an independent clause° to express important ideas in the sentence, and it contains dependent clauses° or phrases° to express ideas of lesser importance. (17d–17g)

suffix A syllable or syllables added to the end of a root word° that modify its meaning. (20c-2, 22d-1)

summary A condensed version of the essentials of ideas originally expressed in a longer version. (31d)

superlative The form of the adjective° or adverb° when three or more things are being compared: *greenest, most quickly*. (12e-1)

syllogism The structure of an argument reflecting deduction°. It has two premises°, the first one an assumption and the second a fact or an assumption based on evidence°. The conclusion, which is about a specific instance, follows logically from the premises. (5e-2)

synecdoche A kind of figurative language that substitutes a part for the whole or a whole for the part. (21b)

synthesis A component of critical thinking in which one makes connections among ideas. (page 114)

tense The time at which the action of the verb° occurs—in the past, present, or future. (8h)

tense sequence The accurate matching of verbs° to reflect the logical time relationships in sentences that have more than one verb. (8h)

thesis A statement of the central theme of an essay that makes clear the main idea of the essay, the writer's purpose, and the focus of the topic. It may also suggest the organizational pattern of the essay. (2e-4, 3c-2)

third person See *person*.

tone The writer's attitude towards his or her material and reader, especially as reflected in the writer's choice of words. (1c-1, 2e-3, 5b-3, 21a)

topic The subject of a piece of writing. A writer should consider both audience° and purpose° in choosing a topic. (2c)

topical paragraph See *paragraph*.

topic sentence The sentence in a paragraph° that contains the main idea of the paragraph. Not all paragraphs have topic sentences. (4a-1)

transition The logical connection of one idea to another in a piece of writing. Transition is achieved through the use of transitional expressions°, pronouns°, parallelism°, and the repetition of key words and phrases. (4b)

transitional expressions Words and phrases that signal connections among ideas and create coherence. A transitional expression lets the reader know how one idea connects to the next. (4b-1)

transitional paragraph See *paragraph*.

transitive verb A verb° that takes a direct object. (8c, 8d)

transitional words See *transitional expressions*.

714

understatement Also called *litotes,* a rhetorical device in which something is deliberately stated as being less than it is. (21b)

unity The close relationship of the parts of a piece of writing to one another. In a college essay, all parts should relate to the thesis° of the essay and all parts of a paragraph° should relate to the topic sentence° or main idea of the paragraph. Also called coherence°. (4a, 4b)

valid A term applied to an argument based on deduction° when the conclusion logically follows from the premises°. Validity has to do with the structure of the argument, not the truth of the premises. An argument based on untrue premises is valid if the conclusion follows from those premises. (5e-2)

verb The part of the predicate° in a sentence that acts or describes a state of being. Verbs change form to show time (tense°), attitude (mood°), and role of the subject (voice°). Verbs can be main verbs° or auxiliary verbs°, and they appear in verb phrases°. Verbs can be described as transitive° or intransitive° depending on whether they take a direct object°. (7d, 8)

verb phrase A verb° and its modifiers°. A verb phrase functions as a verb in the sentence. (7d, 8a)

verbal phrase A group of words that contains a verbal°—an infinitive°, participle°, or gerund°—and its modifiers°. Verbals function as nouns° or modifiers° rather than as verbs°. (7d)

verbals Verb parts functioning as nouns°, adjectives°, or adverbs°. Verbals include infinitives°, present participles°, past participles°, and gerunds°. (6c)

voice An attribute of a verb° showing whether the subject° acts (active voice°) or is acted upon (passive voice°). (8j)

webbing See *mapping.*

writing process A series of stages in which a writer gathers and shapes ideas, organizes material, expresses those ideas in a rough draft, evaluates the draft and revises it, and edits the writing for technical errors, and proofreads it for typographical mistakes or illegibility. See planning°, shaping°, drafting°, revising°, editing°, and proofreading°. (2, 3)

715

INDEX

A degree symbol (°) after an index entry signals that the term is defined in the Glossary of Grammatical and Selected Composition Terms. An entry in boldface italics (***advice, advise***, for example) is discussed in the Usage Glossary. Section numbers are in boldface type and page numbers in regular type. The listing **6a**: 142 thus refers you to page 142, which is in Section 6a.

a, an, **6a**: 142. *See also* Articles
Abbreviations, **30h,i**: 500–504
  for academic degrees, **30h**: 501
  acronyms, **23b**: 411, **30e**: 496
  commas with titles and degrees, **24h**: 436
  in dates and times, **30h**: 500–501
  in documentation, **30i**: 502–4, **32g-2**: 563, 564, 565, 566, 568
  of money units, **30h**: 502
  of months, **30i**: 504
  of organizations and agencies, **30h**: 501
  for parts of a book or play, **32k-l**: 564
  periods with, **23b**: 411
  scholarly, **30i**: 503
  of states, **23b**: 411, **30h**: 502, **30i**: 503–4
  symbols as, **30h**: 502
  of titles of persons, **30h**: 501
-able, -ible spellings, **22d-1**: 397
about, for doubtful information, **23d**: 412, **29b-4**: 479
Abridged dictionaries, **20a-3**: 360–61
Absolute phrases°, **7d**: 163, **19d-1**: 347
Abstract language, **20b-2**: 365–66
Abstract nouns°, **6a**: 141
Abstracts°
  bibliographic citations, **32g-2**: 571–72
  in computerized databases, **32e-8**: 556
  in scientific reports, **34d-3**: 653
Academic degrees
  abbreviations of, **30h**: 501
  punctuation with, **23b**: 411, **24h**: 436
Academic writing, **1c-2**: 10
  appropriate tone, **21a-1**: 372
  language standard, **21a-2**: 373
  topic selection, **2c-1**: 17–18
accept, except, **22c-1**: 389
Acronyms°
  capitalization, **30e**: 396
  periods and, **23b**: 411
Active voice°
  avoiding unplanned shifts to passive, **15a-2**: 284–85
  in different academic disciplines, **34a-2**: 619
  and passive voice, 205–7
  revising passive to, for conciseness, **16a-2**: 304–5
A.D., **30h**: 501
Addition
  conjunctive adverbs showing, **6f**: 148
  revision activity, **3c-1**: 51
  transitional expressions for, **4b**: 84
Address, direct. *See* Direct address

Addresses
  abbreviations in, **30h**: 502
  commas with, **24h**: 436, 437
  numbers in, **30j**: 506
ad hominem fallacy°, **5f**: 136–37
Adjective clauses°, **7e-2**: 167–68
  commas with, **7e-2**: 168, **24e-1**: 429
  expanding basic sentences with, **19d-1**: 347
  reducing to phrases, **16a-3**: 307
  restrictive and nonrestrictive, **7e-2**: 168, **24e-1**: 429
  subordination of, **17**: 323
Adjectives°, **6e**: 146–47
  vs. adverbs, **12**: 247–57
  avoiding pronoun reference to, **10c-2**: 224
  changing nouns to, **12f**: 256–57
  commas between, **24d**: 426
  comparison, **12e**: 253–55
  as complements°, **7c-1**: 159, **12d**: 251–52
  coordinate, and commas, **24d**: 426
  demonstrative, **6e**: 147
  descriptive, **6e**: 146
  expanding basic sentences with, **19d-1**: 347
  indefinite, **6e**: 147
  interrogative, **6e**: 147
  irregular comparative forms, **12e-2**: 254–55
  limiting, **6a**: 142, **6e**: 146, 147
  modified by adverbs, **6f**: 148, **7c-2**: 160–61, **7e-2**: 167, **12**: 248, **12b**: 249
  as modifiers, **7c-2**: 160
  numerical, **6e**: 147
  possessive, **6e**: 147
  proper, **6e**: 146, **30e**: 491
  regular comparative forms, **12e-1**: 253–55
  relative, **6e**: 147
  suffixes for, **20c-1**: 369
  verbals functioning as, **6d**: 145, **7d**: 164, **8a-1**: 179
Adverb clauses°, **7e-2**: 167
  commas with, **7e-2**: 167, **7f-4**: 173, **17**: 322, **24b-1**: 420–21
  elliptical, **7e-2**: 170
  expanding basic sentences with, **19d-1**: 347
  introductory, **24b-1**: 420–21
  subordination of, **17**: 322
Adverbs°, **6f**: 148–49
  vs. adjectives, **12**: 247–57
  -ally, -ly endings, **12**: 247, **22d-1**: 397, **22e-3**: 406

716

Adverbs° (cont.)
  comparison, **12e**: 253–55
  conjunctive, **6f**: 148, **14b**: 273, **14e**: 278–79, **25c**: 445
  descriptive, **6f**: 149
  expanding basic sentences with, **19d-1**: 347
  irregular comparative forms, **12e-2**: 254–55
  as modifiers, **7c-2**: 160–61, **12a–12b**: 249
  modifying adverbs, **6f**: 148, **7c-2**: 160–61, **7e-2**: 167, **12**: 248, **12b**: 249
  not modifying linking verbs, **12d**: 251–52
  regular comparative forms, **12e**: 253–55
  splitting infinitives, **15b-3**: 290
  verbals functioning as, **6d**: 145, **7d**: 163, 164
ad verecundiam fallacy, **5f**: 137
***advice, advise*, 22c-1**: 389
***affect, effect*, 22c-1**: 389
Afterwords, bibliographic citations, **32g-2**: 567–68
aggravate, irritate
Agreement°, **11**: 230–45. *See also* Pronoun agreement; Subject-verb agreement
ain't
aisle, isle, **22c-1**: 389
all
  as hyphenated prefix, **22e-2**: 404
  as indefinite pronoun: pronoun agreement, **11n**: 244; subject-verb agreement, **11f**: 238
***all ready, already*, 22c-1**: 389, **22c-3**: 395
***all right*, 22c-3**: 395
***all together, altogether*, 22c-1**: 389, **22c-3**: 395
***allude, elude*, 22c-1**: 389
***allusion, illusion*, 22c-1**: 389
-ally, -ly, **22d-1**: 397
***a lot*, 22c-3**: 395
Almanacs, **32e-5**: 545
altar, alter, **22c-1**: 389
although, **14d**: 276
A.M., P.M., **23b**: 411, **30h**: 500
Ambiguous placement of modifiers, **15b-1**: 288–89
Ambiguous pronoun reference, **10a**: 222, **10c**: 224–25
Ambiguity as logical fallacy, **5f**: 137–38
American English
  edited, **21a-2**: 373
  history of, **20**: 355–56
American Psychological Association (APA) documentation style, **32d-4**: 540, **34c-3, 4**: 646–50
among, between
amount, number
Amounts, subject-verb agreement with, **11j**: 240. *See also* Measurements; Numbers
an, and
Analogy°
  false, **5f**: 135–36
  as introductory device, **4e**: 107
  as paragraph development pattern, **4d**: 102–3
  in the social sciences, **34c-2**: 642
Analysis°
  of cause and effect, **4d**: 103, **5d**: 130–31
  and critical thinking, **5**: 114
  in the humanities, **34b-3**: 621–25

to introduce a quotation, **31e-4**: 529
as paragraph development pattern, **4d**: 100
in the social sciences, **34c-2**: 642–43
-ance, -ence spellings, **22d-1**: 397–98
and, **6h**: 151, **17**: 317
  pronoun agreement with antecedents joined by, **11l**: 243
  agreement of verb with subjects joined by, **11c**: 234–35
  with *who, whom,* or *which* in parallel clauses, **18c-4**: 335
  See also Coordinating conjunctions
***and/or*, 29e-3**: 485
Anecdotes as introductory device, **4e**: 107–8, **33**: 595
angel, angle, **22c-1**: 390
-ant, -ent spellings, **22d-1**: 397–98
Antecedents°, **6b**: 142
  of adjectives clauses, **7e-2**: 168, 170
  clear references to, **10a**: 222
  collective nouns as, **11o**: 245
  indefinite pronouns as, **11n-1**: 244
  of *it, that, this,* and *which*, **10c-3**: 225
  and pronoun agreement, **11**: 242–45
  remote, **10b**: 222–23
  and subject-verb agreement, **11g**: 239–40
  of *who, which,* or *that*, **7e-2**: 168, **10f**: 228–29, **11i**: 239–40, **17**: 322–23
Anthologies, articles from bibliographic citations: APA style, **34c-4**: 649; MLA parenthetical-references style, **32g-2**: 565–66; MLA note style, **34b-4**: 639
  documentary note references, **34b-4**: 635
any, subject-verb agreement, **11f**: 238
APA style, **32d-4**: 550, **34c-3,4**: 646–50
Apostrophes, **27**: 457–61
  in contractions, **27c**: 460–61
  misuse of, **27b**: 459–60
  for omitted letters or numbers, **27c**: 460–61
  with plurals of letters, numbers, symbols, and words used as terms, **27d**: 461
  in possessive forms, **27a**: 457–59
anybody, any body*; *anyone, any one
anyplace
anyways, anywheres
Appeal to ignorance, **5f**: 137–38
Appeal to the person, **5f**: 136–37
Appositives°, **7c-3**: 161–62
  emphasizing with dash: **29a-1**: 475
  final, introduced by colon, **26a**: 452
  nonrestrictive, commas with, **7c-3**: 161, **24e-2**: 430
  pronoun case forms, **9b**: 213
  as sentence fragments, **13c**: 268
Appropriate language, **21a**: 371–77
  nonsexist, **21a-3**: 373–75
  unslanted, **21a-5**: 377
  vs. slang, colloquial, and regional language, **21a-4**: 376–77
  standard for, **21a-2**: 373
  tone of, **21a-2**: 372–73
apt, likely, liable
Archaic usage, **20a-1**: 358
are, hour, **22c-1**: 390
Argumentation, **1a**: 3, **1b-2**: 5. *See also* Logical fallacies; Persuasive writing
Arguments, circular, **5f**: 136

Articles° (*a, an, the*), **6a**: 142
  dropped, in citations of periodicals, **32g-2**: 570, 571
  ignored, in alphabetizing bibliographic entries, **32g-2**: 562, 565
  inadvertent omission of, **15e-3**: 299–300
  with newspaper names, **30f**: 498, **32g-2**: 571
  repeated in parallel forms, **18c-3**: 334
Articles (in publications)
  abstracts of, **32e-8**: 556
  bibliographic citations: APA style, **34c-4**: 649, 650; MLA parenthetical-references style, **26b**: 454, **32g-2**: 566, 569–71, **33**: 613; MLA note style, **34b-4**: 639, 640
  documentary note references, **34b-4**: 635, 636
  indexes to, **32e-6**: 550–52
  parenthetical references, **32k-1**: 584
  titles of, quotation marks for, **28b**: 468–69
Artificial language, **21d**: 380–84
Arts, reference works on, **32e-5**: 547
Art works
  bibliographic citations, **32-g**: 574
  titles of, italics for, **30f**: 497
as
  pronoun case after comparisons with, **9e**: 218
  as subordinating conjunction, **14d**: 276
ascent, assent, **22c-1**: 390
as follows, colon after, **26a**: 453
Asides
  dashes for, **29a-3**: 476
  parentheses for, **29b-1**: 478
as if, subjunctive mood with, **8i-2**: 204
as, like, as if
assent, ascent, **22c-1**: 390
assistance, assistants, **22c-1**: 390
Assumptions, unstated, **5e-2**: 134
assure, ensure, insure
as though, subjunctive mood with, **8i-2**: 204
as to
Atlases, **32e-5**: 545–46
Audience°, **1c**: 8–11
  general reading public, **1c-1**: 8–9
  instructors as, **1c-2**: 10
  for research paper, **32c**: 536–37
  specialists, **1c-3**: 10–11
  and writing situation, **2b**: 15
Authorities
  false or irrelevant, **5f**: 137
  quoting from, **31e-2**: 526
Author names
  in bibliographic citations: APA style, **34c-4**: 648, 649–50; MLA parenthetical-references style, **32g-2**: 563–64, **33**: 611, 613; MLA note style, **34b-4**: 637, 638; scientific style, **34d-4**: 658
  in documentary notes, **34b-4**: 635
  in introductions to quotations, **31e-4**: 527–29
  in parenthetical references, **32k-1**: 580, 582–83
Auxiliary (helping) verbs°, **6c**: 144
  be and *have,* **8c**: 188
  and future tenses, **8c**: 188
  modal, **8a-1**: 178, **8c**: 188–89
  with present participle, **8a-1**: 179
  in progressive forms, **8g**: 195
  in verb phrases, **8a**: 177
awful, awfully
a while, awhile
Awkward placement of modifiers, **15b-3**: 289–91

Background information as introductory device, **4e**: 107
bad, badly, **12d**: 251
bad, worse, worst, **12e-2**: 255
Balanced sentences°, **18b-3**: 333
Balancing subordination and coordination, **17g**: 328
Bandwagon fallacy, **5f**: 137
bare, bear, **22c-1**: 390
barely, **12c**: 249
Base form° (of verb). *See* Simple form
B.C., **30h**: 501
be
  in academic writing, **8c**: 187
  as auxiliary verb, **6c**: 144, **8c**: 188
  in expletive constructions, **11e**: 236
  forms of, **8c**: 187
  as main verb, **8c**: 186–87
  with present participle, **8a-1**: 179
  in subjunctive mood, **8i**: 203–4
because, **14d**: 276
  after *reason . . . is,* **15d-2**: 296
been, being
being as, being that
beside, besides
better, had better
between, objective case with, **9a**: 212
between, among
Biblical references, **26b**: 453
Bibliographic notes, **32k-2**: 585
Bibliographies. *See also* References Cited list; References list; Works Cited list
  abbreviations in, **32g-2**: 563, 564, 565, 566, 568
  card preparation, **32g-1**: 561–62
  in the humanities: MLA Works Cited, **26b**: 454, **32d-4**: 540, **32g-2**: 562–74, **33**: 611–13; with MLA note-style references, **34b-4**: 637, 638–40
  in the natural and technological sciences, **34d-4**: 658
  as a research tool, **32e-5**: 546–47
  in the social sciences (APA style), **34c-4**: 647–50
Bibliography cards, preparing, **32g-1**: 561–62
Biographical reference works, **32e-5**: 546
Biology, style manual, **34d-4**: 657
Block structure, for comparison and contrast, **4d**: 101, 102
board, bored, **22c-1**: 390
Body paragraphs. *See* topical paragraphs
Book reports, **34b-3**: 626
Book titles
  capitalization, **30e**: 495
  italics with, **30f**: 498
Books
  bibliographic citations: APA style, **34c-4**: 649, 650; MLA parenthetical-references style, **32g-2**: 563–69, **33**: 611; MLA note style, **34b-4**: 635, 638
  in library collections, **32a-7**: 552–54
  parts of: abbreviations for, **32k-1**: 584; numbers in, **30j**: 507
  titles: capitalization of, **30e**: 495; italics for, **30f**: 498
bored, board, **22c-1**: 390
both . . . and. See Correlative conjunctions

Brackets, **29c**: 481–82
  for insertions into quotations, **29c**:
    481–82, **31e-1**: 525
  with parentheses, **29c-2**: 482
Brainstorming°, **2d-3**: 24–26
brake, break, **22c-1**: 390
breath, breathe, **22c-1**: 390
bring, take
British spellings, **22c-2**: 394
broke
Buildings, names of, **30e**: 494
Bureaucratic language°, **21d-5**: 383–84
burst, bust
Business
  reference works on, **32e-5**: 547
  obtaining research information from
    firms, **32e-2**: 542, **32e-3**: 543
Business writing, **35**: 659–68
  letters, **35a**: 659–60; block paragraphing,
    4: 73; for job application, **35b**: 660–61;
    salutation, **26b**: 454
  memos, **35d**: 662–63
  resumes, **35c**: 662
but, **6h**: 151, **17**: 317
but, however, yet
but that, but what
buy, by, **22c-1**: 390

calculate, figure, reckon
Call numbers, **32e-7**: 552
can, **6c**: 144; **8c**: 188
can, may
Canned rhetoric, **2c-2**: 19
can't hardly, can't scarcely
canvas, canvass, **22c-1**: 390
capital, capitol, **22c-1**: 390
Capitalization, **30**: 487–96
  after colons, **26a**: 453
  of first word of sentence, **30a**: 487–89
  in formal outline, **2e-5**: 41
  guide, **30e**: 492–96
  of interjections, **30d**: 491
  after interjection with exclamation point,
    24b-3: 422
  of listed items, **30b**: 489–90
  of proper nouns and adjectives, **30e**:
    491–96
  with quotations, **30c**: 490
  of titles, **30e**: 495; in APA references,
    34c-4: 649; in scientific references,
    34d-4: 658
Card catalogues, **32e-7**: 552–55
Card-stacking, **5f**: 137
Case°, **6b**: 142, **9**: 209–20
  in appositives, **9b**: 213
  in comparisons with *than* or *as,* **9e**: 218
  in compound constructions, **9a**: 210–12
  before gerunds, **9g**: 218–19
  with infinitives, **9f**: 218
  after linking verbs, **9c**: 214
  matching noun and pronoun, **9b**: 213
  who, whoever vs. *whom, whomever,* **9d**:
    215–17
  See also possessive case
Case studies, in social sciences, **34c-3**:
  643–45
Cause, subordinating conjunctions showing,
  7e-2: 166
Cause-and-effect analysis
  in critical thinking, **5d**: 130–31

  guidelines, **5d**: 130–31
  as paragraph development pattern, **4d**:
    103
  post hoc, ergo propter hoc fallacy, **5f**: 136
CBE (Council of Biology Editors) *Style*
  Manual, **34d-4**: 657–58
-cede, -ceed, -sede, **22d-1**: 398
censor, censure
chairman, chairperson, chair
Chapter numbers, **30j**: 507, **32k-1**: 584
Choice, subordinating conjunctions showing, **7e-2**: 166
choose, chose, **22c-1**: 390
Chronological order°, **2e-2**: 32
  and cause-and-effect relationships, **5d**:
    130
  in narrative paragraphs, **4d**: 97
  post hoc, ergo propter hoc fallacy, **5f**: 136
  in process description, **4d**: 98
  sentences arranged in, **4c**: 93
Chronological resume, **35**: 668
Circular arguments and definitions, **5f**: 136
CIS, **32e-3**: 543
Citations. *See* Documentation
cite, site, **22c-1**: 390
City names
  in publication data, **32g-2**: 563
  with state names or abbreviations, **23b**:
    411, **24h**: 436, **30h**: 502
Clarifying sentence°, **4a**: 76
Classification°, as paragraph development
  pattern, **4d**: 100–101
Clauses°, **7e**: 165–70
  coordination and subordination of, **17**:
    316–28
  parallel, **18**: 331, **18b**: 332–33
  punctuation with, **7f-2,3,4**: 173
  reducing to phrases, **16a-3**: 307
  and sentence types, **7f**: 172–73
  See also Adjective clauses; Adverb
    clauses; Dependent clauses; Indepen-
    dent clauses
Clichés°, **21c**: 379–80
Climactic order°, **2e-2**: 32
  in paragraphs, **4c**: 91–92
  of parallel phrases and clauses, **18b-2**: 333
Climactic sentences°, **19d-2**: 348
Closed (unhyphenated) words, **22e-2**: 404
cloths, clothes, **22c-1**: 390
coarse, course, **22c-1**: 390
Coherence°
  combining techniques for, **4b-5**: 86–87
  in essay, **3b**: 48
  among paragraphs, **4b**: 87–88
  within paragraphs, **4**: 75, **4b**: 83–88
  with parallel structure, **4b-4**: 86
  with pronouns, **4b-2**: 84–85
  with repetition of key words, **4b-3**: 85
  with transitional expressions, **4b-1**: 83–84
Collections, works in
  bibliographic citations: APA style, **34c-4**:
    649; MLA parenthetical-references
    style, **32g-2**: 565–66, 571; MLA note
    style, **34b-4**: 639
  documentary note references, **34b-4**: 635
Collective nouns°, **6a**: 141
  pronoun agreement with, **11o**: 245
  verb agreement with, **11g**: 238
Colloquial language°, **20**: 355, **20a-1**: 358,
  21a-4: 376–77

Colons, **26**: 451–55
  in biblical references, **26b**: 454
  in bibliographic citations, **26b**: 45, **32k-1**: 583
  capitalization after, **30a**: 488
  before lists, **25e-2**: 447, **26a**: 453
  in memos, **26b**: 454
  misuse of, **26c**: 454–55
  before quotations, **26a**: 451–52
  after salutations, **26b**: 454
  before summaries, **26a**: 452
  in time expressions, **26b**: 453
  between titles and subtitles, **26b**: 453
Combining sentences
  for conciseness, **16a**: 306
  coordination and subordination, **17**: 316–29
  to correct a comma splice, **14d**: 276–77
COMCAT, **32e-7**: 555
Comma fault°. *See* Comma splice
Commands
  end punctuation for, **8**: 202, **19b**: 344, **23a**: 410, **23e**: 412–13
  in imperative mood, **8**: 202
  with implied subject, **8**: 202, **13a**: 263
  for variety and emphasis, **19b**: 344
Commas, **24**: 415–41
  with academic degrees or titles that follow names, **23b**: 411, **24h**: 463
  in addresses, **24h**: 436
  after adverb clauses that precede independent clauses, **7e-2**: 167, **7f-4**: 173, **17**: 322, **24b-1**: 420–21
  to clarify meaning, **24h**: 435–37
  after conjunctive adverb at beginning of sentence, **14e**: 279
  with contrasts, **24f**: 432
  between coordinate adjectives, **24d**: 426
  before coordinating conjunctions that join independent clauses, **7f-2**: 172, **7f-4**: 173, **14c**: 275, **17**: 318, **24a**: 416–18
  in dates, **24h**: 435
  with dependent clauses, **7f-3**: 173, **13a**: 263, **14d**: 276
  with direct address, **24f**: 432
  with interjections, **24b-3**: 422
  with interrupting elements, **24f**: 431–32
  after introductory elements, **14d**: 276, **24b-1,2,3**: 420–22
  in letters, **24h**: 436
  misuse of, **24j**: 439–41
  overview of uses, **24**: 415
  in names, places, and addresses, **24h**: 436
  in numbers, **24h**: 437
  with nonrestrictive elements, **7c-3**: 161, **7e-2**: 168, **7f-4**: 173, **10f**: 229, **14d**: 277, **17**: 323, **24e**: 427–30
  and other punctuation: exclamation point, **23e**: 413, **24g**: 434; parentheses, **29b-4**: 479; question mark, **23c**: 412, **24g**: 434
  with parenthetical expressions, **24f**: 432
  with quotations, **24g**: 433–34
  role of, **24**: 416
  with series items, **24c**: 423–24
  with states names or abbreviations that follow city names, **23b**: 411, **24h**: 436, **30h**: 502
  before tag questions, **24f**: 432

  with transitional elements, **4b**: 83, **14e**: 278, **24f**: 432
Comma splices°, **14**: 271–79
  avoiding, **24a**: 418
  correcting: with coordinating conjunctions, **14c**: 275; by revising an independent clause as a dependent clause, **14d**: 276–77; with semicolon or period, **14b**: 274, **14e**: 278–79
  leading causes, **14a**: 273
  recognizing, **14a**: 272–73
Common knowledge, **31b**: 511
Common nouns°, **6a**: 141, **30e**: 491–92
Communicating, **1a**: 3
Company names
  capitalization of, **30e**: 493
  subject-verb agreement, **11k**: 241
Comparative° forms, **12e**: 253–55
  in compounds, **22e-3**: 406
  redundant, **12e-1**: 254
Comparison°. *See also* Contrast
  and analogy, **4d**: 102–3
  comparative and superlative forms of adjectives and adverbs, **12e**: 253–55
  complete, unambiguous, and logical, **15c-2**: 298–99
  conjunctive adverbs showing, **6f**: 148
  elliptical, **7e-2**: 170
  as paragraph development pattern, **4d**: 101–2
  with *than* or *as*, **9e**: 218
  transitional expressions for, **4b**: 84
complement, compliment, **22c-1**: 390
Complements°, **7c-1**: 158–59
  adjectives as, **7c-1**: 159, **12d**: 251–52
  faulty predication, **15d-2**: 296
  noun clauses as, **7e-2**: 170
  nouns as, **6a**: 141, **7c-1**: 159
  object, **7c-1**: 159
  subject, **7c-1**: 159, **8c**: 186–87, **11g**: 239
Completeness, in scientific writing, **34d-2**: 652
Complete predicates°, **7a-2**: 156
Complete subjects°, **7a-1**: 155
Complex sentences°, **7f-3**: 173
  to correct comma splices or fused sentences, **14d**: 276
  subordination in, **17**: 322–28
  tense sequences in, **8h-1**: 197–99
Composing, **2e**: 30. *See also* Drafting, Shaping activities
Compositions, **2a**: 14. *See also* Essays; Papers
Compound-complex sentences°, **7f-4**: 173
  coordination and subordination in, **17g**: 328
Compound constructions, pronoun case forms in, **9a**: 210–11
Compound predicates°, **7a-2**: 156
  as sentence fragments, **13c**: 268
Compound (coordinate) sentences°, **7f-2**: 172, **17**: 317–20, 328
  commas with, **7f-2**: 172, **7f-4**: 173, **14c**: 275, **17**: 318, **24a**: 416–18
  to correct comma splices and fused sentences, **14c**: 275
  illogical, **17c-1**: 319
  for occasional effect, **17b**: 318–19
  overuse of, **17c-2**: 320
  revising strings of, **19a-2**: 342

Compound subjects°, **7a-1**: 155
  agreement with verbs, **11c**: 234–35
  pronoun case form, **9a**: 210–11
Compound words
  capitalization of, **30e**: 496
  plural forms, **22d-4**: 401–2
  possessive forms, **27a-4**: 458
  prefixes with, **22e-2**: 404
  hyphenation rules, **22e-3**: 405–6
Computer disks, storing word processing
    output on, **3f**: 72
Computerized databases, **32e-8**: 555–57
Computer software, bibliographic citations,
    32g-2: 573
Concerts. *See* Performances
Concession
  subordinating conjunctions showing,
    7e-2: 166, **17**: 323
  transitional expressions for, **4b**: 84
Conciseness, **16**: 302–14
  avoiding nouns formed from verbs, **16a-4**: 308
  eliminating empty words and phrases,
    16b: 311–13
  eliminating unneeded words, **16b**: 309–13
  reducing sentence structures, **16a-3**:
    306–7
  revising expletives, **16a-1**: 303–4
  revising passives, **16a-2**: 304–5
  revising redundancies, **16c**: 314
  using strong verbs, **16a-4**: 308
  See also Wordiness
Concluding paragraphs, **4e**: 109–11
  content not included in formal outlines,
    2e-5: 41
  devices for, **4e**: 109
  in job application letters, **35b**: 661
  in research paper, **33**: 607
  what to avoid, **4e**: 110
Conclusions
  in deductive reasoning, **5e-2**: 133
  qualified, **5c**: 126
  in scientific reports, **34d-5**: 654
Concrete details, developing paragraphs
    with, **4a-2**: 81–2
Concrete nouns°, **6a**: 141
Concrete words°, **20b-2**: 365–66
Conditional relationships
  subjunctive mood and, **8i-1**: 203
  subordinating conjunctions showing,
    7e-2: 166, **17**: 323
Conference proceedings, bibliographic cita-
    tions, **32g-2**: 568–69
Conjectures, subjunctive mood for, **8i-2**:
    204
Conjunctions°, **6h**: 151–52
  inadvertent omission, **15e-3**: 299–300
  in titles, **30e**: 495
  See also Coordinating conjunctions; Cor-
    relative conjunctions; Subordinating
    conjunctions
Conjunctive adverbs°, **6f**: 148
  in comma splices and fused sentences,
    14b: 273, **14e**: 278–79
  joining independent clauses, **6f**: 148, **25c**:
    445
  placement of, **14e**: 279
  punctuation with, **14e**: 278–79, **25c**: 445
  as sentence modifiers, **7c-2**: 160–61, **12**:
    248
Connotation°, **20b-1**: 363–64

conscience, conscious, **22c-1**: 390
consensus of opinion
Content notes. *See* Notes
continual, continuous
Contractions
  apostrophes in, **27c**: 460–61
  appropriate uses, **27c**: 460
  double negative and, **12c**: 250
  vs. possessive pronouns, **27b**: 259–60
Contrary-to-fact statements, subjunctive
    mood for, **8a-1**: 203
Contrast
  as clue to word meaning, **20c-2**: 370
  conjunctive adverbs showing, **6f**: 148
  as paragraph development pattern, **4d**: 101–2
  set off with commas, **24f**: 432
  set off with dashes, **29a-2**: 476
  transitional expressions for, **4b**: 84
Coordinate adjectives°, **24d**: 426
Coordinate sentences. *See* Compound
    sentences; Coordination
Coordinating conjunctions°, **6h**: 151
  to correct comma splices and fused
    sentences, **14c**: 275
  linking independent clauses, **7f-2**: 172,
    7f-4: 173, **14**: 271, **14c**: 275, **17**: 318,
    24a: 416–18, **25b**: 444–45
  meaning and function, **17**: 317
  parallel forms with, **18c-1**: 333, **18c-4**: 335
  in a series, **24c**: 424
Coordination°, **17**: 316–20, 328
  balancing with subordination, **17g**: 328
  and compound sentences, **7f-2**: 172
  defined, **17**: 316
  for effect, **17b**: 318–19
  illogical, **17c-1**: 319
  overuse of, **17c-2**: 320
  to show relationship, **17a**: 318
Corporate authors
  in bibliographic citations: APA style,
    34c-4: 650; MLA style, **32g-2**: 564; old
    MLA style, **34b-4**: 638
  in documentary note references, **34b-4**:
    635
  in parenthetical references, **32k-1**: 583
corps, corpse, **22c-1**: 390
Correlative conjunctions, **6h**: 151
  agreement of pronoun with antecedents
    joined by, **11m**: 243–44
  agreement of verb with subjects joined
    by, **11d**: 235–36
  with parallel forms, **18c-2**: 334
could, **8c**: 188
council, counsel, **22c-1**: 390
couple, couple of
course, coarse, **22c-1**: 390
Cover page format, **33**: 590–91
Critical thinking, **5**: 113–38
  evaluating cause and effect, **5d**: 130–31
  and reading, **5a,b**: 114–24
  recognizing and avoiding logical fallacies,
    5f: 135–38
  understanding reasoning processes, **5e**:
    131–34
  using evidence, **5c**: 125–29
Criticism, benefiting from, during writing
    process, **3c-4**: 60–63
Cumulative sentences°, **19d-2**: 348
Cutting, revision activity, **3c-1**: 51. *See also*
    Wordiness

721

-d, -ed. See -ed, -d
dairy, diary, **22c-1**: 390
Dangling modifiers°, **15c**: 293
Dashes, **29a**: 474–76
  with asides, **29a-3**: 476
  for broken-off speech, **29a-4**: 476
  with contrasts, **29a-2**: 476
  with explanations, **29a-1**: 475
  with other punctuation, **29a-3**: 476
  vs. parentheses, **29b**: 477
data
Databases, computerized, **32e-8**: 555–57
Dates
  abbreviations with, **30h**: 501
  doubtful, **23d**: 412, **29b-4**: 479
  numbers in, **30j**: 506
  punctuation of, **24h**: 435, 437
Days of the week, capitalization of, **30e**:
  495
Deadwood°, **16b**: 310–13. *See also*
  Wordiness
Decimal figures, **30j**: 506
Declarations, emphatic, **23e**: 412–13
Declarative sentences°, **7**: 154
  varying with other types, **19b**: 344
Deduction°. *See* Deductive reasoning
Deductive reasoning, **5e-2**: 133–34
  comparison with inductive reasoning, **5e**:
    132
  in general-to-specific paragraphs, **4c**:
    90–91
  and position of topic sentence, **4a-1**: 77
  summary, **5e**: 134
  syllogisms, **5e**: 133
Definitions
  circular, **5f**: 136
  in dictionary entries, **20a-1**: 357–58
  emphasizing with dashes, **29a-1**: 475
  as introductory device, **4e**: 107
  as paragraph development pattern, **4d**:
    99–100
  in the social sciences, **34c-2**: 642
Demonstrative adjectives, **6e**: 147
Demonstrative pronouns°, **6b**: 143
  antecedents, **10c-3**: 225
  plural, subject-verb agreement, **11a**: 232
Denotation°, **20b-1**: 362–64
Dependent (subordinate) clauses°, **7e-2**:
  166–70
  in complex sentences, **7f-3**: 173
  in compound-complex sentences, **7f-4**:
    174
  elliptical, **7e-2**: 170
  introduced by *if* and *unless*, **8i**: 203
  introductory, **19d**: 349, **24b**: 420–21
  noun, **7e-2**: 170, **24j**: 439–40
  restrictive and nonrestrictive, **7e-2**: 168,
    7f-4: 173, **24e-1**: 429
  revising independent clauses as, **14d**:
    276–77
  as sentence fragments, **13a,b**: 263–66,
    14d: 276
  subordination of, **17**: 322–28
  tense sequences in, **8h-1**: 197–99
  use of *who, whoever* or *whom, whomever,*
    9d-1: 215–17
  See also Adjective clauses; Adverb
    clauses
Description, **1a**: 3, **4d**: 97–98
Descriptive adjectives°, **6e**: 146

Descriptive adverbs°, **6f**: 149
descent, dissent, **22c-1**: 390
dessert, desert, **22c-1**: 391
Details, developing paragraphs with, **4a-2**:
  81–82
Development patterns, **4d**: 96–103
  analogy, **4d**: 102–3
  analysis and classification, **4d**: 100–101
  cause-and-effect analysis, **4d**: 103
  comparison and contrast, **4d**: 101–2
  definition, **4d**: 99–100
  description, **4d**: 97–98
  example, **4d**: 99
  narration, **4d**: 97
  process, **4d**: 98–99
  RENNS, **4a-2**: 81–82
device, devise, **22c-1**: 391
Developmental paragraphs, **4**: 73. *See also*
  Topical paragraphs
Dewey Decimal System, **32e-7**: 553
Dialect
  expository writing and, **21a-4**: 376–77
  usage label, **20a-1**: 358
DIALOG Information System, **32e-8**: 556
Dialogue, broken-off, **29a-4**: 476, **29d-2**:
  484. *See also* Direct discourse
  punctuation with, **24g**: 433–34
Diction°, **20b**: 362–66, **21a**: 371. *See also*
  Language; Tone; Words
Dictionaries, **20a**: 356–62
  abridged, **20a-3**: 360–61
  biographical, **32e-5**: 546
  information in entries, **20a-1**: 356–58
  as a research tool, **32e-5**: 546
  specialized, **20a-4**: 361–62
  as a spelling aid, **22b-1**: 386
  unabridged, **20a-2**: 359–60
Dictionary form° (of verb). *See* Simple form
  (of verb)
die, dye, **22c-1**: 391
different from, different than
Direct address
  improper use of *you,* **10e**: 227
  words of, set off with commas, **24f**: 432
Direct discourse°
  commas with, **24g**: 433–34
  quotation marks with, **28a-3**: 466–67
  shifts to indirect, **15a-4**: 286–87
Direct objects°, **7b-1**: 157–58
  case form, **9**: 210
  and transitive verbs, **8d**: 190–91
Direct questions°, **23c**: 411–12. *See also*
  Questions
Direct quotations°, **28**: 464. *See also*
  Quotations
Direct titles, **3c-2**: 52
Discourse
  in the humanities, **34b-1**: 620
  punctuation with, **24g**: 433–34, **28a-3**:
    466–67
  shifts between direct and indirect, **15a-4**:
    286–87
Discovery draft, **3b**: 46–47. *See also* First draft
Discussion section, in scientific reports,
  34d-3: 654
disinterested, uninterested
Displayed lists, **30b**: 489
Displayed quotations, **28a-1**: 465
  format, **28a**: 465, **33**: 596–97; 681
  parenthetical references with, **32k-1**: 581

722

Dissertations, bibliographic citations, **32g**: 572
Division°. *See* Analysis; Word division
do, forms of, **8c**: 187
Documentation°, **31b**: 512–13
  abbreviations in, **30h**: 502, **30i**: 502–4, **32g-2**: 563, 564, 565, 566, 568
  to avoid plagiarism, **31a**: 512
  concept of, **31b**: 512–13
  in the humanities: MLA parenthetical-reference style, **32g-2**: 562–74, **32k**: 579–85; MLA note style, **34b-4**: 631–40
  in the natural and technological sciences, **34d-4**: 656–58
  note references, **34b-4**: 631–38
  parenthetical references, **32k**: 579–85; with ellipses, **29d-1**: 483
  selecting an appropriate style, **32d**: 539–40, **34a-2**: 618
  simplified, **34b-4**: 633–34
  in the social sciences (APA style), **34c-4**: 647–50
  unnecessary, **31a**: 511
Documentation notes. *See* Notes
Documentation style°. *See* Documentation
dominant, dominate, **22c-1**: 391
done
don't
Double comparatives, **12e-1**: 254
Double negatives°, **12c**: 249–50
Doublespeak°, **21d-4**: 383–84
Double superlatives, **12e-1**: 254
Drafting°, **3b**: 46–49
  defined, **2a**: 13, **3**: 44
  getting started, **3a**: 44–46
  and introductory paragraph, **4e**: 106
  reading compared to, **5a-2**: 116
  of research paper, **32j**: 577–79
  of thesis statement, **2e-4**: 33–36, **32h**: 575–76
Drama. *See* Plays
Drop test, for pronoun case, **9a**: 211, 212, **9b**: 213, **9d-1**: 216–17
due to
dye, die, **22c-1**: 391

each
  agreement of pronoun with, **11l**: 243
  agreement of verb with, **11c**: 234
Economics, reference works on, **32e-5**: 547
-ed, -d, for past tense, **8a-1**: 178, **8b-1**: 181, **22d-1**: 397
ed., eds., **32g-2**: 564, 565, 566
Edited American English°, **21a-2**: 373
Edited book, bibliographic citations, **32g**: 564, **33**: 611
Editing°, **3d**: 63–70
  checklist, **3d**: 63–64
  defined, **2a**: 13
  vs. revising, **3c-1**: 51–52
Editions, in bibliographic citations, **32g-2**: 567
Editorials, bibliographic citations, **32g-2**: 571
Effect, subordinating conjunctions showing, **7e-2**: 166
effect, affect, **22c-1**: 389
-ei-, -ie-, spelling rules, **22d-2**: 399
either. . .or. See Correlative conjunctions
either-or fallacy, **5f**: 137

Elements of writing. *See* Writing.
elicit, illicit, **22c-1**: 391
Ellipses, **29d**: 482–84
  for broken-off speech, **29d-2**: 484
  for omissions from quotations, **29d-1**: 482–84, **31e-1**: 526
Elliptical clauses°, **7e-2**: 170
Elliptical constructions°, **15e-1**: 298
  to reduce clauses, **16a-3**: 307
elude, allude, **22c-1**: 389
eminent, immanent, imminent, **22c-1**: 391
emigrate from, immigrate to
Emphasis, **19**: 340–52
  with added modifiers, **19d**: 346–49
  conjunctive adverbs showing, **6f**: 148
  with dashes, **29a-1**: 474–76
  with inverted word order, **19e**: 350–51
  with italics (underlining), **30g**: 499
  with repetition, **19f**: 351–52
  with sentence fragments, **13d**: 269
  and subject choice, **19c**: 346
  with varied sentence lengths, **19a**: 341–43
  with varied sentence types, **19b**: 344
Emphatic declarations, **23e**: 412–13
Emphatic order. *See* Climactic order
Emphatic resume, **35**: 667
Empirical evidence, **34d-1**: 651
Empty words and phrases, **16b**: 311–13
-ence, -ance spellings, **22d-1**: 397–98
Encyclopedias, **32e-5**: 545. *See also* Reference books
Endnotes, formatting, **34b-4**: 632. *See also* Notes
End punctuation, **23**: 410–13. *See also* Exclamation points; Periods; Question marks
ensure, assure, insure
-ent, -ant spellings, **22d-1**: 397–98
enthused
envelop, envelope, **22c-1**: 391
Envelopes, business format, **35**: 665
-er, -est endings, **12e-1**: 253–54
-es, -s endings, **8a-2**: 179–80, **11a**: 232–33
Errors, in quoted material, **29c-1**: 481–82. *See also* Proofreading
Equivalent grammatical form, **18**: 330. *See also* Parallelism
Equivocation, **5f**: 137–38
especially, specially
Essays
  bibliographic citations, **32g-1**: 572
  form of, **2e**: 30
  length of, **2a**: 14
  ordering ideas in, **2e-2**: 32
  revision checklist, **3c-3**: 54
  thesis statements, **2e-4**: 33–36, **4e**: 106–7
  titles of, **3c-2**: 52–53, **28b**: 468–69, **28d**: 471
  unity in, **3b**: 47
  See also Papers; Writing process
et al.
  in bibliographic citations: APA style, **34c-4**: 648; MLA style, **32g-2**: 564
  in parenthetical references, **32k-1**: 582
etc.
Etymologies, **20**: 355–36
  in dictionary entries, **20a-1**: 357
  specialized dictionaries for, **20a-4**: 362
Euphemisms°, **21d-3**: 382

Evaluation
  and critical thinking, **5**: 114
  of evidence, **5c**: 125–26
  in reading, **5b-3**: 120–23
  of sources, **5c**: 128, **32d-2**: 538, 539
Evaluative reading, **5b-3**: 120–23
every
  agreement of pronoun with, **11l**: 243
  agreement of verb with, **11c**: 234
everyday, every day, **22c-3**: 395
everywheres
Evidence°
  guidelines for using, **5c**: 125–26
  primary, **5c**: 126–28
  secondary, **5c**: 128
Exact words, **20b**: 362–66
Exactness in scientific writing, **34d-2**: 652
Examples
  as cause of comma splices or fused
    sentences, **14a**: 273
  as clue to word meaning, **20c-2**: 370
  emphasizing with dashes, **29a-1**: 475
  for paragraph development, **4a-2**: 81–82,
    4d: 99
  in parentheses, **29b-1**: 478
  transitional expressions for, **4b**: 84
except, accept, **22c-1**: 389
Exclamation points
  with commands, **8**: 202, **19b**: 344, **23e**:
    412–13
  with emphatic declarations, **23e**: 412–13
  with exclamations, **19b**: 344
  with interjections, **6i**: 152, **24b-3**: 422
  with other punctuation, **23e**: 413, **24g**:
    434; dashes, **29a-3**: 476; parentheses,
    29b-5: 479; question marks, **23c**: 412
  overuse of, **23f**: 413
  in quotations, **24g**: 434
Exclamatory sentences°, **7**: 154, **19b**: 344
Experts
  false or irrelevant, **5f**: 137
  interviewing, **32e-2**: 542
  quoting from, **31e-2**: 526
  as a source of secondary evidence, **5c**:
    128
Explanations. *See* Examples
Expletive constructions
  overuse of *it,* **10d**: 226–27
  revising for conciseness, **16a-1**: 303–4
  subject-verb agreement, **11e**: 236–37
Expletives°, **6j**: 152–53
explicit, implicit
Expository writing°, **1a**: 3, **1b-1**: 4–5. *See
  also* Informative writing
Extended definitions°, **4d**: 99–100

-f, -fe, plurals of words ending in, **22d-4**:
    401
Facts
  books of, and almanacs, **32e-5**: 545
  conditions contrary to, **8i-1**: 203
  vs. opinions, **5b-3**: 122–23
fair, fare, **22c-1**: 391
Fallacies. *See* Logical fallacies
False analogy, **5f**: 135–36
False authority, **5f**: 137
False dilemma, **5f**: 137
farther, further
Faulty parallelism, **18**: 331
Faulty predication°, **15d-2**: 295–96

fewer, less, **12e-2**: 254
Figurative language, **21b**: 377–78
figure, calculate, reckon
Figures. *See* Numbers
Films
  bibliographic citations: MLA
    parenthetical-references style, **32g-2**:
    574; MLA note style, **34b-4**: 639
  documentary note references, **34b-4**: 636
  reference works on, **32e-5**: 550
  titles of, italics for, **30f**: 497, 498
Final draft
  proofreading, **3e**: 70–71
  of research paper, **32i**: 579
Final thesis statement, **2e-4**: 34. *See also*
  Preliminary thesis statement
fine, find
Fine arts, reference works on, **32e-5**: 547
Finite verbs°, **8a-1**: 179
First draft, **3b**: 46–48
  of research paper, **32i**: 578
First person°
  conventions for use in various disciplines:
    humanities, **34b-2**: 621; natural and
    technological sciences, **34d-2**: 652;
    social sciences, **34c-2**: 643
  shall with, **8c**: 188
  subject-verb agreement, **11**: 231
Focus
  of essay, **2b**: 15
  of sentence, **19c**: 346
Focused freewriting, **2d-2**: 23–24, **3a**: 46
Footnotes, formatting, **34b-4**: 633. *See also*
  Notes; Parenthetical references
for, as coordinating conjunction, **6h**: 151,
  17: 317, **24a**: 416–17
Foreign words and phrases
  American English and, **20**: 355–56
  in italics (underlined), **30f**: 497, 499
  plural forms, **22d-4**: 402
formally, formerly, **22c-1**: 391
Formal language level, **21a-1**: 372–73
Formal outlines, **2e-5**: 39–43
  conventions, **2e-5**: 39–41
  parallel structures in, **18e**: 337–38
  for research papers, **32i**: 577, **33**: 592–93
  topic vs. sentence type, **2e-5**: 41–43
Formal tone, **2e-3**: 33
former, latter
forth, fourth, **22c-1**: 391
Fractions
  figures vs. spelled-out form, **30j**: 506
  hyphenation of, **22e-4**: 406
  slash with, **29e-2**: 484–85
Fragments. *See* Sentence fragments
Freewriting, **2d-2**: 23–24
Fused sentences°, **14**: 271–79
  correcting: with coordinating conjunc-
    tion, **14c**: 275; by revising an indepen-
    dent clause to a dependent clause, **14d**:
    276–77; with semicolons or periods,
    14b: 274, **14e**: 278–79
  leading causes, **14a**: 273
  recognizing, **14a**: 272–73
Future perfect progressive tense°, **8g**:
    196
Future tense°, **8**: 192, 193
  formation of, **8c**: 188
  and simple form of verb, **8a-1**: 178
  and tense sequences, **8h-1**: 198, 199

Gathering ideas, **2d**: 20–30
  brainstorming, **2d-3**: 24–26
  freewriting, **2d-2**: 23–24
  keeping an idea book, **2d-1**: 21–22
  keeping a journal, **2d-1**: 22–23
  mapping, **2d-5**: 28, 29
  reading, **2d-6**: 28, 30
  using journalist's questions, **2d-4**: 26–27
Gender°
  appropriate use of masculine pronoun, **11n-2**: 244–45, **21a-3**: 374
  pronoun agreement, **11**: 242
  sexist language, **21a-3**: 373–75
gender, sex
Generality, levels of
  in formal outline, **2e-5**: 40
  grouping ideas by, **2e-1**: 30–31
General indexes to periodicals, **32e-6**: 550–51
Generalizations
  and deductive reasoning, **5e**: 134
  hasty, **5f**: 135
  and inductive reasoning, **5e**: 132–33
General sense, as clue to word meaning, **20c-2**: 370
General-to-specific arrangement, **4c**: 90–91
General words, **20b-2**: 364–66
Geographical names. *See* Place names
Geology, style manual, **34d-4**: 657
Gerund phrases°, **7d**: 163–64, **24j**: 440
Gerunds°, **6d**: 145
  possessive case before, **9g**: 218–19
  present participles as, **8a-1**: 179
given, giving
goes, says
gone, went
good and
Going along with the crowd, **5f**: 137
good, better, best, **12e-2**: 254, 255
good, well, **12d**: 252
gorilla, guerrilla, **22c-1**: 391
got, have
Government agencies, abbreviations of, **23b**: 411, **30h**: 501
Government publications
  bibliographic citations, **32g-2**: 568
  as a research tool, **32e-3**: 543
Grammar, **6**: 140
Group possession, **27a-6**: 459
Guide to Reference Books (Sheehy), **32e-5**: 544

had best, had better
had ought, hadn't ought
hanged, hung
Hard copy, **3f**: 72
hardly, **12c**: 249
Hasty generalization, **5f**: 135
have
  as auxiliary verb, **6c**: 144, **8c**: 188
  forms, **8c**: 187
  as main verb, **8c**: 188
have, got
have, of
he, him, his, avoiding sexist use, **11n-2**: 244–45, **21a-3**: 374
he, she, he or she
hear, here, **22c-1**: 391
Helping verbs°. *See* Auxiliary verbs
Highly formal level of language°, **21a-1**: 372
himself, **9h**: 220
himself, herself

History, reference works on, **32e-5**: 547–48
hole, whole, **22c-1**: 391
Homonyms°, **22c-1**: 389–93
hopefully
hour, are, **22c-1**: 390
however, as conjunctive adverb, **14e**: 278–79
human, humane, **22c-1**: 391
Humanities, **34b**: 620–40
  documentation: MLA parenthetical-reference style, **32g-2**: 562–74, **32k**: 579–85; MLA note style, **34b-4**: 631–40
  methods of inquiry, **34b-1**: 620
  types of papers, **34b-3**: 621–30
  writing purposes and practices, **34b-2**: 621
  writing traditions, **34a**: 615, 616
Hyphens, **22e**: 403–7
  in bibliographic citations, **32g-2**: 564
  in compound words, **22e-3**: 405–6
  at end of line, **22e-1**: 403
  in mixed numbers, **29e-1**: 485
  with prefixes and suffixes, **22e-2**: 404–5
  in spelled-out numbers, **22e-4**: 406, **30j**: 505
Hypotheses, in scientific method, **34d-1**: 651

I, capitalization of, **30d**: 491
-ible, -able spellings, **22d-1**: 397
Idea book, **2d-1**: 21–22
Ideas
  gathering, **2d**: 20–30
  grouping, **2e-1**: 30–31
  ordering, **2e-2**: 32
  repetition for emphasis, **19f**: 351–52
  shaping, **2e**: 30–43
-ie-, -ei-, spelling rules, **22d-2**: 399
if, as subordinating conjunction, **14d**: 276
if clauses, in subjunctive mood, **8i-1**: 203
if, whether
Ignorance, appeal to, **5f**: 137–38
Ignoring the question, **5f**: 136
illicit, elicit, **22c-1**: 391
Illogical coordination, **17c-1**: 319
Illogical predication°, **15d-2**: 295–96
Illogical subordination, **17f-1**: 326
illusion, allusion, **22c-1**: 389
immanent, imminent, eminent, **22c-1**: 391
immigrate to, emigrate from
Imperative mood°, **8**: 202, **15a-3**: 286
Imperative sentences°, **7**: 154, **19b**: 344. *See also* Commands
implicit, explicit
Implied subjects, **8**: 202, **13a**: 263
Implied topic sentence, **4a-1**: 79
including, no colon following, **26a**: 453, **26c**: 454–55
imply, infer
Incomplete sentences, **15e**: 297–300
  elliptical constructions, **15e-1**: 298
  incomplete comparisons, **15e-2**: 298–99
  inadvertent omissions, **15e-3**: 299–300
  sentence fragments, **13**: 260–69
incredible, incredulous
Indefinite adjectives, **6e**: 147
Indefinite pronouns°, **6b**: 143
  agreement: with personal pronouns, **11n**: 244–45; with verbs, **11a**: 232, **11f**: 237–38
  as implied subjects, **8**: 202
  possessive form, **27a-1**: 458

Indentation
  in bibliographic lists, **32g-2**: 562, **34b-4**:
    637
  of displayed quotations, **28a-1**: 465
  in formal outlines, **2e-5**: 40
  of notes, **32b-4**: 632
  to signal paragraphing, **4**: 73
Independent (main) clauses°, **7e**: 165; **7e-1**:
    166
  colons after, **26a**: 451–53
  comma spliced or fused, **14**: 271–79
  conjunctive adverbs joining, **6f**: 148, **12**:
    248, **14e**: 278–79, **25c**: 445
  coordinating conjunctions joining, **14c**:
    275, **17**: 316–20, **24a**: 416–18
  modified by adverb clauses, **7e-2**: 167
  revising as dependent clauses, **14d**:
    276–77
  semicolons between, **14b**: 274, **14e**:
    278–79, **25a,b,c**: 443–45, **25e**: 446
  and subordinated information, **17**: 322–28
  in various sentence types, **7f**: 172–73
Index cards
  for bibliographic data, **32g-1**: 561–62
  for note taking, **32f-2**: 559–60
  as a research tool, **32d**: 537
Indexes to periodicals, **32e-6**: 550–52
Indicative mood°, **8**: 202, **15a-3**: 286
Indirect discourse°
  quotation marks not used with, **28a-3**:
    467
  and unmarked shifts to direct, **15a**:
    286–87
Indirect objects°, **7b-2**: 158, **9**: 209
Indirect questions°, **23a**: 410–11
Indirect requests, **8i-3**: 204
Indirect sources, parenthetical references,
    32k-1: 584–85, **33**: 597
Indirect titles, **3c-2**: 53
individual, person, party
Induction°. *See* Inductive reasoning
Inductive reasoning, **5e-1**: 132–33
  compared with deductive reasoning, **5e**:
    132
  and position of topic sentence, **4a-1**: 78
  in specific-to-general arrangement of
    paragraph, **4c**: 91
  summary, **5e-1**: 132
Inferential meaning, **5b-2**: 119–20
Infinitive phrases°, **7d**: 163–64, **24j**: 440
  introductory, comma with, **24b-2**: 421
Infinitives, **6d**: 145, **8a-1**: 179
  objective case with, **9f**: 218
  repetition of *to* in parallel forms, **18c-3**:
    334
  split, **15b-3**: 290
  and tense sequences, **8h-2**: 200
Informal language level°, **21a-1**: 372–73
Informal outlines, **2e-5**: 38–39
  for research paper, **32i**: 576–77
Informal tone, **2e-3**: 33
Information
  background, **4e**: 107
  sending for, **32e-3**: 542–43
  for which documentation is not required,
    31b: 511
Information services, bibliographic
  citations, **32g-2**: 573
Informative writing°, **1b-1**: 4–5
  in the humanities, **34b-2**: 621

thesis statements, **2e-4**: 34–35
  topical paragraphs, **4**: 74
Inquiry, methods of
  in the humanities, **34b-1**: 620
  in the natural and technological sciences,
    34d-1: 651
  in the social sciences, **34c-1**: 640–42
inside of, outside of
Instructor as audience, **1c-2**: 10
insure, assure, ensure
Intensive pronouns°, **6b**: 143, **9h**: 220
Interjections°, **6i**: 152
  capitalization of, **30d**: 491
  punctuation with, **6i**: 152, **24b-3**: 422
Interpretation papers, **34b-3**: 625–26
Interrogative adjectives, **6e**: 147
Interrogative pronouns°, **6b**: 143
  case forms, **9d**: 215, **9d-2**: 217
  vs. relative pronouns, **13a**: 264
Interrogative sentences°, **7**: 154, **19b**: 344.
    See also Questions
Interruptions
  dashes with, **29a**: 474–76
  in parentheses, **29b-1**: 478
Interviews
  bibliographic citations: MLA style, **32g-2**:
    572, **33**: 613; old MLA style, **34b-4**: 639
  conducting, **32e-2**: 542, **34c-1**: 641–42
  documentary note references, **34b-4**: 636
in to, into, **22c-3**: 395
Intransitive verbs°, **8d**: 190–91
Introductions
  bibliographic citations, **32g-2**: 567–68
  in scientific reports, **34d-3**: 653
  See also Introductory paragraphs
Introductory devices. *See* Introductory
    paragraphs
Introductory elements
  commas after, **24b**: 420–22
  for variety, **19d**: 349
Introductory paragraphs, **4e**: 106–9
  content not included in formal outline,
    2e-5: 41
  devices for, **4e**: 107, **33**: 595
  in job application letters, **35b**: 661
  what to avoid, **4e**: 109
Invention techniques°. *See* Gathering ideas
Inverted order
  dates, **24h**: 435
  for emphasis, **19e**: 350–51
  names, **24b**: 436
  and subject-verb agreement, **11e**: 236–37
Irony°, **21b**: 378
irregardless
Irregular adjectives, **12e-2**: 254–55
Irregular adverbs, **12e-2**: 254–55
Irregular verbs°, **8a-1**: 178
  principal parts, **8b**: 181, **8b-2**: 182–85
  tenses, **8**: 193
Irrelevant authority, **5f**: 137
irritate, aggravate
isle, aisle, **22c-1**: 389
Issue numbers, **32g-2**: 570
is when, is where (faulty predication),
    15d-2: 296
it
  in expletives: **6j**: 152–53, **10d**: 226; and
    subject-verb agreement, **11e**: 236
  in idiomatic expressions, **10d**: 226
  indefinite use of, **10c-4**: 226

overuse of, **10d**: 226–27
  as a pronoun: checking for clear antece-
    dent, **10c-3**: 225; possessive form,
    22c-1: 391, **22c-4**: 396, **27b**: 459
Italics (underlining), **30**: 497–99
  added to quotations, **29c-1**: 481
  for emphasis, **30g**: 499
  for foreign terms, **30f**: 499
  for letters and words used as terms, **27d**:
    461, **28c**: 470, **30f**: 497, 499
  for names of ships, aircraft, and
    spacecraft, **30f**: 497, 498–99
  for scientific names, **34d**: 658
  for titles, **28b**: 469, **30f**: 497–98
it's, its, **22c-1**: 391, **22c-4**: 396, **27b**: 459
-ize

Jargon°, **21d-2**: 381–82
Job-application letters, **35b**: 660–61, 666
Joint possession, **27a-6**: 459
Journal articles
  abstracts of, **32e-8**: 556
  bibliographic citations: APA style, **34c-4**:
    650; MLA parenthetical-references
    style, **32g-2**: 569–70, **33**: 613; MLA note
    style, **34b-4**: 640
  documentary note references, **34b-4**: 636
  indexes to, **32e-6**: 550–52
Journalist's questions, **2d-4**: 26–27
Journal keeping, as a source of ideas, **2d-1**:
  22–23

Key words
  repetition of, **4b-3**: 85
  research use, **32d-3**: 538–39
kind, kind of, sort, sort of
know, no, **22c-1**: 391

Labels
  sexist, **21a-3**: 375
  for word usage, **20a-1**: 358
Language
  appropriate, **21a**: 371–77
  artificial, **21d**: 380–84
  bureaucratic, **21d-5**: 384
  clichéd, **21c**: 379–80
  colloquial, **21a-4**: 376
  euphemistic, **21d-3**: 382
  evasive (doublespeak), **21d-4**: 383–84
  figurative, **21b**: 377–78
  jargon, **21d-2**: 381–82
  levels of formality of, **21a-1**: 372–73
  pretentious, **21d-2**: 381
  regional (dialectical), **21a-4**: 376–77
  slanted, **21a-5**: 377
  specialized (jargon), **21d-2**: 381–82
  specific and concrete, vs. general and
    abstract, **20b-2**: 364–66
  tone of, **1c-1**: 9, **2c-3**: 33, **4e**: 106, **5b-3**:
    120–21, **21a-1**: 372–73
  See also Words
Language level, **21a-1**: 372–73
Languages, capitalization of, **30e**: 494
later, latter, **22c-1**: 391
latter, former
lay, lie, **8d**: 190–91
lead, led, **22c-1**: 391
Learning
  and reading, **5a-2**: 115–18
  and writing, **1**: 2

learn, teach
least, **12e-1**: 253
leave, let
Legal writing, numbers in, **29b-3**: 479
less
  comparative use, **12e-1**: 253
  and *fewer,* **12e-2**: 254
lessen, lesson, **22c-1**: 391
Letters (of the alphabet)
  with formal outline items, **2e-5**: 40
  with list items, **24c**: 424, **29b-2**: 478
  omitted, apostrophes for, **27c**: 460–61
  used as letters: italics for, **30f**: 49, 497,
    499; plural forms, **27d**: 461
  with year of publication, **34c-4**: 648
Letters (correspondence)
  bibliographic citations, **32g-2**: 571, 572
  business format, **4**: 74, **35a**: 659–60
  commas in, **24h**: 436
  of job application, **35b**: 660–61, 666
Letter writing, to start writing, process, **3a**:
  46
Levels of meaning, **5b**: 118–23
Library papers. *See* Research papers
Library of Congress classification system,
  32e-7: 553, 554
*Library of Congress Subject Headings
  (LCSH),* **32e-7**: 554
Library resources
  card catalogues, **32e-7**: 552–55
  computerized databases, **32e-8**: 555–57
  indexes to periodicals, **32e-6**: 550–52
  reference books, **32e-5**: 544–50
  use of, **32e-4**: 543–44
lighting, lightening, **22c-1**: 391
likely, apt, liable
Limiting adjectives°, **6a**: 142, **6e**: 146, 147
Limiting sentences°, **4a**: 76
Limiting words, ambiguous placement of,
  15b-1: 288–89
Lines, in a poem or play, **30j**: 507, **32k-1**:
  584
Linking verbs°, **6c**: 144
  agreement with subjects, **11g**: 239
  be as, **8c**: 186–87
  complements, **7c-1**: 158–59, **12d**: 251–52
  faulty predication with, **15d-2**: 296
  subjective case, **9c**: 214
Lists
  capitalization of items in, **30b**: 489–90
  colon preceding, **25e-2**: 447, **26a**: 451–52,
    453
  parallel structure in, **18e**: 338, **30b**: 489
  run-in, punctuation of, **24c**: 424, **29b-2**:
    478
Literal meaning°, **5b-1**: 119
Literary works
  analysis of, **34b-3**: 621–25
  reference works on, **32e-5**: 548
  parenthetical references to, **32k-1**: 584
Literature Cited lists, **34d-4**: 658. *See also*
  Bibliographies
little, less, least, **12e-2**: 255
Location, subordinating conjunctions
  showing, **7e-2**: 166. *See also* Spatial order
Logical fallacies°, **5f**: 135–38
  ambiguity, **5f**: 137–38
  appeal to ignorance, **5f**: 137–38
  appeal to the person (*ad hominem*), **5f**:
    136–37

Logical fallacies° (*cont.*)
  avoiding in concluding paragraph, **4e**: 110
  bandwagon (going along with the crowd), **5f**: 137
  card-stacking (special pleading), **5f**: 137
  circular argument, **5f**: 136
  either-or (false dilemma), **5f**: 137
  equivocation, **5f**: 137–38
  false analogy, **5f**: 135–36
  false or irrelevant authority (*ad verecundiam*), **5f**: 137
  hasty generalization, **5f**: 135
  non sequitur, **5f**: 136
  post hoc, ergo propter hoc, **5f**: 136
  red herring, (ignoring the question), **5f**: 136
  self-contradiction, **5f**: 136
  taking something out of context, **5f**: 137–38
loose, lose, **22c-1**: 392
Loose sentences°, **19d-2**: 348
lots, lots of, a lot of
-ly ending, **12**: 247, **22d-1**: 397, **22e-3**: 406

Magazine articles
  bibliographic citations: APA style, **34c-4**: 650; MLA parenthetical-references style, **32g-2**: 570; MLA note style, **34b-4**: 640
  documentary note references, **34b-4**: 636
  indexes to, **32e-6**: 550–51
  titles of, quotation marks for, **30f**: 498
Main clauses°. *See* Independent clauses
Main point, in summary, **31e-1**: 520. *See also* Topic sentences
Main verbs°, **6c**: 144
  be as, **8c**: 186–87
  forms of, **8a**: 177–80
  have and *do* as, **8c**: 188
  principal parts of, **8a-1**: 177–79
  -s form, **8a-2**: 179–80
man, avoiding sexist use of, **21a-3**: 374
many, more, most, **12e-2**: 255
Mapping°, **2d-5**: 28
Maps
  atlases, **32e-5**: 545
  bibliographic citations, **32g-2**: 573
Masculine pronouns, avoiding sexist use of, **11n-2**: 244–45, **21a-3**: 374
Mass nouns°, **6a**: 141
may, **6c**: 144, **8c**: 188–89
maybe, may be, **22c-1**: 392, **22c-3**: 395
may, can
Meaning
  clarifying with commas, **24i**: 438
  levels of, **5b**: 118–23
  preserving in summary, **31d-2**: 521
  See also Word meaning
Measurements
  commas between, **24h**: 437
  figures for, **30j**: 507; hyphenated to unit, **22e-3**: 406
  symbols for, **30h**, 502
meat, meet, **22c-1**: 392
Mechanics°, **30**: 487–507. *See also* Abbreviations; Capitalization; Italics
media
Medium level of formality° (language), **21a-1**: 372–73
Memos, **35d**: 662–63
  colon in, **26b**: 453

Message
  as element of writing, **1a**: 3
  in memo, **35d**: 663
Metaphors°, **21b**: 377–78
Metonymy°, **21b**: 378
Microfilm records
  catalogues, **32e-7**: 555
  indexes to periodicals, **32e-6**: 550, 551
might, as modal auxiliary verb, **8c**: 188
mighty
Mild commands, **8**: 202, **19b**: 344, **23a**: 410
mind, mine
miner, minor, **22c-1**: 392
Misplaced modifiers°, **15b**: 288–91
Mixed constructions°, **15d-1**: 294–95
Mixed metaphors°, **21b**: 378
Mixed sentences, **15d**: 294–96
MLA Handbook for Writers of Research Papers (Bigaldi and Achtert), **32g**: 562
MLA style. *See* Modern Language Association (MLA) style
Mnemonic spelling aids, **22b-2**: 387
Modal auxiliary verbs°, **8a-1**: 178, **8c**: 188
Modern Language Association (MLA) style
  for first page of report, **33**: 591
  prior to 1984 (old MLA style): bibliographic citations, **34b-4**: 637, 638–40; documentary notes, **34b-4**: 631–37
  for parenthetical references, **32k**: 579–85
  recent changes, **32d-4**: 540
  for tables, **33**: 599
  for Works Cited list, **32g-2**: 562–74
Modifiers°, **7c-2**: 160–161
  dangling, **15c**: 293
  defined, **12**: 247
  misplaced, **15b**: 288–91
  negative, **12c**: 249–50
  nouns as, **12f**: 256–57
  positioning, **19d-2**: 348–49
  restrictive and nonrestrictive, **24e**: 427–30
  squinting, **15b-1**: 289
  for variety and emphasis, **19d**: 346–49
  See also Adjectives; Adverbs
Money, sums of
  figures and symbols for, **30h**: 502, **30j**: 507
  subject-verb agreement, **11j**: 240
Months
  abbreviations for, **30i**: 504
  capitalization of, **30e**: 495
Mood° (of verb), **8**: 177, 202–4
  avoiding shifts in, **15a-3**: 286
moral, morale, **22c-1**: 332
more
  comparative use, **12e-1**: 253–54, **12e-2**: 255
  subject-verb agreement, **11f**: 238
most
  subject-verb agreement, **11f**: 238
  superlative use, **12e-1**: 253, 254, **12e-2**: 255
Moving material, revision activity, **3c-1**: 51
ms.
much, more, many, **12e-2**: 255
Multiauthor works
  bibliographic citations: APA style, **34c-4**: 648, 649; MLA parenthical-references style, **32g-2**: 565–66, **33**: 611, 613; MLA note style, **34b-4**: 638
  documentary note references, **34b-4**: 635
  parenthetical references, **32k-1**: 582

Multivolume works
  bibliographic citations: MLA parenthical-
    references style, **32g-2**: 566–67; MLA
    note style, **34b-4**: 639
  documentary note references, **34b-4**: 635
  parenthetical references, **32k-1**: 583
Musical compositions
  bibliographic citations for recordings and
    performances of, **32g-2**: 574
  titles of, italics for, **30f**: 497, 498
must, **8c**: 188–89
myself, yourself, himself, herself
Mythology, reference works on, **32e-5**: 549

Names of persons
  with academic degrees or titles, **23b**: 411,
    24h: 436, **30h**: 501
  capitalization of, **30e**: 492
  inverted, **24h**: 436
  nicknames, **28d**: 471
  using to develop paragraphs, **4a-2**: 81–82
  See also Author names
Narration, **1a**: 3, **4d**: 97
Narrowing an assigned topic, **2c-2**: 18–20,
  32b: 533–36
Nationalities, capitalization of, **30e**: 494
Natural sciences. *See* Scientific writing
Negative modifiers, double, **12c**: 249–50
neither. . . nor, double negative with, **12c**:
  249. *See also* Correlative conjunctions
never, avoiding double negative with **12c**:
  249–50
Newspaper articles
  bibliographic citations: APA style, **34c-4**:
    650, MLA parenthetical-references
    style, **32g-2**: 570–71, **33**: 613, **34b-4**:
    639, 640
  documentary note references, **34b-4**: 636
Newspaper names, **30f**: 498, **32g-2**: 571
Nicknames, **28d**: 471
no
  double negative with, **12c**: 249–50
  homonym of *know*, **22c-1**: 391
Nominative. *See* Subjective case
none, double negative with, **12c**: 249–50
Nonessential elements°. *See* Nonrestrictive
  elements
Nonfinite verbs°, **8a-1**: 179
Nonrestrictive elements°, **24e**: 427–30
  commas with, **7e-2**: 168, **7f-4**: 173, **17**:
    323, **14d**: 277, **24e**: 427–30
  use of *which* with clauses, **7e-2**: 168, **10f**:
    228–29
Nonsexist language°, **11n-2**: 244–45, **21a-3**:
  373–75
Non sequitur fallacy, **5f**: 136
nor, **6h**: 151, **17**: 317
  pronoun agreement with antecedents
    joined by, **11m**: 243
  verb agreement with subjects joined by,
    11d: 235–36
not
  contractions of, **12c**: 250, **27c**: 460
  double negative with, **12c**: 249–50
Notes
  content: APA style, **34c-4**: 647, with MLA
    parenthetical references, **32k-1**: 580,
    32k-2: 585, **33**: 611
  documentary (old MLA style): formatting,
    34b-4: 632–33; first references, **34b-4**:

635–37; second and subsequent
  references, **34b-4**: 638; text references
  to, **34b-4**: 631; when few sources are
  used, **34b-4**: 633–64
Note taking, **32f-2**: 558–60
  to avoid plagiarism, **31b**: 512
  recording bibliographic data, **32g-1**:
    561–62
nothing, double negative with, **12c**: 249–50
nothing like, nowhere near
not only. . . but (also). *See* Correlative
  conjunctions
Noun clauses°, **7e-2**: 170
  punctuation with, **24j**: 439–40
Noun determiners. *See* Articles
Noun markers. *See* Articles
Noun phrases°, **7d**: 162, 163
Nouns°, **6a**: 141–42
  abstract, **6a**: 141
  as appositives, **7c-3**: 161–62
  collective, **6a**: 141, **11g**: 238, **11o**: 245
  common, **6a**: 141, **30e**: 491–92
  as complements, **6a**: 141, **7c-1**: 159
  concrete, **6a**: 141
  formed from verbs, **16a-4**: 308
  infinitives as, **8a-1**: 179
  mass, **6a**: 141
  matching pronoun case to, **9b**: 213
  modified by adjectives, **6e**: 146, **7c-2**: 160,
    12: 248
  as modifiers, **12f**: 256–57
  as objects, **6a**: 141
  plural forms, **6a**: 141, **11a**: 232–33
  possessive forms, **6a**: 141, **27a-1,2**: 458
  present participle as, **8a-1**: 179
  proper, **6a**: 141, **30e**: 491–96
  as subjects, **6a**: 141
  suffixes with, **20c-1**: 368
  verbal phrases as, **7d**: 163–64
  verbs functioning as, **6d**: 145
nowheres
Number
  avoiding shifts in, **15a-1**: 283
  of nouns, **6a**: 141
  of personal pronouns, **9**: 209
  pronoun agreement, **11**: 242–45
  subject-verb agreement, **11**: 230–41
  of verb, **8**: 176
Numbers, **30j**: 505–7
  combined with words, hyphenation with,
    22e-4: 406
  commas with, **24h**: 437
  decimals, **30j**: 506
  doubtful, **23d**: 412, **29b-4**: 479
  in formal outlines, **2e-5**: 40
  with list items, **24c**: 424, **29b-2**: 478
  omitted, apostrophes for, **27c**: 461
  prefixes with, **22e-2**: 404
  spelled out, **30j**: 505–6, followed by
    numeral, **29b-3**: 479; hyphenation of,
    22e-4: 406
  used as terms: italics for, **30f**: 497, 499;
    plural form, **27d**: 461
  using to develop paragraphs, **4a-2**: 81
  See also Fractions, Page numbers, Roman
    numerals, Statistics, Volume numbers
Numerical adjectives, **6e**: 147

o, oh, **30d**: 491
Object complements°, **7c-1**: 159

Objective case°, **9**: 210
  with infinitives, **9f**: 218
  in prepositional phrases, **9a**: 212
  whom and *whomever*, **9d**: 215–17
Objects°, **7b**: 157–58
  awkward separation from verb, **15b-3**: 291
  direct, **7b-1**: 157–58, **8d**: 190–91, **9**: 210
  indirect, **7b-2**: 158, **9**: 209
  of infinitives, **9f**: 218
  noun clauses as, **7e-2**: 170
  nouns as, **6a**: 141
  of prepositions, **6g**: 149, **9a**: 212
Observation, in the social sciences, **34c-1**: 641
Obsolete, usage label, **20a-1**: 358
off of
of, have
of, off, **22c-1**: 392
OK, O.K., okay
Omissions. *See* Incomplete sentences
Omitted elements
  apostrophes for, **27c**: 460–61
  proofreading for, **15e-3**: 299–300
  in quotations, ellipses for, **29d**: 482–84
on account of
one. . .who, which, that, subject-verb agreement, **11i**: 239–40
only, placement of, **15b-1**: 288–89
Onomatopoeia°, **21b**: 378
Operas
  bibliographic citations of performances of, **32g-2**: 574
  titles of, italics for, **30f**: 497, 498
Opinions, vs. facts, **5b-3**: 122–23
or, **6h**: 151, **17**: 317
  pronoun agreement with subjects joined by *or,* **11m**: 243
  verb agreement with subjects joined by *or,* **11d**: 235–36
Ordering ideas, **2e-2**: 32
Organization names
  abbreviation of, **23b**: 411
  capitalization of, **30e**: 493
ought to, **8c**: 188
Outlining, **2e-5**: 37–43, **32-i**: 577–78. *See also* Formal outlines
outside of, inside of
Oversimplification, **5d**: 130–31
Oxford English Dictionary (OED), **20e-2**: 359–60, **32e-5**: 546
Oxymoron°, **21b**: 378

Padding°. *See* Deadwood
Page numbers, **30j**: 507
  in bibliographic citations, **32g-2**: 565, 568, 569–70, 571
  with line numbers, **24h**: 437
  in parenthetical references, **32k-1**: 580–81, 583
  typing on research paper, **33**: 595
Paintings. *See* Art works
Pamphlets, titles of, **28b**: 468
Papers, **2a**: 14
  humanities, **34b-3**: 621–30
  natural and technological sciences, **34d-3**: 653–56
  social sciences, **34c-3**: 643–47
  See also Essays; Research papers
Paragraph development°. *See* Development patterns

Paragraphs°, **4**: 73–112
  arranging sentences in, **4c**: 90–93
  coherence of, **3b**: 48, **4b**: 83–88
  concluding, **2e-5**: 41, **4e**: 109–11
  defined, **4**: 73
  development of, **4a-2**: 81–82, **4d**: 96–103
  and essay form, **2e**: 30
  indentation of, **4**: 73
  in job application letters, **35b**: 661
  introductory, **2e-5**: 41, **4e**: 106–9
  ordering ideas in, **2e-2**: 32
  revision checklist, **3c-3**: 54–55
  showing relationships among, **4b-6**: 87–88
  special types, **4e**: 106–12
  successful, characteristics of, **4**: 75
  transitional, **4e**: 111–12
  unified, **4a**: 75–82
Parallelism°, **18**: 330–38
  for coherence in paragraphs, **4b-4**: 86
  with coordinating conjunctions, **18c-1**: 333
  with correlative conjunctions, **18c-2**: 334
  faulty, **18**: 331
  in formal outlines, **2e-5**: 41, **18e**: 337–38
  in lists, **18e**: 338, **30b**: 489
  of phrases and clauses, **18b**: 332–31
  between sentences, **18d**: 335
  repetition of words with, **18c-3**: 334
  of words, **18**: 330, **18a**: 331–32
Paraphrasing°, **31c**: 513–19
  avoiding interpretation, **31c-1**: 514
  avoiding plagiarism, **31c-3**: 515–19
  guidelines for, **31c-3**: 517
  and summarizing, **31d-4**: 522–24
  using one's own words, **31c-2**: 514–15
Parentheses, **29b**: 477–80
  and capitalization, **30a**: 488
  with interrupting material, **29b**: 477, **29b-1**: 478
  with numbers or letters before run-in list items, **29b-2**: 478
  with numerals repeating spelled-out numbers, **29b-3**: 479
  with other punctuation, **29b-4,5**: 479–80, **30a**: 488–89; brackets, **29c-2**: 482; question marks, **23d**: 412, **29b-4**: 479
Parenthetical documentation°
  APA style, **34c-4**: 647–48
  content notes with: APA, **34c-4**: 647; MLA, **32k-2**: 585
  functions of, **32k-1**: 580
  MLA style: **32k**: 579–85; articles in books, 584; authors with same last name, 583; authors with two or more works, 582–83; corporate authors, 583; indirect sources, 584–85; multiauthor books, 582; multivolume works, 583; multiple sources, 584, parts of a literary work, 584; works cited by title, 583
  scientific style, **34d-4**: 657–58
Parenthetical expressions, commas with, **24f**: 432
Parenthetical references. *See* Parenthetical documentation
Participial phrases°, **7d**: 164, **19d-1**: 347
  introductory, comma after, **24b-2**: 421
Participles
  tense sequences with, **8h-2**: 200
  as verbals, **6d**: 145
  See also Past participles; Present participles

730

Parts of speech, **6**: 140–53
  adjectives, **6e**: 146–47
  adverbs, **6f**: 148–49
  articles, **6a**: 142
  conjunctions, **6h**: 151–52
  dictionary information about, **20a-1**: 357
  expletives, **6j**: 152–53
  interjections, **6i**: 152
  nouns, **6a**: 141–42
  prepositions, **6g**: 149–50
  pronouns, **6b**: 142–43
  verbals, **6d**: 145–46
  verbs, **6c**: 144
  See also main entry for each part
party, individual, person
passed, past, **22c-1**: 392
Passive constructions°, revising for conciseness, **16a-2**: 304–5
Passive voice°, **8**: 205
  avoiding shifts to, **15a-2**: 284–85
  as cause of dangling modifiers, **15c**: 293
  misuse of, **16a-2**: 305
  revising to active, **16a-2**: 304–5
  uses of, **8j**: 206–7, **16a-2**: 305; in scientific disciplines, **34a-4**: 619–20, **34c-2**: 643; **34d-2**: 652
Past participles°, **8a-1**: 177, 178
  of irregular verbs, **8b-2**: 183–85
  with passive voice, **8**: 205
  phrases with, **7d**: 164
  of regular verbs, **8b**: 180, **8b-1**: 181
  as verbal, **6d**: 145
Past perfect progressive tense°, **8g**: 196
Past perfect tense°, **8**: 193, **8f**: 195
  and tense sequences, **8h-1**: 198
Past progressive tense°, **8g**: 195
Past subjunctive, **8i**: 203
Past tense°, **8**: 192, 193, **8a-1**: 177, 178
  of irregular verbs, **8b-2**: 183–85
  with past subjunctive, **8i**: 203
  of regular verbs, **8b**: 180, **8b-1**: 181
  and tense sequences, **8h-1**: 198, 199
patience, patients, **22c-1**: 392
peace, piece, **22c-1**: 392
per
Percent symbol, **30h**: 502
percent, percentage
Perfect tenses°, **8**: 193, **8f**: 194–95
Performances, bibliographic citations, **32g-2**: 574
Periodicals, articles in
  abstracts of, **32e-8**: 556
  bibliographic citations: APA style, **34c-4**: 650; MLA parenthetical-references style, **32g-2**: 570; MLA note style, **34b-4**: 640
  documentary note references, **34b-4**: 636
  indexes to, **32e-6**: 550–52
Periodic sentences°, **19d-2**: 348
Periods
  with abbreviations, **23b**: 411
  to correct comma splices and fused sentences, **14b**: 274, **14e**: 278–79
  at end of statements, mild commands, and indirect questions, **23a**: 410–11
  with quoted poetry, **29e-1**: 485
  with other punctuation: ellipses, **29d-2**: 483; exclamation points, **23e**: 413; parentheses, **29b-5**: 479; question marks, **23c**: 412

Person°
  avoiding shifts in, **15a-1**: 283–84
  and case, **9**: 209
  pronoun agreement, **11**: 242
  review, **11**: 231
  subject-verb agreement, **11**: 230–31
  of verb, **8**: 176
personal, personnel, **22c-1**: 392
Personal knowledge, **31b**: 511
Personal pronouns°, **6b**: 143
  cases, **9**: 209–10
  possessive forms, **27b**: 459–60
  subject-verb agreement, **11a**: 232
Personification°, **21b**: 378
Persuasive writing°, **1b-2**: 5–6
  checklist, **1b-2**: 6
  in the humanities, **34b-2**: 621
  thesis statements, **2e-4**: 35–36
  topical paragraphs, **4**: 74–75
Philosophy, reference works on, **32e-5**: 549
Photocopying
  of sources, **32f-2**: 560
  of a draft needing revision, **32j**: 578–79
photocopy, Xerox
Phrases°, **7d**: 162–64
  absolute, **7d**: 163, **19d-1**: 347
  empty, **16b**: 311–13
  gerund, **7d**: 163–64, **24j**: 440
  introductory, **19d-2**: 349, **24b-2**: 421
  nonrestrictive vs. restrictive, **24e-1**: 429–30
  noun, **7d**: 162, 163
  parallel, **18**: 331, **18b**: 332–33
  reducing clauses to, **16a-3**: 307
  reducing to shorter phrases or single words, **16a-3**: 307
  as sentence fragments, **13c**: 267–68
  between subjects and verbs, **11b**: 233–34
  translated, **28c**: 470
  verb, **7d**: 162–63, **8a**: 177, **15b-3**: 291
  verbal, **7d**: 163–64, **13c**: 267
  See also Prepositional phrases, Infinitive phrases, Participial phrases
Physics, style manual, **34d-4**: 657
Place, transitional expressions for, **4b**: 84. *See also* Spatial order
Place names
  capitalization of, **30e**: 493–94
  commas with, **24h**: 436
Plagiarism°, **31a**: 511–12
  avoiding: in note taking, **32f-2**: 559; in paraphrases, **31c**: 515–19; in summaries, **31d-3**: 521–22
  and documentation, **34a-2**: 618
  See also Documentation
plain, plane, **22c-1**: 392
Planning°. *See also* Gathering ideas
  gathering ideas, **2d**: 20–30
  as stage of writing process, **2a**: 12–14
  thinking, **2b**: 14–16
  topic: narrowing a, **2c-2**: 18–20; selection, **2c-1**: 17–18
  writing situation, **2b**: 14–15
Plays
  bibliographic citations of performances, **32g-2**: 574
  references to parts of, **24h**: 437, **30j**: 507
plenty
Plurals°, **22d-4**: 401–2
  of compound words, **22d-4**: 401–2

731

Plurals ° (*cont.*)
  of foreign words, **22d-4**: 402
  of letters, numerals, symbols, and words
    used as terms, **27d**: 461
  possessive forms, **27a-3**: 458
  -s and *-es* endings, **11a**: 232–33
  subjects connected by *and*, **11c**: 234–35
  that retain singular form, **22d-4**: 402
  of words ending in *-f* or *-fe*, **22d-4**: 401
  of years, **27d**: 461
plus
P.M., **23b**: 411, **30h**: 500
Poetic usage, **20a-1**: 358
Poetry
  quotations from, **28a-3**: 466; capitaliza-
    tion in, **30a**: 489; slashes in, **29e-1**: 484
  titles of, quotation marks for, **28b**:
    468–69
Point-by-point structure, for comparison
  and contrast, **4d**: 101–2
Political science, reference works on, **32e-5**:
  547–48
Positive form of adjectives and adverbs °,
  12e-1: 253, **12e-2**: 255
Possessive adjectives, **6e**: 147
Possessive case °
  apostrophes in, **27a**. 457–59
  instead of nouns as modifiers, **12f**:
    256–57
  before gerunds, **9g**: 218–19
  of nouns, **6a**: 141; avoiding pronoun
    reference to, **10c-1**: 224
  of personal pronouns, **9**: 210, **27b**:
    459–60; vs. contracted forms, **22c-4**:
    396
Postal abbreviations of states, **30h**: 502,
  30i: 503–4
post hoc, ergo propter hoc fallacy, **5f**: 136
practical, practicable
precede, proceed, **22c-1**: 392
Predicate adjectives °, **7c-1**: 159
Predicate nominatives °, **7c-1**: 159
Predicates °, **7a-2**: 156
  in clauses, **7e**: 166, 167
  compound, **7a-2**: 156
  simple, **7a-2**: 156
  in sentence outlines, **2e-5**: 39
  See also Complements; Objects; Verbs
Predication, faulty, **15d-2**: 295–96
Predicting, during reading, **5a**: 114–15
Prefixes °, **20c-1**: 366, 367–68
  hyphenated, **22e-2**: 404–5
  spelling, **22d-3**: 400
  and word division, **22e-2**: 404
Prejudice, **5b-3**: 122
Preliminary thesis statement, **2e-4**: 34, **32h**:
  575
Premises °
  contradictory, **5f**: 136
  in deductive reasoning, **5e-2**: 133
Prepositional phrases °, **6g**: 149, **7d**: 163
  instead of nouns as modifiers, **12f**:
    256–57
  case of pronouns in, **9a**: 212
  expanding basic sentences with, **19d-1**:
    347
  as sentence fragments, **13c**: 267–68
  between subject and verb, **11b**: 233
Prepositions °, **6g**: 149–50
  inadverant omission of, **15e-3**: 299–300

objects of, **6g**: 149, **9a**: 212
repetition of, in parallel forms, **18c-3**: 334
Present participles °, **8a-1**: 179
  phrases with, **7d**: 164
  in progressive forms, **8g**: 195, **6d**: 145
Present perfect progressive tense °, **8g**: 196
Present perfect tense °, **8**: 193, **8f**: 194–95
  and tense sequences, **8h-1**: 198, 199
Present progressive tense °, **8g**: 195
Present subjunctive, **8i**: 203
Present tense °, **8**: 192, **8e**: 193–94
  -s form, **8a-2**: 179–80
  and tense sequences, **8h-1**: 198, 199
Pretentious language °, **21d-2**: 381
pretty
Prewriting strategies °. *See* Gathering ideas
Primary evidence °, **5c**: 126–28
Primary research, **34c-3**: 645–46
Primary sources °, **32**: 531, **34a-1**: 617
  in the social sciences, **34c-3**: 646
principal, principle, **22c-1**: 392
Principal parts of verbs, **8a-1**: 177–79
  of *be, do,* and *have,* **8c**: 187
  of irregular verbs, **8b-2**: 182–85
Problem-to-solution arrangement, **4c**: 92
Process description, **4d**: 98–99
Process, writing. *See* Writing process
Progressive forms (of verbs), **8a-1**: 179
  tense, **8**: 193
  use, **8g**: 195–96
Pronoun-antecedent agreement °, **11**:
  242–45
  with antecedents joined by *and*, **11l**: 243
  with antecedents joined by *or* or *nor*,
    11m: 243
  with collective noun antecedents, **11o**:
    245
  with indefinite pronoun antecedents,
    11n-1: 244
  using masculine pronoun appropriately,
    11n-2: 244–45
Pronoun case °. *See* Case
Pronoun reference °, **10**: 221–29
  avoiding indefinite use of *you,* **10e**: 227
  avoiding overuse of *it,* **10d**: 226–27
  choosing *who, which,* or *that,* **7e-2**: 168,
    10f: 228–29, **17**: 322–23
  making pronoun refer to a definite
    antecedent, **10c**: 224–25
  making pronoun refer to a single antece-
    dent, **10a**: 222, **10c-2**: 225
  placing pronoun close to antecedent, **10b**:
    222–23
  See also Pronoun agreement
Pronouns °, **6b**: 42–43
  antecedents of, **6b**: 142, **10**: 221–29, **11**:
    242–45
  case forms, **6b**: 142, **9**: 209–20
  as cause of comma splices and fused
    sentences, **14b**: 273
  demonstrative, **6b**: 143, **10c-3**: 225, **11a**: 232
  inadvertant omission of, **15e-3**: 299
  indefinite, **6b**: 143, **11a**: 232, **11f**: 237–38,
    11n: 244–45, **27a-1**: 458
  intensive, **6b**: 143, **9h**: 220
  interrogative, **6b**: 143, **9d**: 215, **9d-2**: 217,
    13a: 264
  modified by adjectives, **6e**: 146, **12**: 248
  personal, **6b**: 143, **9**: 209–10, **11a**: 232,
    27b: 459–60

Pronouns° (*cont.*)
  reciprocal, **6b**: 143
  reflexive, **6b**: 143, **9h**: 220
  using for coherence in paragraphs, **4b-2**:
    84–85
  See also Pronoun agreement; Pronoun
    reference; Relative pronouns
Pronunciation
  dictionary information, **20a-1**: 357
  homonyms, **22c-1**: 389–93
  and spelling, **22c-4**: 395–96
  and word division, **22e-1**: 403
Proofreading°, **2a**: 13, **3e**: 70–71
  for comma splices, **14a**: 272
  for omitted words, **15e-3**: 299–300
  for sentence errors, **15**: 282
  for spelling errors, **22a**: 385–86
Proper adjectives°, **6e**: 146, **30e**: 491
Proper nouns°, **6a**: 141
  capitalization of, **30e**: 491–96
  prefixes with, **22e-2**: 404
Proverbs, **21c**: 380
Punctuation
  apostrophes, **27**: 457–61
  brackets, **29c**: 481–82
  colons, **26**: 451–55
  commas, **24**: 415–41
  dashes, **29a**: 474–76
  ellipses, **29d**: 482–84
  exclamation points, **23e, f**: 412–13
  hyphens, **22e**: 403–6
  parentheses, **29b**: 447–80
  periods, **23a,b**: 410–11
  question marks, **23c,d**: 411–12
  quotation marks, **28**: 464–72
  semicolons, **25**: 443–47
  slashes, **29e**: 484–85
  See also main entry for each mark
Purpose°
  of reading, **5a-1**: 115
  of writing, **1a**: 3, **1b**: 4–6, **2b**: 15; research
    papers, **32c**: 536–37; scientific papers,
    34d-2: 652
  and thesis statement, **32h**: 575

Qualification, of evidence, **5c**: 126
Question marks
  with direct questions, **23c**: 411–12
  for doubtful dates or numbers, **23d**: 412,
    29b-4: 479
  with other punctuation: dashes, **29a-3**:
    476, exclamation points, **23e**: 413;
    parentheses, **29b-4,5**: 479; quotation
    marks, **24g**: 434
Questionnaires, **34c-1**: 641–42
Questions
  case of *who* and *whom* in, **9d-2**: 217
  direct, **23c**: 411–12
  ignoring (red herring fallacy), **5f**: 136
  with interrogative pronouns, **13a**:
    264
  as introductory device, **4e**: 107, 108
  journalist's, **2d-4**: 26–27
  in reading, **5a-2**: 116–17
  requests phrased as, **23c**: 412
  in a series: capitalization of, **30a**: 488;
    question marks with, **23c**: 412
  tag, commas with, **24f**: 432
  for variety and emphasis, **19b**: 344
quiet, quite, **22c-1**: 392

Quotation marks, **28**: 464–72
  with direct quotations, **28a**: 464–67
  misuse of, **28d**: 470–71
  not used with displayed quotations,
    28a-1: 465, **32k-1**: 581
  single, **28**: 464, **28a-2**: 466
  with titles, **28b**: 468–69
  with words used in a special sense, **28c**:
    469–70
Quotations°, **31e**: 524–29. *See also*
    Documentation, plagiarism
  accuracy of, **31e-1**: 525–26
  appropriate use of, **31e**: 524–25
  capitalization of, **30c**: 490
  displayed, **28a-1**: 465, **32k-1**: 581, **33**: 597
  with errors in original, **29c-1**: 481–82
  with explanatory words, commas with,
    24g: 433–34
  guidelines for, **31e-4**: 528
  from indirect sources, **32k-1**: 584–85
  insertions into, brackets for, **29c-1**: 481–82
  introduced with colon, **26a**: 451–52
  introduced with *that,* **24g**: 434
  as introductory device, **4e**: 107, 108
  long: avoiding, **31e-3**: 527; displaying,
    28a-1: 465, **32k-1**: 581
  omissions from, ellipses for, **29d**: 482–84
  in paraphrases, **31c-2**: 514–15
  parenthetical references with, **32k-1**:
    580–81
  of poetry, **28a-3**: 466, **29e-1**: 484, **30a**: 489
  within quotations, **28a-2**: 466
  selection of, **31e-2**: 526
  working in smoothly, **31e-4**: 527–29

Races, capitalization of, **30e**: 493
Radio programs, bibliographic citations,
    32g-2: 573
rain, reign, **22c-1**: 392
raise, raze, **22c-1**: 392
raise, rise, **8d**: 190–91
rarely ever
Reaction papers, **34b-3**: 626
Readers, **1a**: 3, **1c**: 8–11. *See also* Audience
Reader's Guide to Periodical Literature,
    32e-6: 551
Reading
  and critical thinking, **5a,b**: 114–24
  to evaluate, **5b-3**: 120–23
  to learn (SQ3R system), **5a-2**: 115–18
  for literal meaning, **5b-1**: 119
  to make inferences, **5b-2**: 119–20
  making predictions during, **5a**: 114–15
  purpose of, **5a-1**: 115
  using for writing, **2d-6**: 28–30
real
really
Reason, subordinating conjunctions show-
    ing, **7e-2**: 166, **17**: 323
Reasoning processes, **5e**: 131–34. *See also*
    Deductive reasoning; Inductive reason-
    ing; Logical fallacies
reason . . . is because, **15d-2**: 296
Reasons, using to develop paragraphs, **4a-2**: 81
reason why
Reciprocal pronouns°, **6b**: 143
Reciting, and learning, **5a-2**: 117
reckon, calculate, figure
Recommendations, subjunctive mood for,
    8i-3: 204

Recordings
  bibliographical citations, **32g-2**: 574
  titles of, italics for, **30f**: 498
Red herring fallacy, **5f**: 136
Redundancies, revising, **16c**: 314
  double comparatives, **12e-1**: 254
  double negatives, **12c**: 249–50
Reference books
  bibliographic citations: APA style, **34c-4**:
    649; MLA style, **32g-2**: 566; old MLA
    style, **34b-4**: 639
  documentary note references, **34b-4**: 635
  library resources, **32e-5**: 544–50
References Cited list, **34d-3**: 654
References list, **34c-4**: 647, 648–50
Reflexive pronouns°, **6b**: 143, **9h**: 220
regarding, in regard to, with regard to
Regional (dialectal) language°
  avoiding inappropriate use, **21a-4**: 376–77
  specialized dictionaries for, **20a-4**: 362
Regular plurals, **22d-4**: 401
Regular verbs°, **8b**: 180
  principle parts, **8b-1**: 180, 181
  tenses, **8**: 193
Reinforcing, **5a-2**: 116, 117–18
Relative adjectives, **6e**: 147
Relative clauses°. *See* Adjective clauses
Relative pronouns°, **6b**: 143
  with adjective clauses, **7e-2**: 167, 168
  antecedents of, **10c-3**: 225
  cases, **9d**: 215–17
  omission of, **7e-2**: 170
  in parallel clauses, **18c-4**: 335
  with sentence fragments, **13a**: 263–64,
    13b: 264
  and subject-verb agreement, **11i**: 239–40
  for subordination, **14d**: 277, **17**: 322–23
  use of *who, which,* or *that,* **7e-2**: 168, **10f**:
    228–29, **17**: 322–23
Relevance, of evidence, **5c**: 125–26
Religion, reference works on, **32e-5**: 549
Religious terms, capitalization of, **30e**: 495
RENNS, **4a-2**: 81–82
Repetition
  for emphasis, **19f**: 351–52
  for coherence in paragraphs, **4b-3**: 85
  with parallel elements, **18c-3**: 334
  pattern of, in cause-and-effect relation-
    ships, **5d**: 130
  unplanned, **16c**: 314
  See also Redundancies
Reports, **2a**: 14
  on books, **34b-3**: 626
  scientific, **34d-3**: 653–56
  See also Research papers
Reprints
  bibliographic citations: MLA
    parenthetical-references style, **32g-2**:
    567; MLA note style, **34b-4**: 639
  documentary note references, **34b-4**: 637
Requests
  implied subject, **13a**: 263
  indirect, subjunctive mood for, **8i-3**: 204
  phrased as questions, **23c**: 412
Research. *See* Research papers; Research
    process
Research logs, **32f-1**: 557–58
Research papers, **32**: 530–85
  audience for, **32c**: 536–37
  bibliographies for, **32g**: 560–74

cover page, **33**: 590–91
documentation style, **32d-4**: 539–40,
  34a-2: 618
drafting and revising, **32j**: 557–79
footnotes or endnotes in, **32j-2**: 585
in the humanities, **34b-3**: 626–30
outlining, **32i**: 576–77
parenthetical references in, **32j**: 579–85
processes involved, **32a**: 532–33
purpose and audience, **32c**: 536–37
sample paper, **33**: 586–613
sample schedule, **32a**: 532
in the social sciences, **34c-3**: 645–47
sources for: evaluating, **32d-2**: 538, 539;
  primary vs. secondary, **32**: 531, **34a-1**:
  617–18; search strategy, **32e**: 542–57
thesis statements for, **32h**: 575–76
topic selection, focusing, **32b**: 533–36,
  32e-1: 540–41
See also Documentation
Research process, **32a**: 533
  basic equipment, **32d**: 537, **32d-1**: 538
  differences among disciplines, **34a-1**:
    617–18
  logging, **32f-1**: 557–58
  in the natural and technological sciences,
    34d-1: 650
  note taking, **32f-2**: 558–60
  preparation for, **32d**: 537–40
  search strategy, **32e**: 540–57
  in the social sciences, **34c-1**: 640–42,
    34c-2: 645–46
  See also Library resources
respectfully, respectively, **22c-1**: 392
Restatement
  as a clue to word meaning, **20c-2**: 370
  introduced by colon, **26a**: 452
  in paraphrases, **31c-1**: 514
Restrictive elements°
  clauses with *that,* **7e-2**: 168, **10f**: 228–29
  commas not used with, **24e**: 427–29
Result
  conjunctive adverbs showing, **6f**: 148
  subordinating conjunctions showing,
    7e-2: 166, **17**: 323
  transitional expressions for, **4b**: 84
Results section, in scientific report, **34d-3**:
  654
Résumés, **35c**: 662, 667–68
reverend, reverent, **22c-i**: 392
Reviews
  bibliographic citations, **32g-2**: 571
  scientific, **34d-3**: 656
Revised draft, **3c**: 50–59
  criticism of, **3c-4**: 60–63
  editing, **3d**: 63–64, **32j**: 578–79
Revision°, **2a**: 13, **3**: 44, **3c**: 50–63
  checklist for, **3c**: 53–56
  reinforcing compared to, **5a-2**: 116
  of research paper, **32j**: 577–579
  steps and activities, **3c-1**: 50–52
  and thesis statement, **3c-2**: 52, **32h**: 575
  using criticism, **3c-4**: 60–63
Rhetoric°, **1**: 2–11
Rhythm
  of parallel elements, **18b-1**: 332
  due to repetition, **19f**: 351
right
right, rite, write, **22c-1**: 392–93
road, rode, **22c-1**: 393

Roman numerals
    for acts of plays, **24h**: 437, **30j**: 507
    changing to arabic in volume numbers,
        32g-2: 567
    in formal outlines, **2e-5**: 40
Root words°, **20c-1**: 366–67
Run-in lists, **30b**: 489. *See also* Lists
Run-on sentences°. *See* Fused sentences

-s, -es endings, **8a-2**: 179–80, **11a**: 232–33
said, pronoun reference with, **10a**: 222
Salutations, in letters, **24h**: 436, **35b**: 661
says, goes
says, said
scarcely, **12c**: 249
scene, seen, **22c-1**: 393
Scholarly abbreviations, **30i**: 503
School courses, capitalization of, **30e**: 494
Science, reference works on, **32e-5**: 549
Scientific method, **34d-1**: 651
Scientific reports, **34d-3**: 653–56
Scientific reviews, **34d-3**: 656
Scientific terms, capitalization of, **30e**: 494
Scientific writing, **34a**: 615–16, **34d**: 650–58
    abbreviations in, **30h**: 502
    documentation style, **34d-4**: 656–58
    method of inquiry, **34d-1**: 651
    purpose and practices, **34d-2**: 652–53
    types of papers, **34d-3**: 653–56
    use of passive voice, **34a-4**: 619–20
    See also Social sciences
Scores, **30j**: 507
Search strategies, **32e**: 540–56
Seasons, not capitalized, **30e**: 496
Secondary evidence°, **5c**: 128
Secondary sources°, **32**: 531, **34a-1**: 617–18
    evaluating, **5c**: 128, **32d-2**: 538, 539
    in the social sciences, **34c-3**: 646
Second person°, **11**: 231. *See also* You
-sede, -cede, -ceed spellings, **22d-1**: 398
seen
-self pronouns, **9h**: 220
Self-contradiction fallacy, **5f**: 136
Semicolons, **25**: 443–47
    in complex series, **24c**: 425, **25d**: 445–46
    between independent clauses: closely
        related, **14b**: 274, **25a**: 443–44; linked
        by conjunctive adverbs or other transi-
        tional expressions, **14e**: 278, **24f**: 432,
        25c: 444; containing commas, **24a**: 418,
        25b: 444–45
    misuse of, **25e**: 445–46
    in parenthetical references, **32k-1**: 584
sense, since, **22c-1**: 393
Senses, appeals to, **4a-2**: 81–82
Sentence combining. *See* Combining
    sentences
Sentence fragments°, **13**: 260–69
    dependent clauses as, **13b**: 264–65
    phrases as, **13c**: 266–68
    intentional, **13d**: 269
    testing for, **13a**: 261–64
Sentence outlines, **2e-5**: 39, 42–43
    for research papers, **32i**: 577, **33**: 592–93
Sentences°
    with adverb modifiers, **6f**: 148
    arranging in paragraphs, **4c**: 90–93
    balanced, **18b-3**: 333
    basic parts, **7a**: 155–56
    capitalization of first word in, **30a**: 487–89

combining, **16a-3**: 306–7
complex, **7f-3**: 173, **8h-1**: 197–99, **14d**:
    276, **17**: 322–28
compound-complex, **7f-4**: 173, **17g**: 328
coordination and subordination in, **17**:
    316–28
with dangling modifiers, **15c**: 293
declarative, **7**: 154
defined, **7**: 154
end punctuation for, **23**: 410–13
exclamatory, **7**: 154
fused, **14**: 271–79
imperative, **7**: 154
incomplete, **13**: 260–69, **15e**: 297, 300
interrogative, **7**: 154
interruptions in: with dashes, **29a**:
    474–76; with parentheses, **29b-1**: 478
length of, varying, **19a**: 341–43
with misplaced modifiers, **15b**: 288–91
mixed, **15d**: 294–96
parallel, **18d**: 335
parallelism in, **18**: 330–38
revising for conciseness, **16**: 302–14
revision checklist, **3c-3**: 55
shifts in, **15a**: 282–87
simple, **7f-1**: 172
structure of, **7**: 154–73, **19d-2**: 348–49
subject choice for, **19c**: 346
testing for completeness, **13a**: 261–64
types of, **7**: 154, **7f**: 172–73; for variety,
    19b: 344
unclear, **15**: 281–300
variety and emphasis in, **19**: 340–52
    See also Compound sentences; Topic
    sentences
Sequence of tenses, **8h**: 197–200
Series (of items)
    commas with, **24c**: 423–25
    questions in, **23c**: 412, **30a**: 488
    semicolons with, **25d**: 445–46
Series (of publications), in bibliographic
    citations, **32g-2**: 568
set, sit, **8d**: 190–91
sex, gender
Sexist language°, **11n-2**: 244–45, **21a-3**:
    373–75
shall, will, **8c**: 188
Shaping°, **2e**: 30–43
    defined, **2a**: 13
    determining role and tone of writer, **2e-3**:
        33
    drafting thesis statement, **2e-4**: 33–36
    grouping ideas, **2e-1**: 30–31
    ordering ideas, **2e-2**: 32
    outlining, **2e-5**: 37–43
Shifts, unnecessary, **15a**: 282–87
    between direct and indirect discourse,
        15a-4: 286–87
    in mood, **15a-3**: 286
    in number, **15a-1**: 282
    in person, **15a-1**: 282–83
    in subject, **15a-2**: 284–85
    in tense, **15a-3**: 285–86
    in voice, **15a-2**: 284–85
Ships, italics for, **30f**: 497, 499
Short stories, titles of, **28b**: 468–69
should, **8c**: 188–89
should have, **22c-4**: 396
should, would
sic, **29c-1**: 482

Similes°, **4d**: 102–3, **21b**: 377
Simple form° (of verb), **8a-1**: 177–78
    and future tenses, **8**: 192, **8a-1**: 178
    with present subjunctive, **8i**: 203
    tense sequences with, **8h-1**: 198
Simple predicates°, **7a-2**: 156
Simple present tense, **8**: 192, 193
    functions of, **8e**: 193–94
    tense sequences with, **8h-1**: 198
Simple sentences°, **7f-1**: 172
Simple subjects°, **7a-1**: 155
Simple tenses°, **8**: 192, 193
since, **13b**: 265
Singular°. *See* Number
Singular nouns, with plural form, **11j**: 241
Singular verbs, *-s* and *-es* endings, **8a-2**:
    179–80, **11a**: 232–33
site, cite, **22c-1**: 390
Slang°
    avoiding inappropriate use, **21a-4**: 376,
        28d: 470
    specialized dictionaries of, **20a-4**: 361–62
    usage label, **20a-1**: 358
Slanted language°, **21a-5**: 377
Slashes, **29e**: 484–85
    with *and/or,* **29e-3**: 485
    with numerical fractions, **29e-2**: 484–85
    with quotations of poetry, **28a-3**: 466,
        29e-1: 484
so, as coordinating conjunction, **6h**: 151, **17**:
    317
Social sciences, **34c**: 640–50
    abbreviations in, **30h**: 502
    APA documentation style, **34c-4**: 647–50
    methods of inquiry, **34c-1**: 640–42
    reference works on, **32e-5**: 549–50
    types of papers in, **34c-3**: 643–47
    writing purposes and practices, **34a**: 615,
        616, **34c-2**: 642–43
some
    comparative and superlative forms, **12e-2**:
        255
    subject-verb agreement, **11f**: 238
somebody, some body
someone, some one
sometime, sometimes, some time
somewhere
sort, kind, sort of, kind of
Song titles, quotation marks for, **28b**: 469
Sources
    evaluation of, **5c**: 128, **32d-2**: 538, 539,
        33: 595
    indirect, **32k-1**: 584–85, **33**: 597
    primary and secondary, **32**: 531, **34a-1**:
        617–18, **34c-3**: 646
    See also Bibliographies; Documentation;
        Library resources
Spatial order°, **2e-2**: 32, **4c**: 92–93
Speaker tags°, **24g**: 433
Specialists, as audience, **1c-3**: 11
Specialized dictionaries, **20a-4**: 361–62
Specialized indexes, **32e-6**: 552
Specialized language, **21d-2**: 381–82; **34a-4**:
    619–20
specially, especially
Special pleading, **5f**: 137
Specific details, developing paragraphs
    with, **4a-2**: 81–82
Specific-to-general arrangement, **4c**: 91
Specific words, **20b-2**: 364–66

Speculation, subjunctive mood for, **8i-1**: 203
Spelling, **22**: 385–406
    American vs. British forms, **22c-2**: 394
    of compounds, **22e-3**: 406
    dictionary aids, **22b-1**: 386
    errors in: common patterns, **22b-3**:
        387–89; proofreading for, **22a**: 385–86;
        in quoted sources, **29c-1**: 481–82
    homonyms, **22c-1**: 389–93
    and hyphenation, **22e**: 403–6
    ie/ei rules and exceptions, **22d-2**: 399
    methods for improving, **22b**: 386–89
    of plurals, **22d-4**: 401–2
    with prefixes, **22d-3**: 400
    and pronunciation, **22c-4**: 395–96
    with suffixes, **22d-1**: 397–99
    visual and mnemonic aids, **22b-2**: 387
    of words with multiple forms, **22c-3**: 395
Split infinitives, **15b-3**: 290
SQ3R system, **5a-1**: 115–18
Squinting modifiers, **15b-1**: 289
Standard English°, **21a-2**: 373
Statements, periods with, **23a**: 410
State names
    abbreviation of, **23b**: 411, **30i**: 504, **32g-2**:
        563
    after city names, commas with, **23b**: 11,
        24n: 436, **30h**: 502
stationary, stationery, **22c-1**: 393
Statistics
    as evidence, **5c**: 125
    as introductory device, **4e**: 107, 108
    numbers, **30j**: 507
Stereotyping
    by gender, **21a-3**: 374–75
    as logical fallacy, **5f**: 135
straight, strait, **22c-1**: 393
Strong commands, **8**: 202, **19b**: 344, **23e**:
    412–13
Style manuals
    APA, **34c-4**: 638
    MLA, **32g**: 652
    in the sciences, **34d-4**: 657–58
Subject complements°, **7c-1**: 159
    with forms of *be,* **8c**: 186–87
    with number different from subject, **11g**:
        239
Subjective case°, **9**: 209, 210
    after linking verbs, **9c**: 214
    who and *whoever,* **9d**: 215–17
Subjects°, **7a-1**: 155
    agreement with verbs, **11**: 230–41
    awkward separation from verbs, **15b-3**:
        290
    in clauses, **7e**: 166, 167
    emphasizing, **19c**: 346
    implied, **8**: 202, **13a**: 263
    of infinitives, **9f**: 218
    noun clauses as, **7e-2**: 170
    nouns as, **6a**: 141
    plural, **11a**: 232–33, **11c**: 234–35, **11d**: 236
    required for completeness, **13b**: 262–63
    shifts in, **15a-2**: 284–85
    after verb, **19e**: 350–51
    See also Subjective case
Subject headings in research, **32d-3**: 538–39
Subject trees, **2e-1**: 31
Subject-verb agreement°, **11**: 230–41
    with collective nouns, **11g**: 238
    with indefinite pronouns, **11f**: 237–38

Subject-verb agreement° (*cont.*)
  with intervening phrase, **11b**: 233–34
  with inverted word order, **11e**: 236–37
  with linking verbs, **11g**: 239
  with -*s* and -*es* endings, **11a**: 232–33
  with singular subjects in plural form, **11j**: 241
  with subjects joined by *and,* **11c**: 234–35
  with subjects joined by *or, nor,* or *not only. . . but (also),* **11d**: 235–36
  with subjects that specify amounts, **11j**: 240
  with titles and company names, **11k**: 241
  with *who, which,* and *that,* **11i**: 239–40
  with words used as terms, **11k**: 241
Subjunctive mood°, **8**: 202–3, **8i**: 203–4
  shifts with other moods, **15a-3**: 286
Subordinate clauses°. *See* Dependent clauses; Subordination
Subordinating conjunctions°, **6h**: 151–52, **7e-2**: 166–67
  and comma use, **24b-1**: 420–21
  correcting comma splices and fused sentences with, **14d**: 276–77
  relationships implied by, **17**: 322, 323
  selection of, **17e**: 324–25
  with sentence fragments, **13a**: 263, **13b**: 264–65
Subordination°, **17**: 316–17, 322–28
  balancing with coordination, **17g**: 328
  choosing appropriate subordinating conjunction, **17e**: 324–25
  to correct comma splices and fused sentences, **14d**: 276–77
  illogical, **17f-1**: 326
  overuse of, **17f-2**: 327
  to show relationship, **17d**: 324
Subtitles, colons before, **26b**: 453
such
such as, to introduce list or series, **26a**: 453, **26c**: 454
Suffixes°, **20c-1**: 366, 368–69
  spelling, **22d-1**: 397–99
  and word division, **22e-1**: 403, **22e-2**: 404
Summaries°, introduced with colon, **26a**: 452
Summarizing, **31d**: 519–24, **33**: 603
  avoiding plagiarism, **31d-3**: 521–22
  condensing, **31d-2**: 521
  guidelines for, **31d-4**: 522–24
  isolating main points, **31d-1**: 520–21
  from long paragraphs, **31d-4**: 522–24
Summary
  conjunctive adverbs showing, **6f**: 148
  transitional expressions for, **4b**: 84
Superlative° forms, **12e**: 253–55
  double, **12e-1**: 254
supposed to, **22c-4**: 396
sure
Surveying, in reading, **5a-2**: 115–116
Suspended hyphens, **22e-2**: 405
Syllables
  accented, in dictionary entries, **20a-1**: 357
  number of, effect on comparative and superlative forms, **12e-1**: 254
  and word division, **22e-1**: 403
Syllogisms°, **5e-2**: 133
Symbols
  vs. spelled-out forms, **30h**: 502
  used as terms, plural forms, **27d**: 461

Synecdoche°, **21b**: 378
Synonyms
  in dictionary entries, **20a-1**: 358
  in paraphrases, **31c-2**: 514–15
  specialized dictionaries for, **20a-4**: 361
Synthesis°, and critical thinking, **5**: 114

Tables, **30h**: 502, **33**: 599
Tag questions, **24f**: 432
take, bring
taught, taut, **22c-1**: 393
teach, learn
Technical terms, in quotation marks, **28c**: 470
Technology, reference works on, **32e-5**: 549. *See also* Scientific writing
Television
  bibliographic citations of programs, **32g-2**: 573
  reference works on, **32e-5**: 550
  titles: of episodes, **28b**: 469; of series, **30f**: 497, 498
Temperatures, **30h**: 502, **30j**: 507
Tense sequence°, **8h**: 197–200
Tenses°, **8**: 177, 192–200
  perfect, **8**: 193; **8f**: 194–195
  progressive forms, **8g**: 195–96
  sequences of, **8h**: 197–200
  shifts in, **15a-3**: 285–86
  simple, **8**: 192, 193, **8e**: 193–94
Term papers. *See* Research papers
Terms, words used as
  italics (underlining) for, **27d**: 461
  plural forms, apostrophes in, **27d**: 481
  subject-verb agreement, **11k**: 241
than
  homonym of *then,* **22c-1**: 393
  pronoun case after comparisons with, **9e**: 218
that
  agreement of verb with, **11i**: 239–40
  checking for clear antecedent, **10c-3**: 225
  implied in elliptical clauses, **7e-2**: 168
  before quoted words, **24g**: 434
  subjunctive mood with, **8i-2**: 204
  vs. *who* or *which,* **7e-2**: 168, **10f**: 228–29, **17**: 322–23
that there, then there, this here, these here
that which
the, **6a**: 142. *See also* Articles
the fact that, **15d-1**: 295
the following, **26a**: 453
their, there, they're, **22c-1**: 393, **22c-4**: 396
theirself, theirselves, themself
them
Themes, **2a**: 14. *See also* Essays
themselves, **9h**: 220
there
  as expletive, **6j**: 152–53, **11e**: 236
  homonym of *their, they're,* **22c-1**: 393
Thesis°. *See* Thesis statements
Thesis statements
  as aid to revision, **3c-2**: 52
  basic requirements, **2e-4**: 34
  drafting of, **2e-4**: 33–36, **32h**: 575–76, **33**: 595
  and drafting of essay, **3b**: 47, 48–49
  and formal outlines, **2e-5**: 41
  in introductory paragraphs, **4e**: 106

they
  avoiding indefinite use of, **10c-4**: 226
  possessive form, **22c-1**: 393, **22c-4**: 396,
    27b: 459–60
Thinking, and writing, **1**: 2–3, **2b**: 14–16.
  See also Critical thinking
Third person°
  -s, -es endings, **8a-2**:179–80, **11a**: 232–33
  subject-verb agreement, **11**: 231
  See also he; it, they
this, checking for clear antecedent, **10c-3**:
  225
through, threw, **22c-1**: 393
thusly
till, until
Time
  conjunctive adverbs showing, **6f**: 148
  of day: colons in, **26b**: 453; numbers, **30j**:
    506
  subordinating conjunction showing, **7e-2**:
    166, **17**: 323
  transitional expressions for, **4b**: 84
  words indicating, **13b**: 265–66
Time order. *See also* Chronological order
Titles of essays and research papers
  as aid to revising, **3c-2**: 52
  avoiding pronoun reference to, **10c-5**: 226
  formatting, **33**: 590–91
Titles of persons
  abbreviations for, **23b**: 411, **30h**: 500
  capitalization of, **30e**: 492–93
  after name, commas with, **24h**: 436
  subject-verb agreement, **11k**: 241
Titles of works
  capitalization of, **30e**: 495; in APA style
    and scientific bibliographies, **34c-4**:
    649, **34d-4**: 658
  compound, **22e-3**: 406
  italics for, **30f**: 497–98
  in MLA-style parenthetical references,
    32k-1: 583
  quotation marks for, **28b**: 468–69, **28d**:
    471
  of scientific reports, **34d-3**: 653
  with subtitles, colons between, **26b**: 453
  in text discussions, **31e-4**: 528
  within titles, **32g-2**: 568
to, too, two, **22c-1**: 393
told, pronoun reference with, **10a**: 222
Tone°
  formal and informal, **21a-1**: 372–73
  determining, **2e-3**: 33
  evaluating in reading, **5b-3**: 120–21
  for general reading public, **1c-1**: 9
  in introductory paragraph, **4e**: 106
Topical paragraphs°, **4**: 73–75. *See also*
  Paragraphs
  arranging sentences in, **4c**: 90–93
Topic outlines, **2e-5**: 39, 41–42
  for research papers, **32i**: 577
Topics°
  narrowing, **2c-2**: 18–20, **32b-1**: 534–35,
    32e-1: 540–41
  selecting, **2c-1**: 17–18, **32b**: 533–36
  and writing situation, **2b**: 14–15
Topic sentences°, **4a-1**: 76–79
  defined, **4a**: 76
  at beginning of paragraph, **4a-1**: 77–78
  at end of paragraph, **4a-1**: 78–79
  implied, **4a-1**: 79

  and limiting sentences, **4a-1**: 76
  to summarize other sources, **31d**: 520
toward, towards
Tracers, in card catalogues, **32e-7**: 553, 554
track, tract, **22c-1**: 393
trans., **32g-2**: 564
Transition°, **4b**: 83–84
Transitional expressions°
  as cause of comma splices and fused
    sentences, **14b**: 273
  for coherent paragraphs, **4b**: 83–84
  punctuation with, **14e**: 278–79, **26b-3**:
    421–22, **24f**: 432, **25c**: 445
Transitional paragraphs°, **4e**: 111–12
Transitive verbs°, **8d**: 190–91
  have and *do* as, **8c**: 188
  objects, **7b**: 157–58
Translations
  of terms, quotation marks for, **25c**: 470
  of works, bibliographic citations, **32g-2**:
    566
try and, sure and
type

Unabridged dictionaries, **20a-2**: 359–60
Underlining. *See* Italics
Understatement°, **21b**: 378
uninterested, disinterested
unique
Units of measurement. *See* Measurements
Unity°
  in an essay, **3b**: 47
  in a paragraph, **4a**: 75–82; development
    and, **4a-2**: 80–82; topic sentences and,
    4a-1: 75–80
unless clauses, in subjunctive mood, **8i-1**:
  203
Unpublished material, bibliographic citations, **32g-2**: 572
Unstated assumptions, **5e-2**: 134
until, functions, **13b**: 265
U.S., **30h**: 501
us, we, in appositives, **9b**: 213
Usage, specialized dictionaries for, **20a-4**:
  362
Usage labesl, **20a-1**: 358
used to, **22c-4**: 396
USSR, **30h**: 501

Validity°, of deductive argument, **5e-2**:
  133–34
Variety, **19**: 340–52
  with added modifiers, **19d**: 346–49
  with inverted word order, **19e**: 350–51
  in sentence length, **19a**: 341–43
  in sentence type, **19b**: 344
Verbal pharases°, **7d**: 163–64
  as sentence fragments, **13c**: 267
Verbals°, **6d**: 145–46
  as nonfinite verbs, **8a-1**: 179
  in sentence fragments, **13a**: 261–62
  See also Gerunds; Infinitives, Participles
Verb phrases°, **7d**: 162–63
  constituents, **8a**: 177
  interrupted, **15b-3**: 291
  with past participles, **8a-1**: 177
Verbs°, **6c**: 144, **8**: 176–207
  agreement with subjects, **11**: 230–41
  awkward separation: from object, **15b-3**:
    291; from subject, **15b-3**: 290

Verbs° (*cont.*)
  finite, **8a-1**: 179
  forms, **8a,b,c,d**: 177–91, **20a-1**: 357
  intransitive, **8d**: 190–91
  irregular, **8a-1**: 178, **8b-1**: 182–85, **8**: 193
  modified by adverb clauses, **7e-2**: 167
  modified by adverbs, **6f**: 148, **7c-2**:
    160–61, **12**: 248, **12a**: 249
  mood, **8**: 177, **8i**: 202–4, **15a-3**: 286
  nouns formed from, **16a-4**: 308
  number, **8**: 176, **11**: 230–41
  objects of, **7b**: 157–58
  person, **8**: 176, **11**: 230–31
  and predicates, **7a-2**: 156
  principal parts, **8a-1**: 177–79, **8b-2**:
    182–85, **8c**: 187
  regular, **8b**: 180–81
  required in complete sentences, **13a**: 261–62
  revising weak to strong, **16a**: 308
  singular, **11a**: 232–33
  before subject, **19e**: 350–51
  suffixes for, **20c-1**: 368
  transitive, **8d**: 190–91
  for weaving quotations into text, **31e-4**: 529
  See also Auxiliary verbs; Linking verbs;
    Main verbs; Subject-verb agreement;
    Tenses; Verbals; Voice
Visualization, **3a**: 46
Vocabulary, increasing, **20c**: 366–70. *See
    also* Language; Tone; Words
Vogue words, **21c**: 379
Voice°, **8**: 177, 205–7
  avoiding shifts in, **15a-2**: 284–85
  preferences in various disciplines, **34a-4**:
    619–20, **34c-2**: 643, **34d-2**: 652
  revising passive to active, **16a-2**: 304–5
Volume numbers, in documentation
  of multivolume works, **32g-2**: 567, **32k-1**: 583
  of periodicals, **32g**: 569–70

waist, waste, **22c-1**: 393
wait on
waive, wave, **22c-1**: 393
ways
we, us, in appositives, **9b**: 213
weak, week, **22c-1**: 393
weather, whether, **22c-1**: 393
Webbing°, **2d-5**: 58
*Webster's New World Dictionary of the
    American Language,* **20a-3**: 360–61
*Webster's Third New International Dic-
    tionary of the English Language,* **20a-2**:
    360
week, weak, **22c-1**: 393
well, better, best, **12e-2**: 255
well, good, **12d**: 252
went, gone
where, were, **22c-1**: 393
what
when
  as interrogative pronoun, **13a**: 264
  as subordinating conjunction, **14d**: 276
where
where . . . at
whether, if
which
  agreement of verb with, **11i**: 239–40
  checking for clear antecedent, **10c-3**: 225
  vs. *who* or *that,* **7e-2**: 168, **10f**: 228–29,
    17: 322–23

which, that
which, who
who
  agreement of verb with, **11i**: 239–40
  possessive form, **22c-1**: 393, **22c-4**: 396,
    27b: 459–60
  vs. *which* or *that,* **7e-2**: 168, **10f**: 228–29,
    17: 322–33
  vs. *whom,* **9d**: 215–16
whoever, whomever, **9d**: 215–17
whole, hole, **22c-1**: 391
Who's Who, **32e-5**: 546
who's, whose, **22c-4**: 396, **27b**: 459–60,
    22c-1: 393
who, whom
will, shall, **8c**: 188, **8**: 192
-wise
Wishes, subjunctive mood for, **8i-3**: 204
witch, which, **22c-1**: 393
Word choice, **20b**: 362–66, **21a**: 371. *See
    also* Language
  for general reading public, **1c-1**: 9
  revision checklist, **3c-3**: 55–56
Word division, **22e-1**: 403, **22e-2**: 404
Wordiness, **16**: 302–14
  empty words and phrases, **16b**: 309–13
  overly long clauses and phrases, **16a-3**:
    306–7
  redundancy, **16c**: 314
  unnecessary expletive constructions,
    16a-1: 303–4
  unnecessary passive constructions, **16a-2**:
    304–5
  weak verbs and nominals, **16a-4**: 308
Word meaning, **20**: 355–70
  context clues, **20c-2**: 370
  denotation and connotation, **20b-1**:
    362–64
  dictionary information, **20a**: 356–62
  with prefixes and suffixes, **20c-1**: 366–69
  specific and concrete vs. general and
    abstract, **20b-2**: 364–66
Word order, inverted, **19e**: 350–51
Word processors, **3f**: 71–72
Words
  closed, **22e-2**: 404
  combined with numbers, **22e-4**: 406
  dictionary information, **20a**: 356–62
  effect of, **21**: 371–84
  meaning of, **20**: 355–70
  initials pronounced as, **23b**: 411
  inserted into quotations, **29c**: 481–82
  introductory, **19d-2**: 349, **24b-3**: 421–22
  parallel, **18**: 330, **18a**: 331–32
  repetition of, for emphasis, **19f**: 351–52
  that call for parallel structure, **18c**:
    333–35
  transitional, **24b-3**: 421–22
  translations of, **28c**: 470
  unnecessary, **16b**: 309–13
  used as words, **28c**: 470, **30f**: 497, 499;
    plural form, **27d**: 461; subject-verb
    agreement, **11k**: 241
  used in special senses, **28c**: 469–70
  vocabulary building, **20c**: 366–70
  See also Foreign words; Language; Word
    meaning
Works Cited list, **32d-4**: 540, **32g-2**: 562–74,
    33: 611–13
Works of art. *See* Art works

would, **8c**: 188
would, should
write, right, rite, **22c-1**: 392–93
Writers, role of, **2e-3**: 33
Writing
  audiences for, **1c**: 8–11
  avoiding artificial language, **21d**: 380–84
  avoiding clichés, **21c**: 379–80
  for business, **35**: 659–68
  elements of, **1a**: 3
  forms of, **1a**: 3
  in the humanities, **34b**: 620–40
  in the natural and technological sciences,
    34d: 650–58
  myths about, **3a**: 45
  purposes of, **1b**: 4–5
  to reinforce learning, **5a-2**: 118
  in the social sciences, **34c**: 640–50
  using appropriate language, **21a**: 371–77
  using figurative language, **21b**: 377–78
  See also Writing process
Writing blocks, **3a**: 44–45
Writing process°, **2a**: 12–14
  choosing a topic, **2c**: 17–20
  distinctions among later parts, **3e**: 70
  drafting, **3b**: 46–49
  editing, **3d**: 63–70
  gathering ideas for, **2d**: 20–30
  getting started, **3a**: 44–46
  overview, **2a**: 13
  proofreading, **3e**: 70–71
  for research papers, **32a**: 533
  revising, **3c**: 50–63

  shaping, **2e**: 30–43
  thinking and planning, **2b**: 14–16
  with word processor, **3f**: 71–72
Writing situation, **2b**: 14–16, **2e-3**: 33
Wrong placement of modifiers, **15b-2**: 289

Xerox, photocopy
Xmas

-y, words ending in,
  adding suffixes to, **22d-1**: 398
  adjectives, **12e-1**: 254
Yearbooks, **32e-5**: 545
Year of publication, in APA style reference
  lists, **34c-4**: 648
Years
  apostrophes with decades, **27c**: 461
  plural form, **27d**: 461
yet, as coordinating conjunction, **6h**: 151,
  17: 317
yore, your, you're, **22c-1**: 393, **22c-4**: 396
you (second person), **11**: 231
  in direct address, **15a-1**: 283–84
  as implied subject, **8**: 202, **13a**: 263
  indefinite use, **10e**: 227
  possessive form, **22c-1**: 393, **22c-4**: 396
yourself
your, you're

Zip codes, **24h**: 436

Photograph © 1986 by Jill Krementz

LYNN QUITMAN TROYKA received her Ph.D. from New York University in 1973. She started teaching in 1960 and joined the faculty of Queensborough Community College of the City University of New York (CUNY) in 1967. There she became a professor (specializing in writing) in 1976. At CUNY she also has taught at the Center for Advanced Studies in Education at the Graduate School and has been a research associate at the Instructional Resource Center.

Currently, Dr. Troyka is editor of the *Journal of Basic Writing,* and she serves on the editorial board of *College Composition and Communication (CCC)* and as a reviewer for *College English* and *Research in the Teaching of English.* Her articles have appeared in journals such as *CCC, College English,* and *Writing Program Administration* and in books from Southern Illinois University Press and Boynton/Cook.

She is the co-author of *Steps in Composition* (Prentice-Hall), now in its fourth edition; author of *Structured Reading* (Prentice-Hall), now in its second edition; co-author of *Taking Action* (Prentice-Hall), a book based on her doctoral dissertation; and editor of *Guide to Writing* (Harper & Row).

Dr. Troyka has been a consultant to federal agencies including the National Endowment for the Humanities, the National Institute of Education, and the Fund for the Improvement of Post Secondary Education; and to testing agencies including the College Board, Educational Testing Service, and American College Testing. She has been a guest lecturer at dozens of colleges and universities. She is a past chair (1981) of the Conference on College Composition and Communication, and she is currently chair of both the College Section of the National Council of Teachers of English and the Division on the Teaching of Writing of the Modern Language Association.

KEY LISTS, GUIDELINES, AND SUMMARIES

Characteristics of Informative and Persuasive Writing *5, 6*
Checklist of Audience Characteristics *9*
Overview of the Writing Process *13*
Ways to Gather Ideas for Writing *21*
Basic Requirements for a Thesis Statement *34*
Pattern for a Formal Outline *39*
Activities During Revising *51*
Revision Checklist *53–56*
Editing Checklist *63–64*
Transitional Expressions *84*
Good and Bad Strategies for Introductory Paragraphs *107, 109*
Good and Bad Strategies for Concluding Paragraphs *109,110*
Universals in Reading to Learn *116*
Checklist for Making Inferences During Reading *120*
Guidelines for Using Evidence *125–26*
Guidelines for Evaluating Cause and Effect *130–31*
Summaries of Inductive and Deductive Reasoning *132, 134*
Subordinating Conjunctions and the Relationships They Imply *166, 323*
Common Irregular Verbs *183–85*
The Forms of *be, do,* and *have 187*
Forms for *sit, lie, rise* and *set, lay, raise 191*
Summary of Tenses, Including Progressive Forms *193*
Uses of the Simple Present Tense *194*
Summary of Sequence of Tenses *198–99*
Case Forms of Personal Pronouns *210*
Case Forms of Relative and Interrogative Pronouns *215*
"Person" Review *231*
Avoiding Sexist Language *245, 374–75*
Summary of Differences Between Adjectives and Adverbs *248*
Forms of Comparison for Regular Adjectives and Adverbs *253*
Irregular Comparatives and Superlatives *255*
Test for Sentence Completeness to Identify Fragments *261*
Causes of Comma Splices and Fused Sentences *273*
Guide for Eliminating Empty Words and Phrases *311–13*

Meaning of the Coordinating Conjunctions *317*
Usage Labels *358*
Techniques for Building Your Vocabulary *367*
Homonyms and Commonly Confused Words *389–93*
Comma Rules for Dates, Names, Places, Addresses, Letters, Numbers *435-37*
Summary of Comma Cautions *440–41*
Capitalization Guide *492–96*
Guide to Underlining *498–99*
Scholarly, Postal, and Month Abbreviations *503–4*
Using Outside Sources *510*
Location List for Documentation Styles *513, 619*
Guidelines for Paraphrases *517*
Guidelines for Summaries *523*
Guidelines for Quotations *528*
Sample Schedule for a Research-Paper Project *532*
Equipment for Conducting Research *537*
Evaluating Sources *128, 539*
Flowchart of a Search Strategy *541*
Formats for MLA *Works Cited* Entries *563–74*
Guidelines for MLA Parenthetical References *579–84*
Guidelines for MLA Content Notes *585*
Major Aspects of Literary Works to Analyze *622*
Questions for an Interpretation Paper *626*
Guidelines for Note Numbers *631*
Guidelines for Endnotes *632*
Guidelines for Footnotes *633*
Guidelines for Bibliographies *637*
Guidelines for Questionnaires *641*
Guidelines for Parenthetical Citations in APA Style *648*
Guidelines for the APA *References* List *648–49*
Guidelines and Format for Job-Application Letters *660–61, 666*
Memo Format *663*
Guidelines and Format for Business Letter and Envelope *664–65*
Sample Résumés *667, 668*
Cue Words in Essay Tests *670–71*